The Cambridge Handbook of Sociocultural Psychology

This handbook provides a representative international overview of the state of our contemporary knowledge in sociocultural psychology – as a discipline located at the crossroads between the natural and social sciences and the humanities. Since the 1980s, the field of psychology has encountered the growth of a new discipline – cultural psychology – that has built new connections between psychology, sociology, anthropology, history, and semiotics. The handbook integrates contributions of sociocultural specialists from 15 countries, all tied together by the unifying focus on the role of sign systems in human relations with the environment. The handbook emphasizes theoretical and methodological discussions on the cultural nature of human psychological phenomena, moving on to show how meaning is a natural feature of action and how it eventually produces conventional symbols for communication. Such symbols shape individual experiences and create the conditions for consciousness and the self to emerge; turn social norms into ethics; and set history into motion.

Jaan Valsiner is a cultural psychologist with a consistently developmental axiomatic base that is brought to analyses of any psychological or social phenomenon. He is the founding editor (1995) of the journal *Culture & Psychology*. He is currently professor of psychology in the Department of Psychology at Clark University. He has published many books, the most recent of which are *The Guided Mind* (1998), *Culture and Human Development* (2000), and *Comparative Study of Human Cultural Development* (2001). He edited (with Kevin Connolly) the *Handbook of Developmental Psychology* (2003). He established the new journal on individual case analyses, *International Journal of Idiographic Science* (2005), and is the editor of *Integrative Psychological and Behavioral Sciences* and *From Past to Future: Annals of Innovations in Psychology* (2007). In 1995, he was awarded the Alexander von Humboldt Prize in Germany for his interdisciplinary work on human development. He has been a visiting professor in Australia, Brazil, Estonia, Germany, Italy, Japan, the Netherlands, and the United Kingdom.

Alberto Rosa is professor of psychology at the Universidad Autonoma de Madrid. He is a member of the Sociedad Espanola de Historia de la Psicologia and the International Society for Cultural and Activity Research, and he has served as vice president for the latter since 2005. In 1987, the Spanish Ministry of Labour and Social Affairs awarded him the Second National Award for research and technical aids to the handicapped. He has taught courses in Argentina, Brazil, Chile, Colombia, Italy, Mexico, and Sweden.

The Cambridge Handbook of Sociocultural Psychology

Edited by

JAAN VALSINER

Clark University

and

ALBERTO ROSA

Universidad Autonoma de Madrid

CAMBRIDGE
UNIVERSITY PRESS

CAMBRIDGE UNIVERSITY PRESS
Cambridge, New York, Melbourne, Madrid, Cape Town, Singapore, São Paulo

Cambridge University Press
32 Avenue of the Americas, New York, NY 10013-2473, USA

www.cambridge.org
Information on this title: www.cambridge.org/9780521854108

First published 2007

Printed in the United States of America

A catalog record for this publication is available from the British Library.

Library of Congress Cataloging in Publication Data

The Cambridge handbook of sociocultural psychology / edited by Jaan
Valsiner, Alberto Rosa.
    p.   cm.
Includes bibliographical references and index.
ISBN-13: 978-0-521-85410-8 (hardback)
ISBN-10: 0-521-85410-5 (hardback)
ISBN-13: 978-0-521-67005-0 (pbk.)
ISBN-10: 0-521-67005-5 (pbk.)
1. Social psychology.   2. Culture.   I. Valsiner, Jaan.   II. Rosa, Alberto.
HM1033.C34   2007
306.01–dc22   2006034612

ISBN   978-0-521-85410-8 hardback
ISBN   978-0-521-67005-0 paperback

Contents

Preface

It is taken for granted that any existing disciplinary field must have handbooks readily available for its students and researchers. This is the first *Handbook of Sociocultural Psychology* to appear with such a title, and so its appearance acts as a sort of landmark for its official constitution as a field. But no volume can give birth to an area of research, at the most it can only signal the crossing of a threshold. When shaping such a volume what the editors do is to surf above the agitated surface of disciplinary tides, making figures which make apparent the force of waves of researchers who have been gathering strength from a long time effort.

Social and cultural life are indissociable from the threads which make up the fabric of the human *Psyche*. The very forefathers of Psychology did not fail in acknowledging this. However, their early insights and contributions were left aside from the mainstream of a fast-growing Psychology. Psychology was quick in recognizing Psyche's biological and social roots but took its time in setting itself into the inquiry of how culture shapes human psychological processes and how cultural change (History) leaves its traces on the working of the mind.

As in any other up-growing contemporary disciplinary field, Socio-Cultural Psychology was a curiosity – it branched out of many traditions of research and received many names. Most of them gather the adjectives Folk, Cultural, Social, and Historical besides the name Psychology in different combinations. Whatever way one chooses to call it, there was always a common concern for the psychological study of distinctly human psychological phenomena, but without losing sight that human phenomena are themselves always also natural and biological.

The very nature of the research field of Sociocultural Psychology makes it a branch of the psychological sciences that continuously needs to cross the disciplinary borders and to collaborate with the social sciences and the humanities. So, to call for a specialised field of Sociocultural Psychology is a sort of oxymoron. Sociocultural Psychology cannot leave aside anything that is human; its challenge is to address its complexity and provide tools for its explanation and understanding. Sociocultural Psychology is both a field of Psychology and a cross-disciplinary endeavour. That is why empirical work has always to be hand in hand with a theoretical concern always shuttling across disciplinary boundaries. Vygotsky's claim for a general psychology was an early demand for not losing sight of the complexity of the task when going into a particular research project.

A handbook always attempts to present as completely as possible the field it covers by gathering significant contributions. This has to be done by selecting topics and authors so that a *Gestalt* of the state of the field can be made to appear. This no doubt is a result of the choosing of the editors who, when so doing, are making an interpretation of the past and present of the discipline, but also cast a message conveying their view about promising possible future developments of the field. An argument, running through the volume as a whole, so arises. And, as it could not be otherwise, sketches a structure of sub-areas, hints to continuities, but also makes apparent gaps and inconsistencies which signal challenges to the future. The result is a figure arising from a patchwork better or not as well knitted together. It is the contrast between figures and the background provided by the other figures which makes the dynamics of the field to exist and set the ground for the dialogues which keep together the common endeavor of the community of researchers, so that the field keeps continuously on the move.

A dynamic disciplinary field arises because of socio-cultural interests on the study of some kind of phenomena. A community of knowledge develops around the cultivation of these interests. This community maps the domain, and when exploring it lays out a network of methods, of paths, crisscrossing the field and so making possible to transit from some regions to others. But roads should not be confused with the landscape. They just scrub on its surface and may leave aside blank spaces in the map, sometimes so much ignored that may not even have the mark *terra ignota* written upon

them. A community of researchers should not be confused with a corporation of logistics only concerned with fast transportation through well-paved roads, so that goods can be speedily made available to the destination market. Researchers are explorers, not caravaneers. If they keep together along well-trodden paths, celebrating being together when traveling, they may enjoy themselves, but they would not make much service to the expansion of knowledge of the field. Orthodoxies may have some advantages when penetrating in a foreign field but can become a deleterious trap when one wants to go deeper into it. An advised traveler pays more attention to the landscape than to the road. But when doing so, a price has to be paid: either one travels slowly paying homage to the rules of the road, or one may crash. When so doing, one behaves as a sort of tourist, taking pictures which are very much like postcards already available in kiosks. The real thrill is in leaving the road, making new paths as moving on the land. But this also has a price. The journey is uncertain and solitary, one may get lost, and perhaps nobody else would find interesting to visit that part of the realm, so that no road (method) would ever be developed to cross through it. Researchers have to balance between getting credit from moving fast along the communication lines for the commerce of knowledge (orthodoxies) and the more risky business of opening new vistas on the phenomena to study.

The authors here gathered are explorers and road builders so the knowledge they produce could be shared. Some are well seasoned and enjoy ample credit, but all of them together, when sharing with us their views, make us contemplate a vista of directions to explore and feel invited to use their methods to go further ahead in our journey. They together form a variegated company coming from different corners of the world, engaged in exploring their disciplinary areas, speaking many different languages, always attentive to what is going on beyond their immediate neighborhood, and eager to enter into dialogue with the others. They were enthusiastic in joining this common enterprise and made the editors feel obliged to them for making the task of putting together this volume both a challenge and a pleasure.

This handbook, as any other human enterprise, has its own history. Its birth was summoned by Philip Laughlin who – with Cambridge University Press – foresaw the actuality of the area and suggested that the time had come to set up the field with a definitive handbook. Eric Schwartz followed Philip in equally enthusiastic support.

We are also deeply grateful for the careful management of the production of the book by Peter Katsirubas, of Aptara, Inc., whose detailed suggestions and work with high-quality copy editors made the editing process a great pleasure. A team of enthusiastic assistants also participated in the editing process. Ignacio Brescó, Marcela Lonchuk, Tomás Sánchez-Criado, Irina Rasskin, and Silviana Rubio dealt with the tedious task of checking references and manuscripts.

Contributors

EMILY ABBEY
Department of Psychology, Box 38A
College of the Holy Cross
1 College Street
Worcester, MA 01610, USA
EAbbey@holycross.edu

AMELIA ÁLVAREZ
Universidad Carlos III de Madrid
Facultad de Humanidades, Comunicación y
    Documentación
Madrid 133
28093 Getafe, Madrid, Spain
amelia.alvarez@uc3m.es

KATIA S. AMORIM
Faculdade de Filosofia Ciências e
    Letras
de Ribeirão Preto – USP
Avenida Bandeirantes, 3900
14.040-901 Ribeirão Preto (São Paulo),
    Brazil
katiamorim@ffclrp.com.br

AYUMU ARAKAWA
Law School
Nagoya University

Furo-cho, Chikusa-ku, Nagoya City, Aichi
    Prefecture
464-8601, Japan
arakawa12a@hotmail.com

GUGLIELMO BELLELLI
Dipartimento di Psicologia
Università di Bari
Palazzo Ateneo
Piazza Umberto I, 1,
I-70100 Bari, Italia
g.bellelli@psico.uniba.it

SHOSHANA BLUM-KULKA
Department of Communication and
    Journalism
Hebrew University of Jerusalem
IL- 91905 Jerusalem 91905,
    Israel
Shoshana.blum-kulka@huji.ac.il

STEVEN D. BROWN
Department of Human Sciences
Loughborough University
Loughborough, LE11 3TU,
    Great Britain
S.D.Brown@lboro.ac.uk

MARIA ALBURQUERQUE CANDELA
School of Education
University of Delaware
Newark, DE 19716, USA
mariacandela@gmx.net

JORGE CASTRO-TEJERINA
Facultad de Psicología
Universidad Nacional de Educación a
    Distancia
Juan del Rosal, 10
Ciudad Universitaria
ES-28040 Madrid, Spain
jorge.castro@psi.uned.es

NANDITA CHAUDHARY
Department of Child Development
Lady Irwin College
Sikandra Road
New Delhi – 110001, India
nanditachau@rediffmail.com

SANG-CHIN CHOI
Department of Psychology
Chung-Ang University
Seoul, Korea
choi@cau.ac.kr

MICHAEL COLE
Laboratory of Comparative Human
    Cognition
University of California, San Diego
    9500 Gilman Drive,
La Jolla, CA 92093,
    USA
mcole@weber.ucsd.edu

WILLIAM A. CORSARO
Department of Sociology
Indiana University
Ballantine Hall 744
1020 East Kirkwood Avenue
Bloomington, IN 47405-7103,
    USA
corsaro@indiana.edu

ALAN COSTALL
Department of Psychology
University of Portsmouth
Portsmouth, PO1 2DY, England
alan.costall@port.ac.uk

ANTONIETTA CURCI
Dipartimento di Psicologia
Università di Bari
Palazzo Ateneo
Piazza Umberto I, 1
I-70100 Bari, Italia
a.curcci@psico.uniba.it

AGNES E. DODDS
Medical Education Unit
Faculty of Medicine, Dentistry &
    Health Sciences
The University of Melbourne
Melbourne Vic 3010, Australia
agnesed@unimelb.edu.au

GERARD DUVEEN
Department of Social and Developmental
    Psychology
Faculty of Social and Political Sciences
University of Cambridge
Free School Lane
Cambridge CB2 3RQ, Great Britain
gmd10@cam.ac.uk

YRJÖ ENGESTRÖM
Center for Activity Theory and
    Developmental Work Research
P.O. Box 26
00014 University of Helsinki
Finland
yrjo.engestrom@helsinki.fi

SILVIA ESPAÑOL
Instituto de Investigaciones
Facultad de Psicología
Universidad de Buenos Aires
Av. Independencia 3065 3°
Capital Federal (cp:C1225AAM)
República Argentina
silviaes@psi.uba.ar

WILLIAM MINTZ FIELDS
Great Ape Trust of Iowa
4200 SE 44th Avenue Des Moines,
    IA 50320, USA
panbanisha@aol.com

ALEX GILLESPIE
Department of Psychology
University of Stirling
Stirling, FK9 4LA, Scotland
alex.gillespie@stir.ac.uk

MIGUEL GONÇALVES
Department of Psychology
University of Minho
4710 Braga
Portugal
mgoncalves@iep.uminho.pt

MICHAL HAMO
Department of Communication and
    Journalism
Hebrew University of Jerusalem
IL- 91905 Jerusalem 91905, Israel

GYUSEOG HAN
Department of Psychology
Chonnam National University
Gwangju, S. Korea
ghan@chonnam.ac.kr

ULF HEDETOFT
Director of the Saxo Institute of
History, Ethnology, Archaeology
Faculty of Humanities
University of Copenhagen, Denmark
Hedetoft@ihis.aau.dk

SOPHIE HENGL
Faculty of Psychology
University of Vienna
Liebiggasse 5
A-1010 Vienna, Austria
s.hengl@gmx.net

BERIT O. JOHANNESEN
Department of Psychology
Norwegian University of Science and
    Technology
NO-7491Trondheim, Norway
Berit.johannesen@svt.ntnu.no

KATHRYN A. KAVULICH
Department of Psychology
White Gravenor Building, 3rd floor
Georgetown University
Washington, DC 20057, USA

AYAE KIDO
Faculty of Education
Kyoto University
Yoshida-honmachi, Sakyo-ku, Kyoto-city
Kyoto, 606-8501, Japan
mi_chu_chu_lm@yahoo.co.jp

CHUNG-WOON KIM
Department of Leisure Studies
Myongji University
Seoul, Korea
cwkim@mju.ac.kr

JEANETTE A. LAWRENCE
School of Behavioural Science
The University of Melbourne
Melbourne Vic 3010, Australia
lawrence@unimelb.edu.au

GIOVANNA LEONE
Dipartimento di Sociologia e
    Comunicazione
Università di Roma La Sapienza
Via Salaria, 113
I-00198 Roma, Italia
giovanna.leone@uniroma1.it

KEREN LILU
School of Education
University of Delaware
Newark, DE 19716, USA
k_lilu@hotmail.com

EUGENE MATUSOV
School of Education
University of Delaware
Newark, DE 19716, USA
ematusov@udel.edu

DAVID MIDDLETON
Department of Human Sciences
Loughborough University
Loughborough, LE11 3TU, Great Britain
D.J.Middleton@lboro.ac.uk

HAZIME MIZOGUCHI
Faculty of Social Welfare
Rissho University
1700 Magechi Kumagaya-city
Saitama, 360-0194, Japan
hazime@ris.ac.jp

FATHALI M. MOGHADDAM
Department of Psychology
White Gravenor Building, 3rd floor
Georgetown University
Washington, DC 20057, USA
moghaddf@georgetown.edu

Piero Paolicchi
Dipartimento di Scienze Sociali
Università di Pisa
Via S. Maria 46
I-56126 Pisa, Italy
paolicchi@dss.unipi.it

Adolfo Perinat
Universidad Autónoma de Barcelona
Facultad de Psicología
Dptoo Psicología Básica, Evolutiva y de la
    Educación
Campus de Bellaterra
ES-08193 Bellaterra, Barcelona, Spain
adolf.perinat@uab.es

Pablo del Río
Universidad Carlos III de Madrid
Facultad de Humanidades, Comunicación y
    Documentación
Madrid 133
28093 Getafe, Madrid, Spain
prio@hum.uc3m.es

Cintia Rodríguez
Universidad Autónoma de Madrid
Facultad de Formación de Profesorado y
    Educación
Cantoblanco
ES-28049 Madrid, Spain
cintia.rodriguez@uam.es

Alberto Rosa
Dpto. de Psicología Básica
Facultad de Psicología
Universidad Autónoma de Madrid
Cantoblanco
ES-28049 Madrid, Spain
alberto.rosa@uam.es

M. Clotilde Rossetti-Ferreira
Faculdade de Filosofia Ciências e Letras
de Ribeirão Preto – USP
Avenida Bandeirantes, 3900
14.040-901 Ribeirão Preto (São Paulo),
    Brazil
mcrferre@usp.br

João Salgado
Instituto Superior da Maia
Av. Carlos Oliveira Campos
4475-695 Avioso S. Pedro
Portugal
jsalgado@ismai.pt

Tatsuya Sato
Department of Psychology
Ritsumeikan University
56-1 Toji-in Kitamachi, Kita-ku,
Kyoto 603-8577 Japan
satot@lt.ritsumei.ac.jp

E. Sue Savage-Rumbaugh
Great Ape Trust of Iowa
4200 SE 44th Avenue
Des Moines, IA 50321, USA
ssavage-rumbaugh@greatanetrust.org

Pär Segerdahl
Centre for Bioethics
Faculty of Philosophy
Uppsala University
SE-75185 Uppsala, Sweden
Par.Segerdahl@bioethics.uu.se

Jordi Serrallonga
HOMINID Human Origins Group
Science Park of Barcelona
Universitat de Barcelona
C/ Adolf Florensa 8
ES-08028 Barcelona, Spain
jserrallonga@ub.edu

Ana Paula S. Silva
Faculdade de Filosofia Ciências e Letras
de Ribeirão Preto – USP
Avenida Bandeirantes, 3900
14.040-901 Ribeirão Preto (São Paulo),
    Brazil

Thomas Slunecko
Faculty of Psychology,
University of Vienna
Liebiggasse 5
A-1010 Vienna, Austria
thomas.slunecko@univie.ac.at

Mark Smith
School of Education
University of Delaware
Newark, DE 19716, USA
mpsmith@UDel.Edu

Noboru Takahashi
Osaka Kyoiku University
Osaka, Japan

David Travieso
Dpto. de Psicología Básica
Facultad de Psicología
Universidad Autónoma de Madrid
Cantoblanco
ES-28049 Madrid, Spain
david.travieso@uam.es

Jaan Valsiner
Frances L. Hyatt School of
    Psychology
Clark University
950 Main Street
Worcester, MA 01610, USA
jvalsiner@clarku.edu

James V. Wertsch
Department of Anthropology
Washington University
St. Louis, MO 63130, USA
jwertsch@wustl.edu

Toshiya Yamamoto
Maebashi Kyoai Gakuen College
1154-4, Koyahara
379-2192 Maebashi, Gunma, Japan
HAE00142@nifty.com

Yuko Yasuda
Faculty of Education
Kyoto University
Yoshida-honmachi, Sakyo-ku,
    Kyoto-city
Kyoto, 606-8501, Japan
yuko-y@kcat.zaq.ne.jp

Tania Zittoun
Institut de Psychologie
Université de Lausanne
Anthropole
CH-1015 Lausanne
Switzerland
Tania.Zittoun@unil.ch

The Cambridge Handbook of Sociocultural Psychology

Contemporary Socio-Cultural Research

Uniting Culture, Society, and Psychology

Jaan Valsiner and Alberto Rosa

An area of knowledge creation can be said to come of age when it becomes integrated through publishing a handbook. The readers are the beneficiaries of that act, initiated by the Cambridge University Press in recognition of the vastly growing and socially important area. The world is filled with symbolic places in relation to which meaningful actions – tourist trips, pilgrimages, homecomings, war efforts, and the like – are undertaken. New cultural places and myths of their meanings are constructed. Countries as well as spouses quarrel about resources, rights of access to them, and public images. Persons feel sad, angry, or jealous in culturally constrained and personally escalated ways. Our human world, in short, is a culturally constituted world of the relationship of the human species with their constantly re-constructed environments.

Since the end of the 1980s, one can observe rapid development of a synthesis of psychology, anthropology, sociology, history, and medical sciences in the field that has become labeled *socio-cultural psychology*. The roots of this new perspective are deeply in the fertile grounds of every-

day social reality. Socio-cultural psychology deals with psychological phenomena that happen because of the socio-cultural aspects of human lives in varied social contexts – peace or war, famine or purposeful avoidance of overweight by dieting, poverty, or affluence. This makes socio-cultural psychology to be a part of human psychology. In parallel, the proliferation of the branch of the social sciences called *cultural studies* has proliferated. As all quickly developing areas, socio-cultural psychology is in need of consolidation of its expertise and creating a solid base for its further development. This Handbook is meant to accomplish these functions.

This present recognition of the area has burgeoning recent history The pioneering effort in the initial promoting of the field was a series of conferences on Socio-Cultural studies (1992 in Madrid, 1996 in Geneva, and 2000 in Campinas), as well as the establishment of the journal *Culture & Psychology* in 1995 (Valsiner, 2001). In its original development, the field of Socio-Cultural Studies was built on the initiatives of Spanish researchers in collaboration with colleagues

1

all over the World (Rosa & Valsiner, 1994; Wertsch & Ramírez, 1994; Mercer & Coll, 1994; Álvarez & del Río, 1994; Wertsch, del Río & Álvarez, 1995). The field of cultural psychology was developed in parallel both in Europe (Boesch, 1989, 1991; Eckensberger, 1995, 1997) and in North America (Cole, 1990, 1996; Rogoff, 1990, 2003; Shweder, 1990; Shweder & Sullivan, 1990; Wertsch, 1991) and is notably interdisciplinary in its focus. No surprise, given such cosmopolitan history, that the present Handbook is profoundly international,[1] with a slightly Mediterranean accent. Added to it is the notable activity theory movement that since 1960s has proliferated in former Soviet Union, East Germany, Denmark, and other European countries and has led to the establishment of ISCAR – and we can see how the socio-cultural perspective has become a prominent force in contemporary social sciences.

Why Such Complex Term – *Socio-Cultural* Psychology?

Why invent (yet another) hyphenated term in the already labels-rich field of the social sciences? General labels that present an area of knowledge are means of communication with others – outsiders to the field – who are expected to provide an audience to the ideas covered by the label (and, of course, social and economic support for the promoters of that label). The new label presents the synthesis of sociological ("socio-...") and anthropological ("...-cultural") research traditions with those of psychology. However, the label is as generally vague as its constituents on both sides of the unifying hyphen.

Culture is a term that operates easily at the common language level of discourse, but proves difficult to define as a scientific term. Kroeber and Kluckhohn (1952) listed 164 definitions, and since then the number of yet other nuanced definitions of the term has further increased. Culture has traditionally been the subject matter of anthropology.

Yet, ironically, it is precisely at the time – 1990s – when psychology re-discovers culture – that cultural anthropology becomes skeptical of the theoretical value of that concept. Likewise, the general notion of "society" in sociology is an imprecise term that unifies many researchers in their direction of focus – but has no explanatory value (Valsiner, 2007).

Psychology is the science of ambiguous kind. It is on the one hand oriented to the study of mental processes (which are most directly accessible in the *Homo sapiens* in contrast to other species), and its effort to make sense of other species have regularly relied on the focus on behavior. As human psychological functions are a result of cultural history intertwined with phylogeny of the species, we can observe some of such phenomena in some other animal species. At the same time, the long process of emergence of human psychological functions in the history of the species is not directly accessible to our investigation. Instead, psychology usually deals with the already emerged forms of the conduct of our contemporary representatives of Homo sapiens. They are fully social – in the sense of their dependence upon the social contexts they create for themselves. Yet they are simultaneously uniquely personal – subjective, affective, and individually goals-oriented.

There is little doubt that speaking, communicating, and higher forms of reasoning, remembering and attending cannot be understood without taking into account social life and, in the case of humans, also show the consequence of the use of cultural devices. But, what about human feeling, perceiving, desiring, performing motor acts and all other forms of behavior? Where can we draw the boundaries between the natural and the cultural? Or – do we need to make such distinction at all? How can this new direction in research build up its conceptual framework that can open new methodological directions for the social sciences? The very frequently uttered (and "politically correct") notion of interdisciplinary nature of sciences would remain an empty phrase unless such new directions are created.

Directions of Inquiry in Socio-Cultural Psychology

Psychology is no longer a juvenile science with a long history in philosophical thought – as Ebbinghaus once claimed. It is a matron science well past its first century of life, and besides all its cyclical ailments, enjoys a very good health, if one looks at its institutional grounding. And – as we show in Chapter 1 – it is also a bastard science that was born as an illegitimate baby to a tumultuous and temporary union of philosophy and *Naturwissenschaften* in the 1870s.

Psychology has of course led to recurrent deconstruction efforts of its theoretical core, as well as to various efforts to eliminate the discipline by downward (to physiology, or genetics) and upward (to texts, cultural models) reductionism. It is certainly not too difficult to eliminate a science by denial of its object of investigation – the *Psyche*. Yet it is clear (see Chapter 1) that reductionist sentiments cannot win in psychology – they can only slow down its development. If a parallel is worthwhile making – psychology in the 21st century can be in a state similar to 17th century chemistry, where painstaking work led to slow replacement of alchemy by science. Much of contemporary psychology – especially in its applied side of "prediction of future" by test scores, and the mystiques of therapies, resembles the actions of alchemists.

However, matters may be different if one looks inside and try to look for what Vygotsky (1926) called "the skeleton" – the core concepts and methods that make sense of the phenomena observed. It is this internal theoretical structure – that acts in a science as analogs of the bones, joints, and muscles – which make it possible to keep upright and move with grace in order to display its products in an intelligible discourse able to describe and explain, with an acceptable level of accuracy, what is going on in real-

ity. This aesthetics of scientific explanation is similar to Einstein's ways of relating his theory with the experimental evidence – instead of the crude accountant's belief in the accumulation of "the data" solving our problems, it is the sheer elegance of crucial empirical evidence that forces the theory constructor to ask for specific empirical studies.

Vygotsky's metaphor – and Einstein's credo – are not easily applicable to the current social sciences where *methodlatry* is still in fashion. It protects itself – it is no longer the case – that once methodological parlance is removed, the knowledge offered collapses in a mass without shape, as happens in mollusks (once their external skeleton is removed). Psychology has devised many methods (often presented as "standardized") and created many constructs as well as developed many applied techniques that are put in use in many different areas of modern life. If their use in social practices proves their adequacy then the selection notion ("survival of the fittest") is put to its ultimate test since it stops further invention.

The Conceptual Map of Socio-Cultural Psychology

The family of perspectives to which the label *socio-cultural* is currently being applied is a result of various historical dialogues within psychology, sociology, and anthropology. Hence it is not a theoretically coherent group, but rather heterogeneous kind. It looks as if it is unified as a concept – yet it is actually a conglomerate of similar, yet not mutually coherent, perspectives (see Slunecko & Hengl, Chapter 2). Their unity comes through their contrast with non-social (individual-specific, or subjective) ways of looking at human beings. The emphasis on "the social" permeates the discourses about "the individual," or "the *Psyche*" (see Chapter 1). Focus on language – which unites persons into language communities – is often taken as the basic human defining feature that is both personal and social at the same time.

Within the complex of the socio-cultural approach, we can distinguish a number of directions:

1. The discursive/conversational tradition (see Castro & Rosa, Chapter 3). This tradition can be viewed as operating at different levels of generality – from macro-social (different discourse types present, or developing, in the history of the given society) to micro-social (analyses of specific discursive phrasing of issues in everyday talk or interview transcripts – see Edwards, 1997). The analysis of conversations – of interpersonal moves using language for particular purposes – borders on this discursive complex (see Hamo and Blum-Kulka, Chapter 20);

2. The semiotic mediational approach. Here the focus is in the construction and use of meanings – created or adopted. Its nearest neighbors are the tradition of social representation (see Slunecko & Hengl, Chapter 2, and Duveen, Chapter 26) and the focus on dialogical nature of the self (see Salgado & Gonçalves, Chapter 30). Simultaneously, the tradition of social representing is a bridge to the macro-social discursive *foci*.

3. The activity tradition. While the previous perspectives emphasized the cultural embeddedness and constructivity of the *Psyche*, the activity-theoretic perspectives focus on the direct mutuality of the persons and their socially organized settings (see Cole & Engeström, Chapter 23). Of course, the action environments of human beings (as well as primates kept in humanized conditions – see Fields et al., Chapter 8) include semiotically marked areas and objects, and people do talking during their acting (as captured by the micro-discursive approach). The symbolic action theory of Ernst Boesch has for decades united the activity and semiotic perspectives (Boesch, 1993, 1997, 2005).

4. The evolutionary readings of cultural histories. Our contemporary psychology is increasingly infested by stories told about how it might be that we as Homo sapiens became as we now are – attached to TV screens, eating freedom fries, and worrying about almost anything we can worry about. Of course the use of evolutionary psychology's explanation of how higher functions of the *Psyche* emerged includes substantial involvement of literary cheating – the stories told need to be not just plausible but also shocking. Yet when the excesses of evolutionary journalism are overlooked, the issue of emergence of cultural meanings and action tools in specific ecological conditions is a necessary and productive sub-field of the socio-cultural research field (see Serrallonga, Chapter 9).

Does this mean that all provinces of psychology belong to the realm of socio-cultural psychology? We believe this is not the case. The study of perceptual illusions, psychophysics, and some forms of learning – to mention just a few examples – do not need to take into account the socio-cultural as a part the phenomena under study. Even if perceptual processes may be fully immersed within the field of symbolic stimuli of cultural kind – like national flags or costumes at festivals – psychology as a whole cannot be lost in the sea of socio-cultural psychology. The type of explanation to offer to these basic psychological phenomena has to be devised in such a way that it can permit a developmental explanation of the transitions between natural basic phenomena and the higher psychological functions of intentionality, without the need of falling in the Scilla of reductionism, or the Caribdis of dualism (for a more detailed argument, see Travieso, Chapter 6).

The reality of all complex biological, social, and biological systems entails the emergence, maintenance, and (at times) demolishing of hierarchical regulatory systems. In case of human psychology it is the capability for willful, intentional actions that is crucial for human living. We experience as we try to move towards some objectives of the future, and may try again, and again – while creating stories in the middle of the ongoing processes of failing to reach our utopias. These stories give color to our striving – experience is movement towards the (yet) unknown on the basis of our narrated personal histories.

Cultural Experiencing of Social Worlds

A theme that multiple authors in this Handbook touch upon is the centrality of human experiencing of the world. Socio-cultural psychology specifically deals with the psychological phenomena that result from the interpretation of experience, and so it deals with meaning-making, the co-construction of knowledge and its keeping and transformation along time. So – there exists a socio-cultural domain that can be distinguished from other psychological phenomena – and that can be investigated in its own right. These phenomena of the socio-cultural domain cut across the boundaries of what currently are diverse psychological sub-disciplinary fields. Thus, we take socio-cultural psychology to be both a part of psychology devoted to the study of psychological phenomena, and a way of going into new ways of doing psychological research. It is neither a separate discipline, nor has it any imperial claims over the rest of psychology.

What is more, socio-cultural research goes well beyond the limits of psychology, penetrating in the field of the social sciences and the Humanities. Socio-cultural psychology dwells in a sort of hinterland between the natural and the cultural. Or, to be more precise, it deals with matter and also with the spirit, or, if we want to exorcise such dangerous word, with that thing German idealists called *Geist* (spirit). As German was the first language within which psychological issues became discussed, the role of the contrast between *Geist* and *Seele* (soul) is of importance. The "spirit" is immaterial – it is not a thing, an entity. It is a process of experiencing our relations with our worlds.

Psychological experiences – not encoded in terms of either "soul" or "spirit" – exist in different animal species, as the so-called instinct of "curiosity" allows us to observe. The impulse to finding out what kind of

thing something "is," and that also produces "surprise" or "fear" when it is found out that has been misunderstood for another, that a mistake has been made. Earliest emergence of sign-mediated relations with the environment can be non-linguistic, yet crucial for living (von Uexküll, 1982; see also Fields et al., Chapter 9). This same phenomenon of mediation of experience takes a different shape in humans. It may make one to understand what words such as "justice," "freedom," or "loyalty" refer to; or what to be Christian, Muslim, Japanese, or member of a class or group "means," to what standards of virtue, honor, decency, or ethics has one to stand up to. Or, referring to more down to earth matters, how to make sense of what is going on in a ritual, or how to understand the movements and sayings of an unfamiliar person coming from a distant culture whose etiquette is unknown to us.

Socio-Cultural Psychology – Its Past, and Needs

It may be relevant to note that Psychology became first institutionalized as a Science of the Spirit, as a *Geisteswissenschaft*. Official histories of Psychology usually fail to tell that the first chair of Psychology (that bore the title of *Völkerpsychologie*) was created in 1860 at the University of Bern for Moritz Lazarus (Jahoda, 1993). He was also the editor – together with Heyman Steinthal – of a journal with the same title, that survived until the beginning of the 20th century. As it is well known *Völkerpsychologie* was also in the title of a series of books written by Wilhelm Wundt (1900–1920). The thematic areas of our present-day socio-cultural psychology were covered a century ago by folk psychology and language studies, as well as by ethnology.

As history tells, the new – calling itself "scientific" – psychology started from experiments on psychological phenomena carried out in physiological laboratories from the 1860s onwards. Wundt's *Grundzüge der Physiologische Psychologie* (1st edition 1873) set the ground for the development of experimental psychology, that was already announced by Hermann Lotze's *Medizinische Psychologie, oder Physiologie der Seele* (1852). For Wundt, Experimental Psychology was a natural science (*Naturwissenschaft*), but never thought that the psychological realm could be exhausted by the use of this approach. He agreed with Lazarus, and also with Wilhelm Dilthey, that it also had to be a "science of the spirit" (*Geisteswissenschaft*). He also went into the pains of offering some epistemological guidance (*Logik*, 1883, 1908) of how to transit from one kind of explanation to another (Jahoda, 1993). It could be said that since these times psychology has failed to integrate the *Naturwissenschaft* focus of its basics with the specifically higher-order phenomena of the *Geisteswissenschaft* kind. The latter were prominently kept in focus by the line of psychological thought that proceeded through the work of Franz Brentano.

THE PROBLEM OF CONSCIOUSNESS

It is usually in the case of phenomena of consciousness that the integration between these two approaches has traditionally failed. Consciousness is the most central of psychological phenomena. No science could exist without empirical verification, and empirical experience is the product of the processes that produce consciousness. These processes are the result of the movements of a natural being in its environment. Conversely, subjects' behavior cannot be studied without the empirical experience of the observer. Since both, subjects and observers, are human subjects a sort of tautology seems to appear. Unless consciousness already exists, the study of consciousness (of the others, or of one's own) is not possible.

EVOLUTIONARY THOUGHT AND UNDERSTANDING CULTURE

Darwinism understood humanity as a product of biological evolution (Fernández, 2005; Richards, 1987, 2002). William James's pragmatism applied to psychology a Darwinian approach and set the ground for an evolutionary psychology that attempted to explain all psychological phenomena

from biological principles, as Thorndike, Woodworth and the Chicago functionalists started to do. Instincts, drives, and motives came forward as devices for the explanation of intentions and meaning (see Danziger, 1985, 1990, 1997). Later on behaviorism resorted to conditional and associative reflexes, the Law of Effect, or a combination of both, to explain how biological needs were the basis upon which social values were learnt, and how the two together could account for the explanation of goal-directed behavior – that was how meaning was portrayed in its more extreme mechanistic views.

Evolutionism had widespread effects on the sciences, psychology, and culture at large. One of them was the development of a new way of understanding the structure and functioning of the nervous system, where psychological functions were taken as having its origin. A British physician, John Hughlings-Jackson, mediated in the polemic between locationists and anti-locationists, offering an evolutionary view of its structure and functioning. This view set the stage for the development of new conceptions such as those of schema (Henry Head, 1926; Bartlett, 1932), and functional organs and functional systems, developed in Russia by Piotr Anokhin (1964) and Alexander Luria.

DUALISMS (AND FIGHT AGAINST THEM) AS EPISTEMOLOGICAL IMPASSES

For quite a long time psychology seemed to be caught in a quandary. It looked as if it had to opt for one kind of explanation *or* another. There was a self-imposed choice – whether to be devoted to the understanding or the vital experiences of individuals, or to discover general laws. The former choice was aimed at understanding particular individuals, leaving aside any attempt of general explanation. The second led to the search for universal explanatory principles that would account for all of the observable behavior. Making choices between these options led psychology to no new solutions – as the inter-individual variability in the empirical domain made it impossible to inductively arrive at generalizations, and the in-depth understanding of the single cases were not expected to provide general knowledge.

As is the case with many *impasses* in science, it is the creation of mutually exclusive opposite categories – "body" *versus* "mind", or "singular" *versus* "general" – that block the road to substantive discovery. It is more than ironic that heated disputes against "dualisms" in psychology recur – insisting usually upon one or another kind of monologic reduction of the complexity to one preferred causal entity (e.g., "person" *or* "the environment," "genes" *or* "the society," etc.) – while it is axiomatically obvious that all psychological phenomena are in principle possible only through the constant process of relating with the environment (i.e., are open systems). Hence, we can consider "the mind" as a generic counterpart of a relation to "the body" – it is the latter that makes all the phenomena of "the mind" possible, as well as becomes modified itself through the vicissitudes of "the mind" as the experiences of anorexics, ascetics, and committers of suicide demonstrate. The "body/mind dualism" is therefore an axiomatic impasse for psychology, while its systemic alternative – *duality* of "the body" and "the mind" as parts of the same whole – could lead to new conceptualizations.

A similar transposition of the opposition idiographic <> nomothetic is in order. Generality of knowledge in psychology is obtainable through the study of particular cases in their systemic organization (Molenaar, 2004; Valsiner, 2006). The fruitful beginning of differential psychology as part of general investigation (Stern, 1911, 1935) has eroded over the last hundred years to become a field of indiscriminate "study of individual differences". A synthesis of the study of unique phenomena in conjunction with general theoretical goals provides us a new version of science – idiographic science (Molenaar & Valsiner, 2005) – that transcends the "*either* general *or* particular" ethos of the previous dichotomy. Dualisms of all kinds are obstacles for science – but so are also fights against dualisms that deny the dualities embedded in systemic parts <> whole relations.

THE PROBLEM OF MEANING – BETWEEN PARTS AND THE WHOLE

Meaning was the hard nut to crack if one were to bridge the Cartesian abysm. And so it was repeatedly attempted by some. *Geist* had to be the result of what happened in the body as a consequence of its encounters with the rest of the world. If these encounters produced sensations and feelings, these had to be either associated, or in some mysterious ways combined (e.g., Wundt's *creative synthesis* and *apperception*) to account for the appearance of abstract ideas or new understandings and thoughts.

Not surprisingly this explanation did not satisfy many, and new approaches were attempted. Action theory enthusiasts – the newest generation of whom one finds also well represented in this Handbook – emphasize the unity of experience. That unity is a form – a dynamic one. Following the course traced by Franz Brentano, Carl Stumpf, Hans Cornelius, and Christian von Ehrenfels advanced the discourse about *Gestaltqualität*. Form, irrespectively of its sensory qualities, keeps being perceived as the same, as it happens when a melody changes pitch, when every one of the sounds that together make the melody, are changed, but the mutual relationship among them keeps constant. In order to explaining this phenomenon, two directions in holistic psychology developed.

First, there were the different Gestalt traditions – the Berlin-based Gestalt Psychology, and Leipzig-based *Ganzheitspsychologie* (Diriwächter & Valsiner, 2007) – where scientists started to think in terms of structuring fields – and borrowing elements of physics, referred to forces, valences, and dynamic equilibria within the field of consciousness, which was taken to be isomorphic with the material/external realm. So, understanding, insights and coming to terms with the encounters with the world, were results of reaching a balanced stable equilibrium. Meaning was a result of this underlying process analogous to physical phenomena. It appeared as a sudden insight of understanding how to act – hence broke the equilibrium – to be embedded in new ones. In contrast, the "Austrian school" of Gestalt discourse – rooted in Brentano but involving Alexius Meinong and his intellectual offspring from the "Graz School" of psychology. Christian von Ehrenfels, and Heinz Werner emphasized the emergence of "higher order forms" in our holistic relating with the world (Karkosch, 1935; Smith, 1988). In any organized – and self-organizing – system the notion of hierarchical order is a basic general axiom on which to build new theories. That order may involve few – or many – levels, be transitive or intransitive (Valsiner, 2006) – it can take a multitude of forms. It can combine *loci* of strict and fuzzy forms of organization within itself. Yet that kind of order is there in a socio-cultural phenomenon, and the task of science is to find out how it functions.

SOCIO-CULTURAL THOUGHT AND SOCIAL TRANSFORMATIONS OF SOCIETY

Ideas usually develop on the shoulders of gigantic social turmoil within societies – wars, revolutions, economic instabilities. World War I and the subsequent revolutions in Russia, Austro-Hungarian Empire, and Germany provided a crucial new beginning for socio-cultural thinking.

Following the Russian revolution of 1917, dialectical-materialism and dialectical-historicism became the official philosophy of the new Soviet state. Materialism, together with historical consciousness, were central concepts not be neglected. The institutional turmoil of the country made possible that young scientists (during a brief period) could produce novel approaches with the tools of knowledge they had available. Following a critical review of the psychology of the time by a number of young thinkers – Lev Vygotsky, Alexander Luria, Mikhail Bakhtin, and others – culture, history, and biology were interconnected within an approach that combined the idea of internalization (taken from psychoanalysis) with that of mediational tool (based on the account of anthropogenesis given by Friedrich Engels) and an evolutionary-developmental approach that combined phylogenesis, history and ontogenesis. This amounted to the emergence of the *cultural-historical school* of Lev Vygotsky and Alexander Luria (van der Veer & Valsiner, 1991).

Precisely a similar turn in psychology was prepared at the same time in post-revolutionary Austria where Karl Bühler published his classic work on *Die Krise der Psychologie* (Bühler, 1927/2000). This direction was carried forth by the Prague Linguistic Circle (where Bühler was one of the members). Meaning was taken as a central category, but coming mainly from the internalization of language and its use in communication and collective activities. Consciousness became then a result of the internalization of (*social*) communication with semiotic materials (*cultural*), accumulated along the (*historical*) past of the cultural group, and so capable of planning ahead and transforming the future. Social, cultural, and historical became the adjectives to be put together with the noun psychology, in the banner that signals this school of thought, that also has Luria's neuropsychology as one of its important contributions.

Curiously enough, *meaning* and *semiotics*, being central concepts of this way of approaching psychology, are taken for granted and are not either defined or explained in the abundant production of those who are usually taken to be main flag-holders of this way of approaching psychology. From both Vygotsky's and Bühler's verdicts on their contemporary psychology we learn about a clear scenario for the future – focus on meaning-construction processes. Such focus was supported by developments in the study of language functions.

DEPENDENCE ON LANGUAGE

Language seems to have been taken as the only way of dealing with meaning and sense. The development of linguistics, and philosophy of language throughout the 20th century has influenced psychology profoundly. Following Saussurean structural linguistics, meaning was taken to be a result of reference, but also a product of the syntagmatic nature of language. Grammatical structure was taken to be the grinding mill for the production of meaning. As Wittgenstein pointed out, any system of knowledge has to be stated in a language capable of capturing the essentials of observational statements, and later on, concluded that everything that we could know about the world was a result of playing with words. Any kind of knowledge, and consequently all our experience, was a result of the language games we play. The linguistic turn was taking shape.

There are two related disciplines that have meaning as its subject-matter: *semiology* and *semiotics*. Their difference in name would deserve an explanation that would go beyond our purposes here. *Semiology* originates from the work of the Genevan scholar Ferdinand de Saussure, and *semiotics* from the contribution of the American logician Charles S. Peirce. Both take the study of signs as its primary focus, but the first soon concentrates in conventional symbols and language, while the second goes into developing a general theory of signs in the form of a semiotic logic. Saussure's legacy has left a deep mark in psychology. For example, Jean Piaget's structuralism is not foreign to the structural logic derived from it, in addition to the indirect influence via linguistics that was alluded above. On the other side, Peircean semiotics have fared rather differently. Appreciated by the best scholars of his time – James Mark Baldwin and William James – but disliked by academic institutions, Peirce left a sophisticated legacy in terms of his semiotics that is being carefully utilized over a century later. Using logic and mathematics as his starting point, he introduced a classificatory system of signs that is useful in our time (see Chapter 10).

By the end of the 20th century the focus on language started to change. No longer were researchers investigating syntax or even semantics of words, but a focus on whole messages (utterances) in the contexts of conversation and discourse became highlighted. Also the meaning of *discourse* started to change. Earlier it had been referring to processes of argumentation and thinking, but now it came to mean the type of speech production – oral or written – which resulted from the language games used in social activities. These language-games, as could not be otherwise, had to do with social practices,

and therefore carried with them power relationships, hidden mechanisms for including or excluding, for valuing or degrading, and so had the capability of shaping the view of the world of any one who became an user of such device (Foucault, 1972). Since there is no other way of making sense of an experience that putting it into words, and words are connected among themselves in a grammar, and also have to be uttered in a discursive form, then there is no way of avoiding using the discursive tools available.

Alternatively, one could say that it is the language (or discourse, or the social structure, etc.) that "uses" a human individual to speak in a particular context. So viewed, meaning resides in social discourses and literary genres that circulate in societies. This theoretical stance turns the social abstract units – texts, discourses, institutions, ideologies – into purposeful and active agents who *act through* the persons. Thus, if one wanted to study a particular meaning, one can easily go for a visit to its "residence" in texts (as cultural historians or literary critics do), or try to capture it when the meanings are wandering from one mouth to another – at a distance (if one plays some of the games of discourse analysis). Persons are merely "carriers" of the agency of social units – in apparent parallels with the promotion of different religions that emphasize the deities' "speaking to" the persons through specific moments of communion.

An opposite move – although not fully contradicting the former – has also been utilized. If one can only make meaning through language, and speaking is the result of the use of bodily structures – a two-way relation is present. Using language is not only an act of vocal movements – or of the expression of scripts–but also an application of rules on how to perform those movements. Why not accept that we all share both – the corporal structures ("hardware") and the rules for their use (the "software")? The history of encounters with the environment (including other members of the species) would then account for these vocal, brain, and cognitive foundations that now come to all us as a free birth gift from evolution. This view, under the assertive powers of Chomsky and Fodor (among many others), has an appeal for those who long for the comfort of a Platonic ideal of truth embodied in the trinity of the world, language and cognitive structures. After having been rubbing against each other throughout the eons of evolution, by now, if properly analyzed their study can show us "the truth" of "how things really are". Namely the true meaning of things is assumed to be already encoded in language, in the brain, and in the cognitive structures. So, it is as if, looking beyond all the sophisticated parlance used, we were gliding back to the beginnings of modernity, to Descartes, and in a new looping towards the past, to Plato and the eternal forms of being.

Whatever the case, the Cartesian rift has proved itself difficult to be crossed. Attempts do abound, but they seemed to be bridge-constructions started from one side, that somehow do not seem to set firm ground on the other. It is as if Auguste Comte's curse on Psychology – explanation of human affairs can only be either in its material or its social nature, but never in the middle of both – had haunted the discipline from before its birth. Reductionism – either physical-biological or social-cultural – becomes the norm for explanations. In this book we hope to overcome that norm.

EMBRACING SEMIOTICS

Contemporary socio-cultural psychology is navigating from activity theories towards semiotics. The latter is of course not new – yet long neglected. This is no moment to go into the deployment of hypothesis about the reasons for this long neglect on taking into account Peirce's contribution for the benefit of psychology (see Houser, 1992; Menand, 2001; Riba, 1995). Whatever the case, a revival of Peirce seems recently to be taking effect in different realms: Philosophy (Apel, 1975; Innis, 2005), biosemiotics and zoosemiotics (Hoffmeyer, 1997a. 1997b; Riba, 1990; Sánchez & Loredo, 2005), and Developmental Psychology (Rodríguez & Moro, 1994). The revisiting of some early contributions of this discipline, that otherwise has also enormously influenced linguis-

tics, with the creation of pragmatics, and its subsequent influence on Psychology (e.g., Bruner), may help to address the second question stated above – whether we can approach the study of meaning and experience before language, in animals and children. If that was the case, we would be in the path that Saussure signaled when he said that the study of why something can come to be a sign, and how does it happen, is a matter that concerns psychology, not semiology. Peirce's Semiotic Logic may be a useful tool for this purpose (Peirce, 1896, 1935, 1982). Chapter 8, 10, 12, and 14 go into the exploration of some of its possibilities.

The Pre-View of the Handbook

This Handbook covers a wide field of contemporary research fields, that are situated in different disciplines – psychology, sociology, education, philosophy, political science, and anthropology – and which strive to build interdisciplinary links. However, as will be evident from the following chapters, building such bridges is not an easy objective. Each of the chapters shows the tentative nature of moving outwards from one's base discipline, towards the domain of the unknown and often untrusted of other disciplines, or of different areas of social practices. As a result, our Handbook – appropriately to the field as it exists nowadays – covers a heterogeneous and multi-voiced discourse. This heterogeneity gives us the trust in the (still) developing nature of the field.

In Part I of the Handbook – *Psyche, Society, and Culture* – we examine the effects of cross-disciplinary collaboration in the creation of this new form of knowledge. It also offers reflections on methodological and theoretical issues, as well as opening new views for future developments. We set up the stage for systematic inquiry of different features of human lives. The myth of the life history of the *Psyche* (Chapter 1) illuminates our way through the savannas of the multitude of socio-cultural approaches.

As will be clear from Chapter 1, the perennial question of causality remains a hot issue in contemporary socio-cultural discussions. In addition to the classical – Aristotelian – discourse about proximal and final causes we bring in new ways of looking at causality that fit the open systemic nature of socio-cultural phenomena, such as systemic and catalyzed versions of causality. The multi-level nature of organization of socio-cultural phenomena entails the need to deal with the direction of causality within the systems – upward (emergence-linked) and downward (regulatory) causality.

All talk about causality is based on some sign system – most often on our language. And language is relatively separate from the language user. In Chapter 2, Slunecko and Hengl give an overview of the centrality of language as the agent who captivates the persons who use it. This reversal of the ordinary expected perspective – PEOPLE USE LANGUAGE → LANGUAGE USES PEOPLE accentuates the mutuality – yet not sameness – of the personal and the social. This amounts to the look at what is "in between" persons, and their environments. The study of *communal codes* – rather than mental representations – is their answer to the methodological question. These codes need to be investigated within their cultural histories.

Castro and Rosa (Chapter 3) emphasize the bounded nature of discursive polyphony – the varieties of discourses are organized by the realities of personal experience. Yet the discourse possibilities are wider than actual experiences – hence discourse can create new meanings for mundane life events. They propose the use of thematic categories to analyze the cultural regulation of experience –

> *"actors" (subjects or elements of the subjectivity in the socio-cultural activity),*
> *"objects" (tools and material or symbolic instruments present in the socio-cultural activity),*
> *"spaces" (places and zones involved in the socio-cultural activity), and –*
> *"time" (past, present or future moments linked to the socio-cultural activity).*

This four-component system allows to look at all kind of strategies implied on the search of the meaning of the human activity: from the behavior of an individual or collective subject facing the action or identity in dialogue with otherness (Simão & Valsiner, 2007), to the formulation of the most complicated and disciplinary theories about the structure of the being and the activity. Psychology's self-reflexivity as a science depends upon the emergence of self-reflexivity in everyday discourses, which, as Castro and Rosa show, is a relatively recent historical accomplishment.

Coming closer to the methodological needs of the socio-cultural research tradition, Sato et al. (Chapter 4) attempt to overcome the a-historic nature of the mainstream psychology's research strategies. What is at stake is the sanctity of the belief in randomization in research process. Instead of belief in "random sampling" – where the systemic connections of the sampled specimens are purposefully lost – we get to see the possibilities of Historically Structured Sampling (HSS). It restores the role of history in the selection process of specimens for further study (Valsiner & Sato, 2006), and recognizes the open-systemic nature of socio-cultural phenomena where histories diverge at bifurcation points and converge at equifinality points.

Part II of the Handbook – *From Nature to Culture* – explores central issues in the natural basis of action, social behavior, communication, and the creation and transmission of culture from a comparative evolutionist approach. Action is the most basic feature of all socio-cultural agents – be they humans or other animals. The boundary between species who are accepted – by us, humans – to "have culture" and others ("have-nots") is highly flexible and is being moved around as the semiotic perspective is transferred from the human semiotics onto the bio-social world. Ecosemiotics (Nöth, 1998) and the focus on semiotic interaction within organisms (Hoffmeyer, 1997a) counter the existing duality of oppositions. The latter takes the notion of signs to the level of intra-cellular processes – maybe a very wide extension, yet informative. It is based on the sign-function nature of making distinctions – if a distinction A|B emerges from the agent's (scientist, or practitioner) whole field {A&B} we can argue that A "stands in for" B (or vice versa). So, a hypothetical biological unit – that we call a gene – "stands in" for the reality of some combination of base pairs in a DNA sequence. Genes – seen such way – are thus signs that represent (and present) the reality of DNA. Likewise, from the dog's point of view, the scientist's ardent concentration upon some images on the computer screen "stands in" for the delay in getting one's access to the contents of cans of food with conspecifics' pictures painted on it.

Making distinctions can be seen to happen in the life of any organism – differentiation of organ systems in embryogenesis is as relevant as "self/other" distinction in our immune systems, or personality. However, after making such distinctions there are two opposite ways of making use of them: *coordination* (of distinguished parts of the same whole), or *subordinating exclusion* (of the incompatible other). The semiotic perspective arrives at a synthesis of the two possibilities – it constitutes a case of *subordinating inclusion*. Here the sign subordinates the full reality of what is denoting to the abstracted features of those that it highlights (A presents only some facets of the A&B), while remaining representative of the whole (A&B).

Looking at the chapters in Part 2 may benefit from understanding of such subordinating inclusion function of comparative-psychological and phylogenetic presentations of the socio-cultural field. Alan Costall (Chapter 5) and David Travieso (Chapter 6) are making their case for presenting the development of human beings as immediately dynamically intertwined with their immediate environments – their *Umwelts* (to use von Uexküll's theoretical language – von Uexküll, 1928, 1982). Costall provides a rigorous and passionate account of how great the need in socio-cultural psychology is to overcome the dualistic heritage of cognitive science. The spirit of John Dewey's coordination of organism-environment relations, mediated by James Gibson's field-

theoretic "directness of experiencing" idea, leads him to question where the contemporary socio-cultural field is going. It seems that the old dualisms prevail – and Travieso's chapter demonstrates that they do. By trying to reduce the notion of cultural mediation to the premises of the Dynamic Systems Theory the focus on qualitative synthesis becomes a hostage.

The critical issue for all such efforts to emphasize the directness of human experiencing is the conceptualization of the qualitative breakthroughs in the process of organism's immediate relating with the world – how higher levels of evolutionarily emerged species can simultaneously be involved in the immediate living within the environment – and physiologically[2] as well as psychologically going beyond that immediate relation. Despite earlier efforts by Wundt (Diriwächter, 2004) and Vygotsky (van der Veer & Valsiner, 1991), the problem of synthesis remains unsolved and understudied. Yet it is the central concern for all social sciences that claim that they study development or emergence. The emergence of the use of mediating devices – tools and signs – in the lives of developing higher species makes that rupture with the immediacy of being possible. Yet our theoretical accounts in socio-cultural psychology have difficulties considering both the immediate and mediated psychological processes together within one scheme. This tension is visible in Travieso's chapter – where, in contrast with Costall's pointing out the ills of "mediationism" – the goal is set to build a mediational framework on the grounds of dynamic systems ideas.

The same problem haunts researchers in the area of comparative psychology and paleo-anthropology. Coming from the former, Adolfo Perinat (Chapter 7) analyzes the ways in which different species communicate, focusing on the question of emergence of referential communication as the evolutionary processes have ascended towards the making of *Homo sapiens*. The issue of intentionality surfaces in this comparison – while the human beings easily accept that they are intentional, they are by far less eager to grant that capacity to other species. Yet the dedicated and enthusiastic researchers of ape language capacities are eager to break that barrier of our armchair conservatism of theoretical allocation of "limitations of the mind" to our nearest biological relatives. They demonstrate ever new and more sophisticated uses of semiotic systems by higher primates who have had the privilege of being research participants in laboratory studies of their socio-cultural potentials for development (see Chapter 8 by Fields et al., also Matsuzawa, 2001).

However, the highly sophisticated laboratory environments of contemporary ape mentality projects are not modeling the realities of actual history of human culture. Neither are our contemporary interlocutors among the bonobos, chimpanzees, gorillas, or orangutans direct analogues of proto-hominids. Creating the narrative of our own history of the species is a demonstration of human semiotic ingenuity that mediational tools make possible for our reflexivity. The knowledge base of paleo-anthropology is filled with various stories of how our ancestors evolved – mostly by becoming bipedal, by becoming obsessed by producing tools, and becoming involved in highly symbolic leisure activities such as making cave paintings and funeral arrangements. Yet most of such stories tell us more about our contemporary story tellers than about our distant past relatives who were lucky to survive the fluctuations of ambient temperatures, roaring predators eager to improve their diets by some proto-hominid delicacies added to their natural consumption, and epidemics of various kinds of illnesses. Taking an *etho-ecological* perspective, Jordi Serrallonga (Chapter 9) points out a number of limitations in these stories, calling for a consistent analyses of possible real behavioral encounters of the early emerging hominids with their contexts. By calling for flexibility in our theoretical creativity, he opens the door for a number of innovative hypotheses of previously little considered assumptions of what was relevant in our history. Maybe it was the graciousness of lions that treated the first experiments of hominids with con-

serving fire as suggestions that better meats are elsewhere – or perhaps all human species can be viewed as benefiting from the invention of distancing devices – such as sandals or their equivalents[3] – between our "natural" bodies and the rough environmental surfaces we inhabit in our habitual bipedalism.

Part III – *From Orientation to Meaning* – includes chapters devoted to the study of how meaning evolves from orientation to the environment via perceptual activities and movement, the progressive conventionalization of the use of objects in interaction, and the insertion in social-cultural networks of meaning. Particular attention is also paid to inter-individual differences, physical challenges, and developmental disorders, as well as to re-mediational strategies for mitigating their possible effects. In Chapter 10, Alberto Rosa develops an account of how to integrate the domains of action and meaning construction through the centrality of semiotically modulated experiencing. It is the case in contemporary socio-cultural psychology that interdisciplinary connections are being actively built (see also Gertz, Breaux & Valsiner, 2007).

Chapters 11 (by Silvia Español) and 12 (by Cintia Rodriquez) take the reader to the realm of human ontogeny, demonstrating how the emergence of uses of signs is supported by the social environments. Following the work of Jerome Bruner, these contributions demonstrate how signs regulate children's creation of meanings in everyday activity settings.

Finally, in Chapter 13 we get an integrative picture of how meaning-making is situated in the full socio-historical matrix of human development by the CINDEDI Group in Brazil, led by Clotilde Rossetti Ferreira. The CINDEDI group has for over the last decade done groundbreaking research on how the immediate child-care environments of *creches*, pre-schools, and schools guide the emergence of semiotic mediating devices and cultural action patterns. Their perspective – looking at the whole field of childhood experiences as constructed jointly by the interaction of the child with people around him/her – provides an example of how practice-based research questions reach theoretical generality and transposability to other contexts.

Part IV – Symbolic Resources for the Constitution of Experience – examines the relationship between institutional life, and the development of the self and identity and their connection with social norms and ethics. The dynamics of the self, its narrative character, and the phenomena which arise when confronted with cultural conditions. Dramas of actuations (see Chapter 14) set up the symbolic directions for human action and interaction. Peer interaction (see Chapter 20) is the framework for constant re-negotiation of meanings and social norms. It feeds into internalization of values – as Chapter 15 (by Sang-Chin Choi, Gyuseog Han, and Chung-Woon Kim) demonstrates the absolute nature of self-worth in the Korean cultural history. The *shimcheong* notion organizes inter-personal relationships in ways that do not require verbal negotiations. Instead, the "deep feeling" into the Other can both make interpersonal harmony possible – or restore it if it has disappeared. The centrality of feelings takes the form of hyper-generalized semiotic fields (Valsiner, 2005). The Korean concepts of such hyper-generalized emotions are a basis for general theory construction of emotional experience.

Yet there are other symbolic resources than words or silences – books, films, and so on – that human beings have created in their history, and use for their identity creation. Tania Zittoun (Chapter 16) focuses on the role of interpersonal guidance of the use of symbolic resources through a scaffolding mechanism she calls the *semiotic prism*. Human lives are filled with expected – even culturally scheduled (e.g., entrance to school, adolescent initiation rites) – ruptures. In addition, dramatic ruptures occur in unexpected ways – close family members become ill and die, accidents happen, and so on. Human cultural conduct sets us all up to be prepared to move ahead in our life courses despite the ruptures. Or even more – the ruptures and the symbolic resources

usable to overcome those can be enabling for emergence of new forms of development. The ambivalence of the human living is captured by Emily Abbey (Chapter 17) who builds a theoretical synthesis of semiotics and Bergsonian focus on irreversible time. Her exposition of the case study of a middle-aged man elaborates Zittoun's focus on the uses of symbolic resources.

Socio-cultural psychology of our time also returns to topics that psychology has lost interest in over decades. The behaviorist legacy – followed by its cognitivist sequel – has overlooked the complex phenomena of human religious feelings and practices. Even as in the beginning of the 20th century most leading psychologists were interested in phenomena of religion, one hundred years later these phenomena are rarely studied. Pablo del Rio and Amelia Alvarez (Chapter 18) return us to one of the most interesting forms of psychological activity – that of prayer. It is a form of self-dialogue (compare with Chapter 30 of Salgado and Gonçalves), and constitutes a basis for personal-cultural making of one's self. The latter – through the angle of mutual constraining – is captured by Jeanette Lawrence and Agnes Dodds in Chapter 19. Contemporary societies – like their historical counterparts – leave little of human self-construction to the free will of the person. The advertising of "do-it-yourself" features in our contemporary worlds are a version of "do-it-as-I say," that is, by giving instructions to the ambivalent and unprepared youngsters, the source of advice acquires social power precisely by way of creating wide constraints for the recipients of the advice. Such wide constraints evoke the need to co-construct their narrowed-down versions. The young can develop new personal cultures in their content – yet with active rigidity of the form that resembles that of the advice givers.

Part V – *From Society to the Person through Culture* – captures the theme of immersion in social-cultural activities. Whether it happens within the classroom, the family, the community, or in specified activity settings such as theatres, political rallies, or encounters of football fans, or in the privacy of one's own bedroom – these settings are the cradle for the constitution of the person. The experiencing person is the constantly variable – context-bound – participant in one's own socio-culturally constituted life. On the side of societies – such settings are the arenas for cultural change and innovation, particularly in the cases in which different cultural groups interact in these settings.

In Chapter 20, Hamo and Blum-Kulka introduce the distinction between *mechanisms of conversation* (the ability to interact) and dialogicality (meaning-making in conversation). Conversation entails *talking-for-talking's-sake*. It is talk as a social activity in its own right, not goals-focused, and not subordinated to any physical activity. This segregation of the talk domain from other activities is heuristically useful – especially if we look at dynamic divergence of talking from the rest of acting, interspersed by the opposite process of convergence of these lines (Gupta & Valsiner, 1999). The study reported by the authors in Chapter 20 was precisely aimed at demonstrating how the conversation system of peer talk becomes liberated from other activity contexts to create new competencies in conversation.

Corsaro and Johannesen (Chapter 21) overview the new sub-field of Childhood Studies that – in contrast to the traditional studies of socialization – is an empirical interpretive ethnographic look into children's social lives in peer group contexts. Children are particularly important targets for socio-cultural psychology as what happens with them is never value-neutral. The history of Child Study or paedology movements in the past shows that on issues of children different dialogues of the adults in the given society are being conducted. Children and their childhoods are expressions of the cultures of which they are members – and the conditions for their creation and functioning of peer relations are conditional on the adults' set-up of "age sets" by some particular sign markings.[4] Developing their ethnographic methods as applied to children's peer groups,

the authors' notion of interpretive reproduction parallels the methodological program of Barbara Rogoff (1990, 2003). Most directly the authors work in dialogue with Keith Sawyer's work on collaborative emergence that is a contemporary version of Muzafer Sherif's classic work on the collective construction of social norms (Sherif, 1936).

The fully constructive nature of culture is emphasized by Eugene Matusov and his colleagues (Chapter 22). By turning the notion of culture from its ontological state (of "being" *as is*) into a living, constantly co-constructive dynamic process (creation of "creole cultures" in classrooms), the authors transcend one of the largest intellectual obstacles in socio-cultural psychology – treating developing processes *as if* these were static essences. Both psychology and anthropology have been caught in that trap of turning fluid phenomena of collective experience into static "snapshots" that lose their inherent dialogic nature. In contrast, Michael Cole and Yrjö Engeström (Chapter 23) take the reader to the "fifth dimension" and show how cultural mediation operates in teaching/learning and work settings. Mediation through negotiations is the primary means of transformation in social groups. Symbolic resources – such as money – enter into human relations in ways that make interpersonal acts in peer groups meaningful. Nothing can be a better empirical demonstration of that than the study of children's thinking and use of their pocket money (Chapter 24 by Toshiya Yamamoto and Noboru Takahashi).

This section is concluded by Nandita Chaudhary's overview of family context as the one where all the different negotiations take place. Continuing on her phenomena-centered look at socio-cultural phenomena (Chaudhary, 2004), she outlines a number of contrast ("Western" versus "Indian", present versus past) which, at closer look, are all hiding the complexity of the issues, while revealing their selected and homogenized facets.

Part VI – From Social Culture to Personal Culture – unites a number of relevant perspectives in contemporary socio-cultural psychology. The theory of dialogical self has gained momentum in the past decade (Hermans, 1995, 1996a, 1996b). As João Salgado and Miguel Gonçalves show in Chapter 30, by assuming the notion of multiplicity of "voices" in the self makes it possible to capture the dynamic nuances of the personal-cultural processes. Social representations are another area of activities within the socio-cultural research domain. The original ideas of Serge Moscovici (1981, 1982) have been developed further in multiple directions in the recent decades, as is evident from the chapter by Gerard Duveen (Chapter 26).

Chapter 27 by Piero Paolicchi is dedicated to the ways in which personal-cultural systems of morality are guided by social orientations. It illustrates the value of treating the complex reality in terms of social representing. Even further complexity of semiotic kind is added by Ulf Hedetoft (Chapter 29) who brings the symbolic nature of political discourse to our attention. It is clear that personal identities are closely linked with duties and rights (Chapter 28 by Fathali Moghaddam and Kathryn Kavulich) which grow out of the collective-cultural history of a society.

Memory is an important socio-cultural function – both for persons and societies. In Part VII of the Handbook we see the ways in which collective and personal memory functions are intricately linked. The chapters in this section deal with memory of public events (Chapter 31, by Bellelli et al.; Chapter 33 by Middleton and Brown) and collective memory (Chapter 32 by Jim Wertsch). The constructive nature of memory – remembering the contributions of Frederic Bartlett – leads to the issue of collectively distributed and socially located mediational devices. The whole social world is filled with collective memory devices – architectural creations in urban settings, monuments, newspaper ads, and so on all work on the collective maintenance as well as eradication of social events in (and from) people's memories.

Gillespie (Chapter 34) provides an overview of four kinds of theoretical standpoints that can be the basis for socio-cultural psychology. The *rupture theories* entail the existence of a moment of qualitative breakthrough – disequilibration – in the life experience that leads to new understandings. The *mirror theories* include the "social other" as a basis for comparison and interlocution. The *conflict theories* imply a struggle – inside the self between its parts, or in relations with the interpersonal others. *Internalization theories* take the tension and conflict assumed by the other theories and situate these as constructive processes in human-social world transaction in development. The result is dynamic distancing of the self from the social world – which actually demonstrates the centrality of the social embeddedness of the self. Developing further George Herbert Mead's theoretical position, Gillespie emphasizes that the crucial feature in human social development is constant exchange of positions within the social structures. In other terms – personal experience is constantly transformed as the person changes one's position vis-à-vis social forms of organization – between being "in" (or "out") of those, or – when "in" – playing a role that can vary from most peripheral (e.g., being a party of an audience of a theatre performance, or of public execution) to the most central (being one of the actors of the scene, or the executioner – or the one to-be-executed). Social roles are distributed, and are constantly being re-distributed – by social organizations, with invitations (at times coercive ones) to join in a crowd, a party, a family, love affair, or – at the height of solitary sociality – a pleasurable personal encounter with a book or a film.

In all these perspectives, what matters is the historical nature of socio-cultural phenomena – that functions for the future. We are here interested in the future – a possible one – for socio-cultural psychology. Having established itself with the birth cry of interdisciplinary nature of its scholarship, the new hybrid needs to demonstrate its intellectual viability by providing answers to questions that have remained unanswered – or even unasked – by psychology, anthropology, sociology, and history.

The Coming of Age of Socio-Cultural Psychology

It seems as if psychology, once reached venerable age, and comfortably seated on the high table with the other sciences, can dispense of its worries for looking scientific, and can go back to the study of some old problems (Cole, 1996). But things never happen twice the same. The gathered life experience helps to approach old problems with newer skills, greater prudence, and lesser worries of embarrassment. Perhaps a new set of methodological initiation rites is needed (see General Conclusions) to replace the hegemony of quantitative or qualitative empiricism.

Of course there is the ever-developing social order for new kinds of knowledge that remains behind academics' deliberations. The family of different perspectives that are subsumed under the socio-cultural approaches label grows as our investigative inquiry progresses towards new dialogues with the nature-focused sciences and social ideologies that attempt to monopolize human cultural phenomena *as if* those were natural. So, we can predict the emergence of *socio-cultural pharmacology* (a sub-discipline that studies the construction and use of meanings in relation to the uses of various new medicines with all their potential side- and interaction "effects"), and *socio-cultural veterinary science* (a sub-discipline that deals with the role of the social environments in the life-worlds of pets, and their medical treatments) – to name just a few potential new areas. Our confidence in the growth of these areas stems from the inevitable expansion of human cultural practices to new domains that were previously considered "purely natural" – our meaning construction capacities make the growth if the field inevitable. That proves our point of the centrality of the socio-cultural approaches in the human lives.

There are now concepts and methods capable of approaching meaning-making, and the elaboration of experience in many different settings for action and with subjects (human and not human) in different developmental or evolutionary moments. This assortment of tools allows one to move at one and another side of the disciplinary boundaries of psychology. Something we cannot be dispensed of, if one has to make sense of how an animal of the genus homo becomes a person, acquires resources to make sense of what goes on around him or her, and makes sense of his/her experience in the complexity of socio-cultural life.

These are reasons why socio-cultural psychology cannot have clear disciplinary boundaries, nor can be happy by being called an inter-disciplinary collaboration. It is a genuinely cross-disciplinary field of research. It has its own voice, but it cannot sing solo. It must be in harmony, and counterpoint with other voices in the choir. Socio-cultural psychology produces empirical research, but also cannot renounce to theoretical and methodological developments. *Methodos* is a Greek work that means road. Roads exist when one knows where is and where to go. But perhaps Cavafy (1911) was right when he said that it is the journey what matters. This book gathers empirical contributions, reviews of the literature and theoretical and methodological contributions. This variety of contributions we believe offer a valuable contribution to the development of this up and coming area of research. New ideas – as Antonio Machado said – create their own path when moving ahead.

Notes

1 Our authors come from 15 different countries.

2 The physiological level of such transcending of the here-and-now situation is modeled by the focus on anticipation of the future in the theories of Piotr Anokhin (1964) and Nikolai Bernstein (1966).

3 Obviously, an underutilized topic for telling the story of human cultural history is that of the gradual distancing of the walking body from the ambience. Hence, possibly the evolution from sandals to high-heeled shoes (for the elegant part of humankind) or army boots (for the other side) creates a new potentially appealing theme for a book on *Walking*

Intelligence (to join their highly commercially adaptive counterparts of *Emotional Intelligence*, and other similar kinds).

4   For example, the U.S. society uses educational institutional meaning sets to define children's age sets – in child psychology journals one encounters designations of "first graders" or "eighth graders" as age set designation – without age markers. A similar – yet semiotically different – distinction is made by talking about "8 year olds" or "13 year olds," or about "circumcized" and "not yet circumcized" age sets (obviously, in societies where circumcision as adolescence transition marker is socially relevant).

References

Albertazzi, L., Jacquette, D. & Poli, R. (Eds.) (2001). *The school of Alexius Meinong*. Aldershot: Ashgate.

Álvarez, A. & del Río, P. (1994). *Education as Cultural Construction*. Vol. 2 of *Explorations in Socio-Cultural Studies*. General editors James Werstch, Pablo del Río & Amelia Álvarez. Madrid: Infancia y Aprendizaje.

Anokhin, P. (1964). Systemogenesis as a general regulador of brain development. In W. A. Himwuich & H. E. Himwich. (Eds.), *Progress in brain research*. Vol. 9 (pp. 54–86). Amsterdam: Elsevier.

Apel, K. O. (1975). *Der Denkweg von Chales S. Peirce. Eine Einführung in dem amerikanischen Pragmatismus*. Frankfurt am Main: Suhrkamp Verlag.

Bartlett, F. C. (1932). Remembering. A Study in Experimental and Social Psychology. Cambridge: Cambridge University Press.

Bernstein, N. (1966). *Ocherki po fiziologii dvizhenia I fiziologii aktivnosti*. Moscow: Meditsina.

Boesch, E. E. (1989). Cultural psychology in action-theoretical perspective. In Ç. Kagitçibasi. (Ed.), *Growth and progress in cross-cultural psychology* (pp. 41–51). Lisse: Swets & Zeitlinger.

Boesch, E. E. (1991). *Symbolic action theory and cultural psychology*. New York: Springer.

Boesch, E. E. (1993). The sound of the violin. *Schweizerische Zeitschrift für Psychologie*, 52 (2), 70–81.

Boesch, E. E. (1997). *Von der Sehnsucht*. Saarbrücken: Privater vor-abdrück.

Boesch, E. E. (2005). *Von Kunst bis Terror*. Göttingen: Vanderhoeck & Ruprecht.

Bühler, K. (2000). *Die Krise der Psychologie*. Göttingen: Verbrück Wissenschaft. [Original work published in 1927]

Cavafy, C. P. (1911). *Ithaka*. http://srs.dl.ac.uk/people/pantos/kavafis_ithaca.html.

Chaudhary, N. (2004). *Listening to culture*. New Delhi: Sage.

Cole, M. (1990). Cultural psychology: A once and future discipline? In J. Berman. (Ed.), *Nebraska Symposium on Motivation*. Vol. 37 (pp. 279–336). Lincoln: University of Nebraska Press.

Cole, M. (1996). *Cultural Psychology*. Cambridge, MA: Harvard University Press.

Danziger, K. (1980). The history of introspection reconsidered. *Journal of the History of the Behavioral Sciences*, 16, 241–262.

Danziger, K. (1985). The methodological imperative in psychology. *Philosophy of the Social Sciences*, 15, 1–13.

Danziger, K. (1990). *Reconstructing the subject*. Cambridge: Cambridge University Press.

Danziger, K. (1997). *Naming the mind*. London: Sage.

Diriwächter, R. (2004). *Völkerpsychologie*: the synthesis that never was. *Culture & Psychology*, 10, 1, 85–109.

Diriwächter, R. & Valsiner, J. (Eds.) (2007). *Striving towards the whole: Creating Theoretical Syntheses*. New Brunswick, N.J.: Transaction Publishers.

Eckensberger, L. H. (1995). Activity or action: two different roads towards an integration of culture into psychology? *Culture & Psychology*, 1(1), 67–80.

Eckensberger, L. H. (1997). The legacy of Boesch's intellectual oeuvre. *Culture & Psychology*, 3(3), 277–298.

Eckensberger, L. H. (2003). Wanted: a contextualized psychology. In T. S. Saraswathi. (Ed.), *Cross-cultural perspective in human development* (pp. 70–101). New Delhi: Sage.

Ehrenfels, C. von (1988). On Gestalt qualities (1932). In B. Smith. (Ed.), *Foundations of Gestalt theory* (pp. 121–123). München: Philosophia Verlag.

Edwards, D. (1997). *Discursive Psychology*. London: Sage.

Fernández, T. R. (2005). Sobre la Historia Natural del Sujeto y su lugar en una Historia de la Ciencia. A propósito de Robert J. Richards y el Romanticismo de Darwin. *Estudios de Psicología*, 26(1), 67–104.

Foucault, M. de (1969/1972). *The Archaeology of Knowledge. And the Discourse on Language.* New York: Tavistock.

Gertz, S. H., Breaux, J.- P. & Valsiner, J. (Eds.) (2007). *Semiotic rotations.* Greenwich, Ct.: InfoAge Press.

Gupta, S. & Valsiner, J. (1999). Coordination of speaking and acting in the second year of life. Mind, Culture & Activity, 6(2), 143–159.

Head, H. (1926). *Aphasia and kindred disorders of Speech.* Cambridge: Cambridge University Press.

Hermans, H. J. M. (1995). The limitations of logic in defining the self. *Theory & Psychology,* 5(3), 375–382.

Hermans, H. J. M. (1996a). Voicing the self: from information processing to dialogical interchange. *Psychological Bulletin,* 119(3), 31–50.

Hermans, H. J. M. (1996b). Opposites in a dialogical self: constructs as characters. *Journal of Constructivist Psychology,* 9(1), 1–26.

Hermans, H. (2001). The dialogical self: Toward a theory of personal and cultural Positioning. *Culture and Psychology,* 7(3), 243–281.

Hermans, H. J. (Ed) (2002). Special Issue on dialogical self. *Theory & Psychology,* 12(2), 147–280.

Hoffmeyer, J. (1997a). Biosemiotics: Towards a New Synthesis in Biology. *European Journal for Semiotic Studies,* 9(2), 355–376.

Hoffmeyer, J. (1997b). The swarming body. In I. Rauch and G. F. Carr. (Eds.), *Semiotics around the world: Synthesis in diversity.* Berlin: Mouton de Gruyter.

Houser, N. (1992). Introduction to Vol. 1. In *The Essential Peirce: Selected Philosophical Writings, 1893–1913.* Bloomington: Indiana University Press.

Innis, R. E. (2005). The signs of interpretation. *Culture & Psychology,* 11(4), 499–509.

Jahoda, G. (1993). *Crossroads between culture and mind.* Cambridge. MA: Harvard University Press.

Karkosch, K. (1935). Über die Anfänge der Lehre von der "Gestaltqualitäten". *Archiv für die gesamte Psychologie,* 93, 189–233.

Kroeber, A. & Kluckhohn, C. (1952). Culture: a critical review of concepts and definitions. *Papers of the Peabody Museum of American Archaeology and Ethnology,* 47(1), i–viii.

Lotze, R. H. (1852). *Medizinische Psychologie oder Physiologie der Seele.* Leipzig. (reprinted, Amsterdam 1966).

Matsuzawa, T. (Ed.), (2001). *Primate origins of human cognition and behavior.* Tokyo: Springer.

Menand, L. (2001). *The Metaphysical Club: A Story of Ideas in America.* New York: Farrar, Straus & Giroux.

Mercer, N. & Coll, C. (1994). *Teaching, Learning and Interaction.* Vol. 2 of *Explorations in Socio-Cultural Studies.* General editors James Wertsch, Pablo del Río & Amelia Álvarez. Madrid: Infancia y Aprendizaje.

Molenaar, P. C. M. (2004). A manifesto on psychology as idiographic science: Bringing the person back into scientific psychology, this time forever, *Measurement: Interdisciplinary research and perspectives,* 2, 201–218.

Molenaar, P. C. M. & Valsiner, J. (2005). How generalization works through the single case: A simple idiographic process analysis of an individual psychotherapy case. *International Journal of Idiographic Science,* 1, 1–13. [www.valsiner.com]

Moody, E., Markova, I. & Plichtova, J. (1995). Lay representations of democracy: a study in two cultures. *Culture & Psychology,* 1, 4, 423–453.

Moro, C. & Rodriguez, C. (1994). Prelinguistic sign mixity and flexibility in interaction. *European Journal of Psychology of Education,* 9, 301–310.

Moscovici, S. (1981). On social representations. In J. P. Forgas. (Ed.), *Social cognition* (pp. 181–209). London: Academic Press.

Moscovici, S. (1982). The coming era of representations. In J.-P. Codol & J.-P. Leyens (Eds.), *Cognitive analysis of social behavior* (pp. 115–150). The Hague: Martinus Nijhoff.

Nöth, W. (1998). Ecosemiotics. *Töid margisüs teemide alalt/Sign System Studies,* 26, 332–434.

Peirce, C. S. (1896). The regenerated logic. *The Monist,* 7, 1, 19–40.

Peirce, C. S. (1935). *Collected papers of Charles Sanders Peirce.* Vol. 6. Cambridge, MA: Harvard University Press.

Peirce, C. S. (1982). *Writings of Charles S. Peirce.* Vol. 1, Bloomington, In.: Indiana University Press.

Riba, C. (1990). *La comunicación animal. Un enfoque zoosemiótico.* Barcelona: Anthropos.

Riba, C. (1995). De ayer y de hoy: Charles S. Peirce (1839-1914). *Anuario de Psicología,* 64, 83–89.

Richards, R. J. (1987). *Darwin and the emergence of evolutionary theories of mind and behavior.* Chicago: The University of Chicago Press.

Richards, R. J. (2002). *The Romantic conception of life. Science and Philosophy in the age of Goethe.* Chicago: The University of Chicago Press.

Rogoff, B. (1990). *Apprenticeship in thinking.* New York: Oxford University Press.

Rogoff, B. (2003). *The cultural nature of human development.* New York: Oxford University Press.

Rosa, A. & Valsiner, J. (Eds.) (1994). *Historical and theoretical discourse. Explorations in socio-cultural studies* Vol. 1 of *Explorations in Socio-Cultural Studies.* General editors James Werstch, Pablo del Río & Amelia Álvarez & Pablo del Río. Madrid: Infancia y Aprendizaje.

Sherif, M. (1936). *Psychology of social norms.* New York: Holt.

Sánchez, J. C. & Loredo, J. C. (2005). Psicologías para la evolución. Catálogo y crítica de los usos actuales de la Selección Orgánica. *Estudios de Psicología* 26(1), 105–126.

Shweder, R. A. (1990). Cultural psychology – what is it? In J. W. Stigler, R. A. Shweder, & G. Herdt. (Eds.), *Cultural psychology* (pp. 1–43). Cambridge: Cambridge University Press.

Shweder, R. A. (1991). *Thinking through cultures.* Cambridge, MA: Harvard University Press.

Shweder, R. A. & Sullivan, M. A. (1990). The semiotic subject of cultural psychology. In L. Pervin (Ed.), *Handbook of personality* (pp. 399–416). New York: Guilford Press.

Simão, L. M. & Valsiner, J. (Eds.) (2007). *Otherness in Question: Labyrinths of the self.* Greenwich, Ct.: Information Age Publishers.

Smith, B. (Ed.), (1988). *Foundations of Gestalt theory.* München: Philosophia Verlag.

Stern, W. (1911). *Differentielle Psychologie.* Leipzig: J. A. Barth.

Stern, W. (1935). *Allgemeine Psychologie auf personalistischer Grundlage.* Den Haag: Martinus Nijhoff.

Valsiner, J. (2001). The first six years: Culture's adventures in psychology. *Culture & Psychology,* 7, 1, 5–48.

Valsiner, J. (2005). Affektive Entwicklung im kulturellen Kontext. In J. B. Asendorpf. (Ed.), *Enzyklopädie der Psychologie.* Vol. 3. *Soziale, emotionale und Persönlichkeitsentwicklung* (pp. 677–728). Göttingen: Hogrefe.

Valsiner, J. (2006). Developmental epistemology and implications for methodology. In. R. M. Lerner (Ed.), *Theoretical models of human development* (pp. 166–209). Vol. 1 of *Handbook of Child Psychology* (W. Damon and R. M. Lerner, Eds.). 6th edition. New York: Wiley.

Valsiner, J. (2007). *Culture in minds and societies.* New Delhi: Sage.

Valsiner, J. & Sato, T. (2006). Historically Structured Sampling (HSS): How can psychology's methodology become tuned in to the reality of the historical nature of cultural psychology? In J. Straub, D. Weidemann, C. Kölbl & B. Zielke. (Eds.), *Pursuit of meaning* (pp. 215–251). Bielefeld: transcript.

Van Der Veer, R., & Valsiner, J. (1991). *Understanding Vygotsky: A quest for synthesis.* Oxford: Basil Blackwell.

Von Uexküll, J. J. (1928). *Theoretische Biologie.* Berlin: Julius Springer.

Von Uexküll, J. J. (1982). The theory of meaning. *Semiotica* 42, 1, 25–82. (original in 1941)

Vygotsky, L. S. (1926). The Historical Meaning of the Crisis in Psychology. A Methodological Investigation. In *Sobranie sochinenii,* vol 1 (pp. 291–483). Moscow: Pedagogika. [English translation in In R.V: Rieber. (Ed.), *The collected Works of L.S: Vygotsky.* Vol. 3. *Problems of the Theory and History of Psychology.* New York: Plenum. 233–344.]

Wertsch, J. (1991). *Voices of the mind.* Cambridge, MA: Harvard University Press.

Wertsch, J., del Río, P. & Alvarez, A. (Eds.) (1995). *Sociocultural Studies of Mind.* Cambridge: Cambridge University Press.

Wertsch, J. & Ramírez, J. D. (1994). *Literacy and Other Forms of Interaction.* Vol. 2 of *Explorations in Socio-Cultural Studies.* General editors James Werstch, Pablo del Río & Amelia Álvarez. Madrid: Infancia y Aprendizaje.

Wundt, W. (1873). *Grundzüge der physiologischen Psychologie.* Leipzig: Engelmann.

Wundt, W. (1883). *Logik.* Vol. 2. *Methodenlhere.* Stuttgart: Enke.

Wundt, W. (1907). *Logik.* Vol. 3. *Logik der Geisteswissenschaften* (3rd Edition). Stuttgart: Enke.

Wundt, W. (1900–1920). *Völkerpsychologie.* 10 vols. Leipzig: Kröner-Engelmann, 1900–1910; 3rd (Ed.), 1911–1920. vol. I : Die Sprache. part I, vol. II: Die Sprache. part 2; vol. III: Die Kunst. vols. IV-VI: Mythus und Religion. vols. VII, VIII: Die Gesellschaft. vol. IX: Das Recht. vol. X: Kultur und Geschichte.

Part I

THEORETICAL AND METHODOLOGICAL ISSUES

CHAPTER 1

The Myth, and Beyond

Ontology of *Psyche* and Epistemology of Psychology

Jaan Valsiner and Alberto Rosa

Psychology is a science overridden by envies and jealousies that are reminiscent of the myth of Psyche, Eros, and Aphrodite (see Figure 1.1).

Psychology – like *Psyche* – is a beautiful bastard. It promises much to young students who flock to specialize in it. Yet at its heart it has been eternally homeless. It has tried to locate its parents in physiology, physics, or even in art – to be rebuffed by all these alleged parents as either not solid enough – or not sufficiently beautiful. So it continues to wander in the World – between societies – looking for its place. At times it finds a temporary place when there is some ideological order for its products – like tests or ways to re-direct blame for various actions between groups in a society. Yet such applied success – selling one's actions while hiding one's soul – does not lead to the latter's discovery of its own identity, unsuccessfully sought after in Pavlov's dogs, Skinner's rats, or (currently) in fMRI pictures. Technology cannot solve intellectual problems – but can only assist.

From Beauty to Science: A Quick Look to *Psyche*'s Past

Psychology seems to eliminate beauty in its making of a science, in the way it regards its subject-matter: *Psyche*. At the beginning Psyche was just a short way of referring to life. For the Ancient Greeks, *psyche* was the vital principle, as *anima* was for the Romans. Things were either animated of unanimated, because they had an *anima* or a *psyche*. Plato, as he did with everything else, decided to give substance to that principle. It was an idea that produced an entity: the Soul, which was a thing that, as all others, was eternal; but that also had the desire, and capability, for reaching beauty and truth. So, Plato created an entity, and provided it with contents and desires. Aristotle, a naturalist, somehow fought against Plato's heritage and went back to the vital principle. But nothing could be the same again. Psyche had already come to the world as an entity. However, Aristotle's Psyche was a peculiar entity that he called an *entelechia*:

Figure 1.1. *Psyche* – the mythological creature. W. V. Hoyer 1806–1873: Psyche. Photo © Maicar Förlog – GML

that is, something immaterial that makes matter be alive, to move, to transform, and to reach goals. When doing so, he was surprisingly modern; he devised an entity that was not a thing, but a set of functions that govern movement and change. Aristotle set the path for the development of theories of action. His influence is still felt, but it had to suffer the burden of Neoplatonic interpretations.

Medieval intellectuals (irrespective of whether they were Jews, Christians, or Muslims) thought of Psyche as a thing: the Soul, an immaterial and immortal entity that had an inner structure that made it have some capabilities for action (faculties). Some of them, as Ibn-Sina did, placed some of these faculties in the brain, a path followed by Renaissance Galenic physicians, such as the Spaniards Gómez Pereira and Juan Huarte de San Juan, and later on by the father of modern dualism – René Descartes. Descartes laid the ground of modern thought, but also made us all pay the price of breaking Psyche into two halves. Some functions could be explained by the material structure of the organs (lower psychological processes), while higher psychological processes (language and reason) resulted from the working of the immaterial *res cogi-*

tans, and so were not accessible to scientific explanation.

This division of Psyche has hindered psychology for centuries. Even the idealistic views of British Empiricism ended up being interpreted as a materialistic associationism based on the connective properties of the Nervous System falling in materialistic reductionism, as Pavlov and some Behaviorists did. On the other hand, the German intellectual tradition (Leibniz, Kant, Herder, Fichte, Hegel) chose to deal with the Spirit, the vital principle, but as something devoid of any material basis. However, they pointed out something important. Spirit is not something to be found solely in live matter, but also in social groups and institutions, in language and nations. It was created and transformed, and affected individual Psyches, making them non identical, with significant differences in different parts of the world, and not because of biological reasons, but because of the different cultural-historical development of societies. History then became a central issue for the explanation of Psyche.

Wilhelm Wundt, the founder of experimental psychology, took into account both profiles of Psyche: the biological and individual, and the collective and social-cultural-historical (Diriwächter, 2004). He also took the pains of sketching ways of connecting these two ways of approaching psyche. There were universal psychological principles – which could be studied in the laboratory – and historical-cultural laws (which had to be elaborated by comparative and historical methods) that were particular specifications derived from the universal principles (Jahoda, 1993).

There was quite widespread consensus in the importance of keeping in sight these two sides of Psyche at the beginning of the 20th century. Janet, Freud, Dilthey, Spranger, Stern, Bartlett, G. H. Mead, Vygotsky, Luria, and K. Bühler were among the psychologists who made contributions to making sense of the unity of the Psyche. Yet after the War World II this concern was, generally speaking, left aside until the last two decades of the 20th century. Currently, it is the social-cultural-historical research that seems to enjoy excellent health, with important contributions to the development of knowledge presented in this Handbook.

Of course the socio-cultural-historical researchers are not alone in developing knowledge. We are a part of a much wider community with whom we share many common concerns. That community exists in a social environment that selectively highlights some theoretical perspectives ahead of others. This is reflected in psychologists' obsession with establishing social positions. Thus, in the beginning of the 21st century, psychology finds itself fragmented, involved in fights between different "schools" ("-isms": behavior<u>ism</u>, cognitiv<u>ism</u>, socio-cultural<u>ism</u>, etc.). All these perspectives use <u>the rhetoric stance</u> of science in their argumentation for their own relevance. They are surrounded by wider, social-ideological "-isms" popular in societies – Marxism, feminism, and so on. This curious habit of creating and using "-isms" leads to the issue of the role of theory construction in psychology.

Two Roles of Scientific Evidence: Knowledge Construction and Group Maintenance

Science is a social practice, carried out by individuals gathered in groups within institutions whose funding comes from public and private agencies. So the knowledge these individuals and institutions produce cannot be thought of as angelically independent of the management policies these institutions develop in order to keep themselves in business. How research groups get funding, researchers are hired, or career promotion works, are not minor issues for the explanation of the type of knowledge they produce, what this knowledge is useful for, and the shape it takes. Therefore, group formation around a perspective in a science is a natural part of the social side of research. Yet the groups can function in ways that retain the primacy of the phenomena, or in ways that concentrate on the primacy of the

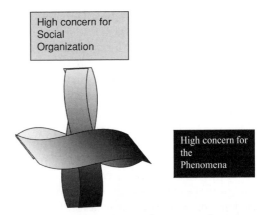

Figure 1.2. Two linkages of science with its realities.

group – moving away from the focus on the phenomena.

These two aspects (the social and the epistemic) are not the extremes of a continuum, so one could say that the research outcome of these institutions can be graded between the highest "pure science" and the lowest service to "corporate interests." The social and the epistemic sides are two intersecting dimensions that shape together the outcome of scientists' work. Figure 1.2 depicts how these two dimensions cross each other in a sort of Möbius' continuous ribbon.

It is easy to see how easily the primary focus of a science may shift from phenomena-centered activities to social group organizational activities. The work of the members of a research institution can drift towards a primary concern for the cohesion, defense, and perpetuation of the group. In the reverse case – centering mainly on the subject matter of study and not paying attention to the social needs of the research community also guarantees fragmentation of the discipline. In either of these moves, nothing seems to change at the beginning, but only a small shift on the accent of gravity. But sooner or later changes may become dramatic. In the latter case the diminishing cohesion and solidarity among the members of the group may end up with a loss of institutional footing, and so seriously affecting the very possibility of keeping in the business of studying their cherished phenomena.

It is then understandable that at times different disciplines re-iterate the need of young scientists to be introduced to the phenomena through immersion (e.g., cultural anthropologists' focus on field experience) or by constant need to know the object of investigation (e.g., ethologists' imperative of knowing the species one works with).

Since scientific inquiry is both an epistemological and social activity, the two parts of the inquiry are necessarily coordinated with one another – at times with tension involved. Under some conditions, the social function of the enterprise can enhance its epistemological function. Under other conditions – it can stifle the latter. Likewise, an event on the epistemological side of inquiry – for example, a new breakthrough in ideas – may feed into the development of the social group relations among researchers.

Theories in Psychology: Intellectual Tools Versus Identity Markers

There are two implicit functions of theories in psychology: (a) theories are *tools* for taking a new look at the phenomena we want to understand; and (b) theories set *mental (and socio-ideological) positions* that are being followed for the reasons of "contributing to the literature", or following a tradition, or getting tenure in an academic institution, or reaching many other socially and personally useful objectives.

Obviously it is only the first of these two functions that has relevance for *Wissenschaft*.[1] The latter is the function of theories that has undoubtedly central relevance for a science's relations with the socio-ideological texture of the given society at the time. Our central point here is the ideal of dominance of the first over the second for a productive historical period in a science, and the domination of the second over the first in case of stabilization of a given discipline in a state of "normal science" in a Kuhnian sense.

Theories as Identity Markers

This function of theories is an outgrowth from the social organization of a particular science within particular institutions at a given historical period. It is an example of appropriation of those theories for the purposes of the social needs of a group within an institution, something that can only succeed when those theories are also useful for the socio-political discourses of the given society at the time (even if only rhetorically). This second function obviously sets the stage for the first one – leading to both quick spurts in the development of the discipline (e.g., the role of "Marxist turn" in psychology in Russia in the 1920s) and to long-term stagnation in the study of some psychological functions (e.g., the role of American behaviorism in the delay of the study of mental functions, from 1910s to 1960s).

Of course, the first function of a theory – as an intellectual tool – may itself become transformed into an ideological position as it advances beyond the efforts of the initiators to make sense, to the efforts of the groups of disciples to follow (rather than further advance) the original ideas. This would constitute a marginal case between theories' functions *a* and *b* – a system of ideas that originally was created to allow for a fresh look at phenomena becomes dissociated from the phenomena and turned into a vehicle for group formation of the clans of scientists. History of psychology gives us ample evidence of how originally intellectually productive theories became fixated upon their own role, entered into various social disputes with others, and became fossilized. Some of such changes happened under the leadership of the originator becoming well established in one's social network (e.g., Freud, Piaget), others in ways quite contrary to the wishes of the originator (Vygotsky). Some idea systems were socially turned into orthodoxies to be followed – the study of behavior became behaviorism, the study of mental phenomena – with its original Würzburgian and *Völkerpsychologie* focus – was turned into cognitivism. Psychology has socially generated "*-isms*" of various kinds – all of which are examples of the second function of theories in that discipline.

The critical question is what value is the rhetoric positioning in organization of any science for actual knowledge creation by that science? What is the actual new knowledge construction (if any) that is made possible by discussions of the benefits of cogniti*vism* over behavior*ism*? Or is such use of "-isms" merely a rhetoric device for looking more valuable within a community of scholars?

Theories as Intellectual Tools

In contrast, theories as tools function in ways that help the researcher set up one's perspective on the phenomena under study in ways that allow investigation of some otherwise overlooked side of these phenomena. Here theories grow due to the research practices – sure, the starting point is a general, set perspective – leading to a specific empirical endeavor. Yet under the conditions of "toolness" of a theory, the theory is changed based on that endeavor. The theory – at some level of its hierarchical build-up – will change as a result of empirical evidence, leading to a new look at the phenomena, changing research practices, providing again a new look, and so on.

The construction – and use – of theories as intellectual tools is predicated upon the notion of *vertical consistency* between assumptions, theories, methods, data, and phenomena within the general cycle of methodology (Branco & Valsiner, 1997; Valsiner, 2000, chapter 5). This notion makes empirical investigation central for theory construction – albeit in strictly limited *loci* of the creation of knowledge. It is the theoretical construction that constitutes knowledge – proven by crucial probes into the empirical domains – not the accumulation of data in some database.

Criteria for Detecting a Shift in the Equilibrium Between These Two Functions of Theories

Dominance fights between "competing" theoretical "systems" (e.g., at times agitated "fights" between self-proclaimed "Piagetians" and "Vygotskians", or between "cognitivists" and "behaviorists") are a first indicator of the loss of the function of theories as tools. For a researcher using a theory – for instance, Vygotsky's theory – to approach a specific issue of understanding, the contrast to some other theorist's (e.g., Piaget's) abstract constructions are merely a contrasting "intellectual mirror" that can be consulted but not used as it does not allow for capturing some desired aspect of the target phenomenon. Hence to spend one's intellectual energies on "fighting for" the adequacy of one "system" over the other is for that researcher a mere waste of time. Not so for others – for whom the different "systems" have acquired the status of social ideology. They would insist upon debates around the issue of dominance of their pet "system" over all others, and may even get to the issues of need of proliferation of "the right stuff" in the society at large. Any deconstruction exercise played out on the grounds of an existing theory – without a corresponding re-construction of the theory – speaks about the use of theoretical discourse for the function of identity negotiation. Thus, "critical psychology" can be "critical" in two ways – demolishing the target theoretical system, or bringing out features that can lead to its improvement. The latter belongs to the theories-as-tools orientation, the former, not.

A second criterion for detecting the turn of the role of theory as a tool to that of a social ideology is the presence of *deconstruction efforts without corresponding re-construction* focus. It is certainly not difficult to analyze a rivaling theoretical "system" exposing its hidden premises and unexpressed meaning nuances. This can be done as a part of dismissal of the target – or with the focus on learning from the deconstruction for one's own re-construction. It is the latter that represents productivity in science. A mere "critical stance" in psychology may display the ills of the discipline – but stop at the doorstep of revitalizing it.

Knowledge Construction and Technological Uses: Construction Versus Use

The question of whether new theories (as tools) are constructed de novo, or merely old ones used (by following them for a local particular purpose) is embedded within a wider societal meaning opposition CONSUMPTION ←→ PRODUCTION. It can be seen that our contemporary societies move swiftly to a dependence upon producing and selling high volumes of standardized and short-term usable consumer products (rather than durable, and repairable, high quality products). There are economic reasons for such reduction of quality (and with them – of skills that could maintain quality, e.g., the extinction of repair facilities for anything ranging from shoes to computers). Instead of repair an object, we replace it – with the resulting distancing from how the object actually works.

The psychological impact of such social change is a strict differentiation of the consuming from the producing orientation in everyday life. Instead of creating a new object (and preparing to do so in a life-long education process) we select and purchase a ready-made one to fit our needs. These ready-made objects are made by others (who know how to make them – but keep that know-how to be accessed by a dedicated few), while the large cohorts of consumers are kept away from the production process.

What Socio-Cultural Perspectives to Psychology Can Contribute?

Updating Psyche's Image

One of the contributions we can make to the effort of furthering the human sciences is to update the image we have of Psyche at the beginning of the 21st century, and how the image so pictured suggests avenues for research, not only in Psychology, but also in other human sciences. This is an ambitious task, and surely futile for many. We want to open the floor to a dialogue and discussion on a matter which we think is of importance.

First, it must be said that we do not see Psyche as any kind of thing, as any kind of substance, but as pure change, as movement, as ongoing dynamics, whose nature has to be explained. So, if we want to call it an entity, it is a virtual entity, a way of referring to how some things move, behave, or act. This is important, because we are going to purposely avoid any kind of substantialism.

Second, we follow a diachronical approach. If Psyche is a way of referring to movement and change, one cannot look at it as any sort of permanent substance, but as something that changes along time. So, time is a basic dimension for the explanation of Psyche. A time that flows throughout evolution, history, and the individual's lifespan.

It is well known that modern science rejects any explanatory power to final causes, keeping efficient causality as the only form of explanation. However, neither biology nor psychology can dispense with the fact that living creatures do not simply respond to stimuli, but actively seek satisfaction of their needs in the environment. This has sometimes been understood as a sort of teleology, as the result of a kind of final cause. The concept of 'function' has been developed in order to transform the final cause of behavior – the goal to be reached in order to restore homeostasis – into an efficient form of causality.

The concept of function is not only a biological or psychological concept. It is also a key concept in mathematics and physics. The expression $y = f(x)$ is also called a function, as well as an identity. Both sides of the sign "$=$" are identical. Natural laws are mathematically expressed through functions. How a particular physical state comes to be can be explained by an equation, or a set of equations, that, for short, we can express also with the formalism $y = f(x)$. Something we could translate into English as "in order to become 'y', 'x' has to fulfill requisites 'f'". But, obviously, 'x' does not do anything (nor can choose whether to do 'f' or not), simply 'f' happens to 'x' in certain circumstances, and then 'y' comes to be. But why in these circumstances and not in others?, why does 'y' happen rather than 'w', for example? The answer must be found in basic natural principles, such as the Second Law of Thermodynamics (which states that energy tends to distribute uniformly within a closed system, until it reaches an equilibrium), or any other universal principle.

If we observe a natural phenomenon, and we want to make sense of how it came to be, or we want to reproduce it, the function clearly states how efficient causes act, what happened so that phenomenon appear, and what we have to do (if we can) in order to reproduce it. Thus, one could say that, in some sense, efficient and final causes collapse into each other, that they are two sides of the same form of explanation. In Nature phenomena are produced by efficient causes, but technology harnesses the knowledge we have of the working of efficient causes in order to produce the desired effects. So it seems that human culture manages to make effective teleological use of efficient causality. But, how can we explain the emergence of such a strange form of causality as teleology?

This question will be answered following a natural path that does not need any type of mysterious emergetism. But, in order to do so, we must to go into what may look like a detour: a consideration of the world of objects. Something that will also be useful to point out why we think that Aristotle's insistence on formal causes should also not be forgotten. Rather than considering a world made of substances, of things and objects given from the start, a dynamic view is in order. The task is to explain dynamically what objects are (any type of objects – from stones to animals, humans, nations and texts), and the way in which objects come to be. This is a central point in the on-going argument, because if Psyche is the *entelechia* that make things move and change, we have to consider first how to make sense of these things.

We know now that Nature is sometimes capable of spontaneously producing order and structure, in apparent (but only apparent) contradiction of the second law of thermodynamics. Namely, order and structure arise in some regions, while disorder (entropy) increases in some others. In the last few decades many natural phenomena of formation of spontaneous order have been observed (e.g., Prigogine & Stengers, 1984), at the same time that new formalisms for their explanation have been devised. The Dynamic Systems Theory is now a powerful device able to produce formalisms for the exploration of such phenomena, and for the production of explanatory models of their functioning (van Geert, 2003; see also Travieso, chapter 6).

According to this view, Nature is capable of producing areas of distribution of energy in which interacting forces create states of spontaneously emerged equilibrium, keeping each other within a certain range of values. This is a state of dynamic equilibrium, where forces interact keeping each other in a sort of locked position. Even if the forces change, the equilibrium is kept by spontaneous readjusting. This stability has a beginning, transforms along time in many different fashions (cyclical, ordered in stages, or with a mixture of randomness and regularity), and have an end. Energy flow and time are the basic factors that affect how long dynamic or static stabilities will remain in existence, and how they may evolve. Within some of these dynamic systems autocatalytic processes may occur, which unleash a system of reactions that end up producing a result much more complex than the received input. The result is the self-organization of a system that already was quite complex; and the spontaneous emergence of novel structures.

SOCIO-CULTURAL PHENOMENA
AS OPEN SYSTEMS

A dynamic system is, by the definition, an open system. It continues to exist because of its exchanges of energy (or information) with its environment (what is outside the system in a state of equilibrium). The shape the change takes, results from environmental inflow and from the previous state of the system, so that the evolution of the system is *iterative*, that is, the path of development it follows depends on its previous state. This has an important consequence: dynamic systems evolve in a non-linear fashion, which means that a factor that influences the system may not have results proportional to its magnitude. Another interesting factor to take into account is that the forces that affect the working of a system do not always have a deterministic character, they may be random events that may affect the course of change in the system, and so producing what is called *bifurcation points*. Finally, there is a moment in which the forces that govern dynamic systems reach a temporal state of equilibrium from which the system does not evolve any further. This final point is called an *attractor*. Examples are the temperature set in a thermostat in an air-conditioning system, the body size of an adult animal, or the linguistic proficiency level of a human speaker in a cultural group (van Geert, 2003).

But isolated systems within an environment are not the only matter of interest to us. Systems are in interaction among themselves, and often there are systems hierarchically nested within other systems, as well as interacting with others in networks. This creates a complex dynamics with very interesting features, since then bifurcation points abound; which may produce, together with the effect of the iterative principle, dramatic changes in the structure and functional properties of the system, in the way it maintains its stability and interacts with others.

From what has been said so far, the structure of an object (or a body) is then the result of a temporal state of equilibrium within its environment, and changes with its new encounters. So shape (form) is also a cause of change, as well as a result of previous encounters. That is why concepts such as affordances and effectivities are useful to relate structure and action.

We may speculate that biological evolution has followed this path of change. That efficient causality has proceeded in the way we have just outlined, and so different attractors and different spaces of stability came to be, which, in turn, started new dynamical processes. If we were not wrong when saying so, we may also add that mate-

rial objects (rocks, water, a cloud in the sky, or a wave in the sea) are dynamic systems in states of equilibrium with different parameters of stability that affect their temporal duration. The same can be said of live matter, of living things, capable of reproducing themselves, as well as acting in their environment in order to keep their negentropic state, their structure, and their internal and external homeostasis. That is, they act as if they were following teleonomic causality models – a rule-governed path to reach a final point.

What Is Psyche? Who Is Psyche?

Now we have some elements to risk formulating an answer to the question of what Psyche is. If we accept what has been said so far, we may say that Psyche is the working of dynamic systems capable of producing movements to maintain their own existence and to reproduce themselves. A very vague and wide definition, that would also apply to many types of spontaneous physical phenomena and life and also applies to groups. If we were to refer to the human Psyche, we may add that Psyche is also capable of setting its own goals for action and even to creating images of the world and of itself as a way of understanding who herself is and what to look for in the future. Namely, Psyche is also capable of setting imagined final causes that would act as stimuli and norms to canalize her own actions, actuations and activities.

Dynamics systems theory is a set of formalisms, it is a sort of language game. It is also a young creature whose very existence cannot be explained without the cooperation of computers (which carry out their lengthy calculations), without a General Theory of Systems (von Bertalanffy, 1950), without the mathematics of complexity, or without Boolean logics, algebra, Arabic number notation and the invention of writing (Havelock, 1991; Olson, 1991; Ong, 1982). It is only when one reaches some proficiency in the use of these tools painfully accumulated by generations throughout time, that one can conceive the possibility that Psyche may be the effect of the working of dynamic systems. One does not immediately perceive Psyche as a dynamic system. Dynamic systems may help to make sense of some of what we sense and feel of the movements of others, and of the results of the operations of our own Psyche. That is, formalisms are useful for science only if they provide us with a rationale to make sense of our own experience, of the experience of everyone, of every individual. This is what makes science to furnish us with truths, because we take something as such when it helps us to make sense of what we experience, to stabilize our image of the world, and so makes our future less unpredictable, allow us to devise ways of solving problems and to plan ahead. Science, together with other forms of epistemic discourse, is among the resources we have to reduce uncertainty and direct our lives.

Science, then, lays on formalisms developed throughout historical time, but also on individual experience. But, what is individual experience?, how can we feel the world and ourselves?, how can we amplify our capacities for experiencing?, how can we communicate these experiences?, how can we be sure that we all experience the world in a similar manner? Answering these questions is of prime importance to ground scientific knowledge, and, above all, the scientific knowledge we have about Psyche, because *these are the phenomena Psyche produces*. When Psychology appeared as a scientific field, this was what it took as its main task: the study of consciousness, which sometimes was, and still is, called Experimental Phenomenology.

Conscious experience has to be described and explained, as cognition and behavior are. Not only because conscious experiences are the stuff our biographies are made of, but also because sometimes it affects the way we move around, how we interpret what is going on around us and, above all, the way we communicate with others, conceive our world and our lives, and gather knowledge and store it for the use of future generations.

So, Psyche is not just a virtual object to be scrutinized. I, myself, am a Psyche. Psychology cannot just explain what Psyche is

or does. It also has to go into what each of us says about what he or she feels about the objects of the world and him or herself, and how she or he feels about what others do. When inquiring into this, surely some differences, but also regularities will appear. And Psychology has to deal with the explanation of both.

Consciousness and Experience

Psychology came to be a science taking consciousness as the field area for research. The so-called founder father of the discipline – Wilhelm Wundt – took "immediate experience" to be the subject matter of psychology. This make Psychology to be an empirical science, but it was one that looked at experience in a peculiar manner. The rest of the empirical sciences were concerned at the study of "mediated experience", that is, experience produced by an object that mediated the perceived experience. These other sciences worked as follows. When an object was being observed the observer's flow of consciousness was stabilised by the presence of the object, and so the human experiences mediated by this object could be recorded. But psychology was not concerned with the observation of experiences mediated by objects, it was concerned by "immediate consciousness"; that is, rather than looking at what you experience when before an object, the focus was in scrutinizing the regularity of the operations that happen in consciousness, which make it possible to have experiences of the world. Obviously any experience is always two-sided, it is at the same time mediated and immediate, has an objective and a subjective pole, and psychology is concerned about the latter.

As Blumenthal (2001) put it,

Consciousness is not a thing-like physical concept. Rather it is an immediate and transient process, the investigation of which amounts to no less than the study of subjectivity. Consciousness is a continuous flow, a constant unfolding of experience, which according to Wundt's findings cannot be separated into discrete "faculties" as has been done in ancient times. (p. 127)

This two-sided nature of experience and the active character of consciousness was the kernel of Franz Brentano's approach.

Every mental phenomenon is characterized by (. . .) the intentional (or mental) inexistence of an object, and what we may call (. . .) immanent objectivity. Every mental phenomenon includes something as object within itself, although they do not all do so in the same way. In presentation something is presented, in judgement something is affirmed or denied, in love loved, in hate hated, in desire desired and so on. (Brentano, 1924, 88)

According to Brentano, our experience of the world, and of ourselves as a part of the world, is a result of what psyche does, of how the three ways in which Psyche acts combine around the object. These are as follows: (a) *presentations* make the object appear in consciousness; (b) *judgement* asserts the reality or unreality, the truth, falseness or degree of probability of what is presented (so the combination of both may result in perceiving, imaging, or remembering); and (c) *phenomena of interest* (positive or negative, such as love or hate) that make the object to be desirable or undesirable.

Experience, so viewed, is not only something that happens in consciousness (although it is true that sunlight happens to penetrate in my consciousness and I can do little to avoid it when being outdoors in a sunny day), but also something that depends of what Psyche does (sunlight may be real or imagined, delicious or painful, missed or resented, etc.). The role of psychology is that of describing and explaining how the encounters between the individual organism and the world (the acts of Psyche) make experience to appear in the consciousness of the experiencer.

The Social-Cultural-Historical Nature of Experience

Experience itself is canalized by the social discourses which flow within a particular socio-cultural context at a time. This makes knowledge and science historically contingent, as well as instrumental for setting new horizons for truth, and methodologies for reaching such evasive and valued commodity. Truth is like an unreachable love, one longs for it, but in spite of partial advances, our seducing efforts never manage to be but partially successful at best. The Eros and Psyche story seems to repeat itself in science.

Nevertheless, social and theoretical discourses furnish our minds and provide us with images of the world, and give sense and meaning to our lives. Psychology also plays this role within the disciplinary division of labor. It provides us with images of what we are, how we perceive, think, or feel. And also who each of us is, or should be, together with models and techniques on how to change if one wants to be successful and lovable. This is so because Psychology, as any other social practice and discourse, is connected to the current concerns of the community it belongs to, as well as with all other social discourses, either scientific or even mythical. It can be no surprise then, that conflicting images of how or who I am, or should be, are very salient when one changes from one social context to another, either in time or space.

There is an interesting consequence of this. Psychology is one of the cultural artifacts for the construction of the self, for constructing images of who I am, for making sense of who my Psyche is. And, as an outcome to this, to give relevance, sense and meaning to my experience, to the world I live in, and so it also provides guidelines on how to act in order to reach one's social and personal goals. Surely one should remember that Moral Science was one of the disciplinary forefathers of the social sciences, and psychology as well.

Viewed in this way, psychology cannot be solely concerned with *what* Psyche is, but also with *who* Psyche is. Perhaps this is one of the reasons for the tension, and dialectics, between theoretical and applied psychology. But this also helps to explain why "what Psyche is", is related to "who Psyche can be" in a particular social-cultural-historical context.

Locating Socio-Cultural Psychology: Levels of Organization

Psychology is the disciplined form of knowledge devoted to the study of Psyche, so it has to be able to approach its subject matter in all its complexity. This is not an easy task. It requires consideration of how experience comes to appear, what are the structures that provide the conditions of possibility for the observed movements and transformations, the form these transformations take and when and how they happen. Psychology faces the task of describing and explaining how the phenomena of experience are produced in the individual consciousness, and to link the production of these phenomena to observable empirical movements, as well as to state principles which would explain the observed regularities. In other words, Psychology cannot renounce to either an etic or an emic approach. Emic experiences are the "material prima" upon which knowledge is elaborated. And etic explanations are indispensable for making possible that emic experiences can make us to conceive the world.

Table 1.1 sketches a theoretical-methodological approach that could be of use for these purposes. The first column maps the different levels of organization – from physical to socio-cultural – which we believe are currently useful for the description and explanation of the kinds of phenomena the etic and emic perspectives focus on. The second column presents the explanatory principles for each of these levels: And the third and fourth columns refer respectively to the experiential and structural aspects of psychological phenomena. Experiences (emic) allow one to conceive the realities (etic) of the world.

The algebraic expression $y = f(x)$ sums up how the emic and etic aspects of psychological explanation relate to each other via a functional explanation, always in an identical relational fashion, although this does not mean that the functional explanation keeps being identical. It changes as the elements that appear in each row describe phenomena of an increasing complexity as one proceeds downwards following the time arrow.

This table tries to capture the evolutionary and developmental nature of psychological phenomena. The down-pointing time arrow depicts how throughout evolution, ontogenesis and history, new emic phenomena appear, and so new mundane entities show themselves in consciousness, and so changing the ways the world can be conceived. Physical forces become stimuli, and then signals, which in turn make possible to feel sensorial qualities, that conform types of objects, which later can be individualized. This is the process that makes possible that along the evolution and development the world shifts its shape, and with it, the conception we have of it and ourselves. Chapters 10 and 14 are devoted to a more elaborate explanation of this process.

And what if we reverse the functional equation? What would happen if we attempt to explain experience by resorting to the causal forces of the encounters of mundane structures, i.e., reversing the equation making it to become $x = f'(y)$? This is no other thing that what scientists do when explaining the experience we have of the world via the creation of counter-intuitive entities (such as atoms, waves, and forces) and the elaborated algorithms for accounting of their interrelationships (see Table 1.2). This move is typical of the so-called naturalistic approach, as opposed to the phenomenological approach presented before.

What way should we take, the phenomenological or the naturalistic? Psychology seems to be caught in a quandary. Either it offers an explanation of experience by resorting to the existence of supposed natural entities, whose existence should depend on some empirical proof (something difficult to maintain once the very idea of experience is taken as a black box that never should be opened). Or the very existence of the world is the result of an elaboration

Table 1.1: Theoretical-methodological approach (1)

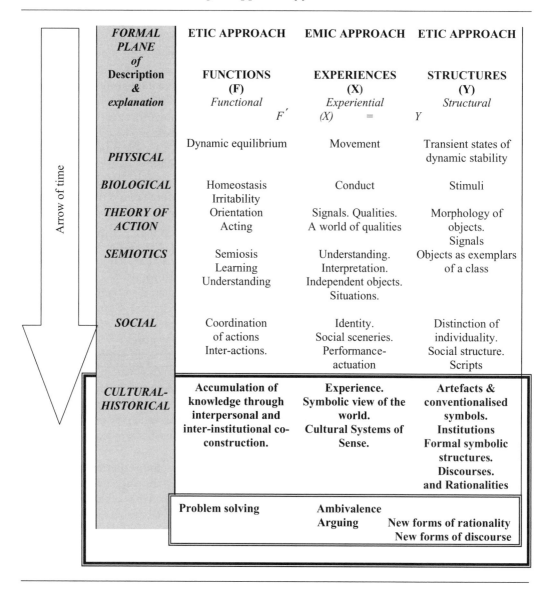

	ETIC APPROACH	EMIC APPROACH	ETIC APPROACH
FORMAL PLANE of **Description** & *explanation*	**FUNCTIONS (F)** *Functional* F'	**EXPERIENCES (X)** *Experiential* (X) $=$	**STRUCTURES (Y)** *Structural* Y
PHYSICAL	Dynamic equilibrium	Movement	Transient states of dynamic stability
BIOLOGICAL	Homeostasis Irritability	Conduct	Stimuli
THEORY OF ACTION	Orientation Acting	Signals. Qualities. A world of qualities	Morphology of objects. Signals
SEMIOTICS	Semiosis Learning Understanding	Understanding. Interpretation. Independent objects. Situations.	Objects as exemplars of a class
SOCIAL	Coordination of actions Inter-actions.	Identity. Social sceneries. Performance-actuation	Distinction of individuality. Social structure. Scripts
CULTURAL-HISTORICAL	**Accumulation of knowledge through interpersonal and inter-institutional co-construction.**	**Experience. Symbolic view of the world. Cultural Systems of Sense.**	**Artefacts & conventionalised symbols. Institutions Formal symbolic structures. Discourses. and Rationalities**
	Problem solving	**Ambivalence Arguing**	**New forms of rationality New forms of discourse**

Arrow of time

of Psyche, and so no entity can be conceived without resorting to a developmental explanation. But do we really have to choose between these two alternatives? Our option is to accept both, and relate them in dialectical form (see Figure 1.3).

By using alternatively the phenomenological and the naturalistic approaches, to explain experience and empirically support explanation in successive steps, we may be able to overcome what sometimes is viewed as two alternative and irreconcilable approaches to knowledge, between which one has to choose because of ontological, epistemological, or ideological reasons.

This way of portraying the evolution of Psyche allows one to locate what is the task of socio-historical-cultural research: *the description and explanation of experience and how it influences action.* But this way of conceiving the task of Psychology also helps to locate the socio-cultural research

Table 1.2: Theoretical-methodological approach (2)

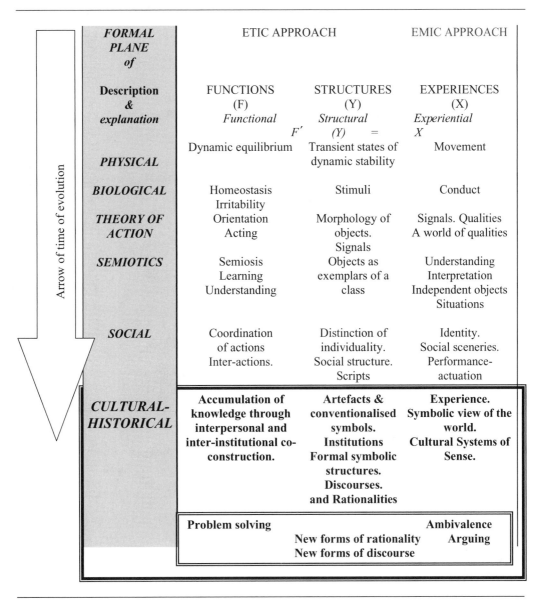

FORMAL PLANE of	ETIC APPROACH		EMIC APPROACH
Description & explanation	FUNCTIONS (F) *Functional*	STRUCTURES (Y) *Structural*	EXPERIENCES (X) *Experiential*
		F' (Y) = X	
PHYSICAL	Dynamic equilibrium	Transient states of dynamic stability	Movement
BIOLOGICAL	Homeostasis Irritability	Stimuli	Conduct
THEORY OF ACTION	Orientation Acting	Morphology of objects. Signals	Signals. Qualities A world of qualities
SEMIOTICS	Semiosis Learning Understanding	Objects as exemplars of a class	Understanding Interpretation Independent objects Situations
SOCIAL	Coordination of actions Inter-actions.	Distinction of individuality. Social structure. Scripts	Identity. Social sceneries. Performance-actuation
CULTURAL-HISTORICAL	**Accumulation of knowledge through interpersonal and inter-institutional co-construction.**	**Artefacts & conventionalised symbols. Institutions Formal symbolic structures. Discourses. and Rationalities**	**Experience. Symbolic view of the world. Cultural Systems of Sense.**
	Problem solving	**New forms of rationality New forms of discourse**	**Ambivalence Arguing**

Arrow of time of evolution

realm within the family of psychological sub-disciplines, as well as it is instrumental for connecting Psychology with other forms of disciplined knowledge. This theoretical-methodological approach is also of use to avoid the dangers of reductionism, or the lack of care in the application of the principle of parsimony.

There is no doubt that, if one takes the naturalistic (etic) approach, any phenome-non chosen from Table 1.2 can be described (and explained) using the methodological tools of an earlier functional explanation (i.e., a human phenomenon as only social, biological, or physical), but this reduction-ist move will unavoidable involve the fail-ure to account for the emic characteristics of the experience under scrutiny – which automatically will be downgraded to an inferior phenomenological and ontological

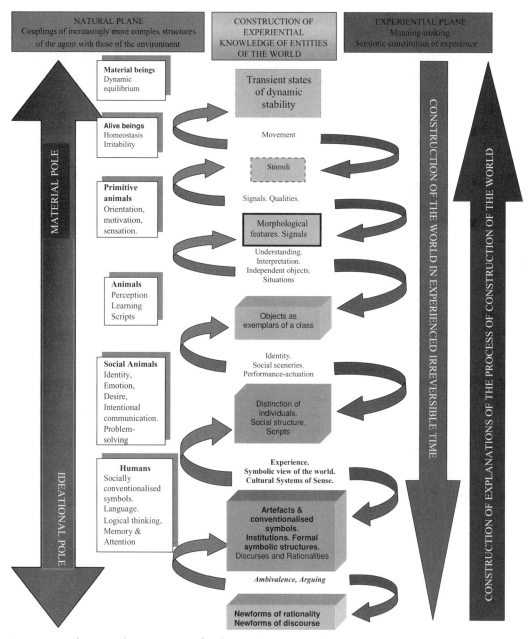

Figure 1.3. The mutual constitution of reality and experience. Co-construction of the world by the dialectics between *explanation* and *understanding*.

status – and so failing to perform the explanatory role depicted in Figure 1.3.

The opposite move, that of offering a higher form of explanation than needed, it is a much easier trap to fall in. The failure to apply the principle of parsimony would also break the explanatory cycle, detaching the studied phenomena from nature and ignoring a part of the task to be carried out.

The socio-cultural and cultural-historical domain is characterized by the centrality of the function of co-construction, and focuses on either artifacts and symbolic forms (the etic approach) or on the agent's (person's or social institution's) views of the world (sense systems). The study of these phenomena requires new epistemological strategies that go beyond the ones well known for the study of other levels (biological, action, or even semiotic levels).

Towards a New Epistemology in Socio-Cultural Sciences

Viewing the practices of dealing with theories in psychology in recent decades, one may think that many psychologists expect theories to be ready-made, finished, and supply immediately applicable "products" that can be linked with their particular empirical needs. If one of those does not fit, it is not repaired (i.e., transformed into a more fitting form), but abandoned in full. It is replaced by selection of another – "pre-packaged" – theory that is tried out in a similar way. Psychologists' work becomes that of consumers' use of theories, not creation of new ones (or transformation of the old ones). It is obvious that consumers' selection between ready-made products cannot innovate the products. Dissatisfaction with these products may lead to a producer to offer a new – yet "pre-packaged" – theory as yet one other of such products. What becomes lost in this is the psychologists' general orientation towards creating their own abstract tools to deal with their needs. The tools are habitually selected, not created. In that selection, major mismatches occur between theories' implicit premises and the nature of the phenomena. As a result, many of psychology's empirical data – especially those created by "standardized instruments" – reduce our understanding of the phenomena studied (or at least do not enhance it).

Socio-cultural phenomena are highly variable. Variability of both kinds – inter-individual (so-called "individual differences") and intra-individual (variability within the person over time and contexts) is all over the place in psychological studies. One can observe its centrality through looking at published papers where standard deviations or other indicators of variation are reported[2] – often will one see these indicators being of magnitude that would render the use of the averages meaningless. Yet the authors – after reporting the variability data – go on and make further claims based on the averages, and differences of averages. These differences may be minimal – yet statistically significant – which for the authors' set mindset is *the* basis for further inductive generalizations.

Of course the generalizations are necessarily futile in such cases – or perhaps coincidentally analogous to whatever may happen in reality. Yet the social prescription of a frame of reference – the inter-individual frame here (see Valsiner, 2000, chapter 5 on frames of reference) – is mis-fitting with the phenomena. For the latter, the dominance of inter-individual variability in the data suggests the adoption of the individual-ecological or individual-socioecological reference frames (which both assume the normal state of affairs in the phenomena to be variable). As a result of reference frame substitution, most interesting psychological phenomena become transformed into the least interesting data – resulting in the loss of the phenomena (Cairns, 1986) and in empirically based generalizations that no longer represent the phenomena.

If the superimposition of the inter-individual reference frame to psychological research efforts is artificial (as we claim here), then why does that practice continue? Muzafer Sherif – years ago (Sherif, 1936) – explained phenomena like this through an analysis of social norm construction. Fixating a reference frame in a science through establishment of a social norm for its use is thus part of ordinary social psychology of human beings.

Many seemingly complicated problems in theoretical domains of different disciplines may have relatively simple solutions. The one for productive use of theory in psychological investigation is simple – *distancing from the social ideologies* (encoded as "-isms" in psychologists' discourse) with a parallel re-focus on the richness of the phenomena from where the empirical data are derived. This idea is not new in psychology – it was eloquently expressed in late 19th century by Conwy Lloyd Morgan in his elaboration of "two inductions" in scientific knowledge construction (Morgan, 1894; Valsiner, 2003).

In terms of the notion of the "methodology cycle" (Branco & Valsiner, 1997; see also General Conclusions here; Valsiner, 2000) that would entail "vertical" consistency between phenomena, basic assumptions, theoretical constructs, and – only finally (but most importantly) – methods developed on the basis of that consistency, completing the whole. This perspective would replace the currently widespread use of "horizontal consistency" – social consensus (or corporationist patenting) based symbolic acceptance or rejection of the many "-isms" that psychology's theoretical discourse uses (behaviorism, cognitivism, feminism, etc.)

A number of implications follow:

1. Quantification is not automatically the rule in deriving data from the phenomena. It may be adequate under circumstances when theoretically validated, and completely unscientific under circumstances where the theoretical construction calls for non-quantitative data derivation. In other terms – theory construction decides what kind of data fit for the given research task, not social consensus of "hardness" (versus "softness") of one or another direction in data derivation.

2. The general social role of the researcher transcends all socio-ideological (or ethnic) backgrounds within which each researcher is inevitably embedded. Thus, neither cognitivist nor feminist perspectives *in themselves* (i.e., because of their "-ism" social function) can produce new knowledge that is of universal value. Yet particular researchers (or groups of researchers) who may build upon one or another sets of assumptions (which may be, for matter of convenience of shorthand reference, labeled "-ist" of some kind) can build new knowledge as long as their goal is general *Wissenschaft*, rather than one or another social position assumption within the current map of the given discipline.

We are fully aware that both of these implications are precisely the opposite of the two prevailing tendencies in contemporary psychology – increased uncritical quantification and proliferation of the practice of social positioning (of researchers and research groups) within the current fields of psychology. Hence it is obvious that we do not find what is considered "new developments" (read: new "-isms") to be intellectually productive for the *Wissenschaft* of psychology. New knowledge is needed – unless the discipline vanishes in its local in-fighting between various "-isms" – and theory construction is central for guiding our current hyperfascination with psychology as "empirical science" into a domain of knowledge where the empirical studies are crucial for key theoretical propositions – rather than "adding to a database". The latter is a business concept – a storehouse – not at all fitting with *Wissenschaft* – the art of making knowledge.

Notes

1   *Wissenschaft* is a German word that is often translated as "Science", but that has a wider meaning. It literally means the 'activity of knowing' that makes one 'to come to understand' what is under scrutiny, also connecting it with other phenomena. Therefore, it refers to any rigorous form of knowledge, and so it does not need necessarily to conform to a canonical definition of science as opposed to e.g. the humanities.

2   This is not necessarily available in all published empirical papers – many omit publishing variability indicators all together.

References

Blumenthal, A. L. (2001). *A Wundt Primer. The operating characteristics of Consciousness.* In Robert W. Rieber & David K. Robinson: *Wilhelm Wundt in History. The Making of a Scientific Psychology.* New York: Kluwer Academic/ Plenum Publishers.

Branco, A. U., & Valsiner, J. (1997). Changing methodologies: A co-constructivist study of goal orientations in social interactions. *Psychology and Developing Societies, 9*, 1, 35–64.

Brentano, F. (1924). Psychologie vom empirischen Standpunkt I. Leipzig: F. Meiner.

Cairns, R. B. (1986). Phenomena lost: issues in the study of development. In J. Valsiner (Ed.), *The individual subject and scientific psychology* (pp. 97–111). New York: Plenum.

Diriwächter, R. (2004). Völkerpsychologie: The synthesis that never was. *Culture & Psychology, 10*(1), 179–203.

Havelock, E. (1991). Oral-Literate Equation: A Formula for the Modern Mind. In D. R. Olson & N. Torrance (Eds.), *Literacy and Orality* (pp. 11–27). New York: Cambridge University Press.

Jahoda, G. (1993). *Crossroads between culture and mind*. Cambridge. MA: Harvard University Press.

Morgan, C. L. (1894). *An introduction to comparative psychology*. London: Walter Scott Ltd.

Olson, D. R. (1991). Literacy and Objectivity: The Rise of Modern Science. In D. R. Olson & N. Torrance (Eds.), *Literacy and Orality* (pp. 149–164). New York: Cambridge University Press.

Ong, W. (1982). *Orality and Literacy. The Technologizing of the Word*. London: Routledge.

Prigogine, I., & Stengers, I. (1984). *Order out of Chaos. Man's New Dialogue with Nature*. Toronto: Bantam Books.

Sherif, M. (1936). *Psychology of social norms*. New York: Holt.

Valsiner, J. (2000). *Culture and human development*. London: Sage.

Valsiner, J. (2003). Comparative methodology as the human condition: Conwy Lloyd Morgan and the use of animal models in science. *From Past to Future, 4*(1), 1–9.

van Geert, P. (2003). Dynamic System Approaches and Modeling of Developmental Processes. In J. Valsiner & K. Connolly (Eds.), *Handbook of Developmental Psychology* (pp. 640–672). London: Sage.

von Bertalanffy, L. (1950). The theory of open systems in physics and biology. *Science, 111*, 23–29.

CHAPTER 2

Language, Cognition, Subjectivity

A Dynamic Constitution

Thomas Slunecko and Sophie Hengl

Language, cognition, and subjectivity – how do they relate? What happens to our understanding of psychology once we analyze this relation? To what extent are we "bound" to language, and, in extension, to discourse? In our attempt to get to the bottom of these questions and to determine the connections lying between language, culture, and the subject, we will be alternating between concrete examples and abstract considerations. We thereby hope to encourage our readers to follow us into more sophisticated epistemological concerns, which are, in our view, of most fundamental value for the elaboration of a genuine cultural psychology.

The premise to our argumentation is quite old: Aristotle already conceived of the human being as *zoon logon echon* – the animal that masters language. In the light of contemporary epistemology, however, we must be very precise about this honorable finding. A speaking animal is not an animal that, at a particular point in its evolution, has been accessorily bestowed with language; rather, this "human animal" – as we find it now regardless of all cultural differences – could never have come into being without it.

To put it the other way: Language cannot possibly be removed from humans without simultaneously having "the human" as such eradicated. Language is constitutive of the speaking animal's being-in-the-world, or in less philosophical terms, language is constitutive of humans' position or situation in the world (compare Fields, Segerdahl, and Savage-Rumbaugh, in this volume, for a reflection on language among primates). We shall dwell on the word "constitutive" at this stage, since it is of major relevance. It would not seem sensible to regard humans as beings, which at a certain point in time develop language, as one would put on a shirt. Rather, humans are simply not to be found outside of language. Indeed, the human being, as we encounter it today, has been brought about by humans' first and utmost cultural medium: language. Language, then, comes forward as the *conditio sine qua no* for such animal, which radically abandons its instincts in order to trust in learning, which moreover puts its faith in the transmission on knowledge as well as on social cooperation.

The 20th century has been filled with echoes to Aristotle's notion of *zoon logon echon*. We would like to cite three of them, which prominently have inspired our work: Making use of the specific capacities of his language, the French psychoanalyst Lacan (1977) defined the human being as "parlêtre" – from parler, to speak and être, to be – thus as "speechbeing," whose self-created environment is primarily linguistic, not biological – a notion that also conveys his key idea that language structures all human experience. Speaking with the German phenomenologist Martin Heidegger, language is the "house of being" (1993: 237). Indeed, language houses us, provides us with a home without which we would not be able to live. Heidegger's metaphor, however, retains a flaw; it could in fact be tempting to think of that house as one we can step out of. Clearly, such thought would be misleading: the boundaries of language are the boundaries of the world (cf. Wittgenstein, 1949, 5.6)

Different Concepts on the Horizon

Cultural psychologists usually do not build on anthropological and philosophical deliberations on human's generic being. Their starting point often rests on a more ostensible finding instead: there exist many languages, not a sole one; and as soon as we step out of our own language, we promptly notice that other languages dispose of concepts for facts, situations or occurrences that we, in our language, would not be able to properly utter. In his semi-academic book "They have a word for it" (1988), Rheingold gathered dozens of examples for such idiosyncrasies, that is, words that have developed in the semantic niches of particular cultures. Some of them are easily accessible to us, for example, the German *Torschlusspanik*, which indicates a possible growing uneasiness or even panic of childless women approaching their forties as they realize they might never have a child. Other examples of this are more difficult to take out of their cultural origin and context: for instance, an

untrained Westerner would be unable to recognize the *wabi* on a teacup made by a master of Japanese pottery. At first, an American eye would maybe see a tiny crack in the cup, but without understanding it as the distinctive, aesthetic flaw that marks the spirit of the moment, in which this very cup was created, and distinguishes this moment from all other moments in eternity. Most Japanese have access to this quality of rough spontaneity in their arts, be it in pottery or calligraphy. As soon as the Westerner starts to see the *wabi*, he or she has already been pulled into the Japanese aesthetic regime and *Weltanschauung*. This last example further demonstrates the extent to which any concept or notion is ultimately and principally intertwined with its semantic web, that is, with its culture. It can only be fully understood within this web. Likewise, my appropriation of a concept such as *wabi* must not be regarded as an isolated event, that is, as if I were merely adding a word to my vocabulary. Rather, such appropriation influences my whole semantic web and forever transforms the way, in which I perceive beauty in human artifacts.

Different Linguistic Structures – Different Worlds

Since the early 20th century, cultural differences between languages have been a major topic of scientific debate in linguistics, anthropology, and psychology. This debate is not about certain notions, which some languages account for and other languages lack (as the ones described by Rheingold). Rather, the emphasis here lies on the *structure* of language. Different languages do not merely articulate the same facts differently; nor do some languages merely detain more differentiated vocabularies than others on certain topics that are of particular ecological relevance to a speech community (the renowned – yet contested – example from Inuit, who possesses several words for snow, may come into mind here). Rather, what becomes cogent is the idea that along with each language, whole different *worlds* open up.

The so-called Sapir-Whorf hypothesis doubtlessly ranges among the most famous theories dealing with the relation between language, thought, and culture. Sapir and Whorf, the figureheads of this debate, stress the inexorable interconnection between our language and our worldview. According to the earlier facet of the hypothesis, "theory of linguistic determinism," language fundamentally determines our world; that is, we can only perceive what is semantically and structurally contained in our language: "Human beings do not live in the objective world alone, nor alone in the world of social activity as ordinarily understood, but are very much at the mercy of the particular language which has become the medium of expression for their society" (Sapir, 1958 [1929]: 162).

The hypothesis' later facet, termed "theory of linguistic relativism," which was further investigated by Whorf (1956), claims that different languages entail different ways of experiencing the world. At this point, we will not enter the widely held discussion on possible – more or less deterministic, more or less relativistic – interpretations of the Sapir-Whorf hypothesis. What we would want to retain, though, is its core idea: language powerfully configures the modes in which we perceive and experience the world. In other words, we all inherit a worldview along with the language we grow up in:

> We dissect nature along the lines laid down by our native languages (...). We cut nature up, organize it into concepts, and ascribe significances as we do, largely because we are parties to an agreement to organize it this way – an agreement that holds throughout our speech community and is codified in the patterns of our language. (Whorf, 1956: 213)

Whorf thereby suggests that content and form of language are interdependent, and more precisely, that conceptual categorizations of reality are, at least partially, determined by the structure of language. For example, English is a highly noun-oriented language; most things we try to define or which we argue about in English would hardly exist in a verb-oriented language. Likewise, English requires a time commitment, which means that every English sentence gives, some way or another, an indication on time – in contrast to, for example, Japanese, which holds a required status commitment. Linguistic structures, therefore, preconceive our worlds and what we know of them. And as we will see later in this paper, when our knowledge of the world changes, language, too, alters its form.

Language is Alive

So far, we have been somewhat neglecting this important aspect of language: language is not static and inert, but on the contrary, well alive and constantly moving about. It is therefore compelling to shift our perspectives on language from horizontal or synchronous considerations to vertical or diachronic ones; when examining the historical transformations languages undergo, we immediately find that each language is a living, relentlessly morphing formation. We also observe that languages have been borrowing terms from each other, in order to convey something they alone could not – or not properly – express, but that still has meaning to the speech community, or that has acquired meaning in the course of cultural exchange. The online encyclopedia *Wikipedia* (www.wikipedia.org) has a special category, which lists foreign notions that have recently been incorporated into the English language. For example, German words such as Zeitgeist, Delicatessen, Doppelganger, Kindergarten, and so on have gained certain autonomy and diffusion in English, but they still comprise an awareness of their linguistic origin, which, in the course of time, will entirely vanish: most of today's English speakers probably do not realize that the term "uncle" stems from the Latin word *avunculus*.

Language, however, does not solely change through such imports from other languages; it also transforms itself from within. It is interesting to note that some semantic domains transform themselves more quickly than others in. For instance, languages replace quite swiftly their taboo words, which therefore are different for every generation. The linguist Steven Pinker (1999) coins this phenomenon with the term "euphemism treadmill": a euphemism is an expression intended to be less offensive, or disturbing, than the word it replaces. When a phrase is used as a euphemism, it often becomes a metaphor, whose literal meaning is dropped. It seems, however, that after a while, a euphemism's power to contain an unpleasant or troubling idea diminishes, and that the negative connotations of the original referents resurface. What used to be a euphemistic description eventually becomes a taboo word itself. For example, *toilet room* was replaced by *bathroom* and *water closet*, which were respectively replaced by *rest room* and *W.C.*; similarly, *funeral director* replaced *mortician*, which replaced *undertaker*. Euphemisms are ubiquitous in economic, military, and political rhetoric – a phenomenon also called "doublespeak" (Lutz, 1987). For instance, "neutralizing the target" or "collateral damage" appears more suitable than "killing people," at least insofar as people's appetite would not be ruined while they watch the evening news; similarly, industry's "overflow" or "runoff" instead of "pollution" attenuate the unpleasantness of its damaging consequences on the environment.

Notions Have Their Destinies

As we have seen so far, words are inscribed in time; they come and go, and this coming and going is all but fortuitous. We shall now turn to an example, which permits us to illustrate the rise of a concept in a culture. Le Goff (1984) elaborates on the invention of the purgatory as concept. He thereby describes the gruesome campaign, which Christianity led against usury during the 12th and 13th century. Usury originally depicts the condition of paying back interest and compound interest charges (in Latin:

usura) to the person who has lent money, the usurer. This practice, which appears so self-evident today, was utterly incompatible with the Christian beliefs of the time, which traditionally regarded God and money as opposites. The charge of interest was thus fiercely condemned and classed as capital sin on five subsequent Vatican Councils. Yet at the same time, a new order was emerging in trade and manufacturing, an economy somewhat at dawn of capitalism, which required some kind of credit institution. So people painfully began to figure out a way of joining the traditional usury prohibition and the new economic prerequisites. During the 13th century, a rescuing concept emerged among the so-called *exempla*, that is, moralizing stories, which were slipped into allocutions and sermons in order to convince the public of the salutary effect of a given measure. This new notion was the purgatory. However familiar it may appear to us, there is no clear mention of the purgatory in the Bible. The purgatory is a new *topos*, which surged out of the pressure of the contradiction between sacred taboos and real requirements. It surfaced in order to circumnavigate the inconvenience of being excluded from heaven when dealing with the profitable formula of lending. The purgatory is an excellent illustration of symbolical dialectic: phenomenologically, it still represents hell; ontologically, though, it is already heaven, since the persons, in our case the usurers, who enter it, can be certain to reach paradise – after a period purifying affliction.

Our example illustrates the idea that notions and language do not randomly float in an empty space. In fact, they are intimately related to socio-historical circumstances, that is, to the overall condition of their culture. Humans appear to invent new concepts in threatening situations and to drop old concepts that have become obsolete. In this sense, cultural psychology may find its own translation of the beautiful sentence from Hölderlin's hymn to "Patmos": "Where, however, danger is, grows the saving power too" (in Heidegger, 1977: 28).

Linguistic Structures Have Their Destinies, Too

Psychologists know that linguistic structures evolve during childhood. It is stunning to observe, for example, how children who just start speaking, universally project souls onto everything; how they therefore employ all things, even lifeless things, as subjects of their sentences; and how they only gradually can be convinced of narrowing the scope of possible subjects to what for adult speakers seems appropriate. As it often happens, cultural-historical development can here be modeled after ontogenetic development; for the history of 'high cultures' has to some extent witnessed the eradication of an animistic world, where a plethora of agents with souls and intentions used to flourish. That world disappeared as soon as the structural-linguistic rule surfaced, according to which correct sentences would only contain humans – and sometimes perhaps animals – as subjects of emotions and actions; stones and trees would only be allowed to feel or to act in poetry, or else, under the safe and well-identifiable characterization as figure of speech, more precisely, as metonymy. Even an extremely powerful shift of world formatting such as the expulsion of animism, thus, also occurs within language. After that shift, poetry remains the only alcove, where trees may figure as subjects in adults' speech. Hence, adults' language is undergoing a kind of disillusionment; its once ubiquitous "sea of souls" is drying up to the extent that today, we as members of a contemporary speech community, perfectly understand who ought to have a soul and therefore may serve as a subject of our sentences. It so appears of interest to note that while we remove subjectivity from objects (e.g., we do not say "the tree has spoken" or "the car wanted"), we actually concede subjectivity to non-material entities, by saying, for instance, "economy is doing good" or "the government has carried out a program." We will come back to this phenomenon of "false entities" later in this chapter, when discussing discourse analysis. For the moment, we shall underline the main idea of this subsection: Language's structures and rules rise and fall much in the same way single terms do.

Language and Subject Formation

We shall now lead the case back to our discipline, psychology, and to one of the paramount semantic-linguistic transformations European mind was ever to experience, a transformation Havelock (1963, 1986) analyzes with remarkable acumen:

> At some time towards the end of the fifth century before Christ, it became possible for a few Greeks to talk about their 'souls' as though they had selves or personalities, which were autonomous and not fragments of the atmosphere nor of a cosmic life force, but what we might call entities or real substances.
>
> . . .
>
> Thereby, the radical change of meaning of the word psyche is of crucial importance: Instead of signifying a man's ghost or wraith, or a man's breath or his life blood, a thing devoid of sense and self-consciousness, it came to mean 'the ghost that thinks', that is capable both of moral decision and of scientific cognition, and is the seat of moral responsibility. (Havelock, 1963: 197)

We must therefore wait for Socrates and Plato in order to encounter the concept of a psyche that holds a sense similar to our contemporary understanding. For the first time then, indeed, the psyche is being depicted as a relatively autonomous inner entity. By opposition to that, Homer's heroes, who came before, were not yet equipped with a monolithic, distinctive inner-world, which would be separated from the outer-world; the Homeric word psyche still designates a general life force rather than a site of thinking and feeling.

Thought and feeling in Homer's heroes do not take place on one invariable location. Homer's terminology of the states of the soul hints at such fragmentation: "Some things happen in the 'thumos', others in the 'phrenes', others again in the 'kradiē', 'ētor', 'ker', still others in the 'noos' " (Taylor, 1989: 118). These notions can be loosely associated with bodily reactions or bodily locations; for instance, *kradiē*, *ētor*, or *ker* are to be identified within the heart region, *phrenes* and *thumos* have survived until now (cf. the English words "phrenic" and "thymus"). In short, these depictions refer to parts of the body, and not yet to the autonomous inner subject. The new concept of psyche that surfaces in Plato's times, gives rise to a radically new perspective: humans now start to possess and control a stable inner-space, an autonomous inner being, which is not immediately touched by outward circumstances. Individuals can now dissociate themselves with certain superiority from the fluctuating, ever-changing external world. Based on this dissociation, inner stability, and distance from what is immediately given, the new *homo metaphysicus* embarks on an unprecedented journey – a more expansive and a more active journey than an animist, absorbed in his local conflicts, could have ever dreamed of (Sloterdijk, 2004: 232).

Distance from the outside by way of an intangible, indestructible inner core: this notion sets an important psycho-political imprint onto the then incipient metaphysical aeon, which roughly begins to manifest itself within language around 500 B.C. – an aeon at whose exit we find ourselves now. In order to be able to start their affair with philosophical metaphysics, Greeks had first to get acquainted with the idea of an eternal, unbreakable soul. Havelock's title – *Preface to Plato* (1963) – is thus perfectly accurate: The success of Plato's philosophy, seminal as is was for the occidental history of ideas, only becomes possible on the basis of a prior formation of such 'metaphysically enabled' or attuned state of the soul in the human being.

Again, we are here not merely dealing with a single word – psyche – and its semantic impact. We are rather dealing with an overall alteration of both the linguistic order and the formation of the subject. The fact that the "discovery" of the psyche, as an independent inner space, involved more than just a change in the semantics of the word *psyche*, can be documented on a syntactical level.

According to Havelock, in the 5th century B.C., Greek pronouns, both personal and reflexive, began to appear in new constellations, for example, as objects of verbs implying cognition ("I think to *myself*"); they furthermore started to be placed in antithesis to the body, which the psyche was supposed to inhabit, or in opposition to body-based emotions. A sentence as common today as "I did not let myself get carried away by my anger" would simply not have been conceivable for the Greeks in Homer's times, since it implies this very autonomy and mastery of the self over emotions. Indeed, it was not only until the middle of the 5th century B.C. that the inner-space established itself in language. Or was it, on the contrary, language that created this inner-space, because the tendency to generate a self-ruled inner being, once articulated, became replicable and extensively multipliable? Does the emergence of a new language of the soul set off the proliferation of souls or, in more modern words, is psychology the one who makes the psyche bloom (cf. Sloterdijk, 1993: 178)?

Who Is the Agent of All That?

We shall now turn to the highly relevant culture-psychological question of who or what could be held responsible for such alterations of linguistic structures and thus for the conceptual transformations of conscience, the soul, and so on. The examples we borrowed from LeGoff and Havelock have pointed up, tacitly, that this task could not be ascribed to single "cultural heroes", that is, culture-making individuals. Though common sense would rapidly connect the cultural changes mentioned above to the life and work of "illustrious men" such as Socrates and Plato, it certainly is more accurate to regard these changes as dissipative creations of many minds among their predecessors, contemporaries, and successors.

We here find ourselves confronted by one of the major methodic discrepancies between traditional and cultural psychology. Cultural psychology, indeed, does not place individuals at the source of its research – as opposed to traditional psychology, which self-evidently always takes the individual as starting point. At all times, cultural psychology considers individuals as resulting from historical circumstances. Hence, it would run against the core logic of cultural psychology to base its epistemology on alleged individual culture-heroes, whose actions and decisions change the course of culture. What must be done instead is to describe cultural drifts, which are much too forceful to be shouldered by a single person. This contention, that is, the sense that single individuals are always the result or in the flow of something, has often repelled those humanists, who think of the subject as one that always has full choice as to start off in any direction he or she wants to. Nevertheless, cultural psychology cannot think in terms of transmission processes, which lie above the level of single individuals. In that sense, even individuals as illustrious as Socrates and Plato are already epiphenomena of a higher non-personal "intelligence," which inscribes itself into the thinking and acting person. Speaking with Sloterdijk (1988: 43), we do not "have" our tradition, the tradition 'has' us. As soon as we awaken to thought, we have always already been "started" by our cultural and linguistic tradition; and when "starting over", the individual does so only on the premise of in his or her "being started" already.

Do We Acquire Language or Vice Versa?

In order to abandon psychology's habit of always taking the fully accomplished, individual subject as the natural starting point (and therefore, as the primary agent of cultural changes), a simple consideration may be helpful – a consideration that leads us back to language – language patently surpasses the single individual. No human develops language alone; we all have entered a seamless stream of linguistic transmission, which has been accompanying human evolution from the start. This is why all theoretical models, which place too much emphasis on the subject and his or her own degrees of freedom when it comes to the construc-

tion of symbolic worlds, are necessarily on the wrong track.

It is part of the same deceptive reasoning to presuppose a neutral notion of "the individual," who – at some point in his or her development, but always already as an individual subject – starts to learn something like language. Still, psychologists have mostly been studying the process by which people acquire language, without bothering to examine the ramifications of language on how people are constituted (notable exceptions being Vygotsky, 1962, or Bruner, 1983, 1990). They start out – at least implicitly – with the idea of some kind of "natural soul," or, cognitively speaking, of a universal mental processor, which achieves language and other cultural competencies as additional instruments; they so omit the constitutive effects these instruments have on the processor. However, if we contemplate the world just as "an indifferent flow of information to be processed by individuals on his or her own terms, [we] lose sight of how individuals are formed and how they function" (Bruner, 1990: 12). "[H]ow individuals are formed" is the crucial moment of this citation, since it explicitly indicates that individuals cannot be presupposed, but that they emerge out of the call, among others, of language.

In fact, borrowing from Bruner's (1993) wording – "do humans acquire culture or vice versa?" – humans are not primarily beings, who dispose of language; rather, they are also beings, who themselves are acquired, modified, or formatted by language, and thus by their culture. Culture is thus constitutive of psyche; and when psychology builds on the individual alone, it always resorts to reduction. There hardly is a more laconic formulation than Geertz's (1973: 49): "there is no human nature apart from human culture." Language and culture – that is, the symbolic arrangements and practices transmitted onto us by the preceding generation – always acquire us first. And for all our lives, we remain open for the "inspirations" that emerge from our "traffic" with them.

We may thus delineate the following conclusion: symbol systems preexist the individuals who grow into them. These systems constitute a set of collective cultural tools, which transforms anyone who starts employing them into a member, a reflection, and an embodiment of that culture. Hence, language "owns" or "has" us; it structures thinking and feeling; it even provides us with formats of subjectivity. We are in this sense always the results of processes, which lie above and beyond us, since we, as individuals, do not choose our cultural and linguistic formats and imprints. We rather find ourselves woven together with them in a net, within which we "live, and move, and have our being" (Acts of the Apostles, 17, 28). Speaking with Heidegger (1962), we are "thrown" into them. In spite of common psychological practice, thus, subjects cannot be starting points for a psychology of culture; they are already epiphenomena of cultural and linguistic environments and circumstances. Individuals certainly move and modify these semantic worlds, as they are the ones bearing them; but as transformed transformers, they themselves are always simultaneously moved and modified.

Language in Contemporary Psychological Research Practice

Keeping these thoughts in mind, we shall now turn to some of the theoretical and methodical domains, which currently set much of social and cultural psychology's agenda. We will specifically fine-tune our previous reflections on the relation between language and culture with respect to discourse analysis, theory of social representations, and metaphor analysis.

Discourse Analysis

At its most basic, discourse analysis is a theory and research practice for studying social practices and the actions that constitute them. Since the 1980s, discourse analysis has developed alternative perspectives on the hitherto predominantly cognitivist accounts of such basic psychological issues as attitudes (Billig, 1987, 1991; Potter & Wetherell, 1987), gender (Marshall & Wetherell, 1989;

Wetherell, Steven & Potter, 1987), memory (Edwards & Potter, 1992), and categorization (Edwards, 1991, 1997). Unfortunately, the notion of discourse analysis as well as the research practice that lays claim to this title are extremely heterogeneous (for an orientation with regard to the different strands of discourse analysis, cf. Potter & Wetherell, 1990; Potter & Edwards, 1993). For the sake of this overview, we will follow the tradition of continental social philosophy and cultural analysis that is heavily inspired by the work of Foucault (1970, 1972, 1977). Discourse as described by Foucault signifies a system of positions, rules, and strategies of speech (or other practices), which characterize and determine a certain social field, establishing which actions and assertions are permissible on this field.

One example for such permissible actions is ready at hand: We, the authors, will possibly have to negotiate the narrative shape of this chapter with our editors, since our writing modus does not fully correspond to the rather impersonal style usually found in scientific handbooks. As many other domains, science is thoroughly regulated as to "who can say what to whom in which form and from which position." These rules, however, remain implicit; they are tacitly embedded in scientists' actions. Nobody can properly spell them out, nobody ever overtly agreed to them. The reflection on these rules and the eventual disclosure of the power relations inherent to them, constitute discourse analysis' focal point.

Discourse constantly though furtively comprises an interplay of power and knowledge, where strategies of knowledge formation and transmission are intertwined with disciplinary practices (compare Castro-Tejerina & Rosa, 2006, in this volume, who apply this very principle to psychology). Even the worldview of a culture *in toto* may be regarded as a "discursive formation," that is, as an output of the "discourse machinery" that pervades und structures this culture. By opposition to the theory of social representations, which we will refer to later in this paper, discourse analysis does not only deal with conceptual atoms in their cognitive solitude; it is mainly concerned with forms of realization, with social practice and performance.

We already mentioned an important discourse analytical argument above – when we referred to the warning against false entities: Language deceives us when leading us to believe in the existence of subjects and objects such as rulers, madness, state, religion, humanity, and so on. It does so by allowing for the linguistic use of these terms as if they were natural entities. As soon as we awake to conscience, we find ourselves in a network of such terms, we assimilate their normative force, and we employ them in order to interpret our initially wordless existence. Discourse analysis, however, considers these "things" only as correlates of specific practices; the semantics of common sense, thus, is illusionary, it corresponds to what Barthes (1972) calls "the mythology of everyday life." For discourse analysts, things such as the state, madness, religion, humanity, freedom, and so on may be understood solely out of the discursive practice that created them at a particular point in time. These things have no essence and continuity as such; if they had, different times and cultures would have no choice but to come to terms with them, that is, to react to their given existence with specific practices. To handle these things does not mean to respond to some continuous natural essentials. Instead, these things (state, religion, madness, etc.) are to be explained out of our discursive practice – and never the other way around. Because madness or sexuality (Foucault's most prominent objects of inquiry, 1965, 1976, 1978, 1985, 1986) are not natural entities, but discursively constructed ones, there is no point for science to go asking people about their attitudes toward these objects. Rather, science has to analyze the discursive practice, by which madness or sexuality emerge in their specific historical appearances. This critique blatantly affects human and social sciences, as long as they thoughtlessly take their starting point from the false entities and overlook the process of their creation. The methodical con-

sequences of that critique are cogent: when asking people about their attitudes, judgments, or opinions on madness, beauty, sexuality, and so on, that is, about their beliefs on false entities – an endemic practice in psychology – all one does is corroborate the faith in false objects. Instead of trying to leave the illusionary circle, one ultimately ends up substantiating and reproducing the dominant discourse and ideology.

Everyday consciousness cannot deter and dispose of the conditions of historical discursive practice, since it is constituted by them. Furthermore, everyday consciousness cannot inform on these conditions, since it is subjected to them. Hence, the research practice of addressing this consciousness directly – that is, of assessing peoples' attitudes on this and that – is a quite narrowsighted strategy. In the more poignant discourse analytical jargon, such strategy rather petrifies die self-illusion regarding false entities, and it perpetuates the disguise and numbness of every day consciousness when facing the forces to which it is exposed. Consequently – and contrary to many hermeneutic approaches – discourse analysis breaks with the intentions and the self-understanding of the interpreted text. It permeates through the overt opinions of the producer of such text, and purposely overlooks what he or she believes to know about the world.

Discourse analysis thus examines the practical routines of our talking and acting together and the changes of these practices over time. It is the particular power of this examination that allows revealing the extent to which false entities (the free market, the government, etc.) and their respective power relations are created in everyday life, for everyday knowledge. It focuses on the questions of how things are displayed, which constitutive features of society are thereby being disclosed or concealed, to which ends (power relations), and to whose profit. Even though discourse is understood as something supra-personal – that is, there is no powerful author of the discourse – the discourse analytical approach is always inherently critical towards power players, and towards science: for science, too, does not sufficiently question its own terms and power acts. This genuinely critical stance – in particular towards science and ideology – may be the reason why discourse analysis has only been reaching psychology's mainstream in very low doses.

For our sketch of cultural psychology, we thus retain an important lesson from discourse analysis: culture preserves and alters its power relations through language. It may be because of this very focus on power relations that discourse analysis sometimes displays a zealous tendency to argue politically too quickly. This happens whenever the critical approach would not move beyond the accusation of single actors. In such a case, we would possibly lose our main focus from view: language inscribes itself into our concerns about the world and concurrently speaks through, or formats, these concerns. Even when analyzing a single person's speech – be it the speech of a president (Ruiseco & Slunecko, 2006) – not all of the findings may be imputed to that person alone, since his or her words always float on discursive constellations, which are older, more sustainable, and more pervasive than his or her intentions.

Social Representations

Similarly to discourse analysis, theory and method of social representations (Farr & Moscovici, 1984; Moscovici, 1988, 2001; Duveen, in this volume; Duveen & Lloyd, 1990; Canter & Blackwell, 1993; Wagner & Hayes, 2005; Flick, 1998) settles the construction of reality onto the site of human communication. In comparison to discourse analysis, however, it alludes much less to power relations and ideology (though there are notable exceptions, among them, e.g., Augoustinos 1998; Wagner, Elejabarietta & Lahnsteiner 1995) – which might be the cause of its more favorable reception within mainstream psychology, especially social psychology, since the 1990s. We would like to dwell on this theory for a while, because

it seems both to convey and yet to overlook some of cultural psychology's concerns.

Basing his theory on Durkheim's (1965) concept of collective representations, Moscovici (1988, 2001) depicts social representations as the outcomes of collective elaborations of social objects. A community's world is composed of social objects (e.g., the social objects at "12 o'clock" in Figure 2.1). New objects start to exist for a group only when they are given a name: it is by designation that something achieves social reality. Once incorporated into a community's repertoire, each social representation is constantly transformed through the continuous stream of language. This transformation and elaboration of social representations takes place in everyday communication processes, and nowadays very much in mass media, too. A social representation's elaboration process never reaches an end; social representations exist through their unceasing production – and they decay when they are no longer of use in a community's representational world.

The emergence of a social representation may be particularly well documented whenever a community's identity is threatened (cf. Figure 2.1). Such challenges, be they social (e.g., integration of refugees), ecological (e.g., the ozone gap), technological (e.g., genetics, technologies of reproduction), and so on call for material as well as symbolical coping strategies. Whereas material coping is being delegated to professionals, e.g., engineers, doctors, and so on, symbolical coping is a matter of the community's discursive performance, which ensures and protects the integrity of its semantic identity (Wagner, 1998). Symbolical coping usually involves the new phenomenon's association with already existing social objects, a procedure called "anchoring": the new or menacing phenomenon is affixed to the present knowledge apparatus of the group, so already acknowledged representations are being activated in order to describe the phenomenon. AIDS, for instance, an altogether mysterious phenomenon in its beginnings, was first anchored in what we would today consider a very rough form into the medical (as a venereal disease) or religious realm (as a punishment from God); it took some time before the social representation of AIDS gained a more precise shape and substance as an immunodeficiency syndrome.

The community's overall "cognitive" strategy thus aims at projecting elements, which belong to an acknowledged source domain, onto an unknown target domain; we employ familiar structures in order to approach the unknown, that is, we chart the unknown with metaphors. Metaphorization – the use of a metaphor – may be described as symbolic immunity response: 'objects', which are too abstract, or too far off the common life world and experience, thus barely accessible, create a "cognitive tension" in the collective. To overcome this tension, already existing concepts are transferred onto these new challenges, which may then be processed, tailored, and made comprehensive. This way, the unusual turns into a tangible picture and becomes a conceivable reality.

Moscovici understands social identity as constituted by a common knowledge on the world's objects and phenomena. The elaboration of this knowledge is the common project of the whole speech community, and it enables any of its members to orient him – or herself, as well as to interconnect with others within that identity structure. Only such shared knowledge, such common code allows for communication and joint action and, thus, guarantees the group's unity and cohesion (cf. Mühlmann, 1996).

Hence, social representationalists, too, know that we grow into specific semantic spaces. They know that we always already stand in a context of collective imagery. Individual experience, then, may only be comprehended in the light of collective experiential spaces; in fact, individual experience cannot be detached from its collective frame of reference. Social representations theory thus attempts to leave methodological individualism behind and to understand social reality as an outcome of complex historical-cultural negotiation

processes. However, research practice often does not keep up the theory's ambitions. It often so happens that, for the sake of feasibility, studies end up isolating both subjects and objects of inquiry. Many empirical studies on social representations question high numbers of independent *individuals* regarding their representations. Not only do they so inevitably find themselves within the one-person-paradigm; worse, they thereby also focus on what individuals *think* instead of their discursive *actions*. Finally – and even more problematic yet – empirical studies often address single, discrete, and sharply defined social objects (e.g., AIDS, the Euro, the ozone gap, genetics); thereby accounting for a certain atomism – as if such representations could be respectively processed in total isolation from others.

Even sudden changes of reality (as the ones illustrated in Figure 2.1), however, do not merely reverberate on such conceptual atoms alone; rather, they shove the whole grammar these conceptual atoms are inscribed in. The impact of the pest epidemic, for instance, which overcame 14th-century Europe and killed at least a third of its population within a few years, did not merely affect the social representations of the plague itself. To a much greater extent, this catastrophe had repercussions on that times' overall Weltanschauung and on its narrative order, that is, on the ways stories could be told in public. This shift can be easily witnessed in those days' literature, most impressively in the 100 stories, which Boccaccio gathered in his *Decameron* (1353/1924). When reading this eminent book, which was written shortly after the plague epidemic, one gets an unmistakable sense of how the firm modus of Christian Middle Ages' story telling broke down in the aftermath of the calamitous 1340s and 1350s. Though one still comes across religious and courtly characters – priests, hermits, nobles, and even a queen – the very narrative is utterly changed. The stories are loaded with a so far unheard of – and certainly unpublishable – irony and blasphemy; they convey lust for life in the present-day existence, sexual desire in particular, in

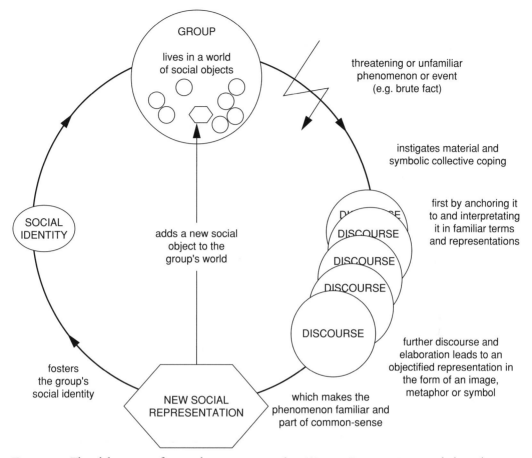

Figure 2.1. The elaboration of a social representation (see Wagner, Duveen, Farr, Jovchelovitch, Lorenzi-Cioldi, Marková, & Rose, 1999).

a hitherto unthinkable manner. All stories converge in one point: from now on, terrestrial existence should no longer be considered as an intermediate stage of suffering on the way to heaven. Instead, life on earth becomes the real thing, humans' last opportunity (Gronemeyer, 1993) to fulfill their wishes and to enjoy themselves. It seems as if the plague had forced humans' reliance on the Christian age's generous God and their confidence in His safe order of things to an end. It seems as if the plague had cracked the symbolic cover of peacefulness and security, under which medieval Christianity had been living for centuries.

Such profound alterations (and also structural linguistic changes like the one we encountered with Havelock) can not be grasped within social representations research practice; for this research practice focuses too much on semantic atoms, that is, on particular representations isolated from the complex web of meanings we call culture. It is thus possible – and actually quite common – to read and apply social representations theory individualistically, atomistically, and cognitively, against Moscovici's primary relational intentions. Social representations are then handled as if they resided in the heads of interacting individuals, as if there were a "distributed view" (Harré, 1984).

In our perspective, such usage undermines what is actually at stake: the notion that social knowledge is always embedded into interactive processes. Social knowledge mainly occurs implicitly – a system of values, ideas, and practices allowing for human orientation, a communal code allowing for the unambiguous designation of the world and its circumstances. This knowledge is like a baldachin, woven by joint speaking and acting, which floats above people's heads – an image corresponding to what Harré (1984) calls an "in between view" of social representations. It is important to note that this baldachin cannot be constructed with an unlimited amount of degrees of freedom, since the social knowledge it stands for constantly lies under ecological pressure. Whenever a system of social representations is not able to work out explanations for a situation that threatens the collective, it gets strained. To use yet other metaphors: human collectives necessarily produce some kind of semantic-linguistic vital coating, or imaginative atmospheres that protect, maintain, and expand their life spaces. Whatever occurs to the collective, it is being processed inside that semantic coating, which must be able to arrange and adjust reality for its inhabitants; as soon as they fail to do so, social representations – and the manner in which they are negotiated – start to reshuffle (Mühlmann, 1996; Slunecko, 2002).

Metaphor Analysis

In the 1980s, the examination of metaphorical structures of thought and speech has been developing – with or without explicit reference to social representations theory – into a genuine research method: metaphor analysis. Lakoff and Johnson's book "Metaphors we live by" (1980) has herein been of major importance. Far from taking a culture-psychological stance, however, metaphor analysis has been originally committed to the cognitivistic approach. Lakoff (1987) and Kovecses (1986) for instance employ the emotion anger in order to demonstrate to what extent the reality of the body underlies representations of emotions. Indeed, many colloquial expressions around anger (e.g., someone is boiling, is about to explode, is losing his cool, is hot under the collar, brimming with rage, etc.) belong to a field of metaphors that have to do with heat, internal pressure, and agitation; they may be summarized as follows: inside the body, a vessel heats up and is about

to burst – a picture that also corresponds to the physiological activity of the autonomous nervous system of an angry person. That is why Johnson (1987) coined such metaphor-based "reasoning" with the term "experiential realism" – a concept, which he then applied well beyond the realm of emotions.

Approaches such as Johnson's experiential realism leave room for "natural" things such as body sensations, which preexist discourse, and which inscribe themselves into discourse. In the cultural psychologist's view, however, this does not mean that emotions are universal – as Ekman, for instance, asserted (e.g., Ekman 1982, 1989), and as Lakoff (1987) partially endorsed. Even if emotions refer to certain physiological activities of the body, they still are social objects, which evolve within discourse. In other words, there are entirely disparate ways, by which emotions and the discourse on emotions can be embedded into a culture's semantic web. Even the so-called basic emotions – if they exist as such – can be enculturated and valued quite differently. Moreover, emotions sometimes appear to be culturally unique and hardly intelligible outside their culture, *fago* in Ifaluk-culture (Lutz, 1988), and *amae* in Japan (Doi, 1973, 1986, 2004) figuring among the most prominent examples. This argument can obviously also be applied to our Western emotional realm: for instance, the feeling of falling in love "western-style" is just as loaded with socio-historical prerequisites; it would not be accessible without the appropriate enculturation.

Hence emotions, too, are neither ahistorical nor acultural; they form part of the previously mentioned symbolic or imaginative atmospheres, which cultures produce through time. Social constructivists, precisely, have actually produced excellent work on the social construction of emotions (Averill, 1982, 1985, 1990), among them, on the invention of an emotion as basic as maternal love (Badinter, 1980), or on the cultural invention of a life phase as basic as childhood (Ariès, 1962; de Mause, 1974). We also find Sheper-Hughes's (1992) fieldwork on the economic and ecological conditions to maternal love, maternity, and bonding in a Brazilian shantytown very instructive.

Considering what we formerly said about discourse, we should particularly not overlook the discursive uses of metaphors: "When we define a certain part of the world metaphorically, this is not just an invitation to *think* about it in a certain way, it is also an invitation to *act* in terms of certain implied assumptions" (Danzinger, 1990: 351). Indeed, everyday knowledge does not primarily strive to represent the world (as it is the case for scientific knowledge), it rather looks for ways of acting in the world. Since metaphorical concepts always allude to specific actions, they are not "models *of* reality," but "models *for* reality" (Geertz, 1973: 93).

We just had developed a short piece of anger's metaphorical thesaurus. Apart from the "heat, pressure, and container" – expressions we mentioned, Lakoff (1987) also identified "madness" or "dangerous animals" as source domains for anger. So when choosing a certain metaphor, one also chooses to stress or to produce some aspects of the "target domain" to the detriment of others. "Highlighting" and "hiding" the target domain's qualities are terms usually employed in that context. As different anger metaphors highlight certain aspects and hide others, they become more or less suitable for distinct occasions. For example, "boiling with rage" is more passive and self-oriented than "to bite her head off," which holds a more active and object-directed connotation. With the help of one or the other metaphor, thus, alternative narratives of causal attribution and accountability may be alluded to (Gibbs, 1994; Edwards, 1997). Metaphors, to conclude, serve talking, they want to suggest practical consequences in communication; they generate and shift communicative realities (Edwards, 1991, 1997).

When it comes to psychological theory formation, metaphors appear as relevant for two reasons. First, the intangibility of psychology's objects requires particular auxiliary forms of illustration. Second, psychology's models are being drawn, sent out, and received in a language that is relatively close to everyday language – by contrast, for instance, to nomothetic disciplines such as physics. Indeed, psychology stands comparatively near to colloquial speaking (it specially likes to refer to new technologies), which, in turn, talks back into theory (Slunecko, 1999). New technologies – as compelling alternative source domains – therefore easily find their way into psychological models. For example, Freud used the source domains of his time when employing hydro-mechanical and electrical metaphors to describe phenomena such as repression and resistance. And had we written this chapter 50 years ago, that is, before the computer age, we would not have been able to speak about soul-*formatting* in the way we have done it in previous sections. Gentner and Grudin (1985) also provide a nice example; they carried out a metaphor analysis on nine issues of the journal *Psychological Review*, beginning at the inception of the journal in 1894 up to an issue of the year 1975. Their chief finding was that spatial and animate metaphors of the mind gradually vanished in the early decades of the 20th century, leaving their place, from the 1950s onward, to system metaphors, often borrowed from mathematics and physics.

Again, we find ourselves confronted with the idea that language does not change erratically from within, but that its changes are tied to the specific social, economic, and ecological characteristics of a speech community. As in Lakoff's model, we once more face the fact that the premises and "real" conditions of the world are being traced into the stream of language. Language, thus, is embedded in real world conditions, but these real world conditions are both natural and cultural (Slunecko: 2002). We here run into fundamental theoretical implications for cultural psychology, which we will return to in the last section.

Applying These Thoughts Onto Cultural Psychology – An Integrative Outlook

In what sense are these thoughts of relevance to a culture-psychological endeavor?

In this last section, we will attempt to transfer our previous reflections onto suggestions for cultural psychology's core research aims and research practice. In so doing, some methodological concerns pertaining to the entire discipline of psychology will come up, too.

Historicity and Contingency of Human Subjectivity

Though controversially debated, Jaynes (1976) offers an impressive account of the historicity of subject formation. He claims that the notion of a reflecting consciousness, which we modern people so much take for naturally granted, is a relatively new one when considering it in an evolutionary perspective. Individual autonomy of thought and decision, willpower, self-reflection, and thus conscience, are historical newcomers, roughly 3000 years old. According to Jaynes, the heroes described in Homer's epics still were not able to decide and act with the kind of consciousness with which we are familiar. Instead, in times of distress they would 'hallucinate', hear the voices of their deities and follow these voices – without the existential doubts and fears we often experience when taking a decision. Their actions were pre-conscious, automatic, they seemed to have no sense of their own agency. Even something as obvious to the modern mind as the connection between the act and the one who commits the act, was by no means evident to the Homeric mind (Snell, 1953). Homer's verses neatly illustrate this relative independence between the deed and the doer. Therein, Achilles does not kill his enemy; instead, "rage falls upon Achilles' arm." This independence relates to the circumstance that the sovereign and monolithic structure of subjectivity has not yet established itself. Rather, acts are being directed and carried out by some partial forces of the soul; whether these forces lie within or outside the person, remains uncertain. If, then, the doer and the deed do not relate as much as moderns would believe, modern notions of merit or guilt also appear to be inapplicable. Interestingly enough, the early Greek interpretation of the relatedness – or rather unrelatedness – between doer and deed better fits into a postmodern, systems theory's world view (e.g., Luhmann 1990, 1991). It so seems as if even an act's attribution to an agent – an utterly basic concept for modern jurisprudence, which always requires to identify a subject that carries the responsibility for an act – were an evanescent moment within cultural development.

We might want to retain this chapter's central thesis: subject formation is historical and contingent – contingent in the sense that subject formation does not occur arbitrarily, but out of an interplay with cultural elements, particularly language, and to a larger extent with all media (Slunecko & Hengl, 2006).

According to Jaynes, people lived in a radically different state of consciousness until the early literary civilizations: In distress, he argues, the speech areas of the non-dominant brain hemisphere (which are silent and seemingly functionless in today's subjects) directly communicated with the auditory areas in the dominant hemisphere – thus giving rise to autosuggestions, which were considered as of divine origin and thus rendered decision-making on the subject's own account unnecessary. This bicameral arrangement starts to collapse around 1000 B.C. Jaynes very much relates this change to the concomitant emergence of a new revolutionary technology, writing, which would radically and permanently alter the relation between humans and language. Especially the Greek vocalic alphabet powerfully modifies the format of subjectivity, by giving birth to a highly autonomous subject. This is because reading and writing of Greek letters amounts to a training program for subjects who rely on visual observation, are capable of abstract thought, and can dissociate from their auditory and social environment to a hitherto unprecedented degree. That shift, which is doubtlessly responsible for the special development of the Western sense of subjectivity, has been extensively analyzed by authors such as McLuhan (1962, 1964), de Kerckhove and Lumsden (1988), Ong (1982), Havelock (1963, 1986), and Scribner and Cole (1981).

At this point, and with the help of the above-mentioned authors, we gather a new element concerning one of the primary questions of this chapter – that is, the question on the agent of all these changes – an element, which Sapir and Whorf did not bear in mind: cognition's dependence on media. The revolutionary Greek alphabet hosts the new psycho-historical aeon. Sense, experience, reality, psyche – all of these ultimately depend on the media we employ, and particularly those media, which drastically change our use of language, such as writing and, later, print. What is known, thought, and said about the world can only be known, thought, and said in function of the media, through which we communicate our knowledge. Under the impact of media-theoretical reflections (McLuhan, 1962, 1964), this thesis affected the shape of linguistic relativity theory in a radical way: what we now might call media relativity theory not only asks for the linguistic fundaments of cognition, it more generally places media, and in particular our media of communication, at the core of an entirely new perspective. Media revolutions are revolutions of meaning, they remodel reality and create new foundations of the world (Gergen, 1996, 2000; for an in-depth elaboration of this argument, cf. Slunecko & Hengl, 2006).

Beyond Universalist and Ahistoric Knowledge Claims and Toward Self-Reflexivity of Psychology as a Science

It is thus of utmost necessity for psychology to ponder on the conditions of subjectivity, rather than conceive of subjectivity as something unalterable, timeless, and natural. One of mainstream psychology's cardinal errors indubitably lies in its ahistoric and cognitivist stance toward subjectivity, i.e., in its belief in an initially "untainted" human subjectivity, a kind of universal mind processor, whose pure (i.e., "unpolluted" by culture) functioning psychology wants to uncover. Yet, human subjectivity does not simply fall from the sky whenever a human is born; for humans are self-generating beings – if not on an individual basis, then most certainly on a cultural one.

If we cannot think the soul's constitution and orientation in its historicity and culturedness, we end up treating the subject as illusory, presumably permanent entity (compare our chapter on discourse analysis), and we neglect the cultural-ideological weight, which has been forming the modern subject as well as the science that studies it. What if the a-historic one-person-paradigm actually incarnated the dominant ideology in the humanities; and what if this ideology required the creation of isolated and isolatable subjects, i.e., subjects, who can be easily detached from their social relations, their local coherences, and their grown lifeworlds; Giddens (1990), for whom this process is closely related to the electronic media, called it "disembedding." Such *disembedded* subjects could then be easily integrated into the new global economic formats, which disregard time and space – and thereby still be convinced of their freedom.

Contemporary Western subjectivity thus is not an indisputable achievement of the history of mind – nor is it a self-evident, completed starting point for psychology as science. Quite to the contrary, subjectivity must be studied in terms of its genesis, its structure, and its effect. Modern subjectivity is neither the "natural" form of self-hood, nor the "natural" relation to the world; it rather corresponds to a particular historical formation, the conditions of which psychology ought to investigate.

This line of reasoning may and should as well be applied to science that needs to become aware of its own principal and inevitable culturedness. For science, too, being shoved and shaped by language, is a historic and contingent endeavor. Thus, psychology as we know it, is the outcome of specific occidental socio-economic and ecological circumstances. Psychology is the product of a very particular cultural setting; as such, it could not have appeared in any other culture (compare Castro-Tejerina & Rosa, 2006, in this volume, who also emphasize the necessity of self-reflexivity for psychology). Psychology's early cross-cultural strive to simply export its questions and methods to different cultures, therefore, was correctly perceived and criticized as a form of imperialism (Schwarz, 1986) and counteracted by indigenous psychological approaches (Sinha, 1998; Yang, 1999, 2000; Yang & Bond, 1990).

Implications for Research Methodology

We realize by now that even the most fundamental Western epistemological convictions, such as the strong division between the knower and the known, that is, between the recognizing subject and the recognized object, is specific to our culture and by no means something "given." Both in theory and in research practice, psychology was in fact incarcerated in this subject-object dichotomy. Actually, dichotomies (e.g., mind-body, nature-nurture, inherited-learned, etc.) have long been blocking psychology's capacities. Indeed, as soon as one accepts such dichotomies, one is henceforth exclusively busy with their consequences.

The problem with mind-body or subjectivism-objectivism has been accompanying us throughout this paper. We have argued that cultural psychology, on one side, needs to clearly dissociate from an objectivistic-naturalistic, ahistorical understanding of its objects and of itself in order to value the originality of human creations. However, we have recurrently come across one of subjectivism's pitfalls, too: the threat of overestimating the individual's as well as the collective's degrees of freedom in the process of cultural creation. We have argued that humans are far from being free and self-determined when it comes to the constitution of symbolic-cultural worlds; these symbolic worlds rather emerge beyond our conscious intentions and ambitions. We all are inspired and formatted through our contemporaries' and predecessors' discourses. Worse still,

subjectivity itself does not remain steady; the historical argument also concerns the very structure of subjectivity. We are so led to conclude that no speaker can be regarded as entirely intentional subject of its speech or writing; the subject rather may be conceived as "medium," which language speaks through. By no means does cultural psychology's paradigm, thus, imply a call for more subjectivity in science. Instead, it involves a change of perspective, away from what subjects think they know towards what speaks through them.

With respect to culture-psychological research methodology, the implications are quite clear: since subjects never can be experts on their own cultural formatting, there is no point in asking them about it – be it with standardized methods or qualitative exploration techniques. For the speaker's intentions are not of primordial concern to empirical cultural psychology, which rather cares for the constituents that lie beyond the intentional realm. Intentions are merely the epiphenomena of a collective "intelligence," which rests in the perpetual stream of speech. Therefore, empirical methods, which aim at "looking through" the speakers' intended contents, are especially promising to psychology's socio-cultural research endeavor. Metaphor analysis, for instance, literally dissolves the text, partitions it into its elementary pieces in order to extract its metaphorical substance from the presumably intended. This extraction allows for the recognition of the deep semantic structures, which underlie our speaking and thinking the world. Yet another approach can be found in the documentary method (Bohnsack, Loos, & Przyborski, 2001; Bohnsack & Nohl, 2003), which is at present starting to reach English-speaking academia. With the help of such methods, we turn our attention onto observations, "which have escaped remark only because they are always before our eyes" (Wittgenstein, 1953, § 415). Instead of exhausting all our research energy by hunting down new facts, we can get "to understand something that is already in plain view" (Wittgenstein, 1953, § 89).

Beyond Objectivism (Realism) and Subjectivism (Idealism)

The theoretical implications we have been discussing may also be applied – though in a slightly modified manner – onto the realism versus idealism dichotomy. Throughout our paper, we were recurrently confronted with the question on the extent, to which we construct our symbolic worlds in accordance with the real world, e.g., with our body physiology (cf. Lakoff in section 3.3.). The idea that our corporeality stands at the basis of our thinking, can also be found in Rosch's research program (1973, 1975, 1978) in a more culture-psychological mode. Rosch asserts that the basic level categories of our thinking, i.e., the ones that are learned first and used more frequently, are 'human-sized'. They correspond to distinctive bodily actions: we sit in chairs and we eat from tables, but we do not perform similar activities with all kinds of furniture. Thus, we end up with the basic level categories chair and table. Hence, our life-world supplies us with propositions regarding its possible articulations. The concept of articulation has been elaborated by Latour (1993, 2004; Latour & Weibel, 2005), who proposes, in a stimulating manner, to walk the way between idealism and realism. According to Latour, humans – as speechbeings – are neither discoverers (that would lead back to the realistic-objectivist approach), nor mere inventors (that would correspond to the idealistic-subjectivist approach). Rather, they are nature's collaborators, co-producers of propositions, in which possible and real being come into human reach (Sloterdijk, 2004: 219).

Cultural psychology, thus, will have to navigate between these two poles of realism and idealism, and avoid the pitfalls of both objectivism (i.e., language depicts reality) and subjectivism (i.e., language creates reality). It stipulates that the degrees of freedom for creating our symbolic worlds are not countless and that cultures do not construct their symbolic representations in an arbitrary way. Rather, they construct them into a pre-structured mold, because the processing of social representations always occurs in concurrence with preexisting characteristics of a community's world. Where should metaphors otherwise come from? They emerge out of the collective's existing source domains repertoire, for example, out of the landscape it inhabits, out of its agricultural practices, its technology, and so on.

As we have argued throughout this chapter, language does not randomly produce new things; language speaks of reality, that is, there is an intimate connection between life world and structures of meaning. For instance, it only became possible to speak of "society" and to conceptualize it in function of the social contract model, once experiences with commercial societies and their main characteristic – contracting – had been sufficiently established to constitute a utilizable source domain. Contractual depictions of society consequently emerged at the same time as trade companies, and then started to compete with traditionally holistic conceptions of society as house or as body.

Everywhere, reality traces itself into the stream of language. Anything that occurs in the real world affects existing representations, and vice versa: language and discourse fundamentally codetermine what we perceive in the world and which propositions we pick. That is why we find the notion of "dynamic constitution" (Slunecko, 2002; Slunecko & Hengl, 2006) very compelling for our attempt to move beyond subjectivist and objectivist pitfalls.

Conclusion

Several theorists are today reflecting on the possibility of a third way, a way that moves between subjectivism and objectivism. Such a middle way would stipulate that it is language, which allows for human worlds to unfold. In his "Phenomenology of the Mind" (1949), Hegel already perceived concepts and terms as active mediators, who both rearrange reality and are being rearranged by reality; as moments and motors of a dynamic process, who express at once what is and what will be. In fact, Whorf (1956) also pointed toward such perspective. Heidegger recounted in a still more radical way the aforementioned shift away from the subject towards language. In one of his most dreadful formulations, he declares that "language speaks and the human being corresponds to language" (1971: 220).

Again, thinkers who value the freedom of the human being might feel menaced by this phrase, because it assumes, unmistakably, language to be the agent, leaving to humans the task of reacting. If it remains consistent, cultural psychology would then have to reply: the mention of the subject's freedom, too, is a heavily cultured one. Freedom had to undergo a long cultural process before being conjured up to the paramount value it today represents. Freedom, in the discourse analytical sense, has now even become a key element of the dominant ideology. Hence, we should not feel too uncomfortable about methodological approaches, which, as they attempt to elude subjectivist pitfalls, bracket the idea of a free individual agency. In our view, the success of a cultural psychology, in any case, heavily relies on our readiness to move our epistemological frame of reference beyond the dichotomies of idealism-realism or subjectivism-objectivism. We have to understand language and discourse as the space, where "everything is carried through" (Wittgenstein, 1953: 30).

And once subjectivity is recognized as something "under construction," it also becomes possible to ponder upon different shapes of selfhood and of relations to the world, that is, it becomes possible to get a feeling for alternatives. This last point is a crucial one, since cultural psychology is not only pointing in a historical direction. We also want to understand what is happening just before our eyes and look for the contemporary re-constitution of subjectivity. The information technologies of our times revolutionize the grammar of subject constitution with much higher speed than the introduction of writing used to. Computers and the Internet literally transfigure the way our minds and intentional worlds are format-

ted (Giddens, 1990; Turkle, 1995; Slunecko, 2003). For cultural psychologists, who want to keep a lucid eye on this logical chief event of today, these certainly are exciting times.

References

Ariès, P. (1962). *Centuries of childhood: A social history of family life*. New York: Vintage.

Augoustinos, M. (1998). Ideology and social representations. Towards the study of ideological representations. In U. Flick (Ed.), *Psychology of the social* (pp. 156–169). Cambridge University Press.

Averill, J. R. (1982). *Anger and aggression*. New York: Springer.

Averill, J. R. (1985). The social construction of emotion: With special reference to love. In K. J. Gergen & K. E. Davies (Eds.), *The social construction of the person* (pp. 89–109). New York: Springer

Averill, J. R. (1990). Inner feelings, works of the flesh, the beast within, diseases of the mind, driving force, and putting on a show: six metaphors of emotion and their theoretical extensions. In D. E. Leary (Ed.), *Metaphors in the history of Psychology* (pp. 104–132). Cambridge University Press.

Badinter, E. (1980). *The Myth of motherhood: A historical view of the maternal instinct*. Tel Aviv: Maariv.

Barthes, R. (1972). *Mythologies*. London: Jonathan Cape.

Billig, M. (1987). *Arguing and thinking: A rhetorical approach to social psychology*. Cambridge University Press.

Billig, M. (1991). *Ideologies and opinions*. London: Sage.

Boccaccio, G. (1924). *The Decameron*. Translation by J. M. Rigg. London: The Navarre Society. (Italian original 1353)

Bohnsack, R., Loos, P. & Przyborski, A. (2001). 'Male Honour': Towards an understanding of the construction of gender relations among youths of Turkish origin. In H. Kotthoff & B. Baron (Eds.), *Gender in interaction: Perspectives on femininity and masculinity in ethnography and discourse* (pp. 175–207). Amsterdam: Benjamins Publishing.

Bohnsack, R. & Nohl, A. (2003). Youth culture as practical innovation: Turkish German youth, 'Time Out' and the actionisms of breakdance.

European Journal of Cultural Studies, 6, 366–385.

Bruner, J. S. (1983). *Child's talk: Learning to use language*. Oxford University Press.

Bruner, J. S. (1990). *Acts of meaning*. Harvard University Press.

Bruner, J. S. (1993). Do we "acquire" culture or vice versa? *Behavioral and Brain Science*, 16(3), 515–516.

Canter, D. & Blackwell, G. (Eds.). (1993). *Empirical approaches to social representations*. Oxford: Clarendon Press.

Castro-Tejerina, J. & Rosa, A. (2006). A sociocultural approach on theorising about psychology. In J. Valsiner & A. Rosa (Eds.) *Handbook of sociocultural psychology*. Cambridge University Press.

Danziger, K. (1990) Generative metaphor and the history of the psychological discourse. In D. E. Leary (Ed.), *Metaphors in the history of Psychology* (pp. 331–356). Cambridge University Press.

de Kerckhove, D. & Lumsden, C. J. (Eds.). (1988). *The alphabet and the brain. The lateralization of writing*. Berlin & Heidelberg: Springer.

de Mause, L. (1974). *The history of childhood*. New York: The Psychohistory Press.

Doi, T. (1973). *The Anatomy of Dependence*. Tokyo: Kodansha International.

Doi, T. (1986). Amae: A key concept for understanding the Japanese personality structure. In T. S. Lebra & W. P. Lebra (Eds) *Japanese Culture and Behavior* (pp. 121–129). University of Hawaii Press.

Doi, T. (2004). *Understanding Amae. The Japanese concept of need-love*. Global Oriental Publisher.

Durkheim, E. (1965). *The elementary forms of religious life*. Translation by J. W. Swain. New York: Free Press.

Duveen, G. & Lloyd, B. (Eds.). (1990). *Social representations and the development of knowledge*. Cambridge University Press.

Duveen, G. (2006). Social representations. In J. Valsiner & A. Rosa (Eds.) *Handbook of sociocultural psychology*. Cambridge University Press.

Edwards, D. (1991). Categories are for talking. On the cognitive and discursive bases of categorization. *Theory & Psychology*, 1(4), 515–542.

Edwards, D. (1997). *Discourse and cognition*. London: Sage.

Edwards, D. & Potter, J. (1992). *Discursive Psychology*. London: Sage.

Ekman, P. (1982). *Emotion in the human face*. Cambridge University Press.

Ekman, P. (1989). The argument and evidence about universals in facial expressions of emotion. In H. Wagner & A. Manstead (Eds.), *Handbook of social psychophysiology* (pp. 143–164). Chichester: Wiley.

Farr, R. M. & Moscovici, S. (1984). *Social representations*. Cambridge University Press.

Fields, W. M., Segwerdahl, P. & Savahe-Rumbaugh, S. (2006). The material practices of ape language research. In J. Valsiner & A. Rosa (Eds.), *Handbook of sociocultural psychology*. Cambridge University Press.

Flick, U. (Ed.), (1998). *Psychology of the social*. Cambridge University Press.

Foucault, M. (1965). *Madness and civilization*. New York: Pantheon.

Foucault, M. (1970). *The order of things*. New York: Pantheon.

Foucault, M. (1972). *The archaeology of knowledge*. New York: Pantheon.

Foucault, M. (1976). *Mental illness and psychology*. New York: Harper & Row.

Foucault, M. (1977). *Discipline and punish*. New York: Pantheon.

Foucault, M. (1978). *The history of sexuality. Vol. I: An introduction*. New York: Pantheon.

Foucault, M. (1985). *The history of sexuality. Vol. II: The use of pleasure*. New York: Random House.

Foucault, M. (1986). *The history of sexuality. Vol. III: The care of the self*. New York: Random House.

Geertz, C. (1973). *The interpretation of cultures*. New York: Basic Books.

Gentner, D. & Grudin, J. (1985). The evolution of mental metaphors in psychology: A 90-year retrospective. *American Psychologist*, 40(2), 181–192.

Gergen, K. J. (1996). Technology and the self. In D. Grodin & T. Lindlof (Eds.), *Constructing the self in a mediated world* (pp. 127–140). London: Sage.

Gergen, K. J. (2000). The self: Transfiguration by technology. In D. Fee (Ed.), *Pathology and the postmodern. Mental illness as discourse and experience* (pp. 100–115). London: Sage.

Gibbs, R. W. (1994). *The poetics of mind: figurative thought, language, and understanding*. Cambridge University Press.

Giddens, A. (1990). *The consequences of modernity*. Cambridge University Press.

Gronemeyer, M. (1993). *Das Leben als letzte Gelegenheit*. Darmstadt: Wissenschaftliche Buchgesellschaft.

Harré, R. (1984). Some reflections on the concept of 'social representations'. *Social Research*, 51, 927–938.

Havelock, E. A. (1963). *Preface to Plato*. Harvard University Press.

Havelock, E. A. (1986). *The muse learns to write. Reflections on orality and literacy from antiquity to present*. Yale University Press.

Hegel, G. F. W. (1949). *The Phenomenology of Mind*. Translated by J. B. Baillie. London: Allen & Unwin.

Heidegger, M. (1962). *Being and time*. Translation by J. Macquarrie & E. Robinson. New York: Harper & Row.

Heidegger, M. (1971). "...Poetically Man Dwells". In M. Heidegger: *Poetry, Language, Thought* (pp. 211–229). Translation by A. Hofstadter. New York: Harper & Row.

Heidegger, M. (1977). *The question concerning technology and other essays*. Translation by W. Lovitt. New York: Harper & Row.

Heidegger, M. (1993). Letter on humanism. In D. F. Krell (Ed.), *Martin Heidegger: Basic writings* (pp. 230–245). Translation by D. F. Krell. New York: Harper & Row.

Jaynes, J. (1976). *The origin of consciousness in the breakdown of the bicameral mind*. Boston: Houghton Mifflin.

Kovecses, Z. (1986). *Metaphors of anger, pride, and love. Pragmatics and Beyond*. Amsterdam: John Benjamins.

Lacan, J. (1977). *Ecrits: A selection*, Translation by A. Sheridan. London: Routledge.

Lakoff, G. (1987). *Women, fire, and dangerous things. What categories reveal about the mind*. Chicago: University of Chicago Press.

Lakoff, G. & Johnson, M. (1980). *Metaphors we live by*. Chicago: University of Chicago Press.

Latour, B. (1993). *We have never been modern*. Harvard University Press.

Latour, B. (2004). *Politics of nature: how to bring the sciences into democracy*. Translation by C. Porter. Harvard University Press.

Latour, B. & Weibel, P. (2005). *Making things public*. Cambridge: MIT Press.

Le Goff, J. (1984). *The birth of purgatory*. Translation by A. Goldhammer. Chicago: Chicago University Press.

Lutz, W. (1987). *Doublespeak: From "Revenue Enhancement" to "Terminal Living": How government, business, advertisers, and others use language to deceive you*. New York: Harper & Row.

Lutz, Catherine, A. (1988). *Unnatural emotions: Everyday sentiments on a micronesian atoll and their challenge to Western theory*. Chicago: University of Chicago Press.

Luhmann, N. (1990). *Essays on self-reference*. Columbia University Press.

Luhmann, N. (1991). Paradigm lost: On the ethical reflection of morality. *Thesis Eleven*, 29, 82–94.

Marshall, H. & Wetherell, M. (1989). Talking about career and gender identities: A discourse analysis perspective. In S. Skevington & D. Baker (Eds.), *The social identity of women* (pp. 106–129). London: Sage.

McLuhan, M. (1962). *The Gutenberg galaxy. The making of typographic man*. Toronto: Toronto University Press.

McLuhan, M. (1964). *Understanding media*. New York: McGraw Hill.

Moscovici, S. (1988). Notes towards a description of social representation. *European Journal of Social Psychology*, 18, 211–250.

Moscovici, S. (2001). *Social Representations: Explorations in Social Psychology*. Edited by G. Duveen. New York: New York University Press.

Mühlmann, H. (1996). *The nature of cultures. A blueprint for a theory of culture genetics*. Vienna: Springer.

Ong, W. (1982). *Orality and literacy. The technology of the word*. London: Routledge.

Pinker, S. (1999). *Words and rules: The ingredients of language*. New York: Basic Books.

Potter, J. & Edwards, D. (1993). A model of discourse in action. *American Behavioral Scientist*, 36(3), 383–402.

Potter, J. & Wetherell, M. (1987). *Discourse and social psychology: Beyond attitudes and behaviour*. London: Sage.

Potter, J. & Wetherell, M. (1990). Discourse: Noun, verb or social practice. *Philosophical Psychology*, 3(2–3), 205–219.

Rheingold, H. (1988). *They have a word for it. A lighthearted lexicon of untranslatable words and phrases*. Los Angeles: Tarcher.

Rosch, E. (1973). Natural categories. *Cognitive Psychology*, 4, 328–350.

Rosch, E. (1975). Human Categories. In E. Warren (Ed.), Advances in cross-cultural psychology Vol. 1 (pp. 3–49). London: Academic Press.

Rosch, E. (1978). Principles of categorization. In E. Rosch & B. Lloyd (Eds.), *Cognition and categorization* (pp. 27–48). Hillsdale, NJ: Erlbaum.

Ruiseco, G. & Slunecko, T. (2006). The role of mythical European heritage in the construction of Colombian national identity. *Journal of Language and Politics*, 5(3), 359–384.

Sapir, E. (1958) [1929]. The Status of linguistics as science. In D. G. Mandelbaum (Ed.), *The selected writings of Edward Sapir in language, culture, and personality* (pp. 160–166). University of California Press.

Scheper-Hughes, N. (1992). *Death without weeping: the violence of everyday life in Brazil.* University of California Press.

Schwarz, B. (1986). *The battle for human nature: Science, morality, and modern life.* New York: Norton.

Scribner, S. & Cole, M. (1981). *The psychology of literacy.* Harvard University Press.

Sinha, D. (1998). Changing perspectives in social psychology in India: A journey towards indigenization. *Asian Journal of Social Psychology,* 1, 17–31.

Sloterdijk, P. (1988). *Zur Welt kommen – zur Sprache kommen. Frankfurter Vorlesungen.* Frankfurt: Suhrkamp.

Sloterdijk, P. (1993). *Weltfremdheit.* Frankfurt: Suhrkamp.

Sloterdijk, P. (2004). *Sphären III. Schäume.* Frankfurt: Suhrkamp.

Slunecko, T. (1999). On harvesting diversities into a dynamic directedness. *International Journal of Psychotherapy,* 4(2), 127–144.

Slunecko, T. (2002). *Von der Konstruktion zur dynamischen Konstitution.* Vienna University Press.

Slunecko, T. (2003). Reality TV und postmoderner Affekt. Ein Laborbericht. In A. Birbaumer & G. Steinhardt (Eds.), *Der flexibilisierte Mensch. Subjektivität und Solidarität im Wandel* (pp. 113–123). Heidelberg: Asanger.

Slunecko, T. & Hengl, S. (2006). Culture and media. A dynamic constitution. *Culture & Psychology,* 12(1), 69–85.

Snell, B. (1953). *The discovery of the mind.* Harvard University Press.

Taylor, C. (1989). *Sources of the Self. The making of modern identity.* Harvard University Press.

Turkle, S. (1995). *Life on the screen. Identity in the age of internet.* New York: Simon & Schuster.

Vygotsky, L. S. (1962). *Thought and language.* Cambridge, MA: MIT Press.

Wagner, W. (1998). Social representations and beyond – brute facts, symbolic coping and domesticated worlds. *Culture & Psychology,* 4, 297–329.

Wagner, W., Duveen, G., Farr, R., Jovchelovitch, S., Lorenzi-Cioldi, F., Markov, I. & Rose, D. (1999). Theory and method of social representations. *Asian Journal of Social Psychology,* 2, 95–125.

Wagner, W., Elejabarietta, F. & Lahnsteiner, I. (1995). How the sperm dominates the ovum – objectification by metaphor in the social representation of conception. *European Journal of Social Psychology,* 25, 671–688.

Wagner, W. & Hayes, N. (2005). *Everyday discourse and common-sense. The theory of social representation.* Basingstoke: Palgrave-Macmillan Publishers.

Wetherell, M., Steven, H. & Potter, J. (1987). Unequal egalitarianism: A preliminary study of discourses concerning gender and employment opportunities. *British Journal of Social Psychology,* 26, 59–71.

Whorf, B. L. (1956). *Language, thought and reality.* Cambridge, MA: MIT Press.

Wittgenstein, L. (1949). *Tractatus Logico-Philosophicus.* London: Routledge & Kegan Paul.

Wittgenstein, L. (1953). *Philosophical investigations, Part II.* Oxford: Basil Blackwell.

Yang, K. S. (1999). Towards an indigenous Chinese psychology: A selective review of methodological, theoretical, and empirical accomplishments. *Chinese Journal of Psychology,* 4, 181–211.

Yang, K. S. (2000). Mono-cultural and cross-cultural indigenous approaches: The royal road to the development of a balanced global psychology. *Asian Journal of Social Psychology,* 3, 241–263.

Yang, K. S. & Bond, M. H. (1990). Exploring implicit personality theories with indigenous or imported constructs: The Chinese case. *Journal of Personality and Social Psychology,* 58, 1087–1095.

CHAPTER 3

Psychology within Time

Theorizing about the Making of Socio-Cultural Psychology

Jorge Castro-Tejerina and Alberto Rosa

A Socio-Cultural Look Upon Psychology

The aim of this chapter is to examine the kind of explanations Socio-cultural Psychology offers as a discipline. Our attempt will be to deploy a self-reflective approach, taking Psychology itself, and specifically its socio-historical or cultural aspects, as the subject matter of our study. In order to do so, Psychology will be considered here as a cultural product resulting from specific socio-historical conditions and demands. We will focus on something that most psychologists tend to leave aside: the fact that Psychology is, like any other product of human behavior, a consequence of situated activities and thus the knowledge it offers is subordinated to a process of continuous cultural and historical transformation.

This chapter, rather than referring to psychological theories concerned with the explanation of behavior, knowledge acquisition, or whatever, will focus on developing a theory about how Psychology develops, about what psychologists can do when deve-

loping theory and practice and, in addition, how their labor affects not only the historical change of the discipline, but also the way people make sense of themselves.

Reflexivity as a Methodological Tool

Before going into the development of our argument, an explanation of the assumptions on which it is elaborated is needed. This requires, first, to refer to the notion of human subject we hold (for a more detailed explanation see Chapter 14) and how an acting human psyche can produce knowledge.

This move is a methodological application of reflexivity (Rosa, 1994; Rosa, Huertas, & Blanco, 1996). We take reflexivity to be a necessary requisite for the consistency of a theory. It is not enough that a socio-cultural psychological theory explains the individual and collective processes of knowledge production, but the explanations provided also have to be compatible with how knowledge production results from historical processes situated in socio-cultural settings. None of these two kinds of processes can be considered in isolation from each other. They are inextricably united and can only be considered separately for analytical purposes. But even when this is done, the theoretical apparatus employed, and the description and explanations produced, have to be careful in providing the slots and interfaces necessary for linking the final product to the complementary side of this two faceted process. The tensions and challenges so posed when these two sides of the endeavor are matched, call for the consideration of particular phenomena otherwise neglected, while they urge to develop transitional categories (Vygotsky, 1926) to bridge the gap between the socio-cultural and individual processes of knowledge construction throughout history.

This chapter focuses on the historical socio-cultural processes of producing psychological theories, and most specifically theories of a socio-cultural kind. So the reflexive approach we have chosen to take requires us to start with some consideration of how psyches are able to produce knowledge, and particularly knowledge about themselves.

A Socio-Cultural View on Cognition

Following the approaches of authors such as Vygotski (1978, 1986) and Leontiev (1979), we are interested in the socio-cultural re-elaboration of biological activity throughout the historiogenetic and ontogenetic processes. The instruments, tools, or mediational signs acquired in socio-cultural interaction will be the focus of our study. Within a specific culture, these artifacts (Wartofsky, 1973; Engeström, 1987) allow human beings to communicate and collaborate – or disagree – with the rest of his/her fellow beings in an effective way.

Communication and language form the backbone of these mediational means. The explicit or implicit function of any linguistic category used in everyday life is to define, explain and control (to adjust and allow the self adjustment of) our own experiencing of the world. Throughout history, these cat-

egories relate to each other through rules which shape specific forms of reason and different rationalities, which develop from, but are not reducible to the rationale of the primary functions of biological adaptation (see Chapters 10 & 14). The adaptative value of every particular cultural rationality is established within a symbolic space – a socio-cultural framework – where the meaning and pragmatic logic of daily life needs to be continuously negotiated, what results in many different ways a human life can be lived and understood. Human activity is always meaningful. It is placed within a normative framework, or as Wittgenstein (1973) said, it is always inscribed in some of the "Language games" which shape the semiotic network of a culture in a specific time and place.

The Argument of the Chapter

It is from this point of view that we will develop our argument. We will start by going into describing how human rationality gets shaped in a socio-historical spiral. It is within the construction of socio-cultural realities, that different levels of self-reflection about human experience appear. The emergence of these levels makes possible human activity to become an object for scrutiny. It is within such process that linguistic categories and social institutions picture collectivities and individuals as active or passive subjects of socio-cultural activities. Our main focus here will be on how culture establishes and distributes levels of self-reflection about human action.

An analysis of the emergence of psychological theories about the socio-cultural phenomenon follows. Psychology is a field of knowledge where different disciplines concerned about the study of the human phenomenon interact. From the first moment of its constitution as a discipline in the 19th century, Psychology became a meeting point for the integration of theories about individual and collective entities, as well as a ground for the development and intertwining of technologies elaborated by Philosophy and the Natural and Social Sciences. The result is a psychological approach to culture (understood as practices oriented towards the construction of meaning), which is responsible of the two main attributes acquired by the subject of modernity, that is, individuality or singularity, and agency or responsibility.

The third section is devoted to follow up how this multidisciplinary heritage produced current psychological approaches to socio-cultural phenomena. The socio-cultural network of contents, reasons, and meanings, which shape subjectivity and permit to make sense of human activity will be examined, together with the clues and tools devised in order to achieve a self-reflective look at any account of what "human subjects" do. This includes Psychology itself, and of course (as it should be expected), our own perspective.

Finally, it will be argued that human behavior always involves, in one way or another, an activity oriented towards establishing the meaning of experiencing. Psychology itself is a part of such activity.

The Inscription of the Human Subject in the Structure of the Socio-Cultural Reality

A discussion on the discursive construction of the category of subject within the socio-cultural framework is the main concern here. This requires focusing on the cultural distribution of semiotic resources for self-reflection on human action, as well as in the stabilization, preservation and change of these resources throughout the processes of socialization and institutionalization, that is, how public discourses formalize, homogenize, and regulate the agent's behavior within socio-cultural practices.

Individuals, as linguistic agents, are themselves constructed by the discursive categories present in their culture. From a semiotic point of view, we are talking about multi-purpose categories susceptible to different linguistic "uses", that is, possible senses and references – when facing new contexts of experience. However, this openness is relative, since the potentiality of linguistic "uses" are actualized according to socio-cultural rules, which act as devices which allow and constrain the possible relationships of the individual with reality[1] within a specific culture.

The Discursive Control of Human Activity

Any dynamic socio-cultural framework produces new meanings, but also sets limits for interpretation. The processes which exercise this controlling function are not very different from the ones that make possible, and regulate, individual enculturation and socialization. They are varied enough as to provide a discursive variety that makes possible a limited "polyphony" of possible interpretations of individual experiences. The social languages of a culture are a resource, but also a constraint, for the socialized individual's interpretation of his or her experience.

Social languages exist in a structured social milieu, with a social hierarchy. This means that there are politics of interpretation, so the political side of the management of these linguistic resources cannot be neglected. Every collectivity, independently of its degree of sophistication, has a series of leaders and elites strategically placed in the social network, who have some degree of management control on the polyphony of discourses.

Bakhtin's notion of *voice* is a useful tool for the examination of the effect on the human subject of all these discursive controls. Wertsch (1991) addressed this point when posing the question "Who is doing the talking?" An utterance, besides being pronounced by a speaker addressing a particular addressee, also borrows categories and ways of speaking belonging to a social language and previously uttered by other voices. Bakhtin called this process *ventriloquation*, which is not only a way of accounting for the individual appropriation of cultural resources, but also is one of the devices for cultural transmission. Of course, ventriloquation is beyond a complete control of the political agenda of social elites, but this does not mean that they do not have enough power to set limits on what meanings are to be taken as legitimate, and so to be privileged to be distributed throughout the socio-cultural network via the institutions developed for this purpose.

Institutions are responsible for what Berger and Luckman (1966) called *objectivisation* – externalization – and *subjetivisation* – internalization – of social knowledge. They organize the life and experience of individuals throughout their whole life: from the very cradle of the vital experience of the individual (the family), passing through the acquisition of the cultural skills explicitly and formally required to become a full member of the social group (the school, where cultural homogenization takes place), and eventually providing the resources and the framework for dealing with their adult life in social, economic and power relationship (workplace, law, courts, state administration). Within all these spheres, certain discourses and social practices get privileged, become legitimized and made official, so that "normality" and "abnormality" eventually appear. As Foucault (1971/1972) explained, institutional support and distribution of some discourses tend to put pressure and coercion on some others.

Institutional distribution usually intervenes in the negotiation of meanings in a conservative or even reactionary fashion, since official and legitimate discourses are necessary tools for the maintenance of institutions. Something which is also valid for the institutions devoted to the production and distribution of knowledge, including science. As Foucault (1971) pointed out, the "will to truth" comes together with the way knowledge is put into practice in a society where is valued, distributed, shared, and also attributed to individuals and institutions. Discourses and institutions mirror each other.

Social structure and power distribution are also issues to be taken into account. Latour (1987) points out the symmetry of the *technogram* of scientific texts (i.e., the structure of theoretical knowledge) and the authors' positions within the institutional *sociogram* of the discipline. And Bourdieu (1991) coined the terms *symbolic capital* and *symbolic power* to refer to the political-academic position of their bearers, and how value is attributed within the *symbolic market*. The best example is the institutional organization of knowledge in schools and universities where modern elites are selected and shaped.

The reproduction of structures of meaning is one of the most important mechanisms of defense used by societies or cultures. It is useful not only to normalize their members' interpretation of reality (what is especially relevant for newcomers into the group, either children or migrants), but also to avoid radical transformations which could put at risk the established socio-cultural order or the very existence of the group as a collectivity with a specific identity. This process is neither simple nor direct. Discourses are not reproduced as if they were faxed from one mind to another. They are resources to be used in the contexts of everyday life, and so they have to be selected, negotiated, re-elaborated, and combined in conflictive intersubjective contexts, and so new discursive categories or meanings emerge, and with them, new tools to make sense of the person's experience in the world. A close scrutiny over the practices which legitimize official discourses, and their continuous updating in the socio-cultural network is of prime importance for the understanding of cultural and historical change. Science is no exception.

Thus, socio-cultural normalization controls the production of possible meanings within a socio-cultural framework. It has provisions for almost any encounter (even with illegitimate discourses and practices) in which changes in the established discourses and social-cultural practices could be considered. There are even some particular institutions which offer self-reflective contexts (e.g., some universities and research centers) where tolerance for a greater polyphony of discourses could be instrumental for the exploration of ordered possibilities of socio-cultural change. But historical change does not only proceed in such a conservative and ordered way. The unavoidable existence of any grade of polyphony of discourses within a social group offers a ground ready for the development of deviant discourses that could end up producing subcultural or even countercultural tendencies. However, if they are to get some success, they have to reach some form of institutionalization, even if this is informal and alien to the institutional fabric nurtured by the discourse of the specific power. Thus, official and alternative discourses are weaved with the same semiotic threads.

No doubt, the tension between preservation of normality and socio-cultural change has effects on how people conceive themselves, that is, on how they use linguistic categories and discourses for self-reflection in an effort to make sense of their lives. When they do so, they have to enter into a dialogue in which categories taken from different discourses and social languages present in the group are borrowed and so new discourses are made possible to appear. This may result in a challenge to official cultural models, and to attempts to revise, resist or eliminate the received legitimacy. If these new discourses get widespread, if the number of people able to appropriate them increases, then a radical rupture may happen, since the distance between the official discourses and alternative ways of making sense of personal experiencing is made apparent. Individuals, then, may realize that cultural (scientific, political, religious...) knowledge is a device for managing and legitimizing what should be considered *normal* or *abnormal*. In extreme cases, this discursive struggle may involve not only a dispute on what is to be taken as legal or official, but also to the very understanding of the structure of reality, and so, to the very consideration of what is to be taken as true or deceiving.

The existence of discursive struggles is a proof that, given the right circumstances, human beings can be sensitive to the effect of discrepancies between discourses, as well as to the politics of discourse management. If this is so, then it becomes possible that discourses on how to deal with alternative semiotic devices (which permit to make sense of experiencing in different ways) may also appear. The question then changes radically.

Now there are discourses not only on how to make sense of experiencing, but also on how to figure out that different discourses take one to make sense of the world in different manners. Discourses, and oneself, become then issues to be considered as detached from immediate experience. When this happens, conditions are served for the idea of *self* to come to the forefront. A sociological and anthropological turn is then in effect.

The Socio-Historical Emergence of Self-Reflective Discourse

What changes is not the fact that any one is reached by the discourses distributed by official institutions. What is new is that now there are also self-reflective discourses available. Then a new rationality appears within this cultural group: a rationality that is able to report that itself is not the only way of making sense of the world, but just one of the possible ways of understanding experiencing. Such rationality did not exist before, it is a result of a historical process that followed a particular path of development that we are still witnessing in the Western and Westernized cultures at the present.

Self-reflection, as a result of self-reflective discourses, is not only the cradle of the idea of the self, but also a feature of Western culture. Havelock (1986) and Foucault (1988) showed how ancient Greco-Latin literature provided spaces for critical self-reflection which produced an assortment of different structures, grammars, and theories of action. These spaces for critical reflection resulted in a sophisticated specific rationality to theorize about the "self," to shape and bureaucratize it, as happened in Roman law. This contrasts to the persistence and immutability of other cultures, which relied on ritualized and cyclic myths with a rigid structure that made very difficult a socio-cultural change of the view of reality to happen. It is when referring to these kinds of cultures that Levy-Bruhl (1963) coined the idea of the collectivism of "primitive mentality", a controversial expression because of its ethnocentric phrasing. His ideas were furthered by his disciple Leenhardt (1971), whose studies forerun the idea of the lack of a consciousness of individuality observed in exotic and illiterate societies, so different to the conceptions of singularity and responsibility (or a self-reflective view about the agent) common in Western cultures. In those societies mythical structures shape human daily actions, providing ready-made immediate decision-making theories, and so leaving little room for the development of self-reflective discourses.

This type of discourses did not percolate into Western cultures, becoming quite widespread, until the end of the 18th or the beginning of the 19th century. It was then when Modernity brought in a new set of related socio-cultural phenomena: the extension of liberalism and industrialism, political revolutions, the crisis of the monarchies and empires, the birth of nation-states, the culture of leisure, intimacy, privacy, and so on (see Ariès and Duby, 1999; Elias, 2000). This was a critical socio-historical moment, closely related to the self-reflective turn to culture and to the development of the idea of the human individual. Such turn made possible that discourses calibrating alternative paths for action and choice among possible vital alternatives started to appear. In short, a complex anthropology – a theory of the human subject – began to unfold. New theories were needed when (and where) the belief that the course of personal life (and history) was determined by Providence started to be shaken (Blanco, 2002). These new theories of the human subject were supported by two pillars: (1) individuality or personal singularity, and (2) responsibility or human agency. The intersection of both attributes defined a singular and independent human subject – either individual or collective – who, at the same time, was distributed, fragmented, and prepared to carry out the multiple socio-cultural functions demanded by the modern scenario. In sum, human individuals had to become competent to deal with socio-cultural polyphony (some times even cacophonies of discourses), at the same time that they become liable for their own actions (see

Gergen, 1991 for the concept of fragmentation and saturation of modern subjectivity).

It is evident that self-reflective discourses about singularity (or individuality) and agency (or responsibility) do not govern individual activities in every socio-cultural context. Certainly, the complexity of Western societies favors the production of self-reflective discourses, but this does not mean that every social agent is continuously in touch with them. This means, that the gap between a *collective mentality* (with a scant articulation of their individual self) and a well developed self-reflective consciousness (which would imply a complex articulation, or even disarticulation, of the individual self) is not an effect of geographical location or historical distance, but also runs between different contexts within the same socio-cultural framework. So, there is no clear-cut historical transition line between one type of mentality (or reason) and another. There are fuzzy limit zones which cross throughout the contexts of different socio-cultural practices within modern groups. A variety of theoretical and practical technologies had then to be developed in order to facilitate transitions between these different contexts. These theories and technologies offer explanations and provide techniques, which include a way of accounting for the transitions between the collective and the individual, and so offer a way of distributing the agency of actions. A schema of the dynamics of this transitional process is shown in Figure 3.1.

So viewed, self-reflective discourses do not only belong to specific socio-historical conditions, but also to particular socio-cultural practices. These are practices which have evolved from what Foucault (1988) called the "caring of the self", that is, the old hedonistic, stoic and Christian formulas for the knowledge and development of the body and the spirit. It was in the Enlightenment and Romanticism of later 18th century that these formulas re-appeared in context of leisure, intimacy and privacy. But they were also essayed in philosophical and scientific contexts where social and individual phenomena were explored and started to be redesigned. The most powerful prescriptions to objectifying, ordering, and administering private and public life in the new emerging nation-states were developed in academic institutions reformed for this purpose.

It was within this context, and precisely in the new fields of knowledge then emerging, where classical anthropological self-reflective theories, still in use nowadays, were constructed and sanctioned. Slowly first, but with increasing determination later, a new psychological field appeared and soon appropriated the treatment of the individual and collective self. From that position, Psychology claimed a role for influencing self-reflective theories. But, of course, once Psychology started to take shape within in its own discursive formations, institutions and practices, could not escape from the rules of administration and circulation that, as stated above, govern any social discourse. So, Psychology cannot avoid Bakhtin's and Wertscht's suspicion that there is neither "neutral and impersonal language" nor possible of "decontextualization" of utterances (Wertsch, 1991). The origins and purposes of any discourse, and Psychology is no exception, have to be found within the socio-cultural framework in which it developed.

It is then clear that the products generated in the disciplinary field of Psychology can only be understood through an analysis of how Psychology, as a disciplined form of knowledge, became culturally important. Or, in other words, by taking into account how culture and the human subject became psychologized themselves (Blanco, 2002). So, an inquiry into how civilization established and transformed devices to control the more basic psychological structures of the human being – such as Norbert Elias's (2000) study on "emotion" – is of great interest. But we need to go further, and focus on how the semiotic and socio-cultural values of self-reflective categories were used to construct psycho-sociological phenomena, such as "emotion".

The links between Psychology and its socio-cultural contexts attracted the attention of researchers influenced by cultural history (see Daniel, 2001). Following Elias, J. Jansz, and P. van Drunen (2004) gathered a series of studies to shed light on the relation between the practical orientation of Psychology – education, mental health, organizations of work, delinquency, and so on – and the particular concerns of Western society during the last three centuries. From a Foucaultian perspective, Rose (1985, 1996) reconstructed the genealogy of Applied Psychology in the United Kingdom, and the role of psychological discourse in the construction of contemporary subjectivity. Danzinger (1990, 1997) explained the origins and cultural importance of the laboratory as an institution in modern scientific Psychology, as well as the historical process of construction of psychological categories. Leary (1990), Soyland (1994), Draaisma (1995), Blanco and Castro (1999), Castro, Jiménez, Morgade, and Blanco (2001), and F. Blanco (2002) explored the metaphorical and rhetorical condition of psychological categories.

All these studies, rather than attempting an epistemological foundation of the discipline, centered on exploring how Psychology became a culturally significant instrument. The resources and limits established by socio-cultural discourses and institutions, and the socio-historical constitution of a human subject defined by singularity (or individuality) and agency (or responsibility) are the foundations on which a genealogy of academic Psychology can be built. It was in the 19th century, when the theoretical, practical, and institutional keys which shaped contemporary Psychology appeared.

A Brief Genealogy of Psychology as a Discourse on Socio-Cultural Phenomenon

The exploration we are about to begin now does not derive from a reconstructive historiographical approach to History of Psychology, nor is an attempt to defend identitarian interests. It results from our conviction that

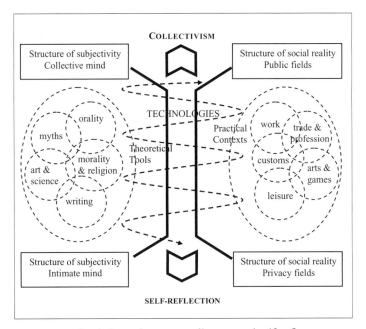

Figure 3.1. The dialectic between collective and self-reflective contexts and their technologies.

any discursive formation should be analyzed through its socio-historical, epistemological, and ethical-political determinants, if one wants to produce a self-reflective explanation of that disciplined realm of knowledge.

Disciplined Psychology as a Discourse Reflecting Upon the Self

The 19th century was an epistemologically crucial period: it was then when "man was invented" (Foucault, 1966). The fixed order of all the creatures of Creation, the representationalism and the taxonomic structuring of knowledge typical of the 18th century were disposed of to be replaced by new hidden forces with a high explanatory potential: origin, causality, and history (Foucault, 1966), which resulted from the discovery of time (Toulmin & Goodfiel, 1965). This new *episteme* made human beings to be the ultimate object and subject of all knowledge. Once a general theory of representation of the world disappeared, the need for inquiring into how human cognition proceeds became crucial for the explanation

of knowledge. "Man became that upon the basis of which all knowledge could be constituted as immediate and non-problematized evidence" (Foucault, 1966, p. 345).

The development of a self-reflective anthropology is the fundamental landmark of 19th century knowledge, and was the main factor for the birth of the Human Sciences. New intellectual interest centered on the understanding and control of the "human phenomenon". From the 1850s onwards, Psychology grew into a key force in the new context of the Human Sciences. A consequence, we believe, of its epistemological capacity to integrate every kind of theoretical and practical knowledge about the human being. Furthermore, Psychology seemed to have been able to gather under the umbrella of its name discourses and technologies fitted to the demands of modernity.

This placing of Psychology in a crossroads of various disciplines devoted to the study of the human phenomenon was a key element for its institutional success, but this was also a burden bought at the price of a chronic epistemological crisis suffered from the very moment of its institutional foundation. Its difficulties in integrating philosophical speculation with the mechanism and materialism of natural sciences of the time are a reflection of the paradoxes and controversies inherent to the theoretical and practical design of the modern subject. Eclecticism and multiple theoretical-practical faces were constitutive conditions of the new Psychology, and still remain to be so (for an analysis of the structure of the different current handbooks of Introduction to Psychology see Castro, Jiménez, Morgade, & Blanco, 2001).

The new *episteme* pictures the modern human subject as beholder of two basic characteristics: individuality or singularity, and agency or responsibility. Psychology attempted to address these features by means of the use of concepts such as *character, will, intentionality, mind, personality, purpose, motivation*, and so on. These categories were applied to ease the tension between free will and creativity (a heritage of metaphysical categories such as *soul*) and determinism or mechanism (implied in the naturalist approaches, and presented in racial and anatomical-physiological terms). Nevertheless, Psychology managed to establish different areas where some theoretical and practical rules were developed as a contribution to the design of modern man. Agency and individuality are two dimensions along which the different areas of classical psychological knowledge can be articulated. Agency or responsibility spans between consciousness (or self-reflection) and the unconscious or the automatisms of behavior. On the other hand, individuality or singularity shapes a second dimension spanning from the particular character of each individual to the collective features of groups. Figure 3.2 distributes the theoretical subdisciplines (circled by a dotted line) and the practical applications (circled by a continuous line) of Psychology, as they were at the end of the 19th century and at the beginning of the 20th century.

Three well-defined psychological areas appear in Figure 3.2. The top – ruled by General Psychology – deals with the psychological processes belonging to an abstract canonical human subject. The bottom – concerned with collective psychological phenomena – started to develop from earlier *Völkerpsychologie*. And the transitional area between the other two is occupied by applied subdisciplines. It was in these latter fields where theoretical arguments arising from the areas of elaboration of psychological knowledge were tested and updated.

This division in three areas was already perceptible in the early 20th century, when there was still some epistemological symmetry[2] in their inter-exchanges. General Psychology consolidated, first, through academic institutionalization (starting with Wundt's laboratory in Leipzig in 1879), and then by developing applied areas as the drift of Dewey's pragmatism towards education or Münsterberg's Practical Psychology towards industrial settings show (Leahey, 2004). However, *Collective psychologies* failed to reach a similar status, perhaps because there the epistemological problems derived from the eclecticism of 19th-century Psychology were more extreme. In addition, there were two well established traditions sharing the field. On the one hand, was the German *Völkerpsychologie*, inaugurated by Moritz Lazarus (1824–1903) and Hajim Steinthal (1823–1899),[3] and continued by Wilhelm Wundt (1832–1920) (see Jahoda, 1992), which was interested in the study of psychological processes common to all human beings. And, on the other, the French characteriological tradition of Hippolyte Taine (1828–1893), Alfred Fouillée (1838–1912), and Gustave Le Bon (1841–1931),[4] devoted to the study of specific psychological processes in particular human groups. In spite of Lazarus and Steinthal's initial confidence in the complementarity of both approaches, their irreconcilable distance was definitely pointed out by Wundt in his *Elements of Folk Psychology* (1916).

Even so, controversies within Collective Psychology[5] may have been eventually fruitful, since they were forerunners in the attempt of offering socio-cultural explanations. The following section studies how this

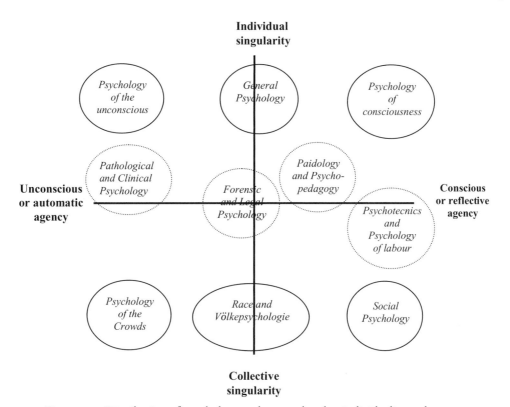

Figure 3.2. Distribution of psychology realms as related to individuality and agency.

contribution was linked to its capacity to integrate very different disciplines.

Collective Psychology: A Multidisciplinary Effort to Link Psyche and Culture

It is a merit of *Collective Psychology* to have taken culture within the regard of Psychology. It is worthy to remind that the first chair with the term "psychology" in its denomination was occupied by Lazarus at Bern in 1860, and held the name of *Völkerpsychologie* (Jahoda, 1992). This was a discipline that gathered concepts and arguments of the Humanities and Social Sciences of the time, including those belonging to disciplines such as Metaphysic, Philosophy of History, Linguistics, Sociology, Law, Anthropology, Biology, and of course, General Psychology.

It is important to remember the role these disciplines, and their representatives, played in the theoretical and practical construction of the socio-cultural structure of modernity. Such structure came to replace the guidelines for behavior of the old monarchies and empires by the means of a new socio-political device: the liberal nation-state. Individuality (or singularity) and agency (or responsibility) became features not only of individuals, but also of collective entities. An intersubjective framework was assumed to underlie any socio-cultural phenomenon, including the nation-state. Its formulation and design demanded theoretical concepts to express the "natural unity" of all members of the collectivity. Scientific rhetoric was used to reinforce the national community and provide political agendas and common future projects in competition with other national groups (see Hobsbawn, 1983; Anderson, 1983; Smith, 1991). But constructing the singularity and agency of the collective subject should not jeopardize the preservation of the singularity and agency of the individual subject, since the distribution of different socio-cultural roles and responsibilities was basic for the protection and progress of the collective.

The idea of social unity appeared first with the concept of *Volkgeist*, especially in the fields of Metaphysics and Philosophy of History (Fichte, Hegel, etc.) and Linguistics (Humboldt, Grimm, Bopp, etc.). From the mid-19th century onwards, the concept of social organism was also operative in Sociology and Law (Comte, Spencer, Le Play, Savigny, Jhering, etc.) and Anthropology and Biology (represented by Tylor, Waitz, Quatrefages, Darwin, Haeckel, etc). Attention should also be paid to the widespread use of the idea of "race" as a way of accounting for collective identity. Race at the beginning was an idealistic and positivist concept, and only later acquired the reductionistic and biological connotations it now has.

By mid 19th century, *Collective Psychology* was a meeting point for the conceptual categories of the emergent Humanities and Social Sciences. It offered a ground to integrate and regulate the conceptual tools of the above mentioned disciplines and authors. Table 3.1 arranges some of these concepts distributed in five fields (subject, place, product, time, and finality).

The elements and categories gathered in Table 3.1 were employed for dealing with multiple theoretical and practical questions in relation to socio-cultural phenomena. They were the bases for the evaluation of specific differences, peculiarities, authenticities, and singularities of human groups. They also defined the degree of agency – consciousness and unconsciousness, activity or passivity – that could be attributed to the behavior of such groups.

By late 19th century and early 20th century, guidelines for intervention started to appear within Psychology. They were technologies addressed to deal not only to understanding socio-cultural singularities but also to tailor the responsibilities of human collectives to the demands of the times. This meant that Collective Psychology was challenged to get in touch with the applied areas of the discipline. Individuality (or singular-

ity) and agency (or responsibility) were the key issues for this test.

Concerning singularity, the goal was to underpin and harmonize the cultural framework of the new nation-states. This task depended mainly on Psychopedagogy and Clinical and Legal Psychology. The former worked as a means of monitoring the incorporation of new subjects to the national community. It had an important role in the process of education for literacy and in the articulation of collective memories, usually the teaching of history, art, folklore, and customs. On the other hand, Clinical and Legal Psychology were in charge of the control and normalization of the "sick", the "degenerated", or marginal individuals and groups, who were viewed as deviant from the official culture, and so considered potentially dangerous.

In relation to agency, the goal was the management of socio-cultural activities and progress. This was a task that also first started within the psychopedagogical context, as it was in charge of the social distribution of basic tools for reaching the civilized and scientific progress of the ideal modern world. But when dealing with the economic structure and the division of labor, new technologies had to be developed to deal with the complexities of socio-cultural articulation. So Psychotechnics and Psychology of Labor started to be instrumental, as nowadays Communitarian Psychology or Sociocultural Animation also are (for a sociocultural approach to the different fields of application of Psychology, see Jansz and Van Drunen, 2003).

Collective Psychology could not match this challenge. The Psychology concerned with the study to the abstract canonical individual human subject surpassed the Psychology concerned with the study the cultural processes and products. Soon *Collective Psychology* started to fade away within Social Psychology, and ended up disappearing without a trace. Nevertheless, some of its concerns were preserved within the work of scholars such as G.H. Mead in the United States or L. Vygotsky, A. Luria, and A. Leontiev in the Soviet Union (see Valsiner and van

Table 3.1: Humanities and Social Science concepts used by Collective Psychology in the second half of the 19th century

	Conceptual Signs or Elements				
	Subject	*Place*	*Products*	*Time*	*Finality*
General Psychology	Personality Intellect/ feeling Will Soul		Logic Ethics	Psychological laws	
Metaphysics and Philosophy of History	Great Man Mentality	Landscape Territory	Customs Religion Art and Science	Historical law Historical stages Eternal return	Cosmopolitism Fraternity Harmony
	Genius/Spirit *Volkgeist* People	Nature	Languages	*Zeitgeist*	Humanity Nationalism
Linguistics	Language Character Race	Geography and Climate	Myths	Stages of language	
Anthropology and Biology	Brain Instincts			Laws of evolution Laws of heredity	Natural selection Survival
	Organism Crowds/Elites	Environment	Folklore Technology	Cultural stages	Civilization Colonialism
Sociology and Law	Society Individual Social classes	Nation-state	Law Institutions Division of labor	Laws of Economics	Order and progress Pacifism Revolution

der Ver, 1996). Meanwhile, General Psychology reached a privileged place in official discourses. It ended up as a background for the regulation of the practical aspects of the discipline, some of which developed technologies to be applied in the socio-cultural realm.

When looking at the past, it can be said that Psychology succeeded in its evolutionary struggle because of its ability for drawing clear institutional, academic, and professional demarcations. This was a process that ran parallel to its increasing theoretical-critical disinterest in socio-cultural and historical reflections. There is little doubt that this capability for self-reflection was given back to the disciplines that, at first, inter-

acted in the field of *Völkerpsychologie* (see Cole 1996).

It seems that Psychology's interest for culture as a constituent part of the human phenomenon faded away as it became institutionally stronger. The ability *Collective Psychology* showed to integrate strong currents of the Humanities and Social Sciences of that time, at the same time that reinforced its apparent power to manage the attributes of singularity and agency of the modern subjectivity, was also the source of its weakness, making extremely difficult to reach a proper systematization. The synthesis it attempted was not achieved, and the field about to be constituted broke into pieces. Eventually, the sign "psychology" was appropriated by generalist and applied approaches addressed to the study of individuals and groups, which left culture aside. However, the socio-cultural perspective did not completely disappear out of contemporary thought. We will deal with some of its lines of continuity in the next section.

Towards a Self-Reflective Proposal About the Analysis of Socio-Cultural Contexts

In spite of its lack of success, *Völkerpsychologie* is currently considered as a forerunner of the contemporary families of Cultural and Socio-cultural-historical Psychology (see Jahoda, 1992; Cole, 1996; Rosa, 2000a and 2000b). These approaches continue to claim that intersubjectivity is a key issue for the constitution of the human phenomena, even if sometimes this means to pay the price of some eclecticism. They also keep alive the interest on the two issues of modernity we have been repeatedly mentioning – individuality (or singularity) and agency (or responsibility) – two attributes referring to decision-making capabilities and to the distribution of socio-cultural functions, for both groups and individuals.

An example of such concern is apparent in Wertsch (1991). For him "the word in language is half somebody else's" leaving the explanation of how this happens to the following Bakhtin quote.

> "It becomes 'one's own' only when the speaker populates it with his own intentions, his own accent, when he appropriates the word, adapting it to his own semantic and expressive intention. Prior to this moment of appropriation, the word does not exist in a neutral and impersonal language (it is not, after all, out of a dictionary that the speaker gets his words!), but rather it exists in other people's mouths, in other peoples' concrete contexts, serving other people's intentions: it is from there that one must take the word, and make it one's own." (Bakhtin, 1981, pp. 293–294, quoted by Wertsch, 1991, p. 59)

The agent must mediate between the individual psychological functions and the available resources offered by the socio-cultural contexts in which s/he inhabits. So there is clearly some room for a decision that can be attributed to the human subject. Cole (1996) also claims the need "to place Culture in the center", what for him means that Culture acts as an agent providing artifacts to impulse and develop individual or collective anthropological structures.

We agree with Wertsch and Cole's views on socio-cultural psychological phenomena. Individual and collective subjects, together with social structures and practices and the mediational artifacts of culture, share the agency of human actions. But our interest here is not going into a discussion on how to develop a psychological theory about socio-cultural life, but to go into an examination of some aspects of how theorizing about Psychology is being performed.

We do not believe that the goal of Psychology as a discipline should (or could) be to explain and control what people may be and do throughout their lives, as the universalist theories of General Psychology and its technological promises for a better world (for some) sometimes do. Our option is take a turn that, as Bruner (1990) stated, makes one to seriously take into account what people say they are and are doing when carrying along in their daily lives.

Furthering Bruner's perspective, we are interested in the study of the kind of strategies humans apply when searching for meaning in what they are doing. And this ranges from the observation of somebody carrying along any daily activity, to the scrutiny of how a scientist proceeds when formulating a hypothesis or struggling to articulate a disciplinary theory about some part of the world – including psychological theories. The socio-cultural (and epistemological) activities carried by scientists (and also by analysts of culture) become, then, a part of the subject matter to study.

In order to approach this goal a self-reflective strategy of analytical decentration is required. A strategy that, on the one hand, resorts to particular theories developed within particular psychological or socio-cultural subdisciplines to describe and explain how meaning-making in context is done. And on the other, struggles to adapt these theories to our goal of explaining the processes of producing accounts of socio-cultural activities, and among the latter, the activity of building theories about socio-cultural psychology.

Any explanatory account of an observed action is done through language, it is a discursive process. So, if explanations are to be taken as the subject matter of an inquiry, some features of language should be taken into account. Linguistic signs reify experiences. The semantic categories in use within a socio-cultural activity, such as an epistemic practice, are the building blocks with which an image of the world is built. This means that any examination of how an explanation is produced requires a genealogical exploration of how the categories employed in such explanation were coined.

Devising an Auto-Reflexive Method

Current socio-cultural psychology dwells in the heritage received from 19th century modern Social Sciences and Humanities. Subject, place, time, product, and finality were the fields which ordered the categories gathered within *Collective Psychology* (see Table 3.1). They are still alive in the current interest of Cultural Psychology for the self, contexts, mediation, artifacts, and socio-cultural integration. On the other hand, Socio-cultural Psychology also keeps alive a concern for accounting for the two main features of modern subjectivity: individuality and agency. These two dimensions will be instrumental for our purposes here. Our strategy will be to relate these two sets of dimensions in order to create some new categories useful for our purposes.

Any current consideration of *individuality* requires the development of a theory of identity. Hedetoft (1995), from the standpoint of Political Science, carried out a research project on national identity in several European countries. His methodology was heavily influenced by Peircean semiotics, and was able to pinpoint several areas where national identity was exercised. Territory

was the central issue, and ethnicity, history, immigration, and confrontations (either in war or sport) acted as pivot elements for exercising national identity. These areas provided a semiotic space where the intersection of political entities and cultural identity had to be negotiated using signs and arguments. Hedetoft's semiotic categories were not far from the above mentioned five classical fields of 19th century *Collective Psychology*, and permits to rearrange them in four thematic categories: *actors, objects* (tools and material or symbolic instruments present in socio-cultural activities), *spaces,* and *time* (past, present, or future events). These four categories are not ordered in any kind of hierarchy. They are thematic categories for the discursive production of acts of identification (or counteridentification) in socio-cultural activities. As it will later be shown, they are useful for the analysis of how Socio-cultural explanations address the issue of individuality.

Any socio-cultural concern about *agency* requires referring to how goals, intentions, or motives are present in individual or collective actions. These are elements which are not independent. They together shape a motivational structure, which in turn cannot be considered independently from a theory of action. Such a theory, when approached from a discursive outlook, as is the case here, needs to take into account how these conceptual elements are arranged, in order to figure out how the explanation provided pictures the way in which action starts and follows a particular course.

Kenneth Burke's *Grammar of Motives* (1969) offers some tools useful for this purpose. For him any explanation of action provided can be characterized as a result of a *dramaturgical action*, which can be portrayed by going into the examination of the functional articulation of five elements: *agent* (whom or what the responsibility of the activity is attributed to), "*agency*"[6] (the means or ways applied to reach the goal), the *scene* (where the activity takes place), *act* (action and the form that it takes), and *purpose* (the aim or goal, the "why" or "what for"). These five functional elements are not independent from each other, they relate among themselves conforming a structure, which then is able to picture the particular grammar of motives articulating the explanation provided.

These five grammatical functions are always apparent in any explanation provided to an observed activity. There are always some beginning conditions that are articulated in the *agent-scene ratio*. From such conditions, the motivational structure employs *"agencies"* to develop a particular *act*. This model assumes that the agent-scene ratio can be preserved or modified continuously during the act. This is a kind of grammar that has the added property of portraying its object in a way that resembles a narrative plot, which implies a program of future.

Hayden White (1973, 1987), when applying a narratological strategy to the examination of History and Philosophy of History, pointed out to how within a narrative, besides the plot and the argument, there is also a moral and an ideology. They together take a particular form which he termed a *historical style*. This concept is defined as a narratological strategy that links past and present, emphasizes some events instead of others, and promotes a desired future to be reached by following some particular means. Joining together Burke and White's contributions, it could be said that the weight of *ideology* is in the *act-purpose ratio*, as this gathers the moral of the story – that is, the theory of change – that runs through the act until the reaching of the purpose.

So far we have devised two set of categories to deal with the two main issues of concern: individuality and agency. Individuality is addressed by a set of categories which can be treated as themes in discourse analysis; while agency is dealt with another set of interrelated functional categories. They together can be taken as two axes conforming a grid for the analysis of current approaches to Socio-cultural phenomena.

At a first glance, the categories of both dimensions may look coextensive. The "agent" is usually an "actor", the "scene" can be identified with the "space", etc. However a specific sign does not always necessarily play the same function in the structure of the activity. In fact, different accounts of an observed activity make possible to uncover different motivational structures in the explanations provided, since each thematic element can play a different functional role. The first dimension is descriptive; it simply pinpoints the presence of actors, objects, spaces, and time. The second, however, deals with the function that these described elements play within the explanation under analysis.

For example: any topic of the category *actor* could work as *agent* as long as it plays the main character of an historical-temporal event – which then plays the function of *act*. But this *actor* could also appear as *"agency"* if it is considered only a vehicle that transports the *act* of certain *spatial* factors, which then would play the function of *agent*. This strategy allows uncovering differences on the functional role given to each element when explaining a particular action. In other words, the method of analysis here presented is concerned on describing how current views on Socio-cultural phenomena can offer explanations about the distribution of agency.

A Catalogue of Ways in Which Socio-cultural Psychologies can Address Agency

The result of the application of this method is the grid presented in Table 3.2, which offers a catalogue of all the possible ways in which the four thematic categories can play a functional role in the explanation of action. The 20 cells so produced present the currently available possibilities for an analyst of socio-cultural activities to attribute meaning to his or her observations. In other words, Table 3.2 acts as a catalogue of current possible ways of producing explanations about how singularities (either individual or collective) interact with agency (can be made accountable of the observed outcomes).

The 20 possibilities presented in the table are interdependent alternatives. A specific

Table 3.2: Thematic categories in a grammar of explanatory functions

	Agent	*Scene*	*Act*	*Agency*	*Purpose*
Actor	1. Entity or subject that performs the activity	5. Entity or subject included in the activity	9. Change or preservation of a subject as activity	13. Entity or subject that suffers or carries the burden of the activity	17. Kind of entity or subject projected or pursued in the activity
Space	2. Physical space that causes the activity	6. Physical space where the activity takes place	10. Construction or destruction of a space as activity	14. Physical space suitable for the appearance of the activity	18. Utopia projected or pursued by the activity
Time	3. Temporal instance that causes the activity	7. Moment when activity takes place	11. Temporal change as activity	15. Temporal space that favors the activity	19. Uchronia projected or pursued by the activity
OBJECT	4. Symbolic or material artifact that causes the activity	8. Symbolic or material product that confines the activity	12. Symbolic or material creation as activity	16. Product that expresses or canalizes the activity	20. Tasks projected or pursued by the activity

thematic element could play different functions in alternative motivational structures. This may be clarified by looking at examples of 19th century Collective Psychology. If we look to Hippolyte Taine's theory (1863), he made geo-climatic or historical environments to play the function of *agents* (and so they could be placed either in box 2 or 3) in determining the character of the collective, which, in this case, would be an *"agency"* (box 13) or even an *act* (box 9). Another author may offer alternative explanations in which the environment may play the role of a background landscape or a momentary *scene* for collective action (and so to be placed in boxes 6 and 7). Or, alternatively, make this *space* to play the function of a *purpose* if environmental change is to be taken as a goal (boxes 18 or 19) pursued by an individual *agent* – the Great Man – or a collective one – the race – (box 1), as Joaquín Costa did (1898).

Of course, a specific thematic element can only carry out one function within the particular instance of the grammar of action under analysis. In that way, if a specific place and period – for example, a *context* according to Cole (1996), or a *cronotope* according to Bajtin (1981) – are defining a *space* and a *time* within an enclosed activity (boxes 6 and 7), they would not be able to carry out any other function in the analysis of the same activity. This, of course, does not hinder that different elements of the same thematic category could carry out several functions at the same time. A good example can be found in Lazarus and Steinthal's *Völkerpsychologie*. In their works, People play the role of *"agency"* (box 13) that permits the expression of *agents* such as the *Volkgeist*, the *collective mentality* or race (box 1), which clearly play the functional role of *actor*. The same process happens when an *object*, with a symbolic meaning, configures a *scene* – a socio-cultural or institutional context – (see box 8) where other material or symbolic *objects* play the functional role of *"agencies"*, that is, myths, art, technology, and so on (box 16). Moreover, these *"agencies"* could express or execute the prescriptions of an *object* playing the role of *agent*, such as social norms may do (box 4). Something which is not too far from explanations sometimes offered by socio-cultural theorists such as Engeström or Leontiev.

Purpose plays a function which we believe is particularly interesting. It illustrates the projection of any thematic element or sign into the future, that is, its conversion into what Hyden White called "ideology" (boxes from 17 to 20). How *purpose* is dealt with is crucial for how a theory of change (or preservation) is presented within the motivational structure. In classical Collective Psychology, *purposes* were apparent in the tension between homogeneity (thematized in concepts such as *humanism, colonialism, civilization*, etc.) and socio-cultural singularity (with terms such as *survival, nationalization, social harmony*, etc.). Issues that are not too far from current concerns about the conflict between globalization and the preservation of cultural, religious, or national identities, which too often result in several forms of fundamentalism, sometimes together with a revival of ethnocentrism and neo-colonialist "manifest destiny" doctrines.

The function "purpose" plays within this grid helps us to notice that every analytical discourse – with its thematical variation and functional arrangement – negotiates in a particular way the tension between stabilization of the socio-cultural activity and its alteration and modification. In the first case, the burden of explanation is in the *agent-scene ratio*, reinforcing the view of actors as responsible for the outcome of their actions, while in the latter the *act-purpose ratio* makes the goal to play a causal role as a feed-forward drive with teleological properties.

These examples make apparent how this method could be useful as a self-reflective methodological tool for the production of socio-cultural explanations, since it calls attention on the need for a detailed consideration of the *ratio* between the elements. The result is that every analyzed instance ends up producing a particular grammar where the different themes are articulated in a particular functional balance.

Final Remarks

The method presented in this chapter takes reflexivity into account as a methodological resource. It is concerned about how the past left us resources for meaning-making, but also about how to use them to prepare a future. This means that any individual, when trying to make sense of what s/he experiences, is always empowered and constrained by the discursive and institutional limits within which s/he works. This is equally valid for a plain person, for a scientific observer or for an academic when devising an explanatory theory. Meaning-making is always a pragmatic and situated activity.

This is one of the consequences of modernity, which postmodern thinkers have been right in pointing out. Epistemological discontent is one of its outcomes. Any attempt to relate singularity and agency cannot avoid involvement with unending levels of reflexivity.

Our attempt here was to offer a tool for the systematization of such a self-reflective endeavor. We offered a sort of map (a meaning-making device) which may be of use for analysts and researchers in their interpretative journey. We believe it can be useful in fixing one's position and course. This grid offers a set of quadrants that have the added property of showing the resources one is working with, and the course followed by others to take us to our current position. Our view of reality is a consequence of this.

This method is also a travel guide. It helps to take a self-reflective approach when producing analysis and devising theories. This map is useful for keeping account of what resources one has available, as well as how to apply them for avoiding inconsistencies. It is also an analytical device for the examination of descriptions and explanations given, and for the theoretical accounts produced. In addition, it makes apparent that we cannot afford to forget the genealogy of the categories which constitute our own current rationality. The meaning and course of our life depends on this.

Maps are always a simplification for interpreting reality. They have a lifespan, and therefore is a mistake to use them as corsets to restrict our movements. The landscape changes, and no course can be set without taking into account the conditions of the sea. No map can forecast future changes either. Maps are tools for orientation, but it is a mistake to ignore the environment when piloting. Although we believe the categories here employed are still useful, there is little doubt that they will surpassed. This will be done by negotiating new waters, visiting new realms, devising new instruments, drawing new maps, and changing cartography itself.

This methodological proposal involves a self-reflective turn, and so helps to be aware of one's own activity and the compromises and commitments one has within the socio-cultural matrix of categories and functions. As it could not be otherwise, this method is itself inscribed within the socio-historical process of searching for meaning. A process which, at least since the beginning of the 19th century, shows our ambivalence between the nostalgia of what we were, and the worry about what we may become.

Acknowledgments

Preparation of this chapter was supported by the grants SEJ2005–09110-C03–03/PSIC and SEJ2005–09110-C03–01/PSIC from the Spanish Ministry of Education and Science.

The authors thank Elena Battaner and especially Ana Pereira for the help received in translating the manuscript.

Notes

1 For a discussion on "reality," see Chapter 14 and the General Conclusions of this volume.
2 In their mutual dialogue, collective psychologies tend to reproduce the classical structure of subjectivity in General Psychology: a rational part devoted to the soul, and an empiricist or experimental part devoted to the study of will, feeling, and sensation or thought. This scheme expanded to the characterization of the collective phenomenon.
3 Lazarus and Steinthal were the most important representatives of the 19th-century *Völkerpsychologie*. They founded the

Zeitschrift fur Völkerpsychologie und Sprach-wissenschaft. The journal comprised a series of articles related to linguistic and cultural products associated with the human development and peculiarity. Wundt admitted this heritage in his *Völkerpsychologie* (Wundt, 1900–1920).
4 Taine, Fouillée, and Le Bon are important representatives of different generations in the development of the French psychosociological thought during the 19th century and the beginning of the 20th. They all gave a fundamental importance to the temperamental heritage in the constitution of the collective psychology of a nation. In any case, there was a clear theoretical evolution since Taine's determinist position in works such as *History of English Literature* (1863), to the irrational vitalism that Le Bon showed in his *Psychology of Crowds* (1895). Fouille's moderate Hegelianism, present in texts such as *Psychological Sketch of European People* (1902), takes a sort of middle position between the other two.
5 *Collective Psychology* will be used here as a general label referring to the late 19th and early 20th century attempts to build a psychological discipline in the crossroads of the social sciences, natural sciences and humanities. It includes German *Völkerpsychologie*, but also other attempts among which the French contribution is particularly outstanding. A review of such contributions can be found in Castro (2004).
6 "Agency" in Burke's methodology must not be confused with *agency* as a feature of the modern subjectivity. Uses of Burke's category in this chapter will always appear in quotes. When the meaning of agency is related to modern subjectivity, it will appear without quotes.

References

Anderson, B. (1983). *Imagined Communities. Reflections on the Origin and Spread of Nationalism.* New York: Verso.

Ariès, P., & Duby, G. (Eds.). (1999). *Histoire de la vie privée. 4.* París: Éditions du Seuil. [*A history of private life.* Cambridge, MA: Belknap Press of Harvard University Press, 1987–1991]

Bakhtin, M. M. (1981). *The Dialogic Imagination: Four Essays by M. M. Bakhtin.* Austin: University of Texas.

Berger, P. L., & Luckmann, T. (1966). *The Social Construction of Reality*. New York: Doubleday.

Blanco, F. (2002). *El cultivo de la mente: un ensayo teórico-crítico sobre la cultura psicológica*. [*The Culture of Mind: a theoretical-critical essay about psychological culture*]. Madrid: Antonio Machado.

Blanco, F., & Castro, J. (1999). La descripción de la actividad epistémica de los psicólogos en los manuales de Historia de la Psicología [The Description of the Epistemic Activity of Psychologists in Handbooks of History of Psychology]. *Revista de Historia de la Psicología*, 20 (3–4), 59–72.

Bourdieu, P. (1991). *Language and Symbolic Power*. Cambridge, Ma.: Harvard University Press.

Bruner, J. (1990). *Acts of Meaning*. Cambridge, Ma.: Harvard University Press.

Burke, K. (1969). *A Rhetoric of Motives*. Berkeley: University of California Press.

Castro, J. (2004). *La Psicología del pueblo español: El papel del discurso psico-sociológico en la construcción de la identidad española en torno a la crisis del 98*. [The Psychology of the Spanish People: The role of psycho-sociological discourse in the construction of Spanish identity around the 1898 crisis] Doctoral Dissertation. Madrid: Universidad Autónoma de Madrid.

Castro, J., Jiménez, B., Morgade, M., & Blanco, F. (2001). La función de los mitos fundacionales en la promoción de una identidad disciplinar para la psicología [Function of Foundational Myths in Promoting of a Disciplinary Identity in Psychology]. *Revista de Historia de la Psicología*, 22 (3–4)., 297–309.

Cole, M. (1996). *Cultural Psychology*. Cambridge, Ma.: Harvard University Press.

Costa, J. (1898/1991). Reconstitución y europeización de España. En *Reconstitución y europeización de España y otros escritos* [Reconstitution and Europeanisation of Spain. In Reconstitution and Europeanisation of Spain and other works]. Madrid: Instituto de Estudios de Administración Local.

Daniel, U. (2001). *Kompendium Kulturgeschichte, Theorien, Praxis, Schlüsselwörter*. Frankfurt: Suhrkamp Verlag Frankfurt am Main [*Compendium of Cultural History: Theory, Practice, Keywords*].

Danziger, K. (1990). *Constructing the Subject: Historical Origins of Psychological Research*. Cambridge: Cambridge University Press.

Danziger, K. (1997). *Naming the Mind: How Psychology found Its Language*. Londres: Sage.

Draaisma, D. (1995). *De metaforenmachine – een geschiedenis van het geheugen*. Groningen: Historische Uitgeverij [*Metaphors of memory : a history of ideas about the mind*. Cambridge, U.K.: New York: Cambridge University Press, 2000].

Elias, N. (2000). The civilizing Process. Oxford: Basil Blackwell.

Engeström, Y. (1987). *Learning by Expanding*. Helsinki: Orienta-Konsultit.

Foucault, M. (1966). *Les mots et les choses, une archéologie des sciences humanes*. París: Editions Gallimard. [Alan Sheridan (tr.). *The Order of Things, an Archaeology of the Human Sciences*. New York: Vintage, 1970]

Foucault, M. (1971). *L'Ordre du discours*. París: Gallimard. [In A. M. Sheridan Smith (trans.). *The Archaeology of Knowledge and the Discourse on Language*. New York: Pantheon, 1972, 215–37.

Foucault, M. (1988). *Technologies of the self: a seminar with Michel Foucault*. Amherst: University of Massachusetts Press.

Fouillé, A. (1902). *L'Esquisse psychologique des peuples européens*. Spanish version *Bosquejo psicológico de los pueblos europeos* [Psychological Sketch of European Peoples]. Buenos Aires: Americalee (1943).

Gergen, K. (1991). *The Satured Self*. New York: Basic Books.

Havelock, E. (1986). *The Muse Learns to Write. Reflections on Orality and Literacy from Antiquity to the Present*. New Haven and Londres: Yale University Press.

Hedetoft, U. (1995). *Signs of Nations. Studies in the Political Semiotics of Self and Other in Contemporary European Nationalism*. Aldershot: Darmouth.

Hobsbawm, E. (1983). "Introduction: The Invention of Tradition". in E. Hobsbawn and T. Ranger (Eds.). *The Invention of Tradition*. Cambridge: Cambridge University Press, 7–21.

Jahoda, G. (1992). *Crossroads between Culture and Mind: Continuities and Change in Theories of Human* Nature. New York: Harvester/Wheatsheaf.

Jansz, J., & Van Drunen, P. (2004). *A social history of psychology*. Oxford: Blackwell Publishing.

Latour, B. (1987). *Science in Action*. Cambridge, MA: Harvard University Press.

Le Bon, G. (1895/1981). *Psychologie des Foules* [The Psychology of Crowds]. Paris: Presses Universitaires de France. English version in http://socserv2.socsci.mcmaster.ca/~econ/ugcm/3ll3/lebon/Crowds.pdf

Leahey, T. (2004). *A History of Psychology*. Englewood Cliffs, NJ: Pearson Prentice Hall.

Leary, D. (1990). *Metaphors in the History of Psychology*. Cambridge: Cambridge University Press.

Leenhardt, M. (1971). *Do Kamo. La personne et le mythe dans le monde mélanésien*. París: Gallimard. [Do kamo: person and myth in the Melanesian world. Chicago: University of Chicago Press, 1979.]

Leontiev, A. (1979). *Activity, Consciousness and Personality*. Englewood Cliffs, NJ: Prentice Hall.

Lévy-Bruhl, L. (1963). *L'âme primitive*. París: Gallimard. [*The 'soul' of the primitive*. New York: Praeger, 1966]

Rosa, A. (1994). History of Psychology as a ground for reflexivity. In A. Rosa y J. Valsiner (Eds.).: *Historical and Theoretical Discourse in Social-Cultural Psychology*. Madrid: Aprendizaje.

Rosa, A. (2000a). ¿Qué añade a la psicología el adjetivo cultural? [What does the adjective 'cultural' add to Psychology]. *Anuario de Psicología*, 31 (4), 27–57.

Rosa, A. (2000b). Entre la explicación del comportamiento y el esfuerzo por el significado: una mirada al desarrollo de las relaciones entre el comportamiento individual y la cultura [Between the Explanation of Behaviour and the Effort after Meaning: a Glance at the Development of the links Between Individual Behaviour and Culture]. *Revista de Historia de la Psicología*, 21 (4), 77–114.

Rosa, A. (2007a). Acts of Psyche. Actuations as symthesis of semiosis and action. In J. Valsiner & A. Rosa (Eds.). *Cambridge Handbook of Sociocultural Psychology* (pp. 205–237). New York: Cambridge University Press.

Rosa, A. (2007b). Dramaturgical actuations and cultural artifacts: making the rationality of the world. In J. Valsiner & A. Rosa (Eds.). *Cambridge Handbook of Sociocultural Psychology* (pp. 293–317). New York: Cambridge University Press.

Rosa, A., Huertas, J. A., & Blanco, F. (1996). *Metodología de la Historia de la Psicología* [A Methodology for the History of Psychology]. Madrid: Alianza.

Rose, N. (1985). *The Psychological Complex*. London: Routledge and Kegan Paul.

Rose, N. (1996). *Inventing Ourselves: Psychology, Power and Personhood*. Cambridge: Cambridge University Press.

Smith, A. (1991). *National Identity*. London: Penguin Books.

Soyland, P. (1994). *Psychology as Metaphor*. Londres: Sage.

Taine, H. (1863). *Histoire de la littérature anglaise* [History of English Literature]. Paris: L. Hachette.

Toulmin, S., & Goodfield, J. (1965). *The Discovery of Time*. New York: Harper & Row.

Valsiner, J., & Van Der Veer, R. (1996). Desde el gesto hasta el self: perspectivas comunes en las sociopsicologías de George Herbert Mead y Lev Vygotski [From the Gesture to the Self: Common Perspectives in the socio-psychologies of George Herbert Mead and Lev Vygotski]. In D. Páez y A. Blanco (Ed.), *La teoría socio-cultural y la psicología social actual* [Socio-cultural Theory and Present Social Psychology], pp. 63–74. Madrid: Aprendizaje.

Vygotsky, L. S. (1926). The Historical Meaning of the Crisis in Psychology. A Methodological Investigation. In *Sobranie sochinenii*, vol 1 (pp. 291–483). Moscow: Pedagogika. [English translation In R. V: Rieber (Ed.), *The collected Works of L.S: Vygotsky*. Vol. 3. *Problems of the Theory and History of Psychology*. 233–344. New York: Plenum. 1997]

Vygotsky, L. S. (1986). *Thought and Language*. Cambridge, MA: Massachusetts Institute of Technology.

Vygotsky, L. S. (1978). *Mind in Society. The Development of Higher Psychological Processes*. Cambridge, MA: Harvard University Press.

Wartofsky, M. (1973). *Models*. Dordrecht: D. Reidel.

Wertsch, J. (1991). *Voices of the Mind*. Cambridge, MA: Harvard University Press.

White, H. (1973). *Metahistory*. Baltimore: The Johns Hopkins University Press.

White, H. (1987). *The Content of the Form*. Baltimore: The John Hopkins University Press.

Wittgenstein, L. (1973). *Philosophical investigations*. New York: Macmillan.

Wundt, W. (1900–1920). *Völkerpsychologie*. 10 vols. Leipzig: Kröner-Engelmann, 1900–1910; 3rd (Ed.), 1911–1920. vol. I : Die Sprache. part I, vol. II: Die Sprache. part 2; vol. III: Die Kunst. vols. IV–VI: Mythus und Religion. vols. VII, VIII: Die Gesellschaft. vol. IX: Das Recht. vol. X: Kultur und Geschichte.

Wundt, W. (1916). *Elements of Folk Psychology*. London: Allen & Unwin.

CHAPTER 4

Sampling Reconsidered

Idiographic Science and the Analyses
of Personal Life Trajectories

Tatsuya Sato, Yuko Yasuda, Ayae Kido, Ayumu Arakawa,
Hazime Mizoguchi, and Jaan Valsiner

Our knowledge, our attitudes, and our actions are based to a very large extent on samples. This is equally true in everyday life and in scientific research.... In science and human affairs alike we lack the resources to study more than a fragment of the phenomena that might advance our knowledge.

Cochran, 1963, p. 1

What is sampling? And why do we need to pay attention to it? Sampling is an inevitable operation in any research project – involving selection of some specimens of a class from the whole class. Yet there is more than mere decision of "whom to select" at stake here – sampling is predicated upon the realities of accessibility of the phenomena for investigation. After deciding what to investigate, researchers plan to how to access the phenomena what they want to know. Social scientists may focus on states, biologists may focus on bushes or animals, and psychologists most likely focus on human beings or their nearest phylogenetic relatives.

Furthermore – psychologists' real interest may be in some special aspect of those human beings – their mental properties for instance. Here is the access limitation involved in sampling – these properties cannot be selected independently of the cooperation by the whole – the real persons who decide to participate in a study (or decline to do so), who cooperate with the procedures (or – undermine those by lukewarm or disruptive participation strategies). Thus, the researcher faces a difficult task – for knowing the selected properties, psychologists should select a particular human being as a whole (because mental properties never appear by themselves) – yet the interests of research are a part of the whole.

Two Ways to Generalized Knowledge

In any research project we have a problem – we can only study some of the members of the set of all of the phenomena – yet we want to arrive at conclusions that cover the whole set. Hence, the issue of how we select what we study is crucial for our knowledge. This issue is subsumed under the general question of sampling. We locate and select

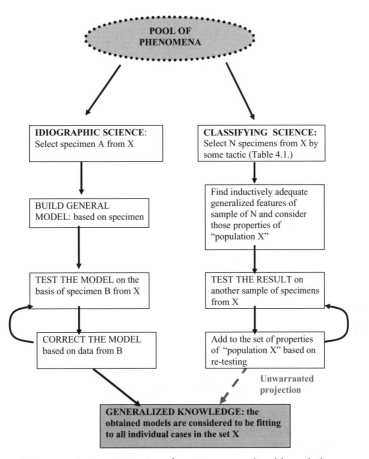

Figure 4.1. Two trajectories of creating generalized knowledge.

a specimen – *a* sample (a singular example) – from the whole multitude of the phenomenological field we want to study. Yet the reasons for selection of any specimens are not in the nature of such individual case. Instead, we use the individual case – or a selected group of individual cases – for creating generalized knowledge (Molenaar, 2004; Molenaar & Valsiner, 2005). Cultural psychology uses ways of generalization that are based on systemic analyses of singular phenomena (Valsiner, 2003a). It therefore leaves aside the set of methodological axioms of classificatory, inductively accumulative ways of arriving at generalization. That latter logic of generalization is inductive in its nature, and requires the creation of collection of specimens ("a sample" – a sub-set of N specimens of all N+N' cases that make up the class X). On the basis of such collections,

formal rules of generalization are set to make claims that are considered to apply to the full class X ("the population"). Hence, we have two lines of thought involved in the process of generalization (Figure 4.1).

The two trajectories make different use of the selections from their common phenomenological field. The trajectory of Idiographic Science (IS) is based on the selection of single cases – together with their structural and/or temporal context – developing a general model that fits the systemic nature of a single case, testing that model on other single cases, and arriving at a generalized model that fits the generic organization of the selected aspect of phenomena. Many sciences are by default limited to this trajectory of knowledge construction – the object of investigation may be present in a singular form (e.g., the Moon that circles the Earth), yet their goal is to generate knowledge about processes that fits phenomena beyond the single case (e.g., empirical "Moon science" is expected to provide generalized knowledge about processes of the formation of the universe, or general geological processes on the Earth).

The second trajectory – we call it that of "Classifying science" (CS) – is built on the assumption that multiple specimens of the same class (category) are needed to arrive at trustable knowledge (and, conversely, a single case does not allow generalization). CS creates collections of specimens – selecting cases from the phenomenological field and treating such sub-set as "a sample."

This tactic of CS leads to the de-focusing of the systemic connections of each of the sampled specimens from the original phenomenological field (Valsiner, 2005). If such connection is irrelevant for the kind of research tasks of a study, this tactic may afford new generalized knowledge about the full set ("population") of the specimens. Yet the critical issue is if the knowledge about the full set is applicable to each and every individual member of that set. This is possible only if the full set is a crisp set (i.e., all its members are of the same quality). If, however, the full set is a fuzzy set – a set where its members belong to it by varying degrees of membership – then the transfer of generalization from population to a generic individual case (see Figure 4.1) constitutes an unwarranted projection.

The trajectory of IS follows the line of classical tactics of generalization in psychology. Wilhelm Wundt is usually credited with being the principal representative of experimental psychology in Germany. As the successor to Herbart and Fechner, and the first to bring the new scientific psychology to real fruition (Wozniak, 1998), Wundt's voice has been historically prominent in the shaping of the discipline. Researchers' aims are to clarify the nature of mental phenomena and they turned adults into objects of psychological analysis quite naturally. The problem of specimen selection would never be focused under such intellectual situation. Phenomena and specimens are inseparable at the start point of scientific psychology – in the course of the whole sequence of study.

Wundt stressed the distinction between psychology and natural science. He pointed out that "two directions for the treatment of experience," should be divided. And he continued:

> . . . one is that of the natural sciences, which concern themselves with the objects of experience, thought of as independent of the subject. The other is that of psychology, which investigates the whole content of experience in its relations to the subject and in its attributes derived directly from the subject. (Wundt, 1896/1897, p. 3)

According to Wundt, the discrepancy between investigation theme and subject was completely alien to psychology such a science. But on the other hand, Wundt's plan of mental phenomena supposed the two levels – the lower and higher mental functions. Wundt claimed that the higher mental processes, involving the truly human, symbolic aspects of experience, can only be understood within a social context, using a non-experimental methodology (Leary, 1982). For the latter, Wundt emphasized a non-experimental methodology and wrote the ten-volume work of *Völkerpsychologie*. However, to say the least, this program was not followed by psychologists including his students. Experimental methodology won psychologists' affections.

However, a parallel epistemological framework arose from experimental psychology – by taking experimentation out of the laboratory and transforming it into large-scale questionnaire studies. In the U.S. context of late 19th century, it was called "child study movement." It found an enthusiastic audience among scientists and professionals as well as the lay public (Drunen and Jansz, 2004). Taine (1876) and Darwin (1877) were pioneers who described the development of their own children using observation methods. But the most influential work was done by the German developmentalist William Preyer (1882).

The usage of the biographical method allowed for the analysis of the development of the individual as well as the institutional and social conditions that influenced the developments (Bergold, 2000). Pioneers tried to describe and understand the developmental phenomena of children. Because they observed only a few children, they were still working within the IS trajectory. Yet the social demands upon psychology led to the proliferation of the second – CS – trajectory. The applied practice of mental testing in France in the 1890s (Alfred Binet) and its parallel focus on "child study" in the United States were building their generalizations upon the CS trajectory. This was put into practice by G. Stanley Hall. Hall learned experimental psychology in Germany and was one of the founders of American psychology. Much of his professional life was dedicated to the area of child study. Within the "child study movement," studies were performed in which parents and teachers acted as researchers' allies.

CREATING NORMS: THE CHILD BECOMES A CLASSIFICATORY OBJECT

Developmental psychology has developed in parallel with child psychology – yet the two areas differ substantively (Valsiner & Connolly, 2003). Child psychology is non-developmental in its nature – it compares children of different ages as homogeneous groups. Educational psychology and experimental pedagogy might also tend to treat children as specimens who form similarity groups (e.g., age sets, school grade grouping: "first-graders," "fifth-graders," etc.). By creating such similarity categories, psychologists moved away from careful look at phenomena and replaced it by comparison of outcomes of psychological functions as those appear in comparison of similarity groups. Thus, the focus on phenomena disappeared. Child psychology started to treat children as a social classificatory object – whose "fit into a category" explained the particular phenomena that were the basis for such fit. History of psychology tells us child psychology established the normative data of development of childhood. Yet the processes of development were no longer in focus of child psychology – a characteristic of the area that

remains this way to our present day (Cairns, 1998; Valsiner, 2006).

In contrast, developmental psychology has concentrated on processes. For example, Arnold Gesell – one of the students of G.S. Hall, was eminently involved in describing ontogenetic progression in children. In his introduction chapter of *The first five years of life*, Gesell (1940) emphasized that concepts such as habit, intelligence, and mental abilities can never explain the ever-changing organization of child. He suggested that the notion of growth be made into the key concept for the interpretation of development. He didn't intend to regard inter-individual differences as static state.

> *There are laws of sequence and of maturation which account for the general similarities and basic trends of child development. But no two children (with the partial exception of identical twins) grow up in exactly the same way. Each child has a tempo and a style of growth which are as characteristic of individuality as the lineaments of his countenance. (Gesell, 1940, p. 7)*

Thus, Gesell himself tried to depict the normative process of behaviors changes for understanding the determinants of growth. Though Gesell recognized the trajectories of infant development, he proceeded to depict the normative development pattern. His interest of infant hygiene made him consider the normative data rather than difference of trajectories.

Danziger (1990, p. 65) undertook an analysis of major American and German psychological journals to show the percentage of empirical studies in which "an exchange of experimenter and subjects roles" occurred. More than 30% of psychological research (1894–1896) in *American Journal of Psychology*, *Philosophische Studien* and *Psychological Review*, the roles of experimenter and subjects were exchange-possible. Though the percentage declined from 31 to 8 over a 40-year period, it still remained in 1930s. One the other hand, in late-coming journals such as *Journal of Educational psychology* (founded in 1910) and *Journal of Applied psychology* (founded in 1917), there were few (almost no) studies in which an exchange of experimenter and subject roles appeared. Danziger (1990) pointed out that individuals were treated as an object of invention rather than as the subjects of experience. His point of view resonates with our view of dissociation of specimens and phenomena. Our look at sampling emphasizes the organism-centered experiences of growth.

What Is a Sample?

The reason researchers want to know about the properties of samples – is for the sake of generalizing to another abstract unit – population. Sampling means a procedure choosing sub-groups or elements from a population according to some criteria. Once the criteria are set, the sampling procedure treats all the sampled specimens as members of a qualitatively homogeneous class.

However, the nature of autopoietic systems – their self-regulation that leads to reproduction – acts in ways contrary to the simple image of taking a number of similar objects out of an urn. At the first glance, a selection of biological materials from biological world seems to be a kind of sampling as well. The selection of materials leads to critical impact to the progress of biological investigation of the transformation of the materials. The typical case of this situation has been shown in the field of genetics at its very beginning. The pioneer of genetics, Gregor Mendel, chose seven characters of garden peas as biological materials during the late 1850s and early 1860s. Yet these were sampled not for the sake of identifying some "essential cause" that remains behind the varieties of peas. He needed to demonstrate the specific ratio of segregation by hybridization – and revealed the duality of genetic encoding through crossing different kinds of peas with one another. He did not find out what the "prototypic" or "true" pea is like – as is the case of much of psychology's sample-to-population generalization effort (see also General Conclusion – on the semiotic experiment). The search for a "true pea" – or for

"the true score" in psychological testing – presumes that such "true" and static abstract entity exists. That assumption itself is untenable in the case of all living systems that exist only through their exchange relations with the environment.

The research directions in genetics since Mendel have concentrated on the sampling of theoretically relevant structured varieties of the biological materials that were selected for investigation. Following along the same lines of thought, the discovery of the structure of DNA by James Watson and Francis Crick in 1953 became possible. It would have been a very different matter if these two youngsters had tried out to randomly sample the different base pairs for their model. The structure of the DNA may be a long chain of base pairs the location and function of many of the sub-sequences may be obscure – but by no means is that structure random. Nor is it possible to study the human genome through assuming that all base pairs make up the "population."

The Meaning of "Population"

Population is a *collection* of specimens of a particular category – be these *people*, or *organisms* of a particular *species* – that are located within some universe. Usually it is defined as a crisp set (where each member of the set belongs to it with full extent of membership). Given the inter-specimen variation [2] within each grouping of biological, sociological, anthropological, or psychological specimens it would be more adequate to define a population in terms of a fuzzy set – where each member of the set belongs to it by some measure of extent of membership (membership function). Populations are heterogeneous classes.

The concept of population eliminates the systemic qualities of the whole. As any collection it is devoid of structure – the specimens belong to a population if the inherent systemic connections between them are eliminated, or de-emphasized. Thus, all the leaves of a given tree form a "population" (of leaves of that tree) only if they are taken separately from their location on the tree. In other terms – a full tree is a tree (= a system uniting all leaves), not a "population of leaves of the tree." The quintessential example of a population of the leaves of the given tree is the collection of fallen leaves in the autumn – leaves can be collected (as a sample that approaches the full population) independently of their history (of locations on the tree). Such leaves become statistical population – an abstraction that approximates the "real" population, but is not the same (nor is it representing the original system). In an example from the human level – a military unit in a war situation (consisting of soldiers of various ranks and roles, all operating as one unit) becomes a "population" after all of its members end up buried in separate graves in a cemetery. All the graves in the cemetery are the "population of the cemetery" – that can be studied in full (i.e., listing each and every member of the population) or by generalizing from a "random sample" of graves to the whole of the cemetery. One can see that the history of the whole – the actions of the military unit – cannot be restored from any version of sampling of the outcomes of their action (i.e., their distribution in the cemetery).

LOGIC OF GENERALIZATION BASED ON THE HOMOGENEITY ASSUMPTION

The basis for using the sample-to-population generalization is the assumption of "homogeneity" of the phenomena under study in their basic essences. If one can believe in the homogeneity of a class, the arbitrary sampling is enough to do any research. But, in fact, un-ignorable variation within the sample (inter-individual or intra-individual) needs to be recognized. For integrating two contradicting concepts – homogeneity and variation – another intervening concept is needed. Usually the variation becomes regarded as "noise" that obscures the "pure essences" of the properties. This look at the reality of phenomena is built on static, a-historical, and essentialist philosophical grounds that are challenged in contemporary psychology (Hermans, 2001,

2002; Valsiner, 1986). Here the "noise" becomes the "essence" of the phenomena – and instead of static ontology researchers begin to look at dynamic equilibria and disequilibria.

The focus on interdependency of persons and environments does not fit well with the notion of random sample. Looking back to the history of science, random sampling is discussed on the context of logical inference. The American semiotician Charles Sanders Peirce insisted that

> *The truth is that induction is reasoning from a sample taken at random to the whole lot sampled. A sample is a random one, provided it is drawn by such machinery, artificial or physiological, that in the long run any one individual of the whole lot would get taken as often as any other. (Peirce, 1896/1957, p. 217)*

Yet it is precisely Peirce who repeatedly demonstrated how science cannot be built solely through the inductive techniques (see Rosa, Chapter 10 of this Handbook), and actually operates through the unity of induction and deduction in the form of abductive inference (Wirth, 1997). It involves the selection of phenomena, formation of hypotheses, and creation of new knowledge at the intersection of deduction and induction through a "leap" of inference.

Randomization is thus a product of an atomistic axiom as applied to complex world. It presumes the independence of each randomized object from one another. If that assumption is applicable, randomization is necessary because the quality of inference should be guaranteed through minimizing imbalances of selection of the specimens. Such inference has aim to understand not sample itself but population. Applicability of this axiomatic may depend upon approximation. For instance, its applicability to the grain growing on various agricultural plots (i.e., the basis of R.A. Fisher's development of variance-oriented statistics) may possibly be claimed. Yet it is an unfeasible assumption when human beings, social groups, or societies are concerned.

The Notion of Sampling in the Natural Sciences

In various biological fields, ecological research has been using sampling frequently. Recently, its importance is noticed in relation to with views of nature preservation, biological resources, and biomass energy. Sampling as well as experimental design has been based on Fisher's "three principles" – local controls, randomization, and replication. A major problem of data sampling in biological field can be explained by how to apply the Fisher's principles.

Selecting a number of individuals of organisms in some areas is an essence of ecological research. Then, the mass of organisms, their growth rate and death rates are needed. However, biological population produces descendants – who are needed for maintenance of the species. Hence, stable living environment causes population to reproduce the stable number of descendants. What matters for our knowledge of the ecological system is the relative balance of individuals who exit the system (hence the need to know the death rate, or emigration rate) with those who enter (by birth, or by immigration). The most popular method of understanding death rate is "mark release." That is, marked individuals are "released" to living environment. Afterwards, they are "re-caught." The death rates are estimated from these individuals. This method is applied to marine and freshwater animals and birds and other animal species.

The practices of the fishing industry can be seen as depending upon the practice of sampling. As it is a productive industry, its well-being is dependent upon controlled catching of fish as well as the affording of the remainder of the fish populations to reproduce themselves. Knowledge of the nature of the fish populations – through sampling – makes it possible to decide upon quotas on catching the fish so that the population would not become extinct – nor grow beyond the conditions afforded by the environment. Yet it is very difficult to estimate the death rate. It is done on the basis of measuring the samples of living organisms over time – as in case of observations of the whale population. Yet the socio-political decisions – establishing hunting quota on one or another species by representatives of *Homo sapiens* – depend on the values give to one or another population size estimate in relation to its decline (= death of numbers of specimens).

Sampling in the Behavioral Sciences

Looking at history of psychology at its independent starting point of scientific study of psychology, random sampling was never taken into account. For example, in Fechnerian psychophysics it wasn't necessary to consider a human being as a sampling unit. Fechner only needed to define the concept of sensation and stimulus. Likewise, Wundt's psychology succeeded with this basic attitude. The focus on the phenomena of the psyche in general did not need the notion of sampling at all.

In the early period of psychology, psychologists focused on the mental states such as consciousness – or on behavior. In either the psychological traditions of Wundt, Külpe, Vygotsky on the one hand, or Pavlov, Bekhterev, Watson, and Skinner on the other, sampling was an unnecessary operation to be performed by a researcher. However, as the subject matter of psychology gradually became to have interests in groups of people – such as school classrooms filled with pupils or army recruits in military training – sampling came into focus (Danziger, 1990). Danziger outlines how temporal trends exist in the use of different categories of research subjects. Academic psychologists are at first the most important group of subjects for psychological research in the 1890s and then show a progressive decline in the next decade (Danziger, 1990). Human beings were replaced by rats and army men – all treated as homogeneous classes rather than individualities. A military unit is a "sample" from the population of the given army as a whole – representing the latter precisely because of its homogeneity. In contrast – a writer, poet, or a painter do not represent any population – their creativity stems from their immediate personal experiences.

Expansion of the areas of research for psychologists into the public domains changed the sampling method of psychology and led to random sampling. The idea of random sampling seems to be imported from social survey. At the U.S. presidential election in 1936, a then-unknown pollster named George Gallup predicted that Roosevelt would win the election, based on a random sample of 50,000 people. On the other hand, the *Literary Digest* poll, which was based on 10 million questionnaires mailed to readers and potential readers (over 2 million were returned) failed to predict the winner. The success of Gallup and the failure of *Literary Digest* highlight random sampling as a proper method for prediction of pubic opinions.

Sampling and Statistical Theories

Sampling theory can be traced to the late nineteenth century. Basic statistical techniques for probability sampling were first proposed by Jerzy Neyman (D'Onofrio and Gendron, 2001). Neyman's seminal work *On the Two Different Aspects of Representative Methods: The Method of Stratified Sampling and the Method of Purposive Selection* was such landmark work (Neyman, 1934). Nevertheless, the importance of representativeness of data wasn't considered before World War II. Although there were some statisticians such as Yule (1929) and Neyman (1934) discussing the random sampling, McNemar (1940, p. 331) lamented that "the sampling inadequacy of so many researches" was "a reflection of the scanty treatment of sampling" in the textbooks on statistical method in United States. He insisted that "a large amount of psychological research must depend upon sampling for the simple reason that human variation exists."

Here we can note that sampling is the method for dissipating the idea of the existence of variation within a population. McNemar (1940) pointed out that at least 90% of the researches in psychology are interested in making an inference about the similarity or difference of two groups. Sampling theory has been valued because the biased interpretation easily occurred in research using hypothetical tests (Marks, 1947). Therefore, McNemar (1940) insisted that the validity of a scientific inference must depend upon the precision of data on which it is based. Interestingly, he used the word "the universe" in spite of "population" so that psychologists' concerns might focus on understanding the universal mental state (not human being or organisms). Securing a representative sample was easily attached to systematic sampling procedures, including random sampling.

In his 1934 paper, Neyman claimed that the method of stratified sampling was preferable to the method of purposive selection. As Smith (1976) notes the importance of the paper to statistical sampling is enormous especially in the area of social survey within a period of 10 years. These 10 years approximately match the age of "inference revolution." The "inference revolution" (dated approximately to 1940–1955; Gigerenzer & Murray, 1987) created a mono-vocal orthodoxy of the inferential techniques and introduced it as standard scientific practice in psychology. Within that orthodoxy, the notion of random sampling occupied a central place.

It is interesting to have a look at how methodology of sampling had attracted psychologists' interest over time. Figure 4.2 shows the number of journal papers include "sampling" in the title before World War II. [3]

Interestingly, journals on educational psychology were the places where sampling issues were discussed very often during this period. Spearman published his "The Sampling Error in the Theory of Two Factors" on the *British Journal of Educational Psychology* in 1924. This paper was one of the earliest papers that use the term of sampling in the title. The period of the 1920s was precisely the time when psychology moved from being a primarily laboratory science to becoming a discipline that tries to be relevant in the public and applied areas of society. As a result, the questions of selection of persons by some criteria became emphasized.

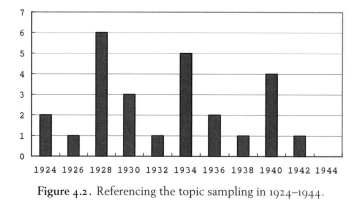

Figure 4.2. Referencing the topic sampling in 1924–1944.

STEPS IN SAMPLING

Usually, the word "sampling" means "sampling the specimen as a unit." Sampling always implies "to sample" – that is, to take – the specimen (a person, an organism, a marble out of an urn) to investigate it for the sake of a general goal. Although we insist that phenomena-oriented sampling is better than specimen-oriented sampling, this distinction is vague and many researchers seem to be familiar with the specimen-oriented sampling, it may be useful to consider the sampling from the prevailing view. Under such assumption, we know there are three steps in the psychological sampling and investigation:

Step 1 – Focus on selected properties (basis for sampling)
Step 2 – Sampling of the human participants
Step 3 – Measuring the selected properties through the cooperation of the participants

Step 2 is critical for sampling – it is here that the focus changes from psychological phenomena of individuals to that of the amorphous character of "the sample." At Step 2, the size and the representativeness of the sample of research participants *in relation to "population"* – rather than their representativeness as to *how well the targeted phenomena are present in each individual* – becomes an issue. It is here where the quality of the target phenomena easily gets lost in the discourse of samples → population generalization narrative. Comparison of samples leads to comparative statements about populations – which cannot easily be translated back to each and every individual case in each of the compared populations (Valsiner, 1986). The notion of samples – and of sampling – is an example of the utilization of elementaristic linear causality schemes (Valsiner, 2000, p. 73). As we will show in this chapter, in the case of sociocultural psychology that scheme of causality is not applicable. Correspondingly, the notion of sampling needs to be transformed.

Changing the Axiomatic Base: Historicity of Life Courses

If psychology tries to understand the individual in her/his generic form(s), we should apart from the philosophy of randomization. If there is anything random in human conduct it is not the position of a particular person within a social structure, but specific features of conduct in the person's movement from the present setting to the next anticipated future state. Even there the randomness is bounded by limits of past history (Valsiner, 1997) and future anticipation (Valsiner, 2003b). At most, we act in quasi-random ways in our search for non-random forms of conduct that grant our adaptation to the not-yet-known future.

We can find it there was a bifurcation point of our concerns on the sampling methodology. Researchers in psychology (especially social psychology) have taken a course to random sampling in the past 50 years.

Other scientists moved along on a different trajectory. According to Egon Brunswik, proper sampling of situations is more important than that of persons (Brunswik, 1947). Brunswik was a fighter against statisticians in those days (see Hammond, 1948). His Viennese background (see Benetka, 1995) made him competently skeptical of the "dust-bowl" statistical empiricism that began to dominate the United States after World War II. Brunswik is one of the eminent pioneers of ecological validity. Recognizing the unity of person-environment relations leads to the understanding of inevitability of sampling of actor<>environment units.

Hence we can see that sampling is a topic with venerable – yet ideologically situated – history in the social sciences. What contemporary science of psychology needs is clarity about how to construct adequate methods for specific research purposes – and not a discussion about whether one or another category of methods is better (or worse) by virtue of their ontology (Valsiner and Diriwächter, 2005).

Types of Sampling

Although the methodology of psychology has been dominated by the principle of random sampling, other sampling methods are being designed. We once considered the different notions of sampling in the social sciences (Table 4.1).

In general, random sampling is regarded as one of the probabilistic sampling techniques. But we want to emphasize here that "random" and "representative" are not same concepts. In purposive sampling, subjects are selected because of some pre-set characteristics. In other words, the selection of participants is made by human choice rather than at random. Purposive sampling is popular in qualitative research. Patton (2002) has proposed the following cases of purposive sampling (Table 4.2).

Here we add the explanations of some of Patton's sampling methods. "Intensity" is a method of picking information-rich cases that manifest the phenomenon intensely, but not extremely. "Politically Important Cases" is a method of picking cases that are important for political reasons. Of course, the scientific and political aspects of researches (especially ones of cultural psychology) are interdependent but are hoped to be reciprocally reinforcing. "Confirming or Disconfirming" is a method of picking cases to seek out confirming or disconfirming evidence. So this may be used second stage of researches. Both taxonomies are organized from the perspective of sampling – it is assumed that the researchers are "drawing a sample" from "a population." So these taxonomies lack a consideration of the nature of human lives – including those of researchers.

The sampling rhetoric implies that the researcher is an omnipotent "boss" of the population – like a Napoleon as general of large armies – who can by select a sample from the whole set of available and equally willing subjects. We know that this is almost never the case – the researcher is not "in control" (but needs to go through complex persuasion techniques to secure subjects' cooperation – Günther, 1998), and the selection process is sequential so that the previously selected subjects may be known to the latter ones. Last but not least – different subjects have their own active reasons for (or against) participation. Sampling is thus a cultural negotiation process. Here, we see culture as the key to any research encounter, and consider human beings as open systems.

Sampling in Socio-Cultural Psychology

Adoption of culture as a central concept in psychology leads to the necessity of taking a new looks at some of the key methodological problems in the discipline (Valsiner, 2001, 2003a). Among those is the systemic nature of human psychological processes that becomes highlighted by the re-insertion of cultural or higher psychological processes into our models of the mind (Sato and Valsiner, 2006).

Cultural psychology is the new synthetic direction in contemporary psychology that emerges from the developmental traditions of Lev Vygotsky, Karl Bühler, and Heinz Werner. It brings back to psychology the

Table 4.1: Different notions of Sampling in the social sciences

Random	A sample of objects is selected for study from a larger group (called population). Each object is chosen by procedures that are designated to be random- it is "by chance" that the objects are selected. Each object in the population has an equal chance of being selected into the sample. Within that sampling mode sub-types exist: cluster sampling (population is divided into clusters, followed by random selection of the clusters), or independent sampling (samples selected from population are mutually free of affecting one another).
Representative	The act of selection is based on the proportional representativeness of the objects in the population. The sample includes a comparable cross-section of varied backgrounds that are present in the population. Sub-types are stratified sampling (first divide the population into sub-groups, then select from these groups) and matched sampling (each object in one group is matched with a counterpart in another)
Theoretical	The underlying theory if the researcher determines whom to select for the study. Our new introduction (HSS) belongs here.
Practice based	A practitioner – a clinical psychologist, teacher, nurse – who wants to do research on their field and experience treats his or her clients as research subjects. Ethical protections of subjects' rights are in place, but the agreement by persons to participate is set up within the field of their indebtedness to the researcher as the provider of some other practically needed services.
One-point breakthrough	Even if researchers hope to access the ideal kinds of subjects, exceptional circumstances and/or special conditions may prohibit that. In such case, the researchers struggle to access anyone who accepts the research proposal-literally fighting against tight access barriers. Undoubtedly such sampling is far from being "non-biased" or "random" yet there is no need to criticize such a sampling as "biased." Depending on the research theme, it's preferable to do something rather than nothing. And it may develop into a version of relational network based sampling as below.
Relational network based	(i.e., the "Snowball Method"): The researcher engages the members of the first selected (and agreeing) participants to bring to the sample the members of their relationships networks. A crude sub-type is quote sampling (researcher may be given a "quota" of how many and what kinds of objects s/he needs to bring into the study.
Convenient	Researchers in University ask students to participate into their research. Cognitive Psychologists like to regard them as adults and developmental psychologists like to regard them as adolescent. And comparative psychologists like to regard them human being. So university students are convenient samples of psychology studies.
Capricious	The researcher takes whoever happens to agree to participate.

Table 4.2: Purposive sampling (from Patton, 2002; p. 243–244)

Extreme or Deviant Case
Intensity
Maximum Variation
Homogeneous
Typical Case
Stratified Purposeful
Critical Case
Snowball or Chain
Criterion
Theory-Based or Operational Construct
Confirming or Disconfirming
Opportunistic Random Purposeful
Politically Important Cases
Convenience
Combination or Mixed Purposeful

crucial role of history. Vygotsky similarly maintained that psychological functions are internalized relations of a social order and are structured by this order. Vygotsky explained that in modern society,

> ... the influence of the [technological and social] basis on the psychological super-structure of man turns out to be not direct, but mediated by a large number of very complex material and spiritual factors. But even here, the basic law of historical human development, which proclaims that human beings are created by the society in which they live and that it represents the determining factor in the formation of their personalities, remains in force. (Vygotsky, 1930, cited in van der Veer & Valsiner, 1994, p. 176)

Cultural psychology requires a theoretical perspective and a rigorous methodology. Focusing on the sampling method, sampling the specimens together with their contextual and historical surroundings is needed. This indicates a return to the practice of sampling of the phenomena – and a move away from the tradition of sampling of specimens. Cultural psychology uses the individual-socioecological reference frame (Valsiner, 2000, p. 73 – see General Conclusions of this Handbook) where the idea of separating

the object of investigation from its contextual surroundings equals elimination of the phenomena one wants to study.

This is the good starting point to innovate new methodology in psychology. To begin with, if not the individual but the process is understood, a new methodology concerning a new sampling is needed. It presumes that the definitive database for any scientific generalization in developmental and cultural psychology is a single case (rather than a sample – Molenaar, 2004; Molenaar & Valsiner, 2005). This is in contrast to the usual sample-to-population generalization in which the systemic nature of the single case is irreversibly lost in the process of generalization. What contemporary science of psychology needs is clarity about how to construct adequate methods for specific research purposes rather than a discussion about whether one or another category of methods is better (or worse) by virtue of their ontology (Valsiner and Diriwächter, 2005).

To summarize, sampling is an inevitable operation in any research project. Any research effort, unless it analyzes the whole realm of the given phenomena, requires some way of sampling. Some specimens of the existing (known) pool of all specimens are selected, which means others are left out. That selection is best accomplished on the basis of the history of the objects of investigation (Valsiner and Sato, 2006). It is the processes of development that result in a variety of histories of the same class of phenomena.

Generalization – Knowing About What? Population or Generic Models?

The issue of generalization is another side of the coin when we consider sampling. Sampling is a tool for generalization – and not a goal in itself. As has been pointed out elsewhere (Valsiner, 2003, 2007), there are two trajectories for generalization – from samples to populations, and from a single case to a generic model (which is further tested on other selected single cases).

Size and representativeness of sample are taken into account for good generalization. Usually one might consider that small size of sample inevitably mean non-representative. But Yin (2003) insists that small sample size doesn't lead to biased sampling.

> A common complaint about case studies is that it is difficult to generalize from one case to another. Thus, analysts fall into the trap of trying to select a "representative" case or set of cases. Yet no set of cases, no matter how large, is likely to deal with the complaint.
>
> The problem lies in the very notion of generalizing to other case studies. Instead, an analyst should try to generalize findings to "theory", analogous to the way a scientist generalizes form experimental results to theory. (Note that the scientist does not attempt to select "representative" experiments.)" (Yin 2003, p. 38)

Yin (2003) proposes to distinguish between "statistical generalization" and "analytical generalization." Statistical generalization refers to the ability to make statistical inferences about a population based on research on a small sample of that population.

Socio-cultural-historical phenomena in cultural psychology are studied with a different type of universality in focus that is available to researchers through analytic generalization. In this sense, our contemporary socio-cultural psychology continues the general traditions of Fechner, Wundt, Külpe, Skinner, and modern cognitive science based on the early mental experimentation (Simon, 1999). The generalization from population to sample trajectory is limited in its knowledge construction power because of its hidden assumption of the average (or prototypic) phenotype allowing us to infer the causality for its generation. This assumption is untenable (Valsiner, 1984, 1986).

Socio-cultural psychology deals with higher psychological functions that are mediated by signs (see Rosa – Chapter 10). Hence the elementaristic forms of causality are not applicable in this area – and we need to return to the historical traditions in the discipline to find alternatives (Valsiner, 2000; Capezza & Valsiner, 2006). As was mentioned above, Wundt accepted the distinction between cultural studies and natural science (Nerlich, 2004). As Diriwächter (2004) suggested, in order to understand higher psychological processes, only historical comparisons, the observation of our "mind's" creations (Beobachtung der Geisteserzeugnisse), could be looked at. So, a trajectory of non-experimental and non-statistical psychology is needed. Assumptions of the statistical paradigm do not afford this kind of approach, and need to be abandoned (Baldwin, 1930). In the first place, the aim of statistical work is to assume a priori separate status for objects that are actually held together by systemic links, thus replacing the real systemic order by a statistically reconstructed artifact (Valsiner, 1986). The statistical route of inductive generalization constructs a reality and consistency in the form of larger, more abstracted and homogeneous objects (Desrosières, 1993, p. 236). The "population" becomes a new created object – to which generalizations are legitimately made. Yet it is impossible to take such constructed sign – "population" – as an equivalent to a structured order of a society. A step further- back projection of generalizations about "population" as if those were generic models that work within each and every individual case within the population is a theoretically unwarranted move (Valsiner, 1986). So it isn't necessary for us to critically examine the premises of statistical methodology in socio-cultural psychology. [4]

Changing the axiomatic is needed and is in the process of happening these days. Cultural psychology might be a promising program because cultural psychology, especially socio-cultural approach, regards persons as systems rather than units. And cultural psychology is one of orthodox (legitimate) heritages of Wundt's Völkerpsychologie which study (the products of) the higher processes.

Development as a Process: Constructing Histories

There has been much inconsistency in maintaining a developmental focus in psychology

(Cairns, 1998; Valsiner & Connolly, 2003). However, that focus is inevitable if one deals with socio-cultural phenomena in their basic form – that of open systems. In the most general sense, the developmental perspective is based on the axiom of becoming which takes two forms:

$$X \text{ —[becomes] —> } Y$$

$$X \text{ —[remains] —> } X$$

The axiom X —[remains] —> X is not the same as the identity axiom of non-developmental perspectives $—X = [is] = X$. Being is conceptualized as an ontological entity, while remaining is a process of maintaining an emerged state of a system is implied. Both becoming and remaining are processes that guarantee both relative stability and change in the case of development. Epistemology of psychology tends to overemphasize the stability of human nature. Here we'd like to appreciate the possibility of change and regard the stability as the result of remaining. If one can find the stability, we ought to seek the conditions that interfere with the process of becoming.

All human development is contingent on the encounters with the world – events influence persons' life. We mean "contingent" as unexpected and/or uncontrollable. It doesn't necessarily mean that contingent life is uncertain life – yet it is life filled with phenomena of ambivalence (Abbey, Chapter 23 in this Handbook). For example, the meaning of events related to reproduction is by no means warrantable. The notions of "love," "justice," and so on are culture-bound, as well as systems of marriage (and notions of concubinage, levirate, etc.), family, and economics (Escobar, 1995; Radaev, 2005). At different age periods the particular features of the relations with the environment differ. The more one ages, the more he/she comes to meet various experiences. Personal life history is constructed through semiotic means and leads to the wisdom of human living.

Furthermore, no one experienced same events similarly to one another. Many dramatic events (viral infections, etc.) may selectively capture one person, but not others. And even if such events occur in some persons, the influences of such events are different for each person. A boy/girl who has to be taken to a hospital may begin to aim in life to become a medical professional, while another might try to avoid any encounter with medical settings. A psychologist who experiences a similar situation reminded him/her of the fact that one lives only once. Someone (e.g., a successful pick-pocket) may encounter a happy event (of success in his activity), and the other (the "donor" of the stolen purse) would not consider the same event happy. Clearly there are many life events – each of which may, or need not, happen. Life is contingent on the conditions of living. Medical sociologist Arthur Frank claims that the patients' onset of illness is somewhat contingent but experience of illness influenced the patients life course (Frank, 1995).

Socio-Cultural Experiences on the Trajectories of Living

Contingent experiences such as illness inevitably play some role in the person's life. It's not a developmental task and of course it's not pure biological necessity. Rather, it is socio-cultural experience within which all persons are guided by the internalized cultural meaning systems. Here, we can regard the socio-cultural events as contingent ones. Even illness isn't eternal. Some contagions are completely eradicated, and new contagion such as AIDS appears. And HIV infection rates are varying in time and place. So being affected by a contagion is principally a socio-cultural experience. Another example is an Amyotrophic Lateral Sclerosis (ALS). ALS, also known as Lou Gehrig's Disease, is a progressive and ultimately fatal neuromuscular disease. So if one would suffer from the ALS, the ALS would severely influence one's life. The person suffering from ALS needs to live in the different way.

Besides medical events like illness, our life events are contingent and no one is in control. For example we cannot control our parents' lives. One child's parents might die when s/he was one year old. The other child's parents would move to a foreign country. Alternatively, we cannot control a relative position of an academic achievement. Suffering from AIDS or ALS influenced one's life. Parents' deaths influence one's life too. However, the developmental theory tends to disregard such contingent events. So we need the new methodology to understand human life from the perspective of contingent events as socio-cultural experiences.

It is important that the event has the historicity in the double meaning that the individual experiences the contingent event. Such events are embedded in historical context and individuals have their own historicity. Socio-cultural psychology is therefore necessarily historical. A sampling method such as random sampling doesn't treat these contingent events. Thus there is a need to create a new way to consider the act of sampling.

It's difficult to sample randomly contingent events because they are just "contingent." We should devise the new sampling methodology so that we might treat the contingent experience as a socio-cultural experience. Suppose one person happened to know (s)he was stricken with mortal illness and researchers should know his/her experience. Handing a questionnaire to fill in is one of the representative methods. We can get the scores on scales such as fear of death. We even compare the scores of the mortal illness and the healthy, if possible. Yet such comparisons tell us nothing about the real transformation of persons over their particular life course trajectories. Contingent events such as suffering deadly disease influence one's total life and transform the structures of human existence. The basic notion of psychological science needs to be built upon idiographic assumptions (Molenaar, 2004; Molenaar & Valsiner, 2005). Sampling should be dependent of the theory and the methodology derived from the method, rather than a direct import from

manuals on methodology. The theory we use here is that of development – looking at human lives not as "variables" but as transforming structures (Valsiner and Connolly, 2003).

A New Philosophy of Method: HSS (Historically Structured Sampling)

Historically Structured Sampling (HSS) is a method of sampling individual cases based on their previous (up-to-now) knowable life course histories analyzed as a series of bifurcation points. It makes it possible to contrast individuals who have arrived at the present state (equifinality point) through vastly different life course trajectories. The notion of HSS relies heavily upon the notion of equifinality that originated in the general systems theory (GST) of von Bertalanffy (1968) and is rooted in the early work of Hans Driesch (1908).

Human psychological structure functions as an open system, not as closed system. A central place in it is given to the notion of equifinality. The notion of equifinality originates in Driesch's biological work. Driesch performed a series of experiments agitating sea urchin cells during division and causing them to fragment. Instead of forming a partial embryo, Driesch found that the cells formed an entire one. Here, the same final state may be reached from the different initial conditions and from different ways. This is what Von Bertalanffy (1968) called equifinality. Despite Driesch's vitalist general philosophy, von Bertalanffy built his organismic perspective on the basis of multi-linear developmental model along similar directions. Equifinality is the basic characteristic of open systems, and unilinearity is merely a special case of multilinearity (within which equifinality dominates).

Von Bertalanffy pioneered the organismic conception of biology from which the GST developed. He regarded living organisms including human beings as not closed systems but open systems (Valsiner and Sato, 2006). Von Bertalanffy (1968) outlined the

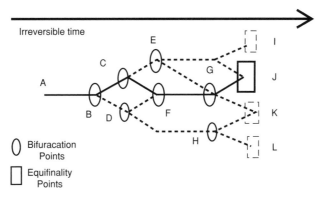

Figure 4.3. Actual life course trajectory and its crucial change possibilities.

principle of the equifinality as crucial for the open systems:

> In any closed system, the final state is unequivocally determined by the initial condition: e.g., the motion in a planetary system where the positions of the planets at a time t are unequivocally determined by their positions at a time to. . . . If either the initial conditions and or the process are altered, the final state will also be changed. This is not so in open systems. Here same final state may be reached from initial conditions and in different ways. This is what is called equifinality, and it has a significant meaning for the phenomena of biological regulation. (von Bertalanffy, 1968, p. 40)

HSS intends to select individual cases for the study through consideration of their historical trajectories moving through a common temporary state (equifinality point). In other words, HSS focus on the individual events and/or states considered as equifinality points (EFP). Equifinality means that the same state may be reached from different initial conditions and in different ways in the course of time. Then researches try to depict multi linearity, that is, trajectories to such EFP. It plays the central role in the selection of cases of developing systems in case of HSS. Any psychological states and/or life events in what researchers have interest are structured historically. The researcher decides which aspects of the historically organized system

are the objects of investigation – the EFP becomes a part of the conceptual scheme in the researchers' thinking (Valsiner and Sato, in press).

Trajectory Equifinality Model (TEM)-Based on HSS

Trajectory Equifinality Model (TEM) is a new proposal to describe human development from the perspective of cultural historical approach. It is important to emphasize that equifinality does not imply sameness – which is an impossible condition in any historical system. Rather, it entails a region of similarity in the temporal courses of different trajectories. After establishing the equifinality point, trajectories should be traced. Depicting the TEM makes it possible to grasp the trajectory with irreversible time (Figure 4.3).

In Figure 4.3, the rectangle J is the supposed equifinality point (EFP) on what researchers focus in their researches. For this EFP, there are many pathways to pass. Seven ellipses "B thorough H" are bifurcation points (BFPs) in this TEM. We can call them *passage points*. Of course, many passage points are both EFP and BFP, but main EFP should be focused along researches' interests. Researchers may find many passage points. But no matter how many points we can find, the natures of all points are not equal. Some points are trivial, and the others are crucial. Some are inevitable, others suggested these points were inevitable.

TEM is the method to describe persons' life courses within irreversible time after researchers' focusing important events as EFPs. We propose some notions for practicing TEM to construct models. The first one is notion of irreversible time and this notion originates in Henri Bergson. Next, bifurcation point (BFP) is a point that has alternative options to go. Last but not least, *Obligatory passage point* (OPP) originated in the context of the sociology of science (Latour, 1988). OPP is a phase and/or event persons inevitably experience. There are two types of OPP, indigenous and exogenous. The former includes species-specific biological transition points – such as cutting of teeth in infancy, menarche, or menopause. The exogenous OPP is set up by the environment and/or custom.

The act of using the HSS and TEM involves the following steps (Valsiner and Sato, 2006):

A) locating the relevant equifinality point (EFP) – as well as all relevant OPPs – in the generic map of trajectories necessarily present for the generic system of the processes under investigation (theoretically based activity),

B) empirical mapping out all particular cases – systems open to study that move through these points, and

C) comparison of different actual trajectories as these approach to the equifinality point by superimposing onto each trajectory a pattern of theoretically meaningful "range measure" – derived from (A) – that specifies whether the given trajectory fits into the realm of selectable cases.

Since EFP depends on the researcher's focus and/or research questions, we set up *polarized equifinality points* (PEFP) for neutralizing implicit value system of researchers. PEFP makes researchers notice the possibility of invisible trajectories.

Examples of HSS: Three Studies that Explicate the TEM

We introduce here three studies using the TEM model that is the basis for the HSS method of sampling. In the case of each of the three – on adolescents' abortion experience, girls' decisions to start making cosmetics, and infertile wives to abandon to continue receiving reproductive treatments – we outline the structures of personal life-decision histories through an analysis of various bifurcation points.

INFERTILITY IN JAPAN

Infertility is a phenomenon that is strongly influenced by the cultural and social context. All over the world, as well as historically, societies have oriented young generations, i.e., married couples, towards childbearing. The inability to bear children has always been marked with negative connotations. This situation is the same in Japan. Couples suffering from infertility have diverse experiences. They select a behavior based on these experiences, which is linked to their goal – such as undergoing fertility treatment. It is important to understand the trajectory of infertile experiences from the viewpoint of persons who have chosen fertility treatment and have also considered adoption. Both, being "conscious of infertility" and "considering adoption" are not merely personal experiences and/or life-course options, but they are historically structured experiences.

Yasuda (2005) interviewed nine couples that had continued to be unable to have children after fertility treatment and who had been considering adoption, in order to evaluate their experiences with infertility. She described the diversity of infertility experiences after fertility treatment along the passage of time, using the descriptive TEM developed in the process of her research. From the interviews, she was able to extract the participants' views on how to deal with the social systems of fertility treatment and adoption.

In this research, trajectories start from the point of beginning fertility treatment. People

Table 4.3: Couples categorized by the transition processes of conduct selection

Type 1	Had become conscious of adoption before ending fertility treatment (Turning Point 1), and had changed over to the adoption option from fertility treatment.
Type 2	Had become conscious of adoption after fertility treatment, but had not attempted adoption because of disagreement between the couple. They had ended fertility treatment (Turning Point 1) and had decided to live without children.
Type 3	Had ended fertility treatment deciding to live without children (Turning Point 1), but later, they had become aware of the possibility of adoption (Turning Point 2), and had tried it.
Type 4	Had ended fertility treatment (Turning Point 1) and later they had become aware of adoption (Turning Point 2). However, they had not been able to realize it. So they had given up trying adoption (Turning Point 3), and had decided to live without children.

continue to have fertility treatment so long as infertility does not end. Some may be aware of adoption. Some others continue to have fertility treatment, whereas others may end treatment and try adoption. In the latter case, Turning Point 1 is observed (Some women end fertility treatment without being conscious of the possibility of adoption. Most may consider adopting children, but some do not select this option because they do not recognize it as a social system for having children). Type 1 individuals become aware of adoption before they end fertility treatment and as a result, they change over from fertility treatment and try this option. This suggests that it is important to let people suffering from infertility know that adoption is one social system for having children. It is also essential to inform the options that are available to them. In fact, most couples said that they wanted help in getting to know methods of adoption that were available to them, because they could not have children, in spite of continuing fertility treatment. They realized that adoption was an option and have persevered with it. Type 2 people were conscious of adoption while undergoing fertility treatment but did not try it. These couples could not agree regarding adoption between the couple, though they continued to live together after ending fertility treatment. Few Type 2 couples considered adoption after they ended fertility treatment. That is to say, the appearance

of Turning Point 2 happens within a wide range of time. Type 3 people had ended fertility treatment, and afterwards they became aware of adoption and have persevered with adoption. Adoption cannot necessarily possible just because the couple wish to do it. Type 4 people did not realize the possibility of adoption and have given up. Giving up adoption is regarded as Turning Point 3 in Yasuda's study.

Three basic experiences were revealed in the interview: "stopping fertility treatment," "considering the possibility of adoption" and "deciding not to adopt." In this study, the nine couples were classified into four types (see Table 4.3).

Obviously, the four categories described above are not static, *a priori* ones. They are the results of dynamic trajectories of nine couples. Therefore, the trajectories could be defined using the TEM. With the intent of understanding the experiences of the couples, including those after stopping fertility treatment, Yasuda focused on the experience of stopping fertility treatments as an EFP, and decided the experiences of considering the possibility of adoption as an OPP and those of deciding not to adopt as a BFP. Yasuda depicted the diversities of their experiences that converged into and diverged from EFP (Figure 4.4, which refines TEM by Sato, Yasuda, and Kido (2004) and TEM by Yasuda (2005), which are derived from the same data. By depicting the data with TEM, they set the EFP as the condition of

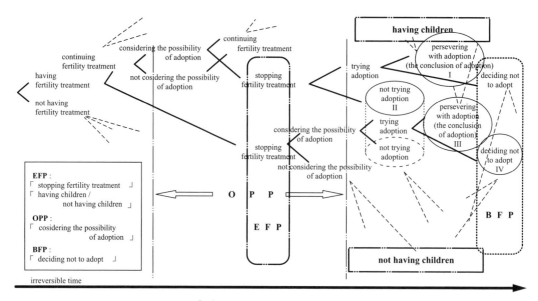

Figure 4.4. Life decision trajectories for infertility issues.

couples that either became parents or not. In other words, they consider a "couple with children" and a "couple without children" as polarized EFPs. Either one of these conditions is neither superior nor inferior to the other, but is considered equal.

Naturally, the decision not to have children should be considered equal to the decision to have children. Namely, the decision not to have fertility treatment and adoption should be equal to the decision to have fertility treatment and adoption. It is important not only to present choices, but also to guarantee the choice of trying nothing.

Figure 4.4 shows the life histories that were told by the couples or the wives. The four heavy circles represent the four categories. However, logically there should be more categories. In this study, Yasuda could identify only four categories partly because of restrictions in participant recruitment method that resulted in a small sample. However, this small sample size did not cause a sampling error. From a different perspective, we can say that we have envisioned the diversity of infertility experiences without participants. There could be many infertility experiences that cannot be understood by certain research techniques. TEM is a method of describing experiences that facili-

tates understanding of the diversity of experiences that cannot be perfectly grasped, but must exist.

In her study, Yasuda (2005) was able to explain the diversity of infertility experiences along the flow of time with TEM that was developed in the process of this study. It sets the stage for potential use of HSS – for further investigation of the infertility-related decisions. By using TEM, she will be able to select participants and adjust the focus of analyses according to the research question: "How do people select fertility treatment?" and "How do people select the social system of adoption as a way of having children?" among others. In fact, the couples could change their mind at any time, and she explained the importance of the sincerity in making these selections. At no time, was it necessary to make a choice, and all possible choices were to be equally respected.

Later she asserts that making choices is not necessarily perfect. For example, adoption cannot be considered as merely a way to have children. To begin with, adoption is basically a social system to ensure children's happiness. Therefore, people trying adoption need to consider not only themselves, but also the children. Further this presents the important consideration even

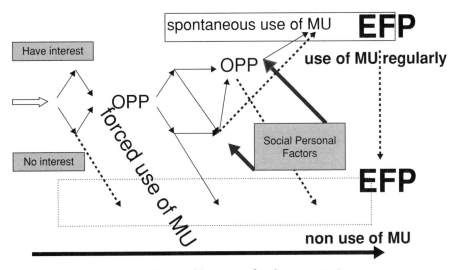

Figure 4.5. Personal histories of makeup use in Japan.

with regard to fertility treatments. While having treatment, people tend to pay attention only to giving birth to children, but they have to think of the children's happiness after they have them. Various factors regarding the selection of adoption must be taken into account.

Regarding fertility treatment, people who start it have a chance to select one treatment over the other. Fertility treatments have progressed as the biological technologies have improved. So, selections also can only be secured under those, and have kept up with the times. Therapeutic procedures such as "host mother," "surrogate mother," and other fertilization techniques have not yet been approved in Japan. Incidentally, it is necessary to examine the ethical meaning of selecting these treatments. Available choices and wishes that can be realized are restricted by social, cultural, and ethical conditions. Therefore, it is important to grasp and depict the diversity of people's experiences within the limits of possibilities. Actually, the social systems that are involved in "fertility treatments" and "adoption" are different. So considering each case with the social systems deliberately is important. TEM is a good scheme for depicting the diversity of infertility experiences, because infertility experiences themselves are embedded in other social sub-system such as "fertility treat-

ments" and "adoption operation." Needless to say, each society and/or culture has a unique way to prohibit or allow such reproductive techniques.

USE OF COSMETICS BY JAPANESE WOMEN
IN THE UNITED STATES
In Japan, most women wear facial makeup, and some Japanese women feel that this is a duty. Most studies concerning women's makeup have focused on women who use cosmetics, and not on those women who do not. Kido's study focused on both groups of women (Sato, Yasuda, and Kido, 2004). The purpose of this study was to clarify the psychological and behavioral process by which Japanese women begin to use cosmetics (or not) and the transition in their use of makeup. Five Japanese women were interviewed and were depicted in the TEM in Figure 4.5. Being forced to use makeup is an OPP point. Society facilitates women's spontaneous use of makeup.

Next, to clarify this transition, Kido (2006) examined women who had experienced acculturation. Five Japanese women who had studied at a college in the United States were interviewed. All the interviews were taped with permission. The content of each interview was clustered into four groups (e.g., "adaptation," "a choice made to express one's qualities") using the KJ

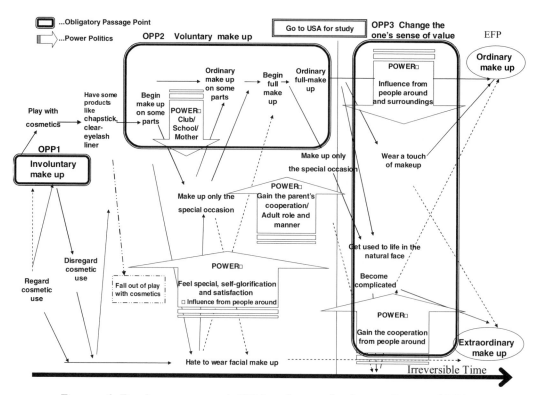

Figure 4.6. Five Japanese women's TEM on the use of makeup in Japan and USA.

method. The KJ method is one of famous idea and/or category generation method in Japan. KJ method is one of famous idea generation methods in Japan. KJ Method is a technique for summarizing information. The original KJ method was developed by Jiro Kawakita in the 1960s (See Kawakita, 1986). In Kido (2006)'s case, all relevant events and facts of cosmetic experiences are written on individual cards and collated. Cards that look as though they belong together should be grouped. This grouping procedure should be repeated and lastly aggregated and abstract catefories are expected to be emerged. After using the KJ method, Kido (2006) depicted their life courses using the TEM (Figure 4.6).

In this model, Kido (2006) found three obligatory passage points (OPPs). When all the interviewees lived in Japan, they felt that they had to use makeup, but could choose not to do so in the United States. Therefore, it seems that in Japan, strong social forces (a form of power politics) almost forced one

to wear makeup. In addition, once a pattern of makeup use was established, it seems to have become a habit.

PSYCHOLOGICAL PROCESS OF ABORTION

Arakawa and Takada (2006) applied the trajectory equifinality model (TEM) to investigate the psychological process of abortion experience because pregnancy and abortion are constrained by time, permitted only up to the 22nd week by "mother's body protection law" in Japan. Therefore, abortion choice is strongly affected by society and culture. Arakawa and Takada (2006) interviewed three young women (21–27 years old) who had terminated their pregnancies.

The results of the interviews are depicted in Figure 4.7.

As illustrated in this figure, the time between "taking notice of unusual physical condition" and "abortion surgery" is strictly limited, and pregnant women had to do and decide several things (discussing with the partner, doing tests by using pregnancy

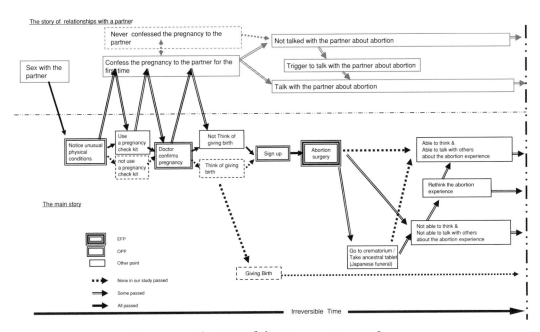

Figure 4.7. The TEM of abortion experience in Japan.

check kits, going to a clinic, deciding if they should give birth or not, signing up, and worrying about their obscure future) before the time limit.

Based on the TEM, Arakawa and Takada (2006) divided such events into two types. The first type is the events in which variety is not tolerated. To terminate their abortion, doctor's diagnosis and signing the certificate of consent are necessary. Besides such institutional constraints (OPP), there are certain other trajectories all of which have to be passed. The first is "using a pregnancy check kit." Arakawa and Takada (2006) pointed out that the reason women hesitate to go to a clinic is because there is no turning back. The second one is "not thinking of giving birth." The reason for this is assumed to be due their age. Although there were alternatives, they did not select them. This shows that non-institutional-constraints also affect the women's choice.

The second type is those events in which variety is tolerated. For example, as far as "talking with the partner about abortion or not" is concerned, some women could talk about their abortion, but other women could not. "The timing that women con-

fess pregnancy to the partner" and "Meaning of abortion experience" also varied. Many responded that "It depends on the relationship with the partner." "Meaning of abortion experience" also depends on creating a positive meaning.

Arakawa and Takada's (2006) study illustrates how TEM reveals the points a woman has to pass, and where she may not have pass. And TEM is suitable for visualizing the social direction, that is, what kind of power in the culture and the society affects women's choices at the decision-making process of abortion. The psychological theories of choices and/or options like TEM should connect theories of social sciences. Amartya Sen, the winner of the Nobel Prize for Economics in 1998, emphasizes the importance of choice.

> *Choosing may itself be a valuable part of living and, a life of genuine choice with serious options may be seen to be - for that reason – richer. (Sen, 1992, p. 41)*

Cognitive science tends to treat decision making as a cognitive process and individual situation might be abstracted. But cultural psychology tries to treat one's living with choosing. Our analytic efforts (depicted in Figures 4.3–4.7) show five TEMs. Yet the appearances of these TEMs are not same. Of course, these are TEMs because they are based on the new sampling practice (HSS). And TEM is versatile so that we can depict the various trajectories.

Conclusion: Re-Thinking Sampling and Re-Building Theories

Sampling is a process of selecting something for inclusion in a research project. Sampling should be done to increase information richness. So we should plan to make a good sampling design. Sample design refers to the means by which one selects the primary units for data collection and analysis appropriate for a specific research question (Handwerker, 2004).

TEM is a strategy for qualitative research similar to the grounded theory (Glaser and Strauss, 1967). But we proposed HSS and TEM as a set of methodologies. HSS and TEM depend on each other. HSS is a sampling method based on the systemic view, while TEM is a way of describing the full life history of the cases that includes both the actualized moves of the past and possible (considered) actions which – for one or another reason – were left within the realm of possibilities. Sampling in this respect equals that of the systems' life histories within the "landscape" of life events. In the latter, both actualized and non-actualized trajectory options can have an impact to the present decisions undertaken to face the future. Our suggested HSS method thus allows for a developmental perspective of the socio-cultural phenomena.

Last but not least, theories are tools that help us look at phenomena (see General Conclusions, this Handbook) – and are not orthodoxies to follow. Our outlining of TEM is to find out how participants make sense of their experiences in order to come to a decision by evaluating the different bifurcation points. This conforms to an explanatory model of conduct. This view is not one of prediction and control, but of bounded indeterminacy.

Notes

1 The best example of such categorical reasoning is in the failure to define intelligence – other than by the method that is classified "intelligence test". The phenomena of intelligence – problem-solving in any everyday context – are lost in the "measuremenbt of intelligence" by way of tests.

2 This is axiomatically granted by the nature of these groupings not as collections of specimens but as open systems where interspecimen variability is constantly amplified.

3 Journals were British Journal of Educational Psychology, Child Development, Journal of Abnormal and Social Psychology, Journal of Applied Psychology, Journal of Comparative and Physiological Psychology, Journal of Consulting Psychology, Journal of Educational Psychology, Journal of Social Psychology; Political, Racial and Differential Psychology, Psychological Bulletin.

4 And not only in that area – the inferential problem of confusing individual generic levels of knowledge with that gained on "populations" is present everywhere in psychology, with possible exceptions of experimental psychology and (some examples of) neuropsychology.

References

Arakawa, A. & Takada, S. (2006). Choosing abortion and its effect on one's life based on a TEM (trajectory equifinality model) analysis. Poster for ISSBD meeting, Melbourne, Australia, July.

Baldwin, J. M. (1930). James Mark Baldwin. In C. Murchison (Ed.), *A history of psychology in autobiography*. Vol. 1 (pp. 1–30). New York: Russell & Russell.

Benetka, G. (1995). *Psychologie in Wien: Sozial- und Theoriegeschichte des Wiener Psychologischen Instituts 1922–1938*. Wien: WUV-Universitätsverlag.

Bertalanffy, L. von (1968). *General systems theory*. New York: Braziller.

Bergold, J. B. (2000). The Affinity between Qualitative Methods and Community Psychology

[40 paragraphs]. *Forum Qualitative Sozial-forschung/Forum: Qualitative Social Research* [On-line Journal], 1(2). Available at: http://www.qualitative-research.net/fqs-texte/2–00/2–00bergold-e.htm [Date of Access: December 25, 2005].

Brunswik, E. (1947). *Systematic and representative design of psychological experiments. With results in physical and social perception.* Berkeley: University of California Press.

Cairns, R. B. (1998). The making of developmental psychology. In W. Damon & R. Lerner (Eds.), *Handbook of child psychology*: Vol. 1. *Theoretical models of human development* (5th (Ed.), pp. 25–105). New York: John Wiley and Sons.

Cochran, W. G. (1963). *Sampling Techniques*, 2nd edition, New York: John Wiley and Sons.

Danziger, K. (1990). *Constructing the subject: historical origins of psychological research.* Cambridge: Cambridge University Press.

Darwin, C. (1877). A biographical sketch of an infant. *Mind*, 2, 285–294.

Desrosières, A. (1993). *Politique des grands nombres.* Paris: Editions La Decouverte.

D'Onofrio, M. J., & Gendron, M. S. (2001). Technology Assisted Research Methodologies: A historical perspective of technology-based data collection methods. Paper presented at the Internet Global Summit: A Net Odyssey – Mobility and the Internet – The 11th Annual Internet Society Conference, Stockholm Sweden.

Driesch, H. (1908). *The science and philosophy of the organism.* London: Adam and Charles Black.

Drunen, P. van & Jansz, J. (2004). Child-rearing and education. In J. Jansz, and P. van Drunen (Eds.), *A Social History of Psychology* (pp. 45–92). Malden, MA: Blackwell.

Escobar, A. (1995). *Encountering development.* Princeton, NJ: Princeton University Press.

Frank, A. W. (1995). *The Wounded Storyteller: Body Illness, and Ethics.* Chicago: University of Chicago Press.

Gesell, A. (1940). *The first five years of life: a guide to the study of the preschool child.* London: Methuen.

Glaser, B. G. & Strauss, A. L. (1967). *The discovery of grounded theory: strategies for qualitative research.* Chicago: Aldine.

Gigerenzer, G. & Murray, D. J. (1987). *Cognition as intuitive statistics.* Hillsdale, NJ: Lawrence Erlbaum Associates.

Günther, I. A. (1998). Contacting subjects: the untold story. *Culture & Psychology*, 4, 65–74.

Hammond, K. R. (1948). Subject and object sampling-A note. *Psychological Bulletin*, 45, 530–533.

Hermans, H. J. M. (2001). The dialogical self: Toward a theory of personal and cultural positioning. *Culture and Psychology*, 7, 243–281.

Hermans, H. J. M. (Ed.), (2002). Special issue on dialogical self. *Theory and Psychology*, 12, 147–280.

Kawakita, J. (1986). *The KJ Method: Seeking Order Out of Chaos* (In Japanese). Tokyo: Chuokoron-sha.

Kido, A. (2006). The TEM (trajectory equifinality model) of the transition of cosmetic use by Japanese women in the United States. Poster for ISSBD Australia.

Leary, D. (1982). Immanuel Kant and the development of modern psychiatry. In W. R. Woodward and M. G. Ash. (Eds.), *The problematic science: psychology in nineteenth-century thought.* (pp. 17–42) New York: Praeger.

Latour, B. (1986). *Science in Action.* Philadelphia: Open University Press.

Marks, E. (1947). Selective sampling in psychological research. *Psychological Bulletin*, 44, 267–275.

McNemar, Q. (1940). Sampling in psychological research. *Psychological Bulletin*, 37, 331–365.

Molenaar, P. C. M. (2004). A manifesto on psychology as idiographic science: Bringing the person back into scientific psychology, this time forever. *Measurement: Interdisciplinary Research and Perspectives*, 2, 201–218.

Molenaar, P. C. M., & Valsiner, J. (2005). How generalization works through the single case: A simple idiographic process analysis of an individual psychotherapy case. *International Journal of Idiographic Science*, 1, 1–13. [www.valsiner.com]

Nerlich, B. (2004). Coming full (hermeneutic) circle: The controversy about psychological methods. In Z. Todd, B. Nerlich, S. McKeown, and D. D. Clarke (Eds.), *Mixing Methods in Psychology – The Integration of Qualitative and Quantitative Methods in Theory and Practice* (pp. 17–36). London: Routledge.

Neyman, J. (1934). On the two different aspects of the representative method: the method of stratified sampling and the method of purposive selection. *Journal of the Royal Statistical Society*, 97, 558–606.

Patton, M. Q. (2002). *Qualitative research and evaluation methods* (3rd. Ed.). Thousand Oaks, CA: Sage Publications, Inc.

Peirce, C. S. (1957). The Principal Lessons of the History of Science. In *Essays in the philosophy of Science*. Indianapolis [original paper from 1896]

Preyer, W. T. (1882). *Die Seele des Kindes*. Leipzig: Grieben.

Radaev, V. V. (2005). *Ekonomicheskaya sotsiologia* [Economic sociology]. Moscow: Izdatel'skii Dom GU-VShE.

Sato,T. Yasuda, Y., & Kido, A.(2004). Historically structured sampling (HSS) model: A contribution from cultural psychology. Paper presented at the 28th International Congress of Psychology, Beijing, China, August 12.

Sato, T., & Valsiner, J. (2006). Historically Structured Sampling (HSS) and Trajectory Equifinality Model (TEM); New methodologies for cultural historical approach. Poster symposium for ISSBD, Melbourne, Australia, July.

Sen, A. (1992). *Inequality Reexamined*. New Delhi: Oxford University Press.

Simon, H. (1999). Karl Duncker and cognitive science. *From Past to Future*, 1, 2, 1–11.

Smith, T. M. F. (1976). The foundations of survey sampling: A review. *Journal of the Royal Statistical Society*, Series A, 139:183–204.

Valsiner, J. (1984). Two alternative epistemological frameworks in psychology: The typological and variational modes of thinking. *Journal of Mind and Behavior*, 5, 449–470.

Valsiner, J. (Ed.), (1986). *The individual subject and scientific psychology*. New York: Plenum.

Valsiner, J. (1989). *Human development and culture: The social nature of personality and its study*. Lexington, MA: Lexington Books.

Valsiner, J. (1997). *Culture and the development of children's action*, 2nd (Ed.) New York: John Wiley and Sons.

Valsiner, J. (2000). *Culture and human development*. London: Sage.

Valsiner, J. (2001). *Comparative study of human cultural development*. Madrid: Fundacion Infancia y Aprendizaje.

Valsiner, J. (2003a). Culture and its Transfer: Ways of Creating General Knowledge Through the Study of Cultural Particulars. In W. J. Lonner, D. L. Dinnel, S. A. Hayes, & D. N. Sattler. (Eds.), Online Readings in Psychology and Culture (Unit 2, Chapter 12), (http://www.wwu.edu/~culture), Center for Cross-Cultural Research, Western Washington University, Bellingham, Washington, USA.

Valsiner, J. (2003b). Beyond social representations: A theory of enablement. *Papers on Social representations*, 12, 7.1–7.16 [http://www.psr.jku.at/]

Valsiner, J. (2004). Three years later: Between social positioning and producing new knowledge. *Culture & Psychology*, 10, 5–27.

Valsiner, J. (2005). Transformations and flexible forms: Where qualitative psychology begins. *Qualitative Research in Psychology*, 4, 39–54.

Valsiner, J. (2006). Developmental epistemology and implications for methodology. In R. Lerner (Ed.), *Handbook of Child Psychology*. Vol. 1. *Theoretical models of human development* (pp. 166–209). New York: John Wiley and Sons.

Valsiner, J. (2007). *Culture in minds and societies*. New Delhi: Sage.

Valsiner, J. & Connolly, K. J. (Eds.), (2003). *Handbook of developmental psychology*. London: Sage.

Valsiner, J. & Diriwächter, R. (2005). Qualitative Forschungsmethoden in historischen und epistemologischen Kontexten. In G. Mey. (Ed.), *Handbuch Qualitative Entwicklungspsychologie* (pp. 35–5). Köln: Kölner Studien Verlag.

Valsiner, J. & Sato, T. (2006). Historically Structured Sampling (HSS): How can psychology's methodology become tuned in to the reality of the historical nature of cultural psychology? In J. Straub, D. Weidemann, C. Kölbl & B. Zielke. (Eds.), *Pursuit of meaning* (pp. 215–251). Bielefeld: transcript.

Van Der Veer, R. & Valsiner, J. (1994). *The Vygotsky reader*. Oxford: Blackwell.

Wirth, U. (1997). Abduction and comic in the sign of the three: Peirce, Freud, Eco. In I. Rauch and G. F. Carr. (Eds.), *Semiotics around the World: Synthesis in diversity* (pp. 895–898). Berlin: Mouton de Gruyter.

Wozniak, R. H. 1998 *Classics in psychology, 1855–1914: Historical Essays*. Bristol: Thoemmes Press.

Wundt, W. (1897). *Outlines of Psychology*. Translated by C. H. Judd. Leipzig: Wilhelm Engelmann; first published in German as Wundt, W. (1896). *Grundriss der Psychologie*. Leipzig: Wilhelm Engelmann.

Yasuda, Y. (2005). Self-reassessment Following Infertility: Branching Selection by Couples unable to have Children after Infertility Treatment. *Qualitative Research in Psychology*, 4, 201–226. [In Japanese with English abstract.]

Yasuda, Y. (2006). A trial to describe the diversity of infertility treatments with development of the Trajectory Equifinality Model (TEM). Poster presentation for ISSBD Australia, July.

Yin, R. K. (2003). *Case Study Research: Design and Methods*. Thousand Oaks, Ca.: Sage.

Yule, G. U. (1929). *Introduction to the Theory of Statistics*, 9th (Ed.) London: C. Griffin.

Part II

FROM NATURE TO CULTURE

CHAPTER 5

The Windowless Room

'Mediationism' and How to Get Over It

Alan Costall

. . . This worldless consciousness might be compared to a room without windows which is hung with innummerable and continually changing pictures. Apparently, the self is assumed to live locked up in this room and to ponder whether "beyond" there is perhaps a "world." Is there such a consciousness, a consciousness epistemologically prior to, i.e., more immediately accessible than, the world?

Duncker, 1947, p. 530

Old ideas give way slowly; for they are more than abstract logical forms and categories. They are habits, predispositions, deeply ingrained attitudes of aversion and preference. Moreover, the conviction persists – though history shows it to be a hallucination – that all the questions that the human mind has asked are questions that can be answered in terms of the alternatives that the questions themselves present. But in fact intellectual progress usually occurs through sheer abandonment of questions together with both of the alternatives they assume, an abandonment that results from their decreasing vitality and a change of urgent

interest. We do not solve them: we get over them.

Dewey, 1910, p. 19

Mediationism extends across two contrasting approaches to theory in psychology, namely, the dominant tradition of individualistic, cognitive theory, and the still *too* loyal "opposition" consisting of various alternative approaches seeking "to ground activity previously seen as individual, mental, and nonsocial as situated, collective and historically specific" (Bowker & Leigh Star, 2000, p. 288). These approaches, despite their important differences, are largely agreed on one thing: we do not, and *could* not, have "direct" contact with our surroundings. Something or other is always supposed to be getting in our way: internal rules and representations, schemas, or prototypes, in the case of standard cognitive theory, or else human labor, discourse, or social representations, in the case of the opposition. And once mediation in general is viewed as an all-pervasive epistemological barrier, even the well-intentioned efforts of adults in helping children discover the meanings of things and in scaffolding their actions can only seem like intrusive ways of preventing those innocent victims from finding out what the world is *really* like.

Now, human life is indeed complicated. Mediation in various forms is widespread, including those representational practices based around the new computer technologies which though *ours* keep being attributed, within cognitive theory, to the computers themselves. Any proper approach to human psychology will clearly have to take mediation in its various forms into account. The problem is *mediationism*, making a fetish of mediation, where the various forms of mediation become abstracted from their concrete circumstances, so that sensible non-disjunctive distinctions turn instead into troublesome dualisms.

The considerable attraction of mediationism has long been that it *seems* to provide solutions to a whole range of problems at the heart of the Western intellectual tradition. Yet the very fact that mediationism appears to constitute such an all-purpose solution is itself part of the problem. The trouble is that we have become so enchanted by mediationism that we seldom bother to look closely at the many different problems that it is supposed to solve. But these problems may, on reflection, no longer be so compelling as they once seemed. The answer, then, might not be to try to solve them, but to get over them.

Mediationism in Mainstream Cognitive Psychology

Within cognitive psychology, mediationism has primarily taken the form of *representationalism:* the appeal to internal rules and representations as a necessary and sufficient basis for explanation within human psychology. Representationalism is widely regarded as the means by which modern psychology finally broke free from the yoke of behaviorism, but, as Fodor (1981, p. 140) has noted, "insofar as the Representational Theory of Mind is the content of the computer meta-phor, the computer metaphor predates the computer by about three hundred years."

"Cognition" has long been – and continues to be – *defined* in terms of representation (e.g., Leeper, 1951; Tomasello & Call, 1997, p. 10). What is (relatively) new is that, since the 1980s, psychology *as a whole* has come, in effect, to be defined as the study of cognition:

> *Put plainly, psychology – including developmental psychology – has been redefined as the study of cognition. Friendship has become social cognition, affect is seen as a form of problem-solving, newborn perception is subsumed under a set of transforming rules, and psychoanalysis is reread as a variant of information processing. Cognition, the feeble infant of the late Fifties and early Sixties, has become an apparently insatiable giant. (Kessen, 1981, p. 168)*

Unfortunately, there are some fundamental problems with representationalism. Most of these were identified many years before the advent of modern cognitive psychology, and they have not gone away (see, for example, Bickhard & Terveen, 1995; Harnad, 1990; Janlert, 1987; Pecher & Zwaan, 2005; Shaw, 2003; Still & Costall, 1991a). One serious problem concerns how we can intelligently apply rules and representations to actual situations. How do we know when they are appropriate? The temptation, for the inveterate representationalist, is to invoke yet another level of representations to deal with this problem of situated action, but this does not make the basic problem go away. It merely defers it. Ultimately, there has to be something beyond representation to get us out of this regress.

Another problem concerns the origins of representations, and how they come to have meaning, and "map" onto the world. In traditional perceptual theory, for example, a profound gulf is assumed to exist between perceiver and world, and internal representations are then invoked to bridge the gap. But although these representations are then claimed to derive from the "past experience" (either of the individual or the species), no sensible explanation is ever provided for how *past* experience could possibly escape the severe limitations deemed to apply to the *present*.

Then there is the very curious status of representationalism as a *scientific* theory. For the modern representationalists are, of course, very keen to invoke scientific evidence in their support. But, in the very process of invoking objective, scientific evidence in the cause of representationalism, they keep managing to saw through the branches on which they claim to be sitting. Here, for example, is Richard Gregory unwittingly engaged in such tree surgery:

> It used to be thought that perceptions, by vision and touch and so on, can give direct knowledge of objective reality.... But, largely through the physiological study of the senses over the last two hundred years, this has become ever more difficult to defend.... ultimately we cannot know directly what is illusion, any more than truth - for we cannot step outside perception to compare experience with objective reality. (Gregory, 1989, p. 94)

At one moment, we are supposed to be perfectly capable of finding out scientifically what things are really like (as when we engage in the physiological study of the senses), and, at the next moment, the objective evidence thus gained is then supposed to convince us that we were trapped all along within a "worldless consciousness" – a "room without windows" (Duncker, 1947, p. 530).

Until now, cognitive psychologists have mainly dealt with such problems in the following unsatisfactory ways:

1. *Handwaving*: insisting that the problems will ultimately be solved, and hence are not really fundamental problems at all (e.g., Johnson-Laird, 1988, p. 34).
2. *Passing the buck:* acknowledging that the problems are indeed fundamental, *so* fundamental that they are evidently "metaphysical" and hence a problem for the philosophers, rather than the concern of serious, no-nonsense, scientists.
3. *The Fodor option*: keeping a reasonably straight face, and presenting the very

strange implications of representationalism as exciting new discoveries (as in the Gregory example, above), rather than the *reductio ad absurdum* they might otherwise be taken to be.

Representationalism is now mainly identified with mainstream cognitive psychology, and even within that field there is growing, if still limited, recognition of its problems, and the need to move on. But, of course, mainstream cognitive psychology is not the only game in town. A wide range of alternative approaches now challenge the decontextualized, individualistic approaches of mainstream cognitive research and theory, and have come to emphasize, instead, the importance of the social and cultural. For such approaches, the foundational problems of cognitive science can seem remote, even quaint. But just as the celebrated overthrow of behaviorism led to a remarkably long bout of complacency among the cognitive psychologists, those of us claiming to have moved safely beyond cognitivism need to reflect upon what we too might have unwittingly retained. Representationalism is deeply ingrained within the Western tradition, and linked to a wide range of longstanding and half-forgotten agendas. It is these agendas that are the real problem, and so we need to be clear what they involve if we are not to find ourselves returning to some form or other of mediationism.

Representationalism in Social Cognitive Psychology

Some of the most influential current approaches within social psychology are frank extensions of individualistic cognitive theory to the interpersonal realm, and so it is hardly surprising that representationalism figures centrally in both. This is certainly true of the "Theory of Mind" approach (ToMism), which has been remarkably influential over the last twenty years, and assumes an explicit dualism between what we can directly observe about other people and their feelings, beliefs, and intentions. First, such mental states are supposed to exist beyond the reach of "observation." This has certainly been a source of concern to some psychologists. Miller, Pribram, and Galanter (1960, p. 6), for example, complained that the subject matter of psychology was "distressingly invisible," and went on to suggest that "a science with invisible content is likely to become an invisible science." Yet most of the textbooks are agreed that having an invisible subject matter need not in itself be regarded as a special problem for psychology since many other more reputable sciences are also mainly concerned with inferring hidden structures (such as genes, atoms, etc.) from empirical evidence (e.g., Harré, 2002). But if psychology can claim to be in good company as a science of the hidden, then we need to be very clear about the unusual extent of the concealment of its supposedly hidden subject. The painstaking inferential leap from diffraction patterns to the structure of DNA bears no comparison to that required, according to the dualist ontology of modern psychology, to bridge the gap between what we can observe about other people and what is going on "in their minds."

The problem of inferring mental structures is usually framed in terms of the "poverty" of the stimulus, the underspecification of mental structure by any possible observations of behaviour. But, according to the dualistic premises of ToM, the stimulus is not just impoverished, it is bankrupt. There is supposed to be *no* logical relation between what we can observe about another person and their intentions and feelings. The consequences are stark for any empirical science of psychology, and, of course, for our everyday dealings with other people. As Hammond and Keat (1991) have put it, if we are really faced with a dualism of body and mind, then "no deductively valid inference can be made from statements about one such 'part' of a person to statements about the other. In particular, one cannot validly infer, on the basis of knowledge of a body, any conclusion about a mind" (p. 205).

No wonder proponents of ToM talk coyly about "mind-reading" (see Costall, Leudar,

& Reddy, 2006). On the assumptions of ToMism, it is truly a *miracle* that we can ever tell what other people are thinking or feeling, or, indeed, know that they have any kind of mental life at all. As Alan Leslie (1987, p. 422), one of the main proponents of ToMism, has put it: "It is hard to see how perceptual evidence could force an adult, let alone a young child, to invent the idea of unobservable mental states." This "hard" task of reading other people's minds is claimed to be soluble, nevertheless, in a perfectly non-mysterious, naturalistic way, thanks to the existence of special representational capacities or modules which are supposed to fill the gap between the observable and the unobservable. Yet, as with similar applications of the representationalist approach in perceptual theory, the postulated gap these representations are supposed to bridge is *so* great there is absolutely no way the knowledge embodied in the representations could derive from either individual past experience or even that favorite *deus ex machina* of recent psychological theory, "evolution" (e.g., Tooby & Cosmides, 1995, p. xvii). Not even natural selection can differentiate between differences that are deemed to make no difference (for an extensive criticism of Theory of Mind, see Leudar & Costall, 2004a).

One of the basic problems here is that cognitive psychology, despite its rhetoric of revolution, has retained the Watsonian, objectivized conception of behavior as *antithetical* to the mental, rather than logically connected (see Costall, 2006a; Leudar & Costall, 2004b). As Harvey Carr rightly insisted, "objectivism" was more appropriate than "behaviorism" to describe Watsonian psychology, since, what was really distinctive about this position was "not a distinction of subject matter (behavior) but the objective view from which it is studied" (Carr, 1915, p. 309). As many of Watson's contemporary critics were well aware, not only was the conception of psychology as the study of behavior widely accepted before Watson tried to cause a stir, but also Watson was committed to exactly the same psychophysical dualism that had led the "introspectionists" to suppose that introspection could be the only proper method for the study of mind:

> *Embedded in the very core of the behaviorist's doctrine is the Platonic distinction between mind and matter; and behaviorism, like Plato, regards the one term as real and the other as illusory. Its very case against dualism is stated in terms of that distinction and is made by the classical metaphysical procedure of reducing the one term to the other. This metaphysical distinction, rather than empirical evidence, is the basis on which behaviorism accepts or rejects data for scientific consideration and on which it forms conceptions for dealing with them. . . . Behaviorism has adopted a metaphysics to end metaphysics.* (Heidbreder, 1933, pp. 267–68)

Watson, who had been a student of John Dewey, claimed he never understood what Dewey was talking about. But Dewey, in contrast, was quickly onto Watson's case:

> *To conceive behavior exclusively in terms of the changes going on within an organism physically separate in space from other organisms is to continue the conception of mind which Professor Perry has well termed "subcutaneous". This conception is appropriate to the theory of existence of a field or stream of consciousness that is private by its very nature; it is the essence of such a theory.* (Dewey, 1914/1977, p. 445)

In addition to retaining this objectivized conception of behavior, cognitive psychology also continues to formulate its basic task of explanation in terms of the classical behaviorist formula of "stimulus and response." Much of modern cognitive theory is, therefore, not an alternative to stimulus-response psychology, but merely the most recent elaboration of that scheme: an attempt, as in neo-behaviorism, to fill the gap: to explain "what is going on" between stimulus and response. People are supposed to be passively stimulated by events in their surroundings, and only then to become active – *and then only subcutaneously* – in interpreting what it all might mean on the basis of stored mental representations. This commitment to the stimulus-response formula is blatant, though hardly noticed,

throughout the modern cognitivist literature, as in this statement from a recent text on Social Cognition:

> *At the individual level, social cognition is the mental "filter" through which objective events and experiences are subjectively represented and remembered.* It is a basic premise of the "cognitive revolution" in psychology that individuals do not respond directly to stimuli from the external environment but to their perceptions and cognitive interpretations of those stimuli. (Brewer & Hewstone, 2004, p. xi, emphasis added)

In fact, this commitment to stimulus-response psychology is extensive not just in mainstream cognitive psychology, but in social psychology as well. For example, Brian Schiffer, in his book on the *Material life of human beings*, also insists that we should go beyond the early behaviorists by constructing models "for elucidating the knowledge and cognitive processes *that connect stimulus and response*" (Schiffer, 1999, p. 8, emphasis added). And, Rom Harré (2002, p. 104), an influential critic of mainstream psychology and exponent of discursive psychology (and who really should know better) has recently given the following example of word recognition to explain how we should theorize more generally within psychology:

> *Instead of the behaviorist pattern:*
>
> *Stimulus (retinal sensation) → Response (perception of word)*
>
> *we must have*
>
> *Observable stimulus (retinal sensation) together with unobservable Cognitive process ('knowledge utilization') → Observable response (recognition of word)*

Another problem for which representationalism has long seemed the obvious solution concerns our susceptibility to errors and illusions. The standard line within psychological theory has been to conclude, on the basis that we (or, more precisely, *non*-psychologists) *sometimes* get things "wrong," that "just-plain-folks" are epistemological dupes. Thus, according to the "social cognition" approach, we can only know about other people in a necessarily indirect and generally hazardous way, given the limited and ambiguous evidence:

> Judgments of such internal states as emotions, personality traits, and attitudes are often extremely difficult. *The person's internal state cannot be observed directly - it must be inferred from whatever cues are available.* (Taylor, Peplau, & Sears, 1994, p. 51; emphasis added)

The problem of limited available information ("the poverty of the stimulus") is compounded by the existence of a host of selective biases in judging other people (Smith & MacKie, 2000, p. 85). Curiously, however, the psychologists committed to this "error paradigm" (as Funder, 1995, has characterized it) clearly regard themselves as somehow immune from these epistemological limitations, and perfectly well placed to assess the hopeless inaccuracies of 'other people' in their attempts to make sense of *other* 'other people'.

Now, although representationalism has always seemed the obvious way to explain such errors, there is a snag. Although its readiness to explain illusion has always seemed one of its most conspicuous strengths, representationalism is too effective. It cannot account for our "failures" to err:

> ...the representative theory of knowledge...satisfied the craving for a real and reliable world...by sequestering all error and untruth in a place apart, the 'subjective' world. It is remarkable that this view has been found attractive and serviceable notwithstanding the fact that at the same time it provides that all that any person can experience or know is his own subjective world – the very stronghold of error. Of course it avails nothing that there is somewhere a real and true realm if it is for ever and completely shut out from the 'subjective'. (Holt, 1914, p. 259; see also Gibson, 1950, p. 159; Holt et al, 1912, p. 4; Wilcox & Katz, 1984)

The "problem of illusion," reappears in a more general and fundamental way within the Western intellectual tradition. For, acc-

ording to the ontology of modern physical science, the very world as we experience and "dwell" in it (Ingold, 2001) must itself be regarded as one grand illusion. Within classical physical science, "nature" came to be defined according to the limits of its methodologies (mechanism, atomism, quantification), to sustain the claim that the new science could explain *everything*. And *everything else* – the so-called secondary and tertiary qualities (sensory and aesthetic qualities and also *meaning*) – was relegated to an alternative, shadowy existence beyond nature, the realm of representation:

> In general, the connections between the experiencing individual and the things experienced – conceived in their physical reality – were reduced to a passive conditioning of states of consciousness by a mechanical nature. Into such a mind was carried . . . whatever in nature could not be stated in terms of matter in motion. . . . The result of this was to force upon the mind the presentation of the world of actual experience with all its characters, except, perhaps, the so-called primary characters of things. Mind had, therefore, a representational world that was supposed to answer to the physical world, and the connection between this world and the physical world remained a mystery. (Mead, 1938, p. 359)

The Cartesian dualism of mind and matter (including the body) certainly protected the claim of the new science to explain everything, but it was also congenial to already long established patterns of thought. The assumption that *we* are not part of nature has its origins in classical Greek philosophy and Christian theology. Now, clearly, human beings pose an increasingly dangerous threat to the continued existence of life on earth, but this is precisely because we are part of this world, even though we mainly act as if we were not. Our presence, however, is not necessarily always malign, whereas the assumption that we do not really belong in this world can be. When, for example, the Yellowstone National Park was established in 1864, in an attempt to preserve that region in a state of "nature," the Native Americans who had been living there for thousands of years were either removed or else confined in reservations. Yet the presence of those people and their sustainable practices of hunting and use of fire were an important component of the very ecology that the authorities had been trying to conserve (Hirsh, 2000; Cronon, 1996; Stevens, 1997).

Until this point, I have been presenting the various problems behind mediationism in the form of a list, and it is already getting long. But this is what is so tricky about mediationism: there are so many underlying problems that we easily lose track of what, exactly, they are, and hence whether they are really the kinds of problems that we should still be taking seriously. So let us engage in some interim stocktaking. Long after the supposed demise of stimulus-response behaviorism, does it really make sense to be framing the problem of psychology in terms of explaining what "goes on" between the stimulus and response? Should we really be framing our theories in terms of a Watsonian, objectivized concept of "behavior"? Is it reasonable to be taking the long-rejected ontology of mechanistic physics as a serious starting point for understanding the place of mind in – or *out* – of nature? After all, physical theory went through a whole series of radical transformations throughout the late nineteenth and twentieth centuries, and no longer needs to eject mind from nature, and thereby "set up" psychology as, in effect, the science of the "unscientific." As the philosopher, Arthur Bentley, nicely put it:

Since the 'mental' as we have known it in the past was a squeeze-out from Newtonian space, the physicist may be asked to ponder how it can still remain a squeeze-out when the space out of which it was squeezed is no longer there to squeeze it out. (Bentley, 1938, p. 165)

There are, however, yet further influential sources of mediationism, and they are intimately interconnected. The first of these is "the spectator theory of knowledge" which treats the knower as essentially an observer rather than an agent. This visual metaphor of knowing posits an aloof God's eye view outside the system to be known:

The theory of knowing is modeled after what was supposed to take place in the act of vision. The object refracts light and is seen; it makes a difference to the eye and to the person having an optical apparatus, but none to the thing seen. The real object is the object so fixed in its regal aloofness that it is a king to any beholding mind that may gaze upon it. A spectator theory of knowledge is the inevitable outcome. (Dewey, 1969, p. 23)

This spectator theory of knowledge, in turn, leads to a conception of knowing as representation or correspondence:

If the knower, however defined, is set over against the world to be known, knowing consists in possessing a transcript, more or less accurate but otiose, of real things. . . . Knowing is viewing from the outside. (Dewey, 1917, pp. 58–59)

This approach to knowledge as "viewing from the outside" is further encouraged by the fallacy of intellectualism, the assumption that true knowing is theoretical (*episteme*) not practical (*techne*), and that it is detached not engaged (Toulmin, 1976, p. 69; see also Falmagne, 1995; Ryle, 1999). To a remarkable extent, cognitive theory continues either to *identify* knowing with highly specific and derivative practices of *abstraction*, such as classification, computation, calculation, or logical inference, or else assimilates everything else to their terms, as in the claim that perceiving is nothing but a process of unconscious inference. Here is a recent example of this commitment to the priority of abstraction that comes, remarkably enough, from a book specifically concerned with "grounding cognition":

Our ability to interact appropriately with objects depends on the capacity, fundamental for human beings, for categorizing objects and storing information about them, thus forming concepts, and on the capacity to associate concepts with names (Borghi, 2005, p. 8).

The primacy given to abstraction is most blatant in modern psychological theory in the form of Theory of Mind, and related "theory" approaches, where we are *all* supposed to be living on the basis of theorizing almost *all* of the time. Yet the very experience of theorizing itself has the strange effect of seeming to remove us from the world and from other people:

> When we think, we shut ourselves within the circles of our own ideas and establish, as it were, a methodological solipsism. We behave as though we were 'pure subjects', observers only, unimplicated in the dynamic relatedness of real existence. (MacMurray, 1961, pp. 20–21)

The still-dominant computer metaphor of cognitive theory continues to be widely regarded as a serious challenge to dualism since "brain and mind are *bound* together as computer and program," or hardware and software (Johnson-Laird, 1988, p. 23, emphasis added). But the metaphor proves to constitute a perverse kind of reaction, and a strange kind of bond. The computer metaphor is an awesome condensation (in the Freudian sense) of most of the important problems behind mediationism. First of all, knowledge and meaning are identified with representation. And then the computer metaphor, far from being antidualistic, implies not only the antithesis of mind and matter, since the software is separable from *any* hardware, but also the antithesis of meaning and materiality, since meaning is located solely within the software as self-enclosed symbols. This is precisely why cognitivism can claim to be "a science of structure and function divorced from material substance" (Pylyshyn, 1986, p. 68).

Furthermore, psychologists have been so enthralled by the software or program aspect of the computer metaphor, that they have hardly bothered to spell out what precisely the *hardware* is supposed to represent, not least, whether it refers to the mind, the brain, or the body. Either way, this hardware is no more than a stimulus-response interface. Certainly, some theorists have invoked aspects of the hardware as part of the computer metaphor, such as the central processing unit, memory stores, and buffers. Yet it is the *ideal* of a computer as a "general purpose machine" – a machine whose function is completely unconstrained by the hardware – that formally underpins the supposed separability of software and hardware. And, according to this ideal, the hardware (as mind, brain, or body) can have no explanatory relevance at all (see Costall, 1991, in press). The computer metaphor, as it underpins modern cognitivism, is the apotheosis of dualism.

Déja vu All Over Again

Mainstream psychological theory, even in relation to so-called social psychology, has remained resolutely individualistic, not just in focusing on the individual person, but in regarding the social as derivative, an "overlay" upon our fundamental, human nature. Within the confines of such approaches, mediationism has derived from a "double dualism" – an epistemological dualism of knower and known and a psychophysical dualism which "conceives empirical reality to fall asunder into a world of mind and a world of matter mutually exclusive and utterly antithetic" (Lovejoy, 1929, p. 3).

Many decades before the rise of modern cognitivism, there was a wide reaction against this dualistic scheme, along with the representative theory of knowledge to which it gave rise:

> The supposition, so long accepted as unchallengeable, that all apprehension of objective reality is mediated through subjective existents, that "ideas" forever interpose themselves between the knower and the objects which he would know, has become repellent and incredible to many of our contemporaries; and the cleavage of the universe into two realms having almost no attributes in common, the divorce between experience and nature, the isolation of the mental from the physical order, has seemed...to be unendurable in itself and the source of numerous artificial problems and gratuitous difficulties.... (Lovejoy, 1929, pp. 3–4)

This revolt against dualism was well motivated by important developments within science itself, not just the new physics but also Darwinian theory with its emphasis on the naturalistic origins of the human mind. Yet, as far as modern cognitive theory is concerned, all this might never have happened. But what about those alternative non-individualist approaches that put the emphasis on the "situated, collective and historically specific" (Bowker & Liegh Star, 2000, p. 288)? Vygotsky has, of course, been an important historical influence on many of these alternative approaches, yet his own contrast between the cultural and biological lines of human development, and the way his developmental scheme prioritizes "intrapersonal" and abstract modes of thought are hardly unproblematic (Still & Costall, 1991b; Wertsch, 1996). And James Gibson, for whom the material conditions of shared experience and knowledge was an important concern (see Heft, 2001), and whose concepts such as "affordance" and "proprioception" provide important resources for a non-dualistic psychology (Costall, 2006b; in press), unwittingly set a number of awkward traps. One of these was his failure to foreground our activity *within* and *upon* the world. His approach remained largely within the schema of knowledge as *perception*. According to Edward Reed, Gibson's radical move was to shift the focus from a passive perceiver, to "the active self *observing* its surroundings" (Reed, 1988, p. 201, emphasis added). But this is not a sufficiently radical move at all. Exploratory activity does not, in itself, *change* things. Indeed, Gibson's account of affordances (i.e., the meanings of things for our possible actions) is itself framed in terms of observation, since, according to Gibson, the central claim of the theory of affordances is that "the "values" and "meanings" in the environment can be *directly perceived* (Gibson, 1979, p. 127; emphasis added). Indeed, even Gibson's concept of 'direct perception' is problematic because it became defined, by contrast, with so many diverse senses of "indirect" or "mediated," including "*socially* mediated," that it is

hardly applicable to human perception at all (Costall, 1988, 1990). Despite his many profound contributions, Gibson's "direct perception*ism*" is thus a counterpart, rather than a real alternative, to mediationism.

So, what about the more recent writings in the broad area of socio-cultural psychology? Well, to a very large extent, we find either socialized reformulations of the traditional, individualistic dualisms, or derivative dualisms, most importantly those between nature, on the one hand, and culture or else history on the other.

First of all, there is wide agreement among the "opposition" about the importance of representation, and the need to understand representation in a non-individualistic way, and with this I have no objection. However, the general line would seem to be that we should go further, and, as in traditional theory, take representation to be *primary*:

> *Where discursive and cultural psychology come together is in the recognition given to the primacy of representation (discourse, mediation, etc), and its location in situated social practices rather than abstracted mental models. (Edwards, 1995, p. 63)*

But what, then, do these representations *re-present*? Just further representations? Once again, we find ourselves in "the room without windows" with just pictures on the walls, though these are now pictures of yet further windowless rooms. Thus, as in *some* versions of social constructivism (cf. Danziger, 1997), a realm of the "socially constructed" interposes itself between us and nature, and through which we cannot reach the world itself:

> *It is not that constructivists deny the existence of external reality, it is just that there is no way of knowing whether what is perceived and understood is an accurate reflection of that reality. (Marshall, 1996, p. 30)*

The long-standing dualism of materiality and meaning also reappears in a social guise, where meaning is not necessarily confined to individual mental representations, but to a separate domain of the symbolic:

> ... *we must not confuse the* material *world, where things and people exist, and the* symbolic *practices and processes through which representation, meaning and language operate. Constructivists do not deny the existence of the material world. However, it is not the material world which conveys meaning: it is the language system or whatever system we are using to represent our concepts. It is social actors who use the conceptual systems of their culture and the linguistic and other representational systems to construct meaning, to make the world meaningful and to communicate about that world meaningfully to others. (Hall, 1997b, p. 25)*

Even researchers studying "*material* culture" generally take a similar line, downplaying the importance of materiality in favor of a separate realm of what is, in effect "*immaterial* culture" (cf. Costall, 1995; Hutchby, 2001; Ingold 2000, 2001; Thomas, 1999). To a remarkable extent, the concept of "culture" is now widely *identified* with representation and the symbolic. Here, for example, is Clifford Geertz's well-known definition of culture:

> *A historically transmitted pattern of meaning embodied in symbols, a system of inherited conceptions expressed in symbolic form by means of which men communicate, perpetuate, and develop their knowledge about attitudes towards life. (Geertz, 1975, p. 89)*

But the basic point is repeated throughout the literature:

> ... *what does representation have to do with 'culture': what is the connection between them? To put it simply, culture is about 'shared meanings'. Now, language is the privileged medium in which we 'make sense' of things, in which meaning is produced and exchanged. Meanings can only be shared through our common access to language. So language is central to meaning and culture and has always been regarded as the key repository of cultural values and meanings. (Hall, 1997a, p. 1)*

> ... *to explain culture is to answer the following question: why are some representations more successful in a human population, more "catching". (Sperber, 1996, p. 58)*

> *Culture emerges from nature as the symbolic representation of the latter. (Ellen, 1996, p. 31)*

How do the socio-cultural *avant-garde* keep backing themselves into these theoretical corners? The fact that there is such a close "recapitulation" of the state of individualistic psychology suggests that we have not entirely avoided many of the problems that have always constrained and distorted traditional psychology. Indeed, much of the good rhetorical effect of social constructivism has itself depended upon a traditional notion of nature – of the *natural* – as fixed, universal, and unaffected by *us*. Furthermore, much of the nuttiness of postmodernism would seem to reflect its failure, maybe refusal, to "get over" the modernist scheme it claims to have undermined (cf. Shalin, 1993).

These problems are compounded by others more specific to the socio-cultural approaches. The first of these is a kind of methodologism where the limitation of a research method comes (as was the case in classical physical science) to define the limits of the object of study. Early anthropology was of necessity "a science of words" (Mead, 1975, p. 5) since there were no means of effectively recording gestures and actions, and indeed many of the traditional practices under study were matters only of recall, having been suppressed by the missionaries within whose train the anthropologists tended to follow. Yet, many current researchers restrict their attention to texts and transcriptions of speech, and although this, in itself, is clearly a matter of choice, they often also come close to implying that the *only* things we ever *do* are with words. And they can prove remarkably evasive when challenged on this point. Here, for example, is Michael Billig's defense of the discourse analysts' emphasis upon talk, based on a deft prevarication between an inclusive and a disjunctive meaning of "action":

> Discursive psychologists might be suspected of only taking words into account and not actions. However, that is not so, for the criticism assumes that in social behavior there is a clear distinction between words and action. This is contested by "speech-act theory," which is a philosophical position underlying much work of conversation analysis ... According to speech-act theory, making an utterance is itself an action; also many actions are performed through utterances. ... It is easy to exaggerate the difference between words and actions, as if the latter were more "real" than the former. (Billig, 1997, pp. 46–47)

A further source of trouble concerns the delicate balance between, on the one hand, demonstrating the importance of the specific socio-historical conditions, and, on the other, going too far, and rendering the subjects of our studies so alien they no longer seem to count as "one of us." An emphasis on differences between people can appear sinister not just on the basis of "race" but also their cultural practices, as became the case for the Vygotsky-inspired expedition to study the "primitive" mentality of Uzbek peasants (see Joravsky, 1989, p. 364 et seq.). Eventually, some residue is identified which is claimed to be immune from "the effects of culture," such as the lower mental functions or the irrational (see Connelly & Costall, 2000). But, as Shweder and Sullivan (1990, pp. 407–408) have pointed out, the basic cognitivist schema of structure and content has also been highly influential, where cultural influences are supposed to be restricted to the *contents* of a biologically fixed *structure*: the central processing mechanism. Although this certainly manages to draw a bottom-line, and ensure some kind of ultimate unity for humankind, it is at the considerable cost of a retreat once again into the dualisms of culture *versus* nature, and culture *versus* biology.

Finally, the dualisms of matter and mind and of biology and culture are institutionalized in the very structure of modern academic disciplines. On the one hand, there are the natural and the engineering sciences and, on the other, the human or social sciences. The natural sciences have abstracted for themselves a "material world" set apart from human concerns, while the social sciences, in their turn, have constructed "a world of actors devoid of things" (Joerges, 1988, p. 220). *Inter*disciplinary efforts to bridge this divide, such as the "environmental sciences," have hardly thrived. They have either fractured along the old divide or else retreated to the safety of "hard science" (see Kwa, 1987).

Getting Over Mediationism

The curious thing about the windowless room of mediationism is that there are so many ways of getting into it. Taking note of those different ways, as I have tried to do in this chapter, is an important first step towards getting over mediationism. At the beginning of the 21st century, the problems behind mediationism really ought no longer to appear quite so vital or urgent as they once did. Paradoxically, it might also help to set the clock back in psychological theory, to well before both modern cognitivism and postmodernism, and return to the remarkable writings of figures such as John Dewey, George Herbert Mead, and even William James, and their emphasis upon the *mutuality*, rather than the duality, of mind and world (Costall, 2004):

> ... traditional theories have separated life from nature, mind from organic life, and thereby created mysteries. ... Those who talk most of the organism, physiologists and psychologists, are often just those who display least sense of the intimate, delicate and subtle interdependence of all organic structures and processes with one another. ... To see the organism in nature ... is the answer to the problems which haunt philosophy. And when thus seen they will be seen to be in, not as marbles are in a box but as events are in history, in a moving, growing never finished process. (John Dewey, 1958, pp. 278, 295)

My purpose in this chapter has emphatically not been to deny or minimize the importance of various kinds of mediation in human existence. I am not trying to argue for some kind of "direct" theory of immaculate perception, or even action. What I have been trying to challenge is the appeals to mediation as a way of bridging the very big gaps that are supposed to separate us from the world, when, paradoxically, mediation, invoked in this way just makes matters worse. It *always* gets in the way. It is these very gaps, opened up by dualistic thinking, that are the problem. Whereas mediationism, given its dualistic premises, can only regard mediation as an impenetrable barrier *between* ourselves and the world, we need to remember that our social practices of mediation are, for better or worse, taking place *in* the world, and actually *changing* it by "constitut[ing] objects not constituted before" (Mead, 1934, p. 78). Indeed, mediationism obscures the very conditions of social mediation. If we are going to make sense of *mediation*, how it originates and is sustained, we will need to find a place in our theories for the existence of both meaning and mediation *before and beyond* the realm of representations and symbols, and take their materiality much more seriously. It is time, once again, for psychological theory to become more worldly, and move beyond the antitheses of nature and history, and of materiality and meaning (Costall, 1995; Costall & Dreier, 2006). We are, after all, *part* of what nature has become.

Acknowledgments

I am very grateful to Ivan Leudar, Patrick Renault, Ann Richards, Cintia Rodríguez, and the editors of this handbook for their helpful comments.

References

Bentley, A. F. (1938). Physicists and fairies. *Philosophy of Science*, 5, 132–165.

Bickhard, M. H., & Terveen, L. (1995). *Foundational issues in artificial intelligence and cognitive science: Impasse and solution*. Amsterdam: Elsevier Scientific.

Billig, M. (1997). Discursive, rhetorical, and ideological messages. In C. McGarty & S. A. Haslam (Eds.), *The message of social psychology: Perspectives on mind in society* (pp. 36–53). Oxford: Blackwell.

Borghi, A. M. (2005). Object concepts and action. In D. Pecher, & R. A. Zwaan (Eds.), *Grounding cognition: The role of perception and action in memory, language, and thinking* (pp. 8–34). Cambridge: Cambridge University Press.

Bowker, Geoffrey C., & Leigh Star, Susan. (2000). *Sorting things out: Classification and its consequences*. Cambridge, MA: MIT Press.

Brewer, Marilyn, & Hewstone, Miles. (2004). Introduction. In M. Brewer & M. Hewstone (Eds.), *Social cognition* (pp. xi–xii). Oxford: Blackwell.

Carr, Harvey A. (1915). Review of J.B. Watson (1914). Behavior: an introduction to comparative psychology. *Psychological Bulletin*, 12, 308–312

Connelly, J., & Costall, A. (2000). R.G. Collingwood and the idea of an historical psychology. *Theory & Psychology*, 10, 147–170.

Costall, A. (1988). A closer look at direct perception. In A. Gellatly, D. Rogers & J. A. Sloboda (Eds.), *Cognition and Social Worlds* (pp. 10–21). Oxford: Clarendon Press.

Costall, A. (1990). Picture perception as 'indirect' perception. In K. Landwehr (Ed.), *Ecological Perception Research, Visual Communication And Aesthetics* (pp. 15–22). New York: Springer-Verlag.

Costall, A. (1991). Graceful degradation: Cognitivism and the metaphors of the computer. In A. Still. & A. Costall (Eds.), *Against cognitivism* (pp. 151–170). London: Harvester-Wheatsheaf.

Costall, A. (1995). Socializing affordances. *Theory and Psychology*, 5, 467–481.

Costall, A. (2004). From Darwin to Watson (and Cognitivism) and back again: the principle of animal-environment mutuality. *Behavior & Philosophy*, 32, 179–195.

Costall, A. (2006a). 'Introspectionism' and the mythical origins of scientific psychology. *Consciousness and Cognition*, 15, 634–654.

Costall, A. (2006b). On being the right size: Affordances and the question of scale. In G. Lock & B. Molyneux (Eds.), *Confronting scale* in archaeology: Issues of theory and practice (pp. 15–26). New York: Springer.

Costall, A. (In press). Bringing the body back to life: James Gibson's ecology of agency. In J. Zlatev, T. Ziemke, R. Frank, & R. Dirven (Eds.), Body, language and mind: Vol. 1: Embodiment. The Hague: de Gruyter.

Costall, A., Leudar, I., & Reddy, V. (2006). Failing to see the irony in 'mind-reading.' Theory & Psychology, 16, 163–167.

Costall, A. P., & Still, A. W. (1989). James Gibson's theory of direct perception and the problem of cultural relativism. Journal for the Theory of Social Behaviour, 19, 433–441.

Costall, A., & Dreier, O. (2006). Doing things with things: The design and use of objects. London: Ashgate.

Cronon, W. (Ed.), (1996). Uncommon ground: rethinking the human place in nature. New York: W.W. Norton.

Danziger, K. (1997). The varieties of social construction. Theory & Psychology, 7, 399–416.

Dewey, J. (1958). Experience and nature. New York: Dover. [Based on the Paul Carus lectures of 1925.]

Dewey, J. (1910). The influence of Darwin on philosophy. In J. Dewey, The influence of Darwin on philosophy and other essays (pp. 1–19). New York: Henry Holt & Co. [First published in Popular Science Monthly, July, 1909.]

Dewey, J. (1914/1977). Psychological doctrine and philosophical teaching. In S. Morgenbesser (Ed.), Dewey and his critics (pp. 439–445). New York: Journal of Philosophy, Inc. [First published in the Journal of Philosophy Psychology and Scientific Methods, 1914, 11(19).]

Dewey, J. (1969). The quest for certainty. New York.

Duncker, K. (1947). Phenomenology and epistemology of consciousness of objects. Philosophy and Phenomenological Research, 7, 505–542.

Edwards, D. (1995). A commentary on discursive and cultural psychology. Culture and Psychology, 1, 55–65.

Ellen, R. (1996). Introduction. In Roy Ellen and Katsuyoshi Fukui (Eds.), Redefining Nature: Ecology, Culture and Domestication (pp. 1–36). Oxford: Berg.

Falmagne, Rachel Joffe. (1995). The abstract and the concrete. In L. M. W. Martin, K. Nelson, & E. Tobach (Eds.), Sociocultural psychology: Theory and practice of doing and knowing (pp. 205–228). Cambridge: Cambridge University Press.

Fodor, J. A. (1981). Representations. Cambridge, MA: MIT Press.

Funder, D. C. (1995). On the accuracy of personality judgment: A realistic approach. Psychological Review, 102, 652–70.

Geertz, C. (1975). The interpretation of cultures. New York: Basic Books.

Gibson, J. J. (1950). The implications of learning theory for social psychology. In J.G. Miller (Ed.), Experiments in social process. New York: McGraw-Hill.

Gibson, J. J. (1979). The ecological approach to visual perception. Boston: Houghton Mifflin.

Gregory, R. L. (1989). Dismantling reality. In H. Lawson & L. Appignanesi (Eds.), Dismantling truth: reality in the post-modern world (pp. 93–100). London: Weidenfeld and Nicolson.

Hall, Stuart. (1997a). Introduction. In Stuart Hall (Ed.), Representation: Cultural representations and signifying practices (pp. 1–11). London: Sage.

Hall, Stuart. (1997b). The work of representation. In Stuart Hall (Ed.), Representation: Cultural representations and signifying practices (pp. 13–64). London: Sage.

Hammond, H., & Keat, R. (1991). Understanding phenomenology. Oxford: Blackwell.

Harnad, S. (1990). The symbol grounding problem. Physica D, 42, 335–346.

Harré, Rom. (2002). Cognitive science: A philosophical introduction. London: Sage.

Heft, H. (2001). Ecological psychology in context: James Gibson, Roger Barker, and the legacy of William James's radical empiricism. Mahwah, NJ: Lawrence Erlbaum Associates.

Heidbreder, E. (1933). Seven psychologies. New York: Century.

Hirsch, Paul D. (2000). Beyond discipline: toward effective partnerships between conservation biologists and ecological anthropologists. Unpublished manuscript, Department of Ecology, University of Georgia.

Holt, E. B., Marvin, W. T., Montague, W. P., Perry, R. B., Pitkin, W. B. & Spaulding, E. G. (1912). The new realism: Cooperative studies in philosophy. New York: MacMillan.

Holt, E. B. (1914). The concept of consciousness. London: George Allen & Co.

Hutchby, Ian. (2001). Technologies, texts and affordances. Sociology, 35, 441–456.

Ingold, T. (2000). The perception of the environment: essays in livelihood, dwelling and skill. London: Routledge.

Janlert, L. E. (1987). Modeling change: the frame problem. In Z. W. Pylyshyn (Ed.), The robot's dilemma: The frame problem in artificial intelligence. Norwood, NJ: Ablex.

Joerges, B. (1988). Technology in everyday life: Conceptual queries. *Journal for the Theory of Social Behaviour, 18*, 221–237.

Johnson-Laird, P. (1988). *The computer and the mind.*Cambridge, MA: Cambridge University Press.

Joravsky, D. (1989). *Russian psychology: a critical history.* Oxford: Basil Blackwell.

Kessen, W. (1981). Early settlements in New Cognition. *Cognition, 10*, 167–171.

Kwa, C. (1987). Representations of nature mediating between ecology and science policy: The case of the International Biological Programme. *Social Studies of Science, 17*, 413–42.

Leeper, Robert. (1951). Cognitive processes. In S. S. Stevens (Ed.), Handbook of experimental psychology (pp. 730–757). New York: Wiley.

Leslie, A. (1987). Pretense and representation: The origins of 'theory of mind'. *Psychological Review, 94*, 412–426.

Leudar, I., & Costall, A. (Eds.), (2004a). Special issue: Theory of mind. *Theory & Psychology, 14*(5), 571–752.

Leudar, I., & Costall, A. (2004b). On the persistence of the 'problem of other minds' in psychology: Chomsky, Grice and 'theory of mind'. *Theory and Psychology, 14*, 603–623.

Lovejoy, Arthur O. (1929). The revolt against dualism: An inquiry concerning the existence of ideas. LaSalle, ILL: Open Court. Danziger, K. (1997). The varieties of social construction. *Theory & Psychology, 7*, 399–416.

MacMurray, J. (1961). *Persons in relation.* London: Faber & Faber.

Marshall, H. H. (1996). Clarifying and implementing contemporary psychological perspectives. *Educational Psychologist, 31*, 29–34.

Mead, George Herbert. (1934). *Mind, self, and society.* Chicago: Chicago University Press.

Mead, George Herbert. (1938). *The philosophy of the act.* Chicago: University of Chicago Press.

Mead, Margaret. (1975). Visual anthropology in a discipline of words. In Paul Hoskins (Ed.), *Principles of visual anthropology* (pp. 3–10). The Hague, Netherlands: Mouton Publishers.

Miller, G. A., Pribram, K., & Galanter, E. (1960). Plans and the structure of behavior. New York: Holt.

Pecher, D., & Zwaan, R. A.(Eds.), *Grounding cognition: The role of perception and action in memory, language, and thinking.* Cambridge: Cambridge University Press.

Pylyshyn, Z. (1986). *Computation and cognition.* Cambridge, MA: MIT Press.

Reed, E. S. (1988). *James J. Gibson and the psychology of perception.*New Haven, CT: Yale University Press.

Ryle, G. (1999). Reason. *Linacre Journal*, No. 3, 71–84.

Schiffer, M. B. (with A. R. Miller). (1999). *The Material Life of Human Beings: Artifacts, Behavior, and Communication.* London: Routledge.

Shalin, Dmitri N. (1993). Modernity, postmodernism, and pragmatist inquiry: An introduction. *Symbolic Interaction, 16*, 303–332.

Shaw, R. E. (2003). The agent-environment interface: Simon's indirect or Gibson's direct coupling. *Ecological Psychology, 15*, 37–106.

Shweder, R. A., & Sullivan, M.A. (1990). The semiotic subject of cultural psychology. In L. A. Previn (Ed.), *Handbook of personality: Theory and research.* New York: Guilford Press.

Smith, E. R., & MacKie, D. M. (2000). *Social psychology*, 2nd ed. London: Psychology Press.

Sperber, D. (1996). *Explaining culture: A naturalistic approach.* Oxford: Blackwell.

Stevens, S. (Ed.), (1997). *Conservation through cultural survival: indigenous peoples and protected areas.* Washington, DC: Island Press.

Still, A., & Costall, A. (1991a). The mutual elimination of dualism in Vygotsky and Gibson. In A. Still. & A. Costall (Eds.), *Against cognitivism.* (pp. 225–236). London: Harvester-Wheatsheaf.

Still, A. W., & Costall, A. (Eds.), (1991b). *Against cognitivism.* London: Harvester Press.

Taylor, S. E., Peplau, L. A., & Sears, D. O. (1994). *Social psychology*, 8th edition. Englewood Cliffs, NJ: Prentice-Hall.

Thomas, Julian (1999). Some problems with the notion of external symbolic storage, and the case of neolithic material culture in Britain. In Colin Renfrew, & Chris Scarre (Eds.), *Cognition and material culture.* Oxford: McDonald Institute Monographs.

Tomasello, M., & Call, J. (1997). *Primate cognition.* Oxford: Oxford University Press.

Tooby, J. & Cosmides, L. (1995). Foreword. In S. Baron-Cohen, *Mindblindness: An essay on autism and theory of mind* (pp. ix–xviii). Cambridge, MA: MIT Press.

Toulmin, Stephen. (1976). *Knowing and acting: An invitation to philosophy*. New York: Macmillan.

Wertsch, J. V. (1996) The role of abstract rationality in Vygotsky's image of mind. In A. Tryphon & J. Voneche. (Eds.), *Piaget-Vygotsky: The social genesis of thought* (pp. 25–43). Hove, East Sussex, UK: Psychology Press.

Wilcox, S., & Katz, S. (1984). Can indirect realism be demonstrated in the psychological laboratory? *Philosophy of the Social Sciences, 1984*, 149–157.

CHAPTER 6

Functional Systems of Perception-Action and Re-Mediation

David Travieso

What comes through in the textbooks, and in the minds of many developmentalists, is that the biological side of human existence lives in the first few chapters, and having dispensed with our biological side, we can now move on to more interesting things.

Esther Thelen (in Port and
Van Gelder, 1995, p. 73)

Socio-cultural psychology is widely known as a theory and research field that stresses the determinant role of social interaction and culture in the development of the higher psychological functions. This primary focus may have the effect of overlooking a detailed consideration of the so-called basic psychological processes, perhaps because of their seemingly independence from the effects of culture and social interaction. This is by no means a minor issue, since there cannot be a theory about how culture and social interaction affect the human psyche without a detailed consideration of the basic principles of psychological functioning.

This chapter aims to offer a view of what has traditionally been called basic psychological phenomena that, on the theoretical side, makes possible to present a view of biological organisms based on natural laws, which is compatible, or can be coupled, with the social organism socio-cultural psychology deals with. This will be done by, first, presenting some current research topics that during the last two decades changed some of our views on the basic principles of psychological functioning, and that resulted in a view of the human organism as following principles of dynamic self-organization, and then, exploring a consideration of the concept of re-mediation, and the practices from it derived, which are one of the privileged arenas where basic psychological processes and socio-cultural phenomena have historically intersected. Revisiting some principles of Luria's functional systems theory, and his neuropsychological approach, will make apparent how some of his main concepts and current practices in neuropsychology can be reinterpreted from a dynamic systems approach.

Paradoxes of Dualism

For a long time, basic research in psychology has been dominated by a dualistic conception in which mind and body were ontologically split apart. My attempt here will be to provide a non-dualistic conception of the human being whose perceptions and actions gradually evolve with his or her encounters with the world and others.

The information processing metaphor is currently the most popular flag holder of dualism in psychology. Many of the followers of this trend would agree with Fodor's (1975) statement that psychology deals with an ontologically monistic subject matter, but methodologically one should behave as if one were a believer in dualism. In other words, mind and body can and should be separated when empirically studied, and how they do relate to each other is a matter to be taken into account later (by looking for neuropsychological correlates, supporting emergentism, or whatever).

Sociocultural psychology has sometimes criticized this "schizophrenian" differentiation (e.g., Blanco, 1995), but in fact the search for a congruent conception of the human being from the biological level to the higher psychological functions has not been among the matters of higher interest for researchers. There is no doubt that engagement in social practices requires the organism to move around, seeing, hearing, and so on, but all these areas have gradually been left out the scope of sociocultural psychology[1] and so when there is a need to refer to these issues knowledge instruments developed from the information processing approach are too often borrowed.[2]

Our first move, then, will be to go straight into a review of basic research carried out from an outlook that avoids dualism and, at that the same time claims (a) that a non-representational organism is not only plausible but probable and (b) that there are ways for bridging the perceived gap between the naturalistic view of the so-called basic processes and the realm of intentionality, meaning and consciousness, that is, between the psychologies which deal with both, explanation and understanding.

Perception-Action: A Way of Conceiving the Basis of Knowledge

One of the first dichotomies in psychology is the contrast between a passive, sensorial face of the individual, and a motor, active face of the same individual that carries within the representational inference, that is, the assumption that behavior is controlled by both symbolic and pre-symbolic mental representations of the environment. Our point here will be, rather than emphasizing the active side of the individual, to highlight how this dichotomy disappears when a perception-action approach is adopted.

J. J. Gibson rejected this false dichotomy by emphasizing that perception can only be considered as a form of action, more specifically, that the end product of perception is not a mental representation but a modulation of an ongoing movement or action. One of his most controversial contributions was the concept of *affordance*, which has also been applied to the social realm (Costall, 1995).One example, the inertia tensor in haptic perception, will be useful to help us understand the extent on which this concept allows a radical redefinition of basic psychological processes.

During the 1990s, the neo-gibsonian research group headed by M. T. Turvey at the University of Connecticut developed a long-term research project in dynamic touch, that is, in haptic perception mediated by what was formerly called propioception (see Turvey, 1996; Turvey & Carello, 1995, for a review). Turvey and colleagues (see Carello & Turvey, 2000) demonstrated that touch is mainly controlled by physical parameters described in mechanics and, more specifically in rotational inertia. The key parameter is the *inertia tensor*, a numerical quantity for the object's resistance to rotation, which is related to its point of rotation and its mass distribution. Obviously, the subject chooses the point of rotation and, at the same time, his muscular effort has to equal, or better, to oppose the potential energy produced by the inertia tensor in order to haptically perceive features like weight, length, form, and so on.

Throughout an enormous amount of empirical data and modeling, Turvey and colleagues demonstrated several important points, above all that we do not perceive primary features of the object, but relational properties described in mechanics.

Let me give an example. Pick up a pen from your desk and hold it between your index finger and the thumb. Start from one tip of the pen, close your eyes, and swing it. Then, do hold the pen by the middle. You will be able feel the difference, and although you could not see the length of the pen, you will be able to feel its size, at least to the extent that you can feel the difference between holding it on one side or in the middle.

In fact, Turvey and colleagues proved in several experimental studies (i.e., Amazeen & Turvey, 1995), using psychophysical matching tasks,[3] that we are able to detect the length and weight of the object almost linearly, and even detect form features. The original task was to match the length of the stick by moving a panel to a distance that the subject judges to be the same as the length of the stick.

It has to be noted that there is no need to suppose a percept conveying the idea of length or form. Then, how could we account for what is going on when performing this task? In other words, what are the proximal stimuli, the receptors, or the transduction process and representation, that allow us to detect these dimensions? The answer clearly goes beyond the representational way of picturing what is going on when this task is being performed. As Turvey and colleagues pointed out, the individual who handles the pen is detecting his or her muscular effort opposing gravity which, at the same time, depends on the mass distribution of the object and the distance of this distribution from the point of rotation, that is its inertia tensor I_{yy}. Since the perceiver fixes

the point of rotation, so s/he is determining the form of perception through his/her own action.

From this point of view, we can say that we perceive because our activity changes in a regular or rather in a lawful way, not because of inputs received from the object or the environment as such, but through the dynamic relationship between our organism and the environment. Thus, the active-passive dichotomy is simply unnecessary. The sensorial and motor sides dissolve and the concept of representation, to the extent that the object does not determine its effect on the organism, cease to be necessary.[4]

It may be argued that touch has always been a tricky field of study, because of its phenomenology, its dual objective and subjective faces (Katz, 1925/1989; Merleau-Ponty, 1957; Schiff & Foulke, 1982), and because it is the result of various biological subsystems, cutaneous and proprioceptive, working together (see Heller & Schiff, 1991 for a canonical description of the haptic system). Then, evidence taken from other sensorial modalities may be useful to test whether this way of accounting for perception holds in other senses.

Vision is one of the privileged areas of research for the information processing approach. This makes most relevant to offer a second example on optic flow which offers an alternative view to the traditional segmentation process (see Marr, 1982) for the analysis of vision, even in the field of artificial vision. Gibson (1979, p. 203) showed that humans are very bad at calculating distances, but paradoxically our 3-D vision, thought to be controlled only by stereopsis and perspective, seems to be very accurate in detecting the so-called time-to-contact. The photographic concept of vision, in which the final product of perception is a static representation, does not seem particularly fitted to account for the visual control of a moving organism in a changing environment (updating online representations for planning and executing actions). In contrast there are dynamic, i.e., temporal indexes in the optic flow – the temporal changes in

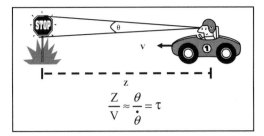

Figure 6.1. Time-to-contact or τ model.

the image – that specify spatial, not depth relations, between the observer and patterns in the environmental optic array (Gibson, 1979).

The classical τ model (Lee & Reddish, 1981) is the best example for time-to-contact or collision models (i.e., Lee, 1998). Figure 6.1 shows how the τ model describes how accurate estimations of the time to contact are possible without the need of knowing the speed of approach, the size of objects or how far they are. Estimations of the time left before contact with an approaching object are possible just by taking into account a single parameter of optic flow -τ-, which is the ratio of the angular size of the object ahead divided by its time derivative, that is, the rate of optical expansion.

Our point again, is that we do not need to perceive depth (the object's distance of the object from the observer) in order to be accurate in detecting collisions. When subjects are asked to catch or kick an approaching object in an experimental setting, or to stop before a barrier, they are able to control their actions as a direct function of this temporal parameter (Lee, 1976). So we have available a parsimonious and elegant formalism for the description and explanation of the above described phenomena.

Needless to say, these parameters, and all the others that are being studied (see Rogers & Effken, 2003 for a summary of recent research in these areas) are models that account for the temporal adjustment of the individual and his or her environment (control over the body is gradually modified as it grows up, and the same can be said for the optic array).

Thus, perception and action are coupled and should be studied together. Perception would not be, as the idealistic view has established in modern thought, a system for copying how reality works, but as Maturana and Mpodozis (1996) put it, it is a type of perturbation to the organism dynamics, triggered by the environment and determined by the actions of the organism.

And what about memory, attention, and the rest of the faculties on which we traditionally rely upon in order to explain the organism's cognitions? How can the individual learn adaptive new abilities without memory storage, attentional mechanisms for selecting parts of the stimulation, and so on? Powerful alternatives to the psychology of faculties are now available, which may facilitate a coherent consideration of the transformation of processes that sociocultural psychology deals with. The answer is the use of formal tools of the branch of science that studies the temporal evolution of systems: the dynamic systems theory.

The Dynamic Approach in Psychology

The dynamic systems theory in psychology is a quite prolific line of basic research in the field of psychological functioning, mainly in perception-action, which presents an alternative view on the behavior of the human subject. This is an approach, in which different disciplines like psychology, biology, physics, and neuroscience merge, and that regards the human being as an open, nonequilibrium system (Kelso, 1995).

There are certain provisos to be made about this definition. First, the dynamic systems approach has both methodological and theoretical constraints. Methodological constraints have to do with the mathematical tools for formalization: *dynamic systems theory*, which restricts the sort of aspects that can be considered within this framework; namely, aspects or variables with numerical values displayed in the temporal dimension. In other words, this approach comes from the naturalistic tradition. Second, in its most radical version, the dynamic systems approach considers that there is no difference between structure and function (or change); but dynamic patterns that evolve on different time scales (Kelso, 1995), an assumption that holds for both animate and inanimate matter. In other words, rather than a materialistic realism, an operational realism where the observer defines the system, both in its spatial and temporal dimensions, is supported. Therefore, the system cannot be defined *a priori*, but through the empirical analysis of sufficient and necessary elements to properly describe the change in time.

This definition of an open system is a consequence of the need for a continuous inter-exchange with the environment in order to keep the system as a differentiated entity. And non-equilibrium refers to the property of continuous shift of relations between elements within the organism. Thus, the system does not have a stable dynamics but it is always changing from one temporarily stable state to another through instabilities.

Taken together, these assumptions and constraints radically change the image of the human being projected by basic research. Following Maturana and Varela (1984), the classical concept of the psychological subject as a processing information unit or, more generally, as an entity having a representation of its environment, is simply impossible because the ecological niche, the environment and even the stimulus, do not specify the changes produced in the subject.

If we take psychological processes to be no other but observer's specifications, there is no place for the consideration of psychological faculties (such as memory, attention, or perception) conceived as independent of any particular task. Likewise, primary qualities or properties of our environment are not "out there" ready to be perceived or known, rather all that happens is a set of encounters between the organism and the environment. And when discussing perception-action, these encounters can be described using physical laws.

As Gibson (1979) said:

> ...the rules that govern behavior are not like laws enforced by an authority or decisions made by a commander; behavior is regular without being regulated. The question is how can it be. (p. 225)

We are now in the position to provide an answer to this question. Biological systems are self-organized, and the theoretical framework that describes the temporal evolution of systems and their behavioral changes is the dynamic system theory.

Rather than attempting the impossible task of summarizing this approach, I will present one key example of the working of a dynamic process, and then continue with a further development of the pen-grasping example.

What is a dynamic process? Generally we may say that it is a system, a set of related elements, with numerical states that evolve in time in accordance with certain rules. A "State" is the form a certain aspect takes in a certain moment, "behavior" is the change of the general state of the system, and the "state space" is the set of states that the system may take, so that its behavior can be described as a set of points in the state space.

An intuitive example is the Rayleigh-Bénard instability, as described by Kelso (1995). It is the description of a fluid heated from below and cooled from above, such as water being heated in a pot. If the temperature difference between the top and the bottom of the pot is small, there is no large-scale motion of the liquid. The heat is dissipated amongst the molecules as a random micro-motion (heat conduction). However as it happens in any open system, when the temperature gradient grows, instability occurs. The liquid begins to move as a coordinated system, random movements are replaced by an orderly, rolling motion. The reason for this collective or cooperative effect has to do with density, but the interesting point here is that the control parameter, the temperature gradient, does not prescribe the code for the emerging pattern. Moreover, the rolling motion can rotate in one direction or the other, and the random starting point, regarded as a cluster of vibratory modes described in the instability equation, is what determines the direction of the movement.

This example is not a metaphor; it is just a description of one of the simplest illustrative instabilities. And the point of presenting it here is to show that there already are formal tools for a description of systems that gradually evolve into more complex forms of behavior without the need of a central unit of control or a commander. This could also be the case of biological and even human beings.

Let us now go back to our dynamic touch example. Pick up a pen and hold it again on one side with an index-thumb grip. If you hold it firmly without movement, you probably cannot perceive its length or weight. But if you hold it at the lower end, the pen will turn upside-down, swinging as a pendulum. Just by touching the pen you can feel neither its size nor its weight, you have to perform movements that make the pen to move. There is no privileged access to discrete patterns of information, nor can you reach knowledge of the value of the inertia tensor of the movement. All that happens are changes in the spatial and temporal properties of the relation between the pen and the hand with temporal variations of forces and spatial positions. All these elements can be described together in a dynamic equation, and the relevant element for establishing the pen's features is the inertia tensor, an unchanging parameter of the equation. Insofar as the pen has no autonomous movement, it is our own movement that varies the values (states) in the equation. And the act of perception is the recognition of different effects as being linked to the parameters of the situation. In other words, if I need more strength to raise the pen, it is because the inertia tensor is higher, which depends on more mass or more distance from the center of mass.[5] Action, then, impregnates all psychological phenomena. The perceptual stability of the world is established through our own movement.

Esther Thelen spent many years studying the development of locomotion and other forms of movement. In her highly productive research group, Thelen and her colleagues proved that the development of motion does not result from a gradual increase of the cortex control on motor acts but rather is a consequence of a gradual refinement of body movements that shape the form of motor control. Instead of learning movements and ordering the body to perform them, the body displays a whole series of movements in terms of amplitudes, strength and frequencies – we see babies flapping, swinging, kicking, holding, and so on, without much control, so that early development is the story of a gradual control of movement aimed at contacting surfaces with the appropriate strength, reaching objects with visual control, an so on.

Development appears then as a changing landscape of preferred but not compulsory behavioral states with varying degrees of stability and instability (Thelen, 1995). Some behavioral states are so stable that they can be regarded as a developmental stage, as the establishment of a function of the organism-in-context.

Her most influential research-project was probably the analysis of locomotive activity in learning to walk. During the 1980s, Thelen's work shook several principles of the development of walking. Previously it was generally held that learning to walk was mainly an issue of neural maturation in which the cerebral cortex, as the agent for purposive behavior, progressively takes control of locomotion. As McGraw (1945) pictured it, the stepping movements seen in the first month or two of life were controlled at a nuclear level along with some advance in sub-cortical centers, and were probably remnants of primitive functioning. The subsequent decline of stepping movements in the following months was thought to be a consequence of cortical inhibitory processes; and, finally, the "onset of cortical participation" could definitely be detected when the child took deliberate steps.

In 1984, Thelen performed a simple but successful experiment in order to test whether changing the conditions for walking affected this behavior. When three-month-old infants, whose stepping behavior had already disappeared under normal conditions, had their legs placed under water (so that they weighted less than in normal conditions), they could step again, but when some weights were added, this behavior disappeared again.

Thelen and Fisher (1982) had previously demonstrated that the infant's stepping behavior was pretty similar to his/her kicking behavior, which continued during the first year when the infant was supine, prone or sitting. So they thought it was unlikely that cortical inhibition or disuse was operating only when the infant was upright. They also observed that the decline in step rate was higher for infants who gained weight faster. Their hypothesis was that stepping had then to be considered as a context dependent dynamic behavior, similar to other infant's movements, and its development could only be regarded as emerging stabilities resulting from previous states of the organism and its interaction with the environment.

Does this means that any organic movement is the result of automatic movements that arise in the intersection of the organic open system and its environment? The next section will show how the gap between basic and higher psychological functions can be bridged by tools of knowledge developed within this new approach. The dynamic systems approach addressed goal-directed movement in a way which is congenial to the study of intentional action, as conceived in socio-cultural psychology.

Current Research Into Intentional Movement: Motor Control and Dynamic Modeling

Before analyzing how motor control deals with intentional movement, it has to be pointed out that, within this tradition, the term intentional is restricted to goal-directed movement, what should not be taken as a reduction of the complexity of intentionality to the type of phenomena studied.

Basic processes of perception-action should be understood in a different light from that of the classical information-processing hypothesis. The implicit idea that the representational organism can judge probabilistic consequences of events, and perform movements that are causally linked to these events, is therefore not appropriate for the description of effective biological movement (Bernstein, 1967). Let us see some of Bernstein's basic ideas concerning how to describe the organism's movements. We will do so following Kelso's (1998) résumé:

1. *Biological movement is goal-directed – instead of being a reflex.* A retrospective cause is not enough to describe this type of movement. Bernstein considered that a motor plan was needed for the prospective control of movement. Probabilistic prognosis instead of retrospective external cause is the causal function of motor acts, which are therefore intentional and can be described as action instead of movement.

2. *The problem of degrees of freedom.* The major biomechanical problem is that movement may have an enormous number of degrees of freedom (variables involved in defining a certain movement: joints spatial axis and muscles), which make their description difficult or unaffordable. In order to reduce the difficulty, Bernstein introduced the idea of synergies: the difficulty is reduced by the interrelation between multiple joints in space and time.

3. *There is a topology or structure for each movement with an associated metric.* In spite of changes in the metrics, topology remains constant for a certain action.

4. *The brain should contain a trace or engram of such a structure, which is responsible for a movement, that then we may call intentional action.*

Although Bernstein's general idea concerning movement is still maintained in current models of motor control, probabilistic prognosis and brain trace are now questioned.

Let me start with a simple example to illustrate the idea of probabilistic prognosis as controlling action. The example is taken from several experiments by Feigenberg (see Feigenberg, 1998 for a summary of his results).

The situation is as follows: an individual is sat facing a row of electric bulbs, each one with a button, and the subject's reaction time for an electric light bulb that is turned on is recorded; results show (1) reaction time decreases when fewer bulbs are presented, given that they are turned on in a random sequence and with equal probability; (2) when one bulb is lighted above the random frequency, reaction time is shorter for that bulb, as it should be expected; (3) but, when a stable temporal series is presented, in spite of unequal probabilities, the reaction time is the same for all bulbs and is equal to the reaction time for a single bulb; (4) Finally, movement preparation in different limbs (arms) shows in EMG recordings when a stable time series is established (Feigenberg, 1998).

However, more complex motor acts, like in changing environments, cannot be efficiently performed in these conditions. As Nam-Gyoon and Turvey (1998) put it, Bernstein was forced to consider probabilistic prognosis given that he considered perception as informing on "what is" over there. But we are taken perception to be something different, as to that what make us capable of informing "what must be done" in these circumstances. How can we merge goal-oriented movement with a non-presentational concept of perception like the one presented above?

An exploratory idea arises from Gibson's concept of information, clearly different to that of the information theory applied to cognitive psychology. Gibson (1966) considered that information is not communication but the coupling of the organism with the environment. Otherwise prognosis would have again to be understood as probability calculus, and motor control will again be regarded as a problem of corrective feedback loops over previously performed movements. Prognosis is a completely different way of approaching the same phenomenon. Perceptual coupling (affordance-effectivity) allows the motor plan to be perceptually controlled (Nam-Gyoon & Turvey, 1998). However, this control is not retrospective; adjustments are made with respect to what will occur (if current conditions persist).

Remember that optic flow, for example, is uniquely determined by the environmental layout and uniquely transformed by changes in the layout and the subject's movements. This time-space structuring imposed on the energy distribution in the environment is what Gibson called information. Optic flow can be informative on future conditions for action, thereby providing a physiology of activity or prospective control (Nam-Gyoon & Turvey, 1998).

This way of picturing information, if accepted, has far-reaching consequences when related to prognosis. Since the brain trace proposed by Bernstein is a device for the explanation of probabilistic prognosis, once the necessity of explaining the latter is overcome (because the very idea of prognosis is dropped), the postulated unobservable brain trace could be made redundant.

As we already mentioned, the light bulbs example is clearly a simplified condition in comparison with the above-mentioned degrees of freedom problem, and the high complexity of biological action. Bernstein proposed synergies as the gateway for reducing complexity. Nowadays, the study of the systemic organization of movement is called coordination dynamics. Its essential principles can, again, be borrowed from Kelso (1998).

1. The motor system can be described as a self-organized system, of the type described in the section on dynamic systems, characterized by synergies, or mutual dependence, or co-evolution between the elements of the involved motor system. The prototype case is perception–action coupling and bimanual coordination (Kelso, 1981; Kelso, DelColle, & Shöner, 1990).

The experiment is as follows. A subject is asked to synchronize movements of the index finger with an auditory metronome in two modes of coordination, on the beat (synchronized) or off the beat (syncopated), for example moving the finger up and down, or tapping on a surface, at the same time as the metronome beats. The metronome frequency is systematically increased or decreased, and several different behavior patterns can be observed. The most prevalent one is the subject switching from syncopation to synchronization at a critical metronome frequency. At higher frequencies synchronization is lost (the relative phase, the position of one finger in relation to the position of the metronome or other finger, breaks up continuously). Finally, near the frequency where synchronization is lost, the relative phase slips but holds for brief periods of time. "There is a tendency to maintain phase attraction, even though the components (hand and stimulus) are no longer one-to-one frequency locked (Kelso, 1998, p. 209). This pattern yields to an elementary coordination equation (see Kelso, 1998): that describes the dynamics of the system through a collective variable, the relative phase between the presentation of the stimulus and the finger movement (whether they are synchronized or there is some delay between them), as described in equation 1. This equation shows how temporal stability can be progressively lost under different parameter values (a detailed description of the coordination equation can be found in Kelso, 1994, 1995, 1998).

$$\phi = \delta\omega - a\sin 2\phi - 2b\sin 2\phi + \sqrt{Q\Psi t}$$

$$(6.1)$$

The equation shows a collective variable "Φ" which is the relative phase between the oscillation of limbs, considered as a function of the two first terms of a Fourier Series, modulated by parameters "a/b" as amplitude modulators – and "$\delta\omega$" as a measure of the differential frequency of the oscillators.

A similar pattern has also been found for bimanual coordination, pendulum-like arm movements, or even coordination between subjects in rhythmic movements (Kelso, 1994; Turvey, 1994).

2. As seen in the previous example, motor system dynamics are described through "collective" or "coordination variables" which, despite being physically implemented, have an informational nature, that is, are mathematical relations.
3. In addition, these motor systems have temporal stability with fluctuations as the means for changing states.
4. The same equations describe several movement coordinations. Therefore, it can be said that coordination dynamics are structures that evolve in a lawful way which can be described mathematically.

The argument so far deployed has focused on presenting a way of accounting for basic psychological phenomena that I believe to be compatible with the conception of the psychological subject a socio-cultural psychology requires. First, it has been shown that the functional organization of the human being can be appropriately described as a self-organized system which progressively evolves to more complex dynamic organization, without appealing to the representational inferences and "the ghost in the machine" that characterized the information processing approach. This functional organization, and its relation to the environment, has been described as perception-action coupling. Second, a formal description for this type of functional organization (the dynamic systems approach) has been presented; this approach highlights the active nature of the individual through a description of the progressive improvements of motor functions. Furthermore, it has also been suggested that the motor control tradition, with its perceptually driven movement analysis, may be a step towards bridging the gap from the analysis of basic processes with the analysis of intentional action through the concept of goal-directed movement.

This way of picturing the transition from movement to goal directedness may pave the way towards bridging the gap between the individual and the social, a gap that perhaps has been more a result of the use of formal instruments and methods rather than deriving from ontological considerations. But a good part of the argument is still to be developed. The next step further is to present a field in which these two research areas merge together: re-mediation. This will be done by revisiting Luria's functional systems theory, and interpreting it from the outlook so far presented, together with some other current developments.

Functional Systems in Brain Functioning

A.R. Luria's well-known functional systems theory establishes a monistic concept of psyche with an explicit link between psychology and biology, together with an explanation of higher psychological phenomena, language, and consciousness as arising from the social dimension. The most relevant issues, for the purposes of our discussion here, are his review of the term *function* and his emphasis on the active nature of human behavior, including neural mechanisms, especially the NCS.

Luria (1979a), like Bernstein, pointed out that behavior cannot be understood by taking into account past experiences, but also through future-oriented plans and goals. He considered that the brain is able to formulate these plans, and that these mechanisms are susceptible of deterministic analysis. Luria addressed the question by discussing the concept of function. Rather than associate one function to any particular organ, Luria pointed out that most psychological functions result from the working of a number of components belonging to several parts of the body apparatus. Functions, then, are carried out by an assembly of organs (a "functional system"), which could be organized in different fashions. In Luria's own words,

> The presence of a constant task (invariable) executed by variable mechanisms (variable), which leads the process to a constant result (invariable), is one of the basic features that distinguishes the work of

the functional system. The second distinctive feature is the complex composition of the functional system that always includes a set of afferent (adjustment) and efferent (effectors) impulses. (Luria, 1979a, p. 28)

> (...) all mental processes like perception and memory, gnosis and praxis, language and thought, writing, reading, and arithmetic cannot be considered as isolated "faculties".... (Luria, 1979a, p. 31)

All of these considerations can, we think, be assumed in our former presentation, probably to an extent impossible during Luria's lifetime. But the most important point is that Luria added the socio-cultural mediation of the biological operations of the organism. In Luria's words,

> The fact that all (functions) are formed through a long lasting historical development, that are originally social, and complex and hierarchical in their structure, and are also based on a complex system of means and methods, ... means that the fundamental forms of consciousness activity should be regarded as complex functional systems. (Luria, 1979a, p. 28)

For Luria, functional systems are based on external elements, like speech, which makes it impossible to understand the working of functional systems when ignored. This also explains why higher psychological processes cannot be localized in restricted areas. As Vygotski (1982) said, the history of development is the history of the construction of psychological systems. These systems are a composition of "natural" functions in order to create new "artificial" functions. The latter are called artificial because they are the result of historically developed forms of action in cultural groups. This is clearly the basis of socio-cultural psychology. External elements, the so-called mediational tools, are essential for establishing the functional connections in functional systems. Luria stressed the example of the brain, in which these external elements establish functional connections between previously disconnected areas.

Luria considered that there are changes in the structure of the functional systems. More specifically, that these processes are never constant or static, but are essentially changed during the development of the child. These changes are described as condensation and automation. Conscious activity includes certain external tools first, and, afterwards, is condensed as an automatic motor ability.

Ontogeny changes the structure of functional systems as well as their interrelation, so that an elementary function in early developmental stages does not only later becomes more complex, but also it does so because it becomes integrated into structurally higher forms of activity, so pushing development ahead.

The model Luria used to describe the operation of functional systems is the auto-regulatory system or feedback loop, which includes afferent as well as efferent elements, so that mental activity takes a complex and active character (Leontiev, 1979).

We cannot conduct an in-depth analysis of the brain units postulated by Luria to understand how the brain works (see Luria, 1979a for a description of his model), but a few words should be said on the auto-regulatory system metaphor, a classic in Soviet psychology.

As mentioned earlier, feedback is a form of probabilistic prognosis that finally drives us to retrospective control (albeit in tiny time windows). As seen before, one form of prognosis that currently fits Luria's theoretical claims is the dynamic theory applied to perception-action systems. Vygotsky (1979, 1982) is also credited with emphasizing that higher psychological functions are originally social or external, and in the course of growth, through interaction with adults, are internalized as auto-regulatory functions.

Once again, this powerful insight has two facets. On the one hand, it opens up the possibility of bridging the gap between the individual and the social, although on the other hand, it introduced a controversial term, *internalization* (for a discussion on this issue, see Lawrence & Valsiner, 1993; Wertsch, 1991; Valsiner, 1992). If functional systems consist of active loops of perceptual and motor elements, what is to be internalized?

It could only be either new regularities arising from encounters with the physical world (either natural or artificial), or patterns of behavior governed by social rules.

Our point is that a dynamic conception of the living individual presents an interesting alternative. Socializing means that the dynamics described so far change or evolve into more complex states in which the system has new coordination properties, and where collective variables change dramatically. When such a system enters into new stabilities, it will never return to a previous stable state. The concept of internalization is simply unnecessary, unless it is used in a metaphorical sense. The functional system changes not because it incorporates a new inner element, but because it evolves into a new stable dynamics, connected with new intervening variables.

What empirical findings are there to develop this understanding of the nature of these changes? Neuropsychology and re-mediation are the empirical and practical realms where social restructuring of functional systems has probably been better described.

Re-Mediation on the Edge From Basic to Social-cultural Functioning

Luria's neuropsychological approach considered that the analysis of functional systems should be addressed to syndromic analysis. Lesions in several cerebral areas, which drive towards different functional disturbances, can alter the functional system as a whole. Each cerebral area involved in the functional system introduces its own value in performance, so that its exclusion will make normal operation impossible, but this does not have to mean that the function could not be carried out at all. There are cases in which it could be fulfilled in a different fashion. This way of picturing the relationship between function and structure can also be applied to the entire body apparatus, so the dynamic system involved in a certain task may either be reorganized in the case of local lesions, or break down when reorganization is not possible.

Normal operation in adults means the socialization of the functional dynamics described above, within the social practices of the group or society in which the individual lives. Indeed, the idea of mediation was intended to refer to activities involving interaction with the environment that are regulated by artificial objects, and conventionalized by social rules.

Therefore, the auto-organized developmental course, described by Thelen (Thelen & Smith, 1994) as context-sensitive, is further led by social interaction towards a homogenization of development and higher psychological functioning among the members of the group, through rearing and educational practices (see Valsiner, 1997, 2000). That is, social integration requires from the subject a pool of functional abilities that can be reached through educational practices starting from different functional-developmental backgrounds.

When referring to the education of children with sensory deficits, Vygotsky (1982) pointed out that education is mainly a homogenization of developmental trends. Thus, the process of enculturation can be viewed as the dialectics between the heterogeneity of developmental mechanisms or processes and the homogeneity imposed by the practices of socialization (Rosa, Huertas, & Blanco, 1993).

Educational technologies in cultural groups are designed for stable and limited forms of biological functions in the human being (Rosa and Ochaita, 1993), and thus different developmental courses, which are more divergent in the case of sensory and motor deficits or mental retardation, may converge in culturally equivalent functions during the enculturation processes, if efficient educational technologies have been devised and remedial education succeeds.

The psychological and educational literature on the physically and psychologically challenged is concerned with providing means to overcoming the difficulties these individuals and groups may have in acquiring some of the functions they need to master in order to reach a successful social integration. The analysis of these practices can be gathered together under the umbrella of the term re-mediation. This term, coined by Cole and Griffin (1983), was defined as

> *... a shift in the way that mediating devices regulate coordination with the environment. (Cole & Griffin, 1983, p. 70)*

Vygotsky, borrowed Adler's concept of overcompensation to emphasize how the urge towards social integration can overcome specific impairments, making them to take novel forms. In other words, the individual overstretches his or her functional systems in order to reach a similar performance to that resulting from normal development. He thus stressed the idea of functional efficiency rather than that of identity of functions, when referring to special education. There are plenty of examples in special education and neuropsychological practices for specific processes of a transition from self-organized systems of perception-action to socio-culturally mediated actions.

Luria (1979b) probably gave very illustrative examples of re-mediation activities carried out together with his colleague Vygotsky. He described how their theoretical position led them to consider that in the absence of language (aphasia), subjects behave in a more primitive manner, a supposition that was proven to be incorrect. In his words

> *This position turned out to be incorrect, as many subsequent investigations have shown. We were greatly oversimplifying both the nature of aphasia and the psychological processing in brain-injured patients. At the beginning, however, these ideas were a strong motivation for assuming that the study of brain injury would lead us to an understanding of the nature of man's higher psychological functions and would provide us a means for understanding their material basis in the brain as well. (Luria, 1979b, p. 128)*

However, this approach led to a powerful insight into the development from self-organized functions to mediation. Luria says, for example,

> We were more successful when we began to observe patients suffering from Parkinson's disease. Parkinson disease affects the subcortical motor ganglia so that the flow of involuntary movement is disturbed. We observed that tremors occurred shortly after patients suffering from this disease started to carry out action. When we asked them to walk across a room, they could take only one or two steps before a tremor set in and they could walk no further.
>
> We realized the paradox that patients (Parkinson disease) who could not take two steps on the floor were able to climb stairs without difficulty. We hypothesized that while climbing stairs, each stair represented a signal to which motor impulses can respond. While climbing stairs, the automatic and successive movement's flux that occurs when walking on a homogeneous surface was replaced by a chain of separated motor reactions. In other words, the motor activity structure was reorganized, and a conscious response to each link in an isolated signals chain replaced the involuntary system, subcortically organized, which drives ordinary walk.
>
> Vigotsky used a simple device procedure to construct a laboratory model of this kind of reorganization of movement. He placed a series of small paper cards on the floor and asked a patient to step over each one of them. A marvelous thing happened. A patient who had been able to take no more than two or three steps by himself walked through the room, easily stepping over each piece of paper as if he were climbing a staircase. We had helped the patient to overcome the symptoms of his disease by getting him to recognize the mental processes he used in walking. He had compensated for his defect by transferring the activity from the subcortical level where his nerves were damaged to the cortical level which was not affected by the disease. (Luria, 1979, p. 128–129)

Neuropsychological practices are thus a privileged ground for the analysis of self-organized systems and socio-cultural mediation. A dynamic systems theory description of functions that are further re-mediated would be the appropriate place for an empir-ical analysis of the specific forms of reorganization produced by external tools during mediation and re-mediation processes.

Luria continued

> We then tried to use the same principle to construct an experimental model of self-regulated behavior, but our experiments were very naive and the results obtained were somewhat inconclusive. (Luria, 1979b, p. 129)

He specifically referred to a set of experiments in which subjects were asked to tap spontaneously or under certain external cues, an experimental condition for which, as shown before, we have now a formal description.

Mediation and the Transit From Basic to Higher Psychological Processes

From the argument so far deployed, it follows that the use of external means in behavior is able to transform the dynamics of movement, and the dynamic system itself, as the internalization metaphor tells. But there is more to this. Social groups, because of their encounters among their own members, with Nature and with other groups, have developed tools for action and social-cultural practices throughout time. The latter include symbolic conventionalized movements and new uses of environmental objects able to attune the behavior of individuals, share goals, and regulate cooperative action. And even more, when these movements are specifically used and transformed in order to communicate among members of a group, they become capable to offering symbolic means for the description and explanation of events and suited to planning ahead what to do in a future. In other words, these symbolic devices are able to go beyond the immediacy of current experience, and so open the possibility of making present what is absent, and so imagine what has already past, or has never happen yet; and so creating experienced time. Having available these new devices (conventionalized mediational tools) for action opens a new realm of possibilities for movement. They still work with the natural regularities describable by the dynamic systems theory, but now inscribed in systems of higher complexity which have to include not only individuals, but also environmental tools, the others, and the symbolic devices for mutual regulation.

So viewed, self-organized dynamic movement seems to have been able not only to transform dynamic systems in increasingly complex stability estates, but also of changing and transforming the uses and even the structure of parts of their environment, and then make use of these new elements to creating new stabilities within themselves. Following Wertsch (1991), we may say that human movement becomes action performed with mediational means, which have been developed throughout the historical development of socio-cultural groups.

Concluding Remarks

As stated in the introduction, this chapter aimed to present a view of the human subject that avoided dualism (mind-body, individual-social, physical-symbolic) and was capable of bridging the gap between the so-called basic psychological processes and the higher processes involving consciousness and meaning. Our means for doing so is to present the reorganization of dynamic systems as a key concept for the description and explanation of perception and movement.

The main claim made here is that the kind of explanation including self-organization and temporal dynamics applied to the development of perception and action may be useful for the explanation of how socialization and enculturation processes develop (Van Geert, 1995, 2003). Social organization provides physical objects with new functional properties (Rodríguez, 2006) as well as it produces new artificial objects which are incorporated into action allowing new functional capabilities which transform the dynamic equilibrium. The outcome is the emergence of new stabilities and instabilities but not reified faculties, co-evolution

but not final states of development. Thus, it is possible to describe social dynamics of cognitive development (Van Geert, 1995) as described by Vigotsky through dynamic modeling (Van Geert, 1994), as well as detect abrupt changes and re-define dynamic systems when functional dependencies are transformed in social interaction. In fact, dynamic systems theory is especially well suited to deal with morphogenesis, through self-organization and the emergence of structure in interactive systems (Port & Van Gelder, 1995, p. 25–27).

I believe that an empirical analysis of these processes should be grounded on an appropriate dynamic description of basic functions, and their temporal development with the use of mediational artifacts in social situations and communication. This is the reason why I believe the basic psychological concepts of Luria and Vigotsky are worthy of being revisited and re-analyzed vis-à-vis current research developments, and so empowering new empirical studies coherently merged with current topics in basic psychological processes. I have no doubt that this endeavor, although at first sight may look far removed from socio-cultural research, will rend useful resources for the furthering of knowledge in socio-cultural psychology.

Notes

1   It is important to mention that this neglect on taking into consideration basic psychological phenomena is a relatively recent phenomenon, probably resulting from result of focusing on some applied areas of research, rather than a historical feature of socio-cultural psychology.

2   Frawley (1997) is a good example of a very meticulous consideration of information processing and Vygotskian approaches somehow eclectically connected.

3   Although a detailed consideration of the issue is beyond the scope of this chapter, it has to be noted that the dynamic systems approach regards psychophysics not as a blind description of the magical communication between two different ontological realms, but

as simple calibration. Psychophysics describes the levels of physical quantities to which we attune.

4   H. Maturana and F. Varela (1984) pointed out that in biological systems it is meaningless to talk of representation insofar as the interactions are "non-instructive" for the organism.

5   The dynamic system formalization of touch implies an illusory effect between weight and size, which can explain the classical size-weight illusion (Amazeen & Turvey, 1995).

References

Amazeen, E., & Turvey, M. T. (1996). Weight perception and the haptic size-weight illusion are functions of the inertia tensor. *Journal of Experimental Psychology: Human Perception and Performance, 22*, 213–232.

Bernstein, N. A. (1967). *The Coordination and Regulation of Movements*. Oxford: Pergamon Press.

Blanco, F. (1995). Cognition as a black box: The blind date of mind and culture. *Culture & Psychology, 1*, 203–213.

Carello, C., & Turvey, M. T. (2000). Rotational dynamics and dynamic touch. In M. Heller (Ed.): *Touch, representation, and blindness* (pp. 27–66). Oxford: Oxford University Press.

Cole, M., & Griffin, P. (1983). A Socio-historical Approach to Re-mediation. *The Quarterly Newsletter of the Laboratory of Comparative Human Cognition, 5*(4), 69–74.

Costall, A. (1995). Socializing affordances. *Theory and Psychology, 5*(4), 457–481.

Feigenberg, J. M. (1998). The Model of the Future in Motor Control. In M. L. Latash (Ed.): *Progress in Motor Control. Bernstein's Traditions in Movement Studies* (pp. 89–103). Champaign, IL: Human Kinetics.

Fodor, J. A. (1975). *The Language of Thought*. New York: Crowell.

Frawley, W. (1997). Vygotsky and Cognitive Science. Cambridge, MA: Harvard University Press.

Gibson, J. J. (1966). *The Senses considered as Perceptual Systems*. Boston: Houghton Mifflin.

Gibson, J. J. (1979). *The ecological approach to visual perception*. Hillsdale, NJ: Lawrence Erlbaum Associates.

Heller, M. A., & Schiff, W. (1991). *The Psychology of Touch*. Hillsdale, NJ: Lawrence Erlbaum Associates.

Katz, (1925/1989). *The world of touch*. Hillsdale, NJ: Lawrence Erlbaum Associates.

Kelso, J. A. S. (1981). On the Oscillatory Basis of Movement. *Bulletin of the Psychonomic Society, 18*, 63.

Kelso, J. A. S. (1994). Elementary coordination dynamics. In P. Swinnen, H. Heuer, J. Massion, & P. Casae (Eds.): *Interlimb coordination: Neural, Dynamical, and Cognitive Constraints* (pp. 301–318). New York: Academic Press.

Kelso, J. A. S. (1995). *Dynamic Patterns. The Self-Organization of Brain and Behavior*. Cambridge: MIT Press.

Kelso, J. A. S. (1998). From Bernstein's Physiology of Activity to Coordination Dynamics. In: M. L. Latash (Ed.): *Progress in Motor Control. Bernstein's Traditions in Movement Studies* (pp. 203–219). Champaign, IL: Human Kinetics.

Kelso, J. A. S., DelColle, & Shöner, G. (1990). Action-Perception as a Pattern Formation Process. In M. Jeannerod (Ed.): *Attention and Performance XIII* (pp. 139–169). Hillsdale, NJ: Lawrence Erlbaum Associates.

Latash, M. L. (1998). *Progress in Motor Control. Bernstein's Traditions in Movement Studies*. Champaign, IL: Human Kinetics.

Lawrence, J. A., & Valsiner, J. (1993). Conceptual Roots of Internalization: From Transmission to Transformation. *Human Development, 36*, 150–167.

Lee, D. N. (1976). A theory of visual control of braking based on information about time-to-collision. *Perception, 5*, 437–459.

Lee, D. (1998). Guiding movement by coupling taus. *Ecological Psychology, 10*, 221–250.

Lee, D., & Reddish, P. E. (1981). Plummeting gannets: A paradigm of ecological optics. *Nature, 293*, 293–294.

Leontiev, A. N. (1979). The problem of activity in psychology. In J. Wertsch (Ed.): *The problem of activity in soviet psychology*. New York: M. E. Sharpe.

Luria, A. R. (1979a). *El cerebro en acción*. Barcelona: Fontanella.

Luria, A. R. (1979b). *The making of the mind*. Cambridge, MA: Harvard University Press.

Marr, D. (1982). *Vision*. San Francisco: Freeman Publishers.

Maturana, H., & Mpodozis, J. (1996) Percepción: configuración conductual el objeto. En H. Maturana (Ed.): *Desde la biología a la psicología* (pp. 27–66). Santiago de Chile: Editorial Universitaria.

Maturana, H., & Varela, F. (1984). *El árbol del conocimiento: las bases biológicas del conocimiento humano*. Santiago de Chile: Editorial Universitaria.

McGraw, M. B. (1945). *The neuromuscular maturation of the human infant*. New York: Columbia University Press.

Merleau-Ponty, M. (1957). *Fenomenología de la percepción*. México: FCE.

Nam-Gyoon, K., & Turvey, M. T. (1998). Optical flow fields and Berrnstein's "Modeling of the Future". In M. L. Latash (Ed.): *Progress in Motor Control. Bernstein's Traditions in Movement Studies* (pp. 221–265). Champaign, IL: Human Kinetics.

Pagano, C. C., & Turvey, M. T. (1995). The inertia tensor as a basis for the perception of limb orientation. *Journal of Experimental Psychology: Human Perception and Performance*, 21, 1070–1087.

Port, R. F., & Van Gelder, T. (1995). *Mind as Motion. Explorations in the Dynamics of Cognition*. Cambridge: MIT Press.

Rodríguez, C. (2006). This volume.

Rogers, S., & Effken, J. (2003). *Studies in Perception and Action VII*. Hillsdale, NJ: Lawrence Erlbaum Associates.

Rosa, A., Huertas, J. A., & Blanco, F. (1993). Psicología de la ceguera y psicología general. In A. Rosa & E. Ochaita (eds.), *Psicología de la ceguera* (pp. 319–361). Madrid: Alianza Editorial.

Rosa, A., & Ochaita, E. (1993). Puede hablarse de una psicología de la ceguera?. In A. Rosa & E. Ochaita (Eds.), *Psicología de la ceguera* (pp. 1–18). Madrid: Alianza Editorial.

Schiff, W., & Foulke, E. (Eds.), (1982). *Tactual perception: A source book*. New York: Cambridge University Press.

Thelen, E. (1984). Learning to walk: Ecological demands and phylogenetic constraints. In L. P. Lipsitt (Ed.), *Advances in infancy research* (vol. 3) (pp. 213–150). Norwood, NJ: Ablex.

Thelen, E. (1995). Time-scale dynamics and the development of an embodied cognition. In R. F. Port & T. Van Gelder (Eds.): *Mind as Motion. Explorations in the Dynamics of Cognition* (pp. 69–100). Cambridge: MIT Press.

Thelen, E., & Fisher, D. M. (1982). Newborn stepping: An explanation for a "disappearing reflex". *Developmental Psychology*, 18, 760–775.

Thelen, E., & Smith, L. B. (1994). *A Dynamic Systems Approach to the Development of Cognition and Action*. Cambridge: MIT Press.

Turvey, M. T. (1994). From Borelli (1680) and Bell (1826) to the dynamics of action and perception. *Journal of Sport and Exercise Psychology*, 16, 128–157.

Turvey, M. T. (1996). Dynamic touch. *American Psychologist*, 51, 1134–1152

Turvey, M. T., & Carello, C. (1995). Some Dynamical Themes in Perception and Action. In R. F. Port & T. Van Gelder (Eds.): *Mind as Motion. Explorations in the Dynamics of Cognition* (pp. 372–401). Cambridge: MIT Press.

Valsiner, J. (1992). Further reflections on Jim Wertsch's Commentary "Internalization: Do we really need it? Unpublished via e-mail network XLCHC, August, 22, 1992.

Valsiner, J. (1997). *Culture and the Development of Children's action*. New York: John Wiley.

Valsiner, J. (2000). *Culture and Human Development*. London: Sage.

Van Geert, P. (1994). Dynamic systems of development. *Human Development*, 37, 346–365.

Van Geert, P. (1995). Growth Dynamics in Development. In R. F. Port & T. van Gelder (Eds.), *Mind as Motion. Explorations in the Dynamics of Cognition* (pp. 313–337). Cambridge: MIT Press.

Van Geert, P. (2003). Dynamic Systems Approaches and Modeling of Developmental Proceses. In J. Valsiner & K. Connolly (Ed.), *Handbook of Developmental Psychology* (pp. 640–672). London: Sage.

Vigotsky, L. S. (1979). *El desarrollo de las funciones psicológicas superiores*. Barcelona: Crítica.

Vigotsky, L. S. (1982). Sobre los sistemas psicológicos. In L. S. Vigotsky: *Obras escogidas, Vol. I*. Madrid: MEC-Visor, 1991.

Wertsch, J. V. (1991). *Voices of the Mind*. Cambridge, MA: Harvard University Press.

CHAPTER 7

Comparative Development of Communication

An Evolutionary Perspective

Adolfo Perinat

It is difficult, if not impossible, to discuss the comparative development of communication except from a phylogenetic standpoint. In this sense, the title of this chapter is redundant. Moreover, the comparative task is highly complicated. Is there any basis for comparison between the forms of communication used by arthropods, anurans, birds, or aquatic mammals, or between human or non-human primates? And if there is, what is it? In an attempt to encompass the great diversity of the forms of communication that exist in the animal world, the definitions that have been proposed inevitably fall back upon generalities, making use of concepts like "transmission of information," "probability of response to a signal," "sharing elements of behavior," or "the means of achieving coordinated action." We are immediately confronted by a further difficulty: each species has evolved forms of communication that make use of the particular properties of its physical environment. Some species use a single dimension: visual, sonorous, olfactory, electrical, or echolocation. Others (the higher species) make simultaneous use of

various dimensions. The type of communication found among organisms with simple nervous systems does not – and cannot – have the same properties and complexity as communication produced by central nervous systems. The immense diversity of communicative "forms" makes it impossible to define even minimally acceptable comparative criteria.

Focusing on the topic of communication from a phylogenetic standpoint always carries with it the idea of a progressive development of communicative capacity. The different modalities of communication have evolved to serve the general function of regulating the (social) behavior of each species within its own ecological niche. Which of these modalities is the best or most efficient is not the issue. However, we humans, looking down from our high point on the evolutionary scale, have pretentiously set ourselves up as the final model and basis of comparison for all species. This viewpoint has given rise, in retrospect, to the concept of an evolutionary trend incorporating the tremendously ambiguous notion of progress. The notion is ambiguous because it mixes two incommensurable conceptual dimensions: (successful) adaptation to a socio-ecological environment, the result of natural selection; and the level of performance of a particular capacity measured on a scale imposed on the other species by man.

Communication is a central phenomenon in the adaptation of each species to its niche. However, we have no information about how it fit into this slow and random process. The narratives of evolution are, in fact, post-factum stories, and we have no criteria on which to base broad comparisons between forms of communication (as they exist today) in taxonomically distant species. What we can do is, starting from the basis of a rudimentary comparison of the psychological apparatuses (or nervous systems) that dot the course of evolution, examine whether these systems correspond to novel characteristics of communication. The term "novel" means that the observable differences can be *grosso modo* translated to a scale of complexity of processing in the nervous system. Later, we will return to study the implications of this general proposition.

In this chapter, I will begin by examining the concept of communication traditionally and currently used in the field of ethology. Second, I will touch on a few landmarks in the evolution of communication in the different species. More than to the rules of communication, I will pay particular attention to the mechanisms that regulate these features since, as I have just suggested, this is where the levels of progressive complexity of processing are found. Third, I will focus on communication in primates, and in particular the anthropoids since, while they do not use language, these animals do make use of forms of communication very close to those of humans (the obligatory final conclusion of any study of comparative communication). Rather than the emergence of language (a highly intricate and nebulous subject), the focus of my final section will be on the sign created by the hominid mind in order to facilitate communication between minds.

General Considerations on the Concept of Communication

A great deal has been written about communication in the animal world. All the general treatises in this discipline dedicate at least one chapter to the topic. In addition there are specific works, such as that of Smith (1977) and those of Sebeok (1968, 1977). E. O. Wilson in his book *Sociobiology* (1975) dedicates considerable space to the topic of communication. More recently we find the monographic work by M. D. Hauser, *The Evolution of Communication* (1996). So how do these specialists define the phenomenon of communication?

The primatologist Stuart Altmann in his book *Social Communication among primates* (1967: chap. 17) lists a number of definitions. After discarding some as being too vague, and others as too restricted, he cites Cherry (1957: 7): "The mere transmission and reception of a physical signal does not constitute communication. (...) Communication is not the response itself but the *relationship* set up by the transmission of stimuli and the evocation of responses" (original italics). Altmann adds a definition of his own: "In short, social communication is a process by which the behavior of an individual affects the behavior of others'." Altmann's definition is the same as the one proposed by classical ethologists which, with certain variations, is also used by Wilson in his *Sociobiology* (1975: chap. 8). Hauser (1996) also transcribes a more eclectic group of definitions of communication, including human communication.

It is possible to identify certain features common to all ethological definitions. At first glance communication involves:

1. The transmission of information.
2. A change of behavior in the receiver.
3. That this change of behavior be adaptive.

To these characteristics we can add

4. An internal processing by the receiver (which also occurs in the sender).

As we shall see later, this is an essential part of our comparative task. Another factor that must be taken into account (the leitmotif of Hauser's treatise) is that communicative forms (songs, calls, postures, language, etc.) have been the object of evolutionary design. It will be illustrative to cite some examples given by ethologists of communicative behavior found in the animal kingdom. These will allow us to understand this apparently simple notion more precisely.

- The sexual encounters of the silkworm moth occur when the female releases a pheromone that is captured in tiny quantities by the male through olfactory organs located in its antennae. The male immediately sets off to search for the female guided by the concentration of the pheromone in the atmosphere (Wilson, 1975).
- The tick, 'that blind and deaf thief of the roads', as Von Uexküll (1956) described it, waits patiently on the branch of a bush for a passing warm blooded animal. The odor emitted by the sebaceous follicles of the mammal and the warmth exuded by its body act as a signal: the tick drops from its perch and burrows into the animal's skin to suck out its meal of blood.
- If any communicative behavior has aroused universal admiration, it must surely be that of the scout bee that returns to the hive and performs a "dance" to inform its companions of the direction of and distance to the location of the flowers – the food source (taken from Von Frisch, 1954).
- Another famous instance of communicative behavior that has been the object of intense study is that of vervet monkeys (Struhsaker, 1967; Cheney and Seyfarth, 1990). The individuals of this species have three distinctive alarm calls in their vocal repertoire corresponding to three different predators: snakes, cats, and eagles. In response to a particular call, the monkeys retreat to safety in the trees (in the case of

a serpent or jaguar) or in the dense ground cover (in the case of eagles).
- Female chimpanzees and other primates in oestrus display a characteristic swelling in the perineal region. Males of the species have been observed to sit facing the female with their legs spread apart exhibiting their erect penis. At times they will even move the penis up and down to make it more visible (De Waal, 1982).

Could all of the above situations be defined as communicative behavior? The ethological definitions of communication (Altmann, Wilson, and others) systematically take their inspiration from the paradigm of the telecommunications engineer: sender → message → receiver, adding a behavioral criteria to guarantee that the relation inherent in the communication exists. This relation is demonstrated when the behavior of the putative recipient undergoes an observable change. The vehicle of such communication is usually called *the signal*: a physical phenomenon (sound, odor, postural change, etc.) that originates in the emitting organism and is captured by the receiver.

However, this concept of a signal is too broad since it could apply to natural phenomena as well as living organisms, for example thunder and the murmur of running water. There is a general principal that any organism is a "signal processing device", but each one is conditioned by evolution to capture and react to a restricted set of signals typical of its socio-ecological environment. In other words, each species lives in a specific semiotic universe (a perceptual world which, in conjunction with the possibilities of action, constitutes what Von Uexküll (1956) called the *Umwelt*). Each species makes use of the signals it processes within itself to organize its behavior. This processing, the result of a long evolutionary history, is what determines the adaptation of the organism. The behavior of the silkworm, the tick, and the bee are characteristic examples of this signal processing.

Information and Communication

Life functions by way of an intense exchange of signals.[1] This endless succession of emitted and received signals can be conceptualized as a semiotic network or *semiosphere* (Hoffmeyer, 1997). However, each species only processes some of the myriads of signals circulating in the semiosphere: the ones perceived by its perception-action system shaped by natural selection. This is the essence of Von Uexküll's concept of Umwelt (Kull, 2001). In other words, each animal lives in its own *semiotic niche* (Hoffmeyer, 1997). Within this niche, the perceptible signals can either be phenomena that form part of the physical environment or signals emitted by other living organisms. It would appear logical to apply the adjective *communicative* only to these and to qualify the rest as merely *informative*. The tick's prey does not communicate anything to the parasite. It is the tick that is *informed* of the presence of its future host by the smell of butyric acid. Another example is the sexual swelling exhibited by female primates: such manifestations are informative signals of a physiological state. Only when these manifestations are orchestrated with postures of approach and presentation can we talk about communication. Yet another example of (surely intentional) communication is the male chimpanzee's exhibition of the penis to females. Conversely, no communicative act occurs when an animal recognizes the trail or odor that another animal has left in passing. *Et sic de ceteris.*

Most of the definitions of communication commonly cited in ethological literature fail to take into account this extremely important distinction between *information* and *communication* (Marshall, 1970). Information requires only a signal processing "device" – an apparatus or organism not necessarily equipped with a nervous system. Information is basically something captured by the receiver, while communication takes place within the relationship established between the emitter and the receiver by means of the signal. This is what Cherry's definition aims to establish. The distinction between information and communication together with the condition that the latter occurs only between organisms of the animal kingdom leads us to disallow expressions such as "the flowers communicate their presence to the bees" or "the murmur of the river communicates the proximity of water to the thirsty animal." This is a metaphorical way of expressing something. If everything is considered to be communication, then communication becomes something irrelevant.

We could add the following condition to differentiate between communication and the mere information circulating within any socioecologic environment: an organism *A* communicates (is an emitter) *when it in some way takes into account* the other *B* which will be the receiver. Here the phrase "when it in some way takes into account" is crucial. This condition would, for example, exclude the case of a mammal passing close to a tick, the presence of which is unknown to it. The same could be said of any prey with respect to the predator that pounces on it by surprise. We may well ask what the scope of this "taking the other into account" is in the case of the silkworm moth or in the case of any other form of communication mediated by pheromones at a distance. I think that a strictly biological, non-mentalist, interpretation of "taking the other into account" is to include in this category the activation of a motivational system in the emitter *E* the function of which is to transmit biologically relevant information to the receiver *R*, for example readiness to engage in a sexual intercourse.

There is a curious example of an interaction called sematectonic communication. The male ghost crab builds a mound in the sand that acts as a signal attracting the female. At the base of the mound is a spiral hole where copulation will take place (Wilson, 1975:187). The male ghost crab does not *think* that constructing the mound will attract the female, nor does he do it *for this reason*: his motivational-sexual system activates and produces this signal, an evolutionary design that differs from the pheromone but is functionally equivalent.

Once we have accepted that communication in the strict sense of the word only occurs between animal organisms, we can move on to examine another of the characteristics referred to earlier. Does communication have to be adaptive for the two communicators or is it sufficient that it be adaptive for just one of them (the emitter or the receiver)? We have already concluded that no communication in the strict sense of the word occurs in the predator-prey interaction (trophic chains): the predator acts by surprise; the prey is suddenly informed of its presence. Becoming a meal for a predator is a failure of the prey's adaptation. The point should be made that interaction should not be confused with communication. It is true that a prolonged interaction – a behavioral exchange – must be "punctuated" by communicative forms that facilitate adjustment of the behavioral actions taking place sequentially, but this does not preclude maintaining the aforementioned distinction. The following observation, which may serve as an example, comes from Arnhem zoo (De Waal, 1982, 37). One of the male chimpanzees displays[2] in front of a rival while holding a stone in one hand. A female chimpanzee comes up behind him, steals the stone, and runs away. There has been interaction but no communication. If a person on the street pushes through a crowd, he interacts with the other people but does not communicate with them.

However, nothing is ever quite that simple. While most of the time, the prey reacts by fleeing to safety, some species use the strategy of "distracting" the predator with postures that make them appear badly injured or dead (Ristau, 1991). Could it be said, therefore, that they are communicating with the predator by using a postural signal that does not reflect a real physiological state? If we apply the condition established above, namely that a motivational system has to have been activated that will result in an adaptive benefit, it could be said that there is communication but that, in this case,

it is adaptive only for the emitter (the potential prey). Another fraudulent use of signals is that of certain female fireflies who mimic the flashes of other firefly species to attract males, which she then devours. Is this not a singular modality of communicative behavior despite being "deceitful"?

This brings us to the notion of communication proposed by behavioral ecologists. Without exception, animals obey the great biological imperative to propagate their genes. As well as doing everything to ensure their own survival, they also endeavor to optimize their own reproductive success: the "selfish gene" strives only to ensure its own propagation in successive organisms. And this is an undertaking governed by an implacable competition: competition for a sexual mate, for food, for a territory, and so on. If at any time collaboration becomes necessary (when parents have to care for the young for example), nature collaborates only to optimize inclusive fitness.[3] Classical ethology maintains that the main function of communication is to coordinate action (cooperation) undertaken for mutual benefit – in other words that it is adaptive for the communicators. "The selfish gene approach to communication" (Dawkins and Krebs, 1978) maintains, on the contrary, that the aim of communication is to "manipulate" the other for one's own benefit. Basically, it is adaptive for the emitter (although it may incidentally be adaptive for the receiver as well). Communication is, in the final analysis, a way of influencing the behavior of the other for one's own benefit in a much more economical way (without expending energy) than the exercise of physical power. In light of these premises, deception and pretense, insofar as they are used to achieve an end, rather than constituting a subversion of communication, are in fact its most common ingredients. This point of view (a cynical one, as Dawkins and Krebs expressly recognize, op. cit.) held by behavioral ecologists is not incompatible with the traditional approach (Hinde, 1981). Besides giving rise to enormously fruitful studies of the evolution of communicative signals in the reciprocal adjustment of the emitter-receiver, it has also opened the door to the existence of deception and misinformation as communication strategies.

From this brief overview of the phenomenon of communication it can be seen that it is not a simple task to define its limits. And neither is it my intention here to impose an impossible consensus on the specialists, who each conceive of it with their own nuances in spite of their common background. But it does seem necessary that we should agree among ourselves here and now at least on the assumptions that we will adopt in this discussion.

The Comparative Proposal

My intention in this chapter is not to compare the communication systems of all the species according to the canons of biology by exploring and detecting homologies, homoplasies, analogies, and other such features.[4] It is, rather, to focus on the psychological aspects of information processing. Communication – emission/reception and the reactions of the participants – is a phenomenon dependent on and subject to an *organization of the nervous system*.

Our starting point is that all animal communication systems (including that of humans) comprise three basic components:

1. the signals that are transmitted,
2. the perceptive-cognitive apparatus of the emitter and that of the receiver, and
3. the behaviors that follow the transmission/reception of the signals.

I propose to adopt the second of these components as the main core of the comparative task. We will study how animal communication systems evolve as the psychological apparatus of the communicators becomes more complex. Within the context of the evolutionary span, I will consider four crucial phases separated by perceptive-cognitive breakthroughs that have decisive repercussions on communication. In the first phase, the organisms lives and communi-

cates in a world merely composed of signals, which are perceived by its "mental" apparatus as unconnected so that the organism's "real world" consists of an array of sensations. The breakthrough into the second phase occurs when the perceptive apparatus is capable of integrating these random and/or sequentially processed signals and creating an *object* – a separate entity to which psychological and not merely physical characteristics can be attributed. The third phase occurs when the mind of the (higher) animals evolves towards a particular type of intelligence (social) that produces complex societies and gives them sophisticated communicative abilities. In the final evolutionary stage, a singular primate manages to create the *sign* opening the door to an extremely complex and novel form of communication: language.

A World of Signals

The communicative forms may be movements that adopt a certain – static (postural synergies) or dynamic configuration; they can be colorations that stand out, luminous flashes, sounds, chemical substances that are released into the atmosphere, etc. Generically we refer to them as "forms" because they adopt a regular profile and, at the same time, the perceptive capabilities of each animal species are predisposed to distinguish them as biologically relevant events. The communicative forms are known by the generic name *displays*. One excellent example is the facial expressions of primates and humans.

The nature of communicative signals is determined by the physical medium of their transmission: air or water. Within each one of these media (particularly air), a huge diversity of conditions exists that has led each species throughout its evolution to develop a specific type of signal. While the air can be the medium for sonorous or pheromonal displays by day or by night, postural displays or coloration are only visible in daylight; in darkness only luminous displays are perceptible. However, even in full daylight, visibility is not the same in the forest as in the open countryside, and the half-light of dawn and twilight also limit visual perception. Visual perception over short distances is possible in an aquatic environment, as is the transmission of sounds or electrical charges. The emission/reception of signals is not only subject to the structural conditions of the environment in which they are produced. For example, the emission of a sound can be attenuated or distorted by the proximity of running water, or by the sounds emitted by other species living in the area. All of these factors constitute the "noise" inherent in the environment in which the signal is transmitted.

The environment in which the species emit their signals includes not only physical conditions but also social and ecological conditions. Other components that make up this environment are the conspecific potential receivers of the signal and others who compete with the emitter for a sexual mate, territory, or food. Individuals of other species, particularly predators who detect their prey by way of the signal it produces or who mimic the signals exchanged by their prey, are also an integral part of the usual living environment. All these aspects constitute what we might call the *social dimension*, in the broadest sense, of the environment. Classical ethology restricted it to the presence of congeners, but in the evolution of the signals of each species (an ongoing evolution) the presence of other organisms that form part of the common environment has been decisive. Communicative forms arise from a set of causes that are capriciously intertwined throughout the natural evolution of the species, always in the interests of optimum adaptation (inclusive fitness).

Many postural displays are variations or transductions of movements that, at the outset, were the inception of terrestrial locomotion or aerial flight; some are derived from grooming practices; and others developed out of defensive or self-protective actions, such as the "teeth baring" characteristic of dogs and cats. Ethology calls these displays *intention movements*. Curiously, the laughter of anthropoids and the human smile appear to have had their origin in the same display reframed as a gesture of non-aggression (Van Hooff, 1972). We might ask ourselves how these "organic productions," many of which are neutral, have become biologically significant, that is, activators of animal perception-action systems, and have thereby acquired the character of signals. The explanation lies in a co-evolution between the species' perception and "behavioral pieces" by virtue of which rough drafts of forms or fragments of functional movements were transposed to the sphere of the regulation of social behavior (communication). These are examples of a typical process that occurs in evolution: functional extension.

The co-evolution of both signals and the perceptive receptor systems tends to favor detection involving a minimum expenditure of time and energy. One consequence of this is that, as physical phenomena, signals are endowed with properties that ensure rapid recognition. This characteristic has to do with the discriminant psychological apparatus, which immediately transfers the information to the motivational systems that trigger action. One property of the signals is that they accentuate contrasts that favor relevance. Animals identify their own species, particularly in the higher species, by way of the body profile or silhouette most probably in conjunction with the characteristic rhythm of locomotion. In other cases, recognition is mediated by the contrasts of coloring on the body. Herring gull chicks studied by Tinbergen (1951) peck on a yellow mark on the beak of their parents to request food. This investigator demonstrated that a white mark on a purple background was just as efficient as the natural mark in triggering the pecking behavior. Another characteristic common to many displays, very probably directed at improving detection and discrimination, is that they tend to be rather stereotyped configurations, making them easily recognizable. The process that gives them this quality was called *ritualization* by J. Huxley. A classic example is the courtship rituals 'engraved' in the nervous system of the species during its natural evolution; it may also have been acquired during the development of the individual. In the latter case it is called *ontogenetic ritualization* (Tomasello and Call, 1997). Among chimpanzees, there are several "ritual ceremonies" that contribute to the cohesion of the group, to mediation in reconciliations, the promotion of alliances, and so on. These are greeting and presentation (see de Waal, 1982).

Still within the general panorama of animal signaling, we can identify certain dimensions in the signals. One of these is the *intensity* with which signals are emitted. Morris (1957) observed that certain animals emit signals (sonorous and postural forms, etc.) at a *typical intensity* (constant). However, other animals produce displays with *variable intensity*, generally characterized by a gradual crescendo. The anal presentation of the primates can be described as being of typical intensity, while their agonistic escalations belong to the second group. Variation in the intensity of displays is a product of evolution that which, at the same time, has sensitized perceptive analyzers and led to a relationship between the intensity and variations in the disposition or motivational state of the individual. Very often, signals of typical intensity tend to be *discrete*, that is, they are emitted at intervals. One example is the rhythmic sonorous calls of toads and owls heard on spring nights.

Another dimension classifies the signals as *unimodal* (those that affect a single receptor channel) and *plurimodal* (affecting various channels simultaneously). The communicative-signaling behavior of an ape (a gorilla) in an agonistic or terrifying situation is mediated by the animal's facial expression and raised hair, its posture, audible sounds, and a glandular secretion that pervades the air in the form of a smell. The channels of emission are numerous, as are the channels of perception/reception. The appearance of plurimodal signals presupposes that the perceptive channels of the animals are capable of mentally integrating an array of sensory inputs. Unimodal signals, such as pheromones or luminescent flashes, are characterized by typical intensity.

While gradual communicative and plurimodal forms carry more information than unimodal forms, this does not necessarily imply the existence of a general law of evolution leading from unimodal to plurimodal forms. This conclusion would be erroneous for various reasons. In the first place, signals evolve within the context of each species. The signals common to the species are those the individuals need to perpetuate themselves and, as such, they have passed the test of efficacy to date. We should not confuse the complexity of the emission/processing of the signal with its adaptation to the socioecology of the species. From our perspective, the "language" of bees is much more complex than the "choirs" of frogs, in spite of the fact that frogs – which are vertebrates with a central nervous system – have a more advanced organization than the insects. Only when we follow the evolution of signals within a single species can we draw the conclusion that later developments are more efficient and advanced than earlier forms. One example of this is the case of human language compared to the other forms of primate communication that preceded it.[5]

Second, from the point of view of energy, emission/reception on more than one channel carries a greater overhead than a single channel, and the expenditure involved in graduating the intensity of such plurimodal forms is also greater. This means that the physiology of the species (or the individual) is an additional conditioning factor. For example, in the competition for the females of the herd, some species of deer engage in bellowing "duels" that rise to a crescendo. The stag that bellows the longest wins the match. The whole display seems to suggest that this expenditure of energy is an indicator (for other males and the females) of the winner's optimal physical reproductive condition or a signal directed to competitors indicating raw strength.

Third, a species may develop and refine a plurimodal or gradual system of communication because, given its living environment, it needs to transmit a greater quantity of information during each instance of communication it produces. The most immediate example of this is human communication. All of this underscores the fact that the evolution of signaling does not obey any general law that specifies "progress from the simple to the complex"; signals evolve within each species and this evolution is the product of interaction between the nature of the species and the socio-ecological environment in all its complexity.

The third dimension that should be discussed is whether the signal is independent of the context in which it is emitted or whether it has any relationship to this context. Many signals are processed in the pure state, that is, in the way an appropriate physical or chemical detector device (such as a telescope, litmus paper, etc.) would process them. Many signals that are discrete and of typical intensity function in this way. Other signals refer to circumstantial phenomena: for example food calls (in the presence of food), alarm calls (when predators are near). The bees' dance and the alarm calls of vervet monkeys are classic examples. The more advanced the degree of sociability, the more likely is it that we will find circumstantial signals. But the complexity of the nervous organization of the species also plays a role – the perceptive apparatus and the cognitive processing. A signal is never presented "in a pure state" to an advanced perceptive cognitive system. The more circumstantial parameters that are incorporated into the emission and processed by the receiving organism, the more probable it is that the subsequent action will be functionally appropriate. The culmination of communicative efficiency is achieved when the receiver incorporates a "representation" of the emitter as one of its own kind and, moreover, a record (memory) of its previous interactions with the other; this occurs among the higher mammals and particularly the primates.

Communication and Perception-Cognition

In the animal world, some signals are informative and others communicative, and they fulfill various vital functions: capture of prey (food), defense against enemies, sexual encounters. The perceptive abilities that make it possible for the organism to process signals play a crucial role. Perception is the threshold of the action, and it has co-evolved with the action in order to exploit the potential of each species' ecological niche (Von Uexküll, 1956; Von Hofsten, 1986). The need to gather information and the urgency for action has led living organisms to develop, throughout their evolution, specific perceptive modalities adapted to the characteristics of their ecological niche. The communicative forms are contained within these modalities.

Most species are equipped with not just one but various sensory detection mechanisms that can serve a single function (for example, sexual encounters). Very often these mechanisms can be used for various functions simultaneously. A typical example of this plurality of function can be found in spiders (Uetz and Roberts, 2002). The perceptual world of spiders is multi-sensorial. They are equipped with vibration-sensitive mechanisms by means of which they detect the prey (insects) trapped in their webs. Some species also detect the proximity of a potential mate by signals of this type. However, spiders more often resort to olfactory detection mechanisms (pheromones, smells), which also fulfill sexual and trophic functions. Their sight is, on the other hand, less evolved. Certain species use it to discern or recognize a sexual mate, and to this end in their displays they shake their legs, which are decorated with eye-catching colors. Note that in the case of spiders, reception of the signal (communicative in this case) is *unimodal* although the receiver can deal with multi-sensorial input. The spider's receptive perception is functionally specialized to detect prey using one modality, to find a mate using another (or the same but with a different type of signal), and so on (Uetz and Roberts, 2002).

Snakes represent another different case. To hunt prey, such as small rodents, they use a series of different sensorial channels: the prey is localized visually or by a heat-detecting organ, pursuit is guided by smell and, once the prey has been captured, the snake functions by touch. "The snake acts as a multichanneled mechanism, where each behavior program is governed by a particular sense channel and where there is no general capacity to translate the information from one channel to the next" (Sjölander, 1997, 2).

The principle is clear: each organism makes use of the perceptive resources developed in co-evolution with the signals or characteristics of its target objects. In the lower animal species the actions are organized in a series together with the signals that trigger them: signal → action, signal → action, and so on. In the higher species, there is prior integration of the information that gives rise (or not) to the action. Natural selection does not give rise to ideal or optimum solutions for functional problems. Each species has opportunistically developed nervous systems connected ad hoc to achieve the essential vital objectives.

An important corollary of this (and a key factor in the domain of comparative communication) is that most of the species in the animal kingdom live in a fragmented sensorial-perceptive universe, so to speak. Until we get to the level of birds and mammals, there is no centralized mechanism providing a representation of the external world that integrates the perceptions entering by different channels. In other words, *the object does not exist*, there is no entity that stands out, is distinguishable from the background, has a silhouette, and individual characteristics. Tinbergen's experimental work with sticklebacks is conclusive: when a rounded or oblong object is introduced into the fish tank, as long as the object is marked with a red patch on the lower side, it triggers an aggressive reaction in the fish (expulsion from the territory (Tinbergen, 1951). Alternatively, the presence of forms that represent a swollen belly caused the stickleback to perform a zigzagging courtship dance. The stickleback reacts to an object marked with a red color or with a bulging curved underside, and not to the male/female fish.

These mechanical or "blind" reactions are known among ethologists as *fixed action patterns*. The fixed action pattern is the most

common modality of reaction to signals among invertebrates and vertebrates below the class of birds. In birds and the higher species we find the beginning of more flexible behavior. This rule also applies to communication: responses to signals are totally stereotyped. At this point, we should ask ourselves not so much whether this is "true" communication, but should rather accept that there are degrees of complexity in communication although, as I said earlier, no scale of comparison exists.

We can investigate what kind of signal processing apparatus animals have, particularly the receivers, and what changes occur at certain points in the phylogenetic tree. The most simple and general schema of a signal processing apparatus consists of: (1) perceptive receivers, (2) a system to evaluate the sensorial input, (3) a system to select the action, and (4) a motor system to execute the response. Stages 2 and 3 can be merged into a single system, which we call the *input-output* organizing system. This schema can be made much more complex by the incorporation of analyzers, different kinds of selector and effector mechanisms, in addition to other meta-evaluators and meta-organizers systems that determine priorities and subroutines for decision making and courses of action (MacKay, 1972). Classical ethologists and behavioral ecologists have proposed – under various names – the existence of this basic schema. Green and Marler (1979) postulated an internal assessment operation that occurs in both the emitter and in the receiver of the signal. Guildford and Dawkins (1991) talk about the receiver's "psychological landscape." Behind the perceptive organs lies "a bewildering complex system of processors, information-stores and decision-makers."

The animals whose response to the signal is of the instinctive automatic type are said to be equipped with a *template*: "a prefabricated repertoire of control patterns suitably matched to the current spatio-temporal features of the field of action" (MacKay, 1972, 15). On the other hand, behavioral ecologists extend the field of the perception and processing of signals to encompass recognition of the emitter/carrier of the signal (kin recognition, mate recognition). However, in the context of the behaviors discussed here, this term has no cognitive connotations. It simply means detection/discrimination of the sender or of a phenomenon being emitted by the sender.

The Encephalization Process and Object Perception

The emergence of birds and mammals was accompanied by a reorganization of perceptive systems, which were for the first-time centralized in the brain. The following is how Jerison (1973) describes this change. During the Tertiary period, the great age of the reptiles, species of this class of organism invaded nocturnal temperate ecological niches. These animals were the forebears of the most primitive mammals. Since the reptilian visual system was inadequate for the distance vision needed by these proto-mammals, their auditory and olfactory system evolved to provide them with this ability. However, an increase in brain mass was required for this new modality of sensorial processing. With the massive extinction of the reptiles, the newly installed mammals moved into daytime ecological niches. And, once again, their visual system evolved towards the system we still have today, namely, cones and rods. In an ecological niche of exuberant vegetation, the interplay of light, shade and sounds makes it very difficult to discriminate functional objectives on the basis of unique signals. The old system of fixed action patterns became obsolete. If they were to survive in that environment, the perception-action system of these new mammals had to evolve. An increase in neuronal tissue laid the anatomical foundation that led to the mammalian brain taking on the function of integrating the impressions coming in on independent sensorial channels which, until that time, had made up a perceptive mosaic. "The effects of that integration would be to identify a pattern of stimulation with an 'object' at a particular position in space [...] A spatial background against which the object would be placed as 'figure' may also be assumed as part of this construction" (Jerison, 1973, 415).

What Jerison is talking about here is the birth of that extraordinary mental construction – the *object*: a "form" that persists in the mind despite changes of location, changes of direction, variations in the way it reflects light, eventual disappearances, and so on. The consequences of this evolutionary conquest are immensely important for communication: the object could be a source of signals. If the object did not exist we could not talk about recognition of the "other/emitter" or of the "other/receiver" even when both are present. What we call recognition in the lower organisms (that is the classes below the birds) is a simple detection or discrimination by way of a signal. From this point on, the communicative signal can be associated/attributed to an organism endowed with qualities ("form" among others) that make possible its identification. In this way the representation of the emitter is born.

One consequence of this evolutionary breakthrough was the construction of an inner representational world with a single centralized reality. What is functionally important for communication is that, together with the attribution of the signal to a specific organism, a centralized system was interposed between the sensorial impressions and the functional activity, thereby introducing a kind of *control* on the latter. Where there had been an automatic response to the signal, what now emerged was flexible behavior (which included inhibition of the action). This represents an initial phylogenetic draft of what in human terms is known as "the decision to act." The way this feature analysis system works is by extracting in an organized manner characteristics of different types, ranging from the most specific (color, silhouette, movement ...) to the most abstract (proximity/distance, similarity/dissimilarity, discontinuity ...) and integrating them all in a final perceptive construct, which is what is usually called a *representation*. Perception has definitively become a cognitive process guided by anticipations, expectations, and assessments, all of which condition the interaction.

Sociability, Cognition, and Communication

The selective ecological pressures that expanded perception towards cognition also had repercussions on sociability. Until this time, all animal social life even the most delicately articulated (that of eusocial insects), had been regulated by signals: olfactory (pheromones), tactile, visual, etc. The psychological construction of the alter – the emitter – presupposed a corresponding breakthrough in the relationship between the partners: *co-presence* becomes a *relationship* between individuals, each one invested with permanent individual qualities that guide the interaction. This gives rise to a social-relational order unheard of until this point in the phylogeny. All these advances initially occurred with the advent of the mammals and reach their zenith in the primates.

Ecological conditions intervened in the evolution towards a communal existence: principally the search for food and defense against predators. Social life – in family units or more extensive groups – offered immense advantages for individual survival. However, it also created the problems inherent in all collective living. This can be clearly seen in the primate species. For this reason Humphrey (1976) suggested that, besides natural intelligence – which primates do not exercise in excess given the stability of their life – a new form of social intelligence had appeared as a result of intense selective pressure. Differences of age and sex exist within the social group giving rise to a hierarchy of individuals each with their own idiosyncrasies. Cooperation (organizing defense and localizing resources, perhaps by way of signals) and competition (for food, sex, hierarchic position) are the typical ingredients of communal living. The larger the group, the more complex it is. According to Dunbar (1996), all this was translated into a new impulse towards encephalization

among the higher primates and, particularly, the hominids.[6]

Social life and communication are two sides of the same coin. The mechanisms that regulated one and the other are highly conditioned by cognition. The mental construction of "that other over there" gave rise, definitively in the primate species, to a situation in which each member of the group individually recognized the others and, in species with the most advanced social intelligence, each one with their particular idiosyncrasies. Monkeys and apes, moreover, know and exploit the relationships between others (third-party relationships) and this allows them to form alliances and calculate the best course to follow with respect to others depending on who their allies are. Friendships, complicity, reciprocal behavior are governed by a "record" that they retain in their memory of daily interactions. Primates are equipped with the capacity for *episodic memory*, that is memory that retains the representation of specific events – situated in a specific place and time – that occur in their daily lives (Donald, 1991).

Socialization is an ongoing process in primates. It acts through social apprenticeship: observation of others, reproduction of behavior (mimicking), trial and error in interactions, and group hierarchy. Companions are the principal source of stimuli and regulation of social behavior. The focusing of attention and learning on individuals potentiated the use of gestures as a means of communication. Postures (corporal attitudes) and facial expressions (supported by a much more refined set of muscles) are the components of this Gestalt we call display. If a primate learns from experience that a particular posture or gesture of a member of its own kind has a high probability of being followed by such and such an attack movement or acceptance of copulation, etc. it serves as an index that allows the animal – observer or receiver – to anticipate the behavior of the other.

The scientific literature relating to the study of primates is full of observations made in their natural habitat (in many cases corroborated by extraordinarily ingenious *in situ* experiments). Altogether, they constitute a fascinating view of the daily social life of the species, in particular the apes, which Tomasello and Call summarizes as follows:

> *'Primates' knowledge of individual group-mates and their various social relation-ships combined with a more generalized ability to comprehend the directedness of the behavior of others in particular situ-ations, makes for a highly complex social field. The combination of these two types of social knowledge is sufficient to enable an individual to determine such things as who it can and cannot attempt to mate with in the presence of which other indi-viduals; who knows where food is; who one can attempt to take food from in the presence of which other individuals; who is about to live the area; who will retaliate if a juvenile is attacked; who is likely to be a strong in a fight; where a frightening object or predator might be located; and who is likely to form an alliance against whom in the future. (Tomasello & Call, 1997, 205)*

One characteristic of primate social cognition is the strategies they use to achieve their ends in alliances, sexual activity, defense, enjoying food without sharing, and so on. The literature on primates is full of anecdotes and observations that illustrate such strategies. Menzel (1974) concealed food in front of one chimpanzee (Belle), who was then led back to her cage. For the first few days, Belle guided the other chim-panzees to the hiding place. However Rock, the dominant male, monopolized the food, pushing Belle away or biting her. On subse-quent occasions, Belle moved away from the hiding place darting back only when Rock was nowhere near. Rock counterattacked by controlling Belle with quick glances or by never leaving her alone. Belle ended up leading the group away from the place she knew the food to be concealed. De Waal (1982) described in great detail the strategies used by a male chimpanzee called Luit who allied himself with Nikkie and the females to 'depose' the leader Yeroen. A short time after this, Nikkie formed an alliance with the females and with Yeroen to dislodge Luit from the dominant position. Another oft cited example is the observation that when monkeys or apes manage to copulate with a female without the knowledge of the dom-inant male, they stifle the screeching cry that would normally accompany this activ-ity. And so on.

Some investigators define these strate-gies as deception or dissimulation. Oth-ers are of the opinion that such strate-gies can be adequately explained by mech-anisms of social learning. If they do rep-resent deception, this would immediately imply what is called "understanding of the other's mental states." To deceive is to lead the other to a false belief and this, by implication, postulates that the deceiver assumes that the other has beliefs (states of knowledge). In other words, the deceiver has a representation of the representations of the other: meta-representations. Primate literature talks about tactical deception, and Byrne and Whiten (1988) attribute (metaphorically) to these minds a Machi-avellian intelligence. The extension of this capacity to the human species falls into the domain of the "theory of mind."

However, do these strategic behaviors involve deception in the human sense of the word? Tomasello and Call (1997) discuss this in detail and maintain – apart from the fact that they represent only occasional epi-sodes – that there are alternative explana-tions. For example, when a male and a female suppress their cries during copulation, this may be because they have prior experience of the aggression they might suffer if they are seen by the dominant male (Premack 1988). In the case of Belle and Rock, it may be that the female learned from experience what Rock's usual reactions were in the pres-ence of food. Applying Occam's razor the rule could be:

1. There is an experience that if A behaves in a particular manner (x), B's subse-quent behavior (x') will have an adverse effect on or frustrate the aims of A. The behavior could then be explained by episodic memory.
2. A anticipates what B will do and does not engage in x while maintaining a

latent intention (plan) to proceed when there is no danger that *B* will prevent him. One important consideration is that, in some experimental situations, the "deceptive" behavior only emerged after many successive attempts, which is a model more like that of learning than a generalized ability to attribute intentions or beliefs. This kind of explanation would imply that primates are simple *behavior-readers*.

The other alternative is to see them as *mind-readers*, that is, individuals that have access to the states of mind of the other: intentions, desires, knowledge, and plans. Byrne and Whiten defend the thesis, at least with respect to the great apes, that these animals have some degree (no matter how small) of access to the minds of others; in other words, that they have the capacity of meta-representation. Tomasello and Call do not rule it out in some chimpanzees raised by humans because it appears to be evident from the way they react. This raises the intriguing problem of whether the "theory of mind" could progress from being a latent state to being activated in the situations of rich stimulation provided by exchange with humans. Fields, Segerdahl, and Savage-Rumbaugh (this volume, chapter 8) show to what extent a group of chimpanzees exposed to intensive contact with humans can develop communicative abilities (based on a proto-intersubjectivity; Perinat, 1993). But this does not presuppose that they have full access to the minds of their caregivers. Neither should we rule out, as Whiten said (1994), that there are grades of mind reading. Communication reaches a peak of collaboration in the species whose members are able to gain access to the minds of others.

Primate Communication

The repertoire of signals used by each primate species, while rather limited, is flexible: different signals can be used to achieve the same objective (in the same context) and, vice versa, the same signal can be used for different objectives (in different contexts). Some of the signals used by primates to regulate social behavior are part of their phylogenetic inheritance, for example, the erect hair of the apes in their aggressive displays, teeth baring, screams of pain or frustration, and so on. They are typical emotional signs. Jane Goodall reported that chimpanzees practically only emit vocalizations when they are emotionally excited (cited by Tomasello and Call, 1997). Our interest will be focused on the signals (gestures, vocalizations) that primates learn in the course of their development (ontogenetic ritualization) and exhibit later in their adult life.

The most typical gestural displays are the aggressive or intimidatory displays. These have been described. Apes very often display this behavior without any apparent immediate target. It can, therefore, be interpreted as a way of asserting the individual's hierarchical category. Chimpanzees have a gesture – called the begging gesture – that involves stretching out an open fisted hand palm upwards; this has different functions: asking for food, asking for grooming and also inviting a third-party to become an ally against an aggressor (De Waal, 1982). Another common gesture, not only among apes but also among baboons, is what is known as side-directed behavior: a female baboon harassed by a male moves towards the dominant male and moves her head looking alternately from one to the other. Young chimpanzees use typical gestures to invite a companion to play: raising one arm above its head, the young primate adopts an expectant posture while looking fixedly at the potential playmate.

Although the begging gesture and side directed behavior may very well be included in the higher category of requesting cooperation, they do occur in the context of social routines. Researchers have encouraged chimpanzees to cooperate with each other, which incidentally poses the problem of the exchange of signals needed to coordinate an action. Crawford in the 1940s and more recently Chalmeau (quoted by Tomasello & Call, 1997) designed the following situation. In front of the chimpanzees they set a box or food dispenser that can only be opened when both animals manipulate it simultaneously in a coordinated manner. After various failed attempts in the course of which each chimpanzee acted independently, they were given additional training and started to coordinate their activity: One waited until the other had a hand on the apparatus or else pulled its companion towards the box. The more well-trained of the two emitted vocalizations, touching its companion until the collaboration was achieved. In another experiment, chimpanzees trained by Savage-Rumbaugh to communicate using a keyboard (lexigrams) were put into two different cages constructed so that one of them had access to the food but could only obtain it using a key that had been given to the other. The chimpanzees used the keyboard intelligently to communicate and resolve the problem. (See Tomasello and Call, 1997, for details). What is extremely interesting is that the chimpanzees stimulated to manipulate the box in a coordinated manner in the first experiment and who managed to exchange signals in order to direct this task, were incapable of coordinating when faced with new tasks of a similar kind. Nor were the chimpanzees trained by Savage-Rumbaugh able to communicate with each other using their own natural means when the keyboard was removed. We will return later to this intriguing limitation.

When they discover food, the individuals of many primate species emit calls to attract the rest of the troop to the feeding place. Rhesus monkeys from Cayo Santiago have an additional peculiarity which is that they emit two different kinds of food calls depending on whether the food found is highly nutritious (such as coconuts) or not particularly valued (Hauser, 1996). In the case of alarm calls, the species that has been studied widely and in the greatest detail are the vervet monkeys (particularly those living in the Amboseli Park in Kenya) mentioned above. More details can be found in the interesting and exhaustive analysis published by Cheney and Seyfart (1990 and other publications) on this subject. The primates' repertoire of gestures and vocalizations are not limited to those discussed here. However, those discussed above are sufficient for the purposes of comparing this signaling behavior with that of humans.

Animal Communication and Human Communication

Human communication is the inevitable reference point for the study of animal communication in general. We explain animal communication in terms of our (psychological) concepts and language. This places us in a serious dilemma: on the one hand we distort the phenomena; on the other we run the risk of banalizing the concepts when they are applied analogically to the animal psyche. Extreme *epistemological caution* must be exercised when analyzing nonhuman communication.

As I stated at the outset, the problem of detecting and decoding signals must be separated from the question of communication per se. In the case of human communication, however, information and communication are inextricably fused to such a degree that it could be said that a human communicates solely to send messages. However, many communicative situations contain little or no actual informative content for example, lovers' conversations or exchanges between a mother and her baby. Nevertheless it could be argued that, even in such situations the listener apprehends the personal feelings and mood of the speaker. In primates, and particularly humans, the musculature of the face has evolved to express a wide range of emotions. These facial expressions are *signals* that serve to regulate social contacts (Trevarthen, 1984). Moreover, in communicative exchanges it is possible that one party may intentionally produce signals to influence the other: facial forms that express doubt or distrust, gestures that indicate a change of turn, and so on. It is even possible that inhibiting a signal could be a way of communicating rejection or indifference to the other party. In short, in the context of human communication, expressive signals not only carry large amounts of information but are also a resource used to intentionally and explicitly transmit mental states.

The level of cognitive (or psychological, or nervous system) processing is crucial when we are distinguishing between degrees of communication. This is what I was indicating when I mentioned the fundamental breakthroughs that have occurred in the course of the evolution of the perceptive-cognitive apparatuses. It is evident that communication based on sign-stimuli causing fixed action patterns differs radically from that of animals capable of incorporating representations of individuals and situations in their mental apparatus. I have suggested that when evolution endows the animal psyche with mental representation, communication undergoes a Copernican revolution. Reaching the level of human communication implies an even higher level: when we communicate we have access to the representations of the people we are communicating with, those they tell us about and those that we attribute to them hypothetically. This is an ability only barely hinted at in primate communication. We transmit/exchange mental representations. This is what Johnson-Laird says in his definition of human communication: "Communication is a matter of causal influence . . . The communicator must construct an internal representation of the external world and then . . . carry out some symbolic behavior that conveys the content of that representation. The recipient must first perceive the symbolic behavior and then from it recover a further internal representation of the state that it signifies" (quoted by Hauser, 1996). This representation has two faces: the *content* and the *intention* that R will recognize this content. Correlatively, the recipient must recognize both things. In apes, the gesture is the vehicle for the content of the representation. The interplay of intentions is more problematic. As can be seen, we are constantly approaching the boundaries of the theory of mind. Is there any opening in this barrier for monkeys and apes? Whatever the case is with these animals, we conclude

that access to representations of the other (and intention includes representation of the objective) constitutes a major milestone in communication.

If we move on to the question of the social regulation which, thanks to communication, is established within the group, we will have to establish some additional conditions. When, for example, the dominant male displays, we suppose that animals X, Y, and Z who are present realize, each one independently, what his plans and intentions are. Do X, Y, and Z know that each one of the others is aware? If the display is aggressive and all the animals escape by getting out of the way, we may conclude that they do. In the case of other kinds of displays with more subtle effects, we cannot be sure that this is the case. Overall, the hypothesis that the relationship between third parties is accessible within the troop of primates leads us to believe that the communicative traffic between two partners gives rise to a representation shared by all the others who observe the exchange. If this were the case, it could be concluded that a fabric of shared representations exists that forms the basis of the regulation of relations within the group. By the same token, shared representations make possible a more efficient kind of communication, potentiating cooperation among other things. In order for concerted action to take place, a shared definition of the situation has to exist: A knows what is required (what it intends to do, anticipates the plan), B also knows the plan. Moreover, A knows that B knows, and vice versa. Furthermore, in order to execute a concerted action some prior signal is needed before the action is undertaken. We have already made the point that this does not happen.

In the literature on animal communication, the concept of *reference* is sometimes slipped in a propos of the dances of bees or the calls of the vervet monkey. There was a time when ethologists had no qualms asserting that these signals were referential. Today they are more cautious in their positions. In order to resolve this question, we must define what it means to "refer to something," although this can only be done on the basis of our human use of language. The reference is like an arrow that points to something. The emitter makes a reference in order to produce a state of knowledge in the receiver by way of a linguistic "text" (code). A signal is not enough. The reference is produced in the context of an intentional communicative act. The receiver recognizes that what is emitted is the representation (of the state of things) evoked by the emitter. Moreover, it is an intersubjective or intermental act of communication. One of its functions is to share representations or meanings.

If we accept this set of conditions, reference is immediately excluded in the case of the bees in spite of the great sophistication of their dance. For the human observer, the bee "points" at an external state of things, but we would never seriously attribute representational and intentional states to the order of insects even allowing (generously) that the worker bee's dance is a code. And the vervet monkeys? Here we will have to argue our case more carefully. The fact that the monkey's alarm calls are different depending on whether the predator is a leopard, an eagle, or a snake can be explained parsimoniously by social learning during early development. In fact there is fairly convincing evidence that this is the case. Cheney and Seyfart (1990) describe the learning process in detail, reporting trials and errors in the alarm calling of young vervet monkeys. At first, these young animals emit many alarm calls at the approach of different animals and even when startled by hanging branches (snakes), but later they start to restrict such calls to actual predators. The association between the appropriate call and the predators is reinforced by very subtle signs coming from the other members of the group. For example, if the apprentice emits the appropriate call in the presence of an eagle, the call is taken up by the others. However, if the young monkey is mistaken, the call is not echoed by its companions. Moreover, Cheney and Seyfart demonstrated using a hidden microphone that the flight reaction of the young monkeys occurred after they saw what the adults were doing, especially the mothers.

However, although the calls effectively evoke the image of the leopard, the snake, or the eagle, we cannot conclude (rather the contrary) that the vervets produce these vocalizations *in order to* evoke this representation, that is, in order to refer to the predators. This would involve attributing to them the intention of creating a state of knowledge. In other words, for there to be reference is not enough that the vervet monkey emit a call so that the others will seek safety, but rather that the call is made *so that the others will know* that there is a leopard, an eagle, or a snake in the vicinity (and that they will consequently seek safety). Today, ethologists accept that the alarm calls of vervet monkeys (and other equivalent phenomena) are only *functionally referential*. A final argument that would destroy the hypothesis that they are referential is the comparative analysis of their ontogenesis in human infants. Space does not, however, permit us to discuss this argument here. This subject is discussed in detail in the context of language acquisition (see, for example, Bruner 1974/75, Perinat, 1986, 1993, 2001).

Finally, I will touch on a rarely discussed topic: the motivation for communicating. In a research project carried out with small gorillas born and raised in captivity (Perinat & Dalmau, 1988; Perinat, 1993), our aim was to compare these animals' communication with that of children and adults engaged in manipulative games (joint action formats to use Bruner's term). For a year and a half, in various observations, we did not manage to record even one shared manipulation (and even less so anything like a game) in spite of the encouragement of caregivers.[7] Nor did we observe any instances of joint attention. Obviously this is not due to the primate's lack of manual dexterity. Reviewing the studies in the field, we noticed that the objects the primates manipulate are branches, sometimes stones, and that manipulation always occurs in connection with food (fishing for termites, cracking nuts) or defense. Likewise, their communicative signals are produced in contexts involving the primary motivations (hunger, sex, aggression-defense) or social intercourse engaged in to satisfy these needs. There is, however, an extension of the primate motivational system towards motor play, which is an innovative source of signaling (Bateson, 1955/1972). The manipulative play does not exist (even involving a single animal) in the gorillas' natural environment.

Our conjecture is that the motivation for concerted action (and consequently for the signaling that establishes the action) is originally subject to the motivation to implement plans of action that revolve around satisfying primary needs. When compared to that of humans, the primate hand has a more limited *psychological field of manipulation of objects*. Communication has not colonized the domain of manual actions. One consequence of this is that coordination is rare in this context. The theory that the mind of monkeys and apes is modularized postulates that in these species the module controlling interaction with the living environment (the natural history module) and the module controlling social life are still closed off one from the other (Mithen, 1996).

At some point in the course of evolution from apes to humans the mastery motivation system expanded thereby facilitating cooperative exploitation of the environment. One aspect of this breakthrough was the innovative use of instruments. The cognitive, social, and communicative systems forged new links that furthered advances in all three systems. In this scenario, cooperation within the family nucleus also received a new impulse to which "the nature and uses of immaturity" of the human infant contributed (Bruner, 1972). The way children depend on adults, their aptitude for social and communicative learning take on a new sense in a phylogenetic context in which concerted action was already playing a driving role in the process of hominization. The cognitive, psychomotor, and motivational systems of apes could have been preadaptations in the Darwinian sense. What was necessary were morphogenetic transformations of the central nervous system to establish connections between all three systems. This would have given rise not only to the creation of a new cognitive schema –

that of the "object-to-be-manipulated" – but also, based on the empathetic relationship between the adult and the child, cooperative play and learning actions would have taken shape, affording the child the benefit of the adult's teaching. At this point, we are talking about nothing more or less than the dawn of culture. All this must have led to the explosion in communicative forms (prelinguistic) seen today in childhood.

In Principio Erat Signum

In the course of this chapter, I have attempted to avoid the term/concept of the sign. Now, however, is the moment to introduce this concept and, incidentally, it will become clear how and why the sign is the opposite of the signal. According to Peirce "a sign or representamen is something which stands to somebody for something in some respect or capacity." As is well known, Peirce posited a distinction between three kinds of sign: icon, index, and symbol. It is important to emphasize that the sign is a sign "for somebody"; it is a *triadic* relationship. In developing his concept of the sign, Peirce used the human mind as a reference. Likewise, the background is human communication. Here – and only here – the relationship between the interpreter and the producer of the sign is intersubjective. However, since this is a purely formal definition, it can be extended to the animal mind and animal communication.

The higher mammals (monkeys and apes) are capable of using signs or, at least, indexes. The vervet monkeys in Amboseli Park have been traditionally harassed and hunted by the Masai people. The Masai bring their herds to graze in the park. The vervets learned to flee from the herders when they heard the animals lowing. Intimidatory and precopulatory postures are also indexes. However, the crucial question is not whether primates recognize indexes (which they do) or any kind of signs *but rather whether they are capable of creating them*. The human mind is capable of *recognizing and creating signs*, whether indexes, icons, or symbols. This is a threshold that has not been crossed by the primate animal mind. The sign is the supreme invention of the human mind. Language is a special kind of sign. Some primate signs belong to the phylogenetic heritage, others originate in intention movements, and others have been assimilated during the animal's development (ontogenetic ritualization). A special case that might fit in here is the assimilation by apes reared by humans of certain signs typical of our species, such as pointing. However, on balance, the ape repertoire is extremely limited and, what is more, no spontaneous incorporation of new signs has ever been observed. Nor have the chimpanzees trained to use lexigrams or American Sign Language ever been observed to create new signs. Moreover, only on very rare occasions have such animals used any of the signs learned from humans to communicate among themselves. Remember that the chimpanzees who were encouraged to open boxes by coordinating manual actions had to be trained to exchange signs. Furthermore, when they were subsequently presented with different tasks requiring coordinated action they were incapable of using these signs (or others). One of the reasons for this is that the chimpanzee's memory is purely episodic so that the use of a sign is memorized as a component part of an event. When the scenario changes, the same sign is not recovered in the new context.

There are, however, anecdotal reports of episodes in which the genesis of a new sign can be glimpsed. D. Fossey reported that a female (Effie) from the group of gorillas she studied was injured in a fight. Her daughter Tuck usually moved to her side to lick her wounds. "The young female would go to her mother and pivot her head around so rapidly that my own eyes could barely follow the motions. After nearly a minute of head twirling, Tuck would begin grooming the wounds intently" (Fossey, 1982: 89). The question we ask is whether Tuck was inventing a sign to initiate an action not included in the usual repertoire. Could this anomalous gesture have been an expression of her intention to do something to alleviate her mother's pain? Or perhaps she did it to fore-

stall any brusque reaction from Effie when she touched her wounds. The conjecture is that Tuck improvised a sign that announced the activity that would follow immediately. De Waal (1982) also mentions observing some idiosyncratic gestures in chimpanzees in Arnhem Zoo. Another exception that confirms the rule is the sentence-like combination of lexigrams created spontaneously by bonobo apes to communicate with their caregivers (Savage-Rumbaugh, Murphy, Sevcic, Brakke, Williams, and Rumbaugh, 1993, chap. 8). This behavior opens up the possibility of the monkeys creating new signs using the basic vocabulary units they have learned. To what extent these sequences of signs can be called 'sentences' or represent the threshold of syntactically correct language is, however, quite a different question.

These are exceptional cases, but they do prefigure the explosion of the sign that occurred in humans. Compare these anecdotes with another case also described by De Waal. The trees in Arnhem zoo were surrounded by an electric fence in order to prevent the chimpanzees from climbing them and eating the leaves. One of the chimpanzees devised a way to climb unscathed into the lower branches by dragging a log to the tree and leaning it on the wire. In a film the chimpanzee can be seen positioning the log and trying to climb into the tree. He fails miserably until another chimpanzee holds the trunk steady for him. However, the climbing chimpanzee has not signaled to request the help of his companion. The second animal's help was given spontaneously after the first chimpanzee's intention movement revealed his plan.

This episode suggests an interesting extension of this line of thought. The same schemas that initiate the action (and afford the onlookers an idea of the plan) we humans can turn into communicative acts by "representing" them (as theatre) and directing the display towards the other while letting him know that he is being addressed. We could speculate that at first the same action, to which is added a signal directed at the other, was the way of proceeding. A later step was to merge the communicative and executive functions in the mime of the representation (drama) transmitting the intention of carrying out the action and inciting the other to join in the action. Now is when the action became an *utterance*. For example, the leader of the troop starts to move, walks a little, stops and waits a moment, looks at the others, moves on, and so on. Could this have been one of the ways by which the sign was inserted into activity or split away from it? This process occurs in the ontogeny of infant communication (Clark, 1978). Merlin Donald (1991) situates it at some point in cognitive evolution between the apes and the emergence of Homo Sapiens. His hypothesis is that, before language – a somewhat tardy arrival on the scene – there must have existed a gestural mode of communication much more advanced than that of our predecessors. Homo, possibly in the Erectus stage, developed the capacity to produce, creatively and intentionally, corporal configurations that translated internal representations into external expressions (mimes). The utility of this new ability in communication and the construction of tools is obvious (although convenient post hoc arguments are never definitive). It is perhaps more convincing to investigate the vestiges and subsequent developments of that capacity in representative art: mime, dance, and ritual. A large number of vocal and postural communications are iconic signs, and their relationship with mimesis is obvious. A specific example is onomatopoeia.

There have been heated debates on the question of whether apes do or do not use symbols in their communication with humans. A symbol is certainly a signifier or a sign: it refers to or substitutes for something else. If we confine ourselves to this formal characteristic, we will conclude happily that the chimpanzee's use of a token or a manual gesture to "mean/signify" banana or other object is equivalent to using a symbol. What must be argued is that a symbol is not merely something that stands for something even when we add that the operation of "standing for" is arbitrary and conventional (terms that

are not synonymous). The symbol is not a rigid signifier but rather something tremendously flexible and ductile. The symbol is arbitrary and conventional because the person who creates it or interprets it can restrict, extend, or remodel its meaning, and can do this creatively in the knowledge that he will be understood. The reason for this is that symbols are inlays embedded in the social fabric of shared meanings (culture). At the same time, the conventionality of the symbol supposes, in the act of its creation, a social intervention, and this is how we connect with its communicative roots: the symbol is born in communication and for communication.

To this theoretical prolegomenon we could add an analysis of how children move little by little, communicating, into the world of symbols (see Perinat, 1993, 1995a, 1995b). But I will condense the discussion by adducing two arguments which in my opinion are definitive. Deacon (1997) put his finger on the heart of the question when he reviewed the studies carried out by the Rumbaughs with their chimpanzees Austin and Sherman. The chimpanzees were initially trained to associate lexigrams with food. The basis of the operation – supposedly symbolic – was that the lexigram stood for the banana or the juice. Lexigrams indicating giving or requesting actions were then added. The animals were then trained to construct noun-verb 'phrases' to request food items. Once this had been achieved, they were encouraged to use the lexigrams in the presence of food items. When the chimpanzees were faced with a certain number of name and verb lexigrams (although limited), the results were chaotic: they combined more than two lexigrams (banana juice give) or two names or two verbs. In a second, extremely laborious, experiment, the Rumbaughs trained the chimpanzees to eliminate the forbidden combinations from their "language." They managed to do this. The chimpanzees learned the primary immediate relationship between the lexigrams and the items, and subsequently that there were other relationships of a higher order between the lexigrams (functionally "words") that governed how they could be combined (something they had not been capable of deducing themselves). Even with a very limited set of token-words and on the basis of training this was an impressive intellectual achievement. What underlies this logical-cognitive operation of combination-exclusion that we humans perform with the words we use?

The key point of Deacon's argument is that the referent (or meaning) to which a symbol points is not wholly encompassed by the fact that the symbol stands for an item but also derives from the fact that the symbols (signifiers) *are related one to another*. The symbols are the knots in the interwoven tissue of meanings that exists within every social group. We grasp the meaning of the symbol precisely because of its "networked" interdependence with all other symbols in a culture. Indeed, culture can be understood as a "symbolic universe." The constitution of the symbolic referent involves two simultaneous operations on different levels: the relationship between the symbol-token and the thing symbolized, and the interrelation between symbols (the network they form). With respect to chimpanzees, Deacon observes that "this shift is initially a change in mnemonic strategy." It is much more, and here we find the second argument. To reveal a second-order relationship is a *recursive operation*, which I postulate represents an impassable frontier in the non-human mind. Recursivity exists because the (human) mind discovers a *relationship of relationships*: the relationship between the symbols which, on another level, are relationships between the symbol and the symbolized. This explains precisely why human language is inaccessible to chimpanzees notwithstanding the highly commendable efforts of the researchers. Although their highly stimulated chimpanzees exhibit quasi-linguistics abilities (Bates, 1993), the comprehension capacity of these animals is limited and their utterances take the form of strings of the basic signs or tokens they have learned, but are devoid of syntax. Their achievements represent a notable performance but cannot be called language sensu stricto because recursivity lies at the core of language. A sentence is not just a carefully regulated combination of words. In a sentence, each word has to be adjusted to those that precede it and those that follow it and, finally, it closes in on itself: the *clause*. The sentence is a relationship between parts that are related one to another in turn. The origin of all "meta" operations is recursivity: meta-representation,[8] meta-cognition, meta-language, and so on. It is profoundly tied up with symbolic play (another behavior out of the reach of chimpanzees). It lies at the heart of consciousness as a mode of introspection. It is the ultimate evolutionary cognitive breakthrough, which has made it possible for language to evolve.

In conclusion, the advent of the sign opened the way towards language. Recursivity – a capacity inherent in syntax – is one of the later milestones in this trajectory. Midway, other crucial processes had to be set in motion to give shape to language as we know it today. Some of these were purely anatomical (neuronal, laryngeal-articulatory, phonatory), while others were psychological (representational, symbolic, intersubjective, and memory capacities), or structural linguistic. As is the rule in all emerging processes, there is a mutual circular relationship that connects them all. Paleoanthropologists, neuroscientists, and evolutionary psychologists toil together on the arduously interdisciplinary task of assembling in the axis of prehistoric times all the pieces of this puzzle in order to discover more about the birth of this fascinating creature – the language that makes us human.

Acknowledgments

I am most grateful to Dr. Josep Call, researcher at the Max Planck Institute for Evolutionary Anthropology, for his comments on the first version of this chapter.

Notes

1   *Biosemiotics* and its subdisciplines, *Ecosemiotics* and *Zoosemiotics* study the functional

relationships between signals and life in all its dimensions. See Sebeok (1972, 2001), Nöth (1990, 1998).

2 The male chimpanzee's aggressive display is an intimidatory postural configuration. The animal's hair stands erect, he emits a series of loud hoots, charges his adversary or the group, runs from one side to another, and bangs on any objects in his way.

3 The number of genes an individual transfers to the following generation as the direct or indirect result of reproduction.

4 Homologies occur when the similarity between a characteristic (morphologic or behavioral) found in two species is due to the fact that they share a common ancestor. When the similarity is the result of convergent evolution, that is, when ecological conditions give rise to the same solution in taxonomically distinct species it is called a homoplasy or analogy. The term anagenesis includes more or less explicitly the concept of progress or improvement in a structure throughout a phylogenetic lineage. For a more detailed discussion of these terms see Hodos & Campbell, 1969, 1990.

5 It is not a general rule that later forms are invariably more advanced than earlier ones because whether a species is more or less complex depends on the problems that it faces, not on the time that it has been evolving. For instance, some animals have lost vision because they live underground; dogs have experienced a 15–20% reduction in their brain size compared to wolves of the same body size.

6 Dunbar found a positive correlation among primates between the size of the social group and relative neocortex size. He later specified that it was not the number of individuals in the group that correlated but rather the quality of their relationships. The quality of these bonds can be seen in the coalitions that form within the group evaluated by way of grooming behavior – "I'll scratch your back, you scratch mine." He concluded that gossip could be a functional equivalent in humans to grooming among primates, a hypothesis supported by the importance given to daily conversation for the cohesion of relationships within a group.

7 Other authors (Gómez, 1989) have managed to get gorillas bred in captivity to perform some manipulations with objects. It is well know that the intensity and fre-

quency of interactions between apes and their human caretakers awakens virtual abilities (see Chapter 8). An interesting question is whether apes can achieve any extension of the *psychological field* that circumscribes the use of their hands. The same question arises in the case of language.

8 If, as suggested here, the higher and general capacity of recursivity is an impassable boundary for the higher primates, metarepresentation and the theory of mind would be typically and exclusively human.

References

Altmann, S. A., (Ed.), (1967). *Social Communication among Primates*. Chicago: The University of Chicago Press.

Bates, E. (1993). Comprehension and Production in Early Language Development. *Monographs of the SRCD*, 58: Nos. 3–4.

Bateson, G. (1955/1972). A Theory of Play and Fantasy. In G. Bateson. *Steps to an Ecology of Mind*. New York: Ballantine.

Bruner, J. (1972). The Nature and Uses of Immaturity. *American Psychologist*, 27: 1–22.

Bruner, J. (1974/1975). From Communication to Language. A Psychological Perspective. *Cognition*, 3: 255–87.

Byrne, R. W. & Whiten, A., (Eds.), (1988). *Machiavellian Intelligence*. Oxford University Press.

Cheney, D. L. & Seyfart, R. M. (1990). *How Monkeys See the World*. Chicago: The University of Chicago Press.

Cherry, C. (1957). *On Human Communication*. Cambridge, MA: M.I.T. Press.

Clark, R. A. (1978). The Transition from Action to Gesture. In A. Lock., (Ed.), *Action, Gesture and Symbol*. London: Academic Press.

Dawkins, R. & Krebs, J. R. (1978). Animal signals: Information or Manipulation?. In J. R. Krebs & N. B. Davies., (Eds.), *Behavioural Ecology. An Evolutionary Approach*. Oxford: Blackwell.

De Waal, F. (1982). *Chimpanzee Politics*. Baltimore: The John Hopkins University Press.

Deacon, T. W. (1997). *The Symbolic Species*. New York: Norton.

Donald, M. (1991). *Origins of Modern Mind*. Cambridge MA: Harvard University Press.

Dunbar, R. (1996). *Grooming, gossip and the evolution of language*. Cambridge, MA: Harvard University Press.

Fossey, D. (1982). *Gorillas in The Mist*. London: Hodder & Stoughton.

Gomez, J. C. (1989). La comunicación y la mani-pulación de objetos en crías de gorila. *Estudios de Psicología*, 38: 11–128.

Green, S. & Marler, P. (1979). The Analysis of Animal Communication. In P. Marler & J. G. Vanderberg., (Eds.), *Handbook of Behavioral Neurobiology*, Vol 3. Social Behavior and Communication. New York: Plenum Press.

Guildford, T. & Dawkins, M. S. (1991). Receiver Psychology and the Evolution of Animal Signals, *Animal Behavior*, 42: 1–14.

Hauser, H. D. (1996). *The Evolution of Communication*. Cambridge, MA: MIT Press.

Hinde, R. A. (1981). Animal Signals: Ethological and Games Theory are not Incompatible. *Animal Behavior*. 29:535–42.

Hodos, W. & Campbell, C. B. G. (1969). Scala Nature: Why is no Theory in Comparative Psychology. *Psychological Review*, 76: 337–50.

Hodos, W. & Campbell, C. B. G. (1990). Evolutionary Scales and Comparative Studies of Animal Cognition. In R. P. Kesner & D.S. Olton., (Eds.), *Neurobiology of Comparative Cognition*. Hillsdale, NJ: Erlbaum.

Hoffmeyer, J. (1997). The global semiosphere. In Rauch, I. & Carr, G. F. (Eds.), *Semiotics around the world*. Vol 2. Berlin: Mouton de Gruyter.

Humphrey, N. K. (1976). The Social Function of Intellect. In P. P. G. Bateson & R. A. Hinde., (Eds.), *Growing Points in Ethology.*Cambridge University Press.

Jerison, H. J. (1973). *Evolution of the Brain and Intelligence*. New York: Academic Press.

Kull, K. (2001). Jacob von Uexküll: an introduction. *Semiotica*, 134: 1–59.

Kummer, H. (1968). *Social Organization of Hamadryas Baboons*. Chicago: University of Chicago Press.

MacKay, D. M. (1972). Formal Analysis of Communicative Processes. In R. A. Hinde, (Ed.), *Non Verbal Communication*. Cambridge University Press.

Marshall, J. C. (1970). The Biology of Communication in Man and Animals. In J. Lyons., (Ed.), *New Horizons in Linguistics*. Penguin Books.

Menzel, E. (1974). A Group of Chimpanzees in a 1-acre Field: Leadership and Communication. Repr. In R. W. Byrne & A. Whiten., (Eds.), 1988. *Machiavellian Intelligence.*Oxford University Press.

Mithen, S. (1996). *The Prehistory of Mind*. London: Thames & Hudson.

Morris, D. (1957). 'Typical Intensity' and its Relation to the Problem of Ritualisation. *Behaviour*, 11: 1–12.

Nöth, W. (1990). *Handbook of Semiotics*. Bloomington: Indiana University Press.

Nöth, W. (1998). Ecosemiotics. *Signs System Studies*, 26: 332–343.

Perinat, A. (1986). *La Comunicación Preverbal*. Barcelona: Avesta.

Perinat, A. (1993). *Comunicación Animal, Comunicación Humana*. Madrid: Siglo XXI.

Perinat, A. (1995a). Prolegómenos para una Teoría del Juego y del Símbolo. *Cognitiva*, 7: 185–256.

Perinat, A. (1995b). 'Juguemos a llamar por teléfono'. Juego Simbólico y Procesos Recursivos en la Interacción Comunicativa. *Substratum*, 3: 77–102.

Perinat, A. (2001). *Psicología del Desarrollo. Un Enfoque Sistémico*. Barcelona: Ediuoc.

Perinat, A. y Dalmau, A. (1988). La Comunicación entre Pequeños Gorilas y sus Cuidadoras. *Estudios de Psicología*, 33–34: 11–29.

Premack, D. (1988). "Does the Chimpanzee have a Theory of Mind" Revisited. In R. W. Byrne & A. Whiten., (Eds.), *Machiavellian Intelligence*. Oxford University Press.

Ristau, C. (1991). *Cognitive Ethology: the Minds of other Animals*. Hillsdale, NJ: Erlbaum.

Savage-Rumbaugh, S., Murphy, J., Sevcic, R. A., Brakke, K. E., Williams, S.L., and Rumbaugh, D. M. (1993). Language comprehension in ape and child. *Monographs of the SRCD*, 58: Nos. 3–4.

Sebeok, T. A. (1968). *Animal Communication*. Bloomington: Indiana University Press.

Sebeok, T. A. (1972). *Perspectives in Zoosemiotics*. Paris: Mouton

Sebeok, T. A. (1977). *How Animals Communicate*. Bloomington: Indiana University Press.

Sebeok, T. A. (2001). Biosemiotics: its roots, proliferation and prospects. *Semiotica*, 134: 61–78.

Sjölander, S. (1997). On the Evolution of Reality – Some Biological Prerequisites and Evolutionary Stages. *Journal of Theoretical Biology*, 187: 595–600.

Smith, W. J. (1977). *The Behaviour of Communicating: An Ethological Approach*. Cambridge MA: Harvard University Press.

Struhsaker, T. T. (1967). Auditory Communication among Vervet Monkeys (Cercopitecus aethiops). In S. T. Altmann, (Ed.), *Social Communication among Primates*. Chicago: The University of Chicago Press.

Tinbergen, N. (1951). *The Study of Instinct*. Oxford University Press.

Tomasello, M. & Call, J. (1997). *Primate Cognition*. Oxford University Press.

Trevarthen, C. (1984). Emotions in Infancy: Regulators of Contact and Relationships with Persons. In K. Sherer & P. Ekman., (Eds.), *Approaches to Emotion*. Hillsdale, NJ: Erlbaum.

Uetz, G. W. & Roberts, J. A. (2002). Multisensory Cues and Multimodal Communication in Spiders. *Brain, Behavior and Evolution*, 59: 222–230.

Van Hooff, J. A. R. A. M. (1972). A Comparative Approach to the Phylogeny of Laughter and Smiling. In R. A. Hinde., (Ed.), *Non Verbal Communication*. Cambridge University Press.

Von Frisch, K. (1954). *The Danzing bees: An account of the Life and Senses of the Honey Bee*. London: Methuen.

Von Hofsten, C. (1986). The Emergence of Manual Skills. In M. G. Wade & T. A. Whiting., (Eds.), *Motor Development in Children*. The Hague: Nijhoff Publ.

Von Uexküll, J. (1956). *Mondes animaux, monde humain*. Paris: Gonthier.

Whiten, A. (1994). Grades of Mindreading. In C. Lewis & P. Mitchell., (Eds.), *Children's early Understanding of Mind*. Hillsdale, NJ: Erlbaum.

Wilson, E. O. (1975). *Sociobiology*. Cambridge, MA: Harvard University Press.

CHAPTER 8

The Material Practices of Ape Language Research

William Mintz Fields, Pär Segerdahl,
and Sue Savage-Rumbaugh

This chapter is about a special population of non-human primates whose abilities and social competencies deserve the attention of cultural studies. Our contribution arises from a long-term investigation of language, culture, and tools in a society of bonobos (*Pan paniscus*) having lived in Decatur, Georgia for the last 25 years. Their names are Kanzi (25), Panbanisha (19), Nyota (7), Nathan (4), Matata (36), Elikya, Maisha (9), and P-Suke (28). In offering our essay to socio-cultural perspectives, we hope, without too strong a challenge to the human-focused goals of socio-cultural psychology, to enrich the multidisciplinary struggle "to explicate the relationships between human [and non-human great ape] action, on the one hand, and the cultural, institutional, and historical situations in which this action occurs on the other" (Wertsch, del Rio & Alvarez, 1996: 11). We seek to innovate emphasizing ethnographic facts of a Pan/Homo society that speak to the socio-historical heritage of Soviet psychology spearheaded by Vygotsky, Leont'ev, and Luria and highlighting the cognitive con-

tinuum of great apes as envisioned by Darwin – and diminishing the emphasis upon the often dramatic but non-useful bipolar debates between linguists and behaviorists. As Denzin reminds us, "theory, writing, and ethnography are inseparable material practices. Together they create the conditions that locate the social inside the text. Those who write ethnography also write theory" (1997: 5). Our goal is to inform culture theory based upon the empirical and ethnographic facts of ape language research.

Background

The history of Ape Language Research (ALR) is a long and exciting one, approaching nearly 100 years of research and intense controversy. Controversy, which to modern sensibilities, is favorably multi-inter-trans-disciplinarian. The multi-disciplinary nature of ALR is its unharvested strength, as its historical practice may be characterized as a hosts of many disciplines talking past one another – linguistics, American psychology, experimental psychology, comparative psychology, behaviorism, paleoanthropology, cultural anthropology, darwinists, neo-darwinists, sociobiology, and primatology, have collided into a stew of definitions, methods, and politics, reacting to the nature versus nurture polarity in rather dramatic and overheated debate. As Premack commented in 1986, "since animal language controversy was blessed with virtually all the classic elements – genetics versus experience, language – specific versus general intelligence, rationalism versus empiricism . . . animal language inquiry ha[s] more to gain from epistemology and philosophy of language than from linguistics" (p. 12). Simply framing the question between either "meaning and truth" or "intentionality and belief" can cause quite a stir. Premack's foresight is pragmatic. His comments reflect an understanding of the problem of the basic first-cause conflict that is operating among the disciplines throughout the academy. Where the school of Vygotsky could have offered some help, a return to an American psychology was underway in the 1960s and the disciplines were too new to be settled beyond political contests.

The significant and critical themes of Vygotsky's theoretical framework offers ape language an important structure: social interactions play a fundamental role in the development of cognition and "that all higher functions originate as actual relationships between individuals." While Vygotsky is talking exclusively about humans, the social development of great apes, within the continuum of evolutionary precepts begs the question: can Vygotskian thought be applied to social groups of chimpanzees? Or to an experimental laboratory society of chimpanzees and humans which features cross fostering of species? One cannot escape the notion of Vygotsky's zone of proximal development (ZPD) and the implications of retrofitting this concept to the work of Itard, Squires, or Kellogg. To the extent that "every function in the child's life development appears twice: first on the social level, and later, on the individual level; first between

people and then inside the child," and thus, "consciousness is an end product of socialization," has enormously broad implications for humanly enculturated non-human primates or canidly enculturated humans (1978: 57).

The ALR of Rumbaugh and Savage-Rumbaugh over the last 35 year has produced strikingly different results than other ALR initiatives. Why the difference in scientific outcomes? The question is based upon two ideas: (1) Chimpanzees are biological preparations to the extent they are products of genes. And therefore, their behavior is genetically telegraphed to expression or (2) behavior can be learned through laboratory techniques of teaching – and learning is controlled by genes. And therefore, chimpanzees in research, zoos, human homes, and the wild are categorically chimpanzees, cognitively equal and the same no matter their cultural origins, pre-and post-natal ontogenies, or the nature of their specific ZPD. Most critical to the discussion of the differences among great apes is Vygotsky's principle, "cognitive development is limited to a certain range at any given age" (1994: 1). This human principle of development is consistent with findings of Kellogg (1931) and Savage-Rumbaugh et al. (1993) regarding non-human development: there exists a critical period in primate development which has lifelong consequences in the individual and thus, the maturing and learning potentials of the individual. If Darwin was a child developmentalist, he would expect to find – the continuum of human and non-human primate cognitive development approximately equates to the biological evolutionary continuum of blood, bone, and tissue across the species.

In the 1980s, while other ALR scientists announced failures, the chimpanzee and bonobo research at Georgia State University (GSU) moved prolifically forward with a variety of successes. The research of Rumbaugh and Savage-Rumbaugh has empirically demonstrated that some apes at the LRC possess the capacity to comprehend spoken English (Savage-Rumbaugh et al., 1993); use symbols to express ideas;

to use grammar and syntax receptively and productively (Rumbaugh, 1977; Savage-Rumbaugh, 1993); to produce Oldowan stone tools (Toth, Schick, Savage-Rumbaugh, Sevcik, & Rumbaugh, 1993); and to vocally speak certain English words (Taglialatela & Savage-Rumbaugh, 2000 Taglialatela, Savage-Rumbaugh, & Baker, 2003). More recently, work underway by Savage-Rumbaugh points to Dennett's question, such that some apes have the capacity to autobiographically report "beliefs and desires about beliefs and desires" and some apes make ethical choices based upon moral rules. One should notice the phrase *some apes.*[1]

Herein lies a critical factor as to why research results varies so dramatically from one chimpanzee lab to another. *Some apes possess the cultural competence for language, culture, and tools. Nature does not provide these competencies.* Only the nurture of enculturation can empower the individual with the cognitive tools upon which human-like language and tools are emergent. So the question arises; how are non-human apes humanly enculturated? The answer is simple: by raising baby chimpanzees as if they are human children. In 1931, Kellogg demonstrated this in his study of *The Ape and Child,* at Orange Park, Florida, where he conducted a co-rearing study of chimpanzee Gua and his human son Donald. The idea and rationale for the research arose from an article describing two young girls in India who were living with animals in the wild. The case and investigative *seque-lae* were published in the *American Journal of Psychology* by Squires in 1927. Kellogg describes it this way:

> Similar to Itard's "wild boy of Aveyron," the wild children were two young girls found in a cave inhabited by wolves. These children behaved as though they were wolves, eating, and drinking like those animals and making no use of their hands except to crawl around on all fours, which was their method of locomotion. Eventually the girls learned to walk upright, although they could never run. One acquired speech, at least a vocabulary of approximately 100 words, but the other child continued only to make grunting noises. Their howling noises at night were never extinguished, nor were their human teachers able to break them of the rather distasteful habit of "pouncing upon and devouring small birds and mammals" (Kellogg, 1931: 162).

Kellogg argued that the wolf children were born of normal intelligence because their adaptation to the wolf environment was exactly what was required of them, and therefore requires intelligence. This hypothesis went against the common notion that feral children were of sub-normal intelligence.[2] To test this idea, Kellogg argued that these human children had learned to be wild and that their wildness was a product of intelligent adaptation to their environment, rather than a product of a cognitive deficiency. Kellogg offered the symmetrical possibility of raising a non-human primate in a human environment with his human son Donald. Thus, a co-rearing study would test this hypothesis by placing a baby chimpanzee in a human home and to be treated as a human to determine if the chimpanzee could acquire human modes of responding.[3] Despite some opposition, Kellogg pushed forward,[4] conducted the study and determined that early rearing experiences shaped the individual. Chimpanzee Gua developed human modes of responding far beyond Kellogg's expectation. With respect to language comprehension, "the ape was considerably superior to the child in responding to human words" (Kellogg, 2002: 1).

Monograph

In 1993, 61 years after Kellogg's famous experiment, Savage-Rumbaugh published her highly acclaimed monograph titled *Language Comprehension in Ape and Child.* The study compared the language comprehension of an eight-year-old bonobo named Kanzi with that of a two-year-old human child named Alia. Whereas Kellogg's *The Ape and Child* was a report on the method of cross-fostering of a chimpanzee infant in a human home and baby Gua's competencies – Savage-Rumbaugh's monograph reports on bonobo Kanzi's competencies without detailed referencing of the ontogeny that produced those competencies. Yet the cultural ontogeny of Kanzi's competencies are addressed in the three findings which attend the major conclusion. The specific aims of the research were to see if Kanzi could understand novel and compound spoken English commands without imitative prompts, contrived reinforcement contingencies or explicit training. The method is simple. Kanzi and Alia were asked to respond to over 600 different verbal instructions. The trials were videotaped. Three observers independently scored the video-data evaluating whether the subjects had accurately responded to meaning of the sentences. The verbal instructions consisted of often odd and novel commands. For example, the subjects were asked:

Turn the vacuum cleaner on.
Give the doggie a shot.
Put the pine needles in the refrigerator.
Go get the ball that is outside.
Pour water on the vacuum cleaner
Open the soap.
Go get some cereal and give it to Rose.
(Savage-Rumbaugh et al., 1993: 111)

The method incorporated 13 different types of verbal commands, increasing in complexity as the trials progressed. Bonobo Kanzi was correct on 72% of the blind and nonblind trials as compared to human Alia who scored 66%. In addition to demonstrating that a non-human primate possessed receptive competence for spoken English with syntax and grammar, Savage-Rumbaugh's report emphasizes three important findings:

1. Language is acquired spontaneously and observationally, not through planned training.
2. Comprehension precedes production and drives language acquisition.

3. Early exposure to language is essential. (Segerdahl, Fields, and Savage-Rumbaugh, 2005: 7).

We emphasize, "these points are still true and important as observations, but today we interpret them in terms of culture. The manner in which Kanzi acquired language shows, we think, that language cannot be abstracted from culture" (Segerdahl et al., 2005: 7). For Kanzi was raised in a bi-cultural environment of a bonobo mother and a human cultural setting.[5] And thus, we reflect these precepts through a cultural contextualization:

1. Language is so deeply intertwined with how we live together that it cannot be learned through planned and explicit instruction. A caregiver may teach a child or ape this or that detail about language, but language as such can never be learned in a planned manner, only by living naturally together.
2. Linguistic expressions have their uses in the culture, and a close familiarity with the culture must develop in the child or ape before she starts using linguistic means herself within these contexts. What would "Yeah!" mean uttered by someone unacquainted with the human practice of asking and answering questions? What would "Hi!" mean uttered by someone who lacks the experience of greeting each other in human ways, for instance, in the street?
3. Culture is not external to us, but constitutes our very way of being. Therefore, a mature ape who has already developed a way of life where human language does not fit in can only to a very limited extent become a being with this language. Consider also the symmetrical impossibility for a mature human to *unlearn* her language. If you want to produce a human who does not possess language, then early exposure to a life without language is just as important as early exposure to language is to normal language acquisition (Segerdahl et al., 2005: 10).

Discussion

Despite the findings of Kellogg and Savage-Rumbaugh, the 1960s debate between linguists and behaviorists continues. It is commonly assumed that either a skill is innate and develops spontaneously, or it must be laboriously learned through special instruction. This sharp dichotomy has played a prominent role in language theory, where Noam Chomsky in his article The Faculty of Language: What Is It, Who Has It, and How Did It Evolve? (Hauser, Chomsky, and Fitch, 2002), and others after him (e.g., Pinker 1994; Bickerton 1995), have argued that since children acquire language spontaneously, and without special training or systematic correction, there must be an innate language faculty that governs human linguistic development. This dichotomy also lies behind a common assumption among people who discuss, or are engaged in, ape language research. It is the assumption that if an ape, that admittedly does not have an innate language faculty, shall learn aspects of human language, then it must learn these aspects through special training.

This idea, that apes need special training to learn humanlike language, governed Herb Terrace's Project Nim. Terrace prepared a classroom for the linguistic education of the chimpanzee Nim and hired a group of teachers who would give Nim that special linguistic education that human children obviously do not need when they acquire their first language. Terrace later reported that the project had been unsuccessful (Terrace, 1979). It therefore seemed that apes might not be able to learn human language. Special training might not counteract the lack of an innate language faculty. Subsequent research (1980–2006) at the Language Research Center (LRC) in Atlanta, Georgia, however, shows that apes can acquire aspects of human language if they were allowed to do it the same way Chomsky observes human children do it, spontaneously and without special training. This was an unexpected discovery even for those of us working at the LRC in the 1980s. Savage-Rumbaugh was unsuccessfully trying to teach the adult bonobo Matata to use lexigram symbols communicatively when one day it was discovered that Matata's adopted son Kanzi had learned to communicate via the keyboard by just being around playing, seeing humans use the keyboard, and hearing them talk (Savage-Rumbaugh et al. 1993, Savage-Rumbaugh, Shanker, & Taylor 1998). This changed the approach to language acquisition at the LRC. Food stopped being used as a reward, and training was replaced with long walks in the forest surrounding the laboratory, during which language was used freely, just as it would be used with a human child: to talk about whatever catches someone's attention, to discuss where to go, or what to do next. Subsequently Kanzi's sister Panbanisha and her sons Nyota and Nathan have acquired language in the same spontaneous manner. Since we do not assume that apes have an innate language faculty, we face the following problem. *How can great apes acquire language spontaneously, if they do not have an innate language faculty?* The answer we have developed is in terms of culture, and it challenges sharp dichotomies between innateness and training, and between language and culture.

Defining Culture

The corpus of anthropological writing is extensive and spans over 100 years. It deals primarily with theory, descriptions of human culture, and, more recently, writing about culture. Reduction of the concept of culture to an operational definition, limited to a few sentences is what experimentalism demands. And anthropology has developed over 300 definitions. Most of these definitions do not stand alone, but requires the anthropological theoretical corpus as a background of understanding. However, the major deficiency for us is the notion of anthropological culture as a uniquely human possession, ignoring the continuum of humans as animals. The reader fortunate enough to have read across a century of cultural writing, at least has an intuitive access to the anthropological meaning of culture. Those readings would run from Tyler and Morgan to Boaz, Kroeber, Radin, Sapir, and Whorf; to Gluckman, Benedict, Mead, Steward, White, and Murdock; to Conklin, S. Tyler, and Strauss; and finishing with Vygotsky, Foucault, Levi-Straus, Turner, Geertz, Shalins, Lakoff, Johnson, Rosaldo, Crapenzano, Shore, and D'Andrade. Just to mention a few. To complicate matters, an entire discipline is theoretically under girded by the technical term 'culture' that is orthographically identical to the lay term "culture." This has lead to misunderstandings. Thus, our reader deserves some illumination on how this essay approaches culture. Robert Murphy offers an accessible definition of culture that broadly corresponds to the corpus of anthropological theory. He writes:

Culture is . . . a set of mechanisms for survival, but it provides us also with a definition of reality. It is the matrix into which we are born, it is the anvil upon which our persons and destinies are forged. (1986:14)

Murphy's definition tells us that culture is about survival and about producing reality, suggesting the notion of realities. And equally important, the idea that the epigenetic cultural matrix to which one is born is inescapable. A certain tyranny of behavioral repertoires facilitated by cognitive closed typology, informing the notion of human specific behaviors. We thicken the discussion as we extend the definition of culture to non-humans, that is, we make no distinction between human and non-human processes of culture, as Murphy and other cultural theorist do. And thus, we argue that culture is much older than *Homo sapiens* and that culture has never been unique to humans. For this essay, we highlight and *hypothesize* the following points about *culture*:

1. Culture is an epigenetic phenomena operating among many classes of living organisms.
2. The radiation of culture is multi-modal with pre- and post-ontogentic influence.
3. Non-human ape culture and human culture are the same dynamic function distinguished, merely, by the differences in ideational content of the culture-function.
4. Culture is topological. (The limits of my world are the limits of my culture.)
5. Culture contours a cognitive structure reflected in neural topologies that controls access to reality.
6. Biology conforms to cultural processes over time, and thus one the many vectors of speciation.
7. The more biologically related, the more culturally related organisms should be except in cases of cross fostering.
8. To the extent that culture is isomorphic with language, we conclude our essay with 12 design features of language, and thus 12 aspects of culture that inform a definition of anthropological notions of culture.

With these ideas in mind, we wish to consider alternatives to the innateness approaches to language and to the notion of the emergence of language without cultural processes – and thus, we consider the challenge of Chomskyism.

A vital component of Chomsky's[6] argument for the innateness of language is his notion of poverty of stimulus. He correctly observes that children acquire language spontaneously, as an aspect of their maturation, but he also assumes that since they do not receive grammatical instruction or systematic linguistic correction, their experience of language is impoverished. His reasonable conclusion, given these premises, is that linguistic development must be predetermined by what is not in human experience: an innate language faculty. Terrace's motivation for educating Nim in a classroom – designed to make Nim concentrate on language and not be distracted by other aspects of life – was very much in harmony with Chomsky's notion of poverty of stimulus. Terrace believed he needed to provide Nim with extra linguistic stimulation, to counteract his lack of innate linguistic forces, but it did him a disservice. The bonobos

Kanzi, Panbanisha, and Nyota acquired language precisely by avoiding special linguistic training, and instead sharing daily life with them in the research. According to Chomsky's notion of poverty of stimulus, Nim's systematic exposure to language ought to have been less impoverished than the bonobos'. But it turns out it was the other way round.

We believe that Chomsky was too quick to interpret his observations of human language acquisition as evidence of an innate and uniquely human language faculty. A comparison between Nim and Kanzi indicates that grammatical instruction is impoverished for the purposes of stimulating first language acquisition, while shared life in culture stimulates a young primate to communicate linguistically. Culture appears to do the job Chomsky thought an innate language faculty must do. Culture might be said to be our language faculty. This motivates reanalyzing the concept of language and conceive of language as an aspect of culture. The widespread tendency to identify language with vocabulary and grammar is in harmony with an urgent task in most modern societies: teaching new generations to read, write and speak foreign languages. Language education is to a great extent a matter of memorizing vocabularies and learning grammatical rules. Shaping a general notion of language on the basis of an educational practice that does not exist universally in human societies, however, is questionable from a biological perspective. Furthermore, since all humans who undergo language education already can speak, the question arises whether this erudite notion is true of language as it is acquired spontaneously by children before school and is used as an integral aspect of real life situations. A new catalogue of design features of language has therefore been developed that departs from the linguist Charles Hockett's (1963) classical catalogue, and that conceptualizes language in cultural rather than grammatical dimensions. When language is seen as an aspect of culture, it becomes more evident that Kanzi's experience of language was an abundance of stimuli, and how his language could develop spontaneously without being innate.

But there is a further aspect of Chomsky's notion of poverty of stimulus that ape language studies indicate is problematic. The notion of poverty of stimulus does not take account of the biological creature that an infant primate is, the topology of experience that comes with having arms that can wave or be stretched out towards others, hands that can grab, gesture and investigate, a mouth that can be happy or aggressive and bite, and eyes that can frighten, express curiosity, or be frightened. This kind of animal is confused with something that engaged Chomsky more in the 1950s and 1960s, namely, mathematically defined automata that are initially in state S_0 and respond to input in formally defined ways. Automata fail to work if they do not have the right internal design, and Chomsky (1957) aroused attention because it seemed he could show that it was necessary to modify the formal machinery to produce all and only the grammatical sentences of English. Automata do not tangibly live. But ape language research cannot disregard the fact that it studies biological creatures, and it cannot disregard how evolution has shaped primate experience and made the great apes and us sensible to the world. That Kanzi acquired language spontaneously by sharing life with humans, although he biologically is less adapted to human language than humans are, supports not only that stimulation in cultural dimensions is abundance of linguistic stimuli. It also indicates that the culture that so profoundly stimulated and changed Kanzi is not an artefact, but can be viewed as our human form of primate culture.

We hypothesize that we share the bulk of the biologically inherited traits that come into play in language with the great apes. We become curious, angry, happy or anguished in similar ways, and turn to others in accordance with related social and emotional patterns (how we tangibly live). The infant's development towards language starts in interactions that center on these common reactions. We form the notion of a broad flexible interface of primate reactions in humans and apes: we respond to each other's physiognomies and movements in related ways. This broad interface of interaction develops over the years and gradually incorporates gestures and uses of words. Evolution has trimmed our primate traits and arranged their orchestration for language somewhat better, but apes too acquire aspects of language if they are exposed to language in broad cultural dimensions.

In spring of 2005, the bonobos living at the LRC in Atlanta moved to the Great Ape Trust of Iowa, where a new facility has been designed to give the apes even better opportunities to explore aspects of human culture and develop any capacities their new environment will stimulate. This will give us unusual opportunities to study a developmental process that does not fit into the traditional opposition between innateness and learning. We call this neglected developmental process, related both to learning and to maturation, *enculturation*. (We remind the reader that we reject the notion of proto-culture or animal culture, and argue for culture as an epigenetic phenomena which is characteristic of many non-human species.)

We hypothesize that children and great apes acquire language through enculturation. Segerdahl's conception of first language acquisition (see Segerdahl et al., 2005) as enculturation departs from cognitivist models of language as an innate faculty of mind as well as from behaviorist models of language as a complex disposition to verbal behavior. It also departs from Tomasello's notion of acquisition of skills through enculturation, since he speculates that the effective factor explaining enculturated apes' remarkable skills is that they always have someone who "points for them, shows them things, teaches them, or in general expresses intentions toward their attention (or other intentional states)" (Tomasello 1999: 35). He reasons as if the apes played the subordinate role of pupils and the humans the leading role of pointing instructors, and as if this pedagogical relation was the genesis of these apes' humanlike abilities. But the whole point of our notion of language acquisition

through enculturation is that teaching and training are absent or play subordinate roles.

We sympathize with our readers and understand that with our idea of enculturation and culture, we create some dysphoria regarding classical notions of learning and the concept of species as a biological preparation with species-specific behaviors. With an eye towards facilitating an understanding of our notions of culture, we suggest the idea of a computer operating system as a metaphor of culture which is "booted up" (acquired) in the cognitive biology of the organism during early ontogeny by the cross-modal experience of living. Once the cultural system has reached a certain critical point in the individual, the "device drivers" exists for learning, and teaching. While we recognize the over reductive quality of this metaphor, we think of students and their struggle to understand anthropological culture. We know many of these students will have had experience with their personal computer capable or running more than one operating system such as DOS, Windows, UNIX, XENIX, and LENIX. There are two significant observations to make: (1) only one operating system can run at a time; and (2) the very different operational character of a computer through the cultural lens of different operating systems. The student will ask, "Where does the cultural operating system that is booted up reside?" The answer is in the matrix of living: the minds, actions, sounds, and experience of living. We suspect the multimodal radiation of culture is a broader spectrum than the receptive competence of eyes and ears; and therefore, mechanism of transmission and the isomorphic power of cultural bites are yet to be identified. Hopefully, with this metaphor, we have armed our reader with more insight into our notion of culture, so that we may speak about Kanzi and his experience with enculturation – and the overemphasis on teaching and learning associated with the concept of post-natal enculturation. We continue with our discussion of learning.

The pupil-teacher relation is only one relation among many, and we did not start up the multifarious life we share with the apes in some propaedeutic practice of pointing, showing, and teaching. Sharing life with young Kanzi meant chasing him, catching and biting him, tickling him, travelling with him, sharing food with him, camping with him, and doing many other things. He would not pay attention to our gestures or react to them in relevant ways unless we had first established this more intimate relation to each other by doing a variety of things together, thereby starting the enculturation process on all fronts simultaneously.

Tomasello assumes that enculturation consists in imposing human culture on the apes: first by over-explicitly pointing and addressing their intentional states, thereby weaving our minds together, and then by demonstrating new skills that they can imitate because pointing has made them see us as intentional beings. Tomasello neglects the importance of the fact that the bonobos' culture is a bi-species culture, what we call the Pan/Homo culture, and that we quite simply do a broad variety of things together every day. What started the bonobos' development was what they already had in common with us in their infancy, a labyrinth of primate ways of moving about and responding to each other and to the environment – what we call the flexible interface of primate reactions – rather than a demarcated pedagogical practice. And once inside this labyrinth of primate experience it gradually expanded, over the years, into the Pan/Homo culture in its present state.

Enculturation, in short, occurs in labyrinths of life, not in referential triangles. It is not a demarcated semi-pedagogical practice that can be used to teach apes about the contents of human life. It is true that we sometimes, when we are indoors carrying out tests, act in a more pedagogical style, and that we occasionally even direct the apes' attention to a boring task by physically turning their heads towards us (as parents do when they want a child's attention against their will). But it is essential that this is an exception: an effect of enculturation rather than its cause.

Since enculturation requires being abundantly stimulated in a broad variety of simultaneous cultural dimensions, the effects of enculturation on the apes abilities are equally broad and must be studied and documented from a number of different perspectives. It can concern communicative capacities such as discussing tomorrow or yesterday, new abilities to use the voice communicatively, new discourse patterns, tool manufacture and tool use, abilities to create and appreciate music, to count or to learn to use new senses, such as touch, where previously vision or hearing were utilized. Our new home is a research instrument designed to provide a comprehensive picture of how a wide variety of humanlike skills can develop spontaneously in great apes through the process of enculturation. Moreover, it is environment in which Kanzi and his family can live, utter, and make and use tools and fulfill their cultural potential. And so we argue, if Kanzi is a cultural being with language and tools, the techniques of cultural anthropology are justified as legitimate techniques of investigation.

Writing Ethnography, Writing Theory

The following is a splicing of ethnographic narratives from the bonobos lives over the last eight years. Interdispersed are the design features of language featured in Segerdahl et al. (2005). It is a sample of effort to demonstrate how ethnographic text might be organized in our future volumes, as well as offering cases in point which may inform how we arrived at these features. As we have quoted Denzin (1997), we make some effort to demonstrate the practical relationship between reporting ethnographic facts and developing theory. In this instance we use synoptic first person narratives within explanations (as opposed to quotes directly from daily notes) to give the ethnographic facts readability and context.

1. *Spontaneity*

Language is acquired without special training or systematic correction, as an aspect of the ape or child's maturation in a humanlike culture.

We suspect that the cultural contouring of an individual begins prenatally. The ontongeny of enculturation is pre- and postnatal event. And thus the modes of culturally responding are being biologically tailored from the moment the individual can sense and respond to the enviornment. This has similarities to the folk-theories such as the Mozart effect. While we do not argue that prenatal exposure to Mozart makes an individual smarter, we suspect it does make the subject different than prenatal exposure to war sounds or the echos of institutional facilties. And one cannot separate the mother's experience from the child in terms of hormones and nutition, particularly stress hormones, both arising from the background radiation of culture and environment. And in this context, language arises spontenously. For language to emerge from intentional training, the poverty of stimulus is a critical issue as Chomsky rightfully points out.

Bonobo Nyota was born (April 4, 1998, 9:00 A.M.) attended by vets and lots of people scurrying around, to my mind doing nothing. Mainly me, I just stood there while Panbanisha, Nyota's mother, endured a long and preeclampsic delivery very unlike other bonobo deliveries. Nyota was born with a seemingly very large head that had been temporarily deformed into a cone by the passage through the birth canal. (most ape babies are born quickly and without much effort to move through the birth canal). I remember how wet and not-so-cute he was at birth. I thought I would love him the minute I saw him but I didn't. When I came to love Nyota as the fierce protective advocate that characterizes me to today, is a point in time I cannot define. Amid the perpetual organization of changing diapers, fixing milk, taking baths, and providing food, warmth, and comfort, I remember very little about me. I was of a mindset that if human language was going to emerge in this little bonobo boy, I had to super-load his experience lest I fail to break through his biological bonoboness and humanely enculturate him. This must be the point I began to love him and the pathology of parenthood took over and displaced the knowledge I had

been trained to bring to this experiment. To make matters worse, Nyota's doctor, Brent Swinson, explained that chimpanzee babies die very easily before the age of three and Brent stressed, "You have to keep him warm and well fed." Something happened to me and I became super-parent organinzing my life around baby rules. I seemed to ignore the fact that I had Sue Savage-Rumbaugh at my side with 25 years of experience. Experience that included a variety of great apes such as Lucy, Washoe, and host of famous great apes and their babies. After all, she did co-rear many baby apes including the world famous Kanzi. With logic gone, no one could tell me anything. I was in a manic race to get Nyota to the promised safety of three years old. To hell with lexigrams, human language, culture, and tools. This was life or death. I now knew what that poor mother and her child must have felt at Laetoli. This is about how one tangibly lives each day. Monsters at every turn that will take your baby and eat you.

One afternoon Nyota (14 months) was taking his nap in my lap while I worked at my computer. Nyota took a nap every afternoon and I attempted to use that time while he was asleep to write. I was working on a presentation that Sue was planning to make at a college near Boston. I was rushing to try and get as much done before Nyota finnished his nap. While I was typing, Nyota awoke. He took his hands and put them on both sides of my face and peered directly into my eyes getting my attention in a very serious way and then crawled over to the talking lexigram board and uttered, "WE IS GOOD HONEYSUCKLE LANA."[7]

(Nyota 1999)

At the moment I was trying to write a few notes on how Nyota used one word expressions like MILK, HUG, and BLUEBERRY and at other times seemed to babble, hitting varieties of lexigrams appearing to be at randon. I asked Nyota, "Do you want to go see Lana? And he responded vocally with a little peep which in the Pan/Homo world signals "yes," (whereas silence indicates "no"). So I packed our backpack and Nyota and I went across the dirt road where troglodytes Lana lived in the Lanson building. Growing near her building was wild honeysuckle. As soon as we got near it, Nyota started pulling toward the plants. It was blooming and he proceeded to eat the blossoms. He picked and ate honeysuckle for nearly 20 minutes. Once he was through eating honeysuckle, Nyota started pointing and directing me back across the road. I followed his directions. Nyota wanted to go back home and finish his nap.

The original communication that spawned our visit to the honeysuckle was a major observational event for me. Fortunately, I had the camera running when Nyota uttered the phrase and I was able to analyze his usage over and over. It was clear to me that Nyota planned his statement to the extent he made sure he had my attention before he made his utterance. Following his utterance he looked at me again to confirm "Did I get it?" And when he confirmed that I understood, he was moving towards the door to the leave the trailer where we lived. It did not surprise me that Nyota used a series of lexigrams, but rather the sequence of behaviors attending the comunicative event that seemed so mature for a 14-month-old child. First, I had never been to Lana's building with Nyota before. I didn't know about the honeysuckle and I didn't realize Nyota knew who Lana was. (Lana is the chimpanzee that Duane Rumbaugh began the LANA project with in 1976. She lives with other troglodytes in a different building from the bonobos.) I believe that Nyota felt he was going to say something to me I might not understand and so he was going to make sure the communication was discrete and careful because he really wanted to eat honeysuckle. This is the spontaneous emergence of a behavior of the communication of language that transcends the development of symbolic competence. From that point forward it seemed that

the ball started moving faster and faster and Nyota's communication moved beyond mere requests for food items to events in which he communicated information to me that I did not know – and I had the distinct impression he knew I did not know. For me, this instance represents how Nyota's language emerged. It happened no matter what I was doing as long as there was opportunity (a lexigram board) and I was open to the idea of responding to his communicative events in authentic and patient manner.

2. Boundlessness

There are no demarcation lines between an ape or child's language development and their life. Acquiring new words is indistinguishable from being initiated into the domains of life where the words have their uses.

Nyota was born into a laboratory unlike other laboratories. We lived and I worked in a 55-acre riverine forest located in a larger 300-acre forests isolated in Dekalb County bounded by the South River about 20 minutes from downtown Atlanta. Our forest was populated with deer, fox, raccoons, beaver, weasels, bear, and wild dogs among the other more common populations of mamals, amphibians, birds, fish, and insects. Our forest was a relatively safe place to travel and many years prior to my work at the laboratory, Savage-Rumbaugh had built locations in the forests. Each forest venue had its unique lexigrams and each site was associated with specific foods and acitivities. These were charming little buildings contructed of various materials, primarily wood. For example, A-Frame is a small a-frame hut close to the large and impressive concrete structure most outsiders would identify as the real laboratory. A-Frame is a very favorite location of Kanzi and Panbanisha provisioned with hot dogs, hamburgers, or coke. Also, associated with this site is fire making and cooking. Another site, Oranges is a location deep in the woods (far away from the concrete lab) associated with the fruit oranges, rocks, and stone tool making. There were a total of 18 sites; however, as we tangibly lived and enjoyed our outings in the forest, the need to name new places arose from living. While our keyboard could not keep up with this dynamic convention, that is the addition of emerging nouns, we developed symbolic placemarkers as shared memory.

One my goals was to teach Nyota how to throw. Bill Calvin (2004) argues that apes cannot aim and throw a projectile at a moving target. Throwing being the use of a tool that arises from the cognitive schema of pointing. Aiming and then following through with flinging an object upon a targeted path with some degree of accuracy is, according to Calvin, an impossible task for apes. I was waiting to teach Nyota throwing when he was old enough. (What ever that meant to me.) One day when Nyota was about 14 months old he uttered on the keyboard, "TURTLE CAR." I inquired if he wanted to go in the car and he responded with his affirmative peep. I assumed that Nyota wanted to travel to Gully Gusher, a location that was similar to a small deck that overlooked a little pond where a big turtle buried itself in the mud. The car wouldn't start, so I decide we would walk. We had our backbpack full of grapes, milk, wipees, diapers, Cliff Bars, and water. As we travelled down a dirt road that led to Gully Gusher, Nyota pointed to the right indicating he wanted to go down the trail that led to Crisscross Corners, (a location associated with blackberries and cheese.) We arrived and there was nothing to eat at the site as we had not requested the forest be supplied with food that day. Nyota began to play and I noticed on the side of the Crisscross Corners building (a shack with verticle members in the configuration of X's), there was a plastic turtle tied up in rope. As I begin to think about the toy turtle and that this is the location Nyota had intended rather than Gully Gusher, Nyota came down from the top of the shack and into my arms indicting, by pointing, that he wanted to travel across the beam bridge to Midway, a location in the middle of the forest and surrounded by swamp. The bridge was difficult to travel because it was eight inches wide and rose

above the ground from varying heights of six inches to four feet. I didn't really want to go (I had fallen off this bridge many times, but never when I carried Nyota); however, I was curious about what Nyota had in mind about this outing. As we began, I noticed the rocks I placed in piles. As a general rule, when I was in the forest, I collected the rocks I saw and placed them in piles. The forest dogs travelled in packs and always ignored us. But when they came too close, I would hurl a rock in their direction and they would silently run away (they never barked, howled, or made any sound). Nyota and I arrived a Midway and there were some very old raisins there which I threw in the swamp and explained to Nyota we couldn't eat those becauase they were rotten. We had been there about a minute when Nyota's hair stood out in the most extreme piloerection making him look as though he were a fat baby. I asked him, "what do you see?" He vocally waaad. And I responded with "do you see something scary out there?" Holding the paper keyboard for him, he uttered "DOG." As I looked up from the keyboard, and as I could feel Nyota's body become very tense and hard, I saw the dogs. There were about eight of them and they appeared to be very close. My pile of rocks was right next to me. I had no anxiety at all. I picked up one of medium size stones and threw in the direction of the dogs hitting a nearby tree. It made a nice impressive thump and the dogs dissapeared. Nyota climbed down from my arms and looked at the rocks. He touched them and placed his hand on top of one of the stones. It seems to me his hand was very small compared to the rock. I commented to Nyota, "Those are our rocks. One day you will be able to throw one and scare the dogs away. But your hand has to get bigger." We went back to Crisscross Corners where Nyota played with the toy turtle that was attached to the rope. This was the turtle he was referring to when he uttered "TURTLE CAR." This is something that had been a part of his experience when he had previously been in the woods with Sue or Liz and I was not there.

3. *Immanence*

The acquisition of language affects all aspects of life. The way speaking primates gesture, act, and coordinate activities is immanent in their language.

Outside our bedroom was a large fig tree. On the back of the trailer was a type of streetlight that illuminated the back of the trailer that was closest to the woods. This light was always our nightlight and it was not too bright in the summer because the large leaves of the fig filtered the pink-yellow light. Each night an opossum climbed up in the tree and looked in the window at us. I kind of like it and thought it a friendly behavior. I created nice stories about our friend the opossum. One night, Nyota decided the opossum was not our friend and *waaad* at the animal. I assured Nyota that there was nothing to worry about. I closed the curtain and we went to sleep. The next morning we went outside to have breakfast on the deck. Nyota left the deck (he is 14 months old and rarely gets two inches from me) to walk around to back of the trailer to the fig tree. He found an old doll's head, probably Panbanisha's or Panzee's when they were babies. He picked up the dolls head, stood up bipedally, and threw at the location of where the opossum had been the night before. The doll's head soared about four feet in the air hitting the fig somewhere close to the ground. I was amazed baby Nyota understood the idea of throwing anything. While he could not actually throw to affect the outcome, I was demonstrating with the dogs, he did in fact understand the schemas. Then he walked back to the deck in a quadrapedal style that Sue calls the gorilla walk (a posture of walking associated with confidence, deliberation, and success) climbed up in his chair, smiled, and ate his breakfast.

Nyota observed me throwing rocks. I never taught Nyota to throw a ball, rock, or any other object. Let me emphasize, I never intentionally taught Nyota how to throw because he started throwing plastic baby heads (and later, rocks) before he had reached an age I thought he was old enough

to teach those kinds of things. Moreover, as he has grown older his skill progressed without mentoring or apprenticeship. Nyota practiced his throwing when the opportunity arose or when he felt like it. Today, Nyota's ability to throw a stone at a target with precision and force exceeds my ability. I do not possess Nyota's level of skill. Nyota throws objects with great power and accuracy. As a seven year old he is rehearsing (as opposed to learning the schemas of throwing) and developing new techniques and challenges to his own initiatives and designs. His bipedal stance is very linear, fluid, and flexible when he is throwing. He has the posture of throwing when he practices. None of the other apes have expressed this level of proficiency in projecting a rock or ball through the air, even though they can all fling and hurl objects. Kanzi has been shown how to pitch which he will do if Sue asks him to, but he does it with a half-heartedness that makes it something different than what Nyota does. Kanzi's and Panbanisha's throwing and pitching a ball or rock always has an arc to it. Nyota can hurl and projectile in a straight line 'straight across the base' so to speak. He hits with accuracy, although he has never hit a person with a stone, he has whizzed one by P-Suke's ear to scare him. Nyota throws with authentic actions as it has arisen from tangibly living. We consider Bill Calvin recent comments:

> Accurate throwing *(not just flinging, which many chimps do, but practicing to hit smaller and smaller targets)* is not usually a set piece like a dart throw or basketball free throw where the idea is to perform the action exactly the same way as your hard-earned standard. *Throwing at a prospect for dinner usually involves something novel: the target is not at the same distance or the same elevation as one of your standards; perhaps it is moving, too. (2004, 94)*

Nyota is a little bonobo boy. He has never had the opportunity to attempt to develop his skill of aiming at a moving target (in fact, he has been discouraged because of concerns of safety for other apes and humans). Soon our laboratory will offer him that opportunity. Calvin suggests that spitting at a moving target (apparently lots of apes can hit a moving target with a mouthful of water) is different at the neurological level because the behavioral synthax of throwing at a moving target involves nested stages strongly reminiscent of grammatical syntax – and spitting doesn't. The question for me, someone who knows Nyota really well, is not whether Nyota will be able to aim at a moving target and hit it with accuracy, but how will Calvin maintain his argument in the face of Nyota's future mature competencies?. Uping the ante is the historical nature of the ape language game.

4. Cultural Creativity and Generality

Linguistic creativity is similar to co-constructed musical improvization. It presupposes, maintains, and transforms a common heritage. The way expressions find new uses in new circumstances is shaped by the culture in which the expressions already are used.

Kanzi and his family use over 384 lexigrams to communicate. These symbols are arranged on three matrices, 16 across and 8 down. A fourth panel has been added for the additions of new lexigrams as real living demands. Nouns and names are impending big additions to our keyboard as we have recently moved to a new laboratory. Just as new spaces required referents, new people require lexigrams if we are to refer to them as other than VISITOR. However, this usage is common among Kanzi and his family. P-Suke (pronounced peace-kay) is a bonobo who came to Kanzi's family from Japan. His arrival some eight years ago required an isolation building which was named the P-Suke Building. The P-Suke building as a lexigram became a destination, as well as, an individual's name. When the caretaking staff must negotiate whether Kanzi wants to go to the P-Suke building or to actually spend some time with P-Suke the bonobo, discussion at the keyboard is required to clarify the matter. Refining a comment is a common event in Kanzi's world because our language use

can be ambiguous, creative, and metaphoric as human usages of language. New expressions and meanings are generated from the common base of parlance and cultural bias arises with all of the lexigrams. For example, the use of the word DOG. All of the apes have grown up with domesticated dogs. The bonobos love dogs and enjoy playing with them. The apes feel safe and comfortable with the dogs especially when we are moving through the forest; however, there are other types of dogs and the apes possess a modified category of dog to refer to those other dogs: BAD DOGS. Bad dogs refers to the wild dogs and they are a category of animal to be avoided, while SNAKE by definition is bad.

Bad Dog

Good Snake

To distinguish poisonous snake from a nonpoisonous one, we must make the reference, GOOD SNAKE. Kanzi, Panbanisha, and Nyota will show dome deference to the GOOD SNAKE as long as Sue, Bill, or Liz are there to insist that it is a good snake; however, Kanzi's mother who does not understand English makes no distinction between good and bad snakes – she kills them all, not matter how we categorize the snake.

When Pär Segerdahl joined the research five years ago, we had planned to add a lexigram for him; however, before we could accomplish generating a new lexigram (there is a lead time for designing and printing) Kanzi and Panbanisha had begun using the food lexigram for PEAR to refer to Pär the person. They did this spontaneously because the English pronunciation of 'Pär' is identical to our pronunciation of the fruit. So we left it that way. We didn't make a lexigram for Pär because Kanzi and Pabanisha had designated one for him. Pär lives in Sweden and comes to lab on planned visits. About

11 months after Pär's first visit, Kanzi uttered PEAR. Not thinking, I responded, "Kanzi we don't have any pears – we have some apples." Kanzi looked at me with a special look we all know when we humans are not getting it. Liz overheard the conversation and said, "I think Kanzi is talking about Pär the person." Kanzi immediately vocalized which we recognize as affirmation (silence represents "NO"). I ran to my office and got a picture of jelly, pears, cheese, and Pär. I took the photograph to Kanzi and said, "Pick the picture you are talking about." Kanzi chose Pär the person. I asked Kanzi, "Do you want me to call Pär and ask him to come visit?" Kanzi and all of the bonobos who were not a part of the original exchange loudly vocalized together the affirmation, which translates to "yes, now you understand." I explained to Kanzi that I would send Pär an e-mail and let him know, which I did. Later that evening Kanzi uttered "PEAR". I told Kanzi that I had talked to Pär and that he said he would come visit in about three weeks. Kanzi did not ask me about Pär again until Pär's day of arrival.

5. Placement

Linguistic communications, even about things remote in space and time, are placed in cultural activities acquired with the first language. The use of clocks makes possible certain forms of talk about yesterday and tomorrow.

Pär lives in Sweden. It is one thing to talk about him when he is in our presence, or three or four days departed; however, nearly a year after Pär's first visit, and right before Pär's next visit, a spontaneous discussion of Pär suggests an historical memory that goes beyond Hockett's displacement. Kanzi also seemed to understand that Pär lives very far away. When I explained that it will take a long time for Pär to get from his home to the lab, Kanzi uttered "CAR." The human context, that is if a human were uttering "car" would suggest that the subject has some undestanding that long distances can be overcome by a car. Cars are a part of Kanzi's world. All of the apes have grown up with cars. We often walk through the forest,

but on cold rainy days, we drive through the forest. I am not arguing that I can empirically show that Kanzi understands car-ness, but merely pointing out that the opportunity to understand what cars are and what they can do is an opportunity that has been available to Kanzi all of his life. He can identify a car in person or in a photograph or video. He can sit in a car and ride. He can open the car-door and close it. He knows to stay in the vehicle until the car stops. He knows he doesn't have to walk if he rides. Does he understand that the car makes a critical difference for a person who lives a long way away? I think so, but I have no proof other than I can predict Kanzi would suggest taking the car if we explained to him that we couldn't go here or there because it was too far to walk. What Kanzi doesn't understand is that the car cannot solve the distance from the lab to Pär's home in Sweden. For Kanzi's world is limited to the 55 acres of the laboratory, what he sees on video, and the fact that most everyone who comes to the lab arrives in a car.

Kanzi understands yesterday and tomorrow, and particularly the lexigram expression LATER. You can ask Kanzi to find his toy he had yesterday, and he will search until he finds the item, ignoring other items that might fit into the category he was asked to find. When Kanzi wants something, you can explain to him that we will do this or have that tomorrow, which certainly results in the cessation of the request. Movever, when tomorrow comes, Kanzi (or Panbanisha or Nyota) will remind you of the promise you made. For example, one Friday night Kanzi asked for "SUGAR CANE." I explained that we didn't have any, but Dan was going to the farmer's market the next day and I would ask him to get some. Kanzi seems to agree this was ok and asked for other foods. The next morning Kanzi looked me right in the eye and uttered at the keyboard "SUGAR CANE." I explained "SUGAR CANE LATER," that Dan had to go to the store first, and that now we were going to have our cereal. Everybody seemed very happy and we moved to the group room to have oatmeal for breakfast. As I was adding blueberries to our cereal, the bonobos ran out to the playyard led by Kanzi and Pabanisha barking at Dan. Dan was on his way to the staff office. I went outside to meet him because the barks had been so serious and it was very unusal for the bonobos to treat Dan this way. I asked, "What are you doing Dan?" He indicatred that he was coming to change his shoes so he could clean the P-Suke building. I said, "When are you going to the farmer's market?" He thought he would go around 10:00 A.M. Kanzi rushed towards Dan with an angry expression. I responded, "I think you better go now." Dan said, "OK, but could he go in the staff office first?" I said that would be fine. The bonobos retreated without protest as Dan moved toward the staff office. As Dan was leaving to go get in the car, Panbanisha picked up a big rock and flung it at him. The bonobos sat down to eat their cereal and watch TV-tapes. About three and half hours later Dan returned in the car and Kanzi ran to keyboard an uttered "SUGAR CANE." As Dan approached the building all of the bonobos were very happy to see him and treated him respectfully as they generally do.

6. *Gestures and Tools*

The entire body, as it functions in activities that may involve gestures and tools, can be perceived as the organ of speech. Recently we moved to our new facility in Des Moines. Our public interface areas where the bonobos can occassionally meet visitors is designed to feature communication. We are in the process of creating technical systems that facilitate the entire suite of communication, discreet and ambient, visual and auditory, production and reception which would be possible through gorilla glass. At the moment we can only communicate with lexigrams, but we cannot hear each other without yelling. The biggest problem is that apes and humans cannot experience group conversations. For the moment it is one person to one person; lexigram to lexigram. I was shocked at how difficult it was for me to communicate with just visual discrete symbols. Through the glass I cannot hear Kanzi's vocalizations. He can barely hear me. I don't have unimpeded views of his facial expression, and especially his eyes because of the glare and distortions in the glass. I cannot touch him nor see his subtle hand gestures. The glass and the backlighting is a partition to Kanzi's entire body as an organ of speech. If he uses chalk to draw a lexigram, I cannot see that without great effort. What I can see are the vivd, beautiful, and colorful lexigrams. For the first time visitor, it is an exciting rich moment. For me this is like listening to Domingo's voice on a Victrola. It is not the rich harmony of expression that I am accustomed to in tangible everyday communication. To understand language in the social environment, linguistic cues are an essential component, as well as, the rapid fire of clarifying what was uttered? For example, Kanzi was sitting in the greenhouse talking to visitors on his keyboard. He uttered "WATER." The visitors turned to me while I was trying to organize some papers and said, "Kanzi wants water?" The inference being to drink. I walked up to the gorilla glass eight inches thick and yelled "Kanzi do you want water to drink or water in your swiming pool?" He was sitting on the edge of his pool which had some water in it and next to a drinking water fountain. Kanzi pointed to the spout of the waterfall which was not turned on. I turn to our guest and told them to tell Sue that Kanzi wanted his waterfall turned on. Ben Beck who was sitting in the lobby listening to me shout through the glass, asked, "How did Kanzi tell you that?" I explained that he pointed to the waterfall spout.

I thought it strange that Kanzi made this request, but I was busy and didn't think about it again until later. In the afternoon, Bill Calvin showed me photographs he had been taking of the apes. And there was Kanzi, all glamourous and beaded with water from the fall as Calvin took shots. Just as I believe Kanzi understands car-ness, I believe I understand Kanzi-ness. Kanzi enjoys being photographed. Kanzi considers being filmed part of his work. He accomplishes his compliance with created twists that have the strong signature of Kanzi-ness. Being filmed with water is just the kind of thing Kanzi would think of (I say this because in my observations of Kanzi over the years, I have seen his creative patterns). Others would argue that it was hot in the greenhouse and Kanzi wanted the cool splash of the fall. Yet I have reason to be suspicious that Kanzi was just merely cooling off – and this harkens back to incident many years ago. Kanzi was about 18 years old. He had a head cold and snot was running down his face, he was hunched over wilting towards the floor – as though he felt terrible. At that time, a generous benefactor had donated money to protect bonobos in the wild. As a gesture of appreciation, we had Kanzi make a sculpture for the donor. A caretaker asked Kanzi if she could take a photograph of him with his sculpture for the visitor. Kanzi agreed. All of the sudden, Kanzi sat up very straight, wiped the snot off his face, picked up the sculpture holding it close to his face, and smiled his giant bonobo toothy-canine smile. Once the photograph was taken, he carefully sat the sculpture down. With his smile gone he returned to his posture of misery.[8]

7. *Medium Independence*

The substrate of meaning is not speech but activities of life. If they can be integrated into the same language activities, other linguistic media than speech, for example, hand gestures, writing, and lexigrams, can fulfill similar linguistic functions.

Despite my reliance upon Kanzi's receptive competence for spoken English and my receptive competence for the meaning in Kanzi's vocalizations, we are still able to quite effectively comunicate through lexigrams, pictures, gestures, and context withinin novel events of exchange. It is often appropriate in communication to be silent, yet actively communicate. One afternoon, Panbanisha (Kanzi's sister, Nyota's bonobo mother) was sitting in the playyard. I walked up to her and asked her how she was doing. She picked up the keyboard and pointed to the lexigram QUIET. I whispered in her ear, "why?" She pointed to the lexigram "MONSTER" and then pointed towards the

woods. After about five minutes, Panbanisha uttered "CAR" and pointed to me. Considering we were still in quiet-mode, I whispered in her ear, "Do you want me to get in the car and go check the woods?" She pointed to the car, which signaled a silent "yes." So I got in the Bronco and drove out into the woods as Panbanisha quietly observed. When I passed A-Frame, I could see up in the distance, something was going on up at Lookout Point. As I drove closer, I saw a man on a motorcycle who was not supposed to be in our forest. Just as I was close enough to speak to him, he drove away. I followed him out of the forest and discovered that our unauthorized visitor had wandered into the laboratory though an opening in a fence that had been created by a fallen tree. When I returned to the play yard, Panbanisha was still silently waiting. I walked up to her and explained it was a man on a motorcycle and I chased him away and everything was ok now. At that point, Panbanisha seemed relaxed, asked for coffee, and we sat down and enjoyed the afternoon together. I asked her, "how is your coffee?" She responded on the keyboard "SUGAR." I inquired, "You want more sugar in your coffee?" Abandoning her silent mode, she sweetly peeped which in the bonobo world indicates affirmative.

8. *Cultural Unity*

Language constitutes a whole in the same sense that a culture constitutes a whole. The unity of language is cultural rather than grammatical. Here is quote directly from our book:

> Consider a young child who learns the numerals for the first time. What does she learn? A language? When she says how much two and two is for the first time, her parents rejoice, 'Oh, you can count,' and not, 'Oh, you can speak such exquisite English.' A child who learns the numerals the first time learns to count in the relevant life situations, rather than to speak a specific language. When the child grows older, however, she will study a foreign language in school. She must now learn the numerals a second time, those belonging to the foreign

language. But this time she does not have to learn to count, or why humans count. She already can count and is familiar with many of its functions in human life. She learned this the first time she learned the numerals. When the language teacher asks questions, she is not testing the ability to count. She is testing the ability to use foreign expression in the familiar practice of counting. When the pupil answers correctly, the teacher exclaims, 'Oh, you speak such fine French.' Not until now, sitting still in school learning the numerals a second time, does the child learn to 'speak a language'. (Segerdahl, Fields, & Savage-Rumbaugh; 2005:74)

And this reminds of many times when Nyota was a tiny baby and learning symbols, but he already *knew* places, things, and activities. And, thus following his gestures, which would lead us from the Trailer to A-Frame or from Midway to Hilltop, I could take Nyota places he wanted to go by following his gestures. On one occasion, I awoke and was looking for my instant coffee. I looked and became frustrated because I had just purchased a new can of the instant latte mix. Nyota indicated he wanted to go outdoors and uttered "GO" on the keyboard. As I carried him, he began to gesture and point, directing our course of travel. He led me to the Deer Site, one of the new locations that does not have a lexigram. There at the site, I discovered my can of coffee. Apparently someone had borrowed it. Nyota picked the can up and gave it to me. In this situation, he was answering my earlier question "where was my coffee" in a world where there was no symbol for the location, nor could he say with his mouth, and the evidence of the answer was in another space. The grammar of living and the knowledge thereof is the essence of the cultural unity that empowered Nyota to answer my question in a world where the answer did not exist in terms of lexigrams.

9. *Non-arbitrariness*

The linguistic sign is arbitrary because something else is not arbitrary: the practice in which the sign is used. It would have been easy to design the lexigrams differently, but unnatural to design uses of signs in the same arbitrary spirit.

Most of the lexigrams used in the history fo the research are arbitrary symbols; however, this issue is more important and critical to methods of ape language investigations of the 1970s and to Hockett's design feature of language than to us. While arbitray symbols offer all linguistic or mathematical systems flexibility, creativity, and generative power – for Nyota's world, there was only one Deer Site, a place where the coffee can was hiding. A tree is not arbitrary nor is a dog or a rock. While humans and non-humans are able to use arbitray symbols, there is nothing fundamentally non-linguistic about iconic symbols, photographs, or the thing or place itself. There is a grammar to the way we live which arises from the cultural logic of tangible world we negotiate by the tools of habit and creative novel invention.

10. *Reflexivity*

To have language is to be able to discuss language, to be able to ask what something is called, to explain what one means.

Reflexivity is all of those things which involve negotiating meaning, understanding requests, checking for reception, creating new names for things, and teaching. All these aspects of reflexiveness are manifest in the accounts above. They are as well, recorded in NHK's video-documentaries Kanzi I, II, and III. An instance of teaching which we recount in Segerdahl et al. (2005) is as follows:

When Nyota was three years old, Pär Segerdahl carried him in the forest according to Nyota's directions. Nyota pointed the way when Pär asked. When they approached one of the halting-places along the track, Pär asked, 'What's this place called then?' Since they did not carry a keyboard, Pär did not expect an answer. He just wanted to say something. However, he felt that Nyota reacted and tried to climb out of his arms. Pär looked up and saw that Nyota placed his index finger on a printed sign, just above the entrance. It was a big version of the lexigram CRISSCROSS. The bonobo Nyota taught the human Pär the name of the halting-place, when the human asked (p. 81).

I chose to emphasize this aspect of reflexiveness because it strongly characterizes the nature of our bonobos' interest in communication. Kanzi and his family understand what it means to not understand or not to know. I have repeatedly observed the apes possess a very high level of interest in facilitating visitors and new employees negotiate their awkward ignorance. I have, all to often, observed humans failing to understand what the apes were offering them, missing salient communications with a visitor attending to eveyrthing but communication – and then seemingly characterizing the bonobos communications as exclusively about requests for foods. Here, Pär is commenting to comment, but Nyota responds authentically and teaches Pär something he didn't know.

11. *Flexible Interface of Primate Reactions*

Humans and apes become curious, angry, happy, or anguished in similar ways, and turn to others according to related social and emotional patterns. The infant's development towards language starts in interactions that center on these common primate reactions. This interface of primate reactions is flexible and can gradually incorporate the use of words.

And thus we come full circle from the wolf children, to human children, and to ape children. Early experience, total submersion into the cultural dynamics of a society shape the organism in its dramatic form; however, we fail to see this dynamic when human children are raised in human society. The exception arises in our attention with respect to the example of the wolf children in a way that we have not as readily detected in ape children. Yet, the cases in point, wolf children and human enculturated apes, clearly demonstrates the flexibility of the interface of primate reaction and emphsizes the enormous plasticity that the pre- and post-natal

ontogenies offers to theories of development. The implications for this dynamic cannot be overstated with respect to the practical implications for treatment of communicative deficiencies in humans.

12. *Moral and Personal Dimension*

Language exists as an ongoing drama between persons. The idea of a neutral observer of language is unclear, since language always is present, for instance, in the practical arrangement of the test situation, negotiation of participation.

The absurdity of ape language research is witnessed in the elegant trials demonstrating Kanzi language competence. It is before, after, and in between those trials where Savage-Rumbaugh is explaining to Kanzi what he needs to do participate in research. The absurdity grows as the language between the trials is far more complex than the language in the trials being tested. The experiment places Kanzi sitting on a cube before a table in which an array of nine photographs of objects or people are placed. Before trial Sue says, "Kanzi you need sit down at your table and look at your picture. Don't look at Sue." During the trials, Sue stands behind Kanzi and asked, "Kanzi, can you give Sue Pears" Kanzi hands Sue the photograph of the pears back over his head facing away from Sue. Then "Kanzi, can you give Sue the picture of Panbanisha?" Kanzi hands the photograph of his sister Panbanisha over his head backwards to Sue. This repeats until we are down to the last photograph. Before Sue can ask the question, Kanzi picks up the photograph and is turning around to Sue. Sue responds, "Turn around Kanzi we are not through." Kanzi turns back around, puts the picture back on the table and then Sue asks, "Kanzi, can you give Sue potato?" and Kanzi politely hands Sue the picture. After the trials, Sue has to answer Kanzi's questions as to whether he can go see Matata or gets some grapes. Sue explains that he has some more pictures to do and that he can go see Matata and get some grapes later. And the trials start again. From an ethnographic perspective, the empirical trials are, in fact, an emic to etic transliterations of aspects of the Pan/Homo society at the LRC. And from this perspective, not nearly as absurd as when the trials are understood and accepted in this context by the academic audience.

Conclusion

The idea of ethnographic accounts with non-human primates is new, and perhaps startleling to ethological and cartesianist perspectives. However, having conversations with apes, *whether they have language or not*, is a fact of our world. How these apes became this way when other population of apes do not appear to have these competencies is easier to understand if one accepts the notion that chimpanzee, bonobos, orangutans, and gorillas are *not* biological preparations with species specific behaviors which would prevent them from acquiring human modes of behaving. One must consider that Vygotsky's idea of zone of proximal development (ZPD) is an effect with continuity within, at least, *Pan* and *Homo*. Kellogg demonstrated this idea in 1931 and it is well understood fact by humans who followed Kellogg, raising ape children, such as The Carpenters, The Gardners, Stephanie Lafarge, The Timerlins, Lynn Miles, Penny Patterson, Sue Savage-Rumbaugh, Liz Pugh, Claudine Andre, and William Fields. When humans raise non-human primates, human modes of responding are quickly evident in the ape child. The ZPD is the critical radius upon which enculturation occurrs. The effects are total and permanent and pre-empt biology. This idea is part of the explanation of why researchers observe so many different outcomes with culturally different groups of chimpanzees or bonobos. Culture is powerful force cross-modally radiating from acts of living individuals with profound and tyrannnical effects upon plastic organsims in immediate post-ontogeny in zone of proximal development. To invert Vygotsky's precept of "Every function in child's life appears twice . . ." (1978, 57), we affirm, if a function and it's isomorphisms are not present in a child's early development, it does not readily appear in the adult.

Notes

1. Between 1932 and 2005, the history of ape baby rearing has passed through the many paradigms of Hayes & Hayes (1951), Gardner & Gardner (1969), Premack (1971b), Fouts & Fouts (1989), Terrace, Petitto, Sanders, & Bever (1979), Miles (1983), Patterson (1978), and Rumbaugh (1993), Savage-Rumbaugh (1986), Savage-Rumbaugh et al. (1993). For a history of ape language see Duane Rumbaugh's book titled *Intelligence of Apes and Other Rational Beings*, 2003.

2. Both girls died at an early age. Like other feral children, the wolf children were judged to be sub-normal in intelligence and it was assumed that their intellectual deficits prevented them from being able to adapt to their new surrounding. This interpretation was common in explaining the problems of adjustment in feral children and was, in fact, the explanation offered by Squires (1927). Kellogg disagree with the interpretation, and in two replies published in the American Journal of Psychology (1931, 1933), he argued that the wolf children learned to be wild animals because that was exactly what their environment demanded of them. He believes in the strong impact of early experience and the existence of critical periods in development, and he maintained that the problem with civilizing feral children was the difficulty of overturning the habits learned early in life Benjamin & Bruce, 1982, p.466). http://www.psy.fsu.edu/history/wnk/ape.html

3. This experiment had been proposed in 1909 by Lightner Witmer based upon the failed attempts to teach adult circus apes human modes of responding.

4. Opponents to Kellogg's research proposal argued that the experiment was inhumane because Kellogg's son Donald was being used as a research subject. Interestingly, no one objected to the separation of Gua from her biological mother as would be the case in 2005.

5. In is important to note that Savage-Rumbaugh intentionally organized Kanzi early rearing as bi-species. This effort ensured that Kanzi would be able to recognize other bonobos

as like himself and to develop normal social behaviors with others of his species. This was a critical feature of the ethics built into the background of the scientific initiative by the investigator.

6   Some have argued that Chomsky has revised his opinions and we are asked why we address his classical positions. Our critique of Chomsky is not about Chomsky and his progress, but rather a recognition that classical Chomskyism continues to influence contemporary multi-disciplinary thinking.

7   Capital letters are used to represent lexigrams on our keyboard. Because our qualitative reporting includes lexigram utterances, as well as vocal utterances, pointing, gestures, and iconic representations, discussions are best illuminated by this convention. When we use all caps, we are referring to a lexigram board event or referring to the lexigram.

8   Anyone who lives with Kanzi and his family know that these descriptions are not appropriately disposed through notion of anthropomorphism. That term is a concept that is used by thinkers who simply do not have direct and extended experience with the matters under discussion. It assumes ideas that have not been factually established to explain away subjective experience with non-humans that would not be used to equally explain away the same types of observations with humans.

References

Bickerton, D. (1990). *Language and Species*. Chicago and London: The University of Chicago Press.

Bickerton, D. (1995). *Language and Human Behavior*. Seattle: University of Washington Press.

Benjamin, L. and Bruce, D. (1982). From Bottle-fed Chimp to Bottlenose Dolphin: a contemporary appraisal of Winthrop Kellogg. *The Psychological Record* 32, 461–482.

Bonner, J. T. (1980). *The Evolution of Culture in Animals*. Princeton: Princeton University Press.

Boyd, R. and Richerson, P. H. (1985). *Culture and the Evolutionary Process*. Chicago: University of Chicago Press.

Bruner, J. (1983). *Child's Talk. Learning to Use Language*. New York and London: W. W. Norton & Company.

Calvin, W. (2004). *A Brief History of the Mind*. Oxford: Oxford University Press.

Chomsky, N. (1957). *Syntactic Structures*. The Hague: Mouton.

Chomsky, N. (1959). Review of *Verbal Behavior* by B. F. Skinner. *Language* 35: 26–58.

Darwin, C. (1859). *The Origin of Species*. London: John Murray.

Dawkins, R. (1976). *The Selfish Gene*. Oxford: Oxford University Press.

Denzin, Norman, K. (1997). Do Unto Others: In defense of the new writing. *Taboo Vol. 1*.

Donald, M. (2001). *A Mind So Rare. The Evolution of Human Consciousness*. New York and London: W. W. Norton and Company.

Fitch, W. T. and Hauser, M. D. (2004). Computational Constraints on Syntactic Processing in a Nonhuman Primate. *Science* 303, 377–380.

Fouts, R. S. and Fouts, D. H. (1989). *Loulis in conversation with cross-fostered chimpanzees*. In Gardner, R. A., Gardner, B. T. and von Cantfort (Eds.), (1973) *Teaching Sign Language to Chimpanzees*. Albany: State University of New York Press.

Fox, R. G. and King, B. J. (Eds.), (2002). *Anthropology Beyond Culture*. Oxford and New York: Berg.

Gardner, R. A. and Gardner, B. T. (1969). Teaching Sign Language to a Chimpanzee. *Science* 165, 664–672.

Gardner, R. A. and Gardner, B. T. (1971). Two-way communication with an infant chimpanzee. In A. Schrier and F. Stollinitz (Eds.), *Behavior of Nonhuman Primates* (vol 4, pp. 117–184).

Guinet, C. and Bouvier, J. (1995). Development of Intentional Stranding Hunting Techniques in Killer Whale (*Orcinus orca*) Calves at Crozet Archipelago. *Canadian Journal of Zoology* 73, 27–33.

Hauser, M. D., Chomsky, N., and Fitch, W. T. (2002). The Faculty of Language: What Is It, Who Has It, and How Did It Evolve? *Science* 298, 1569–1579.

Hayes, K. J. and Hayes, C. H. (1951). The Intellectual Development of a Home-Raised Chimpanzee. *Proceedings of the American Philosophical Society* 95, 105–109.

Hirata, S., Myowa, M., and Matsuzawa, T. (1998). Use of Leaves as Cushions to Sit on Wet Ground by Wild Chimpanzees. *American Journal of Primatology* 44, 215–220.

Hockett, C. F. (1963). The Problem of Universals in Language. In: Greenberg, J. H. (Ed.),

Universals of Language. Cambridge, MA: MIT Press.

Kellogg, W. N. (1931). Humanizing the Ape. *Psychological Review* 38, 160–176.

Kellogg, W. N. (2002). *The Ape and The Child: A Research Project Conducted At Orange Park Florida (1931–1932)*. Retrieved December 15, 2005 http://www.psy.fsu.edu/historywnk/ape.html

Kellogg, W. N. and Kellogg, L. A. (1993) *The Ape and The Child: A Research Project Conducted At Orange Park Florida (1931–1932)*. New York: Whittlesay House.

Pinker, S. (1994). *The Language Instinct*. New York: William Morrow.

Miles, L. H. (1983). Apes and Language: The Search for Communication Competence. In *Language and Primates: Perspectives and Implications* edited by J. de Luce and H. T. Wilder. (Springer-Verlag), New York. 43–61.

Murphy, R. (1986). *Culture and Social Anthropology: An Overture*. 2nd (Ed.), Englewood Cliffs, NJ: Prentice-Hall.

Patterson, F. G. (1978). The Gestures of a Gorilla: Sign Language Acquisition in Another Pongid Species. *Brain And Language* 572–97

Premack, D. (1986). *Gavagai! Or the future history of the animal language controversy*. Cambridge: MIT Press.

Premack, D. (1971a). Language in Chimpanzee? *Science* 172: 808–822.

Premack, D. (1971b). On the assessment of language competence in the chimpanzee. In A. M. Schrier and F. Sollnitz. (eds). *Behavior of Nonhuman Primates*. (Vol 4, pp. 808–822)

Rumbaugh, D. M. (1977). *Language Learning by a Chimpanzee: the LANA Project*. New York: Academic Press.

Rumbaugh, D. M. (2003). *Intelligence of Apes and Other Rational Beings*. New Haven: Yale University Press.

Rumbaugh, D. M., von Glaserfeid, E. C., Warner, H., Pisani, P., Gill, T. V., Brown, J. V., Bell, C. L., Exploring the Language Skills of Lana the Chimpanzee. *International Journal of Symbology* 4, 1–9.

Savage-Rumbaugh, E. S. (1986). *Ape Language*: From Conditioned Response to Symbol. New York: Columbia University Press.

Savage-Rumbaugh, E. S, Fields, W. M., and Taglialatela, J. (2000). Ape Consciousness-Human Consciousness: A Perspective Informed by Language and Culture. *American Zoologist* 40, 910–921.

Savage-Rumbaugh, E. S, Fields, W. M., and Taglialatela, J. (2001). Language, Speech, Tools and Writing. A Cultural Imperative. *Journal of Consciousness Studies* 8, 273–292.

Savage-Rumbaugh, E. S., Murphy, J., Sevcic, R. A., Brakke, K. E., Williams, S. L., and Rumbaugh, D. M.,(1993). *Language Comprehension in Ape and Child*. Monographs of the Society for Research in Child Development, serial no. 233, 58(3–4).

Savage-Rumbaugh, E. S., Shanker, S. G., and Taylor, T. J. (1998). *Apes, Language and the Human Mind*. Oxford and New York: Oxford University Press.

Segerdahl, P. (2003). Conversation Analysis as Rigorous Science. In: Prevignano, C. L. and Thibault, P. J. (Eds). *Discussing Conversation Analysis. The Work of Emanuel A. Schegloff*. Amsterdam and Philadelphia: J. Benjamins.

Segerdahl, P., Fields, W., and S. Savage-Rumbaugh. (2005). *Kanzi's Primal Language*. London: Palgrave/Macmillan.

Shanker, S. G. (1994). Ape Language in a New Light. *Language and Communication* 14, 59–85.

Shanker, S. G. (2001). What Children Know When They Know What a Name Is. *Current Anthropology* 42, 481–513.

Shanker, S. G. (2002). The Generativist-Interactionist Debate Over Specific Language Impairment: Psycholinguistics at a Crossroads. *American Journal of Psychology* 115, 415–450.

Shanker, S. G. and King, B. J. (2002). The Emergence of a New Paradigm in Ape Language Research. *Behavioral and Brain Sciences* 25, 605–656.

Squires, P. C. (1927). 'Wolf Children' of India. *American Journal of Psychology* 38, 313–315.

Taglialatela, J. P. & Savage-Rumbaugh, E. S. (2000). Vocalization production and usage in language-competent, captive bonobos, (Pan paniscus)." [abstract] *American Journal of Primatology* 51 (Supplement 1), 95.

Taglialatela, J. P., Savage-Rumbaugh, E. S., and Baker, L. A. (2003). Vocal Production by a Language-Competent *Pan paniscus*. *International Journal of Primatology* 24, 1–17.

Taylor, T. J. (1992). *Mutual Misunderstanding. Scepticism and the Theorizing of Language and Interpretation*. Durham and London: Duke University Press.

Taylor, T. J. (1994). The Anthropomorphic and the Sceptical. *Language and Communication* 14: 115–127.

Terrace, H. S. (1979). *Nim*. New York: Knopf.

Terrace, H. S., Petitto, L. A., Sanders, R. J., and Bever, T. G. (1979). Can an Ape Create a Sentence? *Science* 206, 891–902.

Tomasello, M. (1994). Can an Ape Understand a Sentence? A Review of *Language Comprehension in Ape and Child* by E. S. Savage-Rumbaugh et al. *Language and Communication* 14, 377–390.

Tomasello, M. (1999). *The Cultural Origins of Human Cognition*. Cambridge, MA, and London, England: Harvard University Press.

Toth, N., Schick, K., Savage-Rumbaugh, E. S., Sevcik, R., and Rumbaugh, D. (1993). Pan the Tool-Maker: Investigations into Stone Tool-Making and Tool-Using Capabilities of a Bonobo (*Pan paniscus*). *Journal of Archeological Science* 20, 81–91.

Toth, N., Schick, K., and Semaw, S. (2003). A Comparative Study of the Stone Tool-Making Skills of *Pan*, *Australopithecus*, and *Homo sapiens*. In: Toth, N. and Schick, K. (Eds.), *The Oldowan: Case Studies into the Earliest Stone Age*. Bloomington, Indiana: CRAFT Press.

Valsiner, J. (1994). Cultural and Human Development: A co-constructionist perspective. *Annals of Theoretical Psychology* 10.

Valsiner, J. and Van Der Veer, R. (2000) *The Social Mind: Construction of the Idea*. Cambridge: Cambridge University Press.

Valsiner, J. (Ed.), (2005). Heinz Werner and developmental science. New York: Kluwer Scientific/Plenum.

Valsiner, J. (2005). Transformation and lexible forms: where qualitative psychology begins. *Qualitative Research IN Psychology* 4(4), 39–57.

Vygotsky, L. S. (1962). *Thought and Language*. Cambridge, MA: MIT Press.

Vygotsky, L. S. (1978). *Mind and Society*. Cambridge, MA: MIT Press.

Vygotsky, L. S. (1994). *Social Development Theory*. Retrieved December 15, 2005 http://tip.psychology.org/vygotsky.html

Wertsch, J., del Rio, P. and Alvarez, A. (1996). Sociocultural Studies; history, action and mediation, in J. Wertsch, P. del Rio & A. Alvarez (Eds.), *Sociocultural Studies of Mind*. Cambridge: Cambridge University Press.

Whiten, A., Goodall, J., McGrew, W. C., Nishida, T., Reynolds, V., Sugiyama, Y., Tutin, C. E. G., Wrangham, R. W., and Boesch, C. (1999). Cultures in Chimpanzees. *Nature* 399, 682–685.

Whorf, B. L. (1956). *Language, Thought, and Reality: Selected Writings of Benjamin Lee Whorf*. edited and with an introduction by J. B. Carroll. Cambridge, MA: MIT Press.

Wilson, Robert, A. (1999) Preface: Philosophy. In R. A Wilson and C. K. Frank (Eds.), *The MIT Encyclopedia of Cognitive Science* (pp. xv–xxxvii). Cambridge, MA: MIT Press.

CHAPTER 9

The End of Myths and Legends About the Biological and Cultural Evolution

A New View in the Knowledge on Hominid Paleo-Ethoecology

Jordi Serrallonga

Introduction

Current studies about the biological and cultural evolution of the first African hominids, and especially those related to the origin and development of the human genus, have often been focused primarily on the always hypothetical cognitive capacities of those bipedal primates. What has been relegated to a second place are the particular ecological conditions that could be reasons for the emergence of various cultural behaviors – or adaptive strategies. The emergence of these strategies has been discussed among archaeologists, paleoanthropologists, and primatologists who want pre-human hominids to take a central stage in the cultural evolution.

Hence, owing to data from the fossil record (archaeology, paleoecology, paleonthology) and from the contemporary record (ethoecology of human and non-human primates) – past *versus* present – in this paper we review some of the hypotheses that, in our opinion, still remain in force in the core of archaeology and paleoanthropology. A discourse that, far from taking away the indisputable merits of human cognitive achievements, will lead us – among other things – to claim the existence of intelligent minds far before the *Homo faber*.

Forest Bipeds: A Life Between Ground and Trees

Until recently (there still are manuals that insist on this) paleoanthropologists linked the origin of the first biped hominids to East African savannah. Nowadays we know this is wrong. Bipedalism and therefore hominids (in the most traditional sense of the term) emerged in the forest patches that, after the gradual dryness that affected East Africa from the Miocene, edged with the new open lands (Pickford & Senut, 2001). This idea changes our conception and analysis of the behavior of Mio-Pliocene fossil hominids, which combined terrestrial bipedalism with the capability of climbing trees (Sabater Pi, Veà, & Serrallonga, 1997, 2003; Serrallonga, Sabater Pi, & Veà, 1998).

But, even though they admit the existence of bipeds in the forests, many specialists still ask themselves the reason for the appearance of this new locomotion model in a forest or mosaic ecological niche. Savannah seems the ideal model to explain such anatomical adaptation: seeing upon high grass, transporting food and tools owing to the liberation of the forelimbs previously used for knuckle walking (walking on the knuckles as is seen in bonobos, *Pan paniscus*, chimpanzees, *Pan troglodytes*, and gorillas, *Gorilla gorilla*), reduced corporal exposition to sun radiations, lower energetic costs, and so on. On the other hand, forest appears to be a less useful model to explain bipedalism since forest pongids from Central and Western Africa are successful quadrupeds.

Thus, shall we believe that bipedalism in forests was a "luxury"? Was it a kind of locomotion that, if it were not due to the vanishing of woods and the success of bipedalism in savannah, would have disappeared? We can take a look at the ethoprimatological record.

In the forests of Central and Western Africa, it can be observed how bonobos and chimpanzees adopt an upright posture and use bipedal locomotion with frequency. This postural or positional bipedalism, as it has sometimes been called to distinguish it from anatomical bipedalism (Serrallonga, Gay, & Medina, 2005), astonishes us because, although the anatomy of bonobos and chimpanzees is obviously quite similar to that of a quadruped (long narrow pelvis, backward position of the foramen magnum, almost inexistent femoral neck, no curvature of the spinal column, and so forth), it manages to be highly efficient. Unlike humans, bonobos and chimpanzees have no abductor muscles to hold the pelvis in a horizontal position while only one leg is resting on the ground (thus allowing us to keep our balance and avoid falling over). Instead, chimpanzees must make a big muscular effort to keep their balance when walking but, in fact, they manage to take strides – even long ones and while running – which are a far cry from the little steps made by some other mammals (e.g., ursids, canids, etc.) when raised up on two legs. These aspects are being studied in the *Pan erectus Project* (Serrallonga, Gay, & Medina, 2005), which is being carried out in the Zoological Park of Barcelona

with a colony of captive chimpanzees (*Pan troglodytes troglodytes*). At this point, we must make it clear that we are not interested in just the biomechanical aspects of bipedalism; rather, one of the main objectives of this research is to study everything that has to do with the functionality of this kind of locomotion in chimpanzees. For example, preliminary results from many hours of observation allow us to state that chimpanzees adopt a bipedal posture in order to transport objects (food and tools) whenever both their hands are occupied. Was not that one of the advantages used to explain the emergence of bipedalism in the core of the savannah? Other functions of the occasional bipedalism exhibited by the captive chimpanzees that have been studied would also be important in the natural context of wild open spaces, that is, vigilance, attack, and defense. These conclusions match the data observed in the ethological recordings of chimpanzees and, especially, bonobos in their natural habitat (Kano, 1992; Goodall, 1986; de Waal & Lanting, 1997).

Our claim is that bipedalism in forests is also adaptive. Those pre-humans who roamed the forests had their hands free to use, produce, and transport tools or to carry food (a more economical kind of movement, in biomechanical terms). They could also gather fruit from low bushes and defend themselves against or attack other individuals – either from their own or another species – more safely and effectively (just to give some examples). And this was when they were on the ground, because their other anatomical adaptations, which were more characteristic of an arboreal primate, also enabled them to move about through the trees. This arborealism, besides being useful for obtaining food, played a key role in another chapter of our ancestors' life: the nesting behavior.

Sleeping in Heights: The Nesting Behavior

When I was just a restless student I asked Donald Johanson, co-discoverer of "Lucy" the famous *Australopithecus afarensis*, his opinion about something that worried me a lot: how did australopithecines sleep, on the ground or upon trees? We must remember that in that moment, by the beginning of the 1990s, Johanson was contrary to all those scientists (for example Brigitte Senut and Christine Tardieu, disciples of his colleague and godfather of "Lucy" Yves Coppens) who affirmed that the famous *Australopithecus*, besides being biped on the ground, was also capable of climbing trees quite easily. Therefore, we should not be surprised for his answer to my question: "Lucy" and her relatives slept on the ground on open air. This answer, he knows, did not convince me at all because I had in mind other primates whose anatomical and ethoecological characteristics are very similar to those of the early hominids. Johanson was not, and is not, the only one to think that the first human ancestors could not be modest mixed arboreal beings but elegant exclusive bipeds. That was especially true with "Lucy" because she was considered by the team of the Institute of Human Origins as the direct ancestor of the genus *Homo* (an opinion nowadays cast into oblivion in favor of *Australopithecus africanus* for some people: Phillip V. Tobias and those who follow him, including me; Lockwood & Tobias, 1999). If, at a time, it was difficult to admit that the origins of the human genus were fossil primates with a half-human half-simian look (sweat and tears were shed by Raymond Dart until he could impose his *Australopithecus africanus* facing the fraudulent *Eoanthropus dawsonii* or "Piltdown Man"; Tobias, 1984), the reticence to admit a life on trees is still palpable. We do not know why, but there is still some fear to link our past to trees: a not enough dignified origin? Most primate species that live in the different arboreal levels in forests would not think the same. Even the Maasai from the Peninj area, who are nomadic cattle-raisers, proud of their lineage, even they do not hesitate to narrate what follows, while we chat by the fire of our camp site in Natron lake: "*Formerly, men did not have huts and lived, as nowadays monkeys do, under the safety and protection provided by trees when the night falls down*" (Serrallonga, 2001). One

way or the other, if there is something we are almost sure of is that, at night, the first bipeds from the Mio-Pliocene did not make their nests on the ground but on the top of trees. We have developed in detail this etho-ecological aspect in already published studies (Sabater Pi, Veà, & Serrallonga, 1997, 2003; Serrallonga, Sabater Pi, & Veà, 1998).

Our closest living relatives, that are bonobos and chimpanzees, make their nests on the top of the trees to spend the night. If we take into account a set of ecological, physiological, anatomical and cultural parameters – an interdisciplinary approach – we can conclude that the first fossil hominids were also forced to build nests upon trees, at least until much later novelties, relevant to camp in the open field, were introduced. Firstly, there were many advantages of nesting upon trees. Trophic pressure in forest areas of Eastern Africa, as it happens in the forests of Central and Western Africa, was much lower than in the open field. In the savannah, the concentration of large herds of gregarious herbivores entailed a high presence of predatory species. At night, hominids, being short of resources to run and having a deficient crepuscular and nocturnal eyesight, contrary to nocturnal hunters (see the case of big felines), would have been an easy prey in a camp site in the open. It is true that some primates have adapted to life in the savannah; the best examples are the representatives of the genus *Papio*, but they are better gifted to run, have greater natural defenses (big fangs) and their physiology of sleep is quite different to that of great apes. Gorillas, chimpanzees, and bonobos show very deep REM phases (Sabater Pi, Veà, & Serrallonga, 1997, 2003), as do humans, and that forces them to sleep on horizontal platforms due to the muscular atony that affects their locomotion muscles. On the other hand, baboons can sleep while sitting and have a light sleep, which allows them to perceive danger more easily (Bert, Ayats, & Collomb, 1967). We can deduce that fossil hominids, with a deep REM sleep, would have preferred sleeping in nests, made of intertwined branches and leaves and located on the top of the trees, in order to avoid being surprised during their resting activities. Even though in savannahs there are also big trees (in fact they are the favorite dormitories for Tanzanian *Papio cynocephalus* from Sinya, in opposition to the rock shelters used by *Papio anubis* from the Natron lake; Serrallonga, Medina, & Galbany, 2005), it should be much better to frequent those woods which edged the savannah during the Mio-Pliocene. As we have stated before, in forests there is a lower trophic pressure: there are no big herds of gregarious mammals and, therefore, there are fewer predators. The fact is that studies on gorillas and chimpanzees from forests show that their only natural enemies, apart from *Homo sapiens*, are leopards (a feline that frequents trees) and eagles that are specialized in hunting small primates . . . far from the greater presence of felines, canids, and hyenids of African savannah. We should not forget that our first ancestors were not much bigger than a bonobo or a chimpanzee.

Then, when did we begin sleeping on the ground? Given that it is related to the next two sections that we are about to tackle, we will give the answer later on.

Homo Faber Versus Australopithecus Habilis: Ethoecology and Archaeological Record

Another myth we can find in archaeology and paleoanthropology manuals is the one related to the *Homo faber* concept (Serrallonga, 1994). It states that the first tools, or technological signs, would be related to the appearance of the human genus (*Homo habilis*). That is a big error. If we resort once again to the ethoprimatological record, we can establish that there are non-human primates, which are capable not only of using but also of making tools. Particularly in the case of chimpanzees, we have been able to establish the use and production of multiple tool types with very diverse purposes (Serrallonga, 2005). If we take into account that chimpanzees and hominids share a common ancestor it is easy to think that, long before the *Homo* genesis, the first forest hominids used and made tools from the raw materials they could find in the woods. Materials like wood, bark, leaves, stems or stalks, which perishable composition prevented them from conservation in the archaeological or paleontological record. Those tools would presumably be efficient for solving problems very similar to the ones solved nowadays by chimpanzees in their natural habitat (gathering food, absorbing water, wrapping up in order to keep warm or protect parts of their bodies, self-defense and defense of the group, communication, etc.). It would be strange that, facing similar ecological conditions, forest hominids had renounced the well-known advantages of the instrumental behavior only because of being pre-humans. This instrumental behavior, undoubtedly, could have been even more frequent than in the case of chimpanzees, given the advantages of bipedalism (in the forest as in savannah) for manipulating and transporting tools.

Even though we are quite sure about our deductions (which depend on the ethoecological record of chimpanzees and other primates) such an approach will always be discussed and put in quarantine by almost the unanimity of our colleagues. Everybody knows science can only advance through objective evidence, through observable and measurable elements. In our case, it is true that we have never found a pre-human in association with small modified branches or fossilized leaves-made sponges. But according to this rule, we could start saying goodbye to these wonderful and fascinating disciplines that are archaeology and paleoanthropology. Why? Because most published hypotheses and conclusions about many aspects of the fossil humans' behavior, based on their cognitive and anatomical capacities, are much more speculative than stating that an australopithecine made wooden bars or nested upon trees. As it happens, we still have never found any pre-human which died with a non-modified stone in its hands (as the ones used by chimpanzees for nut cracking) as neither have we heard a conversation between Neanderthals. If paleoanthropologists are conceited about working with measurable data (detection of the language association areas in endocranial casts, a good vocal apparatus, etc.), paleontologists have also good measurable data about the anatomy of the australopithecines (with regard to their hands, for example, and their encephalic capacity). Why believe ones and not the others? Is it a matter of scientific credibility or a straightforward matter of anthropocentrism? Undoubtedly, it is the second case. It is still hard to admit that an australopithecine presented cognitive abilities to manipulate and make tools (something we can daily observe in the chimpanzees of Gombe, Tai, Mahale, etc.; Whiten et al., 1999). However, we listen enraptured to the discussions about whether *Homo neanderthalensis*, *Homo erectus* or maybe *Homo habilis* were the first ones to chat about how had the hunting day gone off. Some researchers observe in the endocranial casts the scientific basis – observable and measurable – that suggests that at least the speaking ability existed in the fossil humans (Tobias, 1997). This scientific basis is perfectly comparable to the one – also observable and measurable – that we all could see in the hands of the fossil prehumans to state that, at least, there existed the capacity to manipulate tools in such hominids. If we take more often into consideration the ethoecological context perhaps we will forget about such unproductive discussions.

However, we think that the existence or not of tool use in the first Mio-Pliocene hominids was related more to the ethoecological context than to a *Homo* versus *Australopithecus* higher or lower cognitive ability. We only need to look at bonobos. In their natural habitat, *Pan paniscus* do not produce tools and use them very little (there are scarce observations of instrumental behavior in bonobos). Then it would have been easy to state, following the same reasoning of archaeologists and paleoanthropologists, that bonobos are less intelligent or less capable anatomically than chimpanzees in the use and modification of tools. But we know it would have been an error, since results obtained with bonobos in laboratory conditions are extraordinary (Schick et al., 1999;

Toth et al., 1993). The point is that bonobos' ecological and ethological context does not force them to make tools in order to solve certain situations. For example, in the case of the sexual behavior, the chimpanzees of Mahale Mountains (Tanzania) modify leaves in order to make a sort of decoy. Males hold an end of the stalk using their teeth and tighten it with one of their hands; afterwards, with their free hand they hit the object, making it vibrate and therefore attracting the females (Nishida, 1980). On the other hand, bonobos' foreplay is based on touches and caresses that, from an anthropocentric and ethnocentric view, could seem more "intelligent" (the reciprocal and well-accepted love games between male and female) than the use of a call by the males in order to obtain the females services (an act which is considered male chauvinistic among *Homo sapiens*).

We will conclude that definitions as the one from the French pre-historian François Bordes, which considers tools to be the element that differentiates humans from animals, are unjustified. Another thing would be talking about technological complexity, diversity and frequency of use . . . then, obviously, the human genus differs from bonobos, chimpanzees and other living primates. But even in such a point, we dare to defend that the beginning of this differentiation was also based more on ecological than on cognitive questions. Hence, we think that the generalization about the first lithic industries as being a consequence of a higher intelligence in the human genus should be qualified and contrasted with the paleoecological conditions of East Africa during the Plio-Pleistocene. The next section deals with this subject.

Savannah: Scavengers and/or Hunters and Stone Tools

The consecutive climatic crisis in the eastern area of the African continent reduced forest spaces even more. Occupying the savannah would not be much attractive for the first hominids. In the forests there was abundance of food, which was concentrated and of good quality. Nutritious fruits were complemented by tender shoots, seeds, fungi, insects, and the hunting of small mammals and other primates (taking into account ethoprimatological observations). The problem of safety, as we have already discussed in detail, was quite well solved. So this situation was a "paradise" for the first hominids, which took advantage of it while they could. On the other hand, savannahs offered the view of an inhospitable landscape: vegetables were scarce and dispersed and the probability of being hunted was higher for an anatomically defenseless primate. But hominids managed to adapt successfully to the ecological change and to life in savannah. How? Well, mainly due to a novelty in their diet which at the same time forced them to develop new cooperation and social-cohesion strategies and also to improve some of the strategies they already had in the forests. This novelty has a lot to do with the appearance of those cultural elements that are thought to be exclusive of the *Homo* genus: the lithic industries.

In too many occasions, and after having presented our works on chimpanzee technological skills, someone from the auditorium has exclaimed ironically: well then, if chimpanzees are so intelligent, why is it that they do not make stone tools as the ones found in those archaeological sites associated with the oldest specimens of the human genus? We always answer this question with another question: Why should a chimpanzee need to make stone tools? In the same way we give answer to those who, also ironically, ask us about why pre-humans did not make stone tools.

There can be no doubt that the *Homo faber* myth has been reinforced by the archaeological confirmation that there did not find industries, that is fossil elements of material culture, before the *Homo* appearance. We want to offer an alternative explanation, related to ecology, to argue the absence of stone tools near the forest australopithecines and the presence of such tools near the first representatives of the human genus who colonized the savannah.

This explanation would be that in the forest there was no need of sharp-cutting stone tools whereas in the savannah there was such a need! Indeed, savannah hominids were forced by the lack of plant foods to substitute nourishing vegetables by animal protein. This animal protein was obtained from the scavenging and hunting of middle and big-sized animals. Therefore, cutting-edge tools were needed in order to cut up the carcasses. That is why stone tools were invented. Not because of *Homo* but because of ethoecology. And, to support our idea, we will use that sort of evidence loved by armchair paleoanthropologists and archaeologists, with no speculations at all. According to these data, savannah australopithecines did use and made stone tools. But let us take one step at a time.

Chimpanzees use their dentition and their jaw-force in order to cut up small animal preys (it would be stupid for them to make decorative and superfluous stone tools, wouldn't it?). The first *Homo* who inhabited the savannah, being much slenderer than panids, were obliged to use cutting tools in order to process the carcasses of the dead mammals. If those mammals were caught or scavenged, that is another point that would require another paper. Then, we think that the change in their habitat and diet was responsible for the cutting stone tools invention. Curiously, the australopithecines that also abandoned the forest environment and inhabited the open lands, facing the same nutritional requirements, also made lithic tools. We find evidence in *Australopithecus garhi*, discovered in Ethiopia (Asfaw et al., 1999). This gracile *Australopithecus* lived in eastern Africa about 2.5 million years ago, just at the time we detect a new drought episode in the east of the Great Rift Valley. Studies about *Australopithecus garhi*'s habitat indeed reveal flora and fauna typical of savannah. But how do we know that this *Australopithecus* made stone tools? Because in association with the paleoanthropological remains, there have been found fauna remains presenting cut-marks which could only have been produced by sharp lithic tools (tools that have not been found yet, therefore the interpretation is indirect) (de Heinzelin et al., 1999). Then, our hypothesis seems to be validated: the origin of the first lithic industries was not related to a change of genus at a biological level but to an ethoecological change.

As usual, some our colleagues do not seem to be willing to accept such reasoning and they support the statement that those cut-marks that are present on the fauna associated with *Australopithecus garhi* could only have been made by a representative of the *Homo* genus. At this point we could turn the tables on them by saying: wasn't it that pre-humans were not able to make lithic assemblages since they have never been found associated with them? Following the arguments of paleoanthropologists and archaeologists there is no reason to deny *Australopithecus garhi*'s responsibility for the cut-marks, given that in association with those Ethiopian cut-marks there has not been found a *Homo* but an *Australopithecus*. And that would be valid even if there existed only one case, but the fact is that there is another flagrant example apart from the data provided by Yves Coppens about the industries association with australopithecines in Ethiopia (Coppens, 1982). It is the case of the *Paranthropus boisei* in Olduvai, Tanzania.

When Mary Leakey discovered in the FLK site in Olduvai the remains of a complete fossil hominid cranium, her husband, Louis Leakey, did not hesitate to name it *Zinjanthropus boisei* – "Zinj Man" – despite its robust, simian look (so massive was its masticating system that they nicknamed it "Nutcracker"). It was 1959 and the lithic industries found by the Leakey in the same paleontological levels where the *Zinjanthropus* (Leakey, 1959) had been found were associated with it. Then, some specialists stated that OH-5 (the inventory symbol for the "Nutcracker") resembled an australopithecine a lot. Few decades earlier, in 1925, Raymond Dart had published the remains of the "Taung Child," the South African hominid named *Australopithecus africanus* ("The South African Ape"). After the academic establishment opposition to the idea of a human origin so close to apes (the "Taung Child" was a mosaic of humanoid features – bipedal locomotion, dentition and neurological organization – and simian features – strong prognatism, small brain, etc.), Robert Broom wanted to reaffirm Dart's theory by looking for more specimens belonging to the same species. And he found them. To be precise, he found the complete cranium of an *Australopithecus africanus* female: "Mrs. Pless" (Sts 5). But on his way Broom also bumped into some hominids, which were similar to australopithecines but much more robust, the *Paranthropus robustus*. Faced with the *Zinjanthropus boisei* finding, some pointed out the great resemblance between the "Nutcracker" and the South African *Paranthropus robustus*. Louis Leakey was reluctant to accept that… he had never looked with favor on australopithecines. Conceding the premises of those who strangely kept relying on the European remains of *Eoanthropus dawsonii* or "Piltdown Man" (found in Great Britain in 1912); he thought the australopithecines were too simian to explain the origin of the human genus. We must remember that the "Piltdown Man" turned out to be the greatest fraud in science history, a very well directed falsification.

In Leakey's opinion, *Zinjanthropus* was the artisan of certain lithic industries made mainly from pebbles – Oldowan culture or pebble culture-, the oldest industries known at that time, and that could only be human's doing. Things changed when only a year later, in 1960, Jonathan Leakey, a child who played looking for fossils in those places their parents thought he could do no harm, found the remains of a hominid much slenderer than *Zinjanthropus* (Leakey, Tobias, & Napier, 1964). The new hominid – gifted with a bigger encephalic capacity- was chronologically situated at the same levels than *Zinjanthropus* and the lithic industries. Therefore, Louis Leakey did not hesitate to downgrade the "Nutcracker" from its first artisan stripes in order to promote the one that Phillip V. Tobias, John Napier, and Leaky himself would name *Homo habilis*. *Zinjanthropus* was overnight considered an australopithecine (*Australop-ithecus* or *Paranthropus boisei*); its cognitive capacities were downgraded to a pseudo-idiot category and, the most serious thing, some people even thought that it had been the victim and prey of the intelligent *Homo habilis*, the first artisan. Since then, every attempt to attribute some of those lithic tools to the "Nutcracker" has been unsuccessful, being that its neighbor was a representative of the human genus, namely, *Homo habilis* (Klein, 1989).

We differ from that opinion. From our point of view, both *Homo habilis* and *Paranthropus boisei* were responsible for the Oldowan culture. And this is not a whim against anthropocentrism but a hypothesis based, once more, on ethoecological matters. Until recently, and based on the dentition striations and the special anatomical characteristics of the masticatory system of *Paranthropus* or robust australopithecines, it has been stated that those hominids were strict vegetarians adapted to a hard foodstuff diet, that is, roots, tubers, grain and nuts. But some researches on paleo-diet, based on the analysis of isotopes from the bones of savannah robust australopithecines, seem to prove that *Paranthropus*, as the first representatives of the *Homo* genus, were also omnivorous (Sillen, 1992; Sillen, Hall, & Armstrong, 1995). It does not matter if they hunted or scavenged; the fact is that, in order to process herbivore mammals' carcasses, they needed cutting stone tools. With no more fear to be wrong than those who consider the capability of stone tool-making an exclusive merit of the human being, we think that the australopithecines, in the same ecological context and therefore facing the same needs as *Homo*, also made stone tools. Exactly the same as what we have seen in the case of *Australopithecus garhi*, it was the savannah and not a genus change what forced both "*Australopithecus habilis*" and *Homo habilis* to make sharp stone tools.

Australopithecines' cognitive abilities should not be underestimated. We are convinced that, little by little, new evidences for these abilities will be found. In a paper published in *Science* Backwell and d'Errico (2001) presented a set of bones modified by *Paranthropus robustus* in Swartkrans (South Africa). According to what is revealed by studies on traceology and experimental archaeology, those modified bones would have been used to perforate termites' nests the same way *Pan troglodytes troglodytes* from Equatorial Guinea (Sabater Pi, 1974) do nowadays in order to feed on such nutritious insects. Even paleoanthropology now seems to aim to do its part by stating that *Paranthropus*' hands were capable of manipulating instruments (Susman, 1998). Up to a point these data could be considered superfluous, although they are of high interest when it comes to increasing the credibility of our innovative approach. So, here comes again the criticism against both armchair and field archaeologists and paleoanthropologists who live with their backs to ethoprimatological studies. Why? Because if we spend some years observing the manipulating abilities of the living primates, we will realize that not only *Homo habilis*' or *Paranthropus*' hands were capable of making and using tools . . . also the hands of an African cercopithecid can do power and precision grips the same as human hands do (Escobar & García, 1997). On one occasion, and faced with this kind of arguments, a well-recognized paleoanthropologist said: "no ethoprimatologist has certainly seen a mangabey or a chimpanzee passing a coin between its fingers from one lateral side of its hand to the other" (Juan Luis Arsuaga, personal communication).

With or without coins, what we think is that the great "adaptive invention" of the savannah was not bipedalism but a cultural adaptation: "the production of stone tools." This capacity would be favored by such bipedalism which, even though it was originated in forests, became really useful for those hominids that colonized the open lands but still took advantage of the trees when the night fell. As we promised, we are going to talk about when hominids started making camps at ground level. This is a new section that will be tightly joined to the beginning of fire control.

Sleeping on the Ground and the Myth of Fire

When did the fire control take place? It is probable that, after contemplating the abundant volcanic eruptions that happened in the Great Rift Valley as well as the natural fires of savannah, some hominids got to conceptualize the great advantages that this element could bring to them. Perhaps they transported a burning branch to the core of the group and then lit other branches. They discovered that by feeding the flames with more fuel they could keep them burning day after day, night after night. In our opinion, the *Homo erectus* were responsible for this discovery. And this happened 1.5 million years ago, exactly the same dating we attribute to the archaeological and paleontological sites we are working in Peninj (Natron Lake, Tanzania). Evidence exists for this 1.5 million years date in the sites of Swartkrans (South Africa) and Koobi Fora (Kenya), although they are controversial. This evidence consists of ashes that, by what some researchers think, show the presence of fires made by *Homo* (Bellomo, 1994). Others think that they are the remains of natural savannah fires, which are almost indistinguishable from those that humans could have controlled (James, 1996). It is true that in neither of the two examples there have been found remains that prove a space preparation such as stone circles or holes excavated in the ground.

With or without proofs it seems that some kind of fire control – that does not mean fire making – happened about 1.5 million years ago. Why? Because around these dates *Homo erectus'* home bases in the open start proliferating and that shows that those hominids could spend several nights in a same site. This with no doubt implies the presence of fire, given that nowadays there is no nomadic ethnic group camping in an open or closed space without lighting a fire. Even *Homo*

habilis and *Homo rudolfensis* being still ignorant of fire, probably looked for the safety of trees where they built nests to spend the night.

Which would be the advantages of using fire? Fire permits protecting oneself from the cold. It also permits processing vegetables and meat in order to make them more tender and edible. It provides light, therefore prolonging the day, and it also promotes communication among the group subjects. But we should not forget another important question: in places such as Peninj or Olduvai (Tanzania), Koobi Fora (Kenya), Melka Kunturé (Ethiopia), and others, fire could have helped to keep savannah predators at bay while hominids rested during the night. Humans have always thought that fire, by definition, frightens animals off. At least this is what we thought before we started working, in the eastern African savannah, with experts on safaris who told us their personal experiences after more than 10 years working in contact with nature (Serrallonga, 2001).

In fact, our interpretations about the predators' respect or fear towards the fires of our ancestors surprised at professional guides of "Ciencia y Aventura" company. In his camps in Serengeti (Tanzania) they has faced in many occasions lion raids on the camping area. This is obviously a serious problem for the hypothesis of camps in the open areas depending on fire control. Indeed, Serengeti lions do not care about fires and they burst into the camps, gnaw the leather boots set out of the tents and loot the camp kitchens. None of these examples of lions' contempt for fire has ended with casualties. The learning ability, and the culture traditions among the lions, what we find interesting to explain the behavior of the camp-raiders of Serengeti.

The philosopher Jesús Mosterín would define culture is social information that is transmitted among individuals of the same species (Mosterín, 1993). For a long time it has been stated that culture was an exclusive gift of humans. Nowadays, and due to Jordi Sabater Pi, Jane Goodall, and others' studies (Whiten et al., 1999), we know that there are many other primate species capable of developing cultural behaviors. A chimpanzee that discovers how to use a stick as a lever in order to open the trunks of rotten trees and then eat the ants from inside will permit the closer subjects learning to develop the same instrumental behavior for the same purpose. This will happen time and again until every individual in the community knows this technique, and they will continue and perpetuate the tradition generation after generation. At the same time, other chimpanzees of close areas, which have never been in contact with the former group, will develop their own traditions, not necessarily related to opening trunks with a lever. In that sense, although in both western and eastern Africa there are wild nuts that can be opened with the help of stones and trunks, only the chimpanzees from western Africa have developed such instrumental behavior in a widespread way (Serrallonga, 2005). This is a culture tradition.

Perhaps what happened in the Serengeti was that lions were initially frightened of fire (agreeing with the thesis of fire as a deterrent element during the different stages of human evolution) but little by little they learnt to overcome this possible fear. And we say possible fear because, by our experience in the savannah, we dare to say that early humans' fires more than dissuading predators worked well to alert them to the location of hominid concentrations. Those early humans would have developed complex social cooperation strategies that, together with more and more efficient weapons and with the light of fires, would have made possible the defense of the group against the attacks from their natural enemies. After some fights, with casualties in both bands, lions would have learnt the lesson and would have concentrated on hunting other animals, the numerous herbivores that, at least, would not be so difficult to catch. Having last this knowledge among predators for hundreds of thousands of years – cultural tradition – when there came ethnic groups as the Sonjo or the Maasai, with bows or powerful spears and knives respectively, lions would have kept

associating fires to "danger, loose humans." On the contrary, with the tourists arrival, season after season the lions of the following generations realized that those pale and different-smelling humans (has anybody thought about how perfumes and *eaux de toilette* are affecting sensitive smells?) did not represent any danger. They even let them play with their boots and warm by their fires.

However, Africa and its tenants have always given us good lessons. Every book of prehistory says that fire kept wild beasts away from humans, and that's why we extrapolated the presence of fire in every human group living out in the open. African field experiences at least force us to reconsider such arguments, and therefore they show us why we should abandon our armchair and library and go to the field.

Contemporary Knives and Axes . . . and the Ecological Hypothesis of the African Acheulean

The lithic tools that are found in the record have been classified by archaeologists under different chrono-cultural names. First of all we find the Oldowan (from 2.7 M yrs), which is characterized by knapped pebbles and small flakes. Afterwards we find the Acheulean (from 1.8–1.6 M yrs), represented by bifacial hand-axes. Following the most traditional view, the Oldowan would correspond to *Homo habilis* and the Acheulean, which involves a more evolved technology, would correspond to *Homo erectus*. But, what happens if we find contemporary Oldowan and Acheulian assemblages together in the same area? Do we have to consider that they belong to two different hominid species? Taking into account an Ecological Hypothesis, we think that in such cases there is only one culture attributable to one hominid species. Those hominids carried out different activities in different places by using different tools, according to the availability and nature of the raw materials found in the environment (Serrallonga, 2005). Perhaps most of the problem lies in the deficient concept of culture held by archaeology.

Let us analyze the definition of culture proposed by the analytical archaeology: "A politetic collection which comprises categories of type artefacts that are found systematically together in assemblages within a geographical limited area" (Clarke, 1984, p. 441). It is evident that the culture concept in prehistoric archaeology revolves around the study of artefacts, of tools, of the material culture. This should not surprise us if we take into account that, in order to reconstruct the first stages of the human history, we only find objective evidence in the material remains excavated in archaeological sites. This is why cultural anthropologists have interpreted the culture concept in archaeology with the following words: "Archaeologists have reconstructed a culture evolution – the course of prehistory – which goes in parallel with the last part of primates' evolution (. . .) They place this evolution in a relative-time sequence based on preserved artefacts; it starts with the first appearance of culture in the Lower Paleolithic (Old Stone Age) . . . " (Diamond & Belasco, 1980, p. 22). A similar idea has been drawn by philosophers, as showed by Jesús Mosterín in his book entitled Philosophy of Culture: "When archaeologists tell us about culture (. . .), they refer to the whole techniques (especially those related to the production of weapons and tools) of these periods" (Mosterín, 1993, p. 17).

Undoubtedly, the archaeologists have inspired philosophers and cultural anthropologists through their most spread traditional working method (the tipology). The idea of a digger wearing tropical clothes, crowned with a pith helmet, and holding a magnifying glass in his hand, examining the stones found in a site. Such stones, once classified in their own drawers, will help setting an idea of a progressive cultural evolution. First, there would be the roughly flaked pebbles of the early Oldowan assemblages, dating back to 2.7 million years ago. Then we would find the hand-axes – or bifaces – of the Acheulean culture. And finally, there would be the specialized microlithic indus-

tries, which characterize the multiple Upper Paleolithic cultures and cultural facies, dating back to approximately 40,000 years ago. Indeed, in archaeology the change from a culture to another coincides quite well with the contrived periodicity that is shown in most prehistory and paleoanthropology manuals. This idea of a progressive and lineal cultural evolution is made up of stages or phases with a beginning and an end: a primitive stadium – an X primitive culture – is abandoned to go into a more advanced stage – a Y advanced culture. But we often do not take into account that historical succession, the cultural evolution, can also have been the result of accumulating socially transmitted information. That is, instead of always going from an X culture to a Y culture, it is highly probable that in some occasions there also happens an X + Y culture, which can later become an X + Y + Z culture.

The time has come to say that, when it comes to defining the culture concept, there exist different points of view coming from various disciplines. For example, cultural anthropology states that "Culture is a learnt set of traditions and lifestyles which are socially acquired by the members of a society, including their ruled repetitive thinking, feeling, and acting (that is, their behavior)" (Harris, 1996, pp. 19–20). A primatologist, Frans de Waal, also gives his definition: "Culture is a way of life shared by the members of a group but not necessarily by the members of other groups of the same species. It comprises knowledge, customs, skills, tendencies and underlying preferences, which come from being exposed to the others and learning from them (. . .)" (de Waal, 2002, p. 38). And philosophy – by Jesús Mosterín – gives us a third definition that, as the one of Frans de Waal, agrees perfectly with our arguments: " . . . in order to be considered culture, something has to satisfy the triple condition of being (1) information (2) transmitted (3) by social learning. That is why we adopt the following definition: culture is information that is transmitted (among animals of the same species) by social learning" (Mosterín, 1993, p. 32).

In view of the last two definitions, we see that archaeologists and paleoanthropologists may have classified into a unique cultural horizon several industry assemblages that could have been produced by hominids belonging to a single or different species, but with no contact between them. It is also probable that we have distinguished, with different culture names, industry assemblages produced by a single hominid group. Certainly, more than once we have catalogued under the terms of different cultures phenomena that are just responses to different ecological needs.

For example, imagine two prehistoric African sites with no paleoanthropological remains, that is, two sites in which there is no direct evidence of the hominid species responsible for them. The first site (A) has not much lithic industry. We only find small flakes in association with animal bones presenting cut-marks, the proof that they were cut up by hominids. Quite far from this site, but situated in the same studied geological area, we locate the second site (B). Here we register many hand-axes – or bifaces – that do not seem to be associated with any other kind of archaeological remain. In this example, typological archaeology might suggest that these two archaeological sites correspond to two different chrono-cultural episodes and therefore were produced by two different hominid species. Just because there are still many people who, from the existence of a more or less complex industry, infer the presence in a certain place of a more or less evolved hominid. Then, in the first site we could have said that simple tools – flakes as tool type – corresponded to an Oldowan horizon, the culture that is assigned to *Homo habilis*, whereas the site with a large number of complex pieces – bifaces as tool type – corresponded to a typical Acheulean horizon. The latter culture is assigned, also by consensus, to *Homo erectus*, which is considered a more evolved hominid, given that it had a greater brain. In short, by a strictly typological study of the tools, prehistorians would consider the first site (A) older than the second one (B), besides assigning to each one their respec-

tive hominid species (the second one more evolved than the first one).

Following our example, now imagine that we had obtained similar datings for both sites and that we had reconstructed certain ecological differences among several zones within the studied geographical area. In this case, we think that there would be no need to identify neither two cultures producing typologically different sites nor two types of hominids making two different industry assemblages. We would simply defend a hypothesis that would explain the differences between one site and the other: an Ecological Hypothesis held on the fossil, ethoprimatological, ethnological and experimental record. In our studied geographical area there could have been different sorts of anthropic activity performed by only one hominid species. Depending on the situation and ecology of the different sites, this single species generated different behavioral responses. Anthropologists will not always be able to recognize those behavioral responses, because of the lack of direct evidence, but in some cases such responses are evident due to the preservation of lithic tools and bone remains. In our case, for example, we would have detected and differentiated two of these behavioral responses that for others would represent two independent cultures:

(1) An activity related to the manipulation and processing of animal resources in places close to lakes and rivers. That would explain the existence of type A sites, that are, settlements with abundance of fauna remains – presenting cut-marks – and some stone flakes that were probably used by hominids in order to cut up the carcasses. We should not forget that fluvial and lake areas are the favorite places for several predator species to catch their preys, taking advantage of them going to drink.

(2) An activity related to the manipulation and processing of vegetal resources, far from the water sources. That would explain the existence of type B sites, where there is a high presence of large bifacial axes and a

total absence of fauna remains. Other residuals that did exist, vegetal wastes, were not preserved as fossils given their perishable nature.

To sum up, following our Ecological Hypothesis, the hominids that lived in this imaginary African region – dated between 1.8 and 1.5 million years ago – could have been *Homo erectus* capable of making Acheulean axes but also knowledgeable about those techniques used in times of *Homo habilis*. The existence of type A sites with Oldowan tools would simply correspond to the survival of still useful techniques, that is, functional techniques such as obtaining simple flakes in order to cut up preys. Therefore, going back to the culture definition we have given before (a culture that is the result of the accumulation of information: $C = X + Y + Z$), we would say that *Homo erectus* were able to produce bifacial axes because of having a technological $X + Y + Z$ knowledge. But that does not mean they had forgotten technological X or $X + Y$ stadiums. Here X would represent the first stage of the hominid lithic technology –the use of anvils and hammers of non modified stone, of which there is no archaeological record. $X + Y$ would be the first technological stage with archaeological evidence, which is obtaining sharp flakes by means of percussion knapping. A similar story is the one of the nut and the XXI century inventor we are about to tell.

We, the *Homo sapiens*, are living in a technological stage that permits us designing and producing a mechanical nut-cracker controlled by powerful computers and complex programs ... nothing to do with a simply knapped pebble. But if someday we travel from our comfortable experimental laboratory to a rainforest spot, even though we are neither *Homo habilis* nor chimpanzees, we will also be able to use a simple non-modified stone in order to crack a nut. It would be difficult and illogical transporting the heavy mechanical nut-cracker to a rainforest where plugging in would be nearly impossible. Could we name this the Robinson Crusoe Effect? In the same way, the bifacial axes of a *Homo erectus* are technically superior to those dated 1 million years earlier in the same area of the African continent but, however, they were inefficient for opening nuts or cutting up animals. That is why, in certain situations, *Homo erectus* used technological elements that could be wrongly considered as more primitive (as precedent cultures or precedent cultural stages).

We believe that archaeologists and paleoanthropologists have been wrong in many occasions when – driven by a lineal and progressive thinking – they have related industries to cultural horizons and then those cultural horizons to particular hominid species. Despite the inexistence of archaeologist evidence, paleoanthropologists often relate the taxonomical identification of their osteological findings to cultures. For example, they relate *Homo habilis* to Oldowan, *Homo erectus* to Acheulean, Neanderthals to Mousterian and anatomically modern *Homo* to Aurignacian. Archaeologists do exactly the opposite. When they do not find the hominids, they talk about their presence from the typological determination of their industries: Oldowan by *Homo habilis*, Acheulean by *Homo erectus*, and so on. This is a great problem. Especially in view of what the Ecological Hypothesis says, that is, that a single hominid species may have produced what until recently we called different cultures, while a culture with archaeological identity may have been produced by several hominid species. We have applied successfully these ecological hypotheses to several archaeological and paleontological sites in the Peninj area (Tanzania), which will be motive of coming publications.

The lesson would be that we, archaeologists and paleoanthropologists, should always bear in mind that we work with a biased fossil record. If we don't want to have a wrong view of the hominids behavior in a certain place, the fossil record – the past – should be contrasted with present data – ethoprimatology, ethnology, and experimental archaeology. Among other things, we should avoid the temptation to attribute the category of fossil directors to some tools, or type artefacts. Fossils directors define cultures the remains of which, at best, only represent a ridiculous percentage of the original sample. Type artefacts – no matter if they are more or less complex-, instead of representing different cultures may respond to diverse behaviors generated by a single primate group in different situations and ethoecological contexts. Let us get into the ethoprimatological record. For example, let us choose at random one of the three cultural zones defined for the chimpanzee (Sabater Pi, 1978; Serrallonga, 2005): zone 3. Would it be tolerable that, instead of speaking globally of the "leaves cultural area," we determined different cultures – hammer culture, spatula culture, drill culture, and so on – only because of finding different type tools?

Let us imagine a future in which an archaeology team studied the *Homo sapiens* of the University of Barcelona. On one hand, they would find very complex type artefacts in laboratories (electronic microscopes, bio-incubators, computers, etc.) and car parks (cars and motorbikes with a stylized design). On the other hand, they would find much simpler type artefacts in classrooms (pencils, papers, chokes, blackboards, pens, etc.) and restaurants (glasses, dishes, bottles, chicken bones, fruit seeds . . .). Every one of us knows that these tools belong to a single culture and to a single hominid species, but, what would happen if those archaeologists kept with some of the classical ideas of the XX and XXI centuries? They would certainly define two or more cultures, depending on the higher or lower complexity of the artefacts found, and they would assign them to their respective fossil hominid species. Nobody would have taken into account that primates (within a species and a culture) use different tools – modified or not, perishable or perdurable, complex or simple, depending on their needs in different ethoecological contexts. Perhaps, the fact of not having taken into account all these aspects is the reason for the archaeologists and paleoanthropologists to keep on making, twice or more, the same mistake. The last section of our story serves as an example.

The Mysterious Case of the Hand-Axes in Europe: Stupid Colonists?

In the Eurasian archaeological sites that correspond to the first colonists, or African emigrants, there are no stone hand-axes but Oldowan tools. Taking into account that these places date from later than Acheulean invention, many authors have stated that those *Homo* who left Africa were less intelligent or worse adapted than the ones who stayed there. In our opinion, ecology has the answer: in the first colonization stage, Eurasian *Homo erectus* did not need stone hand-axes but Oldowan industries. We should not forget that, apart from lithic industries, the first hominids certainly produced an assortment of tools from perishable materials as wood, leaves, lianas, furs, entrails, and so on, which, obviously (apart from rare exceptions), have not been preserved in the archaeological record. Some of these tools could be much more complex than Acheulean hand-axes. That's why the presence or absence of lithic tools seems irrelevant to us when it comes to judge the degree of technical development of a certain hominid. Definitely, in our opinion there is no reason to think that the first colonists who, from Africa, stepped on Eurasian territory – Dmanisi (Georgia), Fuente Nueva (Granada), Monte Poggiolo (Italia), Gran Dolina (Burgos), and so on – were less intelligent than the ones who stayed in Africa, making hand-axes. Perhaps hand-axes were not as useful when those pioneers spread across the new territories. But, did they appear later on? Yes, they did. Perhaps in the exact moment they started being necessary.

The Solution: A Paleo-Ethocological View

As we have defended in the present paper, in our opinion the best and only method to fight myths and legends about biological and cultural evolution of our species is through interdisciplinary studies and discussions. It is not a question of denying the exceptionality and singularity of the human genus. It is a question of claiming the use of a paleo-ethoecological view for the study of our lineage evolution, as we do with any other species of the animal kingdom (to which we belong).

Acknowledgments

We thank our sponsor, Ciencia y Aventura (www.cienciayaventura.com), for funding this study. We are especially grateful to Jaan Valsiner and Alberto Rosa (eds.) and Anna Albiach (Universitat de València).

Note

This paper is an extended version of the publication: Serrallonga, J. (2004). Ecología, comportamiento y paleo-etoecología homínida: una revisión crítica sobre la evolución biológica y cultural de los primeros homínidos africanos, *Estudios de Psicología*, 25(2), 129–147.

References

Asfaw, B., White, T., Lovejoy, O., Latimer, B., Simpson, S., & Suwa, G. (1999). *Australopithecus garhi*: A new species of early hominid from Ethiopia, *Science*, 284, 629–635.

Backwell, L. R. & d'Errico, F. (2001). Evidence of termite foraging by Swartkrans early hominids. *PNAS*, 98(4), 1358–1363.

Bellomo, R. V. (1994). Methods of determining early hominid behavioral activities associated with the controlled use of fire at Fx Jj 20 Main, Koobi Fora, Kenya. *Journal of Human Evolution*, 27, 173–195.

Bert, J., Ayats, H., Martino, A. & Collomb, H. (1967). Le sommeil nocturne chez le babouin *Papio papio*: Observations en milieu natural et données eléctrophysiologiques. *Folia Primatologica*, 6, 28–43.

Clarke, D. L. (1984). *Arqueología Analítica*. Barcelona: Ediciones Bellaterra.

Coppens, Y. (1982). Qui fit quoi. *Bulletin de la Société Préhistorique Française*, 79(6), 163–165.

Diamond, S., & Belasco, B. (1980). *De la cultura primitiva a la cultura moderna*. Barcelona: Editorial Anagrama.

Escobar, M. & García, C. (1997). La importancia de la mano y de la manipulación en la adaptación de los primates. In F. Pel & J. Veà, *Etología. Bases biológicas de la conducta animal y humana* (pp. 317–346). Madrid: Ediciones Pirámide.

Goodall, J. (1986). *The chimpanzees of Gombe. Patterns of behavior*. Cambridge: Belknapp Press of Harvard University Press.

Harris, M. (1996). *Antropología cultural*. Madrid: Alianza Editorial.

de Heinzelin, J., Clark, J. D., White, T., Hart, W., Renne, P., WoldeGabriel, G., Beyene, Y., & Vrba, E. (1999). Environment and behavior of 2.5-Million-Year-Old Bouri Hominids. *Science*, 284, 625–628.

James, S. R. (1996). Early hominid use of fire: recent approaches and methods for evaluation of the evidence. In O. Bar Yosef, L. L. Cavallidr Sforza, R. J. March & M. Piperno (Eds.), *The Lower and Middle Palaeolithic (Colloquium IX of XIII International Congress of Prehistoric and Protohistoric Sciences)* (pp. 65–75). Forli: Abaco.

Kano, T. (1992). *The last ape. Pigmy chimpanzee behaviour and ecology*. Stanford: Stanford University Press.

Klein, R. G. (1989). *The Human Career. Human biological and cultural origins*. Chicago: The University of Chicago Press.

Leakey, L. S. B. (1959). A new fossil skull from Olduvai. *Nature*, 184, 491–493.

Leakey, L. S. B., Tobias, P. V., & Napier, J. R. (1964). A new species of the genus Homo from Olduvai. *Nature* 202, 7–9.

Lockwood, C. A. & Tobias, P. V. (1999). A large male hominid cranium from Sterkfontein, South Africa, and the status of *Australopithecus africanus*. *Journal of Human Evolution*, 36, 637–685.

Nishida, T. (1980). The leaf-clipping display: a newly-discovered expressive gesture in wild chimpanzees. *Journal of Human Evolution*, 9, 117–128.

Mosterín, J. (1993). *Filosofía de la Cultura*. Madrid: Alianza Editorial.

Pickford, M. & Senut, B. (2001). The geological and faunal context of Late Miocene hominid remains from Lukeino, Kenya. *C. R. Acad. Sci. Paris, Sciences de la Terre et des planètes*, 322, 145–152.

Sabater Pi, J. (1974). An elementary industry of the chimpanzees in the Okorobikó Mountains, Río Muni (Republic of Equatorial Guinea), West Africa. *Primates*, 15(4), 351–364.

Sabater Pi, J. (1978). *El chimpancé y los orígenes de la cultura*. Barcelona: Anthropos.

Sabater Pi, J., Veà, J. J., & Serrallonga, J. (1997). Did the first hominids build nests? *Current Anthropology*, 38(5), 914–916.

Sabater Pi, J., Veà, J. J. & Serrallonga, J. (2003). Nesting behavior in African hominids of plio-pleistocene: a multidisciplinary approach. In J. J. Veà, J. Serrallonga, D. Turbón, J. M. Fullola & D. Serrat (Eds.), *Primates: Origin, Evolution, Behavior*. Barcelona: Parc Científic de Barcelona. 82–90.

Schick, K. D., Toth, N., Garufi, G., Savage-Rumbaugh, E. S., Rumbaugh, D. & Sevcik, R. (1999). Continuing investigations into the stone tool-making and tool-using capabilities of a Bonobo *(Pan paniscus)*. *Journal of Archaeological Science*, 26, 821–832.

Serrallonga, J. (1994). Homo faber, el fin de un mito. Etología y Prehistoria, una aproximación al Presente para reconstruir el Pasado del útil. *Pyrenae*, 25, 31–49.

Serrallonga, J. (2001). *Los Guardianes del Lago. Diario de un arqueólogo en la tierra de los maasai*. Barcelona: Mondadori.

Serrallonga, J. (2005). No estamos solos: chimpancés y australopitecos habilidosos. In F. Guillén (Ed.), *Existo, luego pienso. Los primates y la evolución de la inteligencia humana* (pp. 171–251). Madrid: Ateles.

Serrallonga, J., Sabater-Pi J., & Veà J. (1998). Nest building behavior in the australopithecines and early *Homo*. A new interdisciplinary hypothesis (ecology, ethoprimatology, paleoanthropology, archaeology and physiology). *Dual Congress 1998*. Johannesburg: University of the Witwatersrand.

Serrallonga, J., Gay, B. & Medina, V. (2005). 'Pan erectus' Project: preliminary results on occasional bipedality in captive chimpanzees *(Pan t. troglodytes)* and their importance for the study of the origin of bipedalism in forest areas. *Folia Primatologica*, 76, 64–64.

Serrallonga, J., Medina, V., & Galbany, J. (2005). Paleoecological reconstruction of *Homo erectus* and *Paranthropus boisei* through the study of living and fossil specimens of the genus *Papio*, Tanzania, East Africa, *Folia Primatologica*, 76, 64–65.

Sillen, A. (1992). Strontium-calcium ratios (Sr/Ca) of *Australopithecus robustus* and associated fauna from Swartkrans, *Journal of Human Evolution*, 23, 495–516.

Sillen, A., Hall, G., & Armstrong, R. (1995). Strontium calcium ratios (Sr/Ca) and strontium isotopic ratios (87Sr/86Sr) of *Australopithecus robustus* and *Homo* sp. from Swartkrans, *Journal of Human Evolution*, 28, 277–285.

Susman, R. L. (1998). Hand function and tool behavior in early hominids. *Journal of Human Evolution*, 35, 23–46.

Tobias, P. V. (1984). *Dart, Taung and the Missing Link*. Johannesburg: Witwatersrand University Press.

Tobias, P. V. (1997). Orígenes evolutivos de la lengua hablada. In C. J. Cela Conde, R. Gutiérrez Lombardo & J. Martínez Contreras (Eds.), *Senderos de la evolución humana*. México: Ludus Vitalis, special number 1, 35–52.

Toth, N., Schick, K. D., Savage-Rumbaugh, E. S., Sevzik, R. A., & Rumbaugh, D. M. (1993). Pan the Tool-Maker: Investigations into the stone tool-making and tool-using capabilities of a Bonobo *(Pan paniscus)*. *Journal of Archaeological Science*, 20, 81–91.

deWaal, F. (2002). *El Simio y el aprendiz de sushi*. Barcelona: Paidós.

deWaal, F. & Lanting, F. (1997). *Bonobo, the forgotten ape*. Berkeley, Los Angeles & London: University of California Press.

Whiten, A., Goodall, J., McGrew, W. C., Nishida, T., Reynolds, V., Sugiyama, Y., Tutin, C. E. G., Wrangham, R. W. & Boesch, C. (1999). Cultures in chimpanzees, *Nature*, 399, 682–685.

Part III

FROM ORIENTATION TO MEANING

CHAPTER 10

Acts of Psyche

Actuations as Synthesis of Semiosis and Action

Alberto Rosa

Truth happens to an idea. It becomes true, is made true by events. Its verity is in fact an event, a process: the process namely of its verifying itself, its verification.

> *William James*, Pragmatism, 1907

Experience, Behavior, and Meaning

Psychology seemed to be condemned to be always searching for an object. Consciousness, behavior, cognition are among the subject matters psychologists have been concerned upon. Some would say that these three objects of inquiry are inextricably linked, while some others argue that one of them is the main character when one wants to explain what Psyche does, and so the others play secondary roles, or sometimes none at all.

Psychology also claims to be a science. Some struggle to convince the audience that it is a natural science, while some others are not reluctant to place it among the social sciences. Whatever the case, if psychology is to be taken as a science of any kind its

final goal would be to provide general laws for the explanation of how its subject matter works.

Whatever the case, there is common agreement on viewing psychology as an empirical science. One should start, first, by gathering empirical experiences on what Psyche does; then, continue coding these observations in the shared conventional categories of psychology, and so producing data; and finally inferring regularities and producing descriptive or/and explanatory models. A well-known process that is no different from that of any other science, whether natural or social. The final product is a set of linguistic expressions which true value depends of how the description and explanation they provide can be validated, again, by experience.

The Puzzle of Experience

So, experience is the cornerstone of any science. No scientific utterance about how a part of the world works can be considered as valid, if it does not match with the experience one has of the natural phenomena to which that utterance refers. But, does experience presents the world as it *really* is? Realists seem to believe so. As Hillary Putnam says (1981), they talk about the world as if they have reached God's point by choosing the right method. If they were right, experience would present phenomena, language would describe the world in words and numbers, logic would be applied to infer regularities, and so a metalanguage could be devised to create more utterances that could be taken to be true or ruled out as false depending if they were in accordance or discordance with the experiences observed. But, is it not the case that experiencing is itself a natural phenomenon worthy of being subjected to inquiry? If this is so, which science should deal with the description and explanation of experience?

Psychology is the one science that cannot take experience for granted. As a matter of fact, it started faring as a science with the specific purpose of studying how experience works (see Wundt, 1896, Introduction). Experience is itself a process to be explained. Experience is a result of the working of Psyche. So Psychology cannot skip the examination of how experience comes to appear, and how it works. And this cannot be done otherwise than resorting to experience itself.

Experience is not just an assortment of *qualia* dancing in the discotheque of the mind. It is for something else, it refers to something beyond the realm of consciousness. As Franz Brentano (1874) said, consciousness is intentional; it is the result of acts carried out by an agent upon something different from the agent and experience itself. Consciousness is immanently objective, addresses something beyond itself, and is to be conscious of something. So experience is constituted. Conscious experience appears as having a sense, as presenting us some meaning, and so permits us to feel, represent and think about the world, our fantasies and ourselves. But how is that possible? How is it that meaning is produced? Is it something that suddenly arises together with experience? Does it precede experience?

Behavior and Sense

The realist view of positivism, as above pictured, takes knowledge to be the result of human construction. Moving away from earlier empirical-criticism, neopositivists thought of knowledge not anymore as something simply gathered, it had to be elaborated. One has to observe and manipulate instances of the world to have experiences, put what one experiences in utterances, manipulate these utterances so that something new could be said about what was observed, and eventually actively search for the empirical verification of what has been stated. These are purposeful actions carried out by human agents.

Human agents are material entities moving around in the world. They change their spatial position all the time. To account for the movements of matter in space was the prime objective of modern science. The success of Newtonian Physics in offering an explanation of movements in terms of gravitation, mass, forces, and so on, was a source of inspiration for modern scientists, psychologists being no exception. However, organic matter seems to be rather exceptional, since it is capable of moving itself without the apparent application of any external force. Animals seem to move following their own initiative, but not in a random manner, they seem to do things on purpose. Somehow, there are some kinds of material beings capable of turning movement into purposeful behavior.

Evolutionism made behavior to be a key issue. What an organism does in its environment has consequences not only for its own survival, but also has effects on the long run. Behavior is central to account for the morphological structures of future generations. So the study of behavior became a key issue within Biology, and Psychology adopted it as one of its own subject matters (Fernández, 2005; Richards, 1987, 2002).

As Functionalists viewed it, behavior is goal directed. Animal behavior always has a sense, it is for something. Anything an animal does has a meaning one could only realize by observing in what it results, even if sometimes future events make that behavior meaningless, when it does not reach the desired results. So, the meaning of behavior is in its outcome, in the future, in what may happen later on. This is what I take to be the key meaning of William James's words quoted at the beginning of this chapter. Meaning is not something given; it is always in the making. Meaning is a result of sense once the goal has been achieved. If a behavior does not achieve its expected outcomes, it becomes meaningless.

This is also the case of the epistemic behavior of scientists. As said above, they have to move around in the world to observe phenomena, to communicate them to others or to themselves (another form of behavior), to reason about they have said, to extract observable conclusions, and finally go back to the field (or the laboratory) and see whether what they have done had some meaning or not; whether what it has been said can be matched with what can be experienced, and so being made true. It seems then, that sense is prior to meaning, and truth is a result of matching the outcome of communicative actions with experiences of the world carried out with a purpose.

Meaning and Rule Related Systems of Sense

Philosophy, linguistics, various systems of logic, and psychology have dealt with the issue of meaning for centuries (see Castañares, 2002 for a brief history of Semiotics; or Gottdiener, Boklund-Lagapoulou, & Lagopoulos, 2002–03, for a collection of classical texts), and have produced very important contributions throughout the 20th century. Saussurian Semiology and Linguistics, Frege's Logic, the linguistic turn after Wittgenstein and his followers' contributions, Kripke's Relational Semantics, Chomsky's Generative Linguistics, and Fodor's Philosophy of Mind are some important milestones in this development. All these contributions rely on the use (or construction) of a given language (either natural

or artificial) and about how the elements of this language relate to each other, because of the structure of its components, the way they relate to each other (connectives, quantifiers, etc.), and the rules that govern these relationships. *Meaning* then, appears as a result of the structure of a language, it appears as a consequence of its syntax, of rules.

This is an extraordinary achievement that has produced very valuable practical applications, as well as a deeper understanding of the processes of meaning-making, language acquisition, and thinking. However, still one may keep wandering whether meaning could exist before language.

From what it has been said so far, it seems that sense is a property of actions, that behavior can be meaningful, and even that truth is a result of the confrontation of different meaning-making behavioral systems.

The object of this chapter is to go into an inquiry of how these different terms relate to each other. How an alive movement (action) produces sense. This will be done by first examining what meaning is, and then going into the intricacies of a theory of action capable of accounting for the appearance of meaningful behavior in alive organisms. Chapter 14 will continue this endeavor by going into the detail of how social life and culture produce new meaning-making systems capable of producing experience of the world, knowledge and truth, and eventually how a morally accountable person may come to being.

What Is the Meaning of *"Meaning"*?

The theories of meaning so far mentioned tell us that meaning has to do with language and how language (or information) units relate to each other. So, if we want to find out what meaning means in a natural language (English,[1] for the sake of the reader) we can start our argument by looking at the cultural device that collects words meanings: the dictionary. Table 10.1 shows

Table 10.1: The meaning of "meaning" and related terms. (Merriam-Webster on line Dictionary: http://www.m-w.com/cgi-bin/dictionary)

Mean (*verb*)	1 **a** : to have in the mind as a purpose – **b** : to design for or destine to a specified purpose or future. 2 : to serve or intend to convey, show, or indicate. 3 : to have importance to the degree of. 4 : to direct to a particular individual. *Intransitive Senses* : to have an intended purpose
Meaning (*noun*)	1 **a** : the thing one intends to convey especially by language. **b** : the thing that is conveyed especially by language. 2 : something meant or intended. 3 : significant quality; *especially* : implication of a hidden or special significance <a glance full of *meaning*>. 4 **a** : the logical connotation of a word or phrase **b** : the logical denotation or extension of a word or phrase
Sign (*noun*)	1 **a** : a motion or gesture by which a thought is expressed or a command or wish made known **b** : signal, **c** : a fundamental linguistic unit that designates an object or relation or has a purely syntactic function **d** : one of a set of gestures used to represent language. 2 : a mark having a conventional meaning and used in place of words or to represent a complex notion. 6 **a** : something material or external that stands for or signifies something spiritual. **b** : something indicating the presence or existence of something else. **d** : an objective evidence of plant or animal disease. 7 *plural usually* **sign** : traces of a usually wild animal.
Sign (*verb*)	1**b** : to place a sign on. **c** : to represent or indicate by a sign. 2 **a** : to affix a signature to : ratify or attest by hand or seal. **b** : to assign or convey formally. 3 : to communicate by making a sign or by sign language. 4 : to engage or hire by securing the signature of on a contract of employment – often used with *up* or *on*. **Intransitive Senses**. 1 : to write one's name in token of assent, responsibility, or obligation. 2 **a** : to make a sign or signal **b** : to use sign language
Sense *noun.*	1 : a meaning conveyed or intended. 2 **a** : the faculty of perceiving by means of sense organs. **b:** a specialized animal function or mechanism (as sight, hearing, smell, taste, or touch) basically involving a stimulus and a sense organ **c** : the sensory mechanisms constituting a unit distinct from other functions (as movement or thought). 3 : conscious awareness or rationality – usually used in plural <finally came to his *senses*>. 4 **a** : a particular sensation or kind or quality of sensation <a good *sense* of balance> **b** : a definite but often vague awareness or impression <felt a *sense* of insecurity> <a *sense* of danger> **c** : a motivating awareness <a *sense* of shame> **d** : a discerning awareness and appreciation <her *sense* of humor>. 5 : consensus <the *sense* of the meeting>. 6 **a** : capacity for effective application of the powers of the mind as a basis for action or response : intelligence. **b** : sound mental capacity and understanding typically marked by shrewdness and practicality; *also* : agreement with or satisfaction of such power <this decision makes *sense*>. 7 : one of two opposite directions especially of motion (as of a point, line, or surface)
Sense *transitive verb*	1 **a** : to perceive by the senses **b:** to be or become conscious of <*sense* danger> 2 : grasp, comprehend. 3 : to detect automatically especially in response to a physical stimulus (as light or movement)

the meanings of word "meaning" and other related terms.

When we look closely at this table some interesting features appear. First, all these words are simultaneously nouns and verbs (that also happens to *signal*, not included in the table); they are actions, or the result of actions. *Meaning* is a purpose, something that is in the mind, that can be hidden (but sometimes shows inadvertently) or is explicitly communicated, but then it needs something to be done (a gesture, a token, a sign) that needs to be conventional (or conventionalized) in order to be understood. It is done for something, either to command something else to act, or to show the importance of something (what does not matter is not meant). It points towards the existence of something that exists, that may be now absent but left a trace we can currently sense, it can even refer to something fictitious via the use of something material that stands for it. And all this does not need to be done through language, but rather this is only one of the ways of signaling, of conveying meaning. Meaning is something that comes after sense, which in turn is captured by the senses, who are capable of capturing it in particular situations. Sense is related to intelligence and understanding, since we can make sense of a situation (of direction, of what something is for), to understand, to grasp, to become conscious. Hence, meaning, sense, sign, signal form a family of terms that are actions and result of actions, that require the existence of a purpose, that signal the existence of things (either "real" or "imagined"), that have to do with sensing, understanding, intelligence, and consciousness, and all that with or without language. Or so the dictionary says.

So, it seems that sense is before meaning. That sense depends of the senses, and meaning comes from the mind, once mind has understood, has become somehow conscious. It is as if the dictionary tells us that psychology should have a lot to say about how sense and meaning come to be. If we accepted this view, our task will be that of figuring out how sense appears, and how meaning can be constructed, rather than starting with a given rationality from which meaning could be derived. And this is exactly what this chapter will attempt to do. To sketch a view of how meaning evolves from sense and eventually constructs rationality. But before going into that, our first move will be to go into an examination of the classics who started to develop

the sciences, which deal with sense and meaning.

The Sciences of Meaning: Semiology and Semiotics

As said in the introductory chapter, two closely related disciplines were more or least simultaneously constituted in two separated places around the turn from the 19th to the 20th century: Semiology by the Genevan Ferdinand de Saussure and Semiotics by the North-American Charles Sanders Peirce.

Saussure defined semiology as "a science that studies the life of signs within society", stating also that "to determine the exact place of Semiology is the task of Psychology." He also took Linguistics to be a part of the more general discipline of Semiology. So linguists should explore what is that makes language so special within the mass of semiological data (Saussure, 1959, p. 16; as quoted by Liszka, 1996). He also thought that signs were a psychological entity, since they are a way to relate an idea with a sign, and when that association becomes conventionalized, the sign can become a collective product. A move that again makes Semiology dependent of Psychology. In other words, for Saussure Semiology was a discipline more general than linguistics, and to account for how something may become a sign would be a task left to psychology.

In contrast, Peirce[2] understood Semiotics as the formal doctrine of Signs (Collected Papers, 2.227) and defined it as "the analytical study of the essential conditions to which all signs are subject" (MS 774: 6), and its object to discern "what *must* be the characters of all signs ..." and "what *would be* true of signs in all cases..." (CP 2.227; Liszka, o.c., p. 1). Peirce placed Semiotics within the Formal Sciences –together with Phenomenology, Ethics, Aesthetics, and Metaphysics, and took Semiotics to be "the science of the general necessary laws of signs" (CP 2.39), and so concerned with how phenomena relate to truth. (Liszka, o.c., p. 2–3). So, Semiotics is a normative science, since it is concerned not only with the description and characterization of signs, but also with how they can be adequately used in research in order to persuade and reach consensus and truth. In other words, Grammar, Logic, and Rhetoric are under the overarching umbrella of Semiotics.

By this placing of Semiotics among the formal sciences, Peirce, rather than passing to Psychology the task of grounding how signs can come to work as such, as Saussure did, provided some formal tools for their use in Psychology. His Semiotics aimed at showing what are the formal conditions that make a sign to act as such, irrespectively of how it is presented (a sound, image, thought, feeling, movement, or a natural event). His goal was to offer principles addressed to setting criteria for the adequate use of signs. So, he provided a sort of methodology (an *Organon*) applicable to all sciences.

Meaning-Making – Peirce's Legacy

This section is devoted to the presentation of a résumé of Peirce's semiotic logic. As it may be expected, the main point to develop here is a set of formalisms and basic concepts, that, for the sake of space, are presented in a rather crude manner, without a detailed consideration of the objections a psychologist may raise to some of Peirce's statements that will be presented below. However, if the reader is patient enough, the constructivist and anti-representationist psychologist may feel more at home (or so I hope) as the chapter proceeds along, once Peirce's concepts are interpreted within the context of a theory of action in the following sections of the chapter.

How Is It That We Are Able to Make Sense of What Is Felt?

Our first goal is to consider how sense (and later meaning) are possible before language, how anyone can get acquainted with things, how empirical experience comes to be. Peirce came to terms with this question by choosing what we now would call a phenomenological outlook. He went into

an examination of the most basic form of awareness, for which he coined the terms of *Firstness*, *Secondness*, and *Thirdness*.

> *My view is that there are three modes of being. I hold that we can directly observe them in elements of whatever is at any time before the mind in any way. They are the being of positive qualitative possibility [Firstness], the being of actual fact [Secondness], and the being of law that will govern facts in the future [Thirdness].* (CP, 1.23)

> *It seems, then, that the true categories of consciousness are: first, feeling, the consciousness which can be included with an instant of time, passive consciousness of quality, without recognition or analysis; second, consciousness of an interruption into the field of consciousness, sense of resistance, of an external fact, or another something; third, synthetic consciousness, binding time together, sense of learning, thought.* (CP, 1.377)

These three categories tell us not only the most basic ways of experiencing, but also allow us to glimpse how time and objects come into being through our encounters with the world. Something that will be revisited later on in this chapter.

Qualities are a result of feelings that appear in our consciousness, but they could be either sensed or imagined. One does not seem to do anything to feel, the feeling seems to appear directly in consciousness.[3] But in order to have a sense of factuality, to be related to something that has some radical otherness to oneself, there must be a resistance to our efforts, a sense of polarity or reaction, of two sides of an instant.[4] When both things come together, then we have the synthetic experience of something real happening, of being; of qualities and resistances being compressed into something, a Thirdness[5] appears that can then be taken as the basis of an experience of something being real. It is the resistance that things offer to our efforts what make their qualities to appear in consciousness, and with the regularities of their appearances, objects come into being in consciousness. The resemblance of this view with

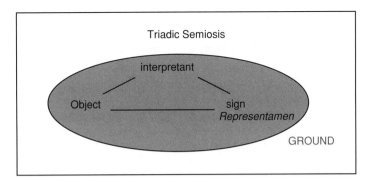

Figure 10.1. Triadic semiosis.

Maturana and Varela's (1987) concepts of structural coupling between an organism and its environment is worthy of being taken into account.

It is through the combination of these three forms of consciousness that meaning-making becomes possible, something that is done through *semiosis*.

Semiosis as a Triadic and Recursive Process

Peirce's semiotics has an important difference to Saussure's semiology that has yet not been mentioned. Saussure established a dyadic relationship between the signifier and the signified: something is a sign of something else because of conventional agreement. Peirce's view includes a third party together with the sign and its object: feeling and processes within the individual that establishes the relationship between the other two; and so semiosis becomes a genuinely triadic process, which then is no other thing than a type of action carried out by an agent. Figure 10.1 presents the basic structure of semiosis.

The difference between Saussure's and Peirce's views is nicely captured by Peirce's definition of sign.

A sign or representamen, *is something which stands to somebody for something in some respect or capacity. It addresses somebody, that is creates in the mind of that person an equivalent sign, or perhaps a more developed sign. That sign which it creates I call the* interpretant *of the first sign.*

The sign stands for something, its object. *It stands for that object not in all respects, but in reference to a sort of idea, which I have sometimes called the* ground *of the representamen.* [CP. 2.228]

This definition of sign[6] deserves to go into a careful examination of its components, particularly of those that appear in italics.

It follows from the definitions of *representamen* that anything that may have some sort of grounded relationship to the object can act as a sign of the latter. The key concept for this relationship is then that of *ground*.

Ground is an aspect in which something can be a sign of something else. One of Peirce's examples is that of 'black' acting as a sign of 'stove' (CP. 1.495). In other words, *ground* is an abstract category capable of acting as a predicate in a statement (e.g., the stove is black), what requires that such category had been previously extracted from experiences,[7] in which that category could be attributed to objects (e.g., a stove, but also to a crow, a piece of charcoal, etc.). This makes *ground* to be both a result of a previous construction by the individual and a consequence of some particular relationship between the sign and its object.[8]

Object at first sight may seem to not need any particular explanation. Objects seems to be out there and this may make us feel is enough, we take their "reality" for granted. But this feeling of immediacy is deceptive. The object may be, for example, this book (which may look pretty real to the reader), but may also be as imaginary as an angel, ether, phlogiston, Don Quixote, or a classless society. Anything can be the object[9] of a sign. What makes it to be the object of that sign is that the sign could represent it, and so making it a sort of entity to which to refer, that Peirce called the *immediate object* of the sign. Nevertheless, for something to be an object it needs to offer some resistance, some limits to the actions exerted upon it (an angel does not allow to perform any possible action – it may be useful as an addressee to which to commission the care of a child left alone, but not as a way of avoiding the wind to blow away a pile of papers, a function easily performed by a rock). It is the latter what makes it to be called *dynamic object*, and therefore to be beyond the particular presentation made by a particular sign in a concrete semiosis. It is thus susceptible to be presented by different signs (e.g., blackness may sign a stove, but the stove may also be signified by hardness, heaviness, hotness, and so on, but dampness, sweetness, or swiftness hardly could play this role).

This way of considering the object makes Peirce to be neither a consensualist nor a naive realist, but a genuine constructivist. So, each particular semiosis presents an immediate object that does not exhaust all the dynamism of the object,[10] which remains open to be signified in different ways (through another phenomenological quality – if the object is a thing; as an unexpected consequence – if the object is a rule, etc.), but not in whatever way, it always has to be *grounded*.

The *interpretant* appears when a representamen denotes an object and so makes possible the understanding that the sign is referring to the object. This makes the interpretant to have the capability of acting as a sign of the object for a subsequent semiosis (see Figure 10.2), and so opening the path for the subsequent recursive semiosis (see below). If the interpretant is a mental state, how can it be psychologically characterized? Peirce usually calls it a feeling, because of its immediacy, but sometimes takes it to be a sort of volitional act (such as standing up following an order), or even as a habit or a rule. This apparent ambiguity, rather than a weakness seems to me one of the strong points

of his position. The psychological status of the interpretant is dependent of the semiosis to which it belongs. If we look to the first semiosis of Figure 10.2, the first interpretant may be a feeling, but the second interpretant may be a movement, and the third a rule. This is a consequence not of a theoretical imprecision, but a consequence of the recursive character of semiosis, which make possible different ways of meaning-making, as it will be shown in due time.

The simple triadic semiosis just presented, is only the basic unit of the semiotic processes. As it has just been said, semiosis have a recursive character. In Peirce's own words:

> A Sign, *or* Representamen, *is a First which stands in a such a* genuine *tryadic relation to a Second, called its* Object, *as to be capable of determining a Third, called its* Interpretant, *to assume the same triadic relation to its* Object *in which it stands itself to the same Object. The triadic relation is genuine, that is its three members are bound together by it in a way that does not consist in any complexus of dyadic relations . . . The Third . . . must have a second triadic relation in which the Representamen, or rather the relation thereof to is Object, shall be its own (the Third's) Object, and must be capable of determining a Third to this relation. All this must equally be true of the Third's Third and so on endlessly. (CP 2.274)*

How Feelings Can Come to Signify Objects

So far, the focus has been on an explanation of the components and the process of semiosis, but how something may become a sign of something else still remains to be explained. A sign is a sort of thing, and so is the object to be meant, irrespectibly of the ontological status of both, the sign or its object. This is a matter of primary importance, since we need to explore the meaning-making process before language. It is here when the categories of Firstness, Secondness, and Thirdness show all their relevance. Table 10.2 show how the different ways in which the

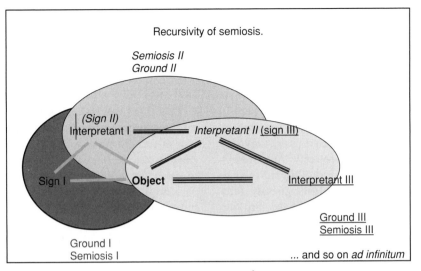

Figure 10.2. Recursivity of semiosis.

phenomenological categories of what acts as a sign can relate to the object and so is able to attribute an ontological status to its referent (as a phenomenon, as a fact, or as an entity). This is done through a cognitive operation that genuinely construct the experience, which always also include some kind of judgment.

Table 10.2 gathers the three trichotomies which form the basis on which Peirce elaborated his 1903 version of his theory of signs (LW, 22–36), and it is an adaptation of Sheriff (1989, p. 67). These trichotomies

refer to all the logical possibilities in which something can be a sign for something else. It is a device to develop a theory of signs that will soon be presented. But before going into that, a review of the meaning of the terms included in each cell is needed.

The first row is devoted to the explanation of how a Firstness (a feeling, a sensorial quality – e.g., brightness) can act as a sign of something else, how an object can be *present*ed. So a feeling of brightness could act, first, as a sign of "brightness itself" (and so being a *qualisign*- a quality that is a sign

Table 10.2: Peirce's *Tricotomies* relate phenomenological or formal categories with ontological or material categories

Phenomenological or Formal Categories		Ontological or Material Categories		
		Firstness	Secondness	Thirdness
Firstness	A sign is:	1 "A mere quality". **QUALISIGN**	2 An "actual existent" **SINSIGN**	3 A "general law" **LEGISIGN**
Secondness	A sign relates with its object in having:	4 "Some character in itself" **ICON**	5 "Some existential relation to that object" **INDEX**	6 "Some Relation to the interpretant" **SYMBOL**
Thirdness	A sign's interpretant represents it (sign) as a sign of:	7 "Possibility" **RHEMA**	8 "fact" **DICENT SIGN**	9 "reason" **ARGUMENT**

of the quality itself, 1), then, be a sign of the presence of something foreign to the perceiver (and so being a *sinsign*, 2), of something real that is out there, and eventually to signify the existence of a real quality that exists in the world (and so to be a *legisign*, a sign of a regularity of the world, 3): there is a real brightness out there. So, a *legisign* is a rule, a law that acts as a sign (in this example *bightness* as a real property "out there") and so stabilizes the world allowing to recognize in the future qualities already felt, and so setting the ground to have familiar experiences – habits. It is only when these experiences (of qualities) are stabilized, that it is possible to start developing the notion of object, as it will be shown later on. Hence, the first row of Table 10.2 tells us how feelings or phenomenological qualities can become properties of something different to themselves. But, as one should expect, that thing different to themselves (reality) has yet to be explained.

The second row states the ways in which Secondness (the feeling of resistance, of presence, of a two-sided instant) can act as a sign that *re-presents* something else. An *icon* (4) is a sign that shares a quality with that it represents (e.g., brightness is a property of light, the sun, a silver plate, and so on, so brightness is an icon that could represent any of these objects – though it has to be taken into account that we have not reached yet the constitution of objects). An *index* is something that shares an existential relation to that object (e.g., daylight always comes together with the presence of the brightness in the sky, or roses always smell, so the fact of a particular smell can act as a sign of the presence of something [a rose], (5). Finally, a *symbol* signals how something that exists (a Second) can be a sign of a previously constituted real relationship (such as daylight can be a sign of brightness, (6). Thus, symbols are regularities of the existence of something that can act as a sign of a previously constituted objective quality or existence. Symbols always point towards previously constituted regularities (legisigns) and, as shown, follow a regularity, they are rules developed throughout encounters with the world, are

conventionalized by experience, but they do not need to be carried upon any sort of language, they can appear as behavior regularities. Thus, this second row has told us how a fact can come to be a sign of something else.

The third row takes us to the realm of interpretation, to how Thirdness can be a sign of something else, how *interpretation* is carried out. A *rhema* is a sign that signals towards a possibility (e.g., it is green, it *may be* something that has greenness – a leave, but perhaps a frog, once leaves and frogs are taken to be real things). It is an interpretation, it cannot be either true or false, it is a sort of hypothesis; it signals the possibility of an abduction (7). In contrast, a *dicent sign* is a sort of proposition (it asserts the presence of something that has some real properties – it is an object that resists one's action, with properties that also resist one's action). If the agent that carry out the semiosis were a bird (e.g, a heron) moving around in a pond, the presence of a green quality could act as a sign of something else (a leave or a frog), and so produce as interpretant a movement, which an observer may take for an exploration (to see whether is one of those things or the other) and if the green jumps away when the agent approaches then it is interpreted as a real frog. So when the heron is chasing the frog is also performing a *dicent sign* (8). Finally, the *argument* is a sign whose interpretation addresses to a lawful systematic connection with other signs. As Peirce says, it is a "sign which, for its interpretant, is a sign of a law" (CP 2.252). If a *dicent sign* elevates interpretation from a hypothesis to a fact, arguments are able to gather *dicent signs* into more comprehensive interpretations. It is now when it can be said that objects can come to exist in consciousness, since they are an assortment of feelings and qualities that come regularly together. An object, then is formed by a set of *dicent signs* (an *argument*, 9) which make possible that feelings and sensorial qualities (already shaped as abstracts categories) could act as symbols for this object, once this is already constituted as something different to the agent's subjective experiences, but that can

Table 10.3: Peirce's theory of signs

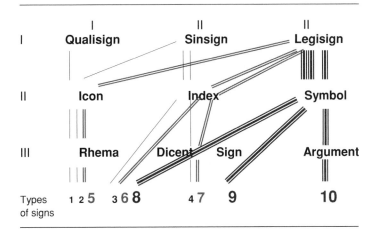

only be taken as existing as a result of the combination of these experiences in (enactive) arguments.

So far, we have been moving through Table 10.2 horizontally from left to right (from cell 1 to 9). When doing so, we have been reviewing all possible ways of signifying, and so using these three trichotomies as a device for the explanation of all the possible ways in which something can be a sign of something else, of how they can *present* something, and *represent* and *interpret* it. But these trichotomies are not yet a theory of signs, but a device for producing a theory of signs.

The reason for this is simple. For something to be a sign that stands for something else, the sign must first become itself a thing in consciousness. Only things can be signs of something else. This assertion has some consequences that will be explored later, since then a distinction could be made between pre-semiotic, quasi-semiotic, and proper-semiotic meaning-making. But, for the time being we will leave this distinction aside, and go straight into Peirce's Theory of Signs.

Peirce's Classification of Signs

Signs are the result of semiosis in which the phenomenological Firstness of signs (first row of Table 10.2) has a capability of pre-

senting a fact (Secondness), so that it can represent it (second row) because of some factual relationship, within some possibilities of interpretation (Thirdness), as they appear in the third row. Hence, the different signs that may come to existence are result of the possible ways in which each of the nine cells within these three trichotomies can vertically combine in triads. But not all the 27 possible combinations are logically possible. The reason for this is that "the presentative aspect of a sign can only been combined with representative aspects which are equal to or lower than the presentative's phenomenological type: the representative aspect of the sign can only be combined with interpretative aspects which are equal to or lower than the representative's phenomenological type" (Liszka, 1996, p. 45). This means that when looking at Table 10.2, only left diagonals are allowed when moving vertically downwards. Table 10.3 explains the structure of the ten types of signs, which result from the type of possible semiosis. The resulting interpretants of these semiosis have the capability of acting as a representamens in subsequent semiosis.

Sign types 1 to 4 cannot ever be linguistic signs, while the others can be so (although they do not need to). Signs 8, 9, and 10 are symbolic, and therefore are one of the basis for cultural transmission of meaning and knowledge. But this does not mean that all symbols must have a cultural nature. A review of these ten types of signs follow.

Sign Type 1. Rhematic iconic qualisign. Is the simplest sign possible. It is any feeling that can refer to an indefinite something else. It is not a factuality, but a quality that can point towards the possibility of something (a brightness felt may signal brightness). It is a necessary step for the other signs that have to rely on this type of sign.

Sign Type 2. Rhematic iconic sinsign. This type of sign is what usually is called an icon. It is a sign that shares some characteristics with its object, and therefore may signify that object; for example, a feeling of brightness acts as a sign of the possible presence of something real that brights.

Sign Type 3. Rhematic indexical sinsign. It is a sign that because of its particular spatial-temporal appearance is signaling (calling attention to) to the possibility of the presence of object; for example, some cricking (of twigs) is a sign of the *possible* presence of something.

Sign Type 4. Dicentic indexical sinsign. It is the next step after the former sign type. If before the sign pointed towards a possibility, now this type of sign signals a certitude. The cricking *is* interpreted as a sign of the presence of something.

Sign Type 5. Rhematic iconic legisign. An already established phenomenic quality (e.g., a display of black spots on a bright surface) is interpreted as a *possibility* of representing something that shares these very same qualities (one feels tempted to say that these qualities are a sign of the *possibility* of the skin of a panther or a leopard – but this is still not possible, since we have not reached yet the stage in which skins or animals have come to be possible to exist in consciousness). It has to be noticed that this sign type opens a new possibility – a quality that may represent many different things that share some common qualities (a mixture of light and shades, skins of different animals, etc.) and so opens the way to the possibility of a conventionalization of one's own experiences, and so making experiences familiar or foreign. It is a legisign, and therefore signals a regularity.

Sign Type 6. Rhematic indexical legisign. It is the next step after the former, but slightly different. It now signals the possibility of the presence of the thing that shares those qualities (the display of black spots on a bright surface signs the *possible presence* of something that shares those qualities).

Sign Type 7. Dicentic indexical legisign. This is a sign that signals something real. The pattern of black and brightness (or the cricking of twigs, or the smell) signals something that is out there (a skin that moves, something heavy moving around). It is a sign that points to the factual presence of a real thing.

Sign Type 8. Rhematic symbolic legisign. With this type of sign we come to a different realm: to that of the possibility of the existence of objects, although we have yet to explain how objects come to exist in consciousness. This is a sign that signals the possibility of an object that shares the features of the perceived qualities (the pattern of colors is a sign of the possibility of a panther –once one knows that panthers exist. There may be a panther).

Sign Type 9. Dicentic symbolic legisign. Now the sign points directly to its object. The perceived quality (color pattern, cricking twigs, and odor) is a sign of something real (of a panther). In fact, a panther is something that moves, that is heavy, that has a peculiar pattern of colors in its skin, that smells in a particular way. That is why a sign of this type has the structure of a statement about a property of its subject; but it is a statement that does not need to be uttered in words, it can be performed in an action (e.g., an emotional expression or/and running away from the object).

Sign Type 10. Argumentative symbolic legisign. These are the type of signs that signal the characteristics of objects through regularities established by habit or convention. Objects appear because of this type of signs. It is an argument because it connects together a set of type 9 signs (e.g., the features which make up skins, and which all together – smells, noise when moving, grunts, and so on – make up panthers to appear as an object of the world).

Once objects are constituted (i.e., once arguments are established), veritative conditions of the other signs can come to existence. They are then capable of signaling features of the world (an object or the possibility of an object) and therefore, able to produce right of wrong interpretations, and so making possible to make mistakes, which may or may not have consequences for the survival of the interpreter. Thus, it is through arguments that the world of objects comes to exist, and how particular experiences get to have some meaning. But arguments do not appear magically, they have to be constructed by encounters with the world that produce experiences of Firstness, Secondness, and Thirdness.

We can discern that the processes of understanding proceed in two ways: (a) moving from signs type 1 to 10, when isolated phenomena are progressively related to each other and eventually forming increasingly complex arguments (and so creating objects and the world at large); and (b) when an experience is able to signal to something else, because it can be connected to arguments, and so particular experiences have a meaning *vis à vis* a world made up of arguments, and so following regularities and having some form of rationality. That is why Peirce's semiotics, and his theory of signs, is not only a catalogue of types of signification, but also a logical machine, a way of explaining how inferences are possible via the interpretative processing of experience that semiosis is. And these inferences happen in action, and not only via the use of symbols, since symbols are themselves a result of previous semiosis.

Semiosis Constructs the Fictional and the Real in Irreversible Time

Peirce's semiotic logic is not only a formalism for the explanation of meaning, but also provides a semiotic explanation of action. And the other way around, experiences get to acquire a meaning as a result of the previous encounters of the agent with its environment. Experiences are the result of recursive semiosis, where the interpretant resulting from a previous semiosis become a new representamen in a subsequent semiosis. Meaning and experience are then developmental phenomena that happen in irreversible time.

But there is more to it. These are classes of signs which exemplars may take very different shapes. They could be sensorial qualities, feelings, movements, sounds, or objects. As previously stated, semiosis are recursive and can become more and more intricate, and so be more and more removed from immediate experience. This is particularly true when symbols are involved, and particularly socially conventionalized symbols, as resulting from the use of language. Speech permits the creation of experiences quite remote from direct phenomenological qualities, or even the creation of entities such as Europe, Apollo, Psyche, atoms, or phlogiston. They are creatures of argumentation, but they furnish our view of the world with images of "real" entities. Some of them are taken to be real, and others fictional.

What is more, our experiences take meaning once we understand them as signs of a "real" or a "fictitious" thing, as true or deceiving, as belonging to the realm of reality or as a result of imagination, which is no other thing that the use of arguments (not necessarily with words) for creating entities. So viewed, the dividing line between reality and fiction is very thin. It has taken our species a very long time to devise science as a method to harness imagination to make sense of experience by creating such estrange creatures such as "the rule of law" "genes," "photons," "entropy," "intelligence," or "electrons" as a way of imaging the inner structure of the world. An effort that along the way has made us to dispose of some other creatures such as "ether," "phlogiston," or "natural moral laws".

What has just been said has also some other consequences worth mentioning. Experience and knowledge are always constructive, poietic (from the Greek verb *poieo*, which means construction and provides the root for the word *poetry*), and also has an aesthetic character (Kant explained perception as a result of what he called transcendental aesthetics). In addition, human experience and knowledge result from active laboring with artifacts and symbols, which conventional uses and meanings change along time; the outcome is that the resulting products – either works of art, techniques, myths, sciences or views of the world – have an inherent historical character, as also the individual experiences that acquire their meaning from them have. Something that deserves a lengthy comment that will be deferred to the end of this volume (General Conclusions).

I believe that the importance of Peirce's legacy is well captured by Karl Otto Apel when he said that "the Peircean program presents the appeal, among others, of making possible the integration of Theory of Knowledge and Natural Sciences, as well as Hermeneutical Sciences, within the framework of a theory of cultural evolution" (1997, p. 14).

Acting and Meaning-Making

The argument so far deployed conceives meaning as the result of establishing a relationship between something (a sign) and something else (its referent) by an agent with some purpose; something that happens according to some formal rules that account for these processes. Meaning is a result of semiosis, which is no other thing than a process that is carried out by an agent for *something different* than the sign, the object, or the agent itself; and this *something different* is what usually is called an objective, a purpose, a *telos*. In other words, a semiosis is an *action* carried out by an *agent* with a *purpose* – three concepts which logically implied each other in an unbreakable triad.

Up to now some central aspects of Peirce's semiotic logic have been examined. These include what can be a sign, what can be an object, and the rules that relate them (i.e., the formal conditions for meaning-making), but neither the agent nor the purpose have yet been subjected to inquiry. This is what will be done in what is left of this chapter.

My goal here will be to examine, first, how the agent and the purpose can come

to existence; second, how they develop into increasingly more complex forms, so they can perform increasingly complex actions and semiosis, which in turn make possible more and more elaborated images of the world; and third, to do it in as much a parsimonious way as the available space allows.

What follows, then, is an attempt to provide some psychological flesh to the bones of Peirce's formalisms in order to offer an explanation to the double process of meaning-making: making sense of the world known by compiling past experiences, and making sense of current experience by relating it to the knowledge of the world one has gathered in the past. This task will be approached following a double strategy: (a) naturalistic, that is, elaborating on how the structures of nature combine into complex systems; and (b) phenomenological, that is, starting from feelings that appear in consciousness.

My attempt here will be to offer a view on the evolutionary path of experience and its counter part, the constitution of increasingly complex patterns of behavior and images of reality. How experience can appear as a property of the functioning of Psyche, and how the working of Psyche let us know about the world. This will be done by inscribing the above presented interpretation of Peirce's semiotics within a theory of action. Something I believe indispensable if one wants to make Peircean Semiotics useful for psychological enquiry. Action theories have a long tradition in Psychology, they started with Aristotle, were amended by Kant, recovered by Brentano, continued by Janet, Piaget, and Maturana and Varela, and continues up to date forming the back-bone of the socio-cultural tradition (e.g., Cole, Engeström, & Vasquez, 1997; Leont'ev, 1978; Valsiner, 1987, 1997; Vygotsky, 1931; Wertsch, 1991, 1998, to mention just a few). The particular theory of action I have chosen for the purposes of this chapter comes from a philosophical essay authored by the Spanish philosopher Antonio González (1997) which I believe is particularly well fitted for my purposes here.

As showed in Chapter 1, Psyche is made up of processes, pure movement belonging to the realm of becoming, not to that of being. If we want to put it in other terms, Psyche is a Heraclitan entity, not a Parmenidean or Platonic creature. Therefore, the task ahead is that of offering a theory about how the processes that make Psyche come to be and produce experience. This will be done through an examination of the simplest forms of experience without taking for granted that neither things, nor the world, not even myself, previously existed as a cognitive subject. Once we had proceeded along this path for a while, we will be able to account for the existence of both: the world and myself.

Movement, Action, and Semiosis

If Psyche is a set of natural processes that makes matter to be alive, we should go first into an examination of the difference between movement and action. Action is made of movements, but movements linked together in peculiar ways. Our first move will be to go into the logical structure of action.

Movements are spatial displacements or structural changes resulting from the application of forces, so that after a first state A, a second state B appears, followed by a third state C, and so on. Movements have a dyadic structure. A produces B, so that it can be said that A is the cause of B; and B the cause of C. However, this does not make that C is necessarily connected to A as belonging to a chain of necessary causal relationships. Other causes different from B may be able to produce the effect C, as causes different from A may also be capable of producing B, given different circumstances. No doubt that the transitive property applies; in this particular case C has been caused by A. But from this it cannot be said that B has been produced by A in order to cause C, so that B were the means to produce C. Only when the latter were the case, we were before an action, not just movement.

If we were to put the $A \rightarrow B \rightarrow C$ movement into a semiotic form, it had to be expressed in dyadic relationships, where A could be taken to be a sign of B, and where the function of object and interpretant collapses together in state B; the same could be said concerning the relationship between B and C. This is what Peirce called a *quasi-sign* (CP5.473) produced in a mechanical way, so that goals are produced by external agencies or automatically predetermined (Liszka, o.c.). In purity it hardly could be said this is a semiosis of the type that interest us here.

What characterizes action vis à vis pure mechanical movement is the existence of a cause-means-goal relationship. In semiotic terminology this could be expressed in terms of sign-object-interpretant. This is typical of natural *teleonomic* processes, where feedforward processes appear (Valsiner, 2005), among which are biological processes. In these cases the triadic relationship is genuine, but not conventional. The actions resulting from this type of relationship are the result of signs belonging to a natural process. Peirce said that these teleonomic semiosis are the result of the working of a *quasimind*, not restricted to humans. Many natural processes,[11] and particularly biological actions and early forms of animal communication fit within this framework.

When the sign relates to its object in a conventional manner, and so produces new interpretants we are before a teleological semiosis, where a "purpose is precisely the interpretant of a symbol" (NEM 4: 244). This requires the presence of a proper mind capable of performing this type of action (Liszka, o.c.): that of contingently relating a sign with an object with a purpose, and also capable of establishing this into a set regularity, into a genuinely new form of behavior that gets started before the presence of this sign. So, teleological semiosis is a form of action that is not a necessary result of natural processes, but develops from them.

The task to be carried out in what is left of the chapter is to examine how teleological action develops from movement and teleonomy. Chapter 14 (Rosa, 2007) will go further in how teleological communicative actuations produce conventional social meanings and culture and, as a consequence, the human Psyche.

Organic Matter as Self-Organized Systems

An organism is a system of organs working together. Each organ has certain capabilities for action. The structures that shape it have a sort of in-built teleonomy; they can couple themselves with the structures that make their environment in some ways, but not in others. It is this capability what provides them with a functionality that makes it able to perform some acts (but not others) on its immediate surroundings. What an organism does in its environment results from the systemic functioning of its internal organs as a result of internal changes of the organism, of changes in the environment, or both. An organism is always active, is in continuous movement, both through adjustments among its constitutive organs, and between them and its environment. It is in the need that heterotrofic animals have of searching for food, and so of moving in their environment where the origin of the development of an intelligent Psyche lies (Fuentes, Quiroga, & Muñoz, 2005; Turró, 1916).

The connection of Biology to Semiotics is a rather recent trend, but also has a long past. As Kull (2001) claims, Jakob von Uexküll interest on building a biology of vital processes which took into account the subject, the living self, already included the seed of current developments that bear the name of Biosemiotics (Emmeche, 1998; Hoffmeyer, 1997, 2001) or Zoosemiotics (Riba, 1990; Sebeok, 1963, 1976). According to this view, "the study of sign systems is simultaneously both biology and semiotics. (. . .) Both biology and semiotics study communicative structures and the sign systems that create them" (Kull, o.c.; p. 3).

Uexküll is best known by his interest on how organisms perceived their *Umwelt* and this determines their behavior. The *Umwelt* is the subjectivized (meaningful) world of the organism, with which the organism relates through functional-cycles (*Funktion-kreis*). The latter is not only a fore-runner of the feed-back concept, but also the mechanism for the construction of the *Umwelt*. His view of biological research was to look at organisms as communica-

tive structures. What an organism can distinguish depends on the structure of the organism and the working of its functional cycles, being the latter responsible for the creation of the *Umwelt*. Taking this idea further, Emmeche (1998) defined life as a "functional interpretation of signs in self-organized material code-systems making their own *Umwelten*" (p. 11).

Everything the organism does in its environment is then a result of its concrete encounters with the environment, but also of systems of acts carried out by its internal organs to adjust among themselves and, all together, with the environment.

That is why each act of the organism is, at the same time, an instantiation of the teleonomic capabilities of the acting global entity that acts and of the structural properties of the elements it encounters – what Gibson (1979) called *affordances*. That is, any act is the result of the interaction between the capabilities for acting of an organ (or organism), its *effectivities*, and the *affordances* of the things it encounters. That is why it can be said that each act shows something of the object on which is applied, of the structure that performs that act, and the way they can get in communication between themselves. Thus, it can be said that there are three aspects in acts that should be differentiated: the organism that carries out the act, the object on which the act is exercised, and the act itself. The three are mutually implied, but also are inseparably united in time.

Time is a dimension of prime importance here, because it is in time where functional cycles do their work, and semiosis get deployed creating new functional structures (Luria, 1974; see also Travieso, 2007), and so making new *effectivities* to appear (Valsiner, 1984).

From Acts to Action

It is on this triad – act, organism, and *affordances* of objects – where the foundations for the next part of the argument here deployed lies. González, paraphrasing Descartes, but also amending him, says that cynics and skeptics may doubt, but there is no possible doubt about acting, because doubting itself is an act (1997, p. 46–49). The act is prior to everything else, because even the possibility of an object and an agent can only appear as a consequence of acting.

It is through acts that things and the agent get actualized (González, 1997). These actualizations are elemental truths that result from the radical otherness of things that the acts present. Acts actualize the properties of things, of the acting agent and of the encounter between the agent and the thing[12]. Acts always come in triadic units – *actions* – that gather these three aspects: the thing, the agent, and the act itself. But not all acts are identical. There are *sensorial acts* that actualize things through sensitive properties – qualities; *affective acts*, that produce an affective tone – an affection resulting from the encounter of the organism with the thing, how the organism has been affected by that encounter; and *volitional acts* or *volitions* which usually show in the shape of bodily movements of approaching or withdrawing from the thing. "These three types of acts are the moments which constitute the *action system*"[13] (González, 1997, p. 87), and in each of these three moments things (and the agent) are actualized in different fashions.

An action system then conforms a unity formed by these three types of acts. This has some consequences worth mentioning. Actions are not mechanical, they do not always produce an identical outcome. The resulting movement is not only a result of the sensorial act, but also of the affections of the organism, which in turn refer to other sensations, affections, and volitions of the organs within the organism. In addition, what the organism could do is also dependent of what the thing on which the movement is applied affords to be done. So, action, from its very beginning, has an ecological character, as well as being inherently *oriented* towards the environment. Things get actualized in ways which always are relative to the state of the organism, which, in turn, reacts to the resulting sensation with a new action, establishing a cycle of action-reaction which Baldwin

(1906) termed circular reaction. Figure 10.3 presents the structure of a simple Circular Reaction in which actions follow each other in time.

As there is shown, actions are objectively oriented to somethings different to the agent that carries it out (an organ or an organism). As Bretano (1874) would say, acts and actions have an immanent objectivity. That is the reason why an ecological approach is indispensable, because the agent and the thing, being different entities, share the agency of movement and action. They are open systems in a relationship of inclusive separation (Valsiner, 1997). Action then is an unit of analysis that crosses the frontier of the membrane of the skin of the agent (Wertsch, 1991).

This conception of action depicts it as a sort of self-controlled automatism acting following the teleonomy dictated by the structure of the active organism and the things it encounters – the *effectivities* of the organs and the organism, and the *affordances* of things (see Travieso, 2007 for a discussion). Actions, then, are the most primitive elements of Psyche, and the only one present in plants and animals with no nervous system, or with primitive nervous systems.

Actions are the basis on which semiosis can be performed, and so are the foundation on which consciousness later will develop. A sensorial act presents qualities (Firstness), an affective act (Secondness) mediates between the quality and the movement carried out in the environment (the volitional act – Thirdness). As Figure 10.4 shows, actions have a teleonomic semiotic character. They can only become semiotic when they are interconnected in higher order units so that recursive semiosis becomes possible. Action is the basic seed for the development of sense and meaning.

What has just been said should not be interpreted as a consequence of some kind of internal representation, and even less as some kind of consciousness, but as something that belongs to the very functional structure of action. If we want to talk of representation, at this moment it only could be a function with a directionality towards

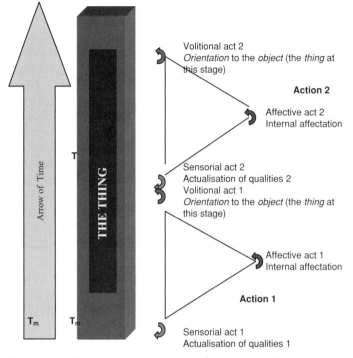

Figure 10.3. Pre-semiotic primary circular reactions. *Orientation* to the object (the *thing*).

something not present, implied in a future that is still removed from what is being done at that very moment. That is why at this level is still impossible to have any kind of associative learning, which would require the mediation of other actions capable of some way of relating what is currently going on with something that happened in another time (past), and so making possible the development of routines addressing an event still to come. This requires the organism to have morphological structures able to support a set of interconnected actions that are no other thing that functional structures arising from repeated encounters with the environment. Chapter 7 (Perinat, 2007) offers a review of how these functions change in evolution.

Intentionality, Actuations, and Dramatic Performances

When the capability of profiting from past events in order to carry out new actions becomes possible, then the instrumental use of former actions in order to achieve a better performance appears, and so a genuine developmental transformation happens. Then actions become capable of connecting among themselves creating a new functional behavioral unit – *actuations*[14] (González, o.c.). Actuations have new properties, they are extended in time, and so they allow making use of past experiences for solving current problems, making possible early forms of *intention* and *understanding* to develop. Thus, actuations are provided with *sense*. This is the earliest form of mediation, when an act or an action become a means that makes possible, and also constrains, the way in which another action can be carried out deferred in time. When this happens the von Uexküll's functional cycle becomes fully operative.

For actuations to develop some requisites have to be fulfilled. First, a certain amount of circular reactions must have happened before; second, there must be a way of maintaining a trace of these repeated actions in

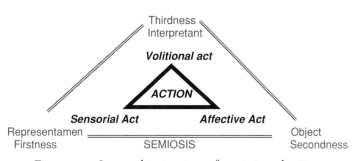

Figure 10.4. Isomorphic structure of semiosis and action.

the structure of the organism beyond the immediate present of each action; and, third, a nervous system capable of keeping these traces active in a more extended time and interconnecting them must exist – something that is already fully developed in birds (see Perinat, 2007).

Actuations are a variant of circular reactions, but now, actions rather that following one another, get integrated into a system, creating a new functional unit (actuation), whose internal structure, following González (1997) we can call *intentional schema*. This schema is not any kind of representation, but a structure of interconnected recursive actions, not only relating to the object, but also related among themselves. Figure 10.5 presents the formal structure of an *intentional schema*.

Intentional Schema

Figure 10.5 presents two actions (actions 1 and 2) that follow each other in two moments in time t_m and t_n in a circular reaction performed on something foreign to the organism (the *thing*). Each of these actions is a system formed by three interconnected acts (sensorial, affective, and volitional). But now, rather than one following each other, the latter relates to the former through a set of actions which constitute the *intentional schema*. This assembly of actions conform together a processing unit capable of producing signs of increasing complexity, at the same time that generates new types of actions which shape psychological processes with particular meaning-making properties. The new structure that so appears has some

properties that are worth explaining with some detail.

When Figures 10.3 and 10.5 are compared it is clearly apparent how in actuations actions overlap with each other along an extended time that goes beyond the present in which an individual action happens. It is not only that a volition (a movement) produces a sensation (that also happened when actions merely follow one another), but that the structure of the relationship between successive external actions changes. New actions of a purely internal (psychological) character appear. The consequence is that the acts that conform the second action are not only acts, but also the result of actions that conflate the second action with elements of the first. I believe this is the origin of the psychological functions, which also have meaning-making capabilities worthy of being examined.

When we look at the first action as it appears in Figure 10.5, we can see how the first and second sensorial acts (the latter is also a consequence of the first volitional act) relate to the first affective act. In purity, this is an action that is the result of a circular reaction – a movement towards the environment that follows another. But now it is not the same as when two isolated actions follow one another (as shown in Figure 10.3). Now the elements of the two actions get intermingled. The first sensorial act (a Firstness – a quality, let us suppose that is the color *green* in the example of Figure 10.7 – green in a frog) here acts as a representamen whose object is the first affective act (a Secondness – a phenomenological presence, the feeling of feeling green) and the interpretant is the first volitional act (a Thirdness) – a movement (of approaching) on the thing. The interpretant of the first action is a volitional act, but this produce *at the same time* a sensorial act (a quality – green again), and so it can be said that approaching the thing is a Thirdness that produces the Firstness that initiates the next semiosis. The outcome of the first semiosis is that the consequence of its interpretant (sensorial act 2 resulting from volitional act 1 – when approaching the thing *green* is felt again) play the role of representamen in the following semiosis.

The second semiosis (represented in Figure 10.5 by a thick line) is the immediate outcome of the first action and the beginning of the second. In this case, the second sensorial act is the representamen, the first affective act is the object and the second affective act is the interpretant. What this semiosis does if one wants to put it into words, is to check whether quality 2 can represent quality 1. The only way of doing this is by relating the green feeling in the second sensorial act with the green felt in the first affective act, something that can only be done by comparing how one has been affected. The result is that sign types 1 and 2 get constituted (there may be green – sign type 1; and there may be something green– sign type 2) what makes possible the semiotic process to start. Sensations, as could be supposed, have an iconic character.

In what it has just been said there are a couple of things that deserve to be commented. First, actions always have a function (a sense), and the function of a circular reaction is to reproduce the result of a first action. This is why the first affective act is the object of the second semiosis just described. But there is another reason for this. The thing is removed from the organism, it only shows as qualities and the affects qualities produce, and the function of the second semiosis is precisely to compare the second sensation with the first, and this can only be done by comparing a new sensation with the affect resulting of the former. The result is an interpretant that is also an affection (affective act 2). There is an interesting consequence of this. Affections are the root of meaning and the constitution of reality. Qualities are the same because they may produce the same affect in me. Both qualities (sensations and affections) are feelings, and share the possibility of acting as signs. They come together, in a sort of double-sidedness, as when one feels being punctured by a needle. In the course of development both have to become distinct, so that one can act predominantly as a sign of the thing (a sensation), and the other a sign of the agent itself (affect). Although the difference between them may not be that simple, as when as one say that a tune is sad or gay, or an object is awkward or lovely.

What it has just been said, is how sensorial processes get started on the way into becoming perceptual processes, once one proceeds to develop higher classes of signs. But before going into how this is possible, we have to proceed ahead with the explanation of how the logical device that the intentional schema is works. This will be done by going into the examination of the next action and semiosis within the intentional schema.

Going back to Figure 10.5, we will focus now on the double lines that connect affective acts 1 and 2 with volitional act 2. As said before, affective act 2 is the interpretant of the last semiosis presented above, and so here acts as representamen of this new semiosis. The object of this new semiosis is again affective act 1, and the interpretant in this case is volitional act 3. Affective acts produce feelings, which at this stage still have no quality in themselves; they are signs of existence – Secondness. This semiosis, then is capable of producing signs of classes 3 and 4. The semiotic structure of this action also has psychological interest: an affective act comes to represent another, and the result is a movement. The consequence is that here we are before the rudiments of the creation of affective structures connected to movements, that is, *emotions*. And with the connection between sensations, emotions, and movements, that is, *desires*. But the semiotic content of emotion and desires will result from the particular semiosis that relate them with particular qualities and volitions, and so would

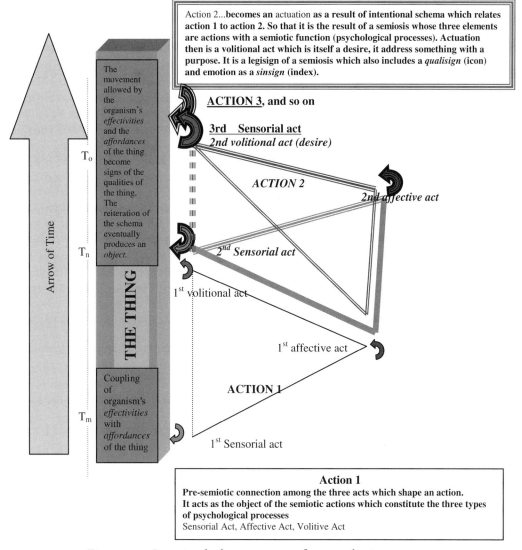

Action 2...**becomes an** actuation **as a result of intentional schema which relates action 1 to action 2. So that it is the result of a semiosis whose three elements are actions with a semiotic function (psychological processes). Actuation then is a volitional act which is itself a desire, it address something with a purpose. It is a legisign of a semiosis which also includes a** *qualisign* **(icon) and emotion as a** *sinsign* **(index).**

ACTION 3, **and so on**

3rd   Sensorial act
2nd volitional act (desire)

ACTION 2

2nd affective act

2nd Sensorial act

1st volitional act

1st affective act

ACTION 1

1st Sensorial act

The movement allowed by the organism's *effectivities* and the *affordances* of the thing become signs of the qualities of the thing. The reiteration of the schema eventually produces an *object.*

T_o

T_n

THE THING

Coupling of organism's *effectivities* with *affordances* of the thing

T_m

Arrow of Time

Action 1
Pre-semiotic connection among the three acts which shape an action.
It acts as the object of the semiotic actions which constitute the three types of psychological processes
Sensorial Act, Affective Act, Volitive Act

Figure 10.5. Intentional schema: systems of actions shaping actuation.

be the consequence of subsequent semiosis belonging to recurrent applications of the intentional schema. Once green is felt again, and produces the same affect, one may feel driven to feel it again or not; to approach or withdraw (being anthropomorphic one may say "one likes or dislikes green"). In addition, this third internal action (and semiosis) re-starts the process of a new circular reaction, since it takes to carry out a new volitional act – a movement. It can be said, that the new volitional act, as it is the interpretant of the semiosis we are now focus-

ing upon, is geared to producing again the same internal affection by acting again on the environment. And this movement opens a new cycle, takes one to a new action (the third action upon the thing in Figure 10.5) which produces a new sensorial act and re-starts a new cycle that again takes the form of another intentional schema. But, before going into that, there is something else that still has to be stated. This latter action-semiosis, as a result of its inscription in the structure of the intentional schema, also has an emergent property. Volitional act 2 is the interpretant of the semiosis we have just described, but also of the semiosis formed by the three elements of action 2, and so it is also the interpretant of the semiosis formed by itself, together with volitional act 1 (that is also sensorial act 2), and affective act 2 (which itself is also an interpretant resulting from another semiosis). This new semiosis then connect qualities (Firstness) with feelings of existence (Secondness), and so produces a new type of Thirdness, that in this case are regularities of experience (habits), which can take the shape of sign classes 5, 6, and 7. Now the felt feeling of feeling green is a sign of something that exists as a real regularity (turning to a naturalistic view, some wavelengths that produce that feeling). If this is so, the new signs so constituted can from now on act as signs of real things that produce the feeling of greenness in me.

The consequence of what has just been said is that the intentional schema is a teleonomic device, but also a meaning-making (semiotic) machine. The outcome of its first application is the construction of the conception of one sensorial quality as a permanent entity referring to things of the environment. And also the construction of a sentiment as a system of affections relating to qualities and volitional acts (movements). Subsequent applications of the intentional schema to the outcomes of earlier actuations will produce sign types 8 and 9 (representation of permanent features of the perceived and felt experience), and so symbols develop. And, after new cycles, eventually sign type 10 (arguments) of increased complexity which gather the above-mentioned features together. The outcome is the constitution of objects, first, and then, situations. It is through the repeated performance of intentional schemas that sensations and sentiments are separated as signs of otherness and selfness.

Intentional schemas produce then a new type of circular reactions, ones that not only are oriented to the environment, but that also transform the representative and interpretative capabilities of the acting organism. These circular reactions are not anymore just a repeated orientation towards a thing, but a developmental device for the mutual development of the functional structures within the organism and the parallel understanding of the objects and situations encountered; the mutual construction of psychological functions and the *Umwelt* through functional cycles. Figure 10.6 shows the basic features of Secondary Circular Reactions, which are a device for internalization of knowledge provided by experience.

An example may help to explain the processes of constitution of objects and situations. Figure 10.7 presents a set of numbered vignettes of events of a story of animals in a pond, explaining in diagrams the semiotic structure of the actions going on. The story, as an external observer would put it, is as follows: "A heron is in a pond. Suddenly it seems to fix its attention into something (fixes its gaze in the same point of space) and moves towards that point. When doing so, a frog jumps away from its previous position, the heron chases it and eventually grabs and swallows it". For the sake of brevity we will suppose that it is the first time that this particular young heron has seen (and tasted) a frog (so it does not know what a frog is), but it is already familiar with the fact that there are many different things that produce in herself the feeling of greenness, that there are edible things that run away from her (and have to be chased), as well as other previous experiences as to feeling hungry, satisfied, restless, tired, and tasting agreeable and disagreeable flavors. What we are going to model now is how this particular heron construct the meaning of *frog* out of a set of experiences. Or in Peircean jargon, how she performs actions that produce sign types 8, 9, and 10; i.e., the stable features typical of frogs, and the (enactive) arguments frogs are made of (how these features together constitute a new type of permanent object – frogs). Once this process is completed, some qualities felt become able to signal the possible presence of a frog, and so what to do to find out whether there is such a thing "out there" or not.

Once the semiosis-actions that constitute an intentional schema have become a functional structure, the organism is able to *make*

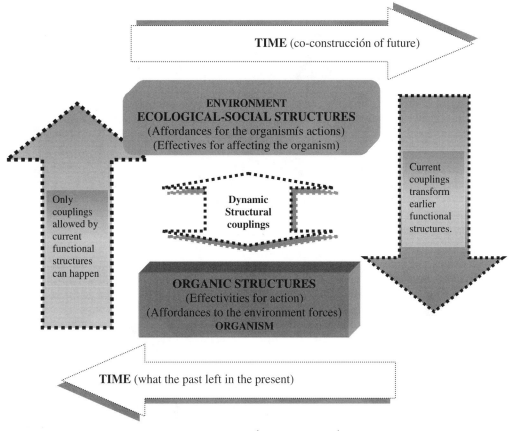

Figure 10.6. Circular reactions cycle.

sense of repeated encounters with the environment. Now there are familiar sensations, and so it becomes possible to profit from past experience, to act with some intelligence. A sensation becomes then capable of presenting something real, which can be interpreted as a sign of the possibility or reality of something else, and so produce new actuations, which have *intentionality*. The organism has now developed new functional structures (intentional schemas) and consequently has increased its *effectivities*. The result is that when carrying out new actuations in its encounters with the environment new *affordances* of the objects are discovered and more and more intentional schemas appear. These circular reactions are then devices for the construction of new dicent signs and arguments (Peirce's sign types 9 and 10).

Actuations Produce Psychological Processes, Objects, Situations, and Actors

The recursive application of the intentional schemas would then provide a formalism for the explanation of the simultaneous development of psychological processes, experiences, and subsequent capability for representations of objects, which also include the rudiments of representations of the agent him/herself.

Following this argument, it can be said that psychological processes result of the production (and later on of the activation) of schemas capable of producing actuations. Then, psychological functions (or faculties as sometimes also called) are no other thing that actuations resulting from the activation of intentional schemas.

1a. A heron, excited by some change in the environment (a change in the display of colors, etc.) orients towards something in the environment.

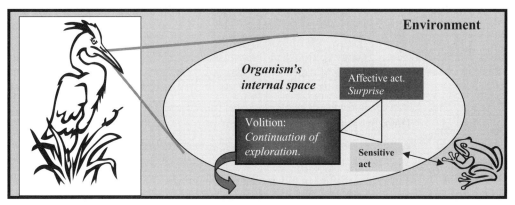

1b. When encountering an unfamiliar thing a set of actions and circular reactions trigger in the heron. The result is a series of events shown in the following vignettes.

2. The volition of previous actions is a movement towards the "thing". When moving the heron feels its own movement and the changes in the position of the thing within the environmental display. Previous functional schemas (of visual exploration, moving around in the pond, etc.) trigger circular reactions.

Figure 10.7. The construction of a permanent object.

3. After essaying different intentional schemas and circular reactions (visual and auditory explorations, movements of approaching and withdrawal), which produce different sensations of the 'thing' (green, patterns of black spots, jumps and changes in position and shape, croaks, etc.), as well as affections resulting from these actions (feelings of its own movements, fatigue, etc.), finally a structural coupling happens: the heron grabs and swallows the thing. Now new sensations (flavors) appear, as well as new affections (satisfaction). The environment has changed, there is nothing else with that peculiar shade of green jumping around, the agent is more tired than before, but also more satisfied. Several steps for the creation of new intentional schemas have been carried out. Green may become a sign for jumping things; green jumping things may produce fatigue and/or satisfaction, etc. Once further circular reactions are performed with similar things, new intentional schemas and actuations develop, and with them the argument of what a frog is develops, as well as the argument of what the situation of being in a pond is. Now green, jumping, or feeling hungry can act as signs of satisfaction, triggering intentional schemas, and providing sensations with a sense.

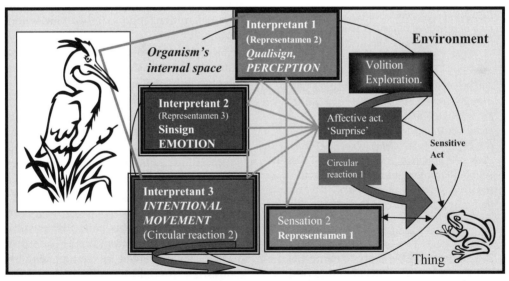

2 & 3 b. The heron's psychological processes when constructing the frog as an object.
Following the first orientation action, a first circular reaction happens, and an intentional schema triggers, followed by further circular actions that essay different intentional schemas. The result is the development of a new intentional schema that eventually simultaneously produces the argument of what a frog is, the qualities and feelings that may act as sign of a frog, and the actuations (scripts) to perform when a sign of something possibly being a frog appears.

Figure 10.7 (*continued*)

So *perception* results from the increased capability of using qualities as signs of other qualities or features of an object or situation. As a consequence of development of intentionality

> *... sensations take a particular sense. Now there is not only a system of properties actualized in a radical otherness, but this system of properties has now a sense [it is something to eat, that signals a familiar taste, that prompts a movement to reach that thing, etc.] ... [S]ensing a system of properties, together with the understanding of sense, is not a simple sensation any more, but what we may call perception.[...]. In perception the sensed properties are organized by a sense and then are 'understood' ... To understand the sense of something is no different as to be able to integrate it into an actuation. (González, o.c., p.115)*

Emotion also results from intentionality and the development of structures of sentiments and their relation to perceptions and movements, which produce encounters with the environment.

> *Instead of mere modifications of the vital tone in a radical otherness to the thing, we have now affections filled with sense. We find, for example, affections of joy or sadness. There are not new affective acts different from those included in an action. They are the same acts , but they now have a sense because they are structured and oriented according to an intentional schema [, ...] we can call them 'emotions'. Emotions are affections with sense.[...] Pure volitions are now oriented desires with a sense. Desire means here an act – the act of desiring. And desires can also have an aversive form, as when something is desired to be avoided. (González, o.c., p. 115)*

Learning would be another name for the semiotic capacity, for the capability of making sense of a sensation that now becomes a percept in a repeated environmental setting, or in a range of variable situations (discrimination, transfer and generalization), and so trigger a script of actuations.

Attention develops from orientation into an attempt of making sense of an unexpected change in the environment (orientation reflex) which then make use of qualities and sentiments in order to perform rhematic semiosis until a dicentic sign can identify what kind of object that novel stimulus can be a sign of.

This no doubt requires the existence of organs capable of performing these tasks, and among them that of a nervous system capable of a highly intricate capacity of performing massive parallel actions, and interconnecting them in lengthier and lengthier structures, which meaning-making capacities increase as far as these structures permit recursive actions and semiosis (see Edelman & Tononi, 2000).

The result is the development of objects (González, o.c.) with a permanence. Rather that an indeterminate otherness that appear in each sensorial act, there is now a continuity between different sensations. Perception makes possible that different qualities perceived in different moments could be interpreted as signs with a similar sense, signaling to the same entity – an object. Objects, then, appear as something permanent that shows through many signs. The consequence is that an understanding of the object's unity of sense appears.

But objects are not the only synthetic result of intentional schemas. Objects come together in situations. What is more, objects acquire a sense within a *situation*, which is a network of actions and actuations within which objects are actualized and acquire a sense (González, o.c.).

Situations include qualities and objects distributed within time and space, and their mutual relations become understandable, once the agent acquires the capability of orienting itself within this particular environment, of behaving intentionally, interpreting the signs received in relation with the desires felt. It could be said that it acquires *scripts* about how to actuate in those situations (González, o.c.). Scripts here cannot be conceived as resulting from a set of symbolic rules for the performance of an actuation, and somehow programmed in the inner processor of an agent (Shank & Abelson, 1977). Rather they would develop from series of action-semiosis triggered by environmental and organismic signs (sensations and affections), and so having their agency distributed between the organism and the environment. However, once situational schemas develop they start to turn into scripts, as the signaling capability of internal signs increase, and so the nature of scripts become increasingly closer to that of a system of rules. If we are concerned about explaining how experience comes to be, the genesis of rules also has to be explained and not simply made to appear as an *ad hoc* explanation. Then, scripts are systems of actuations upon objects included in situations, which make each object within the situation (and the situation itself) to have a sense. The qualities of the objects, and the affections in the organism, are signs for the orientation of behavior, for the establishment of intentions.

Actuations and scripts have sense and a rationale (González, o.c.), they are governed by a semiotic logic, from which a situational rationale develops throughout the history of encounters between the organism and its environment. It is a mundane rationale, constructed by acting upon things, by turning actions into actuations, actuations into scripts, and so developing rules for behavior that widen the *Umwelt* making objects and situations to appear. It is the mastering of this rationale what makes the organism to *know* how to act, and so actions get organized in systems of actuations adapted to particular environmental conditions. This makes actuations to have a historical rationale that also is local and situated, always bounded to the organism's *Umwelt*. Acts (sensorial of affective) become then signs for the orientation of actions, and actions included into systems of actuations make possible through interpretation the emergence of intentionality, sense and experience.

Actions and actuations include processes that happened at both sides of the skin. They are devices for equilibration between the external and the internal. The constitution of objects and situations (unities of sense) is not possible without the simultaneous construction of cognitive structures within the organism, of intentional schemas, of their combination and discrimination of their components, of the refining of perception, emotions, and desires. That is, of the elaboration of increasingly complex psychological processes capable of becoming instrumental to each other. The consequence is a progressive construction of the effectivities of the agent, a development of its capabilities for actuation in the situations within its *Umwelt*.

Once intentions and motives are established; once the actual behavior does not immediately follow the teleonomy dictated by the morphological structures of the objects in the environment and the organs, but becomes mediated by learned intermediate actions which offer resources and set constraints for actuation; then it can be said that some actuations become instrumental to some others; that structures constructed in past actuations become capable of combine among themselves in novel situations and so producing new senses, new actuations in the search of equilibration between the agent and its environment. This is the beginning of the transition between teleonomy and teleology, between actuating and dramatic performing, between an agent and an actor.

This transition from agent to actor is a consequence of the construction of situational scripts, which evolve from the combination of intentional schemas in earlier actuations (González, o.c.). These scripts also have a semiotic nature. They are actuations guided by semiosis, capable of increasing their complexity as intentional schemas for the understanding of situations develop. Together with this, the construction of some understanding of the agent itself as an object with some kind of otherness is also underway. The agent feels the consequences of its movements, but also its emotions (actions referred to itself, which relate actions in different moments of time), and desires. Emotions, that have the function of assessing the consequences of earlier volitions, are capable of acting as signs, and therefore are a necessary requirement for the production of desire and the performing of actuations. Emotion (that is a kind of interpretant) can act also as a sign of the existence of another kind of object – the subject of behavior, the actor. Something that happens in a lengthy evolution both in phylogeny and ontogeny.

The Others Turn Actuations Into Dramaturgical Scripts. *The Influence of the Social*

Actuations evolve into the performing of scripts, at the same time as the agent becomes an actor. An actor is much more than an agent that carries out actuations. What s/he does is not just simply the result of the triggering of an automatism, s/he performs for an audience a script, which also has a dramaturgical sense, that is addressed not only to an object, but to some others. That performance includes some form of pretence, some intention of influencing others. The development of scripts, the transformation of actuations into performances, the change from agent to actor, is something that happens in social life. So we have to turn to the social realm as the next step in the argument.

Organisms do not act alone in an inert environment. They are always within a swarm of life. They are either predators or victims of predators, they need others for mating, they compete with their co-generics for resources, and sometimes they belong to a group or have some form of transient ties with their offspring and mates. So, the others are not just another kind of thing in their environment, but also objects that act, and so one not only has to act upon them, but also interact with them. That is why they have to be made intelligible by constituting them as objects. However, since they resist one's actions beyond the affordances of their physical structure (they run away from me, or charge against me), their constitution as understandable objects also needs to constitute their own behavior as one of their features to be made intelligible. Then, intentional schemas about how to act *vis à vis* the actions and actuations of other alive things have to be constructed. In other words, some kind of understanding of the other's intentions has to be reached, so that one's own behavior can get to some

sort of dynamic equilibrium with that of the other. If one fails to do so, survival is at risk. Now the question is not only what I learned from past experience about how to understand what can I do with this moving object, but also what can I do with what this living object is doing now. Or even better, how can I understand from current signs what the other desires to do, so I may have some advantage in acting in advance. When this happen is when intentional communication develops (for a more detailed explanation, see Perinat, 2007; Riba, 1990).

This is a process which evolves from emotional expression and the development of patterns of behavior which usually are described as anger, threats, fear, submission, and so on, as it can be witnessed when a group of birds or mammal predators interact when competing for devouring a prey. These movements are actuations whose goal is achieved before the performance of the scripts is completed. So that uncompleted aggressive movements turn into threats, and threatening behavior changes into movements communicating anger. As Darwin (1872) described, emotional expression evolved from adaptative communicative behavior. New functional scripts so develop. The goal changes from immediate attack, to signaling the other that one is about to attack, or even to showing that one is getting irritated by the behavior of the other. Then, this actuated script changes from being an actuation to the performance of a script that signals intentions addressed to another, that now is taken as being another actor. It becomes an instrumental actuation, which also has a dramaturgical side. It is a sort of pretence, which looks for influencing the behavior of the other. The situation then starts to change into a sort of social scenery in which actors play their roles adapting their scripts in the ongoing drama of competence for the environmental resources.

Rivière and Sotillo (1999) take this interrupted scripts that change their functionality as one of the origins of the development of communicative symbols. *Suspension* of the ongoing functionality and its substitution by a new function is the key process for the development of symbolic communication, meta-representation, and a theory of mind. When the functionality of these actuations change, when it is *suspended* in the middle of being performed, they become able to take a new sense. Once this happens, the road to the development of conventional meaning is open.

Concluding Remarks. Semiotic Actuations as the Source of Ecologically Developed Teleological Functions

This chapter has centered on the examination of the development of experience. It has focused on an examination of what meaning is, on the intricacies of its production, on how meaning evolves from the sense of actions carried out by alive beings. The experience examined in this chapter is an enactive experience, it is the experience that *presents* the world, it is the experience that results from alive movement that produces the development of an agent and its change into actor, at the same time that the environment becomes intelligible, changes into a meaningful *Umwelt* where the organism learns what to do, so that its behavior follows a rationale. It is the kind of experience that exist before communication and language comes to the scenery. It is the basis on which human experience develops, but it is not still fully developed human experience.

This chapter has dwelled on how movement turns in action, and the latter into actuations, so that meaningful objects, situations and the lived *Umwelt* can appear. This is only a part of journey in the explanation of the production of experience. Full human experience judges what is present by relating it to something absent. It relates what actual feelings *present* with *re-presentations* of the absent (of an imagined past, a present or a future) vehiced on other actual feelings. For this to be possible other types of mediation, different to the ones this chapter presented, have still to develop. Communication between actors has still to be able to produce conventional signs, so that,

first, a mutual regulation of behavior can appear. One has to recognize oneself as an object among others, so that communication with oneself can become possible, and self-consciousness can appear. This is only possible through the mediation of conventional signs developed in social life. It is only then when a full-fledged representation of the world can appear. For this to happen, the sensorial *Umwelt* has to turn, first, into a *social Umwelt*, and then into an *imagined world* that extends well beyond what actual sensations present. Once this process is completed, it is when truth can come to existence. It is then when an utterance (a result of a communicative action mediated by conventional signs) can refer to what actual feelings present to us, and so open the way to contrasting utterances among themselves.

When this process is completed, experience are not any more just right or wrong interpretations of the signs sensed in a situation, which make one to behave efficiently or to make mistakes. Then truth or falsehood can appear, behavior can be termed moral or immoral, and the notion of a morally accountable person could come into the stage. It is when all this process is completed that truth can be created, as William James stated in the quotation at the beginning of this chapter. Meaning, truth and moral are so the result of a social and a historical process, which intricacies have to be disentangled. Chapter 14 (Rosa, 2007) will go into the detail of the development of these processes.

This chapter has centered on episodes previous to the developments referred in the previous paragraph. They are processes that go on in pre-human, but also human, creatures and they cannot be skipped when accounting for the development of experience. It has been a story about how movements turned into intention, and later into desires and intelligent behavior. The open system nature of the relationships between the organism and the environment (Bertalanffy, 1950) was a central issue in this process. The processes that happen inside the organism evolved as a consequence of the teleonomic properties of the structural coupling between the different organs that together compose the organism, and of the organism as a whole with the parts of the environment it encounters. The result is the carrying out of a set of actions that are open to the influence of the history of contingencies suffered, once the internal processes of the organism (affections) become capable of keeping activated a sort of primitive memory of the results of earlier encounters with the environment. Then some actions can become mediational means for other actions to be carried out. The result is that teleonomy and contingencies shape together the functional capabilities of the organism. The recursivity of action and semiosis is a key factor in this process. Intentional schemas develop as a combination of different kinds of actions that together create new senses, and start developing a grammar of action, a rationale that combines actions into actuations and so start to make parts of the environment familiar, and thus creating objects, situations and eventually a meaningful lived *Umwelt*. Psychological functions such as perception, emotion, attention, learning, or problem solving develop as intentional schemas and turn into actuations and scripts. Simultaneously the organism transforms itself first into an agent, and then into an actor.

Actuations are the key issue in this process. They gather together behavior, emotion, and cognition and so they produce consciousness. They come from intentional schemas that gather actions together in a new functional unit, and later on develop into scripts. Social interaction and communication affect this process from the very beginning. The temporal structure of body movements gets culturally shaped in social interaction (see Chapter 11; Español, 2007); the objects included in the social situations for interaction take particular conventional senses (see Chapter 12; Rodríguez, 2007); and the social matrix of meanings which shapes the environment where a young human individual develops, which is the cradle for the construction of a lived and a social *Umwelt* (see Chapter 13; Rosetti-Ferreira, Amorim, & Silva, 2007).

Actuations are teleonomic processes that relate the organism and the environment. They are also the key process for the construction of internal psychological processes. By their recursive operation they shape psychological functions throughout its history of contingent encounters with the environment. It is in these contingencies, once they are of a social communicative nature, where the seed for the development from teleonomy into teleology lies. But this is a story to be told in detail somewhere else (see Chapter 14 and the General Conclusions).

Acknowledgment

Preparation of this chapter was supported by the grant SEJ2005–09110-C03–01/PSIC from the Spanish Ministry of Education and Science.

Notes

1 There are no substantial differences in the meaning of the words referring to "meaning" in Roman languages and English.

2 Quotations of Peirce's work will be done as follows: CP, refers to the Collected Papers; MS, to the Annotated Catalogue of the Papers of Charles S. Peirce; LW, to his Semiotics and Significs: Correspondence between C.S. Peirce and Victoria Lady Welby; and NEM, to The New Elements of Mathematics.

3 "[W]hatever is in the mind in any mode of consciousness there is necessarily an immediate consciousness and consequently a feeling... [T]he feeling [is] completely veiled from introspection, for the very reason that it is our immediate consciousness... [A]ll that is immediately present to a man is what is in his mind in the present instant. His whole life is in the present. But when he asks what is the content of this present instant, his question always comes too late. The present is gone by, and what remains of it is greatly metamorphosized." (CP. 1.310)

4 "Besides Feelings, we have Sensations of reaction; as when a person blindfold[ed] suddenly runs into a post, when we make a muscular effort, or when any feeling gives way to a new feeling... Whenever we have two feelings and pay attention to a relation between

them of whatever kind, there is the sensation of which I am speaking." (CP. 6.19)

5 "This is a kind of consciousness that cannot be immediate, because it covers a time, and that not merely because it continuous through every instant of that time, because it cannot be contracted into an instant. It differs from immediate consciousness, as a melody does from one prolonged note. Neither can the consciousness of the two sides of an instant, of a sudden occurrence, in its individual reality, possibly embrace the consciousness of a process. This is the consciousness that binds life together. It is the consciousness of synthesis." (CP. 1.381)

6 Peirce's definitions of sign abound. Besides the ones included in the text, the following adds new meanings to this concept:

[a sign is] anything which is related to a Second thing, its Object, *in respect to a* Quality *in such a way as to bring a* Third thing, *its* Interpretant, *into relation to the same object* ... *(CP 2.92)*

7 How this is possible will be explained later on in the text.

8 In Peirce's words: "If a Sign is other than its Object, there must exist, either in thought or expression, some explanation or argument or other context, showing how – upon what system or for what reason the Sign represents the Object or set of Objects it does" (CP 2.230). This takes us to the concept of argument which will be developed later on in the text.

9 An object may be a "single known existing thing or thing believed formerly to have existed or expected to exist, or a collection of such things, or a known quality or relation or fact, which single object may be a collection, or a whole of parts, or it may have some other way of being such as an act permitted whose being does not prevent its negation from being equally permitted, or something of a general nature desired, required, or invariably found under certain general circumstances." (CP 2.232)

10 In Gibsonian language it could be said that each perceptual act does not exhaust all the possible affordances of the object.

11 "thought is not necessarily connected with a brain. It appears in the work of bees, of crystals, and throughout the purely physical world" (CP 4.551), quoted by Liszka (o.c.).

12 I have chosen to use "thing" rather than "object", as a way of separating the radical otherness of primitive experiences from objects as entities of the world. The reason is that "objects" are the result of a development that needs to be explained, while "the thing" is a primitive undetermined "otherness" that presents in acts.

13 All quotations from González are my translation.

14 Actuación in Spanish gathers together the meaning of actuation and performance in English, and so includes within it a dramaturgical sense. The use González gives to this term allows to differentiate two phases of its development: first actuations as a sort of developed automatism and, second, its transition towards a communicative dramatic performance in a social milieu.

References

Apel, K. O. (1975/1997). *Der Denkweg von Charles S. Peirce. Ein Einführung in den americanischen Pragmatismus.* Frankfurt am Mein: Suhrkamp. Spanish versión: *El camino del pensamiento de Charles S. Peirce.* Madrid: Visor, 1997.

Baldwin, J. M. (1906). *Thought and Things: A study of the development and meaning of thought, or genetic logic: Vol. I. Functional Logic, or genetic theory of knowledge.* London: Swan Sonnenschein.

Bertalanffy, L. von (1950). The theory of open systems in physics and biology. *Science,* 111, 23–29.

Brentano, F. (1874). *Psychologie von Empirische Standpunkte.* Leipzig: Dunker und Humbolt.

Castañares, W. (2002). Sign and Representation in Semiotic Theories. *Estudios de Psicología* 23(3), 339–358.

Cole, M., Engeström, Y., & Vasquez, O. (1997). *Mind, Culture and Activity.* New York: Cambridge University Press.

Darwin, C. (1872). *The expression of Emotions in Animals and Man.* Spanish version by Tomás R. Fernández: La expresión de las emociones en los animales y el hombre. Madrid: Alianza (1984).

Edelman, G. M. & Tononi, G. (2000). *The Universe of Consciousness. How matter becomes Imagination.* New York: Basic Books.

Emmeche, C. (1998). Defining life as a semiotic phenomenon. *Cybernetics and Human Knowing* 5 (1), 3–17.

Español, S. (2007). Alive Movement in Symbol Formation. In J. Valsiner & A. Rosa (Eds.):

Cambridge Handbook of Sociocultural Psychology (pp. 238–256). New York: Cambridge University Press.

Fernández, T. R. (2005). Sobre la Historia Natural del Sujeto y su lugar en una Historia de la Ciencia. A propósito de Robert J. Richards y el Romanticismo de Darwin. *Estudios de Psicología* 26(1), 67–104.

Fuentes, J. B., Quiroga, E., & Muñoz, F. (2005). Una primera aproximación a las posibilidades de desarrollo de la teoría del origen trófico del conocimiento de Ramón Turró. *Revista de Historia de la Psicología* 26 (2–3), 181–189.

Gibson, J. J. (1979). *The ecological approach to visual perception*. Boston: Houghton Mifflin.

González, Antonio (1997). *Estructuras de la praxis. Ensayo de una filosofía primera*. Madrid: Trotta

Gottdiener, M., Boklund-Lagapoulou, K., & Lagopoulos, A. (2002–03). *Semiotics*. London: Sage.

Hoffmeyer, J. (1997). Biosemiotics: Towards a New Synthesis in Biology. *European Journal for Semiotic Studies* 9(2), 355–376.

Hoffmeyer, J. (2001). Life and reference. *Biosystems* 60, 123–130.

James, W. (1907). *Pragmatism*. Cambridge, MA: Harvard University Press, 1979.

Kull, K. (2001). Jakob von Uexküll: An Introduction. *Semiotica* 134, 1–43.

Leont'ev, A. N. (1978). *Activity, consciousness, and personality*. Englewood Cliffs, NJ: Prentice-Hall.

Liszka, J. J. (1996). *A General Introduction to the Semeiotic of Charles Saunders Peirce*. Bloomington & Indianapolis: Indiana University Press.

Luria, A. R. (1974). *El cerebro en acción*. Barcelona: Fontanella.

Maturana, H. R., & Varela, F. J. (1987). *The Tree of Knowledge: The Biological Roots of Human Understanding*. Boston: Shambhala.

Peirce, C. S. (1931–1958). *Collected Papers of Charles Sanders Peirce* (8 vols.). Charles Hartshorne, Paul Weiss, and Arthur Burks (Eds.), Cambridge, MA: Harvard University Press.

Peirce, C. S. (1967). *Annotated Catalogue of the Papers of Charles S. Peirce*. Richard S. Robin (Ed.), Amherst: University of Massachusetts Press.

Peirce, C. S. *Semiotic and Significs: The Correspondence between Charles S. Peirce and Victoria Lady Welby*. C. S. Hardwick (Ed.), Bloomington: Indiana University Press.

Perinat, A. (2007). Comparative development of communication. In J. Valsiner & A. Rosa (Eds.): *Cambridge Handbook of Sociocultural Psychology*. New York: Cambridge University Press.

Putnam, H. (1981). *Reason, Truth and History*. Cambridge: Cambridge University Press.

Riba, C. (1990). *La comunicación animal. Un enfoque zoosemiótico*. Barcelona: Anthropos.

Richards, R. J. (1987). *Darwin and the emergence of evolutionary theories of mind and behavior*. Chicago: The University of Chicago Press.

Richards, R. J. (2002). *The Romantic conception of life. Science and Philosophy in the age of Goethe*. Chicago: The University of Chicago Press.

Rivière, A. & Sotillo, M. (1999). Comunicazione, sospensione e semiosi umana: Le origini della patrica e della comprensione interpersonale. *Metis* 1, 45–72. Spanish versión "Comunicación, suspensión y semiosis humana: Los orígenes de la práctica y de la comprensión interpersonales". En Angel Rivière: *Obras Escogidas (vol. 3). Metarrepresentación y semiosis*. Madrid: Editorial Médica Panamericana (2003).

Rodríguez, C. (2007). Object use, communication and signs: The triadic basis of early cognitive development. In J. Valsiner & A. Rosa (Eds.), *Cambridge Handbook of Sociocultural Psychology*. New York: Cambridge University Press.

Rosa, A. (2007). Dramaturgical actuations and cultural artifacts: making the rationality of the world. In J. Valsiner & A. Rosa (Eds.), *Cambridge Handbook of Sociocultural Psychology*. (pp. 293–317). New York: Cambridge University Press.

Rosa, A. & Valsiner, J. (2007). General Conclusions. In J. Valsiner & A. Rosa (Eds.), *Cambridge Handbook of Sociocultural Psychology*. (pp. 692–707). New York: Cambridge University Press.

Rosetti-Ferreira, M. C., Amorim, K. S., & Silva, A. P. S. (2007). Development through Social Matrix of Meaning. In J. Valsiner & A. Rosa (Eds.): *Cambridge Handbook of Sociocultural Psychology*. (pp. 279–292). New York: Cambridge University Press.

Saussure, F. (1959). *Course in general Linguistics*. New York: McGraw-Hill.

Sebeok, T. A. (1963). Communication in Animals and Men. *Language* 39, 448–466.

Sebeok, T. A. (1976). *Contribution to the doctrine of signs*. Bloomington IN: Indiana University Press.

Shank, R. C. & Abelson, R. P. (1977). *Scripts, Plans, Goals, and Understanding*. Mahwah, NJ: Lawrence Erlbaum Associates.

Sheriff, J. K. (1989). *The Fate of Meaning*. Princeton: Princeton University Press.

Travieso, D. (2007). Functional systems of perception-action and re-mediation. In J. Valsiner & A. Rosa (Eds.): *Cambridge Handbook of Sociocultural Psychology*. (pp. 124–139). New York: Cambridge University Press.

Turró, R. (1916). *Orígenes del conocimiento. El hambre*. Barcelona: Minerva.

Valsiner, J. (1984). Construction of the zone of proximal development in adult-child joint-action: The socialization of meals. *New Directions for Child Development* 23, 65–76.

Valsiner, J. (1987). *Culture and the Development of Children's Actions*. New York: John Wiley & Sons (2nd Edition, 1997).

Valsiner, J. (2005). Soziale, emotionale Entwicklungsaufgaben im kulturallen Kontext. In *Enzyklpädie der Psychologie (Vol. 3). Soziale, emotionale und Persönlichkeitsentwicklung*. Göttingen: Hogrefe.

Valsiner, J. & Rosa, A. (2007a). Introduction: Social-Cultural Research: Culture, Society, and Psychology. In J. Valsiner & A. Rosa (Eds.): *Cambridge Handbook of Sociocultural Psychology* (pp. 1–20). New York: Cambridge University Press.

Valsiner, J. & Rosa, A. (2007b). The Myth and Beyond: Ontology of Psyche and Epistemology of Psychology. In J. Valsiner & A. Rosa (Eds.). *Cambridge Handbook of Sociocultural Psychology* (pp. 23–39). New York: Cambridge University Press (pp.)

Vygotsky, L. S. (1931/1995). Historia del Desarrollo de las Funciones Psíquicas Superiores. In L. S. Vygotsky: *Obras escogidas (Vol. III)*. Madrid: Aprendizaje/Visor. (pp. 11–340).

Wertsch, J. V. (1991). *Voices of the Mind*. Cambridge, MA: Harvard University Press.

Wertsch, J. V. (1998). *Mind as Action*. New York: Oxford University Press.

Wundt, W. (1896). *Outlines of Psychology*. New York: G. E. Strecher.

CHAPTER 11

Time and Movement
in Symbol Formation

Silvia Español

Language is usually taken to be the human symbolic system par excellence, but this does not necessarily means that it is the best window from which to observe the development of the symbolic function. Jean Piaget (1945) was aware that the social signs – formed by arbitrary and conventional signifiers – that conform language are not as fertile ground for the observation of symbol formation as are the more idiosyncratic and motivated products of fictional play. Following the same argument, Ángel Rivière (1984) emphasized that enactive symbols – forms of action in which the link between signifier and signified is not arbitrary but motivated – provide a window with a privileged view for the study of symbol formation.

Daniel Stern (1985) also observed that although children become members of a cultural group through the acquisition of language, they do so at the risk of loosing the crossmodal wholeness and richness of their original experience. An infant's experience comes from multiple sensory modalities, but when linked to a word, that experience is anchored to only one modality and so becomes isolated from the original

sensory flow, since language fractures the original experience and freezes its temporal flow (Valsiner, 1992). When a child perceives a yellow solar light spot on the wall – Stern says – s/he experiences intensity, warmness, shape, brightness, movement and other crossmodal qualities of this spot. To be able to conserve this flexible perspective, the child needs to ignore particular properties (such as color) that specify sensory channels through which the spot is experienced. He/she must not be aware that it is a visual experience. And this is exactly what language will force him/her to do: "*look* at that *yellow* sunlight." The conventional linguistic version buries the sensorial flow of the experience, which can only reappear when certain conditions prevail over the linguistic version: as happens in certain contemplative or emotional states, or before a work of art whose aim is to evoke experiences that defy verbal categorization. However, even though language, in its ordinary use, buries the flow of global experience stemming from multiple modalities, in its poetical form it is able to evoke experiences that go beyond its expressive capabilities (Stern, 1985).

These features of language suggest the need to go beyond the first manifestations when focusing on the study of the symbol function in children. However this does not mean leaving aside the consideration of the functions it carries out, because in developmental linguistics, as Jerome Bruner (1990) states, *function usually precedes form*, and so it is in children's actions and gestures where we can anticipate functions traditionally associated with language. Moreover, and this will be my attempt here, it is in the actions and gestures of infants where we find the prolongation of previous functions, connected to the qualities of movement, that predominate in the earliest moments of development. My first step will be to clarify what I mean by *movement*, highlighting its intimate connection with emotion. But before that, I would like to remind the reader of some well-known hallmarks of developmental psychology.

Ritualization in the Origin of Gestures and Pretend Play

The application of pragmatics to the studies on language acquisition in the 1970s made clear that preverbal children were able to communicate. And, in parallel, *action* and *social interaction* became central in the explanation of development. The pre-verbal child could ask or declare through gestures; and these gestures, as Vygotsky (1931) observed, stemmed from the transformation of action in contexts of social interaction.

Researchers observed that some actions oriented towards the world – such as grabbing, touching or giving something – when performed in communicative contexts, suffered two substantial changes: first, the re-orientation of the action towards the other that interprets and completes it; and second, the transformation of the form of the action, becoming abbreviated or exaggerated, until it transforms itself into a gesture. In this manner, actions, such as touching or giving an object, evolve into communicative gestures (such as pointing or showing), giving rise to the so-called deictic gestures (Clark, 1978;

Lock, 1978; Español & Rivière, 2000). These gestures, which do not vary when changing their referents (i.e., one does not point differently when signaling the moon, a piece of bread or a ball), generally emerge towards the end of the first year of life and anticipate the imperative and the declarative functions of language. In spite of the central role that ritualization plays in the explanation of the formation of gestures, it was also sustained that some gestures – the so-called conventional and representative gestures – are acquired through imitation (Tomasello & Camaioni, 1997).

In turn, the study of pretend play also suffered the impact of the communicative breezes. On the one hand, it was observed that some inadequate action schemes that characterize second-year pretend play are sometimes used with communicative aims (Iverson, Capirci, & Caselli, 1994), and, what perhaps is most relevant, some ideas from the socio-historical school were recovered, and so social interaction was incorporated as the undercurrent without which symbolic genesis is not possible. The Piagetian tradition of describing the process of ritualization in pretend play was continued, but now bringing to light the participation of adults in this process (Bates, 1979; Español, 2001, 2004; Kavanaugh, 2002; Mc Cune & Agayoff, 2002; Mc Cune-Nicolich, 1977).

The term ritualization has been used in different ways. In the literature on gesture formation, it refers to the way in which deictic gestures are shaped so that the patterns of actions are abbreviated or exaggerated making them adequate only for achieving a communicative goal. In the Piagetian tradition of studies on the formation of symbols, ritualization is a part of the development of representation, allowing a gradual differentiation between signifier and signified; it refers to the performance, repetition, and combination of schemes of action carried out, removed from their adaptive contexts, and so submitted to deforming assimilation.

This double meaning of the term *ritualization* is not irrelevant: it denotes that the transformation of *action* was (and still is) a key for understanding the genesis of communicative and symbolic abilities. However, it is not rare that in Psychology alternative modes of approaching a question co-exist at a given time. This is the case of the information-processing cognitive approach that offered a representational explanation both for communication and fiction in childhood (Baron-Cohen, 1991; Leslie, 1987; Lillard, 1993; Smith, 2002). According to the most radical version of this view, representation substitutes action, computation prevails over interaction, and pre-programmed mechanisms play the role of the genesis of novelty during development. It was even postulated (in the case of Leslie) that the "decoupled representations" that characterize pretend play result from innate and programmed mechanisms that are triggered during the second year of life. However, the representational approach had the virtue of suggesting a link between fictional play and the development of children's Theory of Mind, so allowing a dialogue between cognitivists and interactionists that led to interesting hybrid postures, such as those offered by Hobson (1993), Rivière (1997), and Gómez (1998).

In sum, transformation of *action* and computation over *representations* are the two main approaches that have attempted to explain the genesis of the first communicative gestures and pretend play. My intention here is to show how, when the focus of attention moves to *movement*, it becomes possible for (a) a finer approximation into the emotional world, (b) a better understanding of how some communicative symbols of the child develop, and (c) a different way of picturing the process of ritualization involved in the genesis of pretend play.

Movement as an Expression of the Vitality Affects

Movement and Action

Movement can be understood as a component of action. However, I will make a distinction between these two concepts on the basis of the predominance of *intention* in the case of *action*, and of *feeling* in the case of

movement. A distinction that needs to be explored in some depth.

First, movement and action are not the same; all action implies movement but the inverse is not true. *Inanimate movement* does not imply any kind of intentionality whatsoever, and therefore it is not an action. Action, on the contrary, is inherently propositive, is determined by intentions, and always tends towards a future. Besides inanimate movement, there is *living movement*, which is the movement of organisms. Alexander Truslit (1938, cited in Repp, 1993) postulated "the law of movement in music," according to which *dynamic* musical information has kinetic properties, so that the underlying movement of music is transmitted to the listener who, after the received auditory information can embody movement to it. This "translation" of sound into movement has no intentionality; it simply occurs. In a different manner, the qualities of the *movements that compose an action* – such as the movements of the arms, hands, legs, and trunk implied in the action of lifting a box – are determined by the *intention* that guides them. Their form, amplitude, and tension would be different if they were directed to lifting another object, such as a piece of paper.

Some movements of the newborn infant are teleonomic in nature, but very early on they start to show some intentional features that indicate that they will soon drift towards action. For example, the suction patterns of newborn infants show that these are not a reflex behavior, but rather a function of the organism. In the act of sucking, the infant – sensitive to the flow of milk – performs different movements with his/her mouth, with which he/she adjusts the pressure of suction in advance, so regulating the flow of liquid (von Hofsten, 2003). In suction, the form, amplitude, and tension of the movements of the lips and tongue are the result of the intention that guides them. The infant even makes attempts at correction – in which the mother participates – with the aim of achieving a better interaction between both parties. We can ask ourselves whether suction also includes "modes of feeling" that participate in the regulation of some of its features such as rhythm. Movements involved in suction are probably the earliest movements in human development that become action. And all action, besides being determined by intentions, also assumes, in a higher or lesser degree, qualities of movement that result from "modes of feeling."

There are other movements of the infant, which are fundamentally determined by the feeling that they express, whether or not guided by some intention. As Henri Wallon (1956, 1982) pointed out, "sensitivity" is connected to motor reactions from the very beginning of human life; the muscular apparatus responds with movements that do not possess orientations or objectives: movements, cries, or vocalizations after an increased arousal. When looking at an infant's arm movements and feet-kicking while excited, the image of progressive attempts at accommodation vanishes, and we are left with movements that simply express a certain feeling. The essential issue is that this primitive level, which can be analyzed solely in terms of levels of arousal, is reorganized in the emotional stage, in which *movement* is a wholly "*exteriorized emotion*" (Zazzo, 1976, quoted in Vila, 1986), oriented towards the other, that will progressively be modeled within the universe of the adult-infant dyad.

Movement, Time, and Feeling

In human life, there are two extreme ways in which "modes of feeling" are responsible for the form, amplitude, and tension of movements. One happens in the inter-exchanges in the adult-infant dyad from the second month of life onwards; the other is one of the most primeval forms of art: dance. Between these two extremes, all the graduations of corporal acts where "modes of feeling" and intentionality combine can be scaled.

Dance is the art of dynamics and design of movement. Dynamics is given by the qualities of movement, its speed, and tension. This is intertwined with its design in space – the shapes the body takes – which through continuous succession gives rise to the temporal form of movement. What the dance spectator sees is mainly a movement (with independence of the story behind the ballet), that can be "read" through the diffuse and alluded meanings conveyed by the temporal and dynamic form. Dance is pure movement distilled by culture.

In the studies of early interaction, the fluency of corporal exchanges that give rise to a feeling of communion or closeness are labeled "face-to-face interactions" and form the basis of what Colwin Trevarthen (1982) called "primary intersubjectivity." In these exchanges, each movement, vocalization, or expression is oriented towards the other while maintaining a prolonged eye contact. The mother's movements do not seem to be motivated by a mere attempt to regulating the baby's state of arousal. Rather, it has to do with a maternal call for social and emotional exchange that finds an immediate response in the infant. The mother's movements and vocalizations show a temporal and dynamic shape that cannot be separated from the "modes of feeling" that flow from her. In dancing, as well as in these early states of communion, movement and feelings merge. What comes to the forefront in both cases is the *essential quality of movement for expressing* what Daniel Stern (1985) calls *vitality affects*, a concept that will permit us to consider afresh view of the emotional world.

Before going further into the argument of this chapter, it is at issue to remind ourselves of the deeply rooted Darwinian hypothesis that a few discrete expressions – seven or eight, solely or combined – explain the whole emotional repertoire of human beings. We tend to think of affective life in terms of discrete categories such as happiness, sadness, fear, anger, and so on, at the same time that we tend to believe that there is an innate facial display that corresponds to each one of these categories. This hypothesis played a crucial role in developmental psychology. The analysis of the emergence of pre-verbal declarative communicative patterns has led to a reconsideration of the importance of emotions and primitive experiences of sharing that Wallon (1956) and Werner and Kaplan (1963) claimed long ago. Currently, the idea that primitive experiences of sharing get shaped in the exchange of (Darwinian) emotional expressions that characterize the first dyadic interactions is widespread. So, it is suggested that infants have resources for emotional expression that project internal states such as happiness, sadness, anger, fear, surprise, dislike, and interest (Ekman & Oster, 1979; Izard, 1979), and that they also have an incipient capacity for imitation, which usually is taken to be the foundation for the capacity of sharing emotions. Imitation then allows for the establishing of a connection between the internal states of the infant's emotional experience and the expression of emotions (Kugiumutzakis, 1998; Maratos, 1998). The origin of the human experience of sharing would therefore be in the play of mutual imitations of emotional expressions.

Vitality affects, on the contrary, blur and extend the emotional world. They are temporal "modes of feeling" that are not reflected in the lexicon of the Darwinian affects. These multiple forms of feeling are profiles of activation in time; they are temporally patterned changes in the intensity of sensation that may be described in terms of *agitation, progressive fleeting, explosiveness, crescendo, outbreak, dilation,* and *faint.* They cover all our experiences: they are in our states and movements, in our actions, and may also accompany Darwinian emotions. They are present in the vertigo of sudden memory, in the retarded movement of a caress, in the fleetingness of a gesture, or in lethargic modes of combing. Laughter can be fleeting or explosive, as can the motion of unbuttoning a blouse be dilated or excited.

According to Stern, the infant perceives these temporal patterns – the succession of tensions and dis-tensions of continuity, regularity, disruptions, or breaches – both through its proprioceptive experience (when carrying out acts such as putting a finger inside his/her mouth), and through parental stimulation from the time of birth. However, his main emphasis is: (1) that the social world experienced by the infant is primarily a world of vitality affects, and (2) that *temporal arts* are the

main vehicle for the expression of these vitality affects. The intimate link between sound and movement, and their temporal character, has led music and dance to be considered as temporal arts (Shifres, 2002; Repp, 1993). Dance directly shows multiple vitality affects and its variants, without the need of recurring to any plot nor to the signs of Darwinian emotions. The choreographer tries to explain a mode of feeling, but does not convey a specific feeling. Music and dance have an exact point in common: what the choreographer and the composer experiment is a mode of feeling, rather than a particular feeling (Imberty, 2002). This is why Stern states that the infant, when seeing a parental behavior – with or without Darwinian signs of emotion – is in the same position as the spectator of an abstract dance performance, or one listening to music.

Diversity, Attunement, and Communion

Vitality affects are crossmodal experiences; they have to do with the global perception of profiles of activation in time that occur in different modalities. They are fragments of time, viewed in the present of variations of sensation intensities that *unite the diverse* (Imberty, 2002). A diversity of sensations coming from different modalities of the broad spectrum of all our experience, from a torrent of light to a torrent of thoughts, says Stern, in which the profile is alike, but the background is completely different. The ability to translate information from one modality to another is crucial for the social development of the infant. This ability lies at the basis of neonatal imitation, which requires the establishment of a correspondence between visual and proprioceptive information (Meltzoff & Moore, 1998). But this also allows the infant to unite the stimulation coming from different channels. In this manner, if a maternal caress is accompanied by some kind of vocalization, the infant will perceive a certain profile of activation in different simultaneous stimulations and will be able to unite the sound of a voice with the caress of a hand, so long

as they have, for example, a similar duration, initial force, and final withdrawal. Both
stimulations (tactile and auditory) will have
the effect of making the same vitality affects
arise.

Vitality affects can hardly be put into
words. They belong to the kind of global
and crossmodal experiences that ordinary
language undermines but that, paradoxically, poetic language is able to express.
They flood the infant's social world, but
they are also masterly expressed in adulthood, and in the plenitude of the temporal arts they are shaped in the dynamics of
sound or movement in time. This is why
researchers interested in the origin of the
temporal arts focus on infancy and trace the
antecedents of music and dance in the interactions between mothers and infants (and
vice versa) (Cross, 2000, 2003; Dissanayake,
2000a, 2000b; Gratier, 2000; Imberty, 1997,
2000, 2002; Stern, 1985, 1995; Trevarthen,
1998, 2000).

Temporal arts are the foremost modes
of expression of vitality affects. *Attunement*
is a primitive way of transmitting them
(Stern, 1985). It is a type of imitation of
some chosen features, while others are disregarded. It is not about a faithful translation of the open conduct, but rather of a
type of matching, frequently cross-modal,
of intensity, temporal or spatial patterns of
some conduct. In this manner, there are
at least six types of matches: (1) absolute
intensity: the level of intensity of conduct
A is equal to the level of intensity of conduct B, whatever its modality, (2) profile of
intensity: the object to be matched is the
changes of intensity in time (for example,
acceleration-de-acceleration), (3) pulsation:
a regular pulsation is matched in time, (4)
rhythm: a pattern of pulsations of unequal
emphasis are matched, (5) duration: the
lapse of the conduct is matched, (6) spatial
pattern: some spatial features of the conducts, susceptible of being abstracted and
transformed into different acts, are matched.
As opposed to imitation, which keeps attention focused on the external shape of behavior, attunement brings out that which underlies behavior, the "character of the shared

feeling," to the focus of attention. That is
why attunement is the predominant mode of
sharing internal states or showing that they
are being shared. The matched external conducts may differ in shape and mode but they
are interchangeable as manifestations of a
recognizable internal state.

During the first months of life, attunement only appears in the maternal stimulations, not in the infant's activity. For example, if the infant hits a doll with a constant
rhythm, the mother falls into this rhythm
but in a different modality, for example,
through her vocal tone. The mother takes
something from the infant's expression and
transforms it into something else, changing
the modality. In this manner, small "analogies" are formed among gestures, sounds, and
corporal movements. Attunement may be
assimilated to imitation, as well as to affective contagion or empathy, in so much as
it shares the possibility of establishing an
emotional resonance. However, its differentiating feature is that it does something different, it recasts the emotional experience
into another form of expression, it refor-
mulates a subjective state. It merges different forms of behavior through non-verbal
"metaphors": it seeks to find the "color" or
"tonality" perceived and shared, using all the
cross-modal capacities the infant possesses
(Imberty, 2002). Attunement treats the subjective state as a referent and the open conduct as possible expressions of the referent,
becoming in this manner one of the essential means through which feelings of communion are established. According to Stern,
mothers begin to perform attunements starting from the ninth month of life of their
infants; but as Johnson and colleagues (2001)
indicate, attunement may appear earlier in
maternal conduct.

The presence of vitality affects and attunement behaviors, that refer to the former,
suggest proto-musical qualities in the dyad
exchange, and therefore, the existence of
early proto-musical capacities in the infant.
These capacities have been reported in numerous studies in the area of the Psychology of Music. For example: (1) the infant
sensitivity (from the first month of life

onwards) to temporal changes of sound features, such as frequency, amplitude and harmony (Fassbender, 1996) and the early detection of changes in pitch, melodic contours, and rhythm (Treuhb, 2000), (2) the production of quasi-musical infant behaviors, such as stereotyped rhythmic movements of the head, arms, and legs (Pouthas, 1996), and (3) the synchronization of vocal and kinetic patterns, and the use of prototypical melodic outlines in order to regulate the infant's state (Papôusek, 1996; Grattier, 2000). Beyond the abundance of existing data, what is relevant for us here is that they highlight, as Dissanayake (2000a) states, the existence of *antecedents of the temporal arts* in the early exchanges of the dyad. I will later refer to the destiny of these antecedents. But before going into that, we must refer to another quality of these early exchanges.

Temporal Organization of Movement

Studies on early interaction show that mother-infant behavioral exchanges have a temporal structure from the very beginning. Sometimes they are clearly separated in time, for example, the mother acts first, then the infant does something, and again, shortly after a pause, the mother does something else, and. These early exchanges have been called "protoconversations," since there is a shared interest of two parties in the exchange of signs and a joint regulation of turn-taking (Murray & Trevarthen, 1984). But it often happens that there is an overlapping of behaviors, so that rather than a set of linked responses to each other, one may think that there is some sort of joint and synchronic performance that requires some anticipation of the stream of behavior from the other party. Murray and Trevarthen (1984) showed the temporal accuracy of these early exchanges. They observed mothers and three-month old infants placed in separate rooms interacting through a TV system that was manipulated so that there was a thirty seconds delay in the mother's response. This disturbance produced a significant uneasiness in the infants, who turned their heads away from the image of the mother, giving only occasional glances at the screen. Trevarthen (1998, 2000) emphasized that it is the ordered temporal nature of corporal movements in early social interactions that permits the sharing of temporal patterns, that allow a mutual tuning of dynamic feelings in the dyad. Another essential aspect of temporal organization is that from the beginning, it is organized in the form of repetition-variation. The mother's behavior uses repetition in all available modalities: vocalization, movements, tactile and kinetic stimulation, that is never repeated identically, but rather with subtle variations (in speed, suspense, in vocal accompaniment). The same game, such as tickling the infant's tummy up to the neck, is repeated again and again, always adding some new variation to its elements (the speed of the fingers, or the delay before the final arousal, or together with vocalizations). This structure, in which each variation is simultaneously familiar and new, is ideal for the identification of invariants in the conduct. The infant comes to know which parts of a complex conduct may be suppressed, and which others must remain for the conduct to be considered the same (Stern, 1985).

Michel Imberty (1997, 2002) links the repetition-variation form of early interactions with musical form and suggests that the former represents the original structure of which the profound reality is re-activated by the latter. Musical repetition, like the repetition of behavioral sequences, generates time and a directionality within time, a present that goes towards something else. It creates a *before* and an *after*, a device through which the composer invites the audience to remember and anticipate. This is done with sufficient margin of uncertainty, so that each time it is insinuated that the repetition may not be performed, that the future might be unknown, that the same expectation may merge with another, which in turn might not be completely different. Repetition so creates a tension, with an expectation of satisfaction (the return to the initial sequence) followed by a more or less marked distension, depending on whether the variation is more or less distant from the initial model. It is the succession of tension-distension what institutes an original time, the primitive experience of *duration*. Repetition allows the infant to understand time through varied and ornamented regularities, which form the universal substratum of music in all cultures. The infant learns to adapt to an ever-increasing number of variations, because repetition becomes predictable and organizes time. Probably, the earliest perception of phenomenological time (Rosa & Travieso, 2002) is found in experiences of repetition-variation: a perception that originates on the borders of change and its counterpart, permanence, as is the case of modes of maternal stimulation combining stability and variation. This primordial experience of time is at the basis of what Ricoeur (1983) calls the temporality of the narrative function. When language appears, it will flow along this pre-existing temporality, producing not only events, but also a narrative with a sense (direction) and a progression created by expectations and tensions.

Movement and Action in Circular Reactions

Circular reaction is a function of living beings. It is the repetition of an acquired cycle whose aim is maintaining or rediscovering a new and interesting result. Fernández, Sánchez, Aivar, and Loredo (2003), following Baldwin's original idea, point out that its logic is that of "try it again," and so it has a continuous dynamic form, being recreated in each trial. This is so because unexpected variations arise in these repetitions and the organism performs corrections that, if successful, integrate novelties into the old structure of the cycle, which therefore becomes modified. Piaget graded the levels of complexity of circular reactions in the distinction between primary, secondary, and tertiary circular reactions.

Primary circular reactions (the infant reproduces interesting results discovered by chance and centered on its own body) are the functional unit in the second stage of sensory-motor development. These variations of movements involve temporal variations of duration, intensity, and rhythm. As Karousou (2003) reviews, in spite of the scarcity of data on the duration and rhythm of early vocalizations, a very early control of pitch has been detected. Infants seem capable of producing variations in pitch.

Secondary circular reactions – or the repetition of interesting results obtained when action befalls on the external environment – appear in the third stage of sensory-motor development. But long before the appearance of secondary circular relations, when infants still cannot control physical objects, adults give contingent temporal responses to infant's actions. Emotional expressions, vocalizations, and movements of the infant are followed by comments and expressive gestures of adults, what make the infant increase its social conducts, and produce the effect of calling for more responses from the adult, and so *social circular reactions* appear. There is no point in distinguishing between primary and secondary social circular reactions, since they always have a secondary character (Rivière, 1986/2003). Most of the dyadic exchanges of the type hitherto described are included in social circular reactions, where a *repetition-variation* pattern leads to a temporarily extended cycle. The *variations introduced in repetition usually involve the quality of movement* (as in the game of tickling the infant's tummy up to the neck), the *speed of movement*, or the *extension of a pattern of expectation* that leads to different *profiles of activation* in each variation. The *synchronization between vocal and kinetic patterns* of maternal stimulation, the *alternation and joint performance of movements*, sounds and expressions in the dyad, the *rhythm* that impregnates them, as well as the possible attunements performed by the mother, make social circular reactions an experience that the infant desires to re-live again and again. They are the privileged niche for the perception of vitality affects, something that is apparent in the pleasure showed by the performing dyad.

As Piaget (1936, 1945) showed, circular reactions provide the path towards instrumental and intelligent action. Secondary circular reactions emerge during the third stage of sensory-motor development. If we consider that every action assumes movement, then it is possible to think that *some of the variations of action are temporal changes of movement* (such as the intensity with which a rope is pulled, or the duration and amplitude of the movement stamped on the object), in addition to the fact that they are often experienced in social circular reactions. It is also feasible that some of the purposeful modifications of action that appear in *tertiary circular reactions* (in the fifth stage of sensory-motor development) may follow the same pattern. In short, what I am suggesting is the possibility of a genetic implication between social circular reactions and the secondary and tertiary circular reactions of the period of sensory-motor intelligence.

Beyond this hypothesis, the truth is that the infant's experiences aroused in social circular reactions are the basis for the development of intentional communication.

Whether referring to social circular reactions or not, research on pre-verbal communication and on the system of the theory of mind has repeatedly shown that the first anticipations of the infant (which are indispensable for communicative development) and the initial experiences of sharing (a necessary condition for the emergence of protodeclarative communication) emerge in early interactions. These are issues that have attracted a considerable amount of research and need not be explored further here. I rather will concentrate on showing how the components on which social circular reactions get shaped are not only a condition for the possibility of future abilities, but also are continually used in specific activities throughout development. They (1) extend towards the incorporation of objects, and participate in the genesis of pretend play, (2) materialize in the creation of symbolic gestures, and (3) lead to particular activities that I will call "temporal play," which merge in pretend play.

The "Externalization" of the Components of Social Circular Reactions

Ellen Dissanayake (2000a) suggests that in the beginning of human societies the elements of temporal arts that qualify the intimate "you-I" dyadic relationship were started by taking them from "out there." She suggests that the extensive neonatal period of human infancy produced a selective pressure for the development of psychological proximity and cognitive mechanisms that ensure longer and improved maternal care. This was the cause of the specific human adaptation – *elaboration* – of parenting behavior typical of primates, such as facial expressions, gestures, and sounds. Elaboration is nothing more than the dynamic, rhythmic and crossmodal modeling of these conducts, that directly lead to a state of mutuality that is inherently pleasant. Dissanayake's argument is that, throughout human evolution, societies appropriated the capacity to respond to such elaborations – repetitions and exaggerations of rhythms and modes – that, through change and novelty, create an expectation and so generate and shape an emotional trajectory. These abilities were then put into use in collective ritual ceremonies from which temporal arts started to develop. Her work focuses on describing the genesis of art throughout the evolution of societies, starting from the cornerstone of the mother-infant states of mutuality, going into the analysis the proto-aesthetic qualities the mother-infant relationship show during the first six months of life, and then moving to the study of the cultural history of temporal arts. Our attempt here will be to follow the ontogenetic drift of these "elaborations" beyond Dissanayake's contribution. This will be done through the examination of some viodeo-taped observations I carried out in the course of a longitudinal study of a child, Habib, with whom

I interacted for a period of 15 months, when he was aged between 9 and 24 months.

The components which constitute social circular reactions (which we may understand here as synonymous to elaborations) go through a gradual process of "externalization" and appropriation by the child. This process is initiated in games of the repetition-variation type that include the use of objects, and where the infant takes an increasingly active role. For example, when Habib was 0; 9 (11), both of us initiated "the game of the little cloud," based on a behavior he frequently repeats and finds pleasant. From some time earlier, Habib enjoyed rubbing his face softly on his pillow (or on any soft object within his reach). I started the game making a series of movements with the pillow while singing; when I changed the rhythm, I also changed the amplitude, speed, and form of my movements with the pillow, which I always finished by placing the pillow on the floor near Habib. Then, he joyfully scuffled his face in the pillow. Together, the intensity of sound and movement went in crescendo and declined towards the end. When he wanted to re-start the game, he pushed the pillow towards me. When he was 0; 9 (25), Habib started to move the pillow when he wanted the game to be repeated. When he turned 1; 0 (13), he moved the pillow from one side to another and shook it; I joined his movements by singing a song. In these kinds of games, frequently played by infants and adults together, the qualities of movement prevail over the actions performed. The temporal organization of sounds and movements and their musical features configure a unity. They will soon be combined with pretend play, but not from the beginning.

Movement in the Genesis of Pretend Play

Development of fictional play implies, fundamentally, the transformation of earlier forms of action. Research on the process of ritualization of action (reviewed above) coincide in pointing out that around twelve months of age, infants learn, in collaboration with adults, the use of objects related to their basic activities (such as eating with a spoon, or drinking from a glass), and that almost at the same time, they start to play functional games with the same objects, but using them in a decontextualized fashion, so their actions do not have the same effects as if they were performed effectively. In this manner, the infant begins to understand the grammar of action, a grammar that underlies the use of instruments. The first decontextualized use of instruments appear briefly and in isolation. But rapidly, the addressee of their actions begin to change (they take the empty spoon up to their doll's mouth or to the adult's mouth; they put the telephone receiver near to the other's ear, etc.).

This is a very interesting moment in development, placed between the first decontextualized use of objects and the beginning of the production of fiction, or in Leslie's (1987) terms, "decoupling." It corresponds with what McCune and Agayoff (2002) call the beginning of fiction, which they distinguish from decoupling or fiction as such. In non-human primates, conducts of deception and simulated actions, such as eating, may be observed in the absence of the objects that support them (Savage-Rumbaugh, 1986), as well as decontextualized uses of objects, such as drinking from an empty cup (Byrne, 1995). But the latter does not seem to be a clear sign of symbolic substitution (Gómez & Martín-Andrade, 2002). Fiction, as I am treating it here, does not only "simulate" something through a decontextualized use of objects, or by performing an empty action, it also implies a breach in what is being learned, producing a profound transformation of the conventional meanings of actions, as well as of the modes of using objects, pretending something to be something else. It is precisely at this transitional moment when the temporal components of social circular reactions, or elaborations, are clearly incorporated.

Soon after the emergence of the decontextualized use of objects, a process of *ritualization* starts, via the expansion of the possible addressees and through the combination of various schemes of action. Around the second half of the second year of life, "scenes" that involve various objects (spoons, plates, cups) and actors (the infant, the adult, dolls, which can play the role of agent or addressee of action), begin to take shape. It is within these scenes that the temporal and dynamic shaping of actions starts. *This is a shaping of the qualities of movement involved in action, through the elements of the temporal arts that characterize primitive social circular reactions; this is an "elaboration" of movement in which the infant actively participates.* When a decontextualized use of objects starts (still with no substitution in their function) sound begins to be included in the action performed (such as "shhhh" when serving from an empty teapot, or "aaammm" when bringing an empty spoon towards the mouth). These sounds, usually incorporated by the adult but rapidly appropriated by the infant, go together with the motor action and resemble the matching of temporal patterns; that is, they can be conceived as attunements. There are also changes in the dynamics of movements (accelerated or delayed, abbreviated or exaggerated) included in the on-going action. Likewise, the repetition-variation form seems to hold the combinations of schemes of action that begin to be performed in a fixed and repetitive manner, that nevertheless allow small variations; for example, combing and perfuming a doll always in the same manner, until (imitating adult behavior) an exaggerated inspiration in a precise moment of the sequence is incorporated, which is then repeated over and over again.

It is within the framework of these "small narrations-in-action" where the first prototypical substitutions of pretend play emerge. Elsewhere (Español, 2004) I suggest that it is possible to sketch the development of pretend play, using a grammar of cases: observing the action (the verb) and the cases where substitutions appear. Such analysis shows that the first substitutions appear in the case of instrument (i.e., combing with a spoon), followed by substitutions in the case of object (a ball of wool replaces food), These are later – at the end of the second year of life – accompanied by the appearance of the first substitutions in the case of agent

and in the case of receiver. The child makes the doll and can speak with or hit another doll. I believe that the elaboration of movement promotes and facilitates the separation between each case and its "adequate object." I suspect that each case of substitution is preceded and surrounded by a dynamic and temporal moulding of the elements involved. Elaboration also has the virtue of introducing temporality in the sequences of actions, providing them with the tension and directionality typical of the narrative function. This temporal modeling of action can also explain why pretend play is so pleasant, since it allows a constant flow of the vitality affects.

Movement in the Creation of Gestures

The gradual externalization and appropriation of elements that shape social circular reactions can also be observed in some of the child's creation of gestures. At the beginning of this chapter, I pointed out that deictic gestures are generally taken to evolve from the ritualization of common actions. In contrast, conventional gestures (such as waving goodbye with the hand) and representative gestures (i.e., moving the arms when referring to a bird) are signs that are modeled by adults and imitated by children. These gestures are active and creative re-productions by the child but none of these are either original nor novel signs. In general, the capacity for creating significant novel forms is thought to emerge with pretend play. However, there can also be creation and novelty in the production of gestures. Rivière (1984/2003, 1990) observed that children, when wanting to communicate with others about absent objects or events, construct new gestures by modifying their actions. For example, by blowing on an unlit lighter when calling on the adult's attention, so the adult would light the lighter for the child to blow the flame out; or by placing a semi-closed fist in front of his face, blowing and gently hitting the mouth with an open hand, saying "puff!" as a way of asking for a balloon. In these enactive symbols, the link between signifier and signified is not arbitrary, but motivated, as is the case of Piaget's symbolic play. But, unlike the Piagetian symbol, these do not involve any type of deforming assimilation. They are small enactive metonymies, where a part of a complex action is selected in order to refer to another part or component of the action, created with a communicative aim.

There are also other ways in which children create original symbolic gestures. For example; Habib, at 1; 6 (24), when seeing his father walking into the room, points to the floor and stamps his feet loudly on the floor while he continues pointing. His father laughs and says "Last night I killed a cockroach in the garage." The gesture of pointing to the floor, where there is nothing, and the stepping (probably an imitation of his father's movements, or of his own excitement when seeing with the fleeting bug) form together a new, motivated gesture, through which the child evokes a past event, an absent cockroach.

The same child, at 1; 7 (25), creates a symbol clearly linked to dance. In numerous occasions, Habib has seen a video in which a flamenco dancer, Joaquín Cortéz, dances accompanied by other dancers. He has frequently imitated the movements of the legs and arms, varying the speeds, passing one hand through the opposite arm, turning his head, going round in circles, and tapping his feet in different directions. On one occasion when he saw the video-player was off, Habib looked at me and moved his arms and hands over his head in a waving manner, imitating the movements of flamenco dancing. My immediate response was: "Do you want to see Joaquin Cortez's video?" The arm movement performed by Habib is not a "natural" movement, but rather a cultural, conventional movement. It forms part of the repertoire of resources that culture offers him for symbolic formation: in the same way as the word "papa"; the patterns of movement "are out there" prepared be appropriated by the child. And Habib does so. And by doing it, he gives a new twist to the relation between movement and action. Because *movement becomes a mediator for action*. The child *transforms movement into a symbolic action*, by using it with a communicative *intention*.

A few days later, Habib performs, with gestures, not a petition but a subtly different act: an invitation. He is 1; 08 (02) and invites his father "to dance." And he does this through peculiar movements that in themselves carry the features of the flamenco dance. While the infant is looking at the video, he turns his head around and looks at his father. The movement is exaggerated (the back of his neck is almost bent) and he extends his neck even more, but his father is not paying attention. The infant stands up straight and, still looking at his father, moves his arm and hand in a perfect sinuous wave, and then, keeps still. His father, standing two meters away, has now seen him and responds with the same *"flamenco-like* movement." Habib taps his feet, in a percussion-like manner, watching his father's feet. His father imitates him. Habib keeps looking at his father's feet for a while, and then comes to where I am and hugs me. He leaves me, looks at his father, and, once again, taps his feet twice. His father responds moving his feet and arms, and the infant runs towards him and hugs his legs.

Habib's invitation shows a clear realization that dancing flows through the dynamics and shape of movements. It has to be noted that the first thing he does is to extend his neck backwards, in a delayed and expanded movement that denotes the dynamics (the mode of feeling) of the observed dance, but not its design. He doesn't find an answer and insists on his invitation, now performing a *flamenco-like* movement. He then goes on with movements which are not global and un-differentiated, but which follow with his arms the soft and extended dynamics of the movements of the flamenco dance, and with his feet, the characteristic percussion-like movement that characterizes this type of dance.

The gesture of demand to see a particular videotape, as well as his invitation to dance, are illustrative of the easiness with which the infant incorporates the movements of a culturally patterned dance. His previous experience with the movements that precede temporal arts and the number of times he has been exposed to the varied and ornamented regularity of flamenco dancing allow him to recognize the prototypical movements of this cultural form of expression, and to perform it with such mastery that it is immediately recognized by the observer. The infant's movements make apparent his embodiment of the culture in which he develops. The infant incorporates a form of movement that is distilled in its culture, a way of moving. The *style of movement*, which varies radically from culture to culture, becomes in this manner a *means for communicative action*.

Temporal Play

So far we focused on the gradual externalization of the antecedents of the temporal arts that make up social circular reactions and how they get transformed into play activities and gestures. My next move will be to show how, towards the end of the second year of life, this externalization goes through a qualitative change. At this time of life a new mode of play emerges, that I will call "temporal play," in which the child and the adult adjust to a *third party* and by doing so, the child reaches a new form of behavior that shows artistic qualities.

Bjorn Merker (2002) distinguished among three basic mechanisms of *timing* or temporal regulation: (1) based on reaction time; (2) based on familiarity; (3) based on the underlying pulsation. The temporal regulation of interactive behaviors between mother and infant, from his point of view, is restricted to reaction time and familiarity. But music employs a special mode of *timing*: the equal subdivision of time through musical pulse. Timing based on an underlying pulsation is the fundamental mechanism of sophisticated musical performance. What is specific to music in the domain of time is its capacity to serve as a vehicle for the temporal synchronization of simultaneous and parallel conducts with extraordinary accuracy, irrespectively of whether they arise from identical or different behavioral patterns.

Even though Merker does not claim that the *timing* of early interactions follow a musical pattern, he suggests that, around the end of the second year of life, infants develop a new mechanism of behavioral *timing* based on the underlying pulse mediated through *musical play* in which, through his/her mother's actions, the infant adjusts his/her timing to a third party: the metric structure of the song or game.

When looking at corporal movements, it is also possible to observe a change from the mutual adjustment that characterized early dyad exchanges towards the joint adjustment of infant and adult with respect to a third party. We have witnessed it in the small flamenco choreography performed by Habib and his father. But it can also be observed in other modalities of interaction.

When Habib is 22 months old, he and I performed a sequence of interactions using a plastic toy spring, in which we do nothing more than perform unison movements with contrasting intensity and speed. Each one of these movements – pressing, stretching, and shaking the spring – is associated with a speed – fast or slow – and intensity – soft, strong, or brusque. This alternated dynamics of movements is accompanied by sounds that adhere to a particular form of movement. Together we settled different spatial lines of performance:

a. some are opposed in their direction (extension-contraction of the spring), that are linked to an expression of seriousness and attention, and the quality of the movement (its slowness and softness) is associated with the sound "shhhhh";
b. others (shaking the spring, which draws vertical waves) are made with sharp and strong movements, and are accompanied by different emotional expressions (Habib's guffaws) and with the sound "taka-taka."

What we do is looking for a stabilized form through the establishment of regularities linked to the movements of the bodies, the direction of the gaze, the transformations undergone by the spring, and the sounds made. And the point of the game seems to be the repetition of the achieved form. In fact, my intentions to transform it into something else, granting it fictional features (for example, my attempts to use the spring as if it were a bracelet) are rejected by the infant. As the sequence goes on, the initial regularities are conserved, but variations are added during their repetition. Strikingly, most of the new movements are introduced by Habib (such as guiding the spring to the back of his neck, rubbing our foreheads with it, etc.). The infant and I jointly perform slow and soft movements, rapid and explosive movements that transport different vitality affects. But the sounds I include in the sequence, which the infant immediately incorporates, can also be seen as attunements of the profile of intensity and duration of the conduct. These attunements grant a feeling of communion, and make interaction go on at another level. The contrast of movement becomes accentuated, and the sequence comes to an end, presenting features of a spatial design (manifested in the form and symmetry of our movements and in the visual lines that create spatial directions) and of a temporal design (the phrase formed by the sequence of spatial designs). That design is repeated over and over again, allowing the incorporation of small variations to the sequence (for an expanded analysis of this observations, see Español, 2005).

This scene recalls earlier experiences, but it is not the case of a dyad that adjusts each other's movements in a non-conscious manner. Quite the contrary, child and adult consciously and deliberately adjust their movements to the physical properties of the object, and the "mode of use" of the spring gets defined by the composition of the movement itself. And at the same time, they both consciously and deliberately adjust to the symmetric and equilibrated form shaped by movements, visual lines, sounds and attunements they have created, as well as to the small variations they incorporate now and then. Thus, movement becomes a fixed unit of behavior that the repetition-variation form has made susceptible of elaboration and embellishment. Infant and adult constrained themselves to the dynamic and design of the movement that they have *objectified* together. The composition of movement is therefore transformed into a third party, to whom both adjust, and therefore, in each performance they keep to its rules, respecting the achieved design. *Movement* has changed into *"temporal play,"* at the same time that it has become a *means for action* in a particular manner. In this case, it is the regulated nature of movement, the consciousness of its design, which makes it possible to install in the dyad the *intention* of recreating over and over again the unit they have created.

Temporal Play and Pretend Play

When the dynamic sequence with the spring finished, Habib performed an advanced pretend play with it. He grabbed, with some difficulty, one of its extremes, leaving one part sticking out from his hand (since the spring tends to roll back, it is not easy for him to hold it in this position, but he insists). Held this way, he supports the tip of the spring on a dish and makes the noise "shhhhh," while he points to a cup that I bring him. Habib keeps sounding "shhhhh" while he pretends he is serving something with the spring. He uses the tip of the spring as a substitute for a recipient from which to serve a liquid, and accompanies his action with the sound that, since a few months ago, he associates with serving a liquid. The child has not chosen the substituted object due to its physical properties because this object would allow or facilitate him to perform the gesture of serving. On the contrary, he must force his movements, since the spring rolls back and tends to get tangled, and is difficult for him to keep the tip straight. However, he insists. This is the only "physically forced" substitution that I have observed in the child. He had the intention of using the spring for "serving liquid," and insists on his intention, in spite of the object's resistance. The infant goes from an action where an esthetical value predominates, to an action where a pretend action predominates, and in this transition, the tendency to ignore the affordances of substitute objects is already anticipated.

During the third year of life, the above-mentioned substitutions of pretend play become more complicated, and double substitutions emerge within the same case, or simultaneous substitutions in different cases (Español, Valdéz, Gómez, Jiménez, Martínez, Cevasco, & Pérez Vilar, 2003). In parallel, the tendency to ignore the affordances of the substitute objects appears. That is, the tendency towards a full substitution, in which anything may be "instead of something else," or representing anything else, becomes strengthened. These substitutions assume the breach of some element of the action, since some elements of action have been radically altered, to the extreme of representing or being acted upon as if they were something different from what they actually are (such as when a peg is fed with plastic chips). It may very well be that temporal play is involved in these radical breaches of the elements of action that allow the infant to take off from his/her immediate reality.

Favio Shifres (a professional musician) and I have observed that during the third year of life musical play appears sometimes in isolation and sometimes in contexts of pretend play. When the latter occurs, it tends to follow the following sequence: "pretend play-musical play-pretend play." In the fictional scene, a triggering element appears, which makes the dyad's attention shift from the *pretended theme* to the *musical component* (for example, the repetition of a rhythmic pattern using an object for percussion). In these cases, the object that provokes musical play *loses the function* it was serving during pretend play, and becomes a simple agency for the musical game. When the musical play dies out, the dyad returns to the pretend play theme, that now incorporates some attributes of the previous musical play. For example, the rhythmic pattern of musical play – thematically abstract – is adhered to the pretended action of dialing a wooden box as if it were a telephone. Musical play irrupts in pretend play, displacing its thematic content, as if it were replaced by semantically vague actions that leave a sort of "floating meaning" in the infant (Cross, 2003), which may later support the temporal organization and the thematic display of the fictional scene (Shifres & Español, 2004).

Pretended play involves toying with the grammar of action, which can be linked with what Bruner (1990) called the predisposition to a narrative organization of experience. But when it is taken into account that pretend play merges with social circular reactions and combines with temporal play, it can also be said that temporal modeling *ornaments* action. It favors its transformation and the detachment of the immediate reality; a temporal modeling that evokes dynamic experiences, that transcends verbal categorization, and that genetically links pretend play with the temporal arts.

Having come to this point, we may trace the route of movement in ontogenesis and its connection with the development of action. In the beginning movement is pure exteriorized emotion, and it becomes temporally modeled, dynamically and cross-modally elaborated in the social circular reactions that predominate during the first half of the first year of the infant's life. Later on, a progressive externalization of the elaboration of movement begins. From the second half of the first year of life onwards, movement elaboration is extended beyond the dyad, incorporating objects and granting them a certain mode of use. About the middle of the second year of life, the dynamic and cross-modal elaboration of movement is linked with the ritualization of action that underlies the genesis of pretend play. This connection, on the one hand, promotes and facilitates the gradual separation between each exemplar of action and its adequate object; and, on the other hand, introduces temporality into the sequences of action, providing expectations and tensions similar to those of the narrative function. In parallel, movement becomes cultured movement, which makes the child embody the manner of moving characteristic of the culture in which s/he develops.

And, recursively, it becomes one of many resources that culture offers for the formation of symbols: culturally-patterned movement, when used with a communicative intention, transforms itself into symbolic action. Later on, towards the end of the second year of life, the composition of movement gets objectified and transformed into a third party, which the dyad adjusts to, and so temporal play appears. Finally, during the third year of life, temporal play (particularly, musical play) is intertwined with pretend play, favoring the taking-off from immediate reality. Each of these moments of the extension of movement beyond the dyad is an occasion for the elaboration of movement "out there," that generates and channels the multiple modes of feeling the vitality affects.

Conclusion

In this chapter, I proposed a new way to approach the ontogenesis of symbol formation: the analysis of movement and its relation to the development of action.

First, I highlighted some of the essential traits of movement, both during the early adult-child dyad as well as in temporal arts. Among others, I discussed the capacity that movement has to express vital affections and modes of temporal organization of movements: alternation, synchrony, and the repetition-variation form.

In the second place, I noted that the social circular reactions – characteristic of the first six months of the infant's life – are, to a great extent, a product of dynamic and cross-modal modeled movement. I suggested that the variations in the quality of movement, the attunements, and the repetition-variation forms that constitute the social circular reactions are elaborations, in the Dissanayake sense, which have the virtue to drive an ongoing flow of the vitality affects. I also suggested a possible genetic implication between the social circular reactions and the secondary and tertiary circular reactions of the sensory-motor intelligence.

Finally, I proposed that the elaborations that compose the social circular reactions undergo a gradual externalization process beyond the dyad. Also, that these elaborations contribute to the symbol formation of the child in various ways:

1. In pretend play: the elaboration of movement is linked to the ritualization of action that starts in the second year of life. The elaboration of movement promotes and facilitates a gradual separation between the exemplar of action and its adequate object, while it provides expectations and tensions similar to those of the narrative function

2. In the creation of gesture: the culturally patterned movement, through which the child embodies the manner of movement characteristic of the culture in which s/he develops, is used with a communicative intention and becomes symbolic action.

3. In temporal play: towards the end of the second year of life, the dynamic and pattern of the movement get objectified and transformed into a third party "out there" to which the dyad adjusts. The movement acquires artistic qualities and becomes action with the dyad's intention of maintaining and recreating it. During the third year of life, temporal play is intertwined with pretend play, which favors an increasingly significant detachment from immediate reality.

All these considerations argue that the process of symbol formation is genetically linked to temporal arts and the vitality affect that the latter bring about.

Acknowledgment

Alberto Rosa has known how to "read" in my writings various ideas that I was not yet able to shape. He has generously made comments and suggestions, both general and specific, without which this paper would not have its present theoretical scope.

References

Baron-Cohen, S. (1991). Precursors to a theory of mind: Understanding attention in others. In A. Whiten (Ed.), *Natural Theories of Mind: Evolution, Development and Simulation of Everyday Mindreading* (pp. 233–225). Oxford: Blackwell.

Bates, E. (1979) (Ed.), *The emergence of symbols: Cognition and communication in infancy* (pp. 69–140). New York: Academic Press.

Bruner, J. (1990). *Acts of meaning.* Cambridge, MA: Harvard University Press.

Byrne, R. W. (1995). *The thinking ape.* Oxford: Oxford University Press.

Clark, R. A. (1978). The transition from action to gesture. In A. Lock (Ed.), *Action, gesture and symbol: The emergence of language* (pp. 231–257). London: Academic Press.

Cross, I. (2000). Music in human evolution. In S. O'Neill (Ed.), *Abstracts of the Sixth International Conference on Music Perception and Cognition.* Keele – UK. 180.

Cross, I. (2003). Music and biocultural evolution. In M. Clayton, T. Herbert and R. Middleton (Eds.), *The cultural study of music: A critical introduction* (pp. 19–30). New York and London: Routledge.

Dissanayake, E. (2000a). Antecedents of the temporal arts in early mother-infant interaction. In N. L. Wallin, B. Merker and S. Brown (Eds.), *The origins of music* (pp. 389–410). Cambridge, MA: The MIT Press.

Dissanayake, E. (2000b). *Art and intimacy: How the arts began.* Seattle: University of Washington Press.

Ekman, P., & Oster, H. (1979). Facial expressions of emotion. *Annual Review of Psychology, 30,* 527–554.

Español, S. (2001). Creación de símbolos y ficción durante el segundo año de vida [Symbols and Fiction in the second year of life]. *Estudios de Psicología* 22 (2), 207–226.

Español, S. (2004). *Cómo hacer cosas sin palabras. Gesto y ficción en la infancia temprana* [How to do things without words. Gestures and Fiction in early infancy]. Madrid: Antonio Machado.

Español, S. (2005). Ontogénesis de la experiencia estética. La actitud contemplativa y las artes temporales en la infancia. [Ontogenesis of aesthetic experience: Contemplative attitude and temporal arts in infancy] *Estudios de Psicología,* 26 (2), 139–171.

Español, S., & Rivière A. (2000). Gestos comunicativos y contextos interpersonales: Un estudio con niños de 10 a 16 meses [Communicative gestures and interpersonal contexts: A study with 10 to 16 months old infants]. *Estudios de Psicología* 65–66, 225–245.

Español, S, Valdez, D., Gómez, E., Jiménez, M., Martínez, A., Cevasco, M., & Pérez Vilar, P. (2003). Casos de sustitución en el juego de ficción [Case-studies of substitution in pretend play]. *Memorias de las X Jornadas de Investigación.* Facultad de Psicología. Universidad de Buenos Aires. II 129–131.

Fassbender, C. (1996). Infants' auditory sensitivity towards acoustic parameters of speech and music. In I. Deliège & J. Sloboda (Eds.), *Musical beginnings: Origins and development of musical competence* (pp. 56–87). New York: Oxford University Press.

Fernández, T. R., Sánchez, J. C., Aivar, P., & J. C. Loredo (2003). Representación y significado en psicología cognitiva: una reflexión constructivista [Representation and meaning in cognitive psychology: a constructivist reflection]. *Estudios de Psicología,* 24 (1) 5–32.

Gómez, J. C. (1998). Do concepts of intersubjectivity apply to non-human primates? In S. Bråten (Ed.), *Intersubjective communication and emotion in early ontogeny* (pp. 245–259). Cambridge: University Press.

Gómez, J. C., & Martín-Andrade, B. (2002). Possible precursors of pretend play in non pretend action of captive gorillas. In R. W Mitchell (Ed.), *Pretending and imagination in animals and children.* (pp. 255–268). Cambridge: Cambridge University Press.

Gratier, M. (1999/2000). Expressions of belonging: Effect of acculturation on the rhythm and harmony of mother-infant vocal interaction. *Musicæ Scientiæ, Special Issue,* 93–122.

Hobson, R. P. (1993). *Autism and the development of mind.* Hillsdale, NJ: Lawrence Erlbaum Associates.

Imberty, M. (1997). Formes de la répétition et formes des affects du tems dans léxpression musicale. [Forms of repetition and forms of affects of time in musical expresion]. *Musicæ Scientiæ,* 1 (1), 33–62.

Imberty, M. (2000). The question of innate competencies in musical communication. In N. L. Wallin, B. Merkerdr y S. Brown (Eds.), *The Origins of Music* (pp. 449–462). Cambridge, MA: MIT Press.

Imberty, M. (2002). La musica e il bambino. [Music and the child] En J. J. Nattiez (Dir.), *Enciclopedia della Musica* (pp. 477–495). Torino: Giulio Einaudi Editore.

Iverson, M., Capirci, O., & Caselli, M. (1994). From communication to language in two modalities. *Cognitive Development, 9*, 23–43.

Izard, C. E. (1979). *The maximally discriminative facial movement coding system.* Newark, DE: University of Delaware Instructional Resource Center.

Johnson, C. O., Clinton, D. N., Fahrman, M., Mazzaglia, G., Novak, S., & Soerhus, K. (2001). How do mothers signal shared feeling-states to their infants? An investigation of affect attunement and imitation during the first year of life. *Scandinavian Journal of Psychology, 42*, (4) 377–381.

Karousou, A. (2003). *Análisis de las vocalizaciones tempranas: Su patrón evolutivo y su función determinante en la emergencia de la palabra* [Análisis of early vocalisations: developmental patterns and their function in the emergence of the word]. Doctoral Dissertation. Universidad Complutense de Madrid.

Kavanaugh, R. (2002). Caregiver-child social pretend play: what transpires? In R.W Mitchell (Ed.), *Pretending and imagination in animals and children* (pp. 91–101). Cambridge: Cambridge University Press.

Kugiumutzakis, G. (1998). Neonatal imitation in the intersubjective companion space. In S. Bråten (Ed.), *Intersubjective communication and emotion in early ontogeny* (pp. 63–88). Cambridge: Cambridge University Press.

Leslie, A. M. (1987). Pretense and representation: the origins of "theory of mind". *Psychological Review, 94*, 412–26.

Lillard, A. (1993). Pretend play skills and the child's theory of mind. *Child Development, 64*, 348–71.

Lock, A. (1978). The emergence of language. In A. Lock (Ed.), *Action, gesture and symbol: The emergence of language* (pp. 3–18). London: Academic Press.

Maratos, O. (1998). Neonatal, early and later imitation: Same order phenomena? In F. Simion and G. Butterworth (Eds.), *The development of sensory, motor and cognitive capacities in early infancy: From perception to cognition* (pp. 145–160). East Sussex: Psychology Press.

Mc Cune-Nicolich, L. (1977). Beyond sensorimotor intelligence: Assessment of symbolic maturity through analysis pretend play. *Merrill-Palmer Quaterly, 23*, 89–99.

Mc Cune, L., & Agayoff, J. (2002). Pretending as representation: A developmental and comparative view. In R.W Mitchell (Ed.), *Pretending and imagination in animals and children*

(pp. 43–55). Cambridge: Cambridge University Press.

Meltzoff, A. N., & Moore, M. K. (1998). Infant intersubjectivity: Broadening the dialogue to include imitation, identity and intention. In S. Bråten (Ed.), *Intersubjective communication and emotion in early ontogeny* (pp. 47–62). Cambridge: Cambridge University Press.

Merker, B. (2002). Principles of interactive behavioral timing. In C. Stevens, D. Burham, G. McPherson, E. Schubert and J. Renwick (Eds.), *Proceedings of the 7th International Conference of Music Perception and Cognition.* Sydney: University of Western Sydney. 149–152.

Murray, L., & Trevarthen, C. (1984). Emotional regulation of interactions between two-month-olds and their mothers. In T. Field y N. Fox (Eds.), *Social perception in infants* (pp. 177–197). Norwood, NJ: Albex.

Papôusek, M. (1996). Intuitive parenting: a hidden source of musical stimulation in infancy. In I. Deliege y J. Sloboda. (Eds.), *Musical beginnings. Origins and development of musical competence* (88–112). Oxford: Oxford University

Piaget, J. (1936). *La naissance de l'intelligence chez l'enfant.* [The origins of intelligence in children] París: Delachaux et Niestlé.

Piaget, J. (1945/1962). *Play, dreams and imitation in childhood* [Trans. C. Gattegno & F. M. Hodgson]. New York: Norton. (Original work: J. Piaget (1945). *La formation du symbole chez l'enfant.*)

Pouthas, V. (1996). The development of the perception of time and temporal regulation of action in infants and children. In I. Deliege and J. Sloboda (Eds.), *Musical beginnings. Origins and development of musical competence* (pp. 115–141). Oxford: Oxford University Press.

Repp, B. H. (1993). Music as motion: A synopsis of Alexander Truslit's (1938) 'Gestaltung und Bewegung in der Musik', *Psychology of Music, 21/1*, 48–72.

Ricoeur, P. (1983). *Time and narrative.* Chicago. University of Chicago Press.

Rivière, A. (1984/2003). Acción e interacción en el origen del símbolo. [Action and interaction in the origin of symbol] En M. Belinchón, A. Rosa, M. Sotillo & I. Marichalar (comp.) *Ángel Rivière. Obras Escogidas*, Vol II, pp. 77–108 Madrid: Panamericana.

Rivière, A. (1986/2003). Interacción precoz. Una perspectiva vygotskiana a partir de los esquemas de Piaget. [Early interaction. A vygotskian perspective from Piaget's schemas]. En M. Belinchón, A. Rosa, M. Sotillo & I. Marichalar (comp.) *Ángel Rivière. Obras Escogidas*, Vol II, pp. 109–142. Madrid: Panamericana.

Rivière, A. (1990). Origen y desarrollo de la función simbólica en el niño. [Origin and development of the symbolic funtion in the child] En J. Palacios, A. Marchesi & C. Coll (Comps.), *Desarrollo psicológico y educación* (pp. 113–130). Madrid: Alianza.

Rivière, A. (1997/2003). Teoría de la mente y metarrepresentación. [Theory of mind and metarrepresentation] En M. Belinchón, A. Rosa, M. Sotillo & I. Marichalar (comp.) *Ángel Rivière. Obras Escogidas*, Vol I, pp. 191–231. Madrid: Panamericana

Rosa, A., & Travieso, D. (2002). El tiempo del reloj y el tiempo de la acción. Introducción al número monogrfico sobre Tiempo y Explicación Psicológica [A time for the clock and a time for action. Introduction to the special issue on 'Time and Psychological Explanation']. *Estudios de Psicología*, 23 (1), 7–15

Savage-Rumbaugh, E. S. (1986). *Ape language*. New York: Columbia University Press.

Shifres, F. (2002). De la fuente de la expresión musical al contenido de la experiencia del oyente [From the source of musical expression to the content of the listener's experience]. En Martínez, I. & Musumeci, O. (Eds.), *Actas de la Segunda Reunión Anual de SACCoM (Sociedad Argentina para las Ciencias Cognitivas de la Música)*. Buenos Aires: Universidad Nacional de Quilmes y SACCoM.

Shifres, F. y Español, S. (2004). Interplay between pretend and music play. *Proceedings of the 8th International Conference on Music Perception & Cognition*, Evanston, IL.

Smith, P. (2002). Pretend play, metarepresentation and theory of mind. In R.W. Mitchell (Ed.), *Pretending and Imagination in animals and children* (pp. 255–268). Cambridge University Press.

Stern, D. (1985). *The interpersonal World of the Infant: A view from Psychoanalysis and Developmental Psychology*. New York: Basic Books.

Stern, D. (1995). *The motherhood constellation: A unified view of aren't-infant psychotherapy*. New York: Basic Books.

Tomasello, M., & Camaioni, L. (1997). A comparison of the gestural communication of apes and human infants. *Human Development*, 40, 7–24.

Treuhb, S. (2000). Human processing predispositions and musical universals. In N. L. Wallin; B. Merkerdr y S. Brown. (Eds.), *The Origins of Music* (pp. 427–448). Cambridge, MA: MIT Press.

Trevarthen, C. (1982). The primary motives for cooperative understanding. In G. Butterworth & P. Light. (Eds.), *Social Cognition* (pp. 77–109). Brighton: Harverster.

Trevarthen, C. (1998). The concept and foundations of infant intersubjectivity. In S. Bråten. (Ed.), *Intersubjective Communication and Emotion in Early Ontogeny* (pp. 15–46). Cambridge: Cambridge University Press.

Trevarthen, C. (1999/2000). Musicality and the intrinsic motive pulse: evidence from human psychobiology and infant communication. *Musicæ Scientiæ*, Special Issue, 155–215.

Valsiner, J. (1992). Making of the future: Temporality and the constructive nature of human development. In G. Turkewitz y D. Devenney. (Eds.), *Time and Timing in Development*. Hillsdale, NJ: Lawrence Erlbaum Associates.

Vila, I. (1986). *Introducción a la obra de Henry Wallon* [Introduction to Henry Wallon's production]. Barcelona: Anthropos.

Von Hofsten, C. (2003). On the development of perception and action. In J. Valsiner y K. Connolly (Eds.), *Handbook of Developmental Psychology* 114–171. London: Sage.

Vygotsky, L. S. (1931/1997). The History of the Development of Higher mental Functions. In R.W. Rieber. (Ed.), *The Collected Works of L.S. Vygotsky*. Volume 4. New York: Plenum Press.

Wallon, H. (1956). La psychologie génétique. [Genetic psychology]. *Bulletin de Psychologie*, 10 (1), 3–10.

Wallon, H. (1982). *La vie mentale*. [Mental life] Messidor/ Editions Sociales, París.

Werner, H. & Kaplan, B. (1963/1984). *Symbol formation*. Hillsdale, NJ: Lawrence Erlbaum Associates.

CHAPTER 12

Object Use, Communication, and Signs

The Triadic Basis of Early Cognitive Development

Cintia Rodríguez

Sigma lives in a world of signs,
not because he lives in the wilderness,
but because, even when he is alone,
he lives in society

Umberto Eco, Signo

The Pragmatic Approach to Language and Objects

Bruner, following Vygotsky, has insisted that "meaning [is] the central concept in Psychology" (1990: 2), and furthermore that "meaning itself is a *culturally mediated phenomenon* that depends upon the prior existence of a shared symbol system" (*ibid.*: 69, emphasis added). In the 1970s, in his studies with babies on language acquisition, Bruner referred to the "pragmatic opportunism" humans demonstrate when solving problems (1983: 7). He concluded that it is not possible to treat language separately from its function, as an autonomous syntax, nor as a semantic or lexical unit. Communication has practical repercussions: we *do* things with words. Without denying the importance of

syntactical form in language, he concentrates almost exclusively upon function:

> [. . .] *the child's acquisition of language requires far more assistance from and interaction with caregivers than Chomsky (and many others) had suspected.* Language is acquired *not in the role of spectator but* through use. *Being "exposed" to a flow of language is not nearly as important as using it in the midst of "doing". Learning a language, to borrow John Austin's celebrated phrase, is learning "how to do things with words.* (1990: 70–71, emphasis added)

In his well-known critique of Chomsky, Bruner distanced himself from the view of language in which syntax is almost exclusively predominant, and where the acquisition of the formal syntactical structure of language is supposed to occur completely independent from knowledge of the world, or social interaction with language speakers. From Chomsky's perspective[1] (1982/1984: 174) where only the underlying rules are important (Bresson & Lebovici, 1989), it is pointless to ask about the communicative exchanges between the child and the people surrounding him/her. As pointed by Chris Sinha, the reduction "[. . .] axiomatic for generative linguistics – of all dimensions of human natural language complexity and creativity to *syntax* has obscured rather than illuminated [. . .] the question of language origins" (Sinha, 2000: 204).

To emphasize the *use* of a language – that is, the pragmatics of speech – is to highlight the variety of its communicative functions. Language acquisition is seen as having a plurality of functions that are themselves linked to a plurality of contexts beyond language without which its uses could not be understood. Hence, Bruner's "pragmatics of speech" refers to "how language interacts with context to achieve its meanings" (1978: viii) [. . .] "*Using* language [. . .] cannot be dismissed as the "mere" performance of an underlying grammatical competence" (*ibid.* p. vii). This means that, in order to understand linguistic meanings, we will also need to take into account meaning as it exists before the acquisition of language and also beyond once it is acquired.

However, the emphasis placed by Bruner on contexts-of-use in relation to language acquisition (1975) has, paradoxically, not been applied to objects. It is as if *language is used*, but *objects* are *not*. Perhaps this happens because the things that are in front of our eyes, such as objects, are the most difficult to see, no matter how important, complex, or necessary they may be. This chapter is devoted to some of those things that escape our notice due to their continuous presence, such as *objects* and their *uses in everyday life*. First, we consider now how the pragmatic perspective was introduced in early development through the acquisition of language.

What Is the Origin of the Pragmatic View That Leads Bruner to Link Meaning and Use in Language Acquisition?

Bruner was influenced by the American philosopher Charles Sanders Peirce, the father of modern semiotics. As he himself states, it was Peirce's writings on mediation through signs, which allowed him not only to understand Vygotsky's claim that consciousness is semiotically mediated (1983: 8), but also to distance himself from Piaget's solitary subject. However, the philosophers Austin and Wittgenstein were probably more influential in his introduction of usage in the explanation of language acquisition. While Peirce's semiotics does not centre on language – one of his most insightful pragmatic maxims states that *everything can become a sign* if there is an interpreter – those of Wittgenstein and Austin do.[2] In order to explain Bruner's theory of language acquisition we will now take a closer look at their influence on the "pragmatic turn" he took during his years in Oxford.

According to Bruner, the idea that the child's interaction with others holds the key to the explanation of language acquisition has different variants. The most recent arises from speech acts. Prelinguistic children already know how to declare and ask without using language, through the use of gestures, intonation, and so on (1982: 175). As Tomasello (2001) reminds us, Bruner was introduced to Speech Act theory in Oxford through Austin's influence (where he left an active legacy: Searle, Grice, or Harré are good examples). However, the origin of speech act theory can be found in Karl Bühler's work:

> [. . .] for all of us there are situations in which the problem of the moment, the task at hand is solved by speaking directly from within the life situation: speech actions [. . .] the feature that must be highlighted in the concept 'speech action', the feature without which it is inconceivable, is that the speaking is completed (or fulfilled) to the extent that it performs the task of solving the practical problem in the situation. Accordingly, the speech action cannot be imagined apart from its provenance (in the vineyard of practical life), its origin is part of it. (Bühler, 1934/1990, pp. 62–63, emphasis in the original)

Bruner was also influenced by the latter Wittgenstein, who stressed that the symbols of language take their communicative significance from the social practices in which they are embedded. For both Austin and Wittgenstein (and Bühler) language is grounded upon forms of life, not something that can be considered in isolation, independent of the multiple functions it fulfils in the lives of its users (Wittgenstein 1953/1958; Carrió & Rabosi, 1962; Bouveresse, 1998).

Bruner's influence on early development studies has continued to grow since the 1970s.[3] Few in the field are surprised to learn that communication exists through well-developed non-linguistic means long before the infant is able to speak. The fact that there are, indeed, well-established conventions and rules governing communication between adults and babies, seriously undermines the Piagetian belief that the beginnings of language are not founded on pre-existing conventions of subject-subject interaction. Bruner's main achievement has been to establish that, in contrast to Piaget, the semiotic function does not emerge from sensorimotor actions of the subject acting in isolation.[4]

Bruner's Two Logics: With Language the Logic of Use, With Objects That of a Direct Relationship

Yet the emphasis placed by Bruner on contexts-of-use in relation to language acquisition has, paradoxically, not been applied to (material) objects. It is as if language is *used*, but objects are not; as though we did things with words, but not with objects. In this sense, two logics are often used: one that stems from pragmatics, when dealing with language and its acquisition, and a quite different one when dealing with objects, where the "pragmatic and semiotic influences" do not manage to reach. Whereas, with language, it is employed the logic of use, with objects that of a direct relationship. The latter is not semiotically mediated, since objects ultimately are supposed to show themselves *as they obviously are*.

Objects are considered in early infancy in a "syntactic" and formal way, thus disconnecting them from their use in everyday life (Rodríguez & Moro, 1998; Moro &

Rodríguez, 2005). In fact, by introducing a pragmatic perspective upon early development, Bruner offers a solution partly coherent with our argument about objects: "the acquisition of a first language is very context-sensitive," meaning that "it progresses far better when the child already grasps in some *prelinguistic* way the significance of what is being talked about" (1990: 71, emphasis in the original). Bruner has never seriously focused on the use of objects and yet if we are to situate language acquisition in its contexts of use, we must do the same with objects. Objects play an important role "in what is being talked about."

This "double standard" exists not only within Bruner's approach but also to some extent with Vygotsky and Saussure: the *logic of social, public use* is applied when dealing with language, but in the case of objects, the *logic of immediate meanings*, of "syntax," of the lack of need for conventions, is applied. With Vygotsky, the problem arises from his dualism of the cultural and the natural lines of development (Van der Veer & Valsiner, 1991); according to such a view, the prelinguistic child exists outside the realm of the semiotic. In the case of Saussure, his semiology is limited to the realm of intentional signs[5] and there is no room for "natural signs" (Castañares, 1985).

Where Does the "Natural" Lie in Natural Signs?

As noted above, Bruner's theory is most strongly influenced by the pragmatics of the linguistic philosophers for whom language is the system *par excellence* from which the world and its circumstances are observed.[6] We have focused on two authors that have had a great influence on the pragmatic stance throughout the 20th century, Wittgenstein and Austin.

If any idea has migrated between disciplines in the Human Sciences, it is the one espoused by Wittgenstein in his *Philosophical Investigations*, when he states that: "For a *large* class of cases – though not for all – in which we employ the word "meaning" it can be defined thus: the meaning of a word is its use in the language" (43).

The meaning of this phrase has been much debated, as well as the limits that "a large class of cases" imposes on the relationship between meaning and use, according to which the meaning of a word is defined by the use we make of it. It might well be that, as José Hierro claims, the end of the phrase has been excessively highlighted (1986: 276): "the meaning of a word is its use in the language," when part of the answer was given by Wittgenstein himself when he concludes that "the meaning of a name is sometimes explained by pointing to its *bearer*" (1953: 43). In our view, there are many misunderstandings on this point in need of clarification, especially since we are referring to early development before language. Here it is not enough to assert that the meaning of a name is (sometimes) explained by pointing to what is named. It might be enough in the case of adults who, from the same cultural parameters, share knowledge about *that which is pointed at*. If I face an adult who does not speak my language, but is part of the Western world, and say "cup" while pointing to a cup, it will probably not be hard for this adult to understand what it is that I am pointing at, and to understand that *that* is called a "cup." This is because she shares with me a universe of knowledge about the conventional uses of this object, a knowledge that is "beneath" words. That is, even though this adult may not know that cups are *called* "cups," he or she lives in a world where cups exist, and hence knows what a cup *is for*; given this knowledge, an educated adult finds it quite easy to place a name. Therefore, pointing to a cup solves the meaning of the word "cup." Wittgenstein's affirmation, "the meaning of a name is sometimes explained by pointing to its bearer" (*ibid.*) is easily applied to this situation. However, it would not be enough to point and name what is being pointed to, if the subject with whom I am communicating does not even partially segment the world meaningfully in the same way that I do. This is precisely what happens to children during their first year of life – they do not segment reality in the

way adults do. Hence, in order to grasp the public meaning of objects it is not enough to just point and name the object. Nor is identifying the object pointed at sufficient since the object is still far too complex. In order for the child to come to understand the *function of what we are pointing at*, language is not enough. We need to accompany language with other semiotic systems, where the uses of objects are also included.

One Thing Is the Production of a Natural Sign; Its Interpretation Is Quite Another

Now we come to our main point. The distance between Saussure's natural *versus* artificial signs (in many ways similar to the Ancient Greek distinction between *symbola* and *semeîon*[7]) has, to our day, been taken to lead to a profoundly misleading conclusion, which extends to the very foundations of the analysis of the subject. Namely, if a sign is *natural* because the relation between its terms is free of convention (i.e., cloud and rain, smoke and fire), then the subject's interpretation of the sign is also taken to be *natural*. But there are no *natural* interpretations. All interpretations are based on previous ones. They are the product of a cognitive construction, of a *certain point of view*, even if many people share this point of view. Take the example of symptoms, these are natural signs (Cronkhite, 1990) but this does not mean that the mechanisms we employ to understand them are also "natural," in the sense they do not involve socially mediated interpretation.

The nature of the production of a sign must not be confused with the nature of its comprehension. Its comprehension implies a consensus with respect to the accepted social meaning granted by a community at a given time (Eco, 1973/1988). Nowadays, it seems obvious to us that if someone has fever it is *because* there is an infection. The relationship is of cause (infection) and effect (fever). What is no longer a cause-effect, however, is the medical knowledge that understands there is a causal relationship between fever and infection. In fact, if there is such a thing as a medical tradition, it is because we need professionals specially trained to read these signs, no matter how *natural* they are.[8]

As is well known, the inhabitants of Pompeii in 79 A.D., in ancient Rome, were buried in ashes when the Vesuvius erupted. This is a dramatic example of how a natural phenomenon – smoke announcing what was to come – does not necessarily lead to adequate "natural interpretations." One must, rather, have at one's disposal a system of signs, a tradition, which allows for the cultural interpretation of a natural fact or event. The people of Pompeii did not interpret the *smoke* coming out of the mountain as a *sign* of danger. For them, *that* smoke did not mean the Vesuvius would erupt. And so the pragmatic effects of such an interpretation did not occur. This is why people stayed in the city instead of running. They were unable to anticipate what was about to happen to them: their disappearance under smoke, rocks, and ashes.

Why Does Psychology Naturalize Objects Instead of Viewing Them From a Pragmatic Perspective?

If we consider in early development what is really happening in relation to the child's use of objects, we see that towards the end of the first year of life, the child begins to use objects according to their social and conventional everyday-life functions. One of the reasons for the lack of interest in introducing the object into the pragmatic mould, and in seeing *how* and through which *processes*, the child reaches this level, may be that the object creates the illusion that it is "one-dimensional" and evident. It is supposed to act as a natural sign that is "naturally" interpreted by the child, needless of communication and semiosis. As the French semiologist Roland Barthes states: when dealing with the object, we are faced with the obstacle of the evident (1985).

The roots of this state of affairs are, certainly, profound. To untangle them would require more space and time than is here available (for a longer explanation see Moro & Rodríguez, 2004). However, a short explanation will help us better understand our point. When psychologists deal with signs in relation to early development, they almost invariably leave *natural* signs aside – there is an obvious connection to the *naturalized* status usually conferred on objects – the signs focused on are usually *intentional* and highly conventional, such as language or the great semiotic systems. These were of interest to Saussure, the philosophers of the linguistic turn, and Vygotsky. In fact, Vygotsky focused, at least towards the end of his life, on language as the semiotic system *par excellence* and certainly this idea of language as the semiotic system *par excellence* is, explicitly or implicitly, still very much present among his followers.

Though Bruner is among these, he considerably improved the situation when he introduced communication and culture in early development. However, the pragmatic perspective he introduces has not extended to the study of "cognitive development" where traditionally (as in the Piagetian approach) objects have always been emphasized. In other words, the attempt to understand how *language* is *used* pragmatically has seldom led also to a similar understanding of how *objects* are actually *used*, namely, in situations that always involve other people.

Communication as Cause of Cognitive Development: The Role of the Object

In the study of early infancy, it is very common for objects to be treated as natural signs that lead to "natural and direct interpretations." This implies that children encounter objects alone, without any communicative or semiotic mediation. The object is rarely placed within a network of interpersonal relationships where its uses affect the ways subjects communicate with each other. Indeed, the psychological literature rarely recognizes the historical, cultural and local nature of the object. After all, the manufactured objects that inhabit many, but not all, of the realities in which children grow up, have been created by someone with a certain intention, with one or various functions. They are also articulated with other objects that have their own functions. All of this is part of the scenarios where the everyday lives of children and their caregivers take place. This neglect is unsurprising given that research on early infancy rarely shares the views characteristic of the analysis of later didactic and educational situations.

Some Clarifications About Triadic Interactions

There is no doubt that early infancy research has often analyzed triadic interactions. We need, however, to introduce a more nuanced reading. The triadic interactions usually analyzed occur at the end of the first year (Trevarthen & Hubley, 1978; Bates et al., 1979), and are related to the child's first intentional behaviors (Piaget, 1936/1977). Recently Tomasello and Rakoczy (2003) have referred to this as the Nine-Month Revolution:

> [...] we may observe that 6-month-old infants interact dyadically with objects, grasping and manipulating them, and they interact dyadically with other people, expressing emotions back-and-forth in a turn-taking sequence. But at around 9–12 months of age a new set of behaviors begins to emerge that are triadic in the sense that they involve a referential triangle of child, adult, and the object/event to which they share attention. Thus, infants at this age begin to flexibly and reliably [...] act on objects in the way adults are acting on them (imitative learning) – in short, to "tune in" to the attention and behavior of adults toward outside entities. (p. 125)

In the triadicity referred to in this quotation the infant is already able to perform intentional communicative behaviors. But such triadicity must itself necessarily emerge from previous triadicities, in which the adult acts as a guide. When Tomasello and Rakoczy claim that before the "Nine-Month Revolution" the infant only relates dyadically – that is alternating between objects and people, but never simultaneously – they are telling only part of the story. The beginning of it is missing, since the adult always acts triadically, it is the adult who "main-

tains" the triadic interaction. What we must seek to understand is how the subtle transfer of intentions, meanings, and semiotic instruments takes place between adult and child, through what the adult "brings in" to the child from the world. Once the child is able to communicate intentionally, at about 9 months of age, the adult does not give up the guidance role, but rather starts combining with the child mutual intentions about the world.

The triadicity that characterizes didactic situations, that is to say when the adult acts as a guide, is generally absent from early cognitive development. This is precisely the period in which humans most need the presence, care, and guidance of others. In spite of the achievements of research into early development, we still know very little about the functioning of the subtle semiotic framework in which the adult acts as a guide who gradually opens up the world to the infant. We know even less when it comes to the complex and various uses that characterize everyday objects. We need to connect early cognitive development and later phases of development, where education and culture are openly dealt with. Among the developmental schools of psychology, we can say Piaget is still favored over Vygotsky when it comes to the ways in which we study the relationship between the infant and the world. Communication as a cause of cognitive development has not yet penetrated the foundations of developmental psychology.[9] Andy Lock has recently pointed out something similar:

> [...] at this age it is the actions of the adults that are of the prime developmental significance [...] if we take the central point from Piaget that infants learn through their actions on the world, then how the world they are learning about is structured becomes of major significance as to what they learn. There are some very important maturational changes going on with respect to infants' psychological makeup at this time, such that a number of new capabilities come "on-line" in the last quarter of the first year of their lives [...] How these abilities are structured as they emerge, and

what it is that they are put to work on,
is crucially dependent on the raw material
they both work on and are forged through.
That is, it is not just the case that infants
act on the world, but that the world itself
is transacted *to them in the way another*
presents it. (2001: 386)

The importance of adult models for the child to acquire language has been strongly emphasized. The school contexts are undoubtedly crucial for children to appropriate the great semiotic systems – reading and writing, drawing, music, calculus, and so on (Mili & Rickenmann, 2004; Martí, 2003; Nogues, Weil-Barais, Villeret, & Bouchafa, 2005; Wirthner & Schneuwly, 2004; Saada-Robert & Balslev, 2004). And, yet, this essential guiding role of adults is completely forgotten when referring to the basic semiotic systems prior to the acquisition of language.

How Many Triadicities Are Necessary to Understand the Role of Education in Early Development? Indexical Gestures Point to Something in the World

In order to illustrate the separation between education and early development, let us turn to a paradigmatic case of triadic interaction, extensively studied in the literature, based on the work of Bates, Camaioni, and Volterra in the 1970s: protodeclaratives. Protodeclarative behavior consists of an action, occurring towards the age of 10–12 months, where a child gives or shows an object to an adult in order to capture her or his attention. The most emphasized aspect of these studies is the protodeclarative gesture of pointing that takes place around the age of 12–14 months. Franco, Perucchini, and Butterworth go as far as claiming that "pointing is not dependent on the adult's social scaffolding, emerging simultaneously with adults and with peers" (1992, quoted by Reddy, 2001). The child, in Franco et al.'s position, points by him or herself; the supportive role of other people is not deemed necessary in this long journey. This conclusion is surprising if we consider that in everyday life adults continuously point and indicate in many ways. The

child lives in a world where other people *continuously perform* indexical signs. The variety of indexical signs is enormous; pointing is only one example. Here we have some of Peirce's definitions of what an index is.

"I define an Index as a sign determined by its dynamic object by virtue of being in a real relation to it" (1904:33).

"A sign which denotes a thing by forcing it upon the attention is called an *index*. An index *does not describe* the qualities of its object" (1896, CP 3-434, emphasis added).

"The index *asserts nothing*; it only says "There!" It takes hold of our eyes, as it were, and forcibly directs them to a particular object, and there it stops" (1885: 162–163 emphasis added).

What still remains unclear is *how* the child reaches the level of development allowing him to read indexical signs as such. We know very little about how adults guide (i.e., correct, give guidelines, modify certain contextual clues, exaggerate, repeat, present themselves as models, introduce segments of practice, frame, suggest, etc.) children to, first of all, understand indexical signs. Later children understand pointing gestures as indicative rather than only as ostensive, until they are able to point with a communicative function. They later use their own indexical gestures privately (Delgado, Gómez, & Sarriá, 1999, 2004), or with a self-reflexive function, in the context of solving problems related to complex conventional uses of objects (Rodríguez & Palacios, 2005). The idea that pointing is spontaneous and does not need to be learned is hardly new. Cassirer, quoting Wundt, claimed that: "The child also tries to grasp the objects that, being too far away, he cannot reach. In this case, the movement of grasping is *immediately* transformed into pointing. It is only after repeated attempts at grasping objects that pointing is established as such" (1964/1998: 137, emphasis added). He even referred to pointing with the hand as "distance grasping."[10]

There is another important fact that is not sufficiently considered: being an indexical sign, the gesture of pointing in its different versions – communicative or private – always indicates *something in the world*, essential for the function of the gesture to be understood. That is, indexical gestures are characterized by the presence of that which they point towards. It is necessary to include that which is being pointed to, *the object in the world that is being indicated*. Otherwise, the gesture cannot be understood. Our insistence on this is due to the failure of early infancy studies to include the world (the object) within a communicative, cultural, and pragmatic frame.

We also still know very little about the *processes* through which children come to understand indicative signs that are less sophisticated than pointing. The function of specific cultural contexts in the acquisition of different indexical gestures is also generally unknown. Wilkins's (2003) studies on Australian adults are very suggestive. They show pointing gestures are not as universal as we tend to believe, and that the nature of *the target of the pointing* – if it is one thing or several, close or far away, or if it implies movement – affects the gesture itself.

Before the Child Produces Her First Symbols and Conventional Uses of Objects, Adults Have Continuously Produced Them

Early development has also not questioned the adult's influence on how children *acquire* the first symbolic uses of objects, forgetting the enormous role played by adults as "manufacturers of the symbols we are." However, some voices that consider *the role of adults* in the birth of these symbols have started to be heard. An example would be Katherine Nelson's consideration of the roots of the first symbols:

> [...] I hypothesize that the first symbolic play involving objects emerges in interactions with a social partner, who uses the object in a pretend action. This hypothesis has not been systematically investigated, however. (1996: 358)

Adults use symbols to fulfill a variety of functions. And children are witnesses to them well before they themselves start producing their first symbols towards the end of their first year (Rodríguez, Palacios, & Vázquez, 2005). Another equally important issue is that when psychologists refer to symbols, they usually treat them as "symbolic play," and, therefore, spontaneous. However, this does not take into account that symbolic uses, with or without an object, carry out numerous functions and are rooted in the conventional uses of the objects (Rodríguez & Palacios, 2005). This is of the utmost importance in the cases in which children present a disability (or a risk of developing one) in their first year of life (Rodríguez, 2003; 2006). A similar process takes place with the first conventional uses of objects. We seem to forget that, from the moment children are born, adults use objects in their daily chores, in a space of public and everyday uses. Children continuously attend to and participate in these "performances" well before they themselves are able to perform the first conventional uses of objects (Rodríguez & Moro, 2002). When it comes to showing/giving an object, children do not just start doing it from one day to the next at the age of ten months (Reddy, 2001). One of the first fully semiotic acts that adults carry out in front of children consists of the ostensive showing of features of the world selectively to the infant.

Does the Adult Play a Role in the Child's Acquisition of Object Permanence?

We cannot end this section without referring to object permanence, another of the great themes in early cognitive development. Ever since Piaget drew attention to this important issue (1937), all work on cognitive development approaches it in some way or other (Bremner, 2001). Piaget insisted upon two things. First, that the permanence of the object is the basis of our representation of the material world. Second, that the child does not discover it through cultural means. Hence, the object is again caught within a narrow "syntax." But we do not want to focus on Piaget just now. We want to emphasize two things. (1) We have not found in the literature any link between object permanence and the conventional and public use of everyday objects. (2) We must explore how the conventional use of the object affects its permanence, which is another way of placing the object within its pragmatic contexts of use (Rodríguez & Moro, 1998a). The adult plays a very active role in this type of permanence.

This leads us to another issue. Children's acquisition of object permanence tends to be viewed independently of adults' actions on the child's world, as though the adult were a stranger to this birth. In fact, adults treat the world – objects – as permanent in front of the child, long before he does it himself. We need to explore how the child is affected by the permanence that others attribute to objects. Thus there is a need to develop research programs that locate this important question in contexts of triadic interaction.

In conclusion, we know very little about the first educational processes of triadic adult-infant-object interaction, where the adult provides the infant with significant clues about how to deal with the world. And we also possess scarce knowledge about how the child appropriates the significant systems proposed by the adult in relation to the selected parts of the world. To better understand the functioning of the pre-didactic triadicity, which we refer to here, we therefore need to develop research on "ongoing *processes* of change" (Lavelli, Pantoja, Hsu, Messinger, & Fogel, 2005; Thelen & Smith, 1994/1998). We also need to introduce in the analysis objects, situations or contexts in their specificity. Objects cannot continue to be considered separately from "commonsense."

The theorists of the embodied mind, as well as the philosophers of the linguistic turn, have also claimed the need to pay attention to "commonsense" as itself problematic. When Overton wonders how the computational approach and the embodied mind approach stand with respect to contexts of meaning, he claims that the computational view postulates a rupture of

the mind from the world of commonsense. Such a banishment of commonsense leads to the separation of "the cultural context from mind; culture [. . .] plays no formative role in the development of mind" (1994: 10). As opposed to this, the claim of embodied mind theory is that the mind is dialogical in character (*ibid*.: 11). When we claim the need to situate the object in a pragmatic perspective, we mean that must be considered from the point of view of commonsense, that is, how it is understood by the child in everyday life in all its complexity. The object is used in the process of communication, with all its imperfections, errors, doubts, changes and shifts of meaning, etc. which affect communication itself.

In the next section, we will illustrate our position by approaching, from a triadic perspective, the role of the adult as guide in providing the child with the semiotic mediators, which allow him/her to incorporate increasingly complex levels of meaning. Children begin, in this way, to appropriate the socially established use of objects (Rodríguez & Moro, 1998; 1998a; 2002; Moro & Rodríguez, 2005), and to perform private pointing and ostensive gestures related to them. Internalizing the semiotic mediators previously used by others, as well as awareness in relation to these public uses (Rodríguez & Palacios, 2005; *submitted*).

Conventional Uses of Objects, Communication, and Cognitive Development

We usually pay least attention to the things that are continuously present in our everyday lives. This is so due to a common misunderstanding: that what lies in front of us is not necessarily obvious. Such is our relationship to objects – since they are always there, we end up not seeing them. This situation is paradoxical, since, in ontogenesis, the process of their appropriation by the child is complex and never immediate.

Previous work (Rodríguez, 2003) referred to the myth of the *evidence of the object*. This myth has to do with how early development studies have rarely questioned the relations children establish with things in everyday life. This situation is possibly based on the idea that objects belong to the physical world, and are, thus, independent of culture, communication, and the social and public uses we make of them. The lack of interest in objects and their daily uses might be related to the scarce attention that psychology tends to pay to the materiality of the ordinary, of the concrete.

The reader is probably wondering what the reasons for this situation might be: Why has knowledge of objects been virtually always viewed as independent from social convention? It is not easy to answer this question since the issue has an enormous repercussion. Namely, it affects how we view the child's construction of knowledge from first months of life onwards, when the encounters between the child and the objects – the world in its materiality – are at stake.

Objects are used for doing things in everyday life. The child does not appropriate the first canonical uses of objects directly, because objects, against all evidence, are "opaque," complex and not obvious. There is a great difference between the object being "seen" or used in a non-standard way, such as pulling or sucking, and the object used in a conventional way. Only in the latter case is the object subject to the rules of shared and socially established use. The fact that objects can be seen or touched does not mean that their *function* is directly visible.

Besides having physical properties, objects also have functional properties of use, which are not obvious, but opaque. *Objects do not say what they are, or what they are for.* Objects do not show their meaning directly. The mediation of signs is necessary for objects to "speak." Children are not born knowing how to use them, nor do they know what their function is. Nor is it enough to look at them in order to know them, because objects do not show themselves being used, someone must do it. Therefore, it is necessary to bring the object – the materiality of the world – within

a pragmatic and communicative perspective. The child needs someone else to perform these uses. She or he is then gradually introduced into the networks of meaning, and relies on the signs provided to be able to read the world. For an object to become a *sign of its use*, many other signs need to have acted upon it. This is an intricate process by which children progressively acquire complex semiotic systems.

Cognitive Development Is "Spontaneous" Because the Object Is Evident

Two great assumptions have traditionally underpinned the way cognitive development has been approached:

1. Early cognitive development is "spontaneous"
2. The meaning of objects (the materiality of the world) is self-evident

The conjunction of both assumptions – early cognitive development is spontaneous because the object is evident – partly explain the relative lack of interest in triadic studies before the child can communicate intentionally. Or in studies concerning the role of the adult as a guide to the social and cultural scenarios that surrounds them going beyond language acquisition. The conception that cognitive development is spontaneous because *the* meaning of the object is self-evident is without doubt a powerful reason for the lack of interest in including the object within a pragmatic perspective.

The situation has not greatly changed from the time Cassirer claimed, when referring to the "mimic language of the North American natives," that very few gestures had a "conventional" origin, since "they mostly consist of *the simple reproduction of patent natural phenomena*" (1964/1998: 139, emphasis added). As opposed to language: "The procedure of highlighting only this feature of pantomimic reproduction of sensitively perceivable given objects, does not seem to lead us towards *language*, considered a free activity and coming from the spirit" (*ibid.*).

From a Pragmatic and Semiotic Perspective, How Do Children Acquire the Conventional Uses of Objects by the End of Their First Year?

At what point and through what semiotic processes does an object become a sign of its conventional use? To answer this we must first tackle other questions related to adult-infant-object triadic interactions, such as:

What signs does the adult employ to *communicate* with the child *about* the *use of objects*? How do these signs operate?

What kinds of uses of objects do children carry out first in the course of development?

How do the uses of adults affect those of children and her development?

In which *semiotic processes concerning the object* does the adult act as a guide?

How does this semiotic performance vary once the child begins to internalize different semiotic systems?

How dependent are these signs on the child's *level of development*? That is, how are the macro and microgenesis articulated?

How do different objects affect the production of signs? And if they vary, *how, when*, and *why* do they vary?

What signs do children rely on first, and, then, later on?

At what stage do the more complex signs start to be effective in allowing for children to *"read" the conventional uses of objects*?

How does communication take place between such different subjects when interacting around objects?

How do the adult's intentions affect the emergence of those of the child?

How many types of uses of objects are there before the child comes to understand their conventional uses? How many different levels of conventional uses are there?

How do symbolic uses rely on conventional ones?

To answer those questions we analyzed the interaction of 6 Spanish and 6 Swiss babies with their mothers and two different objects. The first was a toy telephone, the second a toy truck that could be loaded, through different types of holes, with up to 6 blocks. As the study was longitudinal, we filmed the children with their mothers at three different stages of development. The first filming session took place when the children were 7 months old, the second when they were 10 and the last session at 13 months. The filming lasted 5 minutes per stage and object. In this study, as in the rest of our studies on triadic interaction, we took the following aspects into consideration:

Our aim was to analyze *processes*, that is, *how* children come to carry out conventional uses of objects, and internalize them. The analyses are *microgenetic*, as we needed an in-depth analysis of real interactions as they are produced in everyday life. This would then allow us to study processes in a more dynamic way. The method is *longitudinal* – we observed the same subjects in 3 moments of their development.

We have only considered a *triadic unit of analysis*, based on child-object-adult interaction, taking place in real time. We have relied on *Peirce's semiotics* for our observational categories. We made this choice for many reasons. The most relevant to our present point is that Peirce attends to signs in general – not just linguistic signs. As he does not exclusively deal with intentional signs, he allows for the inclusion of objects and their uses within a semiotic reading. The object becomes a sign of its use at a certain stage of development.

As stated above, our interest is in microgenesis, that is, the *processes* by which *signs* are used within triadic interaction. It means that we look microgenetically at the three poles of interaction: the adult, the child and the object, *at the same time*. We do so in real time and through real situations of interaction.

We expected that the *use the adult made of the object* while facing a baby of 7 months would not be the same as when facing one of 10 months, nor one of 13. We also expected *communication about the use of the object* to be different at the three different moments in time. The child would obviously also not *use the object* in the same way, nor would she *communicate* with the adult *about* the object in the same manner. Therefore, we expected the whole triangle would vary throughout time. This was the object of our analysis: *how the triadic whole varied* during the 5 minutes of interaction, and from one session to the next with a Spanish (Rodríguez & Moro, 1998) and a Swiss population (Moro & Rodríguez, 2005). In the next section we present some of our results very briefly.

The Appropriation of Conventional Uses: A Complex Process. Not "A Simple Imitation"

If we come to the conclusion that the meaning of the material world is not obvious, one-dimensional, or evident, this is because when observing children we find that *objects do not have the same meaning* for them as they do for us.

Objects can be used in many ways, conventional and non-conventional. Before the child carries out cultural and conventional uses, she makes many types of uses of objects. The early uses obey basic rules, which in turn obey more primitive meanings, of iconic and indexical nature.

Children's uses of objects are related to the mediation of signs that *refer to those uses* that adults make of them. This has allowed us to understand that children do not just start imitating adults' conventional uses of objects from one day to the next. It is a rather long drawn-out, to-and-fro process of appropriation of meaning, of interaction and communication through the object between adult and child. Children progressively come to understand *aspects of the use* of objects. Conventional meanings are *gradually* configured. This process is very much dependent on the signs that adults display when communicating with children about what to do with ordinary objects. Children are able to "read" the public uses of objects thanks to the signs provided by adults. By relying on these signs, children are themselves able to

penetrate these spaces of meaning, and pose themselves the same goals adults do.

For example, none of the 7-month-old infants spontaneously carried out the conventional use of any of the available objects (the telephone and the truck). They only carried it out when the adult performed a *demonstration*, so introducing the child to the use of the object, whether it is conventional or symbolic. The adult tries to introduce the child to her own intentional network and this sometimes works.

At this moment of development, children only rely on certain kinds of signs produced by adults. Pointing gestures, which are much more complex than ostensive signs, are not understood by children as indicative. For example, when the adult persistently points to one of the holes of the truck in order for the child to introduce the block he holds, no child is able to interpret the gesture in those terms. No child takes the block and guides it towards the hole pointed by A, and no matter how many times the adult *demonstrates* how to put blocks inside the truck, no child imitates him/her. Children read the indexical gestures of adults as ostensive gestures, and not as gestures that indicate a *direction with respect to the use of an object*.

From 10 months of age on, the situation with the same objects is quite different, but not always. Even though in some cases an entrance is made into the conventional uses of the object, these uses are not systematic, nor always produced. The child frequently returns to uses characteristic of previous stages. In some cases, during the same sequence of film, children perform all types of uses, from more basic and undifferentiated uses (non-conventional) up to the specific use of these objects (conventional or symbolic). At this moment, children already know how to read the communicative indexical signs of the adult as such; that is, as a direction in relation to a use expected of *this* object with respect to the *other* object. This "reading" obviously helps them to carry out the conventional uses. But they do not always do so.

Therefore, children start to make conventional use of the telephone and the truck, in the latter case, by putting the blocks inside. Here we would like to highlight two aspects. The first conventional uses of the telephone are produced with the receiver (they raise the handle to their ear in many ways), but it is not until they are 13 months that they start to follow the succession of uses that characterize "making a phone call," such as dialing, holding the receiver to their ear and vocalizing at the same time, or handing the receiver to the adult so that she may use it. This leads us to suggest that the introduction to conventional uses (in this case, symbolic) is not produced suddenly, but gradually. The other aspect we would like to highlight is that by inserting the blocks in the truck, as the toy is meant to be used, the objects disappear – and children never search for them at 7 months. However, they do look for them when they are 10 months old, encouraged by the adult, who insists in many ways that the "object exists, even though we cannot see it," that it is *permanent*. As indicated above, adults live in a world of permanent objects, long before objects become permanent for the children. Hence, we also suggest that the adult plays an important role in the child's acquisition of object permanence. In the 13-month-old infant this "where is the block?" search disappears, indicating that since they already "know" it is there, that it is permanent, they do not need to look for it.

When they reach 13 months of age, children also employ "easier alternative strategies" to insert the blocks. For example, instead of inserting the block through its hole, they open the back door and insert them through there, as this requires less effort. The adult never uses these strategies, since they imply some sort of "cheating." This also indicates that children are more flexible in their ability to reach the desired goal.

When we began our research, we knew that the two objects presented are used for different things, whether in a symbolic space (making a telephone call) or in a conventional use (inserting the blocks into the truck and taking them out again). However, we were very much surprised by another fact we had not previously considered: different objects provoke semiotic mediators with different communicative functions. Therefore, *communication* (the signs employed in communication) *between subjects* is not produced in a vacuum, but is affected by the *type of object* around which the communication revolves.

Conventional Uses of Objects, Consciousness, and Private Gestures

We would not like to end this chapter without mentioning a study in process (Rodríguez & Palacios, 2005; *submitted*) in which we analyze the triadic interaction of Nerea, a girl with Down syndrome within a family context. At the beginning of the study Nerea was 12 months old. At that stage, she never took the initiative in carrying out the conventional use of the object, which consisted of inserting hoops of different sizes around a pivot. She was only able to introduce some hoops *after* her mother had performed for her several displays of signs: encouraging her, performing *multiple exaggerated ostensive* signs, presenting herself as a model, performing *immediate demonstrations*, and later returning to *distant demonstrations*, *pointing* time and again. Her *pointing* gestures were *immediate*, since she touched the object being pointed at the pivot, and they were *multiple*, because *she pointed repeatedly*.

Here we come to our main point. At 18 months of age, Nerea relies on various *private gestures*, that is, *ostensive* (Moro & Rodríguez, 2005) and *pointing gestures*, with a new reflexive function: communicating with herself. Ostensive and indexical signs had previously employed by her mother with a communicative function to indicate where she had to introduce the hoop. She relies on her own *private ostensive* and *pointing gestures* – she points with one hand towards the pivot and then tries to insert the hoop with the other.

It is not possible to understand the meaning of the *private pointing gesture* without also understanding what is being pointed at in the specific context. One has to include the object pointed at within a world of meanings, not just in relation to the gesture itself (the meaning of the gesture). These gestures become meaningful when they are connected to their contexts, in this case, with the conventional uses of objects. Once the conventional use is constituted, the use "guides" the gesture. Previously the opposite process was true, where it was the adult who, through gestures, contributed to the child's awakening to and configuration of meaning with respect to canonical uses of objects.

Initially in development, the other person directs gestures towards the child, trying to attract his attention towards something in the world, or to make him/her perform a specific action upon the world. At first, children do not usually understand these gestures: "if gesture, then modify something in the world". As we have described, they later come to understand the gesture the other directs towards them as linked to the expected use of the object. Even later on, the child uses the gesture, not with a communicative but reflexive aim – to "indicate to herself what she has to do" – with the degrees of consciousness it implies. In this way, they are correcting their thoughts with respect to the conventional use of the object, as a way of perfecting their own use and their own thoughts about such use. This is what happens to Nerea who, at 18 months of age, directed the gestures to herself as a means of "external thought" in a context where she had not yet *completely* mastered the conventional use of the object. Although she controlled the goal to be performed, she had serious difficulties in controlling the *means* by which that goal could be achieved. These gestures help her to "think the situation out" and to perfect the means she must apply.

So, the permanence granted by the conventional use of the object based on its materiality, as well as the permanence granted by the public use of gestures, imply that they are susceptible of being used as semiotic tools that help one to think about complex situations. They become, therefore, instruments that entail progressive degrees of consciousness. Such a form of consciousness, based on the ability to "turn on itself" (Bronckart, 2000; 2002), as communication

with oneself, and made of a network of signs (Vygotsky, 1934/1985), may be used to search for solutions in the context of object use, such as the case of Nerea.

It is communication with oneself. It is not about dialogue because the girl cannot yet talk. This is accomplished by the encounter between signs and the world, which allows one to read it. This encounter never occurs in a social vacuum.

Conclusion

Our objection to the "naturalistic view of the object," prevalent in early infancy studies, is that it excludes from cognitive development the social and functional dimension of objects. This in contrast with other Social Sciences where "things" have a "social life" (see Appadurai, 1986/2005; 1996). According to the naturalistic perspective, there is a directness, a spontaneity in the encounter between child and object. This view is based on the idea of the existence of a literal, obvious, direct, material reality, which can be approached only from *one* point of view – *God's point of view*, paraphrasing Putnam (1994). Such a "syntactic" view of the object ignores the complex reality of its everyday use (Costall, 2006). It is foreign to the cultural and educational influence of others on children's cognitive development.

In the first part of this chapter we discussed Bruner's work in the 1970s, influenced by the philosophers of the linguistic turn. He introduced the idea of "pragmatic opportunism" which humans use when solving problems. Language, therefore, cannot be treated merely as syntax and separate from its function. This "pragmatic wave" has continued to have considerable influence on research on language acquisition to this day. Nowadays nobody is surprised by the fact that there is well-developed non-linguistic communication before the child is able to talk, or by the suggestion that this communication influences and makes possible the development of language.

We went on to question the paradox that while contexts of use are given great importance in relation to language acquisition, this pragmatic orientation has not been duly applied to objects. It is as if objects were not part of our daily life, as if they were foreign to functions and public conventions of use, as if we "do not do things with objects." It is as if objects were not at all related to the cultural immersion of the child from her birth.

To try to find the reason for this absence of link between objects and cultural signs, we asked ourselves where the *natural* in natural signs lay. We briefly explore different semiotic perspectives (the Ancient Greeks, Saussure, Peirce, Eco), concluding that psychology has focused primarily on intentional, conventional signs and has left "natural" ones aside. But its greatest mistake has been confusing the *forms of production* of signs and their *interpretation*. It has ignored that natural signs can only be interpreted through conventional rules. Our complain fits very well with Alan Costall's (in this volume) when he refers to the dualism matter/mind and biology/culture as they are "institutionalized in the very structure of modern academic disciplines". He stresses that the natural sciences have abstracted for themselves a 'material world' set apart from human concerns, while the social sciences, in their turn have constructed "a world of actors devoid of things" (Joerges, 1988, quoted by Costall, this volume).

We have therefore stressed that objects are usually treated by researchers of early infancy as *natural* signs that bring about natural, spontaneous and direct interpretations. We then went on to claim that the construction of knowledge is triangular. This means the child holds an indirect relation with his environment, one that is, instead, mediated through the semiotic systems adults produce. The encounter between the child and the world is thus mediated by different systems of signs (Vygotsky, 1934/1985). The triadic interactions usually analyzed in early infancy tend to be exclusively those in which the child communicates intentionally with another about something in the world. But we need to look at triadic interactions long before the child begins to communicate intentionally in this way. Therefore, the unit of analysis for the construction of human psychological processes has to be triadic. In other words, without communication and education, cognitive development simply does not – *could* not – take place. Our claim is not new. Vygotsky stressed the triadic nature of human knowledge, and so does Sinha when, following Karl Bühler, says that "joint reference is the criterial basis for the emergence of symbolization" (2005a: 321).

In the last section, based on our own work on triadic adult-infant-object interaction, we highlighted the importance of longitudinal, microgenetic and qualitative research, based on the *processes* of construction, not only on their results. The Peircien approach to signs we have adopted, allows us to unity a semiotic analysis with the materiality of objects, to understand the kinds of meanings individuals are using at each moment in relation to the function of objects, and how children construct the shared public meanings of objects through communication with adults. Hence, from a certain stage of development onwards at the prelinguistic level, objects become for children "signs of their use." This work leads us to see the everyday object as irreducible to natural signs that lead to "natural" interpretations. It follows then that "[. . .] the world of imagination and symbolization is *not discontinuous from the material world*, but practically intertwined with, and ontologically embodied in this world" (Sinha, 2005b, stresses added). Objects as important protagonists in early cognitive development, when seen from a pragmatic perspective, are also part of the network of signs, culture and education.

In the previous section we also referred to a study in process of the functions of private pointing gestures and private ostensive gestures related to the conventional uses of objects in the case of a girl with Down syndrome. We concluded that pointing gestures and ostensive gestures first had a communicative function, as the adult often communicated with the child by pointing to things, events, etc. However, later on they ended up having a reflexive function, since the child used such gestures to guide or correct her/his own actions. The guidance thus provided by the adult through pointing and ostensive gestures, that is, external regulation turns into internal regulation when the child uses the same gestures with the same function to "think externally." Private gestures become "tools of thought." Consciousness is thus produced; signs are reflexively turned upon themselves (Rodríguez & Palacios, *submitted*). This helps the child to find a solution to difficulties when carrying out a conventional action upon the object. Applying signs to other signs – private pointing and ostensive gestures to the objects as conventionally used – means that the circle that began with others' semiotic regulations is thus closed. When children are able to use signs with a self-regulatory function, they can master their own destiny, by opening new degrees of freedom in the significations of acts.

Acknowledgments

I would like to thank Alan Costall and Vasu Reddy for their help, patience, and comments on different versions of this chapter.

Notes

1   The term "linguistic competence" was introduced by Chomsky in 1955, in one of the founding texts of the "cognitive revolution." In this text, Chomsky attempts to counter the thesis of linguistic behaviourism, according to which language is learned through trial and error, conditioning, reinforcements, and so on. He believes the speed with which the main linguistic structures are acquired cannot be explained in terms of learning, but is indicative of the existence of an innate and universal "linguistic disposition." Linguistic competence designates this disposition. Competence implies that there is a "mental organ" in the structures of the human mind/brain, which grants each individual an ideal and intrinsic capacity to produce and understand any given natural language. Even though the existence and properties of this innate organ are still currently affirmed, they have not been the object of any attempt at scientific validation (Bronckart & Dolz, 2002).

2   This exciting issue deserves more space and attention than we can offer here. We will just point out that 20th century philosophy has centred its reflection on language, leaving aside the meanings that do not follow its safe path. Nathan Houser (2002), an expert on Peirce, affirms that when pragmatism is connected essentially to language it becomes *pragmatics*, which is different. This occurred from the 1930s onwards, with the influence of the immigrants from the Circle of Vienna in the United States. The intellectual influences Morris was exposed to, the American pragmatists and most of all Peirce, were responsible for Morris' insistence on adding a third pragmatic dimension to the division of syntax and semantics proposed by Carnap. According to Houser, the encounter between Morris and Carnap gives pragmatics a profound linguistic turn. This turn does not coincide with the wider concern with meaning that must necessarily go beyond the margins of language. This linguistic turn that takes place in the first third of the 20th century has profound effects in our discipline. It affects, as we can see in Bruner's work, much of the foundations of infant development (Rodríguez & Moro, 2002).

3   We are far from the situation John Shotter faced in 1970s England, when he observed mothers and pre-linguistic children solving problems in interaction, but did not know how to quantify and present the data in a rigorous, scientific manner: "[...] we were still somewhat at sea, aware that we were not able to present experiments or testing hypotheses as such, that we were not able to present measurements or 'objective data'. It was clear that there was something here of great importance not captured in previous, more hard-nosed approaches, but we did not know how publicly to present what we were observing. We badly lacked a leader and protector. Jerry [Bruner]'s arrival in England [and the creation between 1972 and 1976 of "a kind of travelling workshop/seminar" connecting Nottingham, Cambridge, Edinburgh and Oxford] "gave us the focus we needed" (2001, 170).

4   Michel Deleau (1990) strongly stresses this idea. Picking up on Henri Wallon's critique of Piaget in the 1940s, he claims that the

conventions characteristic of semiotic functions cannot be the product of an individual discovery by a solitary subject.

5 Saussure makes his position clear in relation to language in his well-known phrase: "Signs that are wholly arbitrary realise better than the others the ideal of the semiological process; that is why language, the most complex and universal of all systems of expression, is also the most characteristic" (1916/1985: 69). But there is another aspect of Saussure that is much less spoken of – he never claimed signs were free of convention, so the social is present in all his semiology. In our reading of Saussure's work (Rodríguez & Moro, 2002) we could say he sees a certain gradation in terms of convention. Language would be the highest, because the relationship between signifier and signified is so conventional that it is arbitrary. Other systems which are also conventional are, nevertheless, less arbitrary. For example, when he speaks of the scale as a symbol of justice, even though the relationship between both is conventional, it is not entirely arbitrary. Saussure states, that we find here "the rudiment of a natural bond between the signifier and the signified." And he justifies this by saying that "[T]he symbol of justice, a pair of scales, could not be replaced by just any other symbol, such as a chariot" (ibid.).

6 Many researchers followed the path initiated by Bruner and became interested in language from the perspective of its usage (Ninio & Snow, 1996; Tomasello & Rakoczy, 2003), or approached early communication from a pragmatic perspective (Guidetti, 2003).

7 There is, since Ancient times, a practical semiotic knowledge connected to the experience of hunters, sailors, doctors, i.e., of those who interpret traces or evidence (Castañares, 2002: 350). In fact, the practical knowledge of doctors – their interest in the particular (Wertsch, 1996/2000) and their reading in terms of indices, of the non-linguistic materiality, as a sign of something – remains intact to our day. Castañares claims this semiotic tradition was passed on to philosophers unlinked to reflection on (or at least not unified with) language. Two traditions are, in this manner, torn apart. One of them is tied to the term semeîon, the other to terms used in the linguistic context such as logos, symbolon, etc. This can be clearly seen in Aristotle, for whom names are all "signifying by convention" and are, thus, symbols. This interpretation fits "the original sense of symbolon: each of the parts or halves of an object that two guests, friends or contracting parts, break, each keeping one part in order to have proof or evidence of the relationship established, so that it can also serve as proof of their own identity" (ibid., translated by us). But when Aristotle refers to semeîon, the aspect of social convention is missing. One of the examples he gives is "It has milk, therefore it has given birth" (ibid.). Semeîon is, hence, more closely associated with what doctors are interested in; with a sense closely associated to that of the words "symptom" or "indication." Its inferential relationship is hypothetical; sometimes fully demonstrative, sometimes not.

8 Daddesio (1994) has also dealt with the difference between the form of interpretation and of production of natural signs. "[...] such natural signs involve much more than the direct apprehension of a simple causal link; they are embedded in a symbol system that makes the correct interpretation of the sign possible. ... I believe, a *fundamental confusion between the manner in which a sign is produced and the manner in which it is interpreted*" (p. 110–11, underlined by us).

9 Nevertheless, what has often been stressed is that when action is not at the core, children are capable of doing many things before the age indicated by Piaget. For instance, according to Philippe Rochat "Piaget's classical theory on child development was wrong to interpret that children's actions are a direct reflection of their cognitive competence. Recent studies on early infancy show that babies know much more than what the observer can grasp when her/his view centres on self-generated actions on objects [...] Babies are active explorers from the time they are born, but clumsy actors who develop relatively slowly" (2001/2004: 171).

10 Some readers may have recognized the influence of these studies on Vygotsky.

References

Appadurai, A. (1986/2005) (Ed.). *The social life of things. Commodities in cultural perspective.* Cambridge: Cambridge University Press.

Appadurai, A. (1996). *Modernity at Large. Cultural Dimensions of Globalization.* Minneapolis: University of Minnesota Press.

Bates, Elisabeth; Begnini, L., Bretherton, I., Camaioni, Luigia; Volterra, Virginia, Carlson, V. Carpen, K. Y. Rosser, M. (1979). *The emergence of symbols: Cognition and communication in Infancy*. New York: Academic Press.

Barthes, R. (1985). *L'aventure sémiologique*. Paris: Seuil.

Bouveresse, J. (1998). *Le philosophe et le réel. Entretiens avec Jean-Jacques Rosat*. Paris: Editions Hachette.

Bremner, G. (2001). Cognitive development: Knowledge of the physical world. In G. Bremner & A. Fogel (Eds.), *Blackwell handbook of infant development* (pp. 99–138). Oxford: Blackwell.

Bresson, F., & Lebovici, S. (1989). Le développement du langage et la genèse de la communication. In S. Lebovici & F. Weil-Halpern (Eds.), *Psychopathologie du bébé* (pp. 191–197). Paris: PUF.

Bronckart, J. P. (2000). El problema de la conciencia como "analizador" de las epistemologías de Vygotski y de Piaget. In S. Aznar & E. Serrat (Coords.), *Piaget y Vygotski ante el siglo XXI: referentes de actualidad* (pp. 15–41). Universitat de Girona. Institut de Ciències de l'Educació: Horsori.

Bronckart, J. P. (2002). La explicación en Psicología ante el desafío del significado. *Estudios de Psicología*, 23(3), 387–416.

Bronckart, J. P., & Dolz, J. (2002). La notion de competence: Quelle pertinence pour l'étude de l'apprentissage des actions langagières? In J. Dolz & E. Ollagnier (Eds.), *L'énigme de la compétence en éducation* (pp. 27–44). Bruxelles: De Boeck Université.

Bruner, J. (1975). From communication to Language. A Psychological Perspective. *Cognition*, 3(1), 255–287.

Bruner, J. (1978). Foreword. In A. Lock (Ed.), *Action, gesture and symbol. The emergence of language* (pp. vii–viii). London: Academic Press.

Bruner, J. (1982/1984). Los formatos de la adquisición del lenguaje. In *Jerome Bruner. Acción, pensamiento y lenguaje* (pp. 173–185). Madrid: Alianza. Compilación de J.L. Linaza.

Bruner, J. (1983). Préface. In J. Bruner. *Le développement de l'enfant. Savoir faire, savoir dire* (pp. 7–9). París: P.U.F. Texts translated and presented by Michel Deleau.

Bruner, J. (1990). *Acts of meaning*. Cambridge: Harvard University Press.

Bühler, K. (1934/1990). Theory of Language. The representational function of language. Amsterdam/Philadelphia: John Benjamins.

Carrió, G., & Rabosi, E. (1981/990). La filosofía de John L. Austin. In J. Austin (1962). *Cómo hacer cosas con palabras*. Barcelona: Paidós.

Castañares, W. (1985). El signo: Problemas semióticos y filosóficos. Tesis doctoral. Madrid: Universidad Complutense de Madrid.

Castañares, W. (2002). Signo y representación en las teorías semióticas. *Estudios de Psicología*, 23(3), 339–357.

Cassirer, E. (1964/1998). *Filosofía de las formas simbólicas. I Lenguaje*. México: Fondo de Cultura Económica.

Costall, A. (2007). The windowless room: 'Mediationism' and how to get over it (this handbook).

Costall, A. (2006). *Doing things with things: The Design and Use of Ordinary Objects*. London: Ashgate.

Cronkhite, G. (1990). Psychosemiotics. In T. Sebeok and J. Umiker-Sebeok (Eds.). *The semiotic web 1989* (pp. 547–586). Berlin, New York: Mouton de Gruyter.

Daddesio, T. (1994). *On minds and symbols*. Berlin: Mouton de Gruyter.

Delgado, B., Gómez, J. C., & Sarriá, E. (1999). Non-communicative pointing in preverbal children. Poster presented at the *IXth European Conference on Developmental Psychology*. Spetses, Greece.

Delgado, B., Gómez, J. C., & Sarriá, E. (2004). Is pointing more than a communicative gesture? A study about the role of pointing in regulating one's own attention. Poster presented at the *18th Biennial Meeting of the International Society for the Study of Behavioural Development (ISSBD)* July. Gante, Belgium.

Deleau, M. (1990). *Les origines sociales du développement mental. Communication et symboles dans la première enfance*. Paris: Armand Colin.

Eco, U. (1973/1988). *Signo*. Barcelona: Labor.

Guidetti, M. (2003). *Pragmatique et psychologie du développement. Comment communiquent les jeunes enfants*. Paris: Belin.

Hierro, J. (1986). *Principios de filosofía del lenguaje*. Madrid: Alianza.

Houser, N. (2002). *Some thoughts about pragmatics (from a Peircean perspective)*. Conference presented in the Faculty of Education. Unpublished manuscript. Universidad Autónoma de Madrid.

Lavelli, M., Pantoja, A., Hsu, H. C., Messinger, D., & Fogel, A. (2005). Using microgenetic designs to study change processes. In D. Teti (Ed.), *Handbook of research methods in developmental science*. Oxford: Blackwell.

Lock, A. (2001). Preverbal communication. In G. Bremner & A. Fogel (Eds.), *Blackwell handbook of infant development* (pp. 379–403). Oxford: Blackwell.

Martí, E. (2003). *Representar el mundo externamente. La adquisición infantil de los sistemas de representación*. Madrid: Visor.

Mili, I., & Rickenmann, R. (2004). La construction des objets culturels dans l'enseignement artistique et musical. In C. Moro & R. Rickenmann (Eds.), *Situation éducative et significations* (pp. 165–196). Bruxelles: De Boeck.

Moro, C., & Rodríguez, C. (2004). L'éducation et le signe comme conditions de possibilité du développement. Un questionnement qui transcende les frontières disciplinaires. In Chatelanat, G., Moro, C. & Saada-Robert, M. (Eds.), *Unité et pluralité des sciences de l'éducation. Sondages au coeur de la recherche*. Bern-New York: Peter Lang.

Moro, C., & Rodríguez, C. (2005). *L'objet et la construction de son usage chez le bébé. Une approche sémiotique du développement préverbal*. Berne-New York: Peter Lang.

Nelson, K. (1996). *Language in cognitive development. The emergence of the mediated mind*. Cambridge: Cambridge University Press.

Ninio, A., & Snow, C. (1996). *Pragmatic development*. Oxford: WestviewPress.

Nogues, L., Weil-Barais, A., Villeret, O., & Bouchafa, H. (2005). Noter pour se souvenir de quantiés discrètes et continues et faire des déductions: comparaison d'enfants en CE1 et en CM2 (8 et 11 ans). Communication présentée dans le colloque Internationale, *Noter pour Penser. Approches développementales et didactiques*. Université d'Angers 27–28 Janvier.

Overton, W. (1994). Contexts of meaning: The computational and the embodied mind. In W. Overton & D. Palermo (Eds.), *The nature and ontogenesis of meaning* (pp. 1–18). Hillsdale, NJ: Lawrence Erlbaum.

Peirce, Ch. S. (1885). *The writings of Charles S. Peirce. Vol. 5*. Bloomington: Indiana University Press.

Peirce, Ch. S. (1896/1931). *Collected Papers*. The Regenerated Logic, Cambridge, MA: Harvard University Press.

Peirce, Ch. S. (1904/1977). *Semiotic and Significs: The Correspondence Between Charles S. Peirce and Victoria Lady Welby*. Bloomington: Indiana University Press.

Piaget, J. (1936/1977). *La naissance de lintelligence chez lenfant*. Neuchâtel-Paris: Delachaux et Niestlé.

Piaget, J. (1937/1977). *La construction du réel chez l'enfant*. Neuchâtel-Paris: Delachaux et Niestlé.

Putnam, H. (1994). *Words and life*. Cambridge: Harvard University Press.

Reddy, V. (2001). Mind knowledge in the first year. In G. Bremner & A. Fogel (Eds.), *Blackwell handbook of infant development* (pp. 241–264). Oxford: Blackwell.

Rochat, P. (2001/2004). *El mundo del bebé*. Madrid: Morata.

Rodríguez, C. (2003). *Hitos en el desarrollo temprano y prevención de la discapacidad*. Published in CD by the organizers of the Congress "Current Perspectives on Special Education." Ciudad de México, September.

Rodríguez, C. (2006). *Del ritmo al símbolo. Los signos en el nacimiento de la inteligencia*. Barcelona: ICE-Horsori.

Rodríguez, C., & Moro, C. (1998). *El mágico número tres. Cuando los niños aún no hablan*. Barcelona: Paidós.

Rodríguez, C., & Moro, C. (1998a). El uso convencional también hace permanentes a los objetos. *Infancia y Aprendizaje*, 84, 67–83.

Rodríguez, C., & Moro, C. (2002). Objeto, comunicación y símbolo. Una mirada a los primeros usos simbólicos de los objetos. *Estudios de Psicología* 23/3, 323–338.

Rodríguez, C., & Palacios, P. (2005). Les gestes privés et les origines de la conscience. Communication présentée dans le colloque Internationale, *Noter pour Penser. Approches développementales et didactiques*. Université d'Angers 27–28 Janvier.

Rodríguez, C., & Palacios, P. (*submitted*). Do Private Gestures (ostensive and pointing) have a self-regulatory function? A case study. In Legerstee, M. & Reddy, V. (Ed.) Monograph in preparation.

Rodríguez, C., Palacios, P. & Vázquez, J. (2005). First symbols in a girl with Down syndrome. Paper presented at the *First ISCAR Congress*. Sevilla 20–24th September.

Saada-Robert, M., & Balslev, K. (2004). Une microgenèse située des significations et des savoirs. In C. Moro et R. Rickenmann (Eds.),

Situation éducative et significations (pp. 135–163). Bruxelles: De Boeck.

Saussure (De), F. (1916/1985). *Cours de linguistique générale*. Edition critique préparée par Tullio de Mauro. París: Payot. [English version: *Course in General Linguistics*. New York: McGraw-Hill, 1966]

Shotter, J. (2001). Towards a third revolution in Psychology: From inner mental representations to dialogically-structured social practices. In D. Bakhurst & S. G. Shanker (Ed.), *Jerome Bruner. Language, culture and self* (pp. 167–183). London: Sage Publications.

Sinha, C. (2000). Culture, Language and the Emergence of Subjectivity. *Culture & Psychology*, 6(2), 197–207.

Sinha, C. (2005a). Biology, Culture and the Emergence and Elaboration of Symbolization. In A. Saleemi, O. Bohn & A. Gjedde (Ed.), *In Search of a Language for the mind-brain: Can the Multiple Perspectives be Unified?* (pp. 311–335). Aarhus: Aarhus University Press.

Sinha, C. (2005b). Blending out of the background: Play, props and staging in the material world. *Journal of Pragmatics*, 37, 1537–1554.

Thelen, E., & Smith, L. (1994/1998). *A dynamic systems approach to the development of cognition and action*.Cambridge: MIT Press.

Tomasello, M. (2001). Bruner on language acquisition. In D. Bakhurst & S. G. Shanker (Eds.), *Jerome Bruner. Language, culture and self* (pp. 31–49). London: Sage Publications.

Tomasello, M., & Rakoczy, H. (2003). What makes human cognition unique? From individual to shared to collective intentionality. *Mind & Language*, 18, 2, 121–147.

Trevarthen, C., & Hubley, P. (1978). Secondary Intersubjectivity: Confidence, Confiding and Acts of Meaning in the First Year. In A. Lock (Ed.), *Action, gesture and symbol. The emergence of language* (pp. 183–229). London: Academic Press.

Van Der Veer, R., & Valsiner, J. (1991). *Understanding Vygotsky. A Quest for synthesis*. Cambridge: Blackwell.

Vygotsky, L. S. (1934/1985). *Pensée et Langage*. Paris: Editions Sociales.

Wertsch, J. (1996/2000). El papel de la racionalidad abstracta en la imagen vygotskiana de la mente. In A. Tryphon & J. Vonèche (Comps.), *Piaget-Vygotsky: La génesis social del pensamiento* (pp. 41–63). Buenos Aires: Paidós.

Wilkins, D. (2003). Why pointing with the index finger is not a universal (In sociocultural and semiotic terms). In S. Kita (Ed.), *Pointing: Where language, culture and cognition meet* (pp. 171–215). New Jersey: Lawrence Erlbaum Associates.

Wirthner, M., & Schneuwly, B. (2004). Variabilité et contrainte dans la construction des significations d'un objet d'enseignement. L'effet d'un outil pour enseigner le résumé d'un texte informatif. In C. Moro & R. Rickenmann (Eds.), *Situation éducative et significations* (pp. 107–133). Bruxelles: De Boeck.

Wittgenstein, L. (1953/1958). *Philosophical investigations*. Englewood Cliffs: Prentice-Hall.

CHAPTER 13

Network of Meanings

A Theoretical-Methodological Perspective for the Investigation of Human Developmental Processes

M. Clotilde Rossetti-Ferreira, Katia S. Amorim, and Ana Paula S. Silva

UBUNTU UNGAMNTU NGANYE ABANTU – People are people through other people

> *Xhosa proverb – Nelson Mandela's mother langue*

Foreword

In this chapter we intend to introduce the *Network of Meanings*, a theoretical-methodological perspective, which is being constructed for the investigation and understanding of the complex processes of human development. Such perspective presupposes development as a time-irreversible co-construction of an active person through the interactions he/she establishes, in specific scenarios, which are socially and culturally organized. Thus, metaphorically, it proposes that development occurs through a network of meanings, of semiotic configuration, composed by organic, physical, interactional, social, economical, cultural, and political elements. Interrelations between those elements create arrangements with specific configurations. They structure, signify, and canalize a set of possible actions, emotions, and conceptions, acting as constraints on the situation, providing possibilities and limits to the persons' behaviors and development. Due to constant changes in some of the involved dimensions, a continuous construction and reconstruction of the nets occurs. Through these, and as a product of the figure and background movements, certain processes and meanings emerge and acquire dominance, while others nestle at a second level, until new events occur in the continuous flow of the situations, rearranging the network. Thus, development is conceived to occur by the continuous (re)configuration of nets. In this process, language, knowledge, and the person's subjectivity are being continuously and reciprocally constituted and transformed. As the goal of the perspective is its use for an analysis of developmental processes, throughout time and across situations, different nets are mapped, reconstructing each stage and capturing the movements, within which changes are identified. Analysis is done, seeking to apprehend new and old behaviors, emotions, and conceptions, searching for the origins of the changes, in order to apprehend the co-constructive processes and persons' mutual transformations in specific situations. In this perspective, interaction has a relevant role, both as a process and as a foreground focus of analysis, as it is through interactions that a set of possible actions and discursive practices (Pinheiro & Spink, 2004) are structured and interpreted. A complex relationship between researcher–researched is conceived, where the object of investigation contributes to constrain the network of meanings in which the researcher is embedded, canalizing the interpretation of the observable events. By this way, data are constructed in the interaction of the researcher with the object of investigation.

Initially, the *Network of Meanings* perspective was elaborated for the study of the insertion of babies into day care. We are now extending its use for the analysis of a wider range of situations, subjects, interactive fields, scenarios, and elements of the socio-historical matrix. Situations involving crisis and transformations are a preferential focus for study, as they favor developmental changes, but also because they usually lead to abrupt emergence of emotions, new concept uses, and conflicts within the social group. By that, changes gain visibility, helping researchers in their efforts at making sense of the situation.

In this presentation of the perspective, a special focus will be given to theoretical issues, that is, to the main concepts, as their uses in various empirical studies have been published elsewhere. Beforehand, some details about the history of its production will be provided.

The Perspective Production Background

Along the last 15 years, settled in the field of Developmental Psychology, we have been working on and investigating human developmental processes, which occur within diverse complex situations. Some were related to babies' adaptation to day care centers (Amorim, Vitoria, & Rossetti-Ferreira, 2000; Amorim & Rossetti-Ferreira, 2005), to the development of individuals involved in criminal acts (Silva, 2003), to children's adoption and fostering (Solon, Costa, & Rossetti-Ferreira, 2005), and to the inclusion of children with special needs at regular schools (Yazlle, 2001; Roriz, 2005).

At the outset, instigated by the increasing and controversial situation of babies' attendance into a daycare center, we focused our studies on early child development in collective educational environments and, more specifically, on the process of integration of babies and families into day care centers.

The group's awareness regarding this issue was the result of multiple queries that emerged throughout the last decades. It was stimulated both by our investigations on children development in daycare center settings, and by the group's active involvement on various intervention activities within regional and national early child care and educational systems, as well as on its direct involvement in the organization of a university daycare center at our Campus.

Supported by a dialogue between theory, research, and practice, typical of our approach, the work in progress challenged us to analyze the encounter between diverse contexts (family, daycare center, work, social policies, health, and educational institutions), in which various persons were directly or indirectly involved, each one with its own perspectives, needs and privileged partners. Moreover, as our research group's characteristic is of being composed by professionals from diverse knowledge fields (psychology, medicine, pedagogy, nursery, nutrition, occupational therapy, among others), the investigated issues were viewed through diverse lenses, making explicit different interpretations, as well as drawing attention to the various controversies and conflicts regarding the studied objects. Our data and debates exposed many divergences and confrontations, which occurred throughout that investigative process.

By being so, and based on cultural-historical assumptions (Bakhtin, 1934/1981, 1990; Volosinov, 1929/;2000; Vygotsky, 1978; Wallon, 1941, 1959a, 1959b; and, Valsiner, 1987), we looked for research approaches able to analyze the complex intertwinement of personal, relational, and contextual elements, which occur during developmental processes. This compelled us to explore different theoretical-methodological perspectives of analysis, looking for research methodologies able to provide innovative, dynamic and inclusive views about those complex issues.

The search for research paradigms able to apprehend and analyze complex phenomena in their multiple dimensions, with an integrated and inclusive way, has been increasingly common both in the biological and social sciences (Kuhn, 1962; Morin, 1990, 1996).

Those views are usually referred to as systemic, although they may vary widely. Some consensual points, however, may be mentioned, such as: the center of attention moves from the individual to the persons in interaction; the focus on the influence of one person over the other is substituted by looking for the interdependence, reciprocity and synergism between/among the various participants in the situation; an interest on an ecological view of the phenomena (as interdependent and in reciprocal transformation with its environment) prevails over the use of laboratory observations which allows a better control of variables.

The author that best represents this ecological and systemic view in developmental psychology is Urie Bronfenbrenner (1979, 1993). He conceives the persons' developmental contexts as nestled structures, which are interdependent and in continuous interaction. Those contexts encompass both policies, ideologies and governmental institutions, which compose the macrosetting and exosetting. As well, microsettings, where face-to-face interactions take place, and mesosettings, where the interference of one setting over the other can be observed, such as the mother's job over her here-and-now interactions with her baby at home or with the caregivers at the day care center. Bronfenbrenner proposed his ecological perspective of human development based on the analysis of various research projects developed by other investigators with large samples and through complex multifactor analyses of events and situations.

However, our research work evolved from ample and diversified data basis, encompassing various short-term case studies with small samples. An effort was made both to approach the situation in its various features, from varied positions and perspectives, and to apprehend the processes of persons and contexts reciprocal transformations. Thus, our search associated to our empirical studies led us to elaborate the *Network of Meanings* perspective (Rossetti-Ferreira, Amorim, & Vitória, 1996, 1997; Amorim, Vitória, & Rossetti-Ferreira, 2000; Rossetti-Ferreira, Amorim, & Silva, 1999, 2000, 2004).

Introducing the *Network of Meanings* Perspective

This perspective proposes development as occurring throughout life span, as time-irreversible co-constructions of active persons (Valsiner, 1994), in the course of the multiple interactions and relations established, within culturally and socially organized environments. Human development would take place, thus, immersed in a semiotic mesh of elements, dialectically interrelated to each other. Aspects of the persons and of the contexts in which they are inserted are thus considered as inseparable parts of mutual constitution.

As the theoretical-methodological perspective name alludes, this approach belongs to a field that highlights the discursive nature and semiotic character of human constitution. Such position attributes a central role to the interaction, to the processes of meaning production and transaction, and to the co-construction of the act of "signific-action." Thus, it emphasizes the primordial role occupied by the dialogical processes and interactive fields.

The Interactive Fields

The relevance of the interactive fields can be tracked back to birth, as the baby's survival is only guaranteed through his/her relationship with the social other. Amongst all species, the human baby is the one who is born with the greatest motor immaturity and incompleteness, being unable to survive by him/herself. An intimate relation with and a continuous investment and assistance of a human social partner are vital for the child's survival and development (Wallon, 1959b).

Despite the recognition of the baby's long-term immaturity, it is understood that the baby-other relationship is dialogically constructed, supported by a phylogenetic optimization of the infant's emotional expressiveness. Hence, since birth, the baby is endowed with a complex biological repertoire, with a certain perceptual, behavioral, and expressive organization, which allows him/herself to establish and get the most out of interchanges with the social others, setting the child as an active partner in the bond formation (Trevarthen, 1986; Meltzoff, 1990; Fogel, 1993; Carvalho, 1998; Bussab & Ribeiro, 1998). Moreover, those infant's competencies are only thought as effective as the social others are capable of being touched by and able to (re)act within the established relations. Thus, it is understood, that the baby–other dyad has phyllogenetically evolved as an interactive system (Carvalho, 1983).

The interconnected nature of those relations allows one to assert that when a baby is born, also a mother, a father, a sibling, a grandparent, etc., are also "born." Moreover, through the ongoing interactions that occur between them, across time and situations, various positions or roles will be taken over, confronted, rejected, and/or negotiated. Hence, it is through those relationships that the baby's and the social other's actions take place and acquire meanings (Rossetti-Ferreira, Amorim & Vitoria, 1997).

Furthermore, those social others act as mediators, by inserting the child in certain contexts and positions. They complement and interpret the baby for the world and the world for the baby. Through the social *other* and his/her movements and languages, the baby's first attitudes take shape (Wallon, 1959b).

At present, in Western societies, the most significant social other at the beginning of life is usually the mother and/or father. Other people, however, often take upon and/or share that role with the parents – as grandparents, stepparents, neighbors, nannies, daycare center caregivers, and so on – through their interactions with the child, within socially and culturally structured environments. Together, those various social others simultaneously favor / promote / limit / restrain certain conditions and directions for the development of the child. Those directions set by the different social *others* can be diverse and even contradictory. They are continuously (re)dimensioned during the persons' socialization process and they result from an interconnected individual and social manner to conceive and objectify the expectations for that specific child.

The infant, however, is not totally submissive to the other and the context. Since birth and throughout life, relations are understood as *co*-constructed by *inter*-actions, that is, by sharing and interdependent situated actions. Those actions are established through dialogical processes, in which each person (including the infant) has his/her behavioral flow continuously canalized and framed by others and by him/herself – through a role coordination process – in specific situations. Within this role coordination, persons in interaction can accept, deny, confront, negotiate and/or recreate the roles/positions. Also, when acting, persons dialogically transform him/herself and their interactive partners, while are transformed by them. Hence, the psychological functions that give them support are modified, remodeling their purposes, while opening new possibilities of actions, interactions and development (Oliveira & Rossetti-Ferreira, 1994, 1996).

The centrality of the social relations for human development is not restricted to the first years of life. Otherness will stay as the arena / motor of the developmental process throughout the person's life. Through multiple experiences with others in varied contexts, where diverse semiotic resources get available, various roles/positions can be reciprocally apprehended, constructed, and transformed by each person. In here-and-now situations, the emergence of roles/positions occur through processes of fusion and differentiation, in a dynamic segmentation and unification of fragments of lived experiences, interlinked with perceptions of the present moment and future perspectives, altogether constrained by the characteristics of the context in which they are inserted.

The Contexts

As mentioned before, the persons' developmental processes always occur within culturally and socially organized contexts. These are constituted by the social environment, with its organizational and economical structure, and guided by specific functions, rules, routines and schedules. Each specific context defines and simultaneously is defined by the persons who are actually or virtually present in it, with their specific characteristics, status, social roles and roles/positions, which contribute for the professional, personal, affective, and hierarchical construction of relationships among the participants. Each context also carries and is embedded in local and general history, which is intertwined with the participants' present goals, values system, prevailing conceptions, beliefs, and future expectations. Thus, the context has a fundamental role as its participants have to occupy certain places and positions – and not others – contributing for the emergence of certain personal aspects – and not others. Hence, it simultaneously favors and restricts the interactions and the developmental pathways that can occur within such context.

As stated by Wallon (1959b), the context can be understood as having simultaneously two functions: one of environment, context or behavioral field ("*milieu*"); and one of condition, means, instrument or developmental tool ("*moyen*"). Through it, the person's field of experience, socially and historically organized, also constitutes an instrument for his/her own development.

Furthermore, it is understood that certain environmental aspects, which are important for a person at a certain age (in order to build abilities or a set of meanings), can be shifted or modified, giving place, at other moments, to diverse aspects of the environment, as new privileged sources of developmental support.

Accordingly, the context (*milieu/moyen*) can only be defined in its relation to the person or a specific group of people who attend it, with certain competencies, interests and goals, at a particular socio-historical moment. Simultaneously, its characteristics evoke actions / emotions / conceptions in those people in interaction, as it exerts a symbolic power over them, thus delimiting and opening up a set of concrete possibilities to the persons' behaviors. Thus, both persons and context are reciprocally and dialectically constituted and transformed.

Hence, within a certain context, people are, at the same time, submitted to environmental characteristics, while simultaneously being actively involved in its co-construction, by accepting, confronting, fighting, denying, and/or negotiating the context restraints and possibilities. Thus, it is not possible to consider the context without the persons in it. People / relationships / contexts are altogether facets that cannot be thought in a disarticulated or fragmented way, as there are no persons without context and no context without interacting persons.

The Person

In Psychology (among other fields) theoreticians, such as Spink (2004), have pointed to the difficulties, contradictions, and troubles brought by the notions of *individual* and *subject*, as these terms assume the human being as a unit (indivisible entity), or as having a fundamental nature, in a certain way autonomous of his/her environment. Departing from a paradigm that highlights complexity and person-other-context interdependence, we have opted for using the term *person*. Its utilization seeks to ensure the non-dissociable processes of person-environment mutual constitution.

As such, the human being is always seen in relation, co-constructed through interactions with the others, within a certain socio-historical context. Thus, the person gets him/herself differentiated and alike in the relational field (Sampson, 1993). The person's own characteristics are constructed within the relational history and acquire meanings within situated and contextualized relations. In the same way, the other is constituted and defined by me and by the other, and at the same time, I constitute myself and I am defined *with* and by the other. It is within this interplay that the process of co-construction of personal and collective identity, throughout lifespan, develops.

That interdependence, typical of the relational processes with the other, sets the person within interactive games, within which a relational net, impregnated and traversed by discourse, opens and/or interdicts possible roles and positions to be taken up. This characteristic indicates the dialogical foundation of the human constitution, as well as the multiplicity of human character. The person is multiple – because multiple and heterogeneous are the various others with which he/she interacts (Hermans, 2002; Hermans & Kempen, 1995; also see Salgado & Gonçalves, 2006; Salgado & Gonçalves, Chapter 26 in this volume). The person is multiple because multiple are the voices that compose the social world and the interactive fields and positions he/she occupies in discursive practices. This multiplicity of voices and positioning establishes dialogue among each other, submitting the person, while simultaneously preserving a gap for novelty and construction of new positions and meaning processes concerning the world, the other and him/herself.

By being so, the persons' characteristics and attributes, who he/she thinks to be, the feeling of being one and unique – although relatively constant throughout time – is frequently questioned and reinstated by the person, chiefly at moments of transformation or crisis. There are strong socio-historical, economic, ideological, and cultural constraints acting over that process. In fact, at present day western middle class societies, it favors a socio-cultural construction that stresses permanence and individualization, sustained by language, routines and institutional documents. That feeling, on the other hand, is also sustained by the concrete existence of a body, and by the person's daily relationships with a group of people (other concrete embodied persons), with relatively stable patterns of interaction, within similar concrete contexts.

The person's singularity can also be analyzed in the discursive practices, where it is expressed by the impossibility of the other occupying the same discursive and spatial-temporal place (Harré, 1998). That necessary differentiation allows the continuous construction of particular and differentiated selves, with attributes and feelings of uniqueness. Hence, despite being social and relational constructions, the process of becoming a person does not imply an absence of singularity.

The Socio-Historical Matrix

The interactive processes established among persons within specific contexts are considered as embedded in and traversed by a socio-historical matrix, which is conceived as being composed by social, economical, historical, political, and cultural elements. It is constituted by discursive aspects interrelated with the socio-economical, political conditions, and power relationships in which people are inserted, interacting and developing.

The socio-historical matrix is, thus, understood as composed by multiple and often opposing life conditions and discursive practices. For instance, we can mention the strong social expectation regarding the mother in way that she should occupy the role of her children caretaking (at least during their first years of life). Simultaneously, there is a huge dynamic movement impelling women toward the work labor force. Each of these are conceived as a miniature arena, where occurs intersection and confrontation among social values with contradictory orientations, derived from diverse social processes and historical periods (Volosinov/Bakhtin, 1929/2000).

Such complexity, encompassing a multiplicity of possible meanings, points of view, affectionate and power relationships as well as discursive practices contain and promote deviation, dispersion, and contradiction. Yet, it reveals that the socio-historical matrix is more fluid, flexible and process-focused in its nature, entailing more malleable constraints on the person's developmental pathways. The recognition of such complexity allows the researcher to apprehend more closely the daily interactions and development vicissitudes (Amorim, 2002; Amorim & Rossetti-Ferreira, 2005).

The multiplicity and fluidity of the socio-historical matrix aspects, however, inevitably leads to ambiguity, confrontations and conflicts between the same person and/or between two or more persons in situated interactions. As such, it calls for continuous negotiation among those people.

Furthermore, the socio-historical matrix is understood as having concreteness in here-and-now situations. Such matrix concreteness can be disclosed, for instance, through the kind of environment in which the child is cared for (home, daycare center) and the person who cares for the child (mother, grandmother, nanny, daycare center caregiver, and so on); also, by the environment spatial organization, routines and discursive practices. Furthermore, through the place where the child is set (lap, floor, baby pram); the child's posture promoted (laying down, sitting, standing); the adult's location in rela-

tion to the child (close, far; beside, on the back); frequency and quality of contact; what is highlighted (the parents, objects, other children); the degree of autonomy given; the way they intercede when the child faces difficulties. Cultural aspects emerge (as also stated by Fogel, 1993) in the body experience, through sensations and movements. Also through the mother's movement when she picks the child up, by the way she touches him/her, her tone and modulation of voice. Chiefly during the child's first years of life, culture and meanings are constructed by the child's body instead of the words. Such concreteness occurs through the dialogical processes established, within specific scenarios.

Thus, it is precisely the persons who will perpetuate, transmit, modify, reconstruct, and create new voices and conditions, within the already existing multiplicity of voices and conditions. This leads us to stress that the socio-historical matrix does not exist outside the persons' relations and lives, impelling us to articulate the micro and macro social levels. As such, it disrupts the traditional split between personal and collective dimensions, asserting that the latter is concretely present in the former.

The socio-historical matrix is thus considered as existing only through a mutual process of constitution, as it helps to constrain the persons' development, while those very same persons give life to it, participate on its constitution, in a continuous and reciprocal becoming. Therefore, it can be said that the person is co-author of his/her own and of the others history and development (Amorim, 2002).

The Multiple Spatial/Temporal Dimensions

As Spink (1999) proposed, the context is defined not only by the social space in which the action takes place; it is also defined by a temporal perspective. Both are part of the same dimension. But time here is not related to time measured by the clock or by the rolling of days, months and years, but rather the internal time, which results from the relationship between the action imperative and the resonance of the collective memories.

The time which defines the context can have different durations and is understood as being imprinted in the vestiges that mark the context, being imprinted in the spaces, contributing to give sense to the situation (Bakhtin, 1990).

In the presented perspective, the role of temporal dimensions in the developmental processes is seen from two standpoints. One refers to the fact that, in the here-and-now situations, temporal evidences can be verified through the presence of a lived history, that is, of a past, which is active in the present. That past, however, is updated by the meanings flow, which contribute in a creative manner to configure the here-and-now. Dimensioned by people, the past and present are articulated with future goals and purposes, (re)constructing the future perspective. Dialectically and recursively, the future perspective continuously favors new senses and meanings that give new senses both to the present and past time. Thus, it is conceived that, in here-and-now, a temporal plenitude exists that is sensible, visible.

As discussed above, when presenting the socio-historical matrix, it is possible to identify more complex signs of historical time, clues of a time march, marks of human creative activity, signs of diverse historical periods, the diversity of superimposed epochs (Bakhtin, 1990).

In order to encompass those different spatial/temporal dimensions, four intertwined time scales were defined: short time, lived-in time, historical, and future-oriented time. The first three ones have been adapted from Spink's (1999) proposition; and the fourth one was later incorporated (Rossetti-Ferreira, Amorim, & Silva, 1999).

The *short, present, ongoing or microgenetic time* involves here-and-now situations, where face-to-face interactions actually take place. It constitutes the level of the intersubjective discursive practices. In this here-and-now scale, the focus is on the functionality of the repertoires used by people for mak-

ing sense. Context, in this scale, requires of a clear description of the interactive situation and of the dialogical inter animation, which is its characteristic. Within that, the behavioral flow of each person is framed and interpreted by the other's verbal and non-verbal actions, through the positions, perspectives or roles and counter-roles mutually attributed to and assumed by them, in social contexts. In it, the various voices activated by the social memories of the other three times get updated and combined.

The *lived-in or ontogenetic time* refers to situated voices evoked by the discursive practices, which are socially constructed during the primary and secondary socialization processes. This corresponds to the *habitus* territory (Bourdieu, 1989), that is, to the dispositions resulting from the affiliation to specific social groups and to the multiple social languages acquired in the process of socialization. Those voices are shared by relatives, relationships and colleagues who have been through similar experiences and contexts.

The long historical or cultural time is the locus of the socially constructed social-cultural imagery of a certain period. It is the time scale of the discursive and ideological formations, which compose the interdiscourse or collective meanings available to people, in order to make sense of the various world phenomena.

Finally, the *prospective, future oriented time* is based on the three other times. Through it, individual and collective perspectives, proposals and goals are created. It is also made up of discursive and ideological formations, as well as of individual and/or shared motives, anticipations, and plans that were constructed through the other time perspectives and, in various ways, constrain the present actions and interactions.

Those four spatial/temporal dimensions are considered as dynamically interrelated, each one sustaining, opposing, confronting and transforming the other, being always updated in the here-and-now situations. Moreover, as various are the interactive people in a specific context, diverse are the temporal meanings that are derived from and referred to in an interaction. Furthermore, due to the ongoing transformations and development, the temporal meanings must be seen in their dynamic transformation, in a figure and background movement, alternating the position and meaning they acquire in the situation.

Regarding this issue, a second time standpoint emerges, that of *becoming*. In it, time is looked upon as an ongoing process throughout the developmental course, which responds to the flow of the situations, bringing the notion of movement, of events in continuous change and reorganization, of transformation and development.

All these things considered, we had to acknowledge that the apprehension of our study object – human development – is only possible if one considers the relations to which this course is articulated with, belongs and is submitted to. Furthermore, if one recognizes its continuous updating process, it cannot be seen as an ascendant evolution, as it always includes both gains and losses, throughout life span.

Thus, the complexity of the developmental processes, with its relational and contextual interconnected characteristics, with its various articulated temporal perspectives, with its flexibility and dynamism, its transformations and limitations, led us to evoke the *network metaphor*. Through it, we recognized that the meanings present in the action of signifying the world, the other, and ourselves structure a semiotic universe in which development occurs.

The Network Metaphor

This proposal is identified with a paradigm of complexity, which is being increasingly used in diverse knowledge fields, social practices and technologies, in order to overcome research models that tried to understand the world based on independent relations between elements and on predictable mechanisms, supposed to be both exact and invariant (Valsiner, 1987; Morin, 1990; Najmanovitch, 1995). As such, the network metaphor was incorporated within our perspective in order to make explicit the multiple articulations, the apprehension of the complexity in which the persons and their developmental processes are immersed.

Such affiliation derives from an understanding that the articulation of elements of diverse orders semiotically configures a situation pervaded by meanings and senses (which can be wider or more restrict, but always polysemic), constraining a set of limits and possibilities onto the situation.

Depending on the moment, the context and the persons' characteristics, besides the ongoing interactions of the people involved, the network configuration makes available or even highlights a certain set of meanings, discursive practices, as well as social roles and positions. Those favor certain possibilities and limits to the persons' actions / emotions / conceptions, which mediate the person's probable course of action in that situation. Dialectically and recursively, the emergence of those actions, emotions, and conceptions lead to changes in some of the involved dimensions. The network is, thus, re-articulated with a reorganization of its configuration, during the interaction flow, leading the person to the attribution of new meanings / senses to the other, him/ herself and the situation. Thus, a continuous reorganization of the network configuration occurs, which promotes new possible courses of action and interaction, hence new potential developmental routes.

This transformation process is understood as fragmentary, product of figure-and-background movements by which certain meanings and processes emerge and acquire dominance, while others nestle at a second level, until a new event occur in the continuous flow of interactions and situations.

The notion of *centers mobility*, one of Levy's (1993) established principles for the comprehension of the networks, has helped us to analyze those movements and fluctuations. It clearly states that the net's centers are movable, skipping from one to another node. By stating this center mobility, however, we do not propose that the network (re)configuration might shift towards any direction, that every and each meaning is possible, and that all configurations are equiprobable. Thus, we do not shoulder a totally relativistic posture concerning meaning processes, discursive practices, and developmental pathways, as we do recognize that there are both limits and possibilities to their mobility and variability.

The *Network of Meanings* as a Developmental Constrainer

The notion of *constraint*, inspired on Waddington's concept (1966) and adapted by Valsiner (1987) helped us to analyze the data obtained through years of empirical studies conducted by our group, which clearly revealed that not all possibilities are set to a person in a specific situation. Therein, in the *Network of Meanings* perspective, constraints are understood as promoting certain configurations that tend to emerge more easily as a figure, while other possibilities remain kept as background. Thus, they simultaneously favor and set limits to the meaning processes, discursive practices and to the persons' positions and development within a situation.

Hence, personal, contextual and cultural-historical elements, in synergic interaction, configure and constrain certain trajectories possibilities and not others. Those constraints canalize actions / emotions / conceptions in certain directions, more than others; promote certain specific social practices; delimit certain zones for the partners' interactions. Thus, the configuration acts impelling the person towards certain directions, acquisitions, and developmental trajectories; while it simultaneously removes him/her from, set limits or even interdicts other directions, acquisitions, and developmental trajectories.

As such, the constraint system, by acting as a regulator of the developing organism-environment system movement from the present to its immediate future, makes it possible to investigate the actions now with their future implications. Also that development is both determined and undetermined in various domains (Valsiner, 1987). Zones of preservation, negotiation and nov-

elty coexist. Thus development can either lead to possibilities for innovation, or be subjected to certain predictable developmental trajectories, preserving both consistency and change throughout life. This proposed framework simultaneously preserves the novelty and plasticity of the developmental pathways, as well as avoids a naïve absolute relativism.

Under those conditions, it is understood that the person, on one hand, is immersed in a semiotic world of discursive practices from which is difficult to escape from and to which the person is in a certain way subjected to. Furthermore, due to the more rigid structure of certain configurations, some situations, positions and behaviors are recurrent and persistent. They can be elicited by strongly constraining elements of the network configuration, which entangle the person in certain reiterative positions, over which he/she has little control. We named this process, which usually is evoked by strong emotions, as *entanglement*.

On the other hand, as mentioned before, this perspective clearly proposes that persons, from when they are born, are not passive towards or totally submitted to those constraints. On the contrary, they are continuously (although not necessarily consciously) and actively involved in negotiating through their own personal way, the positions to be attributed to and/or assumed. Moreover, due to the discursive practices polysemy, the person has a relative possibility of choosing and guiding his/her own actions in certain directions, more than others, within the network configuration constraints. This possibility preserves a relative opening for the transformation of the person's developmental route.

Networks, Sheds, Meshes, and Webs

As stated above, each person's developmental routes can only be focused by considering the interactive and situated processes he/she establishes within specific contexts, pervaded by the socio-historical matrix. Consequently, it is impossible to consider the development of just one person, in isolation, as development is an interconnected process, which involves various participants and the reciprocal interactive situations established among them.

The network metaphor is particularly useful to apprehend this process, as it allows expressing the development of various persons in interaction, and of the situation as a whole, in reciprocal constitution, and not the linear development of each person, as has been traditionally done in Developmental Psychology.

This implies the necessity to take into account, during an investigation, that each interactive person has lived varied previous experiences, and thus brings onto the situation diverse life histories, different plans, and future expectations. Each partner occupies diverse social roles and discursive positions, and acts and interacts in different ways in the role coordination. As such, it is understood that each person is embedded in a particular configuration of the network of meanings. And, that through the intersubjective dialogical processes, the diverse networks get articulated, with many intersections and superpositions. This is equivalent to what Levy (1993) calls multiplicity of knots in a network. Hence, it is not possible to say that there is one single network. There are always multiple networks, weaving a mesh, with many intersection points.

So, the metaphor stresses that there is not only one network of meanings, but various nets articulated among them, interlinking and interlinked by nodes, which are weaved in a mesh, composing a web with diverse common points. Such a notion allows a disruption with the traditional interior / exterior, micro / macro dichotomies, as it is understood that each node is articulated to wider networks and, simultaneously, a node can be constituted by smaller nets.

Thus, at once, people are understood as immersed in, constituted and submitted by the mesh, while actively contribute to constitute it and to constrain possible pathways to his/her own development, the others persons development and the situations.

Conflicts, Confrontations, and Crises

This conception of network also allows us to say that, for each person, the networks are configured with certain specificities, marked by the person's previous personal experiences, besides the present and future perspectives, within a situated role/positioning play. Each person has to face with and negotiate a set of meanings and discursive practices that are attributed to him/her and that he/she attributes to him/herself, to the other and to the experienced situations. Hence, the probability of coincidence of frames or interpretations of two or more interacting people is virtually none, considering that one can never assume exactly the other's same role/position and actions. Furthermore, each one carries diverse personal components.

Therefore, those differences can lead to disagreements and conflicts, which might or not be overcome in the ensuing process of negotiation. Consequently, as our perspective conceives that development occurs in and through situated interactions established with other partners, and as in those interactions, a confrontation of actions, emotions, motivations and meanings usually occurs, development is here conceived to occur through conflicts and crisis, in which contradiction acts as a component of the process of constitution of people and situations.

The Network of Meanings and the Developmental Processes

Multiple developmental trajectories are possible to be conceived based on the adopted assumptions, especially on the notion of constraint, which at each moment and situation sets some limits and possibilities for the person's development. Developmental trajectories can also follow unexpected courses, due to the continuous reconstruction of the nets in the continuous and changeable life flow – a principle named *metamorphosis* by Levy (1993).

Independently of the course followed, not all potential trajectories will be brought about. So, as some pathways will not be run through, various potential abilities and capacities will not be acquired. Or else, their acquisition might begin, but changes in the person's developmental life conditions can modify its course. Other abilities and capacities might never be set even as a possibility, with no chances of development.

Thus, our developmental perspective is close to those systemic conceptions that recognize the various interconnections and associations among the elements, their relations of proximity and subordination. As such, the perspective points out that the apprehension of the object of study – developmental processes – is only possible if considered through the inter-relations within which it is articulated, belongs to or is subdued to, in here-and-now situations. It proposes that, besides assessing and identifying the various elements involved in the developmental process, one should apprehend the diverse interconnections and associations between them, their intertwinements.

In that way, one can establish a basis that should apprehend the continuous changes in meanings, actions, feelings, and thoughts that occur in the person's daily life, while simultaneously considering the persistence and difficulties involved in those transformations. One can establish a basis to deal with wider and local aspects in an articulated and integrated way; a basis to deal with novelty and repetition, which pervades the person's constitution processes and his/her relation with the environment and culture.

Final Comments

As discussed above, the *Network of Meanings* perspective was initially used to analyze adaptation processes, which occur between babies, families, and caregivers during the infants' entry into a daycare center. Later, the study of a varied set of subjects, interactive fields, scenarios, and socio-historical matrix was required to test the limits of the perspective. Presently, the perspective is being used for the analysis of other issues, such as the social and school inclusion of children with special needs, the development of

individuals involved in criminal acts and the integration of children in foster and adoptive families.

It is clear for us that the diverse topics of the presented perspective are not new on the field. Since the beginnings of the Developmental Psychology, diverse authors have also been seeking and struggling to apprehend the developmental processes in their complexity and dynamics. Alike them, this perspective highlights the complexity of the developmental processes, in order to make explicit the various and heterogeneous constituents of the processes. Moreover, the focus on complexity was used to emphasize the intrinsically interrelation among those constituents and their continuous up-dating processes. As such, it was designed to call attention to the whole thread of events, actions, interactions, retroactions, incidents, within which it congregates contradictions, behavior's maintenance, unexpected unfoldings.

Its quality, as described above, makes explicit that it makes possible to talk about, investigate, and understand development by overcoming polarities between biological, psychological, and social aspects; between universality and singularities, permanence and rupture, determinism and indeterminism, emotion and cognition, body and mind, internal and external, semiotic and concrete, autonomous and subjected to. Our goal is to work accepting and considering contradictions, giving way to dialectical complementarities among them.

Despite this goal, it is here understood that the *Network of Meanings* perspective should not be considered as an instrument through which one can apprehend the totality of a situation. As stressed by Morin (1990), complexity is not a synonym of completeness or wholeness. The approached issues can never be exhaustively studied and understood, as new topics can emerge, reconstituting the meanings constructed by the investigation processes. There are aspects at the borders that cannot be seen, felt or thought (at least, by using our contemporarily available techniques); there are even transformations of the situation within the social processes, that can lead to transformations in the developmental processes comprehension. What we are willing here is to establish a dialogue, assuming a position that keeps the movement in that dialogue, linking theory to methodology, epistemology, and human ontology.

References

Amorim, K. S. (2002). *Concretizações de discursos e práticas histórico-sociais, em situações de freqüência de bebês a creche.* Unpublished PhD Thesis. USP, Brazil. http://www.teses.usp.br/teses/disponiveis/17/17148/tde-09012003-151152/.

Amorim, K. S., & Rossetti-Ferreira, M. C. (2005). When a child becomes ill: The sociohistorical matrix in meaning–making and practices. In A. U. Branco & J. Valsiner (Ed.) *Communication and metacommunication in human development,* (pp. 127–149). Greenwich: Information Age Publishing Inc.

Amorim, K. S., Vitoria, T., & Rossetti-Ferreira, M. C. (2000). *A Rede de Significações como perspectiva para a análise do processo de inserção de bebês na creche. Cadernos de Pesquisa, 109,* 115–144.

Bakhtin, M. (1981). Discourse in the novel. In M. Bakhtin *The dialogical imagination. Four Essays.* Austin: University of Texas Press. (Original work published 1934).

Bakhtin, M. (1990). *Creation of a prosaics.* Standford: Standford University Press.

Bourdieu, P. (1989). O *Poder Simbólico.* [The symbolic power] Lisboa: DIFEL.

Bronfenbrenner, U. (1979). *The ecology of human development.* Cambridge, MA: Harvard University Press.

Bronfenbrenner, U. (1993). The ecology of cognitive development: Research models and fugitive findings. In: R. H. Worzniak, & K. Fisher (Eds). *Scientific Environments* (p. 3–44). Mahwah, NJ: Lawrence Erlbaum.

Bussab, V. S. R., & Ribeiro, F. L. (1998). Biologicamente cultural. In, L. Souza, M. F. Q. Freitas, & M. M. P. Rodrigues (Orgs). *Psicologia: reflexões (im)pertinentes* (pp. 175–193). São Paulo: Casa do psicólogo.

Carvalho, A. M. A. (1983). O desenvolvimento da criança. *Pediatria Moderna, 5,* 269–280.

Carvalho, A. M. A. (1998). Etologia e comportamento social. In, L. Souza, M. F. Q. Freitas, & M. M. P. Rodrigues (Orgs). *Psicologia: reflexões (im)pertinentes* (p. 195–224). São Paulo: Casa do Psicólogo.

Fogel, A. (1993). *Developing through relationships: Origins of communication, self and culture.* Hertfordshire: Harvester Wheatsheaf.

Harré, R. (1998). *The singular self: An introduction to the psychology of personhood.* London: Sage.

Hermans, H. J. M. (2002). The dialogical self as a society of mind. *Theory & Psychology, 12*(2), 147–160.

Hermans, H. J. M., & Kempen, H. J. G. (1995). Body, mind and culture: The dialogical nature of mediated action. *Culture & Psychology, 1*(1), 103–114.

Kuhn, T. S. (1962). *The structure of scientific revolutions.* Chicago: University of Chicago Press.

Levy, P. (1993). *As tecnologias da inteligência: o futuro do pensamento na era da informática.* Rio de Janeiro: (Ed.) 34.

Meltzoff, A. N. (1990). Foundations for developing a concept of self: the role of imitation in relating self to other and the value of social mirroring, social modeling, and self practice in infancy. In D. Cichetti, & M. Beeghly (Eds.). *The self on transition* (pp. 139–164). Chicago: University of Chicago Press.

Morin, E. (1990) *Introdução ao pensamento complexo.* Lisboa: Epistemologia e Sociedade.

Morin, E. (1996). *Ciência com consciência.* Rio de Janeiro: Bertrand do Brasil.

Najmanovitch, D. (1995). Redes. El Linguage de los Vínculos. Buenos Aires: Paidós.

Oliveira, Z. M. R., & Rossetti-Ferreira, M. C. (1994). Coordination of roles: A theoretical-methodological perspective for studying human interactions. In N. Mercer, & C. Coll (Orgs.). *Teaching, learning and interaction – volume 3 Explorations in socio-cultural studies* (pp. 217–221). Madrid: P. del Rio.

Oliveira, Z. M. R., & Rossetti-Ferreira, M. C. (1996). Understanding the co-constructive nature of human development: role coordination in early peer interaction. In J. Valsiner, & H. Voss (Eds). *The structure of learning processes* (pp. 177–204). Norwood, NJ: Ablex.

Pinheiro, O. & Spink, M. J. P. (2004). Discursive practices and democratic participation: negotiating language use in mental health services. *Journal of Health Psychology, 9*(1): 55–71.

Roriz, T. (2005). *A inclusão social e escolar de crianças com necessidades especiais, sob a óptica dos profissionais de saúde.* Unpublished master dissertation. University of São Paulo.

Rossetti-Ferreira, M. C., Amorim, K. S., Silva, A. P. S. (1999). The network of meanings which structures and canalizes interactions, interpretations and comments. *Culture and Psychology*, 5, 3, 341–353.

Rossetti-Ferreira, M. C., Amorim, K. S., & Silva, A. P. S. (2000). Uma perspectiva teórico-metodológica para análise do desenvolvimento humano e do processo de investigação. *Psicologia: Reflexão e Crítica*, 13 (2), 281–293.

Rossetti-Ferreira, M. C., Amorim, K. S., & Silva, A. P. S. (2004). Rede de Significações: alguns conceitos básicos. In M. C. Rossetti-Ferreira, K. S. Amorim, A. P. S. Silva, & A. M. A. Carvalho (Orgs.). *Rede de Significações e o estudo do desenvolvimento humano* (pp. 23–34). Porto Alegre: Artmed.

Rossetti-Ferreira, M. C., Amorim, K. S., & Vitória, T. (1996). Emergência de novos significados durante o processo de adaptação de bebês à creche. *Coletâneas da ANPPEP*, 1, 4, 111–143.

Rossetti-Ferreira, M. C., Amorim, K. S., & Vitória, T. (1997). Integração família e creche – O acolhimento é o princípio de tudo. *Estudos em Saúde Mental*. Ribeirão Preto, F. M. R. P. – USP, p. 107–131.

Salgado, J., & Gonçalves, M. (in this book, at Chapter 26). The dialogical self: Social, personal, and (un)conscious.

Sampson, E. E. (1993). *Celebrating the other: a dialogic account of human nature*. New York: Harvester Wheatsheaf.

Silva, A. P. S. (2003). *Continuidade e mudança no desenvolvimento: trabalhando narrativas de homens envolvidos com a prática de delitos*. Unpublished PhD. thesis, University of São Paulo, Brazil.

Solon, L., Costa, N. R., & Rossetti-Ferreira, M. C. (2005). Narratives of late-placed children about their adoption process. *First Inter-national Society for Cultural and Activity Research Congress – Book of Abstracts*. Vol. 1. Sevilla: Akron Gráfica.

Spink, M. J. P. (1999). Making sense of illness experiences. In: M. Murray & K. Chamberlain (Eds). *Qualitative Health Psychology* (p. 83–97). London: Sage.

Trevarthen, C. (1986). Form, significance and psychological potential of hand gestures of infants. In J.-L. Nespoulous, P. Perron & A. R. Lecours (Eds.). *The biological foundation* (pp. 149–202). Hillsdale.: Lawrence Erlbaum Associates.

Valsiner, J. (1987). *Culture and the development of children's actions*. New Jersey: John Wiley & Sons.

Valsiner, J. (1994). Irreversibility of time and the construction of historical developmental psychology. *Mind, Culture and Activity*, 1 (1–2), 25–42.

Volosinov, V. N. (1929/2000). *Marxism and the philosophy of language*. Cambridge: Harvard University Press.

Vygotsky, L. S. (1978). *Mind in society*. Cambridge: MIT Press.

Waddington, C. H. (1966). *The strategy of the genes*. London: Allen & Unwin.

Wallon, H. (1941). A criança e o adulto, em M. J. Werebe e J. Nadel-Brulfert (Org.) (1986) *Henri Wallon* (p. 68 – 71). SP: (Ed.), Ática.

Wallon, H. (1959a). O papel do *outro* na consciência do *eu*, em M. J. Werebe e J. Nadel-Brulfert (Org.) (1986) *Henri Wallon* (p. 158–167). SP: (Ed.), Ática.

Wallon, H. (1959b). Os meios, os grupos e a psicogênese da criança, em M. J. Werebe e J. Nadel-Brulfert (Org.) (1986) *Henri Wallon* (p. 168–178). SP: (Ed.), Ática.

Yazlle, C. (2001). Pré-escolas convivendo com a paralisia cerebral: uma análise do processo de inclusão/exclusão. Unpublished master dissertation. University of São Paulo, Brazil.

Part IV

SYMBOLIC RESOURCES FOR THE CONSTITUTION OF EXPERIENCE

CHAPTER 14

Dramaturgical Actuations and Symbolic Communication

Or How Beliefs Make Up Reality

Alberto Rosa

Experience, Beliefs, Consciousness, and the Real

Experience is a tricky word. It refers to what the senses present, and thus refers to how one gets to know the real. But it also means what one does in order to know, the actions one carries out to test knowledge, the changes in one's own behavior so that reality can be felt in different ways. As a consequence of that, not only might reality appear to the experiencer in different versions – thus somehow casting shadows on the reliability of the senses, but the very behavioral and cognitive subject – the experiencing person – also changes. S/he gains abilities for managing experiences and testing the knowledge that has emerged up to the present.

So experience changes what is taken to be real, but also the subject's functional capabilities. It makes beliefs about the real to appear as separate from what the senses present. The consequence is the development of consciousness – the capability of producing conceptions of the real, related but not exclusively dependent of what the senses present.

In sum – experience, beliefs, consciousness, and the real are inextricably bounded together. They are the core of what we take to be our being in the world and what make us able to have ideas about what the world and ourselves are like. The task of this chapter is to attempt to disentangle this tetrad of concepts by producing a sort of narrative essay about the natural history of their evolution. Part of the journey has already been traveled. The chapters in Part III of this Handbook have been concerned with how meaning and intelligence came to existence, about how the environment becomes an intelligible *Umwelt* (Chapter 10, Rosa, 2007), how movement turns into symbols (Chapter 11, Español, 2007), how the use of objects becomes conventionalized in shared play (Chapter 12, Rodríguez, 2007), and how the social milieu within which children develop provide a social and cultural sense to what they do and feel (Chapter 13, Rosetti-Ferreira et al., 2007). All these chapters have centered on how this process is double sided – it involves both the development of new functions in the organism, as well as the growing understanding of the milieu by that organism. This dual process involves mutual creation of both – the actor and the understanding of situations.

The purpose of this chapter is to go a step further, examining, first, how communication in hierarchically organized groups offer the possibility for the production of conventional symbols, and so open the path for humanization; and then explore how conventional symbols come to appear, so that a subjective representation of situations can be taken to be real.

The approach taken here will proceed along lines different to any kind of dualism, which when separating matter and spirit presents consciousness and objects as belonging to two different ontological realms. The argument to be deployed here will proceed along the lines already drawn in Chapter 10 (Rosa, 2007). It will go into the examination of how beliefs develop from dramatic actuations within a social *Umwelt*. How social communication produces conventional symbols capable of changing the behavior of others and of the actor her/himself, to convey to others (mediated through symbols) what is being felt, or even of reporting what is absent, removed from what is being presented now by the ongoing actuations. The past, the possible and the future can so appear as a consequence of the development of conventionally mediated communicative actuations, which then makes one to become capable of imagine a reality beyond what is actually felt in the present. A representation of reality can then be produced, which later has to be examined by a painstaking series of confrontations of experiences. A lengthy and complicated process which inner alleys have to be disentangled, in order to be able to explain not only how beliefs, reality and truth can be taken to existence, but also what psychological processes could account for their coming to life.

The attempt here is to go ahead into the exploration of how experience, and thus a subjective construct of reality, come into existence. A statement that may need some clarification. Experience is what make us to feel what is around us, and so presents us with a version of reality. But reality is much more than understanding what to do when some signals are felt, is to take those signals as signs of real entities around ourselves (another entity taken to exist as resulting from signals). So reality results from the belief on the real existence of entities which have a radical otherness *vis à vis* the agent who holds that belief. This makes necessary to explain what a belief is, how it unfolds, and how it can be taken to be real or unreal, true or false.

Beliefs and Actuations

Beliefs are psychological entities. They are outcomes of the acts of Psyche. Beliefs develop from actuations. Actuations are assemblies of actions gathered together in intentional schemas (Rosa, 2007), that make possible to understand stimulation, and when combined in scripts allow intelligent behavior to be deployed in particular situations within the *Umwelt*.

Actuations are a product of the combination of actions that have a semiotic structure, and so produce understanding. Purposeful actions are enactive semiosis of a teleonomic character (see Chapter 10). They are made out of bodily movements and can be examined following Peirce's semiotic logic. They interpret a situation; they are an understanding of what to do and thus can be taken to be a form of problem solving, of enactive thinking. So understood, actuations make possible an understanding of the simultaneous development of action and meaning-making, that is, how psychological functions and familiarity with the environment develop together.

The story so far told went only as far as to the explanation of intelligent behavior. However, we need to go beyond this point. Our goal is addressing how experience emerges. To reach this point we need to go into detail of how one can create not merely an understanding of the current situation, but also to represent to oneself what one is facing, as an instance of what really is out there, beyond what I am feeling at this particular moment. In other words, the task at hand is how the inner space of consciousness develops. The space within which what is felt is understood as a sign revealing the presence of something real existing beyond the body boundaries of the perceiver; or even as a sign of the real existence of the perceiver itself, as a real entity with a reality beyond what one feels of his/herself. So, consciousness is the space where one has experiences about otherness (including oneself as another to be made intelligible), and so constitutes a representation of what objects, myself, situations, or the world at large are.

Going a step further, consciousness is also what makes possible to seed the doubt about whether what one is doing is well-aimed or mistaken, right or wrong, good or evil. Or even, whether the experience felt is a true or false representation of the real. Experience, then, is what makes the real a possible object for knowledge, but we know well that experience may also be deceiving.

Experience is something one takes at first glance as something immediately given, as having a significance immediately felt *vis à vis* the ongoing stream of consciousness (James, 1890). Consciousness and experience are sometimes pictured as a sort of mystery resilient to the efforts of science to disentangled it, as a sort of *sancta sanctorum* of humanity, the inner core of human agency, where understanding lies (Searle, 1984), or the stage of a phantasmagoric Cartesian Theatre (Dennet, 1991) where the soul (or an inner homunculus) contemplates the plays performed by the mind when running into the world, even if these ways of picturing conscious experience are later discarded by these very same authors through elaborate argumentations.

The story here to be told is not only that of the production of experience and the development of consciousness, but also that of a change in the distribution of agency. How mechanic causality turns, first, into feed-forward teleonomy and, later on, into teleology. In other words, how a natural being gains control over its actions, by developing functional capabilities and so making intentionality, intelligence and reason to appear. It is the transition from movements caused by external environmental forces, to the development of needs and desires, and eventually the capabilities that make possible moral feelings and thinking to appear.

The first stage in this journey of exploration is to go into a search within the cradle for the development of subjectivity and consciousness – communication within a group. This will be done by continuing the story already started in Chapter 10, where it was left there, in a social group of animals before humanity (and language) appeared. Later on we will go into the development of conventional symbols for mediating social communication and the new psychological functions these means make possible to emerge. Eventually a hypothesis will be advanced about how these new functions (together with these conventional symbolic means for communication) make up at the same time experience, consciousness, and beliefs about what is real.

Social Life as the Cradle for Subjectivity

Social life offers advantages for the survival of individuals, but there is no advantage without a price to be paid. When living in a group new problems (of a social nature) appear. In order to be successful in this scenery new abilities are required. Now it does not suffice to have intentional schemas for distinguishing an object from another, a member of a group from a stranger, or about what a particular bodily movement means. Nor even schemas of how a member of the same species behaves are enough. One has to become able to identify who is who, how each particular individual behaves, how to understand signs from the actuations of the others so that one could understand when a desire can be fulfilled or there is the possibility of some painful consequence to follow. One has to become able to make sense of what another member of the group is about to do, as well as how to perform in order to influence the behavior of the other, or to speedily avoid its consequences. When this can be proficiently done, a mutual regulation of behavior can happen.

An external human observer would say that whether an individual is above or below the hierarchical social scale is an important issue, since somebody's social position affords different actuations upon the same individual from other actors placed in different steps of the social hierarchy. However, social hierarchies are the result of dynamic processes always on the move, so that whatever depiction of it is a sort of frozen construction always susceptible to become quickly outdated.

Each individual of the group interactuates with the other members of the pack. But in order to do so, each one of them has to be distinguished from the others; they have to become distinct objects. Thus, each member of the group needs developing intentional schemas about each other individual within the group, as well as scripts to apply in social situations where a group of actors interactuate (see Chapter 10). The result is that the mutual adjustment of the behavior of all the members of the group, of their schemas and scripts, produce a dynamic equilibrium in the system of behaviors within the group that can be termed as *social norms*. These norms (which can be modeled as a set of rules) result from an evolutionary process that shapes at the same time both the social *Umwelt* of each actor and the psychological processes that go on within each actor's psyche.

This way of presenting an *etic* account of social life may not be exactly symmetrical to the *emic* understanding of the members of the group. One has to become able to identify each individual, to figure out how to act vis à vis every other member of the group, and to comply with the mutually attuned patterns of interaction. So social norms (Sherif, 1936) are not abstract rules one has to learn to comply with, but a sort of network of individual scripts in a delicate equilibrium that can easily be broken, but when this happens, a new state of equilibrium is soon reached, as when a leader is deposed.

In a group such as this, its members can be taken to be full-fledged actors, with a sense of their own role in an on-going drama, where social norms often do not allow to reach what one desires. Social life is not an idyllic neighborhood. Behind immediately visible appearances, each member of the group has desires of its own, which not always can be fulfilled without making somebody else upset. So, the most possible alley is to keep conforming to the rules, and when an occasion appears for the desire to be realized to take advantage of it. This sometimes makes appear dramatic actuations that often are termed as instances of tactical deceiving, and taken to be a sign of the development of a theory of mind (see chapters 7 and 8; Perinat, 2007; Fields, Segerdahl, & Savage-Rumbaugh, 2007).

The natural environment includes many different objects, each of them with different affordances. Trees to be climbed or to hide behind them, birds or frogs whose presence and noises may signal the presence of water, objects to eat, and predators to keep away from. There are also members of the same species. Some of them are familiar, and others not, because when one runs into them they behave in unexpected ways, and so produce orientation responses (surprise) and prompt circular reactions to test their affordances (curiosity). The members of the group are well known. Some can be playmates, or equals with whom one can compete for food or attention. Others are rather remote and not allow to be disturbed in what they are doing. There are also some others who are desirable, but cannot be tampered or even approached, since it happens that when one attempts to do this is rebuffed by someone who behaves like the Lord of the land. He takes the lead of the group when moving from an area to another, is the first to face an external threat, rebukes anyone who disputes his food or attempts to approach his sexual mates, and sometimes fight with others who attempt to break the *status quo*.

But one has its own feelings: hunger, thirst, or emotions that make one to be restless before some particular objects and events, which make one to be curious, attracted, or afraid. There is also some sort of excitement that makes one to be particularity oriented towards some members of the group (frequently of the opposite sex). These inner states are internal signs that may make one to feel restless and particularly prone to orient oneself to some signs from the environment, and to disregard others. It is as if one was looking for something, as if searching for something meaningful vis-à-vis that internal signal, an object with features that match the *ground* for the semiosis started by an emotion (which then acts as a representamen). When one runs into a something that does so, then that thing becomes object of desire. Desire itself appears within an intentional schema or a script emotionally tinting the object, and making it to appear as something attractive, as a sort of magnet that attracts one as an external force one can make nothing to resist.

Social life is not easy. If one is hungry and finds many acorns under a tree and rejoices this finding, the noises and jumps one makes act as a signal for others to come and find out what is going on, and then join in eating. If there are enough acorns, this goes in good harmony. But if food is scarce, a fight would start and very soon a pecking order is established, and those who may try to brake it will be rebuked. This is done sometimes by brute force, but others just by threatening it. Often aggression is interrupted when one quickly withdraws from the disputed food, so that aggressive movements get suspended before an actual fight brakes on. What started to be movements for attacking, change into movements to signal that one is ready for a fight, so that the other may choose whether to fight or flight. Just the sight of a powerful other showing signs of anger, may suffice to understand what may be about to come, so that actual fighting fades away before starting because of a mutual understanding of each other intentions, and so social norms prevail, or sometimes are broken and reformed.

Fear of the powerful does not prevent one from the effect of affects. Objects of desire keep their power of attraction. As much as the powerful afford the urge of keep-

ing away from him, an attractive object of desire may act in ways as to either sign its un-affordability, or its affordance for one approaching her. But signs have to be understood, and understanding is the result of a semiosis in which internal feelings always play a role, and so communication is often misinterpreted. Whenever the case, attention to the desirable triggers a set of action-semioses governed by intentional schemas that makes one to perform actuations and scripts more and more elaborated as one learns how to deal with these situations. These feelings are, so to speak, genuine and pure. They are not pretended or faked. There are no hard feelings afterwards either. Ambivalence may appear, but once the balance is turned, there are no regrets. Since neither the future nor the past exist in this kind of individual's phenomenal world, there is only a continuous present where everything presents itself anew again and again. Only intentional schemas keep traces of the past, so that one can profit from past experience to better know what to do before a stimulus so that it may be interpreted as a signal. But no advanced planning can be made, since there is no way one can control the workings of its actions. They are teleonomically triggered by the signals received, either from the environment, or from the workings of one's own organs. There is no way one can purposefully make present what is absent. One's internal processes can only proceed following the signals interpreted. But this teleonomy is also constructive, always triggered by the constraints of each particular circumstance in which an actuation is carried out, although their repetition and attunement to changing circumstances produce variations of intentional schemas. When many of them are put together in scripts, these rather than a stereotyped set of movements are more like an assortment of variations on a theme which can be rearranged and adapted to the signals received in particular situations, so that the observed behavior is simultaneously customarily, creative and smooth.

The teleonomic (but also constructive) character of action-semiosis, actuations and scripts for performing, makes the actor to accumulate resources (scripts) to face new situations, and so to be increasingly more prepared to deal with novel situations, since they can trigger old schemas and scripts, as well as so providing possibilities for creating new ones. Novel situations provide opportunities for linking schemas in creative ways. This is what makes possible tactic pretence to appear.

Tactic pretence and deceiving capabilities are often taken to be a sort of turning point in psychological capabilities, as if it were the emergence of a capability for reading the mind of somebody else. How can this rather surprising ability appear? The following narrative will essay a semiotic explanation on how the "Machiavellian intelligence" of apes (Byrne & Withen, 1988; see also de Waal, 1982) develops.

A young male feels attracted to a young female. This may result either because sexual arousal in the male or the female (or both) triggers approaching actuations, which may take many shapes (as a consequence of earlier constructed scripts), from a plain approaching movement, to the presentation of their sexual organs to the attention of the other. But this is risky. The dominant male will not permit such monkey business with members of his harem. So the mutually attracted couple has to learn (often painfully) how to cheat the Lord of the pack. Fear of him and attraction to the other alternate in a dance of movements expressive of their conflicting affections and actuations, which produce signals which if adequately read by the dominant male most surely will produce a threat or a punishment, or may also be misread, for example, as a signal that something threatening is approaching the group, so his attention gets distracted and focuses on somewhere else, and so opens an opportunity for the kind of success the couple desires.

Along this process mutual attunement of movements, actuations and scripts happen. Each of the three performs movements in order to influence the movements of the others. Each movement becomes a signal for an already known actuation, and for its attunement to the new circumstances. And bit by bit, some actuations become instrumental for others within the ongoing script of the developing drama. Movements, as a result of the temporal attunements between each other, get transformed into intentional actuations and performances, so that volitional acts resulting from vitality affects turn into communicative actuations (see Chapter 11; Español, 2007 for a more detailed account). The result is that rather sophisticated scripts develop. Affects arise before an object that becomes an object of desire, a feeling of weariness makes to pay attention to the dominant male, which in turn provokes fear and an expression of fear. If this results in a threat from the dominant, it may produce affects that surpasses the feeling of attraction, and so attention will be withdrawn for the object of desire, which then disappears from the scene. But it may also happen that the dominant male is distracted with something else, or that misreads the signal of fear of him as aroused by something else, and so goes into exploring what is going on, and so inadvertently leaving free leeway. Then the structure of the field changes, and the way is open to obtaining the object of desire. If so happens, a script for cheating is underway into being shaped.

All this does not mean that the individual has a plan, an internal representation of what to do, of who is who, or of who is himself. It simply performs at each moment of time actuations in an intelligent manner. It behaves with an understanding of what to do, performing abductive[1] actuations (taking advantage of previous experiences) which are shaped in such a way that also makes apparent an understanding of what to do by using the resources for actuation so far developed, what also includes an understanding of its position within the group – a sort of enactive protoidentity in the making. If one were to say that animals have a type of representation, of awareness of what is going on, it is an enactive representation (Bruner, Olver, & Greenfield, 1966), or better, the capability of understanding what is presented (rather than re-presenting anything). This is what Liszka (1996) calls a *presentative* capacity, typical of the *quasi-mind* of animals, which are able to understand and behave with intelligence in their *Umwell*, but that also are incapable of planning their behavior in advance, because they do not have the means to do so, as it will be discussed below.

Table 14.1 presents a summary of the natural evolution of psyche before language and humanization appears. As there can be seen, both the organism and the environment get mutually structured following the transformation of agency from lineal causality to teleonomy and then to the emergence of teleology. This table refers to some of the contents already presented in Chapters 1 and 10, as well as to what it has so far been presented in this chapter.

Mediation and Meaning-Making When Performing Actuations

The Limits of Teleonomic Semiosis

Animals are capable of profiting from experience, of learning, of identifying signals as meaningful, as referring to an object or an event, and so to react intelligently, or to negotiate chains of actuations addressed to a goal (see Chapter 8, Fields et al., 2006). They are able to signal their fears and desires, and so influence the others, and sometimes even to disguise their purposes and deceive. When looking at the phylogenetic past of the human kind (Rosa, Gomila, & Vega, 2004) it seems as if an increased awareness of what is going around in the environment of the organism developed and, together with this, the capability for figuring out what to do in different circumstances, and even to solve unfamiliar problems. In sum, perception, emotion, learning, communication, and thinking are psychological functions that reach considerable sophistication in animals, and are always linked to changes in their morphological organic structures, and particularly to their nervous system.

This is the result of a lengthy series of couplings between the morphological structures of the organism and those of the environment. The outcome is a mutual constitution of a structured environment and

of internal processes within the agent. Signals that trigger an actuation for coupling the organism with some part of the environment slowly evolve into becoming signs of external permanent entities. The result is that the animal reacts to many different signals as if they had the same meaning, as if they were coming from the same real entity (greenness, croaking, and jumping are all signs of the presence of a frog). And so the observer can infer that the agent is discriminating an object from another. In order to do so lengthier and lengthier internal processes (chains of schemas, actuations, and scripts) have to happen within the skin of the animal in order to explain its sophisticated behavior. This no doubt requires the existence of specialized organs shaped through evolution, which can support these operations in the form of structural couplings among themselves, so they make possible successful encounters with the environment. The correspondence between the increase in behavioral capabilities and the growth in complexity of morphological structures (particularly the central nervous system) support this claim.

Acts and Actuations

Actions and actuations start as a result of acts, and acts are no different that an automatic reaction to a break in a dynamic equilibrium. Something that can happen at either side of the skin or in both. The search for a dynamic equilibrium takes the shape of actions, actuations and scripts; depending both on the morphological and functional structures previously developed. This makes any behavior to be a consequence of a change in the state of the equilibrium, and inevitably tied to changes in the environment and the agent. So the actor can only perform according to the known scripts, as prompted by the signs received. When so doing it can profit from past experiences, is able to deal with the familiar, as well as to try to make sense of new stimuli by carrying out Semiosis-actions that attempt to assimilate the novel to the already known. But it cannot control its own processes, always subjected to

Table 14.1: Evolution of the co-construction of agency and psychological functions in relationships of inclusive separation

Acting Entity	Agency	Description	Explanation	Functionality	Functions	External Elements
Disordered matter	External	Change and movement resulting from the application of external forces	Lineal (mechanical)			Energy
Auto-organised matter	External-Internal:	Internal dynamics to keep the dynamic equilibrium Open system Inclusive separation	Dynamic System	Maintenance of equilibrium	Feed-forward mechanisms	Energy. Dynamic forces. Attractors
Alive being	Acts	Internal dynamics capable of producing changes to keep the internal equilibrium	Dynamic System-Functional	Homeostasis	Irritability	Forces, dynamic forces
Primitive animal (agent)	Action	Goal-oriented behaviour A change in the internal or external dynamics of the system organism-environment produces movements of the organism to keep equilibrium	Functional-Teleonomic	Discrimination of needs and stimuli Approach-withdrawal	Orientation Motivation Sensation	Stimuli
Higher social animal (actor)	Actuation and scripts Dramaturgical actuations	Movements expressing internal states Exploratory movements on the environment External changes may act as signs of a possibility of change in internal states Distinction between means and ends (a movement can be changed to serve a different function)	Teleonomic-Teleological	Interpretation of experience Protosemiotic (contingent, not socially conventionalised symbols)	Learning Perception Intentionality-Desire Emotion Communication Problem solving Phenomenological awareness Social roles	Objects, Individuals & Groups

new signs that first orient its attention, and then trigger actuations and scripts. It lives in a structured and understandable environment, but always in the present. It is able to understand what is present, but not re-present what is not present. The past cannot be remembered, nor can a future be imagined. For this to happen some sort of representational capacity has first to develop. This is the limit of teleonomic semiosis in "quasi-minds". A subjective space can only appear once the capability for making use of social conventional[2] signs appear. However this can happen in some animals given some circumstances (see Chapter 8, Field et al., 2007), once they have mastered the use of conventional symbols.

By this stage mediation and meaning are fully fledged developed. Scripts not only order actuations in a sequence, but make some actuations to be instrumental for others. Objects appear as a result of the transformation of qualities into symbols; i.e., the capability of performing enactive dicentic legisigns. This makes the object to be the result of enactive arguments (see Chapter 10). Then, what is it left to become human?

A possible answer is the development of new psychological functions capable of changing teleonomy into teleology. Something that happens through a variation of the already acquired capability of changing the sense of an actuation or a script for something different than before, so that the course of a chain of teleonomic causalities addressed to a particular goal gets interrupted and takes on a different functionality. The result of this move is the creation of novel uses for already familiar objects and movements. And this also has an evolutionary path.

From Teleonomy to Teleology

The argument so far deployed resorted to rather few elements: acts, actions and semiosis, recursively structuring themselves in complex systems, as a consequence of the performances of circular reactions resulting for disequilibria, and supported by the mutual couplings of morphological struc-

tures within the limits of the skin. Emotional expressions in social inter-actuations show the way in which the change from teleonomy into teleology happens. An affect develops into an emotion, which acts as signal for oneself to actuate, but it also signals to others what one is going to do, and opens the way for the other to prepare, and so inter-actuations get regulated at distance, and the path for intentional communication opens. Intentional signals so developed.

A similar process happens when the natural teleonomy of an object changes because an intentional actuation, such as when chimps use twigs as tools for digging into termites' nests, or when piling boxes to make platforms for reaching bananas (Köhler, 1925). When this happens the first instrumental use of objects as tools is in the making, and the first wails of the birth of culture can be heard.

Nowadays hardly anyone disputes the existence of animal protocultures, nor the capability of animals for profiting of the use of cultural tools not only for improving their capabilities for actuation and performing scripts, but also for going rather a long way into the path of becoming humanized (see Chapter 8, Field et al., 2007). The latter seems only to happen when they are raised among humans, and go into inter-actuations with humans using human tools for communication and cooperation. The use of bodily movements, pictures or vocal signs as conventionalized symbols for communication provide them with the possibility of making present the absent, and so with imagination, memory and the capability of maintaining purposes through time. Their own functional structures seem to develop beyond what happens when they live free in nature. Their morphological structures seem capable to be stretched into supporting some functional structures that only seem to appear in members of the human species when they are also socialized in cultural groups.

How far this stretching can proceed into the development of functions which so far are taken to be only a privilege of humans is still an open matter subject of a heated discussion, in which the relative importance of morphological and functional structures are at stake. What does not seem to be under discussion is that the threshold of humanity is in double articulation, in the capacity of using tools for making tools, and in using communicative signs to refer to the very act of communicating. But this is no more than joining together two already existing abilities:

a. The capability of changing the use of actuations and natural objects (so transforming teleonomy to open the door for teleology); and
b. The ability to perform circular reactions in novel situations, and so allowing the possibility for recursivity to proceed further.

These are dynamic phenomena with a long evolutionary history before the appearance of the genus *homo*.

Humanization

Social communication is a key issue for experience to appear. It is in communication where the function of actuations within scripts may change. This is something worthy of being analyzed in some detail.

Motor Actuations and Emotion

Communicative actuations are motor movements addressed to some other in order to affect their behavior. Their early origin is in emotional expression (see Chapter 10). Emotions develop from affective acts into bodily movements signaling the sense of an actuation. They signal to the agent and to others what actuation is about to come.

Emotions are multifaceted. On the one hand they are internal actions consequence of the working of the organs of the organism, and play an important role in the regulation of the working of the system (Scherer, 2004). On the other hand, they are made of affective semiosis which end up producing volitional acts (Chapter 10), that is, they prepare

and direct actuations. This is a consequence of what is felt, which then is emotionally tinted as desirable or undesirable, evaluating objects and events (Scherer, 2004), and so producing appraisals of objects or situations and making motivation to appear (Frijda, 2004).

So they have a double semiotic capacity, one addressing the object that produces the emotional reaction, and another turned upon the agent and acting as semiotic component and so playing a role upon the ongoing actuations. This role is very important – is that of shaping the directionality, of providing sense to the actuations to be performed. In addition, emotions are instrumental in the monitoring of the internal state of the organism and its interaction with the environment, as well as communicating the direction of the ongoing actuation (Scherer, 2004).

So viewed, communicative actuations, as any other type of actuation, depend on the shaping of intentional schemas, where sensorial, emotional and volitional actions (movements) are combined in a structure, which provides sense and significance to what the agent does. So bodily movements for communication would have no sense without the directionality provided by affections and emotions, which then are a central psychological component of meaning-making (see Valsiner, 2005). Emotions, then signal towards something still not present, to what may happen afterwards.

A motor actuation is then provided with sense, it is addressed to a goal. When this goal is to change somebody else's behavior, by using some previously acquired motor ability in a novel manner, then we are before the beginning of a conventional gesture, a conventional symbol.

Suspended Actuations

Communicative signs evolve from volitional acts (movements) which change their functionality. They are interrupted when being performed, and rather than being taken to its end are used to influence the behavior of another. So they take the form of a sort of metonymy. They are *suspended* actuations (Bates, 1976; Rivière and Sotillo, 1999). An example provided by Rivière (1984) may help to clarify this issue

> *Pablo (18 moths) came with a lighter. He made sure he captured my attention and, then, showing the lighter, carried out several times the action of blowing. (...) Pablo insisted, repeating the sequence of touching my leg, calling me, showing and blowing, while looking at me. Then I understood (...). I took the lighter and lighted it. Pablo's smile indicated that he was understood. He had managed to communicate the desired effect. (p. 145, my translation, emphasis in the original)*

When this happens something very important appears: the capability of using an old resource for something completely new (see Perinat, 2007). An actuation formerly included in a script is taken out of context and used for a different purpose (Pablo liked to play the game of blowing the flame of his daddy's lighter). Now the meaning of the blowing the lighter is "daddy light it!" To be able to reach to this point, a lengthy process of development must have happened. What is of interest here is how these movements for communication become segregated from the script to which they belong, and come to the forefront, and so becoming themselves objects to be understood, to be made intelligible. Then they become susceptible to new uses.

For this to happen, the movements that mediate communication have first to be distinguished from other types of actuation, they have to be taken as new things to understand. Communicative actuations and scripts have to become themselves the target for attention, they have to be taken as a new kind of objects with some particular affordances (now of a social nature) – which afford one to perform some actuations, but not others. One has to turn them into a representamen of what to do, or what not to do, and so to act as signs for subsequent action-semiosis and actuations. This is a process that goes along throughout chains of circular reactions now carried out not upon objects

on the environment, but upon the actuations of actors – when one actuate upon another, through the mediation of a particular bodily movement.

Such is the case of gestures and vocalizations (Wundt, 1973; Valsiner & van der Veer, 1996; see also Chapter 11, Español, 2007). Both the attempted outcome of the communicative actuation (what wants to be communicated) and the mediating actuation (the gesture or vocalization that so become the signs which make communication possible) have to become things to be understood. This requires the construction of schemas for actuation from which many types of signs develop, what eventually leads to the appearance of conventional signs that now are artificial, specially transformed for their use in communication.

When this happens, two new kinds of objects appear:

a. communication as a type of dramaturgical actuations within scripts, and
b. communicative symbols as means for communication.

Then the recursive use of the same type of instrumental means to influence the course of communication becomes possible. One can produce and respond to communicative actuations, and even more, the possibility of developing means of communicating about the regulation of communication itself opens, and so the seeds for the development of arguing are planted.

Development of Mediational Actuations for Communication

This can only happen when a concrete communicative actuation becomes itself a detached object capable of acting as a symbol (Werner & Kaplan, 1984), that is, when it has been, first, detached as something to be understood; second constituted as a permanent object (i.e., subjected to the process of being the subject of an argument – see Table 10.3); and, third, subjected to conventionalized use within situations of social communication. This requires the repeated development of various intentional schemas, so that the resulting actuations may become enactive dicents signs, capable of eventually producing an argument that constitutes the sign itself as an independent object. So, the very process of producing a communicative symbol includes within the possibility of double articulation: the capability of turning outcomes into means for new outcomes. This developmental process is a continuation of the processes so far explored, but, in addition, it makes completely new processes to appear.

Communicative actuations mediated by these new objects (communicative symbols) open completely new vistas, and make new problematic realms to appear. These symbols are themselves objects, and so they are objects that result from the production of enactive dicents and arguments (their use is learned by practicing in communication). They are, first pragmatically constituted, then conventionalized, and finally acquired by newcomers to the group when inter-actuating in a particular environment in which the hosting group has constructed their own *Social Umwelt*.

The function of communication is to regulate mutual actuations in social intercourse and cooperation when performing actuations upon the environment. Communication is itself a type of performing actuation, and so subjected to the possibilities of structural coupling between the inter-actuating actors, and between them and the natural objects of the environment. Thus, communication mediated by artificial symbols develops its own grammar of action. A grammar that on the one hand follows the natural teleonomy of the inter-actuating morphological structures (of the inter-actuating organisms and the elements of the environment), but also of the structural *affordances* of the mediating symbols.

Actuations and scripts always have a teleonomic nature, they result from the structural coupling of the organism and the environment (or between two inter-actuating organisms) and so they are proportional to the possibilities for coupling, they follow a ratio. There is no doubt that not all coupling possibilities are fulfilled, but only those that are functional for reaching dynamic equilibria. This makes actuations and scripts to follow a rationale, so that it can be said that animal behavior within an environment follow some rules, that a grammar of action develops along its encounters with the part of the environment that constitutes its *Umwelt*. The rules that make this grammar are a result of the development of behavior, and so they do not explain all the possibilities of action, but only those actually exercised along the past of organism's life. Thus the exercise of new coupling possibilities may expand the rules of this grammar. When performing actuations mistakes can happen, because of interpretative errors or operational mishaps, but this cannot take one to say that an action or a performance is true or false, neither that it is moral or immoral. They simply follow a teleonomic rationale. They are actuations addressed to produce favorable outcomes and avoid unfavorable ones, which signal in the form of affections. That is why it can be said that performing actuations are driven to obtain pleasure and avoid pain. Something that since Antiquity has been taken as the seed for the development of morals (González, 1997).

The Social Affordance of Mediational Symbols

Conventionalized symbols are objects which require their users to accommodate to them in order to handle them successfully. The functional structure of each particular symbol has some particular *affordances*, but beyond the physical affordances of the symbolic object itself, what is at stake concerning its communicative capabilities is the social *affordances* it provides (Costall, 1995). Communicational symbols afford to regulate the others' performing actuations, as well as allowing the others to regulate one's own performing actuations. Or rather, it is the change of the actuation of the others what artificial symbols afford. But things now get complicated. As said before, a newcomer into a group enters into a new physical and socio-cultural environment for him or her, but that environment is already understood as a *Social Umwelt* by the hosting group. This *Umwelt* is not only made of familiar objects filled with sense, but also of communicational devices, social norms and practices from which socio-cultural activities get a meaning. The hosting group's *Umwelt* is not made only of objects, but also of symbols, rituals, hierarchies, etiquette, and so on, which are meaningful because there has previously been a mutual attunement of the abilities of the members of the group and the development of those cultural devices. They are the result of a historical process. In order to communicate with the members of the group, the new-comer has to attune him/herself with that socio-cultural environment so that s/he ends up making it also a part of his/her own *Umwelt*, at least to some extent.

The newcomer has to master the use of objects and symbols, pragmatically, semiotically and semantically. Something that can only be done by participating in socio-cultural practices. When this is being done many mishaps may happen. Some members of the group may resist complying with changing their actuations because of one's inadequate use of communicative symbols. Some others may do so but only in some particular circumstances, when it fits within some on-going scripts and complies with the grammar of inter-actuations developed within the group, that is, with its social norms. It may even happen that the inexpert newcomer is rebuked because inadvertently braking social norms. The newcomer, in order to become accepted as a member of the group has to orient him/herself within the shared environment of the group in the same way as his/her hosts, so that objects, movements, and symbols could be interpreted in similar ways.

Social actuations, communication, and language are all different forms of motor actuations regulated by different kind of rules, which are not completely independent to each other. The grammar of the use of symbolic means for communication shares some of its features with the natural grammars of actuation (since communication is

itself a form of actuation), but also has the peculiarities inherent to the particular structure of the artificial symbolic means developed in the social practices of the group and the pragmatic capabilities of their use in that particular group. Since phylogenetic evolution surely has left its traces in the very morphological structure of the actuating human agents, and their environments also share many characteristics (but not all of them), there is no doubt that there must be many common features in the grammars of all languages. However, the physical, cultural and historical diversity of different social *Umwelten* also guarantee many grammatical differences between them.

Conventional Symbols and Agency

As the argument so far presented in this volume shows, there is a continuity in which lineal causality turns into teleonomy, and this rather than produce a necessary path of development, takes a particular one among many possible others as a result of the contingences of existence, and so producing the development of some particular abilities and not others. When disequilibrium happens, there may be alternative ways in which a mutual coupling between the environment and the organism's structures can be afforded in order to reach a new state of dynamic equilibrium. A new state of equilibrium which does not have to be necessarily optimal, but that can be satisfactory enough (Valsiner, 1997), so that some alternative functionalities may appear. Or, in other words, teleonomy sets restrictions as well as offers means for the further development of action and actuation, and open possibilities for different goals to be settled. The *Trajectory Equifinality Model* (Chapter 4, Sato et al., 2007) is a device that helps to picture how teleonomy, by being subjected to contingences, opens the way to the possibility of teleology to arise. Conventional symbols are a consequence of this.

Artificial symbols are a landmark for a new distribution of agency. Now teleonomy can start to be harnessed, and contingences can start to be governed. New functionalities can be made to appear as a result of the co-construction of new symbols in communication, and so new contingencies can be made to appear, although most often they offer unexpected outcomes and collateral effects. Whatever the case, agency then is not anymore only a result of natural contingencies. By using conventional symbols actors become capable of starting managing the received teleonomies in their on-going performances, and so acquire some agency for the government of their own future and that of Nature. Teleology is starting to take shape, and the actor is on the way of becoming an author.

Conventional Symbols Overcome the Tyranny of Presence

Future can only appear because of the working of imagination. The past also cannot be recalled without the ability of making present what is absent. This is a result of imagination – a product of symbolic actuation. A statement that requires some clarification.

Imagination can only exist by the use of symbolic representations. Mental images (imagery) are one of the resources imagination uses. Piaget and Inhelder (1966) defined mental images as the interiorized imitation of accommodative action. Images, so conceived, are no different to the capability of an enactive dicent symbol to produce a set of semiosis-actuations referring to an enactive argument that makes the object to exist as a structured otherness. So viewed, images are operational constructions resulting from previous intentional schemes and actuations. They are a result of intentional actuations which take a symbolic function capable of stabilizing what has been felt into permanent objects and situations.

That is why a quality, or an affect or movement, can act as signs – what Liszka (o.c.) called the presentative character of signs. But when semiotic capabilities develop (as they do in the higher vertebrates – birds and mammals), these signs can be combined among themselves, and so the capability of producing enactive presentations

makes possible that images (a natural symbol) develop. This makes possible a limited form of imagination to appear. An imagination that only can proceed as prompted by sensed qualities, affects and movements, but that still is able to maintain a steady course of action towards the achievement of a goal, unless an external event interrupts the chain of action-semiosis that shape a performing actuation, so opening the path to new ones. When the latter happens, new semiosis (actions triggered by the irruptive event) set the path for new actuations. If this disruptive event, rather than being the result of uncontrollable environmental contingencies can be managed by the agent, then the possibility for a self management of intentionality is open. This is something that will be explored later.

The Role of Imagination

This conception of imagination does not require any type of phenomenological images, nor any assortment of phenomenological qualia to be taken into account for its explanation. However, psychophysics, experimental phenomenology, and the psychology of perception and attention are addressed to the study of sensorial thresholds and how one attends to and understands environmental changes. These subdisciplines, when performing experiments with humans, cannot avoid to refer to some kind of introspective data, where qualitative phenomenological qualities are reported. It seems as if the psychological processes of action-semiosis at some stage of their development produce some kind of phenomenological awareness, which sometimes parallels behavioral awareness, and some other times does not. However, phenomenological awareness is not a necessary condition for semiosis-action to happen and to show its influence on actuations, as subliminal perception and unconscious learning show (for a review, see Froufe, 1997).

Conventional symbols cannot exist if before they have not been an image. They have to be constituted first as imaginary objects carried upon an argument composed by intentional schemas. Objects are themselves a semiotic construction resulting from intentional schemas (see Chapter 10). They can only be made to exist by producing an image, which itself is no other thing that a set of actuations. So viewed, imagery and imagination provide the bridge between a presentative quasi-mind and a fully representative mind. This is the case of gestures (either motor or oral) and, later, of words. Once they are constituted as such, they can be incorporated into the complexities of actuations. They can appear within the on-going chain of actuations within scripts, and so act as interruptive events to change the sense of actuations, or to help to keep a steady course in spite of other distracting stimuli. It is only when such events can purposely be managed to happen, that the wanderings of imagination can be harnessed, and so it can be turned into a means for directing *attention*, calling to already known means for performing scripts, or dramaturgical actuations and problem solving.

From Images to Words

This is what conventionalized communicative symbols do in social life. Gestures and words are objects which mediate communication. The others provide one with a sign that interrupts the on-going recursive semiosis, and so orienting actuations in a particular direction, as well as provoking new semiosis now mediated by the present conventional communicative symbols which the agent will increasingly be proficient in handling. The actor has to learn to understand the sense of the symbol in his/her ongoing actuations, as well as how to make use of them to affect the actuations of others, and her/his own actuations. For this to be possible to happen, the conventional symbolic object has first to be populated with sense.

> "The word of language – is half alien [chuzoye – not belonging to me and unknown – in Russian] word. It becomes "one's own" when the speaker inhabits it with his intention, his accent, masters the

> word, brings it to bear upon his meaningful and expressive strivings. Until that moment of appropriation [prisvoenie in Russian] the word is not existing in neutral and faceless language (the speaker does not take the word from a dictionary!), but [it exists] on the lips of others, in alien contexts, in service of others' intentions: from here it has to be taken and made into one's own." (Bakhtin, 1934/35; published in 1975, p. 106. English version, 1981, pp. 293–294)

When a newcomer arrives to a group, as when a child is born, s/he becomes a part of the *Social Umwelt* of his/her caregivers. Each of the elements that shapes that social Umwelt has received a set of particular functions within the group. Each natural object, each particular artifact, each particular action, noise or movement is for something, has a particular teleology distilled along the temporal evolution of the group. So, in order to become a member of the group, the child not only has to couple him/herself with those natural things, but also has to master the conventional use of these objects, with their sense, with the teleology historically distilled within the evolution of group norms. S/he has to construct the images, gestures, words and utterances and join the practices which give meaning to the natural and cultural elements of the environment so that it becomes his/her own Umwelt. S/he becomes humanized by sharing a particular *Socio-Cultural Umwelt*. The turning of movement and motor actions into social actuations (Español, 2007, chapter 11), the acquisition of the meaning of objects (Rodríguez, 2007, chapter 12; Rodríguez & Moro, 1999), the mastering of the use of language, or the acquisition of social norms and moral development (Paolicchi, 2007, chapter 27) are examples of how socio-cultural milieus shape both the structure of the perceived environment and the functional psychological structures of the individual members of the group.

Vygotsky (1934) claimed that this capacity for regulating one's actions starts being managed by others by the use of speech, and that only later on the actor becomes proficient enough to be able to use these very same means to regulate his or her own actuations. This requires oneself to be taken as another, as an addressee of one's own communicative actuations (Vygotsky, 1934; Ricoeur, 1990), that is, the construction of some sort of image of oneself as an object among others, as an agent and as an actor whose performances can be regulated by the use of those conventional communicative symbols. An image of the self can then start to be developed.

Verbal Utterances, Arguments, and Reason

Conventional symbolic objects mediating communication are a result of imagination. But now these products of imagination are under use in communicative actuations. Actuations on the environment follow some regularities, they have a rationale set by the possible ratio of relations between the possibility of mutual couplings between the organism and its *Umwelt*, a rationale that takes a particular form as it has being actualized by the contingencies happened in the past (see Chapter 10, this volume).

Things get even more complex once one take into account the affordances of conventional symbols (both physical and social). Contextual pragmatics of the use of these symbols makes them to change their function, make new symbols to appear and new rules for their use to develop. So the rules for how to use these symbols together when communicating (sintaxis), how to make them to have some sense vis à vis the on going performing actuations (semiotics), and when and with whom to use them (pragmatics), become more and more intricate. The intersection of these rules (in their origin intentional schemas turned into social norms) creates the possibility of a shared sense in the use of these symbols, of the objects to which they refer to, and of the scripts whose performance they regulate.

Communicative actuations in a group are a particular form of actuations, and as such, they also follow a rationale, but now this rationale gets more intricate, since it also reflects the way communication happens in the group. Its social norms, its hierarchies and practices leave a mark in the structure of social communicational rules, as Michel de Foucault (e.g., 1969/1972) emphasized.

Social norms themselves may also be symbolically coded and declaratively transmitted. They may even be presented in explicit discourses sometimes purposefully devised for transmitting these norms. When this is the case, the result is that a network of mutual regulation comes into operation. Now symbolic actuations and scripts get also regulated by a communicational grammar inscribed within the grammar of the social performing actuations carried out within the group, at the same time that they all are subjected to a mutual transformation through time.

Artificial symbols for communication become then elements in linked actuations within chains of performing scripts regulated by grammatical rules. This makes something completely new to appear – *utterances*. When this happens imagination goes into a qualitative transformation. Not only objects can now be represented, but also actions and events. Words can represent the absent, and utterances can combine them following the rules of the communicative grammar, and so making possible to represent events and entities impossible to witness in direct presentations. New arguments (now supported on words connected by the grammar of communication and action) can be deployed, and so new objects can be created, and so abstractions increasingly deprived of sensorial qualities (such as concepts, explicit norms, etc.) and sometimes even imaginary (mythical entities) are, first, made to appear in language, then to be represented through imagery in a figurative shape and, eventually, sometimes even taken to be real.

When this ability is mastered a past event can be recalled, and voluntary memory appears; problem solving can be performed via representation before actually performing actuations on the environment, and so thinking and planning can develop;

and one's own actions can become a subject to think upon, attention can be controlled and self reflective consciousness becomes possible. Past and future can then be imagined, and even the present can be conceived as a transient state in a flow of time. Actuations can be represented in speech as events, and scripts as stories. And everything that is noticed to happen may get interpreted and communicated, to another or to one self, by using the help of a spoken argument.

In sum, communicative actions, now mediated by symbolic conventional objects (words) incorporated into communicative actuations and scripts regulated by the rules of a historically developed grammar[3] can not only re-present anything in language, but also report it to somebody else, and argue about the accuracy, convenience or goodness of different representations. When this process is already in motion *reason* appears on the stage.

Reason then is not a set of transcendental rules. It is the result of natural action on the natural and social cradles where life develops. It is a result of the mutual coupling of morphological structures when struggling to keep themselves alive. It collects together the accumulated experience of evolution and social history. It is a formidable device for survival. But it is also subjected to the tributes paid to past contingencies, of both the evolutionary path of the species, and the history of the group.

Reason, as Piaget emphasized, is a distillation of actuations in search of equilibria. It is made of actions, schemas, and rules. But also of understanding, sense-making, communication, production of conventional means of communication, and regulation of actuations. It is not transcendental. It is the result of encounters of organisms and their surroundings (natural and social) in order to reach an understanding capable of producing intelligent behavior. Reason can be modeled as a set of propositional rules which govern actuations. But it is also inevitably bounded to spatial and temporal situations in which the actor lived. To brake these limits. Reason has to go beyond the application of these

rules. But for this to happen, rules have to be turned upon themselves. Utterances have to refer not only to actuations, but also to other utterances. Then a propositional logic, that goes beyond the formulation of judgments, can be developed, and the formidable capabilities of symbolic reasoning be stretched. But for this to happen something else has to appear in the scenery playing a decisive role – culture. But it is too early in this volume to go into some detail in its examination and how it affects human behavior. The General Conclusions of this volume will go into the examination of how culture can make reason to turn into *rationality*, reality into the *world*, desires and moral rules into *ethics*, and the actor into a *person* capable of authoring his/her own life.

Table 14.2 presents a summary of the development of higher psychological functions, together with changes in agency and the mutual transformation of the environment and the human subject. As there can be seen, the highest psychological functions can only appear as a result of socio-cultural processes which involve not only groups, but also groups in collaboration or competition. This make these higher functions to take particular shapes as a result of the contingencies of concrete historical processes.

Consciousness Creates Reality

The argument presented throughout this chapter is that reality makes itself apparent in consciousness through experiences, and these are as much a result of these encounters as to how psyche works. As a result of experiences, beliefs about what reality is develop. So these beliefs are not independent of what psyche does when encountering things of the environment. Until now, I have gone into some detail about how psychological functions develop, and new representational means get produced, following the principles of a theory of action-semiosis presented in Chapter 10. But little has been said about what experiences and beliefs are. Experience and

Table 14.2: Evolution of the co-construction of agency and human higher psychological functions in relationships of inclusive separation

These developmental processes can only happen within the double dialectics of human development in a socio-cultural environment, and the historical change of socio-cultural groups when interacting among themselves. This double dialectics is shown in the table by alternating socio-cultural (in italics) and individual agents.

Acting Entity	Agency	Description	Explanation	Functionality	Functions	External Elements
Group	*Social Practices*	*Collective conventionalised ways of acting for the maintenance of the stability of the group*	*Functional-Teleonomic*	*Coordination of actuations, actions, behaviour and movements*	*Artefacts Cultural symbols Norms and rules Social Practices*	*Individuals*
Human individual (author)	Conventionalized actuation	Actuations shaped by socio-cultural conventions Actuations which carry out social tasks	Teleonomic-Teleological	Capability for representing situations in the absence of objects	Language Logical thinking Intersubjectivity & Subjectivity Self-Consciousness Planning Will Memory & Attention Persona Morality Reason	The group
Metagrupal Interacting groups	*Competition/ collaboration*	*Conflicts of conventions and development of new conventionalizations*	*Teleonomic-Teleological*	*Negotiation of conflicts and cooperation*	*Increasingly decontextualized social discourses and symbolic systems Meta-rules & rationalities History*	*Other groups*
Rational agent	Activity	Dramaturgical actuations when rules are in conflict or no rules are fitted for problem solving	Teleological	Problem solving Creation of criteria for truth	Rational creativity Theoretical & metatheoretical discourses Rationality Ethics	Otherness as object for one's ethical responsibility

belief seem to be intertwined when encountering reality, and reality also seems bounded to the other two terms. This chapter aimed at disentangling these terms. We have gone quite a way in this task, but a discussion of these terms is still to be done.

What Is Experience?

John Dewey (1917) took experience to be a pivot term between what he called the old and the new philosophy. According to him, experience is not just a matter related to knowledge, but a result of the relationship between an alive being and its physical and social environment. It is not something primarily physical which may later be tainted with subjectivity, it refers to an objective world to which human action and sufferings belong and is modified because of human reactions. It is not something just referring to what happened in the past (what was felt); rather, vital experience is experimental, it represents an effort for change, a projection towards the unknown, a march towards the future. Instead to be subjected to particularities, experience takes into account connections and continuities. Conscious experience cannot be separated from inferences. Experiences and thinking cannot be taken as opposites anymore.

If we accept Dewey's position, experience is not a category to be taken for granted as the foundation of knowledge about the world. Experience does not present anything in a ready form to be later subjected to the working of reason. There are many kinds of experiences, and all of them involve intelligence, understanding and some kind of thinking. Experience is a process. Rather than talking of experience, we should go into the pains of studying the varieties of experiencing. It is by experiencing that we get to know the real. But experience never presents what is real out there without any trace of what I do when encountering those things. Nevertheless I have the feeling that I am encountering something real. I shape ideas (representations), and I communicate to others and to myself what I take to really be out there. How can this be done?

From Experiences to Beliefs and Reality

It is by experiencing that we make our conceptions about what reality is, that is, our beliefs about the real. But what is a belief? According to Peirce (CP 5: 308–410) a belief is the establishment of an habit. Beliefs are rules for action, and different beliefs are distinguishable because of the different ways of acting they produce. So experiences are as much a result as a cause of beliefs. Some habits of actuating (intentional schemas) produce some experiences (interpretants), which are ways of understanding carried on upon movements (volitional acts resulting from an action-semiosis), upon things of the environment (inert objects, other actors, or myself). These movements can be a physical displacement of a part of the body, or some physic-chemical process of the body. They can either apply some force upon an object, or just to produce a gesture or a set of noises. Whatever the case, the resulting movements are not just physical actions, are also interpretations, understandings, resulting from the working of psyche, of natural intelligence. Gestures and utterances sometimes are able to produce movements of others (or myself), which can be greatly disproportional to the physical impact of the flow of energy upon which the message is transmitted. They can have the effect of changing the actuations of the addressee (often myself), to affect the course of his/her behavior. Conventional signs are able to produce other habits which in turn produce other experiences and make different beliefs appear. And the process can go on along many different cycles of action-semiosis, so producing a sort of successive kaleidoscopic presentations of reality, or rather, of beliefs about reality, of understandings of what reality is.

It has to be clarified that the habits Peirce talked about where misread by the behaviorists (Riba, 1995). The habits Peirce meant had a triadic (not a dyadic) structure. They were not just associations pairing stimuli and responses, but semiotic triadic processes that put together in a basic unit of analysis (semiosis) physical encounters, knowledge, and interpretation.

So experience and beliefs cannot be disentangled at the beginning. A reaction before a change in the environment (such as an orientation effect) it is at the same time as much an experience felt, as a belief that something potentially harmful may be about to happen. But experiences and beliefs start to separate from each other when utterances start describing experiences in words, and so re-present in a new medium what was presented before. And even more when utterances refer to previous utterances, and so produce arguments about what was presented and understood. When this happens argumentation and verbal thinking are on the move. Reason is already on the stage and a new kind of belief appears. Then it is possible to differentiate between this new kind of beliefs and the former ones. The former can be taken to be just experiences, and the latter experiences upon experiences which we may call, if we want, proper beliefs. But they are not different in nature, both are forms of actuation. The difference is not only in the number of layers of actuations mediating between different kinds of experiences, but it is mainly on the kind of re-presentational means producing the resulting experience: motor actuations, feelings, images, or words. One may say that beliefs are always ways of make sense of experiences by producing statements about what happened, or about what some reality is beyond particular experienced events. So viewed, beliefs are but a kind of experiences – those that can be communicated, and so capable of having some effect on directing the actuations of others, or oneself. Beliefs are then communicative experiences capable of directing motor actuations.

Beliefs are the result of actuations. They translate experiencing in utterances and so have the virtue of freezing the flow of experience in an inert product. Once a belief is uttered, experiences are presented as an outcome, as something presenting the virtues of the real, and so making reality stable and predictable. Words are able to substantiate experiencing, and so producing an environment of stable entities, whose changes in the future could be forecasted, so that the uncertainty of life could be faced more easily. Something which is a continuation of the mutual co-construction of the functional capabilities of the agent and the Umwelt (von Uexküll, 1928).

Beliefs are creatures of argumentation. It is through processes of argumentation that beliefs about what reality is can develop. This is no news. Chapter 10 (Rosa, 2007) went into explaining how Peirce's semiotic logic offers formalisms for explaining how feelings (either sensorial or affective) through recursive chains of action-semiosis make qualities, objects and situation to appear. So viewed, it is the working of psyche (the encounters between the organism and things in its environment) what makes objects and situations (reality) to be constructed as a result of the processes of producing arguments (Peirce's sign type 10). This is applicable not only to the production of the reality out there, but also to what is in here – myself as an object and the processes that go-on within me. The objectivity to which Dewey (o.c.) referred cannot leave the subject of experiencing or believing aside. Reality and the experiencing agent are made together, so that both together are the objective world (see Figure 14.1, and also Figure 1.3).

Consciousness

Consciousness is a contested term both in Psychology and Philosophy. Sometimes it is taken to be a kind of realm where Being reveals itself, and some others it is pictured as just a sort of epiphenomenological phosphorescence with no role whatsoever on what psyche does. Other times it is taken to be just a part of the working of psyche, since it is the unconscious that takes care of much of the job.

The argument so far here developed takes one to conceive consciousness as referring to experiencing, believing, arguing, and thinking. And so consciousness furnishes us with ideas and feelings about reality, ourselves, the desirable and the undesirable, beauty and

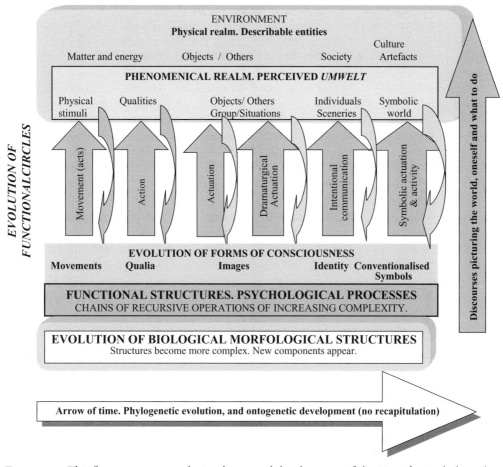

Figure 14.1. This figure attempts to depict the mutual development of the *Umwelt*, psychological functions and phenomenological representations in consciousness via the working of functional circles of actions and actuations between the organism and its environment.

ugliness, what is right and what is wrong, and so makes us capable of projecting the future and, together with this, morally accountable.

If consciousness is the outcome of the processes of experiencing, believing, arguing, and thinking, has it being existing for ever since the origin of life? Does it make sense to speak of consciousness as opposed to the unconscious? To answer these questions is not going to take long, since my aim here is not getting into a theoretical discussion, but stating what my position is as a result of what it has been here said so far.

Consciousness is the continuation of the processes of acting and meaning-making, but consciousness is also judging beliefs as true,

doubtful or false; dramaturgical actuations to be right or wrong; and experiences to be beautiful or ugly. Consciousness is holding believes about reality and one's self, and so it makes possible to direct one's own conduct (and that of the others) by communication through conventional symbolic means. It is mainly the use of these symbolic means in communication what makes consciousness separate from the unconscious.

Sometimes several kinds of consciousness are distinguished, such as (a) phenomenological consciousness (awareness of what is going on around me, or in me), (b) self-reflective consciousness and, related to this, (c) moral consciousness.

Phenomenological consciousness is nearly synonymous to experience. But not all experiences can be conscious. At this point of the argument one must be ready to admit that may be there are ways of experiences impossible to put into images or words. Sometimes aches and pains seem to appear and fade away, somehow going back and forward through the foggy limits of consciousness, making them to be hardly noticeable, and very difficult not only to describe to somebody else, but also to oneself. They are feelings which are in the limits of the unspeakable, and sometimes beyond that. We can only report (to ourselves or to others) what we can separate from something different, what we can somehow picture as distinct, and often this distinction appears in the very act of attending to what is going on when experiencing or when scrutinizing one's own experiencing, or even when putting that experience into words. This can be no surprise. As Peircean semiotics states objects appear as a result of the signaling capabilities of feelings, and so is the case of the objects that appear in consciousness. Phenomenological consciousness can be clear when habits for producing images are already developed, when words are available to report what is felt, when schemas for communication are ready for use. When this happens the stream of consciousness flow smoothly and we feel at home within reality. When it does not we have no way of producing conscious experiencing. The unconscious then is a sort of shadow experiencing beyond the explainable that cannot be put into words, nor even represented by images. It is not only ineffable, but also shapeless. It is the result of action-semiosis before symbols. It cannot be put into words, since words could not exist but as a result of semiosis elaborated upon these early type of signs.

The unexpected then produces surprise or fear (interpretants) and one feels urged to flight or scrutinize it, so it can be made understandable, to assimilate it to an image previously shaped or to produce a new one. But does this means that we have some kind of basic presentational (or representational) units, so that the real (outside or inside the skin) can be presented in consciousness? Philosophers of the mind and many psychologists interested on the study of consciousness are familiar with the term *qualia*. For them consciousness is populated by qualia, unspeakable qualities which resist any attempt to be described. They are private and incommunicable, and they provide the flesh of the experiences through which reality (and ourselves) appear before consciousness. If they were right, there would be a sort of basic units of experience which would make up any possible way of being conscious of anything. But what about expanding the amount of qualia one can experience? One can only appreciate an outstanding Bordeaux, a good extra virgin olive oil, a delicious curry sauce, or a moving interpretation of Schubert's string quintet by educating one's own senses. By being able to make new qualia to surge into consciousness. How is this possible? No doubt this has a lot to do with sensorial receptors, psychophysical thresholds and so on, but is it that new qualia can appear somehow out of the blue?, is it that they are kept somewhere in an unconscious storehouse, so they could be retrieved and put into place when the adequate stimulus comes and one learns how to sort out both physical stimuli and qualia of consciousness? Dennet (1991) says that qualia are imagined by the working of the mind. I believe that Peirce gave a similar solution, but also a more detailed and feasible explanation. Signs types 1, 2, and 3 (see Chapter 10, this volume) are the result of a series of semiosis-actions which result in providing new interpretants (signs for new semiosis to come) so that new qualia can be produced and so objects can become more and more rich when present in consciousness. That is what intentional schemas do (see Chapter 10, this volume) and so they make new forms of experiencing to appear.

Phenomenical consciousness is then a result of action-semiosis, but also of conventional symbolic representation (images and words). It is through acting and meaning-making that qualities appear, objects and images can be formed, conventional symbols can be constructed, and communication can be established. Once these abilities are developed enough, self-consciousness can argue whether beliefs are true or not. Then experiencing turns into experimentation, testing whether beliefs when directing experiencing can be reported as referring to the same reality or not, and so putting the process of truth-making into the move.

Self-consciousness cannot exist without communication and argumentation mediated by symbolic means. It is the result of a multi-layered semiotic process which eventually can produce arguments conveyed in a language regulated by rules which allow and constrain reporting experiences, directing processes of experimentation, arguing about the communication of reported experiences, and so creating voices and ventriloquating voices (Bakhtin, 1981; Wertsch, 1991) in public or inner dialogues which make up self-reflective consciousness (Vygotsky, 1934).

So viewed, moral consciousness is but a form of self-reflective consciousness. Social norms can be ventriloquated and so made present in the polyphony of inner dialogues. Dramatic actuations can then become a matter to be judged and so moral feelings appear as interpretants, making one to feel good or bad vis à vis the judged behavior. And beyond this, moral arguments can be developed and so an increased refinement of moral sentiments becomes possible.

There is one last point to be made. As stated before, Peirce characterized beliefs as habits, and so made them susceptible to be compiled into a sign (one of the kind of legisigns). Vygotsky (1934) also stated that inner speech is abbreviated and takes a predicative form that very often makes it inaccessible to introspection, as the researchers of the Würzburg School discovered over one century ago. Argumentation can be performed very rapidly and accurately well beyond the reach of conscious experience. This is also the case of motor schemas such as learning to ride a bike or driving a car, even if these schemas were learned through a long and painful conscious effort. If one tries to recover an awareness of the actuations being carried out, the ongoing behavior looses smoothness and unexpected mistakes can appear. Consciously controlled actuations can become automatic and unconscious (Leont'ev, 1978).

Final Remarks, Culture, Rationality, and Ethics

Consciousness is a result of the meaning-making capabilities of organisms, but it is also the beginning of a new cycle in the development of psyche. Once it is on the stage, two sorts of realms appear: the objective and the subjective. One learns that not everything one takes to be real happens to be so, that consciousness does not always coincide with reality, and that there are parts of reality not accessible to consciousness. But, it starts to be clear to one self that nothing can be conceived without somehow being taken into consciousness.

Subjectivity is the result of acting. But conscious subjectivity cannot exist without intersubjectivity, without others from which to disentangle oneself, to communicate and to argue with. It is in intersubjectivity where socially conventionalized symbols appear, where self-consciousness develops, and where reality and myself can be separated.

Social life is the cradle of self-consciousness. It provides not only situations for experiencing, but also symbolic tools for producing and communicating beliefs. The social groups accumulate conventional symbolic representations of the real and the human, beliefs about what is real or not, beliefs about who one is, or what was the origin of the group, beliefs about what part of the real can be experienced and what is beyond any kind of experiencing. These beliefs are produced and transmitted from one generation to the other. They are often taken to be true, and some others challenged and subjected to discussion. These beliefs are kept in many ways, from tools that shape and give sense to actuations, to icons, symbols, norms, and narratives. They, together with the social practices which make up social life, constitute the socio-cultural realm of human life.

It is through arguing in socio-cultural life where beliefs about what is taken to be real can be challenged, where social norms and moral can be surpassed by on-going events, where traditional ways of behaving, of conceiving one self can become under scrutiny, and so new ways of making true a belief can appear. When this happens, history is on the move. Reason can start to be turned into rationality, the real into conceptions of the world (knowledge), moral into ethics, and human actors can attempt to be the authors of their own life – and become persons.

Acknowledgments

Preparation of this chapter was supported by grant SEJ2005–09110-C03–01/PSIC from the Spanish Ministry of Education and Science.

Notes

1 By abductive actuations, I mean actuations that attempt an enactive understanding of the situation. As explained in Chapter 10, an actuation involving signs of a *rhematic* character can prompt circular reactions so that a *dicentic* semiosis could be produced, from which an interpretation (right or wrong) of the situation can be reached.

2 Conventionalization can be either individual or social. The former is present in learning and the latter is at the basis of the development of cultural symbols.

3 I take the discussion of whether the grammar of language is innate or the result of a social-historical process to be as misguided as the discussion of what part of the variance of human behavior can be attributed to genetics or the environment. It seems to me more feasible that the evolution of morphological structures in the organism has never been independent of what the organism does in its environment, as the Baldwin effect states. That the morphological structures of the organism shape what it can do is no news, and I fail to see how this fact can affect the line of argumentation here deployed.

References

Bakhtin, M. (1981). *The Dialogical Imagination. Four Essays*. Austin: University of Texas Press.

Bates, E. (1976). *Language and Context*. New York: Academic Press.

Bruner, J., Olver, R. R., & Greenfield, P. M. (1966). *Studies in Cognitive Growth*. New York: John Wiley and Sons.

Byrne, R. W. & Withen, A. (Eds.), (1988). *Machiavellian Intelligence*. Oxford: Oxford University Press.

Costall, A. P. (1995). Socializing Affordances. *Theory & Psychology*, 5, 467–482.

de Waal, F. (1982). *Chimpanzee Politics*. Baltimore: The Johns Hopkins University Press.

Dennet, D. (1991). *Consciousness Explained*. London: Penguin.

Dewey, J. (1917). The need for a Recovery in Philosophy. In R. J. Bernstein (Ed.), *John Dewey: On Experience, Nature and Freedom: Representative Selections*. New York: Bobbs-Merrill, 1960, 19–69.

Español, S. (2007). Alive Movement in Symbol Formation. In J. Valsiner & A. Rosa (Eds.), *Cambridge Handbook of Sociocultural Psychology*. New York: Cambridge University Press.

Fields, W. M., Segerdahl, P., & Savage-Rumbaugh, S. (2007). The material Practices of ape language research. In J. Valsiner & A. Rosa (Eds.), *Cambridge Handbook of Sociocultural Psychology* (pp. 169–186). New York: Cambridge University Press.

Foucault, M. de (1969/1972). *The Archaeology of Knowledge. And the Discourse on Language*. New York: Tavistock.

Frijda, N. H. (2004). Emotion and Action. In A. S. R. Manstead, N. Frijda & A. Fischer (Eds). *Feelings and Emotion*. Cambridge: Cambridge University Press, 158–173.

Froufe, M. (1997). *El inconsciente cognitivo. La cara oculta de la mente*. Madrid: Biblioteca Nueva.

González, A. (1997). *Estructuras de la praxis. Ensayo de una filosofía primera*. Madrid: Trotta.

James, W. (1890). *The Principles of Psychology*. New York: Holt.

Köhler, W. (1925). *The Mentality of Apes*. New York: Harcourt Brace.

Leont'ev, A. N. (1978). *Activity, Consciousness and Personality*. Englewood Cliffs: Prentice-Hall.

Liszka, J. J. (1996). *A General Introduction to the Semeiotic of Charles Saunders Peirce*. Bloomington and Indianapolis: Indiana University Press.

Peirce, C. S. (1931–1958). *Collected Papers of Charles Sanders Peirce* (8 vols.) Charles Hartshorn, Paul Weiss, and Arthur Burks

(Eds). Cambridge, MA: Harvard University Press.

Paolicchi, P. (2007). The institutions inside. In J. Valsiner & A. Rosa (Eds.), *Cambridge Handbook of Sociocultural Psychology* (pp. 560–575). New York: Cambridge University Press.

Perinat, A. (2007). Comparative Development of Communication. In J. Valsiner & A. Rosa (Eds.), *Cambridge Handbook of Sociocultural Psychology* (pp. 140–163). New York: Cambridge University Press.

Piaget, J. & Inhelder, B. (1966). *L'image mentale chez l'enfant*. Paris: Presses Universitaires de France.

Riba, C. (1995). De ayer y de hoy: Charles S. Peirce (1839–1914). *Anuario de Psicología, 64*, 83–89.

Ricoeur, P. (1990). *Soi-même comme un autre*. Paris: Éditions du Seuil.

Rivière, A. (1984). Acción e interacción en el origen del símbolo. In J. Palacios, A. Marchesi y M. Carretero, Psicología Evolutiva (vol. 2). Madrid: Alianza Editorial, pp. 145–174.

Rivière, A. & Sotillo, A. (1999). Comunicazione, sospensione e semiosi umana. *Metis 1*, 45–76.

Rodríguez, C. (2007). Object Use, Communication and Signs: The Triadic Basis of Early Cognitive Development. In J. Valsiner & A. Rosa (Eds.), *Cambridge Handbook of Sociocultural Psychology* (pp. 257–276). New York: Cambridge University Press.

Rodríguez, C. & Moro, C. (1999). *El mágico número tres. Cuando los niños aún no hablan*. Barcelona: Paidós.

Rosa, A. (2007). Acts of Psyche. In J. Valsiner & A. Rosa (Eds.), *Cambridge Handbook of Sociocultural Psychology* (pp. 205–237). New York: Cambridge University Press.

Rosa, A., Gomila, A., & Vega, J. (2004). La evolución de la mente. Algunas consideraciones metodológicas y substantivas. *Estudios de Psicología* 25 (2), 205–215.

Rosetti-Ferreira, M., Amorim, K., & Silva, A. P. S. (2007). Development through Social Matrix of Meaning. In J. Valsiner & A. Rosa (Eds.), *Cambridge Handbook of Sociocultural Psychology* (pp. 277–292).New York: Cambridge University Press.

Sato, T., Yasuda, Y., Kido, A., Arakawa, A., Muzoguchi, H., & Valsiner, J. (2007). What kind of Sampling in Socio-Cultural Research? In J. Valsiner & A. Rosa (Eds.), *Cambridge handbook of Socio-cultural Psychology* (pp. 82–108). New York: Cambridge University Press.

Searle, J. (1984). Panel Discussion: Has Artificial Intelligence Research Illuminated Human Thinking?. In H. Pagels (Ed.), *Computer Culture: The Scientific, Intellectual and Social Impact of the Computer*. Annals of the New York Academy of Sciences, 426.

Scherer, K. R. (2004). Feelings Integrate the Central Representation of Appraisal-Driven Response Organization in Emotion. In A. S. R. Manstead, N. Frijda & A. Fischer (Eds.), *Feelings and Emotion*. Cambridge: Cambridge University Press, 136–157.

Sherif, M. (1936). *Psychology of social norms*. New York: Holt.

Valsiner, J. (1997). *Culture and the Development of Children's Action*. New York: John Wiley and Sons.

Valsiner, J. (2005). Soziale und Emotionale Entwicklungsaufgaben im kulturellen Kontext. In J. Asendorpf & H. Rauh (Eds.), *Enzyklopädie der Psychologie. Vol. 3. Soziale, emotionale und Persönlichkeitsentwicklung*. Göttingen: Hogrefe, 677–728.

Valsiner, J. & van der Veer, R. (1996). Desde el gesto hasta el self: perspectivas comunes en las sociopsicologías de George Herbert Mead y Lev Vygotsky. In D. Páez & A. Blanco (Eds.), *La Teoría Sociocultural y la Psicología Social Actual*. Madrid: Fundación Infancia y Aprendizaje, 63–73.

Von Uexküll, J. J. (1928). *Theoretische Biologie*. Berlin: Julius Springer.

Vygotsky, L. S. (1934). Thinking and Speech. In R. W. Rieber & A. S. Carton (Eds.), *The Collected Works of L. S. Vygotsky. Vol. 1. Problems of General Psychology*. New York: Plenum, 39–285.

Werner, H. & Kaplan, B. (1963/1984). *Symbol Formation*. Hillsdale: Lawrence Erlbaum.

Wertsch, J. (1991). *Voices of the Mind*. Cambridge, MA: Harvard University Press.

Wundt, W. (1973). *The language of Gestures*. The Hague: Mouton.

CHAPTER 15

Analysis of Cultural Emotion

Understanding of Indigenous Psychology for Universal Implications[1]

Sang-Chin Choi, Gyuseog Han, and Chung-Woon Kim

Emotions are culturally constructed. Culture tells people what they should feel and experience and how to express it in a given situation. Even if the biological bases of emotion may be universal – yet the forms of their meanings differ. In this sense ability to experience emotion is culturally developed (Ratner, 2000).

Understanding culture requires the understanding of emotions – and vice versa. This understanding requires the knowledge about how people experience emotions in each context, how their emotions are expressed and communicated to each other in the relationships, and the functions of emotions in each culture. Such importance of emotion is well recognized in anthropology (e.g., Lutz, 1988; Menon & Shweder, 1994; Rosaldo, 1980). In the present work, we will briefly review psychological studies of emotion in the broad area of cultural psychology. Following this, we will present an analysis of indigenous emotional state prevalent among Koreans as an exemplar of illustrating cultural psychological analysis of emotion. Finally, we will discuss the indigenous analysis in broader context and the implications it has for psychological research in general.

Psychological Research on Emotion in Different Cultures

In the field of cultural psychology,[2] study of emotion has been a persistent topic. This does not mean there is a coherent thread running in all those research. Depending upon the orientation taken by the researchers, diverse findings have been reported. We will briefly discuss three trends over the decades in this area of research.

First generation of emotion research in the context of culture tried to find universals of basic emotions, especially in facial expression of emotions (see Ekman, 1972 for review). The culture was a force operating in inhibiting or masking the display of innate biological emotions. As such, interest in culture is secondary to that of emotion. This research tradition draws heavily on Darwinian evolution theory in showing universals of basic emotions. Emotions here are biologically evolved phenomena for survival that transcend the boundaries of cultures. The issue centers around the numbers and the kinds of basic emotion. At most, culture is regarded as a moderator of innate emotions.

The research tradition that followed the universalist paradigm tried to describe commonalities and differences in emotional experience among different cultures (see Mesquita & Frijda, 1992 for a review). The existence of taken for granted universals and the differences were the area of new discoveries. Accumulation of differences in emotions across the cultures led to various attempts to use various theoretical frameworks (e.g., individualism-collectivism, collective self-construal theory) to account for the cross-cultural differences. These theories postulate to what extent emotional experience can vary between societies, and why, trying to shed a light in understanding the way in which culture shapes emotions. Antecedents (societal values, motivations), and corollaries (ideas, self-concepts, or self-construals) and consequences of emotional experience are investigated and compared across cultures (see Kitayama & Markus, 1994).

Despite their contributions to literature, the research in this tradition has to tackle with critical issues. One is the issue of ecological fallacy, treating individuals in a given culture as homogenous people and comparing them with another group of people treated also as homogenous. A number of scholars have pointed out this critically (Hermans & Kempen, 1998; Valsiner, 1986). Yet, the solution has not been given yet. Even recent method of unpackaging culture (Whiting, 1976) is not immune to this criticism. Unpackaging means picking out psychological constructs assumed to play an important role in social behavior (including emotions) and operationalizing it to differentiate cultures (Rodriguez-Mosquera, Fischer, & Manstead, 2004). So the inclusive concept of culture is replaced by a specific construct of interest. The researchers use it as an explanatory variable for observed social behaviors.

The problem with this method is twofold. Since the culture is an inclusive concept, the difference in the observed behavior is still affected by numerous other factors the researchers opted not to consider. It can never be clearly stated that the unpackaged variable is solely responsible for the difference. Second problem is the shift between cultural level to individual level. To counter the criticism of ecological fallacy, that is to allow individual difference to exert influence, the researchers measure the differences at the cultures level by using scales that are fit for the study of inter-individual differences. That is, instead of assuming that Korea as a unified collectivist culture, Korean participants are treated as such due to their high score on collectivism score. Using mediational analysis (Baron & Kenny, 1986), the researchers may show that culture plays still important role after the mediational role of inter-individual difference has been accounted for. Giving a same title to the variable of interest to individual level and culture level is convenient but it need not be justifiable. It will be more appropriate to give different names to each, for the mechanism of characterizing individual is conceptually different from the mechanism of group or culture level to avoid confusion (e.g., Triandis, 1995).

Second critical issue is the problem associated with the approach treating emotion as entity. Entity type approach is very common in psychology while field type approach is very sparse (Valsiner, 2001). Entity type approach treats emotion as intrapsychic phenomenon affected by situational factors (Parrot, 2000; Ratner, 2000). It cannot be denied that emotion is experienced intra-individually. It is "I" who experiences certain kind of emotion at any moment. This does not mean emotion is generated within "I," as if purely intraindividual phenomenon. Although it is I who is experiencing sadness, it is because I am mistreated by my brother. So I am justifiably sad. If somebody is not sad in such situation, he or she may be "strange" person or there is some good reason for not being sad. People experience most emotions (happy, sad, angry, sorry, etc.) in interpersonal settings. Treating emotion as intrapsychic phenomena tells us little about the function of emotion in relation to the other and about the culture.

Most of the important emotions are interpsychic phenomenon. Social events make us feel them. I don't make up or generate emotion except unusual settings (i.e., using drugs). Even purely hedonic pleasure not involving others in the setting (e.g., reaching a solution of difficult problems) implicates culture's value system. In this sense, culture plays central role in emotional experience. The meaning of situation and the proper emotion being experienced all constitute culture itself. Psychologists in the field of cultural psychology all seem to agree on this constitutive view of culture and emotion (see Harre & Parrot, 1996). Nevertheless, most approach to emotion largely remains intrapsychic. It seems to be a result of Cartesian philosophy deeply ingrained in modern psychology. It is no doubt that there is the biological basis for emotional experiences. The biological basis makes affect possible (see Frijda, 1986; Valsiner, 2001). However, the actual nature of such experience should be defined through person's relationships with the social world. Emotions are "temporally embodied self-feelings which arise from emotional social acts person direct to self or have directed toward them by others. Emotions are lodged in social acts and self-interactions" (Denzin, 1983, p. 404, cited in Valsiner, 2001). It is this process aspect of emotion to which psychologists paid little attention. Emotions have been largely treated as some end- (or by) products of events.

EMOTIONS AS INTERPSYCHIC PHENOMENA
Lutz (1982, 1988) found that emotional words are statements about the relationship between a person and a situation where another person(s) is involved among South Pacific tribal society. This is striking to emotional words in Western society where they usually refer internal feeling state. Lutz gave Ifaluk people (3500 people residing in northern Luzon of Philippine) emotional words and asked them to sort the words to find clusters and dimensions. Various emotional words are grouped, as a result of applying a hierarchical cluster analysis, into five basic situations such as good fortune, danger, loss, and connection with others, human error, and complex and misunderstood events. Multidimensional scaling analysis showed also that two dimensions are operating in terms of eliciting situations: that is, the pleasant-unpleasant consequences of the situation and the strength-weakness of ego in relation to the other.

Numerous analysis of emotional words disclosed in West that two most important dimensions are pleasant/unpleasant dimension and active/passive level of activation (Osgood, May & Miron 1975). The two dimensions are all internally referenced dimensions. It is important to note that Ifaluk's dimensions are socio-situational and the Western dimensions are intrapersonal. Gerber (1975) reported from Samoa that the hedonic dimension of pleasant/unpleasant contains consequence of evaluation of meeting social virtue unlike purely hedonic emotional feeling state of Western people.

Ethnological studies of emotion in various societies are valuable in that they show clearly how and why emotion is culturally constructed in each society, and that the function of emotions in life is different across societies. Therefore, they warn against mechanistic comparison of emotion magnitude or its (non)existence in different society. Menon and Shweder (1998) studying an *Orissa* town of India provide the value of cultural psychology of emotion. According to them, the people in the town have a complex theory of emotion system (the *rasa* theory) which was formulated between 200 B.C. and 200 A.D. People believe experiencing different types of emotions is a way to transcend the mundane world, for which activities for dancing, drama, and poetry reading serve. For them, emotions are not separated from reason and they are active medium for self-refinement to break out of *samsara*, the endless cycle of rebirths and redeaths.

For them, experience of happy feeling is brief and nothing to celebrate. Happiness is an immature emotion only suitable for children.

Ethnological findings show how emotions differ across societies. The lived experience of emotion is compelling. Contrasting the catalogues of emotional terms, comparing the magnitude of certain emotion, and investigating how the antecedents and consequences of emotion differ could serve some function but cannot satisfactorily show how the emotions are lived in each society. If self-pride (or self-esteem) is not frequent or low in one society, it is so for some good cultural reasons. In the Western society, it reflects internal feeling state while in some other societies, it reflects external state of events (see Heine, Lehman, Markus, & Kitayama, 1999).

Cultural Emotions: The Subject of Cultural Psychology

Cultural psychological works on emotion have been reviewed briefly above. The recent trend takes it for granted that each culture has different system of emotion; not only the differences of characteristics of emotion, but the function of each emotion in broader social relationship, and the emotional milieu of each culture. In discussing culturally constructed nature of emotion, Ratner (2000) characterizes emotions in quality, intensity, behavioral expression, the manner in which emotions are managed, and organization or system of emotions. Cultural psychology of emotion may differ in any of those characteristics. It is not yet clear what cultural emotion is. The term is being used very loosely. Nonetheless, it is important to sort through studies conducted within the loose domain of cultural emotions. This will provide what is known now and needed in the future. Roughly, three types of research can be identified.

First type involves research trying to characterize emotional culture of certain tribe or country. Early research in the tradition of psychological anthropology falls in this category. Many studies discovered some indige-nous emotional concepts which seem to reflect some characteristics of the local society. Heelas (1996) provides good sketches of those indigenous emotions. Javanese emotion *Sungkan*, for example, refers to a feeling of respectful politeness before a superior or an unfamiliar equal, an attitude of constraint, a repression of one's own impulses and desires, so as not to disturb the emotional equanimity of one who may be spiritually higher (see Geertz, 1960 on Javanese). This emotion thus reflects strict hierarchy of the Javanese society. This type of research, mainly conducted by anthropologists through participatory observation, is important for it provides understanding of emotion in its cultural context. One drawback is that it may oversimplify the emotional characteristics of the local culture. For example, from a number of ethnography and anthropological studies, we say "... the Germans authoritarian, the Russians violent, the Americans practical and optimistic, the Samoans laidback, the Japanese shame-driven ..." (cited from Geertz, 2000, pp. 12–13). Identifying certain emotion as characterizing such large group of people is more often a gross simplification, stereotypical, and even dangerous. Those characterizations reveal less about the target culture but more about the social psychology of laypeople. Usually this characterization is not intended but a result of getting a grasp of such anthropological investigation. Despite their invaluable contribution, this type of research has limitation unavoidable due to participatory observational nature of fieldwork. As outsiders approach the local culture in limited duration, penetration to the local culture is unavoidably limited and the attempt of interpretation is vulnerable to misinterpretation (see Freeman, 1983 on M. Mead's report of Samoans and also Enriquez, 1994 on outsider's report of Filipinos). Also, it is difficult to get a comprehensive picture of emotional life especially when intricate phenomena is involved, many of which even locals are not able to articulate. For example, anthropologist Rosaldo (1993, p. 18) writes 13 years after publishing the field report on Ilongot society that "my earlier understandings of

Ilongot headhunting missed the fuller significance of how older men experience loss and rage. Older men prove critical in this context because they – not the youths – set the processes of headhunting in motion. Their rage is intermittent, whereas that of youths is continuous. In the equation of headhunting, older men are the variable and younger men are the constant."

Second type would be those studies comparing certain emotional types cross-culturally to see relative prevalence or strength of emotion. This type of research is usually conducted with some theoretical frames such as individualism and collectivism. For example, Markus and Kitayama (1991, 1994) proposed that among independent-self construal society, self-focused emotion (pride, ambition, happy, sad, guilt, etc.) is more typical while in interdependent-self construal society, other-focused emotion (shame, compassion, sympathy, shyness, etc.) is more typical. This line of research is important in that it provides comparative overall scheme of understanding different cultures' emotional characteristics. However, this line of research is often subject to ecological fallacy and is unable to catch the dynamics of emotional life in those societies. This research tradition reflects the entity type approach. Acknowledging this weakness, researchers try to further divide a whole national culture into subcultures (Oyserman, Coon, & Kemmelmeyer, 2002; Vandello & Cohen, 1999). The results may be closer to reality but complications are inevitable (see Oyserman et al., 2002 and Takano & Osaka, 1999). Still this attempt is not free from the ecological fallacy attack but also it does not deal with dynamism issue at all.

The third type of attempt is the insider's analysis of own cultural emotions. Perhaps best known is the analysis of *amae* in Japanese society by Doi (1973). Few studies have been reported that can be classified to this type. Enriquez (1994, chap. 4), credited for popularizing the term of indigenous psychology, also published an intriguing analysis of the concept of *kapwa* as the key mentality of Philippine people. Enriquez and Doi, being insiders and shrewd observers, are able to put together relevant indigenous terms to give penetrating psychological analysis of their own societies. *Amae* is dependent indulgence mentality expressed behavior in close relationship (to be discussed later), which could be easily taken as immaturity and also puzzling to an outsider from West. Although *amae* property is natural for children in every society, it is observable among adults only in Japan. It is a complex relational emotion operating in particular context. The work on *amae* requires both insider's experience and more importantly theoretical mind. Understanding of *amae* or *kapwa* is very useful to insiders and as well as to outsiders. It can provide more accurate and comprehensive picture of the local minds not only to the outsiders but to the insiders too. Also, it can shed new light upon more general understanding of human psychology that has been missed or neglected previously. It also invites research interest from insiders. It makes the familiar unfamiliar and inspires fresh look at the society (Shklovsky, 1969, p. 15). Inspired from Doi's analysis on *amae*, much work has been reported to discuss whether *amae* mentality represents Japanese society (see Befu, 1993; Gjerde, 2000; Hamaguchi, 1985). Much more work needs to be done in this third type. Following analysis is another one in that direction.

Cultural Psychology of Affective Process: Shimcheong *Psychology*

Korean society is replete with episodes that are puzzling to both insiders and outsiders. Following episode is just one such sample. "At a bus stop in a rainy day, a mother was waiting with an umbrella for her son's arrival from school. When the son got off from the bus, he got angry on seeing his mother and say blatantly, "You shouldn't have come out here with the umbrella for me." The mother replied, "OK, My son, sorry about that".

Superficial contents of this discourse are constituted by a complaint made by the son about his mother and an apology made by the mother. However, the episode tells more about Korean psychology of interaction. The son must be grateful for the considerate behavior of his mother. Nonetheless, the son hides his real gratitude by getting angry with his mother. The mother also conceals her disappointment at her son and simply apologized to him. Often, the strength of bond in close relationships is reinforced by expressed emotions that are opposite to the real and hidden emotions.

To understand this kind of interactional episodes and relationship working, understanding of *shimcheong* psychology is critical. Literally translated as 'affectional state of mind', *shimcheong* plays central role in Korean social relationship. Building up interpersonal relationships on deep *shimcheong* means to become one in flesh and spirit. We propose that the *shimcheong* psychology is not only critical for understanding of Korean people but also functional in shedding light on understanding of emotion in general psychology. Here, full-blown treatment of *shimcheong* psychology is not adequate. We provide necessary terms and analysis of *shimcheong* psychology for current purpose and defer fuller explication in a separate paper (see Choi & Kim, 1998a).

Meaning of Shimcheong

The Korean word '*shim-cheong* (心情)' consists of two characters, '*shim*' meaning mind and '*cheong*' meaning feeling. Together *shimcheong* means general affectional state of mind. The word *shimcheong* can be used as a generic term referring to all mental states. Such usage, however, is very limited in conversation but it implies that mind state is very important among Koreans. This may be sharply contrasted to Samoans who do not care much about mind states (i.e., motive, intention, etc.; Ochs, 1988 see also Lillard, 1998 for other societies). *Shimcheong* is most widely used to refer the aroused affective state precipitated by the other's actions in close relationships. However, this affective state alone as such is either engendered or activated by interpersonal events, does not qualify as *shimcheong*. In order for this affectional state to acquire the psychological

quality of *shimcheong*, one condition needs to be satisfied. The condition is that at least one party thinks that they have developed a good faith one another and, therefore, he or she can expect some caring mind from the other, which apparently is not shown by the action of the other. When *shimcheong* is aroused, it could be either positive or negative. In the previous case, it is negative. On the contrary, if the other's action far exceeds one's expectation, positive *shimcheong* would be felt. *Shimcheong* could be experienced by both parties but each with different reason. Also, *shimcheong* can be experienced by only one party; the other party may not be at all aware of this. This is very likely for each party tends to take benign perspective for one's own behavior, not realizing the possibility that the other may suffer from his/her own 'neutral' act. Once *shimcheong* is aroused, the interactional exchange does not further the depth of relationship. It is because the person in the aroused mode of *shimcheong* tries to readjust the entire relationship psychologically. *Shimcheong* works as a causal ground to reinterpret past exchanges as well as upcoming exchanges between the two parties. *Shimcheong* needs to be settled down for the relationship to develop further.

Phenomenological Process of Experiencing Shimcheong

PRECONDITIONS

Interactions between strangers or acquaintances do not incur *shimcheong*. *Shimcheong* becomes the issue in close relationship or in a sustained relationship where parties feel some intimacy and some trust one another. People start feeling this state of relationship as they employ more frequent use of 'we' and share activities together; meeting often and showing care and concern for one another. In such interpersonal relationship, feeling of communal bonding develops and the parties become '*woori*' where individual boundary gets blurred (Choi & Choi, 1994). *Woori* is literally translated as 'we' or 'our' and is best characterized for a family relationship where mind-to-mind bonding, caring, and sharing are all taken for granted.

Through mutual caring and concern, each party feels he or she is regarded worthy of such caring from the other party. Self-serving act is discouraged (even individual act such as Dutch-pay is not tolerated in *woori* relationship) but its motive typical in social exchange theoretical frames (Homans, 1961; Kelley & Thibaut, 1978) is generally fulfilled through turn-takings of other-serving behaviors.

SHIMCHEONG INCIDENTS

When the rule of fair exchange of other servings is perceived to be violated by one party (A), the other party (B) gets suspicious about the faith and caring mind of person A. This incident would be termed as *shimcheong*-hurting event. The mental state of *shimcheong* becomes a matter of concern in dynamical sense. A metaphor of a pebble thrown into a placid lake would suit here. The wave caused by a pebble is amount to *shimcheong*. *Shimcheong* is the fluctuating state of affectional mind. *Shimcheong* is not a specific emotional feeling such as sadness, happiness, or anger. It is a quality of mind state, a *ganzheitlich* mind experience one is going through here and now (Krueger, 1926; see also Diriwächter, 2004). It will eventually subside down like wave in the lake but with some consequential change in the relationship. Whenever it becomes an issue of concern, it requires adjustment of the level of *wooriness* (oneness in one extreme to separatedness in other extreme). Although *shimcheong* becomes the issue mostly in cases of unmet or undermet expectation, *shimcheong* of gratitude can occur in cases of overmet expectation. However, the dynamic and significance of *shimcheong* is more fully represented in the *shimcheong* hurt experience.

SHIMCHEONG CALCULATION –
INTROSPECTIVE ANALYSIS

When B sees A's behavior outrageously out of expectation, B will feel strong emotions such as anger or fury. B will react immediately in scornful manner. Strong emotion tends to precipitate immediate action and does not ignite *shimcheong* mode of mind. If B thinks A's behavior is apparent proof

of distrusting and even betraying B, B may get furious, place strong challenge against A, and cut off the relationship. *Shimcheong* is not an issue here. However, this is unlikely in a valued relationship or in an ascribed relationship such as a mother and a daughter-in-law. More typical experience in a close relational interaction is affective feeling that something is not right. For example, husband action of not visiting wife's home during holidays is contrary to wife's expectation. The action may not be outrageously wrong and may be understood considering limited amount of time available. But the action may not seem right, putting the wife in uneasy feeling state.

People tend to mull over those not apparent and somewhat ambiguous uncomfortable feelings caused by the expectation that was not met. Those *shimcheong* hurting incidents put B goes through reflectively the past exchanges between the two. Through this introspective analysis, the other-serving behaviors or caring behaviors exchanged are now examined for balancing. This balancing is subjective analysis where a self-serving bias is likely to operate. B will come up with inferences about A's state of mind toward B. B feels disappointment and sorry for A. The positive feelings B enjoyed in the *woori* relationship with A such as self worthiness, being secured and supported, and so on are turned into feelings of resentment and fury due to the feeling of having been disregarded, deserted, and even deceived. At this stage, cause of *shimcheong* is attributed outwardly to the instigating party. A typical analysis in this stage would be like "why is A (who hurts my *shimcheong*) doing this to me?" "what is me to A?" "what is my self-worth to A?" Overt conflict between A and B is likely when opportunity arises. When no such opportunity is given, further semiotic process of *shimcheong* is to develop intrapsychically (Valsiner, 2001).

SHIMCHEONG SCRIPTS – EXTROSPECTIVE
ANALYSIS

If negative mind, motivations, or no caring mind, either conscious or unconscious, of the person A is judged to be involved, particularly under A's awareness, B will reevaluate their *woori* sentiment and the worth of one's own self to A. For Koreans, due recognition and regard from the other in the relationships contributes to a greater extent toward the ongoing feeling of self-worth than does the solitary achievement of valuable attributes (status, wealth, etc) of one's own. Thereon, the secondary stage of *shimcheong* starts. In this reviewing process, realistic perspectives about one's own self as an object of observation and self-other relationship as objective reality are consciously sought. Individuals use culturally prescribed *shimcheong* scripts to judge the legitimacy of felt *shimcheong*. *Shimcheong* scripts prescribe when person should feel *shimcheong* aroused and hurt. They are consensual cultural grammar evaluating exchanges of countercannonicality. The self-serving tendency in the initial stage is thoroughly scrutinized. This process can occur intrapsychically (with *shimcheong* scripts) and interpsychically (with the other persons). Now, the target of evaluation becomes the self who has played some active role in the relationship. "The involved I" gets criticized not having been keen to the distrustfulness of the other and it becomes ridiculed and pitied upon. A part of responsibility for the other's distrust or uncaring befalls on the self. That is, the primary outward affective feeling appeared in the early phase of *shimcheong* occurrence recedes gradually with the passage of time. The secondary inward emotion conduced with self-conscious reevaluation of the *shimcheong* incidents looms up along with self-narrative form of *shimcheong* explanations about why and how this secondary emotion is brewed up in the innermost locus of mind. *Shimcheong* emotion and mind thus can be said to have been explicated and articulated by the aid of self-narratives about one's own experience. Often the explicated attempt of *shimcheong* experience is not fully accepted in its authenticity. This unresolved *shimcheong* remains active prompting such self-complaints as "I can't sleep! The more I think about it, the more I get resentful." Thus *introspective* explanation about *shimcheong* experience in narrative form is checked against and adjusted with *extrospective* analysis of objective reality as the *shimcheong* mind gets clarified.

Along the same lines – the communication of *shimcheong* experience also takes the narrative form of self-confessions about one's own introspective resonance of one's own experiencing mind and emotions. In other words, *shimcheong* experiences take the form of *monological* self-story. At the same time, the process of *shimcheong* experience is *dialogical* in the sense that *shimcheong* matters only in the context of 'inter-self' and 'inter-mind' relationship between persons interpersonally involved (Choi, Han, & Kim, 2004; Hermans, 1996, 2001). The matters of 'What are you for me' and 'What am I for you' make the starting point of *shimcheong* crux (*shimcheong* entanglement).

RELATIONAL SELF

Cross cultural studies have shown clearly that relationship with other people carries more importance to East Asian people, characterized as having interdependent self-construals, than to the Euro-American people (Ho, 1996; Markus & Kitayama, 1991; Triandis, 1989, 1995). The importance of relationship is reflected in the more flexible, variable, and concrete self-concept (see I. Choi & Y. Choi, 2002; Rhee, Uleman, Lee, & Roman, 1995; Suh, 2002). Although those studies provide interesting contrasts of self, they all posit the concept of self as entity. It is argued, however, that entity-like self is more germane to Western self and phenomenological mind self is more germane to Korean self (Choi & Kim, 1999a, 2002). This term of phenomenology captures the *shimcheong* crux where the notion of self gets highlighted suddenly. Self becomes a matter of contemplation in the relational context especially when one is put in the *shimcheong* experience. The awareness of self, especially the feeling of self-worth, is contingent upon the treatment of the other party-in-relationships; the self is relational in this sense. If the other party shows caring mind and support meeting one's expectation, the feeling of self-worth can sustain. If not, the feeling is shaken. One of the most miserable experiences is "getting ignored" by the other in relationship. This feeling makes people furious for it signifies "I am not worthy of such mind" "I am nobody to him/her." As long as the relational self is concerned, what is important is not "what I have" or "who I am," but "what is my worth to the other person in the relationship."

MIND EXPERIENCE

Life is full of various experiences; some sad, some happy, some hurtful. Among them, mind experiences are those resonate in the heart frequently because the person has gone through it with heart. One has lived through them with agony or/and delight and they have become constituents of oneself. Mind experience is not simply passive lived experience but an experience in the construction of which the person has played an active role. It is the experience consolidated through self reflection of related episodes. For a mundane experience to become a mind experience, the person should be the target of contemplation by oneself. The entire life path gets reviewed with fateful perspective (this is referred to *shinse* in Korean vernacular). It is subjective phenomenological experience objectified through reflective process. Consequently, mind experience is not only a rational account of a life event, but also deep feeling that permeates the episode. Each mind experience becomes a lasting episode for life. It provides understanding for one's taking and deservingness in life. The person always carries it around and occasionally refers to it when the situation precipitates them. Once constructed, it serves like an affective schema – similarly to a cognitive schema (Bartlett, 1932). It is activated when the situational context resembles it or cues it. When activated, it puts the person in empathic state with the own self or with the other. Mind experience is phenomenologically varying 'here and now' experience. It provides source and criteria to articulate ambiguous feeling into *shimcheong* narrative. *Shimcheong* precipitates and may consolidate into mind experience.

Self-explanatory narratives about the 'how and why' of activated *shimcheong* are fed into self experience of one's own *shimcheong*, constraining it into self-conscious and contextual emotion. Mind experience can be characterized as *Ganzheit*-experience operating always as a totality (Krueger, 1926). Going beyond the Gestalt experience of perception, people try to make good sense out of piecemeal or ambiguous episodes into ganzheit experience (Diriwächter, 2004). The episode synthesized through life reflection becomes one experience of totality supplying the repertoire of mind experience.

MIND PSYCHOLOGY OF KOREANS

Although modern psychology deals mainly with behaviors, psychologists as well as laypeople are comfortable in talking mind, for example, motives, intentions, personalities etc. Ethnologists report not every culture considers mind important. For example, Samoans do not care much about the intentions (Ochs, 1988). While Samoans may be placed in one extreme, Koreans may be placed in the other extreme, and the Westerners in the middle. For Koreans, intentions and motives are more important than the behaviors. People readily lift responsibility of behavior from the actor once they understood the situational constraint operated against actor's intention or motive (Choi & Nisbett, 1998). That is, Koreans understand in general that social behaviors do not necessarily reflect the actor's true mind. Choi and Kim (1999a) aptly summarize this as: mind is the social currency in Korea – whereas in the West it is behavior.

Although people allow behaviors to be varying from situation to situation, they value stability and consistency of the mind. Mind is not an abstract concept in Korea but carries more of relational context. When the term of mind (as *Maum* in Korean vernacular) is mentioned in conversation, it refers more often to relational concerns such as caring, neglecting, feeling sorry, and remorseful than to cognition. Loyalty and caring mind is the core of the relational mind. Koreans believe strongly the agentic property of mind. As the owner of mind, individuals should be able to exercise control over his or her mind in order not to yield to tempting and treacherous situations (Choi, 2004). The individual is to exercise control over a variety of minds constantly evolving over time (Choi, 2004; Choi & Yoo 2002). Not only the minds are changing as the situational constraints are imposing, but also the individual changes the mind on his or her own will. Individuals are owner of their agentic mind in the latter sense. The agentic mind represents the degree of self-control and determination.

Most unique, however, to Korean psychology is the admission of authentic mind. Authentic mind is true inner mind brewing up beyond one's conscious control. This mind is regarded as pure and truthful for it is not something the owner can control. *Shimcheong* is such kind of authentic mind brewed up in relational setting. The person is not responsible for his or her *shimcheong* and mind even though it comprises of contents unfavorable to others involved in the close relationships (Choi & Kim, 1998a; Choi, Kim, & Kim, 2000). When the others realize such brewed up *shimcheong* from the partner, they do not resent but tend to review past episodes to understand the authentic mind of *shimcheong*.

SHIMCHEONG DISCOURSE

Communicating mind experience between the parties may be called as *shimcheong* discourse. *Shimcheong* discourse plays an important role in relationship development because it is believed to convey truly authentic mind among Koreans. In daily conversation, Koreans are very conscious of maintaining harmony and tend to refrain from disclosing inner mind especially if doing so disrupts the interactions. *Shimcheong* discourse serves to fill the gap between outer conforming behavior in interaction and inner authentic mind. Engaging in *shimcheong* discourse is significant itself for it signifies relational flow may be in jeopardy, demanding prompt attention. Intentionally ignoring this cue will hurt the relationship. *Shimcheong* dialogue is usually called for when one party's action is likely to be mistaken as uncaring action to the other. This dialogue can be invited openly by one party or can

be solicited implicitly. A typical case of former is when a boss acted out that might have hurt the subordinates' mind. The boss takes them out for a drinking party in an attempt to soothe the subordinates' hurt *shimcheong*. The latter case may take the form of request like "please show some regard for my *shimcheong*!" This person is not making a call on his or her interaction partner to activate cognitive abilities, in the sense of 'theory of mind', and to put her/himself into the position of person A. Rather it is a request for the activation of an emotional, affective mutuality. The pre-requisite for *shimcheong* dialogue is presupposed feeling of 'we-ness.' In a 'we-ness' relationship then, one has to always be prepared to respect the *shimcheong* of the other. In consequence, the statement "I don't understand your *shimcheong*" actually means "I *don't want* to understand your *shimcheong*." This statement destroys the 'we-ness.' Calling on *shimcheong* obliges the partners to confirm the 'we-ness' and to view the problem from the perspective of mutuality (Choi & Kim, 1998b).

Without *shimcheong*, 'we' is mere an aggregate of individuals. Studies have shown that we-ness in Korea is marked by such communal feeling (Choi & Choi, 1994). *Shimcheong* augments we-ness feeling and we-ness feeds into *shimcheong*. In fact, "the exchange of *shimcheong* discourse is itself confirming that the interactants are in we-ness relationship and conveying their private minds are intersubjectively shared. It also confirms they are in the relationship of disclosing authentic mind" (Choi, 2000, p. 118).

The partner in *shimcheong* dialogue could be the person who is responsible for brewing up *shimcheong* or a third party. In case where a third party is the partner, the third party is likely to be the person who has experienced similar situations. So the partner is able to readily empathize with the *shimcheong* narrator. *Shimcheong* has to be justified from the canonicality criterion; otherwise, it will backfire to put blame on the person as narrow minded. In *shimcheong* discourse every guard for the sake of self presentation or persuasion would be laid off.

The initiating form of *shimcheong* exchange is likely to be non-verbal, for *shimcheong* talk is off the routine talk, disclosing a need of serious conversation. When one party shows the sign, the other should notice it and invite to engage in *shimcheong* discourse. During the dialogue, attending to the illocutionary functions of the words outspoken is more important than taking lexical meanings of the words per se (Choi & Kim, 1999a, 1999b). For instance, Koreans often ask, "Where are you going?" or "Did you take a meal?" when they come across with a friend. In this type of exchange, what Koreans try to convey to the friend is their concern of and care for their partner. When exposed to a wide range of modes of *shimcheong* discourse from partners, Koreans perceive their behavior as a delivery or a pour-out of *shimcheong* and base their own behavior on the logics of *shimcheong* rather than those of rationality. The conceptual constructions of mind and *shimcheong* are quite unique in the Korean culture in this sense.

When parties engage in *shimcheong* discourse, the mode of communication takes quite different properties from the normal discourse where the logic of fact (based on rationality) prevails. Both parties think conveying inner mind would clear up most misunderstanding. During the dialogue of exchanging own narrative, each party's mind experience is felt into other in the ambience of empathic concern. Mind experience gets fully articulated into *shimcheong* narrative during the dialogue through questioning, confessing, verifying, and readjusting. The person feeling *shimcheong* starts *shimcheong* conversation with the specific behaviors and articulates the interpretive meaning of the behavior and questions "what am I to you." Arguments may occur for clarifying the facts and one's position in case of misunderstanding but do not persist long. Table 15.1 summarizes the two types of discourse.

SUMMARY

Shimcheong is a dynamic mind state occurring in close relational context. When the other' caring mind in relationship is per-

Table 15.1: Relation-oriented *Shimcheong* logics vs. Individuality-oriented Fact logics

Shimcheong Logics	Fact Logics
Interdependency oriented	Autonomy oriented
Private	Public
Sharing mind	Individualizing mind
Intersubjective	Objectivity
Affectional mind	Cognitive mind

ceived falling below the other's expectation, one's *shimcheong* emerges and becomes the focal issue of the relationship. At initial stage, the person feeling *shimcheong* reviews the history of exchanges with the other. The person assesses oneself in relationship context with the partner upon experiencing his/her behavior not meeting ones expectation. Through reflecting upon the event in the context of relationship, one arrives at the conclusion that like anybody else in such situation one can't help feeling that one is betrayed, or distrusted. The resultant feeling and blame for it is more likely directed against the other. At second stage, the person takes a perspective of reflecting oneself from outward. This perspective places ultimate burden of responsibility on the self and its lot (*shinse*). In this stage of analysis of self-involved events, cultural *shimcheong* scripts are used to validate the mind experience, which is likely result in construction of *shimcheong* narrative. *Shimcheong* involves the process of evaluating emotion felt within me, clarifying the feeling of delicate and somewhat weak but not easily dismissible. This weak affective state gets clarified and intensified after interpretative reflection (Valsiner, 2001).

In this process of reflection, the person actively takes hermeneutical interpretation of event from one's own perspective as well as from other's. The seemingly trivial mind state becomes great significance thru semiotic mediation of which process is, unknown to others, much like self-talk. Because of this hermeneutics mediation involved, a seemingly insignificant event to a third party may be inscribed as mind experience. *Shimcheong* is an authentic mind justifiably reviewed according to cultural script with the other or a third party.

Indigenous Psychology for Universal Implications

Culture and Epistemological Understanding for Shimcheong

Korea, China, and Japan share a great deal of Chinese lexicons because the Chinese system of writing was adopted and practiced for several hundreds years. The Chinese letter signifying heart (the letter in two forms; 忄 or 심방변 is inserted in most characters and words dealing with relationships and mind of many different sorts. For example, it combines with other characters to make up most of the words referring to the emotions (i.e., happy, anger, love, hate, shame, etc.), various affective state of relationships (mere acquaintance, close relationship, long relationship, shallow relationship, broken relationship, generous relationship, unmet expectation, etc.), attitude, personality, volition, and other mental states as well. Use of language influences the way people think and communicate (cf. Sapir-Whorf hypothesis). Having languages of so many lexicons containing mind component in its letter is certainly related to the habitual practice of inferring mind from behaviors among East Asian countries especially among Koreans. This behavioral tendency carries great importance in cultures that emphasize relational harmony over individual striving, politeness over self-assertion, group achievement over individual achievement, abstinence over show-off, and self-discipline over self-indulgence. Not only the reading is frequent but also the showing behavior is often practiced in subtle form. This practice is often puzzling to outside observers. In an attempt to understand this, Hall (1976) proposed a scheme of high vs. low context culture of communication. East Asian countries are depicted as high context culture where the interpretation of spoken or written expression has to be contextual (see also, Gudykunst, Ting-Toomey, & Nishida, 1996). Depending upon the context, same expression could mean completely different things. In Korea, the words said are only behavior manifested. Often, more important is the way the words are said (that is, the context, the paraverbal, and the nonverbal) which tips what the other really wants to say. It is unlikely that people infer the other's mind in relationship of mere acquaintances. Interaction history allows more accurate deciphering of mind from the text spoken. Therefore, direct deciphering of the text into mind irrespective of context will be a problematic practice in Korea.

Why has knowing *shimcheong* and its communication become so much important? Understanding of this question requires understanding of weltanschauung of Korean people. Comparative philosophy proposes that relationalism is at the heart of the weltanschauung of East Asians where philosophical traditions of Confucianism, Taoism, and Buddhism are still dominantly observed (cf. Hansen, 1983; Shin, 2005). Perhaps the ontological epistemology of Western society is best expressed in Kantian notion of *Ding An Sich*. It postulates entity or substance existing on its own. The focus of attention lies on the entity and entity search. The whole enterprise of building science and knowledge construction is major consequence of such epistemological weltanschauung. On the contrary, relational epistemology of East Asia posits nothing is solely in existence and carries its own entity. Everything is related each other and must be looked at that way. Therefore, attentional focus is equally placed on the context and on the focal stimuli. This view applies to matters, events, and human affairs. For example, the value of a precious stone (i.e., diamond) is not inherent in it. It varies depending upon many factors; who holds it, where it is located, etc. To understand its value, the context plays vital part. Same logic holds for human affair. The talent or personality of a person greatly depends on the relational context in which the person is situated. A person may be mediocre in a group of strangers but may turn out highly talented in family. Therefore, individual talent is not as important as his or her relationships with other people; who he or she is in relationship and what reputation one is developing in the relationship.

Key concepts of the prevalent philosophical traditions in the East Asia also reflect this relational epistemology. The most cherished book by Confucius himself is *the Book of Change* (周易). The book contains many sign characters composed of symbols and their meanings. Each symbol has own meaning of being good-bad, yin-yang, heaven-earth, or male-female. Nevertheless, the place and relational status in a character override the meaning of each symbol to determine the property of the whole character. Another important lesson the book provides is that nothing stays stable long. *The Book of Change*, composed long before Confucius era, is still widely used to foretell what kind of change is likely to come by in the future. People resort to it to get prepared for the future.

Perhaps not so apparent at surface but critical reflection of relational epistemology is the concept of *tao* (道), the truth. In Confucianism and Taoism, absolute truth such as platonic *idea* is not of concern. *Tao* is not abstract ontological substance or *idea* to be found. *Tao* is written simply as road to walk on. It is the road to guide life activities. In Confucianism, *tao* is operating in different facets in each of significant human relationships. It is loyalty in boss-subordinate, filial piety in father-son, discrimination in husband-wife, faith in friendship, and orderliness in adults-youngsters. They constitute the five cardinal moralities to uphold. They all serve to maintain each type of relationship ideal. The word *ren* (仁)summarizes best the Confucian morality. *Ren* is the spirit of benevolence toward another. It states approaching others empathetically and treating them with the dignity they deserve (Fingarette, 1972). Persons become honorable being by acquiring *doug* (德). This can only be achieved by practicing the different facets of *tao* with the spirit of *ren*.

Tao in Taoism is something inherent in the nature beyond description, unlike *tao* in Confucianism. Despite immense difference between Taoism and Confucianism, both philosophies postulate *tao* as the guiding principle of life and espouse relational epistemology in foundation. According to the most cherished scripture of Taoism written by Laozi, "*tao* of nature is always beneficial and *tao* of noble man works without causing strain or conflict among people" (*The Laozi*, chap. 81). The pinnacle of relational epistemology is the Buddhist's theory of relatedness. According to the theory, everything is related and constructing each other. Causality of linking cause and effect is futile attempt. The graphical image of *Indra Net* represents this view well. *The Net* is hung in the palace of nirvana. Every corner of the cell in the net is located a gemstone. Each gemstone reflects every other gemstones in the net. Since other gemstone reflects the rest too, every gemstone is reflecting the whole including its own in multitude. Because of this complex reflection and their relatedness in world, nothing stays stable and everything changes all the time. Co-construction is the correct way representing causality at work. Ontology of *being* is replaced by epistemology of *becoming*.

The comparative epistemology is manifested not only in thinking style (Nisbett, 2003), but also in emotional life. The issue of emotional life is not what the emotions are (as in the West) but how emotions are managed in life. Confucius philosophy puts forth the principle of mind cultivation as most important (B-Y. Choi, 2003). The philosophy was fully blossomed into forming the doctrine of "*mindology* or the study of working mind" in Korea. The mindology is regarded to be the unique Korean contribution to the Confucian philosophy (Yoo, 2003). Although the mindology has equipped with highly sophisticated explanatory system of mind, it is not pursuing scientific validity of such theoretical system but it asks people to cultivate mind to the degree that brewing up authentic mind no longer pose any problem to the self and the society. Confucius himself seemed to have reached such state of mind in the age of 70 (*The Analects*, chaps. 2–4). It is important to note here that the role of authentic mind in people's life. Cultural norms place great restraints on behaviors in collectivistic societies (Triandis, 1995). Therefore, it is very likely that people show greater level of conforming behaviors desired in the situations. But they do not necessarily correspond to the mind of actor. This conformity may be mistaken as if portraying the people totally under control of situation. This mind is considered foremost important and takes ultimate responsibility of playing social actions. This authentic mind is an inner voice to be heeded in a flux of situational demands. The words or behaviors do not necessarily manifest this mind. Not only has the society developed the norm of situational conformity but also the norm of respecting the authentic mind. The operation of shimcheong communication is the mechanism whereby social actors maintain their individuality in intricate web of relationship, avoiding becoming a straw person.

Understanding of Shimcheong From Existing Literature

In order to clarify the cultural emotion of *shimcheong*, we will examine several concepts having similar features to it from existing literature. We will note similarities and differences.

EMPATHY

Closest Western psychological concept to *shimcheong* is empathy. Empathy was earlier on proposed as the key concept linking independent individuals, making social life possible (Stein, 1917; see Zabinsky & Valsiner, 2004). Empathy is defined as an affective response that stems from the apprehension or comprehension of another's emotional state or condition and that is identical or very similar to what the other person is feeling or would be expected to feel (Eisenberg, Losoya, & Spindrad, 2003; Hoffman, 1982). Batson (1990, p. 339) adds another-oriented response with the perceived welfare of another, which is tantamount to the

caring mind. This concept has been widely regarded as the key leading to altruistic behavior, therapeutic dialogue, and intersubjectivity. Batson, Klein, Highberger, and Shaw (1995) found that empathic concern produces an increased valuing of a target's welfare. This leads the observers to act in ways that benefit the target, even when doing so contradicts usual principles of justice, such as equal treatment for all. Thus, in empathic relations, welfare of another person becomes an increasingly important goal. This increase in valuing of the target can even generalize to other members of the group to which the target belongs (e.g., AIDS patients, homeless persons), and produce more positive evaluations of those groups.

Empathy is analogous to *shimcheong* expanded into relationship general where two parties need not share history of interaction. Herein lies also important distinctions of *shimcheong*. Caring mind is not preconditioned in empathy. It may come about as a response to the plight of the other one encountered. Empathy is subject to the harshness of the condition the suffering party is experiencing and to the dispositional quality of the perceiver. Also, empathy is an emotional state experienced independently from moral judgment; person may feel compassionate and sympathize with the sufferers without moral inhibitions. *Shimcheong* is elaborated narrative after reflection upon the transaction screened through cultural norms (*shimcheong* scripts). Empathy transcends limited operational sphere of *shimcheong* while *shimcheong* is more interaction involved, culturally structured and morally constrained. More important difference between the two is on epistemological ground. Empathy is the concept constructed for theoretical necessity in society where ontological epistemology is prevalent. To quote, "we not only learn to make us ourselves into objects, as earlier, but through empathy with 'related natures,' i.e., persons of our type, what is 'sleeping' in us is developed. By empathy with differently composed personal structures we become clear on what we are not, what we are more or less than others." (Stein, 1917, p. 116 cited from Zabinsky & Valsiner, 2004). Thus, empathy serves both for the communication with others and for the understanding of self. On the other hand, *shimcheong* is a cultural construct in a society where relational epistemology is prevalent.

Closely related to the empathy is the concept of *emotional convergence* (Anderson & Keltner, 2004). This concept is proposed to explain the increasing similarity among partners in their emotional responses over time in close relationship. In close relationship, partners share emotional similarity to events. Three reasons are speculated for this similarity. First, it coordinates the attention, thoughts, and behaviors among individuals to deal better with the impending situational calls (i.e., alarming, threatening) to the collective. Second, emotional similarity makes parties to understand each other better. When people experience similar emotions, they tend to perceive each other's perceptions, intentions, and motivations more adequately. Third, people feel close and more comfortable with others when they share similar emotions. Thus, people feel more solidarity and cohesion. In empirical test of this theory, they had assessed emotional similarity (individually felt emotions in three different discussion sessions) twice six months apart among sixty heterosexual couples. For those 38 couples remained in the romantic relationship, the similarity increased sufficiently for positive emotions and negative emotions too. Interestingly, those same-sex roommates they met in college dormitory also showed increased level of emotion similarity after nine months of co-residency. In addition, it was shown that persons living with depressed people for three months were more likely to themselves become depressed (Howes, Hokanson, & Loewenstein, 1985).

Emotional convergence looks somewhat similar to *shimcheong*. It is quite different concept, however. Emotional convergence is simply increased similarity between two separate emotional individuals. Therefore, even a harmful emotional convergence is utterly possible. For example, emotional convergence in furious battle of couple is deadly for the relationship. *Shimcheong* is not such strong direct emotional experience. It is a state filtered through self-perspective taking and hardly remains such a strong state of emotions. Emotional convergence remains as in the intraindividual level while *shimcheong* is dynamically interindividuals.

AFFECT ATTUNEMENT

Stern (1992), a psychoanalyst, provides an important concept for the understanding of empathic process. He points out the role of various gestures, kinetic movements, and nonverbal activities in conveying emotional states. Depending upon the gestural movements of the speaker, the listener experiences different emotive state. If one conveys feeling of love in bursting manner, the other feels intense. If one conveys feeling of love in easy manner, the other feels comfortable. Stern names this kinetic affectional state as *vitality affects*. Through vitality affects, interactants exchange their affectional state. Not only exchange of affection, but accommodating the other's affectional state occurs. This accommodative process is what he calls *affect attunement*. In tuning affect, people imitate consciously and unconsciously the other's affective movement by employing different modalities such as facial expression, bodily movement, or verbal imitation (Stern, Dore, Hofer, & Hoft, 1993). Most important function of this tuning process is that both parties achieve interpersonal communion; that is, both experience "to be with," "to share," "to participate in," and "to join in" (Stern et al., 1993). Communion means to share in another's experience without altering their behavior. This function is different from the function of communication. The essence of communion is the immanent feeling of connectedness. In other words, a state of intersubjectivity is achieved through affect attunement. Stern (1992) further proposes that this intersubjectivity serves as the platform of self-development. Both concepts, affect attunement and vitality affects, are distinctive contribution to the understanding of how relational affection or empathic state is experienced.

Another term resembling affect attunement has been proposed. Hatfield, Cacioppo, & Rapson (1992, pp. 153–4) term empathic experience as emotional contagion. It is "the tendency to automatically mimic and synchronize facial expressions, vocalizations, postures, and movements with those of another person and, consequently, to converge emotionally." Mimicry produces parallel emotional states in observers, this lead to greater feeling of rapport. Recent lab study (Chartrand & Bargh, 1999) manipulated mimicry by having confederate mimic (or not) the physical actions of their partner during a 15 minutes interaction. Those in the mimicking condition reported greater liking for the confederate and perceived their interaction went smoothly. LaFrance (1979) found that when participants in an interaction had greater liking for one another, they display greater posture similarity.

Affect attunement and emotional contagion share similar properties useful to understand empathic state and *shimcheong*. Affect attunement deals more with unconscious process emphasizing modalities of actions while emotional contagion deals more with emotional state being experienced. They provide a descriptive picture of empathy, how empathic state may come about in interactional settings. They are more pertaining to empathy than to *shimcheong*. To engage in *shimcheong*, empathic state is needed but *shimcheong* is more *complex psychological system*, to use Vygotskyian term. It starts with felt mind oneself, and dialectical processes of interchange taking place in intrapsychically and interpsychically. So, infants have no difficulty in showing affect attuning behaviors and experiencing communion with mothers but they have no *shimcheong* experience yet.

AMAE

A Japanese psychoanalyst proposed understanding the psychology of *Amae* is the key for the understanding of Japanese people (Doi, 1973, 1996).[3] *Amae* is the mental state of "indulgent dependency," rooted in the mother-child bond. *Amae* is experienced by a child as a "feeling of dependency or a desire to be loved," while the mother vicariously experiences satisfaction and fulfillment through overindulgence and overprotectiveness of her child's immaturity. Significant social relationships such as teacher-student, supervisor-subordinate are patterned after the primary mother-child relationship in Japan.

Amae and *shimcheong* both operate in close relationships where each party has communal feeling so that one is entitled for caring mind to some extent from the other party in the relationship. Communication based on either *amae* or *shimcheong* is exclusive, private, nondiscriminating, and tolerant (Doi, 1973). Given that, there are many differences as well. *Amae* is "dependency" mind while *shimcheong* is mutually "interdependency" mind. *Amae* is occasional mind pops up into interaction while *shimcheong* is constantly operating either in the backstage or in the frontstage. Both become the issue or phenomena experienced occasionally. However, *amae* is a more static state of mind not necessarily instigated by some event. *Shimcheong* is more dynamic state of mind operating constantly in the background and is ready to become the issue whenever interactional expectation is not met. *Amae* is the psychology modeled after the mother-child relationship while *shimcheong* is transcending the primary relationship. Unlike *amae*, *shimcheong* goes through elaborate analysis of interactional history, as discussed previously.

Most ethnological emotions reported are of mental states, some are simple as pleasant and others are complex as *amae* of Japan or *metagu* of Ifaluk society (Lutz, 1988). Once aroused, they are reflecting intrapsychological state of relative duration, either positive or negative. *Shimcheong* is not such stable emotional state of particular valence. It is dynamic operation of minds: it puts the whole mind into a state of agitation to be settled down. Inherently it can be positive or negative. *Metagu* serves as the primary inhibitor of misbehavior in both child and adult among Ifalukian. *Shimcheong* is not like that but a mode of mind state and communication.

Implications for Universal From Particulars

Among the values of studying cultural psychology, we would point out two. First, it provides clues of understanding the psychology of locals. It shows how different and similar they are but most importantly how those peculiarities tie together to make sense in that local culture. This is important understanding because fragmentary findings make the locals more or less misunderstood and strange. In discussing *amae*, Doi (1973) relates how the other Japanese psychologies (such as *jibun, enryo, ninjo, tannin*,[4] etc.) can be tied together with *amae*. Similarly, Choi (2000) relates some indigenous concepts depicting social behaviors such as *shimcheong, cheong, nunchi, hahn*, and *pingye*[5] together to illuminate working psychology of Korean people. It is important task to integrate various indigenous concepts together to provide proper understanding of the locals. Otherwise, the understanding is fragmentary often portraying them as exotic people.

Second value of cultural psychology is that the findings may illuminate the locality of previously universal psychology and provide insight into more comprehensive understanding of human minds. A number of studies have served this. Lutz (1982) broadened understanding of emotion by showing how ideology plays in emotion. She obtained her insights from the fieldwork in the Ifaluk society. Shweder and Bourne (1984) showed how the construction of person is varying in different cultures from fieldwork of *Orissa* society in India. Shweder (1994), in discussing emotion concepts, argued that the contribution of so-called Western thought to (an imaginary) worldwide dialogue is the idea that minds mediate emotions. This insight can be extended across the mental domain (see also Greenfield, 1994). Enough

has been discussed with regard to the first value. The remaining discussion is on this second value of *shimcheong* psychology.

CULTURAL VARIATION OF MIND AS MEDIATOR OF SOCIAL BEHAVIOR

Phenomenon of *shimcheong* psychology shows that cultures differ in the extent of providing the importance of mind as mediators. Role of mind (as mediator of behavior in social events) in psychological understanding differs culture to culture. For example, in Samoa, the role is minimal. Act is judged by the act itself, intention is not important (Gerber, 1975, 1985). But, in West, intention is important; the current development of psychological science manifests it. In Korean, it is even more important than in European American. Discussing ethnopsychologies of other cultures in contrast to the Euro-American (EA) ethnopsychology, Lillard (1998, p. 25) states: "many other cultures do not appear to appreciate the mind as a mediator in events but understand person–world relations to be much more direct. In this limited sense, adults in other cultures resemble the younger participants in Piaget's (1932) moral reasoning experiments, looking only at how many glasses were broken (the world event) not whether they were broken as a by-product of being good or naughty (the intent)... The person is connected to the situation, but the mind is not perceived as an important mediary. Adults in other cultures certainly must realize that people sometimes entertain views that differ from reality, but they may not tend to elevate such understandings to the status that EA adults do." She notes that even within the EA tradition, the concept of mind has changed to the current playing a more central role. Apparently, the *shimcheong* psychology of Korean people shows far more important role is given to mind by the Koreans. Deeds and pledges devoid of authentic mind are often committed by some distinguished persons in public. But the responsibility is not carried out full. Perhaps, a representative case is the pledge given by the former presidential candidate who vowed to the public not to run again if failed. The public did not take the words seriously and elected him on the next election.

CAN SHIMCHEONG BE A UNIVERSAL PHENOMENON?

Concerning the phenomenon of Japanese *amae*, sociologist Vogel (1996, p. 200) went so far as to argue that "I see *amae* as the universal basic instinct, more universal than Freud's two instincts, sex and aggression." Doi (1996) would agree; he asserts that the psychic feeling of feeling emotionally close to another human being is not uniquely Japanese – only the rich, semantic meaning of *amae* is unique to Japanese culture. Doi asserts that European languages lack an equivalent word to *amae*. His argument is that the lack of an equivalent word implies lack of social recognition and need of feelings of dependency and the desire to be loved in the West. It is very likely that European American's preoccupation with independence prevents them from admitting the need for indulgent dependency expressed by *amae* positively influencing personal relationships but also other hierachial relationship.

As discussed above, *shimcheong* and *amae* share similarity such as practice in close relationship setting and affectional caring. What is universal about such indigenous concepts as *shimcheong* or *amae*? We have good lesson here. The meaning of universal is not in the sense of 'all encompassing' but rather in the sense that it is one of many particulars: that means, universal particulars or particular universals. The *shimcheong, amae,* and *empathy* are all universal phenomena which are at the same time particular, as the way in which the individual phenomenon relates to each other can be completely different in each cultural context. To clarify this point, a metaphor is pertinent of the musical construction of chords. Every tone is universal but the chords are different, as the relationship of individual tones varies immensely according to musical tradition and practices resulting in distinctive ethnic music (Choi & Kim, 1998b). Likewise, the phenomenon of

authority may be universal but the symbolic and conceptual constructions that relate to the phenomenon can be different according to social practice. The symbolic construction of authority in Korea may be different to the Frankfurt School's understanding of the authoritarian personality. The phenomena of *shimcheong* and *amae* can also be seen in Western societies, and are to this extent universal. They are, however, at the same time culture specific where the conceptual relationships between the individual phenomena and their social practice are concerned. In other words, such phenomena are elaborated, conceptualised and linguistically specified in each cultural context, where as in Western societies they are concealed and pushed to the edge of discourse.

More specifically, when *shimcheong* is mentioned as the characteristically indigenous concept of Korea, it means: first, Koreans are highly sensitive to *shimcheong* phenomena and show its importance in their social interactions. Second, Koreans define, understand, and evaluate personal relationships in terms of *shimcheong* frameworks. Third, they have developed particular sets of communicative grammars and frameworks relating diverse feelings based on *shimcheong*. Fourth, communicative modes of *shimcheong* such as discourses and pour-out of *shimcheong* are well developed and elaborated. Because *shimcheong* is culturally mediated emotional state, a higher mental function developed out of natural lower mental function (Vygotsky, 1981) through socialization, children as well as foreigners have difficulty in understanding the phenomenon.

Regarding the term indigenous, Azuma noted appropriately that the term reflects a view of culture as "circumscribed, fixed, and internally homogeneous" (2000, p. 9). Therefore, it is likely that characterizing a culture with such indigenous terms as *shimcheong* or *amae* may inadvertently reify the target culture. No nation retains its traditional culture intact in this age of globalization (e.g., Gjerde & Onishi, 2000; Han & Shin, 2000). It is an important task of cultural psychologist to keep the term viable and germane by scrutinizing evidence and counterevidence. It is mistake to regard indigenous terms as confining to a local culture. Often unacknowledged, but true value of those terms is when they disclose the parochial property of so-called *nonindigenous* terms. Understanding of *shimcheong* can serve such function.

FUTURE TASK FOR CULTURAL PSYCHOLOGY

Consistently observable theme in the studies of cultural emotions in Asian countries is that relational emotions are more frequent and more important than individualistic emotions. For these cultures, emotions exist "out there" within the inter-minds rather than within the intra-mind. Therefore, it is consensual that relational emotion carries more weight in Asian countries than in EA countries (Markus & Kitayama, 1991; Kitayama & Markus, 1994). This distinction is interesting but more important task lies ahead. Postulating an emotional entity (happy, depressed, *amae*, or interpersonal emotions, etc.) to capture a society is always simplification and often subjects the society to a target of ridicule. Culture is not a static entity; therefore, characterizing a society with a particular emotional term is highly misleading, even dangerous. It is not sufficient to show how the social meaning of particular emotion differs across cultures or to show how certain emotion is more pronounced. Most important pitfall of cross-cultural psychology is that it tends to provide very static picture of each society. Often this picture encounters strange data set (Kashima, Yamaguchi, Kim, Choi, Gelfand, & Yuki 1995; Takano & Osaka, 1999). Collectivistic society may be collective but individual members still manage their individuality in that society. Comparative characterization (i.e., more collective or less individualistic) is generally more accepted but still provides no knowledge to the process operating in that society.

Culture must be viewed as a field where many elements (humans, things, events) are engaged in constant processes (Lewin, 1936; Valsiner, 2001). Therefore, more important task for cultural psychology of emotion is to show how emotion is lived through for individual members to manage their individuality as well as collectivity. Society allowing collectivity or groupness while suppressing individuality is not a viable society that can last long enough. Any viable society allows delicate balancing of collectivity and individuality in daily life. It is this psychological process we need to understand (Greenfield, 1998). It is in this sense that psychology of *shimcheong* shows an exemplar of cultural emotion and where future research effort needs to be directed. Important task for psychological study of cultural emotion is to understand this *field and processes* where affective state is turning into emotional experiences through culturally mediated activities.

How does a relational emotion state turn into cultural emotion of shimcheong, characterizing Korean society? Answering to this question, we may borrow from Vygotsky. Vygotsky proposed that psychology is socio-historically constituted (see Ratner, 2000; Valsiner & Van Der Veer, 2000; Vygotsky, 1978, 1981) and every psychological function is semiotically mediated to form complex psychological system (Vygotsky, 1985, pp. 343–344). *Shimcheong* as the cultural emotion of Korean people is such a complex system where cognition and affection is inseparable, they are interacting whole, as a ganzheit, to experience *shimcheong*. Among the main tenets advocated by *Ganzheit* psychology (see for more details Diriwachter, 2004), holism and feelings are especially relevant to *shimcheong*. *Ganzheit* psychologists define the whole in terms of the processes of experience. Parts are interwoven each other to shape up an experience. An experience is a totality, not a simple accumulation of its parts. *Ganzheit* psychologists also posit feelings as the primary experience of this totality (Krueger, 1928/1953, p. 204, recited from Diriwachter, 2004; see also Zittoun, 2004 for Janet's similar position). As we get to explain a personal experience of feeling, we get more vivid and stronger feeling. To understand *shimcheong* psychology, the whole experience should be treated as a unit; the interacting parties, their relationship history, the level of intimacy, the precipitating event, the feeling, and the ensuing analysis. It all starts with feeling tones (mostly uncomfortable ones) which are to be elaborated. Through this elaborating process, the experience undergoes a synthetic transformation from own-understanding to other-understanding. The principle of creative synthesis operates in a *shimcheong* experience; the primitive totalities (negative feeling tone) transform into more elaborated totalities (Valsiner, 2001). In fact, the *shimcheong* psychology provides a complete exemplar for the *ganzheit* perspective. Satiated with elementalistic approach in psychology, *ganzheit* psychology now gains renewed interest from psychologists (Diriwächter, 2004; Zabinski & Valsiner, 2004). It deals with meaningful life experience as a unit of analysis.

The word *shimcheong* works as semiotical mediation to transform the immediately felt affective state into cultural emotion of *shimcheong and to allow shimcheong discourse taking place*. Through this mediation, interactants are able to sustain their individuality (their authentic mind) and at the same time, they are able to reassure their sentiment of being *woori* relationship. *Shimcheong* becomes the essential feature of Korean psychology where communality and individuality coexist both strongly. Culture becomes medium for its members who can cultivate self in the field (Fuhrer, 2004).

Bruner (1996, p. 160), on writing the psychology's next chapter, states "the next chapter will be about intersubjectivity-how people come to know what others have in mind and how they adjust accordingly... a set of topics... central to any viable conceptions of a cultural psychology." *Shimcheong* is the mode of intersubjectivity where not only cognitive modality but also affective modality is synthetically interrelated in ganzheit form. Prior discourse on intersubjectivity has

been primarily centered on the cognitive modality. Representative example would be the theory of mind (ToM). The theories about ToM are primarily concerned with how one recognises the thoughts and intentions of the other (Perner, 1991; Wellman 1990, 1993). It is also interesting to note that the discourse on intersubjectivity is not only cognition centered but also self (or identity) centered in the West (Bruner, 1996; Hermans, 1996, 2001; Stern, 1992). This reflects the ontological epistemology of Western society discussed before. In fact, epistemologically different conception of intersubjectivity is manifested as *shimcheong* in Korea and as *empathy* in West. Empathy represents linkage among the individuals in the cultural tradition of 'I-self-identity' in which 'being concerned with oneself' and 'being concerned with the other' are seen as functionally equivalent (Choi & Kim, 1998b). On the other hand, *shimcheong* represents confirmation of we-ness in the cultural tradition of 'woori-shimcheong.' It is important to note that the foremost function of *shimcheong* psychology is to foster harmonious relationship without sacrificing individuality. It achieves this function through dialectical affective process going beyond cognitive understanding. Perhaps, *shimcheong* psychology throws an important task for understanding intersubjectivity going beyond cognition.

We presented a cultural psychological analysis of an indigenous emotion. The German term of science, *Wissenschaft*, a fusion of *Wissen* (knowledge) and *Schaffen* (creation/making or construing), allows, through the development of appropriate terminology, search for other construction possibilities (Goffmann, 1959). Social scientists should understand the underlying process of cultural construction of social phenomena and acknowledge the particulars of their constructs. There can only be 'polyphonic cultural psychologies' where cultural psychological discourses are presented as comparative studies between indigenous theories (cf. Geertz, 1993; Lutz, 1988; Staeuble, 1996). Only then, they can legitimately seek for universalities. The foremost value of cultural psychology lies there.

Notes

1 Correspondence should be directed to Dr. Gyuseog Han, Dept. of Psychology, College of Social Sciences, Chonnam National University, Gwangju, S. Korea, 500–757. Email is ghan@chonnam.ac.kr

2 Cultural psychology is very loose field for it now serves as an umbrella covering all the psychological works related to culture, regardless of orientation taken by the researchers (for different orientations see Berry, 2000; Greenfield, 1998).

3 It is not proper to discuss here whether Doi's statement is right or wrong. Interested reader should read discussions on this subject (see Gjerde, 2001).

4 These terms represent analogous meaning of one's share (*jibun*), *remote concern* (*enryo*), *interpersonal affection* (*ninjo*), *and outsiders* (*tannin*) *respectively*.

5 These terms represent analogously interpersonal affection (*cheong*), situation reading tact (*nunchi*), repressed anger (*hahn*), and excuse making (*pingye*) respectively.

References

Anderson, C., & Keltner, D. (2004). The emotional convergence hypothesis: Implications for individuals, relationships, and cultures. In L. Tiedens & C. W. Leach (Eds.), *The social life of emotions*. pp. 144–163. Cambridge: Cambridge University Press.

Azuma, H. (2000). Indigenous to what? *International Society for the Study of Behavioral Development Newsletter*, 37, 9–10.

Baron, R., & Kenny, D. (1986). The moderator–mediator variable distinction in social psychological research: Conceptual, strategic and statistical considerations. *Journal of Personality and Social Psychology*, 51, 1173–1182.

Bartlett, F. C. (1932). *Remembering : a study in experimental and social psychology*. Cambridge: Cambridge University Press.

Batson, C. (1990). How social an animal: The human capacity for caring. *American Psychologist*, 45(3), 336–346.

Batson, C. (1991). *The altruism question: Toward a social psychological answer*. Hillsdale, NJ: Erlbaum.

Batson, C., Klein, T., Highberger, L., & Shaw, L. (1995). Immorality from empathy-induced altruism: When compassion and justice conflict. *Journal of Personality and Social Psychology*, 68, 1042–1054.

Befu, H. (1993). Nationalism and *Nihonjinron*. In H. Befu (Ed.), *Cultural nationalism in East Asia: Representations and identity* (pp. 107–133). Berkeley: University of California, Berkeley, Institute of East Asian Studies.

Bruner, J. (1996). *Culture of education*. Cambridge, MA: Harvard University Press.

Chartrand, T., & Bargh, J. (1999). The Chameleon effect: The perception-behavior link and social interaction. *Journal of Personality and Social Psychology*, 76, 893–910.

Choi, B-Y. (2003). *Psychology of mind cultivation*. Presented at the Special Symposium by Korean Society of Social and Personality Psychology, Chung-Ang University. Seoul, S. Korea.

Choi, I., & Nisbett, R. E. (1998). Situational salience and cultural differences in the correspondence bias and the actor-observer bias. *Personality and Social Psychology Bulletin*, 24, 949–960.

Choi, I., & Choi, Y. (2002). Culture and self-concept flexibility. *Personality and Social Psychology Bulletin*, 28, 1508–1517.

Choi, S-C., & Yoo, K. J. (2002). *Mind models of Korean people: Folk psychological and Neo-Confucianism conceptions of mind*. Paper presented at the 2nd International Conference of Central Asian Association for Korean Studies, May 10–11, Seoul National University, Korea.

Choi, S-C. (2000). Hankookin shimleehak [Korean psychology]. Seoul, Korea: Jung-Ahng University Press.

Choi, S-C. (2004). The rule of justice and the way of heart: An analysis of Western and Eastern conception of social relationship. *A Keynote Address in the XXVIII Int. Congress of Psychology*, 8–13, August, Beijing, China.

Choi, S. C., & Choi, S. H. (1994). We-ness: A Korean discourse of collectivism. In G. Yoon, & S. C. Choi (Eds.), *Psychology of the Korean people* (pp. 57–84). Seoul: Dong-A Publishing & Printing Co., Ltd.

Choi, S. C., & Choi, S. H. (2001). Cheong: The socio-emotional grammar of Koreans. *International Journal of Group Tensions*, 30(1), 69–80.

Choi, S-C., Han, G., & Kim, K. (2004). Monological and dialogical nature of intersubjective emotion of shimcheong. Presented at a symposium "The dialogical nature of affective processes: Empathy reconsidered." In the *3rd International Conference on Dialogical Self.* August 28. Warsaw, Poland.

Choi, S. C., & Kim, C-W. (1998a). "Shimcheong" psychology as a cultural psychological approach to collective meaning construction. *The Korean Journal of Social and Personality Psychology*, 12(2), 79–96.

Choi, S. C., & Kim, C-W. (1998b). Does the multiple self need an identity?: Concerning alternative constructions of the 'self.' Presented at the 4th Congress of the International Society for Cultural Research and Activity Theory, Aahus (Denmark), 7–11 June.

Choi, S. C., & Kim, J-Y., & Kim, K. (2000). The Structural relationship analysis among the psychological structure of Cheong (Sweet Cheong, hateful Cheong), its behaviors, and functions. *The Korean Journal of Social and Personality Psychology*, 14(1), 203–222.

Choi, S. C., & Kim, K. (1999a). A conceptual exploration of the Korean self. *The Korean Journal of Social and Personality Psychology*, 13(2), 275–292.

Choi, S. C., & Kim, K. (1999b). The Shimcheong psychology: Psychological characteristics, interactions, and development of Shimcheong, *The Korean Journal of Psychology*, 18(1), 1–16.

Choi, S. C., & Kim, K. (2002). A Conceptual Exploration of the Korean Self: In Comparison with the Western Self. In K-S Yang, K-K Hwang, P. Pedersen, & I. Diabo (Eds.), *Progress in Asian social psychology: Conceptual and empirical contributions* (chapter 2). Greenwood.

Crocker, J., & Wolfe, C. (2001). Contingencies of self-worth. *Psychological Review.* 108(3), 593–623.

Diriwächter, R. (2004). Ganzheitspsychologie: The doctrine. *From Past to Future*, 5(1), 3–16.

Doi, T. (1973). *The Anatomy of dependence.* New York: Kodansha International. (Amae no kozo, Japanese text, published in 1966).

Doi, T. (1996). Forward. (pp. xv–xvii). In D. Shwalb & B. Shwalb (Eds.), *Japanese childrearing: Two generations of scholarship.* New York: The Guilford Press.

Eisenberg, N., Losoya, S., & Spindrad, T. (2003). Affect and prosocial responding. In R. Davidson, K. Scherer, & H. Goldsmith (Eds.), *Handbook of affective sciences.* pp. 787–803. Oxford: Oxford University Press.

Ekman, P. (1972). Universals and cultural differences in facial expressions of emotion. In J. K. Cole (Ed.), *Nebraska symposium on motivation.* Lincoln, NE: University of Nebraska Press.

Enriquez, V. G. (1994). *From colonial to liberation psychology: The Philippine experience. International Edition.* Manila, Philippine: De LaSalle University Press.

Fingarette, H. (1972). *Confucius-The secular as sacred.* New York: Harper Torchbooks.

Freeman, D. (1983). *Margaret Mead and Samoa: The making and unmaking of an anthropological myth.* Cambridge: Harvard University Press.

Frijda, N. H. (1986). *The emotions.* Cambridge: Cambridge University Press.

Fuhrer, U. (2004). *Cultivating minds: Identity as meaning-making practice.* London: Routledge.

Geertz, C. (1960). *The religion of Java.* New York: Free Press.

Geertz, C. (1993). *Local knowledge.* London: Fontana Press.

Geertz, C. (2000). *Available light: Anthropological reflections on philosophical topics.* Princeton: Princeton University Press.

Gerber, E. (1975). *The cultural patterning of emotions in Samoa.* Ph.D. diss., University of California, San Diego.

Gerber, E. (1985). Rage and obligation: Samoan emotion in conflict. In G. White & J. Kirkpatrick (Eds.), *Person, self, and experience* (pp. 121–167). Berkeley: University of California Press.

Gjerde, P. F. (2001). Attachment, culture, and amae. *American Psychologist*, 56, 826–827.

Gjerde, P. F., & Onishi, M. (2000). Selves, cultures, and nations: The psychological representation of "the Japanese" in the era of globalization. *Human Development*, 43, 23–33.

Goffman, E. (1959). *The presentation of self in everyday life.* Garden City, NY: Doubleday.

Gopnik, A. (1993a). How we know our minds: The Illusion of first-person knowledge of intentionality. *Behavioral and brain sciences*, 16, 1–14.

Greenfield, P. (1994). Independence and interdependence as developmental scripts: Implications for theory, research, and practice. In P. M. Greenfield & R. Cocking (Eds.), *Cross-cultural rootes of minority child development.* pp. 1–37. Hillsdale, NJ: Erlbaum.

Greenfield, P. (1998). Culture as process: Empirical methods for cultural psychology. In J.

Berry, Y. Poortinga, & J. Pandey (Eds.), *Hand-book of cross-cultural psychology. Vol. 1.* pp. 310–346. Needham Heights, MA: Ally & Bacon.

Gudykunst, W., Ting-Toomey, S., & Nishida, T. (1996). *Communication in personal relationships across cultures.* Thousand Oaks, CA: Sage.

Hall, E. T. (1976). *Beyond culture.* Garden city, NY: Doubleday.

Hamaguchi, E. (1985). A contextual model of the Japanese: Toward a methodological innovation of Japanese studies. *Journal of Japanese Studies, 11,* 289–321.

Han, G., & Shin, S-J. (2000). A cultural profile of Korean society: From vertical collectivism to horizontal individualism. *Korean Social Science Journal, 27*(2), 69–96.

Hansen, C. (1983). *Language and logic in ancient China.* Ann Arbor: University of Michigan Press.

Harre, R., & Parrott, G. (1996). *The emotions; social, cultural and biological dimensions.* London: Sage.

Hatfield, E., Cacioppo, J., & Rapson, R. (1992). Emotional contagion. In M. Clark (Ed.), *Review of personality and social psychology. Vol. 14. Emotion and social behavior.* pp. 151–177. Newbury Park, CA: Sage.

Heelas, P. (1996). Emotion talk across cultures. In R. Harre, & G. Parrott (1996*). The emotions; social, cultural and biological dimensions.* pp. 171–199. London: Sage

Heine, S. J., Kitayama, S., Lehman, D. R., Takata, T., Ide, E., Lueng, C., & Matsumoto, H. (2001). Divergent consequences of success and failure in Japan and North America: An investigation of self-improving motivations and malleable selves. *Journal of Personality and Social Psychology, 80,* 599–615.

Heine, S. J., Lehman, D. R., Markus, H. R., & Kitayama, S. (1999). Is there a universal need for positive self-regard? *Psychological Review, 106,* 766–794.

Hermans, H. (1996). Voicing the self: From information processing to dialogical interchange. *Psychological Bulletin.* 119(1), Jan. 1996 31–50.

Hermans, H. (2001). The dialogical self: Toward a theory of personal and cultural positioning. *Culture & Psychology, 7*(3), 243–282.

Hermans, H., & Kempen, H. (1993). *The dialogical self: Meaning as movement.* San Diego, CA: Academic Press.

Hermans, H., & Kempen, H. (1998). Moving cultures: The perilous problems of cultural dichotomies in a globalizing society. *American Psychologist, 53,* 1111–1120.

Ho, D. Y. F. (1998). Interpersonal relationships and relationship dominance: An analysis based on methodological relationism. *Asian Journal of Social Psychology, 1,* 1–16.

Ho, D. Y. F. (1996). Indigenous psychologies: Asian perspectives. *Journal of Cross-Cultural Psychology, 29,* 88–103.

Hoffman, M. (1982). Development of prosocial motivation: Empathy and guilt. In N. Eisenberg (ed), *The development of prosocial behavior* (pp. 281–313). New York: Academic Press.

Homans, G. (1961). Social behavior: Its elementary form. (Rev. ed) New York: Harcourt.

Howes, M., Hokanson, J., & Loewenstein, D. (1985). Induction of depressive affect after prolonged exposure to a mildly depressed individual. *Journal of Personality and Social Psychology, 49,* 1110–1113.

Kashima, Y., Yamaguchi, S., Kim, U., Choi, S.-C., Gelfand, M. J., & Yuki, M. (1995). Culture, gender, and self: A perspective from individualism-collectivism research. *Journal of Personality and Social Psychology, 69,* 925–937.

Kelley, H., & Thibaut, J. (1978). *Interpersonal relations: A theory of interdependence.* New York: John Wiley and Sons.

Kitayama, S., & H. Markus (1994). *Emotion and culture: Empirical studies of mutual influence.* Washington, DC: American Psychological Association.

Krueger, F. (1926). Ueber psychische Ganzheit. In *Neue psychologische studien, Bd. 1,* 1–121.

Krueger, F. (1928). The essence of feeling. In M. Reymert (Ed.), Feelings and emotions: The Wittenberg symposium (pp. 58–86). Worcester, MA: Clark University Press.

Krueger, F. (1928/1953). Das Wesen der Gefuhle. In E. Heuss (Ed.), *Zur philosophie und psychologie der Ganzheit: Schriften aus den Jahren 1918–1940* (pp. 195–221). Berlin, Germany: Springer Verlag.

La France, M. (1979). Nonverbal synchrony and rapport: Analysis by the cross-lag panel technique. *Social Psychology Quarterly, 42,* 66–70.

Lewin, K. (1936). *Principles of topological psychology.* New York: McGraw-Hill.

Lillard, A. (1998). Ethnopsychologies: Cultural variations in theories of mind. *Psychological Bulletin, 123,* 3–32.

Lutz, C. (1982). The domain of emotion words on Ifaluk. *American Ethnologist, 9,* 113–128.

Lutz, C. (1988). *Unnatural emotions.* Chicago: University of Chicago Press.

Markus, H. R., & Kitayama, S. (1991). Culture and self: Implications for cognition, emotion, and motivation. *Psychological Review, 98*, 224–252.

Markus, H. R., & Kitayama, S. (1994). The cultural construction of self and emotion: Implications for social behavior. In S. Kitayama & H. Markus (Eds.), *Emotion and culture: Empirical studies of mutual influence* (p. 89–130). Washington, DC: American Psychological Association.

Menon, U., & Shweder, R. (1998). The return of 'white man's burden'. In R. A. Shweder (Ed.), *Welcome to middle age!* Chicago, IL: University of Chicago Press.

Menon, U., & Shweder, R. A. (1994). Kali's tongue: Cultural psychology and the power of shame in Orissa, India. In S. Kitayama & H. Markus (Eds.), *Emotion and culture* (pp. 241–185). Washington, DC: American Psychological Association.

Mesquita, B., & Frijda, N. (1992). Cultural variations in emotions: A review. *Psychological Bulletin, 112*, 179–204.

Nisbett, R. (2003). *The geography of thought*. New York: Free Press.

Nisbett, R. E., Peng, K., Choi, I., & Norenzayan, A. (2001). Culture and systems of thought: Holistic versus analytic cognition. *Psychological Review, 108*, 291–310.

Ochs, E. (1988). *Culture and language development*. Cambridge: Cambridge University Press.

Osgood, C., May, W., & Miron, M. (1975). *Cross-cultural universals of affective meaning*. Urbana: University of Illinois Press.

Oyserman, D., Coon, H. M., & Kemmelmeyer, M. (2002). Rethinking individualism and collectivism: Evaluation of theoretical assumptions and meta-analyses. *Psychological Bulletin, 128*, 3–72.

Parrot, W. (2000). *Emotions in social psychology*. Philadelphia: Psychology Press.

Peng, K., & Nisbett, R. (1999). Culture, dialectics, and reasoning about contradiction. *American Psychologist, 54*, 741–754.

Perner, J. (1991). *Understanding the representation of mind*. Cambridge, MA: MIT Press.

Piaget, J. (1932). *The moral judgment of the child*. New York: Harcourt Brace.

Ratner, C. (2000). A cultural-psychological analysis of emotions. *Culture & Psychology, 6*(1), 5–39.

Rhee, E., Uleman, J. S., Lee, H. K., & Roman, R. J. (1995). Spontaneous self-descriptions and ethnic identities in individualistic and collectivistic cultures. *Journal of Personality and Social Psychology, 69*, 142–152.

Rodriguez-Mosquera, P., Fischer, A., & Manstead, A. (2004). Inside the heart of emotion: On culture and relational concerns. In L. Tiedens & C. W. Leach (Eds.), *The social life of emotions*. pp. 187–202. Cambridge: Cambridge University Press.

Rosaldo, M. (1980). *Knowldege and passion: Ilongot notions of self and social life*. Cambridge: Cambridge University Press.

Rosaldo, R. (1993). Culture and truth: The remaking of social analysis. Boston, MA: Beacon Press.

Shin, Y-B. (2005). *Lectures: My reading of Oriental classics*. [Gangui], Seoul: Dolbyugae.

Shweder, R. (1994). In S. Kitayama & H. Markus (Eds.), *Emotion and culture: Empirical studies of mutual influence* (pp. 89–130). Washington, DC: American Psychological Association.

Shweder, R. A., & Bourne, E. J. (1984). Does the concept of the person vary cross-culturally? In R. A. Shweder & R. A. LeVine (Eds.), *Culture theory* (pp. 158–199). Cambridge: Cambridge University Press.

Sklovsky, V. (1969). Die Kunst als Verfahren. In J. Striedter (Hrsg.), *Russischer Formalismus*. Munchen: Wilhelm Fink.

Staeuble, I. (1996). Historische und kulturelle Psychologie: In H. Gundlach (Hrsg.), *Untersuchungen zur Geschichte der Psychologie und der Psychotechnik*. Passau: Profil.

Stein, E. (1917). *On the problem of empathy*. Trans. W. Stein.: Washington, D. C. ICS Publications.

Stern, D. (1992). The role of feelings for an interpersonal self. In U. Neisser (Ed.), *The perceived self: Ecological and interpersonal sources of self-knowledge*. Cambridge: Cambridge University Press.

Stern, D., Dore, J., Hofer, L., & Hoft, W. (1993). Affect attunement: The sharing of feeling states between mother and infant by means of inter-model fluency. In, T. Field & N. Fox (Eds.), *Social perception in infants*. Norwood, NJ: Ablex Publishing Corporations.

Suh, E. M. (2002). Culture, identity consistency, and subjective well-being. *Journal of Personality and Social Psychology, 83*(6), 1378–1391.

Takano, Y., & Osaka, E. (1999). An unsupported common view: Comparing Japan and the U.S. on individualism/collectivism. *Asian Journal of Social Psychology, 2*, 311–341.

Triandis, H. C. (1989). The self and social behavior in differing contexts. *Psychological Review, 96*, 505–520.

Triandis, H. C. (1995). Individualism and collectivism. Boulder, CO: Westview Press.

Valsiner, J. (1986). *The individual subject and scientific psychology*. New York: Plenum.

Valsiner, J. (2000). *Culture and human development*. London: Sage Publications.

Valsiner, J. (2001). *Cultural developmental psychology of affective processes*. Invited lecture at the 15. Tagung der Fachgruppe Entwicklungspsychologie der Deutschen Gesellschaft fur Psychologies, Potsdam, Sept. 5.

Valsiner, J., & Van Der Veer, R. (2000). *The social mind: Construction of the idea*. Cambridge: Cambridge University Press.

Vandello, J. A., & Cohen, D. (1999). Patterns of individualism and collectivism across the United States. *Journal of Personality and Social Psychology, 77*, 279–292.

Vogel, S. (1996). Urban middle class Japanese family life, 1958–1996: A personal and evolving perspective. (pp. 177–201). In D. Shwalb & B. Shwalb (Eds.), *Japanese childrearing: Two generations of scholarship*. New York: The Guilford Press.

Vygotsky, L.S. (1978). *Mind in society: The development of higher psychological processes*. Cambridge, MA: Harvard University Press.

Vygotsky, L.S. (1981). The genesis of higher mental functions. In J. V. Wertsch (Ed.), *The concept of activity in Soviet psychology* (pp. 144–188). Armonk, NY: Sharpe.

Vygotski, L. S. (1985a). *Die psychische Systeme*. In L. Vygotski, Ausgewählte Schriften. Bd. 1. Köln: Phal-Rugenstein.

Wellman, H. M. (1990). *The child's theory of mind*. Cambridge, MA: MIT Press.

Wellman, H. M. (1993). Early Understanding of mind: the normal case. In S. Baron-Cohen, H. Tager-Flusberg & D. J. Cohen (Eds.), *Understanding other minds: Perspectives from Autism* (pp. 10–39). Oxford: Oxford University Press.

Whiting, B. (1976). The problem of the packaged variable. In K. Riegel & J. Meacham (Eds.), *The developing individual in a changing world* (*Vol. 1*, pp. 303–309). The Hague: Mouton.

Yoo, K. J. (2003). Toegye's Simhak (Learning of Mind) and Confucian proprieties. *Journal of History for Korean Thoughts, 21*, 271–300. [Korean]

Zabinski, B., & Valsiner, J. (2004). Affective syntesis of the other through the self: A new look at empathy. Paper presented at the 3rd International Conference on Dialogical Self. Warsaw, Poland, August, 28.

Zittoun, T. (2004). Janet's emotions in the whole of human conduct. *From Past to Future, 5*(1), 24–39.

CHAPTER 16

The Role of Symbolic Resources in Human Lives

Tania Zittoun

A person using a symbolic resource is a person using a novel, a film, a picture, a song, or a ritual, to address an unfamiliar situation in her everyday life. This person is thus not simply *having* the cultural experience of watching that film or hearing that music, or even not solely of remembering it: she has that experience, or remembers it, *in relation to something else*, located in her social world or in her inner life.

For example, when Paul comes back from work feeling tensed and irascible, and immediately listens to his preferred punk band, he is using that music as symbolic resource to modify his mood, and possibly, to prepare himself for a nice evening with Julie. After having been told that she would have to spend three months in Spain, Julie surprises herself reading Spanish novels, watching Spanish films and developing an interest for Spanish music. Julie is using these various cultural elements as symbolic resources to develop some representations about the Spain awaiting her, and to envisage possible futures. Hence, using a symbolic resource is something we all do, at times in a very unaware way – when we start to hum "I'm

singing in the rain" because some pleasant idea popped in our mind while we were walking through a spring shower – or sometimes, in a more explicit way – when we discuss a romantic films we have seen with friends and relate them to personal events.

The Concept of Symbolic Resource and Its Use

Although the notion of symbolic resources designates a familiar phenomenon, it has only recently been the object of a systematic theoretical enquiry (Zittoun, Duveen, Gillespie, Ivinson, & Psaltis, 2003; Zittoun, 2001, 2006). This notion aims at offering a theoretical understanding of people's uses of cultural artefacts, or semiotic tools, as developmental resources when they face new, unpredictable situations. In this first section, I sketch the historical background of the notion of symbolic resource, and highlight its potential for socio-cultural psychology.

Cultural psychology is developmental, and thus examines the processes by which a person changes in her evolving environments. Its emphasis is on the mediated nature of the transactions taking place between the person and world. Throughout their lives, people are exposed to unpredictable events generating uncertainty – events which are partly imposed on them, partly created by them. People do not always have the relevant knowledge or skills, the experience or the social support to face ruptures, or turning points (Erikson, 1968/1994) such as being in a country in war, moving place, becoming a parent, etc. However, culture presents people with material tools (wheels, computers) and semiotic tools (words, images, melodies) that enable dealing with such uncertainties. More particularly, semiotic tools encapsulate other people's experiences and interpretations of the world, in various times and places. Such semiotic tools might thus support the transition processes of turning the unfamiliar into manageable environments.

I will consider two sorts of cultural elements. *Cultural elements* as books, movies, pieces of art, and pictures are made out of semiotic configurations of various codes (musical, graphic, verbal, etc.), bounded by a material support. *Symbolic systems* such as religious, political, or ethnic systems are also organizations of signs, including texts or rules of reference, objects and places for rituals, and "wardens," or authorities that fix the system's boundaries (Geertz, 1972; Grossen & Perret-Clermont, 1992).

There are three important conditions for something to be considered a *symbolic resource*:

(1) A person must be *using* such a cultural element (e.g., a picture, a song, a film) or part of such a symbolic system (e.g., a religious metaphor), with some intention, that is, in relationship to something that is at least partially exterior to that cultural element (its "aboutness").

(2) The notion is restrained to uses of symbolic resources in situations normally not contained by the cultural element, that is, beyond the immediate cultural value or meaning of that cultural element (e.g., Julie does not listen to the song for its melody, but to feel closer to Paul).

(3) Additionally, the notion of symbolic resource refers only to the cultural elements that require an "imaginary" experience – the creation of a sphere of experience beyond the here and now of the socially shared reality (the "musical space" of a song; the sacred space of a ritual; the vicarious experience enabled by fiction, an "as-if" experience, see Abbey, this volume, Chapter 17).

A symbolic resource is not just a cultural object that can potentially be used as resource (for example Baltes, 1997). It is rather the fact of being used that turns a cultural device into a symbolic resource. A symbolic resource is to an artefact or symbolic system, what an utterance is to language (Bakhtin, 1979; Wertsch, 1998), or what a used "instrument," is to a potential "tool" (Grossen, 1999; Rabardel & Waern 2003). The notion has also to be distinguished from that of cultural scheme, or model, as these are meant to organize canonical situations in a smooth and automatic way (see for example, Strauss and Quinn, 1997 on marriage), whereas symbolic resources are by definition used "out of place." Third, contrarily to earlier definition (Zittoun et al., 2003), it seems theoretically fruitful to limit the study of symbolic resources as proposed here to *imaginary* experiences, that *clearly* present themselves as inviting to 'as-if' or vicarious experiences. I will thus not consider information-based resources (e.g., a geographical documentary), or processual resources (e.g., an argumentative style) (see e.g., Neuman & Bekerman, 2001; Psaltis & Duveen, 2006). Finally, a perspective focused on the persons' unique use of artefacts radically differs from cultural, social or cognitive approaches to films, the mass media or television (Forrester, 2000; Livingstone, 1998; Livingstone & Lunt, 1994): it does not refer to analyses in terms of "gratifications," "effects," or "influences" of media (e.g., Fiske & Hartley, 1978; Nelmes, 1996).

Historical Background of the Notion of Symbolic Resources

The notion of use of symbolic resource is, first, rooted in cultural psychology as it has developed over the past 20 years, mostly in the Anglo-Saxon world (Bruner, 1990, 1996; Cole, 1996; Valsiner, 2000; Wertsch, 1991). The notion is an offspring of the idea of cultural tool – material or ideational – in Vygotsky (Vygotsky & Luria, 1994). Cultural tools, or instruments, mediate the relationship of humans to the world, to others, and to themselves. Researchers inspired by Vygotsky have explored such "mediating structures" (Hutchins, 1995). Some, following Bakhtin (1979), have emphasized the role of language, or language genres, as semiotic mediations (Bronckart, 1985; Wertsch, 1991). Others have focused on various sorts of artefacts – primary (tools to do things), secondary (tools that comment on how to do these things), and tertiary artefacts (that open a distinct reality) (Cole, 1995, 1996). The notion of symbolic resource aims at capturing the dynamics through which semiotic devices are used, with some intention (Bruner, 1990; Valsiner, 1998).

Second, the notion has an origin in French anthropology and sociology. Levi-Strauss (1962) observed people engaging in symbolic *bricolage*, using bits and pieces of the symbolic and material means available to them, to confer meaning to events. Sociologists also emphasize the logics of users of cultural goods: people often use new manufactured objects in a very unpredictable way, according to their needs and the context (De Certeau, 1980; Perriault, 1989).

Third, the notion of use has a psychoanalytical origin in the work of Winnicott (1971, 1989), who observed the emergence of the children's capacity to "use" their mother, and then transitional objects and the potential space of cultural experiences. Use, here, is an emotional investment in an object, which can then acquire some psychic function: it externally supports and transforms feeling and thinking (see also Green 1969, 2000; Segal, 1991; Tisseron, 2003).

The notion of symbolic resource carries echoes from these various anchorages. It is a notion grounded in a semiotic understanding of human activity, in line with cultural psychology, some trends in anthropology, and psychoanalysis. It is a form of dialogical psychology (Grossen, 1999; Hermans & Kempen, 1993; Marková, 2003), emphasizing intrapsychological mediated dialogue (see also: Abbey & Davis, 2003; Benson, 2001; Josephs, 1997, 1998; Salgado & Gonçalves, this volume Chapter 30; Valsiner, 1997, 1998), or mediated interactions (Gillespie, 2005b, this volume, Chapter 34). It focuses on the knitting of social and cultural determinations and individual meaning-making. Finally, it acknowledges the centrality of emotions and the role of the unconscious in symbolic thinking (Janet, 1934; Freud, 1908).

Theoretical Relevance of the Notion in Socio-cultural Psychology

Socio-cultural approaches face recurrent issues. The notion of symbolic resource offers alternative routes to approach these. First, scholars regularly face the psychological/social divide (Cole, 1996), as the internalization/appropriation debate has shown (see Lawrence & Valsiner, 1993, 2003; Lightfoot & Cox, 1997; Matusov, 1998; Shweder, 1995; Tomasello, 1999; Toomela, 1996a, 1996b; Valsiner, 1998; Wertsch 1993). The notion of symbolic resource is located exactly there, where the person turns a socially shared element into a psychologically relevant resource; uses of symbolic resources necessarily constitute a bridging between inner world and shared reality.

Second, socio-cultural psychologies have recurrently signaled the danger of "losing the subject" (either reducing her to a cognitive structure, or dissolving her in the social) (Grossen, 1999; Valsiner, 1997). Here, a symbolic resource is always used by an intentional person, for whom that cultural element has a particular meaning in a given situation; the subject is thus restored. Third, dialogical approaches drawing on Bakhtin

(1979) are confronted with a methodological problem: how to identify, in a person's externalization, all the infinity of sources that are echoed, or answered to? The notion of symbolic resource offers a powerful analytical tool, for it enables us to trace the transformation of cultural elements as they exist for the community into a persons' unique externalization of these, which carry the trace of the psychic work through which they have been used.

Using a Symbolic Resource: A Model

Studying people's uses of symbolic resources offers a new access for investigating processes of change in people's lives. People are indeed most likely to mobilize cultural elements as symbolic resources when they face situations that question the taken for granted. What are the semiotic dynamics through which symbolic resources will help the person to reduce uncertainty, and to open new possibilities? In this section, I give a model for the analysis of uses of symbolic resources. I will show how symbolic resources participate to psychological development because of their mediation of three basic psychological processes: intentionality, inscription in time, and distancing.

Aboutness of Symbolic Resources

A cultural element that a person uses as a symbolic resource is always put in relationship with something that exceeds the cultural experience it offers: the experience of the person in her world. As with other cultural tools, when a symbolic resource is used, it can produce meaning or action about self, about others, and/or about the socially shared reality. A novel can be used "about" *self* when it is used to deepen one's understanding of oneself, to experience new aspects of self, or to change oneself. Jack London (1913) narrates the story of Martin Eden who aimed at educating himself and becoming a writer through patient and systematic readings; fiction becomes here a means to change his own identity and his

social position. Choi, Han, and Kim (this volume, Chapter 15) similarly mention culturally designed uses of drama to change one's emotions. A novel can be used as a way to connect, to cooperate, or to share some experience with *others* – as when two friends discuss their readings, which will then become part of their relationship. Famous literary or philosophical friendships, such as the one between Jean-Paul Sartre and Simone De Beauvoir exemplify such uses of symbolic resources. A symbolic resource can be used to understand a contemporary historical or political *world* situation. Watching *South Park* can be used as resource to develop a new perspective on current politics. Hence, symbolic resources are cultural elements which, when used by the person, become *about* something else, with some intention (Zittoun et al., 2003).

Time Orientation of Symbolic Resources

As with all semiotic dynamics, uses of symbolic resources have a location within the flux of time (Valsiner, 2001). For one part, cultural experiences always require some knitting of past and future in the present. In order to "understand" the cultural experience, one has to mobilize memories of past impressions and feelings to nourish images, words, and melodies (Vygotsky, 1928); one also has to mobilize cultural knowledge (about narrative, musical or cinematographic genres) to create some expectations about what will come next. For the other part, the *aboutness* of the use is also located in time. One can see a film set in Paris, and remember one's own *past* trip to Paris. Before traveling to Ladakh, tourists watch films such as *Little Buddha* that enable them to shape a representation of their *future* (Gillespie, 2005c). Finally, symbolic resources can be used to support a current, enduring experience. In his movie *The Dreamers* (2003), Bertolucci shows a love triangle over a couple of weeks, in the Paris of the 1960s, during the glorious years of the French cinema. The young people are continuously watching films together, quoting these, and playing out some of their scenes.

Films – and especially *Jules et Jim*, a classical love triangle (Truffaut, 1962) – are here symbolic resources through which the young people are creating the *enduring present* of their love affair.

Level of Mediation of Symbolic Resources

Psychic life is possible through semiotic mediation, or symbolic elaboration, that turns perceptions, impressions, affects, intuition, actions, desires, into thoughts, or representations. It is through semiotic elaboration that these experiences can be linked to one's memories and understanding, that is, become part of semiotic dynamics and thinking. Semiotic elaboration is partly done through the mobilization of our knowledge and memories, but can also be supported by the semiotic environment – as for example, as when one realizes being sad while listening to sad music: the music, provides with an organization of semiotic means that enable distancing from sadness. It is because cultural experiences provide us with external means to support such elaboration of experience that symbolic resources can be "used" at all. Symbolic resources can thus enable to take a more or less distant position towards one's immediate and embodied experience. They can thus bring to various "levels" of distancing, each progressively less dependent on the specific experienced situation, or more generalizable (Janet, 1934; Valsiner 1997, 1998, 2005; Werner & Kaplan, 1963; Zittoun, in press, b). Following Valsiner's propositions (2004), four levels of distancing can be proposed.

A person can be in a state of diffuse feelings and impression. At a first level of mediation, the symbolic resource can group those here-and-now, embodied experiences, reflect them, and enable a person to identify them. Hence, Emma Bovary and her lover are watching the sky on the boat back home after a romantic escape: "The moon rose, and they greeted it with no lack of phrases, finding the planet melancholy and full of poetry. She even began to sing: 'Un soir, t'en souviens-t-il? Nous voguions' <footnote 1>, etc."(Flaubert, 1857/1999, p. 279). Here,

Emma uses this song as symbolic resource to contain, reflect, and fix the diffuse melancholy, sadness, and anxiety she shares with her lover and which are diffracted onto the landscape. It mediates a first level of reflection that enables the acknowledgement of a state of experience.

At a second level, semiotic mediations offered by a symbolic resource can help to identify and label a specific current state of mind or situation. Hence, Emma Bovary finds herself in an incomprehensible state of exaltation after her first intimate meeting with a man; she then recalls romantic novels she used to read, which make her realize: *she has a lover!* She thus articulates in a symbolic manner her experience, which makes it thinkable and communicable.

At a third level, symbolic resources can be used to define class or categories of behavior or events, or attributes of self. Again, Flaubert makes a point at showing us that Emma Bovary has used all her religious and romantic readings to build a distinction between "friendly, but boring marital relationships," and "fascinating, exciting, adulterous passions." Based on these two categories, Emma aims at defining herself as belonging to the type of "passionate lovers". At this third level, the world and herself become classifiable and organized.

At a fourth level, symbolic resources can be used to define and clarify higher-level rules and principles or commitments. Such commitments have the power to organize categories (level 3), or to sustain specific actions (level 2). Hence, Emma Bovary seems to have used her romantic reading to develop the overarching principle that "life is not worth living without passion," which leads her to see herself as a martyr (a category to define self at level 3) and to commit suicide (a specific conduct at level 2).

At each level, thus, the semiotic mediators offered by the symbolic resource meet some aspect of Emma's experience, and represent it in a transformed, more distant way: from an embodied state, to contained and fixed emotional patterns; from these, to a labeled situation; from the latter, to categories grouping various experiences of self and the world; and from categories to orienting values. Symbolic resources offer such distancing possibility, because they create an imaginary sphere where personal, unique experiences meet culturally elaborated versions of other people's comparable experiences (Zittoun 2004) – as signs can, more generally, integrate first person and third person perspectives (Gillespie, this volume, Chapter 34).

Generativity of Symbolic Resources

The tri-dimensional model artificially separates various modalities of uses of symbolic resources. In fact, people using symbolic resources usually combine dimensions and modalities of uses. The outcomes of such combinations can be extremely diverse. Emma Bovary's uses of symbolic resources are particularly dramatic: although they first open alternative lives (the young countryside woman lives new adventures), they quickly bring her to a point where she has no other option but to kill herself (at the end of the novel, she has lost her lover and ruined her husband; inspired by her readings, she drinks poison). Yet uses of resources can also be highly generative. A generative use of resources usually moves across a wide range of modality of uses. For example, Julia, a fan of a British pop-band, the *Manic Sreet Preachers*, uses their songs as resources to soothe her in a mourning period (*about* self); she then uses this music as a means to meet other fans (*about* others). Also, she realizes that the lyrics of that band have some political meaning; trying to understand them, she starts to see the world in a new way (*about* the social world). The uses also vary on the time perspective: Julia first uses the songs, that speak about mining areas in England, to think about the place where she grew up (*past*-orientation), before using them for making plans for her *future* (which professional position might bring her to improve this region). The songs finally enable here to progressively distance herself from her experience. The sad melodies first contain and reflect her sad and fuzzy feelings (level 1); she then realizes that the lyrics

seem to name her feelings and re-present them to her (level 2); the lyrics also give her a position in the world: she is a revolted person, the world contains injustices (level 3); finally, they bring her to define political values that will guide her actions (level 4). At each of these changes of modality of uses, Julia picks up new symbolic resources (novels or poems mentioned in the lyrics) to support her moves. These uses of resources are highly generative: they bring her to new transitions and open up new possible situations of choices and uses of resources (Zittoun, 2006).

The Study of Symbolic Resources in Changing Lives

Symbolic resources are of interest for many researchers aiming to understand the role of culture in human lives. These are especially relevant to examine the trajectory of people inhabiting contemporary societies. In such societies, there is no overarching meaning system that provides people with meaning for important events in their lives; people have to discover how to deal with their striving for sense on the basis of available cultural devices (Zittoun 2005, 2006). Even more, such society diffuse the idea that people are responsible for their life trajectories and for the sense they confer to it, as discussed by Lawrence and Dodds (this volume, Chapter 19).

In our current work on symbolic resource, we have defined *a unit of analysis* for human development: we examine *ruptures* in people's lives – that is, events that question what the person holds as taken for granted – and the subsequent process of *transition*, through which the person engages in restoring some sense of personal integrity, regularity, and continuity, and reduces uncertainty. In our analysis, transitions appear to engage three interdependent processes: identity redefinition and repositioning, skills and knowledge acquisition, and meaning making. Ruptures and transitions can be caused by a wide diversity of events, but we are interested only in these that are perceived as such by a person, and following which she engages in active uses of her resources (Perret-Clermont & Zittoun, 2002; Zittoun et al., 2003; Zittoun, 2005, 2006). This section is organized by a distinction between different classes of ruptures. I examine symbolic resources used by people perceiving their own life as interrupted, symbolic resources used to mediate interpersonal relationships, symbolic resources used to work on one's relationship to a changing environment, and finally, to support one's moves from between environments. In each case, I first indicate studies led by explicit mention of the notion of symbolic resource. I then mention descriptions of uses of symbolic resources in the social sciences and in literature, thus indicating directions for further studies.

Symbolic Resources and One's Life Trajectory

Symbolic resources might be used to address personal ruptures – a person matures, develops new ideas, or has an accident that questions who she is. Becoming a parent is an important change in the course of a life, which will affect bodies, couples, and one's responsibilities. In a study on the transition to parenthood (Zittoun, 2004a, 2005), I have shown two types of symbolic resources used by future parents that help them to define a name for their coming child: on the one hand, traditional cultural elements transmitted through generations, such as naming principles or repertoires of names; on the other hand, names taken from films, songs, novels, the Bible, places, or events. These symbolic resources appeared to support the whole process of transition to parenthood. They would be used to link current changes with a personal and collective past, to generate representations about possible events, and to shape representations of the child to come and of oneself as parent. These symbolic resources appeared to contain complex emotions, ambivalent feelings, and unconscious thoughts about death and life. In some cases, the resources were used to keep these thought apart, where in some other cases it enabled the person to work through them. It appeared that people

engaged in *bricolage*, combining traditional symbolic resources (e.g., religious naming rules), and some resources taken from the media (e.g., a fiction character). The former are often linked to inclusive systems of orientation; they can thus help to represent one's own changes in time (e.g., becoming a father) within a collective definition (e.g., a lineage) (Zittoun, 2004b; 2005).

In the scientific literature focused on individual change in adolescence and youth, researchers have examined the role of objects and cultural elements as resources. Fuhrer (2004), Fuhrer and Josephs (1999), and Habermas (1996, 1999) have shown young people using familiar and preferred objects as they leave home, to support and define their identities, for their soothing functions, and to negotiate their relationship to their social worlds. Csikszentmihaly and Larson (1984) noticed the emotional functions (as dissipative structures) of literature in difficult moment of youth. Heath (1996, 2000), Hundeide (2003, 2004), Kamberlis and Dimitriadis (1998), and Lightfoot (1997) have given detailed analysis of the use of objects, music, narratives, "styles," in adolescents' identity creation, socialization, and learning. Abbey and Davis (2003) have analyzed how rap music can be used to support autodialogue in adolescents' identity processes.

Symbolic Resources in Interpersonal Interactions or Relationships

Symbolic resources might be precious to support a person's real or imaginary relationship to specific others: to facilitate a common project, to get closer to someone, to keep a relationship alive or to accept its disappearance. Analyzing people's discussion as they watch *Dallas*, Liebes and Katz (1990) showed how the serial was used as way to confer meaning to their own relationships. A social scientist, Fonyi (1994) interviewed psychoanalysts about their uses of literature and art in their practice. Some analysts use the fact that patient's discourse awake in them particular echoes of cultural experiences, to guide their interpretations; other use novels and arts to increase their knowledge of the variety of human lives; other prefer to keep cultural experiences as way to switch off their practices. In all these cases their analyst are using novels, music or paintings as symbolic resources to work out their relationship with their patients.

Finally, symbolic resource might play important emotional and meaning function in terms of interruption of relationship. A young woman having dramatically lost her brother found a great support in Khalil Gibran's book *The Prophet*. She thus explains how the verse, "The deeper the sorrow carves into your being, the more joy you can contain" helped her to overcome her sadness (Zittoun, 2006). Similarly, in his *Book of Illusions* (2002), Paul Auster narrates the story of a man deeply affected by the sudden death of his wife and children in a plane crash. Eventually, he becomes fascinated by the silent movies of an unknown and forgotten moviemaker. The narrator's long descriptions of these films and of the story of the moviemaker appear to enable him to realize and transform his own feeling of loss of his close ones. Uses of symbolic resources might thus offer, as the process of artistic creation (Aberbach, 1989) or other forms of semiotic mediation (Josephs, 1997, 1998), individualized forms of mourning or working through losses (as all transitions imply).

Symbolic Resources and Modification Within One's Sphere of Experience

A person lives in various settings that she holds for relatively stable or predictable. Her family life, her experience at school or at work, can be called her "spheres of experience." These spheres of experience can be disrupted, for example because new technologies are brought in the work place (Perret & Perret-Clermont, 2001). Such ruptures are often imposed, and require meaning work. They can question the position of a person within a given structure or social networks, or the meaning of her actions. They can also affect the circulation of devices that might be used as symbolic resources.

A literary critic, Najmambali (2004) analyzes the success of new romantic novels in Iran, which she links to societal changes. Young people engage their transition to adulthood with claims over new forms of sexualities, whereas the adult society does not have the means to control these. The novel offers a space to give shape to these claims and needs, and for reflecting upon their possible consequences. Similarly, collective historical re-enactments in Poland, although an old tradition in Eastern Europe, became widespread in the end of the nineties (Zagórska & Tarnowski, 2004). Their role as symbolic resources can be examined in relation to the countries' difficult integration in the European Union.

Literature and cinema abundantly explore the importance of access to, and use of cultural elements as symbolic resources under authoritarian states. At times, literature is a symbolic resource to maintain one's sense of humanity and relationships to others (Levi, 1985); at others, developing a particular care for books becomes a way to externalize one's disapproval of the current situation (Hrabal, 1976; see also *Fahrenheit 451*).

Symbolic Resources and Moving to New Spheres of Experience

Many ruptures experienced by people are due to their own geographical and social moves and relocations. People change settings of activity or sphere of experience, which questions who they are, what they can do, and what that change means. We have examined the process of transitions of young people coming back from a religious school to the secular world, using the Bible, but also novels and films to confer meaning to the rupture itself (Zittoun, 1996, 2006, in press, a). Gillespie has shown how people traveling to Ladakh use films, pictures, and guidebooks to understand the world in which they find themselves (Gillespie, 2005c, 2006). Immigrant populations are in similar situations: in order to confer meaning to the new situation, they can try to use symbolic resources transmitted in their families, or available around them (Zittoun & Cesari, 1998).

The problem of people's transitions from one sphere of experience to another one is of great social and political relevance. Research on children of migrants has shown how culture might or not be used as symbolic resources in new context, for questions of loyalty to one's group (Dinello & Perret-Clermont, 1988). In the therapy of migrants, ethno-psychoanalysts create a setting that supports operations of bridging between the patients' traditional symbolic systems and the demands of the host society; pivotal objects becomes symbolic resources taken from the traditional system, that can be used in the new setting (Nathan, 1993, 2001).

Artists and novelists have frequently accounted for the important role of cultural elements as resources for social mobility, or as resources when one is propelled to a new setting. In the best-seller *The Beach*, the narrator finds himself in a highly dangerous and unknown island; from this point on, his description of the event become shaped by, and intermeshed with, memories of Vietnam War films (Garland, 1997). Many autobiographic novels insist on the emancipatory role of literature, enabling social relocation. *Kaffir Boy* is for example the narrative of an illiterate, starving inhabitant of a South African slum, who, through his becoming literate and access to literature, eventually migrates to North America (Mathabane, 1986).

The Lost Use of Symbolic Resources: Meaning and Emotion

Four types of ruptures have been distinguished on the basis of external criteria. Focusing on the intrapsychic, interpersonal relationships, one's relationship to a social group, or to a societal state, these types correspond to four possible levels of description of the psychosocial world (Doise, 1982). An analysis in terms of symbolic resources requires a focus on the perspective of the person and her interiority, which is a systemic whole. Symbolic resources work because they are connected into one's emotional and embodied experience. Yet they are likely to generate distancing effects, to change one's intention or time perspective, and through the elaboration of emotions and the creation of new perspective, to generate more ruptures. Above, Julia's initial use of songs as resources was a mean to mourn her grandmother's death (interpersonal rupture); yet the songs bring her to new feelings and understandings of the world. She then decided to join groups of politicized music fans (rupture of spheres of experience).

Studying symbolic resources thus calls our attention to the interdependence of various phenomena often held as distinct. Analyzing autobiographic narratives, we have thus shown how people such as Carl Rogers (Zittoun, 2003) and Malcolm X (Gillespie, 2005a) used literature to transform themselves and to operate important social and symbolic moves (i.e., leaving religion and becoming a psychologist; or quitting a hustler life to become the minister of the nation of Islam). This then led them to change their new sphere of experience (i.e., proposing a new theory, or a new political discourse).

Finally, in this section, we have seen that literature and cinema identify the importance of symbolic resource in personal emotional elaboration, mourning, the definition of collective values in social change, and meaning making when one's personal is in radical mismatch with the socially shared culture. Such issues are raised by modern societies, through the extension of the life course, technological and political transformations, migrations, and the rapid alteration of life styles. However, studies in psychology and the social sciences that investigate changes mostly focus on the work of identity, socialization, and communicative strategies. In contrast, the notion of symbolic resource offers a precious entrance to emotional and meaning making dynamics. These are central for the understanding of how a person can maintain a sense of integrity and continuity, while changing enough to develop beyond a rupture. They thus deserve a full status in socio-cultural approaches addressing change in life.

A Developmental Understanding of Symbolic Resources in Human Lives

From a developmental perspective, two questions can be raised: how does one learn to use symbolic resources? And how does a person's modalities of using symbolic resources change over life?

Learning to Use Symbolic Resources

Learning to use symbolic resources is quite likely to be an extension of the acquisition of early symbolic function in infant, and of language in children. Psychologists from various orientations seem consensually to admit that early symbolic acquisitions require regular patterns of shared and culturally defined actions with adults, that will progressively be internalised by the child, thus provoking qualitative changes in her possible thinking and actions in the world (Moro & Rodriguez, 1998; Nelson, 1989, 1996; Piaget, 1945, 1951; Valsiner, 1997). To summarise these dynamics, a *semiotic prism* can be proposed (Zittoun, 2006, Figure 1). Ontogenetically, this prism includes the infant, a state of the world, a reflecting parent and a symbol with which the parent will reflect the child's recognition of the state of the world (Fonagy, Gergely, Jurist, & Target, 2002; Green, 2002). Basic symbolic abilities are fundamental for later uses of symbolic resources. It is also quite likely that later uses of symbolic resources will emerge within similar interactive pattern. In short, the transformation of cultural experiences into usable symbolic resources is likely to occur *when two persons interact on a regular basis about a symbolic object, and come to an acknowledgement of what that designates (the shared and objective referent) and a mutual acknowledgement of the fact that it does personally mean/feel for each of them (within each person's internal, embodied representational and emotional world).*

When parents read a goodnight story to their child, or sing her a lullaby when she is anxious, they create such a semiotic prism encompassing them, the child, the story or the lullaby, and the emotional state of the child (reflected by the parents, perceived by the child, adjusting in a feedback loop). The child who then asks for her preferred lullaby or goodnight story is already a user of a symbolic resource: she uses that element as a way to regulate her emotion, open an imaginary space, in the comforting and mediating presence of her parents. The parents might, or might not, acknowledge the function of that use. The child might then be confronted with a multitude of such semiotic experiences, in which the parents might be replaced by other adults, or peers. Hence the pole "other" of the semiotic prism is changing, until it might become a generalised Other pole; the mediating position of these others or the generalised others will eventually be internalised by the child. Mother singing rhymes to their babies (Nelson, 1996; Tucker, 1981) or telling them traditional tales (Mathabane, 1986), father supporting their child's reading taste (Lloyd, 1999; Oz, 2004), parents commenting on their children's television watching (Livingstone, 2002; Tisseron, 2000), teachers accompanying children in their discovery of stories (Henri, 2003; Tucker, 1981), pictures (Fasulo, Girardet & Pontecorvo, 1998), or the Bible (Zittoun, 1996) can support such semiotic dynamics. Eventually, these mediations and the presence of others will be internalised, and the child will take a progressive distancing from cultural experiences (Lawrence & Valsiner, 2003). The developmental hypothesis proposed here is thus that the internalization of such interpersonal semiotic dynamics, or semiotic prisms, will enable further uses of cultural elements as symbolic resources (see Gillespie, this volume Chapter 34 for another account of the semiotic dynamics involved).

It is likely that in good enough conditions, and independently of socio-economical factors, people develop a way to relate to stories, images, symbolic objects, and to link these with one's experience in the world. Social or cultural differences can affect *what* will become a symbolic resource – a traditional

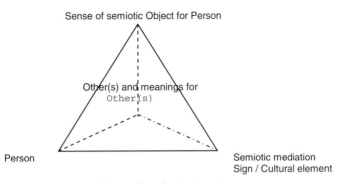

Figure 16.1. Semiotic prism.

tale, one's preferred videotape, a painting in a museum – but not *how* these will be used.

Transformations of Uses of Symbolic Resources

Modalities of uses of symbolic resources are likely to change through life, along two developmental lines that are difficult to separate. On one side, there is a change in a person's whole structure of thinking and remembering over time, which is due to biological maturation, but also, diversification of her life situations, and of the breadth and depth of her social, cognitive, emotional and symbolic experiences. On the other side a person might also develop a specific reflectivity on what she does, or can do, with symbolic resources.

From the developmental angle, modalities of symbolic resources will depend, first, on one's abilities to think associatively, to think in concrete terms or to think abstractly, and to imagine the state of mind of others (Bennett, 1999; Harris, 2000; Piaget, 1945, 1951). Second, uses of symbolic resources are heavily dependent on memory. It seems that memories of younger children do not necessarily have the same features than those of older people (Kavanagh, 2000). Autobiographical literature highlights the embodied quality of childhood memories: places, colours, lights, temperatures, and emotions. Memories of older life might become much more abstract, as synthesis of many similar situations. Third, uses of symbolic resource depend on one's socialisation to media and cultural objects. Very young children might not master the graphic convention necessary to understand a story or a cartoon; a young child might have difficulty to understand character's intentions that are contradictory with their actions (Tucker, 1981). Fourth, uses of symbolic resources will depend on personal needs, which are partly socially shaped, partly idiosyncratic. On the one hand, psychosocial development will confront people to typical transitions. Children becoming siblings might have particular anxieties and fantasies about death and sexuality (Mitchell, 2003), for which some tales might offer good potential symbolic resources. Starting school might call for symbolic resources to stand the frustrations imposed by a highly normative life. Adolescence might incite uses of symbolic resources for personal and social identity definition, or to give space to otherwise invading emotions. Young adulthood requires symbolic resources to support meaning making as one defines life commitments (Zittoun, 2006). On the other hand, people are different, and change through time: at some point, children or adults need to be reassured about their understanding of their world; at others, they might want to explore new possibilities and horizons (Tucker, 1981; Zittoun, 2006). At times, people use symbolic resources to expand or reinforce their social networks – for example, when children can discuss about the film they have all seen (Kavanagh, 2000; Livingstone, 2002); at others, they use them to explore or fill loneliness (Taylor, 1999). Hence, various modalities of uses of symbolic resources (different combinations on the three dimensions of uses) can be more typical at some ages, or in some moments of life. However, progressively, one can expect people to experience a wide range of uses of symbolic resources.

Reflexivity of Uses of Symbolic Resources

People can be more or less reflectively using symbolic resources. In what follows, different degrees of reflectivity are proposed. All along this hierarchy, uses are likely to support some psychological change. People can use symbolic resources with different reflectivity in different contexts and at different moments.

First, people can have cultural experiences and appreciate these experiences for the direct and immediate impression they cause, or meanings they carry. A movie is seen because it is "good fun," a painting is nice because it is "well done" or has beautiful colors, and so on. In such *a degree zero* of uses a person would not have to be aware that the cultural experience is relevant within her sphere of experience. This does not mean that the experience is less significant; but the shaping of the experience occurs without distancing.

Second, people mostly have a vague sense that having cultural experiences do affect them, make them feel things and change them. We can call *quasi use* this vague acknowledgement: seeing a good movie and feeling good afterwards, or listening some music and realizing one's state of mind.

Thirdly, *intuitive uses* indicate an acknowledgement, even if not clearly conscious, of one or many effects of having a cultural experience or remembering it. Bringing objects back from holidays, with the intention of conferring them a memorial value, or putting homely objects on the walls can be seen as intuitive uses of symbolic resources. People seem in effect to guide conduct on the basis on a minimal understanding that symbolic resources might maintain memories, support self-continuity, and so on.

Fourth, uses of symbolic resources can be said to be *deliberate* when a person is actively looking for a cultural element that might be used as a resource to achieve a certain end. This requires her to be, more or less consciously, aware of the functioning of resources and their possible effects. Examples would be people calling upon a vignette from a text or the Bible or a movie to choose among possible conduct (Zittoun, 2006). Deliberate uses can be slowly developed out of progressive reflective understanding of intuitive practices, or can be systematically trained, as is the case in groups of Bible readers.

Fifth, deliberate uses might become object of one's reflectivity. In such *reflective use*, a person might clearly know that she does such uses, and reflect upon her uses and the changes these enables. A person aware of the impact of using symbolic resources, deliberately looking for them, might also start to transform existing elements or ways to use them (such as in mixing music), or creating his own resources (writing poems).

Deliberate and *reflective* uses can be called *expert uses* of symbolic resources. These enable planning and exploring possibilities, in relation to what the person is currently facing. Such uses achieve the full symbolic functions of cultural elements: personally relevant *aboutness*, inscription within a time perspective, and changes of level of mediations. Even though *zero*, *quasi*, and *intuitive* uses do support psychological dynamics and might enable new conduct, *reflective* uses are likely to be the most transformative, as they can accompany the process of reorganizing systems of orientation and linking symbolic resources to concrete situations, so as to develop new perspectives on one's conduct.

A Social Understanding of Symbolic Resources in Human Lives

Uses of symbolic resources are always culturally, institutionally, and socially located (Grossen, 2000; Perret-Clermont, Perret, & Bell, 1991), and therefore constrained.

For economical, geographical, political or social reasons, a person's access to cultural elements might be reduced. Yet it seems that socio-economic factors do not predict how these symbolic resources are used (Livingstone, 2002; Zittoun, 2006). Rather, it is important to question the frames of activity (or spheres, or fields) *in which* the person is embedded. These might indeed legitimate or prohibit some uses of symbolic resources (Duveen, 2001). Gender differences in uses can be seen as reflecting such forces: lonely women have constituted the first readership of fiction (Rieger & Tonard, 1999); at school, boys would avoid "girlish" readings in front of their peers – yet it has been suggested that boys raised by their mother alone often develop stronger links to literature (Kundera, 1986; Tucker, 1981; Zittoun, 2006). Girls might be using resources in a more narrative way as a result of socialisation (Gilligan, 1982), but such differences disappear under stressful conditions (Tisseron, 2000). Also, in a given school setting, girls might feel unauthorized to display their understanding in some types of gendered interactions (Duveen & Lloyd, 1990; Psaltis & Duveen, 2006).

Spheres of activity can also render legitimate, or not, some uses of resources *out* of their own frame. For some orthodox Jews, it might be impossible to use their knowledge of biblical texts to give meaning to everyday struggles out of the religious milieu (Lawrence, Benedikt, & Valsiner, 1992; Zittoun, 2006).

Finally, societal forces (political, economical, ideological) can impinge on these spheres of activities: they can impose or prohibit access to cultural elements (through cultural monopole or censorship, or control of circulation); they can control the uses made out of these resources (controlling interpretations and critics); they can endanger the social and psychological space in which these resources are used (by controlling interpersonal or group communication about symbolic resources; by imposing forms of life that prevent people to become absorbed in worlds of imagination; by condemning symbolic thinking).

Intersubjective and Psychological Constraints on Uses

Using a symbolic resource requires a form of thinking that acknowledges emotions, is analogical and metaphorical, and has similarity to Freud's dream work (1900, 1901). Reflecting on one's uses of symbolic resources might be done through verbal language (but also through other semiotic forms). In that sense, interactions that encourage narrative reasoning around cultural experience might support such uses. Children who go to the museum with mothers that give them *narrative* accounts (stories) of painting, rather than *paradigmatic* ones (causal and argumentative explanation, Bruner, 1986), develop a better memory and can recall these narratives easier (Tessler, 1986; Tessler & Nelson, 1994, quoted in Nelson, 1996). Narrative comments develop children's memories and understanding of time. Such styles of talking and thinking are *not* the one that is encouraged by schools, which promote paradigmatic forms of thinking. Various socio-cultural groups may develop different ways of talking about and referring to cultural experience (Ochs & Capps, 2001), encouraging school-like forms of discourse.

Partly linked to such social and interpersonal conditions, uses of symbolic resources are also restrained by intra-psychical constraints. First, uses of symbolic resources rely on the mobilization of memories and images. These must have some aliveness, that is, be representational and emotional, in touch with both a person's conscious and unconscious thoughts, and on the other side, her experiences of the real world. Traumatic events or psychic pain can endanger this aliveness. In such cases, experiences can resist semiotic mediations (they are "indigestible") (Bion, 1977; Kaës 1994, 1996; Tisseron, 2003). Second, uses of symbolic resources require clear boundaries between a person's zones of experience – her inner life, what belongs to the shared reality, and what belong to the imaginary zone, where the cultural element and her inner life meet. Such boundaries are necessary for avoiding acting out fictional ideas, or for distinguishing one's feelings from feelings created by the cultural experience (Winnicott, 1971, 1989). Personal breakdowns, stressful events, or forms of interpersonal or societal influence, can distort these boundaries. Third, to be transformative, these processes need to be located in time: they need to be connected to memories, and to have a future orientation. If memories are not accessible (when they are repressed or cleaved), or if the person's sense of integrity is too fragile to be imagined in an "as-if" world, such processes cannot take place (Tisseron, 1996).

Methodology and Further Directions

How should one study symbolic resources? To capture the uniqueness of personal uses of symbolic resources, methodologies have to preserve the perspective of the user, and the dynamic, temporal nature of semiotic dynamics. The methodological principle is simple: the researcher has to identify resources mentioned by people, the cultural elements at their origin, and the events about which these have been used. Analysis will identify the transformations and semiotic work at stake, and the constraints exerted upon these.

Reconstructive methods are powerful to elaborate descriptions of uses of symbolic resources that took place in the past. Reconstructive methods work with data based on people's externalization linked to uses of symbolic resources. The analysis aims at reconstructing what cultural elements people have met, internalized, and used as resources. *Interviews* have been used to reconstruct elaborations during the transition to parenthood or in youth (Zittoun, 2004, 2005, 2006). Symbolic resources are often captured by indirect ways. The interview schedule can be designed to bring people to talk about concrete occasions of uses of symbolic resources. For example, students can be asked about the objects they brought with them in their new accommodations; parents are asked about name

choices. It is often while evoking things *about* which the symbolic resources have been used, that these are mentioned (rather than when talking about books or films) (Zittoun, 2004, 2005, 2006). *Historical* data can be used: diaries can be seen as forms of externalizations, and combined with other archival sources to recreate the cultural environment of a diarist (Gillespie, 2005b; Zittoun, Cornish, Gillespie, and Avelling, in press). *Observational* data might be exploited as well: people can be observed interacting in settings in which they mobilize symbolic resources (Zittoun, 1996); people can also develop introspective technique to think their own uses of resources (Zittoun, in pressd, b2006). Uses of symbolic resources can then be studied as case studies, or compared: on the base of the uses, of the resources, or of the users' trajectories (see Chapter 4, this volume; Valsiner & Sato, 2006).

The study of uses of symbolic resources offers a new perspective on semiotic dynamics and change. It offers tools for studying everyday learning, in and out of formal settings. It also proposes a way to apprehend the "user" of films, books, and cultural elements. It might contribute to the exploration of children, youth, and adult learning, to the study of migration and transition to new cultural communities. It helps us to examine interactions between the individual and the societal. It raises questions about the development and the evolution of symbolic resources in the life course, and about the social and interpersonal settings that might support or hinder them. It also questions the boundaries between normality and pathology in using resources. In this chapter, we have seen that symbolic systems and artefacts have as major property the fact that they encapsulate human meaning and experience; people are constantly striving for meaning, especially in moments of change. However, it appears that social sciences are still unable to account for how cultural tools participate in people's personal meaning making, and emotional elaboration as part of psychic transformation. Studying symbolic resources might contribute to such understanding.

References

Abbey, E. & Davis, P. C. (2003). Constructing one's identity through music. In I. E. Josephs (Ed.), *Dialogicality in development* (pp. 67–86). Westport, CT: Praeger.

Aberbach, D. (1989). *Surviving trauma. Loss, literature and psychoanalysis.* New Haven/London: Yale University Press.

Auster, P. (2002). *The Book of Illusions, a novel.* New York/London: Faber & Faber.

Bakhtin, M. M. (1979/1986). *Speech genres and other late essays* (trans: V. McGee). Austin: University of Texas.

Baltes, P. B. (1997). On the incomplete architecture of human ontogeny. Selection, Optimization and Compensation as foundation of developmental psychology, *American Psychologist*, 52, 366–380.

Bennett, M. (Ed.), (1999). *Developmental psychology: achievements and prospects.* Philadelphia /London: Psychology Press.

Benson, C. (2001). *The cultural psychology of self.* London: Routledge.

Bion, W. R. (1977). *Seven Servants. Four works by W. R. Bion.* New York: John Aronson.

Bronckart, J. P. (Ed.), (1985). *Le fonctionnement des discours: un modèle psychologique et une méthode d'analyse.* Lausanne: Delachaux & Niestlé. [The functioning of discourse: a psychological model and a method of analysis].

Bruner, J. S. (1986). *Actual minds, possible worlds.* Cambridge, MA: Harvard University Press.

Bruner, J. S. (1990). *Acts of meaning.* Cambridge: Harvard University Press.

Cole, M. (1995). Culture and cognitive development: from cross-cultural research to creating systems of cultural mediation. *Culture & Psychology*, 1, 25–54.

Cole, M. (1996). *Cultural psychology. A once and future discipline.* Cambridge, MA/London: The Belknap Press of Harvard University Press.

Csikszentmihaly, M. & Larson, R. (1984). *Being adolescent. Conflict and growth in the teenage years.* New York: Basic books.

De Certeau, M. (1980/1984). *The practice of everyday life* (Translated by S. Rendall). Berkeley: University of California Press.

Dinello, R. & Perret-Clermont, A.-N. (Eds.) (1988). *Psychopédagogie interculturelle.* Cousset (Fribourg): DelVal & Université de Neuchâtel. [Intercultural psychopedagogy].

Doise, W. (1982). *L'explication en psychologie sociale.* Paris: Presses Universitaires de France. [Explanation in social psychology].

Duveen, G. & Lloyd, B. (Eds.) (1990). *Social representations and the development of knowledge.* Cambridge: Cambridge University Press.

Duveen, G. (2001). Representations, identities, resistance. In K. Deaux & G. Philogene (Eds.) *Social representation: Introductions and Explorations.* Oxford: Blackwell.

Erikson, E. H. (1968/1994). *Identity: youth and crisis.* New York/London: W. W. Norton.

Fasulo, A., Girardet, H., & Pontecorvo, C. (1998). Historical practices in school through photographical reconstruction. *Mind, Culture and Activity*, 5, 4, 253–271.

Fiske, J. & Hartley, J. (1978/2003). *Reading television* (extended version). London/New York: Routledge.

Flaubert, G. (1857/1999). *Madame Bovary. Life in a country town* (Trans. G. Hopkins). Oxford: Oxford University Press.

Fonagy, P., Gergely, G., Jurist, E. L., Target, M. (2002). *Affect regulation, mentalisation, and the development of the self.* New York: Other Press.

Fonyi, A. (1994). *Lire, écrire, analyser. La littérature dans la pratique analytique.* Paris: L'Harmattan. [Reading, writing, analysing. Literature in psychoanalytical practice].

Forrester, M. (2000). *Psychology of the image.* London/Philadelphia: Routledge.

Freud, S. (1900/2001). The interpretation of dreams. In J. Strachey (Ed. and Trans.), *The standard edition of the complete psychological works of Sigmund Freud* (Vol. 4–5, pp. 1–630). London: Hogarth.

Freud, S. (1901/2001). On dreams. *The standard edition of the complete psychological works of Sigmund Freud* (Vol. 5, pp. 631–678). London: Hogarth.

Freud, S. (1908/2001). Creative writers and daydreaming. In J. Strachey (Ed. and Trans.), *The standard edition of the complete psychological works of Sigmund Freud* (Vol. 9, pp. 141–153). London: Hogarth.

Fuhrer, U. (2004). *Cultivating minds. Identity as meaning-making practices.* Hove/New York: Routledge.

Fuhrer, U. & Josephs, I. E. (Eds.) (1999), *Persönliche Objekte, Identität und Entwicklung.*

Göttingen: Vandenhoeck & Ruprecht. [Personal objects, identity and development].

Garland, A. (1997/2004). *The Beach*. London: Penguin.

Geertz, C. (1972). Religion as a cultural system. In C. Geertz (1973), *The Interpretation of culture, selected papers* (pp. 87–126). New York: Basic Books.

Gillespie, A. (2005a). Malcolm X and his autobiography: Identity development and self-narration. *Culture & Psychology*, 11, 77–88.

Gillespie, A. (2005b). G. H. Mead: Theorist of the social act. *Journal for the Theory of Social Behavior*, 35, 1, 19–39.

Gillespie, A. (2005c in press). Time, self and the other: The striving tourist in Ladakh, north India. In L. Simao and J. Valsiner (Eds.) *Otherness in question: Development of the self*. Greenwich, CT: Information Age Publishing, Inc.

Gillespie, A. (2006). *Becoming other: From social interaction to self-reflection*. Greenwich, CT: Information Age Publishing, Inc.

Gilligan, C. (1982/1983). *In a different voice. Psychological theory and women's development*. Cambridge, MA & London: Harvard University Press.

Green, A. (1969). La lecture psychanalytique des tragiques. *Un oeil vivant: le complexe d'Oedipe dans la tragédie* (pp. 10–47) Paris: Éditions de Minuit. [A psychoanalytical reading of tragic].

Green, A. (2000). *André Green at the Squiggle Foundation*. (Ed.) J. Abrams. London: Karnac Books.

Green, A. (2002). *Abrégé de psychanalyse*. Paris: Presses Universitaires de France. [Short guide to psychoanalysis].

Grossen, M. (1999). Approches dialogiques des processus de transmission-acquisition des savoirs. Une brève introduction. *Actualités psychologiques* (Institut de psychologie, Lausanne), 7, 1–32. [Dialogical approaches of the processes of transmission and acquisition of knowledge. A short introduction].

Grossen, M. (2000). Institutional framings in learning and teaching. In H. Cowie, V. D. Aalsvort & N. Mercer (Eds.). *Social interaction in learning and instruction: the meaning of discourse for the construction of knowledge* (pp. 21–34). Amsterdam: Pergamon Press.

Grossen, M. & Perret-Clermont, A. N. (Ed), (1992). *L'espace thérapeutique, Cadres et contextes*. Neuchâtel (Switzerland)/Paris:

Delachaux et Niestlé. [The therapeutic space. Frames and contexts].

Habermas, T. (1996/1999). *Geliebte Objekte: Symbole und Instrumente der Identitätsbildung*. Frankfurt: Suhrkamp. [Loved objects: symbols and tools for identity construction].

Habermas, T. (1999). Persönliche Objekte und Bindungen im Prozess der Ablösung vom Elternhaus. In U. Fuhrer & I. E. Josephs (Eds.). *Persönliche Objekte, Identität und Entwicklung* (pp. 109–133). Göttingen: Vandenhoeck & Ruprecht. [Personal objects and attachments in the process of separation from the parental house].

Harris, P. L. (2000). *The work of the imagination*. Oxford/Malden, Ma: Blackwell.

Heath, S. B. (1996). Ruling places: Adaptation in development by inner-city youth. In R. Jessor Colby, A., & Shweder, R.A (Eds.), *Ethnography and Human Development, Context and Meaning in Social Inquiry* (pp. 225–251). Chicago: University of Chicago.

Heath, S. B. (2000). Seeing our way into learning. *Cambridge Journal of Education*, 30, 1, 121–132.

Henri, C. (2003). *De Marivaux et du Loft. Petites leçons de littérature au lycée*. Paris: P. O. L [About Marivaux and Big Brother. Little stories about literature at college].

Hermans, H. J. M. & Kempen, H. J. G. (1993). *The Dialogical Self. Meaning as movement*. San Diego: Academic Press.

Hrabal, B. (1976/1992). *Too loud a solitude* (transl. M. H. Heim), San Diego/New York: Harcourt Brace.

Hundeide, K. (2003) Becoming a committed insider. *Culture & Psychology*, 9, 107–127.

Hundeide, K. (2004). A new identity, a new life-style. In A.-N. Perret-Clermont, C. Pontecorvo, L. Resnick, T. Zittoun & B. Burge (Eds.). *Joining Society: Social interaction and learning in adolescence and youth* (pp. 86–108). Cambridge/New York: Cambridge University Press.

Hutchins, E. (1995). *Cognition in the wild*. Cambridge, MA/London: MIT Press.

Janet, P. (1934/1935). *Les débuts de l'intelligence*. Paris: Flammarion. [The beginnings of intelligence].

Josephs, I. E (1997). Talking with the dead: Self-construction as dialogue. *Journal of Narrative and Life History*, 71, 1–4, 359–367.

Josephs, I. E. (1998). Constructing One's Self in the City of the Silent: Dialogue, Symbols, and the Role of "As-if" in Self-Development. *Human Development*, 41, 180–195.

Kaës, R. (1994). *La parole et le lien*. Paris: Dunod. [The word and the link].

Kaës, R. (Ed.), (1996). *Contes et divans. Médiation du conte dans la vie psychique*. Paris: Dunod). [Tales and couch. The mediation of the tale in psychic life].

Kamberlis, G. & Dimitriadis, G. (1998). Talkin' Tupac: Speech Genres and the Mediation of Cultural Knowledge. In C. M. Carthy, G. Hudak, S. Allegretto, & P. Saukko (Eds.), *Sound Identities: Popular music and the cultural politics of education*. New York: Peter Lang.

Kavanagh, G. (2000). *Dream spaces. Memory and the museum*. London/New York: Leicester University Press.

Kundera, M. (1986/1988). *The art of the novel*. (Trans. L. Asher). London/Boston: Faber & Faber.

Lawrence, J. & Valsiner, J. (1993). Conceptual roots of internalisation: from transmission to transformation. *Human Development, 36*, 150–167.

Lawrence, J. & Valsiner, J. (2003). Making Personal Sense. An Account of basic Internalisation and Externalisation Processes. *Theory & Psychology, 13, 6, 723–752*.

Lawrence, J., Benedikt, R., & Valsiner, J. (1992). Homeless in the Mind: A Case-History of personal Life in and out of a Close orthodox Community. *Journal of Social Distress and the Homeless, 1, 2, 157–176*.

Levi, P. (1985/1991). *Other people's trades* (Trans. R. Raymond Rosenthal). London: Abacus Sphere Books Ltd.

Levi-Strauss, C. (1962/1966). *The Savage Mind*. Chicago: The University of Chicago Press. (Trans. G. Weidenfeld & Nicolson Ltd).

Liebes, T. & Katz, E. (1990/1994) *The Export of meaning: Cross-Cultural Readings of Dallas* (2nd ed). Cambridge: Polity press.

Lightfoot, C. (1997). *The culture of adolescent risk-taking*. New York/London: Guilford Press.

Lightfoot, C. & Cox, B. D. (1997). Locating competence: the sociogenesis of mind and the problem of internalization. In B. D. Cox & C. Lightfoot (Eds). *Sociogenetic perspectives on internalization* (pp. 1–21). Mahwah: Lawrence Erlbaum Associates.

Livingstone, S. & Lunt, P. (1994). *Talk on television: audience participation and public debate*. London: Routledge.

Livingstone, S. (1998). *Making sense of television. The psychology of audience interpretation*. London / New York: Routledge.

Livingstone, S. (2002). *Young people and new media: childhood and the changing media environment*. London: Sage.

Lloyd, T. (1999). *Reading for the future. Boys' and fathers' views on reading*. London: Save the Children.

London, J. (1913/1994). *Martin Eden*. London: Penguin.

Marková, I. (2003). *Dialogicality and social representations: The dynamics of mind*. Cambridge: Cambridge University Press.

Mathabane, M. (1986). *Kaffir boy-Growing out of apartheid*. London: Pan Books.

Matusov, E. (1998). When solo activity is not privileged: participation and internalization models of development. *Human Development, 41, 326–349*.

Mitchell, J. (2003). *Siblings, sex and violence*. Cambridge: Polity.

Moro, C. & Rodriguez, C. (1998). Towards a pragmatical conception of the object: The construction of the uses of the objects by the baby in the prelinguistic period. In M. D. P. Lyra & J. Valsiner (Eds.), *Construction of Psychological Processes in Intepersonal Communication* (pp. 53–72). Child development within culturally structured environements, Vol. 4. Norwood, N.J.: Ablex.

Najmambali, A. (2004). The morning after: travail of sexuality and love in modern Iran. *International Journal of Middle East Studies, 36, 367–385*.

Nathan, T. (1993)....*fier de n'avoir ni pays, ni amis, quelle sottise c'était*. Grenoble: La Pensée Sauvage. [...Proud to have neither land, nor friends, how foolish it was...]

Nathan, T. (2001). *Nous ne sommes pas seuls au monde*. Paris: les empêcheurs de penser en rond. [We are not alone in the world].

Nelmes, J. (1996/2002). *An introduction to film studies* (2nd Ed.). London/New York: Routledge.

Nelson, K. (Ed.), (1989). *Narratives from the crib*. Cambridge, MA/London: Harvard University Press.

Nelson, K. (1996). *Language in Cognitive development. Emergence of the mediated mind*. Cambridge: Cambridge University Press.

Neuman, Y. & Bekerman, Z. (2001). Cultural resources and the gap between educational theory and practice. *The Teacher's College Record, 103, 3, 471–484*.

Ochs, E. & Capps, L. (2001). *Living narrative. Creating lives in everyday storytelling*. Cambridge, MA/London: Harvard University Press.

Oz, A. (2003/2004). *A tale of love and darkness.* London: Chatto & Wintus.

Perret, J.-F. & Perret-Clermont, A.-N. (2001). *Apprendre un métier technique dans un contexte de mutations technologiques.* Fribourg (Switzerland): Éditions universitaires de Fribourg [Learning a technical trade in a context of technological mutation].

Perret-Clermont, A.-N., Perret, J.-F., & Bell, N. (1991). The social construction of meaning and cognitive activity in elementary school children. In L. B. Resnick, J. M. Levine, & S. D. Teasley (Eds.), *Perspectives on socially shared cognition* (pp. 41–62). Washington D.C.: American Psychological Association.

Perret-Clermont, A.-N. & Zittoun, T. (2002) Esquisse d'une psychologie de la transition. *Education permanente. Revue Suisse pour la Formation Continue*, 1, 12–15. [Sketch for a psychology of transitions].

Perriault, J. (1989). *La logique de l'usage: essai sur les machines à communiquer.* Paris: Flammarion. [The logic of use: essay on the communicating machines].

Piaget, J. (1945/1994). *La formation du symbole chez l'enfant. Imitation, jeu et rêve, image et représentation.* Lausanne: Delachaux & Niestlé. [The formation of symbol in the child. Imitation, play and dream, image and representation].

Piaget, J. (1951). *Play, dreams and imitation in childhood.* Melbourne/London/Toronto: William Heinemann Ltd.

Psaltis, C. & Duveen, G. (2006). Social relations and cognitive development: The influence of conversation types and representations of gender. *European Journal of Social Psychology*, 36, 407–430,

Rabardel, P. & Waern, Y. (2003). Editorial. From artefact to instrument, *Interacting with computers*, 15, 641–645.

Rieger, A. & Tonard, J.-F. (Eds.). (1999). *La lecture au féminin. La lectrice dans la littérature française du Moyen Age au XXème siècle.* Darsmtadt: Wissenschaftliche Buchgesellsgaft. [Feminine reading. The woman reader in French literature, from Middle Age to the 20th century].

Segal, H. (1991). *Dream, Fantasy and Art.* London/NY: Tavistock/Routledge.

Shweder, R. A. (1995). The confession of a methodological individualist. *Culture & Psychology*, 1, 1, 115–122.

Strauss, C. & Quinn, N. (1997). *A cognitive theory of cultural meaning.* Cambridge: Cambridge University Press.

Taylor, M. (1999). *Imaginary companions and the children who create them.* New York/Oxford: Oxford University Press.

Tisseron, S. (1996). *Secrets de famille mode d'emploi.* Paris: Edition Ramsay. [Family secrets – instructions].

Tisseron, S. (2000). *Enfants sous influence. Les écrans rendent-ils les jeunes violents?* Paris: Armand Colin. [Children under influence. Do screen make youth violent?]

Tisseron, S. (2003). *Comment Hitchcock m'a sauvé la vie.* Paris: Armand Colin. [How Hitchcock saved my life].

Tomasello, M. (1999). *The Cultural Origins of Human Cognition.* Cambridge/London: Harvard University Press.

Toomela, A. (1996a). How culture transforms mind: A process of internalisation. *Culture & Psychology.* 2, 285–306.

Toomela, A. (1996b). What characterises language that can be interiorised, *Culture & Psychology*, 2, 319–322.

Tucker, N. (1981). *The child and the book: a psychological and literary exploration.* Cambridge: Cambridge University Press.

Valsiner, J. (1997). *Culture and the Development of Children's action. A Theory of Human Development* (2nd Edition). New York/Chichester: John Wiley and Sons.

Valsiner, J. (1998). *The guided mind. A sociogenetic approach to personality.* Cambridge, MA/London: Harvard University Press.

Valsiner, J. (2000). *Culture and human development.* London/Thousand Oaks, CA: Sage

Valsiner, J. (2001). Process structure of semiotic mediation in human development. *Human Development*, 2 & 3, 84–97.

Valsiner, J. (2005). Soziale une emotionale Entwicklungsaufgaben im Kulturellen Kontext. In J. Asendorpf (Eds.). *Soziale, emotionale une Persönlichketisentwicklung.* (Vol 3) Entwicklungspychologie – Enzyklopädie der Psychologie (pp. 677–728). Göttingen: Hogrefe. [Social and emotional developmental tasks in cultural context].

Valsiner, J. & Sato, T. (2006). Historically Structured Sampling (HSS): How can psychology's methodology become tuned in to the reality of the historical nature of cultural psychology? In J. Straub, D. Weidemann, C. Kölbl & B. Zielke (Eds.), *Pursuit of Meaning* (pp. 215–251). Bielefeld: Transcript. Vygotsky, L. S (1928/1971). *The psychology of art.* Cambridge (MA)/London: MIT Press.

Vygotsky, L. S. & Luria, A. (1994). Tool and symbol in child development. In R. van der

Veer & J. Valsiner (Eds.), *The Vygotsky Reader* (pp. 99–174). Oxford: Blackwell (Based on a 1930 English-language manuscript given by Luria to Michael Cole).

Werner, H. & Kaplan, B. (1963). Symbol formation. An organismic-developmental approach to language and the expression of thought. New York/London/Sidney: John Wiley and Sons.

Wertsch, J. V. (1991). *Voices of the mind*. London,/ Sidney/Singapore: Harvester Wheatsheaf.

Wertsch, J. V. (1993). Commentary [on Lawrence & Valsiner, 1993]. *Human development, 36*, 168–171.

Wertsch, J. V. (1998). *Mind as Action*. New York / Oxford: Oxford University Press.

Winnicott, D. W. (1971/2001). *Playing and reality*. Philadelphia/Sussex: Bruner-Routledge.

Winnicott, D. W. (1989). *Psycho-analytic explorations*. (Ed.) By C. Winnicott, R. Shepherd, M. Davis. London: H. Karnac.

Zagórska, W. & Tarnowski, A. (2004). *Historical re-enactment in young adulthood: experiences and psychological functions*. Poster presented at the XVII Biennial meeting, Ghent (Belgium), July 11–14.

Zittoun, T. (1996). Non sono tutti fascisti. Immagini di sé e degli altri nei ragazzi della scuola ebraica. *La Rassegna Mensile di Israel*, 62 (3), 155–187. [They aint' all fascists! Images of self and other in children from a Jewish school].

Zittoun, T. (2003). The hidden work of symbolic resources in emotions. *Culture & Psychology*, 9, 313–329.

Zittoun, T. (2004). Symbolic competencies for developmental transitions: The case of the choice of first names. *Culture & Psychology*, 10, 161–171.

Zittoun, T. (2005). *Donner la vie, choisir un nom. Engendrements symboliques*. Paris: L'Harmattan. [Giving life, choosing a name. Symbolic begetting].

Zittoun, T. (2006a). *Transitions. Development through symbolic resources*. Greenwich (CT): Information Age Publishing, Inc.

Zittoun, T. (2006a). Difficult secularity: Talmud as symbolic resource. *Outlines, 3*, 59–75.

Zittoun, T. (2006b). Processes of interiority. In L. Simão & J. Valsiner (Eds). *Otherness in Question: Development of the self*. Advances in Cultural Psychology: Constructing Development. Greenwich, CT: Information Age Publishing, Inc.

Zittoun, T. & Cesari Lusso, V. (1998). Bagage culturel et gestion des défis identitaires. *Cahiers de psychologie, 34* (Université de Neuchâtel), 1–63. [Cultural baggage and dealing with identity challenges].

Zittoun, T., Cornish, F., Gillespie, & Avelling, E.-L. (in press). Using social knowledge: A case study of a diarist's meaning making during World War II. In W. Wagner, T. Sugiman & K. Gergen (Eds.). *Meaning in Action: Constructions, narratives and representations*. New York: Springer.

Zittoun, T., Duveen, G., Gillespie, A., Ivinson, G. & Psaltis, C. (2003). The uses of symbolic resources in transitions. *Culture & Psychology*, 9, 415–448.

CHAPTER 17

Perpetual Uncertainty of Cultural Life

Becoming Reality

Emily Abbey

Of Poetic Motion

Reading a poem can be a complex experience, for in the unfolding of metaphor, literal senses of words are drawn out of reasonably fixed and predictable places into relationship with those imagined. These literal senses are drawn out through various *uncertain* encounters within the metaphor. For instance, as one reads "Paper birch tree and the poet/ In August, still wrapped by winter" uncertainty arises between what on strictly literal grounds are unrelated, for example, the poet and winter. To overcome such uncertainty, meaning reaches from the literal into the imagined realm, where the "poet" and "winter" are joined, and meaning expands into a quiet, sometimes painfully kept, reserve of the art-maker. Note, however, in overcoming the confusion of juxtaposed literal senses, meaning becomes somewhat "uncertain" itself. It is neither purely imagined *nor* literal, but rather, something more. Meaning is the *motion* of these senses, and it transforms through their tension.

Day-to-day meaning shares similar complexity, for at every moment, our literal sense of *what is* in the here-and-now is drawn out of its reasonable security into relation with the imagined, where it is opened to senses more inventive and vaguely defined. As in the poem, meaning is drawn into the imagined through its encounter with *uncertainty*, though in this case, the uncertainty is due to the unknown future. Like the poem, this uncertainty is overcome through imagined senses – the person's expectations of *what could be* that guide toward this unknown terrain. As in the poem, however, this suggests that in overcoming the uncertainty of an unknown future, meaning becomes somewhat "uncertain" itself. It is neither purely imagined *nor* literal, but rather, something more. Meaning is *the* (poetic) *motion* of these senses, and like the metaphor, meaning transforms through their tension.

Endurance and Irreversibility

The parallels between metaphor and the sign that this paper will discuss apply to the extent that one accepts the temporal embeddedness of human meaning-making. By temporal embeddedness, it is meant that each experience humans have is made novel by its unique position within the temporal order. At the center of this sense of embeddedness is Henri Bergson's notion of time-as-duration (*durée*.) This notion of duration served as a key innovation for thinking about process and movement in the transition from 19th century philosophy to 20th century science (e.g., Prigogine & Nicolis, 1971), and much of developmental psychology (e.g., Baldwin, 1915; Piaget, 1962; Vygotsky, 1994) borrows from the notion. The concept of pure duration expresses the circumstances in which the ego "lets itself *live*" (Bergson, 1913, p. 100, emphasis original), resisting the tendency to *separate* past and present conscious states from one another, and instead, allowing them to merge into an experiential whole. As the ego endures, this experiential whole is *ever-changing*, for at any moment, it holds increasingly more of the past. In time understood as pure duration, any action thus becomes tinged with novelty by virtue of the fact that the experiential whole of which it is a part has necessarily grown larger, even from just moments ago.

Time-as-duration may be intuitively appreciated. Nonetheless, the irreversibility of our experiences is indeed somewhat counter-intuitive. Such a sense of time-as-pure-duration is confounded easily as humans often (perhaps *most* often) ignore endurance and instead speak, write, and theorize *as if* the ego were restrained and the past and present *kept separate* from one another. "We set our states of consciousness side by side," Bergson writes, "in such a way as to perceive them simultaneously, *no longer in one another, but alongside one another*" (Bergson, 1913, p. 101, emphasis added). This separation of the past and present amounts to confusing time-as-duration with the notion of time-as-space. "In a word, *we project time into space*," Bergson goes on to explain, "we express duration in terms of extensity, and succession thus takes the form of a continuous line or chain, the parts of which touch with-out penetrating one another" (Bergson, 1913, p. 101, emphasis added). When pure duration is confused with 'extensity' in space, time literally becomes nothing more than a shelf for experiences, which are *reversible*.

Between the Present and Future

EPHEMERAL AND UNCERTAIN

Accepting the notion of time-as-pure-duration suggests, in turn, at least two modifications to our usual understanding of experience. For one, while it is likely humans readily acknowledge a sense of ongoing change – for example, to notice fluctuations in one's mood – this usual acknowledgement will likely have to be pushed further to appreciate fully the "radical" nature (Bergson, 1944, p. 3) of change suggested by pure duration. A pure duration of the ego suggests an ephemeral world, shifting forms at a speed greater than we may usually assume as the experiential whole grows continuously. Bergson's example of two views of an unmoving object that are made from the same perspective can be used to illustrate this point. Typically, we might suggest that the second of two such views does not constitute an instance of change unless it was made from a different angle, or in different lighting. Yet, from the perspective of pure duration, these two views are unique, because the second, though similar in all other respects, is part of a different (i.e., richer) experiential whole.

Equally central, the notion of pure duration suggests future experiences remain unknowable until the moment they happen. As before, while humans may readily accept that there is no way to know what comes next, it is perhaps unlikely this acknowledgement fully appreciates the extraordinary enigma suggested by pure duration. We may assume that we cannot know what will transpire in a day, a week, or even a few hours. Yet, as the ego endures, the experiential whole is continually reformed, and thus the next moment of our lives remain unknowable until – at the given moment of living – its unique experiential whole emerges.

The Boundary Zone

Given the swiftness of experiential shifts in irreversible time, the person can be said to live not in an elongated 'stable' present, but rather, at the *boundary* of an infinitesimally small here-and-now and unknown future. In irreversible time, any notion of the present, as we may commonly mean it, can perhaps better be understood as merely a *boundary marker*, useful in delineating what is now known (the past) and through its realization – stipulation of the known – introduces the next experience as part of the unknown future (Matte Blanco, 1975, 1988). As depicted below, (see Figure 17.1) our lives happen within what can be described as a *boundary zone* of the just barely known moment and the unknown future.

Upon comparison of such a boundary zone with a notion of the "present," one thing that can be appreciated is its instability. Part of the here-and-now and the future simultaneously, the boundary zone is an ambiguous space that cannot be defined in certain terms. From the perspective of irreversible time, humans live with the uncertainty of transition – they are neither within "the present" nor "the next moment" but between the two.

Demands of the Present and Future

Humans use signs to provide some sense of order within their fast moving experiences. Yet, at the temporal boundary, semiotic processes can be conceptualized in ways that are not immediately appreciated from alternate perspectives. Within the boundary zone, the person is tied to the present *and* future. As such, each contextualization of a sign speaks to <u>what is</u> *literally* the case in the infinitesimally small here-and-now *and* simultaneously to the person's *imagined* possibilities for the next encounter with the environment – his or her expectations for <u>what could be</u> in the unknown future (Josephs, 1998; Josephs, Valsiner, & Surgan, 1999).

Unity of the Literal and Imagined

The functional value of this guiding is straightforward – through imagining possible futures, the person builds a bridge between the here-and-now and the unknown that eases the discontinuity of that transition by preparing for whatever comes next before it even happens. These suggestions are, indeed, reflective of the person's social and cultural context; for instance, the same literal sense, "that is rock-and-roll music," offers some individuals the imagined prospect of "excitement" but others a sense of "danger." Less straightforward, perhaps, is this unity between the literal and imagined, as it breaks a boundary well-maintained in some modern epistemological traditions.

To the degree that the literal and imagined are often seen as dichotomously opposed to one another, sign use within irreversible time is, instead, an example of Vaihinger's (1935) claim that the "fictitious" and "real" are often combined. In a widely applicable illustration of this coordination, Vaihinger points to the notion of "free will" as something that is inherently impossible (i.e., humans are *not* free), yet "free will" – a *fictitious* notion – nonetheless serves as the basis from which the "real" laws of a land are derived:

> *we have: (1) the impossible case; the existence of free beings, or, in shorter form, the statement that men are free. – (2) the necessary consequences (that flow from this impossible case); the laws according to which free beings act; these follow necessarily from the existence of free beings. – (3) the equation of something (with the necessary consequences flowing from the impossible case); the laws, according to which actually existing men ought to act, are equated (in the form of a demand) with the laws which necessarily follow from the (unreal or impossible) existence of free beings. Thus an impossible case is here imagined, the necessary consequences are drawn from it and, with these consequences, which also must be impossible, demands are equated that do not follow from existing reality. (Vaihinger, 1935, p. 259, emphasis added)*

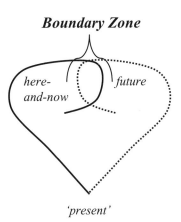

Boundary Zone

here-and-now   *future*

'present'

Figure 17.1. Boundary zone between here-and-now and unknown future.

Vaihinger's claim can also be taken a step further. Vaihinger can be seen as not merely pointing to the possibility of coordination between the fictitious and real, but to an atypical direction of such interaction. Rather than assuming the "real" has some *a priori* status, Vaihinger suggests it is actually arrived at *through* what is unreal. As in the above quotation, the "real" laws that structure the lives of humans are arrived at through the necessarily unreal claim that human thought and action are unbounded.

Meaning as Poetic Motion

One situation in which the literal and imagined *are* allowed close company, and remain visible as they hold it, is the poem. In fact, meaning in the poem and in our daily lives may be relatable. As discussed briefly at the start, at the base of such a comparison is the common circumstance of uncertainty. In the poem, uncertainty is created by juxtaposed literal senses. Our lives, in turn, are uncertain given the ever-changing experiential whole as the ego endures. Also grounding such a comparison is the fact that in the poem and our lives, uncertainty is overcome through reliance upon imagined senses. Given these commonalities, the following section looks in greater detail at the

relation of the literal and imagined within the poem. It then turns to see how the poem might inform our understanding of meaning-making in irreversible time, and the actions of the sign at the temporal boundary.

The Poem

Wallace Stevens' *"The Snow Man"* will be used in this explication; the reader is encouraged to refer back to the poem when useful:

The Snow Man[1]
One must have a mind of winter
To regard the frost and the boughs
Of the pine-trees crusted with snow;

And have been cold a long time
To behold the junipers shagged with ice,
The spruces rough in the distant glitter

Of the January sun; and not to think
Of any misery in the sound of the wind,
In the sound of a few leaves,

Which is the sound of the land
Full of the same wind
That is blowing in the same bare place

For the listener, who listens in the snow,
And, nothing himself, beholds
Nothing that is not there and the nothing
    that is.

As one reads the poem, it is, of course, possible to suggest many interpretations. One interpretation, for the purpose of this analysis, is that the reader encounters (among others) literal senses of "someone viewing a winter scene" and that of an "ordinary person." Between these two, there lies a foundational uncertainty, for these literal senses of meaning find no way of relating to each other on their own.

It is only as imagined senses enter that meaning begins to overcome this uncertainty. This work of the imagined upon the literal is perhaps similar to what Paz (1995) intends when he offers that poetry confuses the usual linearity of language. In metaphoric action, meaning is no longer simply moving from one literal sense to the next, but rather, circles upon itself. "Language is naturally linear...in a poem, linearity twists back on itself...," Paz writes, "the straight line...is replaced by the circle and spiral..." (Paz, 1995, p. 4). In this twisting dance, the usual focus of words becomes circumvented or transcended. This imagined sense *opens* the literal, yet not to anything and everything, as there are only some directions the metaphor can run.

The imagined is necessary for metaphoric meaning but not sufficient. It is true that in metaphoric action, without the imagined, the literal senses cannot be joined. Yet, literal senses are nonetheless necessary, for without them there can be no meaning at all. Importantly, and central here, is the fact that meaning finds its understanding by reaching beyond literal senses *while not abandoning them*. Thus, it is possible to suggest that meaning overcomes the confusion of juxtaposed literal senses by becoming somewhat "uncertain" itself. It is neither purely imagined *nor* literal, but rather, something more. Meaning is the tension-filled *motion* of these senses.

This notion of motion emphasizes the complexity of meaning in the poem. It is not possible, on the basis of what is suggested here, to think of meaning as "certain" or "fixed." Rather, meaning in the poem remains somewhat fluid – and needs this indeterminacy for the metaphor to make its point clearly. In addition, an awareness of meaning-as-motion is important, for it is through these tensions between the literal and imagined that meaning transforms; for instance, in Stevens' poem, the "wintry mind" and the "ordinary person" become a notion of "the simple beauty of the world accepted for what it is."

The notion of meaning-as-motion also highlights an ever-present *ambiguity* that gives *fullness* to meaning inside of metaphor. Ambiguity is itself distinguishable from the literal and imagined senses, which could be described as giving the poem meaning that is "formed" in some way. This form may be a "wintry mind" and "a man," or more developed as an "acceptance of the world." Yet, in either case, the meaning is describable, and maintains a certain discreteness. In contrast, ambiguity is a "present formlessness," akin in some ways, to Alexius Meinong's understandable-yet-not describable objects like "the golden mountain" or "round triangle." In poems, ideas almost melt into one another, and the ambiguity of these transitions gives an exquisite sense of fullness to meaning; for instance, in Stevens' poem, it is as the landscape moves into a human, and the human moves into the landscape that meaning most deeply understands itself.

The Sign

How might the poem inform our understanding of meaning-making in irreversible time? As expressed earlier, acting at the temporal boundary, the person encounters continually the uncertainty of an unknown next moment, and to overcome this uncertainty, meaning reaches into the imagined, constructing a sense of *what could be* that guides the person forward. These imagined expectations for what could come next "open" meaning by taking it beyond what is possible only in the here-and-now, while also not extending it infinitely. To overcome the uncertainty of the temporal boundary, meaning must reach beyond literal senses, in fact, the imagined is so much a part of guiding toward the unknown – and in that sense, part of the general function of meaning as giving order to experience – that it would be hard to call it such without its presence.

It is exactly here that drawing parallels to the poem becomes important. In such reaching into imagined senses, how can one best characterize meaning? Meaning requires the imagined, yet it is equally important that it does not abandon the literal, for without this sense, there can be no meaning at all. Thus, on the basis of parallels with the poem, it is possible to suggest that meaning overcomes the uncertainty of an unknown future by becoming somewhat "uncertain" itself. It is neither purely imagined *nor* literal, but rather, something more. In our lives, meaning is the tension-filled *motion* of these senses.

As was the case in the poem, acknowledgement of motion suggests that everyday meanings are perhaps well characterized as flexible and somewhat fluid constructions. Meaning needs this indeterminacy, in order to cope with an ever-changing world. Likewise, an awareness of meaning-as-motion is important, *for it is through these tensions that meaning transforms itself.* This sense of tension, and its transformative possibilities, can be extended from the metaphor into the lived reality of the person through Lewin's (1936) depiction of the structure of the individual's life space in terms of positive and negative valences. It is possible to suggest that as one moves forward in irreversible time, each present encounter with the environment holds an *ambivalent* relation to the anticipated future encounter with the environment – meaning moves in the action of *overcoming this ambivalence* of *what is* literally the case, and the imagined sense of *what could be* (see Abbey & Valsiner, 2004).

In addition, meaning-as-motion highlights an ever-present *ambiguity* that gives *fullness* to meaning, not only in metaphor, but in our daily lives. As motion, meaning contains a certain *formlessness* that asserts itself, while nonetheless remaining indescribable. Such "formless forms" have been seen as the highest order of semiotic mediating devices (see Valsiner, 2005 for hypergeneralized feeling fields), emerging in the process of affective generalization (Baldwin; Vygotsky, 1925/1971) and allowing for the preservation of aesthetic experiences. This ever-present *ambiguity* in meaning is there on account of the blending of one literal sense into the next through an imagined sense of *what could be.* T.S. Eliot, fittingly in the current focus, describes a similar *smoothness of relation* as something highlighted in the poetic mind. He writes that situations the "ordinary man's mind" would find unrelated the "poet's mind" links easily:

When a poet's mind is perfectly equipped for its work, it is constantly amalgamating disparate experience; the ordinary man's experience is chaotic, irregular, fragmen-tary. The latter falls in love, or reads Spinoza, and these two experiences have nothing to do with each other, or with the noise of the typewriter or the smell of cooking; in the mind of the poet these experiences are always forming new wholes. (Eliot, 1932, p. 247)

As humans use signs at the temporal boundary, even the transition from anger to joy is fluid, as one idea blends into the next through an imagined sense. The ambiguity of such meaning-as-motion provides *fullness* – distinguishes that which simply has meaning, from that which is meanin*gful.*

Meaning-As-Poetic-Motion

The parallels between daily life and the poem suggest, most centrally to this piece, that meaning overcomes the uncertainty of the unknown future by becoming somewhat "uncertain" itself. It is neither purely imagined *nor* literal, but the (poetic) motion of these senses. In addition, these parallels suggest that meaning transforms by overcoming the tensions between the person's here-and-now relation to the environment, and his or her expected future relation to the environment. Based on the poem, development can be seen as a process driven by overcoming the uncertainty between literal and imagined senses.

Meaning-as-motion highlights an ever-present *ambiguity* in meaning, on account of the blending of one literal sense into the next through notions of *what could be.* Even in being nearly indescribable, this ambiguity provides the *fullness* to the idea that is there in each moment of our meaning-making.

Last, and most broadly, these parallels suggest meaning can be seen as *constantly transforming* through tension. In irreversible time, overcoming one tension by arriving at a new sense of *what is* simultaneously introduces a new unknown, and thereby, creates another tension to be overcome – *ad infinitum.* Human lives are uncertain, and as such, it would appear that the meanings we use to provide order are neither static nor fixed, but rather, continually becoming reality, hand-in-hand with experience as the ego endures.

An Illustration of Poetic Motion: Daniel's Story

The paper now turns to illustrate the *poetic motion* of the sign in more detail. It does so by considering such motion as one man struggles to change his story, becoming something more than he previously was by imagining possible futures. As brief synopsis of what follows, a few years before the interview on which this illustration of poetic motion is based, a man, here called Daniel, had reached a point in his life where he didn't feel like continuing. From an objective standpoint, his appeared the "good" life, as it was rich with family, professional success, and community service. Yet from Daniel's viewpoint, his life seemed almost completely unreal. He describes feeling that his identity was a façade, a remainder left behind after years of draining emotional content out of experience. In crisis, he found that he did not see the point of continuing in this hollow and for him, "fabricated" life. Daniel, thus, began an elongated contemplation of how he might shift course. In this contemplation, glimpses of meaning-as-motion and its transformation through tension become acutely visible.

Daniel's Story

Daniel was born near the end of World War II, as the second of three brothers, and his childhood years were spent in a family that, like many others in the country, was both glad to have the war behind and more than ready to focus attention on the immediate business of raising children. His father, who immigrated to the U.S. as a child, gradually worked through corporate ranks to provide a dependable income, while his mother dutifully tended the needs of the three small children, her home and husband. For the first 16 years of life, there was a certain comfort in the predictability of Daniel's life, yet in his last year of high school, an event occurred that replaced this relative sense of security to which he had grown accustom, with a sense of confusion and uncertainty just as powerful.

In the middle of an otherwise ordinary night, Daniel's brother, two years his junior, simply stopped breathing. No cause of death was ever determined, and the event, which would have been hard in any family, proved to be an exceptional challenge for Daniel's, for by habit, they did not deal openly with emotions. The summer immediately after the death, family members dispersed to different locations, all trying to cope in their own ways. Daniel, remaining home alone, found an intense and near over-whelming pain. Of this time, Daniel recounts, *"I slept with all the lights ... and the radio on ... I couldn't stand the dark and ... silence because of the death...."*

For Daniel, the passing of his brother was the event that marked the beginning of nearly four painful decades, putting him into what he describes as *"that place of long-term suffering."* The autumn following this event, at what he can acknowledge as the real beginning of his "suffering," Daniel describes how he began pulling away from the world, trying to live with as little feeling as possible, showing emotions to himself only in private.

Daniel married his first wife at 22 and describes the bond between them as built on a powerful sense of partnership, rather than the seemingly treacherous territory of emotional intimacy. Though he acknowledges that he loved her, Daniel points out that the foundation of their relationship day-to-day lay not in passion, but in their ideological unity, and the joint projects they took on together. *"We were great work partners"* Daniel recalls of this woman. They made a collective decision to protest the ongoing Vietnam War by 'living off the land'. Over a decade, they lived in a small log cabin, where they made clothes by hand and cooked over a wood-fueled fire. In the spring – shadowed by an energetic Golden Retriever – they would walk through the woods, drilling into Sugar Maples to collect running sap later boiled into maple sugar; in the fall, they stowed garden produce in root cellars to furnish the table all winter. Together, amidst successfully petitioning against the proposed building of a nuclear power plant, and creating an oral history of the town, they eventually had a child.

For nearly 13 years, this simple, yet productive life sufficed, but around his midthirties, Daniel explains that – in the context of his own emotional withdrawal – he became attracted to another woman. Looking back, he now sees this attraction as a move to artificially compensate for what he had hidden from himself. As he puts it, "*I actually remarried because I craved . . . connection and I thought this woman brought all this emotional content.*" In his second marriage, the horizons brightened for a time and Daniel had a second child, stopped drinking, and experienced a good deal of professional success. Yet, as he now sees it, nothing had "really changed," for seeking emotions artificially in someone else was a far cry from coming back to life emotionally himself. He describes his thirties and fourties as a time of continued desire for separation from the world – where with humor and humility he offers that the amount of time he spent in "up and away" places physically was an all too fitting "metaphor" for his desired psychological reality:

> *I spent most of my free time on the roof because you couldn't get me there, on a ladder . . . that is actually a good metaphor for my life, I was always seeking an elevated state, where nobody could get at me. Um, literally, I used to climb towers when I was young, climb ladders, walk on roofs, climb mountains, anything that would get me up and away . . . was important.*

During these decades, Daniel describes a process of trying to control what happened in his life far beyond the realm of what was reasonable. "*I would have told you what's going to happen next . . . Monday through Thursday* [and] *what I am doing . . . July . . . 23rd–27th*" Daniel says. He goes on to articulate the extreme planning for all contingencies he tried to exercise during these years, saying, "*I would permit decision making by thinking through the consequences, I had four . . . possible responses to everything, in case the first one didn't fit, I'd have the second one ready, if that one didn't*

work, I'd go to the third or the fourth. . . ." In his story, it seems that a difficult and destructive interplay began to occur, where the more Daniel tried to control life irrationally, the more he would experience an equally intense frustration of the world not going according to "his plan." These frustrations, seemingly found at every corner in such a rigid framework, created a continued sense of the world as a *painful* place. Thus, his control actually *furthered* the sense of needing to withdraw emotionally.

As Daniel moved into his early fifties, he had two healthy children, a successful career, lived in an affluent community, and possessed many artistic talents. By an objective account, his life was a "good" one, yet for Daniel, paradoxically, it seemed that rather than growing, there had been shrinking, and after these decades, almost nothing *felt* real. In a part of the interview where his voice takes on a decidedly softer tone, he says that with year 55, he arrived at a crisis of identity where everything he was seemed a *façade*. In my understanding, this sense of façade is best described as a *remainder* left behind after years of draining the emotional content out of experience in an attempt to avoid feeling pain. For Daniel, there was a sense that he was still *alive* as a being, but his experiences as that being were so thoroughly washed of emotions, and therefore vitality, that this identity could no longer be recognized as "real," "*Nothing in my life was true or real, it was all fabrication, it was all invention. . . .*"

The sense of a façade seems to be a version of *narrative foreclosure*, where one has the sense that his or her life story has come to an end, though he or she continues living – a "*kind of living death, a death of life*" (Freeman, 2000, p. 83). At 55, perhaps catalyzed by the end of his second marriage, Daniel recounts how he felt a lack of will to continue, and contemplated taking his own life.

Poetic Motion: Imagined Senses Through Prayer

In the weeks, months, and eventually years that followed this crisis, Daniel explains how he began saying a prayer – the serenity prayer – throughout the day. He comments about the extent to which the prayer became part of his daily life. *"The serenity prayer is so important,"* Daniel says, *"'let me accept the things I cannot change and* [have] *the courage and wisdom to tell the difference.' It defines my whole life."* Daniel began to use the prayer not in a strictly ritualistic activity, but as a *symbolic resource* (Zittoun, 2003, 2005, 2006 this volume), in a passionate attempt to resolve his crisis of identity. In the context of what has already been described, it seems the serenity prayer offers a critical counterpoint to the control-oriented mindset (and the ensuing frustrations), which had encouraged continued emotional enfolding and through which, over decades, the façade had been formed.

As Daniel describes his use of the prayer, instances of poetic motion become acutely visible. In these instances, this prayer acts as an imagined expectation for how the world *could be*, and through the tension between this sense and the literal, meaning as a whole transforms. Take for example, a volunteer experience Daniel had in a hospital for disabled and underprivileged children – a hospital sorely in need of more resources. Daniel begins with his immediate here-and-now literal sense of the situation, which was one of anger and frustration: *"I felt angry . . . some kids . . . have such a struggle and they sit in this very small and insignificant hospital."* He continues describing his immediate control-oriented sense: *"I wanted to go out and stop every car that cost more than 50K and force . . . them to sell it right there on the street and give all the money to the hospital."* Yet, in the same breath, Daniel narrates how the serenity prayer suggests an imagined possibility of an alternative notion: *"I thought, 'hmm, that's not real charity . . . that's believing that I am somehow in charge of the world.'"*

Here, meaning is motion, a tension between the literal here-and-now sense, "it should be this way" and the imagined expectation of the prayer "but maybe you cannot control it." And through this tension meaning transforms: *"I realized that, first off, peo-*

ple who want to spend that much money on a car, that's their choice." He continues, *"I can't change that . . . but what I can do is find more time . . . to just work at the hospital, which is my job . . . ."* From a place that was focused on one set of ideas, and filled with anger and frustration, meaning thus moves into ideas that are quite different and colored by a sense of calm.

Meaning-as-motion is also visible in Daniel's recounting of another daily life event – a trip to the grocery store. In this account, he describes an encounter that took place in a summer resort community, where often tension arises as tourists bring a 'fast paced' lifestyle to what is arguably a slower context. Daniel recounts being in line at the grocery store, and seeing the woman ahead of him begin screaming at the clerk. Daniel goes on to point out how the woman became *"nastier and nastier"* toward this clerk. His literal here-and-now sense of the scene is one of judgment, he says, *"She looked like a New York socialite . . . she just looked like a summer touristy person pushing her weight around."* At the same time, however, he recounts how the serenity prayer began to suggest the possibility of an alternative focus. Through the tension of the immediate here-and-now ego-centered relation with the world "that woman *shouldn't* be acting this way" and the imagined suggestion "but you cannot control how she acts," Daniel says, *"then I just let it go . . . ."* In this tension, meaning again grows from a situation of intolerance and anger, to one of lighthearted tone.

Changing Stories

In these examples, meaning can be seen as the motion of literal and imagined senses. And through the tensions these senses hold with one another, meaning transforms. Through such transformation, moment by moment, Daniel builds what he calls a new "meaning world," and with it, an authentic self. This self inhabits what Daniel refers to as "the world of mysticism," and it stands in contrast to what he has named "the world of experience and things." The latter is the locus of control-oriented thinking, of judgment and ego-centered experience. The former, in contrast, is comprised of tolerance and acceptance. *"If I am washing the dishes, I am washing the dishes,"* Daniel explains, *"If I am eating, I am eating, if I'm sleeping, I'm sleeping, if I'm showering, I am showering."* To be sure, in the world of mysticism, there is a decided lack of emphasis on control. Daniel says, *"I am not thinking about what I am going to do... or worried about my money...."* For Daniel, these "two worlds" of meaning coexist. He offers the following statement on this point: "[the world of mysticism] *doesn't mean you exit all those things,* [things of the world of experience and things] *they are still there...."* Yet, what seems true is that the world of mysticism provides an alternate outlet of experiences.

The emotional tone of each "meaning world" seems to hold the key in understanding how prayer – and these small moments of poetic motion – may link with the broader scale revival of self-authenticity that Daniel says he has experienced in the past two years since this crisis. As he points out, the world of "experience and things" is about control, and he finds great pain as the world does not go according to his plan. *"I will pick up every problem, every pain associated with that,"* Daniel says, *"I will be disappointed, I will be crushed by events and by situations."* In contrast, in the "world of mysticism," where he does not try and control, these pains literally disappear.

Recall that the façade was constructed through draining emotions from experience in response to pain. Now though, with the construction of the world of mysticism where as Daniel puts it, *"nothing harms me,"* emotions can experienced freely. Daniel explains this in his own words, saying, *"I take the value off of everything... it doesn't mean that I become emotionless, it actually means that I become more deeply emotional about everything."* Thus, the "world of experience and things," through which the façade grew, now has a critical counterpart – the "world of mysticism," where emotions can be deeply felt, and through such feeling, the sense of an authentic self begins to emerge.

Constant Uncertainty of Cultural Life

At some moment, it may be interesting to ask why the genre of poetry remains a critical aspect of human lives – and how much of the answer (speaking broadly) may be that in reading poems, we find a space where meaning freely expresses itself. Though in our daily lives, we may by habit or for reasons of security become accustomed to ignoring the duality, ambiguity and motion of meaning, the poem resists this tendency. As Freeman describes, part of the purpose of poetry is to speak "about what is absent in presence; it's about what's often missing from the ordinary experience by virtue of its being 'denied' or 'threatened by circumstances'" (Freeman, 2002, p. 174).

The 'literal' and 'imagined' can be seen as a dynamic field of analysis[2] in socio-cultural psychology to the extent that when human semiotic actions are viewed within irreversible time, the sign cannot be understood with reference to the immediately fleeting here-and-now alone. In an ephemeral world, humans are doing something to organize experience, yet that organizer, the sign, itself bears the mark of the temporal flow, itself becoming motion, and perpetually transforming through those tensions.

Acknowledgments

The author wishes to thank the following intellectual companions: Ingrid Josephs, Joao Salgado, Mark Freeman, Jaan Valsiner, Tania Zittoun, and Daniel.

Notes

1 "The Snow Man," copyright 1923 and renewed 1951 by Wallace Stevens, for *The Collected Poems of Wallace Stevens* by Wallace Stevens and renewed 1982 by Holly Stevens. Used by permission of Alfred A. Knopf, a division of Random House, Inc.

2 An extended notion of *'unit* of analysis.'

References

Abbey, E. & Valsiner, J. (2004 December). Emergence of meanings through ambivalence [58 paragraphs]. *FQS: Forum Qualitative Sozialforschung* [On-line Journal], 6(1), Art. 23. Available at http://www.qualitative-research.net/fqs-tests/1-05/05-1-23-e.htm

Baldwin, J. M. (1915). *Genetic theory of reality.* New York: G. P. Putnam's Sons.

Bergson, H. (1913). *Time and free will.* London: George Allen & Co.

Bergson, H. (1944). *Creative evolution.* New York: The Modern Library.

Eliot, T. S. (1932). "The Metaphysical Poets." In Selected Essays, 1917–1932. New York: Harcourt, Brace & Co.

Freeman, M. (2000). When the story's over: Narrative foreclosure and the possibility of self-renewal. In M. Andrews, S. D. Sclater, C. Squire, & A. Treacher (Eds.), *Lines of narrative: Psychosocial perspectives.* London: Routledge.

Freeman, M. (2002). The presence of what is missing: Memory, poetry, and the ride home. In R. J. Pellegrini & T. R. Sarbin (Eds.), *Between fathers and sons: Critical incident narratives in the development of men's lives.* New York: The Haworth Clinical Practice Press.

Josephs, I. E. (1998). Constructing one's self in the city of the silent: dialogue, symbols and the role of 'as-if' in self-development. *Human Development, 41,* 180–195.

Josephs, I. E., Valsiner, J., & Surgan, S. E. (1999). The process of meaning construction. In J. Brandtstatder and R. M. Lerner (Eds.), *Action & self development* (pp. 257–282). Thousand Oaks, CA: Sage.

Lewin, K. (1936). *Principles of topological psychology.* New York: McGraw-Hill Book Company.

Matte Blanco, I. (1975). The unconscious as infinite sets. London: Duckworth.

Matte Blanco, I. (1988). Thinking, feeling and being. London: Routledge.

Paz, O. (1995). *The double flame: Love and eroticism.* New York: Harcourt Brace & Co.

Piaget, J. (1962). *Play, dreams, and imitation in childhood.* New York: Norton.

Prigogine, I. & Nicolis, G. (1971). Biological order, structure, and instabilities. *Quarterly Journal of Biophysics, 4,* 107–148.

Stevens, W. (1997). *Wallace Stevens: Collected Poems & Prose.* New York: Literary Classics of the United States, Inc.

Vaihinger, H. (1935). *The philosophy of 'as if'.* (C. K. Ogden, Trans.). London: Kegan Paul, Trench, Trubner & Co., Ltd.

Valsiner, J. (2005). Affektive Entwicklung im kulturellen Kontext. In J. B. Asendorpf (Hrg.), *Soziale, emotionale und Persönlichkeitsentwicklung.* Göttingen: Hogrefe.

Vygotsky, L. S. (1925/1971). *Psychology of art.* Cambridge, MA: MIT Press.

Vygotsky, L. S., & Luria, A. R. (1930/1994). Tool and symbol in child development. In R. Van der Veer and J. Valsiner (Eds.), *The Vygotsky reader.* Oxford: Blackwell.

Zittoun, T., Duveen, G., Gillespie, A., Invison, G., & Psaltis, C. (2003). The uses of symbolic resources in developmental transactions. *Culture & Psychology, 9,* 415–448.

Zittoun, T. (2005). *Transitions. Development through symbolic resources.* Advances in Cultural Psychology: Constructing Development. Greenwich, CT: InfoAge.

Zittoun, T. (2006). The role of symbolic resources in human lives. In J. Valsiner & A. Rosa, (Eds). *Cambridge handbook of sociocultural Psychology.* Cambridge: Cambridge University Press.

CHAPTER 18

Prayer and the Kingdom of Heaven

Psychological Tools for Directivity

Pablo del Río and Amelia Álvarez

The Directive Functions of Behavior

Introduction: The Psychology of Sense and the Psychology of Meaning

Religion provided human beings with a stable, effective, and extensive frame for living along history: both social and internal world, normative and emotional behavior have been under its constant influence. In spite of this, its status in Psychology is peripheral and almost illegitimate.

We should perhaps return to Durkheim, who argued that before pronouncing on the rationality or empirical foundation of the object of religious belief we must acknowledge the existence of psychological religious experience. People *hold* representations of religion and *perform* religious actions, so that the religious fact *(le fait religieux)* becomes a legitimate field of study (Durkheim, 2003). These actions and representations require explanation, but their existence is the point of departure for research, the constitution of the empirical fact. James (1902) and Greely (1987) talked mystical states of consciousness. Likewise, Hood (1975) and Lukoff (1985, 1998) approached ecstatic experiences as "real" experiences, that is, as legitimate topics of research and study. Such perspectives, indeed, agree with the more general approach of Ornstein (1977), who argues that experiential events and intuition should be included on an equal footing with rationality in the domains of consciousness.

The study of religious experience is not absent in the current research agenda of psychology, however its presence is marginal and marginalized: in Western psychological literature religion is mainly found in clinical contexts, suggesting that it is more related to pathology and psychological abnormality[1]. And yet religion can certainly not be ignored as a relevant empirical psychological fact in cultural *normality*, even in the West. As McCullough, Larson, Koenig, and Lerner (1999), on the basis of Gallup poll data, point out, 60% of North Americans pray at some time, of whom 97% believe their prayer to be heard or answered, and 86% believe their prayers make them better people.

Such presence of religious practices thus suggests that, in order to understand the human psyche, it may be more advantageous to include prayer and religion in psychological normality – as Vygotsky (1989)[2] argued – than to circumscribe them to pathology.

The mind of this rational species that adds, subtracts, and multiplies also does other things, such as praying or writing poetry, even though its routes to consciousness and rationality may at first sight appear irrational: as Vygotsky (1980) pointed out, the child accedes to the "algebra of the mind" via the unlikely and colorful route of pretend play.

The fact that we scientists place limits on research into directive processes does not mean human beings can live without them. Although scientific explanations about directive functions in general and religious experience in particular have consistently been dodged, in the meantime life goes on and people decide and behave with very limited guidance from science, or even with no guidance at all. As Unamuno noted: "in practice in our lives, rarely do we have to wait for definitive scientific solutions. Men have lived, and still live, according to the most fragile of hypotheses and explanations, and even without any at all" (Unamuno, 1910, p. 2).

Hence the relevance of the fundamental question raised by Durkheim (2003): What is the *function* of religious behavior? Or, in the words of the Spanish philosopher Miguel de Unamuno "Why do so many men believe?" (Unamuno, 1986, p. 25).

The current resurgence of religious and animist phenomena in a wide variety of modalities (del Río & Álvarez, 1995a; 1995b; Rodrigues & del Río, 2000) suggests that they are still living cultural architectures. Little is known, though, about the psychological mechanisms – religious and non-religious – at work in the rich and varied cultural architectures of directivity, and a research agenda is urgently needed, with the aim of providing a scientific explanation of these mechanisms.

Directive Functions in the Cultural-historical Perspective

THE PSYCHOLOGY OF ORIENTATION TO REALITY AND THE NATURAL HISTORY OF THE SIGN

The difficult and conflicting relationship between knowledge and mastery of nature, on the one hand, and of the human being, on the other is at the origin of the modern sciences. At the beginning of the 16th century, the Spanish humanist Acosta proposed a classification of sciences that drew a distinction based on these two dimensions: social and moral (human) sciences, and natural sciences. As the historian Elliot points out, this would be the origin of the modern classification of sciences that dates from the discovery of America to the present day. For Acosta (1962), the primacy of scientific progress should correspond to the former group, since it is they that should set the agenda for the latter; knowledge of man is proposed as the prior framework for guiding knowledge about things.

The first modern materialist approach to human evolution inverted the sense proposed by Acosta and focused on *homo faber* and his capacity to produce tools for mastering his environment. Vygotsky turned again to that initial course, stating that the most relevant tools for a materialist psychology are those that permit human beings to master themselves, to construct themselves: the *psychological tools* (Vygotsky, 1930/1984/1999). Thus, human progress can be valued both for its success in action towards the outside, and for its effectiveness in action towards the inside.

The concern with self-control led Vygotsky to his particular preoccupation with directive processes (del Río, 2004), starting out from a biofunctionalist perspective (del Río & Álvarez, in press a). Vygotsky's approach to the psyche confers a central role to action, and emphasizes the distinction between the involuntary character of the animal's actions – guided by instincts – and human actions – mostly of voluntary or directive nature, guided by intentionality.

The word "directivity," widely employed subsequently by Vygotskyan psychology, has an origin linked to psychological models, which initially conceive of the human subject as *directly* oriented to objects.

However, the term directivity has a dual meaning that may render it ambiguous. It refers first to the fact that the organism has *direction*: it directs itself towards something; and secondly, to the fact that the pre-human directive mechanism is *direct*, immediate, whilst in the human being, and thanks to the use of social and instrumental mediators, it becomes *indirect*, as Vygotsky stressed (1930/1984/1999). In the experiments carried out by Luria and his colleagues (Luria, 1978) on the genesis of executive action, children were provided with verbal, social, and instrumental mediations. These mediators permitted children to control their own action and direct their own behavior *indirectly*, that is, to *re-direct* their actions. This mediated directivity or re-directivity, characteristically human, through which – as Vygotsky (1926/1982/1990) would say– human beings condition themselves to liberate themselves from the direct dictates of stimuli in the medium, is what generally comes to be called directivity in the cultural-historical tradition. Therefore, direct involuntary action develops into indirect and self-controlled voluntary action.

In the cultural-genetic perspective, just as the cognitive logic of presentation is reconstructed in the logic of re-presentation, the logic involved in direction is reconstructed in the logic of re-direction. The concept thus implies the reconstruction of the animal functional edifice of orientation within a new logic of re-presentation and distribution of stimuli and of re-direction of actions. No longer is it the internal innate connections of an isolated individual organism and the external dictatorship of environmental stimuli under the logic of the present – of presentation – that govern human life, but rather the web of new functions originated by these new external connections.

What constitutes this new behavioral logic, this new architecture of the direction

of life? How does it emerge and change? How does it develop?

Vygotsky argued that psychology needed to emulate the natural sciences and, just as they had compiled the "natural history" of species, it should compile an "evolutionary history" of psychological instruments, a "natural history of the sign" (1930/1984/1989). It is important to recall that Vygotsky attributes *functional value* not only to the classical internal abstract functions (attention, memory, etc.), but also to the external forms and strategies of action made possible by cultural operators, which merit consideration as *functions in their own right*. In this sense, his proposal of drawing up a natural history of the sign would in fact be equivalent to tracing the natural history of the higher mental functions insofar as they are mediated historically by culture[3]. Following this logic, activities normalized in cultural history, such as prayer, meditation, expiation rituals, military training of motor control, theatre or drama, to mention but a few, would merit reclassification as higher psychological functions. Outside Psychology, an intensive and extensive movement in social sciences are pursuing a similar goal: Foucault's technologies of the self (1969), Elias' social history of the control of emotions (1978), Febvre's *histoire des mentalités* (1953), are just some examples of this. In our view, although a growing work is dedicated to *cultural history*, the task of linking this history to the historical development of psychological higher functions is still pending, and the Vygotskyan endeavor of establishing an objective history of human cultural evolution with a parallel approach to the evolutionary natural science has not been accomplished. On the one hand, while the Humanities have made great efforts in the study of the psycho-cultural tools Vygotsky would include in his natural history of the sign, these efforts cannot be ascribed to the tradition of natural science, and neither, therefore, to the perspective of "natural history" (i.e., of evolutionary natural science). And on the other hand, when cultural-historical psychology itself has undertaken the study of the cultural operators from which the mental functions would be formed, it has generally done so in relation to present-day operators, without a systematic historical analysis. Moreover, in those exceptional cases in which such an historical and evolutionary approach is present, researchers have focused more on certain cognitive operations that Vygotsky would situate in his "psychotecnics of the intellect,"[4] such as the operators and operations involved in verbal reasoning, arithmetic or spatial representation (Davidov & Andronov, 1979; del Río, 1987; Hutchins, 1996; Zaporozhets, Zinchenko, & Elkonin, 1964). The result is that, as Zinchenko (1995) points out, cultural-historical research has practically ignored the directive cultural architecture that would be situated in the terrain of the "psychotecnics of feelings." Thus, we lack an evolutionary and historical approach to what would be a "cultural engineering" of directive psychological functions in the framework of natural/cultural science proposed by Vygotsky.

An assumption implicit in the Vygotskyan methodological proposal of psychotechnics is that psychological functions are linked to a real, material space, and that mind (brain) and environment are ecologically related. As a good biological functionalist, Vygotsky did not accept permanent presences in the consciousness – remember James's (1890) conception of consciousness as a flow rather than a state. A bio-ecological interpretation of Vygotsky's theory implicitly proposes a thesis convergent with a large part of most current functionalist cognitive approaches, and which within our perspective of the *Syncretic Zone of Representation* could be formulated as follows: *the problem of representations refers to the cultural design of presentations* (del Río, 1990). The *SZR* model thus follows Vygotsky's explanatory proposal on the genetic origin of psychological functions as situated in the environment. The thesis of situatedness can be extrapolated also to directivity – the psychological management of the future – in accordance with the following principle: the design of a cultural system capable of directing one's own behavior and managing one's own emotions, involves building a cultural system of external psychological instruments that prepares, in the present, states of emotional and directive consciousness which will be activated in the future. These ideas have been intuitively put into practice throughout history by popular cultures and religions, as "concrete psychologies."

DIRECTIVE FUNCTIONS FOR A "CONCRETE PSYCHOLOGY"

Vygotsky's "concrete psychology" (Vygotsky, 1989) emerged in a frontal manner in his early work (Vygotsky, 1971), and then in more dispersed – though persistent – fashion, through occasional reflections on play, tales, art, religion, and so on (del Río & Álvarez, in press b). However, current neo-Vygotskyan approaches are somewhat reluctant to embrace the topics and ideas of this "second" Vygotsky. The problem here is that the script of concrete psychology bequeathed by Vygotsky is an incomplete and heterogeneous sketch – by comparison with the relatively explicit model he leaves in abstract psychology and the classic intellectual functions – and that, consequently, later researchers must enter the new territory with fewer clues and methodological support.

A full and systematic consideration of the directive approach to Psychology goes beyond what is realistically possible in the space of this chapter. It would require going back not only to Vygotsky, but further, to the historical bedrock, and recalling the functions that were proposed as alternatives or complements to the classic intellectual functions. It would also require a thorough search in current psychology in order to identify directive functions that might be classified under other headings, such as the so-called executive function. Moreover, it is imperative not to disregard the real, concrete psychology of everyday life, insofar as it constitutes the foundation for the study of what humans do to define their life scripts and culturally regulate their behavior.

The mental functions and processes involved in directivity have largely already been described; indeed, their descriptions in general date from the inception of psychology: *Voluntary attention; executive* and *voluntary action; decision or purpose; free will; long-term conscious orientation*. These functions are related to functional dimensions such as *identity, affectivity, or morality*.

Galperin (1976) or Zaporozhets (1967) related *voluntary attention* and mediated perception with the interaction between receptive and active dimensions of the human "functional circle": that is, the general mechanisms of orientation of the human mind as a functional system of higher mediated functions. *The executive function*, and what James (1890) called *voluntary action* deals with conscious human behavior and with nothing less than the problem of free will, or of human capacity for exercising liberty. Current approaches in neuropsychology on the executive function, though having its origins in Vygotsky, via Luria (1966; 1978), have largely stripped it of its directive and intentional content (Rodríguez Arocho, 2004). However, from its origin it belonged to the active dimension of the functional circle, to which it added voluntary attention and the perceptual receptive dimension. *Decision or purpose* link the intellectual and the directive, the objective and the subjective, the world and personal action and it is not reducible to cognitive planning, problem-solving or thinking – which would be closer to meditation – nor to conscious processing. Decision is not always meta-decision or lucid decision; it is frequently scarcely more than a direct struggle between stimuli – recall Spinoza's thesis. Freedom is not *indeterminacy* of behavior, but conscious *determination* or the capacity for self-determination – *free will*. *Long-term conscious orientation* covers psychological processes mediated by cultural operators and so makes possible for human beings to plan, to make decisions and to keep individual or collective long-term lines of action in the environment. This concept would link in with analeptic (life history) and proleptic (life project) narrative orientation, and involve decision and purpose in the symbolic and narrative *imaginarium* of individual or societies.

This brief and informal enumeration is far from exhaustive, and does not pretend to offer an inventory of any kind. The systematic study of directive functions remains almost in the same indefinite state it was when psychology first emerged as a discipline. Operational descriptions of a more cognitive nature, such as in relation to planning or execution, are indeed valuable, but tell only part of the story of the directive mind, and its cultural ecology has remained practically unexplored.

Despite this heterogeneous and partial state of the matter, the scenario facing the researcher is an exciting one. As it was in the time of Vygotsky, who approached both the more instrumental abstract functions (his "psychology of intellect"), and the directive functions (his "concrete psychology"). He dealt, for example, with primitive resources for resolving inertia situations in decision-making – akin to those of "Buridan's ass" – such as drawing lots or making decisions about real life based on oneiric experiences; with situated external psychotechnical resources that scaffold the mnemonic of decision-making[5]; with tragedies – such as *Hamlet* – that make it possible to capture and transmute feelings; and even with fable, which would permit the construction of a moral narrative of feelings to guide the emotions and the social direction of behavior (Vygotsky, 1930/1984/1999; 1931/1983/1995; 1971; 1980; 1989).

These functions – traditionally associated with intentionality, orientation and action – coincide only partially in their most instrumental aspects with those that current cognitive neuropsychology indicates for executive action (planning, execution, self-regulation, maintenance, spatio-temporal segmentation, and sustained mental productivity). With a more global and systematic orientation, neuropsychology is now making substantial progress (Damasio, 1999; Sacks, 1996) towards this territory, thus contributing to the necessary restoration of equilibrium in research that we suggested above.

The feelings of disorientation, uneasiness, and anxiety induced by cultural change that affect today's societies call for scientific efforts to recover the dynamic integrity of the psychological system. In a "strong" reading of the functional approach, systemic integration requires the *means* (cognitive) functions to be systematically subject to, or articulated by, the *ends* (directive) functions. In a complementary direction is the cultural-genetic view, according to which, just as the cultural architecture of instrumental mediations has been able to develop the powerful human cognitive functions, this same architecture would be responsible for the development of varied and effective directive functions and, above all, of a *specific psychological logic of human orientation* that has complemented and reconstructed the animal directive mechanisms.

Inevitably, certain aspects of directivity appear with great frequency in almost all areas of psychology, and a review of these references and their significance would be an objective in itself, which we clearly cannot take on here. We would simply point out that, as a rule, these aspects appear without any consideration of their bio-functional dimension, but rather as *etic* concepts of an abstract nature.

An abyss thus opens up between the biological material organism and the scientific constructs for explaining its orientation and action, which would belong, in line with a long tradition of dualism, either to the sphere of rational choice or to that of emotional drive, with no communication between the two. The path which leads from organic to mental postures, positions or movements is not a well-trodden one – indeed, it is somewhat overgrown, despite the convincing expeditions made along it at various times by sociogenetic and sociocultural approaches such as those of Wallon or Vygotsky. More recently, general neuropsychological approaches to orientation and emotion (Damasio, 1999; Sacks, 1995) or to the relationships between *embodiment* and religion have gone some way to clearing this path anew (Nikkel, 2005; Varela, Thompson, & Rosch, 1991).

Approaches from philosophy, anthropology, and thinking on religion open up a fascinating and relatively unexplored area of knowledge for the psychologist into which we cannot venture too far here. We would simply point out that *emic* constructs such as that of *virtue* – with no apparent objective value for the scientist – remain efficient in everyday life as cultural mechanisms of orientation, and have throughout history been responsible for the construction of highly refined programs of practice and instruction in the majority of religions. The foundations of such mechanisms can be found in Wallonian theory, a clear antecedent of current theories of *embodiment*; Wallon's theory establishes continuity between the postures of the body and those of the psyche (Wallon, 1934). We should also mention the concept of *talante*[6] in the work of the Spanish philosopher López Aranguren (1994), which includes affective and reflexive dispositions developed through cultural cultivation of temperament and personality, as the individualized idiosyncratic "way of being" and "orienting" oneself.

Following this argumentation, any convincing approach to human orientation should be capable of avoiding dualism and defining a functional system that can integrate situated and symbolic functions in a harmonious fashion; a system that takes jointly into account the cultural network of situated material operators (see later the concept of *operator* we propose) and the dense complex of symbolic operators. The result will constitute the threads of directive experiences – including religious experiences – that weave the cultural fabric of the mind.

But if we are to take advantage of the Vygotskyan conception in this recovery of directivity, it will be necessary to make some corrections to the way his work is generally being interpreted. First of all, we must recover the deep biological and ecological roots that nourish his theory – the hallmark of biofunctionalist science. The distancing from organic and biological processes for which cultural-historical theory has been criticized may have more to do with the recent developments of this theory: it is hard to find such distancing in the biofunctionalist

Vygotsky or the neuropsychological Luria. We should recall that for Vygotsky's functional model, the higher functions develop dynamically upon the very fabric of the natural functions. This principle will be taken into account in our analysis of the cultural reconstruction of the directive functions.

FUNCTIONAL CONGRUENCE AS THE BASIS OF THE DIRECTIVE SYSTEM

How does cultural genetics reconstruct the mechanisms of orientation and direction of the powerful biology inherited by humans from the higher mammals? Answering this question requires us to define religious directivity, making explicit, albeit minimally, the biological foundations – organic, ethological – of prayer, the natural functions lying at the origin of the higher mental functions that adopt the form of religious psychological activity.

The notion that the higher functions are constructed on direct and immediate operations through mediated operators is, as already mentioned, one of the axioms of the cultural-genetic approach. As would be expected, this thesis is potentially in line with some of the positions within the new evolutionary psychology that seeks to identify for each new mental function the organic, ethological and neurological base on which the higher function is built. Only then can the mechanism of mediation be defined avoiding it being a mere abstraction. Mediated processes re-channel and reconstruct the natural mechanisms, which, at the same time, provide the conditions and potentials for the architectures of mediation.

As Griffin and Baron-Cohen (2002) suggest, far from being in opposition to one another, the thesis of psychological evolutionism and that of sociocultural evolution can be articulated, as long as the logic of evolution that permits humans to move from one evolutionary structure to another can be made explicit. Elsewhere (del Río, 2005), we have proposed the concept of *evolutionary congruence* as a general criterion for establishing the functional viability of a given course of psychological change, to highlight the fact that not all the courses of development pro-posed, and even imposed by society and culture, are equally possible and appropriate. In our opinion, the most viable are those best adjusted to the great universals or features of what we might call "the functional personality of the species," the logic of its organic functional system. The new designs proposed by culture will be more successful the better they combine the two processes – biological and cultural – of evolution. And there will be greater need of congruence for functions concerned with achieving *ends* (directive functions) than for instrumental functions that provide the necessary *means* or knowledge (cognitive functions). Recent developments in evolutionary psychology appear to pay more attention to ethological mechanisms, and are thus more in line with this functional requirement of evolutionary congruence or harmony (Dennett, 1998).

The assumption of evolutionary congruence applied to religious behaviors means that what we call the spirit is constructed *from* the body, not *against* the body – and even in those cases in which it struggles against the body, in order to subjugate it to a plan of behavior guided by a religious agenda, it uses the organism as a means of support. This is clearly reflected in the ascetic practices of the more sophisticated religions: Christian detachment or the *karma* of Buddhists are attained through an ascetic program of discipline and focusing of the body. Here, the directive functions would follow a path analogous to that of the cognitive functions: as shown in experiments, mental operations such as multiplication are built based on manipulative activities (Zaporozhets, Zinchenko, & Elkonin, 1964).

This chapter can do no more than to outline this problem, highlighting what cultural-genetic psychology considers to be the two pillars of orientation of our species: orientation to *objects* (Luria, 1972/2002); and orientation to *social others*, described by Wallon and Vygotsky in their respective socio-genetic approaches. Orientation to others has in the most recent phylogenetic stage acquired a special characteristic: combined with the consequences of De Vore's hypothesis (anticipation of birth brought about by bipedestation), social orientation has converted care of the "unfit" or disabled into the human formula for survival, so that the social distribution of functions and shared individual incapacity is to be viewed as capacity for the species, and survival of the fittest individual turns into survival of the fittest community (del Río, 1990).

These two orientations, social and objectual, would constitute the foci for the set of directive operators for the distributed mind, and would open up the two large avenues for the development of the cultural-historical evolutionary designs of directivity in general and religious directivity in particular. We can assume, therefore, that underlying spiritual processes these two basic orientations of the ethology of the species could be found.

The Methodological Problem. Mediational Ecology

We should therefore start out from the basic orientations of the species looking for cultural formulas through which the logic of natural behavior has evolved towards others with the help of social and instrumental mechanisms of mediation. This means first of all defining the new processes of orientation and the previous processes on which they are based. Secondly, it requires the analysis of the social and cultural operators that serve the new processes. In our line of research, this involves sketching an "ecology of the spirit," drawing up a map of the resources for orientation (situated and symbolic) operating in a given culture or for a particular person.

Embodiment in Vygotsky and the Cultural Ecology of Directivity

The psychological logic of culturally reconstructed human orientation is therefore, in our view, an *eco*-logic. Insofar as it has its source in the Vygotskyan approach to mediation, it is of eco-bio-functionalist origin, and stipulates that the functions of the organism be *materially linked to their environment* (del Río & Álvarez, in press a). The requirement is explicit in Vygotsky's theory: "The soul is localized and, thus, it is materialized and mechanized. Moving and activated by the body, the soul must itself be bodily" (1930/1984/1999, p. 189). We hold that the unit of analysis of the psychotechnical act should be *operation*: an action mediated by an *operator*. An operation would thus involve the use of operators, an operator being a material element ecologically and culturally accessible outside (or inside, if it has been interiorized) that permits us to activate and control (i.e., to *operate*) a mental function. An important assumption is implicit in the Vygotskyan methodological proposal of psychotechnics: the intentional, conscious, and directive use of mediations. The unit of analysis is not reaction but operation. One could say that it is Pavlov (the researcher) who rings the bell to the dog - which reacts- in the laboratory. In everyday human life, though, the *subject rings the bell for himself*, operates the operator. The subject organizes the operators that become an *organ*, a psychological device. In our view, a theoretical and methodologically coherent application of the natural history of the sign and the Vygotskyan theory of mediation would therefore require, at the research level, an ecological identification of the operators and operations that activate and control the corresponding higher mental functions. At the level of action it would imply the design of the appropriate operators and operations and their conscious localization and situation, their cultural *mise-en-scène*.

Externally oriented operators and internally oriented operators. At a first developmental level – more accessible from natural functions – external directive mediators permit human beings to redirect and control their behavior from the outside. Symbolic markers and presences in everyday life (such as stone crosses) external rituals (such as standing up when the teacher or another authority figure enters, saluting the flag, donning the gown before an academic event or a trial, covering oneself on entering a church, or removing one's hat when a funeral cortège passes) aid performance of the appropriate psychological action, activating it from the context.

Analogously, in order to understand and master themselves from their interior, human beings need to delve into themselves, and for this they use other types of directive psychological instruments that articulate analysis of the reality and of the situation with analysis of oneself, and of oneself in the situation. These more individualized instruments – personal organizers, diaries, poetry, prayer – direct subjects towards the interior of their consciousness and permit them to evaluate and operate their own thoughts and feelings.

The "natural *history* of the sign" proposed by Vygotsky would in our view thus require an analysis of the role of operators in the context of the *new organism-environment relationship* and the new form of mediated orientation created by culture. In practice this would involve the development of a *psychological ecology* of the external (and, where applicable, more or less internalized) cultural operators that transform mental operations. Each culture may be considered as a community psychofunctional system; as such, it has developed a specific network of instrumental or social mediators, a "psychological toolbox," containing tools that are only partly interiorized by the individuals in that community: the library, the flag, the press and television, history, and so on. Likewise, each individual possesses his or her own internal functional system and external cortical system, of functional extensions – and along with it a personal and characteristic ecology of his/her situated mind. In order to identify these functional architectures or cultural neuropsychologies, researchers should address the internal diagnosis and mapping of the mind in combination with the external mapping and psychotechnical analysis of the operations and mechanisms set in motion by cultural operators (del Río, 2002). In this regard we can identify two directive ecologies:

1. *Situated ecology*. The mechanism of cultural *mise-en-scène* (del Río & Álvarez, 1999)

shapes human spaces not only for facilitating physical activity, but also for orienting mental activity. Inhabited territories have become shaped for directing action and perception by means of new extended functions mediated by cultural operators. Thus, religious operators such as prayer are inserted into the directive ecological environment and so spatio-temporally situate actions: prayers or verbal and gestural invocations on getting up, going to bed, leaving the house or going on a journey; crossing oneself on entering a football field or passing a church, and so on.

2. *Imaginary ecology*. As well as being *situated*, human culture is a *symbolic* culture (even though the symbolic media may be, in turn, anchored in the situated *mise-en-scène*). A great deal of our research has been devoted to the systematic analysis of the content of the symbolic culture in its directive sense, i.e., which reality appears in the media, and consequently, which reality is *proposed* to the subjects of a culture. In general terms, the description of the content of one given culture has been one of the core concepts in the anthropology of human cultures, in philosophy and in psychology, (cfr. Wundt's *Völkerpsychologie*, 1900–1920). The concepts of semiosphere (Lotman, 1990), rhetorical framework (Valsiner, 2002), or that of *Weltanschauung* from classical Philosophy, contribute nuclear ideas of a global nature for understanding the general symbolic orientation of a culture. In our approach, we attempt to operationalize this symbolic orientation through the study of the specific "cultural diets" to which subjects from different generational cohorts are or have been exposed, and which may have constituted their "*Weltanschauung*": the generational *imaginarium*. The concept of *diet* has been applied for us to define – in the tradition of natural history, that is involving the recollection of specimens, knowledge of ecological distribution and structure, and content analysis – the accumulated consume and appropriation in development of cultural contents (Álvarez & del Río, 1999). It has also been used effectively to characterize

the child's accumulative consumption of television content (Huston & Wright, 1998; Wright & Huston, 1995; del Río & Álvarez, 1993), and we consider its cultural-historical operationalization extremely useful for identifying the repertoires of symbolic content of the general population – the "cultural imaginarium" – and for analyzing the mechanisms and operators underlying it (del Río, Álvarez, & del Río, 2004).

The Religious Ecology of the Kingdom of Heaven: The Scenario and the Toolbox

THE LOCUS OF RELIGIOUS CONSCIOUSNESS

Situated religious operators can be mobile and "portable" – accompanying the subject as a cultural prosthesis attached to the skin, like a medallion or a cross hung around the neck – or situated in "shells" (Álvarez, del Río, & Guerrero, 1979; Moles, 1974), such as the work desk, the bedroom, or the car.

In the shell pertaining to the desk or the bedroom we generally find the "stabilizers" of situated consciousness, the operators (photos or images, relics hung from the rear-view mirror in the car, etc.) that permit the functional flow of consciousness to be structured on a stable cultural ecosystem, with the same quality of permanence as the habitat of an animal, but also with the psychotechnical power provided by the cultural mise-en-scène of perception-action.

As Vygotsky proposed, operators of perception and action act by inserting themselves in the context and, "stowing away," so to speak, in the natural psyche of the here-and-now with elements that are materially in accord with the physical habitat, but which in mental terms come from other spatial-temporal contexts. And this initial quality in fact makes possible a further, even more complex quality. Not only are elements from other contexts situated in the present physical habitat, but the same mechanism permits some of these elements to assume the form of bridges to other full contexts, worlds, or scenarios – just as the monolith in 2001, A Space Odyssey opens a "gateway to the stars." Likewise, the kingdom of heaven, ancient

Rome or a here-and-now situation projected to another place or another country become accessible through the creation of imaginary contexts. The logic of cultural mise-en-scène permits us to insert into the present context not only isolated elements, but also entire contexts and other worlds. This quality of hyper-mediational dovetailing permits the articulation of situated mediations and those of the imaginarium; the latter are inserted in the biological natural ecosystem as contextual bridges or gateways (the television screen, books, oral narratives, and so on).

The perceptual habitat is redesigned, then, as an articulated complex of cultural scenarios. These loci make up a whole set of mediators designed to constitute an articulated system that is presented or re-presented in accordance with the logic of cultural mise-en-scène (del Río & Álvarez, 1999). But in addition to the extensive repertoire of elements or operators that can be situated in personal and social spaces, and which take us to other places or bring such places to our perceptual field, different cultures have developed operators and scenarios that transport us to our interior: "specific spaces for the conscience," such as shrines, churches, sanctuaries, chapels, and so on, visited at certain times (religious festivals) or on pilgrimages (Santiago, Jerusalem, Rome, Mecca, etc.).

OBJECTS, GESTURES AND VOICES IN RELIGIOUS CONSCIOUSNESS

The use of objects, gestural communication, and totemic and dramatic performance constitute historical forms of making entities from the beyond present in the here and now. All institutional cultures, and clearly all religions, have developed functionally efficient systems for inducing states of consciousness by means of a system of operations and the operators and scenarios that these require. We cannot even begin to list all of them here, even in summarized form. Given their more significant association with the final section of this chapter, their central role in religious directivity and their essential implication in prayer, we shall refer here to voice and speech.

The Vygotskyan perspective seems to fit like a glove the use of speech in religious activities. Social and private speech are articulated, so that community rites and locutions are appropriated, made private and interiorized, giving rise to the "internal life" that is assumed to be the province of the spirit. The use of the two levels, community and personal, is equally reinforced by religious practices. And in this system of religious ecology, locutions (prayer) provide the connecting thread – both when shared in institutional and ritual contexts and when used individually. Prayer is such a vertebral aspect of so many human cultures that it might well be considered a *leading activity* in the majority of them.

The Ecology of the Kingdom of Heaven

Throughout history, the great religions have arrived at two types of mediated functional organization of spiritual activity, so that we can distinguish the "popular" and "expert" levels. Both types of organization are highly refined, and have attained an undoubted effectiveness, though each following a different logic of behavior and consciousness management. But despite their diverse degrees of complexity, both provide a practical solution to the problem of conscious living: they offer a stable model of the world and provide an explanation of the inexplicable; they are capable of making evident invisible entities beyond the visible, of evoking past events and anticipating future ones by means of cultural mediators rooted in the present. They are therefore systems that permit us to recover the stability of the world in the cultural ambit of the higher functions, just as it became stable at the level of natural functions thanks to organism-context functional evolutionary adaptation (von Uexküll, 1909). All religions propose a *Weltanschauung*, a general framework for interpreting reality, and this representational framework is anchored in an effective way on the direct or presentational world by virtue of an adequately designed cultural ecology of the spirit.

LIVING IN THE KINGDOM OF HEAVEN WITH ONE'S FEET ON THE EARTH: POPULAR RELIGIOUSNESS

Although in a broad sense popular religious life is lived "under the eye of God," God leaves a fair degree of room for practical matters. In the everyday life of most believers the profane takes priority, and religion is not, so to speak, "professionalized." Instead, people's religious feelings manifest themselves only in some strategically situated instances, at key ritual and existential moments in both the community and personal spheres. This allows the religious worldview to be present in a reasonably economical fashion: life on earth prevails, but certain strategic "celestial inserts" confer convenient spiritual meaning on the earthly kingdom, without substituting it. Operators of external rather than internal orientation predominate, and the latter are mostly rooted in narrative and situated representations.

At this level of religiousness we find operators on the weekly and annual agenda within the framework of a ritually shaped and repeated narrative. Catholicism has its Sunday mass, the rosary on Saturdays or in the month of May, Christmas, Easter, Ascension, Whitsun; most religions mark critical moments of the daily routine – prayers on rising and at bedtime, crossing oneself on leaving the house, and so on – and of the life cycle: births and giving a name to a baby, weddings, deaths, and burials. These specific presences are anchored in strategic spaces responsible for the *mise-en-scène* of the kingdom of heaven on earth through the articulated employment of operators and *loci* on two levels. One of these involves the activation of religious operations, certain operators being placed in the scenarios of everyday activity (icons, images, crucifixes, photos on the sideboard, in the car, on the work desk or workbench, and so on, or the actual incorporation of prayer in such places); the other involves the facilitation of specific time slots (such as the Sunday service) or specific spatial slots (churches, shrines, stone crosses) for the evocation of the religious *imaginarium* and religious practice.

LIVING IN THE KINGDOM OF HEAVEN AS
IF WE WERE NOT ONLY ON EARTH:
EXPERT RELIGIOUSNESS

At the second level, religious cultural mediation becomes specialized and the stuff of experts; we might speak of a professional, systematic psychological ecology. The day, the week, the year are literally *replete* with systematized mediations for living constantly imbued with religious awareness; the figure of God and divine personages have a virtual but situated presence that makes them true competitors with the living figures making up the social networks of distributed consciousness. This dense mesh superimposes the life of the spirit on the basic cultural framework; that is, the kingdom of heaven becomes ecologically omnipresent in everyday space and time by means of a tightly-packed network of psychological anchorages. On contemplating the earthly kingdom through this cultural mesh of the celestial kingdom, the worldly sphere takes a perceptual and directive back seat. The monasteries of the great religions have literally constructed a "protectorate" of the kingdom of heaven on earth, a life medium corresponding to a *mise-en-scène* for bringing about the presence of the spirit in all the spaces and times of the earthly life of monks.[7] Such external omnipresence propitiates permanent religious awareness: among the set of religious operators, those more clearly addressing the interior, such as meditation and certain sophisticated forms of prayer, hold a prominent position in the psycho-ecology of these specialized settings.

The two above-mentioned levels act partly in parallel and partly in articulated fashion: the experts guide the novices. As we can see in the all the major religions, the professionals of the second level perform as "social operator" for those of the first level.

Psychological Tools for the Spirit

RELIGION AS A SOCIAL WORLD

Two world dimensions (earth and heaven) correspond to two social relations: with others and with virtual others. The world of others is socialized and humanized; the social basis of psychological higher functions postulated by Vygotsky and Wallon finds in virtual social others a firm psychological foundation. The dialogic aspect that characterizes our deepest experiences highlights the social nature of human emotion, as Wallon (1934) argued. And the tendency to address oneself to a more powerful "Other" from whom we expect help, emotional support or guidance appears to be a universal of human behavior. In situations of conflict, doubt, anxiety, danger, or, on the other hand, of joy and fulfillment, there is a seemingly natural and fairly generalized need to express desires and share feelings. By its very nature, communicative expression requires someone to whom we can address our words (orders, requests, or pleas). In the case of a religious person this social canalization of our directive system is expressed towards the transcendent Other, and flows through the channels of religion. In other cases it is manifested in quasi-impersonal invocations, but it is rare for such invocations not to be addressed to someone (or something), however virtualized they may be.

PRAYER AS THE TOOL FOR LINKING
HEAVEN AND EARTH, HUMANS AND GOD

Words are the tool for establishing a dialogue with this transcendent Other, and also for talking to oneself and directing one's own actions in tune with that Other. According to Vygotsky and Luria (1994), the directive speech of parents, and subsequently of the child to him/herself, convert the child's activity into executive action (Luria, 1972/2002). This leading role is fulfilled by speech not only in childhood, but throughout the life span, and verbal operators – oral and written – are the connecting thread for constructing the general directivity of life, in both situated and symbolic settings.

META-OPERATORS OF RELIGIOUS
CONSCIOUSNESS: MEDITATION AND THE
INNER LIFE OF THE SPIRIT

In the same way as reading-writing and complex semiotic systems have provided the instrumental basis for more advanced representational and cognitive processes, religious meta-consciousness makes use of stories, images, parables, rites, and myths to create a rich internal imaginary symbolic world. These mediators do not address only the rationality of representation and thought, but seek to activate postural feelings and responses and emotional states of consciousness; all aimed at transforming perception, comprehension, emotional response, decision, and execution.

Expert use of activators of directive consciousness directed towards the inside is generally referred to as *meditation*. This is not a purely religious process, since meditation is also involved in a large part of non-religious systemic and directive processes of awareness. However, having been swept to the margins of psychology's rationalist agenda, it tends to be perceived as a specifically religious process.

A general-purpose reading/writing-based operator is the diary (dialogue with a virtual self or other). The diary is one of the most effective tools for individualizing and stabilizing consciousness: it articulates the subject's past and future and provides ecological support for the identity. A dialogic operator comparable to the diary has traditionally been the letter (as could be the e-mail and SMS today), though these have a more enactive and less reflexive character. In general, written operators for regulating everyday activity, such as personal organizers, or life histories (CVs, memoirs, and so on) would bring the user up to the "expert" level.

Fortunately, users can turn to other more socialized and accessible operators – generally speech-related, such as chatting and round-table discussion – that feed narrative and identitary consciousness and permit us to braid our own story in a distributed fashion with those of others (as *inter-narratives*). It is through chatting and informal or round-table discussion, especially at rites of passage where our networks of "significant others" are present (christenings, weddings, funerals, etc.), that we keep up to date the articulation of our personal story with those of others, and weave the plot and meaning of our life.

Meditation can be activated and regulated through dialogue, by others and from out-side, and this is its commonest modality in religiousness at the popular level, in which it is triggered by means of sermons, parables, narrations, or scenifications. But it can also be self-regulated by means of external operators. The relationships between this expert level of meditation and thought are difficult and conflictive, as the thought and rationality component may come to dominate the dialogic and sentimental process. Unamuno, in the phase in which he was most involved with religion – that which is the object of the analysis we shall discuss below – writes of this clash between thought and meditation, and of how he commonly turned to expert operators of the culture:

> *Mental prayer eludes me. My bookish habits are such that I only conceive of pious thoughts and propositions by reading, as a commentary on what I read, and I am forced to crystallize them by writing them down. Study in order to write! Such is the goal of intellectualism: to think in order to produce thoughts! It is the terrible vicious circle of our economy transferred to the world of the spirit. We do not think for our own sake, for our own salvation; we do not meditate, we think. [. . .] We meditate while praying, we think while reading. Meditation is really considering with love, through concentration and withdrawal, a mystery, a real mystery, trying to penetrate unto its essence of love, its life-giving centre; thinking is establishing relationships between different ideas. The highest degree of meditation is ecstasy; the highest degree of thought is the construction of a philosophical system. Meditation makes one better and more saintly; thinking, more wise. [. . . .] I have been a great talker because I needed to talk out my thoughts, and words themselves stimulated that in me, I thought aloud. By striving to transmit my ideas to others I formulated them, and discovered myself, and developed them. Hence my impertinence in always being the one to speak, in interrupting but not wanting to be interrupted, in always choosing the topic of conversation and then turning it into a monologue. I thought, but I did not meditate. That's why I sought company and shunned solitude. Now I'm starting to meditate on what I have thought, to examine its*

roots and its very soul, and that's why now
I cherish my solitude. (Unamuno, 1986,
pp. 181–182)

Unamuno raises here an important problem for research methods. The mechanisms that activate prayer may be perceptible only from within it; that is, they may diverge somewhat from pure rationality. We are not talking about operators of an objective process, such as multiplication or subtraction, whose impact can be appreciated on external entities or representations, but about a subjective one, which affects subjects themselves and their internal mental states. These processes that are set in motion are not only less visible, but may also be incommensurable with rationality, so that only from those mental states activated by prayer is it possible to perceive or accept certain visions, certain mythical or dramatic forms of perceiving the world. As Unamuno argues, "prayer is the only source of a possible understanding of the mystery" (Unamuno, 1986, p. 170). "I lost my faith by *thinking about dogmas*, about the mysteries as dogmas; I recover it by *meditating on the mysteries*, on the dogmas as mysteries" (op. cit., pp. 183–184).

In any case, given the role of language, in the form of both speech and writing, in prayer and meditation, the analysis of its religious use is methodologically unavoidable. Neurological examination of the effects of meditation on brain development is possible (Lutz, Greischar, Rawlings, Ricard, & Davidson, 2004),[8] and the process of meditation should also be accessible through analytical psychological techniques. As we shall see in the following section, the analysis of spoken and written protocols thus emerges as a strategic method, for the study of both directivity in general and that of religious activity in particular.

Protocol Analysis as a Tool for Research on Mental Operations

Mental Operations and Verbal Protocols

The cognitive assumption of mental processing rests implicitly on the notion that thinking proceeds through the processing of internal mental representations that are not accessible to direct analysis but only to analysis through plausible simulations and replicas with external technologies that emulate them. The consideration of external representational phenomena (such as speech, notes, or instrumental and technical manipulations) as linked to the processing of internal mental representations opens a door to the external analysis of mental processes from the cognitive perspective. In the 1980s, K. Anders Erickson and Herbert A. Simon proposed "thinking aloud" and the verbalizations that accompany the performance of tasks as legitimate *data* for research (Erickson & Simon, 1980, 1984, 1998). With this endorsement of verbal protocols, cognitive psychology extends its methods of scientific observation of conscious activity and attributes validity – as Vygotskyan psychology had done, but for different reasons – to external cultural operators. And cognitive researchers, who had previously disregarded clinical, introspective, and interpretive methods based on subjects' verbalizations about conscious content, now consider verbalizations as *objective material* of analysis.

The application procedures of protocol analysis accept three kinds of report (Erickson & Simon, 1986): spontaneous speech aloud; thinking aloud (as subjects perform the task); and retrospective reports (reporting what they were thinking while doing the task). Erickson and Simon's aim was to infer thinking processes from the verbal behavior registered during the execution of problem-solving tasks, on the assumption that all overt responses can be considered as a reflection of internal processes, which would be only partially expressed (the responses would be a subset of that internal processing: we do not say everything that goes on in our heads, only a part of it). This overt response can also be considered as an external process totally or partially distinct from internal processing (verbal responses would constitute a set that was complementary to internal processes).

Verbal responses can thus be treated in the same way as motor or physiological responses. They accompany the internal processes externally, and account for them in various ways.

Protocol Analysis From the Perspective of Cultural Mediation

In one way or another, verbal expressions may thus constitute a correlate, by means of speech or writing, of mental processing. As is well known, the Vygotskyan approach had already, long before, endorsed the experimental validity of verbal protocols, though the explanation for granting validity to the protocols was a different one: rather than simply assuming that verbal manifestations externalize internal processing, it was postulated that, in the genetic sequence, external processing becomes an indirect – mediated – form, characteristic of higher processes. And this mediated process would later be internalized together with speech: external social speech passes to external private speech, and then to internal private speech (Vygotsky, 1930/1984/1999). Erickson and Simon (1998), in their debate with Smagorinsky (1998) about the sociocultural and information-processing perspectives in relation to the protocol analysis, defended a convergence of the two perspectives.

What these authors quite reasonably argued from the start was that data from a verbal response to a test or questionnaire are no "harder" or more legitimate than the verbalization that accompanies the thinking process prior to "the response"; simply, the former is specified by the instructions in the test application procedure and the latter is not. On accepting verbal productions other than the specific response to instructions as pertinent, these authors legitimate two classes of evidence that they propose to recover methodologically for the provision of "hard data": protocols of thinking aloud, and retrospective responses to the tests. Nevertheless, they do exclude from this group of objectivizable verbalizations the classic introspective report of self-observers trained in introspection.

According to the cultural-genetic tradition, the thinking process makes use of external and internal operators (notably speech) that should be registered and analyzed for a faithful description of that process. The objective perception and assessment of the process followed by subjects in response to instructions will therefore be substantially affected if we subtract from their analysis the indirect and external operations and operators they employ for reaching their final response. The vindication of at least one of these cultural operators (speech out loud, or voiced speech) by a part of cognitive psychology thus constitutes a meeting point with the eco-cultural approach we outlined in the previous section, and should be welcomed by both perspectives, the cognitive and the cultural-genetic.

The general presuppositions of protocol analysis permit the same method to be shared by different theoretical models of processing, according to Erickson and Simon. And to some extent this is true, as we pointed out in relation to the Vygotskyan theory, but then the *method itself should change and extend its meaning*. This occurs with Vygotsky's theory on thinking and language (Vygotsky, 1930/1984/1999; 1934/1982/1987). From the Vygotskyan perspective, verbalizations are the actual operators of the processing: "the child not only speaks about what he is doing, but for him speech and action are in this case *one and the same complex psychological function*, directed toward the solution of the given problem" (Vygotsky & Luria, 1994, p. 109).

EVERYDAY LIFE PROTOCOLS FOR A CULTURAL PSYCHOLOGY
The cultural-genetic perspective on verbal protocols involves at least two extensions with respect to the initial cognitive advance made by Erickson and Simon, which indeed they also defend (1998).

The first of these extensions would consist in applying the cognitive vindication of verbal protocols not only to laboratory or psycho-diagnostic situations, but also to everyday situations; in this way, methodological accessibility would be extended to mental processes that are the object of folk psychology.

From the Vygotskyan approach and its thesis of social and instrumental mediation, the methodological problem is not restricted to the analysis of the internal or personal meaning of verbalizations; a problem structurally linked to it consists in explaining the external and cultural meaning of verbalizations. For the cultural-historical perspective, the two explanations cannot correspond to totally different units and levels of analysis without losing the genetic meaning of the process of their construction. As a consequence of this, we would not be able to escape mind-culture dualism, and the problem of "the effects" of the latter on the former would remain for ever insoluble. Vygotsky's proposal in the face of this problem is expressed in the well-known basic thesis of his "double-formation law": intrapsychological processes (thinking, mediated deep feelings – in sum, the so-called "higher functions") proceed from interpsychological processes. What is individual and internal in adulthood originated as social and external in the child. It is upon social and cultural artefacts and operators – in general more embedded in folk psychology and everyday scenarios than in formalized processes appropriate for the laboratory – that we subsequently construct those operating at the individual and mental level.

Bearing this in mind, the sociocultural perspective permits us to go one step further in the line of the methodological recovery of verbal protocols – the second extension – going *into the wild* (Hutchins, 1996) to seek them. If we consider speech as the initial external scaffolding of processing, and adopting a Bakhtinian perspective, we can accept that speech operators are acquired by the subject as "speech genres" (Bakhtin, 1986), as complete expressions that are relatively socially and institutionally typified and ritualized – linked to activities and situations, and therefore corresponding to the

logic of the *drama* and *mise-en-scène*, and accessible to the eco-cultural analysis of psychological operations (del Río & Álvarez, 1995a, 1999). It follows that we can study highly typified social speech acts as meaningful objective material which incorporates a given psychological operator and which, therefore, constitutes a *normalized psychotecnics*, socially standardized for producing certain mental processes or states. The normalization of the *multiplication table* induced by school would be one example, in the field of Vygotsky's "psychotecnics of the intellect"; *The Lord's Prayer* would be another, in the field of his "psychotecnics of feelings". From a perspective of cultural ecology, we can select significant verbal protocols in the natural history of the sign – normalized in cultures as operators – whose use is taught and extended in the process of formal and informal education.

VERBAL PROTOCOLS OF ABBREVIATED
MENTAL ACTIONS AND INSTRUMENTALLY
SOCIALLY/DISTRIBUTED MENTAL ACTIONS
From the genetic Vygotskyan perspective on the sequence of development of the higher functions, speech is considered as the principal operator of thinking, in an "outside to inside" development process (other's speech→private external speech or addressed to oneself→abbreviated internal speech). We think, then, because we communicate: we do not communicate because we think. First comes speaking with others, dialogue, then speaking with oneself. From the perspective of eco-cultural psychology, the tool we apply to the protocols of the individual subject should thus be comparable with that which we employ with the protocols corresponding to shared and extended speech, and even to folk culture and the mass media. Therefore, and to continue with the same examples of normalized cultural operators, we should attribute the same methodological importance to the multiplication table sung in class or *The Lord's Prayer* recited all together in church as to their more individualized and interiorized developments: the interiorized multiplication table or personal prayer

transferred to private speech. It is external social operators that came before mental calculation and individual and personal prayer: the personal verbalization a subject directs towards him/herself (on mentally multiplying or praying) fulfils an inward role in functional continuity with those of sung arithmetical operations in class or communal prayer focused outwards.

These external and internalized processes, already well known and studied for intellectual operations, have been much less studied for directive operations. And yet, Vygotsky and Luria's early research on the activation and control of mental operations through words focused first of all on directive processes and the verbal control of executive actions (Luria, 1973, 1979). Vygotsky (1931/1983/1995) distinguished three levels in the cultural system of verbal control of thinking and socioculturally acquired action: *inter-psychological* (someone gives me orders, I obey); *extra-psychological* (that person who gives me orders becomes myself through external speech); and *intrapsychological* (external orders to oneself become internal by means of internalized speech). But this sequence from reaction to operation is reversible: the subject who is undergoing a moral or emotional conflict, just like the subject faced with a complicated mathematical operation, resorts to the earliest stages of verbal mediation, and we can find him/her once more talking or praying aloud, discussing it with a friend or relative, or even furiously talking "to himself" in the street.

As Vygotsky (1931/1983/1995) or Galperin (1992 a, b) pointed out, the methodological advantage of the double-formation law of mental actions (from the social to the individual sphere, from the external to the internal plane) resides in the fact that internal processes become accessible to researchers in their external stages of constitution. Even after their formation, the interiorized part of processes can be elicited externally in situations – spontaneous or designed by the experimenter – in which the cognitive or emotional charge obliges the subject to resort once more to the initial external mediators. As Davidov and Andronov (1979) pointed out, abbreviated or "reduced" mental actions, automated in mental gestures, maintain an extremely synthetic relationship with language. Gesture and word act as triggers of automated mental algorithms which, after prolonged interiorization and practice, develop in an independent way.

Rather than constituting a complication and involving a loss of information, this problem of variability in interiorization becomes one more methodological tool, highly effective in the analysis of protocols. A psychotechnical resource that can provide us with extremely rich information on the external and internal mechanisms of mediation. All verbalizations, then, are significant, though not all in the same way.

The importance of the cultural-genetic relationship between internal psychological process and verbalization is thus quite clear: utterances are both symptom and operator of mental processes. The methodological problem, however, lies in establishing an accurate framework of psychological operations insofar as their processing is socially distributed, and distributed, moreover, among the external instrumental operators (psychological tools) and internal operators – of which verbalizations are just a part, no matter how important that part may be. Psychological processes are, furthermore, throughout the life span, at different degrees of appropriation and interiorization, and therefore of internal abbreviation of externally extended operations. The (highly advisable) privacy of one's own thoughts or feelings, in addition to the enormous evolutionary and contextual variety of the functional distribution of mental operations, means that each protocol analysis has a specific value, though in all cases its methodological utility appears to give it a firm advantage. We shall leave our analysis of this question here, though not without stressing the crucial importance of this methodological encounter between the information-processing perspective and the cultural-genetic approach.

An Analysis of The Lord's Prayer as a "Psychotecnics of Feeling"

Miguel de Unamuno: Diary, Meditation, and Prayer as Existential Levers

The Spanish philosopher Miguel de Unamuno[9] (1864–1936) managed to combine throughout his life agnostic philosophical-scientific thinking and cultural and religious feeling. More out of critical demand and loyalty to both than out of methodological artifice, the two continually clashed in his mind in a painful struggle between the cognitive mind and the directive psyche ("When I prayed, my heart recognized the God my reason denied", 1986, p. 23). Unamuno's own religious experience thus becomes a unique case of extraordinary relevance for the exploration and understanding of religious feeling.[10] As regards the role of religion as a mechanism of direction of human activity, his short novel "Saint Manuel Bueno, Martyr" (Unamuno, 1933) is revealing on his position. The novel tells the story of a priest – a non-believer in his heart of hearts – who uses religion as an instrument for making his parishioners live more humanly, which turns him into a saint even before his death. Right up to the end of his life, Unamuno would grapple with the contradictions between science and religion, between reason and feelings, refusing both to believe and not to believe, without resolving the conflict, and focusing on the existential problem of the human tragedy of living knowing that we have to die (Unamuno, 1913).

Unamuno died in 1936, two years after Vygotsky and without any knowledge of him, but in many places in his work we find clear echoes of the Vygotskyan spirit. Thus, his philosophical thinking confers existential entity upon cultural makings, which would play the role of consciously shaping the life project of the human being and of communities and societies. He established a generative connection between "reading ourselves", "writing ourselves," and "being ourselves." This is a point of view that would lead him to attribute greater cultural-historical existence – more psychological impact on history – to Don Quixote than to Cervantes, and to consider the novel as an instrument for the construction and materialization of consciousness.

Unamuno also considered the diary, or meditation and prayer as instruments for generating consciousness. His approach to cultural instruments as the cornerstones of the construction of consciousness, though not strictly cultural-genetic one, is nevertheless in strong accordance with that perspective.

In the following section we shall examine the personal use Unamuno makes of three of these instruments. We could have considered the novel, as the cultural operator most characteristic of his work (Álvarez & del Río, 1999; Unamuno, 1990), since Unamuno undoubtedly wrote his life like a novel, and his novels as archetypes of life. However, we feel that prayer, being the most generalized tool of religious directivity, is for the purposes of this chapter a better option. Prayer emerges in Unamuno not only as something that he experienced, but also as an object of analysis and meditation, and is reflected as such in his diary. Three central religious operators are thus considered in our analysis of Unamuno's *Diario Íntimo*: the *diary* itself, as an "expert-level" instrument of consciousness; *meditation* (more expert than popular when its operators are written; more popular than expert when they are spoken); and *prayer* (*The Lord's Prayer*).

As we argued above, for the purposes of orientation of the human organism, mediated deep feelings are just as crucial to the control processes of this direction as thinking. Unamuno, in extending the ambit of philosophy beyond the strictly rational, finds himself impelled to extend the ambit of the mental processes covered by philosophy, and considers thinking and meditating equally necessary: "Meditation makes one better; thinking, wiser" (Unamuno, 1986, p. 181). Furthermore, this distinction is extended to the written cultural instruments for thinking and meditating, and it was in this connection that Unamuno referred to people who speak like books and books that speak like people.

On reading Unamuno we can witness his efforts to analyze and integrate the two processes, thinking and meditation, analysis and narrative. But his efforts to integrate prayer were less fruitful. Prayer appears to have been, in the intellectually mature Unamuno, a primitive religious throwback to his childhood, which, when it seemed he had got over it, re-emerged by surprise, unsettling and stimulating his intellectual life, and contributing to the onset of the profound religious crisis reflected in his diary:

> *While in Munitibar, when Ceferina was going through that difficult labour, I went out onto the road, and all I could think of to do was to pray. In that situation all those vain doctrines of mine were no use at all, and prayer welled up from the bottom of my heart [. . .]. And I didn't understand what I was witnessing, my ears closed to the voice that was speaking inside me. [. . .] . . . a thousand explanations in reason I sought in the subtleties of psychology, and I didn't want to see the truth, which, impelled by pity, revealed itself in me. (1986, pp. 13–14)*

Unamuno recounts this experience several times in his *Diario Íntimo*, and it may indeed have had a significant impact on his process of religious re-conversion.

An Analysis of The Lord's Prayer

In the process of building up a picture of the cultural psychotecnics of human directivity, the research we have been undertaking in the last few years involves, on the one hand, field studies on situated operators of the ecology of the spirit, and on the other, content analysis on cultural repertoires of symbolic ecology (Álvarez and del Río, 1999; del Río and Álvarez, 1999; del Río and Fuertes, 2004; Fuertes and del Río, 2004). Below we present a sample of the work on the psychotecnics of the spirit which we began a few years ago (del Río, 1997), and which we believe has the virtue of operating at the situated and symbolic levels simultaneously; at that of popular religiousness anchored in speech, on the one hand, and at that of expert religiousness, anchored

in written meditation, on the other. The sample selected involves an analysis of the most famous of Christian prayers, *The Lord's Prayer* – whose invocations form the first *corpus* of analysis – considered through the feelings-thoughts reflected in Unamuno's meditations in his *Diario Íntimo*; all Unamuno's entries referring to the invocations of *The Lord's Prayer* constitute the second *corpus* of analysis.

As regards the *first content* of the analysis – the actual statements in *The Lord's Prayer* – we should explain that we chose it for its status as a nuclear operator, a summarized compendium of the most basic religious perceptions and psychological postures of Christianity. Articulated as a sequence of entreaties and invocations that can be inserted in the key moments and scenarios of the day or of life, it permits the activation of the principal ideas, metaphors, and emotional evocations of the Christian *Weltanschauung*. Given its extremely widespread and intense use, this prayer can be considered to be as normalized in Christian directivity as is the multiplication table in Western academic knowledge. From the mediational point of view, each phrase of *The Lord's Prayer* would act as a mental handle that evokes representations and feelings in the mind, through the mechanism of the abbreviation of private speech characterized by Vygotsky (1934/1982/1987). In mental abbreviation, one part activates the whole; one phrase (such as when we say "Somewhere in La Mancha . . ." or "Once upon a time . . ." we evoke the whole of *Don Quixote*, or the narrative structure of the tale), a single word, or even a mental gesture, evokes or triggers a whole complex of meanings.

Concerning the *second set of content*, Unamuno's meditations on *The Lord's Prayer*, we should point out that they are taken from the diary he kept in the years around 1900. The content of five of these notebooks – covering the period from the onset of his religious crisis, in 1897, to January 1902 – is what makes up the *Diario Íntimo*, published for the first time in 1970 (the quotations in the present analysis are taken from the seventh reprint, 1986). Unamuno finally got over the crisis-recovering his religious faith- after a long struggle with an agnosticism rooted in his scientific rationalism, by that time well established.[11] The fact that Unamuno recorded his meditations in a diary during this sensitive period has given us access to a particularly valuable cultural protocol. Unamuno himself wrote about the role of the diary as a cultural instrument of self-awareness, about its effectiveness for permitting the subject to "read himself." Writing in a diary would certainly not be the only occasion for meditation in a person as pensive as Unamuno recognized himself to be, even if, according to his testimony, his own diary includes a significant proportion of his meditations. He tells us, in fact, that he would take notes on the ideas that came to him during the day, to record them later in his diary or use them in his writings, which makes him a kind of self-compiler of protocols. Furthermore, his meditations seek support in, and at the same time reflect, the oral and written meditations of other authors, whom he usually quoted when they had activated one of his thoughts.

The aim of the present analysis is first to identify the psychological mechanisms triggered by the invocations in the words of *The Lord's Prayer*. The second goal is to identify those mechanisms of which a subject expert in meditation and self-awareness is conscious. The third goal is to identify the processes and operators involved in these mechanisms. To this end we have distinguished three categories of analysis:

1. *Evolutionary congruence*: basic mechanisms of natural orientation and culturally reconstructed mechanism of orientation (referred to as EC) that permit the passage from the natural function to the mediated higher function.
2. *Operators based on social mediation* (referred to as Social Operators: SO).
3. *Operators based on instrumental mediation* (referred to as Instrumental Operators: IO).

Each statement of *The Lord's Prayer* is accompanied by all the meditations

recorded in Unamuno's *Diario Íntimo* on that same statement. The reader will find the statement from The Lord's Prayer [in square brackets], followed by Unamuno's meditations on it (below and further to the right) and, thirdly, the comments resulting from our analysis, with an indication in brackets of the mechanism or operator considered. We should point out that they do not necessarily follow the order in which they appear in the prayer.

The Lord's Prayer as a Cultural Reconstruction of Orientation

The Lord's Prayer is the Christian prayer par excellence, being, according to the gospels, that which Jesus Christ himself spoke to his disciples when they asked him to teach them how to pray. The most well-known and complete version is the one that appears in the Gospel of St Matthew (Matthew 6, 9–13). The words Unamuno used in Spanish[12] are those from the traditional version, which in English correspond to those of the King James Bible: "Our Father which art in heaven, Hallowed be thy name, Thy kingdom come, Thy will be done on earth, as it is in heaven. Give us this day our daily bread, and forgive us our debts, as we forgive our debtors. And lead us not into temptation, but deliver us from evil."

Basing ourselves on what we have said up to now and as an introduction to the analysis of a verbal protocol on *The Lord's Prayer* – archetypal *normalized psychotecnics* of Christian prayer – we shall discuss Unamuno's reflections on religious meditation from his *Diario Íntimo* (1986).

Human Species as Human Family

[Our Father]

[. . .] The prayer does not say Our God, *but rather* Our Father. *(Unamuno, 1986, p. 201) [. . .] Father! This is the revelation of Christ, for nowhere in the ancient law does God appear as a father. (op. cit., p. 54) [. . .] this is the living idea of Christianity. God is Father, is love. And he is our Father, not my Father. (op. cit., p. 19)*

Unamuno highlights here that Christianity (the New Testament as opposed to the Old) extends the bio-etho-social mechanism of paternity to all human relations.

From a mediational perspective, considering humankind as a family indeed appears to be a good psychotecnics of thinking and of feeling. The extension of the family metaphor to the conception of gods is a widespread phenomenon in the myths and religions of the majority of cultures – creating man in God's image is the reverse of creating gods in man's image. *The Lord's Prayer's* first invocation activates the family metaphor, to which parables in the Gospels so often refer. This *basic family model* (SO) accompanied by other verbal-conceptual operators (SO: parents, brothers, and sisters) introduces a perceptual mediation in relation to *others*, elevating them above tribal belonging, which permits the consideration of any human being not just in terms of their quality as a member of one's tribe or of another tribe, but as a member of the *gens* community.

Unamuno appeals to one of the universals of the human condition (EC): shared consciousness, especially in maternal and paternal symbiosis. As a verbal instrument (IO), the invocation "Father" is a psychological handle for moving into a "postural set" and expresses an attitude of shared consciousness with a superior symbiotic member: on saying "Father," the person who says it becomes a child; the instrumental mediator evokes the virtual social mediator (IO→SO). Private speech with a virtual Other conceived as a father activates in the adult the same reactions that accompany the family relationship with a father in childhood, and allows the adult to relive the feelings of attachment, submissiveness, respect, love and devotion characteristic of childhood. If we consider development purely as a cognitive advance, the return to earlier (i.e., "inferior") stages of development may appear dysfunctional. However, the case of the directive functions is a different one, since it is in the psychic posture of childhood that the most valuable qualities for activating the shared and socially distributed

mind survive. Having a permanent virtual and omnipresent super-father permits us to maintain that state and activate the reactions and feelings of the child, in adulthood. As the Gospels say: "[...] Except ye be converted and become as little children, ye shall not enter into the kingdom of heaven. Whosoever therefore shall humble himself as this little child, the same is greatest in the kingdom of heaven" (Matthew 18, 2–4).

The Constitution of the Spiritual World

[which art in heaven]

[...] on earth, in the kingdom of reality, as in heaven, in the ideal kingdom. (op. cit., p. 19)

Unamuno equates "heaven" with the world of the mind and of representations, with the world of ideas. In the historical development of religions, which converges with stages in which the earthly world is organized in kingdoms, this becomes the Kingdom of Heaven. In science and technology, instrumental mediations of intellectual and cognitive processes contribute to creating and activating the representational space of consciousness and invisible conceptions and theories, giving it existential entity; religious mediations do the same in the sphere of sentimental and directive processes: from the religious perspective, "heaven" is the perceptual opposite of the earth, the world of representational consciousness as against that of presentational perception.

The "Kingdom of Heaven" could well be, therefore, as Unamuno suggests, a focusing towards the world of our consciousness. In psychological terms, it involves adding, to the visual field or natural presentational scenario, the "field of time" (as Vygotsky would say), which extends the former and at the same time transcends it (EC). The invocation in *The Lord's Prayer* of *which art in heaven* (IO) thus activates the new representational field of consciousness – the internal representational model – as a framework from which to consider the direct and real, presentational world. In relation to inducing self-awareness and meta-consciousness, the idea that it is easier to behold our deepest self through the eyes of God than through our own eyes highlights the importance of recourse to an omnipresent virtual Other (SO) whom we could not deceive. Profound faith permits this mediational mechanism to act with all its power, preparing the psyche for renouncing the defensive rationalizations so commonly examined by psychoanalysts.

In physical religious spaces the *mise-en-scène* focuses the eyes – and through them the consciousness – towards that interior space through external correlates, such as stained glass windows or altarpieces. The architecture and art of religious spaces constitute highly refined mediational complexes (IO) which provide spiritual, representational, processes with presentational anchors.

Moral Directivity: Between Reasoning and Feelings

[but deliver us from evil]

It is not the same to do good as it is to be good. It is not enough to do good, one must be good. [...] The morality of the world is concerned only with the act, not the agent; [...] With civilization, evil spreads, becomes scattered, it is spilt in small doses through each little act. [...] There are fewer murders, but more looks of contempt and malice, more words of scorn, more expressions of arrogance. [...] It is better to be good even if you occasionally do bad things, than to be bad and do good, apparent good. (op. cit., pp. 92–95) [...] God hates the sin and loves the sinner; man loves the sin and hates the sinner, takes advantage of the crime and condemns the criminal. (op. cit., p. 137)

The distinction between sin and sinner to which Unamuno refers is an essential one: mediational efforts are addressed to making visible not "the evil one," but rather, "evil" *per se*. And the other distinction he makes is between the evil act and evil itself, between a *pragmatic* view of evil that reduces it to the judgment of acts, and a *socio-sentimental* view, which is what he actually refers to

as religious. Unamuno does not find virtue in good external actions if they are not the expression of internal goodness; nor does he find evil acts so condemnable if they are not accompanied by internal badness. This is a perspective that tends more towards constructing what is human on the basis of the universal of prosociality (EC), than on the basis of the universal of pragmatic action. Habermas (1983) postulated a convergent idea on expressing his doubts about whether moral development reduced to mere ethical rationality – moral judgment à la Piaget-Köhlberg – actually makes possible *moral conduct*, or *doing good*.

This approach places greater emphasis on the psycho-functional development of goodness (constructing good people) than on rational knowledge and instrumental control of correct behavior. In terms of human development, it is much more important that the person acquire virtues, sentiments for doing moral actions than cognitive skills for making moral judgments. This is how things have been understood by religions, which "scenify" and emphasize the prescription of "correct behavior" through situated and narrative symbolic dramatizations, more than through the fostering of a supposed normative, pragmatic, or rational capacity.

The psychological orientation towards goodness is activated by the invocation *but deliver us from evil* (IO), moving the mind towards the activation of thinking+feeling in relation to goodness and badness, and not towards the act or agent (the evil act, the evil person).

[Thy kingdom come]

When has any Protestant attained the freedom of the Catholic mystics? They fall into either the slavery of the letter or the nihilism of reason. (op. cit., p. 53)

Unamuno once more juxtaposes rational truth and existential truth: The kingdom of God entails the sharing of human feelings, rather than mere adherence to a rational prescription.

And he points once again to an idea that seems to evoke the two kinds of mediation characteristic of the human species conceptualized by the cultural-genetic approach: social mediation – based on natural orientation to others – and instrumental mediation – based on natural orientation to objects (EC).

> [...] to ask for it is to ask for death, since only through death shall we achieve it. (op. cit., p. 184)

Asking for the Kingdom of Heaven to come equates in the Christian view, as Unamuno suggests here, to asking for death. Indeed, the death-consciousness contrast pervaded Unamuno's religious and existential thought throughout his life. Only departure from this world or material realm that confuses our ideas will permit the other kingdom to impose itself. The new representational world of consciousness (EC) that was evoked with the *which art in Heaven* appears, once again, through the *kingdom come* (IO). Unamuno felt the essential contradiction in mystical thinking, which considers life as a passage to and a preparation for the authentic life that comes after death. There is a profound longing for the world of the spirit, and this longing finds its way out in the model of life as drama and as a dream – expressed in Calderón's *La vida es sueño* ("Life is a Dream," 1635/1992): life as a play that prefigures other realities and as a dream from which we have to wake. Through the eyes of religious faith, the visible, real world loses legitimacy to the invisible world of the spirit.

> [Thy will be done on earth, as it is in heaven]
>
> The entire value of the prayer is wrapped up in this request. We ask God for what in any case has to be, that his will be done. (op. cit., p. 211) [...] Thy will be done! From here we move to human omnipotence, the ability to do everything we want [...]. (op. cit., p. 99)

The acceptance of our fate as one that is well-intentioned and good, decided by the Father and with an inevitable happy ending, constitutes a powerful mechanism for substituting the other type of submission to reality: the instinctive mandate in the species (EC). This acceptance of reality so patent in the animal thus meets religious belief. We are able to accept any reality that presents itself thanks to a new ascetic and conscious route: that of total detachment or absolute surrender to "the arms of God," as the Spanish mystic Santa Teresa wrote; when we reach this point all is perfect, all is fine. The Buddhist quest for perfection pursues a different aim, but is similar in its psychological mechanism. In the mystic state of abandon, rather than guessing previously what has to be done (as in mechanisms of mediation through the magic of oracles, sortilege, or omens), anything that occurs is accepted *a posteriori*, and even *a priori*, as good, as the will of God, from the religious narrative.

First, the individual is liberated from social dependence through a supra-dependence. On using a virtual super-other (SO), the real "others" lose strength. Unamuno follows the path of this virtual social supra-mediation to achieve individual autonomy.

And second, Christianity, especially the form which follows the mystic path of San Juan de la Cruz and Santa Teresa, seeks detachment from the world – and with it the acceptance of any situation – through the extreme tightening of emotional bonds, complete fusion, abandoning oneself with love into the arms of God. It is perhaps here that we find the most distinctive feature of Christian mysticism with respect to other religious paths which, equally expert in the development of directive consciousness, consider ascetic perfection to lie in the total elimination of any trace of emotional attachment.

Postural and Situated Operators: Verbal Anchoring of Presences and the Ecological Cementation of Intentions

> [Hallowed be thy name]
>
> Let praises be sung only of Thee, and let all things refer to Thee [...]. (op. cit., p. 19)

In animist thinking, the word is to some extent the thing, or can act magically on the thing. If we mention an unfortunate event, we can provoke it. If we invoke something, we cause it. Offending the name – in speech or in writing – of family members – father, mother – or of gods or saints has a similar importance for religious thinking. Through the physical presence of objectual operators, the human being acts on virtual presences by means of the laws of animal presentational behavior (EC).

Acceptance of the pre-eminence of the name of God, like other acts of verbal animism ("giving one's word," promising, swearing, cursing (mal-e-*diction*), blessing (bene-*diction*), and so on), attempts to link, in an animistic way, verbal and present actions (and their object, the word) with mental actions, actions on the plane of the soul. Furthermore, the verbal invocation of God's name is accompanied by an ethological ritual of submission to a pre-eminent Other (EC). In order to guarantee the psychological posture before God, the pre-eminence of the instrumental operator that leads to God has to be ensured (IO→SO).

The invocation "hallowed be thy name" works here as a verbal handle (IO+SO) for this attitude. In general, religious rites of adoration and other fervent acts of praise associated with them would cover the same function, either verbally or through etho-motor posture and gestures that cultivate *internal postures.*

[And lead us not into temptation]

Let us not trust our own strength, for he who loves danger dies in it. (op. cit., p. 20)

The concept of temptation and the effort to extricate oneself from it expresses the conflict between the demands of the pre-sentational natural and instinctive world and those of the culturally reconstructed world of consciousness. Here, human extension of the natural functions becomes conflic-tive and painful; the substitution of instincts by new directive mechanisms is difficult, because the former are still effective and the latter only attempt to become so (EC).

Religious directivity exerts pressure and demands the materialization of intentions and goodwill. In Christian thinking, mental (or "spiritual") actions are considered as real, but at the same time, it is understood that if one does not possess the will to convert good decisions into action, one is not vir-tuous. It is accepted that consciousness, in order to be good, must be effective (ideo-*motor*), voluntary, executive; that is, that the decisions of the kingdom of heaven (of the plane of consciousness) must be effec-tive in the earthly realm (the presentational plane) and the religious mode (of "grace") must thus be effectively capable of sub-stituting the non-religious or animal mode (of sin).

But, as we said above, quoting Spinoza via Vygotsky, the problem of decision is to remember decisions and execute them; and it is therefore the external mediations designed for achieving decision that consti-tute the cultural architecture of the higher function of voluntary behavior. The disem-bodied, purely spiritual view of religious moral decision tends to neglect the ecologi-cal body of the soul (its mediated operational architecture). A similar oversight occurs in some of the more abstract models of execu-tive action.

Christian thinking is in this respect clearly contradictory. Despite the fact that Chris-tianity makes theologically responsible the soul and its internal powers (the will), Chris-tian ascetic thinking has nevertheless devel-oped a potent architecture of external cul-tural mechanisms (of everyday rituals in civil and religious life) for externally scaffold-ing internal directive processes, whose study would require a complete cultural ecology (IO, SO). And the orientations of saints and doctors commonly express the same idea ("keep order and order shall keep you", said St. Augustine).

Religious Catharsis

[Give us this day our daily bread]

[. . .] for the bread of God is he which cometh down from heaven, and giveth life unto the world . . . I am the bread of life . . . (John 6, 33, 35) (op. cit., p. 178)

Equating Christ with bread (Eucharist) implies a fusion of the mediational mechanisms of animism (objectual magical action). The Eucharist constitutes an exceptionally powerful cultural construction of catharsis, and one of the best examples of psychotechnics of feeling. This is due to the fact that it brings together the two principal directive mental features that distinguish the functional system of the species at its "natural" level – its social orientation and its orientation to objects (EC). The two dimensions, social and objectual, are mediated by the same operator – the consecrated bread/body of Christ – which, so to speak, merges the social mediation and the instrumental mediation (SO+IO).

[forgive us]

Everything that can be said against auricular confession by those who are most opposed to it and most deeply repelled by it I have already said myself, and still repeat, but I still feel myself drawn to the confessional. It strikes me that the more superstitious I find it, the more it attracts me. Yes, because the more superstitious and vulgar and fetishistic, the more humiliation to be found in submission to it, the greater is the humility in accepting it. (op. cit., p. 140)

Penitence and forgiveness (the sentiment of reconciliation and of being forgiven implied in the invocation *"forgive us"*) are basic processes in religious behavior that culturally extend a natural social ethogram (EC). The state of psychological maladjustment of the new human consciousness, of discontentment with one's own psyche or mental state – at either the individual or collective level – seeks and designs socio-cultural mechanisms of *purification* and catharsis for the recovery of homeostasis. It might be said, in accordance with the socio-genetic thesis based on the inherited social psyche, that individual homeostasis in the human being is a social homeostasis: recovering compliance with one's own consciousness is equivalent to recovering compliance with others (EC). It should also be stressed that the reflexological architecture of forgetting (in this case of forgiveness from social guilt) occurs not through the "erasure" of connections, but rather through their de-hierarchization – they are subjected to new connections that restructure them and change their value. In the logic of mediation, this implies that instead of erasure, humans resort to rituals that "overwrite" the guilt or rewrite it, producing the erasure, not through elimination, but as the *effect of a mediation* of the guilt (guilt+forgiveness) – which confers on it a new meaning (IO). The new structure becomes more powerful than the previous guilt by means of rites for inducing cognitive-sentimental catharsis that are present in all cultures (such as the ritual of "burning" at some point of the year all the sins accumulated in the past twelve months).

It is for this reason that Unamuno argues that the state of purification after passing through sin is more human than was the state of grace prior to sin (op. cit., p. 80). The mediational architecture permits an understanding of the reasons for this reflection on the state of discontentment towards oneself or on reconciliation with oneself, which Unamuno carries out from within Christian faith. It is, moreover, this instrumental-social purification mechanism that permits consciousness to perceive and re-present to itself the state of psychological unease (impurity) and well-being (purity), as well as re-presenting the sense of the ritual itself addressed to the recovery of the previous state (purification). The ritual of auricular confession which is the subject of Unamuno's meditation accentuates socially (SO) and instrumentally (IO) the invariants of the process of expiation, of humiliation.

The profound involvement of religion and theatre in purification rites in Indo-European cultures (Hindu and Greek, for example) expresses an apparently paradoxical mental phenomenon: that the mechanism of accentuating the fall constitutes a necessary ritual for purification as the path to a deeper state of purity (sentimental homeostasis). In this line, in the Catholic Christian perspective, forgiveness not only permits the purification for returning, so to speak, to a state of repaired goodness, imperfect goodness, a necessary evil for rubbing out sin, but gives access to a deeper perception of the state of "purity": access to "grace." There thus emerges the paradox that, although without sin forgiveness is unnecessary, without forgiveness grace does not seem to be accessible psychologically.[13] Hence, the Christian view establishes original sin to ensure that this basic mental state of sinner is present in all human beings; such a functional relationship between purity and impurity, grace and sin was indeed deeply rooted in the religious thinking of Spain's *Golden Age*. In contrast to an illusory and perhaps non-human vindication of a life totally free from mistakes or defects, the saying "from great sinners, great saints" would express this mental experience that only sin allows us to truly value "grace." In this view, it would be the error-correction mechanism itself that makes perceptible the process of approaching (more than reaching) truth, which remains always as a dynamic and interactive process, a cybernetic process more akin to biology than to logic. In the Vygotskyan instrumental mediational perspective, it is also the operation with instrumental operators that permits us to perceive and experience the operation and its mental product. Adding or multiplying are made apparent only when operating with the abacus or the multiplication table.

Conclusion

In this chapter we have attempted to explore from cultural-genetic psychology a path towards a type of psychological phenomenon – such as prayer – that has up to now been hidden behind a "veil of mystery," to use Vygotsky's expression from his analysis of *Hamlet* (1971). We trust that this will help at least somehow to bring back into the fold of Psychology those processes we refer to here as directive functions, even more characteristic of the human condition and the "higher mind," than the cognitive or intellectual functions, as Vygotsky (1931/1983/1995), and Lewin (1926) before him noted.

Acknowledgments

We should like to express our thanks to Alberto Rosa for his comments on the draft. Thanks also to our translator David Weston, for his efforts to maintain the quality of the text in spite of the ambiguities in the original.

Notes

1   Gallup polls (1987) have shown an increase in percentages of people who report: mystical experiences (from 35% in 1973 to 43% in 1986), contact with the dead (from 27% in 1973 to 42% in 1986), ESP (from 58% in 1973 to 67% in 1986), visions (from 8% in 1973 to 29% in 1986), and other unusual experiences. Clinically, the figures are lower: in a survey, psychologists reported that 4.5% of their clients over the past 12 months brought a mystical experience into therapy (Allman et al., 1992, quoted by Lukoff, 1998): "Cases where a focus of therapy involves a religious or spiritual problem are not very easy to find. A systematic analysis of case reports involving religious or spiritual issues in the Medline bibliographic database from 1980–1996 located only 364 abstracts which addressed religious or spiritual issues in health care. This was from a database containing 4,306,906 records from this period (Glazer, National Library of Medicine, personal communication, May 1997), indicating that a shockingly low .008% of published articles in the major medical health care database address religious and spiritual issues (. . .). These figures are probably more indicative of the types of problems that mental health professionals like to write about."

2   "The task of psychology is to study the reactions of the personality, i.e., relations of the type dream = regulatory mechanism. The role of religion, etc. Every (social) ideology is matched by a psychological structure of a specific type – but in the sense of subjective perception and vehicle of ideology, in the sense of the construction of strata, layers, and functions of the individual person. Cf. Kaffir, Catholic, worker, peasant. Cf. my ideas – [relationship] of a structure of interests to the social regulation of behavior. Cf. [A blank space is left here in the manuscript. There are

four question marks in the margin.] (Vygotsky, 1989, p. 65)

3 "As a logical consequence of admitting into the system of psychological categories the use of signs as being of decisive importance to the history of the development of higher mental functions, external symbolic forms of activity such as verbal communication, reading, writing, counting, and drawing are also involved. These processes have traditionally been considered as auxiliary with respect to internal mental processes, and separate from them, but from the perspective we have outlined they are admitted into the system of higher mental functions as equivalent to all other higher mental processes." (Vygotsky, 1930/1984/1999, p. 37)

4 The concept of psychotecnics was at the time of Vygotsky related to the technics of evaluation of psychological functions (as today is mostly used and understood) but also to the psychological *external* technics used to perform the tasks involved in measuring those functions, such as tokens or signs for mnemotechnics. In tune with his own theory on the mediational role of instruments and social others in the development of functions, Vygotsky talked about *psychotechnics of intellect* to refer to the mediational processes involved in acquiring and internalizing cognitive functions, and *psychotechnics of feeling* to refer to the mediational processes involved in acquiring and internalizing directive functions.

5 "We can do nothing in relation to our soul," said Spinoza, "if we do not remember it". Indeed, the decisive role of memory in research on intentions indicates the extent to which they are always linked to a given memory apparatus which must subsequently put them into practice" (Vygotsky, 1931/1983/1995, p. 262).

6 Personality has been approached in Psychology related to global archetypes, such as temperament (more of hereditary and physiological nature) and character (more linked to experience and to education). *Talante* is a term for describing character in a more social and *situated personality* manner. Philosophy's concepts such as the *self and its circumstances* (Ortega) or the *being here* – Dassein – (Heidegger) echo the biofunctionalist organism-medium cibernetic relation, and would be closely related to the postural personality – the tonic and movement organic founda-

tion supporting mental functions (Wallon, Damasio).

7 The monastery of Santa Catalina in Arequipa, Peru, is an example within the Catholic religion – one among many religions and many historical stages – of such organization: houses, streets, squares, and all the facilities of earthly life (washhouse, workshops, kitchens) are within the confines of the cloister, a veritable fortress of the Kingdom of Heaven, in which the residents, some of whom were born there, spent their whole life in the ante-room of what they expected would be the definitive Kingdom of Heaven.

8 Lutz, Greischar, Rawlings, Ricard, and Davidson (2004) have demonstrated that long-term Buddhist practitioners self-induce sustained electroencephalographic high-amplitude gamma-band oscillations and phase-synchrony during meditation. These data suggest that mental training involves temporal integrative mechanisms and may induce short-term and long-term neural changes. This research has important implications for the cultural-genetic perspective, and supports Vygotsky and Luria's thesis on brain neoformations as an effect of the development of cultural forms of behavior. According to the strong Vygotskyan interpretation of the concept of function, we would be talking here about a higher psychological function due to a cultural fact (religion).

9 Miguel de Unamuno spent his childhood and youth in his native city of Bilbao. The rest of his life was spent in Castile – first Madrid, where he took his degree, and then in Salamanca. He became Professor of Greek at Salamanca and served as Rector of the University from 1901 – with a break of six years due to his being exiled as an opponent of the military dictatorship of Primo de Rivera during the reign of Alfonso XIII – until his death in 1936, the year the Spanish Civil War broke out. Despite the fact that he was not a philosopher in the strict sense of the term – he did not bequeath a "closed" system, and in was in fact mistrustful of the concept – all Unamuno's work is pervaded by philosophical reflection, with strong existentialist and tragic overtones (indeed, one of his works his entitled "The Tragic Sense of Life") shared by many Spanish intellectuals pertaining to the *Generation of 98* (Álvarez y del Río, 1999).

10 Unamuno's search is contradictory but authentic and painful. It starts out from a

deep skepticism (*skepsis* as search), expressed in phrases such as "Dreams give us faith, death gives us science," but also from the awareness that research into the human condition involves dealing with the unexplained void that is the meaning of life. He contemplates religion from philosophy and psychology, but also lives it profoundly, striving to practice his motto for the human being – *think high, feel deep*: "It seems incredible that I should write these things and then rebel against them. Am I not sincere when I write them? Or am I not sincere when I rebel against them? Or is it that in me there are two I's, one who writes these lines and another who rejects them as delirium?" (1986, pp. 138–139). More than seeking a compromise in an intermediate point, Unamuno appears to force the extremes of religion and his own conflict: "This is enough to drive anyone mad. Sometimes a diabolical idea comes to me, and it is to consider this whole crisis, all this call of grace, as a psychological experiment, as self-experimentation, and to tell the story of a conversion. Isn't that the same as committing a crime so as to describe the criminal state of mind, or becoming an alcoholic to describe alcoholism?" (op. cit., pp. 153–154). "Be careful not to get carried away by a sinful curiosity, a spiritual lust for new emotions" (op. cit., p. 91). Unamuno is quite guarded about emotional sensations and experiences as relevant to religious experience, and he discards them as superficial to true religious feeling. Unamuno's search is contradictory but authentic and painful. It starts out from a deep skepticism (*skepsis* as search), expressed in phrases such as "Dreams give us faith, death gives us science," but also from the awareness that research into the human condition involves dealing with the unexplained void that is the meaning of life. He contemplates religion from philosophy and psychology, but also lives it profoundly, striving to practice his motto for the human being – *think high, feel deep*: "It seems incredible that I should write these things and then rebel against them. Am I not sincere when I write them? Or am I not sincere when I rebel against them? Or is it that in me there are two I's, one who writes these lines and another who rejects them as delirium?" (1986, pp. 138–139). More than seeking a compromise in an intermediate point, Unamuno appears to force the extremes of

religion and his own conflict: "This is enough to drive anyone mad. Sometimes a diabolical idea comes to me, and it is to consider this whole crisis, all this call of grace, as a psychological experiment, as self-experimentation, and to tell the story of a conversion. Isn't that the same as committing a crime so as to describe the criminal state of mind, or becoming an alcoholic to describe alcoholism?" (op. cit., pp. 153–154). "Be careful not to get carried away by a sinful curiosity, a spiritual lust for new emotions" (op. cit., p. 91). Unamuno is quite guarded about emotional sensations and experiences as relevant to religious experience, and he discards them as superficial to true religious feeling.

11 When asked about his religious position (What religion are you?), he declared himself incapable of replying, and scarcely of clarifying the question a little. Two verses from one of his sonnets (The Atheist's Prayer), however, might be seen as summarizing his stance: "Hear my prayer Thou, God who does not exist […] Inexistent God, for if you should exist, I would also truly exist."

12 "Padre nuestro que estás en los cielos, santificado sea el tu nombre, venga a nos el tu reino, hágase tu voluntad así en la tierra como en el cielo. El pan nuestro de cada día dánosle hoy, y perdónanos nuestras deudas, así como nosotros perdonamos a nuestros deudores y no nos dejes caer en la tentación, más líbranos del mal."

13 A similar paradox can be found in the argument of Roger Shank (1982), who defined truth as an error corrected enough times: truth is more the process than the product. Attaining directive "truth" requires, as in the case of cognitive "truth," a "process" approach, rather than a "product" approach. The rite of expiation leads not simply to a recovery of the badly repaired "broken vase," but to the sight, for the first time and thanks to this rite, of the Other and oneself in another, deeper state of consciousness.

Acknowledgments

We should like to express our thanks to Alberto Rosa for his comments on the draft. Thanks also to our translator David Weston, for his efforts to maintain the quality of the text in spite of the ambiguities in the original.

References

Acosta, J. de. (1572/1962). *Historia natural y moral de las indias* (2nd Ed.). México: Fondo de Cultura Económica.

Álvarez, A., & del Río, P. (1999). Cultural mind and cultural identity: Projects for life in body and spirit. In S. Chaiklin, M. Hedegaard, & U. J. Jensen (Eds.), *Activity Theory and Social Practice: Cultural-Historical Approaches* (pp. 302–324). Aarhus: Aarhus University Press.

Álvarez, A., del Río, P., & Guerrero, F. (1979). *La vida en el Barrio*. Sevilla: Prosevilla.

Bakhtin, M. (1986). *Speech genres and other late essays*. Austin: University of Texas Press.

Calderón de la Barca, P. (1635/1992). *La vida es sueño*. Madrid: Club Internacional del Libro.

Damasio, A. R. (1999). *The feeling of what happens: Body and emotion in the making of consciousness*. New York: Harcourt Brace.

Davidov, V. V., & Andronov, V. P. (1979). Origen de las acciones ideales: condiciones psicológicas de las mismas. *Infancia y Aprendizaje, 10*, 21–36.

del Río, P. (1987). *El desarrollo de las competencias espaciales: el proceso de construcción de los instrumentos mentales*. Unpublished doctoral dissertation, Universidad Complutense de Madrid.

del Río, P. (1990). La Zona de Desarrollo Próximo y la Zona Sincrética de Representación: El espacio instrumental de la acción social. *Infancia y Aprendizaje, 51–52*, 191–244.

del Río, P. (1997). Signos para la razón, signos para la emoción: pistas para el análisis cultural de protocolos. *Comunicación y Cultura, 1–2*, 85–118.

del Río, P. (2002). The external brain: Ecocultural roots of distancing and mediation. *Culture and Psychology, 8*(2), 233–265.

del Río, P. (2004). El arte es a la vida como el vino es a la uva. El papel del arte en la educación a la luz de la genética cultural. *Cultura y Educación, 16*(1–2), 43–64.

del Río, P. (2005). De bestias, personas y máquinas. Riesgo e incongruencia en el desarrollo humano. Invited address. *IV Jornadas de Desarrollo Humano y Educación*, Alcalá de Henares, 6–9 September.

del Río, P., & Álvarez, A. (1993). *Programas infantiles de televisión: Analisis de líneas actuales y diseño estratégico de alternativas*. Unpublished Research Report. Departamento de Estudios de TVE.

del Río, P., & Álvarez, A. (1995a). Directivity: The cultural and educational construction of morality and agency. Some questions arising from the legacy of L. S. Vygotsky. *Anthropology and Education Quarterly, 26*(4), 384–409.

del Río, P., & Álvarez, A. (1995b). Tossing, praying and reasoning: The changing architectures of mind and agency. In J. V. Wertsch, P. del Río, & A. Álvarez (Eds.), *Sociocultural studies of mind* (pp. 215–247). Cambridge, MA: Cambridge University Press.

del Río, P., & Álvarez, A. (1999). La puesta en escena de la realidad cultural. Una aproximación histórico cultural al problema de la etnografía audiovisual. *Revista de Antropología Social, 8*, 121–136.

del Río, P., & Álvarez, A. (in press-a). Inside and outside the *Zone of Proximal Development*. An eco-functional reading of Vygotsky. In H. Daniels, M. Cole & J. V. Wertsch (Eds.), *The Cambridge Companion to Vygotsky*. Cambridge, MA: Cambridge University Press.

del Río, P., & Álvarez, A. (Eds.) (in press-b). *Escritos sobre arte y educación creativa de Lev S. Vygotsky*. Madrid: Fundación Infancia y Aprendizaje.

del Río, P., Álvarez, A., & del Río, M. (2004). *Pigmalión. Informe sobre el impacto de la televisión en la infancia*. Madrid: Fundación Infancia y Aprendizaje/MEC.

del Río, P., & Fuertes, M. (2004). ¡Cámara! ¡Acción! Un análisis de la confrontación de la tipología industrial y la tipología dramática en el proceso de construcción de la realidad por el cine. *Cultura y Educación, 16*(1–2), 203–222.

Dennett, D. C. (1998). *Brainchildren: Essays on designing minds*. Cambridge, MA: MIT Press.

Durkheim, E. (2003). *Les formes élémentaires de la vie religieuse*. Paris: Presses Universitaires de France.

Elias, N. (1978). *The Civilizing Process. The History of Manners, Vol I.* (E. Jephcott, trans.). Oxford, Blackwell/New York: Urizen Books.

Erickson, K. A., & Simon, H. A. (1980). Verbal reports as data. *Psychological Review, 87*, 215–251.

Erickson, K. A., & Simon, H. A. (1984). *Protocol analysis. Verbal reports as data*. Cambridge, MA: Bradford Books/MIT Press.

Erickson, K. A., & Simon, H. A. (1998). How to study thinking in everyday life: Contrasting think-aloud protocols with descriptions and explanations of thinking. *Mind, Culture & Activity, 5*(3), 178–186.

Febvre, L. (1953). *Combats pour l'histoire*, Paris: Armand Colin.

Foucault, M. (1969). *L'Archéologie du savoir*. Paris: Gallimard.

Fuertes, M., & del Río, P. (2004). El viento se llevó lo qué. Un análisis de la creación cultural y la construcción narrativa en el cine. *Cultura y Educación*, 16(1–2), 181–201.

Galperin, P. Ia. (1976). *Vredenie v Psijologuiv*. Moscow: Moscow University.

Galperin, P. Ia. (1992a). Linguistic consciousness and some questions of the relationship between language and thought. *Journal of Russian and East European Psychology*, 30 (4), 81–92.

Galperin, P. Ia. (1992b). Stage-by stage formation as a method of psychological investigation. *Journal of Russian and East European Psychology*, 30 (4), 60–80.

Greeley, A. (1987). Mysticism goes mainstream. *American Health*, (January/February), 47–49.

Griffin, R., & Baron-Cohen, S. (2002). The intentional stance: Developmental and neurocognitive perspectives. In A. Brook, & D. Ross (Eds.), *Daniel Dennett: Contemporary Philosophy in Focus* (pp. 83–116). Cambridge, UK: Cambridge University Press.

Habermas, J. (1983). *Moralbewusstein und Kommunikatives Handeln*. Frankfurt am Main: Suhrkamp.

Hood, R. W. (1975). The construction and preliminary validation of a measure of reported mystical experience. *Journal for the Scientific Study of Religion*, 14, 29–41.

Huston, A. C., & Wright, J. C. (1998). Mass media and children's development. In I. Sigel, & K. Renninger (Eds.), *Handbook of child psychology: Vol 4. Child psychology in practice* (pp. 999–1058). New York: John Wiley and Sons.

Hutchins, E. (1996). *Cognition in the wild*. Cambridge, MA: Harvard University Press.

James, W. (1890). *Principles of psychology*. New York: Henry Holt.

James, W. (1902). *The varieties of religious experience*. New York: Longmans, Green.

Lewin, K. (1926). Vorbemenkungen über die psychische Kräfte und Energien und über die Struktur der Seele. *Psychologische Forschung*, 7, 294–329.

López Aranguren, J. L. (1994). *Obras Completas, Vol I: Filosofía y Religión*. Madrid: Trotta.

Lotman, Y. M. (1990). *Universe of the mind. A semiotic theory of the culture*. London & New York: I. B. Tauris.

Lukoff, D. (1985). The diagnosis of mystical experience with psychotic features. *Journal of Transpersonal Psychology*, 17, 155–181.

Lukoff, D. (1998). From spiritual emergency to spiritual problem: The transpersonal roots of the new DSM-IV category. *Journal of Humanistic Psychology*, 38(2), 21–50.

Luria, A. R. (1966). *Higher cortical function in man*. New York: Basic Books.

Luria, A. R. (1972/2002). Language and organization of psychological processes. Lecture in the Department of Psychology, Moscow State University, 13th December, 1972. In K. Kashirskaya (Ed.), & M. Cole (Trans.), *A memorial Disk for A. R. Luria's 100th Anniversary of the Birth*. CDRom. The Fith Congress ISCRAT. Amsterdam, 2002.

Luria, A. R. (1973). The frontal lobes and the regulation of behavior. In K. H. Pribram, & A. R. Luria (Eds.). *Psychophysiology of the frontal lobes* (pp. 3–26). New York: Academic Press.

Luria, A. R. (1978). Investigaciones sobre la acción consciente en la primera infancia. *Infancia y Aprendizaje*, 1, 24–28.

Luria, A. R. (1979). *Iazik i Soznanie* (Language and consciousness). Moscow: Moscow State University.

Lutz, A., Greischar, L. L., Rawling, N. B., Ricard, M., & Davidson, R. J. (2004). Long-term meditators self-induce high-amplitude gamma synchrony during mental practice. *PNAS*, 101 (46), 16369–16373.

McCullough, M. E., Larson, D. B., Koenig, H. G., & Lerner, R. (1999). The mismeasurement of religion: a systemic review of mortality research. *Mortality*, 4, 83–194.

Moles, A. (1974). *La communication*. Paris: Marabout.

Nikkel, D. (2005). Humanity and Divinity as Radically Embodied. Paper presented at "Science and Religion: Global Perspectives", June 4–8, Philadelphia (www.metanexus.net).

Ornstein, R. E. (1977). *The Psychology of Consciousness*. New York: Harcourt Brace Jovanovich.

Rodrigues, D., & del Río, P. (Eds.) (2000). *The Religious Phenomenon: An interdisciplinary approach*. Madrid: Fundación Infancia y Aprendizaje.

Rodríguez Arocho, W. (2004). Una aproximación al estudio del funcionamiento ejecutivo y el lenguaje en el trastorno por déficit de atención e hiperactividad desde su complejidad. *Revista IRICE*, 18, 51–68.

Sacks, O. (1996). *An Anthropologist on Mars.* New York: Random House.

Shank, R. (1982). *Dynamic memory.* Cambridge, MA: Cambridge University Press.

Smagorinsky, P. (1998). Thinking and Speech and Protocol Analysis. *Mind, Culture & Activity,* 5(3), 157–177.

Unamuno, M. de (1910). *Mi religión y otros ensayos breves.* Madrid: Renacimiento.

Unamuno, M. de (1913). *Del sentimiento trágico de la vida en los hombres y en los pueblos.* Madrid: Renacimiento.

Unamuno, M. de (1933). *San Manuel Bueno, mártir, y tres historias más.* Madrid: Espasa Calpe.

Unamuno, M. de (1986). *Diario íntimo.* Madrid: Alianza.

Unamuno, M. de (1990). *Cómo se hace una novela.* Madrid: Alianza [o.v. 1927].

Valsiner, J. (2002). *Comparative study of human cultural development.* Madrid: Fundación Infancia y Aprendizaje.

Varela, F., Thompson, E., & Rosch, E. (1991). *The embodied mind: Cognitive science and human experience.* Cambridge, MA: MIT Press.

von Uexküll, J. (1909). *Umwelt und Innenwelt der Tiere.* Berlin: J. Springer

Vygotsky, L. S. (1926/1982/1990). Prólogo a la edición rusa del libro de E. Thorndike "Principios de enseñanza basados en la psicología". In A. Álvarez, & P. del Río. (Eds.), *L. S. Vygotsky. Obras Escogidas, Vol. I. Problemas teóricos y metodológicos de la psicología* (pp. 143–162). (Trans. José María Bravo). Madrid: Visor Distribuciones.

Vygotsky, L. S. (1930/1984/1999). Tool and sign in the development of the child. In R. W. Rieber. (Ed.), *The Collected Works of Vygotsky, Vol 6. Scientific Legacy* (pp. 1–68) (Trans. Marie Hall). New York: Kluwer/Plenum.

Vygotsky, L. S. (1931/1983/1995). Historia del desarrollo de las funciones psíquicas superiores. In A. Álvarez, & P. del Río. (Eds.), *L. S. Vygotsky. Obras Escogidas, Vol. III. Problemas teóricos y metodológicos de la psicología* (pp. 9–340). (Trans. Lydia Kuper). Madrid: Visor Distribuciones.

Vygotsky, L. S. (1934/1982/1987). Thinking and Speech. In R. W. Rieber, & A. S. Carton. (Eds.), *The Collected Works of Vygotsky, Vol 1. Problems of General Psychology* (pp. 3–68) (Trans. Norris Minick). New York and London: Plenum.

Vygotsky, L. S. (1971). *The Psychology of Art.* Cambridge, MA: MIT Press.

Vygotsky, L. S. (1980). Fragmento de los apuntes de L. S. Vygotsky para unas conferencias de psicología de los párvulos. In D. B. Elkonin, *Psicología del juego* (pp. 269–276). Madrid: Pablo del Río Editor.

Vygotsky, L. S. (1989). Concrete human psychology. *Soviet Psychology,* 27 (2), 53–77.

Vygotsky, L. S., & Luria, A. (1994). Tool and symbol in child development. In R. van der Veer & J. Valsiner. (Eds.), *The Vygotsky Reader* (pp. 99–176). Oxford, UK: Basil Blackwell.

Wallon, H. (1934). *Les origines du caractère chez l'enfant.* Paris: Presses Universitaires de France.

Wright, J. R. & Huston, A. C. (1995). *Effects of Educational TV Viewing of Lower Income Preschoolers on Academic Skills, School Readiness, and School Adjustment. One to Three Years Later: A Report to Children's Television Workshop.* Austin, TX: Center for Research on the Influence of Television on Children (CRITC).

Wundt, W. (1900–1920). *Völkerpsychologie,* 10 volumes, Leipzig: Kröner-Engelmann.

Zaporozhets, A. V. (1967). *Vospratie i deistvie* (Perception and action). Moscow: Prosveschenie.

Zaporozhets, A. V., Zinchenko, V. P., & Elkonin, D. B. (1964). The development of visual-motor thinking during the preschool age. In A. V. Zaporozhets, & D. B. Elkonin. (Eds.), *The psychology of preschool child* (pp 208–231). Cambridge, MA: MIT Press.

Zinchenko, V. P. (1995). Cultural-historical psychology and the psychological theory of Activity: Retrospect and prospect. In J. V. Wertsch, P. del Río, & A. Álvarez (Eds.). *Sociocultural studies of mind* (pp. 37–55). Cambridge, MA: Cambridge University Press.

CHAPTER 19

"Myself, the Project"

Sociocultural Interpretations of Young Adulthood

Jeanette A. Lawrence and Agnes E. Dodds

"Twenty-one today" has lost much its traditional significance. Many young people experience the responsibilities and privileges of adulthood much earlier, so that a 21st birthday has become a less significant rite of passage than a driver's license or adult Id Card. Contemporary social institutions make different demands on young people, as they address new-found agendas for identifying their adult status (e.g., in terms of education and welfare provision: Davis, 2003; Puyat, 2005).

Young people, nevertheless, are not simply the pawns of changing government and corporate policies. They impose their own agendas on social structures by their cross-national fashions, consumer power, technological skills, and willingness to risk. They jockey between institutions, working to construct a life of their own: a life that expresses their changing aspirations and adjusts to the changing conditions of social life. They know what they are trying to achieve, and are more aware of what it takes to be autonomous than their counterparts of earlier generations (Furstenberg, Rumbat, & Settersten, 2005).

For contemporary researchers, any reasonable account of the exchanges between young adults and their social worlds must be able to track through the multiple levels of change that absorb the attentions and energies of persons and institutions. Since sociocultural theories identify themselves by their explanations of personal phenomena that are at the same time social (Lawrence & Valsiner, 2003), they are obliged to synthesize accounts of changes in social life with accounts of changes in personal, psychological life (see Valsiner & Rosa's introduction to this volume). It is not sufficient to work with parallel social and personal models. Sociocultural psychology needs to address how the social *is and becomes* psychological and how the psychological *is and becomes* social.

As Sawyer (2002) argued so cogently in his critique of sociocultural theories, sociocultural models of personal development falter to the extent that they neglect to incorporate appropriate accounts of social structures. Attempting to explain macro sociological phenomena in terms of the psychology of small groups clearly is in danger of "displacement of scope" (Sawyer, 2002, p. 300). Falmagne (2004, p. 822) makes a similar criticism of the failure of contemporary self theorists to effectively imbed their theorizing in "a broad macro-level systemic model of the social world."

The points made by Sawyer and Falmagne are well taken, and present a salutary note for sociocultural theorists. There is, however, a corollary. Macro-level theories falter to the extent that they do not incorporate models of the processes by which social meanings functionally become psychological. Just as it is not sufficient to project psychological processes onto social structures (Sawyer, 2002), it is not sufficient to assume that social meanings and practices are automatically absorbed into psychological processes (Lawrence & Valsiner, 1993). A sociocultural approach of the "weak" type (Sawyer, 2002, p. 293) that accepts the idea of separate ontologies for personal and social worlds, is obliged to specify how the two entities connect. Taking an alternative, practice-based position adhering to inseparability is faced with justifying its own reductionism and neglect of psychological reality (Sawyer, 2002; Valsiner, 1998).

Although finding appropriate models and methodologies for the dialectical force of macro and micro structures on each other has always plagued developmental psychology (Riegel, 1979), it is particularly hard to deny their distinctiveness, but interconnectedness, when the developing person is an adult rather than a child. Adults are constantly dealing with society in novel ways, seeking to establish and maintain their own identities and places in the world (Shanahan 2000). While researchers may have some limited success in glossing over the dialectical nature of children's personal-social interaction in terms of the processes of acquiring cultural concepts, in the case of adults, it is crucial to account for the conflicting activities of distinct mentalities and wills and the externalized expressions of their intentions (McDougall, 1945/1908).

Treating early adult experience as a historically significant arena for the rapprochement between social and psychological processes, we propose that Beck and Beck-Gernsheim's (2002) sociological theory of *Institutionalized Individualism* appropriately sets the macro scene for a sociocultural account of young adult personal life. They identify the social forces that have emerged in recent history, and demonstrate how these forces demand particular modes of response from people dealing with them. The responses they require are particularly pressing for young people who have to make their way through social structures where the rules of engagement have been changed (Furlong & Cartmel, 1997).

We further propose that Valsiner's (1987, 1989) processes of *mutual constraining* forge a needed bridge from these macro-level social processes to micro-level psychological processes that make sociocultural forces and meanings into effective parts of individualized development. Mutual constraining describes the processes by which the social penetrates the psychological and the processes by which the psychological penetrates the social.

A back-and-forth shuffling of initiating and responding actions contributes to the transformation of both personal and social experiences. To illustrate these dialectic processes of change, we draw on young adults' experiences of late modern social life. The experience of teaching young adults has been for us a rich source of examples of the construction of Do-it-Yourself (DIY) personal life projects that Beck and Beck-Gernsheim (2002) see as the personal response to the demands of life in late modernity. DIY constructions made by individuals, however, take the analysis deeper into institution-by-person encounters in which they are both elicited and expressed. These encounters are always open to action initiated by the person as well as by the institution, with each side trying to move things in their own preferred direction. The living encounter, then, has potential for modifying the institution's position as well as the person's DIY constructions. The outcome is never totally predictable.

Setting the Macro Scene: Social Life in Late Modernity

The historical period starting roughly in the mid twentieth century is described by Giddens (1991) and Beck and Beck-Gernsheim (2002) as "late modernity," in which life is dominated by the global market economy. The labor market shapes the fortunes of individuals at all levels of employment and unemployment, and across urban and rural settings (Herriot & Scott-Jackson, 2002). This market-dominated macro environment imposes many constraints on the experience of young people in particular.

Life is lived globally. Alliances and nations constantly shift in their composition and in the reach of their activities into individual lives. Socio-politically, the global village clutched in the grasp of nationalized powers is the volatile environment that people view daily on television and the internet. For young people, access to globally marketed resources has become a major differentiating factor in how well they live (Chatterjee, Bailey, & Aronoff, 2001; Lansdown, 2004). For instance, internet downloading disseminates the same music for young enthusiasts regardless of nationality, if they have access to it.

Life is detraditionalized. With social institutions in upheaval or meltdown, traditional values, routines, and expectations are severely modified. Western young adults, released from traditional early marriage, for example, have to find their own way of expressing the intensity of their intimate relationships. If they chose marriage, a young couple has to devise its own ceremonies. Where, in what clothes, by whom, with what kinds of vows are among the choices to be made with prolonged anxiety. If they chose not to marry while still committing to a long-term partner, they need some way to express that commitment: some non-traditional statement that nevertheless marks the passage. Their public statement often takes the form of a joint rental contract, housing loan or purchase of a puppy. These statements are used in place of the outcomes of formal marriage.

Life is uncertain. With the breakdown of traditional means of defining one's life and knowing one's place, young people have to find their way through experiences for which they have few if any authoritative guidelines. Previously stable structures are in flux and do not, for example, supply bridges for the transition from child to adult services (Davis, 2003). Even the high achieving university student debating with academics on Wednesday, on Friday becomes the casual server turning up on time, wondering whether her services will be required that day.

In the world of employment specifically, many forms of work previously open to young people are no longer available to those not possessing an academic edge. Graduates with basic degrees find that government departments outsource middle-level work. Less qualified young people find that unskilled jobs have dried up or gone offshore to cheaper labor forces. Work has become a precious commodity. In Australia, gaining stable employment takes up to two years of casual labor for many young people to achieve (Teese, 2005). In Sri Lanka, the drive to increase educational levels for young people raised the number of tertiary graduates from 2% in 1953 to 21% in 1997. The fallout is massive pressure on the labor market, because work aspirations that rise with the qualifications do not match the type of work available for the young (Hettige, 2005).

Life demands choice. With a particular focus on the social dislocation forced by the marketplace economy, Beck and Beck-Gernsheim's (2002) analysis places at the centre of social life, the choices each individual is forced to make when dealing with institutions. It is not simply that there are fewer resources to go around, or that there are fewer opportunities. The means of access to jobs, along with the means of accessing welfare support are firmly closed to all but individuals. Collectives find little tolerance in this marketplace (Ferguson, 2001). If the person aspires to the commodities and opportunities on offer, s/he is compelled to act personally (to enlist, to join, to buy).

In Australia, a traditionally socialist society, the government has recently formalized individual choice into a system of industrial relations replacing unionized negotiation by individualized contracts. The system is explicitly designed to reduce the power of the collective and to ensure that pay and conditions are negotiated by the individual and the employer. Here the pressure falls on the young and inexperienced.

Successful entry to the workforce are so endemic to adult life, that Dwyer and Wyn (2001) interpret its achievement as stretching adulthood downward into the earlier teen years, because independent choice is a major marker of being adult. At the same time, prolonged educational and economic constrictions mean that more young adults are financially dependent on their families for longer, stretching adolescence and emerging adulthood upward well into the thirties (Arnett, 2004).

Living is paradoxical. The person moves between institutions, filling in forms and attending to regulations that are constantly being reviewed and updated. S/he is forced to deal with each department or company as a single decision-making unit, disconnected from other people, and assumed to be disconnected from the person expected to appear at the next institution.

> *In developed modernity – to be quite blunt about it – human mutuality and community rest no longer on solidly established traditions, but, rather, on a paradoxical collectivity of reciprocal individualization. (Beck, 2002, p. xxi)*

Part of this paradoxical twist resides in the interdependence of young people and social institutions. We add that the paradox is deeper, because social institutions also are liable to change when the person is reciprocally agentic. While government and commercial organizations may seem disinterested in people's needs and desires, they are not the impregnable fortresses they appear. Their defined boundaries, once tested, show their substance to be more like plastic than barbed wire. A knowing consumer, potential employee, or student may petition for a range of compensations and special concessions. Furthermore, in the deregulated market economy, s/he may get them. The opportunities of the social system can release individualized creativity that may also bring about radical systemic change. Beck and Beck-Gernsheim interpret this as a positive sign of social restructuring and renewal.

Within such fluid and volatile social structures, the person has to stand at the center of social action, and also at the centre of his or her own uncertainty. Choice is a part of everyday life. Effectively this means that the routes through social institutions are full of challenges and possibilities to be taken up and used. For the novice adult, in particular, the choices may seem endless, and the constructive effort required to push out the boundaries dependent on resolve and action. As one student, Sophie commented about her future prospects, "I need excellent marks to get into the desired area of practice (i.e., successful job), but I'm not motivated enough to study to achieve those marks. I can't become highly motivated because I feel so lost and out of control – work and study, and friends all holding me back, keeping me in the same place."

Sophie understood that any achievements were dependent on her own efforts, but she simply could not make the move. The juxtaposition of challenge and threat produced inertia.

Institutionalized Individualism

The processes of creating an identity and a personal place in social institutions: the processes of "Individualization" are critical experiences of the transition to adult privileges and responsibilities. Among multiple approaches to contemporary individuality (e.g., Budgeon, 2003; Côté & Levine, 2002; Shanahan, 2000), the individualization processes that Beck and Beck-Gernsheim specify have direct relevance to a sociocultural perspective, because the institutional-personal exchanges that drive late modern society have their genesis in the social world, but are given meaning and impetus in personal consciousness.

A canny applicant, for instance, looks for loopholes in publicized regulations. For a price (e.g., to venture or risk), but with much to be gained, it is reasonable to try to extract something novel from the system: better credit card repayment conditions, a longer extension for an assignment, hours off work for sporting commitments. In the vernacular, "You can't be hanged for trying."

Beck never envisaged this individualized activity as socially isolated. Although choice is thrust upon people, that choice is socially elicited and, in turn, elicits social action. Nor does Beck's individualization theory fit with an exclusively individualistic account of personal development. His theory is, in fact, *"Institutionalized individualism" (Individualisierung;* Beck, 2002, p. xxi), whereby the activities of individuals are always socially situated and are always identified in terms of relations with the social institutions that organize their lives. Public organizations, in particular, deal with people in terms of the role or specific detail that concerns their particular organization's function.

> To the extent that society breaks down into separable functional spheres that are neither interchangeable nor graftable onto one another, people are integrated into society only in their partial aspects as taxpayers, car drivers, students, consumers, voters, patients, producers, fathers, mothers, sisters, pedestrians, and so on. Constantly changing between different, partly incompatible logics of action, they are forced to take into their hands that which is in danger of breaking into pieces: their own lives. (Beck, 2002, p. 23)

Here Beck clearly invests the individual with the task of integrating the self across "functional spheres." Because institutions are disconnected from each other within the disintegrating society, there is no other agent who can bring coherence to the various parts of an individual life. Psychologically speaking, in the process of making different responses, gestures and decisions, the person is contributing to the development of a personal identity. "While I may be only a patient to this hospital, I am also a father, an executive, and someone who is accustomed to being consulted about what happens to me. I expect the staff to discuss my condition with me." Thus, a personal identity and pattern of interaction is progressively constructed and affirmed in its expression in multiple person-by-institution encounters. In a real sense, "institutionalized individualism" describes the activities of the person.

Leading a Life of Their Own: Young Adult's DIY Constructions

In the popular press and everyday wisdom, young people celebrate the removal of traditional pathways of achievement. Gone are the "historical recipes" that mandate how they should live their lives. Even when freedom may be "risky" and "precarious," it is preferable to traditional bondage. With the breakdown of distinctions that previously were entrenched in class and gender, more people than ever before are able to exercise personal autonomy.

> (W)hat is historically new is that something that was earlier expected of a few – to lead a life of their own – is now being demanded of more and more people and, in the limiting case, of all. The new element is first, the democratization of individualization processes, and second (and closely connected), the fact that basic conditions in society favour or enforce individualization (the job market, the need for mobility and training, labor and social legislation, pension provisions etc.). (Beck & Beck-Gernsheim, 2002, p. 8)

Borrowing Hitzler's (1988) concept of *Bastelbiographie*: "Do-it-yourself biography," Beck and Beck-Gernsheim develop the imagery of the life task of contemporary persons as constructing personal life projects. This amounts to "leading a life of one's own," with that life synthesized across social institutions and in spite of societal dissolution. Individuals make life-directing choices, acting on their own volitions, and integrating their social behaviors across situations and times. These self-constructed biographies displace the traditionally expected biographies sanctioned for particular groups within their collectives. Patterns of consistent and also exceptional choices gain coherence and meaning as "*My* biography, my life project, my story." The first emphasis of the DIY life project is personal ownership: "Mine." Being dependent on personal choice and action, these complex constructions demand attention and effort, are liable to evolve in different forms, and can be quite idiosyncratic. Current fascinations with body studs and tattoos, along with body building regimes speak to this personalized work of constructing oneself. Admittedly, these fascinations follow fashionable trends, but they also become statements about a person's active creation of personal attributes.

The second emphasis is that the products are complex projects rather than simple activities, because they are progressively assembled out of a range of experiences. They are constructive and integrative, encompassing multiple times and situations. Scripting personal narratives and stories (Maguire, Ball, & Macrae, 2001) carries a similar meaning of layered and coordinated self-development. One could say that the product and the processes intertwine as the constructive work continues.

The third emphasis is on the temporary, tentative quality of the DIY project. The project, physical or conceptual, usually has the sense of work in progress, because time and effort are distributed across opportunities and tasks. It has little sense of completeness or permanency, and is achieved only tentatively. As Côté (2000) point outs, identity formation becomes a crucial personalized accomplishment. It is not surprising, then, that young adults faced with a multitude of possibilities want to keep their options open for as long as possible, and to form tentative, revisable identities (Bauman, 2002). Tentativeness is particularly experienced by young women encountering the double standards of the freedom afforded them in rhetoric and the highly disparate actualities available experientially. While they are expected to pursue careers

and achieve their market potential, affordable and trustworthy child care is often beyond their financial reach. The way to handle identity and lifestyle constructions is to move at one's own pace, and to take charge of one's own choices and actions.

To engage in the project work, then, is like walking a tightrope, with its attendant possibilities of "slippage," "collapse," "DIY breakdown" (Beck, 2002, p. 3). If such negative experiences do eventuate, the contemporary person is given the unwelcome consolation of knowing that they are experiencing a personal failure in experimenting with a "life of my own" rather than systemic inadequacy (Côté, 2000). There is little escape from that attribution, because social organizations conspire to target the individualization processes when assigning responsibility.

Côté (2000) also contributes to the sense of the tightrope quality of the biographical work, by his mostly positive note about the young person's ability to build up "*identity capital.*" Identity capital is a personal commodity whereby young people who have a stable sense of self and appropriate social and technical skills are able to use these attributes and accomplishments as "passports into other social and institutional spheres" (p. 209). Educational achievements, physical attractiveness, self efficacy and cognitive flexibility are but a few of the characteristics and skills that can be accrued for use in different circumstances. Conversely, without the requisite identity capital that helps one negotiate a way through personal and social obstacles, the tightrope experience can lead to dissolution of the self.

Nevertheless, the social system that so quickly attributes blame to the bankrupt, the drop-out, or the under-achieving relative also has to take some responsibility for putting pressure on people to make the individualized choices that cut the person adrift from any supportive collectives. The project that may seem to be solo work when one is in the midst of it, is culturally imbedded. The culture, even if in disarray, provides the meanings and values against which to judge choices. Chandler, Lalonde, Sokol, and Hallett (2003) demonstrate how young people with inadequate strategies for interpreting their own continuity stumble, because they lack a sense of a self that allows them to link up the future with the past. They cannot see themselves as viable entities existing beyond the problematic moment. Devoid of realistic future selves whose well-being is at stake, they throw it all away. For Chandler and his colleagues, as well as for Marcia (2003) as an identity theorist, this critical sense of a continuing self is not a solo acquisition. The development of a personal identity is tied to the young person's place in a continuing culture, and it is here that Chandler and his colleagues fill out the picture of how DIY constructions can go wrong.

Particularly for young people from close collectives (West Coast Canadian First Nations Bands), personal continuity is tied up with the continuity of the community. When communities break down people are at greater risk of loss of identity, and there is a heightened incidence of youth suicide. Individualism is personally and socially costly, because it has no base. Chandler's work, then, is illustrative of Beck's position. Beck sees all late modern societies as breaking down leaving the person standing alone. Chandler demonstrates that individual young people can be lost in their aloneness. The aloneness furthermore is most strongly felt by those whose cultural identity comes from a collective.

The marketplace boldly steps in by offering some young people resources to fill the gaps left by broken down community ties, or so it wants people to believe. By paying a fee and committing to the ideal of self-development, one may engage a personal coach or trainer. Many products and schemes are advertised as able to inspire or organize personalized efforts to bulk up one's muscles, one's confidence, and oneself.

This DIY constructive work, from a sociocultural perspective, epitomizes the paradoxical situation in which contemporary young adults find themselves. They have no choice but to establish and maintain a personal identity and a personal life-style within prevailing constraints. The complex activity of constructing one's personal biography simultaneously contributes to the construction (in some cases, deconstruction) of the very constraining social system. Whenever one person beats the odds and makes a personal gain, she opens up the way for other individualized encounters with institutions. The institution may shore up the loopholes, tighten the criteria for interacting with it, or alternatively, relax those criteria, making the next person's encounter either more difficult or easier (Valsiner & Lawrence, 1997). The system changes. The systemic effect of such micro-level engagements, for example, can be seen in Rosa Parks' refusal to give up her bus seat for a white passenger. One woman's resistance to the boundary conditions ultimately provoked change in segregated transport.

Illustrative DIY Constructions

The comment on her own achievement by one teenage single mother particularizes the radical break with expected norms that allowed her to use a life skills program (YouthWorks) to better her life circumstances. Joanne was a participant in Budgeon's (2003) study of individualization in English young women. The interviewer asked her why she became involved in the program: "What was there about it that you thought was good for you?" Joanne acknowledged her escape from the expected trajectory of a young single mother:

> When I fell pregnant with Jason a lot of people said "she's not going to do anything with her life. Now she's ruined her life." But it was like I wanted to get more grades so I've got more things to aim for so I though I may as well do this. I'm not doing anything else and I should try my hardest at it and it did work out because I got a job through it. (Budgeon, 2003, p. 55)

At age 19, Joanne pulled life for herself and her two year old son out of the expected pathway. The choice and the activity were hers, and the skills program made it possible for her to overcome the usual boundaries for someone in her circumstances. Instead of working in a factory like her cousins, she was working in a photography studio. As Budgeon (2003, p. 56) noted, "For Joanne, the violation of an anticipated trajectory produced a positive outcome." She made an escape from the expected, but an escape that she fashioned herself, by taking up and using an opportunity to gain confidence to follow a different route that dramatically "violated" the expected, ". . . so I haven't done none of what they're saying young women are doing" (p. 56).

Our examples of young adults' personalized life projects come from advanced undergraduate psychology students in Australia. We asked them to identify their personal goals for the next five years. They typed their open-ended comments into a computer program, *"Living as a young adult."*

As well as identifying three personal five-year (short-term) goals, the students made open-ended comments on whether or not they were achieving these goals, whether there was anything likely to get in the way, and what they were doing about either proceeding to their goals (those without obstacles) or "What do you think you'll do about the things(s) in the way of achieving your five-year goals?" (those with obstacles).

One 21-year-old student, Brett, gave a clear statement of his priorities and their barriers, in answer to the question, "What in your life experience has influenced the organization of your life now?"

The divorce of my parents has brought me to hold social support and stability far more highly than I might have. My lack of a scientific background has compromised my current career-oriented goals. Having a partner means that everything I do in life takes them and the effect on them into consideration.

Brett's goals were to "become a qualified beer brewer, travel, be financially stable." In response to the question about possible obstacles, he generated a list of interrelated constraints focused on his financial needs that were complicating his ability to gain the qualifications to meet these career and lifestyle goals.

My lack of academic background in my chosen field, the fact that I have already undertaken an undergraduate course (limiting financial support from the government), lack of finances to pay for up front fees. Travel costs. Finding a place at which I want to study.

The obstacles, however, did not deter Brett from his dream. His strategies clearly expressed the kind of concentrated, manipulative action that belongs to a Beck-type DIY life project. His list pointed to his plan to proactively engage with the relevant organizations and people, "Find loopholes. Talk to industry experts for advice. Search out every option. Save money." This "find loopholes" strategy clearly expresses the kind of individualized action back on institutions that lies behind Beck's macro-level analysis.

Tran, a 22-year-old Vietnamese woman listed her five-year goals for which she felt there were no obstacles: "Start a challenging, fulfilling career. Meet someone special enough to start a family. Travel to various, at least 3 continents." Tran's response reads like the expression of a rehearsed and readily retrieved list. She knew what she wanted to achieve. The strategies for achieving these goals not only focused on herself, but also expressed a formula for moving forward in various domains of her life with the same personalized pursuit.

Researching and getting practical experience on what I want to do and where I want to do it. Getting only into relationships that I think will last and where I can be my complete self. Setting time and making verbal commitments to travel overseas with friends.

Tran identified the set of self-determined choices and activities that she believed would lead to the fulfillment of her goals. She would either open-up or cut-off a range of possibilities, including relationships, in order to pursue her agenda.

Although Brett and Tran were not specifically aiming to upset social expectations like the less fortunate Joanne, they clearly expressed personal ownership of their future and the means they envisaged using to ach-ieve what they wanted. Their comments convey the sense of lives under construction and moving forward.

Sociocultural Connections

It can readily be seen that Beck's Individu-alization theory has a natural affinity with sociocultural accounts that see change com-ing from dialectical interactions between personal and social worlds. We see Beck's position as a clear macro-level invitation to develop a micro-level account of how young adults actually piece together their DIY biographies in restricting yet pliable social environments. The macro-level analy-sis actually demands a complementary anal-ysis of the personal take-up of opportunities, and the forms of personal actions that issue in personal and institutional adaptations.

Moscovici (1976) saw how personalized reciprocal activities are provoked by such challenges. His comment of 30 years ago is particularly applicable to today's social con-ditions.

> Our society is an institution which inhab-its what it stimulates. It both tempers and excites aggressive, epistemic, and sex-ual tendencies, increases or reduces the chances of satisfying them according to class distinctions, and invents prohibitions together with the means of transgressing them. (Moscovici, 1976, p. 149)

This comment conveys the tensions and con-tradictions laid before people like second-hand wares on a market stall. They are dis-played with all their inconsistencies. They surprise as they entice. They demand imag-inative selection.

The personal-institutional situation is vol-atile, and that volatility and its outworkings can be addressed by weak sociocultural the-ories (Sawyer, 2002, p. 293), because they admit separate ontologies. Any interaction between these separate entities is dialectical, to the extent that social and psychological mentalities act upon each other and create

something new to each of them in the pro-cess. As a consequence, the social world that Beck describes does not fit well with a socio-cultural approach that denies the distinctive-ness of psychological processing. Choice and action are individualized responses to varied possibilities. In fact, it is difficult to see how a sociocultural model with inseparability at its core could take up Sawyer's challenge of paying due attention to the macro condi-tions of young adults' social encounters. The dialectical mechanism of change is missing. "Inseparability does not allow the sociolo-gist to account for the constraining power of external forces, for macrosociological pat-terns, for history, or for material conditions" (Sawyer, 2002, p. 289).

Embracing separate ontologies, however, demands showing how the social and the personal contribute to each other's life history and development. Valsiner and Lawrence (1997) proposed a model of adult development where lasting, ontogenetic development is dependent on the person's active progression through various social institutions. Novel transforming activities emerge in the psychology of the person, as they do in the collective consciousness that directs action in the culture's institutions. People take up the challenges thrown out by the formal regulations and informal arrange-ments which both "temper and excite" per-sonal responses, simultaneously "prohibit-ing" and "giving the means of transgressing," in Moscovici's (1976) terms.

Specifically in relation to the Beck model, the dialectical exchange involved in pro-cesses of mutual constraining describes how such institutional challenges and opportu-nities are actualized in people's life expe-riences. These exchanges situate and con-cretize particular activities in cultural history and in personal experience (Riegel, 1979). DIY projects are built up within and across specific events. Specific instances of inter-acting with the social world generate new powers (or sometimes, new weaknesses) as the person gives those instances meaning. The meaning and the coherence is capable of being developed in pre-action planning, within the dialectical encounter, or in post-action integration.

Beck and Beck-Gernsheim give glimpses of the effects of historico-cultural limitations on specific lives (e.g., in their treatment of the paradoxical situation of modern young women, reproduced from Beck-Gernsheim, 1983), but the theory generally wants an explanation of how persons and institutions actually act upon each other in concrete situations.

In the examples of DIY life projects we have described, there is a definite place for the intra-personal, psychological processes by which personal intention motivates and drives responses to institutional demands and provisions. Joanne, for example, took herself out of the expected forms of behavior of teen-age mothers by the outworking of her personal goals: "What I wanted" led her to action. Her intentions were put into practice: "I thought I may as well do this . . . try my hardest." The student examples also invite further analyses of how loopholes can be found in the kinds of limiting situations Brett expected to meet, and how Tran would actively choose through various experiences, the pathways that would serve her goals.

We are given only one side of the story in each of these cases. What does the skills program do when Joanne or others arrive, with baby? High schools, for instance, have to make substantial institutional adjustments to accommodate girls returning to study with their babies, setting up special child-care facilities and timetables. In contrast to this kind of institutional responsiveness, we may ask how swiftly and effectively government departments will act to repair any loopholes that someone like Brett finds in order to exploit existing student funding opportunities. Universities have similarly responded to the plagiarism that the internet offers enterprising students by commissioning computer programs for detecting creative borrowing. Constraining is bi-directional, and the responses made to constraining forces can be either positive or negative in their outcomes, just as they can be predictable or novel.

Person-by-Institution Mutual Constraining Processes

Two lines of theorizing come together to suggest how constraining processes work in human experience: cognitive psychology's account of problem-solving in a Gibsonian environment (e.g., Norman, 1988), and Lewin's (1936) field theory (see Valsiner, 1987). In both lines, a *constraint* is identified as something that sets boundaries around a situation to be processed by persons, specifying the limiting features to which they must respond.

With its complementary Gibsonian concept of *affordance*, the constraint has been useful for explaining how and why people act in particular ways, for example, in using physical objects. Norman (1988) demonstrated how door handles, knobs and hinges influence the way people perform routine activities. If household appliances were shaped differently, we would pick up, pour and store them in distinctly different ways. For example, a chair is designed to afford sitting. Modern forms of seating (e.g., backless, sloping stools, and exercise balls) exert specialized force on sitting persons to make them position their backs and legs in particular ways. Structural features also limit the use of seating objects for other purposes (e.g., standing on sloping stools invites disaster). Users must function within the parameters that define productive use. By the same token, many novel and creative inventions directly emerge out of violations of the understood parameters of an object or situation, for example, turning junkyard rubbish into objects d'art. No less obvious, however, are the non-material processes used for turning social parameters into personal advantages.

For his consciously social perspective on constraining activities, Valsiner (1987) built on Lewin's (1936) account of social boundaries. Particularly applicable here are Lewin's concepts of fuzzy boundaries that limit a person's life field or space, especially the conditions for joining a social group. In his analysis, Valsiner provides a nice preview of the type of personalized transformations that we believe Beck's model suggests. Someone wishing to join a club, is turned away, frustrated by the club's entry conditions. If this person enters into Lewin's *boundary zone* by adding his name to the waiting list, he loosens the boundaries. Significantly according to Valsiner, he changes the membership conditions for himself.

> The person who is in the process of joining the club changes the boundary of club membership for himself *while moving to become a member, but not for any other person (neither those who are already members, nor for those who remain non members). (Valsiner, 1987, p. 93, original emphasis)*

He, for example, may progressively chip away at the entry requirements, violating the very conditions that exclude him (e.g., age or race). He may falsify his credentials, turn up at every meeting, or pester club officers with an endless stream of applications.

If he succeeds and creates a chink in that barrier for himself, we add, he also changes the nature of the barrier for others. Once the boundary conditions are loosened or breached, the precedent and its memory make further breaches all the more possible. Just as Rosa Parks' action set in train a nation-wide change, the actions of one black teacher, Sadie Delany poked a chink in the racial barriers to teaching in the early 20th century white New York school system. She appeared on the first day of school without disclosing her ethnicity, having previously avoided an interview. They needed a teacher. She was there. Any rejection would be totally public. "Once I was in, they couldn't figure out how to get rid of me" (Hearth, Delany, & Delany, 1993, p. 120). She changed the membership barriers for others in the act of changing them for herself. She created a precedent, by the public trace of her triumph over the official conditions.

This kind of "loophole-making effect" of the person's action is developed further in the Valsiner and Lawrence (1997) account of adult development. Change comes out of cycles of reciprocal constraining encounters.

The culture and its agencies may provide signs and rituals that give life within that culture meaning, but that meaning is constructed anew, when the person takes over the cultural material into personal forms of thinking. These intra-psychological constructions vary in personal interpretations that range from something very similar to the accepted cultural schema to its transformation in a person's thinking that effectively expresses a fundamentally oppositional view.

By way of illustration, Funder (2002) reports the verbal exchange between a GDR official and a woman, Julia, in line for unemployment benefits. Julia asked someone else in the queue how long he had been unemployed. This provoked an altercation when the official overheard and corrected her, "You are not *unemployed*, you are *seeking work.*"

> Julia wasn't daunted. "I'm seeking work," she said, "because I am unemployed." The woman started to shout so loudly the people in the queue hunched their shoulders. "I said, you are not unemployed! You are seeking work!" And then almost hysterically, "There is no unemployment in the German Democratic Republic!" (Funder, 2002, p. 104)

While the power differential is frustrating for "cultural deviants" like Julia, it sometimes happens that the very institutions that stress strict boundary conditions, unofficially make provision for personal escape routes (Lawrence, Benedikt, & Valsiner, 1992). The history of cultures abounds with examples of moratoria, let-out clauses, and tacit acceptance of deviants within strict collectives as they make room, for instance, for socially awkward saints or idiots (Weinstein & Bell, 1982). When a person takes up such outlying possibilities, or even more radically, creates a unique possibility, as in the Parks and Delany examples, the person is reciprocally constraining the institution.

Limiting forces are imposed, interpreted, and re-imposed by active, bi-directional constraining, where we emphasize the present continual sense of constrain*ing* (Lawrence &

Valsiner, 2003, p. 727). Bi-directional testing and limiting occurs as the cultural tools of sanctified and taboo objects, accepted procedures and regulations, schemas and concepts are given fresh meanings and semiotic value. The tools in the cultural toolkit (Cole, 1996) are inherently plastic and amenable to re-interpretation, precisely because they are given meaning by persons. It is this feature of mutual constraining processes that gives a way of situating (in Riegel's 1979 terminology, "concretizing") the micro-level activities of persons and social institutions, so that they function as effective driving forces of macro-level change. Macro changes impose upon specific, micro interactions. Specific, concretized interactions impose on institutions, and either immediately or cumulatively issue in macro change.

Student/Teacher Mutual Constraining in the Contemporary University

Recently, we have been experiencing this form of reciprocal constraining in university students' approaches to learning. We interpret our exchanges about teaching and learning procedures as our instances of institutional encounters with young people's DIY constructions. The cases of Brett and Tran are illustrative of the personal priorities that students bring to their studies. Varied expressions of those personalized constructions in cycles of bi-directional constraining have issued in changes in our teaching arrangements.

Current students frequently talk about the difficulty of trying to balance work, lifestyle and study. In their market-dominated world, undergraduate and professional training takes longer and costs more than it did a few decades ago. More students work longer hours in paid work, finding that work opportunities are more precarious and less under their control than was the experience of previous cohorts of students. Simultaneously, more students are aspiring to the higher grades needed to scale the next hurdle of entry to graduate programs, with

tougher academic entry requirements (Hettige, 2005).

We began taking notes of instances of mutual constraining that arose as we designed and taught a developmental psychology course around the theme of personal and social change across the life-span. We found ourselves being constrained to adjust the teaching style to students' styles of using learning resources.

Our university, like many others, expects that PowerPoint shows now will be made available to students on the intra-net system. In response, some lecturers reproduce all their slides on paper. Others make them available prior to the lectures. Educationally, we prefer to use interactively in class printed materials that are a mixture of reproductions of slides and additional information and questions. They do not simply replicate the slides. We ask students to make their own notes about orienting questions, and we extend the PowerPoint text and graphics material with example cases, explanations and answers to students' questions.

Some students made quite forceful petitions that the slide shows be available in advance of the class. They argued that it gave them greater control over scheduling their time and classroom note-taking. Our responses to this active lobbying forced us to stand back and reflect, re-defining for ourselves and the students our teaching and learning philosophy and strategies. We were committed to interactive and accumulative learning that exploits varied modes of presentation. Consequently, we explicitly identified our aims and cut out any excess, distracting features in the existing materials. We matched slides and handouts more closely to each other, without directly replicating them. We made a commitment to provide the slides immediately after the lecture and to link them specifically to the class interactions (e.g., providing feedback on questions students had worked on in previous classes, integrating significant points across various lectures). By being constrained, we were becoming clearer, more focused and crafting a new form of learning package. We were not, however, simply complying.

The new materials represented a synthesis of opposing criteria.

Once they realized what was happening, students saw that they were being constrained to take a more active role in their engagement with the material and the teaching style. By responding to student demands, but with our own interpretations, we were entering into reciprocal constraining. Those students who did not take up the opportunities afforded by the package, could continue their own DIY learning agendas, but their individualized adjustments actually placed greater demands on them. By not joining in the collective learning experience we were creating, they found themselves with more material to absorb before the exam, because their own strategies were now disassociated from the new synthesis.

Constraining Out of Internalization/ Externalization Processes

In relation to these examples of institutional-personal encounters and the others we have presented, mutual constraining describes the dialectical processes by which change is generated. Obviously such an account of constraining activities depends on the assumption of separate mentalities. The intentions underlying mutual constraining exerted on institutions by the person may be immediately generated *in situ*, but as we have demonstrated, they may also be planned in advance, or be generated afterwards. Actions and verbal exchanges externally expressed in the social phenomenal world are the outcomes of intellectual synthesizing of originally social material, whether they are generated on the run or in quiet reflection. Behind the dynamic constraining are the psychological processes of internalization and externalization.

In line with a soft-edged socioculturalism with separate ontologies, the personal side of reciprocal constraining is generated by the psychological processes in which social material is made personal (Lawrence & Valsiner, 2003). Social messages that are conveyed verbally, in action, or by numerous forms of public communication are either accepted or rejected by the person. Social messages and models available in society's institutions are sufficient to give meaning that allows participation in diverse activities (Shore, 1996, p. 51), but the person is able to re-create those meanings to allow either overt conformity, or, instead, radically non-conforming novelty. Surrendering one's seat on a bus, for example, once it is personally interpreted as an act of racial capitulation rather than of social convention, is no longer tolerable.

The synthesis and re-interpretation of material, once social now personal, is the person's own construction, as we observed in the cases of Joanne (Budgeon, 2003) and our students. When the newly personalized material is fed back in the service of self-preserving and self-developing constraining activities, it again becomes social, but with a different significance. For example, our reflections on the students' proposals for new teaching styles on our part generated proposals for new learning strategies on their part. Once externalized, it was a new socially available possibility. Such academic reflections and theorizing are able to generate further possibilities that take the effect of the encounter further into the macro system, by feeding into the dialogues of university committees and papers.

In this account of mutual constraining processes, we have not developed a thorough description of these internalization/ externalization processes (see Lawrence & Valsiner, 1993; 2003; Valsiner, 1989; Valsiner & Lawrence, 1997). The focus here was explicitly on showing how reciprocal activities link the sociological theory to sociocultural psychological theory.

Conclusion

As sociologists, Beck and Beck-Gernsheim (2002) were not specifically trying to explain either personal reflection or personal development. Yet, by proposing their theory of individualized individualism, they describe a social world that elicits the kind of reflections and expressions that contribute to development. Personal responses take the macro scene away from any social passivity. The outworking of psychological processing that we have proposed as a complementary analysis involving socially situated encounters allows the person to participate, to construct, and to be changed in the process.

We are claiming that a sociocultural model of the dialectical interactions between young adults and social institutions finds an appropriate macro-level theory of contemporary social life in Beck's institutionalized individualism. In return, a sociocultural approach that treats these dialectical interactions as personal by institutional mutual constraining provides the macro-level theory with a complementary micro-level analysis. Focusing on social-personal encounters and the psychological processing surrounding these encounters, brings the broad dimensions of the sociological theory down to the concrete situations by which Riegel (1979) saw adult development being worked out. He saw change as the outcome of dialectical exchanges between the different dimensions of life, specifically social-structural and personal-psychological dimensions. We have proposed how the mutual constraining that institutions and persons exert upon each other in concrete situations issue in change for both. In short, the macro-level sociological theory and the micro-level sociocultural theory have a natural affinity and enrich each other in explaining how the changes that occur are at the same time social and personal.

Developing these complementary accounts, we deliberately focused on the developmental period of young adulthood, in part, because Beck and Beck-Gernsheim describe the forces of late modernity that impinge on the fortunes of young people. From a development perspective, in their transitional life experiences, young adults are in the business of establishing new ways of dealing with social institutions that are widely recognized as demanding agentic responses. Career paths, intimate relationships and personal identities need to

be established. What is constructed and reconstructed for oneself (the DIY project) in and across specific negotiations has its effects in long-term, ontogenetic change for the individual, but also for the interacting culture and its institutions.

The culture is no less intrusive in the lives of young adults than it is in the lives of children who are being initiated into cultural ways of life. The materials for constructing a life project are social, and the life project is constructed in dynamic person-by-society interaction. Young adults are engaged in DIY activities through their choices and actions, but these DIY constructions are never solo works, as Beck so clearly understood. The tools and meanings made available to them are neither static nor predictable. There is no indisputable script for "This is what you do now," "This is the next task in your life." There is simply the demand to choose and to do. Even privileged young people have to grab hold of opportunities and create others or to be left behind, as the experience of Tran and Brett demonstrates.

DIY constructive work may appear to be neo-liberalism in new clothes, but Beck and Beck-Gernsheim disabuse that assumption. The freedom of late modernity is as full of tension and hard work as it is precarious. Sociocultural mutual constraining aptly picks up the tension and the back-and-forward shuffling that can provide explanations to move Beck's world beyond deconstruction to the reconstruction that is his positive anticipation. When asked about the type of values and ethics that may emerge from the world of his late modernity, Beck answered: "In the old value system, the ego always had to be subordinated to patterns of the collective. A new ethics will establish a sense of "we" that is like a co-operative or altruistic individualism." (Beck & Beck-Gernsheim, 2002, pp. 211–212)

References

Arnett, J. J. (2004). *Emerging adulthood: the winding road from the late teens and twenties*. New York: Oxford University Press.

Bauman, Z. (2002). Individually, together. Fore-word to U. Beck, & E. Beck-Gernsheim, (2002). *Individualization* (pp. xiv–xix). London: Sage.

Beck, U. (2002). A life of one's own in a runaway world. In U. Beck & E. Beck-Gernsheim, E. (2002). *Individualization* (pp. 22–29). London: Sage.

Beck, U., & Beck-Gernsheim, E. (2002). *Individualization*. London: Sage.

Beck-Gernsheim, E. (1983). Vom "Dasein für andere" zum Anspruch auf ein Stück "eigenes Leben" – Individualisierungsprozesse im weillichen Lebenszusammenhang. *Soziale Welt*, 3, 307–341.

Budgeon, S. (2003). *Choosing a self: young women and the individualization of identity*. Westport, Conn.: Praeger.

Chandler, M. J., Lalonde, C. E., Sokol, B. W., & Hallett, D. (2003). Personal persistence, identity development, and suicide. *Monograph of the Society of Research in Child Development*, 68 (2, Series No. 273).

Chatterjee, P., Bailey, D., & Aronoff, N. (2001). Adolescence and old age in twelve communities. *Journal of Sociology and Social Welfare*, 28(4), 121–159.

Cole, M. (1996). *Cultural psychology: A once and future discipline*. Cambridge, MA: Harvard University Press.

Côté, J. E. (2000). *Arrested adulthood: The changing nature of maturity and identity*. New York: New York University Press.

Côté, J. E., & Levine, C. G. (2002). *Identity formation, agency and culture*. Mahwah, NJ: Lawrence Erlbaum & Associates.

Davis, M. (2003). Addressing the needs of youth in transition to adulthood. *Administration and policy in mental health*, 30(6), 495–509.

Dwyer, P., & Wyn, J. (2001). *Youth, education and risk: Facing the future*. London: Routledge/Falmer.

Falmagne, R. J. (2004). On the constitution of "self" and "mind." *Theory and Psychology*, 14(6), 822–845.

Funder, A. (2002). *Stasiland*. London: Granta.

Ferguson, H. (2001). Social work, individualization and life politics. *British Journal of Social work*, 31, 41–55.

Furlong, A., & Cartmel, F. (1997). *Young people and social change: Individualization and risk in late modernity*. Buckingham: Open University Press.

Furstenberg, F. F. Jr., Rumbat, R. G., & Settersten, R. A. (2005). On the frontier of adult-hood: Emerging themes and new directions. In Settersten, R. A., Furstenberg, F. F. Jr., & Rumbat, R. G. (Eds.), *On the frontier of adult-hood: Theory, research and public policy* (pp. 3–25). Chicago: Chicago University Press.

Giddens, A. (1991). *Self-identity and modernity*. London: Polity.

Hearth, A. H., Delany, S., & Delany, A. E. (1993). *Having our say: The Delany sisters' first 100 years*. New York: Kodansha International.

Herriot, P., & Scott-Jackson, W. (2002). Globalization, social identities and employment. *British Journal of Management*, 13, 249–257.

Hettige, S. T. (2005). Demographic and economic pressures to move: Youth aspirations and livelihood opportunities for youth in the liberal economic environment of Sri Lanka. In F. Gale & S. Fahey (Eds.), *Youth in transition: The challenges of generational change in Asia* (pp. 227–241). Bangkok: Regional Unit for Social and Human Sciences in Asia and the Pacific, UNESCO.

Hitzler, R. (1988). *Kleine lebenswelten – Ein Beitrag zum verstehen von kultur*. Opladen: Westdeutscher Verlag.

Lansdown, G. (2004). *World youth report, 2003*. New York: United Nations.

Lawrence, J. A., Benedikt, R., & Valsiner, J. (1992). Homeless in the mind: A case-history of personal life in and out of a close orthodox community. *Journal of Social Distress and Homelessness*, 1(2), 157–176.

Lawrence, J. A., & Valsiner, J. (1993). Conceptual roots of internalization: from transmission to transformation. *Human Development*, 36(3), 150–167.

Lawrence, J. A., & Valsiner, J. (2003). Making personal sense: An account of basic internalization and externalization processes. *Theory and Psychology*, 13(6), 723–752.

Lewin, K. (1936). *Principles of topological psychology*. New York: McGraw-Hill.

McDougall, W. (1945/1908). *Social psychology*. London: Methuen. Originally published in 1908.

Maguire, M., Ball, S. J., & Macrae, S. (2001). Post-adolescence, dependence and the refusal of adulthood. *Discourse: Studies in the Cultural politics of education*, 22(2), 197–211.

Marcia (2003). Treading fearlessly: A commentary on personal persistence, identity development, and suicide. *Monograph of the Society of Research in Child Development*, 68 (2, Series No. 273), pp. 131–138.

Moscovici, S. (1976). *Society against nature: The emergence of human societies*. Atlantic Highlands, N.J.: Humanities Press.

Norman, D. A. (1988). *The psychology of everyday things*. New York: Basic Books.

Puyat, J. H. (2005). The Filipino youth today: Their strengths and the challenges they face. In F. Gale & S. Fahey (Eds.), *Youth in transition: The challenges of generational change in Asia* (pp. 191–205). Bangkok: Regional Unit for Social and Human Sciences in Asia and the Pacific, UNESCO.

Riegel, K. F. (1979). *Foundations of dialectical psychology*. New York: Academic Press.

Sawyer, R. K. (2002). Unresolved tensions in sociocultural theory: Analogies with contemporary sociological debate. *Culture and Psychology*, 8(3), 283–305.

Shanahan, M. J. (2000). Pathways to adulthood in changing societies: Variability and mechanisms in life course perspective. *Annual review of Sociology*, 26, 667–692.

Shore, B. (1996). *Culture in mind: Cognition, culture and the problem of meaning*. New York: Oxford University Press.

Teese, R. (2005). For which young people do schools work really well? In S. Richardson, & M. Prior (Eds.), *No time to lose: The wellbeing of Australia's children* (pp. 240–254). Melbourne: Melbourne University Press.

Valsiner, J. (1987). *Culture and the development of children's action: A cultural-historical theory of developmental psychology*. New York: John Wiley & Sons.

Valsiner, J. (1989). *Human development and culture*. Lexington MA: D. C. Heath.

Valsiner, J. (1998). Dualisms displaced: From crusades to analytic distinctions. *Human Development*, 41, 350–354.

Valsiner, J., & Lawrence, J. A. (1997). Human development in culture across the life span. In J. W. Berry, P. R. Dasen, & T. S. Saraswathi (Eds.), *Handbook of cross-cultural psychology. Vol. 2. Basic processes and developmental psychology. 2nd ed.* (pp. 69–106) Boston: Allyn & Bacon.

Weinstein, D., & Bell, R. M. (1982). *Saints and society: The two worlds of Western Christendom, 1000 to 1700*. Chicago: University of Chicago Press.

Part V

FROM SOCIETY TO THE PERSON THROUGH CULTURE

CHAPTER 20

Apprenticeship in Conversation and Culture

Emerging Sociability in Preschool Peer Talk

Michal Hamo and Shoshana Blum-Kulka

Our aim in the present study is to explore young children's conversations as a unique linguistic, social, and cultural phenomenon, by investigating the relative salience, contexts, affordances, structures, and functions of conversation in preschoolers' peer interactions. Previous research on children's conversations has been carried out from two perspectives: the developmental perspective of child-language study, focusing on the acquisition of conversational skills and competencies; and the socio-cultural perspective of sociolinguistics and ethnography, focusing on the social functions of conversation. We will briefly review these two traditions, and then draw on both in analyzing naturally occurring peer conversations of young Israeli children. Our approach to child discourse combines two perspectives: on the one hand, as strongly argued by Corsaro and Johannesen (this handbook) we view the joint, moment by moment process of the creation of childhood peer culture as a central feature of childhood; on the other hand, differing from Corsaro and Johannesen, we consider the collective creation of fictive and non-fictive realities in here in space

and now in time as a major site for individual developmental gains. Viewing these two processes as simultaneous requires a balanced view, one that considers the cultural and developmental as complementary aspects of childhood, for the children as much as for the researcher. Our discussion of children's conversations is hence done from a double perspective, as an arena for meaning-making within childhood culture, as well as an opportunity space for the mastering of conversational skills (Blum-Kulka, 2005; Hamo, Blum-Kulka, & Hacohen, 2004).

Our analysis aims at documenting the emergence of conversation from two points of view: the first focuses on the move from activity-related talk to talk as an activity in its own right, namely conversation; the second, on the ways children accomplish one of the major functions of conversation – sociability. The theme of sociability is further linked to issues of enculturation – to what degree are the discursive resources activated in these children's conversations culture specific? Can we detect patterns of peer enculturation towards culturally colored ways of speaking? We shall conclude by discussing the unique nature of children's conversations.

Conversational Skills in Child Discourse[1]

Within child-language research, the salient perspective on children's conversations has traditionally been developmental, focusing on the acquisition process of a wide range of conversational skills. We propose to distinguish between two major clusters of skills[2]: one relating to the *mechanisms of conversation*, i.e., the ability to interact, and the other to joint meaning-making in conversation, i.e., *dialogicity*. Each of these two clusters is divided to micro- and macro-levels.

The development of the mechanisms of conversation has been studied primarily by adopting the analytic framework of Conversation Analysis and applying it to child discourse. The main micro-level mechanism of conversation is the turn-taking system. Mastering it includes developing skills such as the ability to project turning relevance places; to apply a wide range of strategies for speaker selection and negotiation; to secure extended, multi-Turn-Constructional-Unit turns; and to maintain a continuous flow of talk, adhering to the principal of "one at a time," that is, no-pause-no-overlap. Such skills develop in interaction foremost with caretakers, and might be, as claimed by Trevarthen, motivated by an innate mechanism for social interaction, which explains infants' readiness to enter into well-timed proto-conversations with their caretakers much before the onset of speech (cf. Trevarthen & Hubey, 1978). Studies of children in the West, where children are treated as conversational partners from birth, indeed show a pattern of early development for turn-taking. By the time they are producing their first words, British and American children can sustain long stretches of well-timed turn-alternations with mothers (Kaye & Charney, 1981; Snow, 1977). When children reach the age of three, they largely follow the rules of turn-taking with each other (Ervin-Tripp, 1979; Katz, 2004), and by four, can draw simultaneously on several resources (such as gaze, syntax, and intonation) for smooth turn-taking and for speaker selection (Gallagher & Craig, 1982). Four to five year old children have also been observed employing adult-like strategies for securing an extended turn, such as manifesting topical relevance and aligning participants for forthcoming conversational storytelling (Blum-Kulka, 2005). Still, the precise timing of adult conversationalists is beyond the reach of young children. Young children may have difficulty in projecting possible turn completion points for their own speech and identifying Transition Relevant Places in the speech of others, and as a result manifest fewer overlaps and longer gaps in their peer conversation (Garvey & Berninger, 1981). Identifying transition relevant places and self-selecting is especially challenging for children in relatively complex participation structures, such as multi-party, intergenerational mealtime conversations (Blum-Kulka, 1997).

While turn-taking skills are all manifested in the moment-by-moment progress of conversation, a different set of skills is at work on a more global macro-level – that of conversation as a whole. This level entails the ability to open and close conversations; the ability to carry out the interactional roles of speaker (i.e., maintaining interest among listeners and seeking their acknowledgement), and of active listener (i.e., asking questions, producing backchannels, etc.), and finally, the ability to exchange these roles with conversational partners, resulting in a balanced and reciprocal participation structure.

The cluster of mechanisms of conversation is focused on skills required for accomplishing the interactive nature of conversation, through cooperation and reciprocity. While micro-level skills of this cluster represent relatively general competencies which form the basis for any interaction, its macro-aspects may be more context- and genre-sensitive. For example, children achieve competence in opening and closing telephone conversations only at the age of five – a finding discussed as related to the unique context-specific nature of this skill (Bordeaux & Willbrand, 1987).

In studies of child-discourse, micro-aspects of the cluster of mechanisms of conversation have received some focused attention, while the investigation of its macro-aspects have been mostly meshed with attention paid to a second cluster of conversational skills, subsumed here under "dialogicity". This cluster focuses on skills required for joint meaning-making in conversation.

Micro-level skills of dialogicity have been studied from a wide range of research traditions, ranging from text linguistics to pragmatics and conversation analysis. Such skills are geared at maintaining content continuity in the moment-by-moment progress of conversation. This happens through cross-turn relevance, accomplished either by a wide range of cohesive devices (sound play, repetition, lexical cohesion, anaphoric reference), or by producing responses which are topically relevant (adhering to the Gricean maxims of conversation), and functionally relevant (second parts of adjacency pairs). Macro-level joint meaning-making goes beyond local relevance and continuity and focuses on skills required for two aspects of joint meaning-making. First, the focus is on skills required for producing coherent, interesting, and sustained conversational episodes, which combine topic maintenance and topic change. Secondly, the emphasis is on skills required for generating context-appropriate social meanings through the use of varied keys and keyings (real, make-believe, serious, humorous, subversive, etc.; cf. Blum-Kulka, Huck-Taglicht, & Avni, 2004), politeness strategies and register and style.

Adult-child interactions from an early age have been one of the major sites for the study of the development of dialogic skills. In both dyadic and multi-party interactions with young children, at the early stages adults tend to take on the bulk of conversational responsibilities, initiating topics, asking questions, providing interpretations, and expanding unclear utterances, as well as challenging children to abide by the maxims of relevance and informativeness (Blum-Kulka & Snow, 2002; Snow, 1984).

The discourse values stressed in such interactions vary with culture. In Jewish-American families, for instance, they encourage *speakership*, calling for children's active participation (Blum-Kulka, 1997). In Japan, in contrast, what is called for is intent *listenership*, whereby children are expected to develop interpretative skills for understanding indirectly formulated speech acts (Clancy, 1986). The focus in these lines of research has been – on the one hand – on the relations between types of adult scaffolding (known as CDS – child directed speech) and language development at large, (i.e., Richards & Gallaway, 1994) and – on the other hand – on cross-cultural variation in language socialization, including variation in the interactional formats through which children become full conversational partners in their culture (i.e., Schieffelin & Ochs, 1984).

More specific evidence on the development of conversational skills comes from studies of peer talk. For example, McTear's (1985) study of natural interaction of a dyad of two girls from the age of four to six identified four developmental trends:

a. extended scope of cross-turn cohesive markers, from repetition and prosodic shifts toward anaphoric pronouns, ellipsis and sentence connectives;

b. enrichment in modes of topic initiation and re-initiation, showing children's growing awareness of the need for other acknowledgement;

c. a move from brief, closed exchange structures to longer and more open, topically and interactionally related sequences; and

d. increased use of remedial devices, testifying to the children's growing ability to monitor their and the other's speech and locate and repair conversational breakdowns.

These trends are supported by further research. Cross-turn cohesion was found to be sensitive to age; in younger children's conversation, it is often maintained by sound play rather than topical cohesion, in line with young children's overall preference for verbal play (Blum-Kulka et al., 2004; Garvey 1975; Keenan, 1974; Kirshenblatt-Gimbeltt, 1979). Yet concurrently, young children were also observed to employ a variety of linguistic means in order to maintain cross-turn coherence in long stretches of talk (Blum-Kulka, 2005; McTear, 1985; Sanders & Freeman, 1998). The use of cohesive markers is also sensitive to context – in an experimental setting with a teacher or a peer, five- to nine-year-old children used ellipsis and lexical cohesion similarly in both settings, but used more logical connectives and anaphoric references with teachers than with peers (Fine, 1978). Enrichment in rate of topic initiation and re-initiation was found to typify second to fifth grade children judged by adults as "good conversationalists" (Schley & Snow, 1992); this feature was also salient in fourth grade children's dyadic conversations with an academically high (rather than low) achieving partner (Schober-Peterson & Johnson, 1993). In another study Schober-Peterson and Johnson (1989) found that for four year olds having a familiar script as topic helped topical elaboration. The developmental path for maintaining conversational coherence across long stretches of discourse moves between second to fifth grade towards higher levels of topical relatedness, as well as towards an increase in manifest attention paid to the other's emotional and/or cognitive perspective (Dorval & Eckerman, 1984; Dumensil & Dorval, 1989, American children). The emotional angle in the last result might be culturally bound, as suggested by the positive value placed by American children-judges on self disclosure and emotional display in their peers' conversations (Hemphill & Siperstein, 1990).

The second aspect of macro-level joint meaning-making focuses on sociolinguistic skills. Sociolinguistic skills, both productive and receptive, rely on various levels of monitoring and meta-awareness, and hence, will be discussed here in conjunction with meta-communicative skills.

The fourth dimension observed by Mc-Tear (1985) in peer talk – namely the use of remedial devices and monitoring, is linked to a rich set of meta-communicative skills. These skills are manifested not only through meta-communicative talk, but also through the ability to recognize breakdowns of the normal order of conversation and to sanction and repair them, and through the ability to evaluate the conversational competence of others by observing their behavior. Children employ repairs of both grammatical and pragmatic aspects from an early age, and exhibit a preference for self-repair similar to the same preference in adult discourse. This preference was also found to grow with age (McTear, 1985). Further meta-communicative skills are manifested in judgments of others' conversations. Fourth to sixth graders exhibit a highly developed ability to distinguish between "good" and "poor" conversationalists, while being sensitive to a wide range of delicate differences.

Interestingly, different clusters of skills were found to play a differential role in children's estimates of what counts as "good conversation" – the macro-aspects of dialogicity are evoked in judgments of competence, while both the micro- and macro-aspects of mechanisms of conversation seem more noticeable in judgments of incompetence. Thus, when observing taped conversations of normal children with normal and slightly retarded partners, children judged the former as "good" mainly on grounds of richness of topic initiations, and the latter "poor" on grounds of the mechanism of conversation, like too many pauses and hesitations and the scarcity of questions (Hemphill & Siperstein, 1990). Adult judgments of children's conversations confirm the importance of macro-dialogicity skills: global evaluations of role-plays of second to fourth grade children were found to correlate with levels of topic initiation, elaborate response, and topic initiations more strongly than with age (Schley & Snow, 1992).

A rich source of information on the use of remedial devices and monitoring in children's conversations comes from studies of pretend-play. Pretend-play also provides the earliest evidence for children's development of sociolinguistic skills, such as register variation and politeness use (Andersen-Slosberg, 1990). Monitoring in pretend-play comes to the fore especially in signaling meta-communicatively frame-shifts in and out of play, in aligning by voice and register with enacted characters and in meta-comments aimed at correcting digressions from the key and register of play (i.e., Aronsson & Thorrel, 2002; Hoyle, 1998; Sawyer, 1997). Even toddlers (2.5 to 3) identify correctly pretend and non-pretend framing (Katz, 2004). Andersen-Slosberg (1990) found that through role-plays, young children exhibit sensitivity to relative status, familiarity, and sex from an early age, varying their register use accordingly, especially in playing familiar scripts, like "family." Work with teenagers has shown that older children acquire the more subtle ability to signal the social functions of language use by choice of language varieties, such as indexing their alliance to youth culture and/or their gender (i.e., Cheshire, 1991; Eckert, 1989; Hemphill, 1989; Hoyle, 1998; Hoyle & Temple Adger, 1998). Other aspects of this socio-cultural angle will be discussed in the next section. A summary of the conversational skills discussed so far is presented in Table 20.1.

The Socio-Cultural Perspective on Children's Conversations

The socio-cultural perspective on children's conversations brings to the fore the *culturally filtered* nature of conversational skills, emphasizing that the specific definition of the scope of normative conversational performance is culture-sensitive and often reflects or echoes underlying cultural norms and ethos. For instance, in adult speech specific patterns of turn-taking phenomena such as high paced speaker change, high paced speech and frequent overlaps have been documented in female discourse (Edelsky, 1981) and in Jewish New Yorkers' high involvement style (Tannen, 1984), and discussed as linked to cultural concepts of social distance and solidarity. Similarly, our concepts of speaker and listener roles are affected by the Western communicative norm which places the onus of accountability for meaning on the speaker rather than on the hearer (Kochman, 1986). Work on children's conversations from this perspective, mainly within the traditions of ethnography, sociology, and sociolinguistics, has focused on conversation mainly as a site for social-relational work and for cultural identity construction. Researchers from these traditions study naturally occurring peer interactions while focusing on issues such as language-bound cultural patterns, power negotiations, social relations in and out of play and gender identities. Thus studies of child culture with an anthropological orientation have shown how participation in peer conversations is important for children's co-construction of specific language bound cultural patterns. Examples of these patterns include food-sharing, peace-making, and exchange rituals among Israeli children (Katriel, 1991), African-American children's unique patterns of dispute (M. H. Goodwin, 1990), and Italian and American children's styles of argumentation (Corsaro & Rizzo, 1990). Studies from a socio-cultural perspective also pinpointed the discursive ways in which children collaboratively co-construct social relationships in play (Corsaro, 1985), negotiate power asymmetries in same sex dyads (M. H. Goodwin, 2002) and re-affirm gender identities (Faris, 2000; Kyratzis, 1999).

Discursive phenomena are addressed by these studies to varying degrees: while some do not focus specifically on talk, others are grounded in detailed linguistic and interactional analysis and highlight language as a major resource in cultural and relational work. This range is mirrored in data collection methods, moving from exclusive reliance on observations and field notes to the integration of recordings, transliterations, and at times transcriptions. Our work is informed by both traditions, and aims at integrating them to the study of naturally occurring peer talk from a double perspective, both developmental and socio-cultural (Hamo et al., 2004).

Table 20.1: Conversational skills

	Mechanisms of Conversation	*Dialogicity*

Micro-level	• Turn-taking abilities:
	  ○ Projecting turning relevance place
	  ○ Producing minimal pauses
	  ○ Applying a range of speaker selection strategies
	  ○ Securing extended turns
		• Cross-turn relevance:
		  ○ Employing a variety of cohesion devices
		  ○ Maintaining topical relevance: Gricean maxims, adjacency pairs, indirectness

Macro-level	• producing a balanced participation structure
	• Appropriately carrying out interactional roles:
	  ○ exhibiting awareness of the need for interlocutors' acknowledgment
	  ○ acting as an active listener
	• Opening and closing conversations
		• Initiating topics drawing on a range of initiation strategies
		• Maintaining lasting topical coherence
		• Allowing for a gradual topical progression (topic shifts)
		• Selecting context-sensitive, appropriate and interesting topics
		• Expanding topics
		• Distancing from the immediate context
		• Marking and identifying keys and keyings
		• Employing politeness strategies and doing face work
		• Employing register and style variation

Meta-knowledge	• Recognizing breakdowns and repairing them • Evaluating the conversational competence of others	

The two lines of research discussed above viewed children's conversations either as a site for acquiring and exhibiting interactional skills, or for accomplishing social and cultural functions. Our claim here is that conversation is a unique phenomenon that cannot be described merely as the sum of the skills it requires, or even by the variety of social functions it may fulfill, but foremost holistically, as a unique social framework and activity type. Adopting such a holistic view in analyzing children's conversations will allow us to unveil how children come to recognize conversation as a unique activity type, learn to divorce it from other activities at hand, and reach an understanding of its macro social function as talk for talk's sake.

The nature and status of conversation as a defined activity type are highly ambiguous (Linell, 1998), and still await a systematic definition. We propose to focus here on a major defining characteristic of conversation: conversation is *talking-for-talking-sake*. It is talk as a social activity in its own right, not subordinate to any physical activity and not goal-oriented, but rather focused on spending time together, enjoying companionship and establishing sociable and communal bonds (Eggins & Slade, 1997; Goffman, 1981, p. 14, fn. 8). Our aim in the present study is to trace the emergence of this activity type in preschool peer interactions, through a focus on two major axes: the move from activity-related to independent talk, and the emergence of sociable talk. We hope to demonstrate that moving from activity-related talk to talk as an independent activity is an important step in becoming competent social agents, and in preparing the ground for the emergence of truly sociable talk.

Data and Method

The naturally occurring peer interactions analyzed in the present study were collected during eight months of fieldwork in two

Israeli preschools in 1999–2000.[3] Children were recorded during free-play time: an hour and a half mid-school day, devoted to free play in the yard, drawing and coloring, book reading, playing on the computer, with building blocks or with dolls etc. During this period, children interacted freely with each other in a variety of participation structures and predominantly without any adult intervention. Three types of recordings were used: (1) child-focused audio recordings of children wearing lapel microphones connected to a tape recorder in a small pouch; (2) setting-focused audio recordings taped by a small tape recorder placed at the center of some activity (e.g., the drawing table); and (3) setting-focused video recordings. Recordings were supplemented by extensive field notes providing contextual and background information. Materials were transcribed using an amended version of the Jeffersonian Conversational Analytic transcription system (see appendix of this chapter for transcription conventions).

Children's talk was mapped using a discursive model developed for describing and analyzing the rich spectrum of peer talk. Interactions were segmented into discursive episodes, and each episode was coded for genre and keying (Blum-Kulka et al., 2004). Following initial results of this coding, the present study focused mainly on discursive episodes identified as conversational, or 'chat'. Such episodes do not have specific underlying structural features (Eggins & Slade, 1997), and were identified using three criteria: (1) talk-focused talk, not subordinate to physical activity; (2) relatively balanced turn-taking and the lack of extended discourse; (3) the lack of global genre-related structural framework, such as narrative, discussion, or conflict.

The Emergence of Conversation: From Activity-Related to Independent Talk

During free play periods in the preschool, children are engaged in a variety of activities: pretend play, joint book reading, playing with building blocks or on the computer, drawing, or coloring. In the course of these activities, they have ample chances to talk with their peers; however, in the vast majority of cases, this talk remains subordinate to the physical activity at hand, or is used to advance pretend play, and only rarely do the children engage in conversation in it own right.

As children play together in the preschool, or draw side by side, they are in a state of co-presence without constant joint attention. Goffman (1981: 134–5) has identified such occasions as "open states of talk," during which focused talk is possible but not necessary, and participants can move relatively freely in and out of conversation. Recent work on classroom discourse of school aged children investigated the complex relations between context, activity and talk in those states, focusing on the opportunities to converse different activity frames offer and on the limits they place on talk, on the use of context as a resource for initiating conversation and on other engagement strategies (Jones & Thornborrow, 2004; Szymanski, 1999).[4] In the following we analyze three segments, each presenting a different relation between activity and talk. We focus on initiation and engagement patterns and on the linguistic and topical characteristics of each segment in order to demonstrate the ways preschoolers gradually move from activity-related talk to independent conversations.

Example 1 is a typical example of activity-related talk. The two children are drawing faces using a computer software; they coordinate their actions through talk by giving instructions ("press here again"), seeking information ("Where is Tet?"), or monitoring and announcing their own actions ("I'm going to make something really nice for you"). The relatively subordinate status of talk in this segment is indexed by the use of highly contextualized and instrumental language, and is evident in the frequent long pauses, indicating that talking is possible but not required, and there is no obligation to maintain the conversational flow.

EXAMPLE 1

10.1.00, "Einit" Preschool, Jerusalem

Participants: Guy, male, 5;11, Mor, female, 5;3, Dani, Male, 5;4.

The children are playing a computer game of drawing faces, using preset options of different facial components based on the Hebrew alphabet (Bet, Kuf, Kaf, Tet, Lamed, and Alef are Hebrew letter names).

1 Guy: axshav tilxeci po. ani yode'a ma ani o- (.) tilxeci po shuv. (.) o↑key↓ ani holex la'asot lax mashehu nora yafe. at ROCA la'asot et kol ha-pircos, et kol ha-parcufim?

   Guy: now press here. I know what I'm d- (.) press here again. (.) o↑key↓ I'm going to make you something really nice. Do you WANT to make all the fice, all the faces?

2 Mor: °ken°.

   Mor: °yes°.

3 Guy: o↑key↓ (1.0) aval↑ (1.0) bet, efo °bet°?

   Guy: o↑key↓ (1.0) but↑ (1.0) bet, where's °bet°?

4 Mor: bet .

   Mor: Bet.

5 Guy: bet, ku:f, (1.0) ka::f (1.37) (tni li liyot) leyad °bet°=

   Guy: Bet, ku:f, (1.0) Ka::f (1.37) (let me be) by ((this)) °bet° =

6 Mor: = EFO TET?

   Mor: = WHERE'S TET?

7 Guy: lamed. (1.3) l:o o↑mer. (1.0) xet. (3.0) alef.

   Guy: Lamed. (1.3) ((I)) do:n't sa↑y. (1.0) xet. (3.0) alef.

8 Mor: alef.

   Mor: alef.

9 Guy: zehu:, ve-nixtov (1.34) <be:t °shuv pam.°> hine. axshav ani elxac, enter. > roca lir'ot ma ikre?< ze ya'ase bet pa'amayi:m (0.84) >ba-sof ve-ba-hatxala< (xiyux) e:: (1.3) krica↑ (8.37) [yafe?

   Guy: that's i:t, and we'll write (1.34) <be:t ° once again.°> There. Now I'll press, enter. >do you want to see what will happen?< it will make bet twi:ce. (0.84) >at the end and at the beginning< (a smile) e:: (1.3) a wink↑ (8.37) [nice?

10 Dani: [ulay] na'ase she-hu (yivke) le-tamid?

   Dani: [maybe] we'll make him (cry) for ever?

EXAMPLE 2

7.3.00, "Einit" preschool, Jerusalem.

Participants: Sigal, female, 4:8, Daniela, female, 5;9, Guy, male, 6;1, Raxeli, female, 4;7, other unidentified girls and a boy.

In an activity celebrating the holiday "Purim," the children stand in line waiting to have make up put on by their friends.

1 Girl1: HA-BA BA-TO::R↑

   Girl1: NEXT IN LI::NE↑

2 Sigal: ani ba-TO:::R.

   Sigal: I'm neX::T.

3 Daniela: Sigal?

   Daniela: Sigal?

4 Sigal: l::evi'a.

   Sigal: l::ioness.

5 Daniela: ma at roca?

   Daniela: what do you want?

6 Sigal: le- levia.

   Sigal: li- lioness.

7 Daniela: <le::viya?> eh, (1.7) tov, az ani cxa ceva shel (. . .)

   Daniela: <li::oness?> eh, (1.7) well, so I need the color of (. . .)

8 Guy: ze, >eze ceva at cixa<?

   Guy: this one, >which color do you need?<

9 Girl2: cahov carix, l- l- levi'a hi be-ceva °cahov°.

   Girl2: you need yellow, l- l- lioness is °yellow°.

10 Raxeli: o be-ceva katom.

   Raxeli: or in orange.

11 Boy1: leviya hi amra, lo?

   Boy1: lioness she said, no?

12 Girl2: lo, hi amra levi'a.

   Girl2: no, she said lioness.

13 Boy1: leviya↑

   Boy1: lione↑ss

14 Guy: HINE, HINE CEVA cahov.

   Guy: HERE, HERE IS yellow color.

15 Raxeli: lo, o ceva cahov o cheva katom.(1.0) o ceva cahov o ceva katom.

   Raxeli: no, or yellow or orange. (1.0) or yellow or orange.

Activity-related talk does offer at times chances for a momentary move from the instrumental and concrete to relatively autonomous talk. In Example 2, the children are applying make up to each other's faces as part of the celebration of the Purim holiday in the preschool. The segment mostly exhibits the same features of the previous example: contextualized instrumental language used to coordinate and monitor the activity at hand. However, in turn 9 the focus of the interaction moves away from the specific task the children are performing, as one of the girls grounds the need for a specific color in a general, decontextualized description of the natural world: "yellow you need, a lioness is yellow." In the course of task-related instrumental talk, the children may often feel the need to ground or justify their actions and suggestions by using explanations, resulting in a local shift from the instrumental to a more general discussion. These local shifts may eventually lead to more extended sequences of non-task-related utterances (Habib, Hamo, Huck-Taglicht, & Blum-Kulka, 2002).

In Examples 1 and 2, the activities the children engage in require coordination through talk, due to their challenging nature (operating the computer and identifying the alphabet) or to their cooperative nature (applying make up on each other). In contrast, in Example 3 the children have been asked to complete a simple monotonous task – to stick small colored stickers on paper cutouts of a flower and a butterfly. As a result, there is little need to pay focused attention to the task or to monitor and coordinate it through talk, and an "incipient floor" is created (Jones & Thornborrow, 2004). There are long pauses during which the children work silently, but from time to time the silence is broken in favor of conversation. Example 3 is the longest and most developed conversation during the entire coloring event. It is initiated by drawing on the physical context as a topical resource, through a noticing remark[5] – a child comments on Dani farting, leading to a sequence of teasing targeting the guilty party. Hair color is first introduced to the conversation as a ground for teasing, using the metaphor of coal for black hair and predicting a change in Dani's hair color (turn 9). The children move from a focused teasing targeting Dani to a general discussion of hair color, using three metaphors: coal, chicks, and the Pokemon cartoon character Pikachu.

EXAMPLE 3

30.3.00, "Einit" preschool, Jerusalem.
Participants: Naomi, female, 5;11, Dani, male, 5;10, Rafael, male, 6;1, Becky, female, 5;7, Alon, male, 4;11, other unidentified boys and a girl.

The children are sitting around a long table and sticking colorful stickers on paper cutouts. Naomi and Rafael are blond; Dani has bright chestnut hair.

| 1 | Boy: ani mic- ani mictae↑r dani aval as-aval asur laasot flocim ba-ga↓n a-ze. | Boy: I'm so I'm so↑rry Dani but it's-it's not allowed to fart in th↓s preschool. |

((7 turns omitted: the children continue to tease Dani, calling him "a farter" and making fun of his too long hair))

9	Boy: [ve-ata carix] ladaat lexa she-od meat iye lexa sear- (lox-) kmo pexam, ve-a-sear shelxa iye pexa↑m. ((laughter))	Boy: [and you have] to know that in a short while you'll have- (lox-) like coal, and your hair will be coa↑l. ((laughter))
10	Boy: >ve-gam ata tiye [pexa↑m<]	Boy: >And you will also be [coa↑l<]
11	Naomi:[>o↑y o↑y<] a- acilu acilu a-axoti↑ i pexa↑m (2.9) (...) ki yesh la sear˙ ((laughter))	Naomi:　　[>o↑y o↑y<] he- help help m- my si↑ster is coa↑l (2.9) (...) because she has hair‿ ((laughter))

((9 turns omitted: the children continue to discuss hair colors))

23	Naomi: LO, ANI efroax. ani, rafael, ani ve-DANI, anaxnu efroxim, ki yesh lanu sear cahov. [cahov.] eze kef lanu↑ =	Naomi: NO, I'M a chick. Me, Rafael, me and DANI, we're chicks, because we have yellow hair. [Yellow.] How great for us↑ =
24	Dani:　　[lo naxon.]	Dani: [you're wrong.]
25	Boy: =L::O, [LI YESH-	Boy: =N::O, [I HAVE-
26	Dani:　　[°lo naxon,°] ze xum bahir im kcat↑ °ceva cahov°	Dani: [°you're wrong,°] it's light brown with a little↑ °yellow color°

27 (1.4) ((background noises))

28 Naomi: lo na:xon↑. li ze axi ((haxi)) cahov. u↑f, be'ecem le-dani en <sear cahov> °(k'tom)°

Naomi: you're wro:ng↑. Mine is the elloest ((yellowiest)). U↑f, actually Dani doesn't have <yellow hair> °(ornge)°

29 Dani: LI yesh rak↑ kca:t ((cahov)). Az ani kcat gam pikachu =

Dani: I HAve only↑ a litt:le ((yellow)). So I'm also a little bit Pikachu =

30 Boy: =°naxon.° ((laughing)) =

Boy: =°right.° ((laughing)) =

31 Boy: =°lo naxon.°

Boy: =°wrong.°

32 Rafael: nu, gam ani kcat pikachu.

Rafael: well, I'm also a little bit Pikachu.

33 Boy: lo naxon, ki le-pikachu en, .h en sear. ((the children laugh))

Boy: wrong, because Pikachu doesn't have, .h doesn't have hair. ((the children laugh))

34 Erez: (1.7) Rafael, Rafael gam ata lo pikachu, aval- (...)-

Erez: (1.7) Rafael, Rafael you're also not Pikachu, but- (...)-

35 Naomi: =axoti pikachu ki yesh la (.) e::m, nu, yesh la, [(xulca cehuba)]

Naomi: =my sister's Pikachu because she has (.) e::m, well, she has, [[a yellow shirt]]

36 Erez: [rak im ticbeu et a-sear be- be-sprey cahov

Erez: [only if you'll color your hair with- with a yellow spray.

37 Child: (1.5) ixs.

Child: (1.5) yuck.

38 Boy: hey, aval rega adain lo-

Boy: hey, but just a second you still do-

39 Naomi: LI MAT'IM LIYOT PIKACHU, .h KI LI YESH SEAR HAXI AROX.

Naomi: I SHOULD BE PIKACHU, .h BECAUSE I HAVE THE LONGEST HAIR.

40 Boy: (1.4) [aval at lo-

Boy: (1.4) [But you're no-

41 Dani: (1.4) [aval le-pikachu] en sear.

Dani: (1.4) [but Pikachu] doesn't have hair.

42 Boy: na[xo:n

Boy: ri[gh:t.

43 Rafael: [rega, exad, ani caho↑v. ((some children laugh))

Rafael: [Just, a second, I'm yello↑w. ((some children laugh))

44 Boy: (ma?) ((some children laugh))

Boy: (What?) ((some children laugh))

45 Girl: e, axoti (..) pikachu ki, ki hi cehuba kula↑

Girl: e, my sister (..) Pikachu because, because she's yellow all over↑

46 Child: (1.6) st-

Child: (1.6) st-

47 Naomi: =lo naxon, im gam az efroax (...) en [[(...)-

Naomi: =wrong, if also then a chick (...) doesn't [[(...)-

48 Erez: [aval kol exad cahov. >le-kol exad (yesh) ta-panim ((et ha-panim)) shelo °cehubim.° < lax po yesh caho:v, (3.0) ve-li↑ yesh [po ve-po.

Erez: [but everyone is yellow. >everyone (has) da ((the)) face °yellow.° < you have here yello:w, (3.0) and I have↑ [here and here.

49 Alon: [LAMA?] <LA-INDYANIM EN.>

Alon: [WHY?] <THE INDIANS DON'T.>

50 Naomi: .h gam LA-[ETYO]PIYO↑T EN↑ (8.0) [E::-

Naomi: .h also THE [ETHIO]PI↑ANS DON'T↑ (8.0) [E::-

51 Dani: [naxon.]

Dani: [right.]

52 Erez: [GAM L-] (5.0) la-aravim en,

Erez: [ALSO TH-] (5.0) the Arabs don't,

53 Dani: gam la-marokaim en. ((giggling))

Dani: also the Moroccans don't. ((giggling))

54 Naomi: GAM LA-SINIM E:- (2.0) EN [°la-sinim yesh°

Naomi: ALSO THE CHINESE E:- (2.0) DON'T [°the Chinese have°]

55 Becky: [savTA SHELI MAROKAIT =

Becky: [my GRADMA IS MOROCCAN =

56	Naomi: =LA-SINIM AVAL YESH-	Naomi: =THE CHINESE BUT HAVE-
57	Dani: (5.0) en la-=	Dani: (5.0) she doesn't-= ((have))
58	Naomi: =AVAL E- (2.0) LANU EN E:- (4.0) enayim meluxsa↑not, aval la-sinim davka yesh.	Naomi: =BUT E- (2.0) WE DON'T ((have)) E:- (4.0) slanted eye↑s, but the Chinese do have them.
59	Boy: rak la-kushim en °ani xoshev.°	Boy: only the Negros don't °I think.°
60	Alon: HE::Y, h- ha-kushim e:- ((laughing))	Alon: HE::Y, t- the Negros e:- ((laughing))
61	Naomi: HEY, ASUR LEHAGID KUSHIM ZE MA'ALIV ET A-ETYOPIM. (6.0) >omrim etyopim bimkom kushim.<	Naomi: HEY, YOU CAN'T SAY NEGROS IT INSULTS THE ETHIOPIANS. (6.0) >you say Ethiopians instead of Negros.<
62	Boy: ata kushi.	Boy: You're a negro.
63	Alon: ata kushi.	Alon: You're a negro.

((7 turns omitted: the children continue to call each other "Negro"))

This humorous argument gradually involves more and more referents – first, the participants themselves, then family members, and eventually, people in the world. The topical shift from the local circle of participants and acquaintances to a general and distant discussion of ethnicities is accomplished in turns 48–49. Erez claims that "everyone is yellow," and Alon counters by evoking the Indians, who are not. From this point on, the children collaboratively enumerate different ethnicities (Indians, Ethiopians, Moroccan, Chinese, and Blacks), noting their skin colors and facial features, a topic which eventually leads them to drift into a discussion of social politically correct norms. Finally, they come full circle and return to a playful teasing mode (turns 62–63).

The initiation and progression of Example 3 draw on relatively advanced conversational skills. Noticing events and objects is a common strategy for topic initiation both in adult talk and in the discourse of school-aged children (Linell & Korolija, 1997; Szymanski, 1999), gradual topic shifts are a salient feature of adult conversations (Linell & Korolija, 1997), and their use was found to contribute to the ability of school-aged children to maintain extended conversational episodes (Schober-Peterson & Johnson, 1993). The children also exhibit highly developed turn-taking and cross-turn relevance patterns: the cross-turn links are based at least on lexical cohesion ("coal">"coal") combined with loose topical relevance (as between turns 10 and 11), and at best, on combining the use of cohesive markers (note the anaphoric use of "it's" in turn 24, referring back to "yellow hair" in turn 23) with full topical relevance (refuting a previous claim while presupposing it, as in turns 26, 31, and 33) resulting in coherent exchanges. A third option used by the children is manifest in turns 48–52: an elliptical structure ("Xs have/have not") serves as a syntactic frame for a rhythmic sequence in which each contribution substitutes a new referent for "X," until Naomi uses the same frame to introduce a topical shift (turns 53–55).

Example 3 demonstrates that such features and strategies, though rare, emerge at an early age, resulting in highly developed, rich, and complex sequences. This complexity is evident in the keyings and themes of example 3. The children move freely between a humorous teasing key (e.g., turn 36), a pretend key (turns 39–41) and a serious key (turns 49–51, 56–59). They gradually move from physically present, immediate referents to distant referents, and from contextualized, concrete language (turn 48) to decontextualized general statements (turns 58, 61). They draw on personal knowledge and acquaintance (e.g., turn 45), as well as on knowledge obtained through cultural texts (turns 49, 56), and merge a general objective stance (turn 53) with personal emotional involvement (turn 55). This richness of theme and keying, combined with the use of advanced con-versational strategies, allows for an extended coherent conversation which functions both as a source of amusement and as a site for exploring the human world while attending to issues of identity, social difference and cul-tural norms and morality.

Accomplishing Sociability

In the following section we shall discuss other rare cases of non-activity-related talk in preschool peer interaction. Each of the three segments presented below develops as an independent conversation while the chil-dren are engaged in some physical activity, and each demonstrates a different pattern of sociable talk in the preschool.[6] We shall focus our analysis of each of the segments on four issues: initiation strategies, participa-tion structure, the relative status of content and form, and sociability and other socio-cultural functions.

In Example 4, Ilan joins his best friend Yuval at the coloring table, and repeatedly attempts to initiate a sociable conversation with him. Each attempt is marked by a par-ticipatory embedding device – summoning Yuval by the use of his name (turns 1, 5, 9), and each attempt relies on a different strat-egy for topic initiation. In the first attempt (turn 1), Ilan mentions a newsworthy item concerning the immediate situation – the fact that he is wearing a lapel microphone; in his second attempt (turn 5) he draws on the more distant realm of children's popular culture, while using a conventional formula for topic initiation ("Do you know that X?"); and in his third, most successful attempt, he initiates a language game, probably echo-ing and paraphrasing an Israeli racist proverb ("a good X is a dead X"). Yuval becomes involved in this game, and the two boys cooperatively develop and expand a highly inventive cohesive sequence, which fulfills the sociable function of talk in its fullest sense: it establishes enjoyable and support-ive co-presence and joint attention, which reaffirm the two boys' friendship, without any transactional aim or referential content.

EXAMPLE 4

3.3.00, "Eynit preschool," Jerusalem
Participants: Ilan, male, 4;11, Yuval, male, 4;7.
Yuval is sitting at the coloring table, Ilan joins him and they both draw.

1 Ilan: Yuval samu li od a-pam. ((referring to the lapel microphone just attached to him by the researcher))   Ilan: Yuval they've put ((it)) on me again. ((referring to the lapel microphone just attached to him by the researcher))

2 Yuval: (1.0) ve-gam li yasimu ax:ar kax. (6.0) ma'ta ((ma ata)) xoshev? le-kula↑m yaSIMU::,   Yuval: (1.0) and on me too they'll put ((it)) la:ter. (6.0) what d'you ((do you)) know? On everybo↑dy they'll PU::T,

3 Ilan: lo le-kulam. hem matxilim me-ha-hatxala yuval.   Ilan: not on everybody. They're starting all over Yuval.

4 (25.0) ((The children draw in silence; voices of other children and of the teacher in the background))

5 Ilan: >Yuval ata ata yodea< she- .h she-ba- seret kasisi xokrim et ha-xa- (0.7) kirot ((xakirot)) ve-shama ((shma)) (.) mi asa zot?   Ilan: >Yuval do you do you know< that- .h that in the movie Kasisi they investigate the in- (0.7) vestigation ((investigation)) and that ((it's)) name (.) who's done it?

6 Yuval: mi?   Yuval: who?

7 Ilan: (3.0) shem ha-xakira ha-zot mi asa zot.   Ilan: (3.0) the name of this investigation is who's done it.

8 (7.0) ((the children continue to draw))

9 Ilan: >yuval< karish tov .h hu karish met.   Ilan: >Yuval< a good shark .h is a dead shark.

10 Yuval: (3.0) ma, karish tov hu karish she-hu me:t?   Yuval: (3.0) what, a good shark is a shark that is dea:d?

11 Ilan: ken. karish tov hu- hu karish °me↑t.°   Ilan: yes. A good shark is- is a dead °sha↑rk.°

12	Yuval: ve-gam krishonit me<u>ta</u>?	Yuval: and de<u>ad</u> sharkinoness ((neologism, female diminutive form of "shark")) is too?
13	Ilan: #krishonit#. ((emphatically, and in a slightly smiling voice)) (1.0) t- ve-gam krishoni<u>t</u> tova hi krishonit me<u>ta</u>. (2.0) 'ta yodea lama? =	Ilan: #sharkinoness#. ((emphatically, and in a slightly smiling voice)) (1.0) t- and also a good sharkinoness is a <u>dead</u> sharkinoness (2.0) d'you know why? =
14	Yuval: = ve-gam tir- tiraksa .h e:::m (.) (kol tova me-) =	Yuval: = and also tir- tirkasa .h e::m (.) (every good is de-) =
15	Ilan: = VE-GAM ve-gam ve-gam xayot, torfot, adam:meta ((adam meta)) (1.0) °hem xayot tovot.° (2.0) hine yuval, axshav ani roce tush axer. =	Ilan: = AND ALSO and also and also <u>dead</u>, carnivorous:animals ((carnivorous animals)) (1.0) °are good animals.° (2.0) here Yuval, now I want a different marker. =
16	Yuval: = kax.	Yuval: = take.

The conversational episode in Example 5 is initiated using a common strategy for topic initiation in both adult talk and school aged children's talk – an announcement (Linell & Korolija, 1997; Szymanski, 1999), through which Hila is describing her actions as noteworthy. This highly contextualized comment gradually leads to an elaborate discussion of Teletubbies costumes, independent from the ongoing activity of drawing. The most striking feature of this discussion is its high degree of mutual alignment and coordination, manifesting to the extreme the nature of talk as a mutual accomplishment. This is evident on all levels of language use. First, on the level of floor management and turn-taking: the episode exhibits characteristics of high involvement style (Tannen, 1984) – high paced talk, high pace of speaker change, short turns, and many overlatches. The conversational floor is highly polyphonic, as almost all the turns are secured using self-selection, and the frequent preference in conversation to return to the previous speaker (Sacks, Schegloff, & Jefferson, 1974) is relatively rare (only 9 of the 31 turns reflect this pattern). It might be argued that these characteristics echo the discursive styles of the target adult cultures of the participants – both the female interactive style (Edelsky, 1981) and the Israeli-Jewish style (Blum-Kulka, 1997).

On the level of sequential organization, collectively built utterances are frequent in the episode and are accomplished using many different strategies: the use of elliptic forms, relying on previous utterances for comprehension (e.g., turns 1–2); sentence completion by an interlocutor (e.g., turns 2–3); and a word search, accomplished precisely in the way documented in adult interaction (C. Goodwin, 1987; turns 19–20). At times, the pattern of collectively-built utterances reflects a high degree of pragmatic competence. Note, for example, turn 9 vis-à-vis turn 7: in turn 7, Hagar did not explicitly say what she did not want to do; Ravit infers this missing piece of information, but instead of simply completing Hagar's utterance, she presupposes it as a given, integrating it into a new piece of information – she too, like Hagar, did not want to buy the Teletubbies costume.

The same features are mirrored in the patterns of dialogicity, both on the micro-level of local contentedness and on the macro-level of topical organization. The episode is highly cohesive, due to a regular use of repetition (e.g., of the phrase "me too," or of the word "stupid" in its various inflections). Thematically, the episode is geared toward establishing and reinforcing a consensus regarding Teletubbies costumes. This is accomplished gradually, as the girls move from establishing the existence of the object of their talk, to stating towards it negative attitudes, both affective and behavioral. They then introduce the attitudes of their mothers, and finally, move to a more general discussion of costumes.

EXAMPLE 5

13.3.00, "Eynit" preschool, Jerusalem.

Participants: Galia, female, 4;7, Ravit, female, 5;0, Hila, female, 4;4, Hagar, female, 4;7, Mixal, female, 4;3, three unidentified girls.

The girls are sitting at the drawing table, coloring.

1	Hila: ani osa (.) <tele:↑tabi::z.>	Hila: I'm making (.) <Tele:↑tubbie::s.>
2	Girl₁: (0.8) YESH BA-XANUYOT	Girl₁: (0.8) THERE ARE IN THE STORES
3	Galia: shel purim ve-raiti teletabiz.	Galia: for Purim and I saw Teletubbies.
4	Girl₁: oish an- ani raiti ba-xanut et ha- (.) teletabiz she-	Girl₁: Oish I- I saw in the store the- (.) Teletubbies that-
5	Galia: (.) GAM ANI	Galia: (.) ME TOO
6	Hila: gam ani .	Hila: Me too.
7	Hagar: she-ha-metumtam lo raciti afilu-=	Hagar: of the stupid I didn't want even-=
8	Galia: =ze metumtam haya (.) be-kol miney .h ha-cvaim shel shel ha-teletabiz ha-=	Galia: =It was stupid (.) in all sorts .h of colors of of the-Teletubbies the-=
9	Ravit: =GAM ANI lo raciti liknot oto, lefaxot she-kanit- she-lo raciti ta- teletabiz ((et ha-teletabiz)) °ha-ele.°	Ravit: =ME TOO I didn't want to buy it, at least that ((I)) bought- that I didn''t want th'Teletubbies ((the Teletubbies)) °those.°
10	Galia: gam aNI: ,	Galia: Me TOO:,
11	Ravit: (.) Le-faxot she-lo raci-=	Ravit: (.) At least that I didn't wan-=
12	Hagar: =ani lo raciti, ve-ima sheli gam e .h gam lo racta she-hi tikne li et ze.	Hagar: =I didn't want, and my mother also e .h also didn't want that she'd buy this for me.
13	Ravit: (0.1) ve-ani lo raciti, ve-ima sheli (....)	Ravit: (0.1) And I didn't want, and my mother (....)
14	Hila: ani ani- ani lo raciti =	Hila: I I- I didn't want =
15	Ravit: =KOL HA-ZMAN HEXLAFTI TAX-= ((taxposot))	Ravit: =I KEPT CHANGING COS-= ((costumes))
16	Mixal: =(...) kanta li et malkat ester↑	Mixal: =(...) bought me the queen Esther↑
17	Galia: (0.1) az lo↓ racit.	Galia: (0.1) so you did↓n't want.
18	Ravit: ani an- (0.1) kant:a li ota:↑m (0.2) et ma she-raciti (ze haya)-	Ravit: I I- (0.1) she bough:t me the:↑m (0.2) what I wanted (it was)-
19	Mixal: =ani. (.) ani afilu lo ra- citi ((raciti)) liknot >lo< °et↑° et h::a	Mixal: =I. (.) I even didn't' wa- nt ((want)) to buy >no< °the↑° the::
20	Hila: °>teletabiz.<°	Hila: °>Teletubbies.<°
21	Mixal: tele>tabi↑z.< ve- ve-ima sheli, afilu, gam lo hirsha li.	Mixal: Tele>tubbie↑s.< an- and my mother, even, also didn't let ((irregular form)) me.
22	Hila: (0.2) lama?	Hila: (0.2) Why?
23	Mixal: >ki kaxa↑ hi lo marsha li.< gam li ve-le-ron >ve-la-axim (sheli.)<	Mixal: >because just like tha↑t she doesn't let me.< Also to me and to Ron >and to (my) brothers.<
24	Ravit: (0.1) le-ro:↑n ima shela marsha la (ve...)	Ravit: (0.1) to ro:↑n her mother lets her (and...)
25	Girl₂: (0.5) IXSA:: ↑ eze metumtamim em ((hem)).	Girl₂: (0.5) YU::CK↑ how stupid dey ((they)) are.
26	Mixal: (.) ve-ron [mitxapeset]	Mixal: (.) and Ron is [dressing up]
27	Hagar: [metumtamim] la'ala.	Hagar: [totally] stupid.
28	Mixal: ve- ron mitxapeset <le-pingwin.>	Mixal: and Ron is dressing up <as a penguin.>
29	Galia: NU:: at at ala::y. ((complaining that Hila is leaning on her))	Galia: COME O::N you you're on m::e. ((complaining that Hila is leaning on her))
30	Girl₂: ani lifa'mim =	Girl₂: I sometimes =
31	Girl₃: =ani mitxapeset (le-ima) shel mor.	Girl₃: =I'm dressing up as Mor's (mother).

It is our claim that the main function of the episode is to construct a homogenous community with shared norms and beliefs, without leaving room for individuating information, in a manner that echoes the centrality of building shared world concepts as a developmental challenge for preschoolers (Corsaro, 1985). This function is accomplished by what Aston (1988) terms matching assessments: a routine by which "Participants provide evidence of affective convergence inasmuch as both parts are preferably built on the same frame of reference … thereby 'showing' rather than 'claiming' agreement" (p. 255–6). This function is manifested most strikingly in what is missing from the episode: in the entire episode, there is no use of second-person pronouns, there is only one occurrence of an information-seeking question (turn 22), no backchannel responses, and no explicit responses to the information each girl presents. The participants register the previously imparted information by presupposing it and moving the text forward. They are preoccupied primarily with constructing *a jointly agreed-upon collective claim*, and do not acknowledge the delicate differences between their potentially unique personal storylines. As a result, the interaction progresses linearly, and all the girls share the same discursive role – that of *co-tellers*. The salience of agreement and the construction of the joint linear argument are also apparent in the almost excessive use of repetition, lending the interaction a slightly mechanical and poetic nature. This is also reflected in the scarcity of informative content – very much like the television show discussed, the joy of conversation here is in the performance and not in the text.

In Example 5, sociability is achieved by emphasizing similarity and agreement. Example 6 demonstrates a slightly different accomplishment of the sociable function of talk. Like the "Teletubbies" episode, the episode exhibits a high degree of conversational competence, both in terms of turn-taking and of cohesion. But the participation structure of the discussion of the social network of the girls in Example 6

is different than that of the "Teletubbies" episode: three girls exchange roles as *main tellers* (Mor in turns 9–14; Dafna in turns 15–23 and 29–33; Naomi in turns 24–28), with their interlocutors taking the role of *an active audience*, by responding with questions and backchannels. The interaction progresses spirally – each girl tells her individual story, while maintaining cohesion and coherence with the previous story. This echoes the adult pattern of story rounds (Linell & Korolija, 1997). This pattern allows not just for manifesting mutual alignment but also for negotiating the tension between sameness and uniqueness – an underlying feature of adult conversation (Gurevitch, 1990; Linell, 1998).

The relatively more balanced and reciprocal participation structure of Example 6 allows for the accomplishment of several social functions: through supportive listenership and mutual interest, the girls foster their social bonds, and by establishing mutual acquaintances and a common social network, they construct a sense of community. But at the same time, they negotiate social boundaries and distinctions through an explicit discussion of participation entitlements (turns 37–40), and work towards gaining social status, power and prestige through name-dropping.

Both Example 5 and 6 are built around high degrees of cooperation and mutual alignment, but these are manifested in two distinct forms: through agreement and joint accomplishment in the "Teletubbies" episode, and through responsiveness and reciprocity in the "slumber party" episode. The differences between the two episodes can be interpreted from two complementing points of view, each focused on one dimension of the double opportunity space of peer talk (Blum-Kulka, 2005). As the "slumber party" participants are older by a year on average than the "Teletubbies" participants, it can be argued from a developmental perspective that the "Teletubbies" episode reflects the partial competence of young girls, who lack in their responsive ability, while the "slumber party" episode represents a higher level of conversational development. From a cultural perspective, the unique structure of the "Teletubbies" episode is not seen as reflecting limited competence, but rather as fulfilling child-specific social functions, such as constructing shared world concepts.

EXAMPLE 6

27.3.00, "Einit preschool," Jerusalem.
Participants: Naomi, female, 5;11, Mor, female, 5;5, Dafna, female, 6;3, Rotem, female, 5;10, unidentified girl.

The girls are playing in a structure called "the girls' structure" ("mivne shel ha-banot") in the back yard. They are using a strainer to strain and clean out sand from the sandbox for their "cooking."

1   Naomi: mi ra'ata a-yom mesibat pijamot?

    Naomi: who saw "Slumber party" today?

2   Mor: [ani::]

    Mor: [I di::d]

    Dafna: [<ani lo] ro'a kol #yo:::::m# ((trembling her voice))>=

    Dafna: [<I don't watch every #da:::::y# ((trembling her voices))>=

3   Rotem: =>gam ani lo<

    Rotem: =>me neither<

    Girl: (. . .)

    Girl: (. . .)

4   Mor: aval en.

    Mor: but there isn't.

5   Dafna: <ani be-yom (shlishi) lo:: #ro'a:::::#> ((trembling her voice))

    Dafna: <I on (Tuesday) do::n't #Wa::::tch#> ((trembling her voice))

6   Rotem: >ve-gam be-yom shishi<

    Rotem: >and not on Friday either<

7   Mor: AVAL BE-YOM SHLISHI ye- i e a axare (.) axare yom sheni a-ba, ba yom shlishi?

    Mor: BUT ON TUESDAY the- i e a after (.) after next Monday, there's Tuesday?

8   Rotem: ken.

    Rotem: Yes.

9   Mor: .h az ax- az be-yom shishi ani olexet le-yom uledet shel il- shel ilon.

    Mor: .h So af- so on Friday I'm going to the birthday of il- of ilon.

10   Naomi: [LO BE-YOM] shishi

    Naomi: [NOT ON] Friday

11   Dafna: [shlishi?]

    Dafna: [Tuesday?]

12   Mor: ke. ((ken)) (.) lo, amarti shlishi, lo- lo shishi =

    Mor: Ye. ((yes)) (.) No., I said Tuesday, no- not Friday =

13   Dafna: =ve-ani be-yom shlishi ulay ba'a el gil ve-le- ve-ani yesaxek im axot shelo. (.) °ki ani makira ota. i ayta po shana she-avra axot shel gil.°

    Dafna: =and I on Tuesday may be going to gil and to- and I'll play with his sister. (.) °Because I know her. She was here last year Gil's sister.°

14   Naomi: KOR'IM LA RO↑N

    Naomi: HER NAME IS RO↑N

15   Dafna: #naxon. # ((laughing voice))

    Dafna: #Right.# ((laughing voice))

16   Mor: E[FO?

    Mor: WH[ERE?

17   Dafna: [ve-ani yesaxek im ron-=

    Dafna: [And I'll play with Ron-=

18   Mor: =EFO RON?

    Mor: =WHERE'S RON?

19   Dafna: ron? ron ba:- ba-kita a↑lef

    Dafna: Ron? Ron is in the: in the first gra↑de

20   Mor: °a°

    Mor: °oh°

21   Dafna: ve-ani yesaxek im >ro↑n< ve-ani yesaxek im °gil.°

    Dafna: And I'll play with >Ro↑n< and I'll play with °Gil.°

22   Naomi: >ani mkira, et a-yeled exad axi metumtam< ba-olam

    Naomi: >I know, one kid the most stupid< in the world

23   Dafna: mi? =

    Dafna: who? =

24   Mor: =ex korim lo?

    Mor: =what's his name?

25   Naomi: ariel noy.

    Naomi: Ariel Noy.

26   Mor: ariel noy?

    Mor: Ariel Noy?

27   Dafna: (.) ani- atem yodim? (0.1) em mor, at yoda↑'at? naxon, elad pontiflo↑ra? az ani mekira gam et ax shel↑o, (0.1) ve-gam, e:m yalda me-a-kita shelo. =

    Dafna: (.) I- you know? (0.1) em Mor, you kno↑w? you know, Elad Pontiflo↑ra? So I know both his bro↑ther, (0.1) and also, e::m a girl from his class. =

28   Rotem: =LO NAXO::N. ani yora alexem, ani yora alexem °[(. . .)]° =

    Rotem: =WRONG. I'm shooting at you, I'm shooting at you °[(. . .)]° =

29 Dafna: [ve-yesh] lo gam axot le-xav- le::-yalda me-akita shelo, ve-ani mkira ota biglal she- ve-ani yoda'at gam ex korim la. vered (.) gam le-axot shela korim no:ga. (0.2) ve-ve-em be-emet bno-bn- °bnot dodim sheli ° (0.1) °em be-emet (0.1) ve-ani mkira ota ve-gam et oded.°

Dafna: [and he] also has a sister to his frie- to::- a girl from his class, and I know her because o- and I also know her name. Vered. (.) Also her sister is called No:ga. (0.2) an- and they are really my cou- cou- °my cousins° (0.1) °they are really, (0.1) and I know her and also Oded.°

30 Mor: mi ze oded?

Mor: who's Oded?

31 Dafna: oded ze a-ax shel elad pontiflora, ve-at ve-at [lo↑ °makira°]

Dafna: Oded is Elad Pontiflora's brother, and you and you [don't °know°]

32 Rotem: [° (..) yesh lo od ax] yesh lo od ax

Rotem: [°(..) he has another brother] he has another brother

33 Mor: gam le-rotem yesh shtey axim (0.2) naxon rotem?

Mor: Rotem has two brothers too (0.2) right Rotem?

34 Rotem: (naxon) yesh li shtey axim.

Rotem: (right) I have two brothers.

35 Dafna: ken aval av-aval aval em aval °lo dibarnu itax mor° (0.2) anaxnu anax-

Dafna: yes but bu-but but but em but °we weren't talking with you Mor° (0.2) we w-

36 Girl: AT LO MAKIRA et elad <pontiflora.>

Girl: YOU DON'T KNOW Elad <Pontiflora.>

37 Dafna: #i gam lo makira et oded (.) ve-et noga ve-vered# ((smiling voice))

Dafna: #she also doesn't know Oded and Noga and Vered# ((smiling voice))

38 Girl: az lama at omeret?

Girl: so why do you say?

The three episodes presented above form a continuum of types of sociable talk, ranging form pure language games to more referential discussions. The role of content in children's sociable conversations changes as we move on this continuum – from insignificance, as in the case of the "Sharkinoness," to playing an important part in negotiat-

ing and establishing social status, as in the case of the "slumber party." The "Teletubbies" episode demonstrates an intermediate position – while content does play a role in establishing socially-agreed norms and attitude, the mechanical nature of the episode, as well as the fact that discrepancies between contributions are not explicitly discussed, may indicate that maintaining agreement and coherence is more important than exploring the issue at hand. This continuum is part of a larger continuum – ranging from the non-verbal proto-conversations of infants (Trevarthen & Hubey, 1978) to the fully competent sociable talk of adults.

Conclusion

In one sense, this chapter can be taken as a further rebuttal of the old stereotype of young children as non-communicators. As we saw, even if they do not do so frequently, young children do engage in sociable talk and can enjoy talk for talk's sake. We focused on a specifically adult-associated form of communication, namely sociable conversation, and showed its modes of emergence in peer talk from two points of view: first, in its move from activity-related to independent talk, and second, in its evolving modes of sociability.

The children in the preschools observed manifest a drive to converse: when the activity at hand allows for engaging in talk-for-talk-sake, they initiate such talk. The drive to converse is even more evident in the findings of Cekaite and Aronsson (2004) who observed conversations in a Norwegian immersion classroom, and found that children with very limited proficiency in the target language applied the few shared linguistic recourses they had to produce humorous sociable talk. This drive can be interpreted as evidence of the impact of culture and modes of enculturation on young children. In many Western countries, including Israel, talking to children from birth and encouraging child participation in multi-party and intergenerational encounters are much practiced and highly valued practices (Blum-Kulka, 1997; Blum-Kulka & Snow, 2002). Alternatively, it can be viewed as supporting the claim that non-goal-oriented sociable talk is a universal phenomenon (Moerman, 1990/1991).

By way of summary, we shall point out some of the major similarities and differences between the preschool conversations of our corpus and adult conversation. Perhaps surprisingly, the two share many characteristics. First, both adult and child conversations are highly context-sensitive and dependent on the affordances and limitations of the social frame of the situation, the activity type, and the task at hand. Some activity types – sitting at the coloring table for preschoolers or at the dinner table for adults – enable participants to move in and out of a state of conversation, and to intermingle it with task-oriented talk, resulting in a wide range of initiation and engagement strategies shared by adults and young children. Second, preschoolers' conversations exhibit many interactive patterns documented in adult conversations, such as collectively built utterances, story rounds, or audience involvement strategies. Third, adult and child conversations often fulfill similar functions – constructing a sense of community, negotiating social status, power and boundaries, establishing shared norms and attitudes and so on, and they often draw on the same thematic resources – popular culture or familiar social networks.

Against the backdrop of these similarities, the most striking difference between preschool and adult conversation is the relative balance of form and content. Either due to their more limited conversational competencies or to the unique norms and needs of their peer culture, preschoolers' conversations tend to be more focused on form, leaving content much less significant than it is in adult talk. This results in highly poetic sequences, and is evident, for example, in the salience of repetition in the conversations analyzed above. The progression from mere repetition (sometimes of just nonsense syllables, as observed for almost three year old twins by Keenan, 1974) to full issue-related or sociable conversations can be taken as a move from a focus on the code as such to a focus on the content. At one end of this continuum joint sound play, repetition, prosody, and verbal routines serve as major resources for mutual engagement; at the other end, prosody interacts with linguistic and pragmatic skills in the co-construction of more adult-like sociable conversations. From the socio-cultural and interactive perspective on pragmatic development adopted here, the important point is that underlying all verbal manifestations of this continuum is the drive for sociability through language and conversation.

Appendix: Transcription Conventions

[words] – overlapping talk
= – overlatch
(0.5) – timed intervals
(.) – intervals of less than 0.2 seconds
(. . .) – incomprehensible words
(words) – transcription doubt
. – a falling intonation at the end of an utterance
, – a continuing rising intonation
? – a rising intonation at the end of an utterance
↑ – a sharp rise in pitch
↓ – a sharp fall in pitch
WORD – high volume
°word° – low volume
word – emphasis
wo::rd – sound stretch
wor- – cut off
.h – in breath
>words< – fast rhythm
<words> – slow rhythm
{word} – unusual pronunciation
#words# – unusual tone, indicated in a comment
word/word/word – rhythmic pronunciation
((comment)) – transcriber's comments

Notes

1   The present article is focused on *conversational* skills and does not review other related clusters of skills. First, basic linguistic competence is naturally assumed as a prerequisite; second, our focus here is on general conversational skills rather than on the related field of pragmatic development, which includes topics like speech acts, indirectness or genre-specific skills, such as storytelling (Ninio & Snow, 1996); and third, we focus on discursive skills with concrete linguistic and

interactive manifestations, rather than on cognitive, emotional and social skills which underlie those discursive phenomena. Such skills (e.g., perspective taking, identity construction, social boundaries negotiation) have received wide attention in the fields of developmental psychology, sociology and anthropology (Corsaro, 1985; M. H. Goodwin, 2002; Hughes & Dunn, 1998; Rogoff, 1990), and go beyond the scope of the present article.

2   For another classification of pragmatic skills see Ninio and Snow (1996); for a similar classification of conversational skills, see Nelson and Gruendel (1979).

3   The present study is part of a large-scale longitudinal study of pragmatic development, designed to provide a context-sensitive developmental account of the acquisition of different discourse genres. This study focused on 20 Israeli target children from the two preschools observed, following them over the duration of three years. The children were recorded during three types of speech events: (1) naturally occurring peer interactions; (2) family mealtimes; (3) semi-structured adult-child interviews. The study also included 20 target children of an older cohort (9–10 year old at the onset of the study), recorded over the same period and in the same speech events. The study further included a cross-cultural component, based on data collected in American preschools. The project was funded by the American-Israeli Binational Science Foundation Grant No. 980031, 1999–2002, and Grant No. 2001070, 2002–2005, and by ISF Grant No. 83201, 2001–2004.

4   Relations between activity, physical context and talk in child language have been explored from two additional perspectives: (1) the discursive literacy perspective, focusing on the emergence of decontextualized language (Habib, Hamo, Huck-Taglicht, & Blum-Kulka, 2002) required for academic discourse; and (2) studies on the interface between talk and physical context, delineating the moment-by-moment embedding of talk in its surroundings through micro-analysis (cf. C. Goodwin, 2000).

5   The physical context may have had an additional contribution to the progression of this episode. It can be argued that the presence of stickers in different colors led to the priming of colors as an organizing scheme and a topical framework. This demonstrates the com-

plex possible relations between context and discourse – a major issue in the study of talk-in-interaction (Hamo et al., 2004).

6   Although sociable talk as an activity type is rare in the preschool, interpersonal functions associated with sociability may often be accomplished through other activity types, in particular joint pretend play. Pretend play – which accounts for a large amount of the free-play time in the preschool – involves the joint project of establishing a coherent imaginary world and cooperatively "acting" in it. As such, it allows for enjoyable companionship, while emphasizing mutual knowledge and shared cultural background. Accordingly, it can be argued that pretend play is a unique child-specific way of accomplishing sociable functions – a claim which merits further research beyond the scope of the present article.

References

Andersen-Slosberg, E. (1990). *Speaking with style: The sociolinguistic skills of children*. London: Routledge.

Aronsson, K., & Thorell, M. (2002). Voice and collusion in adult-child talk: Toward an architecture of intersubjectivity. In: S. Blum-Kulka & C. Snow (Eds.), *Talking to adults* (pp. 277–295). Mahwah, NJ: Lawrence Erlbaum Associates.

Aston, G. (1988). *Learning Comity: An approach to the description and pedagogy of interactional talk*. Bologna: Editrice Clueb.

Blum-Kulka, S. (2005). Modes of meaning making in young children's conversational narratives. In: J. Thornborrow & J. Coates (Eds.), *The Sociolinguistics of narrative* (pp. 149–170). Antwerp: John Benjamins.

Blum-Kulka, S. (1997). *Dinner Talk: Cultural patterns of sociability and socialization in family discourse*. Mahwah, NJ: Lawrence Erlbaum Associates.

Blum-Kulka, S., Huck-Taglicht, D., & Avni, H. (2004). The social and discursive spectrum of peer talk. *Discourse Studies, 6*, 307–328.

Blum-Kulka, S., & Snow, C. (Eds.), (2002). *Talking with adults: The contribution of multi-party talk to language development*. Mahwah, NJ: Lawrence Erlbaum Associates.

Bordeaux, M. A., & Willbrand, M. L. (1987). Pragmatic development in children's telephone discourse. *Discourse Processes, 10*, 253–266.

Cekaite, A., & Aronsson, K. (2004). Repetition and joking in children's second language conversations: Playful recyclings in an immersion classroom. *Discourse Studies*, 6, 373–392.

Cheshire, J. (1991). Variation in the use of *ain't* in an urban British English dialect. In: P. Chambers & J. K. Trudgill. (Eds.), *Dialects of English: Studies in grammatical variation* (pp. 54–73). London: Longman.

Clancy, P. (1986). The acquisition of communicative style in Japanese. In: B. B. Schieffelin & E. Ochs. (Eds.), *Language socialization across cultures* (pp. 213–251). Cambridge: Cambridge University Press.

Corsaro, W. A. (1985). *Friendship and peer culture in the early years*. Norwood, NJ: Ablex.

Corsaro, W. A., & Johannesen, B. O. (2006). The creation of new cultures in peer interaction. In: J. Valsiner & A. Rosa. (Eds.), *Cambridge handbook of socio-cultural psychology* (pp. 458–459). Cambridge: Cambridge University Press.

Corsaro, B., & Rizzo, T. (1990). Disputes in the peer culture of American and Italian nursery-school children. In: A. Grimshaw. (Ed.), *Conflict talk* (pp. 21–67). Cambridge: Cambridge University Press.

Dorval, B., & Eckerman, C. O. (1984). Developmental trends in the quality of conversation achieved by small groups of acquainted peers. *Monographs of the Society for Research in Child Development*, 49, Serial #206.

Dumesnil, J., & Dorval, B. (1989). The development of talk-activity frames that foster perspective-focused talk among peers. *Discourse Processes*, 12, 193–225.

Eckert, P. (1989). *Jocks and burnouts: Social categories and identity in high school*. New York: Teacher College Press.

Edelsky, C. (1981). Who's got the floor?. *Language in Society*, 10, 383–423.

Eggins, S., & Slade, D. (1997). *Analyzing casual conversation*. London: Cassell.

Ervin-Tripp, S. (1979). Children's verbal turn-taking. In: E. Ochs & B. Schieffelin. (Eds.), *Developmental pragmatics* (pp. 391–414). New York: Academic Press.

Faris, C. S. P. (2000). Cross-sex peer conflict and the discursive production of gender in a Chinese preschool in Taiwan. *Journal of Pragmatics*, 32, 539–569.

Fine, J. (1978). Conversation, cohesive and thematic patterning in Children's dialogues. *Discourse Processes*, 1, 247–266.

Gallagher, T. M., & Craig, H. K. (1982). An investigation of overlap in children's speech. *Journal of Psycholinguistic Research*, 11, 63–75.

Garvey, C. (1975). Requests and responses in children's speech. *Journal of Child Language*, 2, 41–63.

Garvey, C., & Berninger, G. (1981). Timing and turn-taking in children's conversations. *Discourse Processes*, 4, 27–57.

Goffman, E. (1981). *Forms of talk*. Philadelphia: University of Pennsylvania Press.

Goodwin, C. (1987). Forgetfulness as an interactive resource. *Social Psychology Quarterly*, 50, 115–131.

Goodwin, C. (2000). Action and embodiment within situated human interaction. *Journal of Pragmatics*, 32, 1489–1522.

Goodwin, M. H. (1990). *He-said-she-said: Talk as social organization among Black children*. Bloomington, IN: Indiana University Press.

Goodwin, M. H. (2002). Building power asymmetries in girls' interaction. *Discourse & Society*, 13, 715–730.

Gurevitch, Z. D. (1990). The dialogic connection and the ethics of dialogue. *British Journal of Sociology*, 41, 181–196.

Habib, T., Hamo, M., Huck-Taglicht, D., & Blum-Kulka, S. (2002). Peer talk: Children's explanations in natural discourse. Paper presented at the joint conference of the 9th Congress of the International Association for the study of Child Language and the 23rd Annual Symposium on Research in Child Language Disorders, Wisconsin-Madison, July 2002.

Hamo, M., Blum-Kulka, S., & Hacohen, G. (2004). From observation to transcription and back: Theory, practice and interpretation in the analysis of children's naturally occurring discourse. *Research on Language and Social Interaction*, 37, 71–92.

Hemphill, L. (1989). Topic development, syntax and social class. *Discourse Processes*, 12, 267–286.

Hemphill, L., & Siperstein, G. N. (1990). Conversational competence and peer response to mildly retarded children. *Journal of Educational Psychology*, 82, 128–134.

Hoyle, S. M. (1998). Register and footing in role play. In: M. S. Hoyle & C. Adgerdr Temple. (Eds.), *Kids talk* (pp. 47–68). Oxford: Oxford University Press.

Hoyle, M. S., & Adger Temple, S. (1998). Introduction. In: M. S. Hoyle & C. Adgerdr Temple. (Eds.), *Kids talk* (pp. 3–23). Oxford: Oxford University Press.

Hughes, C., & Dunn, J. (1998). Understanding mind and emotion: Longitudinal associations with mental-state talk between young friends. *Developmental Psychology*, 34, 1026–1037.

Jones, R., & Thornborrow, J. (2004). Floors, talk and the organization of classroom activities. *Language in Society*, 33, 399–423.

Katriel, T. (1991). *Communal webs: Communication and culture in contemporary Israel*. New York: State University of New York Press.

Katz, J. R. (2004). Building peer relationships in talk: Toddlers' peer conversations in childcare. *Discourse Studies*, 6, 329–446.

Kay, K., & Charney, R. (1981). Conversational asymmetry between mothers and children. *Journal of Child Language*, 8, 35–50.

Keenan, E. O. (1974). Conversational competence in children. *Journal of Child Language*, 1, 163–184.

Kirschenblatt-Gimblett, B. (1979). Speech play and verbal art. In: B. Sutton-Smith. (Ed.), *Play and learning* (pp. 219–238). Philadelphia: University of Pennsylvania Press.

Kochman, T. (1986). Strategic ambiguity in Black speech genres: Cross-cultural interference in participant-observation research. *Text*, 6, 153–70.

Kyratzis, A. (1999). Narrative identity: Preschoolers' self-construction through narratives in same-sex friendship group pragmatic play. *Narrative Inquiry*, 9, 427–457.

Linell, P. (1998). *Approaching dialogue: Talk, interaction and contexts in dialogical perspectives*. Amsterdam: John Benjamins.

Linell, P., & Korolija, N. (1997). Coherence in multi-party conversation: Episodes and contexts in interaction. In: T. Givon. (Ed.), *Conversation: Cognitive, communicative and social perspectives*. Amsterdam: John Benjamins.

McTear, M. (1985). *Children's conversation*. Oxford: Blackwell.

Moerman, M. (1990/1991). Exploring talk and interaction. *Research on Language and Social Interaction*, 24, 173–187.

Nelson, K., & Gruendel, J. (1979). At morning it's lunchtime: A scriptal view of children's dialogues. *Discourse Processes*, 2, 73–94.

Ninio, A., & Snow, C. (1996). *Pragmatic development*. Boulder, Colorado: Westview.

Richards, B., & Gallaway, C. (Eds.), (1994). *Input and interaction in language acquisition*. Cambridge: Cambridge University Press.

Rogoff, B. (1990). Apprenticeship in thinking: Cognitive development in social context. New York: Oxford University Press.

Sacks, H., Schegloff, E. A., & Jefferson, G. (1974). A simplest systematic for the organization of turn-taking for conversation. *Language*, 50, 696–735.

Sanders, R., & Freeman, K. E. (1998). Children's neo-rhetorical participation in peer interaction. In: I. Hutchby & J. Moran-Ellis. (Eds.), *Children and social competence: Arenas of action* (pp. 87–115). London: The Palmer Press.

Sawyer, R. K. (1997). *Pretend play as improvisation*. Mahwah, NJ: Lawrence Erlbaum.

Schieffelin, B., & Ochs, E. (Eds.), (1984). *Language socialization across cultures*. Cambridge: Cambridge University Press.

Schley, S., & Snow, C. (1992). The conversational skills of school-age children. *Social Development*, 1, 18–35.

Schober-Peterson, D., & Johnson, C. J. (1989). Conversational topics of 4-year-olds. *Journal of Speech and Hearing Research*, 32, 857–870.

Schober-Peterson, D., & Johnson, C. J. (1993). The performance of eight- to ten-year-olds on measures of conversational skillfulness. *First Language*, 13, 249–269.

Snow, C. (1977). The development of conversation between mothers and babies. *Journal of Child Language*, 11, 423–452.

Snow, C. (1984). Parent-child interaction and the development of communicative ability. In: R. Schiefelbush & J. Pickar. (Eds.), *Communicative competence: Acquisition and intervention* (pp. 69–107). Baltimore, MD: University Park Press.

Szymanski, M. H. (1999). Re-engaging and disengaging talk in activity. *Language in Society*, 28, 1–23.

Tannen, D. (1984). *Conversational style: Analyzing talk among friends*. Norwood, NJ: Ablex.

Trevarthen, C., & Hubley, P. (1978). Secondary intersubjectivity: Confidence, confiding and acts of meaning in the first year. In: A. Lock. (Ed.), *Action, gesture and symbol: The emergence of language* (pp.183–229). London: Academic Press.

CHAPTER 21

The Creation of New Cultures
in Peer Interaction

William A. Corsaro and Berit O. Johannesen

In sociology and anthropology a new field of childhood studies has emerged in contrast to what is known traditionally as socialization. Although there are a variety of approaches to socialization, it is a "concept that has been much employed by sociologists to delineate the process through which children, and in some cases adults, learn to conform to social norms" (James, Jenks, & Prout, 1998: 23). Childhood studies reject the notion of socialization as a starting point for studying how cultural meaning emerges in children's activities, arguing instead for approaches that share an appreciation of the importance of collective, communal activity – how children negotiate, share, and create culture with adults and each other (Corsaro, 1992, 2005; James, Jenks, & Prout, 1998; Mayall, 2002). From this perspective, it is possible to distinguish empirically *descriptions* of meaning production and *reflections* on various constraints to meaning production. Some of these constraints are related to societal expectations on children's behavior and cultural participation. By shifting the focus, we can see how children contribute to cultural reproduction and change.

In our work we have offered the concept of *interpretive reproduction* (Corsaro, 1992, 2005). Interpretive stresses innovative and creative aspects of children's participation in society. Children's agency in this participation is collective in that it is embedded in the communal production of cultural routines, which are a major aspect of children's peer cultures. In a series of studies we have shown that children collectively produce and participate in their own unique peer cultures by creatively appropriating aspects of the larger culture to address their own peer concerns and meanings in their everyday lives (Corsaro, 1985, 1992, 1994, 2003, 2005; Johannesen, 2004). Reproduction calls attention to the fact that children do not simply internalize society, but actively contribute to culture and cultural change. The term reproduction also implies children are, by their very participation in society, constrained by their location in the social structure and by forces of social reproduction. In this sense, children and their childhoods are expressions of the cultures of which they are members (Corsaro, 2005; also see Qvortrup, 1991).

A key aspect of childhood studies is that children and their childhoods are worthy of study in their own right. This appreciation of the conceptual autonomy of children and childhood has led some childhood theorists to separate their work from disciplines and theoretical approaches which are primarily concerned with individual development (James, Jenks, & Prout, 1998). This position is understandable in that many developmental psychologists who stress the importance of children's agency and feel social and cultural context is important, still argue for the primacy of individual change. We believe, however, that research and theory in childhood studies, most especially work on children's peer cultures, can benefit from integration with recent work in sociocultural psychology. This work, although still with a primary aim of understanding individual development, rejects both the notion of the individual as the basic unit of analysis and the belief that development depends on internal construction or internalization of external knowledge (Rogoff, 1995). We also believe, in turn, that sociocultural theory can benefit from theory and research in childhood studies and the notion of interpretive reproduction.

Interpretive Reproduction and Sociocultural Theory

As Wertsch (1995) has argued Vygotsky saw "mediated action" as a basic unit of analysis and believed that all action must be interpreted "as involving an irreducible tension between mediational means and the individuals employing these means" (p. 64). From this perspective, individuals do not act alone, but rather agency is seen as "individual-operating-with-mediational means" and the focus is on collective actions in sociocultural and historical context (Wertsch, 1995). Further, mediational means do not simply facilitate collective actions, but often transform them bringing about redefinitions of cultural processes and knowledge as well as change at the individual level. It is this change at the individual level, an "altering of

the entire flow and structure of mental functions" (Wertsch, 1995: 63) which most interests students of human development in the sociocultural tradition. Our interests, however, are primarily redefinition and creativity in peer culture on the collective or interpersonal level and how children's use of mediational means contribute to such creativity.

Mediational action as discussed by Wertsch (1995) fits well with interpretive reproduction's emphasis on the importance of cultural routines. Cultural routines are repetitive everyday activities collectively produced by members of a culture. The habitual, taken-for granted character of routines provides children and all social actors with the security of belonging to a social group. This very predictability empowers routines, providing frameworks within which sociocultural knowledge can be produced, displayed and interpreted (Corsaro, 1992, 2005). These frameworks are similar to mediated action in that they are self-organized and based on a shared understanding of the activity taking place ("what actors are doing"). This understanding is not necessarily explicit, but embedded in the perception of intentional objects, space, and time. Within this phenomenological perspective, children do not so much use mediational means or tools, rather the mediational means express the mediated action and how children produce themselves as cultural beings within nested cultural routines.

The notion of interpretive reproduction also parallels theoretical work in the sociocultural tradition by Barbara Rogoff (Rogoff, 1995, 1996, 2003). Here again units of analysis in studying development and change are a key issue of similarity with a shared focus on collective activities in sociocultural context. Rogoff argues that changes "are neither exclusively in the individuals nor exclusively in their environments, but a characteristic of individuals' involvement in ongoing activity" (1996: 273). Peer cultures are produced, shared, and refined through children's activities with peers and adults. The nature or degree of children's involvement in these activities changes over time given children's shared experiences with others in specific activities. For example, children's shared history with peers in creating and refining routines or other aspects of peer culture contributes to changes in the nature of the peer culture, children's interpersonal relations and friendships, and in individual cognitive, social and emotional development. Rogoff develops the idea of children's involvement or participation in sociocultural activity with the concept of "participatory appropriation" which refers to "the process by which individuals transform their understanding of and responsibility for activities through their own participation" (1995: 150).

We share this notion of appropriation as a process of participation, but participation in shared collective action or cultural routines over time. Such participation in collectively produced cultural routines surely contributes to children's individual development. However, our focus from the perspective of interpretive reproduction is not on individual development, but rather on the creative production of shared peer cultures which results from appropriation through participation in collectively produced cultural routines. In short, our focus remains squarely on the nature of cultural processes that are at the very heart of childhood. Furthermore, we argue that it is not just the individual who is being prepared for future events in Rogoff's sense, but also members of the peer group itself of which the individual child is a participating member. Thus, children are not only creating a peer culture through their collective participation in shared routines, they are also becoming more aware of what it means to be a peer. In the process they are forging a group identity as well as developing differing levels of affiliation with members of their peer group.

For purposes of this chapter we define peer culture as a stable set of activities or routines, artifacts, values, and concerns that children produce and share in interaction with peers (Corsaro, 2005; Corsaro & Eder, 1990). To demonstrate processes of children creating peer cultures and establishing group identities we consider the involvement of children of various ages in three

different types of shared peer activities: ritualized sharing, improvised fantasy play, and shared acts of resistance to adult authority. We also consider the nature and development of affiliation or friendship in these and other shared features of children's peer cultures.

Ritualized Sharing

We are well aware that the range and nature of children's collective activities are affected by a host of cultural factors (including economic production, family structure, customs, beliefs about child rearing and age-grading, social policies related to child care, and schooling, among others, see Rogoff, 2003; Valsiner, 2000). Cultures vary widely in how they organize the lives of young children. Some children are primarily in the care of mothers, while others are cared for by older siblings or in groups of mixed age peers, while still others spend considerable time in child care and early education institutions. Therefore, preschool age children will have various opportunities for sustained interaction with siblings and peers. In modern societies, most especially in Europe children as young as 18 months spend considerable time together in child care and early education settings. In such settings in France, Italy, the Netherlands, Norway, and the United States researchers have documented toddlers' production and participation in shared peer routines (Corsaro & Molinari, 1990; de Han & Singer 2001; Katz, 2004; Løkken, 2000; Mussaiti & Panni, 1981; Stamback & Verba, 1986). These routines often develop spontaneously and demonstrate ritual sharing and joy. Over time, some of the routines are expanded and refined, expressing complex organizational features and even negotiations about the correct enactment of the routines among the toddlers and between toddlers and caretakers.

Løkken (2000) documented Norwegian toddlers making music together and creating what she termed a "bathroom society" by rhythmically banging plastic cup, boats, and their hands together as they sat on a bench in the bathroom of a child care center. These orchestrated actions were expanded by two girls singing "Oh we are us. We are us." Løkken notes that the singing, "communal, playful actions, vocalizations, and smiles in general were part of this piece of 'music' performed by the four children, living through a 'We' in vivid present" (Løkken, 2000: 540). Here we see common objects, spaces, and events (using the bathroom) transformed through mediated action into a shared routine of the children's collective creation. The singing of "We are us" is one of children's ways of marking the routine as a shared event of their own creation.

Corsaro and Molinari (1990) describe several routines among toddlers in an Italian *asilo nido* providing care and educational experiences for children from 6 months to 3 years of age. In the "curtain" routine several children run to a window and wrap themselves in the curtain, laughing loudly and drawing the attention of other children. When other children join, they first push those children inside the curtain and laugh, and then join their playmates inside. In some variations of the routine a child inside the curtain runs away crying out for help, saying he is being chased by a wolf. He goes to hide behind a cupboard and is pursued by the others who, upon finding him, push each other and laugh. The children then return to the curtain again hiding themselves and then a different child cries for help and runs to the cupboard to hide.

This routine has two interrelated components: disappearance-reappearance play, and fantasy play involving the identification of and fleeing from a threatening agent. In the first component the children create a situation similar to games like "peek-a-boo" that most of them probably played with parents (Bruner & Sherwood, 1976). The second component involving displays of fear of a threatening agent like a wolf, witch, or monster is similar to a play routine "approach-avoidance" Corsaro (1985, 2005) identified in a more elaborate format among older (3 to 5 year old) American and Italian children in preschool settings. Approach-avoidance in turn can be seen as a precursor to

more structured games with rules (Corsaro, 2005). However, for the toddlers the play is all about shared excitement and fear and through the activities themselves they create a shared routine in the peer culture.

In a second routine, "the little chairs," the toddlers arranged and then walked on top of small chairs from one part of a room to another in the child care center. Almost all of the children in the center participated in this routine at some point over the school term. The play took on embellished variation over time as children extended the length of the line of chairs creating curves rather than a straight line, pretended to lose their balance but did not fall, and passed other children in front of them. The routine also gave the children a sense of control in the setting as the teachers allowed this normally seen, and possibly dangerous, "misuse" of the chairs to occur as long as the children were careful in their play. Aware of the teachers' concern certain older children reminded younger ones to be careful and admonished peers for pushing or moving chairs from the line.

The simple participant structure of these cultural routines among toddlers correspond to a central value of peer cultures; doing things together. Adults, including many scholars of child development, tend to view children's activities from a "utility point of view," which focuses on learning and social and cognitive development. Young children do not know the world from this point of view. "For them," argues Strandell, "the course of events of which they are part has an immediate impact on their existence here in space and now in time" (1994: 8) Thus, we need to appreciate young children's culture productions on their own terms – as culture processes often without reflective awareness that are shared and appreciated in the course of production and always open to embellishment and change.

Improvised Fantasy Play

There is a vast research literature on young children's fantasy play, most of which explores the importance of such play for children's social, cognitive, and emotional development (see Goldman, 1998; Sawyer, 1997; Singer & Singer, 1990 for reviews). Our interest here is addressing how the content and collective production of fantasy play contribute to shared peer culture. Corsaro (1985; also see Corsaro, 2003) was one of the first to argue that fantasy play was a basic routine in the peer culture of preschool children. By videotaping and analyzing fantasy play episodes among various groups of children over long periods, Corsaro (1985) identified children's communicative strategies in producing fantasy play and underlying plots or themes in the play. For example, Corsaro (1985, 2003) found that such play occurred in particular areas of preschools (such as block areas, around sand tables, and in areas were play materials like blocks and Lego were available) and that children had shared histories and built friendships that were closely connected to their collective participation in fantasy play.

Corsaro found that much of the fantasy play was highly complex and often implicit and produced "in frame" in an emergent fashion without the children's reliance on references to shared scripts or plans for action. In short, fantasy play is often constituted totally in the social interaction itself. This complex, improvised feat is accomplished by children's use of paralinguistic cues (voice, pitch, intonation), orchestrated manipulation of play objects (toy animals, blocks, sand, Lego), verbal descriptions of actions, repetition of speech and action, and semantic tying and expansion (see Corsaro, 1985: 192–219, 2003: 91–110 for detailed examples).

Corsaro (1985, 2003) documented three underlying themes in much of the children's fantasy play: danger-rescue; lost-found; and death-rebirth. Although these themes can also be seen in fairy tales and popular children's media, Corsaro found that the children never produced actual sequences from such sources and few references to characters or events from children's media or literature. These themes were somehow extracted from such sources, used as shared knowledge implicitly, and were stretched and embellished in fascinating ways. For example, the children often used highly complex strategies for negotiating how one could talk or indicate they were dead in death-rebirth themes given the fact that "You can't talk if your dead" (see Corsaro, 2003: 103–107).

Building on Corsaro's work and linking it to linguistic anthropology, most especially the area of metapragmatics, Keith Sawyer (1997) develops further the improvisational nature of children's fantasy play. A key aspect of metapragmatics, notes Sawyer, is what Silverstein (1993) called "indexical entailment," meaning that utterances often index potential directions that interaction may proceed. Sawyer views metapragmatic entailment effects as poetic, "because they derive from the line-by-line structure of the interaction" (1997: 45). These poetic performances in children's pretend play are part of shared culture in that they are created in an improvised fashion through what Sawyer calls "collaborative emergence" (1999, 2002).

By collaborative emergence, Sawyer means that narratives in children's pretend play are improvised and collectively produced phenomena. In this sense they are like cultural routines we described earlier in that they provide frameworks for producing, displaying, and interpreting sociocultural knowledge. In these routines of fantasy play narratives are "collaboratively emergent" from improvised dialogue for several reasons:

(1) they are unpredictable and contingent;
(2) they are not the conscious creation of any one child but emerge from the successive actions of all participants;
(3) they are collective social products and cannot be equated with any child's mental schema; and
(4) because improvisational discourse allows for retrospective interpretation, the emergent narrative cannot be analyzed solely in terms of a child's goal in

an individual turn, because most often a child does not know the meaning of her or his turn until other children have responded (Sawyer, 2002: 340–341).

In his work, Sawyer has focused on describing the improvised and emergent nature of children's pretend play and its implications for individual development. Regarding individual development Sawyer links his argument to Bakhtin's notion of heteroglossia. For Bakhtin heteroglossia captures the diversity of artistically organized voices in novels in that "the novel can be defined as a diversity of social speech types and a diversity of individual voices, artistically organized" (as quoted in Sawyer, 1997: 173). Sawyer (1997) maintains that children move from monoglossic social speech primarily with caretakers until around age 3 and then over the period of 3 to 6 years of age, through the repeated collective production of pretend play with peers, children develop heteroglossia (see Corsaro, 1997: xiii).

Sawyer's notion of collaborative emergence is insightful and draws attention to the improvisational complexity of children's fantasy play. However, he does not develop fully the contributions of collaborative emergence for the creation of shared culture in early childhood. He does note that certain of the children he studied repeated various themes in their play, preferred particular play materials, and developed friendships centered around pretend play (Sawyer, 1997). He also provides examples where children draw from shared knowledge of media in their play, but modify, extend, and embellish characters and scripts through improvisational collaboration. Still we do not have analyses of the production of shared culture in the peer group through meaning production in the shared practice of pretend play over time. Instead, Sawyer focuses more on developmental outcomes noting that children produce less improvisational fantasy play around age 6, because it has served its developmental purpose. However, Corsaro has argued that this position may fail to take into account that children's skills

in such play may wither away without continual practice, and the full appreciation of the novelty and complexity of such play for childhood culture may be underappreciated or taken for granted (Corsaro, 1997: xiv).

In later work, Sawyer (2002) addresses children's narrative practices and takes as a point of departure that children, through their play, produce quasi-narrative storylines. These products have similarities to well-formed narratives in a text genre sense, but are rarely fully formed. In focusing on children's narrative *practices* rather than the products of fantasy play as text, Sawyer supports the notion of the irreducibility of children's collectivity. By focusing on the narrative genre of text as the means to measure children's narrative abilities, however, Sawyer lets the significance of children's cultural production slip away.

Through his notion of collaborative emergence Sawyer, as we noted above, focuses on children's turn-by-turn interaction and the dialogic strategies they use to negotiate narrative performances. Johannesen (2004) used similar strategies in a longitudinal study of Lego play among Norwegian 5- to 6-year-old children. A closer look at one characteristic of fantasy play talk observed by both Sawyer and Johannesen will serve to contrast the instrumental perspective carried out by Sawyer with the perspective of interpretive reproduction.

Within the fantasy play reality, children let toy figures talk and act or they embody different characters of play themselves. These characters of the play reality often negotiate the interpretation and the direction of the unfolding events as they enact them. Sawyer names this kind of in-frame acting and negotiating implicit metacommunication

The term implicit metacommunication intimates two levels of communication expressed by the characters involved. Bakhtin's notion of "dialogism" adds to our understanding of such levels. He used the term to "refer to the two-leveled nature of improvised dialogue" (Sawyer, 2002: 330). The two levels are constituted by the narrator and the author of the story respectively. During implicit metacommunication within children's fantasy play the voice of the play characters and the voice of a narrator are combined in a dialogic manner. The story is acted out at the level of the narrator, and the author's voice is distributed among the children. An example from Johannesen's (2004) research, where Lego characters negotiate unfolding present tense action through past tense utterances, illustrates the described dialogism of fantasy play.

The situation unfolds in the Lego reality where one dragon and two monkeys are surrounded by an emerging jungle. Odin and Simen are the children involved.

Simen: *You know .. it was a .. the monkey met a bad guy ...*

The dragon in Odin's hand turns bad and rushes towards the monkey.

Odin: *Ah-ah-ah!* (growling)

But the monkey hides in a jungle

Simen: *No you did not find us .. we were in the jungle .. the monkey ...*

The dragon manipulated by Odin withdraws and switches places with another monkey holding a spear. Odin now in the person of the monkey makes monkey growling sounds and comes running towards the jungle.

Odin: *Ah-ah-ah!*

Where it too faces a certain resistance.

Simen: *No .. you wanted .. you were ...*

The monkey reaches the jungle in spite of the protests, and they go on to discuss what will happen next.

Odin: *I found you.*

Simen: *No!*

Odin: *Yes 'cause this monkey knew where the jungle was .. and he knew ...*

Simen: *But they were not .. you did not know where this jungle was .. it was another jungle ...*

And they reach a certain agreement.

Odin: *I knew where the jungle was .. but I did not find you inside the jungle.*

And the monkey starts making monkey sounds again.

Aaah—ah—aaah!

The example starts with a monkey confronting a bad guy. The event takes place through the narration, and a bad dragon comes flying at that very moment. But he does not find the prey he is after. The jungle seems impenetrable and the dragon withdraws. Now a second monkey comes running, confronting the first one who is hiding in the jungle. This one felt sure he knew the location of the jungle as well as the monkey in it. But then he could not find the right jungle after all and when he did the hiding monkey was nowhere to be seen.

This episode shows clearly how the Lego characters argue and negotiate the actions they are performing and thus exemplifies what Sawyer calls implicit metacommunication. Sawyer argues convincingly that the narrative structure resulting from such fantasy play is generated in an improvised manner between the children taking part in the play episode. But he also makes a further claim, namely that the outcome of the improvised play is totally unpredictable until the play episode has ended. The resulting narrative structure is built from "below" in a turn-by-turn process where "– one child proposes a new development for the play, and other children respond by modifying or embellishing that proposal" (Sawyer 2002:

340). The outcome Sawyer looks for in accord with his narrative measuring stick, is typically a temporal structure of motivating events, tension, and release of tension. The implicit metacommunication with its combination of the narrator's and author's voices gives the narrative its poetic texture (2002: 326) and the dialogic tension between the children's individual proposals creates the ambiguity which makes the outcome totally unpredictable.

This assumption of an unpredictable outcome is an important point in Sawyer's notion of collaborative emergence. The researcher can at no point during the children's play identify the narrative structure with any certainty. The structure is known only when the play-episode is over and the children seem to switch to other activities. Paradoxically then, to be able to stick to the open ended turn-by-turn dialogic process as the analytic focus of collaborative emergence, Sawyer needs to identify the narrative episodes from a point outside the practice. He does this by assuming that the narrative ends with the end of the children's play in a particular episode.

Contrary to an instrumental and external-to-the-practice perspective, Johannesen (2004) in her Lego study chose to enter the practice of fantasy play in the terms of the practice itself. One way to do this is to consider the in-frame reality as voiced by the play characters as a real world, and the voices as real voices expressing real experiences.

By following the movements of the dragon and the monkeys in the above example, we are let into the world of monkeys and dragons, as are the playing children, and we see that the actions negotiated and carried out by the Lego characters express these characters' perceptions of a shared world or event. The negotiations at hand express the experiences of a bad dragon chasing his prey and the experiences of a monkey preyed upon and hiding. Each of these perspectives within the jungle and surrounding area carry certain expectations; someone preyed upon should try not to be found and someone preying should keep at it and not give in easily. If he does someone will fill this empty position before long.

Earlier we have pointed to approach-avoidance play as a precursor to more structured games with rules. We also discussed the observed combination of disappearance-reappearance episodes and fantasy play involving a threatening agent in the play carried out by toddlers and preschoolers. When we experience fantasy-play from the perspective of the Lego characters we become even more aware of the continuum between hide and seek and other disappearance-reappearance play and the themes of fantasy-play observed by Corsaro. In games of hide and seek the children themselves embody the chaser and the ones chased upon while in fantasy-play the positions are materialized and instantiated by the play characters.

Sawyer claims that the play content reaches its completion when single play episodes end. The longitudinal study of meaning production among Lego playing children however, shows that the shared reality of the Lego characters remains intact, even when the characters are stacked away from one week to the next. The play-reality not only persists but becomes increasingly complex as the characters plan and experience recurring episodes of danger-rescue and other themes over time in the history of shared play. These recurrent experiences materialize in the enduring relational identities of characters, artefacts, and of the participants of play.

It is true that episodes acted out within the reality of play can seem unpredictable from a perspective external to the practice itself, just like Sawyer observed. But this is due to the fact that plot-*lines* are not at the core of this cultural production. It is not the *line* of the plot which is confirmed and re-enacted with every recurring event and every rebirth, it is the tension between positions constituting a *relational* plot structure.

What constitutes the dialogical tension inherent in the negotiations of the play characters is not the mixture of unpredictable ideas brought about by the individual children taking part. Rather the tension inheres in the linguistic and bodily cultural routines of fantasy-play constrained by local conditions. This tension opens a space where the individual bodies taking part in the routine constitute themselves as participants creatively interpreting and reproducing cultural deep structures.

Challenging Adult Authority

Some researchers argue that numerous studies which document how children and youth challenge and mock adult authority in their play and other activities suggest that this behavior may be a universal feature of child and youth cultures (Corsaro, 2005: Schwartzman, 1978). Until recently it is the oppositional nature of preadolescent and adolescent peer cultures which have received the most attention. Some of these studies record mischief like knocking on doors and running and making prank phone calls (Fine, 1987). Such antics have probably been passed down from generation to generation. In an historical study, Nasaw (1985), described how young boys selling newspapers (newsies) had various strategies to trick adults into buying papers such as loudly announcing false or misleading headlines, or claiming they had been working all day and just had one paper left, and other techniques to avoid giving back full change after a purchase. Nasaw also documented how newsies went on strike against the major New York publishers Joseph Pulitzer and William Randolph Hearst in 1899 in protest of a rise in the prices of papers. The publishers did not take the strike seriously at first, but after growing public support for the newsies, they gave in and offered a settlement. As Nasaw notes, by "unionizing and striking to protect their rights and their profits, the children were behaving precisely as they believed American workers should when treated unjustly" (1985: 181). Other researchers have shown that the oppositional aspects of youth culture, though highly creative, can have less positive effects and even contribute to processes of the social reproduction of class inequality (Willis, 1981).

More recently several researchers have documented that opposition to adult authority and control appears in the preschool years and is a major feature of childhood culture. Here we see the actual processes of children creating culture as these examples seldom involve the passing down and embellishing of strategies learned from older children. Instead children confront certain organizational or conventional rules or restrictions of preschools or day care centers that they find unfair, arbitrary, and in some cases illogical. Corsaro has documented children's strategies for getting around these rules in preschools in the United States and Italy. In line with Goffman's (1961) work on adults in total institutions like asylums or prisons, Corsaro refers to these strategies as *secondary adjustments* and the children's creation and sharing of secondary adjustments as composing the *underlife* of preschools.

Take, for example, rules in most preschools that prohibit children from bringing toys or other personal possessions from home to school. These rules exist because children often get into disputes when playing with such possessions and because the particular toy or possession may be broken. To avoid such organizational problems teachers prohibit the bringing of such items or severely restrict their presence in the school. In Corsaro's (1985) early work he found that children got around the rule by smuggling small objects to school that they could hide in their pockets like matchbox race cars, tiny dolls, and other small toys. However, the smuggler almost never played with the toy alone, but showed it to another child and then the two or sometimes more kids played with the forbidden object surreptitiously or so they thought. Actually, teachers often observed what was going on, but overlooked it as long as the children did not fight over the toy.

In such instances the children were very careful in their play, returning the smuggled object to their pockets when a teacher passed and smiling at their playmates. It became clear after awhile that "getting around the rule" was just as important as having and playing with the forbidden object. Here we clearly see collective cultural production by the young children. First, surely the children did not get the idea to bring the small toys from parents, as it is extremely doubtful that a parent would say, "So the teacher says not to bring toys, well take something like your small dolls that your can conceal and fool the teacher." No, the kids come up with the idea themselves and then, of course, it can and is passed on to other kids. Second, as we noted teachers often overlooked the violations and even admired the creativity of the children's productions. In some cases, they even changed school rules in line with the children's secondary adjustments by allowing sharing days when children were encouraged to bring their toys to school. Thus, the children not only create their own cultures, but bring about change in the adult culture. This point has strong evolutionary backing as can be seen in research on Japanese macaques (Kawamura, 1959). Kawamura reports that juvenile macaque first developed novel techniques related to food washing and eating among themselves and then these techniques were propagated upward to adults. In addition the speed of propagation of the techniques was faster among the juveniles than it was among the adults (1959: 46).

Corsaro (1985, 1990, 2003, 2005; Corsaro & Molinari, 2005) found that children's secondary adjustments applied to a whole range of conventional (as opposed to moral) rules which restricted children's behavior. For example in American and Italian preschools there are rules about cleaning up and putting away play materials at different times of the day such as before snack, lunch, outside, and nap time. Kids do not like this rule and some even find it illogical. Corsaro (1985) overheard two boys who said "Clean up time is dumb, dumb, dumb. We could just leave our trucks here and play with them after snack time." The result is that children come up with a plethora of ways of avoiding clean up including relocating (moving to another area as soon as the announcement of cleanup is made); pretending not to hear the announce-

ment (which delays the start of cleaning up so the children have less work to do); and using personal-problem delays (having some other pressing business that is more important). The last of these strategies is very inventive and involves things like feigning an injury, pretending to be dead as part of fantasy play, or having to go to the bathroom among many others (Corsaro, 1990).

Corsaro (1990, 2003, 2005) documented a wide range of strategies to deal with the many conventional rules children run up against in preschools. In Goffman's terms the children form an underlife which is an important element in peer culture that enables them to work the system and collectively avoid the main force of or get around adult rules completely. Other researchers have also documented this aspect of children's cultures in societies where respect for adult authority is deeply ingrained in children at an early age. For example, Kathryn Hadley (2003) found that Taiwanese kindergarten children used complex word play to both resist and accommodate the Confucian values that their teachers introduced to them. By manipulating and playing with adults' names and class names, the children collectively resisted the teachers' rules to act respectfully towards adults. Again the collective production and symbolic sharing of aspects of the rule violation is central here. As Hadley notes using "word play to resist the value of being a good student could not be accomplished, however, without a parallel enactment of the very skills that characterize a good student. Understanding word structure, vocabulary and word placement were 'good student' skills that facilitated the delivery of a disrespectful word play" (2003: 204).

Overall, children's secondary adjustments are innovative and collective responses to the adult world. By sharing a communal spirit as members of peer cultures in creating, producing, and sharing in the underlife of the organization (here preschools and kindergartens) children come to experience how being a member of a group "affects both themselves as individuals and how they relate to others" (Corsaro, 2005: 152–153).

By creating and using secondary adjust-ments, children come to see themselves as part of a group and subculture (a peer group a culture of students), which is sometimes aligned with other groups and in other cases opposed to other groups (teachers and adult culture). Again we see how routines in peer cultures create frameworks that serve as tools or mediated action in creating culture.

Creating Peer Cultures, Creating Friendships

In this discussion we have had space to con-sider three of many features of children's creation of new cultures in peer interac-tion: toddlers' non-verbal and verbal play routines, children's improvised fantasy play, and children strategies and secondary adjust-ments to challenge and get around adult rules. These are only a few aspects of the highly complex nature of children's produc-tion of peer cultures that have been doc-umented in research from the perspective of childhood studies (Corsaro, 1985, 2003; 2005; Evaldsson, 1993; Goodwin, 1990; Schwartzman, 1978; Thorne, 1993). We have stressed the collective and processual nature of children's peer cultures. In so doing we argue for the study of culture creation as an active, performative process. Children col-lectively share in and build social relations with adults and especially each other in the creation of peer culture. The nature of these relations is not always cooperative and often can involve conflict and disagreements (Cor-saro, 1994, 2003; Corsaro & Rizzo, 1988; Evaldsson, 1993; Goodwin, 1990). However, such conflict often invigorates the shared peer cultures and can transform emerging peer relations to close and often enduring friendships.

We have not directly discussed children's friendships in this review. However, like peer cultures we see friendships as socio-cultural productions deeply ingrained in shared col-lective action. In this process approach, friendship formation "involves recognizing its developmental fluidity *along with* its gen-esis as a socio-cultural promoted construc-

tion and explaining its temporal flow with the main current (system) of socio-cultural promoted activities and skills" (Winterhoff, 1997: 227). This process approach to friend-ship can be contrasted with the outcome approach in which friendships are seen as static entities which are the reflections of the stage like development of underlying con-ceptions (Corsaro, 2004; Winterhoff, 1997).

In our review of research on culture cre-ation by toddlers we noted the importance of shared non-verbal and verbal routines. These routines often take form and gain shared significance through the cooperation of particular playmates who feel a special sense of community that we see as early friendship relations. These relations do not reflect a fully formed underlying conception of friendship, but they do promote the devel-opment of representations of friendship as related to communal sharing in the emer-gent peer culture.

Over time through shared negotiating in building shared themes in fantasy play chil-dren often establish and extend friendship relations. In fantasy play verbal routines are central in constituting the different levels of reality involved. Such routines are self-organizing and constrained from within the play by the shared mood and emerging focal content. Verb tense, personal pronouns, and voice quality are all aspects of verbal rou-tines and index a shared focus. The emerging focus in its turn indicates whether the voices to be heard are to be received as characters of the fantasy world or child participants. In the group of Lego-playing children mentioned earlier in Johannesen's (2004) research we can see how to perform such verbal Lego routines in a consistent and proper way relate to emerging friendship structures and relations.

Unlike the dragon and the two monkeys discussed earlier, some Lego characters never actually act or speak themselves. Instead they are only mentioned as third person per-spectives. This is the case when the three children Odin, Simen, and Dan are looking for thieves to put in a prison just built by Dan. These thieves are important to the rela-tional structure of the Lego reality, but they are not associated with the horizon of participants because no child lends voice to them. In other words, their presence in the Lego reality is not reflected in a participant structure of opposing positions. On the contrary, the horizon of participants is unanimously supporting the idea of throwing the bad guys in prison. When Dan says in a play episode, "Let's hurry and throw them in jail," we strongly feel a sense of community between the participants and the morally respectable Lego characters alike in the effort to control the evil forces.

But then, when Simen encourages Odin to "throw the bad guys in *his* [Dan's] prison," and Dan say "we must throw them in *my* jail," a certain structure between the participants emerges. The phrases "his prison" as well as the "my jail" are uttered within the mood of the Lego reality. But no Lego character is directly referenced in this exchange. Rather the "his" and the "my" refer to Dan who just finished building the prison. Thus, a differentiation between Dan and the other two boys occurs within the frame of the Lego mood, but without really having anything to do with the actual events taking place in the Lego reality.

Shortly after, Dan spots a bomb in the box of Legos and hands it to Simen. Odin places it on the prison as part of a stockpile for throwing at the bad guys should they attack. The mood is still that of a communal effort against some third person bad guys. But the stockpile of bombs seems to get Dan worrying and he says, "I am not one of the bad guys." Dan can not at the same time be part of the unanimous participant horizon trying to capture thieves, and one of the thieves within the Lego reality. In short, Dan's uncertainty of how his role might develop creates some inconsistency in the verbal routine. This inconsistency in the shared focus of the play blurs the difference between Lego reality and participant structure.

Two basic aspects of fantasy play, namely the horizon of participants and the fantastic reality, are of topical interest in these short episodes. In the first episode we sense a structuring of the horizon not stemming from the Lego reality. Rather the structure is related to the fact that Dan has built the prison. In the second episode the differentiation between Lego reality and horizon of participants is blurred. The mood of the Lego reality seems to envelop Dan and the Lego figures alike and confuse participant positions and Lego positions.

When Odin reassures Dan in an overly friendly voice "no Dan, you are the kindest guy ever," the impression is that Dan lacks a certain competence in carrying out the routines of Lego play. Odin's very attempts to assure Dan and keep him in the play frame at the same time signals that Dan does not share the taken-for granted skills he, Odin, has established with Simen.

This impression is confirmed with another instance of overstated positive feedback. It occurs as Dan starts to climb the box of Legos. Climbing the box has nothing to do with the production of play content between the children, and is not really a relevant thing to do in the situation. Simen watches Dan, he then turns to Odin, points at Dan, and exclaims: "Wow! Dan is good! He is balancing." Simen's approval of Dan was directed as much or more to Odin. Now Odin replies knowingly and in a low voice "not like me . . . and you." A participant structure of Simen and Odin as the experts and Dan, as the novice whom they try to help, starts to emerge. The notion between Odin and Simen of practicing Lego in a manner similar to each other, but different from Dan, is part of a growing friendship awareness among the two boys. An awareness that can be traced also in the differentiation between Dan and the other two in the prison episode.

We can trace the origins of a special sense of community between Odin and Simen within the Lego play by going back and taking a closer look at how these three boys practiced Lego together prior to our small episodes. Three weeks earlier the three of them were in the process of establishing an island with a strong defense against some Lego bad guys. Then all of a sudden a very funny monkey came driving by in his car and started to fool about. Dan was manipulating and lending voice to this monkey. The other Lego characters tried hard to make the monkey withdraw, but without succeeding. Eventually Simen and Odin abandoned the Lego reality and started to discuss their whereabouts together outside of the school area instead. Overall, these examples capture the complexity of interconnecting levels of the actual practice of fantasy play with Lego on the one had and the development and cultivation of friendship on the other.

As we have noted resistance of adult authority and control is always a collective practice which generates a strong group identity among children. Often particular children work together in developing complex strategies to get around particular rules they find as both constraining and arbitrary. In doing so children at times develop close friendships in their shared creativeness and feelings of control in evading various adult rules.

For example, in one American preschool Corsaro (1985; 2003) studied children encountered rules about the use of objects and space that they felt were particularly bothersome. Two boys in particular, Peter and Graham, often ran up against rules related to the teachers' conception of inside and outside play. Running, chasing, and shouting were considered inappropriate behaviors inside the school. Also Peter and Graham and several other boys were especially irritated by an additional restrictive rule. Because many of them seldom played indoors during the first month of the school term, the teachers closed the outside area for the first 45 minutes of free play. The hope was that this rule would prompt the boys to become more active in indoor play activities.

The rule was successful to a certain degree, but it also led the boys, especially Peter and Graham, to devise a number of ingenious secondary adjustments. For example the two boys attempted to extend family role play in the playhouse in interesting directions. On several occasions Peter and Graham suggested to other children that the play house was being robbed and convinced the others to be the robbers while they took the role of police. The police then chased the robbers from the playhouse and throughout the inside of the school. When the teach-

ers reminded the children that there was no running inside the school, Peter and Graham claimed that they needed to run to catch the thieves who robbed the playhouse. Faced with this response, the teachers often compromised and allowed the children to continue their play, but told them to confine the chase to an area near the playhouse (Corsaro, 2003: 145).

Inspired by their success, Peter and Graham, came up with other plots that required physical play. For example, Graham suggested that the playhouse had caught fire and ordered all the children to flee the burning structure while he and Peter, as brave firefighters, put out the roaring blaze. In a final example, the two boys concocted an impressive scenario in which Peter crawled into the playhouse growling loudly and scratching at the children who were inside pretending to eat their dinner. Peter also grabbed food from the table and knocked over a chair. At this moment, Graham arrived and announced that Peter "was a wild lion who had escaped from the zoo." Graham in the role of lion trainer chased Peter all around the school before capturing him to the applause of other kids who were playing nearby and had joined in the chase.

Again the teachers wanted to know what was going on and warned the children about running around and not using their "inside voices." Graham was ready for this admonishment, however, and quickly explained how the lion (Peter) had escaped the zoo and threatened the other children. Having saved the day, Graham now explained to the teachers that he would return Peter to his cage in the zoo and order would be restored. By this time the teachers had become suspicious of the escapades of the two boys, but they just smiled and accepted Graham's resolution of the problem with a promise that the lion would stay put until outside time.

These examples demonstrate how a particular aspect of children creating culture – here devising secondary adjustments to get around particular adult rules – led to a stronger bonding and deeper friendship among these two boys. Peter and Graham realized they had developed a reputation for devising these interesting plots and dramas among both their peers and the teachers. In the process their innovative collective practices were infused with shared positive emotions toward one another that are clear elements of children's early friendships.

Conclusion

In this chapter we have considered children creating culture by focusing on children's collective production of specific peer routines at different ages and in certain types of activities. We have stressed the importance of such cultural production in regard to "meaning making" in the moment of children's shared experiences in childhood. In this sense culture creation is the central feature of childhood and not simply practice for socialization or development. Surely, such culture creation contributes to child development, however, analyzing it only in developmental terms reduces its complexity and misrepresents its importance and immediacy in the everyday lives of children. In the process of creating peer cultures children transcend individual development and even individual identities and agency. In creating culture, children share collective cognitions and meanings of their ongoing lives. As we have discussed the creating and sharing of children's culture over time also has strong emotional elements which are the basis of friendship relations. Friendship is thus a process of doing things together, sharing positive emotions, and anticipating and supporting the desires and needs of others. The direct, intensive, and longitudinal study of children creating culture is essential to the documentation and understanding of childhood experiences in their own right and on their own terms.

Our position thus stresses the collectively produced unique cultures of childhood which have some overlap, but are clearly separate and segregated from adult culture. Such separate cultures develop within adult controlled institutions at very young ages as demonstrated by our review of research on shared routines among toddlers. These routines, and all routines of peer cultures, depend on the creative use of communicative systems, which among toddlers require orchestrated bodily movements, laughter, and verbalizations. Even among these very young children once such routines are collectively produced and shared, there is the tendency to protect them from adult control or restriction. This tendency is all the more remarkable because the routines often involve appropriating elements of the adult culture, but for use in different and creative ways from which they were intended.

Creative use by peers of materials provided by adults was also very evident in our discussion of preschool children's fantasy play. Here we argued for the importance of shared "meaning making" in the moment through highly improvised play dependent on the children's language routines and definitions and mutually recognized manipulation of play materials like Lego. In the meaning producing process of fantasy play children often confront a resistance between fantasy and reality in the bodily and linguistic aspects of the play routines. While different lines of fantasy sequences are signaled through improvisational linguistic and bodily actions children must often step out of fantasy to the reality of negotiating rules on how materials are to be used and the role of certain objects in the play. Therefore as the improvised routines of the fantasy play are carried out they continually produces the division between fantasy and reality and thereby crate a new field of experience for those taking part.

We believe that improvised play of this type involves skills that are collectively or communally developed and honed through repeated play routines that are quite different than internalized rules which are typical of more formal games. The innovative quality of improvised fantasy play is thus something that may be unique to the cultures created in early childhood. The skills involved seem indeed to diminish with lack of use as children's play becomes more formalized in games with rules. Thus, again we see the importance of studying these play routines as valuable creative and meaning making structures in their own right and part of cultures created by children.

Finally, the notion of separate and innovative peer cultures is captured by the collective actions and interpretive reproductions of children and youth in their resistance to certain types of adult rules. Conventional or organizational rules (as opposed to moral rules) are often part of adult attempts to supervise children in adult controlled spaces and organizations in which children spend a great deal of their childhoods. When children see these rules as arbitrary or unfair, they do not simply protest their existence. Rather they collectively create what we have termed secondary adjustments (Goffman, 1961) which are often innovative, creative, and successful in their intent by children and youth to display their group identity and reach group goals. We provided examples of such resistance to adult rules across time and cultural space and argued that such resistance is a clear manifestation of interpretive reproduction in children's cultures. Such resistance through collective produced secondary adjustments have a range of outcomes including children's recognition of why a rule may be necessary (reproduction of adult culture) to adults' recognition and accommodation to the children's secondary adjustments (change in the adult culture).

Overall, children's creation of their own peer cultures shows the importance of taking children's childhoods seriously as times of shared creativity and forging of strong communal bonds. Thus children are full participants in their own and adult cultures and not merely future adults. In this sense we come to recognize that the future of childhood is based on the understanding of peer cultures children produce in the present.

References

Bruner, J., & Sherwood, V. (1976). Peekaboo and the learning or rule structure. In J. Bruner, A. Jolly, & K. Sylva (Eds.), *Play: Its role in development and evolution* (pp. 277–285). New York: Basic Books.

Corsaro, W. (1985). *Friendship and peer culture in the early years*. Norwood, NJ: Ablex.

Corsaro, W. (1990). The underlife of the nursery school: Young children's social representations of adult rules. In G. Duveen & B. Lloyd (Eds.), *Social representations and the development of knowledge* (pp. 11–26). Cambridge, England: Cambridge University Press.

Corsaro, W. (1992). Interpretive reproduction in children's peer cultures. *Social Psychology Quarterly*, 55, 160–177.

Corsaro, W. (1994). Discussion, debate, and friendship: Peer discourse in nursery schools in the US and Italy. *Sociology of Education*, 67, 1–26.

Corsaro, W. (1997). "Forward" to R. Keith Sawyer. *Pretend play as improvisation*. Mahwah, NJ: Lawrence Erlbaum.

Corsaro, W. (2003). *"We're friends, rights?: Inside kid's culture*. Washington, D.C.: Joseph Henry Press.

Corsaro, W. (2004). Process approaches to children's friendships: What we know and where we are going. *International Society for the Study of Behavioural Development Newsletter*, 46, 14–16.

Corsaro, W. (2005). *The sociology of childhood* 2nd edition. Thousand Oaks, CA: Pine Forge Press.

Corsaro, W., & Eder, D. (1990). Children's peer cultures. *Annual Review of Sociology*, 16, 197–220.

Corsaro, W., & Molinari, L. (1990). From *seggiolini* to *discussione*: The generation and extension of peer culture among Italian preschool children. *International Journal of Qualitative Studies in Education*, 3, 213–230.

Corsaro, W., & Molinari, L. (2005). *I compagni: Understanding children's transition from preschool to elementary school*. New York: Teachers College Press.

Corsaro, W. & Rizzo, T. (1988). *Discussione* and friendship: Socialization processes in the peer culture of Italian nursery school children. *American Sociological Review*, 53, 879–894.

de Hann, D., & Singer, E. (2001). Young children's language of togetherness. *International Journal of Early Years Education*, 9, 117–124.

Evaldsson, A. (1993). *Play, disputes, and social order: Everyday life in two Swedish after-school centers*. Linköping, Sweden: Linköping University.

Fine, G. (1987). *With the boys: Little league baseball and preadolescent culture*. Chicago: University of Chicago Press.

Goffman, E, (1961). *Asylums*. Garden City, NJ: Anchor.

Goldman, L. (1998). *Child's play: Myth, mimesis, and make-believe*. New York: Oxford University Press.

Goodwin, M. (1990). *He-said-she-said: Talk as social organization among black children*. Bloomington, IN: Indiana University Press.

Hadley, K. (2003). Children's word play: Resisting and accommodating Confucian values in a Taiwanese kindergarten classroom. *Sociology of Education, 76,* 193–208.

James, A., Jenks, C., & Prout, A. (1998). *Theorizing childhood*. New York: Teachers College Press.

Johannesen, B. (2004). On shared experiences and intentional actions emerging within a community of Lego-playing children. Paper Presented at the Third International Conference on the Dialogical Self. Warsaw, Poland.

Katz, J. (2004). Building peer relationships in talk: Toddlers' peer conversations in childcare. *Discourse Studies, 6,* 329–346.

Kawamura, S. (1959). The process of sub-culture propagation among Japanese macaques. *Primates, 2,* 43–60.

Løkken, G. (2000). Tracing the social "style" of toddler peers. *Scandinavian Journal of Educational Research, 2,* 163–176.

Mayall, B. (2002). *Towards a sociology of childhood: Thinking from children's lives*. Philadelphia: PA: Open University Press.

Mussati, T., & Panni, S. (1981). Social behavior and interaction among day care center toddlers. *Early Child Development and Care, 7,* 5–27.

Nasaw, D. (1985). *Children of the city*. New York: Anchor.

Qvortrup, J. (1991). Childhood as a social phenomenon – An introduction to a series of national reports. *Eurosocial Report No. 36.* Vienna, Austria: European Centre for Social Welfare Policy and Research.

Rogoff, B. (1995). Observing sociocultural activity on three planes: Participatory appropriation, guided participation, and apprenticeship. In J. Wertsch, P. Del Rio & A. Alvarez (Eds.), *Sociocultural studies of mind* (pp. 139–164). New York: Cambridge University Press.

Rogoff, B. (1996). Developmental transitions in children's participation in sociocultural activities. In A. Sameroff & M. Haith (Eds.), *The Five to Seven Year Shift* (pp. 273–294). Chicago: University of Chicago Press

Rogoff, B. (2003). *The cultural nature of human development*. New York: Oxford.

Sawyer, R. K. (1997). *Pretend play as improvisation: Conversation in the preschool classroom*. Mahwah, NJ: Lawrence Erlbaum Associates.

Sawyer, R. K. (1999). The emergence of creativity. *Philosophical Psychology, 12,* 447–469.

Sawyer, R. K. (2002). Improvisation and narrative. *Narrative Inquiry, 12,* 319–349.

Schwartzman, H. (1978). *Transformations: The anthropology of children's play*. New York: Plenum.

Silverstein, M. (1993). Metapragmatic discourse and metapragmatic function. In J. Lucy (Ed.), *Reflexive language* (pp. 33–58). Cambridge, England: Cambridge University Press.

Singer, D., & Singer, J. (1990). *The house of make-believe: Play and the developing imagination*. Cambridge, MA: Harvard University Press.

Stamback, M., & Verba, M. (1986). Organization of social play among toddlers: An ecological approach. In E. Mueller & C. Cooper (Eds.), *Process and outcome in peer relationships* (pp. 229–247). New York: Academic Press.

Strandell, H. (1994). *What are children doing? Activity profiles in day care centres*. Paper presented at the XIII World Congress of Sociology, Bielefeld, Germany.

Thorne, B. (1993). *Gender play: Girls and boys in school*. New Brunswick, NJ: Rutgers University Press.

Valsiner, J. (2000). *Culture and human development*. Thousand Oaks, CA: Sage.

Wertsch, J. (1995). The need for action in sociocultural research. In J. Wertsch, P. Del Rio & A. Alvarez (Eds.), *Sociocultural studies of mind* (pp. 56–74). New York: Cambridge University Press.

Willis, P. (1981). *Learning to labour: How working class kids get working class jobs*. New York: Columbia University Press.

Winterhoff, P. (1997). Sociocultural promotions constraining children's social activity: Comparisons and variability in the development of friendships. In J. Tudge, M. Shanahan & J. Valsiner (Eds.), *Comparisons in human development: Understanding time and context* (pp. 222–251). New York: Cambridge University Press.

CHAPTER 22

"Culture Has No Internal Territory"

Culture as Dialogue

Eugene Matusov, Mark Smith, Maria Alburquerque Candela, and Keren Lilu

There is a growing consensus among educators that attention to the notion of culture is important for promoting democracy, equity, and quality of education. It has been demonstrated that the teachers' and students' cultures can clash in the classroom, negatively affecting educational processes (Heath, 1983; Philips, 1993). Often this phenomenon is explained using an essentialist approach focusing on pre-existing cultures. In this chapter, we will discuss problems with essentialist approaches and explore an alternative, dialogic, approach to the problem of "cultural mismatch."

There are at least two different types of approaches to the notion of "culture" that are used in educational research and practices. According to an essentialist view, culture is seen as a central preexisting factor – a way of doing things and communicating among each other distributed in a particular social group – that frames our relations with culturally different others. It is assumed that cultural differences can sometimes cause breakdowns in relations, particularly between culturally diverse groups. The other perspective can be called a constructivist and

dialogic approach that sees culture as one of the several explanations for breakdowns in relations among people.

We argue that the essentialist type of approaches to culture, although useful at times, can lead to unilateral pedagogies while the dialogic approach to culture promotes collaboration and dialogue among the teacher and the students (and beyond). One important issue we will address here is the question of what culture is and how culture emerges from breakdowns as an alternative view to cultural differences creating or causing breakdowns. This can be an important theoretical shift, for it transforms the way educators deal with problems of cultural diversity in research and practice.

Essentialist Approaches to "Other Communities" in History and Education

Historically, there have been several major essentialist approaches of how to deal with the issue of culture in education. Before the notion of "culture" fully emerged by the end of the 19th century (accidentally or not, concurrently with the establishment of mass schooling) as an explanation for systematic human differences in behavior of groups, racial subspecies theories dominated Western discourse about differences. According to these theories (varying in details), the human species consists of several biological subspecies (races) with European subspecies intellectually at the top, and the other human subspecies comparatively being limited (either totally or partially within the group population). For example, the term "mulatto," commonly used in French and Spanish colonies, referred to people of mixed races (Black and White). The Spanish word "mulato" (literally "a little mule") came from the word "mule" emphasizing unnatural breading of different species – a sterile hybrid offspring of female horse and male donkey (Hochschild, 2005). In these racial approaches, behavioral differences among different groups were explained by biological limitations (Gould, 1996). Because of the biological limitations of intellect in non-European subspecies, guidance, if needed, has to be "biologically sensitive" (i.e., it does not make sense to teach a cat calculus!) – formal education for inferior subspecies was recommended to be segregated, limited (often to training skills useful for slave owners), or not provided at all.

Already by the end of the 18th century, it became clear for some Western progressive intellectuals and activists that biological approaches to human group differences were an ideological cover-up for slavery, murder, oppression, and exploitation that was increasingly at odds with the ideology of democracy emerging in new bourgeois Western societies (Anderson, 1991; D'Souza, 1995; Hochschild, 2005). Western imperialism and power domination were redefined, explained, and justified in historical and cultural terms – new historico-cultural deficit approaches were raised (Hochschild, 1998). Non-European (and some European-like Eastern and Southern European) societies became to be seen as culturally and historically primitive and backward. These historico-cultural deficit approaches were

based on universal progressivism and social Darwinism (Hofstadter, 1955). According to universal progressivism, cultural differences between human societies were explained by an unevenness of historical development among (and even within) societies (all the while relying on teleological understandings of societal progress). The Western societies were seen as historically ahead of many other societies whose primitive cultures represent the historical past of Western societies (see, for example, Vygotsky, Luria, Golod, & Knox, 1993). Because of their historico-cultural superiority, Western societies were not only justified but morally obligated to dominate and guide historically backward and culturally deficient societies (see, for example, Luria, 1976).

It is important to mention here that this dominance, guidance, and patronage were often viewed as temporary phases of development of a culture within the historico-cultural deficit approaches. Historico-cultural deficits were seen to be remedied by social engineering the environment of the culturally inferior societies and through formal education. When in the early 1960s, Jerome Bruner, a well-known and well-respected US psychologist and educator, testified in the US Congress to advocate for a "War on poverty," he used his experiments with rats deprived of "natural" environmental stimulations to justify the establishment of the Head Start program for children of color and poverty (Bruner, 1998). Making parallels between the cognition and behavior of rats, raised in sterile conditions, and the cognition and behavior of children of poverty and color in the United States sounds absurd, invalid, and disrespectful now. The problem was not so much that the rats in psychological labs were used to model human psychological processes, but it was in the fact that the rats-psychologists relations in the United States (or dog-psychologist relations in the Tsarist and Soviet Russia) were used to guide human (power) social relations.

However, against the backdrop of biological approaches to human behavior and cognition, deficit approaches emphasizing cultural and environmental deprivation appeared to be more progressive and less racist, sexist, and classist than biological approaches (Boykin, 1986). It was argued that educationally, cultural deficits can be addressed through educational remediation and enrichment (see, for example, Bereiter & Engelmann, 1966 for such efforts).

Probably due to the defeat of colonialism around the globe and the Civil Rights movement in the 1960s, deficit approaches were increasingly put under attack. In the 1970s and onward, in the social sciences, critique of deficit approaches led to the emergence of new approaches that argued that the problem that many groups face in school (and other Western-based institutions) is due to cultural differences and Western historical dominance and hegemony rather than in the unevenness of societal development and progress (Bradley & Bradley, 1977; Cole & Bruner, 1971; Heath, 1983; Labov, 1972; Ogbu, 1978; Ryan, 1971). Out of all approaches oppositional to biological, cultural, and environmental deficits, so-called "cultural mismatch" approaches are probably most powerful and widespread (and the most coherently oppositional to the deficit approaches). According to cultural mismatch approaches, all cultures have rich "funds of knowledge" (Moll, Amanti, Neff, & González, 1992); however, conventional schools utilize and privilege only mainstream middle class cultures (Heath, 1983; Vogt, Jordan, & Tharp, 1987). Conventional middle-class-oriented schools and the students from non-mainstream communities have different cultural expectations, values, norms, and tools. When the different cultures face each other, they often go on a collision course without even knowing that the collision is caused by a cultural mismatch. Since mainstream middle-class-oriented schools have more power over the students from non-mainstream, less powerful, communities, the collisions are often publicly defined and framed in terms of blame and deficits (Rogoff, 2003). The cultural mismatch approach guides educators to appreciate, value, and utilize students' home cultures and provide forms of instructions that are congruent with the students'

cultural ways of learning (cf., the concept of "culturally responsive pedagogy" Ladson-Billings, 1994). We argue that although cultural mismatch approaches are pedagogically more sound than deficit approaches, they are also faced the problem of being essentialist like deficit ones (cf. discussion of the European history of the colonialist/Orientalist discourses in Said, 1979). The following example can help both illustrate the cultural mismatch approach and reveal its theoretical and practical limitations.

Problem of Cultural Mismatch: "Look at ME!"

In order to demonstrate and analyze the essentialist nature of the cultural mismatch approaches and the problems this poses, we present a case of a communicational breakdown between a White Afrikaans teacher and 10-year-old Black child of Sotho descent who is in his first days of classes at an all-Black student private school in a Black township outside Pretoria, South Africa. In this area of Guateng province in the Republic of South Africa (and in the township and in the school), the majority of the Black population is Sotho. Zulu is the next largest group. The whole episode that we videotaped in South Africa in 2003 lasted only less than 2 minutes.

At the beginning of the school year in January, all students in the school have an assembly at the large open school field for sport games and physical education each morning, before summer heat sets in and before other classes start. The fourth grade class sits on the grass in four rows while their White Afrikaans teacher stays in front of the rows of the students and provides her guidelines about upcoming sport activities. At some point, the teacher notices that one of the boys has long pants. She wonders why and wants to make a point to him that next time he comes to school he should wear short pants because of school policy. While talking with the child the teacher notices that the Black student is putting his head down and not looking at the teacher when she is speaking to him. The white teacher repeatedly demands that the Black student look at her while she is talking to him (she repeatedly asks him to "look at me! look at me!"). The more she demands this, the more he puts his head down and remains silent. Although she tries to be helpful and friendly to him by using a soft voice, and using welcoming and non-threatening words like "dear," "please," and "sweety," reassuring him that "nobody's going to shout at you," and providing her reasoning for her demand, she apparently cannot establish eye contact with the boy.

White Teacher (talking to the Black boy in long pants): Where're your short pants, sweety? (going around the rows of the children sitting on the grass close to the boy)

WT (yelling at other children): Hey! Hey!... Stop it!

WT (back to the boy): Where are your short pants? Don't you have any shorts? What school were you at last year? Matsefu, don't you have any other short pants? (The boy puts his head down.)

WT: Listen, Mark, dear... Look at me! Look at me! Look at me!... Look at me!

WT: Tomorrow, put on any short pants, OK?

WT (showing at another boy): Stand up, Meseti. You see, Meseti got anything on [i.e., he is wearing short pants]. You see Meseti?

WT: Nobody's going to shout at you.... please, please put on short pants, OK? Fine.

WT: (continues talking to the boy): Either you fasten your shoes properly or you take them off, please!

WT: (yells to everybody): And everybody sees they [shoes] are fastened properly! You'd hurt your ankles if you don't fasten them.

Afterwards, we interviewed a Black teacher from the school about the incident and found out that it is common in African Sotho communities for children to look down when an elder talks to them to show their respect. He also talks about confusion for the Black youth to communicate in places where white people are in charge (explicitly mentioning the school).

Black Teacher: ... it would not be proper to look at someone straight at upper, straight in the eye. We just look down and short... in a way, you're showing respect by doing that. But now as we... what happens... there is that mixture of conscience [?]. There will be a time we get confused.... "Where do I draw the line? When should I do?... When I want to look straight into the face and when should I look down?" Then as time goes on you can actually [draws a line in the air]... actually decide now: if I'm talking to talk to this person, this is what I'm going to do; but if I'm talking to this person this is what I'm going to have to do. Yeah. So, um... That's why I'm saying... with most of kids who are living, [growing up] in an urban environment... they're sort of [unclear]... but then if finally they're moving in and out... it happens in rural... rural areas... you get that confusion now... Cause when they go out in those rural areas, the kids will be expected to do something different. But it also depends on how long they stay and [?]... to see where... this difference, difference comes in.

He also tells that Sotho and Zulu African traditional communities are different in this regard. In Sotho traditional communities youngsters are expected not to look directly at the elders, while in Zulu traditional communities they are expected to look directly while elders talks to them.

It is clear from the episode that the Afrikaans teacher is not aware of these cultural differences and assumes that the Sotho boy does not look at her directly because he feels threatened by her. For that reason she seems to use a tender voice and gentle addresses to the boy like "sweety" and "dear." She insists to him that she is not shouting at him. Although we did not interview her afterwards, she probably feels uncomfortable when the student she talks to does not allow establishing his eye contact with her. She appears to be aware of her own discomfort in this interaction and deliberately attends to how to fix this discomfort by making the student establish eye contact using several strategies. She is aware of breakdown in their interaction – she cannot simply deliver her message of intent that the boy needs to have short pants instead of long pants in future – but she seems to feel that she is forced to focus on changing the way their interaction is organized. However, her attempts to change the organization of their interaction were failing. It is difficult to say how the Sotho boy interpreted the event but it is very reasonable to assume that he also took an active stance to it. This situation seems to be very similar to one observed and described by Philips when White Anglo teachers felt uncomfortable when they could not establish their eye contact with some Native American students when addressing them (Philips, 1993). However, unlike American White teachers observed by Philips, the South African Afrikaans teacher does not seem to consider the boy disrespectful, challenging, and aggressive.

Textbooks on multicultural education often recognize this and similar cases as examples of "cultural mismatch": the teacher and the student come from two distinctively different pre-existing cultures and the teacher is probably unaware of the cultural nature of the child's behavior and misinterprets it as, for example, the student's shyness or fear (in our case) or aggressiveness and disrespect (in Philips's case). These multicultural education textbooks recommend that teachers learn about students' home and their own cultures to become aware of potential cultural differences and mismatches. This awareness can help avoid the teacher's blaming or developing adversarial relations (see, for example, Nieto, 1996). However, using an essentialist cultural interpretation for relational breakdowns may or may not be helpful for the teacher. While the essentialist cultural interpretations may help the Afrikaans teacher and other educators avoid blaming the child for being disrespectful by

not looking at her when she speak, it does not guide what educators should do after the realization of the mismatch. Indeed, what should the teacher do in the case when he or she *needs* to see the student's eyes directly when talking to the student, while the student *needs* to hide his or her eyes when a person of authority talks to him or her?

The realization of mismatch between the teacher and student's pre-existing cultures puts the teacher into the dilemma of promoting either children-run or adult-run educational unilateralism as described by Matusov and Rogoff (2002). The dilemma is between whether to adopt the child's home culture over her own discomfort (i.e., to allow to the child to put his head down while the teacher talks to him) – *or* to force the child to adopt her home culture over his discomfort (i.e., to demand, as the teacher in our case did, that the child looks directly at the teacher while she is speaking). The proponents of children-run unilateralism argue that school exists for children and not for the teacher and it is the teacher's obligation to make the students' learning as comfortable and effective as possible by making the teacher's instruction "culturally sensitive" (Bean, 1997; Ladson-Billings, 1994; Lee, 2003; Rueda & Dembo, 1995; Rueda & Moll, 1994; Tharp, 1982). It is believed that the alternative would be to enforce the teacher's mainstream culture in the classroom and in turn, promote the *status quo* of educational, social, economic, and political inequalities.

The proponents of adult-run unilateralism argue that the students from non-mainstream and often economically and politically disadvantaged communities need to learn how to successfully navigate and operate in mainstream institutions that White middle-class teachers represent. Accommodating to the students' home cultures and not teaching the mainstream ways of doing things can potentially do a lot of disservice to the students, their future, and to their communities at large. In the view of adult-run unilateralism proponents, if school is committed to social justice, it should focus on directly teaching the "master's tools" to students from disadvantaged communities

(Delpit, 1995; Ogbu, 2003). Finding any compromise between the children- and adult-run unilateralisms is especially difficult in such cases like eye contact or dialogic turn taking or ways of talking and thinking since it is difficult if not impossible to do two (or more) "ways of doing things" at once or even in alternation (Heath, 1983; Kaplan, 1966; Michaels & Cazden, 1986; Philips, 1993; Rogoff, 2003; Rogoff, Mistry, Göncü, & Mosier, 1993).

It appears that both children- and adult-run unilateralisms are unsatisfactory. The children-run unilateralism disregards the comfort of the teacher and the teacher's culture and community and does not prepare students from disadvantaged communities for how to deal with the mainstream institutions in future. Adult-run unilateralism disregards the comfort of the student and his/her home community and his/her ways of being and learning, does not promote sensitive guidance, and accepts the power status quo. Also, although adult-run universalism can promote institutional success for some individual students from disadvantaged communities. It cannot promote success for an entire disadvantaged group as a whole because many mainstream institutional practices are based on competition and discrimination (i.e., "zero sum game" where success of one is failure of another) (De Lone, 1979; Labaree, 1997; Varenne & McDermott, 1998).

Applying Latour's (1987) framework that he developed in his study of science practice, the essentialist approach to culture can be called "ready-made culture" (Matusov, Pleasants, & Smith, 2003). It assumes that the cultures pre-exist each other and their mismatches cause interactional breakdowns similar to the described above. We define "interactional breakdown" similar to the field of family psychology (Helfer, 1987) as a dramatic event (Bakhtin, 1986; Bakhtin & Emerson, 1999) in which the smooth flow of interaction becomes impossible and participants are forced to shift their attention from their messages to the interaction itself and their relations (Matusov, St. Julien, & Hayes, 2005). The essentialist approach to culture (i.e., the "ready-made culture" approach) assumes that cultures and cultural differences pre-exist the interaction and cause the breakdowns.

We have found several problems with the "ready-made" essentialist approach to culture. First, as we already mentioned, it does not guide educators what to do with cultural mismatches because both unilateral solutions (and even their combination and/or alternation) are not satisfactory. Second, the essentialist approach cannot explain why cultural mismatches sometimes do not automatically produce interactional breakdowns. Third, the essentialist ready-made cultural approaches cannot explain the emergence of new cultures and cultural dynamics in general. Finally, it cannot explain the phenomenon of why, under a careful historical analysis, any culture and cultural practice is never a monolith and, on a close look, consists of many cultures that it is incorporated in past (like any language or authorship of any text).

Dialogic Framework to Cultural Breakdowns

In order to develop an alternative non-essentialist approach to interactional breakdowns in the classroom, we have turned to the existing literature and educational practices for insights. We specifically were attracted to the literature that talks about relational rather than essentialist nature of interactional breakdowns.

We found important insights of why differences in cultural practices may not be responsible for interactional breakdowns. Bateson (1987) criticized the classical notion of information (more exactly, the smallest unit of information) developed by Turing, Weaver, and Shannon, the main founders of the cybernetics, as any difference codified as 0 and 1 in the computer language. Bateson argued that information should be defined as "difference that makes a difference" (Bateson, 1987: 381) – one difference in objects is not enough for emergence of information (it is possible to find similar ideas in Mead, 1956 who defined the notion of "meaning" as subject's reaction to the action of others). The other difference is the difference in subjects that the first difference in objects produces on the participants. Thus, according to Bateson, any information is always objectively subjective. Without the participants making an active response to the difference in the object, there is no information. Information is always mediated by human relations for a difference in objects to become information for humans.

Applying this idea to interactional breakdowns in the classroom, we can say that, although a difference in ways of doing things is necessary precursor for interactional breakdowns (one difference), it is not sufficient for causing a breakdown. The breakdown is constituted by the active response of the participants to this difference. In our South African case, the response of the participants was in the Afrikaans teacher's efforts to make the student look at her while she was talking to him (e.g., "sweety," "Look at me!," "nobody's going to shout at you") and in the Sotho boy's actions of putting his head even more down as the teacher talks to him. The Afrikaans teacher and the Sotho boy together co-construct "the second difference" (in Bateson's terms) that together with "the first difference" in their ways of doing things (i.e., relational difference in their behavior when the teacher looks at the boy when speaking while he is not) constitutes an interactional breakdown event.

Another big insight that became a part of the title of our article came from work of the Soviet philosopher Bakhtin who made an important statement defining culture as boundary and relationship,

> One must not . . . imagine the realm of culture as some sort of spatial whole, having boundaries but also having internal territory. The realm of *culture has no internal territory*: it is entirely distributed along the boundaries, boundaries pass everywhere, through its every aspect, the systematic unity of culture extends into the very atoms of cultural life, it reflects like the sun in each drop of that life. Every cultural act lives essentially on the boundaries: in this is its seriousness and its significance; abstracted from boundaries, it loses its soul, it becomes empty, arrogant, it disintegrates and dies. (Bakhtin & Emerson, 1999, 301)

Bakhtin's revolutionary statement suggests that it is not difference in cultures that creates interactional breakdowns but, conversely, interactional breakdowns constitute boundaries and create cultures. This seems to mean that "culture" is a certain interpretative frame (among other possible interpretative frames) that is used to manage interactional breakdowns in a certain way. Let's consider an example to illustrate this point.

I may notice that when I talk with another person, the person moves toward me. He makes me uncomfortable and aware of the situation so I move back from the person. The person keeps moving toward me while we are talking and I keep moving back, away from him. I can make several plausible interpretations about this situation. For example, I can think that the person is power hungry and tries to dominate me by violating my private space. Or I can think that the person is probably shortsighted and needs to move closely to see me better. Or I can think that the person violates my private space to rob me. Or I can think that the person cannot hear me well. Or I can think that the person wants to tell me something private. Or I can think that the person is sexually attracted to me and tries to make an advance. Or, finally (among many more other possibilities) I can think that the person comes from "another culture." By "another culture," I mean that we belong to different stable social groups systematically practicing different norms for proximity (Rogoff, 2003). Each of my listed interpretations affords different possible actions and relational stances toward the person in response to my interpretation: to run away, to fight, to call the police, to move closer, to look at the person sexually, to respect the person, to stop the interaction, to hate the person, to like the person, to blame the person, to give advice, to negotiate our common space, to ask the person why they are coming closer to me, and so on. Thus, seeing our interactional breakdown as cultural calls for certain expectations and negotiation on my part.

Using "culture" as an interpretative frame for an interactional breakdown also implies that in future I should expect similar and other types of breakdowns on a regular basis not only with this person and me but between any person from his/her community and my community. Notice that my and his/her communities are also defined through the breakdowns. Similarly, in the case of "Look at me," Afrikaans and Sotho communities are defined through interpretation of many different interactional breakdowns in the past and anticipation of many more breakdowns in future. When interactional breakdowns cease to continue or cease to be recognized as cultural or cease to be expected, cultural and communal boundaries disappear together with the cultures and communities themselves ("culture has no internal territory"). That is why the notions of culture and community are so illusive and non-essential. When anthropologists crossed all definitions of what it means to be "French" circulating among French nationalists in Canada, they got nothing in common (Linger, 1994). However, even though that the "French" distinction has nothing in common in definition, this does not mean that the French-non-French distinction does not have real – social, economic, political, and psychological – consequences for people in Canada.

Using Bakhtin's framework, it is possible to say that Canadian Frenchness emerges from interactional breakdowns and interpretative frames even though these frames may not be always consistent and coherent with each other, as the anthropologists have shown. Similarly, being an immigrant in the United States from the Soviet Union, I (Eugene Matusov, the first author) was recognized as a "Jew" in the USSR (and still in Russia when I visit it) and as a "Russian" in the United States. I am "essentially the same" but my boundaries are constituted by interactional breakdowns with others are

different in the United States and in the USSR/Russia.

Boundaries constituting cultures and communities are not static but rather relational, dynamic, conflictual, and communicative. In other words, boundaries are dramatic and dialogic,

> If we had not talked with others and they with us, we should never talk to and with ourselves... Through speech a person dramatically identifies with potential acts and deeds, he plays many roles, not in successive stages of life but in *a contemporaneously created drama*. The mind emerges. (Dewey, 1925, 170)

Thus, "culture" is a certain dramatic dialogic discourse about dramatic events of interactional breakdowns. From a dialogic perspective, it is impossible to avoid breakdowns in human relations. The issue becomes how to manage these breakdowns in a better educational way. The dialogic approach is based on the key premise that the teacher cannot and should not solve the breakdown in a *unilateral* way (i.e., only by the teacher) but rather through a collaborative dialogue (Bakhtin & Emerson, 1999). From the dialogic perspective, the question of "what should I, as the teacher, do in case of an interactional breakdown" is a trap into unilateralism (cf. Mayo, 2000). Furthermore, a teacher's submission or passive accommodation to the students' ways of doing things in response to interactional breakdown over and above the needs of the teacher or others in the classroom or the classroom environment more generally would be a form of children-run unilateralism.

In past we developed a dualistic approach to the notion of "culture" (Matusov, Pleasants, & Smith, 2003) based on the dualistic approach to science developed by Latour (1987). Latour argues that there are two mutually related views of science practice: ready-made-science and science-in-action. The ready-made-science perspective, familiar from many depictions in popular and scientific literature, describes the past of science as the established product of past

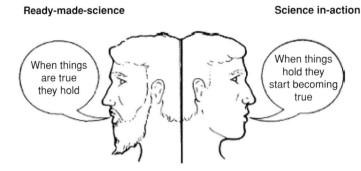

Figure 22.1. Double-face Janus of science (Latour, 1987: 12).

activity (illustrated by the "old face" with the beard on Figure 22.1). It describes science practice as the process of discovery of pre-existing facts. In contrast, science-in-action describes the present practice of science as the unfolding process of active negotiation of the consequences of the actions of the scientists (illustrated with the "young face" without a beard on Figure 22.1),

The "old face" of ready-made-science would say, "When the truth is achieved people become convinced." The "young face" of the science-in-action would reply, "When relevant people become convinced, things start becoming true." Now, Latour argues that the process of "convincing relevant people" is not simply a matter of following some criteria or methodology of science, as positivists and some recent US politicians believe, or of some group conformity processes, as some psychologists may suggest, but rather itself a complex, hybrid practice cycle involving many institutions as within as outside of the science itself (Latour, 1987; Latour & Woolgar, 1979).

Latour argues that these two perspectives are both needed because it is impossible to move forward in science practice (i.e., science-in-action) without assuming that certain devices work and certain "true" statements exist that do not generate controversies among relevant participants (i.e., ready-made-science). A statement from one "face" becomes unproductive, if not plainly wrong, when it actuated within the realm of the other "face." When, on the one hand, any well-established statement and any work-

ing device are challenged, the science-in-action perspective is unproductively shifted into the realm of ready-made-science (as it often occurs in the US political contemporary debates about teaching the theory of evolution versus teaching about "intelligent design" in US public schools). When, on the other hand, a scientific statement and any device in question are viewed as a discovery of pre-existing truth, the ready-made-science perspective is unproductively entered into the realm of science-in-action (as it has occurred in classic positivism). As Latour and Woolgar painstakingly show in their sociological research of a biology lab, the ideology of ready-made science portraying the science as a process of discovery of preexisting truth does not describe or guide well the scientific process of truthmaking-in-action. The latter is exactly what we see as a problem in education dealing with the issue of cultural differences in the classroom. In the classroom, cultures are in making that is why a ready-made approach to culture is not useful and often counter-productive.

Similarly to Latour, Matusov, Pleasants, and Smith (2003) argue that when we describe the stable use of a cultural interpretative frame for recursive interactional breakdowns, the traditional ready-made-culture perspective is useful. However, when we are interested in describing cultural dynamics or prescribe designs for a "new culture" (cf. in Spanish "la cultura vivida," Moll, 2000: 256), the dialogic culture-in-action perspective should be used (Figure 22.2).

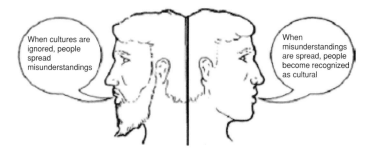

Figure 22.2. Double-face Janus of culture: Dualistic approach to culture based on pragmatic relativism.

This new dualistic,[1] pragmatically relativistic, approach to human phenomena emerged in a dialogic opposition to essentialism. In our view, an essentialist approach often makes two mutually related errors. The first error is to assume that anything that is not firmly rooted in its material object (e.g., a social construction) cannot be truth. However, as we have discussed above, from the fact that there is nothing in common in the definitions of French made by different French Canadian nationalists, it does not mean that French ethnicity does not exist in Canada. A social construction can be as real as a material object – it can kill, it can cure, it can provide resources.

The second error of essentialism is to assume that truth is always and fully grounded in its object. For example, an essentialist would probably claim that the fact that the Roman numeral system is a cultural artifact is *solely* rooted in the way how ancient Romans quantified their practices (i.e., an essentialist definition of culture is "a way of doing things in a community"). However, we argue that the Roman numeral system can be recognized as cultural only when there is a breakdown of translation from another numeral system, for example, Arabic. In other words, its culture-ness and artifact-ness comes as a surplus of encountering another numeral system in addition to how ancient Roman quantified their practices. When, for example, it is written on my TV screen that Stanley Kubrick's movie Spartacus was produced in MDCD, I do

not understand "when exactly" the movie was produced. For me, the Roman number MDCD is not woven into network of historical and (auto)biographical events like Arabic numbers are. After consulting Internet website, I have to translate the Roman number into Arabic using a formula: $M = 1000, D = 500, CD = 400, 1000 + 500 + 400 = 1960$. The Arabic number 1960 is woven into my network of chronologically organized historical and (auto)biographical events so I know "when exactly" the movie Spartacus was produced (e.g., I, the first author, was born in 1960, so the movie Spartacus is as old as I am). Without the breakdown requiring a translation, the Roman numerical system is not cultural but "the way of counting" – the ancient Romans did not need to translate their numbers but perceived them directly within their networks of quantitative practices. For the ancient Romans, their numeral system was *the* numeral system and not the *Roman* numeral system. The qualifier "Roman" comes only after the two numeral systems met together and required translation. Bakhtin made a similar point, "There used to be a school joke: the ancient Greeks did not know the main thing about themselves, that they were *ancient* Greeks, and they never called themselves that. But in fact that temporal distance that transformed the Greeks into *ancient* Greeks had an immense transformational significance: it was filled with increasing discoveries of new *semantic* values in antiquity, values of which the Greeks were in fact unaware, although they themselves created them" (Bakhtin, 1986, 6).[2] Similarly, ancient Romans were probably unaware of the conventional and constructionist nature of their numeral system that they *created* (rather than *discovered*).

The essentialist approach is a ready-made approach and as such it can be very useful. Speaking metaphorically, when one reads a novel, one should see only the novel's characters, their deeds, and relations and not the sentences, words or letters or punctuation signs that help the characters emerge in the reader mind. Focus on the sentences, words, letters, and punctuation signs, would easily distract the reader from the character and, thus, from the novel itself. When one is dealing with stable practices it makes sense to see their culture-ness solely in its object. When a modern person sees the Roman number XXIV, he or she recognizes the pattern of $10 + 10 + (5 - 1) = 24$ as if the pattern is solely rooted in the Roman number and not in an interaction between the Roman and Arabic numeral systems. Switching the attention to this interaction may distract the one's attention from comprehension of what the Roman number XXIV is "really means." A ready-made approach reifies translations and relations among practices and people in the object. This reification (or "blackboxing" in Latour's terms) is not an error or an illusion, as some constructivists claim, but a pragmatically useful strategy to manage our attention in an activity (Wenger, 1998). The useful and necessary strategy of reification transforms into an error of essentialism only when it is treated as the reality in addressing dynamic processes and unstable practices and relations. However, we argue that for education often dynamic processes, unstable practices and relations are in the center focus of the educators.

Clifford calls for a new view of culture-in-action in anthropology based on dialogic translation of "conjunctions" ("borders" in Bakhtin's terms or "breakdowns" in our terms).

The anthropology I have in mind is no longer part of a unified "science of man," a science which sorted out the world's cultures, synchronically and diachronically, from a privileged standpoint at the end, or cutting edge of history. Rather I want to affirm another strand of anthropology which points toward more tentative, dialogical, but still realist, ethnographic histories: a work of translation which focuses not so much on cultures as on conjunctures, on complex mediations of old and new, of local and global (Clifford, 2000, 97).

According to the culture-in-action perspective, "*cultures*" are a dialogically recognized[3] pattern [a frame] of dramatic breakdowns that have temporal and spatial stability, heterogeneity, and synchronicity (among probably other features). To be viewed as "*cultural*," the breakdowns have to have temporal stability because they are recognized and expected to occur on a recursive basis. When breakdowns do not reoccur on a systematic basis, they cannot be viewed as "*cultural*." For example, from a fact that I did not understand a person only one time, I probably won't jump to a conclusion that my lack of understanding is due to a cultural difference between us. Similarly, they have to occur between certain stable social groups to be seen as "*cultural*"; otherwise breakdowns would be interpreted probably in personal, non-cultural terms. For example, systematic breakdowns of translations of feet into inches for some people are not seen as "*cultural*" because these breakdowns are not systematically distributed across different social groups. However, systematic breakdowns across meters and feet can be seen as "*cultural*" – American versus European – because different social groups use different measure systems causing breakdowns. Cultural explanations of breakdowns become stronger when there are diverse breakdowns that have the same temporal and spatial stability. In other words, when different types of breakdowns (e.g., in language, in eye contact, in personal space) systematically occur with the same two groups, it becomes easier to view them as "*cultural*" rather when only one type of breakdown systematically occurs between two groups. Otherwise, the differences may be too idiosyncratic and too difficult to discriminate as "*cultural*" within complex, ongoing social interactions. For example, breakdowns causing by some people's snoring in others, who can't sleep because of the snoring, more unlikely be seen as "*cultural*" than breakdowns caused by deafness or blindness. Deafness and blindness create much more comprehensive and heterogeneous system of breakdowns to constitute distinctive cultures (Mudgett-DeCaro, 1996) than snoring (at least for the historical "*now*"). Finally, when breakdowns occur systematically in the same time (synchronously) for the participants, the breakdowns can be viewed as "*cultural.*" However, when breakdowns occur systematically in different time (diachronically) for the participants, especially for the same group of people, the breakdowns can be viewed as "*historical*" (i.e., the boundary between "*the present*" and "*the past*" is created). For example, the "striking difference" in bodily proximity of male friends on US photos in the 19th century and in the second part of the 20th century is viewed as a "*historical change*" in US male intimacy in the context of male friendship (Deitcher, 2001).

Instead of viewing the interactional and relational breakdowns as communicational nuisances that should be avoided, minimized, or repaired in the classroom, the culture-in-action approach views the relational breakdowns as sites of many opportunities for dialogue and for co-constructing new ways of participating with each other (i.e., genuine teaching and learning, Mayerfeld Bell, 1998). Through this dialogue a "*new culture*" of the classroom community (i.e., a new communal way of communicating and doing things) can emerge. We will offer the notion of "creole community" as a collaborative way of solving cultural breakdowns (Matusov & Hayes, 2002; Matusov, Pleasants, & Smith, 2003; Matusov, St. Julien, & Hayes, 2005). We will illustrate the dialogic approach by providing examples from how a Black South African teacher in the same school (cited as the Black Teacher interviewed above) dialogically deals with breakdowns in his classroom and how the first author dealt with relational breakdowns in his undergraduate classroom for preservice teachers.

Building "Creole Communities" in Education

Here we consider how "creole communities" emerge and how the teacher guides and, to a certain degree, designs this emergence. We follow the definition of "creole community" developed by Matusov, St. Julien, and Hayes (2005: 3): "We refer to the notion of 'community' to emphasize mutual solidarity and affinity among the participants" (Cole, 1996; Durkheim, 1966). We use the term 'creole' to refer to a holistic community where boundaries between diverse and distinguished cultural groups are neither fully erased nor fully maintained. This creole community is united yet preserves the diversity of participants' cultures, backgrounds, immediate and long-term goals, values, and so on." We argue that successful teachers often develop creole communities in their classrooms in response to perceived interactional and communicational breakdowns instead of using an essentialist perspective of pre-existing cultures.

Our following analysis of an educational practice building creole communities reveals that when the teacher is faced with and recognized a recursive interactional breakdown, instead of asking him or herself the question "how can I solve it?," the teacher seems to attempt to share the problem with the students in a public forum. By engaging the students with the problem, the teacher avoids the trap of unilateralism inherent in the essentialist ready-made-culture approaches. The teacher does not just state the perceived problem to the students but also often explores the negative consequences of the problem as it affects or would affect their joint life in the classroom. The teacher works hard to makes sure that all the students understand the problem and its consequences, perceive it as important and serious, and accept as their own through their response to the teacher's bid for having the presented problem as their shared problem. The teacher also makes clear that the solution of the shared problem is impossible without the students' and the teacher's active participation. By this process of sharing the problem with the students, the teacher creates a new, problem-based solidarity in the classroom.

This problem-based solidarity is organized around the realization by all members of a group (not necessarily a community yet) that they are all engaged in the same problem, the solutions for which depend on coordinated efforts by all members of the group. This type of solidarity around a common problem is very different than solidarity around a common vision, oppositional solidarity or cooperative solidarity based on division of labor because, unlike in those types of solidarity, the problem-based solidarity does not require any consensus about the organization of the community that pre-exists the participants' commitment to the new community (Durkheim, 1966; Fullan, 1993; Matusov, 1999; Matusov, St. Julien, & Hayes, 2005; Matusov & White, 1996; Sherif, 1988). Such common vision of some practice, or common opposition to somebody or something, or a division of labor that pre-exists the community, upon which the community is based, and, to some extent, are "above the community" and above the individual members being a rigid structure precluding full negotiation of the community practice and relations. Solidarity based on a shared problem is rooted in each individual member's needs and their realization of a co-dependency in addressing these needs. For the problem-based solidarity to start forming, the participants do not even need to agree fully with each other about the definition of the problem or its solution – but only on the fact that they have a common problem and that its solution depends on active participation of all members of the group (this group may not necessarily be considered a "community" yet). The shared problem creates a "boundary object" (Star & Griesemer, 1989) or "interobjectivity" (Latour, 1996) or "intersubjectivity without agreement" (Matusov, 1996) that coordinates all the participants. The problem-based solidarity allows the participants to participate legitimately and actively in the mutual process of goal defining.

Below we consider two examples of a teacher building creole communities. In both cases, the teacher shared the problem of the breakdown with the students, the students responding by accepting the problem as legitimate and important and sharing ownership of the problem. In both cases, the teacher discussed consequences of the problem with the students and they negotiated a solution together. In the first example, the teacher identified the shared problem and suggested the "solution" which (although it does not work) triggers a new problem-based solidarity and a new practice in the classroom that helps to address the problem. In the second example, a new practice emerges in the classroom as a result of the teacher's discussion of the shared problem without any suggestion for a solution.

"Please Try to Listen to Each Other"

In the same South African school that we described above, we videotaped a few lessons taught by very experienced Black science teacher Mr. Moyo who was born, raised, and got his teacher education in Zimbabwe (the same Black Teacher cited in the interview above). In this particular economics lesson at the beginning of the new school year, Mr. Moyo wanted to discuss with his seventh grade students what things should be considered a "need," a "means," or a "want." About 40 students in the rather small classroom were sitting in several long rows facing the blackboard. He posed the question to his students, "What things would you identify as needs?" They brainstormed and volunteered ideas (such as "education," "air," "shelter," "sunlight," "God," "money," "food," "love," "transportation"), which Mr. Moyo wrote on the blackboard for further discussion. Then he focused the students on each item listed on the blackboard to get a consensus if it is not a "need" or a "want." As soon as Mr. Moyo noticed any disagreement among the students, he asked the opponents to elaborate on their opinion and the rest of the class to judge their reasoning until a class consensus was reached. Sometimes he asked guiding questions to the students or offered comments to make the students' reasoning more evident for themselves and the rest of the class. The class worked in a certain rhythm, alternating between discussing issues at hand among a group of classmates around them and presenting their ideas to the teacher and the whole class. According to our videotaped observation, all students, without exception, actively and sometimes very passionately participated in the discussions. We could not hear all discussions of the students because of "learning noise" (the teacher's term) – often the students talked about the class topic at once – but from their contributions that we could hear and their non-verbal behavior, we judged their high engagement in the lesson.

However, this class work was not without problems. The class discussions were not always "naturally" synchronized. At times when one student was ready to present a group idea to the teacher and the class and was allowed to take the class floor by the teacher, some other groups continued their heated discussions of the issues among themselves. Also, sometimes the students, attentively listening to a student addressing the whole class, split again into informal groups for discussions in reaction to a presented point even though the student having the class floor did fully not finish his point yet. In our eyes and eyes of the teacher, the weak public forum and public platform presented a serious threat to the effectiveness of the discussion and the lesson at large. We did not see any evidence that the students, themselves, were aware of the problem: they did not try to silence the class when they spoke publicly and did not try to silence each other when a student was speaking to the whole class. The teacher dealt with the problem recursively as the problem became more and more apparent in the teacher's eyes.

Mr. Moyo started discussing if "education" was "a need" or "a want." The students got really excited about this topic, with about half saying yes and about half saying no. Their voices rose and became louder, and they started talking at the same time, amongst themselves. Mr. Moyo had to tell them to raise their hands in order to get

them to listen to one student at a time. After each student that Mr. Moyo called on spoke, there was a surge of agreements, disagreements, and comments from the other students in the class. Mr. Moyo called on one student who was raising his hand, but students were still talking to each other. He said, "Ah...Please try to listen. If you want to say something which is going to be heard by everyone, you must listen when others are speaking." This student then starts speaking again, and the class becomes silent, but about half way through what he was saying, the other students started discussing and talking to each other again. Mr. Moyo then looked out at the rest of the class and said, "Now...I think *we are having a problem here*. (Student's Name), you address yourself to the class." Again, the teacher's comment made the class silent and attentive to the student. Mr. Moyo seemed to move from an ad hoc dealing with the problem to a public recognition of the problem for the class. So far he still had full responsibility for solving the problem.

Mr. Moyo then turned back to the student, and started a new conversation with the class. He reaffirmed that the class should hear ideas from everybody and that the whole class should arrive at a consensus at the end. They started discussing whether "money" is an economic need or want for people and once again the students were getting excited and were all speaking at the same time. Mr. Moyo looked at the students and said, "Now remember...if you have to say something, you must make sure others are listening...if you just shout it, then you're just wasting your time." He pointed at a student who raised her hand and she could speak in silence. By making this move, the teacher apparently abandoned his attempts to solve the problem unilaterally by just attracting their attention to the problem. He provided two reasons for why the students should listen to each other: (1) to have a reciprocal obligation to listen to others if you want to be listened when you talk to the class and (2) to not waste time by shouting because no one can listen if everyone shouts. Up to now, it is possible to claim that the problem remained unshared with the students despite the teacher's growing efforts to share the ownership for the problem with the students.

As they continued to discuss the money issue, some students were raising their hands while some were still shouting out what they wanted to say. When Mr. Moyo called on a student who raised his/her hand, the students were quiet as they were speaking. When the student was coming to the end of what he or she was saying, the rest of the class started talking all at once again in reaction to what was said. This seemed to be fine with the Mr. Moyo. This showed complexity of the problem because at certain time when the class floor was not occupied by any one speaker, splitting into small discussion groups was effective and legitimate in the teacher's eyes (as he pointed out in his post-lesson interview).

At some point, the teacher decided that the class had had enough small group discussions to generate a productive whole class discussion and he called on a student who was raising his hand and sitting in the first row (next to the teacher) and asked the class to listen to him, "Let's listen to him." The student tried to make a point that money is an economic need for people. To make this point, the student said that without enough money, a person has to rely on the government, which seemed to be bad according to the student. The class reacted on the student's point actively: some in disagreement and some in agreement. The noise grew again. Mr. Moyo asked the student: "Who is the government, by the way? Huh? Who is the government who is supposed to give you shelter, who is supposed to give you food...?" (friendly, smiling at student). Student responded (through the class noise) by that the government is the people. Mr. Moyo turned to the entire class: "I suppose you heard what he said." Many students replied, "Nooo...." Mr. Moyo told to the class: *"It was a good point. What? You say 'no'? Why? You were talking...it's not a bad thing, to talk...the main thing is that you all listen. He said a good point here."* Mr. Moyo looked at the class with surprise and confusion. He

showed them that he was confused that they did not hear, because they should have if they were quiet when others were talking; he also recognized that the reason they did not hear was because they were talking to each other at the same time. Again, the class became quiet. One student asked, "What did he say?" The student repeated and several students raised their hands in response – it was clear that the students agreed with the teacher that the student's point was really good and important (although they might disagree with it). More students began raising their hands to get the class floor at this moment and one more time the students could hold the class floor in silence while the others were listening. We also noticed that the students lowered their hands when they actively listened to the classmates taking the class floor. Sometimes they raised their hands again and sometimes they did not immediately do so after the classmate finished speaking to the class. Although, we could not rule out completely the possibility that the students simply and unconditionally complied with the teacher's request to be silent during a classmate's talk to the entire class, we found it difficult to use compliance as the sole explanation for the changes in the students' behavior we observed since their compliance was conditional and situational involving their own judgment. It was much more plausible to explain the students' new behavior by their understanding and acceptance of the new problem to listen to their classmates when they took the class floor.

The teacher continued his efforts to share the problem with the students and promote the value of listening to each other, especially when one student was talking to the entire class. It became evident that more and more students started visibly enjoying the whole class discussions as they more and more listen to each other. The teacher gave the students respect by telling them that what they were doing was not "bad thing" (i.e., talking), which also showed them that he liked that they discussed and conversed with one another. But at the same time he was showing them that they could miss some really good ideas and points, and that it was important to listen to each other. As Mr. Moyo was saying, "the main thing is that you all listen. You missed a good point here," and the students became very quiet.

Guided by the teacher the class continued developing how to balance small group discussions, whole class discussions, listening, and giving a student the class floor. Mr. Moyo brought up the question, "What is money? Let's just try to get to understand, what is money?" One student answered, and when she was finished talking, all of the students started talking at the same time to each other, in agreement or disagreement with the student who just spoke. They were talking to each other about the question Mr. Moyo posed – what is money – and were voicing their ideas. Mr. Moyo stood and let the students discuss among themselves for about 15 seconds. He stood and watched, giving the students a chance to talk with each other. He then pulled them back to the lesson, saying "I don't know what you were all saying, a lot of people were talking here and unfortunately I only heard what she said. If you want to say something you are thinking, something which is in your mind, put up your hand like her so everyone can hear." As he was saying this, everyone was silent. And when he called on a girl to speak, the other students were quiet until she was finished. Then there was a wave of talking again – apparently discussing in small groups what she just said. Mr. Moyo did not try to interrupt their discussions.

We would consider this situation to be a type of interactional and relational breakdown because the constant talking while others were speaking was a problem for Mr. Moyo, a problem that he shared with his students. Moreover, each time he acknowledged the problem, there was a break in the flow of the lesson. However, this seems to be more of a "continuous" or "ongoing" breakdown, for it kept repeating. This was not one incident, rather it continued happening. It was the beginning of the year and Mr. Moyo was trying to establish the way he expected his students to interact with each other in class. The process started but was far from being finished. We wonder how long it would take for this issue to be resolved, or if it continued to be an issue. As the teacher told during his post-lesson interview, a big part of his curriculum at the beginning of the year with a new class of students was to build a learning community that had its own ways of regulating how students discuss learning issues in the class. Our observations of his other classes with students he worked with for a longer time suggested that he successfully solved similar breakdowns with his students in the past. However, even at the end of the lesson, new practices of communal self regulation such as the students' raising hands, becoming quieter, listening, lowering hands when a classmate took the floor, recognizing when it was time for small group discussion and when it was not, and so on became evident and took shape.

In Mr. Moyo's classrooms, we observed many breakdowns that were brought to a public forum. Many of them were recognized and publicized by the teacher but some were recognized and publicized by students. For example, in a lesson on measurement, a student was expressing a problem he had with something that the teacher was saying. The student brought to the teacher's attention that they were not sure what units were. The teacher then asked the students if they understood what he was saying. The students did not give Mr. Moyo a positive answer, rather they shook their heads and mumbled no. The teacher was apparently taken by surprise. Mr. Moyo was going on with his lesson and was not prepared for the students to have trouble with units. He had the assumption that his students knew what units were; they, on the other hand, were very unclear. Mr. Moyo then decided to change to something else so that they were "all in line," and asked the students if that were ok. The students showed that it was ok, and they all started discussing a different topic that was more familiar and a building block for understanding the unit of measurement. In this interaction, the students and the teacher worked through a problem together and made sure that everyone felt good about it. Mr. Moyo had to stop in the middle of what he was doing and what he had planned, and think of something else to do with them on the spot. There was a breakdown in the lesson for about a minute when this was happening. Mr. Moyo then was able to change what he was doing and introduce something else that the students could relate to, in order to help them understand. The way he solved the issue and handled the student's confusion was successful; when he switched to something else, the students started participating more freely and answering his questions. By the end of their discussion, they were clearer on what units were. In a follow-up interview to us, Mr. Moyo was very pleased with this episode as the students become more responsible for their own learning and helped him better guide them. Student-initiated breakdowns are welcome in Mr. Moyo's classroom and recognized as important contributors for a development of a collaborative creole culture in the classroom.

Doodling in the Classroom

This case was somewhat similar to the situation in which South African Afrikaans teacher faced when dealing with Sotho student who did not look at her while she was talking to him. In this case, the teacher was also uncomfortable with the student's behavior. The setting was a small seminar of 21 undergraduate students of the Elementary Teacher Education program on Cultural Diversity issues in teaching that involved a teaching practicum in afterschool program in a local Latin-American Community Center (see for detailed description of the similar class and program Matusov, St. Julien, & Hayes, 2005). The instructor, the first author of the paper (Eugene), noticed that one of the students named Anna was systematically drawing pictures during class discussions (one of the main instructional formats of this seminar). Although Anna seemed to follow the discussions and actively participate in them, the instructor felt distracted by her "doodling" (as she later called it). Anna clearly monitored the instructor's movements in the classroom and tried to move her drawing away when Eugene

came to her proximity. Other students also noticed the development and apparently were puzzled how to read it. Eugene felt as if the student did not like the classroom discussions and activities, was bored and tried to smuggle extracurricular activities in the classroom to entertain herself, a behavior not different from the resistant behavior of Black Caribbean girls in British classrooms described in Fuller (1984). For a while, Eugene did not make any attempt to stop Anna's drawing, waiting for the development of a stable and clear pattern of her ambivalent behavior: she seemed to acknowledge the illegitimacy of her drawing in the class but still continued drawing on a systematic basis (see also Corsaro and Johannesen, Chapter 21, this volume, for discussion of resistant behavior by students). Her cover up of the activity was also inconsistent: she moved the drawing away when Eugene was coming closer to her but she did not try to hide it when she knew that Eugene noticed her drawing from distance (she chose to sit at the most distant desk cluster from the instructor). Eugene did not know what to do: to change his guidance to be more responsive and sensitive to Anna's needs or to request Anna to stop her distracting drawing in the classroom. After about a month into the semester, the instructor decided to discuss the problem of his own discomfort with the entire class, posing it as a teaching dilemma. He asked the students what they would do if they noticed a student drawing pictures during lessons on a systematic basis in their future classroom when they become teachers.

As soon as everybody heard the question, they looked at Anna whose face became red. The instructor acknowledged that Anna was one of such students but the issue was not about Anna (which was only partially true) but about what the teacher should do. He offered the students what the teacher might think about the doodling student. Together they developed a list of the teacher's possible concerns including ones that the instructor (Eugene) had. Eugene shared his concerns about Anna's drawing distracting him from his instruction. Then the instructor said that since the class had such a student, Anna, in the classroom, it was a good idea to ask her if it was true that she was bored, disinterested, inattentive, and tried to smuggle extracurricular activities to entertain herself. Anna explained that she was drawing pictures in the class because it helped her concentrate and prevent her from daydreaming. She said that she was a person who needed to multitask and keep her hands busy to stay focused. The instructor asked her why she was hiding her drawing when he was coming closer to her and she explained that she was not sure that her behavior bothered him or not and whether the instructor saw it as legitimate. She said that she got mixed nonverbal messages from him in past and was a bit nervous about how Eugene considered her behavior.

The classroom discussion went on about what the instructor should do in case of having in class a student like Anna and how to separate this case from another case when a student was not attentive and indeed smuggled an entertaining activity to class. Initially the class decided that since Anna's doodling was a distraction for Eugene, their instructor, and, hence, she should stop doodling. But then Eugene pointed out that her drawing indeed had been a distraction for him because he had been afraid that she doodled because of her disinterest in the subject and poor quality of his guidance. Since it was apparently not the case, he felt that Anna's doodling would be much less of a distraction for him, if at all, from now on. Besides, he continued, doodling helped Anna to concentrate and better participate in the lesson. The class reconsidered their decision and suggested that it might be okay for Anna to openly draw during the class discussions or the instructor's presentation. After the class, Anna posted on the class web the following message,

> I just wanted to thank Eugene for letting me know today that it's ok for me to doodle and draw in class. Since I was little, I have always needed to be doing something while I am sitting – whether it is in class or just watching TV. Some of my teachers in the past have thought it was rude, but it is not because I am bored

or not listening. In fact, like Eugene mentioned, it helps me concentrate and focus better. It is when I am not drawing that I stare out the window, ignore the teacher, daydream, or fall asleep. I think some teachers need to understand that there are many kids who need to multitask in order to stay focused. Thanks for understanding Eugene (Class webtalk, 10/10/2002).

It was interesting that it was not the case at all that the instructor allowed Anna to doodle in his classroom but rather she (and other students) interpreted their communal consensus that emerged in the class as being sanctioned by Eugene. Another student reinterpreted the event as if the instructor knew from the beginning the solution of the problem.

> I thought it was great that Eugene allowed for Anna to doodle in class today. Most teachers never really think out its effects, and automatically think it is a bad thing. For Anna though, this really is the opposite and doodling has a positive effect on her learning. It allows her to stay focused without shutting out everything else that is going on around her. I really think it is a good thing that Eugene looked at Anna's doodling and saw it as good influence on her learning (Class webtalk, 10/10/2002).

The fourth author of the paper, who was also a student for this class, remembered that she also thought that, from the beginning, Eugene knew that Anna's doodling was good for the students and developed a lesson around that rather than was trying to solve the problem in their classroom. This phenomenon has been described by Latour (Latour, 1987; Latour & Woolgar, 1979) who noticed how quickly a "science-in-action" event was remembered by participating scientists as a "ready-made-science" event. An emergent collaborative, co-constructive dramatic event of legitimizing doodling in class was remembered as unilateral, preexisting, transmission of knowledge. This phenomenon represents a certain challenge for teacher education because it is apparent that the students did not recognize their instructor's learning, classroom drama, problem sharing, and collaborative management of uncertainty.

As an important consequence of this dramatic event, however, a third student got an idea of how to use doodling for management of her own lack of attention in classes.

> You know what I think I am going to have to try the doodling thing. Sometimes I find it hard to pay attention in my classes, because it is so easy to get distracted. Maybe I should try the doodling and see if I am able to focus a little better. I was always afraid that someone would think that I wasn't paying attention if I doodled, but in class today, I realized that it is ok to doodle. I'll have to try it and see if it helps me any. (Class webtalk, 10/15/2002)

After the discussion a few students started bringing color markers for doodling. These students reflected on their use of doodling: whether and when it was distracting for them and when it was helpful. The doodling topic generated many fruitful discussions on cultural diversity in the classroom and on promoting sensitive guidance. The instructor found that doodling was not distractive at all when it had clear meaning for him. It was interesting that when the students had to interview children at the Latin-American Community Center (LACC) as a part of their course assignment, they found that offering the LACC children the opportunity to draw during the interviews helped the children to keep focused on the interview and not become tired too soon. Not only new classroom practices emerged from this event of instructor's sharing his pedagogical problem with his students, but also new classroom solidarity emerged. The new solidarity was evident in the fact that many students who did not have classes immediately after the class stayed together and continued arguing issues that we discussed in our class. As students wrote after the class.

> My favorite part about the class is that it is so open to everything – opinions, laughter, doodling, games, group work, parties, and so on we're not really a class

anymore – we're more like a group of friends. I see you girls at parties and walking to and from classes. I see mark all over campus and occasionally see Eugene on his way to Brew HaHa [campus café, Eugene's favorite place]. I think the level of comfort we have in the class really facilitates learning because we are not afraid to voice our opinions or ask questions, whether it be in class or on webtalk. (Class web, 12/15/2002)

Instead of a Conclusion

Gutierrez, Rymes, and Larson (1995) argue that the only true interaction between the teacher and the students can be achieved through creation of "the third space" of classroom dialogue. They defined the first space as the monologic official discourse of the teacher, in which the students have a passive, peripheral, (or nonexistent) role. The second space is the students' space excluding or even counteracting the teacher. Both two spaces are unilateral. Although, Gutierrez, Rymes, and Larson talk about the third space as being "in the middle ground" (p. 447), in our view, it is actually outside of the teacher-run versus student-run unilateral continuum (see Matusov & Rogoff, 2002; Rogoff, Matusov, & White, 1996 for more discussion of this point). A compromise or combination of the first and the second spaces does not create the third space. The third space has new relational and activity qualities involving mutuality, collaboration, and dialogue between the teacher and the students. Similarly, Bhabha (1994) describes third space as existing along borders and consisting of negotiation of "incommensurable differences." The third space generates a new approach to the relationship between the teacher and the students.

Similarly, the culture-in-action approach to interactional breakdowns is also based on the creation of mutuality, collaboration, and dialogue. When we asked Mr. Moyo, the South African science teacher, what he would do in the shoes of an Afrikaans teacher who apparently felt uncomfortable when some Black students did not establish their eye contact with her while she was talking with them, Mr. Moyo told us that he would share his problem of discomfort with the students so that they together could discuss it and figure out what to do. Thus, the culture-in-action approach presupposes a symbolic "we" (i.e., "*we* will discuss and figure out *together*") even before an actual "we" has been built in the classroom. He rejected the unilateral solution guided by the ready-made-cultural perspective that traps the teacher in the unilateral continuum of "my culture" versus "their culture." The teacher's proleptic, taken-for-granted, "we" is aimed at designing a new creole community in the classroom. The teacher cannot, may not, and does not need to envision a solution for the perceived interactional breakdown on his own, in advance, without classroom dialogue with his students. Any attempt by the teacher to solve the problem of the breakdown leads to unilateralism and away from building a creole community in the classroom.

We hypothesize, although without having any direct data yet, that a creole classroom community cannot be self-contained and limited to the classroom walls. A new emerging classroom culture can affect both the teacher's institutional mainstream culture and the students' home cultures. Participation in a creole culture probably forces its members to negotiate new and old ways of doing things in other communities in which they participate. For example, the students of Mr. Moyo may bring their newly emerging skills and practices of listening to each other in other classrooms with other teachers in the school that may (or may not) disrupt the teachers' ways of doing things and lead to new interactional and relational breakdowns. These possible breakdowns, in their own turn, may lead to fruitful (or confrontational) teachers' discussions about the nature of the breakdowns and how to solve them at the teacher lounge with Mr. Moyo (or without him), which again may (or may not) affect school policy and culture at large. Similar ripple effects can occur at the students' homes and even at Mr. Moyo's home. This plausible hypothesis of an emerging

creole classroom culture having a ripple-effect awaits a new investigation.

Another hypothesis is about students' meta-learning in the third space – the students' learning how to promote the third space in future with different communities by themselves. We call this learning "meta-learning" because it is "above" ("meta" in Greek) students' regular learning, for it is important relational learning of how to participate in a genuine classroom dialogue and in a newly developed creole classroom culture. Does students' socialization in the third space of classroom public dialogue about a shared problem, emerging from interactional breakdowns promoted by the teacher, guide the students how to promote the third space with other people in their future relationships? Can a creole community within the third space, within a space of actively making culture-in-action, reproduce itself through its members (i.e., students)? So far, we have negative evidence for that. Recall please that Eugene's undergraduate students apparently did not recognize their collaborative solution of the "doodling" breakdown and believed that Eugene had had the "good" solution from the beginning. They did not seem to recognize the process of culture-in-action but saw ready-made-culture (like many scientists in Latour's and Woolgar's study of a science bio lab could see only ready-made-science in their past science-in-action practice Latour, 1987; Latour & Woolgar, 1979). It can be that, like Latour's scientists, Eugene's preservice teachers have a gap between their espoused and in-action theories (Argyris & Schön, 1978). Maybe as teachers, through socialization in the third space organized by Eugene in their class, his students have learned how to promote genuine dialogue about interactional breakdowns in their future classrooms (even though, they may describe the process differently, in ready-made terms, afterwards). Alternatively, socialization in the third space can lead to meta-learning about how to promote it overtime – Eugene's students might not simply have enough time to be socialized in their new creole classroom culture in order to meta-learn how to promote creole cultures by themselves. Finally, it can be that socialization itself is not enough for meta-learning the third space and students have to learn how to promote the third space and culture-in-action in their own future classrooms through specially designed instruction and curricula. Future research can resolve this issue.

Our study contributes in elaboration on how the third space can be created by the teacher in the classroom through transformation of interactional breakdown into a shared *ontological* problem for the entire classroom. Since breakdowns disrupt the flow of interaction and relations between the teacher and the students (or among students sometimes as well), the problems they potentially can generate are not just intellectual but ontological – involving the participants' "whole-person" commitment, action, and ethical deeds here and now. The participants cannot simply "walk out" from their breakdown (their "inaction" is also a certain action as it is evident from Eugene's initial attempts to "overlook" Anna's doodling and from Anna's and the classmates' making sense of the act of the teacher's "overlooking") as it is possible in purely intellectual problems. We may hypothesize here that the theme of the third space (i.e., genuine classroom dialogue) is always involved shared ontological problems. Some of these shared ontological problems can come from interactional breakdowns and some (like, for example, in study by Gutierrez, Rymes, & Larson, 1995) can come from other sources (e.g., deep relevancy and high urgency of the academic topic for the students). It is possible to argue that dialogic pedagogy (Matusov, 2004) of the third space is based on a teacher-designed process of "sharing," "problematizing," and "ontologizing" the socially desired academic curricula (cf. Lave, 1992).

Notes

1   Elsewhere we discussed Latour's and our own use of the term "dualism" (Matusov, Pleasants, & Smith, 2003). In contrast to Descartes' essentialist dualism, our dualism is pragmatic (i.e., goal-oriented) and relative (i.e., based on an observer). Descartes' dualism was essentialist because it was unconditional: humans are half-machines, half-soul. Similarly, we argue that Vygotsky's dualism was essentialist because it was unconditional: human development is intertwine of the natural and the cultural or intertwine of psychological and social (Matusov, 1998). In contrast, our dualism is conditional, "Our dualistic approach to the notion of culture, like Latour's approach to science and quantum physics' approach to electrons, is relativistic because it heavily depends on the observer's research focus. However, these relativistic approaches are also *pragmatically relativistic* because they focus on most useful descriptive models – on the purpose of the observer – and abandon the question of 'what is really true' understood outside of pragmatics of human activity. Electron is both a particle and a wave. Culture is both ready-made and in-action" (Matusov, Pleasants, & Smith, 2003).

2   It is possible to claim that ancient Greeks in their early historical phase did not know even that they were *Greeks* in our modern sense as a name of ethnos. The etymology of the Greek work "barbarians" suggests that it comes from phonetic mimicking of incomprehensible speech of foreigners, "bar-bar-bar-bar" (similarly the Slavic work for German "немец" coming from "немой" literally means "mute"). This implies that ancient Greeks saw only themselves as fully human, which what the word *Greek* was probably meant for them.

3   As Said (1979: 54) pointed out correctly, this discursive recognition of the breakdowns can be unilateral, "A group of people living on a few acres of land will [arbitrary] set up boundaries between their land and its immediate surroundings and the territory beyond, which they call 'the land of the barbarians'. . . . I use the word 'arbitrary' here because imaginative geography of the 'our land-barbarian land' variety does not require that the barbarians acknowledge the distinction." However, despite the discursive unilateralism – its objectivization and finalization of "the barbarian others", – it also addresses the others, provokes their response, and involves them in the discourse and, thus, although possibly unwillingly, becomes dialogic.

References

Anderson, B. (1991). *Imagined communities: Reflections on the origin and spread of nationalism* (Rev. and extended Ed.). New York: Verso.

Argyris, C., & Schön, D. A. (1978). *Organizational learning: A theory of action perspective.* Reading, MA: Addison-Wesley Pub. Co.

Bakhtin, M. M. (1986). *Speech genres and other late essays.* Austin: University of Texas Press.

Bakhtin, M. M., & Emerson, C. (1999). *Problems of Dostoevsky's poetics* (Vol. 8). Minneapolis: University of Minnesota Press.

Bateson, G. (1987). *Steps to an ecology of mind: Collected essays in anthropology, psychiatry, evolution, and epistemology.* Northvale, NJ: Aronson.

Bean, M. S. (1997). Talking with Benny: Suppressing or supporting learner themes and learner worlds?*Anthropology & Education Quarterly, 28*(1), 50–69.

Bereiter, C., & Engelmann, S. (1966). *Teaching disadvantaged children in the preschool.* Englewood Cliffs, NJ: Prentice-Hall.

Bhabha, H. K. (1994). *The location of culture.* London; New York: Routledge.

Boykin, A. W. (1986). The triple quandary and the schooling of African-American children. In U. Neisser (Ed.), *The school achievement of minority children: New perspectives* (pp. 57–92). Hillsdale, NJ: Lawrence Erlbaum Associates.

Bradley, L. A., & Bradley, G. W. (1977). The academic achievement of Black students in desegregated schools: A critical review. *Review of Educational Research, 47*(3), 399–449.

Bruner, J. (1998). *The cultural psychology of self construction.* Paper presented at the The Fourth Congress of the International Society for Cultural Research and Activity Theory, Aarhus, Denmark.

Clifford, J. (2000). Taking identity politics seriously: "The contradictory, stony ground . . . " In P. Gilroy, L. Grossberg & A. McRobbie (Eds.), *Without guarantees: Essays in honour of Stuart Hall* (pp. 94–122). London: Verso.

Cole, M. (1996). *Cultural psychology: A once and future discipline.* Cambridge, MA: Harvard University Press.

Cole, M., & Bruner, J. (1971). Cultural differences and inferences about cultural processes. *American Psychologist, 26*(10), 867–876.

D'Souza, D. (1995). *The end of racism: Principles for a multiracial society* ([Pbk. Ed.). New York: Free Press.

De Lone, R. H. (1979). *Small futures: Children, inequality, and the limits of liberal reform* (1st Ed.). New York: Harcourt Brace Jovanovich.

Deitcher, D. (2001). *Dear friends: American photographs of men together, 1840–1918.* New York: Harry N. Abrams.

Delpit, L. D. (1995). *Other people's children: Cultural conflict in the classroom.* New York: New Press, distributed by W.W. Norton.

Dewey, J. (1925). *Experience and nature.* Chicago: Open Court Publishing Co.

Durkheim, E. (1966). *The division of labor in society.* New York: Free Press.

Fullan, M. (1993). *Change forces: Probing the depth of educational reform.* London, New York: Falmer Press.

Fuller, M. (1984). Black girls in a comprehensive school. In M. Hammersley & P. Woods (Eds.), *Life in school: The sociology of pupil culture.* Milton Keynes, UK: Open University Press.

Gould, S. J. (1996). *The mismeasure of man* (Rev. and expanded. Ed.). New York: Norton.

Gutierrez, K., Rymes, B., & Larson, J. (1995). Script, counterscript, and underlife in the classroom: James Brown vs. Board of Education. *Harvard Education Review, 65*(3), 445–472.

Heath, S. B. (1983). *Ways with words: Language, life, and work in communities and classrooms.* Cambridge, UK: Cambridge University Press.

Helfer, R. E. (1987). The developmental basis of child abuse and neglect: An epidemiological approach. In R. E. Helfer & R. S. Kempe (Eds.), *The battered child* (pp. 60–80). Chicago: University of Chicago Press.

Hochschild, A. (1998). *King Leopold's ghost: A story of greed, terror, and heroism in colonial Africa.* Boston, MA: Houghton Mifflin.

Hochschild, A. (2005). *Bury the chains: Prophets, slaves, and rebels in the first human rights crusade.* Boston: Houghton Mifflin.

Hofstadter, R. (1955). *Social Darwinism in American thought* (Rev. Ed.). Boston: Beacon Press.

Kaplan, R. B. (1966). Cultural thought patterns in inter-cultural education. *Language Learning, 16*(1–2), 1–21.

Labaree, D. F. (1997). *How to succeed in school without really learning: The credentials race in American education.* New Haven, CT: Yale University Press.

Labov, W. (1972). *Language in the inner city: Studies in the Black English vernacular.* Philadelphia: University of Pennsylvania Press.

Ladson-Billings, G. (1994). *The dreamkeepers: Successful teachers of African American children*. San Francisco: Jossey-Bass.

Latour, B. (1987). *Science in action: How to follow scientists and engineers through society*. Cambridge, MA: Harvard University Press.

Latour, B. (1996). On interobjectivity. *Mind, Culture and Activity, 3* (4), 228–245.

Latour, B., & Woolgar, S. (1979). *Laboratory life: The social construction of scientific facts*. Beverly Hills, CA: Sage Publications.

Lave, J. (1992). Word problems: A microcosm of theories of learning. In P. Light & G. Butterworth. (Eds.), *Context and cognition: Ways of learning and knowing*. (pp. 74–92). Hillsdale, NJ: Lawrence Erlbaum Associates.

Lee, C. D. (2003). Toward a framework for culturally responsive design in multimedia computer environments: Cultural modeling as a case. *Mind, Culture and Activity, 10* (1), 42–61.

Linger, D. T. (1994). Has culture theory last its minds? *Ethos, 22* (3), 284–315.

Luria, A. R. (1976). *Cognitive development, its cultural and social foundations*. Cambridge, MA: Harvard University Press.

Matusov, E. (1996). Intersubjectivity without agreement. *Mind, Culture, and Activity, 3* (1), 25–45.

Matusov, E. (1998). When solo activity is not privileged: Participation and internalization models of development. *Human Development, 41* (5–6), 326–349.

Matusov, E. (1999). How does a community of learners maintain itself? Ecology of an innovative school. *Anthropology & Education Quarterly, 30* (2), 161–186.

Matusov, E. (2004). Bakhtin's debit in educational research: Dialogic pedagogy. *Journal of Russian & East European Psychology, 42* (6), 3–11.

Matusov, E., & Hayes, R. (2002). Building a community of educators versus effecting conceptual change in individual students: Multicultural education for preservice teachers. In G. Wells & G. Claxton. (Eds.), *Learning for life in the 21st century: Sociocultural perspectives on the future of education* (pp. 239–251). Cambridge, UK: Cambridge University Press.

Matusov, E., Pleasants, H., & Smith, M. P. (2003). Dialogic framework for cultural psychology: Culture-in-action and culturally sensitive guidance. *Review Interdisciplinary Journal on Human Development, Culture and Education, 4* (1), available online: http://cepaosreview.tripod.com/Matusov.html.

Matusov, E., & Rogoff, B. (2002). Newcomers and oldtimers: Educational philosophy-in-actions of parent volunteers in a community of learners school. *Anthropology & Education Quarterly, 33* (4), 1–26.

Matusov, E., St. Julien, J., & Hayes, R. (2005). Building a creole educational community as the goal of multicultural education for preservice teachers. In L. V. Barnes. (Ed.), *Contemporary Teaching and Teacher Issues* (pp. 1–38). Hauppauge, NY: Nova Publishers.

Matusov, E., & White, C. (1996). Defining the concept of open collaboration from a sociocultural framework. *Cognitive Studies: The Bulletin of the Japanese Cognitive Science Society, 3* (4), 11–13.

Mayerfeld Bell, M. (1998). Culture as dialogue. In M. Mayerfeld Bell & M. Gardiner (Eds.), *Bakhtin and the human sciences: No last words* (pp. 49–62). London: Sage.

Mayo, C. (2000). The use of Foucault. *Educational Theory, 50* (1), 103–116.

Mead, G. H. (1956). *On social psychology*. Chicago: University of Chicago Press.

Michaels, S., & Cazden, C. B. (1986). Teacher/child collaboration as oral preparation for literacy. In B. B. Schieffelin & P. Gilmore. (Eds.), *The acquisition of literacy: Ethnographic perspectives* (pp. 132–154). Norwood, NJ: Ablex.

Moll, L. C. (2000). Inspired by Vygotsky: Ethnographic experiments in education. In C. D. Lee & P. Smagorinsky. (Eds.), *Vygotskian perspectives on literacy research: Constructing meaning through collaborative inquiry* (pp. 256–268). Cambridge, UK: Cambridge University Press.

Moll, L. C., Amanti, C., Neff, D., & González, N. (1992). Funds of knowledge for teaching: Using a qualitative approach to connect homes and classrooms. *Theory into Practice, 31* (2), 132–141.

Mudgett-DeCaro, P. (1996). On being both Hearing and Deaf: My bicultural-bilingual experience. In I. Parasnis. (Ed.), *Cultural and language diversity and the deaf experience* (pp. 272–288). New York: Cambridge University Press.

Nieto, S. (1996). *Affirming diversity: The sociopolitical context of multicultural education* (2nd. Ed.). White Plains, NY: Longman Publishers.

Ogbu, J. U. (1978). *Minority education and caste: The American system in cross-cultural perspective*. New York: Academic Press.

Ogbu, J. U. (2003). *Black American students in an affluent suburb: A study of academic disengagement* Mahwah, NJ: Lawrence Erlbaum Associates.

Philips, S. U. (1993). *The invisible culture: Communication in classroom and community on the Warm Springs Indian Reservation.* Prospect Heights, IL: Waveland Press.

Rogoff, B. (2003). *The cultural nature of human development.* New York: Oxford University Press.

Rogoff, B., Matusov, E., & White, C. (1996). Models of teaching and learning: Participation in a community of learners. In D. R. Olson & N. Torrance. (Eds.), *The handbook of education and human development: New models of learning, teaching and schooling.* (pp. 388–414). Malden, MA: Blackwell Publishers Inc.

Rogoff, B., Mistry, J., Göncü, A., & Mosier, C. (1993). Guided participation in cultural activity by toddlers and caregivers. *Monographs of the Society for Research in Child Development,* 58(8), v-179.

Rueda, R., & Dembo, M. H. (1995). Motivational processes in learning: A comparative analysis of cognitive and sociocultural frameworks. In M. L. Maehr & P. R. Pintrich. (Eds.), *Culture, motivation and achievement* (Vol. 9, pp. 255–289). Greenwich, CT: JAI Press.

Rueda, R., & Moll, L. C. (1994). A sociocultural perspective on motivation. In H. F. O'Neil Jr. & M. Drillings. (Eds.), *Motivation: Theory and research.* (pp. 117–137). Hillsdale, NJ: Lawrence Erlbaum Associates.

Ryan, W. (1971). *Blaming the victim.* New York: Vintage Books.

Said, E. W. (1979). *Orientalism* (1st Vintage Books. Ed.). New York: Vintage Books.

Sherif, M. (1988). *The Robbers Cave experiment: Intergroup conflict and cooperation.* Middletown, CT: Wesleyan University Press.

Star, S. L., & Griesemer, J. R. (1989). Institutional ecology, "translations" and boundary objects: Amateurs and professionals in Berkeley's museum of vertebrate zoology, 1907–39. *Social Studies of Science,* 19(3), 387–420.

Tharp, R. G. (1982). The effective instruction of comprehension: Results and description of the Kamehameha Early Education Program. *Reading Research Quarterly,* 17(4), 503–527.

Varenne, H., & McDermott, R. P. (1998). *Successful failure: The school America builds.* Boulder, CO: Westview Press.

Vogt, L. A., Jordan, C., & Tharp, R. G. (1987). Explaining school failure, producing school success: Two cases. *Anthropology & Education Quarterly,* 18(4), 276–286.

Vygotsky, L. S., Luria, A. R., Golod, V. I., & Knox, J. E. (1993). *Studies on the history of behavior: Ape, primitive, and child.* Hillsdale, NJ: Lawrence Erlbaum Associates.

Wenger, E. (1998). *Communities of practice: Learning, meaning, and identity.* Cambridge, UK: Cambridge University Press.

CHAPTER 23

Cultural-Historical Approaches to Designing for Development

Michael Cole and Yrjö Engeström

The goal of this chapter is to summarize theory and research descended from Vygotsky and his followers that takes seriously the idea that practice is essential for testing and improving theory. We refer to this approach as "cultural-historical activity theory" (CH/AT) (Cole, 1996; Engeström, 1999; Engeström, Miettinen, & Punamaki, 1999; Roth, Hwang, Goulart, & Lee 2005).

This approach to theory and practice, which is frequently traced back to Marx, was clearly articulated by Vygotsky, for whom the use of Marxism in psychology was a life-long concern:

> *Practice pervades the deepest foundations of the scientific operation and reforms it from beginning to end. Practice sets the tasks and serves as the supreme judge of theory, as its truth criterion... The most complex contradictions of psychological methodology are transferred to the ground of practice and only there can they be solved. There the debate stops being fruitless, it comes to an end. (Vygotsky, 1927/1997: 305–306)*

In the century since Vygotsky wrote these ideas, mainstream psychology, which has generally accorded culture only a peripheral role in human nature, has firmly institutionalized precisely the division between theory and practice ("basic *versus* applied research") against which Vygotsky was arguing. Nevertheless, we believe that Marx and Vygotsky were correct – the implementation of theory in practice is not a marginal scientific goal in the study of human development – it is essential to understanding the complex interplay of different life processes, *"in life,"* not just in theory. As Engeström (1993: 98) put it, "The epistemology of activity theory transcends the dichotomy between theory and practice."

Cultural-Historical Activity Theory (CH/AT)

Cultural-historical activity theory (CH/AT) brings together ideas associated with the names of L. S. Vygotsky, A. R. Luria, and

A. N. Leontiev. It has been common in recent years to emphasize differences between Vygotsky and Luria, on the one hand, and Leontiev on the other (van der Veer & Valsiner, 1991). According to such interpretations, Vygotsky and Luria are best associated with the principle that the distinguishing characteristic of specifically human psychological functions is that they are culturally mediated: "The central fact of human existence is mediation" (Vygotsky, 1997: 138). By contrast, so the story goes, Leontiev believed that his colleagues overemphasized the cultural mediation of thought and underemphasized the embeddedness of thought in human activity. It might be argued that a significant disagreement exists to this day among those who consider Vygotsky and his colleagues as a starting point for constructing a theory of human development and those who start with Leontiev (1978). According to this line of interpretation, those who follow Vygotsky have focused attention on processes of mediation, adopting "mediated action" as a basic unit of analysis (Wertsch, del Rio, & Alvarez, 1995; Zinchenko, 1985). By contrast, followers of Leontiev are said to choose "activity" as a basic unit of analysis (Engeström, 1987; Kaptelinin, 1996).[1]

The basic impulse underlying a CH/AT approach is to reject this either/or dichotomy. Instead, adherents of a CH/AT perspective argue that whatever their disagreements, Leontiev (1981) readily acknowledges the constitutive role of cultural mediation in his account of activity while Vygotsky insisted on the importance of activity as the context of mediated action (1997). In similar fashion, one sees contemporary scholars who are seen as somehow in opposition with each other on this fundamental point adopting an "and/both" not an "either/or" approach. So, for example, James Wertsch argues for "mediated action in context" as a basic unit of analysis while Yrjö Engeström argues that "the activity is the context" and (as we shall see) pays great attention to principles of mediated action in both his theory and in his empirical research. While the presumably opposing views weight different aspects of the dynamic system of development differently, or view them from a slightly different perspective in their overall approaches, they treat activity and mediation as two aspects of a single, whole in human life world.

Some Basic Principles Used in CH/AT-Inspired Intervention Research

Keeping in mind that there are a variety of views on important issues among those identified as CH/AT theorists, the following are some theoretical principles generated from this position that have been tested in the intervention studies we review in this chapter.

1. *Mediation through artifacts.* The initial premise of the Russian cultural-historical school was that human psychological processes entail a form of behavior in which material objects are modified by human beings as a means of regulating their interactions with the world and each other. As A. R. Luria put it, artifacts incorporated into human action not only "radically change his conditions of existence, they even react on him in that they effect a change in him and his psychic condition" (Luria, 1928: 493).

As a result of acquiring this "cultural habit of behavior," human beings begin to regulate themselves "from the outside." This characteristic of human behavior gives rise to the *method of double stimulation.* An early application of this method was to provide an adult suffering from Parkinsonism with bits of paper, by means of which he was able to walk across a floor (Luria, 1932). It has subsequently been widely used in designing methods for re-mediating the behavior of adults with brain damage, or mentally retarded children (Amano, 1999; Luria, 1979). As we see below, it has become a central principle guiding research on the development of work practices among adults (Engeström, 2005). We will discuss double stimulation in more detail later in this chapter.

2. *Activity as the essential unit of analysis.* The complementary basic premise of the cultural-historical approach, adopted from Hegel by way of Marx, is that the analysis of human psychological functions must be situated in historically accumulated forms of human activity. Unfortunately, the meaning of the term, activity, no less than the term culture, is a bone of contention among scholars from different disciplines and national traditions.[2] According to A. N. Leontiev,

> *Human psychology is concerned with the activity of concrete individuals, which takes place either in a collective – that is, jointly with other people – or in a situation in which the subject deals directly with the surrounding world of objects – for example, the potter's wheel or the writer's desk. [. . .] With all its varied forms, the human individual's activity is a system in the system of social relations. It does not exist without these relations. The specific form in which it exists is determined by the forms and means of material and mental social interaction* (Verkher) *that are created by the development of production and that cannot be realized in any way other than the activity of concrete people.* (1981, 47)

Unfortunately, the USSR was not a place where social scientists were easily permitted to conduct research on the wide range of activities that the theory specified as its basic units of analysis, let alone the larger social system. Although restricted, the early Russian CH/AT theorists demonstrated that at least in some institutional settings it was possible to make activity a genuine object of study while at the same time paying close attention to the processes of mediation with which activity is mutually constituted. Contemporary research has enormously broadened the range of activities and institutions to which scholars have been able to turn their attention (Hedegaard, Chaiklin, & Jensen, 1999; Engeström, Lompscher, & Rückriem, 2005).

3. *The cultural organization of human life.* Implied, but not made prominent in our discussion of mediation and activity is that both concepts imply the centrality of culture to human life. Culture is present in the form of the tools, signs, rituals, and so on that mediate human activity. It is simultaneously present in all the symbolic forms that have accumulated over the social group's history, whether that history is of long or short duration. Lotman (1989) referred to this totality of meaning making materials, the "semiosphere," which he defined as "the semiotic space necessary for the existence and functioning of languages."

In some forms of intervention, culture is treated as a locally emerging activity system involving a briefer stretch of history such as the participants at English football matches or in an afterschool club (Nocon, 2004). In this latter case, the term "idioculture" is especially helpful. Adopting Gary Alan Fine's useful notion:

> *An idioculture is a system of knowledge, beliefs, behaviors, and customs shared by members of an interacting group to which members can refer and that serve as the basis of further interaction. Members recognize that they share experiences, and these experiences can be referred to with the expectation they will be understood by other members, thus being used to construct a reality for the participants.* (Fine, 1987, 125)

4. *Adoption of a genetic perspective.* As Wertsch (1985) points out, Vygotsky used the notion of "genetic" in the sense of seeking the origins of current phenomena by studying the history of the phenomena in question.[3] This general principle has several implications for CH/AT-inspired intervention research, depending upon the nature of the intervention involved.

A) Interventions Must Last for an Appropriate Amount of Time. An important implication of a commitment to the use of genetic methods with respect to formative interventions is that they are unlikely to be brief forays into the field followed by an intense period of data analysis and writing, as is often the case with laboratory experiments. Rather, the duration of the experiment must be appropriate to the time course of the "formative" (developmental) processes under examination. In the examples to be reviewed here, the formative experiments/interventions lasted for a period varying between several months and several years.

B) *Taking account of chronological age*. In so far as one is interested in psychological analysis, it seems obvious that intervention strategies need to take into account the chronological age of the participants whose activity is under study. It makes a difference if one is seeking to test the efficacy of a new form of curriculum with preschoolers, high school students, or working adults. In addition to the obvious fact that as children grow from birth to maturity, and the capacities of adults change as they grow older, early CH/AT theorists suggested that it is helpful to conceive of conventional age periodization in terms of the idea of its leading activity.

According to Elkonin (1971), traditional development stages are best conceived of in terms of the kinds of activity that dominate the lives of people at a given age. Associated with each leading activity is a particularly potent source of motivation. As Leontiev summarized the idea,

> Some types of activity are the leading ones at a given stage and are of greatest significance for the individuals' further development and others a subsidiary one. We can say, accordingly, that each stage of psychic development is characterized by a definite relation of the child to reality that is the leading one at that date and by a definite type of leading activity. (Leontiev, 1981, 395)

Although the terminology differs somewhat according to the particular writer, a rough correlation between typical stages of development with canonical stage theories would read roughly like the following:[4]

- The initial leading activity is coordination with the group into which one is born.

- The "preschool era" in conventional textbooks is the era when play is the leading activity.
- During what is conventionally referred to as middle childhood, formal learning becomes the leading activity.
- Late childhood and Adolescence are delicately referred to as the age when peer relations become the leading activity.
- Maturity, roughly past the age of 18–19, has work as its leading activity.

Vygotsky, Luria, and Leontiev, were of course, conducting research on the leading activities that were being institutionalized in the USSR at the time. This work was hampered both by the fact that serious research on the world of work was ideologically restricted and by the age-graded segmentation of people's lives in the country where they lived. On a world scale, schooling is not universal nor is being part of an industrialized political economy. It is no surprise, then that evidence from various parts of the world demonstrates important cultural variations in the timing and content of leading activities in different societies and markedly different forms of organizing labor, factors that are of obvious importance in the design of formative interventions (Gaskins, 1999; Rogoff, 2003).

What is constant despite such variation is that the organization of people's activities is arranged in such a way that the cultural knowledge that is made manifest in everyday activities of young (or inexperienced) people is simultaneously the form of the leading activity characteristic of the social group. A leading activity represents a sociocultural group's notion of the behaviors and sequences of behaviors that *should* be manifested by anyone who is reaching the age or level of experience where "that can be expected."

5. *Social origins of higher psychological functions*. Vygotsky argued that all means of cultural behavior (behavior mediated by cultural artifacts) are social in their essence. They are social too, in the dynamics of their

origin and change, as expressed in what Vygotsky called "the general law of cultural development":

> *Any function in children's cultural development appears twice, or on two planes. First it appears on the social plane and then on the psychological plane. First it appears between people as an interpsychological category and then within the individual child as an intrapsychological category.* (Vygotsky, 1981, 163)

While Vygotsky was writing specifically about children, the same principle applies at any age. If we combine the idea of leading activities and the idea that developmental change is promoted by having people with different kinds of knowledge and ability engage jointly in a variety of culturally organized, sanctioned activities, it produces an apparently clear design strategy: create interventions in which more knowledgeable and less knowledgeable people and their cultural tools engage each other. The issue then becomes *how* do they engage each other?

6. *The ethical and strategic contradictions of intervention research.* Consideration of the social circumstances most conducive to promoting developmental change makes it clear that in using a particular theory, with its particular judgments about potential desirable futures, one is not "just testing out a theory." By virtue of the intervention's location at the level of a culturally organized activity it is partially constitutive of that activity. The values of intervention researchers, by virtue of their infusion into those activities, become a part of the ensuing developmental process. As we shall see, different research strategies can usefully be seen as different responses to the dilemma of needing to influence the futures of others as a means of testing CH/AT theory.

In short, the relationship between researchers and other intervention participants needs to be a part of the analysis. It must also be kept in mind that nonresearcher activity participants are themselves likely to be distinguished by age, social status, authority, and degrees of experience with respect to the activity, to name but a few relevant characteristics. The "formative process" is itself a form of joint mediated activity in which critical analysis of the notion of "more capable peer" should be part of the analysis.

Consequently, a CH/AT approach to implementation research requires researchers to attend not only to their theory and data, as one does in the study of genetic effects among fruit flies. In addition it is also necessary to attend to the quality of that practice as it is evaluated by the community that plays host to the intervention. Without the community's support, the intervention, no matter how well it works out "in theory" will ultimately fail. The medical dictum remains fully in force: Do no harm. There is an ethical dimension to practices that involve one person's intervention into the lives of others.

Example Intervention Studies Combining Theory and Practice

It is not possible in a chapter of this length to provide an exhaustive account of the body of formative-experimental research that places cultural mediation and activity at its conceptual center. Such an account would take systematically into consideration a number of ingenious interventions that were carried out during the middle decades of the 20th century, many of them by researchers inspired by Kurt Lewin's ideas. Similar in many ways to CH/AT, Lewin's version of genetic field theory encouraged culturally informed implementations, but employed a vocabulary from social psychology where culture is rarely used, but the relevant concepts appear in the form of "norms" and "values." Sherif and Sherif's (1956) text on social psychology, for example, provides a wide example of studies focused on the role of norms, values, and conventions as key constituents of the small group structures. Social Psychologists of this kind clearly rendered their central ideas empirically testable through the construction of specially designed social settings and theoretically motivated changes in those settings (such as the famous Robber's Cave experiment). This research, along with various lines of action research needs to be revisited for the rich insights concerning intervention research centered on questions of culture and development that they can provide.

However, our focus here is on intervention research that grows out of the CH/AT tradition. Recognizing that space does not permit us the luxury of deep and broad coverage simultaneously, we have chosen to highlight three research programs that differ in the cultural and historical circumstances in which they were carried out, the particular populations and institutions that are the focus of the intervention, and the CH/AT principles that they highlight as a guide to their intervention strategies. We conclude by placing this research in the overall landscape of culturally informed developmental interventions. Their combination appears to provide an interesting way to "triangulate" on the role of culturally organized activity in human development.

The Elkonin – Davydov Teaching/Learning Interventions[5]

Perhaps the domain where Russian CH/AT ideas have been most frequently put to the test using formative experimentation is the intervention research program initiated and instituted by D. B. Elkonin and V. V. Davydov (Davydov, 1988 a, b, c; Zuckerman, 2005).[6] Through their influence at the Russian Institute of Psychology in the Academy of Pedagogical Developmental Sciences they were able to organize several multi-year formative experiments, sometimes referred to as "teaching/learning" experiments, as a means of implementing state mandated school reforms (Kaminski, 1994; Markova, 1979; Yanchar, 2003). This line of work is still being expanded by Elkonin and Davydov's

Russian students (Zukerman, 2003) and several non-Russian scholars (Hedegaard & Lompscher, 1999; Schmittau, 1993a, b).

Two theoretical propositions lie at the heart of the Elkonin-Davydov approach, which entail additional CH/AT principles when theory and practice are combined. First, there is the position, championed especially by Davydov, that knowledge formation follows the path of "ascending from the abstract to the concrete" that is intimately linked to the particular conceptual content to be mastered. This general epistemological approach is derived from the way in which Karl Marx formulated a comprehensive, concrete theory of capitalism from the abstract "germ cell" or "kernel" of the commodity as a contradictory unity of use value and exchange value (see Ilyenkov, 1982). Davydov (1988) summarized how this method could be a powerful strategy of learning and teaching in the following terms:

When moving toward the mastery of any academic subject, schoolchildren, with the teacher's help, analyze the content of the curricular material and identify the primary general relationship in it, at the same time making the discovery that this relationship is manifest in many other particular relationships found in the given material. . . . When schoolchildren begin to make use of the primary abstraction and the primary generalization as a way of deducing and unifying other abstractions, they turn the primary mental formation into a concept that registers the "kernel" of the academic subject. This "kernel" subsequently serves the school children as a general principle whereby they can orient themselves in the entire multiplicity of factual curricular material which they are to assimilate in conceptual form via an ascent from the abstract to the concrete." (Davydov, 1988b, 22–23)

Second, and closely related to the first, is the idea of leading activities, reformulated in terms of the sequencing of the curriculum across grade levels to take account of age-expectant activities and associated sources of motivation (Elkonin, 1971). In the Elkonin-Davydov approach these two ideas are combined such that the logical sequence of curricular content is meshed with leading activities in order that what children need to learn in order to fill in their initial, general, but empty abstractions as they rise to more complex forms of concrete reality also satisfies needs associated with the leading activities that will motivate them to engage in the hard work of dealing with problems for which they need to come up with new solutions.

Davydov argued that the process of ascending from the abstract to the concrete leads to a new type of theoretical concept, to theoretical thinking, and to theoretical consciousness. By "theory" he meant "an instrumentality for the deduction of more particular relationships" from a general underlying relationship, not a set of fixed propositions (Davydov, 1988, Part 2:23). The classic example that inspired Davydov is Ilyenkov's (1982) analysis of commodity, the contradictory unity of use value and exchange value, as the germ cell of the socio-economic formation of capitalism.

In summary, the Elkonin-Davydov teaching/learning curriculum was designed in each subject matter area in such a way that it was structured around theoretical concepts appropriate to that domain and that classroom life was organized to insure that the forms of activity and concrete materials were used in an optimally motivating and intellectually effective way. This curriculum has been implemented in a number of subject matter domains from which we have chosen to emphasize mathematics as an example because it is particularly well worked out and has attracted the attention of mathematics educators in many parts of the world (Davydov, 1988; Schmittau, 2003).

The Example of Mathematics

As applied to the domain of mathematics, the Elkonin-Davydov curriculum is designed to provide students with the clearest possible understanding of the concept of real number. This initially abstract concept needs to be introduced at the very beginning of instruction and then must be "filled in" with a great variety of concrete instantiations of the initial germ cell/abstraction. Davydov describes the general principles of this "filling-in" process as follows:

> The children's assimilation of the basic idea of the concept of real number should begin with the mastery of the concept of quantity and with the study of the general properties of the quantity. Then all kinds of real numbers can be assimilated on the basis of the children's mastery of the modes whereby those properties are concretized. In this case, the idea of real number will be "present" in the teaching of mathematics from the outset. (1988b: 67)

Choosing real numbers and measurement of quantity as the germ cell of mathematics education contrasts sharply with the curriculum in other countries that begins by teaching children to count and to support their mastery of the basic arithmetical operations through the introduction of a wide variety of empirical examples. The Elkonin-Davydov approach also involves a wide variety of empirical examples. But they are organized to serve as concrete manifestations of the initial, "germ cell" abstraction of quantity. And, importantly, learning about quantity and relative quantity precedes the introduction of concepts of number, counting, and arithmetic.

In order to realize these ideas in actual curriculum units, the iconic Elkonin-Davydov mathematics curriculum begins roughly as follows: Initially the children are asked to compare the quantity embodied in various pairs of objects and to say whether the amounts (length, volume, etc.) are equal or not equal and if unequal, which is greater in the aspect of quantity involved. The differences between the objects are sufficient so that the children can easily make this judgment.

Then they are shown pairs of objects that are relatively similar in quantity so that they must pick up the object pairs and place them next to each other such that they are aligned at one end and then look to see whether the other ends match – when both ends match, the objects are "equal in length," and so on. Many examples are given using various object attributes until the children can make such comparative judgments automatically, as an operation.

Next the children might be presented a new set of problems with objects that cannot be physically moved and aligned such as two line segments on two blackboards at opposite ends of the room and asked to compare them in length. The operations that worked earlier are no longer usable: the child cannot pick up bookcases or line segments made of chalk and carry them across the room in order to line them up. Now the role of the teacher is to arrange for the children to work on the problem together until, perhaps with some intervention by the teacher, they come up with using the idea of a mediating tool such as a piece of string or a stick that is the same length as one of the chalk line segments. They can then carry the mediating "yard stick" across the room and make the comparison as before, but now through the mediated action of measuring.

Now the idea of measurement as the ratio of the length of the mediating tool to the object(s) being measured is introduced. At first the examples picked are whole numbers but later they will be fractions or even irrational numbers. As Jean Schmittau (2003), who has conducted a good deal of work Davydov's theory and methods comments, when, in later grades, the children are introduced to fractions and irrational numbers, they are not required to reconceptualize number, unlike curricula that start with counting whole numbers, where an entirely new set of operations is needed each time a new concept of number is introduced. Schmittau provides additional examples, extending her observations to multiplication and division that students encounter in later grades, to affirm the effectiveness of Davydov's germ-cell theory approach. Zuckerman (2005) shows how this approach produces results that compare favorably with alternatives using contemporary international testing standards.

Expanding on the Elkonin-Davydov Approach

The conceptual structure and sequencing of the curriculum is not a magic bullet that students master and teachers implement with ease. First, it is important to emphasize that the special conceptual structure of the curriculum is complemented by extensive use of graphic devices (including simple algebraic equations, and varied opportunities to make physical models that embody the mathematical relations involved). Second, children are not expected to be independent learners at the start of the process. In fact, the ability to work collaboratively, to create intellectual divisions of labor in the service of allowing every participant to solve the problem, is assumed to require nourishing along with the particular conceptual content involved (Rubtsov, 1991; Zuckerman, 1994).

This approach also requires that children be motivated to tackle the issues that are laid before them, the socially inherited cultural tools of the academic disciplines. In her research at a Moscow school that was the center of developmental education research during Elkonin and Davydov's lifetimes, Zuckerman (1994, 2003) has focused particularly on organizing instruction so that it was both motivating to the students and cognitively organized in the theoretically appropriate way. This challenge could be met, she believed, if instruction could be organized so the child learned the "tasks, methods, and means and devices of the actual kinds of social activity in which he can be expected to engage in later life" (pp. 4–5). In a manner reminiscent of Dewey, she argued that to produce appropriate and sufficient internal motivation, the assignments should draw upon "the context and structure of the kinds of activities that children can expect to engage in later" (p. 5).

Over and above being motivated and mastering domain specific content, success in the curriculum, because it is focused on creation of theoretical knowledge, depends upon children engaging in active inquiry and an ability to reflect upon their own problem solving efforts – an ability that it is fashionable to refer to as metacognition in the current literature on cognitive development (Hartman, 2001).

The purpose and the entire methodology of the Elkonin-Davydov curriculum is "to develop educated, knowledgeable students who have mastered the cultural values of the past, yet are capable of overcoming the confines of cultural traditions by going beyond generally accepted solutions and frameworks to solve novel problems" (Zuckerman, 2003, 195). But consider what this means, even in the classroom. It is the rare teacher, never mind the rare statesperson, who wishes to be questioned at every turn about the "cultural values of the past." After all, $2 + 2$ equals 4, and to question why is to display stupidity, or its often misidentified cousin, ignorance. A theoretically founded, inquiry-based educational curriculum is designed precisely to develop incessant questioning, a critical, reflective person who produces novelty through mastery and who risks being judged a fool.

Davydov's work was initially a key inspiration for the Finnish group of activity theorists who have expanded the use of the theory to the world of work. Foundational ideas of developmental work research were systematically laid out in Engeström's book *Learning by Expanding* (1987, 1998). Subsequently, the work led to an intervention toolkit based on the principle of double stimulation.

Developmental Work Research: Focusing on the Method of Double Stimulation

Vygotsky described the idea of double stimulation as follows:

> The task facing the child in the experimental context is, as a rule, beyond his present capabilities and cannot be solved by existing skills. In such cases a neutral object is placed near the child, and frequently we are able to observe how the neutral stimulus is drawn into the situation and takes on the *function of a sign. Thus, the child actively incorporates these neutral objects into the task of problem solving. We might say that when difficulties arise, neutral stimuli take on the function of a sign and from that point on the operation's structure assumes an essentially different character.*

> *By using this approach, we do not limit ourselves to the usual method of offering the subject simple stimuli to which we expect a direct response. Rather, we simultaneously offer a second series of stimuli that have a special function. In this way, we are able to study the process of accomplishing a task by the aid of specific auxiliary means; thus we are also able to discover the inner structure and development of higher psychological processes. (Vygotsky, 1978, 74–75)*

The application of the method of double stimulation by Russian psychologists tended to focus on individual behavior of children or medical patients who were provided with potential tools to carry out tasks that were beyond their current capabilities (for a concise summary of early studies, see Luria, 1979). An extension of this idea to collective behavior with adults indicates how the basic logic of the method can be extended as a tool of intervention research.

The Finnish developmental work researchers have used a generalization of the method of double stimulation as a key element in their intervention research, focused on development of adult work practices (Engeström, 2005). They create what they term "Change Laboratories," temporary activity systems that are set up within existing organizations (e.g., hospitals, schools, factories, banks).

The events that transpire in the Change Laboratory are organized to position the intervention as a "tool" chosen by the subject (the people working in that institution) as a means of solving some perceived problems in the ongoing regime of work. At this high level of abstraction, the Change Laboratory occupies the role of the "mediating artifact" within a socially organized, group with which to engage in the "cultural

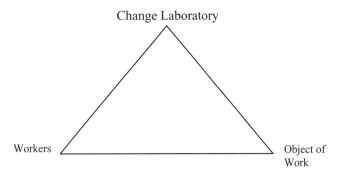

Figure 23.1. Basic mediational triangle with the Change Laboratory in the Position of the mediator.

habit of behavior" (Vygotsky, 1929). In its abstract form, a Change Laboratory can be represented by the archetypal mediating triangle (Figure 23.1). But the Change Laboratory is not a stick or a word, or a pencil, it is a complex set if artifacts and procedures organized to serve as a tool for practitioners to change the conditions of their work. Engeström has diagrammed the prototypical layout of a change laboratory space in the following diagram (Figure 23.2).

A central element within a Change Laboratory-as-auxiliary stimulus is a set of three writing surfaces, each of which has three "layers" representing the past, the present, and the future. Each set of three-layered writing surfaces is used for representing the work activity in a different way. One is called a "mirror" that is intended to represent to the participants critical examples of their current difficulties as manifested in recordings of particularly problematic situations and disturbances in routines as well as novel innovative solutions. This surface represents the 'first stimulus' in Vygotskian terms.

The second set of writing surfaces represents a conceptually mediated image of the participants' situation using models such as Engeström's expanded triangle of systems of

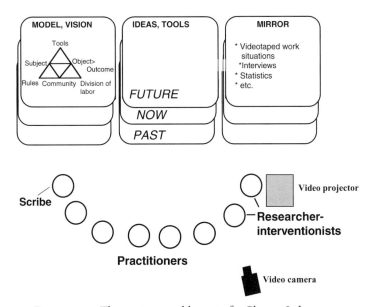

Figure 23.2. The prototypical layout of a Change Laboratory.

activity (Engeström, 1987, p. 78). Conceptual models are filled by participants with specific contents and used as tools for interpreting the contradictions behind current troubles in a more systematic, historically specified and generalizable way. Engeström refers to this as the "model/vision" space, where people use models of their past and present circumstances to envision how the future might be organized to differ in intended ways from the present and past. This surface represents the "second stimulus" in Vygotskian terms.

The third surface, physically located in the middle of the first two surfaces, is for recording the participants' ideas about the sorts of tools that might be used to deal with their problematic situation and to record intermediate, partial, solutions. Here participants might record schedules or flowcharts of their work processes, diagrams of organizational structures, ways of categorizing responses to interviews, etc. Engeström notes that in this intermediate zone, they might try out their ideas by making up simulations or by engaging in role-playing. The participants in a Change Laboratory (including practitioners, a scribe selected from among them, and the researcher/ interventionists) ordinarily sit at tables where they can see the three writing/ drawing surfaces, watch videotapes of their prior interactions, and see and interact with each other. The videotaping is important because videotaped work situations are typically used as material for the "mirror" part of the laboratory sessions. Each session is also videotaped for research and to facilitate the reviewing of critical laboratory events in subsequent sessions.

The Finnish researchers organized this array and sequence of mediating tools on the theoretically reasonable assumption that "as the participants move between the experiential mirror and the theoretical model/vision, they also produce intermediate ideas and partial solutions, to be tested and experimented with" (Engeström, Virkkunen, Helle, Pihlaja, & Poikela, 1996: 12). As this sequence is implemented, the practitioners move from a recognition of their past and currently conceived problems and arrive at a new vision of those problems and their solution, a model and plan for future action.

Engeström and his colleagues refer to such sequences as cycles of "expansive learning" that are induced by interacting with the world through the Change Laboratory. Overall, a cycle is likely to require ten or twelve weekly sessions followed by one or two follow-up sessions a few months later. Then it is time to begin the process once again, leading, in successful circumstances to a "spiral of development." One cycle often leads to the next one, and within the cycles there are smaller cycles of problem solving and learning.

The researchers do not envision this process of development as a smoothly flowing, seamless sequence. It is, rather, always bedeviled by contradictions, breakthroughs, "double binds," adjustment, and resistance. But it is a process that embodies, however imperfectly, the collective agency of the practitioners involved.

Change Laboratory interventions have been conducted in dozens of variations since the first prototypes were tested in 1995. The initial focus on a single organizational unit as a spearhead of development has been complemented with "Boundary Crossing Laboratories" with participants from multiple collaborating organizations (Engeström, Engeström, & Kerosuo, 2003) and "Competence Laboratories" which put frontline practitioners and their managers in intense dialogue with one another (Ahonen, Engeström, & Virkkunen, 2000; Virkkunen & Ahonen, 2004).

Change Laboratories are judged by their practical outcomes. These outcomes are not primarily understood in terms of traditional cognitive variables. Practitioners are interested in actual changes in their work practices, including new objects, tools, rules, and divisions of labor. Thus, the creation and practical testing of the "care agreement" toolkit for the negotiated collaborative care of patients with multiple illnesses and multiple caregivers in the Helsinki area may be judged in terms of the actual utility of the artifacts named "care agreement," "care map" and "care calendar" (Engeström, 2001). These tools, when used by practitioners, are judged by their potential to reduce gaps, overlaps, and fragmentation in the care of concrete patients. They are materially palpable learning outcomes.

Collective learning outcomes in Change Laboratory processes may also be assessed using such indicators as transformations over time in the quality of discourse within the community of practitioners. Thus, the Change Laboratory process conducted among the teachers of a middle school led to a qualitative shift in the way the teachers talked in their meetings about students. The researchers followed the Change Laboratory process and the subsequent implementation of its results for a period of 18 months. At the beginning, the teachers talked about their students in predominantly negative terms, as lazy and incompetent.

"Half of the students will be like that, they'll skip the whole idea. I have an oral presentation assignment at the moment, one student has held a presentation, and others have skipped it. This is what they will always do."

Toward the end of the process, positive talk about students as energetic and competent increased radically and remained at a high level.

"Well, I thought about someone, for example in my class, that she or he at least will definitely not do it. And then there have been these positive surprises, the person has actually produced a project, and a good one, too. Students who have otherwise been doing pretty poorly, and have been absent a lot and so on, they have actually shaped up really well."

Interestingly enough, negative talk did not disappear but stayed also at a relatively high level of frequency. The authors call this "expansion by enrichment" (Engeström, Engeström, & Suntio, 2002).

Another way to assess the outcomes of Change Laboratory interventions is to trace the formation and implementation of novel theoretical concepts. A Change Laboratory conducted in a commercial bank led to the construction of what the researchers characterize as "a perspectival concept" in which the practitioners envisioned and represented two desirable systems of their work, a near-future one and a more distant future model. Crucial to such collective concept formation is that the future models are named, depicted with the help of systemic models, and elevated to concreteness by means of identifying and actually implementing practical steps toward their realization (Engeström, Pasanen, Toiviainen, & Haavisto, 2005).

Designing and Implementing Activities as Idiocultures: The 5th Dimension

A distinctive characteristic of a good deal of American intervention research within the CH/AT tradition is that it takes cultural variation and the social creation of social inequality as a central concern, drawing upon anthropological and sociological ideas about culture and context to design and implement interventions. The notion of culture that informs this line of work is an amalgam of American cultural anthropology (D'Andrade, 1984; Goodenough, 1994) and the ideas of the original Russian CH/AT theorists and their successors (Cole, 1996); culture is treated as a special kind of medium, constituted of ideal/material artifacts assembled as part of the behavioral patterns manifested in social practices along with their associated values and beliefs. On any given occasion ("according to the context") a subset of these resources is recruited as instruments for achieving the objectives of those involved. The design challenge, from this perspective, is to create new kinds of activities that promote the desired form of development and are suitable for a given social group at a particular time and place.

The particular intervention we describe in detail is called a 5th Dimension. At the most abstract level, a 5th Dimension intervention can be represented by a triangle (see Figure 23.3), with the 5th Dimension

UNIVERSITY   COMMUNITY

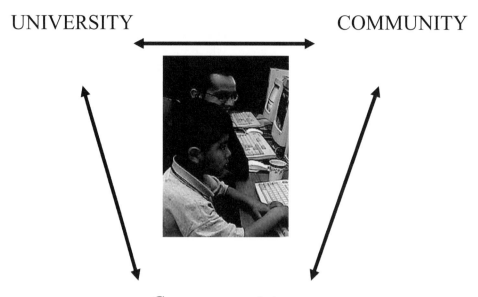

Common activity

Figure 23.3. The basic organization of joint activity between a university and a community institution.

Activity System mediating the interaction of two institutions; a university (or college) and another organization in its community.

At a next level of abstraction, each part of the overall system can be differentiated (see Figure 23.4).

These two diagrams make it clear that the 5th Dimension is a medium for joint activity between two institutions that collaborate in its implementation and ongoing care. What is hinted at, but not clear in the diagram, is that when we move to the level of implementation, the spatial symmetry of the triangular design architecture obscures an important reality: as an idioculture, the 5th Dimension has to be located *somewhere*. As a rule, that "somewhere" has been in a community institution that cares for K-6 children after school, but 5th Dimensions have also been implemented at the local university in some cases. For purposes of simplicity, we focus on implementations of 5th Dimensions that are physically located in a particular community organization with joint participation by children and adults from both of the cooperating institutions.

The Social-Ecology of 5th Dimensions

Most, but not all, 5th Dimensions have been implemented during the after school hours with the overall goal of providing children development-enhancing experiences, particular activities associated with intellectual and social development (Cole, & the Distributed Literacy Consortium, 2006; Vasquez, 2002). Consequently, 5th Dimensions are, from the perspective of participants, suspended in the temporal gap between school and home while at the same time they are mediating between a local community institution and a University that is both inside and outside the community (as indicated by the eternal rhetoric of town-gown relationships).

A conspicuous characteristic of the community organizations that host children after school is that their resources are sufficient to keep children off of the streets and out of trouble, but they rarely have the resources to make their activities rich in developmental/intellectual potential. Yet, they espouse intellectual development (coded as education) as a major goal.

This combination of attributes suggests the basis of reciprocity between university and community organizations that motivates their collaboration in creating 5th Dimensions. From a University perspective, the community organization that provides space and regularly present children also provides the university and its students a laboratory setting needed by their students. From the perspective of a community organization, the University is providing it valued resources to accomplish its goals.

Designing the Joint Activity

We concentrate here on the design of the joint activity and the way in which it provides tests of various theoretical principles. From what has been said so far, the following characteristics of the joint activity emerge.

1. It is voluntary, at least in the sense that the state does not require children to go to afterschool programs, and within those programs, no one requires the children to participate in the 5th Dimen-

sion. Children come and go as they please.

2. It involves the mixing of leading activities because afterschool is a time in the day when children are often allowed to play, yet adults want them to be learning. In addition to mixing play and education, it emphasizes affiliation because the social and emotional bonds between undergraduate children provide a powerful foundation of their participation in the 5th Dimension.

3. It is multi-generational in three important senses. First, when speaking of the children and the undergraduates, age and educational expertise differentiate the participants. Second, when speaking of researcher/professors and children, the undergraduates are an "intermediate" generation with whom it is attractive and easy for the children to interact. Third, when speaking of length of participation in the idioculture of the 5th Dimension, the children are often of an older, and more experienced, generation of the members, than the undergraduates so they are the more capable peers.

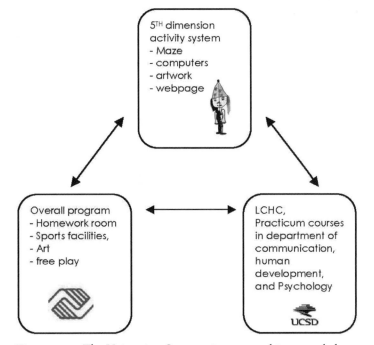

Figure 23.4. The University–Community partnership expanded to include its constituent parts.

4. It occurs across a span of as many years so long as it continues to be sustained. This long time span allows one to study cycles of activity as they are influenced by such factors as changes in the school calendar, the continuities and discontinuities in participation structures, secular changes in technology, financial support, etc. It is also possible to study several levels of the activity system ranging from the minute to minute interactions within the 5th Dimension, to changes in children over months and years, undergraduates over quarters and semesters, the overall structure of the joint activity over its supporting institutional arrangements over years.

Describing the Ideal-Type

A major expectation is that the particular activity system that arises under the constraints described thus far will differ from each other in a myriad of ways. However, over time it seems possible to discern a more or less stereotypical description of a 5th Dimension in a given U-C Partnership system of the sort one might use in a description made available to parents. The following description has been used in several publications for this purpose (e.g., Brown & Cole 2004).

The 5th Dimension is an educational activity system that offers school aged children a specially designed environment in which to explore a variety of off-the-shelf computer games and game-like educational activities during the after school hours. The computer games are a part of a make-believe play world that includes non-computer games like origami, chess, Boggle, and a variety of other artifacts.

College or university students enrolled in a course focused on fieldwork in a community setting play, work, and learn as the children's partners. In assisting children, the students are encouraged to follow the guideline: Help as little as possible but as much as necessary for you and the child to have fun and make progress. The presence of college or university undergraduates is a major draw for the children.

As a means of distributing the children's and undergraduates' use of the various games, the 5th Dimension contains a tabletop or wall chart maze consisting of a number of rooms, initially 20 (see Figure 23.5). Each room provides access to two or more games, and the children may choose which games to play as they enter each room.

Games are played using "task cards" written by project staff members for each game. They fulfill several goals. They are designed to help participants (both children and undergraduate students) orient to the game, to form goals, and to chart progress toward becoming an expert. They provide a variety of requirements in addition to the intellectual tasks written into the software or game activity itself. These additional requirements routinely include having participants externalize their thinking and learning or reflect upon and criticize the activity, sometimes by writing to someone, sometimes by looking up information in an encyclopedia, or by teaching someone else what one has learned.

There is an electronic entity (a wizard/wizardess/Maga, Golem, Proteo, etc.) who is said to live in the Internet. The entity writes to (and sometimes chats with) the children and undergraduates via the Internet and they write back. In the mythology of the 5th Dimension, the electronic entity acts as the participants' patron, provider of games, mediator of disputes, as well as the source of computer glitches and other misfortunes.

Because it is located in a community institution, the 5th Dimension activities require the presence of a local "site coordinator" who greets the participants as they arrive and supervises the flow of activity in the room. The site coordinator is trained to recognize and support the pedagogical ideals and curricular practices that mark the 5th Dimension as "different"– a different way for kids to use computers, a different way of playing

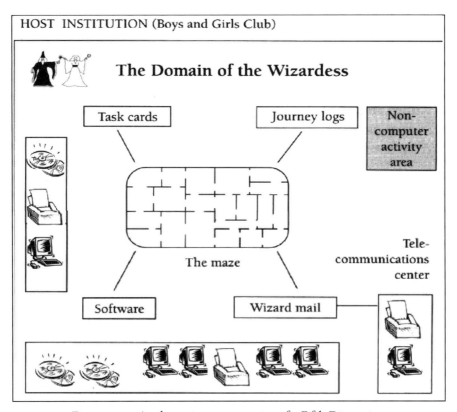

Figure 23.5. A schematic representation of a Fifth Dimension.

with other children, and a different way of interacting with adults.

Evaluating the Intervention

There have been a great variety of analytical methods used to evaluate the usefulness and shortcomings of CH/AT principles in the design of 5th Dimensions (Blanton, Moorman, Hayes, & Warner, 1997; Cole, & the Distributed Literacy Consortium, 2006; Mayer, Schustack, & Blanton, 1999). These methods include specially designed tests that sample forms of knowledge and skill that make up the explicit content of the activities, questionnaires, indices of the monetary support provided by both the University and Community institutions, videotaped records of extended episodes of interaction between undergraduates and children engaged in various local practices, and data mining of stu-

dent fieldnotes, which number more than 26,000 between 1990 and 2005.

The specific data sources used by different implementers of a 5th Dimension (approximately 40 different research groups from different parts of the world) depend heavily upon the expectations of their local communities, the professional criteria of the academic disciplines they answer to, the specific interests of the investigator, and the resources available to them (see Cole, & the Distributed Literacy Consortium, 2006 or consult www.uclinks.org/Resources for access to detailed reports).

Looking first to the activity systems as a whole, perhaps the most obvious result is that the idioculture that forms is highly sensitive to local constraints and resources. No two 5th Dimensions, even when implemented by the same researcher with the same group of students in two community organizations of the same kind in highly similar communities, look like replicas of each other. Many common features are evident – the mixture of play and education, a friendly, but often-contentious welter of overlapping social interactions, the presence of some common games and routines. But within a period of months, if not weeks, each idioculture takes on its own characteristics, a blend of values, norms, and practices characteristic of the local institution (its staffing, architectural structure, its location in the community, etc.) and its University partners (who may be from backgrounds in education or linguistics, sophomores or seniors, predominantly of one ethnic group or several, etc.).

Tracing implementations in widely disparate conditions quickly reveals that some 5th Dimensions have failed to survive initial meetings between universities and potential community sponsors. Others have been implemented and run successfully, only to cease operation after less than a year as a result of inability to satisfy institutional imperatives that went undetected in the startup phase (for example, the inability of staff to keep track of the turnover of undergraduate participants owing to a university employing a quarter system combined with strict regulations about the presence of "strangers" at an afterschool program). Others have continued to a point where the two collaborating institutions discover that they do not really share a common vision of a good developmental environment for children or when the level of continuity in staffing (on either the university or community side) is inadequate, degrading the quality of the ensuing activity. Still others have continued for several years, but coincidence of several "risk factors" (decreased funding, loss of key personnel in two or more parts of the system) have led to their demise despite their recognized value. Finally, many implementations prosper and increase in scope, sometimes "giving birth" to new generations of 5th Dimensions. At the time of this writing, 28 years after the experiment began, dozens of 5th Dimensions and their associated university-community superstructures are in operation.

In evaluating the success of the design principles for promoting children's development, the logic of evaluating developmental processes and the logic of evaluating developmental products have, from the beginning, been in constant tension. Whenever there is voluntary participation there is the probability that selection factors are in play. However, in some socio-ecological circumstances plausible comparison groups can be constituted and wherever this has been possible, 5th Dimensions have been shown to improve academic achievement of a variety of kinds. From a CH/AT perspective, this information tells us little about the *process* of development, but it does provide evidence sought by the University and the Community that the outcomes of whatever processes are at work meets their criteria for the *products* they are seeking. Without such evidence, it is more difficult to coax support from University and Community administrators.

Some investigators have combined a strategy of giving tests that are interpreted as objective measure of performance changes with analyses of field notes and videotapes that provide evidence about the processes that produce the test results. When such analyses have been carried out, they reveal the ways that organization of 5th Dimension idiocultures routinely encourages the kinds of mediated joint activity between more and less capable peers that results in mastery of intellectual content, motivation to solve difficult problems, and increased skill at collaboration-in-the-service-of-learning that provide plausible explanations for changes in tested performance.

In short, 5th Dimension idiocultures routinely create an institutionalized version of a zone of proximal development for participants. Unlike the educational and pretend play interactions discussed by Vygotsky, in the 5th Dimension there is often creative confusion about who the more capable peers might be (for example, when novice undergraduates encounter children highly skilled in playing educational computer games about which they know nothing). But the general culture of collaborative learning that is created within the 5th Dimension appears to serve the development of all.

There have been several kindred interventions strategies used by American CH/AT theorists to design interventions that seek to incorporate cultural variation associated with the culture of a local social group into the design of activities. Thus, for example, Carol Lee has re-organized classroom discourse in high-school literature classes where students are predominantly African-American using literature in which distinct African-American speech genres are prominent as the starting point of the curriculum (Lee, Spencer, & Harpalani, 2003).

Assessing CH/AT in Practice

We began by introducing an approach to culture and human development that prizes the testing of cultural-historical, activity-based approaches in practice. We end by comparing the three research programs we used as examples and by discussing how a CH/AT approach fits into the broader landscape of culturally informed developmental interventions. Each of the three examples uses a distinctively different mixture of CH/AT principles in the design and implementation of its intervention strategies as researchers seek to grapple with the specific cultural, institutional, and historical circumstances in which their interventions take place.

The Elkonin-Davydov research program came into existence during the 1960s in the USSR and was directed at changes in formal education. It is distinctive for the heavy emphasis it places on the *conceptual content* that it seeks to develop, its focus on developing theoretical thinking, and its use of the idea of leading activities in organizing instruction that is motivating for its students. The starting point of this kind of intervention is a philosophical and historical reconstruction of the logic of the subject matter as a means of choosing the starting point and the logical sequencing of the curriculum. The intervention then requires that its imple-

menters develop age-appropriate activities that embody the "genetically primary" starting points and its subsequent concretizations mediated by algorithmic schemas and models. These activities and the mediating tools they employ must maintain children's interest while constantly challenging them to go beyond already-mastered stages of domain-relevant knowledge to discover and elaborate ever-more varied and complex generalizations appropriate to the conceptual domain.

As reported by Davydov and his colleagues, their mathematics curriculum, when properly implemented, engenders in children a theoretical approach to the subject matter that produces high levels of achievement as indicated by their ability to master higher levels of the mathematics curriculum at an earlier age and to generalize the knowledge they acquire to novel problems. Similar claims have been made for the teaching of grammar, a notoriously difficult subject to teach in elementary and middle school students (Markova, 1979).

Notably absent from reports of this research during the Soviet era were reports of what other aspects of children's behavior may have changed as a result of this curriculum. Rubtsov (1991), for example, demonstrated that children's understanding was improved by organizing presentation of problems to groups of children in such a way that their conceptual development was enhanced when the distribution of problem elements induced children to discover critical features of the conceptual content through collaborative problem solving. But Soviet classrooms were renowned for the rigid discipline and use of teacher-led pedagogical methods that one might think inimical to theoretical thinking.

Research in the Elkonin-Davydov tradition conducted following the demise of the USSR has done a good deal to reveal consequences of their instructional methods that they, themselves, did not highlight. Zuckerman (2003), for example, emphasizes the fact that implementation of the Elkonin-Davydov method does indeed engender a theoretical approach to learning in children, but that this theoretical approach entails marked change in classroom discourse such that children directly challenge their teachers to come up with theoretically appropriate justifications for *their* statements about (say) a mathematical proof. Noting the reflective attitude that this form of curriculum develops in children, Zuckerman comments that "Developing reflection is as dangerous as experimenting in nuclear physics and genetic engineering, with an outcome just as uncertain" (2003: 195).

Zuckerman's comment raises the question of culture and development in a way quite different from that illustrated by the Elkonin-Davydov curriculum – what are the cultural norms in society such that such a curriculum can be implemented on a broad scale? Observations in classrooms around the globe reveal that encouraging intellectual challenges from their students is not widespread (Hiebert et al., 2003). It requires that teachers have strong command of their subject matter and are well trained in the use of the Elkonin-Davydov approach including its encouragement of reflective theoretical thinking. When such conditions are met, however, the results appear as impressive as those reported by Davydov and his Russian colleagues (Schmittau, 1993a, b).

Particularly worth mentioning in this regard is an application of the Elkonin-Davydov approach as reported by Hedegaard and Chaiklin (2005). Their work took place in a poor, Latino area of New York City in an afterschool setting and was focused on concepts from the social sciences. While no appropriate comparison is possible to similar children engaged in standard curricula, Hedegaard and Chaiklin report the same kinds of ability to make use of conceptual models and to generalize learning to novel examples that are reported by Davydov, Schmittau, and others. Aside from the fact that it took place in an afterschool setting which afforded less hierarchical relations between teachers and children, a notable aspect of this work was that it used locally significant concrete exemplars to fill in the abstractions the children were encouraged to master, thereby showing it is possible to combine local culturally valued knowledge with universal conceptual content to the benefit of the children's intellectual development.

Despite, its successful demonstration of the utility of CH/AT principles in practice, the Elkonin-Davydov research program has yet to gain wide acceptance. This outcome, as we shall see, is relevant to evaluating the other two research programs that have been the focus of our attention.

The Change Laboratory came into being as part of a research program focused on adult work. It is distinctive in its focus on using the principle of dual stimulation as a method of providing adult workers with tools to become agents of change within their own workplaces. The Change Laboratory interventions currently face at least two intertwined challenges. First, the diffusion, generalization, and sustainability of the outcomes of single laboratories are problematic. Traditional social science notions of generalizability and sustainability easily lead to the expectation that forms of intervention and their outcomes should remain essentially unchanged over time and across sites, at the very least, for a given kind of work and institutional setting. From a CH/AT perspective, this is clearly a misguided expectation; culturally organized social innovations are dynamic systems of activity that require constant reconfiguration to stay alive. But how are researchers supposed to trace, document and assess such dynamic processes of generalization and sustained development?

A second challenge arises from the very core of the method of dual stimulation. Vygotsky and his colleagues saw dual stimulation as the basic mechanism of formation of voluntary action and will. In contemporary parlance, they sought to understand the role of agency in development. In a manner that bears clear analogies to dilemmas facing the Elkonin-Davydov formative experiments, it is likely that the most important outcomes of Change Laboratory interventions are changes in the collective agency of the participants, understood as their ability to challenge existing conditions and to initiate change processes. These change processes, if they became general, would shake the foundational assumptions of their institutions – the workplace in the case of the Change Laboratory, the School in the case of the Elkonin-Davydov curriculum. From a methodological point of view we need to understand how the formation of new kinds of collective agency can be conceptualized and empirically identified. And from a larger, societal, point of view we need to understand the cultural-historical conditions that will permit such forms of collective agency to become general in society.

In addition, the successes of the Change Laboratory in Finland, a country which retains a relatively strong notion of social welfare in a world increasingly dominated by neo-liberal forms of economic and political organization, raise the question of how even the research program carried out there can be generalized to countries such as the United States where privatization and short-term profit dominate work practices. As we have emphasized, the kind of formative interventions demanded by the logic of CH/AT research must be carried out over significant periods of time and involve significant expenditures. By contrast, the typical managerial consulting practices in the United States are short term and increasing the collective agency of the workers is unlikely to win the consultants an invitation to return. Once again, the macro sociocultural features of the society place clear restrictions on potential generalization of demonstrably successful applications of theory in practice.

The same dilemmas, in somewhat different form, confront projects such as the 5th Dimension, which arose as a means of creating inter-institutional joint activities focused on the design and implementation of developmental enrichment activities for children in the afterschool hours. It highlights the creation of idiocultures that bring together several CH/AT principles such as the method of dual stimulation and leading activities to create zones of proximal development. Like the Change Laboratory interventions, the principle that every instantiation of the

intervention will be, in principle, different in various ways from very other instantiation creates difficult problems of appropriate description and evaluation. It also deals with the issue of agency; who initiates the university-community collaborations? Whose voice dominates discussions of the activities that are the basis of joint activities between supporting institutions? Like the Elkonin-Davydov project it must struggle to create forms of activity that are appropriate to the (various) age characteristics, but unlike the Elkonin-Davydov project it does not restrict itself to well specified conceptual domains, opting instead to provide a variety of contents embodied in a variety of age-appropriate games and problem solving tasks in order to deal with the enormous variety of its participants.

While there is little doubt that 5th Dimensions more or less routinely succeed in creating genuine zones of proximal development for their participants, this project shares with the Change Laboratory severe challenges concerning how to describe and evaluate the dynamic, always-in-change characteristics of the activity systems it creates. Current social science norms expect unambiguous quantifiable descriptions such as those provided by standardized tests or measure of "output." But the voluntary nature of participation and the always-variable nature of implantations, dependent on their contexts, defy such standardized assessments. And, like the Change Laboratories, those who would use the 5th Dimension to challenge CH/AT theories turn to "real life" measures of effectiveness: Does the community provide resources to continue the collaborations between university and community? Do 5th Dimensions generalize from their institutions of origin? Are they taken up (generalized to) distinctly different social, cultural and economic circumstances? And if they are, do they remain "the same" despite the changes in content and context?

Taken as an ensemble, these three formative interventions indicate the fruitfulness of a theory-practice methodology using CH/AT principles. At the same time, each faces challenges to its own sustainability. Those challenges are, to a certain extent, specific to the problematic conditions that each was designed to address (e.g., poor education, difficulties in the organization of working life). But common across all three kinds of formative interventions is resistance that arises when their successes come into conflict with the larger social conditions that underlie the social problems they were designed to transcend. It is at this point that each intervention can be recognized as a form of critical theorizing about existing conditions in the societies they are a part of. Each reveals ways in which the explicit ideologies of modern industrialized bureaucratized societies espouse values (guaranteeing all children high quality education, creating effective, fulfilling environments for adult work) that they systematically undermine. Finally, each provides society with alternatives that satisfy their society's values, showing that while there is a way to solve explicitly stated social problems, there is, in a deep sense, a lack of will to do so.

Notes

1 There are also different branches of the Russian activity theory tradition, with adherents of Rubenshstein (Abulkhanova- Slavsakaya, 1989) claiming a more authentically Marxist theory of activity than that proposed by Leontiev and his students. Presumably those inspired by Rubenshtein would have their own tradition of designing environments for developing human life but we do not know that literature well and will restrict ourselves to the use of activity following from the tradition of Vygotsky, Luria, and Leontiev.

2 The Russian word, "deyatelnost" is generally translated from the German term, Tätigkeit.

3 "To understand behavior, one must understand the history of behavior," an aphorism that expresses this idea admirably, was attributed to the educational psychologist, Pavel Blonsky by Vygotsky (1978).

4 It is a mistake to interpret leading activities under the assumption that when a new leading activity begins to dominate, the prior ones disappear, as occurs in some treatments of classical stage theories. Old stages don't go

away, they shape and are shaped by future, emerging, constraints (Cole & Subbotsky, 1993; Griffin & Cole, 1984).

5 The Russian term, *obuchenie*, is often translated as education. We prefer the somewhat awkward translation, teaching/learning, because both sides of this interactive process are implicated in the Russian term. There is a more general term in Russian, *obrazovanie*, which is a closer equivalent to the English term, education.

6 The approach developed by Davydov and Elkonin has been given different names since its inception in the 1960's. Early on it was referred to as "teaching/learning based on content-related generalizations," then as "educational activity" and later as "developmental education."

References

Abulkhanova-Slavskaya, K. A. (1989). To Sergei Rubinstein birth centenary: A profile of Sergei Rubinstein's life and work. *Soviet Journal of Psychology, 10*(5), 16–28.

Ahonen, H., Engeström, Y., & Virkkunen, J. (2000). Knowledge management – the second generation: Creating competencies within and between work communities in the Competence Laboratory. In Y. Malhotra (Ed.), *Knowledge management and virtual organizations* (pp. 282–305). London: Idea Group Publishing.

Amano, K. (1999). Improvement of schoolchildren's reading and writing ability through the formation of linguistic awareness. In Y. Engeström, R. Mietinen, & R.-L. Punamäki (Eds.), *Perspectives on activity theory* (pp. 183–205). Cambridge: Cambridge University Press.

Blanton, W. E., Moorman, G. B., Hayes, B. A., & Warner, M. L. (1997). Effects of participation in the 5th Dimension on far transfer. *Journal of Educational Computing Research, 16*(4), 371–96.

Brown, K. B., & Cole, M. (2004). A utopian methodology as a tool for cultural and critical psychologies: Toward a positive critical theory. In M. Packer & M. Tappan (Eds.), *Cultural and critical perspectives on human development* (pp. 41–65). Albany, NY: SUNY Press.

Cole, M. (1996). *Cultural psychology: A once and future discipline*. Cambridge, MA: Harvard University Press.

Cole, M., & Subbotsky, E. (1993). The fate of stages past: Reflections on the heterogeneity of thinking from the perspective of cultural-historical psychology. *Schweizerische Zeitschrift fur Psychologie*, 52(2), 103–113.

Cole, M., & Distributed Literacy Consortium (2006). *Creating and sustaining alternative educational activities: Diversity as a tool for educational design*. New York: Russell Sage.

D'Andrade, R. (1984). Cultural meaning systems (1984). In R. A. Shweder & R. A. LeVine (Eds.), *Culture theory: Essays on mind, self, and emotion* (pp. 88–122). New York: Cambridge University Press.

Davydov, V. V. (1988a). Problems of developmental teaching. *Soviet Education*, 30(8), 15–97; 30(10), 3–77.

Davydov, V. V. (1988b). Problems of the child's mental development. *Soviet Education*, 30(8), 44–97.

Davydov, V. V. (1988c). The concept of developmental teaching. *Journal of Russian and East European Psychology*, 36(4), 11–36.

Elkonin, D. B. (1971). Toward the problem of stages in the mental development of the child. *Soviet Psychology*, 10, 538–553.

Engeström, Y. (1987). *Learning by expanding: An activity-theoretical approach to developmental research*. Helsinki: Orienta-Konsultit.

Engeström, Y. (1993). Developmental studies on work as a test bench of activity theory. In S. Chaiklin & J. Lave (Eds.), *Understanding practice: Perspectives on activity and context* (pp. 64–103). Cambridge: Cambridge University Press.

Engeström, Y. (1999). Learning by expanding: Ten years later. Introduction. *Lernen durch Expansion*. Marburg: BdWi- Verlag.

Engeström, Y. (2001). (Ed.), *Activity theory and social capital. Research Reports 5*. Helsinki: Center for Activity theory and Developmental Work Research, University of Helsinki.

Engeström, Y. (2005). *Developmental work research: Expanding activity theory in practice*. Berlin: Lehmanns Media.

Engeström, Y., Engeström, R., & Kerosuo, H. (2003). The discursive construction of collaborative care. *Applied Linguistics*, Special Issue 24(3), 286–315.

Engeström, Y., Engeström, R., & Suntio, A. (2002). From paralyzing myths to expansive action: Building computer-supported knowledge work into the curriculum from below. In G. Stahl (Ed.), *Computer support for collaborative learning: Foundations for a CSCL community* (pp. 318–324). Mahwah, NJ: Lawrence Erlbaum Associates.

Engeström, Y., Lompscher, J., & Rückriem, G. (Eds.). (2005). *Putting activity theory to work: Contributions from developmental work research*. Berlin: Lehmanns Media.

Engeström, Y., Miettinen, R., & Punamaki, R.-L. (Eds.). (1999). *Perspectives on activity theory*. Cambridge; New York: Cambridge University Press.

Engeström, Y., Pasanen, Toivainen, H., & Haavisto, V. (2005). Expansive learning as collaborative concept formation at work. In K. Yamazumi, Y. Engeström & H. Daniels (Eds.), *New learning challenges: Going beyond the industrial age system of school and work* (pp. 47–77). Osaka: Kansai University Press.

Engeström, Y., Virkkunen, J., Helle, M., Pihlaja, J., & Poikela, R. (1996). The Change laboratory as a tool for transforming work. *Lifelong Learning in Europe*, 1(2), 10–17.

Fine, G. A. (1987). *With the boys: Little League baseball and preadolescent culture.* Chicago: University of Chicago Press.

Gaskins, S. (1999). Children's daily lives in a Mayan village: A case study of culturally constructed roles and activities. In A. Goncu, (Ed.), *Children's engagement in the world: Sociocultural perspectives* (pp. 25–60). New York: Cambridge University Press.

Goodenough, W. H. (1994). Toward a working theory of culture. In R. Borofsky (Ed.), *Assessing cultural anthropology* (pp. 262–273). New York: McGraw-Hill.

Griffin, P., & Cole, M. (1984). Current activity for the future: The zo-ped. In B. Rogoff & J. V., Wertsch (Eds.), *Children's learning in the zone of proximal development: New directions for child development (No. 23)*. San Francisco: Jossey-Bass.

Hartman, H. J. (Ed.), (2001). *Metacognition in learning and instruction: theory, research and practice*. Boston: Kluwer Academic Publishers.

Hedegaard, M., & Chaiklin, S. (2005). *Radical-local teaching and learning: A cultural-historical approach*. Aarhus: Aarhus University Press.

Hedegaard, M., Chaiklin, S., & Jensen, U. J. (Eds.). (1999). *Activity theory and social practice*. Aarhus: Aarhus University Press.

Hedegaard, M., & Lompscher, J. (Eds.) (1999). *Learning activity and development*. Aarhus: Aarhus University Press.

Hiebert, J., Gallimore, R., Garnier, H., Given, K. B., Hollingsworth, H., Jacobs, J., et al. (2003). *Teaching mathematics in seven* countries: *Results from the TIMSS 1999 video study*. Washington, DC: U.S. Department of Education.

Ilyenkov, E. V. (1982). *The dialectics of the abstract and the concrete in Marx's 'Capital'*: Moscow: Progress.

Kaminski, P. H. (1994). Claiming our voices: A teaching/learning experiment. *Journal of Feminist Studies of Religion*, 10(1), 44–56.

Kaptelinin, V. (1996). Computer-mediated activity: Functional organs in social and developmental contexts. In B. Nardi. (Ed.), *Context and consciousness: Activity theory and human-computer interaction* (pp. 45–68). Cambridge, MA: The MIT Press.

Lee, C. D., Spencer, M. B., & Harpalani, V. (2003). "Every shut eye ain't sleep": Studying how people live culturally. *Educational Researcher*, 32(5) 6–13.

Leontiev, A. N. (1978). *Activity. Consciousness. Personality*. Englewood Cliffs, NJ: Prentice Hall.

Leontiev, A. N. (1981). The problem of activity in psychology. In J. V. Wertsch (Ed.), *The concept of activity in Soviet Psychology* (pp. 37–71). White Plains, NY: Sharpe.

Lotman, Y. M. (1989). The semiosphere. *Soviet Psychology*, 27(1), 40–61.

Luria, A. R. (1928). The problem of the cultural development of the child. *Journal of Genetic Psychology*, 35, 493–506.

Luria, A. R. (1932). *The nature of human conflicts*. New York: Liverwright.

Luria, A. R. (1979). *The making of mind*. Cambridge, MA: Harvard University Press.

Markova, A. K. (1979). *The teaching and mastery of language*. Armonk, NY: Sharpe.

Mayer, R. E., Schustack, M. W., & Blanton, W. E. (1999). What do children learn from using computers in an informal, collaborative setting? *Educational Technology*, 39(2), 27–31.

Nocon, H. D. (2004). Sustainability as process: Community education and expansive collaborative activity. Educational Policy, 18(5), 710–732.

Rogoff, B. (2003). *The cultural nature of human development*. New York: Oxford University Press.

Roth, W.-M., Hwang, S., Goulart, M. I. G., & Lee, Y. J. (2005). *Participation, learning, and identity: A dialectical perspective*. Berlin: Lehmanns Media.

Rubtsov, V. V. (1991). *Learning in children : Oorganization and development of cooperation actions*. New York: Nova Science Publishers.

Schmittau, J. (1993a). Connecting mathematical knowledge: A dialectical perspective. *Journal of Mathematical Behavior*, 12(2), 179–201.

Schmittau, J. (1993b). Vygotskian psychology and dialectical logic: A psychological-epistemological foundation for contemporary pedagogy. *The Review of Education*, 15, 13–20.

Schmittau, J. (2003). Cultural historical theory and mathematics education. In A. Kozulin, B. Gindis, S. Miller, & V. Ageyev. (Eds.), *Vygotsky's educational theory in cultural context* (pp. 225–245.). Cambridge, UK: Cambridge University Press.

Sherif, M., & Sherif, C. W. (1956). *An outline of social psychology*. New York: Harper.

van Der Veer, R., & Valsiner, J. (1991). *Understanding Vygotsky*. Oxford: Blackwell.

Vásquez, O. A. (2002). *La Clase Mágica: Imagining Optimal Possibilities in a Bilingual Community of Learners*. Mahwah, NJ: Erlbaum.

Virkkunen, J., & Ahonen, H. (2004). Transforming learning and knowledge creation on the shop floor. *International Journal of Human Resources Development and Management*, 4, 57–72.

Vygotsky, L. S. (1929). The problem of the cultural development of the child, II. *Journal of Genetic Psychology*, 36, 414–434.

Vygotsky, L. S. (1978). *Mind in society*. Cambridge, MA: Harvard University Press.

Vygotsky, L. S. (1927/1997). The historical meaning of the crisis in psychology: A methodological investigation. In R. W. Rieber & J. Wollock. (Eds.), *The collective works of L. S. Vygotsky, Vol. 3 : Problems of the theory and history of Psychology* (pp. 233–243). New York: Plenum.

Vygotsky, L. S. (1997). The problem of consciousness. In R. W. Rieber & J. Wollock (Eds.) *The collective works of L. S. Vygotsky, Vol. 3 : Problems of the theory and history of Psychology* (pp. 129–138). New York: Plenum.

Wertsch, J. V. (1985). *Vygotsky and the social formation of mind*. Cambridge, MA: Harvard University Press.

Wertsch, J. del Río, & Alvarez, A. (Eds.) (1995). *Sociocultural studies of mind*. New York: Cambridge University Press.

Yanchar, S. C. (2003). On methodological innovations in imagery research: Beyond the learning experiment? *Journal of Mental Imagery*, 27 (3 & 4), 258–261.

Zinchenko, V. P. (1985). Vygotsky's ideas about units for the study of mind. In J. Wertsch.

(Ed.), *Culture, communication, and cognition: Vygotskian perspectives.* New York, NY: Cambridge University Press.

Zuckerman, G. A. (1994). The child's initiative in building up cooperation: the key to problems of children's independence. In J. J. F. ter Laak, P. G. Heymans, & A. Podol'skij. (Eds.), *Developmental tasks: Towards a cultural analysis of human development* (pp. 125–140). Dordrecht: Kluwer Academic.

Zuckerman, G. A. (2003). The learning activity in the first years of schooling: The developmental path toward reflection. In A. Kozulin, B. Gintis, V. S. Ageev, & S. Miller. (Eds.), *Vygotsky's educational theory in cultural context.* New York: Cambridge University Press.

Zuckerman, G. A. (2005). The D. B. Elkonin-V. V. Davydov system as a resource for raising the competence of Russian schoolchildren. *Problems of Psychology,* (4) 84–95

CHAPTER 24

Money as a Cultural Tool Mediating Personal Relationships

Child Development of Exchange and Possession

Toshiya Yamamoto and Noboru Takahashi

In this chapter, the process through which children develop within cultural and historical contexts, while pragmatically participating in the concrete human relationships surrounding them and forming their life-world, is investigated from the process of appropriating money as a cultural tool. When dealing with the issues of money and possessions, a review of prior research shows that those issues are not framed in the scope of the concept of *homo economics*, the individualistic internal knowledge, and the relationships in terms of market exchange. In terms of sociology and anthropology of the legal systems, the tangible findings of our research on the pocket money given to the children in Japan, Korea, China, and Vietnam are mainly employed to demonstrate that the sense of possession can be established as multiple consciousness of relationships. Within these relationships, the sense of possession incorporates more than a subject. Any human being who lives in a market- and exchanges-based society leads his or her life integrating the logic of market exchange into the life-world which is based on non-market exchange relationships.

Any discussion of the significance of money as a mediational tool that children master should not be isolated from the formation of such non-market exchange relationships. Based on these, the fundamental structure that makes those non-market exchange relationships and market exchange relationships possible is the set of wider interpersonal relationships unified by the cultural psychological concept of mediation.

Beyond the Premises of Homo Economics

People live, having different desires. Those desires vary and seemingly have no end. Meanwhile, the means of satisfying those desires – especially material needs – involve use of goods and services, which are the objects of such desires. How can those almost unlimited human desires be satisfied with limited resources? This is the fundamental issue of economics.

Today, the most influential school in economics would be the neo-classical school.

The neo-classical economics is based on two premises (Uzawa, 1989). First, each individual can use or exchange the scarce resources such as goods and services which he or she possesses in the most desired way, following his or her subjective value criteria (utility). Second, the fundamental economic agent that comprises the economics is the abstract *homo economics*, and each individual selectively acts rationally based on the subjective value criteria, which are expressed by his or her preference.

As a matter of course, the premise of *homo economics* who take actions for maximizing utility (homo economics as a rational utility maximizer) has been a target of controversy (e.g., Lea 1994). In general, psychologists disagree about humans as rational beings. More precisely, they demonstrate that the rationality in the narrow sense of the term is not viable – as the actions that are against such rationality are legitimate. Nevertheless, their arguments do not always mesh with those of economists, because, for many economists, rationality is not substantive but merely means the logical premise, which is set up for the purposes of economic theory (e.g., Friedman 1953).

Children and Economics

Experimental studies about children's economic activities have been carried out from the viewpoints of economics and economic psychology. That is, those studies were conducted to find out if children would behave as the logic of economics assumes – in other words, how "rationally" children would behave in economic decision making. For example, the bargaining behaviors that children exhibited in dictator games and ultimatum games disclosed that children take actions that are similar with those of adults (Harbaugh, Krause, & Liday, 2003; Murnighan & Saxon, 1998). Those researches demonstrate that children behave rationally even when they are young, and their knowledge becomes more consistent with age, improving the level of rationality in economic decision making.

However, children's economic activities in daily life appear not to be based on the rationality. The ethnographic study about marbles played by children in England (Webley & Lea, 1993a) indicates those children exchange marbles, following the scarcity-based principle of exchange, while intentionally carrying out disproportionate exchanges, such as giving marbles as a plead of friendship to a new classmate. Moreover, various kinds of phenomena of "treats" are observed among children in Korea (Oh, Pian, Yamamoto, Takahashi, Sato, Takeo, Choi, & Kim, 2005). These studies imply that the social function of establishing and maintaining interpersonal relationships and the economic activities are closely tied and children take actions based on the principles that deviate from the rule of *homo economics*. Therefore, the valid research strategy for us is not to accept the premise of the rationality of economic activities for finding its presence (or absence) in children. Instead, we inquire how children become independent from parents and develop interpersonal relationships in different cultural environments – all united by economic nature of human activities. From these, the first maxim of developmental psychology for money is derived as follows.

The first maxim: Developmental psychology for money is not predicated on *homo economics*. Rather, it inquires for the foundation for the structure of human relationships that make exchange and possession possible.

Beyond Children as *Individuals*

When they look at the relationship between children and money, developmental psychologists have been approaching most systematically their understanding of money and various economic concepts as an issue of the knowledge which is established within individuals. Particularly, concerning economic knowledge and understanding about a function of money, psychologists interview children, and, from children's responses, they find out children's knowledge, and their way of reasoning is classified into several stages based on the Piagetian framework (Berti & Bombi, 1988; Sevón & Weckstrom, 1989; Strauss, 1952).

Concerning the understanding about individual economic phenomena, the domains such as the understanding about selling and buying prices have been analyzed most systematically (Furnham & Cleare, 1988; Jahoda, 1979). Jahoda (1979) found out three stages based on the results of the role-playing and interviews with children concerning selling and buying and an income source for a shop clerk. Beyond the merely descriptive analysis, Jahoda links the ability to consolidate various kinds of knowledge into a consistent system with Piaget's cognitive development stages. Inter-domain conflicts and equilibration engender a higher level of understanding.

Similarly, with many of Piagetian tasks, cultural differences are found among these kinds of understanding (Jahoda, 1983; Leiser, Sevón, & Lévy, 1990; Ng, 1983). Jahoda (1983) demonstrates that Zimbabwean children (who do not have direct experiences of selling and buying commodities but see their parents make and sell commodities) understand the relationship between selling and buying and a shop clerk's wage as well as its system more quickly than European children do. Likewise, children in Hong Kong where economic activities are bustling understand banking systems more quickly than Western children do (Ng, 1983). Those facts indicate that children's understanding about economic systems neither exists as architectonic knowledge that children build up independently from their life-worlds, nor separates from their life-worlds.

Another theme in which understanding about economic events cannot be separated from children's real life is the causes of poverty and wealth and children's attitudes toward them (Dittmar, 1996; Emler & Dickinson, 1985, 2004; Furnham, 1982; Leahy, 1981; Leiser & Ganin, 1996). Such studies roughly have two theoretical directions. One direction is based on Bourdieu's argument on social strata reproduction (Bourdieu, 1979). According to Bourdieu, social strata reproduce themselves through categorization of consumption style differences and social worlds as well as internalization of value systems. Cultural assets that comprise children's life-worlds differ with the social stratum or culture. Under such circumstances, children build up their thinking about the social world.

Another direction is influenced by the social constructivism (e.g., Moscovici 2001). Based on Moscovici's theory of social representation (see also Duveen, Chapter 26, this volume), understanding about the causes of being rich and poor and the attitudes toward them are neither the knowledge which exists within individuals nor the substance which exists externally. Rather, they are socially constructed and shared as predominant statement. From this viewpoint, comparisons among social strata and cultures become inevitable. In fact, research that intends to explain the causes of poverty and wealth find out the differences among strata on one hand and the potency of predominant statement in the culture beyond strata on another hand. According to Furnham (1982) in which interviews about the causes of poverty and wealth were held with students in England, the relatively rich public school students and the state school students who are financially below the middle class, public school children tend to attach weight to individualistic explanation about the causes of poverty while state school children attach weight to society-conscious explanation. On the other hand, according to the study of American junior and senior high school students, children in any economic status give reasons such competence of and efforts by individuals instead of social factors, while children who belong to lower economic status tend to be more positive about the possibility of eliminating poverty thanks to social changes (Leahy, 1981). According to the comparative researches conducted in 15 countries which mainly consist of European countries, children who belong to the middle-class strata accept present situations as a whole, and children in a more individualistic country (Israel – except for the kibbutz) give value to individualistic explanation about the causes of the rich and poor, while children in Yugoslavia which was a socialist country give explanation focusing on social structure (Leiser & Ganin, 1996; Leiser, Sevón, & Lévy, 1990).

Based on those results, in one aspect, children's understanding about economic systems could be handled as the knowledge that is built up internally within children, but, evidently, it is not independent from the societies and cultures in which children grow, and its analysis should be carried out holistically. From these, the second maxim of developmental psychology for money is derived as follows.

The second maxim: Developmental psychology for money does not focus on the process for a child of acquiring internal knowledge as an individual. Rather, developmental psychology for money discusses such knowledge is built up in association with the worlds that children experiences in life.

Possessions and Money Beyond Market Economy

From the viewpoint of market economy, money is neutral in the following two senses. First, money can be exchanged for any equivalent. Second, money autonomously exists away from any specific human relationships. Thanks to this neutrality of money, possessions also can be arranged in one-dimensional order by money. In other words, meanings based on specific human relationships can be abstracted from possessions so that they can be neutral.

However, money and possessions bear polysemy, which cannot be described only by a one-dimensional value structure. In our life, we find many things hold "subjective" values and those values differ from market values they have (Belk, 1988, 1991). The characteristics indicative of possessions having "subjective" values can be summarized as follows (Belk, 1991)

1. unwillingness to sell for market value,
2. willingness to buy with little regard for price,

3. nonsubstitutibility,
4. unwillingness to discard,
5. feelings of elation/depression due to object, and
6. personification (such as giving a name to an object).

Memory-laden objects including gifts, family photographs, souvenirs and mementos, heirlooms, antiques, and monuments are typical examples (e.g., Belk 1991; Dittmar 1992). We can find numerous examples that indicate possessions carry subjectively important meaning for individuals. For the aged, roles are given to possessions in providing control and mastery – moderating emotions, cultivating the self, symbolizing ties with others, constituting a concrete history of one's past (Kemptner, 1989). On the other hand, loss of possessions due to theft or disaster accompanies strong sense of loss and depressing feeling (Belk, 1988). After all, as theoreticians such as James and Simmel pointed out, those of mine (possessions) are extensions of self as well. "...a man's Self is the sum total of all that he CAN call his, not only his body and his psychic powers, but his clothes, and his house, his wife and children, his ancestors and friends, his reputation and works, his lands, and yacht and bank-account. All these things give him the same emotions." (James, 1890, pp. 291–292) "material property is, so to speak, an extension of the ego, and any interference with our property is, for this reason, felt to be a violation of the person." (Simmel, 1950, p. 322) In the case of children, their structures of self and their ways of perceiving their possessions as their extensions differ from those of adults (Furnham & Jones, 1987; Yamamoto, 1991a; Yamamoto & Pian, 1996). When elementary school children are asked if their parents can control their possessions, children in lower grades tend to give more positive replies. This tendency is found regardless if they live in European countries such as England (Furnham & Jones, 1987) or in Asian countries such as Japan (Yamamoto, 1991a) and China (Yamamoto & Pian, 1996). Additionally, children in higher grade levels tend to reply that they have discretion to determine who can use their belongings. This tendency also can be found in both Europe and Asia. However, as described later, the structure of self, in other words, interpersonal relationships, and its structure have culture-specific characteristics and thus cognition of mine greatly varies.

Although people have the strong notion that money is free from specific human relationships and abstract, they keep away from using it in some cases. A typical example is money as a gift (Webley, Lea, & Portalska, 1983). In the case of a gift, a sender gives an item for which the sender made efforts in making or selecting it, and a receiver accepts it. In the specific relationship between a sender and a receiver, a gift exists as a symbol which represents a specific effort (or goodwill) of a specific person (Csikszentmihalyi & Rochberg-Halton, 1981). Money transposes the value built on a specific individual relation and/or experience onto the criteria used for all other items and grade such values, therefore, money is shied. The problem of gifts has been discussed extensively in anthropology (e.g., Godlier 1999; Mauss, 1954). As discussed later, gifts are not simply based on the relationships between individuals, but form by themselves a system with norms within and between groups. In this sense, the interrelationship among gifts, exchange, and money should be understood in a broader context.

In addition to its use as a gift, money is avoided to use as a return for the goods or help given by neighbors (Oh, personal communication; Webley & Lea, 1993b). In Korean farm villages, when help is given by a neighbor to a resident, it is common to give help to the neighbor in return. But, if the resident is a part-time farmer, giving help by labor becomes difficult. In that case, some start to pay for the labor in return. This also means such family is losing its role as a full member of the community of mutual collaboration (Oh, personal communication). This kind of exchange is not carried out based on market-economy principles, but based on communal exchange rules (Mills & Clark, 1982). Although money is avoided in some cases due to its neutrality, it is not neutral (versatile in its use) all the time. According to the excerpts from Webley, Lea, and Portalska (1983), European currencies were usually used to purchase ordinary goods and native money was used for purchasing wives in West Africa. From the end of the nineteenth century through the beginning of the twentieth century, in America, income earned by labor of a household wife in a lower economic stratum was regarded as the extension of her housekeeping, and the income was appropriated for the purchase of daily necessities, while her husband income was used as the money which circulates in market economy, such as an investment (Zelizer, 1989). Two important points here are (1) money does not hold the neutrality which allows it to be exchanged with for anything, but has specific application and specific meaning in some cases, and (2) such meaning is not fixed but varies historically and culturally. From these, the third maxim of developmental psychology for money is derived as follows.

The third maxim: Money and possessions are not the issues that can be grasped within and explained by a neutral money-goods exchange system in market economy. Rather, they should be understood in the context of the cultures and histories of the societies where people are living.

Pocket Money as a Research Tool to Investigate Money for Children

Many school-aged children in Western countries, and Eastern Asia, get pocket money (or allowance) from their parents as payment for household chores or simply as an entitlement and buy something they need (Furnham, 1999, in the UK; Mortimer, Dennehy, Lee, & Finch, 1994, in the US; Furnham & Kirkcaldy, 2000, in Germany; Lassarres, 1996, in France; Piang & Yamamoto, 2001, in China; Yamamoto, Takahashi, Sato, Piang, Oh, & Kim, 2003, in Korea; Yamamoto & Piang, 2000, in Japan). In order to learn the relationship between money and children in the society with an advanced money economy, an analysis of their ways of receiving and using pocket money serves as an effective clue. Nevertheless, many of previous researches have been descriptive, focusing on the age when children start to receive pocket money, the amount they receive, if that is periodical, for what it is used, and so on.

From 2003 through 2005, we carried out the questionnaire surveys over children age 10, 13, and 16 in Japan, Korea, and Vietnam (Takahashi, 2005; Takeo, 2005). Concerning the versatility of pocket money they receive, Japanese and Korean children rated the use of pocket money for a CD, a movie, Karaoke, or an arcade game favorably more than Vietnamese children, which apparently reflects the social and economic differences. However, Korean children rated the use for treating a friend to a snack or a meal, or lending it to a friend favorably more than Japanese and Vietnamese children, which cannot be explained by economic conditions alone. As Oh et al. (2005) indicates in their analysis on treats in Korea, treats have a wide variation in Korea, and the aforementioned result reflects the importance of such treats for maintaining peer relationship.

The items which they buy with their pocket money can be classified in Japan by age as follows: (1) those which parents buy when children are young, but children buy with their pocket money when they grow old (e.g., sweets, snacks, and drinks), (2) those which parents pay regardless of children's age (e.g., buying books which are necessary to do homework, and paying traveling expenses), and (3) those which none pay when children are young, but children pay when they grow old (e.g., Karaoke, buying audio CDs, and buying snacks for friends). This reflects the change in children's commitment to their societies and accompanies the changes of their relationships with parents. This does not mean a simple story of children's independence from their parents. Rather, it means the practical meaning of pocket money for children changes, bearing inseparable relationships with their parents and peers and containing such changes.

Based on the three maxims which have been introduced, in the environments which carry social and cultural meanings (maxim 2), children learn how to use money as the tool which has specific meaning to a subject (maxim 3). Additionally, it comes into existence based on human relationships, such as culture-specific parent-child or peer relationships (maxim 1).

From these, the fourth maxim of developmental psychology for money is derived as follows.

Although money is regarded as a neutral tool in market economy, it is a cultural tool in the societies of concrete human relationships with their own culture and history. Children gradually appropriate the meaning of money as a cultural tool and participate in the society through its mediation.

Money and Cultural Development of Self: From Perspective of Possession

We have discussed the limitation of describing human beings as *homo economics*, who have internal economic knowledge as individuals and money as impersonalized neutral one, which functions within money-goods exchange system in market economy. In the following two sections, referring the findings of our studies and related notions of sociology of law and anthropology, we discuss the possibility to expand our theoretical framework.

The legal notion of modern ownership is conceptualized based on the basic principles that mine is at my discretion, and the notion is configured as the impersonalized neutral title, which does not depend on any specific relationships nor personality. According to sociology of law, however, the notion of modern ownership is never universal (Kawashima, 1981). First, even among the adults who live in market-economy society, only few understand the concept of modern ownership correctly, and many of their possession behaviors do not follow it. Even in the world of adults, the concept of modern ownership is normative concept for settling legal disputes and does not sufficiently explain actual behaviors of individuals. Second, the concept of modern ownership itself is the one that is specific to modern society, and it was established historically when the modern market-economy society rolled out.

As sociologists of law emphasize (e.g., Matsumura 2005), the phenomenon of possession becomes viable only when the control over an object is accepted by others (Yamamoto, 1991b). In other words, it is comprised of relationships among three elements at least: a subject of possession, an object for possession, and others (Issacs, 1967). Additionally, when the transcendental element, such as parents, authorities, and laws, which mediates those relationships normatively becomes stably viable, possession establishes as an institution (Yamamoto, 1997, 2000). Therefore, we should understand possession as the multiple consciousness of relationships among subjects over objects, and thus the meaning of and behavior toward possessions vary when their relationships vary by society.

Children do not have the notion that their possessions are completely at their discretion (Furnham & Jones, 1987, in England; Yamamoto, 1991a, in Japan; Yamamoto & Pian, 1996, in China): When parents ask to dispose their possessions, younger students cannot refuse their intervention (Yamamoto, 1992 Yamamoto & Pian, 1996). Children's pocket money is also a part of their possessions, and they usually accept the control by adults while using and managing it. We can say that their consciousness of pocket money as possessions is mediated by the adults' will. This is rooted in the nature of possession in general as multiple consciousness of relationships (Yamamoto, 1992). Its consciousness differs in children's age, family settings, region, and culture, and these differences determine the direction of the development of self of children in the specific cultural contexts. The investigation on the content of this multiple consciousness of relationships is one of our major tasks for understanding children's development within cultural and historical contexts.

Though children's understanding of possession is different from the legal concept of possession in the modern low, they do have and develop their own consciousness of possession. In fact, children before age 2 both in western and eastern societies already begin to respect other's control over some objects such as toys their peers have (Yamamoto, 1991b; Bakeman & Brownlee, 1982). In addition, they will refuse other's intervention toward their possessions in some contexts: In Japan, more than half of the second grade children in elementary school consider that "I do not need to follow my friend's opinion in disposing my belongings if I have no fault" (Yamamoto, 1991a), and many reply "my teacher should not restrict the use of my pocket money". Their criteria of judgment change, depending not only on who makes intervention but also on what is the object for possession. In Japan and Korea as well as among Koreans in China, parental intervention and control over children's possessions is stronger in the case of pocket money than other belongings (Yamamoto, 1992; Yamamoto & Pian, 2000).

While children's judgment on the right of the control of their belongings varies by the other person and possessions, it changes in different cultures as well. Japanese elementary school children think differently about the right of disposition, depending on whether the other person is their parents or their friends; they often acknowledge parental intervention though not the intervention from friends. Such difference is smaller in the case of Han children in Beijing in China (Yamamoto & Pian, 1996). About 50% of Chinese Korean children in Jinlin Sheng accept the right of their teachers' intervention about the usage of their pocket money, while very few Japanese children accept the intervention – a finding that remains the same from elementary school children to senior high school students (Pian & Yamamoto, 2005). Children's acceptance of parental intervention greatly varies by region and tribe, and the pattern of age-derived change also varies (Pian & Yamamoto, 2005).

Possession for children is not the neutral or impersonalized concept, which is included in modern ownership, but the practical understanding for handling real possessions in their life-world, while incorporating intentions of others, such as parents. Their consciousness about possession reflects concrete human relationships in each culture, and it changes with children's age, corresponding with the structural change of their life-world. It represents the developmental process to be adults in each culture, and therefore it is the cultural development of self.

Money and Children's Life-World

In market-economy society, money is used as an abstract marker of value and serves as a general tool for exchange. But when we analyze real exchanging behaviors, we should not understand the notion of money and exchange in such a narrow sense. Our exchanging activities in daily economic life like shopping or wage labor are included in the concept of market exchange, which are a dominant style for the transfer of possessions in market-economy society. The principle of exchange in market economy is characterized as impersonalized exchange, in that any given two possessors of goods and money mutually and instantaneously transfer their equivalent possessions. On the contrary, according to the discussion of exchange in anthropology, the dominant way to transfer possessions in so called a primitive society is based on the specific personalized bond without being mediated by money and its style is one-sided gift and the like, which is different from this kind of market exchange in terms of quality.

Exchange is the resource transfer among people or/and groups, and gift theory of Mauss (1954) and economic anthropology of Polanyi (1977) analyzed the phenomenon of various pattern of resource transfers in human society, including exchange mediated by money in broader perspectives. These studies tell us the existence of various patterns of exchange, which are different from the one in the modern market, as well as the fact that a system of market exchange only has a limited place in those historical and cultural variations of exchange. Several basic concepts in anthropology such as the

obligation to reciprocate (Mauss, 1954), reciprocity, redistribution and market exchange (Polanyi, 1977), should be useful to explain the various resource transfer principles and the quality of social integration based on those principles.

The principles of non-market exchange have an important place even in modern market society so that many behaviors of adults in the matured market-economy societies are controlled by these principles. Concrete human relationships or bond both at home, which is a fundamental setting for one's happiness, and in workplace, which is the main field of one's socio-economic activities, are greatly influenced by the principles of non-market exchange like reciprocity which is advocated by anthropology (see previous sections). We cannot exchange money directly with love, friendship, or trust. That is true for national welfare and education systems governed by nation in which money is spending for supporting their life or education. Money functions as a mediator that supports human relationship or communities based on the non-market exchange principle. Therefore, we should understand "the process of appropriating money as a cultural tool" for children who mainly live in the non-market-economy setting, such as home and school, is the processes of generating life-world based on non-market exchange principles while integrating market exchange principles.

School-aged children begin to understand basic concepts needed in market economy such as selling and buying (Jahoda, 1979), and banking (Ng, 1983) in spite of there being cultural differences of the developmental speed. But even toddlers show basic understanding of exchange: Children in China and Japan around age two begin to take exchange-like behaviors and to try to resolve or prevent conflicts with friends (Yamamoto & Zhang, 1997). Under the circumstances where local communities steadily protect children like in Cheju Island in Korea, some two-year-old children go for shopping alone (Yamamoto et al., 2003). Of course, they may not understand "shopping" as money-goods exchange in market economy but understand it as mere barter. However, they do establish their life-world while using money as a cultural tool, and begin to make relationships with others through exchange.

Then, what do children learn about money in their life-world and what do parents desire them to learn? Parents of school-aged children in Western countries and Eastern Asia give pocket money to them. Main reason to give pocket money and their way of intervention vary in different cultures (Takahashi, 2005; Yamamoto & Pian, 2001). For example, Japanese parents in a provincial city, Nara, sometimes cited educational reasons, such as "to help children learn how to use money correctly" (Yamamoto, 1992). Meanwhile, the Korean parents who live in China tend to mainly cite practical purposes such as expenses for school busing and lunch for children (Yamamoto & Pian 2001). In both cases, their main concern is if children use their pocket money properly, which means the issue is to learn the cultural and ethical meaning of money, and not "how to use money well to exchange." When asked the adequacy of various kinds of use of money such as buying a snack, buying a meal away from home, and paying for tuition, children's evaluations considerably varied depending on their culture, and the pattern will moderately change with age. This means that they do not perceive pocket money as a merely neutral exchange tool but attach meaning as the tool for accomplishing a specific purpose (Yamamoto & Pian, 2000, in Japan and Chinese Korean; Sato, Takahashi, & Takeo, 2005, in Japan and Korea). And the pattern of evaluations is almost shared by both parents and children (Yamamoto & Pian, 2001). We are able to find the cultural meaning of money in this pattern, which generating children's life-world, and the pattern is one of the most important aspects of the meaning of money as a cultural tool.

Concerning the cultural meaning of money, *ogori* (treats)[1] are the topic that discloses remarkable cultural differences in the East Asia. *Ogori* means the behavior of paying for others and the contrary concept of *warikan* (so called "going Dutch"): For example, a child went to shop with her friend and bought some sweets for both herself and her friend. Another child invites his friends to a restaurant at his birthday and paid their fee.

From region to region, the extent and frequency of *ogori* as well as evaluation of *ogori* based on a norm vary. Japanese take the most negative attitudes against *ogori* among children among East Asian countries (e.g., Oh 2003). Contrarily, the Korean families in China consider buying foods and sweets for a friend is better than using money for himself or herself (Yamamoto & Pian, 2001). Additionally, in Korea as well, importance is placed on *ogori* as affirmative actions, and patterns of *ogori* among children is diversified, encouraging children to treat each other in various ways (Oh et al., 2005). Such difference between Japanese and the Chinese Korean cannot be explained well by the development of individualism due to the development of market economy. For example, the minority group members in China, the Tai farmers in Yunnan are deemed to be the most collectivist and the progress of market economy in their villages is deemed to be slower than other regions. However, splitting a bill seems to be popular in their relationships just like in Japan, and they are negative toward *ogori* even though they do not deny *ogori*, which implies continuity with the neighboring country, Vietnam (Yamamoto, 2006).

These cultural differences also correspond with the differences in positioning *ogori* based the relationships among adults. Therefore, it can be deemed that adults hand such meaning down on to children, and through this patrimony, adults bequeath to children the cultural configuration for building friendships.

Appropriation of money is neither the acquisition of mere abstract exchange technique nor the acquisition of understanding of money as an impersonalized, neutral mediator for exchange. On the contrary, appropriation of money is to master cultural meaning of money as a medium of making and maintaining human relationships.

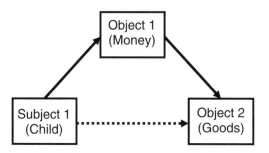

Figure 24.1. Money Mediated Relationship between Subject and Object.

Expanded Structure of Mediation

Based on these discussions, the fundamental structure of the multiple consciousness of relationships, which contains the personality-based relationship with historicity and cultural nature, will be illustrated as the "expanded structure of mediation," for the purpose of defining the building unit of our analysis. Due to the nature of psychology, what is discussed here is the structure of the life-world, which is represented by the viewpoint of an individual. Therefore, we analyze an individual, which is simultaneously emerged with the relationships, as a major objective for our analysis.

As our discussion about children and money indicate, money functions as a practical tool for children to be involved in transfer of their possessions. When this is interpreted that children work on commercial goods as an object using money as the tool, this can be depicted by Vygotsky's triangle (Vygotsky, 1997) as shown in Figure 24.1. However, in this kind of illustration of mediational relationship, another subject cannot be represented, although she or he is always involved in when a child does his or her shopping, that is, such illustration misses the other party in inter-individual relationship. This missing relationship can be expressed when Object in Figure 24.1 is replaced with Subject 2 (e.g., shop clerk). Additionally, the relationship that represents viable exchange between money and commercial goods can be expressed when those two are integrated like Figure 24.2.

This structure of mediational relationships represents more than one subject in the structure, which Vygotsky's triangle cannot depict successfully. The child and the shop clerk are mutually mediated in playing dual roles of the subject and receiver in the passive and active relationships. Cole (1996) incorporates the relationship of those two into his argument about mediation. He overlayed the triangle structure of mediation which an adult interprets the world mediated by text on the mediational relationship by which a child is committed to the world using the adult as a mediator, and thus he depicted the scheme that the child him or herself obtains the new interpretation of his or her world mediated by text.

We should not forget Bakhtin, who first placed importance on another mediational relationship about the commitment to the world through mediation by others as the true nature of human mental activities, using the concept of voice (Bakhtin, 1981). Wertsch (1998) gave attention to this argument and tried to develop Vygotsky's idea. In addition to the simple planar mediational relationship, he tried to approach toward the power relationship structure, which is found in a conversation between a teacher and a student.

There exist two types of mediational relationship discussed here. One is the object-mediated relation (S1-O-S2), where a subject uses an object as a mediator to

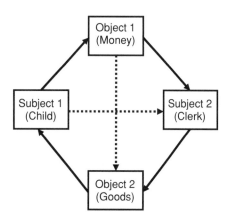

Figure 24.2. Schematic Representation of Exchange as Dual-Mediated Behavior.

work on another subject. Another is the subject-mediated relation, where a subject uses another subject as a mediator (S_1-S_2-O) to work on an object, or vice versa (S_2-S_1-O). Then, we comprehend that Figure 24.2 indicates these two types of mediational relationship are structured, accompanied by another complication. In other words, a subject(S_1) uses an object(O_2) as a mediator to work on another subject(S_2) and this subject(S_2) is mediated by the object(O_1) which represents the S_1's willingness and works on to him or her(S_1) using an another object(O_2) as a mediator (S_1-O_1-S_2-O_2-S_1). This dual-mediated behavior, in which object-mediated and subject-mediated behaviors are integrated, become viable for a child age around two, and this makes exchange behaviors possible (Yamamoto, 1997).

However, this mediational structure is not sufficient to understand the pocket money of children. For example, the relationship of *ogori* among children is not possible only in the world of children. Willingness of parents works on it, which has influence like norms over children in their building up relationships with other children. When the third element is added as the mediational element functioning as norms, we can obtain the minimum necessary elements to depict children's social behaviors, and this is schematized as "expanded structure of mediation" (Figure 24.3). As shown in this figure, society does not become viable only with bilateral relationship but becomes viable with trilateral relationship, incorporating the third party which transcends two parties (Imamura, 2000), and there, institutionalized inter-individual relationship can come into view (Yamamoto, 1997).

Engeström's expanded triangles (Engeström, 1987 – see also Chapter 17, this volume) integrates this transcendental norm-like elements to evolve Vygotsky's mediational relationship. As the feature of these triangles, it practically arranges different ontological aspects such as a group and an individual. Compared with these, our scheme indicates the basic structure where

an individual works on an object or the other through mediation of the transcendental third element, and behavior of an individual necessarily generates a group in each time. Our intension is not to draw a social system itself, but to draw the relational individual who practically participates in a social system and dynamically generates, maintains and changes the social system.

As discussed so far, the expanded structure of mediation contains various kinds of mediational relationship, and no elements become viable as the fixed substance which is independent from others. Any element becomes viable in interdependent relationship while containing the overall features of such relationship or serving as a mediator. The structure of a subject for possession and exchange becomes visible only in such mediational relationship. Additionally, the mediational relationship like this always wobbles and becomes viable dynamically as certain gestalt when necessary, and exists as the mutually mediational relationships between the two subjects.

In conjunction with the establishment of this gestalt, the third element dynamically generates when necessary as the element which serves as a mediator to mediate these mediational relationships as a whole. And when the element appears steadily as the regulator which regulates respective subjects, we can find a relatively stable system there. The will of parents, rules, and consciousness of norms fit this third element in researches on pocket money. Using this expanded structure of mediation, we can sort out the noteworthy points in analyzing the pocket money phenomenon.

Conclusion

In this chapter, the basic framework has been proposed to discuss the relationship between children and money in developmental psychology researches. At first, through the review of previous researches, we summarized the following four maxims of developmental psychology for money:

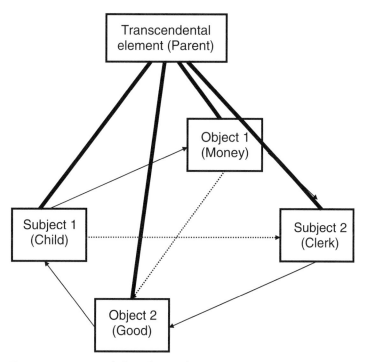

Figure 24.3. Expanded Mediational Structure as Representing Child's Shopping.

First, it is not predicated on the *homo economics* as rational economic decision-makers. But, rather, it inquires for the precondition for it, that is, the foundation for the structure of human relationships which make exchanges and possessions possible. Second, in analyzing children's understanding and knowledge of money, such understanding and knowledge should be always discussed in association with children's life-world, instead of separating from it. Third, it is not predicated on a neutral money-goods exchange system in market economy, but should be analyzed in the social context with its own cultures and histories. Fourth, based on those three points, developmental psychology for money inquires how children would appropriate money as a cultural tool and change their participation in their societies through the appropriation and, additionally, how they would form new culture through implementation of such activities, instead of inquiring how children would understand money as a neutral

tool which functions in a market economy system.

Next, based on the results of the interviews and questionnaire surveys we so far conducted over children in the Eastern Asia, characteristics of money for children were sorted out and the significance of the researches on money for children was discussed from a broader viewpoint which treats the problem of possessions and gifts as well. Money that children possess cannot be differentiated by dichotomy such as mine or not mine, as the concept of possession in the modern law system intends. Rather, it belongs to "me" and "my parents" simultaneously, and the distinction dynamically swings between the two extreme. While the structure of the dynamic parent-child relationship differs by culture, the selves of children which are peculiar to respective cultures are formed. Second, money for children does not represent the neutral tool in market economy which can be converted into any kinds of commercial goods equivalent with the value of money, but it is the culturally valued tool whose applications are prescribed and reflect norms of parents, which are peculiar to respective cultures. Based on those discussions, the following conclusion was drawn: Our society which formed itself by mediation of money cannot always be explained simply by a market economy framework. Rather, as a backdrop to it, the life-worlds whose characteristics vary by cultures exist, and not only children but also adults live in those life-worlds. Therefore, money as a mediational tool does not represent a mere neutral one but a cultural tool.

To conclude, the schema which serves as a building block for analysis was proposed to appropriately describe the mediator-like characteristics of money as a cultural tool. This schema is described by the rectangle which is comprised of two triangles, each of which represents the mediational relationship for a subject when reaching out to an object (commercial goods) by mediation of money and the mediational relationship for the subject when concurrently working on to another subject via money. With this, various situations related with money can be described in terms of relationships among a subject, an object, another subject, and a mediational tool without confining themselves to those of shopping. Additionally, in order to illustrate that this entire mediational structure is controlled by the cultural norm which is another mediational argument, an expanded mediational structure was proposed. This schema of pyramid-shaped mediational structure serves as an effective tool for analyzing the children-money relationships, and, at the same time, for cultural psychology of differences, this schema can be used as a tool for analyzing development of individual children without isolating the individuals themselves from social relationship. Cultural psychology of differences provides an arena where the researchers from different cultures collaborate and study the relationships between money and the children of mutual cultures, and it is dynamic and generative attempts through analyses of such collaborative researches to internally describe the human relation structures of different cultures as well as the cultural norms which make them possible, while externalizing those cultural differences.

Note

1 Treats can be translated into "han-teog" in Korean and "ogori" in Japanese, but the nuance of the words are different. "Han-teog" usually means treating dinner between adults, and does not include everyday practice of treating foods and sweets between children, though the latter is frequently observed and is positively evaluated by Korean people. On the other hand, "ogori" is used for both situations, while the attitude toward "ogori" for Japanese people is relatively negative. We neutrally use the word "ogori" in this chapter for the practice of treating in general.

References

Bakeman, R., and Brownlee, J. R. (1982). Social rules governing object conflicts in toddlers and preschoolers. In Rubin, K. H. and Ross, H. S., (Eds.), *Peer Relationships and Social Skills in Childhood* (pp. 99–111). Springer-Verlag.

Bakhtin, M. M. (1981).*The Dialogic Imagination: Four Essays by M. M. Bakhtin.*, (Ed.), M. Holoquist; trans. C. Emerson and M. Holoquist. Austin: University of Texas Press.

Belk, R. W. (1988). Possessions and the extended self. *Journal of Consumer Research* 15: 139–168.

Belk, R. W. (1991). The ineluctable mysteries of possessions. In Rudmin, F. W., (Ed.), *To Have Possessions: A Handbook of Ownership and Property. Journal of Social Behavior and Personality.* 6, 17–55.

Berti, A. E. and Bombi, A. S. (1988). *The Child's Construction of Economics.* Cambridge: Cambridge University Press.

Bourdieu, P. (1979). *La Distinction: Critique Sociale du Jugement.* Paris: Editions de Minuit.

Cole, M. (1996). *Cultural Psychology; A Once and Future Discipline.* The Belknap Press of Harvard University Press.

Csikszentmihalyi, M. and Rochberg-Halton, Y. (1981). *The Meaning of Things: Domestic*

Symbols and the Self. Cambridge: Cambridge University Press.

Dittmar, H. (1992). *The Social Psychology of Material Possessions: To Have is To Be.* Hemel Hempstead: Harvester Wheatsheaf.

Dittmar, H. (1996). Adolescents' economic beliefs and social class. In Lunt. P. and Furnham, A., (Eds.), *Economic Socialization of Children.* Cheltenham, UK: Edward Elgar.

Emler, N. and Dickinson, J. (1985). Children's representations of economic inequalities: the effect of social class. *British Journal of Developmental Psychology,* 3,191–198.

Emler, N. and Dickinson, J. (2004). Children's understanding of social class and occupational groupings. In Barrett, M. and Buchanan-Barrow, E., (Eds.), *Children's Understanding of Society.* Hove: Psychology Press.

Engeström, Y. (1987). *Learning by Expanding: An activity-theoretical approach to developmental research.* Helsinki: Orienta-Konsultit.

Friedman, M. (1953). *Essays in Positive Economics* Chicago: University of Chicago Press.

Furnham, A. (1982). The perception of poverty among adolescents. *Journal of Adolescence,* 5, 135–147.

Furnham, A. (1999). Economic socialization: A study of adults' perceptions and uses of allowances (pocket money) to educate children. *British Journal of Developmental Psychology,* 17, 585–604.

Furnham, A. and Cleare, A. (1988). School children's conceptions of economics: prices, wages, investments and strikes. *Journal of Economic Psychology,* 9, 467–479.

Furnham, A. and Jones, S. (1987). Children's view regarding possessions and their theft. *Journal of Moral Education,* 16, 18–30.

Furnham, A. and Kirkcaldy, B. (2000). Economic socialization: German parents' perceptions and implementation of allowances to educate children. *European Psychologist,* 5, 202–215.

Godlier, M. (1999). *The enigma of the Gift.* Cambridge, UK: Polity Press.

Harbaugh, W. T., Krause, K. and Liday, S. G. (2003). Bargaining by children. *University of Oregon Economics Department Working Papers.*

Imamura, H. (2000). *Koueki suru Ningen: Zouyo to Koukan no Ningengaku [Homo Communicance: Philosophical Anthropology of Gift and Exchange].* Tokyo: Kodansha.

Issacs, S. (1967). Property and possessiveness. In Talbot, T. (Ed.), *The World of the Child: Birth to*

Adolescence from the Child's Viewpoint. Garden City. New York: Doubleday & Co.

Jahoda, G. (1979). The construction of economic reality by some Glaswegian children. *European Journal of Social Psychology.* 9:115–127.

Jahoda, G. (1983). European 'lag' in the development of an economic concept: A study In Zimbabwe. *British Journal of Developmental Psychology,* 1, 113–120.

James, W. 1890. The Principles of Psychology, vol. 1. New York: Henry Holt.

Kemptner, N. L. (1989). Personal possessions and their meanings in old age. In Spacapan S. and Oskamp, S., (Eds.), *The Social Psychology of Aging* (pp. 165–196). Thousand Oaks, CA: Sage.

Kawashima, T. (1981). *Shoyukenpou no Riron [Theory of Property Law].* Tokyo: Iwanami Shoten.

Lassarres, D. (1996). Consumer education in French families and schools. In Lunt, P. and Furnham, A., (Eds.), *Economic Socialization of Children.* Cheltenham, UK: Edward Elgar.

Lea, S. E. (1994). Rationality: the formalist view. In Brandstätter, H. and Güth W. (Eds.), *Essays in Economic Psychology.* Berlin: Springer.

Leahy, R. J. (1981). Development of the conception of economic inequality: II. Explanations, justifications and concepts of social mobility and change. *Child Development,* 19, 111–125.

Leiser, D. and Ganin, M. (1996). Economic participation and economic socialization. In Lunt, P. and Furnham, A., (Eds.), *Economic Socialization of Children.* Cheltenham, UK: Edward Elgar.

Leiser, D., Sevón, G. and Lévy, D. (1990). Children's economic socialization: Summarizing the cross-cultural comparison of ten countries. *Journal of Economic Psychology,* 11, 591–614.

Matsumura, Y. (2005). Shoyuken no Sinrigaku [Psychology of ownership]. In Sugawara, I., Sato, T. and Kurosawa, K. (Eds.), Hou to Shinri no Furontia [*Frontiers of Law and Psychology*], 1, 35–57.

Mauss, M. (1954). *The Gift: Form and Functions of Exchange in Archaic Societies.* London: Cohen and West.

Mills, J. and Clark, M. S. (1982). Communal and exchange relationships. In Wheeler, L. (Ed.), *Review Personality and Social Psychology III.* Beverley Hills: Sage.

Mortimer, J. T., Dennehy, K., Lee, C. D. and Finch, M. D. (1994). Economic socialization in the American family. *Family Relations,* 43, 23–29.

Moscovici, S. (2001). *Social Representations: Explorations in Social Psychology*. New York, NY: New York University Press.

Murnighan, J. K. and Saxon, M. S. (1998). Ultimatum bargaining by children and adults. *Journal of Economic Psychology*, 19, 415–445.

Ng, S. H. (1983). Children's ideas about the bank and shop profit: Developmental stages and the influence of cognitive contrasts and conflict. *Journal of Economic Psychology*, 4, 209–221.

Oh, S. (2003). Kodomono Kozukai- Kaimono ni Miru Nikkan no Kotonaru Ronri[Different logics under shopping behaviors and pocket money among Japanese and Korean children]. *AERA Mook: Shinrigaku ga Wakaru [Introduction to Psychology]* (pp. 94–96). Tokyo: Asahi Shinbun.

Oh, S., Pian, C., Yamamoto, T., Takahashi, N., Sato, T., Takeo, K., Choi, S. and Kim, S. (2005). Money and the life worlds of children in Korea: Examining the phenomenon of Ogori (treating) from cultural psychological perspectives. *Maebashi Kyoai Gakuen College Ronshu* 5:73–88. http://www.kyoai.ac.jp/college/ronshuu/no-05/oh.pdf

Pian, C. and Yamamoto, T. (2001). Kodomo no Okozukai to Oyakokankei: Oya tono Mensetsuchosa kara [Children's pocket money and their relationship with parents: From the interviews with parents]. In Sogon, S. (Ed.), *Bunka Tokuiteki Youiku Kodo to Kodomo no Kanjo Seigyo Kodo no Hattatsu: Sono Nittyu Hikaku [Culture Specific Parenting Style and Development of Children's Emotion Regulation: Comparison Between Japan and China]*. Report for Grant in Aid of Ministry of Science and Education, 1998–2001.

Pian, C. and Yamamoto, T. (2005). How does children's pocket money become "my money"?; For understanding development of children's self-consciousness and "my money." *Paper presented at the first ISCAR conference*, in Seville.

Polanyi, K. (1977). *The Livelihood of Man*. New York: Academic Press.

Sato, T., Takahashi, T. and Takeo, K. (2005). Okane wo Meguru Kodomo no Seikatsusekai: Seoul (5)[Children's money and their lifeworld: Seoul(5) an analysis of items about value judgments on pocket money]. In Nihon Shinri Gakkai Dai 69 Kai Taikai Hppyo Ronbunshu [*Collected Papers for 69th Congress of Japan Society of Psychology*].

Sevón, G. and Weckstrom, S. (1989). The development of reasoning about economic events: A study of Finnish children. *Journal of Economic Psychology*, 10, 495–514.

Simmel, G. (1950). *The sociology of Georg Simmel*. Wolff, K. H., trans. and (Ed.), New York: Free Press.

Strauss, A. L. (1952). The development and transformation of monetary meanings in the child. *American Sociological Review*, 53, 275–286.

Takahshi, N. (2005). Money as a cultural tool: Results of Japan, Korea, and Vietnam. *Paper presented at the Joint Conference of Psychology in Japan and Vietnam* in Hanoi, August 2005.

Takeo, K. (2005). Self-formation through the medium of allowance: Results of questionnaires research in Japan, Korea, and Vietnam. *Paper presented at the First ISCAR Conference* in Seville.

Uzawa, H. (1989). *Keizaigaku no Kangaekata [The Way of Thinking in Economics]*. Tokyo: Iwanami Shoten (Japanese).

Vygotsky, L. S. (1997). The instrumental method in psychology: Problems of the theory and history of psychology. In *The Collected Works of L. S. Vygotsky*, vol. 3 (Translated by Rene van der Veer). New York: Plenum Press.

Webley, P. and Lea, S. E. (1993a). Towards a more realistic psychology of economic socialization. *Journal of Economic Psychology*, 461–472.

Webley, P. and Lea, S. E. (1993b). The partial unacceptability of money in repayment for neighborly help. *Human Relations*, 46, 65–76.

Webley, P., Lea, S. E. and Portalska, R. (1983). The unacceptability of money as a gift. *Journal of Economic Psychology*, 4, 223–228.

Wertsch, J. V. (1998). *Mind as Action*. Oxford University Press.

Yamamoto, T. (1991a). "Shobunken" ni Kansuru Shogakusei no Shoyu Ishiki to Shinriteki Jiritsu [Possession consciousness in schoolchildren, and psychological weaning: why do Japanese children go against confusion principles?] Nara Joshi Daigaku Bunbakubu Kyoikugakka Nenpo [*Annual Report of Educational Research Nara Women's University*], 9, 93–113.

Yamamoto, T. (1991b). Yojiki ni Okeru "Sensen no Sontyo" Gensoku no Keisei to Sono Kinou [Establishment of the principle of "respect for occupancy" and its function in early children's group: On the problems of ontogeny of possession]. Kyouiku Shinrigaku Kenkyu [*Japanese Journal of Educational Psychology*], 39, 122–132.

Yamamoto, T. (1992). Shogakusei to Okozukai [Primary school students and their pocket money]. *Hattatu* 51:68–76. Kyoto: Minerva Shobo.

Yamamoto,T. (1997). *Yisuiban dao Liangsuiban Yinger Jiaoshe Xingwei yu Jiaohuanxing Xingwei de Xingcheng: Zhongri Yingyouer Suoyou Xingwei de Jieguo jiqi Fazhan Yanjiu Zhi Yi.* [*Development of Possessive Behavior and it's Cognitive Structure in Early Childhood; A Cross Cultural Study between Japanese and Chinese Children*]. Doctoral Thesis, Beijing Normal University, Beijing, China.

Yamamoto, T. (2000). Murehajimeru Kodomotachi [Developmental process of forming play group in early childhood: Autonomous group and tree-pole structure]. In Okamoto, N. and Asao, T., (Ed.), *Nenrei no Shinrigaku* [*Psychology of Age*] (pp. 103–142). Kyoto: Minerva Shobo.

Yamamoto, T. (2006). Chugoku Shisanbanna Taizoku ni Okeru Souki Kyouiku Ishiki [Consciousness of early education in Dai people in Xishuan-Banna, China]. In Ichimi, M., (Ed.), Kaken Houkokusho Higashi Ajia Shokoku ni Okeru Soki kyoiku no Genjo to Kadai ni Kansuru Kokusai Hikaku Kenkyu [*International Comparative Studies on Current Situation and Problems of Early Education in East Asian Countries*]. Report for Grant in Aid of Ministry of Science and Education, 2002–2004.

Yamamoto, T. and Pian, C. (1996). Guanyu Xiaoxuesheng "Suoyou" Yishi Fazhan de Yanjiu [The development of primary school students' concept of possession]. *Xinri Fazhan yi Jiaoyu* [*Psychological Development and Education*], 12, 8–13.

Yamamoto, T. and Pian, C. (2000). Bunka to shite no Okozukai mataha Tadashii Mahotsukai no Sodatekata [Culture as pocket money, or "how to foster 'true' wizard]." *Nihon Kaseigakkaishi* [*Journal of Home Economics of Japan*], 51, 1169–1174.

Yamamoto, T. and Pian, C. (2001). Okozukai wo Toshite Mita Kodomo no Seikatsu Sekai to Taijin Kankei Kouzou no Minzoku, Chiiki hikaku Kenkyu: Kitsurin-sho Chosenzoku, Kitsurin-sho Kanzoku, Shanghai-shi Kanzoku, Nara-shi Nihonminzoku no Hikaku kara [Comparative study of children's life-world and the structure of human relationships revealed by their pocket money: Data from Korean and Han in Chilin, Han in Shanghai, and Japanese in Nara. In Sogon, S. (Ed.), *Bunka Tokuiteki Youiku Kodo to Kodomo no Kanjo Seigyo Kodo no Hattatsu: Sono Nittyu Hikaku* [*Culture Specific Parenting Style and Development of Children's Emotion Regulation: Comparison between Japan and China*]. Report for Grant in Aid of Ministry of Science and Education, 1998–2001.

Yamamoto, T., Takahashi, T. and Sato, T. (2003). Okane wo Meguru Kodomono "Itsudatsu" to Kinsen Kyoiku [Children's 'derogation' and money education]. *Nihon Kyouiku Shinri Gakkai Sohkai Happyo Ronbunshu* [*Paper presented at 45th Congress of Japanese Society of Educational Psychology*].

Yamamoto, T., Takahashi, N., Sato, T., Pian, C., Oh, S. and Kim, S. (2003). Okane wo Meguru Kodomo no Seikatsusekai ni Kansuru Hikakubunkateki Kenkyu: Cheju-to Chosa Houkoku [Children's money and their life-world in Jeju Island: A field research from cultural psychological perspectives]. *Maebashi Kyoai Gakuen College Ronshu* 3:13–28. http://www.kyoai.ac.jp/college/ronshuu/no-03/yamamoto.pdf.

Yamamoto, T. and Zhang, R. (1997). Yisuiban dao Liangsuiban Yingyouer Jiaoshe Xingwei yu Jiaohuanxin Xingwe de Xingcheng [Negotiating and exchanging behaviors concerning possession in early childhood: a study of the structure and it's development of possessional behaviors in Japanese and Chinese children(1)]. *Xingri Kexue* [*Psychological Science*] 20:318–323.

Zelizer, V. A. (1989). The social meaning of money: "Special monies."*American Journal of Sociology* 95:343–377.

CHAPTER 25

The Family

Negotiating Cultural Values

Nandita Chaudhary

The family is understood as a central social group for developing individuals in all societies across time. The economic reasons for togetherness of family members are as significant as the social, political, and emotional ones; all these contribute to cohesiveness and cooperation within and among families. The idea of the family in any cultural location is a driving force behind policy and social evaluation of individual and collective action. It is a dynamic, ideal construction rather than an empirical fact gathered from statistical averages. The experience of being within a family has been critical to the study of growth and development of children, since it is a primary agent identified for research along with social class, race, nationality, and others. One of the key myths about the family is that it is almost always treated as having a universal, unchanging structure without reference to variation in time and space (Burman, 1994).

Different cultures are known to carry different convictions about family life. In India, the family is believed to be a "natural social unit." Within the Hindu theory, family life is seen much more appropriately as an 'activity' rather than an "entity." Hindu Indians believe in the principles of *dharma* or appropriate conduct at every level of social life; wherein it is not convention, but natural laws that are believed to operate according to context-dependent moral obligations relative to particular contexts (Menon, 2003). However, in India, plurality is more the norm than an exception. Alongside the plural ideologies that coexist by way of ethnic, religious, and regional differences at the collective level, individuals actively negotiate with patterns of culture to make their own interpretations and conduct their lives. Thus, we can see how ideology and reality are constantly intersecting to provide us with corresponding images of worship and violence, of prayer and pretence, or of wealth and want. It is the personal and collective reconciliations with apparent contradictions that become the hallmark of family life in the context of such plurality. This chapter will address some principles and practices of being part of a family, with specific focus on the family in India. Additionally, discussion will also approach the issue of methodology in the study of cultures, especially with reference to preferring families as opposed to individuals as the unit of study in certain kinds of research.

Family as a Critical Social Juncture

Care of the new generation is one of the critical tasks for the family. It provides the decisive junction of individual expression on the one hand, and society and state on the other (Pernau, 2003), actively maintained and perpetuated by politico-legal policy in the modern world, wherein the family becomes an important unit for the transaction of state policy, social justice, and economic planning (Uberoi, 2003). Although the family has always been an important institution, the legal and administrative responsibilities that have been assigned to the family by the modern state, are probably unprecedented. Prior to the industrial revolution in Europe, women and children received low wages for their work and the call for a "family wage" was an important claim during the revolution, as a consequence, men became primary wage earners in the family (Gittins, 1985). The American nuclear family provides an instance of the "minimal structure and functional essentials" of the human family, as a specific type of small social grouping (Parsons & Bales, 1955: 354). It was Goode (1963) who placed the claim for the worldwide progression of the family towards a conjugal form (with the exception of India, where he found the family to be particularly problematic to generalize about) after studying families in five different regions of the world. Contemporary forms of the family have challenged these claims, as family size drops below the one visualized at that time.

Modern society is convinced of the fact that existing childcare arrangements are responsible for the future of a society. Therefore, "good parenting" in the form of advice to couples about nutrition, health, autonomy and health care among other issues, are seen as a "vital resource to foster appropriate moral reasoning within the child" (Burman, 1994, 71). In the colonial times in India, British rulers were divided regarding the position of the state on intervention in cultural practices. Some proposed radical intervention whereas others preferred to keep out of private, family matters. Gradually, the law came to be seen as an instrument of social reform. Although liberal ideas about women's status, for example, could be partly attributed to the interface with the British (Azad, 2003), in their own policy, as an example, they actively encouraged gender inequality in inheritance of property in peasant communities in order to keep land holdings within manageable socially connected units (Pernau, 2003). Women, whether they were wives or sisters, were kept outside of the inheritance of landed property to prevent the fission of land holdings that was likely to result in administrative complications. Widow re-marriage was allowed (and even encouraged) within the family as levirate marriages (between a widow and her husband's brothers), primarily so that land (and perhaps children as potential inheritors) would stay within the family (Chowdhury, 1994). The concept of the Indian joint family can also be attributed to British rule, as a result of the "engagement of the colonial administration with indigenous systems of kinship and marriage, notably with respect to the determination of the rights in property and responsibility for revenue payment" (Uberoi, 2003: 1062). The idea was borrowed from Ancients texts on the Indian family and used towards administrative advantage and streamlining of payment of taxes for the British government. The idea of the "joint family" was therefore deliberately constructed around an antiquated source and subsequently became an important influence on social groupings for economic reasons.

Coexisting with these dominant trends in the Indian subcontinent, matrilineal groups have existed for centuries. The *Nairs* of Kerala and *Khasis* of the Northeastern region are two such communities that did not follow the prevalent patriarchal system. The structural ideal of the family was also defied in the *devadasi* tradition in central India, where young women were enrolled as devotees in temples for the purpose of worship in the form of classical dance. The *devadasis* were venerated women who were reasonably free from the demands of the predominantly patriarchal society. However, all these practices (matriarchy, others) came under severe strain in the colonial attempts at homogenizing the natives for smooth administration. Heterodoxy was not easy to govern, and this has had many consequences for social groups over the decades of foreign rule in India. In a recent study on school enrolment, it was found that the *devadasi* women in the sample had far more egalitarian relationships with their husbands, but communicated a desire "to be like the rest" (The World Bank, 2005).

The "idea" of the family is ridden with sentiment and nostalgia in almost every society of the world (Mintz, 2005), and people of the world believe that positive family experiences are essential for well-being. Perhaps for this reason, it becomes an important intersection between individuals and society and a significant process in self-awareness. The family could be seen as one of the structures that operate on individual psychology to guide as well as limit the constructive process of internalisation (Lawrence & Valsiner, 1993) thereby providing that critical link between an individual and collectivity.

The Economic Dimension of Togetherness

The economic dimension of family cohesiveness is important to consider. At every step, the social organization of resources has determined the structure of the family that would "best fit" the social organization. The economic function of the family was perhaps the foremost among the others: status, education, protection, religious training, recreation, and affection (Ogburn, 1933). There is no denying that togetherness would also be driven by socio-psychological factors. As an example, the inclusion of older people in family life by actively giving them social roles is a consequential aspect of personal adjustment in the Indian family. These roles are often derived from the idealized course of life outlined in ancient texts (Menon, 2003). The strategy is often to act "as if" the person continues to be a functional member with an important role within the social and economic unit (Chaudhary, 2004), irrespective of the real contribution. Often this inclusion extracts a heavy price on individual adjustment to older people, but the rewards are many. Although care of the aged is increasingly becoming recognized as a social issue in need of state intervention for the homeless and abandoned, living among family is still believed to be "natural" for the ageing person and therefore the most appropriate solution.

Contributions, earning, and expenditure are essential domains of family activity, and much energy and effort goes into planning and discussions about these issues. Economists for their part view the family primarily as a little factory (Bergstrom, 1997) and children are part of the commodity production and sharing that is envisaged as an economic activity of the household. Such formulation presents a highly constrained notion of family life and rests on several assumptions about a society within which such a family lives (Foster, 2002). It is important to consider that a range of factors influence family life, among them are socio-personal factors, taxation laws, health policy, residential features, to name a few. All these impinge upon the ways in which family functioning is negotiated, and it is essential for any formal analysis of family activity to also consider multiple dimensions.

The modern, corporate world with its high salaries and geographic mobility has imposed several challenges to the traditional constitution of the Indian family. Time will tell whether the ideal of a large network of people living and working together, children growing up with multiple caregivers, or sharing spaces without many boundaries, will succumb to these pressures for nuclearization, or whether there will be creative adaptations of traditional ways and means, as has been the case for centuries (Trawick, 2003; Uberoi, 2003).

The Idea of the Family

The condition of human beings is inextricably bound to created ideas and situations, and to having moved far beyond the limitation of genetic material. Perhaps this is true also with reference to the family as a unit; that it is not only the functional imperatives due to which the family sustains, but also the "idea" of and the social discourse about family life (Burman, 1994) that is critical in determining its survival. These ideas (of the family) have grown abundant and survived the test of time through the pressures of different regimes and ideologies. As Stratton (2003) states, "Our ideas of family have built up over thousands of years as family forms have slowly developed to meet the needs of survival and society" (p. 336). Claims of evolutionary psychologists have supported the cooperation of related members as survival tactic that has been learnt over time and become incorporated in human dynamics and functionalists have assumed that the universality of the family and its continued centrality is based on the dynamics of co-operation and exchange of resources.

Previous generations therefore influence our idea of a family. In Western society, for instance, the notion of family is deeply linked with the 'folk image' of a stable group with well-defined roles both within and outside the homes, men worked outside the home, and women cared for the children and the home. This image persists despite the fact that only around 6% of families actually fit this image (McGoldrick, 1998) and as in any cultural location, real people often defy the neat categorization of social science.

Families also carry stories about themselves over the years that assist in constructing and reinforcing continuity. In some parts of the world, the idea of the "individual" has become juxtaposed against the idea of the family and more and more people are choosing to live alone. In India, in contrast, the idea of the family as an ideal unit is so strong that in most cases, a person leaves the family of origin only under three circumstances, marriage (especially for women), study, or employment, at all levels of the economic scale. Young women who choose not to marry usually stay on with their parents; there is little or no question of moving out of the home to seek an independent life and home as a single person. In many homes, such an eventuality would not even come up for discussion by either generation. Thus, it is important to understand that the notion of the family (whether it is a statistically supported or not) is an important force in evaluating demographic patterns. It would not be wrong to say that close associations among generations, the co-residence of different ages and multiplicity of members is an ideal for the Indian family, unlike its counterpart in the West. When couples live alone, their answers to questions about family are inclusive of parents and siblings, even if they do not live together. The family in India is therefore defined

> [...] not so much as a specific type of household formation, but as an ideology and code of conduct whereby the relations of husband and wife and parent and child are expected to be subordinated to a larger collective identity. This ideology finds constant affirmation in Indian cinema. (Uberoi, 2003: 1077)

While discussing the family, it is imperative to understand the dynamic construction of what has been termed as an "ideal-type" in the Weberian sense (Eshleman, 1991, 4); not as a perfect system, but an elucidation based on abstract, "pure" characteristics that represent the end, rather than the middle of any continuum. One of the main responsibilities of social functioning is to perpetuate social structure, whether through social sanction or legislation. The articulation of the ideal-type of the family is a means for perpetuating the positive notion of the family rather than its statistical average.

Social forces linked with family living have been the concern of ancient society as well. In ancient India, life in the household was meant to provide a social and spiritual atmosphere for the liberation of self-awareness and not just for continuation of the society. The ways in which epics, myths and stories may be used by ordinary people, will however, be plural, and sometimes even prescriptive, whether this was intended or not. The historic transformations in European society half way through the 21st century displayed changes in family size (with the popularity of the birth control pill) and alterations in the concepts governing social life like "society for singles" or "temporary partnerships" or as "living apart together" (Reifeld, 2003: 225). These changes spread far and wide and became symbolic of the new world, free of outdated, bourgeois ideas. State policy to protect the family, especially the mother (As in Article 6 of the Federal Republic of Germany) also becomes the reason for intervention and a mechanism for control, thereby causing unprecedented transformations in the family. Across the Atlantic, the family and the idea of childhood in America are deeply tied to idyllic images of freedom and opportunity with each emerging generation believing that life in the past was a better one (Mintz, 2005). In present times, like the 2004 elections in the United States, family values became a topic for the clever manipulations of public discourse and political dispute. Although America believes that it is a child-friendly society, it is true that Americans themselves are deeply ambivalent about children, especially as a result of the breakdown of norms of family, gender relations, reproduction, and age. The "youthquake" of the 1950s and 1960s resulted in centralizing issues of youth in confrontation with adults. The present generation of adults might even be showing some hostility towards its youth preoccupied with hip-hop (Mintz, 2005).

In ancient Indian society, the family was understood more as a phase of life, an activity rather than a structural imperative. Participation in family life was seen as a transient, albeit crucial step in the personal evolution of individuals who passed through the course of life in stages from the dependency of an infant to the isolation of old age.

Family Systems

The family has been widely attended in the human sciences, often as a factor in the development of this or that; sometimes as a system in need of repair due to its dysfunction, occasionally as a power structure where adult-child interface is analyzed. Certainly, it is a central "niche" for the emergence of a developing person in every culture. Developmental psychology has perhaps overused the family in general and the mother in particular, to identify sources of variation that could be ascribed in the explanation of differences in developmental outcomes in children. The dynamic organization and authority structures within the family have also been studied to have distinct consequences with specific reference to children.

The family as a whole constitutes a dynamic adjustment between different sets like adults and children, grandparents and parents, household helpers and parents, children and helpers, siblings, boys and girls, and so on.

Although one may not go so far as Whitaker (1979) in saying that in a metaphorical sense, "there are no individuals in this world – only fragments of families" (cited in Olson & DeFrain, 1994: 16), there is no denying that the family persists as one of the strongest affiliations for individuals in every society. Over the developmental span, people often (not always) shift away from families of origin. Those that are newly created often carry a strong resonance with the one left behind. Family systems theory has attributed people's adjustments in relationships to patterns experienced in families of origin. The process, timing, and nature of the movement from the natal family to independent living or a partnership, if it occurs is also culturally organized. There are conventions about the timing and appropriateness of the move. A single mother living with her 21-year-old daughter in urban Germany would come under criticism from her friends for limiting her daughter's personal life. Such a situation in India would attract comments IF the daughter moved out! In India, adult children move away from families only if they get married (and that too only for women, men often stay on with their parents) or for work. The support and companionship with a secure and dependable group of people would be taken as sufficient reason for the continuance.

The structuring of relationships works at every level; with children, adults, ethnic groups, the elderly and people with disability, among others. Families that stay together are fast disappearing in present times. Much work has been undertaken to try to assess the reasons for break-up. In doing so, some dimensions of strong families became visible; these were the families that stayed together through all odds. Some of the features of such families (Olson & DeFrain, 1994, 23) were clustered under the qualities of cohesion (commitment to each other and spending time together), flexibility (ability to withstand stress and spiritual well-being), and communication (positive communication and appreciation and affection). In my assessment however, these dimensions are dominated by an "internal" orientation with reference to family dynamics, the family as it is defined by its members. Perhaps such a list would include the linkages and relationships of families with other people, families, and social institutions in order to better represent cultural diversity, and the 'external' pressures for the identity and persistence.

Family as a Unit of Study

At this juncture, it is pertinent to introduce the discussion about methods of research. It has largely been assumed that research investigation can and should proceed with the individual as a unit of examination and analysis. I would like to argue here, that in certain communities, taking the individual as an undisputed unit for study in every research situation is often misplaced. In Indian communities, for instance, it is extremely difficult (if not impossible) to get isolated attention of and audience with a single person, especially while doing research with rural and semi-urban communities. Gender dynamics and restrictions on women's mobility create further hurdles in long interview sessions that insist on undivided attention. Dyadic interactions and exclusive attention on a single task are not common and often insistence on the same can lead to suspicion from the community. Kurtz (1992) states that in India, the "normative subject" at any given time consists of a constellation of people and not an individual (p. 107). Anyone who has successfully completed fieldwork with Indian communities will vouch for the fact that on the whole, people are open, friendly, curious, and forthcoming. Although this is a great advantage in gaining access and working with families and children of all ages, there is a need to resolve the issue of "clustering" of onlookers, enthusiastic participants (Chaudhary, 2005) and distracted respondents. Interview questions are often answered by people other than the targeted person; may be a neighbor, a mother-in-law or even a daughter who is identified as literate and therefore more "capable" of answering questions of importance. The participant herself (or himself) may find it difficult to keep in one place in a dyadic conversation since this is very unusual. In such situations, where family members, neighbors, curious passers-by, and of course many children naturally cluster around a researcher(s), it is often sensible to expand the unit of study to include the others rather than assume that they will fade into the background. The natural unit of study would therefore, also be the family or other group (as in focus group discussions).

In a recent study of schooling among the poor, attempts were made to identify reasons for low participation in schooling in selected communities in three states in India. The project was planned with the family as a unit of study since it was argued that family circumstances and not the individual child, sibling, mother, or father would ultimately decide whether the child would reach the school and stay there (Chaudhary & Sharma, 2005). Asking any one isolated person selected questions would not have been an appropriate strategy. For the purpose of identifying the factors supporting schooling, therefore, we focused on those families where, despite poverty, low access to schools and many other situational difficulties, children were attending classes. The features of these families were then studied to explore the supporting and inhibiting factors. The findings of the study revealed interesting results at every level, family circumstances, community services, and availability. Interestingly, it was birth order and not gender that emerged as the strongest factor keeping a child at home. Among these families, mostly the first-born child was kept at home as a substitute caregiver for younger children, companion at work or assistant in chores at home, whether it was a boy or a girl. The younger children were in many cases, free to attend school. Similarly, a supportive father seemed to be a key factor for schooling, whereas substance abuse by fathers emerged as a strong inhibiting factor among others. Some of these conclusions would have been much more elusive through interviewing of individuals, since it was during the detailed study of the families rather than answers to questions that these findings emerged (Chaudhary & Sharma, 2005).

The Self and the Family: Social and Personal Dynamics

Individual existence is only one of the levels at which human dynamics can operate. The social and personal are interdependent domains and yet somewhat different realms of human functioning governed by diverse, specific forms of organization (Valsiner & Litvinovic, 1996). Further, social activity could also operate at different levels depending upon the importance of the specific social unit in a given culture. The continuum of human groupings is thus flanked by the single individual at one end and humanity on the other. In between are the many layers of sociality, differently organized in different cultures. Caste is and example of a culturally specific grouping to which membership is ascribed. Social class, religious groups, fra-

ternities, and sororities are other instances of other such collections. For those who choose to attend church regularly, for example, it would be an engaging arena in which much discussion and exchange of views would take place. The family forms another significant level of social activity. Belonging to the family "implies" the sharing of a value system, resources, space and time.

In Hindu belief, the discussion of self-other dynamics, and the gradual changes in relationships, is of critical importance to the understanding of human nature. Several texts are devoted to discussions and debate about the dilemma of human existence, the uncertainty of the future and potential isolation of the individual psyche. The life cycle of a person is believed to be organized around principles of fluctuating self-other dynamics. Contrary to popular belief, the Hindu notion of a "person" is deeply individualistic. The "real person" or *aatman* (soul) is believed to be manifested in a human form that is essentially limited in its perception, and therefore easily deceived by manifest reality. This notion is further developed in Buddhism where the self is believed to be a non-entity, created by the misleading machinations of the language of the self. The provenance of all human suffering can be attributed to this error of judgment.

Hinduism takes a different view of the self as an essential quality of an individual that follows through its course of evolution. A human life cycle is believed to be only one part of the cycle of the soul, whose journey is largely unknown to ordinary people. During the human life span, there are believed to be transformations in the basic form of relationships between the self and other, thus making the formulation fundamentally individual in character, in its gradual travel towards ultimate absorption into the cosmos, the final dissolution of the self or *moksha*. This changing organization of personhood is well demonstrated in the notion of *dharma* or recommended conduct in Hindu belief. This is not a universal code of conduct that would apply in all situations; different contexts, ages, stages of life would be governed by different principles of *dharma*.

Such codes of conduct – *dharma* – are presumed to inhere in all generic categories: from country (*rajya dharma* or moral code of the country) to the genus (*jati dharma*), to the lineage (*kula dharma*), to gender (*stri dharma*, women's *dharma* or *purusha dharma* or men's *dharma*), and finally to the single person (*svadharma*, the *dharma* right for one's station or nature) (Menon, 2003: 435).

Apart from situational determinants and social forces, a person's individual developmental stage is also believed to suggest which set of actions are uplifting. The young (*brahmachari*), the householder (*grhastha*), the gradually ageing (*vanaprastha*), and the ascetic (*sanyasi*), all have different objectives to fulfill (Badrinath, 2003), and are to be guided towards an appropriate life by principles of *dharma*. Renunciation is a gradually involving theme, starting from intense dependence at birth to the unfolding interdependence of family life followed by adult independence leading to the preparation for the ultimate sacrifice; the sacrifice of others, material goods, and finally, perhaps the hardest of all, the *tyag* or abdication of the self itself. There is no suggestion that the last stage is the highest in terms of importance; first place is almost always given to the *grhastha*, the life in the family; also because without experiencing the closeness, forfeiture may not be as special. True renunciation is believed to lie in the sacrifice of the feeling that "this is mine." It is only when a person juxtaposes the intensity of closeness with the conscious effort to sacrifice, and that too the most precious gifts of all, the self, that the depth of self-awareness is believed to be understood. The importance of family life is highlighted in the following passage, "Just as all living beings are able to survive owing to the loving care of their mothers; likewise all other stages of life are possible because of the support the households provide" (Badrinath, 2003: 120, 123).

Hindu ideology therefore, can never be unitarily scaled on the continuum of independence/interdependence; each individual's life is believed to range between one end of the imaginary continuum to the other; the ensuing tensions as a result of this apparently fluctuating ideology is the substance of many of the epic writings of Ancient India. In this passage, we are able to understand that social organization is clustered into these levels as significant layers of activity. The *kula* or lineage, that is the family across time and space, is the manifestation that is recognized by the local social reality. The family is thus believed to consist of past members, future generations and members at a given time, who are all believed to be tied together for the purpose of sustaining the gradual evolution of individual persons temporarily (but not insignificantly) in connection with each other.

Parents, Siblings, and Others: The Language and Relationships in the Family

The words chosen to address people not only suggest particular patterns of social relationships, they also assist in creating and sustaining patterns of social activity that constitutes culture. This provides yet another illustration of how events both contain and create reality. Higher order social phenomena are actually created through communication and mutual influence that contribute towards the creation of patterns of collectivity (Sherif, 1936). Such is the linkage between kinship terminology and family dynamics.

Kinship terminology is deeply reflective of the degree of detail that any society requires in the mapping of relationships. On the basis of an analysis of kin terms in America, Schneider (1980/1968) was able to chart relationships between two basic categories, those of "blood" being considered natural and permanent; and those by marriage, believed to be essentially cultural and therefore more contingent in character. In all languages in India, kin terminology is elaborate. Kin terms proliferate as default terminology for all relationships, within or outside actual ties (of blood or marriage) between people, for both real and fictive kin relations. The semantic organization of terminology has also been found to be linked with marriage practices, for instance where three distinguishable forms of marriage were discovered to be coupled with the three language families (Trautmann, 2003).

The use of first names to identify people is mostly avoided, and people feel more comfortable addressing others using a sensitively chosen kin term that may also be explained if the need arises. For the category of ambiguous relationships, people are likely to adopt the English terms of Uncle, Aunty, Madam, or Sir (as a vestige of the colonial past) rather than first names or a title. Such a form of address (title with name) would not be appropriate in most social situations and is used primarily in the event of a formal address or letter writing. This serves to illustrate family relations and kin terms are well established and fundamental to social encounters. This terminology serves as an active template for addressing (and therefore I propose, also affiliating with) other people, whether they are related or not. The usage of kin terms helps also to comprehend the organization of social relationships in terms of gender, hierarchy, potential restriction on inter-marriage (such as calling a person within the exogamous unit of the village a brother or sister), and distance. The complexity of language use is further displayed in the discourse strategies that are also found to vary depending upon each of the critical factors that determine personal positioning in relationships (Chaudhary, 2004). However, the discussion of these is beyond the scope of this paper.

The Indian Family: The Spiritual Evolution of the Individual?

The idea of India is far older than the unwieldy nature of its contemporary society. Plurality and heterogeneity are the norm where nature and culture display a captivating diversity in the manifest ways in which

people live. Writing about the travel from his home state to Punjab at the other end of the map, Guha considers:

This (the state of Punjab) lies at the other end from my own state of Karnataka. But it is not just geographical distance that distinguishes them; there is also language, and landscape, and culture, and cuisine. The people of the two states speak, look, dress and eat differently. Karnataka and Punjab are as different as France and Latvia. The latter duo form part of a loose confederation called European Union; while the former are bound together by a stronger and more rigorously defined political entity known as the Republic of India. . . . Damaged and riddled by corruption and diminished by inefficiency . . . that India somehow hangs together somewhat, and that it has lasted so long, is a modern miracle. (Guha, 2005: 4)

Trying to collect "Indian-ness" as a way of being is an unattainable task. More recently, several authors have attempted to theorize about the unifying forces within the nation state, but are largely confounded by the cohesion threatened by economic inequality, religious plurality, and external threat. Perhaps the persistence of each of these factors also contributes to the consolidation of the idea of India; internally however, heterodoxy remains the norm rather than the exception (Sen, 2005). In discussing family life in India, I have taken the position to "illustrate" rather than attempt a "representation" of plurality. It is perhaps an impossible task to assemble all the different patterns of the family in India.

In organizing a collection of narrated stories from the Indian subcontinent, Ramanujan (1994) classifies stories in six discernible domains: stories centered around animals, men, women, families, fate, death and divinity, funny and clever stories, and stories about stories. Given the importance of oral narratives (particularly in a culture that has been predominated by orality) in community life of India, the nomenclature that Ramanujan uses is noteworthy. While discussing stories about families, he remarks that these include tales about,

> [...] sisters, brothers, brother-sister pairs, sons-in-law, mothers-in-law, couples, co-wives (wives of two brothers), mothers and sons, fathers and daughters appear in all their complex inter-relations. Not only bonds of affection, but rivalry, incest, betrayal, and cruelty are explored in family tales. (p. 4)

In the world of folk tales, therefore, the principle of ideal-types (mentioned earlier) does not prevail and the narratives seem to carry the diversity and contradiction of everyday life. Perhaps narratives take their cues from real manifestations rather than ideal constructions. Ramanujan (1994) proceeds to elaborate:

> [...] folktales are a potent source of psychoanalytic insights, for they concentrate on close family ties and childhood fantasies. For instance, ambivalence towards parents is expressed in a number of symbolic ways. ... As these tales are told to children in the context of the family, they are a part of the child's psychological education in facing forbidden feelings and finding a narrative that will articulate and contain if not resolve them – for the storytellers as well as their young listeners. (p. 27)

The central binding force of the Indian family is the belief in its centrality in the life of an individual. The affiliations of family relationships are presumed to be life-long, and socialization of young children directs strong interconnectedness (not necessarily inter-"dependence") as the norm. While understanding Hindu theory about the family life, it may be far more appropriate to understand it as an "activity" rather than an "entity."

As discussed in an earlier section, the stage of family-life has been given central space in epic works. For the one *living within the family* (thereby suggesting that rules would be different for a person choosing to opt out), the rules of *grhastha* or the household, were very clear (Badrinath, 2003).

Speaking about the epic myth of Ancient India, the author continues:

> The Mahabharata *is concerned that every person overcomes divisions – divisions within the self, and the divisions between self and the other, created by* wrong *perceptions of the self and of the other and of the relation between the two. Not rituals but overcoming self-division; not prescriptions but self-knowledge; not the artificial complexities but the simplicities of life, are the* Mahabharata's *concerns for the individual, for the 'one living in the family', grhastha, above all. (Badrinath, 2003:115, emphasis mine)*

The binding force of the family is not contingent upon individual will, interdependence between its members and changing content, but "obligation" and the assumed unchanging abstract form of the family, independent of time and space. Members of a family remain united by means of duties that are held to be sacred and not merely civil. For example,

> No matter what the character or circumstances of a father or a mother may be, their children owe to them certain duties. Similarly, parents owe to their children certain duties. Protection, loving care, a disciplined upbringing and honest advice, are the duties of parents towards children. Obedience, holding them in honour, and looking after them in old age are the duties of children towards them. (Badrinath, 2003: 124)

Perhaps this is the reason behind the belief that family care is the best for the child even in the event where a mother goes out for work. Other family members (sisters, grandparents, helpers) are seen as best alternatives for the care of young children. Institutional care of groups of children is largely believed to be in violation of the primary needs of a young child (Kapoor, 2005). This belief is very similar to Chinese ideology where:

> Acceptance of dependency within a society that observes the norm of reciprocity creates the most decisive support for the favourable

attitudes towards the elderly. The emphasis on mutual obligation throughout the life cycle coupled with the necessity of repayment eliminates the need for the elderly to justify their need for care and respect on an individual basis. As a result, dependency in old age is viewed as unpleasant but inevitable. (Davis-Friedmann, 1983, 13)

The family unit is presumed to have an organic link to the larger society. Answerable not only to itself and individual members, there are duties to be fulfilled toward society by being kind, hospitable and charitable towards other people, animals and elements of nature. The concept of *rna* (debt) to one's ancestors, to teachers, and debt to society. Each *rna* carries an expectation, to ancestors by raising a family of one's own, to teachers by spreading knowledge further, and to society by leading a civil and disciplined life. The tensions that are created by the presumed levels of social activity (for instance if interests of one group are in conflict with those of another) are again the substance of the abundant content of ancient and folk culture. There are several stories that deal with the inadequacy in "performing" duties due to the interference of human feelings and subjectivity. However, this does not imply the assurance of care or the absence of anxiety linked with child care (Kapoor, 2005) or old age (Vatuk, 1990) or disadvantage of any kind. These are ideal constructions that guide social activity and are not lawful binding.

The care of the young child of employed parents from India has become cause for international travel to all parts of the world. The phenomenon of "roving grandparents" (Anadalakshmy, 2005: 11), suggests that grandparents of today constantly move from one continent to another enthusiastically attending the arrival, award or graduation of a grandchild.

At every major airport, one runs into these roving grandparents. They stay in one place for three months at a time, six months at most. We need to create a new terminology in the social sciences to address the situations arising out of the phenomenon of Indian immigrants to the new world, long-

ing for the support system of an extended family and more often than not, having their mothers present in the home, for every new arrival (p. 11).

The sense of companionship with another person is so intense on occasion (in the Mahabharata for instance) that injury to the enemy is at the same time argued as injury to the self, not only in the collective, but also in the "personal' sense. This powerful inclusion of the "other" in the self is not appropriately understood when it is labeled as "collectivism"; it is perhaps more fitting to understand it as a "spiritual" belief in the inclusion of others in the self and vice versa (Chaudhary, 2004). Perhaps the construct of *advaita* or collective personhood may help to understand the particular essence of collectivity implied here. The notion of *advaita* is a non-dualistic belief in the existence of eternal *brahman*, the source of everything and the *atman* or the unchanging consciousness of the self, which is manifestation of the quality of the eternal. One can see the merit of the distinction between convention and moral rule so well articulated in Menon (2003), where she suggests that for the Indian, almost everything is believed to be governed by natural law, except maybe traffic rules (perhaps because of the high incidence of negotiability on Indian streets). We can extend this formula to the "belief" in the family as well. The family in India is assumed to have indisputable "natural foundations" (Badrinath, 2003, 131), not just a matter of convention that may or may not be. The course of life is supposed to flow out of this basic formula for community living. The intense pressure for entering the stage of *grhastha* is something every young person encounters as a natural course of events; the intensity of the push for marriage is felt even among Indians living in other parts of the world that are sometimes the substance for dramatic description (Jain, 2005).

Addressing moral dilemmas to showcase the complexity of human existence was a strategy well in place in ancient India. The epic war of *Mahabharata* rages between two related families, the *Kauravas* and *Pandavas*;

with the leading warrior of the *Pandavas* being faced with the distress of having to raise weapons against those whom he saw as his own family. The dilemma is raised, discussed and then guided by the intervention of Lord Krishna in the famous passages of the *Bhagvatgita* (Rajagopalachari, 1999).

In the understanding of self-other relations in the Indian family, it is "incorporation" of the group by the individual, as well as the individual by the group, rather than simple identification that seems to be operating. It is common to encounter the absence of family as a source of distress for an average Indian. In the case of childhood, for instance, the "embeddedness of children within the group" continues to be an important feature of social life of Indians (Raman, 2003, 90). Indian community living and public spaces are open to children and very few events might be out of bounds for them. Family life and vertical heterogeneity is the norm. Adolescents spend far more time with the family in India than in other countries (Verma & Saraswathi, 2002; Verma & Sharma, 2003), raising a question regarding the validity of the experience of an "adolescence" phase in the life-cycle of an individual (Saraswathi, 1999). It is the continuity between childhood and adulthood (Kumar, 1993), participation, presence and importance of other people, the value of externality and sociality instead of inwardness, particularly during childhood and young adulthood, that characterize the ideal way of life. Identification with a group implies an un-critical assumption of individualism in its picture of fundamentally separate but associated entities. In this cultural location, however, developmentally, the child and the group are not merely associated by resemblance; the child's ego is constituted through being contained within the group. The child has a sense of his action taken on behalf of or even by the group contained within him. There is a simultaneous "encompassing and a sense of being encompassed" (Kurtz, 1992:103). The group is the thus primary player in the consolidation of the individual sense of self of a child.

Dumont also talks of the issue of containing and being contained by as being a part of understanding principles of hierarchy in the Indian context (Dumont, 1980), as does Trawick (1990). The contained self represents the embedding that is done of the "other" into the self-structure, just as the individual is embedded into the family system, they carry the other within them (Trawick, 2003). Within this ideal construction sustains a degree of diversity that sometimes brings the conclusion under question. What about diversity, poverty, and social discord? There are serious differences between the experiences of being a member in a family depending on the social group to which one belongs. For the child on the street, for instance, how does one evaluate the family's expectation for work even by a young child? Would it still be presumed to be inter-connectedness? Certainly one can take a position that the young child is being exploited here. Is the child believed to be so much a part of the self that she can be exploited for hard labour or beggary? How does one reconcile with such manifestations of self-other relationships or family life in a culture that is largely promoted as organically linked within its people? While addressing cultural reality, there are many difficulties faced as a result of social subjugation and hierarchy that are essential to recognize in order not to be swayed into a false positive bias about any nation, culture or community.

Regarding family matters and children's socialization, concerns like weaning, feeding, and toilet training, just did not seem critical (Anandalakshmy & Bajaj, 1981; Raman, 2003) while gender and age related behaviors and social conduct were important issues. Participation of children in work is considered natural, and children of all ages care for their younger siblings and help with household work, although this is more applicable for the poor as well as the female child (Anandalakshmy, 1996). We see here a fundamental difference between the acceptability of working for the family with the contemporary view of the child in more affluent societies (Jenks, 1996). Dube (1998) argues that the dynamics of kinship is central to understanding social organization in India, and within the family, the relative position of an individual, with considerations of age, gender and generational position, are critical to access as entitlement to power, authority and resources. This makes family, by its very dynamics, a location for power struggles and conflicts among members. Ironically, the Indian family, because of the intense closeness becomes the site for exploitation due to the protection from effective legal action (Banerjee, 2003; Trawick, 2003; Vindhya, 2003). This protective layering of social activity at the level of the family is indeed yet another evidence for the dynamic organization of family life, within which loyalty and devotion are seen as basic features of membership, whatever the reality may be. When gender relations are assessed, it seems almost impossible to understand gender dynamics without its intersection with kinship and family matters (Dube, 1998). It seems contradictory that the easy-going fluidity of family life, particularly in rural and semi-urban communities where boundaries between households is not so clear (Chaudhary, 2004), also harbors episodes like violence against women, abuse of children and disregard of the elderly that go quite unattended in terms of public attention and action (Vindhya, 2003). All this plurality coexists with attempts to package and present Indian family life in general and Indian childhood in particular, as a period that is blissfully indulgent and central to the lives of people; certainly such efforts of glorification (Chandra, 1996) fail to capture the essential plurality of Indian family life (Raman, 2003). In a tradition where the female form is revered and even worshiped as the essential constituent of nature, violence against women and young girls remains a distressing feature of social reality, perpetuated by caregivers. In one study of rape, it was found that 75% of the girls were between 7 and 18 years of age and as many as 43% of the criminals were related (Karlekar, 2003: 1133). This is despite the fact that much of the crime within families is not even reported. The continuance of this pattern is something that will need more than just demographic analysis, legal laxity or history to explain its mani-

festations; one needs to search deeper under the skin, through literary and other sources to understand why we as a people, feel compelled to sometimes hurt that which we worship (Gandhi, 2005).

Another important dimension of Indian family life is the developmental sequence of sociality. An individual is believed to pass through phases of life that are governed by principles of conduct *dharma* as mentioned earlier. There is by no means a uniform prescription of sociality through life. The young child is believed to be completely dependent, the young student, should have devotion to the teacher and to the process of learning, the householder should be dedicated to the pursuit of wealth and care for the family, the older person it is believed, must prepare for departure, and therefore gradually distance the self from the world of relationships and material pleasures. Thus, by no means can Indian society be considered uniformly interdependent or independent. In the course of human life, the individual is believed to be "essentially incomplete" (Trawick, 1990: 244) and deeply confounded.

On the 9th of March 2005, a young man and his distraught wife, residents of New Delhi, first poisoned their two young children and then took their own lives. The news item said that he was bankrupt and could not manage the debts that had piled up. His feeling of responsibility towards the members of his family, his wife and two children pushed him towards this "family suicide" as it was labeled in the newspapers. Such intense commitment to the care of the family can only be driven by forces that are as intensely protective; that they can design to destroy. Durkheim's (1897/1997) work on suicide closely linked social structure to forms in which suicide is manifested, demonstrating that prevalent social reality predisposes individuals towards certain reactions in self-sacrifice. Bankruptcy, like anywhere else in the world, leads to distress and despair, sometimes even to suicide. News reports in Delhi, however, declare an added dimension, where adults first smother the lives of their children before taking their own. In one instance, the child was a 21 year-old woman! The despairing news of this phenomenon (Chauhan, 2005) is perhaps the collective price that society has to pay for its own (perhaps over-emphasized) preoccupation with the duties of a householder. The children were victims of misplaced devotion and sense of responsibility that their parents felt towards them.

Concluding Comments

Searching through theory and research of the family from ancient and contemporary readings has been quite illuminating. On the one hand, the ideal family strikes us as a haven for childhood and trusting, everlasting relationships; on the other hand, contradicting the very premise of the search for truth and happiness, families for some become the source of abuse and exploitation, even death. Dealing with the mystifying contradictions is not an easy task and one searches for coherence and direction from established expressions of the past. A past that is also (naturally) fraught with difficulty and dissent. As Simmel (1904) suggests, perhaps the evidence of the contradiction is testimony to the importance of the issues under discussion. If the family were not a critical domain; if women were not idolized; if children were not adored, maybe there would have been no reason to violate them in the first place. The process of modernization may indeed be responsible for the exaggeration of traditional pathologies of Indian family life (Singer, 1968). This dual form of the family "as at once a site of oppression and violence and a 'haven in a heartless world'" (Uberoi, 2003: 1084) has been the subject of several scholarly works on the Indian family.

To end this chapter, two vows of Hindus have been chosen, the vow of marriage chanted by the man and woman along with seven symbolic steps before embarking on a life together, and the other, the promise between a teacher and student. Both these prayers are resoundingly heard. It is nearly impossible to argue for reconciliation between these extremes of human existence, except to offer to open them for discussion and debate.

> With these seven steps, become my
> friend.
> I seek your friendship. May we never
> deviate
> From this friendship.
> May we walk together.
> May we resolve together.
> May we love each other and enhance each
> other.
> May our vows be congruent and our
> desires shared.

The vow between a teacher and students read as follows:

> May we together protect each other. And
> together, nourish each other.
> May we gain strength together.
> What we have together learnt and
> studied,
> may it in splendour and force glow.
> May we never have for each other
> repugnance and dislike.
> (Badrinath, 2003: 136)

References

Anandalakshmy, S. (2005). Parenting as a fine art. Keynote address at the Asia-Africa seminar on Parenting through the lifespan: Challenges and opportunities. February 16th–18th 2005. M. S. University of Baroda, Vadodara, India.

Anandalakshmy, S. (1996). The girl child and the family. New Delhi: Department of Women and Child Development, Ministry of Human Resource Development, Govt. of India.

Anandalakshmy, S. & Bajaj, M. (1981). Childhood in the weavers community of Varanasi. In D. Sinha (Ed.), Socialization of the Indian child. New Delhi: Concept.

Azad, N. (2003). Gender and family: State intervention in India. In M. Pernau, I. Ahmed & H. Reifeld (Eds.), Family and gender: Changing values in Germany and India (pp. 198–223). New Delhi: Sage.

Badrinath, C. (2003). The householder, grhastha in the Mahabharata. In M. Pernau, I. Ahmad, & H. Reifeld (Eds.), Family and gender:

Changing values in Germany and India (pp. 113–139). New Delhi: Sage.

Banerjee, N. (2003). The marginal families. In M. Pernau, I. Ahmad, & H. Reifeld (Eds.), *Family and gender: Changing values in Germany and India* (pp. 278–295). New Delhi: Sage.

Bergstrom, T. C. (1997). A survey of theories of the family: In M. Rosenzweig & O. Stark (Eds.), *Handbook of population and family economics* (pp. 21–79). New York: Harper Collins.

Burman, E. (1994). *Deconstructing developmental psychology*. London: Routledge.

Chandra, N. (1996). Constructing a national popular: The Hindu India in *Amar Chitra Katha* (1970–91). Unpublished M. Phil. Dissertation, Jawaharlal Nehru University, New Delhi.

Chaudhary, N. (2005). Researching communities: Travails of working with Indian communities. *Cross-cultural Psychology Bulletin*, 43 (4), 5–13.

Chaudhary, N. & Sharma, N. (2005). From home to school. *Seminar*, 546, 14–20.

Chaudhary, N. (2004). *Listening to culture*. New Delhi: Sage.

Chowdhury, P. (1994). *The veiled women: Shifting gender equations in rural Haryana*. New Delhi: Oxford University Press.

Chauhan, A. Driven to despair. Times of India, March 14th. 2005. http://timesofindia.indiatimes.com/articleshow/1050309.cms. accessed on April 10th 2005.

Davis-Friedmann, D. (1983). *Long lives*. Cambridge, MA: Harvard University Press.

Dube, S. (1998). Land of poverty: Memoirs of an Indian family 1947–1977. London: Zed Books.

Dumont, L. (1980). *Homo Hierarchicus: The caste system and its implications*. Chicago: University of Chicago Press.

Durkheim, E. (1897/1997). *Suicide*. Columbus: The Free Press.

Eshleman, R. J. (1991). *The family: An introduction* (Sixth edition). Boston: Ally & Bacon.

Foster, M. E. (2002). How economists think about family resources and child development. *Child Development*, 73 (6), 1904–1914.

Gandhi, R. (2005). *Muniya's light: A narrative of truth and myth*. New Delhi: Roli Books and IndiaInk.

Gittins, D. (1985). *The family in question*. London: MacMillan.

Goode, W. J. (1963). *World revolution and family patterns*. London: The Free Press of Glencoe.

Guha, R. (2005). The colours of India. *The Hindu Sunday Magazine*, April 10, 2005.

Jain, A. (2005). Is Arranged Marriage Really Any Worse Than Craigslist? http://www.aldaily.com. Accessed on April 11th 2005.

Jenks, C. (1996). Suffer little children: A sociological analysis of changing attitudes to child abuse in the late twentieth century. In G. Pfeffer and D. K. Behera (Eds.), *Contemporary Society: Childhood and Complex Order* (pp. 182–213). New Delhi: Manak Publications.

Kapoor, S. (2005). Alternate care for infants of employed mothers. Unpublished doctoral dissertation, Department of Child Development, Lady Irwin College, University of Delhi.

Karlekar, M. (2003). Domestic violence. In V. Das (Ed.), The Oxford India companion to sociology and social anthropology (pp. 1127–1157). New Delhi: Oxford University Press.

Kumar, K. (1993). Study of childhood & family. In T. S. Saraswathi & B. Kaur (Eds.), *Human development and family studies in India: An agenda for research and policy* (pp. 67–76). New Delhi: Sage.

Kurtz, S. N. (1992). *All the mothers are one: Hindu India and the cultural reshaping of psychoanalysis*. New York: Columbia University Press.

Lawrence, J. A. & Valsiner, J. (1993). Social determinacy of human development: An analysis of the conceptual roots of the internalisation process. *Human Development*, 36, 150–167.

McGoldrick, M. (1998). *Re-visioning family therapy: Race, culture, and gender in clinical practice*. New York: Guilford.

Menon, U. (2003). Morality and context: A study of Hindu understandings. In J. Valsiner & K Connolly, (Eds.), Handbook of human development, (pp. 431–449) . London: Sage.

Mintz, S. (2005). *Huck's raft: A history of American childhood*. Cambridge, MA: Harvard University Press.

Ogburn, W. F. (1938). The family and its functions. In W. F. Ogburn (Ed.), *Recent social trends*. Chapter 13. New York: McGraw Hill.

Olson, D. H. & DeFrain, J. (1994). *Marriage and the family: Diversity and strengths*. Mountain View, Ca.: Mayfield Publishing Company.

Parsons, T. & Bales, R. F. (1955). *Family, socialisation and interaction process*. Glencoe, IL: The Free Press.

Pernau, M. (2003). Introduction. In M. Pernau, I. Ahmad, & H. Reifeld (Eds.), *Family and gender: Changing values in Germany and India* (pp. 9–34). New Delhi: Sage.

Rajagopalachari, C. (1999, 36th Edition). *Mahabharata*. Bombay: Bharatiya Vidya Bhavan. First Edition: 1951.

Ramanujan, A. K. (1994/1991). *Folk tales from India*. New Delhi: Penguin.

Raman, V. (2003). The diverse life-worlds of Indian childhood. In M. Pernau, I. Ahmad, & H. Reifeld (Eds.), *Family and gender: Changing values in Germany and India* (pp. 84–111). New Delhi: Sage.

Reifeld, H. (2003). State interest in the family: Social change and social policy in Germany. In M. Pernau, I. Ahmad, & H. Reifeld (Eds.), *Family and gender: Changing values in Germany and India* (pp. 224–241). New Delhi: Sage.

Saraswathi, T. S. (1999). Adult-child continuity in India: Is adolescence a myth or an emerging reality? In T. S. Saraswathi (Ed.), *Culture, socialization and human development: Theory, research and applications in India*. New Delhi: Sage.

Schneider, D. M. (1968). 1980/1968. *American kinship: A cultural account*. 2nd edition. Englewood Cliffs, NJ: Prentice-Hall.

Sen, A. (2005). *The argumentative Indian: Writings on Indian history, culture and identity*. London: Penguin.

Sherif, M. (1936). *Psychology of social norms*. New York: Harper & Brothers.

Simmel, G. (1904). The sociology of conflict. *American Journal of Sociology*, 9, 490–671.

Singer, M. (1968). The Indian joint family in modern industry. In M. Singer & B. Cohen (Eds.), *Structure and change in Indian society* (pp. 423–452). New York: Wenner-Gren Foundation.

Stratton, P. (2003). Contemporary families as contexts for development. In J. Valsiner & K Connolly (Eds.), *Handbook of human development* (pp. 333–357). London: Sage.

The World Bank. Snakes and ladders: Factors influencing successful primary school completion for children in poverty contexts. Discussion paper series, report no. 6, South Asia Human Development Sector, New Delhi: The World Bank, 2004.

Trautmann, T. R. (2003). Patterns of marriage. In V. Das (Ed.), *The Oxford India companion to sociology and social anthropology* (pp. 1105–1126). New Delhi: Oxford University Press.

Trawick, M. (1990). *Notes on love in a Tamil family*. Berkeley: University of California Press.

Trawick, M. (2003). The person behind the family. In V. Das (Ed.), *The Oxford companion to Sociology and Social Anthropology*. New Delhi: Oxford University Press.

Uberoi, P. (2003). The family in India: Beyond the nuclear versus joint debate. In V. Das (Ed.), *The Oxford India companion to sociology and social anthropology* (pp. 1062–1103). New Delhi: Oxford University Press.

Valsiner, J. & Litvinovic, G. (1996). Processes of generalisation in parental reasoning. In S. Harkness & C. M. Super (Eds.), *Parents' cultural belief systems: Their origins, expressions and consequences* (pp. 56–82). New York: The Guilford Press.

Vatuk, S. (1990). To be a burden on others: Dependency anxiety among elders in India. In O. M. Lynch (Ed.), *Divine passions: The social construction of emotions in India*. Berkeley: University of California Press.

Verma, S. & Sharma, D. (2003). Cultural continuity amid social change: Adolescents' use of free time in India. In S. Verma & R. Larson (Eds.), *Examining adolescent leisure time across cultures* (pp. 37–51). San Francisco: Jossey-Boss.

Verma, S. & Saraswathi, T. S. (2002). Adolescence in India: Street children or Silicon Valley millionaires. In B. B. Brown, R.W. Larson, & T. S. Saraswathi (Eds.), *The world's youth: Adolescence in eight regions of the globe* (pp. 105–140). Cambridge: Cambridge University Press.

Vindhya, U. (2003). Private crimes and public sanction: Violence against women in the family. In M. Pernau, I. Ahmad, & H. Reifeld (Eds.), *Family and gender: Changing values in Germany and India* (pp. 322–348). New Delhi: Sage.

Whitaker (1979). is cited in Olson and DeFrain as mentioned in the text.

Part VI

FROM SOCIAL CULTURE
TO PERSONAL CULTURE

CHAPTER 26

Culture and Social Representations

Gerard Duveen

The main aim of the theory of social represen-
tations is clear. By focusing on everyday com-
munication and thinking, it hopes to determine
the link between human psychology and mod-
ern social and cultural trends.

Moscovici, 1988, p. 225

Culture as a Field of Representations

Since the inception of work on social representations nearly half a century ago, there
has been a persistent interest in the articulation between these representations and the
broader field of culture, as Anne Parsons's
(1969) pioneering studies indicate. In part,
her investigations explored the forms of systematic misunderstanding that arise when
expressions of mental states grounded in one
specific culture are projected into a different cultural context. In one of her studies,
she examines the reasons for the failure of
her attempted treatment of a South Italian
immigrant to the United States through a
psychoanalytically based psychotherapy. In
her reflections she focuses on her failures

in grasping Mr. Calabrese's communicative
actions, both in the sense of understanding
what he was saying in relation to his own cultural context (including the specific context
of being an immigrant to the United States),
and in the sense of understanding how his
cultural resources were being employed to
make sense of what she said and did. Such
forms of misunderstanding are now familiar,
but they can be no less instructive for that.
Parsons herself explores the ways in which
different meanings are constructed or connoted in the course of such exchanges, and
as she demonstrates, the meanings of utterances always refer back to a very specific
context. While she herself does not elaborate a semiotic analysis of the context, we
could extend her analysis by noting that
utterances are always particular instances of
forms of semiotic mediation, and that the
context which is so important for their comprehension is always the broader network of
mediational forms which enable the signifiers of particular signs to be related to their
signifieds. As we have argued before (Lloyd
& Duveen, 1990), one of the functions of
representations is precisely to provide the

framework through which signifiers and signifieds can be associated in a meaningful
way, to reduce what Saussure called the arbitrariness of the sign. Such a perspective also
allows us to comprehend how misunderstanding arises when signifiers are associated
with signifieds through a different representational context. Anne Parsons, for instance, records the conflict that arose around
Mr. Calabrese's hostile feelings towards his
wife. From her permissive and professional
perspective, such feelings should have been a
focus of therapeutic concern, while from his
perspective the norms were different, "even
if a marriage is difficult you keep quiet about
it in order to preserve the institution of marriage as such" (Parsons, 1969, pp. 327–8).

But what has just been said about representations could just as easily be said of culture, indeed one might define culture as the
totality of forms of semiotic mediations and
their associated practices available within a
community. At the beginning of her recent
essay on *Social Representations in the Field
of Culture* Denise Jodelet (2002) remarks
on the significance of Durkheim as a common source for both the notions of social
or collective representations and of culture
as a concept in the social sciences. As she
notes, Durkheim's sources for his work on
representations were ethnographic materials related to traditional societies, and that
his work had, as she puts it, "posed the
question of the relation between the individual and the collective in the functioning
of thought" (Jodelet, 2002, p. 112, my translation). Within the Durkheimian tradition,
which has been one of the central sources
not only for the theory of social representations, but also for much thinking about the
notion of culture itself, society can be understood as consisting of representations.

But is this common ancestry sufficient to
justify an elision between these two terms
and consider "culture" and "social representations" as synonymous? Even to pose the
question in this way suggests the absurdity of
such an idea, with its clashing category error.
And yet without wishing to sustain any such
equivalence between these terms, it is nevertheless interesting to observe two comple-

mentary movements within recent thinking
about both these concepts which underlines
not only their common ancestry, but also
increasingly common fields of interest, one
might even say frames of analysis. On the one
hand, recent research on the theory of social
representations has emphasized the need
both to distinguish between levels and types
of representations, as well as the significance
of their thematic origins (cf. Moscovici,
1988, 2000; Marková, 2003). On the other
hand, recent work in cultural psychology
has drawn from the Vygotskyian perspective a concern with the cultural framing of
everyday interactions between people as the
focus for analyzing the forms of semiotic
mediation which are seen as the expression
of cultural forms in psychological life. On
the one hand, then, the theory of social
representations has been reaching back to
connect with some of the basic and fundamental structures (which Moscovici, following Holton, has described as *themata*)
which could be said to characterize culture in its broadest and most general sense,
while on the other, recent cultural psychology has been concerned with analyzing the close-at-hand as the arena in which
cultural forms are most accessible. Given
these complementary movements in recent
research, it is hardly surprising that the relations between culture and social representations have been a focus for a number of
important contributions (cf. Jodelet, 2002;
Valsiner, 2003; Valsiner and Van der Veer,
2000). If these emerging common points of
interest and concern hold the promise of
a productive engagement between cultural
psychology and the theory of social representations, we should also note that while
the terms "culture" and "social representations" appear to refer to different levels of
analysis, nevertheless whatever it is that we
take to be connoted by the term culture only
becomes accessible through the observation
and analysis of specific representations. But
again, this methodological note is not sufficient to elide the difference between these
two terms. The crucial difference remains
one of scale and scope. As an analytical concept, the term "social representation" carries

a dual meaning. On the one hand, it refers to a system of values, ideas, and practices related to a specific object, while also referring to the process through which such representations are formed, a sense more closely conveyed in English by *social representing* (cf. Duveen & Lloyd, 1990). This latter meaning, with its focus on process, already conveys a more dynamic sense than is often found in the use of the term culture. But representations (both in the substantive sense as well as process) always occur within a broader context of other representations which may also contribute towards the ways in which meanings become organized within specific representations. For instance, in her study of representations of Zen Buddhism in both Japanese and British contexts, Saito (1996) notes that while her Japanese respondents (even those not active practitioners) produced a coherent, well-structured account of this aspect of their local culture, while the British followers of Zen produced more fragmented images which were relatively isolated from other social practices within their local culture. What formed a part of the everyday experience and context for the Japanese, appears differently in the British context where it has a more exotic quality precisely because it has been differentiated from more familiar everyday experience.

Culture, then, can be taken as referring to a broader network of representations held together as an organized whole by a community. Social representations, in this sense, can be seen as particular cultural forms, and the analysis of social representations will always refer back in some way to the cultural context in which they take shape. I have already illustrated this idea in relation to Anne Parsons's work, but one might also consider the way in which Moscovici (1976) traces the emergence of representations of psychoanalysis within different social groups in France to the particular contexts in which they are generated. Indeed we could go further and suggest that it is through changing social representations that cultures themselves undergo change and transformation. Not only is it the case that all representa-

tions – even those which seem most deeply embedded in our culture – can at some point become the active focus of representational work leading to their transformation, but also what we might call cultural representations can themselves change through influences operating within the communicative practices of a community, that is, sociogenesis (cf. Duveen and Lloyd, 1990) may lead to cultural change.

Types of Social Representations

For Moscovici social representations are considered as the form of collective ideation which has appeared in the context of the modern world. Whereas pre-modern civilizations are generally characterized by unitary structures of power, authority and legitimation, the modern world is, rather, characterized by a diversity of forms of belief, understanding, and practice in which different social groups construct their own understanding of social processes and social life, in short, their own representations which may not only distinguish one group from another, but can also be the source of conflicts between them. Thus in relating his theory to the work of Durkheim he is not so much concerned with the terminological question of whether these representations are more accurately described as "social" or "collective," as in distinguishing the modes of construction and functioning of representations in the modern world. Representations are the products of patterns of communication within social groups and across society as a whole, and thus, importantly, are also susceptible to change and transformation. While acknowledging the significance of the Durkheimian concept of collective representations, he also marks his distance from the French sociologist by describing his concept as too static (Moscovici, 1984, p. 17; cf. also the discussion in Duveen, 2000), referring to a stable and settled order within a society. By introducing the idea of social representations he aims to capture the dynamic processes of change and transformation in the representations which circulate in the modern world. From this point of view, stability is only ever provisional, reflecting a particular moment in a more general process of transformation in which the social influences embedded in patterns of communication achieve a certain balance and closure.

Expressing a similar idea in a slightly different context Piaget wrote that "sooner or later reality comes to be seen as consisting of a system of transformations beneath the appearance of things" (Piaget & Inhelder, 1971, p. xiii). Or to paraphrase Karl Marx, we might say that all that is solid *can* melt into air, and then re-crystallize in a different form.

Moscovici defines a social representation as:

> a system of values, ideas and practices with a twofold function; first to establish an order which will enable individuals to orient themselves in their material and social world and to master it; and secondly to enable communication to take place among the members of a community by providing them with a code for social exchange and a code for naming and classifying unambiguously the various aspects of their world and their individual and group history. (Moscovici, 1973, p. xiii)

We can, then, think of social representations as structures of semiotic processes. However, while the socio-cultural tradition stemming from the work Vygotsky has emphasized the importance of semiotic mediation as the process through which sign usage organizes psychological activities, Moscovici's attention is not so much focused on the way in which individual signs operate as with the question of how ensembles of signs are held together in a structured and organized way so as to constitute a particular image of an aspect of social reality in which the arbitrariness of signs can be reduced and meaning and reference secured for a particular community. Social representations, then, are collective structures which are both established through communication as well as enabling communication to take place among members of a social group through the exchange of signs with common or shared meanings.

A corollary to this definition is that the realities in which we live are constituted by social representations. Defined simply as structures in this way, however, we would not be able to distinguish between different types of social representation, between, for example, a common idea emerging from the informal talk among a group of friends at a table in a café and the more pervasive and resilient representations of madness which exclude and isolate the mad. If there is a need to distinguish between different types of social representations, there is, as yet, no clear and settled means of identifying which aspects or dimensions of social representations might enable such distinctions to be made. This remains a rather open question within the theory, and indeed, Moscovici himself has offered more than one suggestion for how this might be achieved.

Perhaps the most familiar of Moscovici's suggestions is his proposal to distinguish between the *consensual* and the *reified* universes, which he sets out in the following terms:

> The division into the consensual *and the* reified *categories is a distinctive feature of our culture. In the former, society recognizes itself as a visible, continuous creation which is imbued with meaning and aims; it speaks with a human voice, is part and parcel of our lives and acts and reacts like a human being. In short, man is the measure of all things. In the latter, which comprise solid, fundamental, immutable entities and where particularities and individual identities are disregarded society fails to recognize itself and its works, which appear to it under the guise of isolated objects. In as much as the scientific disciplines are linked to these objects, scientific authority is able to impose this way of thinking and experiencing on each of us, prescribing in each case what is and what is not true. Under such circumstances, things thus become the measure of man.*
>
> The contrast between these two universes is psychologically powerful. The border between them splits collective reality, even physical reality, in two. Obviously science is the mode of knowledge corresponding to the reified universes and social representations

the one corresponding to the consensual universes. The former attempts to construct a map of the forces, objects and events unaffected by our desires and consciousness. The latter stimulates and shapes our collective consciousness, explaining things and events so as to be accessible to each of us and relevant to our immediate concerns. (Moscovici, 1981, pp. 186–7)

While this distinction remains interesting for the way it articulates how modern societies construct a specific way of representing different types of knowledge (cf. Duveen & Lloyd, 1990), nevertheless as a general proposal for distinguishing between types of social representation this proposal remains too limited. Partly because it derives from Moscovici's original interest in the processes through which scientific knowledge becomes absorbed into the world of everyday life (which was the inspiration for his pioneering study of social representations of psychoanalysis, Moscovici, 1976), and partly because it does not address questions about how different types of social representation might differ in their structure and functioning.

A second, more recent proposal is presented in the context of another broader discussion, this time of the relations between the so-called *primitive* mentality and the mentality of modern societies. Here Moscovici proposes that:

A great deal of ink has been poured over this difference between a "primitive mentality" and a "civilized" or "scientific" mentality. In fact it seems to me to refer to the difference between belief and knowledge, so important but so little understood, as can be established by reading Wittgenstein's (1953) late reflections on belief. In my opinion a great many misunderstandings would be dispelled if the following suggestion were to be accepted: The difference with which we are concerned takes on a new meaning when we pay attention to the distinction between:

(a) common representations whose kernel consists of beliefs which are generally more homogenous, affective, imperme-

able to experience or contradiction, and leave little scope for individual variations; and

(b) common representations founded on knowledge which are more fluid, pragmatic, amenable to the proof of success or failure, and leave a certain latitude to language, experience, and even to the critical faculties of individuals. (Moscovici, 2000, p. 136)

This distinction already has a greater utility insofar as it offers a clearer characterization of the qualities which distinguish at least these two types of representations. Although in this chapter Moscovici does not immediately extend this argument, it would be in keeping with his general approach to add that this distinction between representations based on belief and those based on knowledge is not limited to a distinction between the mentalities of different epochs or of different levels of society, but, rather, can be seen as a distinction between types of representation which circulate today within our own cultures (cf. Moscovici's comments on Bartlett's discussion of Lévy-Bruhl, Moscovici, 1990). Yet this distinction, too, is also limited, primarily because it does not yet include any clear discussion of the functional aspects of these representations, of the modalities through which they circulate or are communicated, or the ways in which they serve to structure different types of social groups, or may be structured by different types of social relations.

The proposal in which these functional aspects of representations become most clearly visible is to be found in Moscovici's (1988) response to Jahoda's (1988) critical commentary on the theory of social representations itself. One point which Jahoda emphasizes is what he sees as a lack of clarity in Moscovici's discussion of the relations between social representations and social groups. In responding to this argument, Moscovici suggests a tripartite distinction between:

(i) Hegemonic representations can become shared by all members of a highly

structured group -a party, a city, a nation- without their having been produced by the group.

(ii) Emancipated representations are the outgrowth of the circulation of knowledge and ideas belonging to subgroups that are in more or less close contact.

(iii) Polemical representations generated in the course of social conflict, social controversy and society as a whole does not share them. They are determined by the antagonistic relations between its members and intended to be mutually exclusive.
(Mosocvici, 1988)

What Mosocvici describes as hegemonic representations correspond to the representational forms closest to those described by Durkheim as collective, and could also be said to be largely representations based on beliefs, since they consist of patterns of values and ideas deeply embedded in the practices of everyday life. As such, these representations are not only extraordinarily stable and resistant to change, but also only rarely become the focus of any sustained reflection, remaining more or less closed systems of meaning. They constitute, as it were, the unreflexive assumptions of a particular form of life, the *fraglos gegeben* as Schütz (1972) described them. On the other hand, both emancipated and polemical representations imply a degree of reflection, of discussion, of argument. In both cases, these representations embrace ideational and evaluative positions which need to be defended and legitimized, while at the same time securing a position within the symbolic world of a society which can provide the locus for the social identity of the group affiliated around these ideas and values. The need to secure legitimation for these positions necessarily means that these representations must be more open to argument or debate. The forms of discourse through which legitimation can be secured may be very varied, from the rigorous procedures of the natural sciences to the peculiar inverted logic of a more or less hermetically sealed religious sect. No doubt these different patterns of legitimation correspond to representations with very different types of presence within the social

world, but insofar as they share a certain openness they also tend towards being constituted as representations based on knowledge (even if what is taken as constituting knowledge may also be as varied as the different patterns of legitimation through which it can be secured). What characterizes these representations, then, is a certain activity of reflection as a social group seeks to establish a sense of closure by legitimizing the view of world embodied by a particular representation.

Reflection in the Genesis of Representations

What I have described here as an activity of reflection is, in fact, a key characteristic of social representations. When he considers the origin of representations, Moscovici notes that the "purpose of all representations is to make the unfamiliar, or unfamiliarity itself, familiar" (2000, p. 37). It is within this context of a dynamic of familiarization that he introduces the concepts of anchoring and objectification as the central processes in the genesis of social representations. It is an elegantly simple idea. Something (an idea, a person, a group, a phenomenon) appears which is initially opaque to the existing structures of meaning, and for this very reason is also troubling. In seeking to give the unfamiliar a place within the known world, some kind of representational work, or activity of reflection, is required, and the traces of this activity can be observed in the communications which circulate around this unfamiliar object. At times, of course, unfamiliarity can be very dramatic and even engender considerable change within existing structures of meaning as it becomes familiarized. If we think, for instance, of the fall of the Berlin Wall we can see both the sense of the dramatic emergence of the unfamiliar as well as the profound transformations in structures of meaning which had seemed, at least since the close of the World War II, extraordinarily stable and resistant to change. Or again, if we consider the emergence of HIV/AIDS we can recognize successive transformations in its representation from being a "gay plague" to a disease controllable by medication as it has become anchored within different structures of meaning (cf. Preda, 2005). Both of these examples illustrate the centrality of representational work or the activity of reflection in the genesis of representations as the unfamiliar is familiarized. Indeed, we could say that what characterizes emancipated or polemical representations as distinct from hegemonic representations is precisely that they are representations which are active centres of reflection in this sense. So familiar were the geo-political divisions of the Cold War, at least in the popular mind, that for decades they seemed part of the given structure of the world. The collapse of the Wall, and the processes which followed, had the effect of bringing this stable and settled representation into question so that they became centres of activity as new representations have emerged. The representational work engendered by the unfamiliar is of course focused on the establishment of a more familiar and stable framing of the object. But this is only one part of the process, for this new understanding still has to be legitimized and, perhaps, defended against alternative interpretations. The activity of reflection evident in the communications around emancipated and polemical representations embraces both aspects of this representational work.

Culture as Representation and the Representation of Culture

Culture is sometimes considered as the discriminating principle through which all members of a community are alike in sharing some set of beliefs, values, and practices, and different from other communities which have their own sets of beliefs, values, and practices. While such a view may be helpful to some degree, it can also be a hindrance. First, it presents culture as a categorical phenomenon, which, like all such phenomena, tends to emphasize differences between cultures while minimizing variations within

cultures. Each culture is viewed as though it were a homogenous entity, free of internal division. But as the discussion of social representations has already indicated, such a view is unsustainable. Societies, certainly modern societies but perhaps also other societies, are always marked by internal divisions, to the point where we might find some justification for claiming that society is a machine for producing difference. Nor can this issue be avoided by suggesting that the term culture refers only to hegemonic representations, since it would be absurd to consider emancipated or polemical representations as somehow not also being cultural forms.

Second, this categorical view of culture can also be a hindrance if it is taken as suggesting that the point of demarcation between one culture and another is a fixed or rigid point. As Bartlett (1923, 1932) pointed out many years ago, even what used to be called primitive cultures were communities which were also often engaged in a variety of forms of contact with other communities rather than being isolated from them. And from that contact new representational elements enter into the life of cultures, which may then be incorporated into their own representational structures. What Bartlett describes as a process of conventionalization is also a process of cultural change. A degree of fluidity between cultures is more the norm than the exception. In the modern world this fluidity can produce seemingly paradoxical situations for a researcher, since what are often presented as comparisons across cultures turn out on closer inspection to be rather studies of how a single more globalized culture is spreading across the world. If people engaged in the market economies of the West turn out to have similar ideas about economic processes to the people engaged in similar activities in the East, is this really a comparison across cultures, or simply an indication that in some important sectors of life both West and East find themselves participating in a common culture?

But this is not to say that there are not real boundaries or borders between cultures – regions where horizons emerge and where some form of representational work or negotiation is required. While there may be a fluidity to cultures, this does not mean that any cultural element can be substituted for any other cultural element. There are points where communication only becomes possible if it engenders a change of some kind. Or to put this another way – a cultural identity is revealed at the point where something can no longer be communicated. As Lucien Goldmann (1976) saw so penetratingly, the identities which emerge in the course of development constrain the representations which individuals or groups might accept. In his terms, the limiting case was one where the conditions for the acceptance of a new representation entailed the dissolution of an existing identity – which means change for the individual, or disbandonment, schism, or re-organization for the group.

Goldmann's argument is important since it links identity to communication, to what it is possible to communicate in a relationship, and what is incommunicable, or where communication itself can lead to change and re-organization. The stability of particular forms of identity is therefore also linked to the stability of the network of social influences which sustain a particular representation – as the balance of influence processes changes so too does the predominant representation, and consequently the patterns of identity which are a function of that representation (cf. Duveen, 1998). We can then consider identity as an asymmetry in a relationship which constrains what can be communicated through it – both in the sense of what it becomes possible to communicate and in the sense of what becomes incommunicable (and potentially a point of resistance), or communicable only on condition of a reworking of that identity (cf. Duveen, 2001). Cultural identities, then, become evident at the point where communication becomes problematic; it is when the implicit sense of culture can no longer be taken for granted that the explicit search for culture begins, This is the point where boundaries or horizons between cultures emerge. For the social sciences, the corollary to this view

is that culture cannot be assumed to be a given property of a community which marks out a difference from another community. Rather, difference or similarity is something which needs to be established and articulated through the analysis of specific and particular situations.

Culture and Time

Culture in the sense in which it is being used here must not only be seen as having structure, but as a structure which has a functional role in relation to the community which is sustained by it, and which also sustains the culture. For the community, its culture is a stabilizing element, and as a structure it acquires stability because it is sustained within a context of some kind – a context of other cultures or the history of the culture itself. The community which sustains a culture, like every other social group, defines itself in part through the oppositions it generates in relation to other communities. "We are like *this*, whereas they are like *that*." But as well as establishing stability in the present, for a culture to sustain a community it also needs to account for the past through which the present has emerged, and project a future to which the present is oriented. While there has been considerable interest in the ways in which social groups and communities represent their past in their collective memories, the future as an orienting perspective for a group has rarely figured in the social psychological literature. Indeed, for the most part, social psychological conceptualizations of the group remain largely static, or, one might even say, timeless, that is, they are seen to exist almost as though they were outside the dimension of time. There is something quite astonishing in the neglect of the dimension of time in the social psychology of the group or of intergroup relations, and it is surely a theme which deserves more attention than it can be given here. For the moment, one can only note its absence in almost every social psychological account of the group. A recent, and rare, exception is in the work of Gina Philogène (2001) who introduces the notion of anticipatory social representations in her account of the changing nomination from black to African American, in which representations formed in the present may anticipate expected (or desired) futures. But there is also an earlier contribution to this theme in the work of Bartlett, which is more immediately germane to the present discussion of the relations between culture and social representations.

Bartlett's early work in psychology was much concerned with questions of culture, or more particularly with analyzing the psychological aspects of cultural processes. In his first book, *Psychology and Primitive Culture* (1923), Bartlett sets out to analyze the specifically social psychological aspects of what he (along with most other writers of this time) reluctantly accepts to describer as "primitive" culture – reluctantly because, of course, the word *primitive* not only inevitably carries with it pejorative overtones, especially when used by an academic representative of a dominant society about a dominated society, but also carries implications of simplicity and lack of sophistication which simply do not do justice to the richness, complexity, and subtlety of cultural forms in what we would now describe as non-literate societies.

Central to Bartlett's account is his treatment of primitive cultures not as the product of a more or less isolated social group which sustains a hegemonic and unchanging culture, but rather he considers such societies as being always in touch with – and hence influenced by – their contact with other social groups, and the culture they sustain as being also something which changes, whether externally through these contacts with other social groups or internally through what he calls the constructiveness of social responses, by which he means the "tendency which produces new modes of social organisation" (Bartlett, 1923, p. 29). As he considers the question of cultural change effected through the contact between peoples, Bartlett also comes to

focus more specifically on what he describes as the "group difference tendencies," which differentiate one group from another, and which "cluster about a group's established institutions and act directly as determining factors of individual social behaviour" (Bartlett, 1923, p. 29). Such group difference tendencies give a direction to the ways in which a group may take up and elaborate novel cultural elements introduced through their contacts with other people, indeed he goes on to argue that "how, as well as what, material is received through contact depends to a considerable degree upon the operation of these differentiating tendencies of social groups" (Bartlett, 1923, p. 155).

In his later, more familiar book on *Remembering* (1932), Bartlett returns to this theme in his discussion of conventionalization, by which he means the process through which "cultural material . . . introduced into a group from the outside . . . suffers change until it eventually either disappears or reaches a new stable form" (Bartlett, 1932, p. 268). In this later, slightly more elaborated version of his argument, what Bartlett described as group difference tendencies in his earlier book have been subsumed into his account of social constructiveness, considered as the most interesting form of conventionalization (the others being assimilation, simplification and retention of details). It is in his discussion of social constructiveness that Bartlett offers one of his most radical suggestions for social psychology. "Every well-established social group," he writes, "possesses not only a structure which has been built up in its past, but also a function, or a group of functions, within the community of which it is a part. These functions have to be expressed in co-ordinated human activity, and all such activity has not only a history, but also a *prospect* (my emphasis)" (1932, p. 275). So clear is this prospect, that one can say of a group that "it inevitably tends to develop in certain more or less specific directions; and if we know enough, we can state in some detail the paths along which it is tending" (1932, p. 275). And he continues by suggesting that "when any cultural features come from outside, they may be transformed, not only by assimilation, by simplification and elaboration, and by the retention of apparently unimportant elements, but positively *in the direction along which the group happens to be developing* at the time these features are introduced," so that "the imported elements change, both in the direction of existing culture and along the general line of development of the receptive group" (1932, p. 275).

For Bartlett, the idea of social constructiveness expresses his conviction that social groups do not simply accept or receive cultural elements from outside, but actively transform them to produce new cultural elements. But this activity of transformation is undertaken in relation to the existing structure of the group, so that elements are drawn into existing projects and reshaped or reworked to make them of service to these projects. And as the quotations from his text indicate, for Bartlett to understand this process it is necessary that we construe social groups having, as he puts it, a *prospect*, a *direction of development* which guides and shapes the absorption and transformation of elements encountered through the groups exchanges or contacts with other groups. In this sense, Bartlett's notion of the social group is not that of a static organization of social relations, values, and practices, but rather he sees the social group as having a dynamic organization in which culture not only provides a stable image of the present and its relation to the past, but also projects the group into a future. We might envisage this notion of the group in terms of a cultural vector which by coordinating past, present and future gives shape and meaning to the life of a group, that is, furnishes the group with a project which determines not only aspects of the behavior and practice of members of the group, but also the ways in which environmental influences are transformed as they become part of the group's repertoire of resources. In short, Bartlett's work can be seen as an argument for the necessity of incorporating the dimension of time into our understanding of the social group, and hence also into our considerations of the relations between culture and representations.

Time, Change, and Cognitive Polyphasia

In Moscovici's work, the theory of social representations has always been oriented to the analysis of social, or cultural, change. That is, he envisions social representations as dynamic structures in which knowledge is constantly being transformed as social groups construct and re-construct their grasp of the social world and their place within it. Like every genetic psychology, the theory of social representations is oriented around the dimension of time as a fundamental parameter of social processes. As I noted earlier, particular representations are only ever the product of the balance of influence processes at a specific point in time. As this balance changes, so too will the representations sustained by these communicative processes. Yet while these points are theoretically clear, there has been relatively little empirical analysis of how representations change. There have been studies in the ontogenesis of social representations (e.g., Lloyd and Duveen, 1990; Psaltis and Duveen, 2006) which have explored the dynamics of specific processes of change within the psychological development of individuals. In these studies children are investigated as they develop within a social world structured by a stable set of representations within their communities, and something similar can be seen in other developmental research within the field of cultural psychology (e.g., Lave, 1988; Rogoff, 1990), even if in these cases it is a stable set of social practices which is considered to provide the structure within which children's developing competencies takes shape. While the study of ontogenesis is a crucial arena for the investigation of specific types of representational change in which the orientation to time is quite clear, it nevertheless rarely reaches the level of sociogenesis, where representations themselves are formed and transformed. As children learn how to play marbles, or come to understand something about the world of gender, or grasp the idea of conservation, or learn to weave using a traditional loom, they are always engaged in some process of construction in which something novel emerges. But the novelty is for the child, since it is the construction of something new in relation to their existing knowledge and understanding, rather than something novel for the culture in which they are growing up. It is the study of sociogenetic transformation which is central for an understanding of cultural change, a focus that can pose particular methodological challenges.

From time to time phenomena emerge in the social world which are recognized as significant and important phenomena, but whose initial unfamiliarity means that the process of familiarization (that is, the sociogenesis of new representations, or, rather, representations of this new object) itself becomes visible and open to investigation. The emergence of HIV/AIDS is one such phenomena of recent times, and research has indeed shown how the representation of this phenomena has undergone considerable transformation in the relatively brief period since the condition was first identified, both within the Western world and within developing societies. In these circumstances successive representations of the same object can be identified either in the public discourse of the mass media, or through the discourse of participants in successive waves of research investigations. Not only does the identification of successive representations of the same object provide data for the analysis of sociogenetic transformation, but, especially where public discourse is available, it also includes much information about the communicative processes influencing these transformations (Alex Preda's, 2005, book is a good illustration of this approach, which broadly corresponds to what Moscovici (1990) has described as "Piaget's Way"). But sociogenetic change can also occur in more subtle ways over much more extended periods of time, and here the social psychological analysis of such change encounters more complex methodological issues which concern first of all the visibility of the phenomenon itself. Characteristically a more synchronic perspective has been adopted to the investigation of such transfor-

mation through a strategy by examining the ways in which the same object becomes represented by different social groups (which Moscovici describes as "Bartlett's Way" or "Vygotsky's Way"). Bartlett's own work provides a good illustration of this approach, as can be seen in his (1923) accounts of how specific cultural elements (and he is mostly concerned with elements of the material culture) move from one primitive group to another. Another example, of course, is Moscovici's (1976) own study of the transformations of psychoanalysis as it becomes represented by different social groups in French society. In this work Moscovici draws on both the responses of participants to a questionnaire investigation as well as on a systematic content analysis of the French media. And it is this content analysis which enables Moscovici to analyze the different communicative practices (propagation, propaganda, and diffusion) through which different representations of psychoanalysis are constructed and projected. If one misses a diachronic perspective in this study, it nevertheless provides elegant testimony to the rich possibilities which a careful and thorough synchronic analysis can provide for understanding the dynamics of sociogenetic transformation.

In the course of his work on psychoanalysis, Moscovici introduces a concept which has come to be seen as both theoretically and methodologically significant for the analysis of sociogenetic transformation (cf. Jovchelovitch and Gervais, 1999; Wagner et al., 1999, 2000). In the course of his research on representations of psychoanalysis Moscovici (1976, pp. 279ff) observed the co-existence of different and even contradictory modes of thinking in his research on psychoanalysis. In moving between these different registers or voices, he notes that people in contemporary societies are "speaking" medical, psychological, technical, and political languages. As he puts it, "the same group, and *mutatis mutandis*, the same individual are capable of employing different logical registers in the domains which they approach with different perspectives, information and values" (1976, p. 286, my translation). By extending this phenomenon to the level of thought he suggests that "the dynamic co-existence – interference or specialization – of the distinct modalities of knowledge, corresponding to definite relations between man and his environment, *determines a state of cognitive polyphasia*" (p. 286, my translation, emphasis in the original). Indeed, he suggests that far from being an exceptional state of affairs, it is probable that the "*coexistence* of cognitive systems should be the rule rather than the exception" (1976, p. 285, my translation). From what he describes as the hypothesis of cognitive polyphasia, Moscovici suggests that research should be concerned with "the analysis of transformations – equilibrium and evolution – of these modalities of knowledge, of the relations which are established between them and their adaptation" (1976, p. 287, my translation), and that more generally social psychology should focus on the "movement of forms of reflection and their order, comparing them with events and factors of *interaction and culture*" (1976, p. 287, my translation, emphasis in the original).

Moscovici's discussion of cognitive polyphasia thus suggests that within the complex of representations characteristic of a social group we can expect to find discontinuities, and even contradictions between different elements, and further, that if we consider the dynamic of the social group we shall see that these different elements are not random collections but that they are organized in systematic ways. Methodologically this proposal is important for the analysis of sociogenetic change, since it alerts us to the probability of finding different elements within the representations of a social group, and to exploring the character of the structure through which they are held together within a system. Hence we need to consider cultures not as finished or complete systems, but rather as systems in constant transformation in which the present can be expected to be not only polyphasic, but also structured around the relations (tensions and contradictions) between the various elements of this polyphasia.

One example of polyphasia can be seen in Anne Parsons's (1969) account of the Southern Italian immigrants to the United States who have converted from the Roman Catholicism of their native culture to a form of Pentacostalism. She identifies many ways in which characteristics of the specific pattern of Southern Italian Catholicism survive or re-emerge within the new forms of Pentacostalism, sometimes even in almost unconscious ways, almost like the Freudian return of the repressed. For instance, within the services of this group she observed the "very frequent repetition by the women of the phrase *santa, santa, santa* (*santa* = saint), sometimes appearing in the more complex form of a series of indistinguishable words beginning with *santa*, but always following a rhythmic pattern and phrase length exactly equivalent to that of *Santa Maria, piena di grazia* . . . or the Hail Mary which is intimately known to every Catholic" (p. 252). Indeed it is in the services that she finds these combinations of the rejected past and the accepted present most clearly expressed. She notes for instance the way in which the sermons characteristically moved through cycles of affirmation, doubt, regression, and resolution, and that as they did so the pastor also shifted his religious style. While the affirmative phases were characterized by a more or less rational and coherent discourse in an identifiably Protestant tradition, the intermediate phases were notable for their expression of anxiety and skepticism through modulations of voice, of body posture, and of cognitive incoherence, or as she puts is "a process of free association or a kind of dramatic role-playing that served to act out a number of mutually contradictory attitudes" (p. 269). In her analysis of this material, Parsons suggests that the ritual of the service is more than just a bipolar structure which combines elements from two distinctive cultural traditions, but that the specific forms of the ritual need to be referred to the context of the social and cultural changes through which this particular group is passing. While Parsons' work predates Moscovici's formulation of the hypothesis of cognitive polyphasia, we can nevertheless see in her account of these Pentacostal immigrants a specific form of polyphasia in which the sociogenesis of cultural change is oriented by the dynamic of the group. While Parsons' research is a synchronic study, it can nevertheless be considered as a genetic study precisely because the orientation to social change allows the present to be understood within the dimension of time.

Representations of Mental Health and Illness in Contemporary India

One last example will serve to bring these threads of discussion together. It concerns a study of changing representations of mental health and illness among contemporary urban middle-class North Indians (Wagner et al., 1999, 2000).[1] Traditional Indian patterns of thought have, or course, a rich set of beliefs about the phenomena of mental illness, which in milder forms can be attributed to an imbalance of the humors and in more serious instances to spirit or ghost possession. These different forms of disturbance are also associated with different forms of treatment, ranging from encouragement and support within the family, through various forms of ritual healing in the temple, up to severe physical treatments of trying to beat the possessing spirit out of the body it has occupied (called in Hindi the *jharphook*). Traditional Hindi society in North India includes arranged marriage, and public knowledge of mental illness in the family is a source of considerable anxiety, since it prejudices the marriage prospects for other members of the family. Over the past few decades Western psychiatric medicine, with its very different forms of etiology and treatment, has also become a stronger presence in the life of these Indian groups, both in the sense of the availability of psychiatric clinics as well as through the media in various forms. Faced with these different and disjunctive representations of mental illness, how do these urban Indians now think and talk about the phenomena of mental illness? To explore

Table 26.1: Characteristics of modern and traditional healing

	Psychiatrist	Traditional healer
Etiology	Unfulfilled desires, fear, shock, pressure, depression	Spirit possession, disequilibrium of humors, etc.
Treatment	Talking, finding the reasons, friendliness, removing ideas, medicine	Exorcism, rituals, sacrifice, medicine
Dominant principle	Psychological agency of the patient	Agency of the causes of the illness, e.g. spirits

Adapted from Wagner et al. (2000).

these questions the participants were interviewed on the basis of a short vignette describing a person engaged in strange patterns of behavior (strange, but stereotypical for this community of the behavior of the mentally ill). This strategy allowed the interviews to range over a number of issues related not only to participants' knowledge of both traditional and psychiatric models of mental illness and its treatment, but also to ask how the participants would respond if someone in their own family were to begin to behave in such ways.

What emerged from the interviews was that the participants could talk knowledgeably about both traditional and psychiatric notions of mental illness (see Table 26.1 for a summary of the characteristics attributed to each of these representations), though it was also clear that in general they had a richer, more elaborated understanding of traditional patterns of belief and a more superficial grasp of modern psychiatry; a difference which was especially marked in their descriptions of the details of forms of treatment.

More interestingly for the present discussion, when they considered the relative merits of different forms of treatment, many of the participants expressed a disbelief in traditional forms and faith in the efficacy of the modern scientific approach of the psychiatrist. For instance, this was one man's view of the effectiveness of different forms of treatment[2]

> Interviewer: Do you think that there is a TECHNIQUE with traditional healers?
> Respondent: NO, I THINK NOT. If a TECHNIQUE would be with them then SUCCESS must be there 100%. But they do not get SUCCESS anywhere, I THINK.

Another expressed the difference between traditional and psychiatric forms of treatment in this way:

> Interviewer: If any member of your family would start to have such a behavior as I told earlier, what would you do?
> Respondent: I would take him to a psychiatrist, who does an up-to-date treatment.
> Interviewer: Would you do anything more?
> Respondent: No, nothing... Once a boy came to me and got ill. The people told me to go for traditional treatment, but I said I would not do it... What would the traditional, the traditional healer do? The jhar-phook? That is nothing!

At the same time the respondents were often very aware of the power of traditional patterns of thought within the extended family, as this woman explains:

> *Because... Look, suppose in my family or maybe in the LONG RUN if it will happen to my child or my daughter-in-law or with me, then all the people who will come will suggest to show him [the ill person] to that maulavi [Urdu word for spirit healer], "in Patna there is a good maulavi. Take him to Biharsharif [a village near Patna] to the shrine." So all minds are of the same kind. Isn't it? So I do this even if I don't want to do it, but I won't get SUCCESSFUL [the patient won't be cured there]. But I do it. And when I am not cured, I go to the DOCTOR at LAST and the DOCTOR does the treatment...*

As these extracts indicate, for many of the respondents it was the claim to scientific knowledge and a practice derived from it which was the source of their preference for a psychiatric representation. As one man put it:

> *These people [psychiatrists] are becoming more successful. They are doing research, and they are improving everything. They improve their MEDICINES and their GENERAL SCIENCE.*

Or as this woman expressed it:

> *It is possible that he [traditional healer] is not able to understand the BAD BEHAVIOUR [of the sick person] and it might increase the sickness. It is just possible that he [sick person] can turn mad or become aggressive [because the healer is treating him in a wrong way]. He [healer] might do it unknowingly. But a PSYCHOLOGIST would move in scientifically and would take ACTION continuously. He would always consider whether his ACTION is contributing towards cure or harming him [sick person].*

While this preference for the psychiatric over the traditional was common, especially among those of the younger generation among the participants, at times respondents were more conscious of the conflict between these different representations, especially when, as in the case of this woman, there was also experience of successful intervention by a traditional healer:

> *As I told you, it happened with my aunt. But I think these things are nothing. Many people die, I have read that in books. Haven't you heard that one ojha (spirit healer) killed somebody beating him to death? That man died. His story is finished. So I have some faith and at the same time I don't believe in them.*

Her final sentence crystallizes something important about cognitive polyphasia as the co-existence of contradictory representations. More generally, though, the preference for the psychiatric was linked to the claims of science and the idea of progress which this enshrines. The polyphasic quality of contemporary representations of mental illness among the Indian middle-class has to be seen within the context of their general vision of the shifts and changes in their society. They envisage India as a country which is developing away from a traditional culture and society towards a more modern form. Development in this context means becoming more like the advanced societies of the West, in which a scientifically based medicine and treatment for the mentally ill serves as a token of this process, providing a bridge, as it were, between the traditional and the modern. In this example the "traditional" elements of Indian representations of mental illness which might have been considered as deeply embedded within the communal life of these societies are being drawn into a more *active* form of reflection and change through this process of cultural contact, communication, and exchange.

We cannot predict how these representations will develop. Perhaps traditional patterns of thought will disappear altogether and simply be replaced by Western psychiatric notions. However, given that we know that even in the West social representations of mental illness retain strong and powerful aspects of our historical patterns of thought (Jodelet, 1991) this seems unlikely. Much more likely is that in India new forms of polyphasia will emerge in which psychiatric notions will acquire a characteristically Indian patterning, just as Denise Jodelet shows us how the representations of mental illness among the villagers of Ainay-le-chateau have been able to assimilate notions derived from modern psychiatry within more traditional patterns of belief. For Jodelet the dynamic at work in structuring the representations of these villagers is the profound need to sustain a distinction between the mad who are resident in the village and the villagers themselves. If they could not make this differentiation between self and other, then these villagers risk finding themselves collapsing into madness. Striving to sustain a sense of difference is what generates their endless inventiveness in elaborating structures through which to construct their understanding of mental ill-

ness. For the Indian middle-classes it is the theme of modernization establishes the fundamental dynamic for this social group as it engages in these changes, and also serves to orient their appropriation of Western psychiatric notions to produce a specific form of polyphasia.

Conclusion

This chapter began with the difficulties inherent in the concept of culture itself, and thus also of establishing a clear relationship between culture and social representations. At best it seems that we can distinguish them by noting that while social representations always bear on specific objects, the term culture refers to a more diffuse body of representations which serve to characterize something distinctive about a community. But this is not a sharp distinction, since, of course, in constructing specific representations social groups may also use elements from this broader repertoire of cultural resources. Further, insofar as culture itself can be considered a set of representations then we can also see that the processes of formation and transformation are similar whether we think of social representations or of cultures. Indeed, the interplay between these two terms is what is central – culture being the sedimentation of sociogenetic changes which appear first as changes in the social representation of a specific object. If we think, for instance, of the position of women in society we can note how great the change has been over the past century, from being excluded even from participation in the political life of society towards a situation structured around complex discourses of equality. As always, change was initiated by a minority seeking to establish a different position, creating as it were novel polemical representations. Over time these have shifted towards becoming emancipated representations, and in important ways now constitute hegemonic representations, so that we can accept that there has been a shift in our culture. No doubt there will be further changes in these representations as the theme of equality is expanded and explored further. But in providing a conceptual frame for considering questions of social and cultural change in this way, the theory of social representations has something significant to contribute to contemporary discussions of cultural psychology. By emphasizing the dynamic aspect of social groups, and thus also orienting the discussion of representations to the dimension of time, and through the concept of cognitive polyphasia, the theory can help to elucidate central aspects of processes of cultural change.

Notes

1   This is not an intuition which is unique to Moscovici. One can find similar ideas in the works of many other psychologists concerned with the genesis of social knowledge, stretching back at least to the work of McDougall and Bartlett, for instance.
2   This research was undertaken in Patna, North India with a group of 39 participants, ranging in age from 20 to 55+ years and including equal numbers of men and women. All of the participants had at least begun University level courses.

References

Bartlett, F. (1923). *Psychology and Primitive Culture*. Cambridge: Cambridge University Press.

Bartlett, F. (1932). *Remembering: A Study in Experimental and Social Psychology*. Cambridge: Cambridge University Press.

Duveen, G. (1998). The psychosocial production of knowledge: Social representations and psychologic. *Culture and Psychology, 4*, 455–472.

Duveen, G. (2000). The Power of Ideas. Introduction to S. Moscovici (Ed. G. Duveen) *Social Representations: Explorations in Social Psychology* (pp. 1–17). Cambridge: Polity Press.

Duveen, G. (2001). Representations, identities, resistance. In K. Deaux and G. Philogène (Eds.), *Representations of the Social* (pp. 257–270). Oxford: Blackwell.

Duveen, G. and Lloyd, B. (1990). Introduction. In G. Duveen and B. Lloyd (Eds.), *Social Representations and the Development of Knowledge* (pp. 1–10). Cambridge: Cambridge University Press.

Philogène, G. (2001). From race to culture: The emergence of African American. In K. Deaux and G. Philogène (Eds.), *The Representation of the Social: Bridging Theoretical Perspectives*, New York: Basil Blackwell.

Goldmann, L. (1976). *Cultural creation in modem society*. Saint Louis: Telos Press.

Jahoda, G. (1988). Critical notes and reflections on "social representations." *European Journal of Social Psychology, 18*, 195–209.

Jodelet, D. (1991). *Madness and Social Representations*. London: Harvester.

Jodelet, D. (2002). Les representations socials dans le champ de la culture, *Social Science Information, 41*, 111–133.

Jovchelovitch, S. and Gervais, M.-C. (1999). Social representations of health and illness: The case of the Chinese community in England. *Journal of Community and Applied Social Psychology, 9*, 247–260.

Lave, J. (1988). *Cognition in practice*. Cambridge: Cambridge University Press.

Lloyd, B. and Duveen, G. (1990). A Semiotic Analysis of the Development of Social Representations of Gender. In G. Duveen and B. Lloyd (Eds.), *Social Representations and the Development of Knowledge* (pp. 27–46). Cambridge: Cambridge University Press.

Marková, I. (2003). *Dialogicality and Social Representations: The Dynamics of Mind*. Cambridge: Cambridge University Press.

Moscovici, S. (1973). Foreword. In C. Herzlich *Health and Illness*. London: Academic Press.

Moscovici, S. (1976). *La Psychanalyse, son image et son public*. Paris: Presses Universitaires de France.

Moscovici, S. (1981). On Social Representation. In J. Forgas (Ed.), *Social Cognition*. London: Academic Press.

Moscovici, S. (1984). The Phenomenon of Social Representations. In Farr, R. and Moscovici, S. (1984) (Eds). *Social Representations*. Cambridge: Cambridge University Press. (Reprinted in Moscovici, 2000)

Moscovici, S. (1988). Notes towards a definition of social representations. *European Journal of Social Psychology, 18*, 211–250.

Moscovici, S. (1990). Social psychology and developmental psychology: Extending the conversation. In G. Duveen and B. Lloyd (Eds.), *Social Representations and the Development of Knowledge*. Cambridge: Cambridge University Press.

Moscovici, S. (2000). *Social Representations: Explorations in Social Psychology*. (Edited by G. Duveen). Cambridge: Polity Press.

Parsons, A. (1969). *Belief, Magic and Anomie: Essays in Psychological Anthropology*. New York: The Free Press.

Piaget, J. and Inhelder, B. (1971). *The Mental Imagery of the Child*. New York: Basic Books.

Preda, A. (2005). *AIDS, Rhetoric and Medical Knowledge*. Cambridge: Cambridge University Press.

Psaltis, C. and Duveen, G. (2006). Social relations and cognitive development: The influence of conversation type and representations of gender. *European Journal of Social Psychology*, 36, 407–430.

Rogoff, B. (1990). *Apprenticeship in thinking*. New York: Oxford University Press.

Saito, A. (1996). 'Bartlett's Way' and social representations: The case of Zen transmitted across cultures. *The Japanese Journal of Experimental Social Psychology*, 35, 263–277.

Schütz, A. (1972). *The Phenomenology of the Social World*. London: Heinemann.

Valsiner, J. (2003). Beyond social representations: A theory of enablement. *Papers on social Representations (www.psr.juk.at)*, 12, 7.1–7.16.

Valsiner, J. and Van de Veer, R. (2000). *The social mind: Construction of the idea*. Cambridge: Cambridge University Press.

Wagner, W., Duveen, G., Themel, M., and Verma, J. (1999). The modernisation of tradition: Thinking about madness in Patna, India. *Culture and Psychology*, 5, 413–445.

Wagner, W., Duveen, G., Verma, J., and Themel, M. (2000). 'I have some faith and at the same time I don't believe' – Cognitive Polyphasia and Cultural Change in India. *Journal of Community and Applied Psychology*, 10, 301–314.

CHAPTER 27

The Institutions Inside

Self, Morality, and Culture

Piero Paolicchi

Homo sum. Nihil humani a me alienum puto.

I am a man. I count nothing human foreign to me.

Terence (185–150 B.C.)

The Human Form of Life: Between Nature and Culture

Mapping the ocean of morality is a hard task. Its extent, its depths, and its many varied seas with their manifold features and conditions require a range of navigational skills, from the knowledge of the compass with its universal cardinal points to the ability of navigating by sight. The boundaries and depth of this ocean are coextensive with the presence in space and time of the species *Homo sapiens*, which has developed a "moral world" as part of its own *Umwelt* and of its very nature. Such world is rooted in survival resources common to other species, but evolved into substantially different forms. Interpersonal and group relationships have grown on long lasting sociality, language on preverbal communication processes, thought on

sensory-motor processes, self-consciousness on awareness, emotions, and feelings on basic approaching and avoiding reactions, meanings on objects, and altruism on caring for the young. All these manifestations are so interconnected that no one of them can be predicated of a species in the absence of the others. Humanness is not and has never been in only one of them but in the whole complex since its first manifestations: the endowment of faculties and motives of our ancestors was already plural, as it is even in other animals. Correspondingly, no collective view of the world is simple and internally undifferentiated: all human communities, even the most "primitive" ones, as anthropological research demonstrates, see the world as consisting of distinct domains like instrumentality and sacredness, religion, and economy.

The universal features of human life (and of life at all), are action and experience. For them to emerge, some force must have already done the whole work from separating the earth from the waters to inspiring some inert material with life, be it a well-formed creature of some God, or the first cell coming out of the primordial soup. They are functional powers of every natural system, issuing from the process of polarization which life itself comes from, and referring not to unity, identity, and stability but to plurality, difference, and change. They enable living subjects to place themselves in a world of opposition and connection, inside and outside, acting and suffering, reciprocally defining and activating one another. Action implies an agent with some constitutive powers such as unity and continuity that keep the effort directed to a not yet present state of the world that could be produced in some conditions by the agent's effort. Acting is going beyond the limits of the world as ruled by its own laws: it is standing as a source of how the world could come to be, not as a consequence of how the world already is. Experience too is dialectically in tension between self- and object-reference: as aptly defined by Dewey (1980), it is intrinsically subjective and transitional. It implies the agent's sense of its power to make something to exist, and of the limit coming out from the resistance of a world that stays there, as a sort of judge, to probe the agent's power.

At the physical level, the judge to face up is the external world's spatial-temporal factuality; at the social level, it is other individuals with their own agency and the conditions arising from the distribution of powers and resources in the community; at the cultural level, it is the "moral universe" of institutionalized values and rules. The specific powers by which humans confront the world issue from the capacity and propensity to make and use semiotic devices. Through these, human beings "can distance from what they are currently doing, consider contexts of the past, imagine contexts of future, and take the perspectives of other persons" (Valsiner, 2000, 51). The duality between subject and environment, which marks the passage from the world of physical forces to the world of life, is dramatically reconstructed as consciousness of self and of the world. Human beings, already involved in practical relations with the natural and social world, enter the new world of culture

with all the newly emerged distinctions and oppositions between self and other, psyche and body, sensible and metaphysical, subjective and objective, true and false, good and evil. It is a world endowed with both a practical order and a moral order.

The new way of relating with the world and with others appears in two co-developed and inseparable forms. First, there is a set of *mores*, or collectively shared and objectively enacted local ways of behaving not directly ruled by biological processes. Secondly, there is *discourse* about the reasons for living in those ways and about possible alternatives. Practices are evaluated not only as effective or ineffective, but also as good or evil, desirable or forbidden. Discourse is not only about observable behaviors and the sensible world, but also about things like gods, souls, the afterlife, justice, rights, duties, and virtues. They are not explicitly formulated by people in everyday life or actually used in every concrete situation, but can be found explicated in philosophical debates or presented in culture myths, folk narratives, proverbs, maxims, and everyday conversations about how people are and behave. Furthermore, they are enacted through participation in everyday practices and special collectively ruled situations as rituals, both accurately controlled by institutional "local guardians of the moral order" (Shweder & Much, 1987), such as parents, teachers, or priests.

Some basic processes keep cultures somewhere within the range they allow. Motivational trends contrary to slaughter and bloodshed are there in the very nature of human beings, just as there are trends towards aggression. Discrimination and generalization represent starting points of sensation, perception, and cognition. A few root metaphors seem to universally underlie knowledge construction processes (Pepper, 1942), and some among the "metaphors we live by" (Lakoff & Johnson, 1980) are likely to be rooted in the very structure of the human body. But the ultimate nature and meaning of the material and immaterial, natural and social world, of what is true and false, good and evil, and their boundaries and relations, are *instituted* by each group, in connection with already existing historical ways of living in the world. Thus moral orders, as complexes of mores and discourses about mores, are ubiquitous, numerous, and deeply diverse, though neither infinite nor totally arbitrary. They are never systems of totally formal or computational tokens, though they are cognitively based and treated as objective facts pertaining to a domain of truth independent from individual preferences. They are not separate from the world of deep motives, affects, desires, and dreams equally entitled to inhabit the human world, so that they are also able to motivate action by activating powerful feelings like indignation, pride, fear, guilt, and shame. They do not tend to converge over time (Shweder, 2003), nor do they develop along a linear sequence through necessary and foreseeable stages; as Piaget (1970) also admitted, languages, cultures, laws, and moral orders, being natural systems, are subject not only to evolution like cognitive structures, but also to revolutions.

As concrete life conditions vary, and human powers and motivations are plural, a lot of different and possibly conflicting wants, strivings, and values stemming from the very roots of human nature and from already established collective ways of life have to be balanced at both the individual and collective level. Moral orders have to answer some questions and solve some problems that are common to all human beings. Among them, there is making up some order in the relationships with the external world, with one another inside kinships and with other groups encountered in the wider world. There is as well the need of tempering anxiety that arises from the dark but fundamental sides of life, like death. And there is the need of balancing the irrepressible human capacity to see new possibilities that violate the sacredness of what is already there in the social world, the "inertia of the already established" (Meyerson, 1948).

Shared habits ready to be used in recurrent situations make interactions coordinated and efficient, and by reducing uncertainty and conflicts, they also protect individuals from anxiety before the unknown and the unpredictable. In time, through their being transmitted from generation to generation, they acquire both the reliability of deeply probed ways of living and the weight of a heritage coming from idealized ancestors' wisdom. The succeeding generations find them "out there" in the world, as objective, natural, and necessary (Berger & Luckmann, 1966). Some among those 'instituted objects' become not simply necessary and self evident routines but sacred forms of relating with others and with the natural and supernatural world, so that doubt about and violations to them raise feelings of anxiety and guilt. In all cultures, these are structured at a basic level by some deep *premises* (Shweder, 2003), or visions of how the world is and of what it is to be human. These usually remain unreflected upon and unexplored, but, if contested or attacked, manifest their rootedness in some core and vulnerable layer of individual and collective identity, or value system, through defensive and aggressive reactions (Noam, 1993; Staub, 1993).

The institutions that incarnate and defend these premises govern action and experience, suggesting the ways in which objects and events have to be evaluated, arranging social resources, ruling everyday encounters and special rituals, imposing sanctions and organizing life course transitions (Valsiner, 2000; see also Whiting & Whiting, 1975). But institutions never satisfy only deep natural or cultural needs. As they solve concrete problems of the relation of human beings with nature and among human beings themselves in concrete situations, institutions are historical in essence, and reflect the dynamics of political, social, economical forces confronting in a given historical period. No universal human necessity can be called upon to support private property or communism of goods as necessary or irreplaceable, because both are connected to historical forms of exploitation and allocation of natural resources. Thus, by supporting current institutions and defending their legitimacy, some groups defend also such goods as richness, prestige, power, and their very existence from dissent and violation. As a consequence, mores and rules not only diverge among societies, but also are never totally shared within the same society.

The "instituted" nature of mores and laws, their essence of something generated by a choice, an "act of will," though by a superior one, make them intrinsically undermined by possible refusal and violation: they are born with the woodworm of doubt, argument, alternative proposals inside. Reflexive agents are able not only to act according to rules: they can judge their actions by such rules, change their actions as a consequence of those judgments, and even criticize and change previously adopted rules. Thus, moral worlds are involved in ongoing debates at the public level, if not about their general presuppositions, at least about the different values that those presuppositions can equally support but that can be conflicting or differently prioritized in concrete situations. Individuals too, in judging and acting, must engage in a personal task of deliberating, through a sort of internal debate, about conflicts between their own and others' points of view, and between their decision in the present situation and the whole story of their former decisions. Moral orders are continually and inevitably exposed to the possible gap between the ways reality is directly given to experience and the ways it is institutionally defined. Institutions are always involved in the never-ending dialectics between the creative and potentially disrupting drives and dreams arising in concrete interpersonal relationships and individual experience, on one side, and on the other side the fact that individuals, groups, and societies can survive only on condition that they create and defend norms and institutions.

In Search of the Truth: Morality and Science

Like any other feature of human action and experience, morality can be described and explained exhaustively, or at least not too reductively with respect to its complex and dynamic essence, as one among the many ways in which human beings continually construct and re-construct their world. Such world has to be endowed with some order that makes reality's flux a meaningful whole with features of unity and continuity, as striving for unity and order is not an optional in human life. No idea of either a culture or an individual as a sort of patchwork or changing kaleidoscopic configuration has resisted investigation in anthropology or psychology. However, unity is always balanced by multiplexity. Individual and collective worlds show a set of different elements, from the use of empirical validity and logic in establishing relationships between means and ends, to "believed-in imaginings" (de Rivera & Sarbin, 1998) and assumptions about witchcraft, demons, and immortal souls. The result is not a logically and empirically validated whole, but one having a "rationale," which is far better represented by meaningful, plausible and convincing narratives, than by logical or experimental demonstrations (Bruner, 1990). At the individual level, it appears in the "experiential logic" by which patients explain their troubles to a therapist (Epstein, 1973) or in the ways in which Colby and Damon's (1992) "moral exemplars" justify their choices; at the collective level, it is the "explanation[s] for a customary practice that makes logical sense – transcultural logical sense – given some arbitrary assumptions that reflect cultural values rather than contingencies in the external environment" (LeVine, 1984: 79).

In western culture, on the contrary, the dominant assumption has been that of a unique and universal truth attainable by following an adequate method (from the Greek *méthodos* = course). In a famous debate with Socrates, Protagoras (Plato, 1992) tried, without success, to argue that at least regarding human facts there could be more than one truth. Since then, throughout the Christian medieval philosophers and then Descartes and Kant, up until their heirs in modern psychology, the truth, also about human facts, has been only one. And the discovery of the truth has been regarded as possible only through resorting to some authority or instrument superior to, and separate from everyday human capacities. From time to time, the Euclidean lever by which we can lift the whole world and grasp the truth about it have been universal Ideas reflected in any apparently different concrete object or God's Revelation, the all encompassing sight of pure Reason or the instrumentally armed eye of positive Science. The so-called Enlightenment project, and its continuation into Positivism (Smith, 1997), is the most recent effort to complete a two millennia-long attempt to stop the varying, dynamic, interiorly differentiated world of action and experience, in order to anchor it to solid, stable, and clearly identified entities endowed with universal structuring power. These were found in the ideas of Science and Progress strictly connected to one another, as traditional religious and philosophical ideas fused with the new religion of Science, giving it the task of explaining and governing the destinies of human individuals and humanity in the whole. The God who creates and governs the world from outside was substituted by immanent forces and laws that take His essential governing features, supporting the idea of human history as progress, which is neither shared by other cultures nor justified by the observation of past and present times.

Variability, widespread in all parts and features of reality, is worked out in two ways. The first is to see it only as an appearance under which universal structures can always be traced; the second is to arrange differences hierarchically as stages in a universal progressive manifestation of the same principles or forces that rule a once and forever "instituted" world. A universalistic world vision overcame the relativistic suggestions coming from historical thought, by resorting to a particular and partial interpretation of Darwin's theory of evolution. Fully rational knowledge, identified with science, is seen as a necessary evolutionary result, civilization is equated to the acquisition of a scientific outlook, and rationality becomes the only reliable criterion for judging also about the human facts. Universality and development allow only directional evaluations of differences, with one side defined as somehow negative: it can be error on the cognitive level, deviance on the practical level, or retardation on the developmental level. Still in the 1980s, the Nobel Prize for Medicine winner Sperry (1983) stated that a unique reference system for social problems can be derived from science's revelation of a frame that "cuts across all cultures, faiths, and national interests, for the welfare of mankind and the biosphere as a whole" based on the axiomatic maxim that "[t]he great design of nature [...] is something intrinsically good that it is right to preserve and enhance, and wrong to destroy or degrade" (p. 22).

A "politics of knowing" whose goal was universal order could be brought about better by a 'divide and rule' strategy of conquering and hierarchically administering the diverse territories of reality. With that aim, the human world was split into the two separate spheres of the individual and society as distinct research objects for different disciplines, thus stressing a separation of sociology and psychology, "which in the short term was perhaps beneficial to the consolidation of the identity of both disciplines, but in the long term will be detrimental to the achievement of coherent explanations of human action" (Smith, 1997, 548).

Moreover, on both sides of the individual and society the same epistemology of separating parts and giving one a dominant structuring function was applied. Inside society, it may be deep structural logics or differentiation/integration processes, power relationships or communication networks. Inside the individual, it may be rationality or affectivity, cognitive powers or powerful irrational motives.

Starting with Durkheim, sociology oriented its efforts to constructing a theory of society and institutions based exclusively on social facts and processes without any infiltration by psychological stuff. Morality becomes a mere function of the social system; the inner Christian or Kantian voice of conscience is reduced to a set of social rules and forms of solidarity, issuing from the exigencies of human coexistence. What did remain to explain was how something like morality could enter the hearts and minds of people. Durkheim's answer (1973) was "through education," and at the same time in the United States, where scientific methods applied to society's regeneration and development was the dominant ideal too, psychology, as interpreted by behaviorists, provided the experimental demonstration of control interiorization, by means of stimulus-response and reinforce theories. The instituted world remains unquestioned, and the word "moral" simply designates the conformity of behavior to the standards of society. A so-called moral decision does not stem from the peculiar elements of the person, or from the intrinsic characteristics of action: it is the product of the controls exercised externally by the group and interiorized by individuals. Fear of punishment, and anxiety produced by its anticipation, are the exclusive factors in the interiorization of control (Aronfreed, 1968).

On the individual side, Freud identified the origin of morality in the unconscious mechanisms of identification with the threatening and guilt provoking, but also powerful and protective, internal image of the Father which, in the form of Super-Ego and Ego-Ideal, comes to speak as the internal voice of conscience. The psyche's more basic, irrational processes do the whole work, and society also appears as governed by some general laws rooted in the deep and stable "nature" of the individual psyche. But in the mainstream psychology of morality, it is the rational individual who remains as the ultimate source of all the complex and manifold ways of relating with the world and with others, largely with independence from the historically varying forms of individualization embedded in specific cultural contexts. In cognitive-developmental theories, it is the mind's processes of rational thinking that structure action in, and experience of, both the natural and the social world. Piaget, and Kohlberg following him, continued and reinforced the tradition of looking for answers to problems of the nature of the Good and of humans' place in the world through the study of an immanent and progressive Nature that as such can

also order and display a hierarchy of values (Vandenberg, 1993). With their monumental works, Piaget and Kohlberg set up the truth function of psychological science as a substitute of tradition, myth and theology, through an interpretation of the whole natural history that assigns to science the goal of completing a – religious or laic – but anyway unique universal evolutionary project.

Fully-developed morality is objectively incarnated in universal criteria of justice like those stated by Kant and Rawls, and is concretely instantiated by those human beings who, given some social conditions, develop general and abstract principles of justice as a universal compass to judge about actions and relationships, laws and social arrangements. Kohlberg stated in the very title of a well-known essay (1971) that he was trying to cross the limit between the 'is' territory of science and the "ought" territory of moral philosophy, and to merge the search for scientific truth with the search animating moral debate, on the assumption that the two tend to meet in some omega point towards which cognitive maturation inevitably pushes the expression of human rationality. This is a point that, however, is hardly seen in our past or present vicissitudes and not less hard to foresee in the future. Not surprisingly, Kohlberg himself could never validate empirically the correspondent highest stage 6 hypothesized by his model.

On Becoming Moral: A Dialectical-Historical Process

In contrast with universal perspectives, proposals of a "historical psychology" (Meyerson, 1948; Vernant, 1982) were slowly but gradually spreading the idea that the mind's processes and products change in space and time, that the very categories of action, thought, person and society vary culturally and historically as parts of broad and deep views on the natural and human world. They are neither scientific categories nor inductive generalizations or discoveries of an individual mind. "They are creations of the collective imagination. They are ideas, *premises* by which people guide their lives, and only to the extent a people lives by them do they have their force" (Shweder & Bourne, 1984: 193).

Also universal morality as understood in mainstream western psychology, if analyzed in a historical perspective, appears as the result of a long and tortuous journey in imagination made by people striving to guide their lives in changing worlds of social relationships and societal contexts. It parallels the development of the autonomous individual from the sociocentric view of the medieval feudal world to the new aristocratic and bourgeois times. The modern individual *faber fortunae suae* (maker of his own destiny), which, already according to Gerth and Wright Mills (1953), is an invention of western urban society, emerges from profound transformations in social life organization, progressive internal differentiation, changes in dimension and organization of groups, increasing interaction with other groups, variability and relativity in status-role and rules systems, as well as in the presuppositions that legitimate them all.

Along with those changes, the "individual versus society" morality emerged in western culture through distancing from the close and concrete relations within kinships and groups, and going towards the ideal of a generalized and abstract universe of Kantian persons who bear equal rights because they are equally invested with reason. Thus, in the 18th and 19th century, the relation of individuals to institutions, usually in the form of the relation of personal rights to social obligations. This is what the debate on morality was about in Western culture, and "the aim was to defend the obligation to obey legitimate authority (that is, authority based on consent) and to defend the right to resist coercive force in the absence of legitimate authority" (Horowitz, 1980, 10). Finding the best way to keep the balance between rights and obligations was necessary because resolving the conflict ultimately in favor of one side should be "to surrender the society either to the Anarch or, at the other extreme, to the Behemoth" (*ibidem*). In that context, the rational individual unfolds as the only

true, *super partes* "moral judge," on the basis of a total analogy between moral and logical thought fully explicated in cognitive theories of moral development. In these, "the sense of justice or injustice has its counterpart in people's sense of logical necessity, derived from the application of basic logical schemes to phenomena" (Rest, 1983: 616).

As morality incarnated in universal criteria of justice is fully rational, and as human beings are at least potentially rational by nature, it can be assumed that "in a creature endowed with the capacity for rational thought, as the capacity is cultivated, the development of moral understanding will tend in the direction of what is most rational" (Shweder, Mahapatra & Miller, 1987, 7).

At this "post-conventional" level, such creatures will be able to 'objectively' define what is right and wrong by seeing things from "nowhere in particular" (Nagel, 1979), and judge both individual actions and social arrangements standing as "prior to society" and its institutions (Kohlberg, Levine, & Hewer 1983). To become fully developed moral subjects, able and then legitimized to "institute," to assign with total justice *unicuique suum* (what anyone deserves), human beings have to free themselves from their internal worlds of non rational feelings and motives and from all relational (and thus non-rational) links to others, be they individuals or groups.

One of the most important consequences of separating the individual from the social world, and cognitive processes from affect, in moral psychology theories, has been a deep impoverishment in the treatment of morality as a fundamental, pervasive aspect of human functioning. Morality refers not to the abstract world of reasoning but to the world of actions and choices, having, at least potentially, deep social and interpersonal implications, and involving both intrapsychic cognitive and affective mechanisms. Morality is worked by some simplified images of human beings, on both the individual and the collective side. Individual moral agents and instituted moral worlds, which are twin living protagonists on the stage in any known culture and in individual concrete experience, are separated and frozen by "scientific" theories to serve as stable, ultimate, and foundational elements. These theories put together into unity the many and often conflicting reasons and values that animate any culture and any individual life.

The debate raised by Kohlberg is too broad and complex to be even schematically synthesized, but it is exhaustively presented in the many readings edited by himself and his collaborators (Kohlberg, Levine, & Hewer, 1983) and by others, with the participation of scholars from different disciplinary fields (Modgill & Modgill, 1985; Wren, 1990; Kurtines & Gewirtz, 1991; Noam & Wren, 1993).[1] Criticisms to the dominant cognitive-developmental theories could be synthesized by saying, as Shweder does about Piaget, that they are "undoubtedly correct but terribly incomplete," as "[t]here's a lot more in the mind of man (sic) than logic and natural science" (1984: 53). Focusing exclusively on a justice concept implies underscoring the connection between moral judgment and early interiorized values in different cultures (Shweder, Mahapatra, & Miller, 1987). It also implies excluding from the definition of fully-developed morality what refers to responsibility and guilt (Paolicchi, 1994), friendship (Blum, 1980) and solidarity (Habermas, 1990), attention to situations and feelings (Gilligan, 1982), and even moral perspectives such those of believers and gentlemen who care not about deliberating correctly what is just, but about finding the force to accomplish what they hold just (Harré, 1983).

On the affective-motivational side, such hypothesized roots of morality as empathy and attachment have been often kept separate from the meaning making process of mapping the world, deeply shaped by the pre-existing maps of the world into which human beings are placed from their birth. Compassion, pitilessness, pride, guilt, and shame probably draw on a limited set of universal moral categories, but underlie a great variety of moral behaviors and values that are culturally and historically constituted (Benson, 2001). Underscoring the self-related motivational aspects of agency and responsibility keeps a gap between judgment and action that was focused early by Blasi (1980) as one of the major limits of cognitive theories. However, theory and research on relationships between judgment, motivation, and action produced very little until exploration was oriented towards moral judgments as part of meanings that they hold on a person's life. This required a coherent theory of self as "a process of structuring thoughts, feelings, and behaviors about oneself, others, and the world at large" (Noam, 1993: 217).

Indeed, most of the subsequent work in moral psychology has been done in order to redefine and enlarge the whole picture of morality as a total human phenomenon. Human beings have come back onto the stage as thinking, sentient and meaning-making agents, living in a web of essential relationships with a moral world which they construct while being in turn constructed by it. It is a world that, consequently, shares with the human psyche the same complexity and dynamics it shows to philosophy and cultural studies. Frankena (1973), reviewing Western moral philosophy, identified not one but two basic principles, justice and beneficence, acknowledged by all theories, and Berlin (1969) argued that the so-called ultimate values are numerous, incommensurable and often in conflict with one another. The same is for cultures, in which Shweder, Much, Mahapatra, and Park (1997), through a comparative analysis, identified at least three frames of meaning-making, or ethics of autonomy, community, and divinity, co-present though differently prioritized. Some relatively dominant patterns can develop and produce general orientations such as those towards individualism or collectivism, rights-based or duty-based moralities, but all include justice, rights, care and welfare, though they are prioritized differently by societies and by groups inside them (Turiel, 2002). Empathy and cognition (Hoffman, 1991), and social and cognitive processes (Bandura 1991) are seen as intertwined in moral development. The Self is defined and studied as multi-voiced (Wertsch, 1991), and culture as a "forum" (Bruner, 1990). Both become places where unending dialogue and confrontation go on, notably about questions of what is good, valuable, and worth living. Neither consists of a totally coherent and hierarchically fixed system of principles and rules, but of a set of interpretive frameworks that leave room for individual creativity and negotiation among individuals.

With time, theoretical and empirical explorations strengthened the idea that morality has to do to both "an interior psychological space" in which individual experiencing and acting is located, and "a cultural field" into which human beings are inserted (Benson, 2001, Chapter 8). In both one finds not one primary source or explaining entity, but a complex and dynamic set of intertwined elements and processes. Thus, in real life situations people cannot help being involved in evaluating also through affective responses that not only give a motivating force to their judgments, but also can reframe the situation and orient differently the judging process. On the other hand, any external "objective" criterion for judging is never totally separable from the cultural system of meaning making in which it is created. Nobody can understand concepts like justice, equality, rights, duties, outside the ways of life, or systems of lived relationships that give them meaning (Wittgenstein, 1953). Consequently, a comprehensive theory of morality has to allow going beyond the distinction-separation between individuals and psychological processes on the one hand, and institutions and social processes on the other. The dialectics that is the essence of both individuals and institutions, as well as of their reciprocal relations, issues only from the intertwining of forces and processes that interact on all levels of human reality, intrapersonal, interpersonal, and socio-cultural. Thus the goal of connecting all the separate parts in a coherent picture is not attainable by simply finding some place for each one as an entity with specific and stable characters, but by deeply reconsidering and reformulating them all in terms coherent with a general theoretical background.

Intentional Selves, Intentional Worlds: The Cultural-Psychological Perspective

Among the recent proposals, a particularly useful way of looking at individuals and institutions, individual judgments and collective frames for judging, and at their relationships, can be searched for by taking seriously the core idea of cultural psychology that cultures and selves are "same stuff." The theoretical tool to accomplish this task appears to be cultural psychology's fundamental concept of *intentionality*, or the assumption "that the life of the psyche is the life of intentional persons, responding to, and directing their action at, their own mental objects and representations, and undergoing transformation through participation in an evolving intentional world that is the product of the mental representations that make it up" (Shweder, 1990: 22).

Intentional agents express their powers in concrete particular instances or configurations of historical-cultural conditions, thus coming to interiorize institutions through personal biographical experience. Institutions grow out of relationships among individuals with some deep psychic structure, and are thus influenced by them while in turn influencing and modifying their psychic structure. Cultures provide frameworks bridging the internal-external dichotomy, as they structure the inner self and enable institutions to operate, so that one can say that in the process "[t]he self becomes institutionalized and institutions become psychologized" (Heelas, 1981, 15).

Cultural psychology aims at examining "the different kinds of things that continually happen in social interaction and in social practice as the intentionality of a person meets the intentionality of a world and as they jointly facilitate, express, repress, stabilize, transform, and defend each other through and throughout the life of a person and the life of a world," so that "[t]here are histories (narratives) that can be written about each, or both – the history of lives and the history of practices and institutions"

(Shweder, 1990: 27). In this light, individuals and institutions are both dynamic and open systems involved in deterministic and indeterministic processes (Fogel, Lyra, & Valsiner, 1997), thus they cannot be causally explicated but only interpreted and reconstructed in their becoming (Meyerson, 1948; Geertz, 1973), which is in itself a story of interpretations. In fact, interpreting is what human beings spontaneously and actively do throughout their whole life in simple and awkward situations, and even small or subtle variations can lead to differences in their judgments and decisions (Asch, 1952, chap. 15). Human beings manifest early in childhood the powers of appropriating and re-constructing the world around them, especially in play (Baldwin, 1911; Oliveira & Valsiner, 1997). And as Berger (1997) reminds us in his lovely book on "redeeming laughter," human eyes are always prone to see some unexpected features in any factual or consensually established reality. They show that power at many different levels, from humor and play, through imagination and art, till to religious thinking, all of which express the inherent human capacity to "transcend," to go beyond the world as already given or defined and see not only how it "is" or "has to be" but also how it "could be."

Reframing self and culture, individuals and institutions in ways that keep them as relational, dynamic, and open systems, as both creating and created, *instituting and instituted*, has direct consequences upon two major issues of moral psychology in a diachronical-historical perspective: those of values transmission across generations and of individual moral development through a lifetime.

While unilinear models of socialization describe it as a direct transmission of values and rules across generations, the major sociogenetic theories stress the idea of transmission as transformation through internalisation (Lawrence & Valsiner, 1993). Children's understandings of rules are drawn from the continuous participation in everyday discourses and practices (Shweder &

Much, 1987; Bhatia, 2000), but the process is never one of simply transmitting values and beliefs. First, conflicting messages, ambiguity, and change are found in all societies, even in the simplest and traditional ones, so that, as Boesch states, "[s]ociety is too heterogeneous, too contradictory in its influences to allow it to have a direct forming influence" (2003, 295–96). Secondly, internalisation is structure-generative, and the central structuring work is done not only by the epistemic self of cognitive theories, but also by the individual's striving to integrate experiences as a unique and personally meaningful biography. The force of instituted worldviews, be they rooted in religious, political, or even scientific premises, have been demonstrated by Milgram's experiments in which "normal" good citizens were induced to hurt other people with electric shocks they believed real (1974). More dramatically, the same forces have been and still are at work in real life processes of recruiting perpetrators of violence all over the world and in any time, from Nazi and other totalitarian systems to recent forms of struggle between confronting fundamentalisms towards reciprocally defined worlds of Evil. But in both experimental and real life contexts – as already Fromm stressed commenting on Milgram's experiments (1973), and many others noticed through historical and psychological surveys (Oliner & Oliner, 1988) – it there stays an ineradicable minority of resisters who refuse the institutional context of justification. And, as Fromm himself added, it is they that support some hope for humanity's future.

Biographical studies on moral development show that it is not a fixed and foreseeable trajectory, but a storied life course. Sudden and deep changes in an individual life are empirically observable though often overlooked in mainstream theory and research. Studies of Colby and Damon (1992) on "moral exemplars," of McAdams, Josselson, and Lieblich (2001) on life transitions, and of Paolicchi (1995) on narratives of volunteering. These studies show that life trajectories are "storied," marked by "turning points" and triggering events, in tension between continuity and consistency on the one side, and openness and change on the other. Moral development theories have to assume in their frameworks that each stage has a different story to tell, as to develop is not to become more rational. Instead, it enters a new frame of mind about self-other relationships, so that at each new developmental level some problems are solved and some new problems arise, opening relational tensions formerly unknown (Kegan, 1982). Moreover, deeper developmental structures and processes are usually governed in a hierarchical way by higher ones, but are never eradicated in both individual and collective systems, thus continuing to play some role in organizing human actions, choices, decisions, and projects throughout the life course. Moral development is not a sort of progressive coming closer to clear-cut criteria for judging and acting: a mature moral judgment frame derives from a whole history of internalized interactions and experiences that can produce as much equilibrium and harmony as tension and uncertainty (Noam, 1993).

Higher stages of cognitive complexity are not equivalent to better, truer, or more mature psychological and social adaptations, and consequently there is no highest knowing level whose products are always correct, appropriate or ultimately worth instantiating. Moral atrocities persist in the most "civilized" cultures. Examples in history, empirical research, and therapy encounters, all point in the direction that moral complexity can be used to justify immoral theories, systems, and actions. Eichmann and many among those who killed or contributed to killing in Nazi Germany and more recent locations of atrocities, were often people capable of complex understanding of social reality. Bandura (1999, 2004) demonstrates that cognitive complexity can be applied in the service of moral de-responsibilization and participation in extreme forms of destructiveness. The growth of rationality and science does not seem to be able to reduce or eliminate hostility and violence towards individuals, groups, and communi-

ties, thus rendering so difficult a multicultural education (Paolicchi, 2000) also in cultures with a high level of 'civilization'. Here too, a "hard times" psychology can spread as a large scale phenomenon, producing deep changes in concrete expressions of hatred and pitilessness by radically modifying the boundaries of personal identity, self-other relationships, and morality, and so opening the way to extreme manifestations of violence (Staub, 1993, 2004).

The idea of a progression towards a necessary final point of arrival actually eliminates both the individual and the collective forms of human life as places of possibility, giving them a once and forever instituted destiny. Moral psychology, if one decides not to go on defining it as a specialized study of some particular entities such as rational minds or adapting organisms, and to take on the task of systematically looking at the dialectical circularity between psychological, relational and social processes, has to take a developmental-cultural, that is a historical stance. It has to put selves, morality, and institutions, like any other object of the human world, in a historical-narrative context of explanation. This means that to say what something "is" one has "to describe its origination ('once upon a time') and its density (its aim, purpose, or function) and to comprehend its current status, in the here and now, as part of a longer story of strivings, achievements, obstacles, growth, adaptations, failures, dormancy, or never-ending cyclical return" (Shweder, 1990, 4).

Dilemmas and Decisions: Morality as Drama

If we look at what went on and is going on in western world, the supposed place of highest moral development, we do not see a linear progress toward a better future regarding selves, institutions and their relationships as central part of morality. After the failure of the Cartesian and Kantian project to give self-consciousness a foundational autonomous role, an *innere Ausland* (inner foreign land, as Freud defined the unconscious) grew in the inmost part of the subject, pursuing its own goals independently from, and even in conflict with, the deliberative processes of consciousness. The great "masters of suspicion" like Marx, Nietzsche, and Freud, caused a theoretical and ethical void by attacking the primacy of conscience, and favored the idea that the only real forces acting on the human stage are economic power, or the body's "will to power" or the Es. In so doing, they lowered the sense of agency and responsibility of individuals, leaving them at the mercy of anonymous powers or of leaders that do not respond to anyone for their decisions. The crisis of the primary, unified, and reality grounding "I" of modern western philosophy and culture activated different ways of coping, from the individual strategies of accommodating to a multiple and fragmented experience of self as described by Proust, Pirandello, and Joyce, to the surrender to the "colonization of souls" (Bodei, 2002) in the overarching order and renewed center of meaning embodied in some "meneur des foules" as theorized by Le Bon and historically acted by Dux, Fuhrers, Caudillos, or Conducators in the 20th century.

The same dialectics between selves and institutions seems to be going on in postmodern cultures of "narcissism" (Lasch, 1979) or of "liquidity" (Bauman, 2000), with multitudes of individuals caring only about the minimal space of their personal desires and goals, or free-floating out of the network of social roles and relationships, or running ahead under the power of pre-modern, even ancient institutions and faiths. As always, stressing the institutional or anti-institutional strivings seems desperately tragic, so that the only solution "has to be articulated by breaking the self-referential circle of the I and reconstructing a We capable of strengthening the social link without attacking the autonomy of individuals" (Bodei, 2002: 265; Author's trans.). Theorists of the fluid, multiple Self underscore the centripetal force that keeps together individual experiences as a unitary and unique life-time, and the suffering provoked by traumatic ruptures in one's own individual story. On the other side, the oppression of the collective "We" is no less hard when it is carried out through soft means of persuasion instead of violence. But every time the Father is dead, no Piagetian polycentric and democratic autonomous morality is guaranteed: a "fatherless society" (Mitscherlich, 1963) often initiates unending fights between rival children or wanderings of people through life troubles with greater freedom but also with greater loneliness and anxiety. In the most "advanced" societies, new technologies threaten the very basic bodily support of life through genetic engineering, while globalization processes make the world more interconnected but also more and more complex, so that individuation processes issue in localisms and nationalisms, collective identities are constructed on processes of ingroup-outgroup conflict, and religious or laic fundamentalisms grow equally in both reigns of the Good and the Evil (Mogaddham & Marsella, 2004). Every moral emphasis, if left to rule the moral field on its own, runs the risk of entering a tragic flaw of annihilating other world visions and even the people themselves.

Maybe some hope there is just because human form of life grew out of a set of distinctive and complementary needs that since its beginning have given rise to a sort of implicit moral pluralism. Due to the way in which morality occurs in human experience, not as abstract reflection on lonely mental exercises, but on matters people really care about in the highly meaningful context of living together in one world, at its core there seems to be a need for "caring" (for oneself, others and institutions) which goes beyond the practical demands of fairness in allotting rights and duties. That is the reason why none of the law systems that our "ethical" species (Paolicchi, 1987) creates can exhaust the human yearning for justice, and a continued state of tension between law and ethics produces what Ricoeur (1990) calls the "tragic dimension of the act."

With a slightly different and denser metaphor, we would say that morality is drama. In its original sense, from the Greek verb *drào*, drama means action and then implies agency. This, in turn, implies the sense of being the source of something of which one takes on responsibility: the Greek word *aitìa* means both cause and guilt, the sense of being at the origin of something and of being called for as responsible for something. Selfhood has been rooted since its beginning not on cognitive distinctions and formal operations, but on an agency and "mineness" experience (Blasi, 1988; Boesch, 2003) that links actions, intentions, goals, results, accomplishments, and their consequences with a deep sense of *relatedness* and *responsibility* to both self and others. Ancient forms of knowledge like myths express such deep dialectics between the ineradicable tendency to actively give form to reality and the disquieting sense that, in so doing, agents take on a burden of a kind of responsibility for the state of the world that will issue from their actions, and for themselves as producers of it.

The Bible is clear on this. Our progenitors became fully human only through violating the Law and thus acquiring knowledge of good and evil. By developing a conscience they were no longer only part of the world, but really existed for themselves (from the Latin *ex-sistere*, to stay apart) with the power of choosing about the world's and one's own destiny. The Snake-Devil was right in telling them that acting that way they would become like God. But one could also say that they acted that way just because they were already like the God who had made them in His image, as capable not only to procreate, but also to create. One could think that God sensed this essential link to His creatures, considering His subsequent decision: they were not struck dead or otherwise annihilated, their punishment was to shoulder the work of constructing the world around them and their destiny within it, with the accompanying burden of uncertainty, anxiety, and responsibility.

Any universalistic, final, and absolute perspective, though deeply rooted in the human need for certainty, does not escape the risk of opening the way to fanaticism or at least to the unconscious defense of the *status quo*, the "already instituted" as the unique and unquestionable view from nowhere. The human condition seems to have no way out between the defensive return to one's own certainties, which so often produces domination and destruction, and the willingness to work together through and about everyone's differences. "We are condemned to either ignoring and annihilating differences, or to working tenuously across them to form always risky bonds of understanding" (Narayan, 1988, 34).

The second alternative could be the "view from manywhere" (Shweder, 2003) that seems more fruitful both morally and cognitively, as it supports co-constructive – instead of other-defeating – relations in both intercultural encounters and interdisciplinary dialogues. Indeed, it does not mean a view from anywhere in which "anything goes," but a view in which, before arriving to *comprehend* (from the Latin word that means to have in one's hands) and judge, the other's point is considered to be worth a second look to be understood: the Latin word *respicere*, which *respect* comes from, means just to look at once more. Even in the position of judging from nowhere, or from absolute knowledge and capacity to "institute" the world, which our culture assigns to the Jewish-Christian God, according to the Talmud (as quoted by Billig), decisions have to be taken by considering many different reasons about what a culprit really "deserves." Even God, in such cases, having to consider both values of justice and mercy, prays to Himself by saying: "May it be My will that My Mercy may prevail over My (other) attributes, so that I may deal with My children in the attribute of mercy and, on their behalf, stop short of the limits of strict justice" (Paolicchi, 1987, 215).

Descending from the heights of Heavenly decisions to the more earthly and real, but often no less problematic and involving decisions, the story from the Talmud can be a wise invitation to reflect on morality in its individual and collective manifestations as something deeply and totally human, including in this category both powers and limits of our specific form of life. Diversity is surely one among them, and like the others it is a resource and a problem. Maybe the best way to manage it is not the distant and cold sight of the Platonic Republic's philosopher-ruler, but the much closer to and involved in everyday human affairs Aristotelian philosopher-citizen. This one knows that in the moral field the Truth, if not plural, is surely many-faceted, and the tools to reach it are not universal principles and strict deductions, but the slow and intricate pathways of *phronesis* or wisdom, marked by never ending debate and reconsideration. In this light, the relationship between the two souls of mind and heart with their multiple "reasons," and between "the instituted" and "the instituting" that inhabit both the individual space of the psyche and the collective world of culture, can become a constructive, heated and healing confrontation, instead of a destructive, cold, and freezing struggle. As the whole picture of human history shows, all of them enrich and support life when they nourish and control one another, but impoverish and destroy it when left alone to govern the individual and collective navigation across the open ocean of life.

References

Aronfreed, J. (1968). *Conduct and conscience.* New York: Academic Press.

Asch, S. (1952). *Social psychology.* Englewood Cliffs, NJ: Prentice-Hall.

Baldwin, J. M. (1911). *Thought and things: A study of the development of thought or genetic logic. Vol. 3. Interest and art.* London: George Allen.

Bandura, A. (1991). Social cognitive theory of moral thought and action. In Kurtines W. M. & Gewirtz J. l. (Eds.) (1991). *Handbook of moral behavior and development.* Vol. 1 (pp. 45–103). Hillsdale, NJ: Lawrence Erlbaum Associates.

Bandura, A. (1999). Moral disengagement in the perpetration of inhumanities. *Personality and Social Psychology Review* (Special issue on evil and violence), 3, 193–209.

Bandura, A. (2004). The role of selective moral disengagement in terrorism and counterterrorism. In Mogaddham F. M. & Marsella A. J. (Eds.), *Understanding terrorism* (pp. 121–150). Washington, DC: American Psychological Association.

Baumann, Z. (2000). *Liquid modernity.* Cambridge: Polity Press.

Benson, C. (2001). *The cultural psychology of self. Place, morality and the art in human worlds.* London: Routledge.

Berger, P. L. (1997). *Redeeming laughter.* Berlin: Walter de Gruyter.

Berger, P. L. & Luckmann, T. (1966). *The social construction of reality.* New York: Doubleday.

Berlin, I. (1969). *Four essays on liberty.* Oxford: Oxford University Press.

Bhatia, S. (2000). Language socialisation and the construction of socio-moral meanings. *Journal of Moral Education,* 29, 149–166.

Billig, M. (1988). *Arguing and thinking.* Cambridge: Cambridge University Press.

Blasi, A. (1980). Bridging moral cognition and moral action. *Psychological Bulletin,* 88, 1–45.

Blasi, A. (1988). Identity and the development of the self. In Lapsley D. K. & Power F. C. (Eds.), *Self, ego, and identity* (pp. 226–242). New York: Springer Verlag.

Blum, L. A. (1980). *Friendship, altruism and morality.* London: Routledge & Kegan Paul.

Bodei, R. (2002). *Destini personali [Personal destinies].* Milano: Feltrinelli.

Boesch, E. E. (2003). Why does Sally never call Bobby 'I'? *Culture & Psychology,* 9, 287–297.

Bruner, J. (1990). *Acts of mind.* Cambridge, MA: Harvard University Press.

Colby, A. & Damon, W. (1992). *Some do care: Contemporary lives of moral commitment.* New York: The Free Press.

de Rivera, J. & Sarbin, T. R. (1998). *Believed-in imaginings. The narrative construction of reality.* Washington, DC: American Psychological Association.

Dewey, J. (1980). *Art as experience,* New York: Putnam. [Orig. pub. 1934]

Durkheim, E. (1973). *Moral education: A study in the theory and application of the sociology of education.* New York: Free Press. [Orig. pub. 1925]

Epstein, S. (1973). The self concept revisited or a theory of a theory. *American Psychologist,* 28, 405–416.

Fogel, A., Lyra, M. C., & Valsiner, J. (Eds.) (1997). *Dynamics and indeterminism in developmental and social processes.* Mahwah, NJ: Lawrence Erlbaum Associates.

Frankena, W. K. (1973). *Ethics.* Englewood Cliffs, NJ: Prentice-Hall.

Fromm, E. (1973). *The anatomy of human destructiveness.* New York: Holt, Rinehart & Winston.

Geertz, C. (1973). *Interpretation of cultures*. New York: Basic Books.

Gerth, A. H. & Wright Mills, C. (1953). *Character and social structure*. New York: Harcourt/Brace.

Gilligan, C. (1982). *In a different voice*. Cambridge, MA: Harvard University Press.

Habermas, F. (1990). Justice and solidarity. In Wren T. (Ed.), *The moral domain* (pp. 224–251). Cambridge, MA: MIT Press.

Harré, R. (1983). *Personal being*. Cambridge, MA: Harvard University Press.

Heelas, P. (1981). Introduction to Heelas P. & Lock A., *Indigenous psychologies. The anthropology of the self*. London: Academic Press.

Hoffman, M. L. (1991). Empathy, social cognition, and moral action. In Kurtines W. M. & Gewirtz J. L. (Eds.), *Handbook of moral behavior and development*. Vol. 1 (pp. 275–301). Hillsdale, NJ: Lawrence Erlbaum Associates.

Horowitz, I. L. (1980). Moral development, authoritarian distemper, and democratic persuasion. In Wilson R. W. & Schochet G. J. (Eds.), *Moral development and politics* (5–21). New York: Praeger

Kegan, R. (1982). *The evolving self*. Cambridge, MA: Harvard University Press.

Kohlberg, L. (1971). From *is* to *ought*: How to commit the naturalistic fallacy and get away with it in the study of moral development. In Mischel T. (Ed.), *Cognitive development and epistemology* (pp. 151–235). New York: Academic Press.

Kohlberg, L., Levine, C., & Hewer, A. (1983). *Moral stages: A current formulation and a response to critics*. Basel: Karger.

Kurtines, W. M. & Gewirtz, J. l. (Eds.) (1991). *Handbook of moral behavior and development*. Vols. 3. Hillsdale, NJ: Lawrence Erlbaum Associates.

Lakoff, G. & Johnson, M. (1980). *Metaphors we live by*. Chicago, IL: University of Chicago Press.

Lasch, C. (1979). *The culture of narcissism*. New York: Norton.

Lawrence, J. A. & Valsiner, I. (1993). Conceptual roots of internalisation: from transmission to transformation. *Human Development*, 36, 150–167.

LeVine R. A. (1984). Properties of culture. An ethnographic view. In Shweder, R. A. & LeVine, R. A. (Eds.). *Culture theory. Essays on mind, self, and emotion* (pp. 67–87). Cambridge: Cambridge University Press.

McAdams, D. P., Josselson, R., & Lieblich, A. (Eds.) (2001). *Turns in the road. Narrative studies of lives in transition*. Washington, DC: American Psychological Association.

Meyerson, I. (1948). *Les fonctions psychologiques et les oeuvres* [Psychological functions and products]. Paris: Vrin.

Milgram, S. (1974). *Obedience to authority, an experimental view*. London: Tavistock.

Mitscherlich, A. (1963). *Auf dem Weg zu Vaterlosen Gesellschaft* [*Towards a fatherless society*]. München: Piper & Co. Verlag.

Modgill, S. & Modgill, C. (Eds.) (1985). *Lawrence Kohlberg. Consensus and controversy*. Philadelphia, PA: Falmer Press.

Mogaddham, F. M. & Marsella, A. J. (Eds.) (2004). *Understanding terrorism*. Washington, DC: American Psychological Association.

Nagel, T. (1979). *Mortal questions*. Cambridge: Cambridge University Press.

Narayan, U. (1988). Working together across difference: some considerations on emotions and political practice. *Hypatia*, 3(23), 31–47.

Noam, G. (1993). "Normative vulnerabilities" of self and their transformation in moral action. In Noam G. & Wren Th. (Eds.), *The moral self* (pp. 209–238). Cambridge, MA: MIT Press.

Noam, G. & Wren, T. (Eds.) (1993). *The moral self*. Cambridge, MA: MIT Press

Oliner, S. P. & Oliner, P. M. (1988). *The altruistic personality. Rescuers of Jewish in nazi Europe*. New York: The Free Press.

Oliveira, Z. M. R. & Valsiner, J. (1997). Play and imagination: the psychological construction of novelty. In Fogel A., Lyra M. C. & Valsiner J. (Eds.), *Dynamics and indeterminism in developmental and social processes* (pp. 119–133). Mahwah, NJ: Lawrence Erlbaum Associates.

Paolicchi, P. (1987). *Homo ethicus*. Pisa: Ets.

Paolicchi, P. (1994). Psicologia della colpa tra pubblico e privato [The psychology of guilt between public and private]. In Castelfranchi C., D'Amico R. & Poggi I. (Eds.), *Sensi di colpa* [*Senses of guilt*] (pp. 274–294). Firenze: Giunti (Ed.).

Paolicchi, P. (1995). Narratives of volunteering. *Journal of Moral Education*, 2, 159–173.

Paolicchi, P. (2000). The use of stories in intercultural education. In Leicester M., Modgil S. & Modgil C. (Eds.), *Education, culture and values*. Vol III, Classroom issues (pp. 145–155). London: Falmer Press

Pepper, S. (1942). *World hypothesis*. Berkeley: University of California Press.

Piaget, J. (1970). *Tendences principales de la recherche dans les sciences sociales et humaines*, Part.I: Sciences sociales. Paris-La Haye: Mouton.

Plato. (1992). *Protagoras*. (Trans. S. Lombardo and K. Bell). Indianapolis: Hackett.

Rest, J. R. (1983). Morality. In Flavell, J. H., & Markman, E. (Eds.), *Handbook of child psychology (4th Ed.)*, vol. 3: Cognitive development (pp. 556–629). New York: John Wiley and Sons.

Ricoeur, P. (1990). Etica e conflitto dei doveri: il tragico dell'azione [Ethics and conflict of duties: the tragic of action]. *Il Mulino*, XXXIX, n. 3., 365–390.

Shweder, R. A. (1984). Anthropology's romantic rebellion against the Enlightment, or there's more to thinking than reason and evidence. In Shweder, R. A. & Le Vine, R. A. (Eds.), *Culture theory. Essays on mind, self and emotion* (pp. 27–66). Cambridge: Cambridge University Press.

Shweder, R. A. 1990. Cultural psychology – what is it? In Stigler, J. W., Shweder, R. A., & Herdt, G. (Eds.), *Cultural psychology* (pp. 1–43). Cambridge: Cambridge University Press.

Shweder, R. A. (2003). *Why do men barbecue?* Cambridge, MA: Harvard University Press.

Shweder, R. A. & Bourne, E. G. (1984). Does the concept of the person vary cross-culturally? In Shweder R. A. & LeVine R. A. (Eds.), *Culture theory. Essays on mind, self and emotion* (pp. 158–199). Cambridge: Cambridge University Press.

Shweder, R. A., Mahapatra, M., & Miller, J. C. (1987). Culture and moral development. In Kagan, J. & Lamb, S. (Eds.), *The emergence of morality in young children* (pp. 1–83). Chicago, IL: University of Chicago Press.

Shweder, R. A. & Much, N. C. (1987). Determinations of meaning: Discourse and moral socialization. In Kurtines W. M. & Gewirtz J. L. (Eds.), *Social interaction and socio-moral development* (pp. 197–244). New York: John Wiley and Sons.

Shweder, R. A., Much, N. C., Mahapatra, M., & Park, L. (1997). The "big three" of morality (autonomy, community, and divinity) and the "big three" explanations of suffering. In Brandt A. & Rozin P. (Eds.), *Morality and health* (pp. 119–169). London: Routledge.

Smith, R. (1997). *The Norton history of the human sciences*. New York: Norton.

Sperry, R. (1983). *Science and moral priority*. Oxford: Basil Blackwell.

Staub, E. (1993). Individual and group selves: Motivation, morality, and evolution. In Noam G. & Wren Th. (Eds.), *The moral self* (pp. 337–358). Cambridge, MA: MIT Press.

Staub, E. (2004). Understanding and responding to group violence: Genocide, mass killing, and terrorism. In Mogaddham F. M. & Marsella A. J. (Eds.), *Understanding terrorism* (pp. 151–168). Washington, DC: American Psychological Association.

Turiel, E. (2002). *The culture of morality. Social development, context, and conflict*. Cambridge: Cambridge University Press.

Valsiner, J. (2000). *Culture and human development*. London: Sage.

Vandenberg, B. (1993). Developmental psychology, God and the Good, *Theory & Psychology*, 3(2), 191–205.

Vernant, J.-P. (1982). *Religions, histoire, raisons*. Maspero, Paris.

Wertsch, J. V. (1991). *Voices of the mind*. London: Harvester Wheatsheaf.

Whiting, B. B. & Whiting, J. W. M. (1975). *Children of six cultures*. Cambridge, MA: Harvard University Press.

Wittgenstein, L. (1953). *Philosophical investigations*. Oxford: Blackwell.

Wren, T. (Ed.), (1990). *The moral domain*. Cambridge, MA: MIT Press.

CHAPTER 28

Identity, Rights, and Duties

The Illustrative Case of Positioning by Iran, the United States, and the European Union

Fathali M. Moghaddam and Kathryn A. Kavulich

A major challenge in socio-cultural psychology is to develop more dynamic accounts of human thought and action (Bruner, 1990; Harré, 2002; Valsiner, 2004). Such accounts need to incorporate the fluid, interactive nature of social processes (Crossley, 2000). The theories and methods of traditional psychology are not adequate for such a challenge, although they are suitable for studying specific reactions of isolated individuals in short time periods, as typically found in psychology laboratory experiments completed in an hour or so (Moghaddam, 2005, chap. 2). Researchers interested in longer-term processes, and in dynamic interactions, must turn to alternative psychologies, as suggested by the critical turn in psychology (Fox & Prilleltensky, 1997).

An important example of topics that need to be studied through more dynamic, process-oriented psychologies is perceived justice, particularly what people believe to be *rights*, what is demanded of others (Moghaddam, 2000), and *duties*, what is owed to others (Moghaddam, Slocum, Finkel, More, & Harré, 2000). Very little

research attention has been given to human rights on the part of psychologists (for the major exceptions, see Doise, 2002), and even less attention has been devoted to both rights and duties (for the main exception, see Finkel & Moghaddam, 2004). The historic nature of rights and duties demands that these topics be tackled through innovative theory and research methods.

Rights and duties are not static, frozen in time; rather, they are negotiable and changing. As individuals and groups interact and experience and influence changes, so too their rights and duties tend to shift through a process of continual negotiation. Indeed, even basic ideas of what constitute rights and duties are plastic and malleable, so that in most cases a right can be re-negotiated and re-defined as a duty, and a duty as a right (for a more in-depth discussion and examples of exceptions to this general trend, see Moghaddam, 2004; Moghaddam & Riley, 2004).

Rights and duties are central to identity, another important topic that requires closer study through more dynamic approaches.

Considerable attention has been given to identity since the 1970s, particularly through research inspired by social identity theory (see Ellemers, Spears, & Doosje, 1999). However, most of this research has given attention to identity in the context of very brief laboratory experiments, where long-term "identity change" cannot be studied. Scant attention has been given to the longer-term processes through which individuals and groups negotiate identities for themselves and others, although a few promising avenues are being explored (e.g., Weinreich & Saunderson, 2003). Such processes can be studied through a number of alternative, scientifically valid (Moghaddam & Harré, 1995), approaches that are now available. In this chapter we provide an illustrative example of an alternative research approach, positioning theory (Harré & Moghaddam, 2004), for studying identity in relation to constructions of rights and duties.

Positioning theory represents a highly promising new approach to studying the dynamic social processes that unfold over time. Positions take shape through patterns of rights and duties that are shared among the members of a particular culture. A position sets the boundaries of what an individual or group can legitimately do within a cultural context. In this illustrative example, we apply positioning theory to examine relations between nations and multi-nation unions, building on the idea that "Institutions and even nations can be positioned in that rights and duties to perform certain categories of speech acts are restricted by the conventions of interaction" (Harré & Moghaddam, 2004, p. 5). Of course, the conventions of interactions are themselves fluid rather than static.

In certain contexts, such as in international relations, the conventions of interactions are continually being challenged; first by nations in minority status who want to escape from their disadvantaged situation, and second by nations that already enjoy majority status but are motivated to improve their situation even further (for more in-depth discussion of intergroup positioning,

see Tan & Moghaddam, 1999). With respect to the positioning strategies used by minority and majority nations, an important research question concerns the possible existence of universals. On the one hand, it could be argued that each international situation and set of relationships between minority and majority nations is unique and needs to be treated as a special, different case. On the other hand, it may be argued that there are certain consistencies in positioning strategies across all different types of situations. The second argument, in support of some universals, is in line with recent theory and research on the psychology of rights and duties suggesting that a number of universals do exist in the domain of rights and duties (Moghaddam, 2004; Moghaddam & Riley, 2004).

Because of the scarcity of psychological research on rights and duties, and the need to adopt innovative approaches in this domain, we provide an illustrative example of how research might fruitfully proceed. The first part of this paper articulates a conceptual framework, presenting the idea of a universal cycle of rights and duties, in the context of a broader discussion on positioning, identity, rights, and duties. In part two, we establish the historical and cultural context of the illustrative example that serves as the focus of this chapter: positioning by the Islamic Republic of Iran (IRI), the United States (US), and the European Union (EU). In part three, we discuss examples of positioning by the different parties. This is followed by a brief concluding discussion.

Conceptual Framework

The point of departure for our conceptual framework, following a long tradition (for background, see Billig, 1991; Harré, 2002; Moghaddam, 2002; Valsiner, 2000), is the observation that humans are intentional beings engaged in ongoing social interactions that are characterized both by change and continuity. The implication we take from this observation is that in order to understand human thought and action, researchers need to examine ongoing social processes. Thus, following in the research tradition set by Allport (1955) on becoming, Goffman (1956) on self-presentation and "face work," and Vygotsky on "psychological synthesis" (see Van der Veer & Valsiner, 1991), identity and other such characteristics should be considered as continually shaping and re-shaping, rather than fixed at any particular time. In this illustrative example, we focus specifically on how nation states attempt to use arguments about rights and duties to develop particular identities both for themselves and for other nation states.

A continuing debate concerning rights and duties focuses on the question of possible universals. A strong set of arguments have been put forward against universals in rights and duties; for example, on the grounds that rights and duties reflect group norms and, of course, norms can and often do differ across cultures (see for example, Louis & Taylor, 2004). From this perspective, there can be an infinite variety of different conceptions and practices regarding rights and duties as there are cultural groups. For example, consider the case of a woman's duty to wear the Islamic veil in countries such as Iran, where the authorities insist that all women are duty-bound to wear the veil in public. This "duty" is transformed to a "right" for some Muslim women in France, where the government sees it as a duty of citizens not to wear the Islamic veil (as well as other conspicuous religious symbols) in state schools. Thus, wearing the veil is seen as a duty by the government in Iran and a right by some Muslim women living in France; not wearing the veil is seen as a right by some Muslim women in Iran and a duty by the government in France. One could argue that, from a "relativist" perspective, whether wearing the Islamic veil is a right or a duty, or even an issue worthy of attention in social and political arenas, depends on group membership, culture, and other contextual factors.

An alternative approach is to argue that although in many cases rights and duties are replaceable and context dependent, there are also important universals in the domain of rights and duties (Moghaddam & Riley, 2004). An example of such a possible universal is the priority given to rights and duties by minority and majority groups in interaction with one another (Moghaddam, 2004). There is an important consistency in behavior on rights and duties across the contexts of Iran and France. In both contexts the majority group, the government authorities who enjoy greatest power, give priority to duties: the duty to wear the veil in Iran and the duty not to wear the veil in France (the duty not to wear the veil in French schools comes under the broader duty not to deviate from the separation of church and state). There is also consistency in that in both contexts the minority group, women who are not following traditional Islam in Iran and those who are following traditional Islam in France, give priority to rights: the right not to wear the veil in Iran and the right to wear the veil in France. Thus, although what is a right and what is a duty can shift across cultures, there is consistency in the priority given to rights by minority groups and that given to duties by majority groups (Moghaddam, 2004).

The fluid dynamic of this relationship is demonstrated by changes in the United Kingdom, when on March 2, 2005, a 16-year-old schoolgirl won the right to wear the Islamic shoulder-to-toe dress in school (Aslam, 2005). The girl had waged a two-year campaign to win this "right" in court, while the authorities had argued that it is her duty to wear the appropriate school uniform. This case demonstrates that a minority that resists can, under certain conditions, change the verdict of a majority; reminding us of the seminal research on minority influence by Moscovici (Moscovici, Mucchi-Faina, & Maas, 1994).

Arguments pertaining to rights and duties are used by minority and majority groups to position themselves and others as "deserving" or "undeserving," "justified" or "unjustified," and so on. In this way, both *personal identity*, one's sense of self, and *collective identity*, and one's sense of one's group, are positioned and re-positioned through a continual process. Such positioning and re-positioning takes place through discourse, which follows *story lines*, established and well-known lines of development. For example, a minority group might narrate a "victim" story line, positioning itself as the target of oppression by more powerful adversaries who are determined to deprive minorities of their rights. On the other hand, a majority group might position itself as the upholder of law and order, determined to see that all groups, even so-called "rogue states," carry out their duties in an honest and fair way.

The positioning "triangle," involving positions, discourse, and storyline, has been used to explore intra-personal, inter-personal, and inter-group relations in a variety of personal, social, political, and business contexts (see examples in Harré & Moghaddam, 2004). One aspect of positioning theory that remains under-developed concerns motives: why should groups position themselves and others? Moghaddam and Riley (2004) found that in relationships between representatives of major powers (Henry Kissinger, U.S. Secretary of State and Mao Zedong, Chairman of the Communist Party of the People's Republic of China; and between Henry Kissinger and Leonid I. Brezhnev, General Secretary of the of the Central Committee of the Communist Party of the Soviet Union (CPSU)), an important motive was to avoid breakdowns in communications and to sustain inter-group harmony. This motive is probably also important in relations between the IRI, the EU, and the US. All three parties face grave risks if the negotiations break down: the IRI could face increased international isolation, and the EU and the US could face the possibility of another country walking away from the Nuclear Non-proliferation Treaty. However, in part because of the enormous imbalance of power between these entities, the situation seems in some ways very different and other motives are probably also involved. One possibility suggested by social identity theory (Tajfel & Turner, 1986) is that these interactions are framed by the social demand for a positive and distinct identity (following Goffman, 1974).

The Illustrative Project and the Historical and Cultural Context of Relations Between IRI, EU, and US

In this section we establish the timeframe of the illustrative project, as well as briefly describe the historical context of the relationship between the IRI, the US, and the EU.

The Current Project

The time period of the illustrative project is from September 1, 2004 through November 29, 2004, a period of particularly intense inter-state tensions between the IRI and the EU, and the IRI and the US. Throughout this period, the IRI, the EU, and the US engaged in strategic positioning on the issue of the Iranian Nuclear Power Development Program. To monitor and assess the positioning strategies adopted by the three parties, we collected data from a variety of Farsi and English language news sources, both domestic and international. The end date of the data gathering activities was the adoption of Resolution 291104 by the IAEA Board of Governors on November 29, 2004, which marked an at least temporary decline in tensions between the three parties.

The Historical and Geopolitical Context

Iran is a country with a long history and legitimate claims to a glorious past around 2500 years ago, but in modern times Iran has suffered political and economic weakness, particularly relative to Western powers. The industrial, economic, political, and social revolutions that transformed, empowered, and enriched Western societies from the 17th century did not much benefit Iran. One reason is that the Qajar dynasty that ruled Iran 1796–1921 was particularly corrupt and ineffective. During the 19th century, the influence of Russia and Great Britain increased in Iran, resulting in important territorial, commercial, and political concessions to these two powers on the part of weak Qajar rulers. Stronger popular resistance to this trend, reflecting some movement toward

democracy, came at the end of the nineteenth century when popular uprising forced the Qajars to revoke an 1891 agreement
giving Britain monopoly over tobacco trade
in Iran. This was the start of lengthy a mass
movement to overthrow the monarchy,
which finally came to fruition through the
revolution of 1978–1979.

The history of Iran in the 20th century
reveals two clear trends relevant to this illustrative project, a first is continued attempts
by foreign powers to influence events in Iran.
The strategic location of Iran, on the cross-
road between east and west and a buffer
against Russian ambitions to have overland
access to the Persian Gulf ports, meant that
Iran would become particularly vulnerable
to occupation. During both the first (1914–
1918) and second (1939–1945) world wars,
Iran was occupied by foreign forces. Also,
the discovery of extensive oil reserves in Iran,
and the increasing importance of oil in the
global economy, strengthened the motivation of foreign powers to try to influence
events in Iran. Thus, in the first half of the
twentieth century Britain, and in the second
half the United States, played a decisive role
in the course of events in Iran, including the
establishment of the Pahlavi dynasty by Reza
Shah in 1926, the replacement of Reza Shah
by his son Mohammad Reza Shah in 1941,
and the *coup d'etat* that brought Mohammad
Reza Shah back to power in 1951. The popular belief, both inside and outside Iran, was
that the "last Shah" had been bought back to
power through a CIA-directed coup (Kinzer,
2003).

A second trend in the history of modern Iran relevant to the current project is
attempts by Iranian leaders to maneuver and
better position themselves in relationships
with Russia, Britain, and the United States,
the major powers that enjoy greatest influence in the region, sometimes by playing
one power against another (Pollack, 2004).
Prior to the Second World War, Reza Shah
Pahlavi attempted to use United States influence as a balance against the British and Russian governments, and his son also relied on
the United States to get British and Russian
forces to leave Iran after the Second World

War. Although the dependence of the Shah
on US backing increased during the 1950s,
1960s, and 1970s, the Shah did turn to other
powers when the US refused to meet Iranian requests. An example particularly relevant to the current project is Iranian reliance
on German rather than American technology to launch a nuclear power program in
the 1970s. Although a slogan of Iran since the
1978–1979 revolution has been "Neither East
nor West: Only Islamic Republic" (indicating a rejection of both communism and capitalism and an embracing of "only Islam"),
the government of the IRI has not hesitated
to try to better position itself between different powers and even to play different world
powers, such as the US, the EU, China, and
Russia against one another. The US trade
embargo that came into effect against Iran
and the ending of direct US-Iran diplomatic
relations following the hostage-taking crisis
has resulted in Iran forging stronger trade
and political ties with other powers, in an
attempt to avoid being isolated.

"Nuclear" Positioning by the IRI, the US, and the EU

In order to better understand the current
situation, we need to consider the beginnings of nuclear power in the late 1930s.
The United States began positioning regarding non-proliferation soon after October
21, 1939, when President Franklin D. Roosevelt appointed a committee to explore
the possibility of building an atomic bomb.
Concerns about proliferation were formalized by The Franck Committee, established
by President Truman in 1945 to advise
the US president and congress on nuclear
issues, "in the absence of an international
authority which would make all resort to
force in international conflict impossible,
nations could still be diverted from a path
which must lead to total mutual destruction, by a specific international agreement
barring a nuclear arms race" (1945). But it
would take almost a quarter of a century
before a first international nonproliferation
agreement was reached. Immediately after

the first nuclear explosion, the so-called "Trinity Test" in new Mexico on July 16, 1945, 69 scientists expressed concern that American cities could also become the targets of atomic attacks (Szilard Petition, 1945), and similar concerns about proliferation were expressed by groups of scientists (e.g., The Atomic Scientists of Chicago, 1945) after the atomic bomb attacks at Hiroshima and Nagasaki in 1945.

The United States government pursued two avenues, the first domestic and the second international, for achieving nonproliferation. First, the Atomic Energy Act (1946) represented the start of a series of domestic steps to prevent information about atomic energy to be transmitted from US sources to anyone outside the official US programs. Second, the establishment of the International Atomic Energy Agency (IAEA) through United Nations Resolution (#810) in 1954 launched serious efforts to prevent proliferation at the international level. The United States was vitally instrumental in the approval by the UN General Assembly of the Nuclear Nonproliferation Treaty on June 12, 1968. This treaty set forth that non-nuclear states would remain non-nuclear and that the IAEA's resolutions would be binding for the signatories. At present a total of 188 parties have joined the Nuclear Nonproliferation Treaty.

Throughout the history of atomic research, however, there has continued to be tension between limitations necessary to prevent proliferation, and the freedoms required for nations to be able to develop nuclear power for peaceful purposes. A major problem is that the research and technology to develop nuclear power for peaceful purposes can be diverted to develop nuclear weapons. Once a country has achieved a high level of expertise in nuclear power technology, such expertise can also then be used for non-peaceful purposes. In this way, the number of countries with nuclear weapons has increased.

By 1968 five countries (USA, USSR, UK, France, and China) already had developed the nuclear bomb. From the perspective of the countries that had not developed the bomb, it seemed that they would forever be at a disadvantage. Would countries without the bomb accept this situation? It seems at least some of them did not, because India and Pakistan have joined the list of declared nuclear countries, and Israel (not a Nuclear Non-Proliferation Treaty (NPT) member) and North Korea (withdrew from NPT in 1/10/2003) are believed to also have developed nuclear weapons. Iran is among the countries accused by the US government of attempting to acquire the nuclear bomb.

The collapse of the Soviet Union in 1991 raised fears about proliferation to other nonnuclear states. The Soviet nuclear material and technology, which had been placed throughout the Eastern European Soviet Republics, were now scattered throughout newly independent countries. From the early 1990s to the present, the United States, through monetary assistance and technical expertise, has worked to limit the possibility of proliferation, but dangers have arisen from alternative, non-Western sources. As of February 2004, Pakistani scientist Abdul Qadeer Khan had confessed to selling nuclear technology to North Korea, Libya, and Iran.

Positioning Strategies

Islamic Republic of Iran

Positioning by Iranian authorities needs to be assessed with due consideration for the political relations of the IRI government with, on the one hand, foreign governments and particularly the US government and, on the other hand, the Iranian population. We also need to consider a range of Iranian political factions operating inside and outside Iran, differing in the degree to which they are anti-American and anti-Western in their ideologies.

A long series of events has resulted in deep distrust and antipathy between US government authorities and the IRI government. These include the pro-Shah policies of successive US administrations prior to 1978, the hostage taking crisis in 1979, the continued US trade embargo against the IRI, the freezing of Iranian assets in the United States, and what the IRI government saw as US support for Iraq in the 1980–1989 Iran-Iraq war. The IRI government has publicly adopted an anti-US position, with Ayotollah Khomeini, the founder of the IRI, famously and repeatedly calling the United States the "Great Satan." The IRI government has sponsored numerous anti-American demonstrations, and the Iranian public has been encouraged to see the US as a source of conspiracies against the interests of Iran. This strategy encompasses both 'benefits' and risks for the IRI government.

Some of the "benefits" of this policy can be understood in relation to the psychological process of displaced aggression, discussed in Freud's (1921/1955, 1930/1961) pioneering work and a continued focus in modern research (Miller, Pederson, Earlywine, & Pollock, 2003). The Iranian population has experienced tremendous difficulties and challenges in the post-revolution era, including a drop in the standard of living for most people, a bloody eight-year war, shortages of essential goods, high inflation and unemployment, and severe shortage of educational opportunities for the approximately 60% of the rapidly rising population that is less than 30 years of age. These extreme difficulties threaten to lead to increasing anti-government sentiments among the Iranian population. The IRI government has managed the situation in part by displacing negative sentiments onto the "Great Satan." This displacement continues to be directed by Iranian government leaders, who point their fingers at the United States as the main source of evil and wrongdoings in the world, and particularly in Iran.

Associated with the displacement of aggression onto the US and other foreign "aggressors" has been increased cohesion within Iran, as well as greater focus on the mobilization of national energies behind more radical, aggressive leadership. By building up the threat of the "Great Satan," more radical forces have been able to sideline their relatively moderate political competitors.

But the strategy of displaced aggression as adopted by Iranian leaders also carries considerable risks. One risk that is particularly relevant to the current discussions is that, having positioned America as the "Great Satan," it now becomes very difficult to justify negotiating with the US. Those Iranian leaders daring enough to suggest the route of negotiation run the risk of being branded as anti-revolutionary and even traitors, by both fundamentalists and the general Iranian population who have received decades of anti-American propaganda from the government-controlled media in Iran. These, then, are some of the special limitations facing Iranian leaders as they attempt to position the IRA vis-à-vis the US and the EU in nuclear discussions.

At the heart of the positioning strategy adopted by Iranian leaders is a strong emphasis on the rights of Iran. Even the so-called "moderate" leaders keep to this rhetorical line, as in the case of the "reformist" Prime Minister Khatemi stating that, "We expect our legitimate right to be recognized and that Iran not be deprived of nuclear technology"[1] and "I have no doubt that the policy of . . . the United States is to deprive Iran of its natural right to access to nuclear enrichment technology for producing fuel." Even in the cases where an Iranian leader expresses awareness of the concerns of Western powers in the nuclear negotiations, the issue of the rights of Iran continue to be highlighted, such as when Foreign Ministry spokesman Hamid Reza Asefi states, "Through talks we can make a bridge between their concerns and our legitimate rights."[2]

Iranian leaders have adopted a number of different tactics to try to bolster the legitimacy of their claims about Iran's rights. A first tactic is to bring into effect the authority of third parties who, according to the IRI, support Iranian rights. Examples of this tactic are:

"The Frankfurt Allgemeine has proposed that Iran's rights for using atomic power be upheld" (IRI News)[3]

"Valeed Jan Balot, Leader of the Progressive Socialists in Lebanon, has backed Iran's right to pursue nuclear power for peaceful purposes"[4]

"The Highest Shia Parliament in Lebanon has condemned the US and European pressures on the Islamic Republic of Iran"[5]

A second tactic is to broaden the focus of attention to other countries outside the IRI-US-EU triangle. On the world stage, IRI leaders argue, the US has a credibility problem and an attack on Iran would make the situation even worse for the US.

"An attack on Iran would harm America's credibility."[6]

There is an implicit dare incorporated in this statement: America could attack Iran, but the consequences would be worse for America. Also, on the world stage, the United Nations and other international bodies are most important, and by implication the US is less important.

"India and South Korea emphasize the role of the United Nations in world peace and development."[7]

A third tactic is to claim that the US government has "bad information." The claim that a government has bad information has particularly powerful implications for the United States, in the post-Iraq invasion era. During the build up to the US-led invasion of Iraq in 2003, the US government built the case for invasion in large part on the idea that Iraq has a large and active program to build weapons of mass destruction (WMD). The case for a "dangerous" Iraqi WMD program was presented in some detail at the United Nations by Colin Powel, the US Secretary of State. However, after the invasion, US weapons inspectors failed to discover any credible evidence of an Iraqi WMD program, putting to doubt the efficiency of the Central Intelligence Agency (CIA) and other US intelligence gathering sources. Added to this, evidence emerged suggesting that the decision to invade Iraq might have been taken in private by the White House at a time when there was not solid evidence for an Iraq WMD program (footnote to the "British memo").

In order to further highlight the issue of US credibility, the IRI media has also spotlighted the mistreatment of Iraqi prisoners by the US military at the notorious Abu Gharib prison, as well as the failure of the US intelligence system to prevent the terrorist attacks of September 11. For example, in an article under the headline, "American claims about Parchin are without any basis" (Parchin is one of the supposed "nuclear sites" in Iran), the claim is that, "The Americans have made a complete mess of information gathering in relation to September 11 and Abu Gharib prison" (IRI News).[8]

The adoption of Resolution 291104 by the IAEA Board of Governors created both an opportunity and a challenge for the IRI government. On the one hand, this agreement lessened external pressure on Iran in the short term and allowed the IRA government to claim that it is cooperating with, and indeed has the support of, the international community. On the other hand, the Resolution, because it represents "cooperation" with western powers, opened up new opportunities for radical elements within Iran to attack the government as collaborating with the pro-US interests and working "against the revolution." For this reason in particular, the interpretation of the Resolution takes on the highest importance and the task of "interpretation" began immediately after adoption. Speaking for the IRI government, Mr. Rowhani (the IRI lead negotiator in talks with the EU) gave the following interpretation, "According to the agreement, the European Union has committed itself to cooperate with the Islamic Republic in the campaign against terrorism and in its efforts to establish peace and security in Iraq, and also to reject all the US accusations against Iran"[9] and that, "Our principles have been respected." In this way, Mr. Rowhani interprets the Resolution to mean that the EU stands with the IRI against the US. In a similar manner, another prominent IRI leader Aftab-e-Yazd stated that "The EU big three ultimately accepted our right to use nuclear technology for civil use. The key point in the latest agreement is that Iran's right to peaceful nuclear activity has been established."[10]

Finally, in considering the IRI position, two broad themes need to be considered. First, the argument that the US is using the nuclear bomb issue as an excuse to try to prevent Iran from making progress in other important spheres. For example, the Supreme Leader, Grand Ayotollah Khamenei claimed that "The world oppressors know Iran does not have a nuclear bomb, but what worries them is that Iran can advance in science."[11] Second, the priority of rights, as stated by Mr. Rowhani, in his interpretation of UN Resolution 291104, "No country can force any other country to stop an activity which is its legitimate right, even for one hour. Therefore, suspension, of any extent and duration, will be a voluntary Iranian decision."[12] The proposition that the IRI has chosen suspension as a right and not as a duty is repeated by government representatives, to suggest that the IRI will later exercise the right to cease suspension, "This demand is illegal and does not put any obligation on Iran. The IAEA board of governors has no right to make such a suspension obligatory for any country"[13] Rohani.

In summary, the IRI has attempted to position itself as collaborating with the EU, in defense of its rights against the US. On the one hand, the IRI focuses on its rights and interprets certain rights as enshrined in the NPT. On the other hand, the IRI rejects US attempts to interpret the NPT through an emphasis on what the US claims to be the duties of the IRI.

Positioning by the USA

Whereas the IRI government gave priority to the rights of Iran, the US gave priority to Iran's duties, but also the duties of the international community. The general theme of this positioning strategy is captured by the White House spokesperson, "Iran needs to comply with its international commitments" (Scott McClellan),[14] and by Vice President Dick Cheney, "We recently were...in a meeting with the board of governors in the International Atomic Energy Agency...there will be a follow-up meeting in November to determine whether or not Iran is living up to their commitments and obligations."[15]

But it is not just Iran that has duties; according to US leaders the international community and the US must also give priority to their duties in the nuclear domain. President Bush stated,

The greatest threat before humanity today is the possibility of secret and sudden attack with chemical or biological or radiological or nuclear weapons/meeting this duty has required changes in thinking and strategy/ there is a consensus among nations that proliferation cannot be tolerated/ for international norms to be effective, they must be enforce.[16]

Similarly, Richard Boucher proposed, "We have a mutual interest in ensuring that Iran abide by its Nonproliferation Treaty obligations not to develop nuclear weapons."[17]

The US has repeatedly attempted to heighten a sense of crisis by linking Iran's nuclear program with the duty of Iran to combat the threat of international terrorism. Richard Boucher argued that "...there's something important...the need for Iran to live up to the international responsibilities that all countries have under Resolution 1373 to fight terrorism...," and again "We have said that there are Al Quaida members in Iran, and that Iran needs to deal with them in accordance with their international responsibilities that all countries have under resolution 1373." Associated with this line of reasoning is the presentation of Iran as a much larger threat than is generally recognized. As John Hulsman (Senior Fellow, The Heritage Foundation) put it, "My great frustration is that I think Iran is the 800lb gorilla in the corner of the room."[17]

The general orientation of the US administration regarding duties reflects categorical thinking, reminding us of the line of argument made famous by President G.W. Bush "you are either with us or against us," "The important thing...is what the Iranians say now...as to whether or not, yes or no, they are going to comply with the requirements of the International Atomic Energy Agency board of directors" (Richard Boucher).[18]

In summary, the US has been positioning the IRI as a threat, and focusing on the duties of the IRI as a member of the international community. By continually referring to international agencies, the NPT, and the international community, the US has attempted to position the IRI as an outsider, and a problem to be solved by the US and others.

Positioning by the EU

The EU has attempted to play the role of "honest broker," the mediator who serves as a fair judge in the interests of all sides. Toward this goal, the EU has claimed to be balancing the rights and duties of the IRI. However, underlying this position has been a balancing of "carrots" and "sticks" in attempts to influence IRI government decision making.

Thus, the EU and related sources have made a number of statements highlighting the rights of Iran. For example, according to a confidential EU document, "to suspend all enrichment and reprocessing related activities in a comprehensive and internationally verifiable manner . . . / we would reaffirm the right of Iran to develop research production and the use of nuclear energy for peaceful purposes without discrimination in conformity with Article 2 of the NPT."[19] Similarly, a Foreign and Commonwealth Office news release states, "The E3/EU recognize Iran's rights under the NPT exercised in conformity with its obligations under the treaty, without discrimination . . . the E3/EU recognize that this suspension is a voluntary confidence building measure and not a legal obligation."[20]

But EU statements concerning Iran's rights are balanced with statements concerning Iran's duties in "areas of concern," as in "non proliferation, fighting terrorism, human rights, and the Middle East peace process. More intense economic relations can be achieved only if progress is reached in the four areas of concern. . . . Iran's nuclear program remains a matter of grave concern" (EU statement),[21] and "I don't think that dialogue has been exhausted on this . . . but

we do need the Iranians to understand that the international community does not find it acceptable that they develop nuclear weapons" (U.K. Prime Minister, Tony Blair).[22]

The EU, then, has been encouraging the IRI to accept "duties," by putting forward the fulfillment of certain "rights" as rewards.

Positioning By the Iranian Opposition

A wide range of Iranian political groups located abroad actively oppose the IRI government. Many of the important opposition groups find their voice in Farsi newspapers published abroad, the most important being *Kayhan* (published in London) and *Iran Times* (published in Washington, DC). Opposition groups attempt to position the IRI government as being willing to abandon Iran's legitimate rights and to "sell out" to the West in order to continue in power in Iran; thus " . . . the Islamic Republic has . . . left the door open for bartering. The Tehran regime does not see the offer so far made by the Europeans, as well as by John Kerry the Democratic candidate to replace George Bush, as sufficient. They want a better offer, particularly with respect to political gains, and most important among their demands is assurance of the continuation of their regime and assurance that there would not be military attacks and attempts at regime change."[23]

The reference here to "bartering" implies a willingness to abandon important principles and is repeated in other articles, such as in a major headline, "Islamic republic: Bartering abroad, pressuring at home."[24] Toward the same goal of discrediting the IRI government, the opposition media took every opportunity to present the IRI government as secretly colluding with the U.S., making a huge fuss when the foreign ministers of Iran and America sat next to each other during a conference in Egypt.[25]

Opposition media presented the adoption of Resolution 291104 as evidence that the IRI government had abandoned Iran's rights, and they did this by reference to a remark made by Ayotollah Khomeini when he was forced to make peace with Iraq after the eight-year Iran-Iraq war. At that time, the Iranian Supreme Leader had said acceptance of the peace agreement was like drinking from a poison cup. An opposition newspaper presented Resolution 291104 as "The second poison cup 'voluntarily' drank" (Kayhan Newspaper, Nov 24, 2004 p. 1–2).[26] In the same article, the two possibilities open to the IRI government are depicted as both being disastrous, "Since America has military forces in the Persian Gulf, Afghanistan, and Iraq, America could easily take economic sanctions against Iran. We have to see what path the Islamic Republic will take if it is faced with such a possibility. Will it act like Saddam and bring the dangers of a military attack on itself, or will it act like act like Ayatollah Khomeini and drink the poison and take the path of Colonel Qadhafi."[27]

Concluding Comment

The illustrative case of positioning by Iran, the EU, and the US has been used to demonstrate how positioning takes place in a dynamic, real world context. We conclude by highlighting two themes that emerge from our discussion; a first theme concerns positioning tactics in a the dynamic flow of intergroup relations. A second theme is the link between our discussion and the wider effort toward achieving a theory of rights and duties.

Regarding the first theme, the dynamic flow of intergroup relations, we find that a variety of sometimes ingenious tactics are used to try to achieve desired positions.

In several cases, tactical arguments involved veiled threats. For example, the IRI leadership reminded the world of its conventional weapons capabilities, as when Iran Times quoted Ali Akbar Rafsanjani in a headline saying "Iran has missiles with a range of 2,000 kilometers."[28] Another form of veiled threat concerns America's problems in managing post-war Iraq, where US soldiers are under attack from insurgents. Speaking at Friday prayers, Ahmed Jannati followed up an attack on America's attempts to "deprive us of nuclear technology" by stating that, "The people of Iraq are not sitting idle and every day they carry out tens of attacks against Americans in different parts of Iraq."[29] Through its historic influence among the Shi'a population in Iraq, the IRI could make life even more difficult for US forces "occupying" Iraq.

The IRI leadership has also attempted to throw Western powers off balance by suggesting that the positions Iran has taken involve a certain level of bluff. For example, after the adoption of Resolution 291104, the *New York Times* ran an article with the title, "Iran hints it sped up enriching uranium as a ploy" (2005), reporting that "Iranian officials have hinted in recent days that they sped up their enrichment of uranium in the past year to put Iran in a better position to negotiate with the West."[30] Such ploys underline the dynamic, fluid nature of positions and the tactics used to achieve them.

The second theme that emerged from our discussion concerns the wider effort to develop a theory of rights and duties. Our contribution weighs in on the side of *positive law*, proposing that rights and duties are invented by humans and reflect changing cultural characteristics, rather than *natural law*, the belief that rights and duties are discovered by humans and derive from divine or natural sources. Within the positive law tradition, our contribution is close to two lines of inquiry in particular: the first is ethological research suggesting a sense of 'fairness' among some animals, the second is an "experiential" approach developed by Dershowitz (2004), in legal studies.

In earlier discussions toward a cultural theory of rights and duties, Moghaddam has proposed that modern rights and duties are rooted in *primitive social relations*, elementary universal behaviors that evolved as part of a repertoire of behaviors necessary for group survival (Moghaddam, 2000; Moghaddam, Slocum, Finkel, More, & Harré, 2000; Moghaddam & Riley, 2004). An example of a primitive social relation is turn-taking, which must be practiced for effective communications and basic cooperative living. Primitive social relations evolve in response to functional needs, rather than abstract ideas, and are later interpreted as rights and/or duties depending on cultural conditions. For example, having or taking a turn, giving others a turn, and so on, can be interpreted as a right and/or a duty depending on a cultural context (in road traffic, in a court of law, in political debates, in filling a political post).

Humans feel there is unfairness when their constructed understandings of rights and duties are violated. In our illustrative example, the IRI, the EU, and the US all point to "violations" that they see, the IRI pointing particularly to "the violated rights of the IRI" and the EU and the US pointing to "the violated duties of the IRI." A sense of unfairness arises in such situations.

Violations of what could be termed perceived "rights and duties" can also lead to negative reactions among some non-human groups. This is suggested by an intriguing study on the brown capuchin monkey (Brosnan & de Waal, 2003). The monkeys were rewarded for returning a token, either with a grape (a more favored food) or cucumber (a less favored food). In a "no effort" condition, the monkeys received a grape without having to return a token. The results indicate that a monkey would become less cooperative when it witnessed another monkey receive a more favored reward for the same effort, or a reward for no effort. This and related studies have led ethologists to speculate about a sense of "right and wrong" that emerged out of functional conditions among animals (Bekoff, 2002).

An emphasis on functional experiences is shared by the legal scholar Dershowitz (2004), who discusses the evolution of rights from what he terms an "experiential" viewpoint. Dershowitz argues that rights arise from injustices, " ... rights are those fundamental preferences that experience and history – especially of great injustice – have taught are so essential that the citizenry should be persuaded to entrench them and not make them subject to easy change by shifting majorities" (p. 81). In discussing his theory of "rights from wrongs," Dershowitz (2004) explicitly adopts an evolutionary approach, arguing that the progress of human rights is characterized by the same

"punctuated equilibrium" and fits and starts that is evident in evolutionary processes generally. Thus, rather than rights resulting from abstract ideas, they arise from the practical experience of dealing with catastrophic "wrongs," unevenly distributed over historical eras.

The argument for a "universal" cycle of rights and duties (Moghaddam, 2004) should be seen in the context of this wider literature highlighting the "functional" or "experiential" roots of behavior. Rather than abstract ideas leading minorities to give priority to rights and majorities to give priority to duties, we see such priorities as arising from functional aspects of the situation. In Dershowitz's (2004) terminology, it is the "experiences" of minorities and majorities that give rise to the particular priorities they show for rights and duties. With changing group status and circumstances, we expect the priorities to change.

Our contention is that future sociocultural research on rights and duties should be integrative and should explicitly and necessarily step outside disciplinary boundaries. In the illustrative example, we adopted positioning theory and methodology, crossing the borders of psychology, linguistics, and micro-sociology. But in developing a sociocultural theory of rights and duties, there is need to go even further afield and to also cross into ethology and legal studies, among other domains.

Notes

1   Associated Press. (2004, October 20). Iran Given Final Nuke Chance. *CBSNews.com*. Retrieved September 27, 2004, from http://www.cbsnews.com/stories/2004/10/21/world/main650631.shtml.

2   Reuters News Service (2004, September 26). Iran Says No Immediate Plan to Enrich Uranium. *ABCNews.com*. Retrieved on September 27, 2004, from http://www.abcnews.go.com/wire/World/reuters20040926-57.html.

3   Islamic Republic of Iran News Agency. Frankfurt Ungemeiner supports Iran's rights in the use of nuclear power. Retrieved Sep 22, 2004. (Translated from Farsi by authors)

4   Islamic Republic of Iran News Agency. Valeed Jan Balot, leader of the progressive Socialists in Lebanon, Backs Iran's rights to nuclear power for peaceful purposes. Retrieved Nov 29, 2004. (Translated from Farsi by the first author)

5   Islamic Republic of Iran News Agency. The Supreme Shi'a Council in Lebanon has condemned the U.S. and European pressures on the Islamic Republic of Iran. Retrieved Nov 29, 2004. (Translated from Farsi by the first author)

6   Islamic Republic of Iran News Agency. Pakistani newspaper: An attack on Iran would harm America's credibility. Retrieved Oct 6, 2004. (Translated from Farsi by the first author)

7   Islamic Republic of Iran News Agency. India and South Korea emphasize the important role of the United nations. Retrieved Oct 6, 2004. (Translated from Farsi by the first author)

8   Islamic Republic of Iran News Agency. Minister of Defense: American claims about "Parchin" are baseless. Retrieved Sep 29, 2004. (Translated from Farsi by the first author)

9   Nuclear Agreement Will Bear Fruit at Upcoming IAEA Board Session: Rowhani. (2004, November 17). *Tehran Times*. Retrieved on October 3, 2004, from http://www.tehrantimes.com/Description.asp?Da= 11/17/2004&Cat=2&Num=002.

10 Nuclear Accord Upsets Iran Press. (2004, November 16). *BBC News*. Retrieved on November 8, 2004, from http://news.bbc.co.uk/go/pr/fr/-/1/hi/world/middle_east/ 4015525.stm.

11 Islamic Republic of Iran News Agency. Leader of the Revolution: The reason for the published propaganda against Iran is because of Iran's great achievements. Retrieved Nov 5, 2004. (Translated from Farsi by the first author)

12 Iran Hints it May Suspend Some Unspecified Nuclear Activities. (2004, October 26). *USA Today*. Retrieved on October 28, 2004, from http://www.usatoday.com/news/world/2004– 10–26-iran-nukes_x.htm.

13 Iran Rejects UN Nuclear Demands. (2004, September 19). *BBCNews.com*. Retrieved on September 19, 2004, from http://news.bbc. co.uk/go/pr/fr/-/1/hi/world/middle_east/ 3670018.stm.

14 Charbonneau, Louis. UN Awaits Iran Nuclear Letter. (2004, November 9). *Reuters*. Retrieved on November 15, 2004 from http://swissinfo.org/sen/Swissinfor.html?site Sect=143&sid=5328349.

15 Debate. Vice Presidential Debate. Case Western Reserve University, Cleveland, Ohio. 5 Oct. 2004.

16 Bush, George W. Speech. President Bush Discusses Strategy Against Proliferation of Weapons of Mass Destruction. (2004, February 11). *Fort Lesley J. McNair National Defense University*. Washington, D.C.

17 Address by State Department Spokesman, Richard Boucher. (2004, October 22). Washington, D.C.

18 McGivering, Jill. US Turns the Heat on Tehran. (2004, September 9). *BBC News*. Retrieved on September 14, 2004, from http://news.bbc.co.uk/go/pr/fr/-/1/hi/world/ americas/3632702.stm.

19 Preparatory Text for European Proposals on Iranian Nuclear Program. (2004, October 23). *Tehran Times*. Retrieved on October 26, 2004, from http://www.tehrantimes.com/Description.asp?Da=10/23/2004 &Cat=4&Num=23.

20 Iran-EU Agreement on nuclear program (14 Nov 2004). Agreement between EU and Iran. Http://www.iaea.org/NewsCenter/Focus/ IaeaIran/edu_iran14112004.shtml.

21 EU Trade Threat to Iran. (2004, September 29). *BBC News*. Retrieved on October 3, 2004, from http://news.bbc.co.uk/1/hi/ world/europe/3149174.stm.

22 Iran Hints it May Suspend Some Unspecified Nuclear Activities. (2004, October 26). *USA Today*. Retrieved on October 28, 2004, from http://www.usatoday.com/news/world/ 2004–10–26-iran-nukes_x.htm.

23 Kayhan Newspaper (2004). The last proposal: Carrot and stick, London, UK. 27 Oct, p. 1. (Translated from Farsi by the first author)

24 Kayhan Newspaper (2004). Islamic Republic: Bartering abroad, pressuring at home. London, UK, 10 Nov, Pp. 1–2. (Translated from Farsi by the first author)

25 Iran Times (2004). The foreign ministers of Iran and America sit next to one another during a conference in Egypt Washington, D.C., Nov 26, P. 1&10. (Translated from Farsi by the first author)

26 Kayhan Newspaper (2004). The second poison cup voluntarily drunk. London, UK, Nov

24, p. 1–2. (Translated from Farsi by the first author)

27 Kayhan Newspaper (2004). The difficult situation of Tehran in the face of the latest ultimatum. London, UK, 29 Sep 2004, p. 1–2. (Translated from Farsi by the first author)

28 Iran Times (2004). Iran has missiles with a range of 2,000 kilometers. Washington, D.C., Oct 8, 2004. pp. 1&10 (Translated from Farsi by the first author)

29 Kayhan Newspaper (2004). Under no circumstance can American take away our nuclear capabilities. London, UK, 13 Oct, P. 2) (Translated from Farsi by the first author)

30 Fathi, N. (2005). Iran hints it sped up enriching uranium as a ploy, New York Times, Dec 6, p. 19.

References

Allport, G. W. (1955). *Becoming: Basic consideration for a psychology of personality*. New Haven: Yale University Press.

Aslam, D. (2005). Victory: Schoolgirl describes her fight to wear Islamic dress. *The Guardian*, March 3, 1–2.

Bekoff, M. (2002). Virtuous nature. *New Scientist*, 175, 34.

Billig, M. (1991). *Ideology and opinions*. London: Sage.

Brosnan, S. F., & de Waal, F. B. M. (2003). Monkeys reject unequal pay. *Nature*, 425, 297–299.

Bruner, J. (1990). *Acts of meaning*. Cambridge, MA.: Harvard University Press.

Crossley, M. L. (2000). *Introducing narrative psychology*. Buckingham, UK: Open University Press.

Dershowitz, A. (2004). *Rights from wrongs: A secular theory of the origins of rights*. New York: Basic Books.

Doise, W. (2002). *Human rights as social representations*. London: Routledge.

Ellemers, N., Spears, R., & Doosje, B. (Eds.), (1999). *Social identity: Context, commitment, content*. Oxford: Blackwell.

Finkel, N., & Moghaddam, F. M. (Eds.), (2004). The psychology of rights and duties: Empirical contributions and normative commentaries. Washington, DC: American Psychological Association Press.

Fox, D., & Prilleltensky, I. (Eds.), (1997). *Critical psychology*. Thousand Oaks, CA: Sage.

Goffman, E. (1956). The presentation of the self in everyday life. Harmondsworth, England: Penguin.

Goffman, E. (1974). *Frame analysis: An essay on the organization of experience*. New York: Harper and Row.

Harré, R. (2002). *Cognitive science*. London: Sage.

Harré, R., & Moghaddam, F. M. (Eds.), (2004). *The self and others: Positioning individuals and groups in personal, political, and cultural contexts*. Westport, CT: Praeger.

Kinzer, S. (2003). *All the Shah's men: An American coup and the roots of Middle East terror*. Hoboken, NJ: John Wiley and Sons.

Louis, W. R., & Taylor, D. M. (2004). Rights and duties as group norms: Implications of intergroup research for the study of rights and responsibilities. In N. Finkel & F. M. Moghaddam. (Eds.), The psychology of rights and duties: Empirical contributions and normative commentaties (pp. 105–134). Washington, DC.: American Psychological Association Press.

Miller, N., Pederson, W. C., Earlywine, M., & Pollock, V. E. (2003). A theoretical model of triggered displaced aggression. *Personality and Social Psychology Review*, 7, 75–97.

Moghaddam, F. M. (2000). Toward a cultural theory of human rights. *Theory & Psychology*, 10, 291–312.

Moghaddam, F. M. (2002). *The individual and society: A cultural integration*. New York: Worth.

Moghaddam, F. M. (2004). The cycle of rights and duties in intergroup relations. *New Review of Social Psychology*, 3, 125–130.

Moghaddam, F. M. (2005). *Great ideas in psychology: A cultural and historical introduction*. Oxford: Oneworld.

Moghaddam, F. M., & Harré, R. (1995). But is it science? Traditional and normative approaches to the study of social behavior. *American behavioral Scientist*, 36, 22–38.

Moghaddam, F. M., & Riley, C. J. (2004). Toward a cultural theory of human rights and duties in human development. In N. Finkel & F. M. Moghaddam (Eds.), *The psychology of rights and duties: Empirical contributions and normative commentaries*. (pp. 75–104). Washington, DC: American Psychological Association Press.

Moghaddam, F. M., Slocum, N., Finkel, N., More, Z., & Harré, R. (2000). Toward a cultural theory of duties. *Culture & Psychology*, 6, 275–302.

Moscovici, S., Mucchi-Paina, A., & Maas, A. (Eds.), (1994). *Minority influence*. Chicago: Nelson-Hall.

Pollack, K. (2004). *The Persian puzzle: The conflict between Iran and America*. New York: Random House.

Tan, S. L., & Moghaddam, F. M. (1999). Intergroup positioning. In R. Harré & L.

Van Langenhove (Eds.), *Positioning theory* (pp. 178–194). Oxford: Blackwell.

Tajfel, H., & Turner, J. C. (1986). The social identity theory of intergroup behavior. In S. Worchel & G. Austin (Eds.), Psychology of intergroup relations (pp. 7-24). Chicago: Nelson-Hall.

Valsiner, J. (2000). *Culture and human development*. London: Sage.

Valsiner, J. (2004). Three years later: Culture in psychology – Between social positioning and producing new knowledge. *Culture & Psychology*, 10, 5–27.

Van Der Veer, R., & Valsiner, J. (1991). *Understanding Vygotsky: A quest for synthesis*. Oxford: Blackwell.

Weinreich, P., & Saunderson, W. (Eds.), (2003). *Analysing identity: Cross-cultural, societal and clinical contexts*. London: Routledge.

CHAPTER 29

Symbolic Politics and Cultural Symbols

Identity Formation Between and Beyond Nations and States

Ulf Hedetoft

In standard textbooks on political theory and concepts, symbolic politics (SP) rarely appears in the table of contents or the index at the back. It is not an officially recognized sub-category of political science – whether we think of political communication, vote-catching strategies, ideological positioning, or policies of legitimation – and the literature on the subject is scarce and scattered across a number of scholarly disciplines (see e.g., Campbell 1992; Edelman 1985; Hedetoft, 1995, 1998; Kertzer, 1988; Sears, 1993; Voigt, 1989). Nevertheless, symbolic politics and its forms of cultural representation, identity construction, and (frequently, at least) populist discourses have gained increasing importance in contemporary political life – as a way to maintain or re-build trust and confidence between politicians and electorates; make or accommodate claims for recognition or equal treatment; justify national/ethnic identities and exclusionary policies; or project yourself as a champion of democracy, civil rights, or universal values – or just as a charismatic personality and moral human being.

In this sense, SP is all about representation, projection, persuasion, signals, and appearance – the opposite (or the complement) of a *Realpolitik* built on interests and problem solving. In another, however, it is concerned, substantively, with moulding identities, building trust and legitimacy, and (re)creating solidarities and homogeneities that are, or are felt to be, under threat – whether from above or below, from within or without. For the same reason, SP is far from being the pacific or inconsequential exercise it may seem to be at first glance. Suspended between spin-doctor strategizing and the vehemence of identity politics, it is the stuff that electoral victories and other political successes are often made of, but which can also develop into a perceived threat to the survival of states – as testified by this passionate admonition by Jean Chrétien, the then Canadian Prime Minister, in a speech from 1996:

> *Our country is sick of symbolic politics, and (. . .) it may die from this disease. In symbolic politics, unlike ordinary politics, everything becomes a matter of black*

and white. Positions are turned into sacred ideals on which no compromise is possible. (...) So I would ask all of us in the next few months to be careful in our assessments and our rhetoric, to avoid emotionally laden language and symbolic politics that could destroy this country. We cannot allow Canada to die of symbolic politics. (Chrétien, 1996)

This is the talk of a political actor facing what seemed to be the imminent break-up of his country due to the separatist politics of Quebecois nationalists and to Native land claims movements, both of which rather successfully deployed cultural symbolism, discourses of authenticity, and charges of victimization at the hands of the Federal government (i.e., the myth-making paraphernalia of nationalism) to further their cause.

Interestingly, the Prime Minister, in spite of cautioning against the destructive consequences of SP, does not totally abjure it, but tries to position it where he sees it as properly belonging – between nationalist separatism and "anti-nationalist rhetoric": "It is a trivialization and banalization of dangerous language to simply say that all nationalism is racism," since "nationalism may be a force used to build social solidarity to achieve common projects ... it is those projects we should judge, not the idea of nationalism ... let us judge nationalism ... by its effects." Or in other words, we all resort to SP (as the very speech itself documents) in our efforts to attract sympathy and support, but this can only be applauded if it produces the desired end result, i.e., a strengthening of solidarity across social, ethnic, and territorial divides – and even where it can only be achieved, as in the Canadian case, through the deployment of a multicultural rhetoric of Canada as a country of "diverse national identities."

In this way, contexts and conditions for SP differ between countries and are shaped differently by history, traditions, political cultures, and handed-down forms of authority and legitimate rule – apart from specific situational variations. What is common to all modern exercises in SP, on the other hand, are their formal properties and main objective: through symbolic meaning production, which naturalizes the relationship between people and politics, nation and state, to cater mainly for vertical solidarity within a particular political community and to cast moral leadership and political values as consonant with the will and emotions of the populace. SP, feeding off the symbolic repertoire and consensual narratives of the ethnic group in question, is hence the political semiotics of national identity in practice – communicated, disseminated political fictions entailing a variety of forms, rationales, and consequences. The rest of this chapter will take a close look at some of these salient features and relations.

The Basis: Fictions of the Non-political State

Symbolic politics normally rests on the practical deployment of a variety of more or less complex signs embedded in the collective cultural and psychological repertoire of nations. Umberto Eco (following Charles S. Peirce) once defined a sign as "everything which can be taken as significantly substituting for something else" (Eco, 1976, 7). Signs – and symbols in particular – are inherently relational, in that they refer to, stand for, and connote a referent which is external to the sign, whose properties may be factually unrelated to the autonomous meaning charge of the sign itself, and which, as Eco points out, "does not necessarily have to exist" (ibid.), except in the collective imaginary of the group in question. Symbolic representations especially are characterized by such a contingent or "non-motivated" link between sign and referent. A "rose," per se, has little to do with "love"; a "lion," as such, is unrelated to "courage"; a red rectangular piece of cloth with a white cross superimposed reveals no trace of Danish nationalism; and "Marianne" is a female name (itself of course a sign) with no inherent association to pride in France or the qualities of "Frenchness." Yet the links are there, and we know, by tacit agreement and conventional use, that a rose "is" a symbol of love, a lion of courage, the red and white piece of cloth of the Danish nation state, and Marianne of French grace and historical continuity. It all seems so natural, although it is embedded in codes – second-order signs – that we need to be able to decipher by means of our cultural competences in order to make sense of it.

SP depends for its success on the same kind of process – a process of osmosis producing, *pace* Eco, "a socially shared notion of the thing that the community is engaged to take as if it were in itself true" (ibid.). It is a meaning-producing exercise steeped in cultural signs and ideal discourses intended to produce consensual agreement – identification – between representers (political agents) and represented (peoples, electorates, ethnic groups). The precondition for such identification is that relations and states of affairs are successfully *naturalized* through narratives and fictions (myths, legends, rituals) of the non-political state (Anderson, 1983/1991; Hedetoft, 1995; Kapferer, 1988). This is the paradox of all SP – as a political activity it is crucially dependent on mobilizing images of the "state of nature," of organic relations, historical continuities, and anthropological invariables – in other words on coming across as the natural articulation of the most fundamental desires and ambitions of people. This can only be achieved through deft cultural engineering, welding signs and referents, discourses and practices, nations and states – in and for themselves contingent links – into imaginary unities, natural nexuses – much as in this classic text by Ernest Renan:

A nation is a soul, a spiritual principle. Two things, which in truth are but one, constitute this soul or spiritual principle. One lies in the past, one in the present. One is the possession in common of a rich legacy of memories; the other is present-day consent (...) The nation, like the individual, is the culmination of a long past of endeavours, sacrifice, and devotion. Of all cults, that of the ancestors is the most legitimate, for the ancestors have made us what we are. A heroic past, great men, glory (...) that is the social capital upon which one bases a national idea. To have common

glories in the past and to have a common will in the present; to have performed great deeds together, to wish to perform still more – these are the essential conditions for being a people. (...) A nation's existence is, if you will pardon the metaphor, a daily plebiscite. ... (Renan, 1882/1990: 19)

This is an example of unconditional celebration of the fiction, here almost a moral fable, of the essential, non-political unity of state and nation. Delivered as a lecture by an academic at Sorbonne, it is not as such a political text, and in that sense more an exemplum of the discursive framing that symbolic politics depends on than of such political discourse itself. On the other hand, appearances are deceiving and this scholarly text, too, can be read as "standing for something else," as a sign of political interests, events, and processes in late 19th-century France, which Renan had in mind as the external referent of his lyrical and empathetic narrative about the grandeur of national identification and of the nation/state as a living organism to be likened to "the individual." And, as in the Canadian example above, this referent is more conflictual and less pacific than the discourse itself might lead one to imagine.

His referent (and his audience was fully aware of it) was the problem of the annexation of Alsace and Lorraine by Germany after the Franco-German war of 1870–71. The argument signifies his conviction that this is a national calamity and that the two regions properly belong to France – in spite of the majority of German-speakers in them (hence, language is consistently downplayed as a marker of national identity). They have the memories, the cults, the ancestors, the heroics, the devotion, even the defeats in common – and in future they have a common "programme to put into effect," as the text has it elsewhere. Here Renan becomes more explicitly political, allows the hermetic textual lyricism to point beyond itself into the "real world" of European politics, and reveals that the use of the core term "plebiscite" is meant in literal as well as a metaphorical sense: he knew that if the people of the regions were asked in a referendum, they would opt for France (as actually happened after the Versailles Treaty in 1919). Or differently put: until reunification, French national unity would not be complete, but find itself in a state of *anomie*.

In this representative text, different national *topoi* (see below) structure a series of signs and meanings which essentialize nationhood and assign to the political domain the auxiliary function of contributing a protective frame of cohesion, identity, progress, and influence for the nation and its valuable ideals. In this way, the symbolic-political narrative is usually equipped with a teleology, which orchestrates perceptions of the community's foundational purpose, mission, and goals – which in turn are very dependent on the political form of the relevant regime (democratic, fascist, imperial, despotic...) and its political culture and institutional structure.

This is in the ideal world, however. In reality, contexts and causes of SP are frequently conflictual and riddled with unresolved tensions, casting either the people (top-down discourses of unreasonable popular demands) or the state (bottom-up discourses of elite failure) as problems for national unity. Conversely, it is precisely on the background of such conflicts that SP is mobilized in order to reinstate order and again "make sense" of the (national) world by calling on time-honored virtues, morals, values, and achievements of the collectivity – or to attempt to forge a new and better community within or across traditional political boundary-lines (which in turn will tap into – or engineer – its own myths, legends, and origins). The success or failure of such discourses depend on the one hand on objective conditions and contextual factors (external relations, power struggles, (in)stability, interest constellations, resources – see the following sections), but also on the degree of rhetorical persuasiveness and leadership projection (charisma and trustworthiness) of core political actors; on timing and strategic orchestration (rational deployment of authority); and on how well the symbolism employed aligns itself with positively perceived images and cultural properties of the nation (traditionalism and continuity). Or differently expressed: on the efficient application to the "naturalist" universe of symbolic politics of Max Weber's three forms of authority: traditional, charismatic, and rational-bureaucratic (Weber, 1948/1994).

Rationale, Modalities, and Contexts of Symbolic Politics

It is already transparent that the rationale of SP is multiple and constitutes a permanent companion of more rationally informed political initiatives in modern political regimes, since it is more directed toward affirming or strengthening *identities* than with the pursuit of *interests*, or differently put, with pursuing interests in the form of normative or value-oriented politics. Generally speaking, SP is therefore more affective than cognitive, more rhetorical than substantive, more normative than pragmatic, and more ideational than material. In functional terms, it is aimed toward the maintenance or creation of political legitimacy, authority, and trust, by means of the astute employment of historical signs, cultural values, traditional *mores* and beliefs, and personalized attributes that resonate with received sympathies and orientations of the target audience. Hence, SP consists of exercises in persuasive communication and political mobilization that reaffirm the organic and justified link between sender and receiver, but also reconstitute the political and cultural boundaries between "us" and "them" (rallying sympathies and mobilizing against threats), or prepare transformations between the state of things now and what is in store for the community in future by convincing the national or ethnic public that political leaders can be trusted with coping with such challenges and that the identity of the national community and its culture will be in the best possible hands.

How these generalities translate into real-life politics is, on the other hand, a question largely dependent on the contextual modalities. It is useful to distinguish between three such modalities, characterizing three qualitatively different relations between "state/politics" on the one hand and "nation/people/ethnic group" on the other.

The *first* is one typified by nation-building interests and mobilizing objectives on the part of political elites, who have an idea of their popular base and ethno-national underpinning, but where this "top-down" idea of national community does not yet – or only partially – resonate with the feelings, interests, or orientations of the addressees. This could be termed nationalism in the *imperative modality* (Hedetoft, 1995). It would correspond with the historical processes that we often refer to as the nationalization of the masses (Mosse, 1975; Weber, 1976; Hroch, 1985; Hobsbawm, 1990), but it is a process that can still be found in the pores of the contemporary world, both in Africa, the Middle East, Russia, and some CIS countries, as well as in terms of transnational ethnic mobilization on the part of self-appointed leaderships who are well aware that their only hope of progress, recognition, and attention in the international order is to be able to have – or claim for themselves – an authentic ethno-cultural constituency. Hence, the discourses of such forms of SP are often characterized by an uneasy blend of ideology, sentimentalism, grandiose narratives and stylized lyricism, formalized ritual, and dogmatic-imperative (even imperial-style) rhetoric, since at best they can speak from a position of power or promise, but not from one characterized by the confidence and security provided by established and recognized legitimacy.

The *second* modality is based on precisely such a situation of recognized legitimacy and trusting relations between state and nation, on full-fledged national identity being a state of socio-psychological normality, and on "banal" manifestations and discourses of loyalty, allegiance, and belonging (Billig, 1995). Such stable contexts, states, or situations usually call for less – or more subdued – forms of SP: they can afford to orient themselves more toward practical problem-solving politics, because the "symbolic" conditioning of the ethnic compact between nation and state is tacitly and permanently assumed, national stability representing the historical end-point of a more turbulent and conflictual identity-forming process. Clearly, no national community is ever completely devoid of or protected from dissension, conflict, or challenge – consensus is never total and domestic peace always relative. Also here, therefore, SP is regularly deployed, to re-affirm identity, strengthen trust, pacify concern, bolster common values, and meet (or foreground) challenges – whether real or imagined – in order to give shape to legitimacy, political conviction, and cultural continuity, e.g., in the face of globalization, immigration, European integration, or other imminent threats. SP is not absent, therefore, but assumes less strident forms, is less hegemonic in political discourse, and can, most importantly, take for granted that a strong and extensive cultural resonance board for identity politics is forthcoming in the population at large, in other words a comprehensive, affectively as much as rationally determined will to invest trust and legitimacy in political leadership and representative government. This is what I have elsewhere termed nationalism in the *indicative modality*.

The *third* modality is different still, and probably the one most propitious for the conduct of SP. It is characterized by contexts in which there is a widespread popular feeling of identity and belonging, but no perception of a corresponding and legitimate political/state overarching structure, no government that the community sees as representative of its own interests, values, history, identity, and future aspirations, and often counteractive political forces at work in the environment that (are seen to) conspire against the attainment of independent statehood. Most often this modality is found in contexts where the factual powers-that-be are experienced as illegitimate, discriminatory, or even racist, pursuing policies that marginalize or exclude ethnic minorities, deprive them of their land, possessions, and other resources, and keep them in a position of subordination in which they have been stripped of their human rights – or at least had them severely constrained. This is nationalism in the *subjunctive modality*. The examples already given, from contemporary Canada and historical France, both conform to some if not all of these criteria and stipulations. Other cases would be the Palestinian struggle for independence, the Kurdish fight for Kurdistan, the Tamil Tigers' wish to achieve separation from the Sri Lankan regime, Taiwan's relations with mainland China, many East European independence movements/aspirations during Soviet rule, the Basque separatist movement, Northern Irish Republican aspirations for the unification of Ireland, and Tibetan and Nepalese movements attempting to emancipate the two small states from the stranglehold of Chinese influence, and many more (see e.g., Mayall, 1990; Nagel, 2004; O'Leary et al., 2001; Taras, 2002).

Common to them all is the dream/aspiration of establishing a full-fledged, authentic, and legitimate nation/state compact, on the basis of a strong sense of identity and commonality and in the face of adverse circumstances and asymmetrical power relations. Hence, political manifestations and political rhetoric cannot but be excessively symbolic, both because they must constantly re-affirm unity and purpose, direct themselves against oppressors, and appeal to the understanding, recognition, and support of the international community in historically laden and affective terms. These are all examples of ethnic nationalism aspiring toward completion in the form of a condition of full and formal statehood, of identities dreaming about transformation into political sovereignty. This is when identity politics is the most emphatic and enjoys the best conditions of sympathy and growth – and hence where SP is most effective and most needed, because the context provides ideal opportunities for combining cultural and political, historical and future-oriented, substantive and charismatic dimensions of SP.

This also explains why SP is most prominent in situations of instability, perceived threat, social *anomie*, or other situations characterized by conflict and tension.

Appealing to cohesion, defense of identity and territory, or historical traditions and cultural homogeneity is clearly most acutely called for when the imagined community is imagined as threatened, in some kind of crisis, or as facing serious and unavoidable transformations. In conformity with these three types of situational contexts it is possible to distinguish between three modes of SP: the SP of *civic discontent and moral emergency*, activated e.g., in connection with responses to immigration, marginalization, the erosion of national sovereignty etc.; the SP of *securitization and existential threat*, triggered by predicaments of war, sudden and thoroughgoing political or economic crises/social cleavages, or natural disasters; and the SP of *systemic change*, drawn on in situations where political regimes are facing serious transformative challenges of a social, economic, or political nature, implying new forms of adaptation and inner cohesion, and hence a "rethink" of identity structures and relations of trust. The three modes are not always clearly distinguishable in political and social practice, where they may overlap and interweave in the interpretive mapping and discursive exercises of citizens and politicians alike. Nevertheless, it is useful to think of them as discrete modes fitting different situations and gradations of "emergency" (see below on "immigration, war, and European integration"), and to a large extent determining how the cultural and aesthetic repertoire at the disposal of SP is deployed in specific contexts. This repertoire will be the subject of the next section.

Cultural *Topoi* and Aesthetic Forms

In very general terms, SP draws on the full range of cultural imagery and historical myths at the disposal of nation states, in line with the teleology of the apoliticizing and essentializing fictions discussed above, based on the normative parameters embedded in the respective political cultures, and with an eye to (re)constructing diachronic continuities of identity across periods and vertical congruities of allegiance between nations and states. More specifically, such "naturalizing" discourses – triggered by their very opposite, as clarified above, that is, situations of impending conflict, emergency, or turbulent transformation – assume different narrative moves/communicative strategies and employ different cultural *topoi*, depending on the contextual specifics and the (imagined) effectiveness of the various repertoires at hand.

As regards the narrative moves, five especially are of interest. *First*, we find narratives of direct *depoliticization*, where "state"/"the political domain" is represented as "nation" – the two components of the nation/state nexus no longer being projected as an organic binary, but in the form of national singularity (Voigt, 1989). "Nation," in other words, discursively invades and absorbs "state," signifying the Political (interests, problems, conflicts, etc.) by conflating the two and making the state "roof" (Gellner, 1983) disappear in the process. This move can rely on e.g. the common linguistic usage (and corresponding forms of perception) of terms related to "nation" in order to represent components or functions of state – "national" frequently means "pertaining to state," and the "United Nations" is properly speaking a misnomer for an international organization characterized by the cooperation of governments. *Second*, we encounter strategies that *humanize and personalize* political messages. Structural and impersonal relations are represented in the form of interpersonal problems or as anthropomorphic constants, as for instance when states are projected or imagined as "families" and "tribal communities," international conflicts as "family feuds," or when political actors are required to display charismatic qualities rather than political ideas and problem-solving initiatives. The *third* move consists of *the idealization* of political objectives and political action – which are transformed from a universe of interests, conflicts, and resource distribution to one inhabited and propelled by noble intentions, lofty ideals, good people, and humanitarian objectives. In the *fourth* narrative we find a world of *moral purpose* and bad intent – this is a darker form of political representation, in which the simplistic dualisms of Good/Evil, Positive/Negative, Us/Them, Wise/Foolish, and so on dominate, where politics therefore is turned into a question of standing up for the right moral principles, having the right moral character, propagating the right values, and where boundary questions in moralized form suffuse the discourse. This is typically the narrative move employed in the SP of foreign policy and securitization (cf. Ronald Reagan's coinage of the "Evil Empire" to stigmatize the Soviet Union) highlight the moral superiority of the western alliance, and of course legitimate a specific course of action (cf. following section), or for that matter Tony Blair's moralizing Christian-Socialist discourses about "doing the right thing." Finally, the *fifth* move comprises narratives of *legitimating* government objectives or practices – the most explicitly political narrative strategy, since it is located at the intersection of apoliticization and instrumentalization, between form and usefulness, between rhetoric and action, and between essentialist substance and external justification – justification, that is, of a politics of real conflict and mundane pursuit of interests which the other dimensions of the total narrative wish to either deny or give a harmonious and natural form.

Clearly, the five moves are not separate narratives, but most often intertwine and synergize within a composite symbolic text – fictions, fables, or myths of state, of political actors, and of honorable / natural intentions which simultaneously naturalize, humanize, moralize, idealize, and legitimate in an endeavor to deploy symbolic-cultural instruments and thus to allay concerns and strengthen socio-psychological identity structures. To this end, a number of standard cultural commonplaces, national *topoi*, are frequently called upon to do service. The most significant – most of which can be traced in the Renan extract above – are Creation (Myths of Origin), Mission & Ideals, Heroes, Golden Age, Rituals & Texts, Memory, Landscape, and the Future (Hedetoft, 1995; Herzfeld, 1992; Kapferer, 1988; Kertzer, 1988; Mosse, 1990; Nora,

1984–91; Smith, 1986). In varying combinations, these are the crypto-religious cultural and ideological reference points of all nation states (whether real or would-be), the aesthetic taxanomies and teleological justification of identification, solidarity, and belonging, and they are invariably operationalized in discourses of SP.

Narratives of Creation signify beginnings, birth, and origins – like the word Nation itself. Mission indicates that we are here for a purpose and to realize certain ideals, as in American ideas of Manifest Destiny. Heroes – whether of war, sport, or everyday life – are personalized incarnations of those norms of sacrifice, dedication, and belief which the nation stands for. The Golden Age is the point in mythico-historical time when the nation prospered, ideals were fulfilled, state and nation worked as a unity, inner peace, and outward victory had been achieved, and which serves as moral booster and role model for the more troubled contemporary period. Rituals & Texts represent the written, handed-down, and practiced foundational scripts of the community (Bhabha, 1990; Boswell & Evans, 1999; Hobsbawm & Ranger, 1983) – like constitutions, anthems, the thoughts of "founding fathers," rituals of commemoration, cultural heritage, and official pomp & circumstance. Memory, as "collective," is the repository of national continuity and ensures unity across ages and generations, while Landscape refers outward to the natural scenery and topographical peculiarities that symbolize the inward distinctiveness and special properties of the community. Finally, Future is a *topos* that manifests the progressive and certain projection of the nation into perpetuity and fits, hand-in-glove, with its assumed teleological mission and destiny.

As indicated, these universal *topoi* can combine and cohere differently according to situation, timing, and intentionality. Together they structure a series of signs and referents that help to essentialize ethnic communities and assign to the political sphere the auxiliary function of contributing to an optimal degree of cohesion, identity,

progress, and influence for the collective community in question. In this way – and because it orchestrates the fundamental destiny and purpose of the political community – this repository of cultural themes and taxonomies is indispensable as an instrument for SP of all variants, for reasons of persuasion, mobilization, pacification, legitimation, or other forms of identity engineering belonging to the art of political communication, and especially so in the three critical modalities discussed in the previous section. Let us now have a closer look at three case examples of SP, illustrating each of these modalities – moral emergency, securitization, and systemic transformation – and the ways the cultural repertoire can be tapped into and prove its worth.

Three Cases: Immigration, War, and European Integration

In principle, *immigration* in both political and cultural terms is a serious challenge to all national communities and states, because it defies some of the foundational assumptions on which nation states are based and which facilitate interaction, trust, and solidarity relations between politics and people: clear boundaries, ethnic homogeneity, a common history and culture, same language, shared socialization and political culture, consensual values, and so on (Goodhart, 2004; Hall, 1998; Hedetoft & Hjort, 2002; Nussbaum, 1996). For the same reason, the inevitable and sizeable demographic movements which nevertheless occur across the political and cultural boundaries structuring our worldviews and social practices must necessarily provide fertile ground for symbolic politics – and for constantly reactivating the cultural stock-in-trade discussed in the previous section by appealing, often in outspokenly populist forms, to the fears, loyalties, and moral habitus of nationalist audiences. Migration, especially when it is sizeable and visible (read: derives from areas where people's external physiological features make them stand out) and can be represented as itself a sign of more comprehensive threats (read: glob-alization...), is thus a universal breeding ground for moral panics, apocalyptic dem-agoguery, and discourses of ethnic purity/ purification – but also for domestic dis-sension and international criticism based on the symbolic politics of universal rights and refugee/minority protection. Immigra-tion (and its corollary, cultural pluralism) thus ruffles the feathers of the national com-pact and its arduously achieved common identity, and triggers a variety of political reactions, debates, discourses, and policy ini-tiatives intended to either mobilize peo-ple around and by means of the national narratives or to sooth the same people by appealing to their humanitarian sympathies and insisting that pluricultural solutions do not have to undermine the unity and cohe-siveness of the community, but should be regarded as both a socio-economic supple-ment and as cultural enrichment.

Indubitably, however, it is the SP dis-courses of the former variant – populist policies of identity appealing to people's national "instincts" – that attract most pub-lic attention and political support (Stolcke, 1995; Wodak & van Dijk, 2000). In these discourses, immigrants are framed as prob-lems which threaten the cohesion and hence future of national communities (Berger, 1998; Parekh, 2000), fail or refuse to "inte-grate" properly, live off welfare benefits rather their own independent income, set up "parallel societies" (also called ghet-toes), represent cultures of crime, violence, and paternalism that run counter to demo-cratic norms, or just do not display the engagement, participation, economic initia-tive, loyalty, and gratitude that are to be expected from newcomers. In the terms of a political rhetoric projecting (even some-times freely constructing) such challenges, the national community must defend itself against cultural encroachments and immi-nent erosion (Ascherson, 2004; Goodhart, 2004). In turn, the result is frequently (and increasingly) rallying cries for more proactive cultural or value-oriented debates, reminding people of the need to come to their senses before it is too late, appeal-

ing to (other) politicians to take immediate action, and providing the moral background for and legitimation of remedial practices in the form of restrictive immigration and repa-triation laws as well as tougher integration measures (Guiraudon & Joppke, 2001). In this way, symbolic politics, normative cultur-alism, and specific political action comple-ment each other in the case of immigration. The following is a small example of such migration-based SP discourse, taken from a debate in the Danish Parliament (April 2002) on a proposal for conferment of citi-zenship to specified immigrants. The speaker hails from the Danish People's Party, which has, more than any other party in Denmark, projected itself on an anti-immigrant agenda and since 2001 has provided parliamentary support for the Liberal-Conservative gov-ernment:

I recently heard about a school prin-cipal from Nørrebro [inner-city area of Copenhagen]. One day she met the father of some Turkish children in her school, accosted him and complained that his chil-dren did not speak Danish: 'When they live in Denmark, they must speak Danish'. The Turkish father looked at her and replied, 'Do we live in Denmark? No, we live in Mjølnerparken [concentration of council housing with a majority of ethnic-minority residents], and here only 2 % of the residents are Danish. No, we do not live in Den-mark.' (...) Indeed, it is becoming a very strange thing to be a Dane in this country, for step by step, bit by bit Danes are being turned into strangers in their own land. It is a historic and national disaster, which is taking place. It is the slow extinction of the Danish people that Parliament is allow-ing to happen. For let us not forget who is responsible for the growing alienation of Danes in Denmark: It is this very Parlia-ment. [The proposal before us is] irrespon-sible, immoral, treasonous. (Danish Parlia-ment, 2002)

The debate as a whole lasted for the major part of two days' session and was liberally spiced with often quite detailed and abstruse references to and interpretations of historical origins, foundational texts, myths of unity,

and cultural values of allegedly Danish heritage, although a majority, not surprisingly,
took issue with the direct attack against Parliament for dereliction of its national duty
and although the political conclusions drawn
by different parties in terms of supporting
the bill or not differed significantly. In fact,
most proved to be in favor of "naturalizing" the 6.163 people that it concretely concerned. Nevertheless, the discursive tenor of
the debate was set by the politics of identity inherent in the quotation and almost all
addressed the cultural concerns and political
charges contained in it on a note of respectful recognition and sympathy as regards
the goal of national unity and the worries about failed integration that it articulates. There was, in other words, if not full
agreement then at least widespread consensus that immigration / immigrants constitute a serious challenge, that emergency discourses are not completely misplaced, and
that policies based on values, traditions, and
the history of unitary identity were called
for. The agenda had clearly shifted from one
mainly focused on instrumental, problem-
solving approaches to integration issues to
one deeply infused with the politics and
negotiations of symbolic identity – a shift
which has been noticeable in a multitude
of countries in the last decade as regards
immigration-related problems.

Immigration as a policy field and a trigger
of symbolic politics of the moral emergency
type is interesting because it straddles the
three modalities of nation/state interaction
presented above in the section on "fictions of
the non-political state": the imperative (the
nationalization of the masses), the indicative
(the banality of successful national identity),
and the subjunctive (the national and/or
political dream of sovereignty). It is mostly
based on the indicative as the point of factual or alleged departure, but on this bases
weaves imperative discourses ("they" must
now be integrated and assimilated, and we
need some tough talk and policies to achieve
this state of integration and new-found cohesion) together with subjunctive ones mainly
targeted at the ethno-cultural core community (if only we were back to the good old

days – alternatively let us do all we can
to reconstitute ourselves as a sovereign and
cohesive entity and return to "banality"). In
this way, the SP of immigration, by conjuring up many small emergencies and moral
panics, works not just as a discourse of conflict and controversy, but also as a constant
unifier, by giving political actors the opportunity to reiterate the basis of commonality
and make full use of the national repository
of cultural symbols.

The case of *war* and warlike situations
is more clear-cut and positions itself differently in relation to the three modalities. This is clearly a case of SP deployed
for purposes of securitization (Campbell,
1992; Wæver, 1993) in situations of more or
less real national emergency/crisis, in other
words of conjuring up the fatal menace to
the existential survival of the nation represented by the enemy, of painting the world
in the binaries of black and white, good
and evil, desirable and undesirable, natural
and unnatural, heroic and terrorist, free and
unfree etc. Here SP is preponderantly imperative and moralistic, not just appealing to but
basically demanding the unconditional loyalty and full national backing of the entire
population, but accompanying such calls for
spiritual, civic, and military mobilization by
extensive rhetorical and propagandistic references to the courage and heroics of the
past, the mission and destiny of the nation,
the uniqueness of the national culture, the
extraordinary virtues of duty, sacrifice, and
suffering of the people, the splendors of the
natural scenery, and not least the semi-sacred
righteousness of the noble cause for which it
is worth fighting. "The nation is the culmination of a long past of endeavours, sacrifice,
and devotion," as Renan approvingly articulated the underlying tenet in the lecture
cited above. War-related SP discourses tap
into this radicalized idealization of the state/
nation nexus in order both to justify the
cause, demand the necessary sacrifices, and
ultimately bolster the vision in the form of
social, economic, and military practice – in
other words transform identity politics into
the *Realpolitik* of both civic cultural emergency (Agamben, 1998; Schmitt, 1934/1996)

and direct military combat. Whenever such discourses are successful and prove their positive effect in terms of the more than ordinarily close bonding and camaraderie between state and people that ensues, the nation is in turn saluted by the leadership responsible for the imperative SP in the first place: "In all my life, I have never been treated with so much kindness as by the people who suffered most. One would think one had brought some great benefit to them, instead of the blood and tears, the toil and sweat which is all I have ever promised. On every side, there is the cry, 'We can take it', but with it, there is also the cry, 'Give it 'em back'" – as Winston Churchill put it in one of his BBC pep talks during the Blitz in 1940 (cited from Hedetoft, 1990, 57; see also Cannadine, 1990).

The difference from most of the SP that we encounter in our normal daily lives is that SP of this nature is not just exclusively imperative and coercive, but it is also devoid of any traces of material recompense or rights-based concessions to the target audience. When borders are exclusionary in an absolute sense and the threat to the political community is treated as mortal, the only promise is usually the hope of collective, not individual survival, and the imagined benefits of that vision. Usually – but not always. The caveat does not imply that people – as either soldiers or civilians – are ever exempt from the threat of extinction or dramatically curtailed rights and opportunities once a state of war has been declared, but that in the contemporary period of "asymmetrical" threats, "homeland security" and "war on terror" (White House, 2002), the issue is no longer the survival of the states involved in conducting the battle (in spite of what the securitization discourses themselves conjure up – otherwise they would not come across as credible – but the degree of success that they might enjoy as regards the objective of stamping out or at least containing the threat they perceive to exist against their vital interests. In this case, therefore, SP is strategically deployed not just to deal with situations of dire threat, but in some way also to construct / conjure up this type of situation by appeal-

ing to ingrained psychological defense mechanisms and authoritarian loyalty structures embedded in the collective national imaginary. This leads to the general question of the new configurations of SP engendered by systemic changes in the global order.

The third case – the SP of European integration – exemplifies this third mode, that of adapting to systemic transitional change (Bjola, 2000; Hedetoft, 1998; Medrano, 2003; Schlesinger, 1992). Clearly, this mode lends itself much less to strident, apocalyptic, and dramatic SP than the first two. Nevertheless, it contains important questions pertaining to political cleavage, strained legitimacy, historical continuity, and especially the "fit" between cultural assumptions and political preferences of elected leaders – all of which impacts identities, loyalties, and future orientations. Adapting to and managing deep-seated institutional and systemic change implies, for political actors, toeing the line between instrumental and symbolic discourses, traditional solutions and innovative trajectories, focusing on interests versus focusing on identity – and hopefully negotiating between the binaries in such a way that politicians maintain political support and legitimacy for courses of action that diverge from orthodox solutions and may, in the short or long run, weaken the foundations on which political identities and structures of allegiance have been constructed. To this end, a balanced and fine-tuned activation of the repertoire of SP cultural instruments (sometimes combined with instrumentally oriented elements) is crucial – not, as in the previous modes, to highlight and exacerbate tensions, menaces, and defensive mechanisms, but to alleviate concern and persuade the general public that both national interest and national identity are in the best possible hands. Unless, of course, we are dealing with external pressures and imposed transformations that occur against the will of political elites and are perceived by sections of the populations too as inimical to their traditional lifestyles, occupational base, or collective self-image. The European integration process, particularly in its supranational or quasi-federal configuration as it impinges on national sovereignty, provides ample illustration of both these scenarios.

As regards the first, SP discourses will tend to highlight the beneficial economic or political aspects of institutional integration, while either downplaying or denying that identities are adversely affected or contending that they are in fact strengthened or supplemented by new layers. Consensual processes and discourses in e.g. Germany, Italy, Spain, and the Netherlands have largely conformed to this pattern, though in different ways and on different historical backgrounds. It tends to be found in Member States which have been predominantly pro-integration countries and where the EU has been viewed as an indisputable political, economic, democratizing, moral, or security-oriented gain. Identity questions have here either been muted or overridden by other concerns (it has been possible to present the concessions on sovereignty as unimportant or even advantageous), or they have been emphasized – like in Germany – as an area where the EU could have a positive bridge-building role toward the reconstitution of legitimate forms of national identity, moral legitimacy, and international recognition. At the same time, relevant debates and discourses in these Member States, more often than not, have been an affair for elites, who on the basis of handed-down authority and decision-making structures have been allowed to identify interests, specify preferences, and define identities in relative isolation from (or with the passive consent of) the popular masses. Hence the need for "strong" (or "thick") activation of communitarian-oriented SP has been moderate in this variation of the first scenario (Delanty, 2002).

It has been in stronger demand in another variant (i.e., that pivoting on the need to build an overarching European Identity, either as a replacement for or more often as a supplement to national identities. Such efforts, inspired by initiatives launched by the first Delors Commission and most legitimate in the EU itself as well as among some of the founding members, crucially depend on successful symbolic politics and attendant cultural referents (Hedetoft, 1997; Shore, 1993; Shore & Black, 1994). On the other hand, these are either not forthcoming or must be lifted and adapted from other repertoires, since "European Identity" is a novel, politically engineered top-down construct in search of a political and cultural community – and not the opposite, a culture looking for an identity and a fitting political "roof." Hence, in keeping with the three modalities set out above in the section on "rationale, modalities, and contexts", one would expect European Identity discourses to align themselves with the nation-building modality and its uneasy shuttling between imperative dictates and cultural nostalgia. And indeed, this prediction proves valid, with the exception that European Identity – positioned at two removes from the targeted popular constituency (the Member States interposing themselves) and having no cultural history or legacy or its own – is forced to tap into and reinterpret cultural symbols of its Member States as properly communitarian and universal, to construct its legitimacy by reference to civilizational origins reaching back to ancient Greece and ancient Rome, or to rely on cultural exchanges and intercultural communications of its own doing and initiative. Or briefly: to depend much more heavily on the third modality of hope, wishful thinking, and signifiers relatively void of specific content and collective meaning than the modern drive toward the nationalization of the masses. "European Identity" thus faces the enormous obstacle of wanting to invade a space where the appropriate cultural symbols needed to substantiate, materialize, and give direction to it at the level of personal appropriation has already been occupied by competitive rivals. For the same reason, as a form of SP it is much less frequently employed these days, because the symbols are either ineffective vis-à-vis the target public or carry different cultural and identity-related consequences than the ones intended.

In the second scenario, embracing EU skepticism or dissent, SP is, for the same reason, not just widely employed but also relatively effective – and it is also here that populist discourses of emergency pop up and defensive reactions are activated, based on images of sovereignty erosion and distrust between elites and people. This opens limitless opportunities for taking advantage of the full range of cultural *topoi*, the EU being cast as an impersonal, distant, bureaucratic, and undemocratic force imposing itself on the will, traditions, and identities of its discrete parts – often with the support of national political actors. Unlike the two first modes, however, the SP of European skepticism or opposition is not based on conjuring up imminent apocalypse or a state of dramatic exception. The threatening Other is here of the gradualist kind, one which slowly (but surely) is undermining the staples of national cohesion and territorial integrity, in the interest of indeterminate forces, representing globalization and a borderless world, at work in the external environment. Hence, this is a pervasively moral universe in which the familiar Collective Good of the nation state is jousting with the anonymous Knight of Darkness, the invisible hand of abstract external power having struck a bargain with domestic actors – and where theories of conspiracy, evil intent, and imperceptible aggression masquerading in friendly guises are therefore rampant. In some respects, these discourses of the enemy share elements with the anti-immigrant SP of moral emergency. This latter also evokes images of elite betrayal and gradual erosion of cultural cohesion. What makes the SP of anti-European (and other transitional) rhetoric special is that it is predicated on images of longer-term, systemic, and supranationally embedded challenges to political identities and cultural normality. However, as the next section will briefly clarify, we also find instances of SP which relate positively to disjunctures of state and nation and the perceived promises of transnationalism.

Alternative Symbolic Politics "From Below"

The types of SP to be surveyed in this section are all "alternative" in relation to those that depend on the factual or wistful-nostalgic form of existing nation/state interactions, somehow transcending or ignoring them in favor of other and better variants of identity and belonging. In this sense they all originate from and are articulated as rights-based voices "from below," manifesting protest, resistance, or complementarity – and hence all primarily fit into the third modality of "subjunctive" allegiance, where imagined identities cut across national and/or state boundaries. There are three main forms of such "transgressive" identity politics corresponding to three configurations of the geopolitics of belonging (Kalm, 2005; Massey, 1994).

The *first* could be classified as policies, positions, and discourses of cultural pluralism and hybridity. It comprises a variety of different approaches and ideological underpinnings, ranging from the interculturalism embedded in the cultural rights program of UNESCO, to a celebration of hybrid forms of cultural mixing, to political multiculturalism, and to cosmopolitan identities based on positive readings of globalization and the (perceived) cultural leveling (or cultural resistance) it carries in its wake. These sub-variants are more or less defiant of existing state forms, more or less "politicized," and more or less institutionally rooted – but they join hands by all feeling constrained by the assumption of cultural and homogeneous essentialism represented by the nation-state framework, while at the same time not wanting to discard this framework altogether but contending that alternative cultural and identity-based scenarios are compatible with nation states understood as open, liberal, and plural contexts of identity formation. Hence they are mainly to be seen as projects of cultural complementarity, most often proposed and pursued in moderately non-politicized forms, preferring discourses that tap evenly into functionalist and symbolic cultural repertoires, while balancing between well-tried cultural registers on the one hand and the cultural idealism of trans-border collaboration and global solidarity on the other. This is, then, the SP universe of Arjun Appadurai's "modernity at large" (1996), Ulf Hannerz' "cultural complexities" (1992, 1996), and Roland Robertson's "cultural globalization" (1992).

The *second* consists of the politics of diasporic identities, "transnational" organization, and virtual networks. Most often these are based on communities of migrants or historical minorities communicating, organizing, and politicking across borders, a type of interface based on perceptions of common identities and interests, and sometimes related to maintaining contact with their real or imagined country of origin (Christiansen & Hedetoft, 2004; Croucher, 2004; Frykman, 2004; Pieke, Nyíri, Thunø & Caccagno,, 2004; Smith & Guarnizo, 1998). These transborder identities and their forms of SP are not, properly speaking, transnational, but rather trans-state, seeing that they organize and communicate on the basis of the perception of a common ethnic/national community that happens to find itself scattered across a number of state borders and political-territorial units. Admittedly, they can be more or less openly in opposition to the polity within which they individually find themselves, be more or less explicitly political in terms of claims-making and resorting to international institutions (Bauböck, 1994; Benhabib, 2000; Kastoryano, 2001; Soysal, 1994), and perceive themselves more or less "at home" (respectively "in exile") where they live their daily lives – but in general terms this is a kind of SP and identity politics which shares with national ideology the assumption of ethnic homogeneity, but where this homogeneous unit has been politically and territorially fragmented: either it does not match any of the political regimes that individual members directly answer to in civic terms, or it relates positively to a state from which members feel exiled or hence "in diaspora" (and which for the same reason is often imagined in idealized terms). Hence the specific forms and agendas of such trans-state SP range from rather non-committal cultural idealism and authentic belonging to vocal policies and discourses of representation, recognition, and rights (Christiansen & Hedetoft,

2004; Kymlicka, 1995, 2001; Taylor, 1994; Toggenburg, 2004). Like the first form, this one by and large accepts the international system and its discrete units, but tries – often by means of "thin" symbolic forms of political and communitarian discourse – to modify its boundaries and tilt its institutional structures in its own favor.

Finally, the *third* form contains the explicitly political and thickly communitarian variants of minority rights, identity politics, and oppositional "indigeneity" clamoring for political autonomy and a new "national" status (Catalonia, Scotland, Nunavut) or independent statehood and international recognition – sometimes across states (viz. the Kurdish example), sometimes within states (viz. the Quebecois example). In this form SP assumes militant and separatist features, wedding culture, identity, and political structure to each other, while basing itself both on the factual disjuncture of state and nation in its present form, and on the ideal of having the two rejoined within a new framework, which is claimed to be at the same time authentic, legitimate, and in accordance with human rights (and sometimes the divine order). This SP of righteous opposition to systemic relationships and institutional incorporation will typically resort to the full range of cultural symbolism, historical roots, and international analogies in its communicative and propagandistic practices. This, therefore, is where symbolic politics can turn ugly and where liberalist countries like Canada may risk choking on it.

Concluding Perspectives

As the term indicates, symbolic politics – discourse as well as social activity – straddles the line between human – psychological and social – scientific concerns, between citizens and power, and between interpretive and positivist approaches to social reality. It lives and thrives in the interstices between nations and states, between the production of meaning and the construction of order, and thus provides a number of "democratic" bridges and mediations between those who are ruled and those who rule. It speaks to and about events and developments at second or third remove from the facts at hand, taps into and works back on the imagination of imagined communities, construing reality and its boundaries (vertical or horizontal, internal or external) to fit changing interests and shifting contexts. In this sense, SP is predominantly about the perpetual construction, adjustment, and maintenance of collective identities – that is, sense– making and functional images of oneself and the world.

Due to its liminal, interdisciplinary, and intersectional position, SP is open to a variety of causal explanations and normative critiques: realist, hermeneutical, historicist, ethno-symbolist, functionalist, constructivist, Marxist, and so on. Basically, it can be seen both as a necessary or desirable democratic exercise in confidence – building and societal security, relying on basic human needs for stability, identity, and order – or as discourses and policies of rational power agents keeping an ever-vigilant eye on their own domestic base of trust and support, and gearing their style, message, and choice of cultural signifiers instrumentally toward this objective. When successful, SP will – no matter how it is understood – produce more or less functional perceptions of national and ethnic homogeneity. When it is not, it will – as the Canadian Prime Minister sensed – engender cleavages, controversies, and mistrust. Whereas there is no end in sight to the normative battle between ethno-symbolists and constructivists, affective and discursive readings, psychologists, and realists, it is much less controversial to conclude that SP can assume both pacific and virulent forms, and is an integral and increasingly significant part of national politics in an age of global change.

References

Agamben, Giorgio, 1998. *Homo Sacer. Sovereign Power and Bare Life.* Stanford: Stanford University Press.

Anderson, Benedict, 1983/1991. *Imagined Communities.* London: Verso.

Appadurai, Arjun, 1996. *Modernity at Large: Cultural Dimensions of Globalization.* Minneapolis: University of Minnesota Press.

Ascherson, Neil, 2004. *From multiculturalism to where?* London: openDemocracy (www.openDemocracy.net), August 19.

Bauböck, Rainer, (Ed.), 1994. *From Aliens to Citizens. Redefining the Status of Immigrants in Europe.* Aldershot: Avebury.

Benhabib, Seyla, 2000. *The Claims of Culture.* Princeton: Princeton University Press.

Berger, Peter, (Ed.), 1998. *The Limits of Social Cohesion: Conflict and Mediation in Pluralist Societies.* Boulder: Westview.

Bhabha, Homi, (Ed.), 1990. *Nation and Narration.* London: Routledge.

Billig, Michael, 1995. *Banal Nationalism.* London: Sage.

Bjola, Corneliu, 2000. The Impact of "Symbolic Politics" on Foreign Policy during the Democratization Process. Paper presented at the *Kokkalis Graduate Student Workshop on Southeastern and East-Central Europe*, John F. Kennedy School of Government, Harvard University, February 12.

Boswell, David & Jessica Evans, (Eds.), 1999. *Representing the Nation: A Reader.* London and New York: Routledge.

Campbell, David, 1992. *Writing Security: United States Foreign Policy and the Politics of Identity.* Manchester: Manchester University Press.

Cannadine, David, (Ed.), 1990. *The Speeches of Winston Churchill.* Harmondsworth: Penguin.

Chrétien, Jean, 1996. *Symbolic Politics.* Speech held at Windsor, Ontario, April 28. Downloaded from www.pco-bcp.gc.ca/aia/default.asp?Language = E&Page = PressRoom&Sub = Speeches&doc = 19960428_e.htm& PrinterFriendly = y).

Christiansen, Flemming & Ulf Hedetoft, (Eds.), 2004. *The Politics of Multiple Belonging.* Aldershot: Ashgate.

Croucher, Sheila, 1994. *Globalization and Belonging.* Lanham and Boulder: Rowman & Littlefield.

Danish Parliament 2002. *Debate on Bill for the Conferment of Citizenship – Bill no. L 151 (Forslag til lov om indfødsrets meddelelse),* April 2. Downloaded at www.folketinget.dk/samling/20012/salen/L151_BEH1_45_1(NB).htm.

Delanty, Gerard, 2002. Communitarianism and Citizenship, in Engin F. Isin & Brian Turner, eds, *Handbook of Citizenship Studies.* London: Sage.

Eco, Umberto, 1976. *A Theory of Semiotics.* Bloomington: Indiana State University Press.

Edelman, Murray, 1985. *The Symbolic Uses of Politics.* Second and revised edition. Urbana: The University of Illinois Press.

Frykman, Maja Povrzanovic, (Ed.), 2004. *Transnational Spaces: Disciplinary Perspectives.* Malmö: IMER/Malmö University.

Gellner, Ernest, 1983. *Nations and Nationalism.* Oxford: Blackwell.

Goodhart, David, 2004. Discomfort of Strangers. *The Guardian,* February 24.

Guiraudon, Virginie & Christian Joppke, (Eds.), 2001. *Controlling a New Migration World.* London: Routledge.

Hall, John, (Ed.), 1998. *The State of the Nation.* Cambridge: Cambridge University Press.

Hannerz, Ulf, 1992. *Cultural Complexity.* New York: Columbia University Press.

Hannerz, Ulf, 1996. *Transnational Connections.* London: Routledge.

Hedetoft, Ulf, 1990. *War and Death as Touchstones of National Identity.* Aalborg: The European Research Programme, Aalborg University.

Hedetoft, Ulf, 1995. *Signs of Nations.* Aldershot: Dartmouth.

Hedetoft, Ulf, 1997. The Cultural Semiotics of "European Identity," in Alice Landau & Richard Whitman, eds, *Rethinking the European Union.* Houndmills: Macmillan.

Hedetoft, Ulf, (Ed.), 1998. *Political Symbols, Symbolic Politics. European Identities in Transformation.* Aldershot: Ashgate.

Hedetoft, Ulf & Mette Hjort, (Eds.), 2002. *The Postnational Self: Belonging and Identity.* Minneapolis: University of Minnesota Press.

Herzfeld, Michael, 1992. *The Social Production of Indifference.* Chicago and London: University of Chicago Press.

Hobsbawm, Eric, 1990. *Nations and Nationalism since 1780.* Cambridge: Cambridge University Press.

Hobsbawm, Eric & Terence Ranger, (Eds.), 1983. *The Invention of Tradition.* Cambridge: Cambridge University Press.

Hroch, Miroslav, 1985. *Social Preconditions of National Revival in Europe.* Cambridge: Cambridge University Press.

Kalm, Sara, 2005. Migration Control Policies as Spatial Organization – Mobility, Power, and Geopolitical Imaginations. *AMID Working Paper* no. 35. Aalborg: Academy for Migration Studies in Denmark.

Kapferer, Bruce, 1988. *Legends of People, Myths of State.* Washington DC: Smithsonian Institution Press.

Kastoryano, Riva, 2001. *Negotiating Identities.* Princeton: Princeton University Press.

Kertzer, David I., 1988. *Ritual, Politics and Power.* New Haven and London: Yale University Press.

Kymlicka, Will, 1995. *Multicultural Citizenship: A Liberal Theory of Minority Rights.* Oxford: Clarendon.

Kymlicka, Will, 2001. *Politics in the Vernacular: Nationalism, Multiculturalism and Citizenship.* Oxford: Oxford University Press.

Massey, Doreen, 1994. *Space, Place and Gender.* Minneapolis: University of Minnesota Press.

Mayall, James, 1990. *Nationalism and International Society.* Cambridge: Cambridge University Press.

Medrano, Diez, 2003. *Framing Europe.* Princeton: Princeton University Press.

Mosse, George, E., 1975. *The Nationalization of the Masses.* New York: H. Fertig.

Mosse, George, E., 1990. *Fallen Soldiers.* Oxford: Oxford University Press.

Nagel, Klaus-Jürgen, 2004. Transcending the National, Asserting the National: How Stateless Nations like Scotland, Wales and Catalonia React to European Integration. *Australian Journal of Politics and History,* 50, 1: 57–74.

Nora, Pierre et al., 1984–91. *Les Lieux de Mémoire.* Paris: Gallimard.

Nussbaum, Martha, 1996. *For Love of Country: Debating the Limits of Patriotism.* Boston: Beacon Press.

O'Leary, Brendan et al., 2001. *Right-sizing the State.* Oxford: Oxford University Press.

Parekh, Bhiku, 2000. *Rethinking Multiculturalism.* Houndmills: Macmillan.

Pieke, Frank, Pál Nyíri, Mette Thunø, & Antonella Caccagno, 2004. *Transnational Chinese.* Stanford: Stanford University Press.

Renan, Joseph Ernest, 1882/1990. What is a nation? [original title "Qu'est-ce qu'une nation?"], in Homi Bhabha, (Ed.), *Nation and Narration.* London: Routledge.

Robertson, Roland, 1992. *Social Theory and Global Culture.* London: Sage.

Schlesinger, Philip, 1992. Europeanness: A New Cultural Battlefield. *Innovation,* 5, 1: 11–23.

Schmitt, Carl, 1934/1996. *The Concept of the Political,* transl. George Schwab. Chicago: Chicago University Press.

Sears, David O., 1993. Symbolic Politics: A Socio-Psychological Theory, in Shanto Iyengar & Wm J. McGuire, (Eds.), *Explorations in Political Psychology*. Durham: Durham University Press.

Shore, Cris, 1993. Inventing the "People's Europe": critical approaches to European community cultural policy. *Man* 28, 4: 779–800.

Shore, Cris & Annabel Black, 1994. Citizens' Europe and the Construction of European Identity, in Victoria A. Goddard, Josep R. Llobera & Cris Shore, (Eds.), *The Anthropology of Europe*. Oxford: Berg.

Smith, Anthony D., 1986. *The Ethnic Origins of Nations*. Oxford: Blackwell.

Smith, Michael P. & Luis E. Guarnizo, (Eds.), 1998. *Transnationalism From Below*. New Brunswick, NJ: Transaction Publishers.

Soysal, Yasemin, 1994. *Limits of Citizenship. Migrants and Postnational Membership in Europe*. Chicago: Chicago University Press.

Stolcke, Verena, 1995. Talking Culture. New Boundaries, New Rhetorics of Exclusion in Europe. *Current Anthropology* 16, 1 (February): 1–24.

Taras, Ray, 2002. *Liberal and Illiberal Nationalisms*. London: Palgrave.

Taylor, Charles, 1994. The Politics of Recognition, in Amy Gutmann, (Ed.), *Multiculturalism*. Princeton: Princeton University Press.

Toggenburg, Gabriel N., 2004. *Minority Protection and the Enlarged European Union*. Budapest: Open Society Institute.

Voigt, Rüdiger, (Ed.), 1989. *Symbole der Politik. Politik der Symbole*. Opladen: Leske + Budrich.

Weber, Eugen, 1976. *Peasants into Frenchmen*. Stanford: Stanford University Press.

Weber, Max, 1948/1994. The Nation, in H. H. Gerth & C. Wright Mills, (Eds.), *From Max Weber: Essays in Sociology*. London: Routledge & Kegan Paul.

White House, 2002. *National Security Strategy of the United States*. Washington, DC: The White House.

Wodak, Ruth & Teun van Dijk, (Eds.), 2000. *Racism at the Top*. Klagenfurt: Drava.

Wæver, Ole, 1993. Societal Security: the Concept, in Ole Wæver et al., *Identity, Migration and the New Security Agenda in Europe*. London: Pinter.

CHAPTER 30

The Dialogical Self

Social, Personal, and (Un)Conscious

João Salgado and Miguel Gonçalves

The old dichotomy between person and society is widely known. Our common sense says that, on the one hand, each and every one belongs to a specific group, community, or society, and, on the other hand, we all know the inescapable feeling of solitude, misunderstanding, and distance from others. Along with many others (e.g., Hermans & Kempen, 1993; Marková, 2003), it is our conviction that a dialogical approach may be used as a way of reconciling these two poles of human life. Within dialogism, each human existence is an existence of addressing Others. As Bakhtin (1984) argues, "to be is to communicate" (p. 187) – in other words, each person is created in and through the communicational activity of addressivity. The ego is no longer the sole instigator of meaning (Jacques, 1991), but at the same time we still need to take into account the singular person as an essential element within a system of relationships. Belonging and solitude are, after all, two sides of the same coin; no one can be lonely without belonging to and being immersed in a given relational context.

With this chapter we attempt a contribution to the development of such a promising theory relating to a dialogical self, in the tradition initiated by Hermans and his collaborators (Hermans & Kempen, 1993; Hermans, 1996; Hermans, 2002; Hermans, 2004). More specifically, we are moved by three distinct, but complementary goals. First, we will try to clarify the basic axiomatic assumptions of dialogism, in order to create a tool for a critical analysis of the dialogical self-theory. Secondly, we will present the basic features of this theory and, taken the axiomatic principles of dialogism, we will reflect about the topics that we consider as major challenges or problems that still need further elaboration. Developments within this framework are growingly stating the need of a more careful analysis of "alterity" and process dynamics (Salgado & Hermans, 2005; Valsiner, 2000, 2002, 2004). As such, our third purpose is to contribute to such a discussion with some reflections about the structural elements of a dialogical self-description and its dynamics, especially its hierarchical organization. This is a rather unfinished business and we will not claim that we have a final answer to these challenges. Nevertheless, it enables us to create a picture of selfhood as a complex and dual phenomenon: personal and social, conscious and not conscious, experiential and semiotic. We believe that a dialogical perspective should have the ambition of achieving a holistic model about human beings, even if it is an impossible utopia.

A Dialogical Account of Psychological Phenomena: Main Axiomatic Assumptions

There is no consensual and clear-cut definition of the basic elements of a dialogical approach to human and social sciences. Moreover, some concepts are used interchangeably (for example, dialogism, dialogicality, dialogue; Linell, in preparation), creating an even more ambiguous territory. As Marková (2003) clearly demonstrates, there is a long tradition of dialogical approaches within several territories (philosophy, anthropology, linguistics, and so many others). Thus, it is easy to understand the reason for divergences within the dialogical-oriented researchers, some favoring Bakhtin, while others focusing on the works of Lévinas (1969) or Buber (1962), just to quote a few.

Nevertheless, we consider it useful to expose our basic ideas about the epistemological and even ontological implications of such an approach. First, our thought tries to follow the promises of the Bakhtinian heritage (Bakhtin, 1981, 1984, 1986). In our view, this singular character of the twentieth century, even if not the first to claim the dialogical properties of human life, created a global framework of analysis that pushed dialogicality to every sphere of human life in a unique way (Marková, 2003). Nevertheless, this strong influence is intermingled with many others within psychology (e.g., Hermans, 2004; Marková, 2003), but also outside our discipline (e.g., Jacques, 1991).

In order to clarify this global orientation, we will propose a brief sketch of the main axiomatic principles of dialogism. These axioms are highly influenced by the work of Linell (in preparation) that reviews this matter in a very systematic and rich way. We will present a rather brief proposal as a small contribution to some clarification of the field, since we are not claiming that dialogism is completely characterized by these principles (see also, Marková, 2003).

These claims do not exclusively emerge from dialogism. For example, the figure-ground distinction is, at least, as old as the Gestalt movement and it has been used by different theoretical orientations (e.g., Bateson's approach to systems theory; see Bateson, 2000). We would say that all the perspectives interested in relations and organization of complex systems somehow share some of these principles. As such, we are not claiming that any of the principles presented here are exclusive of dialogism, because they intersect and live in a complex cultural background of dialogue. What may be different is the assemblage and simultaneous coexistence of the principles.

The Relational Primacy: Relationships as the Beginning

For dialogism, every form of human life or every human process of knowing is basically relational. We could extend this principle, at least, to every form of life. In fact, every living being establishes a relationship with their surrounding environment, through which some kind of differentiation is achieved. In other words, differentiation emerges through a contrast that simultaneously unites and separates. This may explain why Holquist (1990) argues that "dialogism's master assumption is that there is no figure without a ground" (p. 22).[1] If this principle may be applied to a biological level of analysis, when considering the psychological properties of a human life, relationships with other people are an essential element to take into account. No human life is possible without this dialogical relationship with others and with the natural world.

Acceptance of this principle would lead psychology to deviate from its traditional Cartesian roots. Assuming a relational stance, it makes no sense to study persons as isolated entities, thus, we should focus on their relational and dynamic qualities. Moreover, if the relational side is favored, the old epistemological problems around solipsism will probably be avoided (see Marková, 2003; Salgado & Ferreira, 2004). The mind is no longer conceived of as a mirror of nature, and so, the pursuit of an isomorphism between our description and the mute ontological level is abandoned.

The Principle of Dialogicality: Monological and Dialogical Relations

As Marková (2003) clarifies, the Bakhtinian approach clearly separates (monological) objects and (dialogical) human beings. An object of the world is non-responsive, while people are clearly responsive and, consequently, dialogical (Marková, 2003). Thus, human knowledge is, in a sense, always dialogical.

Thus, it seems important to distinguish between two kinds of relationships. On the one hand, we have *monological relationships*, characterized by an interaction with "something" from which we do not expect any kind of communicative reaction. Mechanical manipulations of objects are typical monological relations. On the other hand, we also have dialogical relationships that occur whenever we are involved in some communicative interchange. Usually, this happens in actual dialogues with other people. Nevertheless, monologicality or dialogicality is not exclusively dependent on the kind of entity we are relating with, but on the kind of interchange that is going on. Thus, Bakhtin would say (1981), it is possible to have a monological relationship in a dialogue with another person – whenever we are completely authoritative, in a way that excludes the other as another human being. Whenever this happens, we usually say that we are objectifying the other, since we are not

recognizing the person as someone who has a subjective life. These kind of experiences may happen in ordinary life, but they are usually more prominent in exceptional situations – usually, horrible ones. As an example, we have the vivid tales of Viktor Frankl's (1984) experiences in concentration camps during the World War II, in which the prisoners were often treated as non-persons or non-dialogical beings:

> *Under the influence of a world which no longer recognized the value of human life and dignity, which had robbed man of his will and had made him an object to be exterminated (having planned, however, to make full use of him first – to the last ounce of his physical resources) – under this influence the personal ego finally suffered a loss of values. If the man in the concentration camp did not struggle against this in a last effort to save his self-respect, he lost the feeling of being an individual, a being with a mind, with inner freedom and personal value. (p. 70)*

In turn, if it is possible to deal with other human beings as if they were objects or animals, the contrary may happen when we are imaginatively dealing with objects "as if" they were people, creating a kind of intersubjective involvement with "things." Nevertheless, the global picture is probably even more complex, since the description of an object may be conceived simultaneously as a monological act (a relationship with a "mute" object) and as a dialogical relationship (which implies a relationship with all the available discourses and praxis toward that same object – see the third and fourth principle, below).

A Dialogical Relationship Implies a Person and an Other: The Principle of Alterity

The most striking feature of a dialogical relationship is its implication of an Other (a person, a group, a community, a society) with whom a given person relates. Whenever it happens – and we claim that it happens most of the time – we anticipate the answer of that Other in the act of enunciating or doing something and our own actions are molded by this intersection (something that Bakhtin referred to as "simultaneity"; see Bakhtin, 1984).

Thus, alterity or "otherness" is a striking feature of human existence and meaning-making. As Marková (2003) claims, a dialogical relationship is always a relationship between an Ego and an Alter, that stands for single or multiple Others. This thesis, although not exclusive of a Bakhtinian approach, is a central point of this framework, leading to the claim that language and human existence are always addressed to someone else (Holquist, 1990). Consequently, addressivity is a major feature of human life. Whenever something is said (or done), it is said (or done) to someone else, absent or present. Thus, the person is always in a process of a new becoming, in a living act of addressing other people. Moreover, the possible meanings of these acts of saying or doing do not lie within the utterance or act itself, due to their constant dependence on the addressed audience. Meaning becomes rather unstable and tremendously relational, since it always has an element of novelty (the changing Egos and Alters involved), which could explain why it is possible to "discover" new meanings in old texts and sayings. In turn, if no one (present or absent, located in the past or in the future) is able to understand the utterance, there is no meaning at all. This resembles the principle of inexistence of private languages (Wittgenstein, 1953), but what we want to highlight is the directionality of a given utterance or act.

It could be argued that relations with objects do not fit this kind of proposal. To refute this possible objection, the notion of "double directionality" of language (Bakhtin, 1981) may be helpful. For Bakhtin, a given utterance about an object is simultaneously addressed towards the object (or, more precisely, addressed towards the specific available discourses about a given object) and towards an addressee (a real or potential interlocutor, the Alter). We would extend this proposal beyond verbal exchanges or explicit acts, claiming that this double direc-

tionality is always present in each communicational and human act. This means that a dialogical approach defends that a meaningful act or utterance is inscribed in a specific system of relationships, even if we are acting upon objects.

It is important to take into account that this principle of alterity does not dissolve personal agency. In fact, it is quite the opposite: through relationships, personal meanings are created, since a given positioning toward the addressees is assumed, creating a specific pattern of relating with. After all, the person is created through this process of relating with others, developing a dialogue through which a self is always in a process of becoming. *I* and *Others* are two opposite poles of existence and this figure-background distinction creates a psychological space. In other words, the necessary relationship defines an Alter, but also a center of experience. Agreement or disagreement, closeness or distance, empathy or antipathy are all possibly brought to being through relationships enacted with another (see Hermans, 2004) – in other words, personal agency is created within relationships.

This means that a dialogical stance refuses to look at knowledge and meaning-making as something founded in the individual mind (Hermans, 2004; Salgado & Ferreira, 2004). Within dialogism, the human mind becomes a dialogical process of communication with others and with oneself (Hermans, 2004). Human knowledge is created through an activity of coordination with others and there is no possibility of creation of meaning without this addressivity.

Contextual Nature of Dialogicality

In order to build a dialogical perspective about psychological phenomena, we should probably take into account that (1) the psychological realm is brought to being through the dialogical properties of our existence, and (2) dialogicality is deeply rooted in a given cultural context (or multiple cultural contexts). The first argument was previously explained, but the last one needs further analysis.

Each human life takes shape in a given natural and social context. Assuming a dialogical stance, meaning arises through an addressivity toward other people. Meanwhile, we are launched to a life where these others already carry specific norms, routines, praxis, that shape our possibilities of relationship. There is a natural and a social (constructed) reality – but nevertheless, a reality, which we have to deal with. The very possibility of establishing a dialogue is dependent on the specific cultural and semiotic devices available that shape its process and content. As Linell (in preparation) argues, a message necessarily implies a context – a specific language, a specific pattern of relationship, a specific routine. In some way, assuming a certain position implies a process of social indexation (Wortham, 2001).

In turn, cultural context are the result of the dialogical and historical becoming of a given society – fluid, ever-changing, inhabited by different games of meaning-making. *Heteroglossia* was the term introduced by Bakhtin (1986) to describe this multiplicity of languages we contact with. In turn, each new participant that enters the game, changes the game, even if it is not a radical transformation. Take the example of our words. As Bakhtin once said, words used are also half given and half created (Bakhtin, 1981). In fact, there is always some element of novelty in a lived dialogical act. As such, the words we use are part of our social heritage, but whenever used by a given person they become recreated, enacted and embodied by someone involved in a relationship that happens in a certain context.

The Dialogical Self-Theory: Opening the Door for a Dialogical Psychology

Presuming those assertions as (some) of the main axiomatic assumptions of a dialogical approach, what would be the implications for psychology? First, we should look for a relational and dynamic point of view, instead of a psychology based in static entities. If human beings and human knowledge are dialogical, we should pursue these features in our descriptions. Second,

mind and personal subjectivity also become social processes. It is no longer possible to assume the traditional dichotomy person-society that leads to the description of these two realms as separate entities in eventual interactions. The person becomes a socialized mind (Hermans, 2002).

To us, probably one of the most serious and successful attempts in bringing a dialogical approach into psychology has been the dialogical self-theory, introduced by Hubert Hermans and his collaborators (Hermans & Kempen, 1993; Hermans, Kempen, & Van Loon, 1992). Strongly inspired in Bakhtin, but also in William James and narrative psychology, Hermans has been claiming a dialogical exploration of the self, in which the personal biography is understood as polyphonic novel.

The Dialogical Self and Its Polyphony

In a way, Hermans is following the arguments exposed by Bakhtin (1984) regarding novels, especially Dostoevsky's work. The special value of novels, argued Bakhtin, is the possibility of exposing different world views and languages. The plot is completely subordinated to a higher task: to explore the dialogicality of our human world and its heteroglot condition. Within a novel, the author is potentially able to expose and create an interchange between those different languages and world views, since they are embodied and voiced by different characters. For Bakhtin, one of the clearest examples of such a novel is Dostoevsky's work, a demonstration that he, as an author, was able to move himself towards different world views. His characters worked as individual consciousnesses, with a specific voice, different from the author's one: "For the author the hero is not 'he', and not 'I' but a full valid 'thou', that is, another and other autonomous 'I'" (Bakhtin, 1984, p. 63).

Consequently, polyphony arises. Several "voices" are able to emerge, each one with a specific view and compromise with life. Moreover, as Bakhtin stressed, each voice always has a social involvement: each character – or each person – is always addressing someone else, positioning herself or himself towards that audience (physically present or not), creating a personal expression of a world view that is always rooted in a specific culture and society: "each word tastes of the context and contexts in which it has lived its socially charged life" (Bakhtin, 1981, p. 365).

Hermans et al. (1992), exploring the implications of this notion of a dialogical polyphony, conceived the self as a "dynamic multiplicity of relatively autonomous *I* positions in an imaginal landscape" (p. 28). Articulating this notion with William James's (1890) distinction between *I* and *Me*, and its narrative reformulation (Sarbin, 1986), they concluded that "the special character of the polyphonic novel leads to the supposition of a decentralized multiplicity of *I* positions that function like relatively independent authors, telling their stories about their respective *Me*'s as actors." (Hermans & Kempen, 1993, p. 47).

Within such an approach, the self becomes a highly dynamic process, since the *I* is always moving from one position to a different one, which may occur in actual dialogues with someone else or in some form of inner dialogue (or autodialogue; Valsiner, 2002). The key feature is the dialogical relationships established between different positions, which create a lived – and sometimes told – narrative.

Critical Aspects: How to Advance the Dialogical Self-Theory

This model has been a major breakthrough for a dialogical approach of the self and, on a larger scale, of psychology itself. In our view, there are two crucial questions brought to discussion with Hermans's contribution. The first is the assertion that we need to conceive the self as self-with-others or a self-in-relationships, while retaining a sense of personal agency and commitment. The second one has to do with the need of a dynamic description of self-processes.

The need to take into account alterity is clearly stated by Hermans (2004): "the other person, or another 'object', are not simply known as objectified realities or internalized objects, but can be known only as they are allowed to speak from their own perspectives. The other as 'alter ego' has two implications: the other is like me (ego) and, at the same time another one (alter)...self-knowledge and knowledge of the other become intimately intertwined." (p. 21)

However, the insistence on the decentered multivoicedness of the self may sometimes blind us to this "otherness" of human condition and to the fact that a dialogical self does not exhaust itself in its multiplicity (Salgado & Hermans, 2005). Some of the most serious and constructive critiques of this perspective have been calling upon our attention for the fact that a dialogical perspective needs to address the question of how a personal agency is achieved within such a multiplicity of voices, and how the conflicts between opposing voices are resolved (Richardson, Rogers, & McCarroll, 1998). Within this framework, a dialogical human being is committed to life with personal responsibility, permeated by "otherness" but only partially decentered, since we are always challenged to assume an ethical or evaluational stance towards others and the cultural background we move in. Consequently, a dialogical self still has to come to terms with the question of personal agency and subjectivity, while taking into account the "otherness" qualities of such processes (Salgado & Hermans, 2005).

The second and related issue is the dynamic and developmental features of a self defined as a system of relations *I-Others*. To state that the self is always in a process of dialogue, means that the person is always facing novelty and always changing along the flow of time. As such, time and development needs to be addressed, theoretically and methodologically. As Valsiner (2004) claimed, within a dialogical conception of self, "the person is constantly involved in the construction, re-location, and re-construction of I-positions" (p. 3). From then on, several questions remain in the open. How stability and personhood are achieved within such a dynamic system? How are micro-changes related with macro-changes?

Taking these challenges into account, we will attempt a contribution to the discussion of some topics involved in these problems. First, the question of "otherness" within a personal and subjective agency calls our attention to the structural elements that are involved in a dialogical description of a human being. This question can be divided in two kinds of problems: (1) "who is being addressed?"; and (2) "how is this experience of addressivity of others subjectively constituted?" Consequently, we will discuss the basic structural elements within a dialogical self. Finally, we will conclude with a discussion of the global dynamic features of the self.

Structural Elements of a Dialogical Mind: How Many Are Needed to Create One?

A dialogical account must take into consideration the subjective side of human life, in a way that self and other are bounded together. In other words, the other must be brought into the self-space, and the other is constitutive of the self. As adults, this means to interact with a full-constituted subjectivity of others' minds, creating a truly intersubjective field of exchange, in a movement of anticipation of their agreements or disagreements. The dialogical self, in a way, becomes an "intersubjective self" (see Stern, 2004). However, it is useful to remember that the basic unit is a relational system of intersubjectivity, and not exactly two independent minds that happen to occasionally interact. In fact, subjectivity, as used here, is the global label for the personal side of the communication process (Salgado & Hermans, 2005).

As such, it would seem reasonable to conclude that subjectivity needs only two elements: the *I* and the multiple audiences or addressees. Nevertheless, several authors have been defending that dialogical relationships involve a third party (Leiman, 2002, 2004; Marková, 2003; for an extensive review and accurate analysis of this complex

problem, see Linell, in preparation). Based on these perspectives, Salgado and Ferreira (2004) proposed a first sketch of how such a triadic structure could be included in the description of an (inter)subjective/dialogical self. In that proposal, the *I* occupies the centre of the here-and-now experience, affectively involved in the process of addressing an *Other* (an *Other*-in-the-self, the not-*I*-in-me; Holquist, 1990). Meanwhile, all this relation is mediated by an "invisible" third party. The relationship with these addressed *potential audiences* is thought to be simultaneous with the process of addressing an interlocutor (another person or group, or oneself), but probably most of the times not noticeable in the actual speech or action of the person. Following this triadic model, in a typical conversation with another "real" person, we will have an intersubjective exchange going on, accompanied by an internal dialogue with other potential audiences, personally relevant and culturally rooted. The *Other* and these *potential audiences* are, in some way, anticipated, their minds are taken into account – in such a way that the resulting utterance or act is a complex act of answering to a dynamic juxtaposition of several questioning voices.

Dialogical Dynamics of the Mind: Social, Personal, and (Un)Conscious

Probably, the most difficult topic of going further in this framework has to do with the difficulties in surpassing our more usual static perspective, focused on macro individual differences. This kind of perspective is still dominant, not only within psychology, but also in western daily thinking. In a way, we are still in the process of killing Descartes of our own minds. As such, even if there are rich examples of dynamic approaches to the dialogical self (e.g., Fogel, Koyer, Bellagamba, & Bell, 2002; Lyra, in press; Valsiner, 2002, 2004), it is still difficult to avoid the "umbrella-like" concepts that create static and drain descriptions of the ever-changing and unstable features of phenomena under analysis. Thus, we are conscious of the difficulty of the task that we are embracing in this section: to contribute to a more dynamically oriented perspective about the self.

Fluidity and Regularities of a Dialogical Self

As Valsiner (2004) argues, an *I*-position changes from moment to moment, each one with a specific voice (see also Josephs, 2002). Imagine the following dialogue between two people (A and B) involved in a romantic relationship that is going through some kind of crisis. They are in the middle of a strong discussion. Then, in a break of the fight, A, in the need of some reassurance from the partner, says in gentle voice "I love you. . . ." At this moment, all A's attention is concentrated on the partner's answer, since in their history B usually answers the same ("I love you too"). Will B answer that? This is a clear indication that A's utterance, while trying to clarify his own position ("I love you, so I want to go on with this relationship," an implicit answer to the discussion that was going on), had the (implicit) intention of getting some reassurance. Thus, by this utterance A specifies a certain affectively charged position towards B (we would say A's experience of the moment) and their global situation. We will call this position $P(A)_1$. At the same, this creates a given (inter)subjective *Gestalt* or field, filled with tension on both sides. In fact, B feels pressured to make a quick decision, clearly, but implicitly understanding A's intention. B is in a position co-relative of (and occasioned by) $P(A)_1$, that will be named here as $P(B)_1$. B answers with an hesitant voice "I *guess* I love you. . ." $[P(B)_2]$. Thus, B does not sense being in the best condition to provide a clearer answer, and avoids a deeper compromise. Hearing this rather ambiguous answer, A is in $P(A)_2$, co-relative of $P(B)_2$, balancing between disappointment, anxiety and hope. Mixed, quick, and inner dialogues (probably not in the form of articulate speech) may happen, since A tries to foresee possible ways out of the situation,

and says "You guess. . . ?", maintaining a soft, but controlled voice. Once again they are in co-relative positions $[P(A)_3 - P(B)_3]$, in a way quite similar to the first one $[P(A)_1 - P(B)_1]$ since A is still searching for reassurance, but yet different, since they may be closer than before (but that depends on the next moment – B's answer).

This entire scenario is charged with a cultural life. For example, A's position is, in a way, a "social role," charged with specific values, motivations, and implicit codes. On the one hand, this "social role" has been necessarily appropriated and enacted in a personal way. On the other hand, it is socially shared, imposing specific restrictions and regularities that make all the communication intelligible (even if ambiguous)

Additionally, this turn-taking, that may last something like 10 to 15 seconds, is a simple example of the complexity of each lived moment. The flow of time and dialogue constantly pushes the person to a new position, in which the past moment has to be solved in the face of an anticipated co-constructed future. Novelty (coming from the world and especially from others) is always arising – in the example, even a possible long silence would be a novelty. In other words, the self always has some necessary fluidity, and its reduction may endanger the global well-being of the person. In fact, many of the so-called clinical disorders may result of a lower degree of flexibility of the system (Hermans & Gonçalves, 1999).

Nevertheless, human life also implies some form of stability. The patterns of positioning and repositioning may have some kind of regularity, creating some sort of self-with-others organization. For example, A may insist quite frequently on this type of reassurance, inclusively changing the meaning of saying "I love you" that may come to be understood by B as pressure. At the same time, the dialogue may evolve to different types of regular positions – other points of quasi-stability of the relational system (e.g., A being indifferent to B; A exploring joyful activities with B). Thus, potentially we have an infinite number of possible voices, but they tend to become organized in some more or less regular patterns of positioning.

However, the most striking aspect is that these macro-regularities must happen in several micro-moments. Thus, the micro-genetic becoming is an essential topic of study if we want to understand the global dynamics of a self-system (Stern, 2004; Valsiner, 2002). Generalizations only make sense if they relate with the particular. This is something that psychology frequently forgets and that needs to be continuously focused within a dialogical framework.

The Dialogical Self as a Multilayered System

Some of the new and fresh contributions to this field argue for the need to distinguish different levels of analysis, which somehow correspond to different levels of self-regulation. The work from Valsiner (2000, 2002, 2004) clearly points in that direction. Meanwhile, some other contributions from other theoretical orientations also pinpoint this need (e.g., Stern, 2000, 2004).

For our purposes, it seems useful to look for the developmental origins of these dialogical/intersubjective capacities of human beings. The idea that infants are born with amazing capacities of communication is widely known and growingly accepted-this being named by Trevarthen as primary intersubjectivity that stands for the ability of a "responsive conscious appreciation of the adult's communicative intentions" (Trevarthen & Aitken, 2001, p. 5). Quickly, around the first year of life, arises what some may call the "true" intersubjectivity, but which is widely known by Trevarthen's naming: secondary intersubjectivity (Stern, 2000; Trevarthen & Aitken, 2001). In this period of life, the relational system baby-adults starts to show clear signs of interattentionality, interintentionality, and interaffectivity (Stern, 2000): the mind of the other is operating also in the toddler's mind (the reciprocal situation is true even before pregnancy), creating a space for what some call the "intersubjective self" (Stern, 2000).

It is not our goal to discuss the controversies around the appropriate label of each phase or the exact features of each period (e.g., age, duration, specific development), but only to make it clear that it is viable – and indeed necessary – to take into account the non-verbal or paralinguistic levels of intersubjectivity. As Bråten (1998) clearly stated, altero-centric participation is a key property of human life from the very beginning, even if still deprived of a symbolical language.

This relational process progressively introduces the child to the socio-symbolic world, leading them to language. This expands the possibilities of dialogical exchange with the child. Nevertheless, the non-verbal levels of regulation of being-with-others will probably still work throughout life, even if only implicitly, as two parallel, mutually influencing but independent processes (Stern, 2004). The analogical knowing of how to be with others, a kind of implicit process, may be translated into the more digital realm of verbal signs. For example, we can explicitly recognize that an audience is smiling at us. However, this can happen in a completely implicit way, and most of the time a great part of our dialogical involvement with the human world is not strictly dependent on the semiotic "translation" of the experience. As the pioneers of the systemic orientation stated long ago, in a relationship there is always a content and a relation (Watzlawick, Beavin, & Jackson, 1967). The words of Richardson et al (1998), following a hermeneutic perspective about our involvement with life, are also appropriate here:

> These undertakings are more a matter of knowing how than knowing what. They are more like knowing how to reassure a child or make love as opposed to trying to execute those routines with one eye on an instructional manual. (p. 505)

The implicit, "knowing how" and intersubjective world is, nevertheless, enriched with verbal language. Following Bråten (2003), this leads to a tertiary intersubjectivity, in which a reflective and recursive intersubjectivity is instituted. In the period between 3 and 6 years old, children are expected to engage in dialogical exchanges in which they clearly symbolically simulate other's minds. Cheating and lying are clear examples of this capacity of moving to the symbolical world of the other and to play with it in order to achieve one's intention.

Thus, drawing the familiar rough line between two global levels of operation within a dialogical self seems useful here: an implicit level; and an explicit conscious, but not necessarily verbal level. These two levels were already implicitly presented in the dialogue between A and B. The verbal and explicit exchanges between them go along with a "dance" of paralinguistic forms, previous history and implicit common knowledge – in other words, explicit signs go along with the felt and implicit minds of me with the other. It is this implicit and felt field that envelopes the exchange of semiotic signs with their actual embodied and experiential nature – and, as such, human semiotics is a matter of feeling (Valsiner, 2005).

Consciousness, Self-Reflection, and Self-Narratives Within a Dialogical Self

Rough as it may be, this distinction between an implicit and explicit dimension of a dialogical self leads us to the problem of (un)consciousness. It may seem counterintuitive to talk about a consciousness within a dialogical framework. The same may be applied to the concept of mind. Is it not true that a dialogical framework claims for the substitution of the Cartesian theatre of the mind? Our answer is that all labels referring to the mental realm are not a problem within a dialogical approach, so far as they are understood in a relational and dynamic way. As Jacques (1991), a French dialogical philosopher, claimed: "consciousness is no longer the architect of the communication relation, but its inhabitant. It realizes and accomplishes itself during the semic building blocks available for communication within an organized community" (p. 216).

Indeed, consciousness here is viewed as a product of dialogical exchanges, somewhat closer to Stern's (2004) notion of intersubjective consciousness as an interpsychic event. This goes along with a great tradition that goes back to Mead (1988), Vygotsky (1978) and so many others that claim for the social and relational constitution of meaning.

Within a dialogical framework, the argument can run like this (see Salgado & Hermans, 2005). First, we are engaged in relationships with others, constituting a dialogical self. As such, the intersubjective field created establishes an *I* in relation with multiple possible addressees. This *I* emerges as a centre of subjective experience and agency, mutually dependent of others. Although interdependent of the alter, this centeredness is vital to the creation of a feeling of subjectivity. However, the personal subjectivity is also compounded by the addressed other and all the internal audiences.

Second, this opens the door for establishing a relationship with oneself, in which the self works as the agent and as an alter. As such, self-consciousness will be made possible. Thus, since we communicate with others, we become capable of self-communication, in which "the self constitutes itself as an *it* which can stand before the inward *I*" (Jacques, 1991, p. 191).

Consequently, thought is dialogue (Hermans, 2004), in a strong sense of dialogue, involving difference, duality, alterity, and culture. The communication process with others animates the inward life of thought that usually is shaped not as a completely articulated speech, but as an inner communication: "the language in which we think is necessarily the language in which we communicate. Thinking alone means speaking to oneself as though to a second self" (Jacques, 1991, p. 191).

As such, the person becomes self-conscious in the process of establishing a relationship with oneself modulated by the relationship with others. This process certainly has implicit, affective, and pre-semiotic features, as happens in the process of relating with others. Much of what happens in communication is not conscious at all. In the process of relation-with, the immediate feelings create a global lived moment of contrasts, in which some details are highlighted and others are obscured. This global and non-symbolical awareness of the moment, however, becomes mediated by signs, structuring the explicit and conscious meanings of what happens (Valsiner, 2005).

The final result is the person as an arena of felt self-discourse, involved in semiotic communication with oneself. While thinking, the person is involved in an interlocutive relationship with oneself. The object may be something else, or it can be the same person again. In the latter case, a lonely process of self-reflection is going on, a process of negotiating with oneself the own image. However, even if the person is discussing with another "real" person her or his behavior the conversation is also fed by this same process of relating with oneself. In other words, all processes of self-reflection entail this inner dialogue.

This ability of objectifying oneself in order to negotiate "what I am" may create a myriad of self-narratives. Regularities and similarities are usually searched for in order to give a clear and coherent account of that diversity. Moreover, the person implicitly or explicitly may come to realize that some stories are very alike, allowing their organization within a certain "role" ("I as psychologist"), personal attribute ("I as a romantic") or taste ("I as a football fan"). These kinds of semiotic categorizations may animate some inner dialogues, but they are more likely to be global and rough generalizations of macro-regularities. Furthermore, it should not be taken for granted that our inner dialogues are shaped by these stable labels. Indeed, it is probably more common to have thoughts where I qualify myself as a person of a certain kind – for example, a thought as "I am so stupid." The most important part is the process of dialogue, and not only the labeling, because whenever that happens two positions are created. In the example, it is very interesting to notice that such a thought, coming from a very critical position, creates a feeling and corresponding position of inferiority (Greenberg, Rice, & Elliott, 1993).

The global scenario is a very dynamic one and not the static picture that we can obtain whenever someone starts to engage in a calm process of self-reflection and narrative construction about my "different selves." For example, "reflecting about my position X" is different from the lived moment of "being X": in the first case, I occupy the position of a self-reflecting agency, in which "being X" is the objectified and negotiated material. Interesting as this may be – in fact it can introduce novelty in the form of new self-relevant signs in the process of semiotic mediation, can be seen happening in psychotherapy (Leiman & Stiles, 2001) – the underlying processes (the relationship with the interlocutor and the inner dialogues that go on, with parts of oneself or with "virtual others") are the key dialogical features to pursue. We think that this is still a major challenge, not only for a dialogical perspective, but for psychology in general, since there is a global tendency of focusing only on the objectified qualities (the contents of self-reflection) of the self.

The Other Side of a Dialogical Self: From the Unconscious to the Supraconscious

The implicit relational processes of a dialogical self, pose the question of unconsciousness and supraconsciousness. First, the automatic, unconscious and non-verbal processes governing the dialogical exchanges with others must be taken into account. In our view, the phenomenal world of the person is structured by those triadic dialogical fields of interchange between I, Other and inner audiences (the previous relational history of the person actualized in the moment). This field shapes and organizes the awareness of the present moment and the kind of orientation we may have towards objects and other people ("ways of being with"; Stern, 2000). Thus, it simultaneously shapes the intrapersonal and the interpersonal space.

Second, the symbolic relational system, a higher hierarchical level of conscious and semiotic regulation of the intersubjective field, also has an implicit dimension. In fact, the sign is embedded in a social instituted "local rationality" (Billig, 1997). It relates the *I* to a larger community, and represents a probable movement towards a supraconscious (see Valsiner, 2005, for a related, but yet different perspective about hyperconsciousness). This dimension is also implicit. The popular saying states that "The fish does not see the water," and, as such, we are comparable to fishes, since we are not aware of the water we move in.

Although embedded in traditional voices, this notion of unconscious is not necessarily equivalent to the classical ones. First, we are dealing with a different concept of unconsciousness. In the fortunate expression of Michael Billig (1997), we are defending a dialogical unconscious, deeply relational and not necessarily intrapersonal. It is not only situated between our ears and buried inside. On the contrary, it is simultaneously personal and social. Second, it is not necessarily a "mental" concept, because it does not imply a clear separating line between different types of mental contents. It refers to experiential contents (and sub-experiential processes) that are more or less unavailable, unspoken or hard to explain, but implicit in the selfhood dynamics of each person. Finally, it is explained in a dialogical way. It is admitted that some positions dominate other potential voices (Hermans & Kempen, 1993; Salgado, 2003). This does not imply that there is a Truth to be discovered in order to obtain the correct picture of the self; it only implies that there are parts of our lives always waiting to be explored.

Moreover, there is still large theoretical work to be done. The global dynamics of such processes are naturally hard to capture, but it is our conviction that they play a major role on the regulation of the personal life. A dialogical version of the unconscious side of our lives has also to do with such issues as the difficulties in assuming a potential I-position in order to avoid painful feelings or with the monologization of some voices towards others (Salgado, 2002, 2003).

General Conclusion

A dialogical approach may seem quite appealing in order to surpass traditional epistemological, theoretical and methodological problems of psychology. In our view, this is a rather promising path for psychology. Nevertheless, we must avoid using it as an umbrella-like perspective, which allows us to maintain the traditional and taken-for-granted individualistic categories available for the description of human beings. To accomplish that we think we must start with a strong effort in the "recycling" of old concepts in a relational and dynamic way – and, at least to us, it seems to be a hard challenge. A dialogical self is a difficult task for a science that highly values a disengaged subject with rational properties within a society that is still largely formatted by individualistic values.

Since its birth, this theory has been evolving in order to create a more dynamic and relational conception of human beings, since it addresses one of the most central psychological topics. In a way, to talk about the self is to talk about what Jacques (1991) would name as the "heart of the subject" – thus, to talk about the global and central topic of analysis within psychology. As such, this theory opened us the door for a dialogical appropriation of psychological phenomena, a path that we may follow in order to create a global picture of the human (dialogical) mind. This said, we do not see this theory as the final end, but only as the starting point of our reflections and studies.

Note

1 We are here using the notion of unconsciousness in a rather loose way, referring to everything that we are not explicitly aware of. However, in a dialogical approach, this notion still needs a larger refinement. One possible

route to take is the distinction between not-conscious (impossible to become conscious), and non-conscious (part of the phenomenal awareness that does not become conscious and semiotically structured) (inspired by Valsiner, 2004). For other possibilities see Valsiner (2005) or Stern (2004).

References

Bakhtin, M. M. (1981). *The dialogic imagination: Four essays by M. M. Bakhtin* (C. Emerson & M. Holquist, Trans.). Austin, TX: University of Texas Press.

Bakhtin, M. M. (1984). *Problems of Dostoevsky's poetics* (C. Emerson, Trans.). Minneapolis, MN: University of Minnesota Press. (Originally published in 1929, revised in 1963).

Bakhtin, M. M. (1986). *Speech genres and other late essays.* Austin: University of Texas Press. (Originally published in 1979).

Bateson, G. (2000). *Steps to an ecology of mind.*Chicago: Chicago University Press. (original work published in 1972).

Billig, M. (1997). The dialogical unconscious: Psychoanalysis, discursive psychology and the nature of repression. *European Journal of Social Psychology, 36,* 139–159.

Bråten, S. (1998). Infant learning by alterocentric-participation: The reverse of egocentric observation in autism. In S. Bråten (Ed.), *Intersubjective communication and emotion in early ontogeny* (pp. 105–124). Cambridge, U.K.: Cambridge University Press.

Bråten, S. (2003). Participant perception of others' acts: Virtual otherness in infants and adults. *Culture & Psychology, 9,* 261–276.

Buber, M. (1962). *I and Thou* (R. G. Smith, Transl.). Edinburgh: T&T Clark. (original work published in 1923).

Fogel, A., Koyer, I., Bellagamba, F., & Bell, H. (2002). The dialogical self in the first two years of life. *Theory & Psychology, 12,* 191–205.

Frankl, V. (1984). *Men's search for meaning.* New York: Simon & Schuster. (original work published in 1946).

Greenberg, L. S., Rice, L. N., & Elliott, R. (1993). *Facilitating emotional change: The moment-by-moment process.* New York: Guilford Press.

Hermans, H. J. M. (1996). Voicing the self: From information processing to dialogical interchange. *Psychological Bulletin, 119,* 31–50.

Hermans, H. J. M. (2002). The dialogical self as society of mind: Introduction. *Theory & Psychology, 12,* 147–160.

Hermans, H. J. M. (2004). The dialogical self: Between exchange and power. In H. J. M. Hermans & G. Dimaggio (Eds.), *The dialogical self in psychotherapy* (pp. 13–28). Hove, East Sussex: Brunner-Routledge.

Hermans, H. J. M., & Gonçalves, M. (1999). Self-knowledge and self-complexity: A dialogical view. *Constructivism and the Human Sciences, 4,* 178–197.

Hermans, H. J. M., & Kempen, H. (1993). *The dialogical self: Meaning as movement.* San Diego, CA: Academic Press.

Hermans, H. J. M., Kempen, H., & Van Loon, R. (1992). The dialogical self: Beyond individualism and rationalism. *American Psychologist, 47,* 23–33.

Holquist, M. (1990). *Dialogism: Bakhtin and his world.* New York: Routledge.

Jacques, F. (1991). *Difference and subjectivity: Dialogue and personal identity* (A. Rothwell, Trans.) New Haven, CT: Yale University Press. (Original work published in 1982).

James, W. (1890). *The principles of psychology* (Vol. 1). London: MacMillan.

Josephs, I. E. (2002). "The 'Hopi in me': The construction of a voice in the dialogical self from a cultural psychological perspective. *Theory & Psychology, 12,* 161–173.

Leiman, M. (2002). Toward semiotic dialogism: The role of sign mediation in the dialogical self. *Theory & Psychology, 12,* 221–235.

Leiman, M. (2004). Dialogical sequence analysis. In H. J. M. Hermans & G. Dimaggio (Eds.), *The dialogical self in psychotherapy* (pp. 255–269). Hove, East Sussex: Brunner-Routledge.

Leiman, M., & Stiles, W. B. (2001). Dialogical sequence analysis and the zone of proximal development as conceptual enhancements to the assimilation model: The case of Jan revisited. *Psychotherapy Research, 11,* 311–330.

Lévinas, E. (1969). *Totality and infinity: An essay on exteriority* (A. Lingis, Trans.). Pittsburgh, PA: Duquesne University Press.

Linell, P. (in preparation). *Essentials of dialogism: Aspects and elements of a dialogical approach to language, communication and cognition.* Unpublished manuscript.

Lyra, M. C. D. P. (in press). Mother-infant communication development and the emergence of self: The contributions of dynamic systems and dialogism. In C. Lightfoot, M.C.D.P. Lyra & J. Valsiner (Eds). *Challenges and strategies for studying human development in cultural contexts*. Greenwich, CT: Information Age Publishers.

Marková, I. (2003). *Dialogicality and social representations*. Cambridge, UK: Cambridge University Press.

Mead, G. H. (1988). *Mind, self and society*. Chicago: University of Chicago Press. (Original work published 1934).

Richardson, F., Rogers, A. & McCarroll, J. (1998). Toward a dialogical self. *American Behavioral Scientist, 41*, 496–515.

Salgado, J. (2002, October). *Dialogical unconscious and psychotherapy: Giving voice to unspoken narratives*. Paper presented at the Second International Conference on the Dialogical Self, Ghent, Belgium.

Salgado, J. (2003). *Psicologia narrativa e identidade: Um estudo sobre auto-engano* [Narrative psychology and self-identity: A study of self-deception]. Maia, Portugal: Publismai.

Salgado, J. & Ferreira, T. (2004, August). *Dialogical relationships as triadic structures: Exploring a possibility*. Paper presented on the Third International Conference on the Dialogical Self, Warsaw, Poland.

Salgado, J., & Hermans, H. J. M. (2005). The return of subjectivity: From a multiplicity of selves to the dialogical self. *Electronic-Journal of Applied Psychology, 1*, 3–13.

Sarbin, T. R. (1986). The narrative as a root methaphor for psychology. In T. R. Sarbin (Ed.), *Narrative psychology: The storied nature of human conduct* (pp. 3–21). New York: Praeger.

Stern, D. N. (2000). *The interpersonal world of the infant* (paperback edition). New York: Basic Books.

Stern, D. N. (2004). *The present moment in psychotherapy and everyday life*. New York: W. W. Norton.

Trevarthen, C., & Aitken, K. J. (2001). Infant intersubjectivity: Research, theory, and clinical applications. *Journal of Child Psychological Psychiatry, 42*, 3–48,

Valsiner, J. (2000, June). *Making meaning out of mind: Self-less and self-full dialogicality*. Keynote lecture presented at the First International Conference on the Dialogical Self, Nijmegen, The Netherlands.

Valsiner, J. (2002). Forms of dialogical relations and semiotic autoregulation within the self. *Theory & Psychology, 12*, 251–265.

Valsiner, J. (2004, August). *Temporal integration of structures within the dialogical self*. Keynote lecture presented at the Third International Conference on the Dialogical Self, Warsaw, Poland.

Valsiner, J. (2005). Soziale und emotionale Entwicklungsaufgaben im kulturellen Kontext. In J. Asendorpf (Eds.), *Enzyklpädie der Psychologie: Soziale, emotionale und Persönlichkleitsentwicklung* (Vol. 3). Göttingen: Hogrefe.

Vygotsky, L. S. (1978). *Mind in society: The development of higher psychological processes*. Cambridge, MA: Harvard University Press.

Watzlawick, P., Beavin, J. H., & Jackson, D. D. (1967). Pragmatics of human communication: A study of interactional patterns, pathologies and paradoxes. New York: Norton.

Wittgenstein, L. (1953). *Philosophical investigations*. Blackwell Publishers.

Wortham, S. (2001). *The narratives in action: A strategy for research and analysis*. New York: Teachers College Press.

Part VII

MAKING SENSE OF THE PAST FOR THE FUTURE: MEMORY AND SELF-REFLECTION

CHAPTER 31

Social and Cognitive Determinants of Collective Memory for Public Events

Guglielmo Bellelli, Antonietta Curci, and Giovanna Leone[1]

There are some events of the past that are recurrently present in the individual's memory and public discourse: they are expressed in the names of streets, monuments, commemorations, conversations, in publications, and history books. They are never isolated, because they organize the knowledge at different levels, from the personal and idiosyncratic one to the "social", public one. They can be a sort of reference point in the time stream of the personal and collective past of social groups, emblems of periods or the most important stages of social life, a sort of bridge between different ways of perception of the self, culture, and society. These memories belong simultaneously to the individual and to social groups: they are salient, either easy or difficult to access, and are shared with other members of a significant social group. In this chapter we deal with these "collective" memories, the factors that affect them, and the psychological/social functions they accomplish. In the last part of the chapter we will discuss the classic construct of "collective memory" first proposed by Halbwachs at the beginning of the 20th century, and will try to explain how this apparent paradox of a memory of an abstract entity which does not exist independently from the individuals is possible.

Memorable Public Events

In a study carried out at the end of 1999, and so at the brink of the new millennium (Pennebaker, Rentfrow, Davis, Paez, & Bellelli, 2000), 1226 people, mostly students, belonging to six different national groups (United States, Japan, Great Britain, Germany, Spain, and Italy), were requested to indicate three events which occurred respectively within the last 10, 100, or 1000 years that they would have included within an history book.

Aside from any difference within each national group, the events which were mentioned as the first three of the last 10 years were the fall of USSR, the Gulf war and the Balkan war. Immediately after these the participants mentioned also non war related events: a very relevant media event such as the death of Lady Diana (especially in Great Britain and in the United States) and other two very important events bound to change the relationship between the two worlds (the European Community) and the forms of human communication (the Internet). Also very important, since it was not mentioned by other countries, was the reference within the Japanese sample to nuclear proliferation and to terrorism.[2]

The last hundred years have been characterized by war: the two world wars (mostly the second one) and the discovery of space are the most important events. Immediately after "war in general" the cold war and the Vietnam War are mentioned. Within the American sample special attention is given to the murder of John F. Kennedy and the Great Depression of 1929. It is particularly significant that only the Japanese and the German sample mentioned the atomic bomb. Within the Italian sample, after the two world wars, the event which is cited as mostly representative of the last ten years and also of the whole century is the fall of USSR.[3] Space and the development of computers are frequently cited by the English sample. Finally, within the list of the most significant events of the century we should note the absence of the Holocaust, which is mentioned only by the American sample at tenth place.

If attention is given to the most representative historical events within the last thousand years, the first three places at the top are the discovery of the New World, the French Revolution and the Industrial Revolution. At fourth place once more the World War II is mentioned (in first place for the Japanese sample). This confirms the importance attributed to this event also by new generations, that did not experience it directly and whose parents were born during a period of peace. The presence of the nuclear bomb was cited by the Japanese sample, since it had an extraordinary impact on the construction of national identity.

Mostly interesting is the intrusion of events such as World War II and space exploration (this last at tenth place within the general list) among the events occurring within the last century or within the last thousand years. Actually their presence is pertinent, since these are memorable events, and 10 and 100 are logically included in the last 1000 years.

Certainly what deserves a special attention in studies like this, based on free rehearsal and the selection of events, is not only the historical knowledge of individuals, but rather their interpretation and evaluation of history. Among the events mentioned in this investigation, beside those already inscribed within official human history, there are other more recent events. The "pastness" is relatively less important than the subjective links with present motives and debates. Therefore we might ask ourselves if the criteria which define an event as memorable are valid for both recent and/or personally experienced events experienced and for past events which occurred a long time ago before one's own birth.

Drawing on Mannheim's (1928/1952) and Halbwachs' (1950) suggestions, Schuman and Scott (1989) have argued that the attribution of importance to national and international events is strictly linked to a personal experience had during adolescence or adulthood. According to the authors any difference between age cohorts becomes a sort of generational memory, representing an intersection of one's own personal history with national history.

By studying the memories of public events within the last 50 years across a large sample of adult Americans belonging to different age cohorts, Schuman and Scott (1989) have highlighted a very impressive similarity as for the answers given in reference to some events, mostly war events (the World War II and the Vietnam War), and other events which have marked the life of American society: the murder of John F. Kennedy, the exploration of space, the fights for civil rights, and the nuclear threat. These events showed very high percentages since they were mentioned both by people belonging to the generation which had experienced them directly, and by people belonging to the generation which had an indirect knowledge of them, since they occurred before their own birth. Therefore, different generations mentioned at least in part the same events. Different reasons were given to support the choice. For instance, young Americans born after the end of the World War II stated that they had answered starting from the consideration of the impact caused by this event on the life of the country and on the consequences that the war produced (i.e., the emergence of the US as a super power). On the other hand those, who were direct witnesses of those dramatic years, expressed their answers according to motivations which were apparently limited to personal episodes happening to them. Nonetheless, according to Schuman and Scott (1989), the difference in the motivations expressed, associated to a content identity, shows that it cannot be the same type of memory. Those who have personally experienced an event tend to focus their memories first of all on the personal meaning that the event has for them. Those who belong to a generation that has not experienced directly a specific public event tend to attribute a more general political meaning to the event. In the first case these memories mix themselves with one's self-biography, since the collectively shared element (the target event) is accompanied by strictly personal meanings and experiences. In the second case, it is right to speak of shared images of the event which belong to a collective representation of the past, as suggested by Durkheim (1898) and Moscovici (1976).

Some years after, by confronting the collective memories of an English sample with those of a north-American sample, Scott and Zac (1993)found that, besides different events, that mostly mirror national specificity (as for instance the Falklands war for the English sample), there was a marked convergence on some events, first of all the second world war. Actually this event gained a growing importance for both populations: different were the meanings associated to it. The experience of the war was a very important motivation for the people over sixty, thus showing the different quality of recent memories, known indirectly, and of past memories, personally experienced during youth. On the other hand, the youngest participants underlined abstract meanings

(to win a fair war, the changes within the world structure and mostly for the Americans the economic growth derived by the war).

In a more recent study, where memories of public events evoked by college students were confronted with those of their parents, Bellelli, Curci, and Leone (2000) found a recency effect for the younger generation and a primacy effect for the older one. In other words, the students' choices were very strongly focused on more recent, "mediatic" events. The older people, on the contrary, selected much more remote and consequential events (Brown & Kulik, 1977) with a marked preference for events which occurred during their own adolescence. The memory patterns of remote and recent events showed very different results. The importance attributed to the target event (evaluated in terms of the impact had on the individual's personal life), appeared as the most relevant dimension of long-term memorization, while this dimension played only a mild influence in short-term memorization. Here, availability in public discourse and the media resulted as the most important determinants.

The Reminiscence Bump

Within the scientific literature on autobiographical memory a well-known phenomenon is the so-called "reminiscence bump". The investigation of individual memories within different phases of life shows that individuals aged over 50 years have a significantly higher number of vivid memories of the events which occurred during adolescence, that is between 12 and 25–30 years. Even those public events which are better recalled occurred during this life timespan. The majority of the Americans who had mentioned the murder of Kennedy were aged between 15 and 25 in 1963 (Schuman & Rieger, 1992; Schuman & Scott, 1989). The same occurred for the Vietnam War: in fact those who mentioned this event were aged between 11 and 31 in 1969. In a similar fashion, among the individuals who mentioned

World War II, the most numerous were those who in 1943 were between 10 and 30 years old. This phenomenon was firstly described by Franklin and Holding (1977) and it has been confirmed by several procedures (Rubin, Rahhal, & Poon, 1998) in an attempt to find an explanation.

Memory theorists suggest that new and distinctive experiences are better remembered. So a possible explanation for the bump makes reference to the unfair distribution, within life, of these experiences: the events which are first experienced are better codified in memory and most frequently rehearsed. But it is during adolescence that individuals have most of their new experiences, especially social ones (student associations, college, flirtations, travel...) and at the same time have their first contact with great public events. According to Rubin et al. (1998) the period between 10 and 30 years of age is characterized by intense change, followed by a long period of higher stability, which makes the period of the reminiscence bump most distinctive. Nonetheless, Fitzgerald (1988), through a content analysis of rehearsed memories, has found that no more than the 20% of them referred to *first time experiences*, thus suggesting that the phenomenon might be entirely linked to distinctive experiences.

Other hypothesis call on the phenomena implied by identity changes: Erickson (1950) has showed that this period is mostly characterized by the construction of a stable personal identity. The sociologist Mannheim (1952) has shed light on the identification with specific social groups and on the formation of generation identity. Several authors (Fitzgerald, 1988; Mc Adams, 1985) have stressed the relevance of this period as the one when the first "personal life story" emerges.

In general, all the studies show a preferential retention of the knowledge of the social world within adolescence and adulthood. According to Conway (Conway & Pleydell-Pearce, 2000; Holmes & Conway, 1999) there are two reminiscence bumps: the first from 10 to 20 years for public events and the second from 20 to 30 for private events. During the first period the focus would be on the memory of external public events, mostly linked to the *zeitgeist* and would mirror the development of social and generational identity. This would answer the necessity to understand and integrate the self within society, thus creating a schema of the *life story*. The second bump would be focused on the memory of private events in a wide range of intimate relationships. The main function to which it seems to answer is to reach intimacy with the significant others and a close social group.

Flashbulb memories are the paradoxical example of the subjective linking between external, public events, and the personal experience of the individual. The target event represents the shared side of the collective memories, while the personal reception context (Larsen, 1988) is the private side of the history: "I was there" (Neisser, 1982).

Flashbulb Memories: The Individual Dimension of Collective Memories

When a relevant shifting occurs in the ordinary life of a social group, individuals belonging to that group keep a shared record of the eliciting event (Neal, 1998). This shifting might be either unexpected and extremely upsetting (e.g., the assassination of John F. Kennedy), or long lasting and embedded within the functioning of the social system itself (e.g., the Vietnam War) (Neal, 1998).

Individuals' memories for relevant social events are often anchored to the recall of personal circumstances in which news were firstly communicated. Brown and Kulik (1977) called this phenomenon flashbulb memory (FBM), referring to a class of vivid, detailed, and long-lasting memories for the circumstances in which people learned about a shocking public event (for instance, the assassination of John F. Kennedy, Malcolm X, or Martin Luther King). In other words, people may retain for a long time not only the original event itself, but also the reception context for this event, that is the place where they were, the time when they learned of the event, the ongoing activity, the informant, the personal reactions and reactions of others, the aftermath of the event (Bohannon, 1988; Brown & Kulik, 1977; Conway, Anderson, Larsen, Donelly, McDaniel, McClelland, Rawles, & Logie, 1994). These memories have been labeled as Flashbulb, because of their extreme vividness and persistence.

However, a different approach to FBM stresses that, far from being indelible as the photographical metaphor would suggest, these recollections might be affected by reconstructions and decay, as any other ordinary memory (Christianson, 1989; Neisser & Harsch, 1992; Weaver, 1993).

Emotional Determinants

According to Brown and Kulik (1977), the two main determinants of FBMs are surprise and importance – consequentiality of the original event. The authors showed a visual display of their model in a flow-chart concerning the formation and maintenance of FBMs. Their model includes a sequence of checks for unexpectedness, consequentiality, and level of rehearsal of the original news, and ends with the formation of narratives varying in elaboration, and referring to the eliciting event as well as the personal circumstances in which people learned of it. In other words, in Brown and Kulik's model, to elicit a FBM, public events must be unexpected and induce a high degree of surprise as a reaction in the public opinion. Furthermore, individuals must consider the events as having a considerable impact on their life, and on the life of the social group to which they belong.

To illustrate, in the United States, the level of consequentiality ascribed to the deaths of Martin Luther King and Malcolm X was substantially different in the two groups of African-Americans and Caucasian participants. The results showed that African-American participants had significantly more FBMs for these events than Caucasian participants (Brown & Kulik, 1977). Brown and Kulik (1977) explained

these results by postulating a special encoding mechanism that is triggered by the original event and that is assumed to make the memories vivid and long lasting (Livingston, 1967). This hypothesis – called special encoding hypothesis – has been subsequently accounted by other authors, who emphasized the role of surprise, importance–consequentiality, and emotional feeling states in the formation and maintenance of FBMs (Pillemer, 1984; Conway, 1995).

In a more recent model tested by Finkenauer and her colleagues (1998) on data collected in Belgium for the death of King Baudouin, the role of cognitive evaluations in triggering FBMs is emphasized. The authors attempted to link the research work on FBM to the research on cognitive determinants of emotion. FBM is considered as a kind of emotional memory, thus the same cognitive processes activated by ordinary emotional experiences are involved in its formation and maintenance (Finkenauer, Luminet, Gilse, El-Ahmadi, van der Linden, & Philippot, 1998). Finkenauer et al. (1998) focused on the novelty and importance–consequentiality appraisals, and tested a model in which novelty is the direct determinant of surprise, while importance–consequentiality yields emotional feeling states. In this model, emotional feeling states and their cognitive appraisals are structurally linked to produce FBMs. The impact of appraisals and emotion operate mainly, however, through the rehearsal of the event. Rehearsal process includes long-term cognitive and social aspects. Cognitive aspects refer to mental ruminations in which thoughts related to an emotional event repeatedly enter consciousness (Martin & Tesser, 1989; Tait & Silver, 1989). Social aspects involve the need to communicate with other people about the emotional circumstances and reactions (Rimé, Finkenauer, Luminet, Zech, & Philippot, 1998). Additionally, for public events, rehearsal involves the attention devoted to the mass media (TV, radio, newspapers, Internet). In the process of formation of FBMs, by rehearsing the original event, people also maintain the memory for the reception context of the news (Finkenauer et al., 1998).

In a study on the memory for the death of French President François Mitterrand, Curci and her colleagues (2001) carried out a deeper analysis of the cognitive antecedents of FBMs, and put forth the theoretical construct of concerns, which is defined as a set of motives or reasons for striving to reach or maintain a given state favorable to the individual (Frijda, 1994). Individuals' concerns might be considered as the most basic antecedents of the emotional experience, as they direct the cognitive appraisals of the original event, and then elicit differentiated subjective feeling states. An event is appraised as emotionally relevant and has an emotional impact on the individual only if it favors or harms the individual's concerns (Frijda, 1994; Frijda, Kuipers, & ter Schure, 1989). The formation and maintenance of FBMs is the outcome of a process of enhancement of the individual's most basic concerns (Curci, Luminet, Finkenauer, & Gisle, 2001).

Social Determinants

The emphasis on the role of emotional factors has been integrated with the consideration of the effects of social processes in the formation and maintenance of FBMs. The impact of a public event is also determined by the degree to which it promotes the concerns of individuals as members of social groups. As individuals, social groups have their own concerns to enhance or preserve, hence different social groups might be differently concerned by the same public event (Ciompi, 1997; Kenwyn & Crandell, 1984). When a political leader dies, citizens of his home country are likely to have been more affected by his politics, therefore they experience the effects of his death much more than people of foreign countries (Curci et al., 2001). Conway and his colleagues (1994) found that UK citizens had more FBMs for Margaret Thatcher's resignation than non-UK respondents, while Er (2003) showed that people living in the area of the Mar-

mara earthquake developed more FBMs for the event than people living in a not affected area, as they directly experienced the consequences of the original event (Er, 2003). Taken together, these findings suggest that group membership is an important predictor of FBMs, since it modulates the impact of the emotional variables involved in the process of formation and maintenance of FBMs.

However, social membership also plays a background effect on FBMs, by characterizing the context in which the news are transmitted in terms of attitudes, knowledge, and shared expectations. Conway introduced the prior knowledge about the event and its protagonists as a crucial variable in his model of formation of FBM for the Thatcher's resignation (Conway et al., 1994). Finkenauer and her colleagues (1998) stressed the impact of the attitudes towards the event and its protagonists, since they affect the way people approach and react to situations. Both prior knowledge and attitudes are predicted to facilitate the organization and assimilation of the incoming information into existing semantic structures in memory (Conway et al., 1994; Finkenauer et al., 1998), thus they appeared significantly liked to the other predictors of FBMs.

The impact of prior knowledge and attitudes is amplified in modern societies which have a greater access to the mass media. In a study on memories of the September 11th attacks, Luminet and his colleagues (2004) predicted a significant deficit in the formation of FBMs for national groups with a lower level of economic development, which reduced their access to the mass media. Indeed, the mass media identify the so-called social availability of a given news item (Bellelli, 1999), which corresponds to the enduring accessibility of information concerning the original event and its antecedents in a given social context, along with the urge to form a precise attitude towards it.

Finally, spontaneous conversations take place in the months and years following a relevant public event, especially among people highly concerned by it. These conversations are either provoked by the mass media, or occur as a reaction to the emotions experienced in social contexts because of the event. In the last case, the phenomenon is called social sharing of emotions, and stems from the attempts the individual makes to reduce the mental discrepancy induced by the emotional experience associated to the event (Rimé et al., 1998). Eventually, spontaneous conversations about socially relevant topics may turn into rumors, as a way through which social groups express their collective emotional needs (Knapp, 1944; Guimelli, 1999).

Social sharing of emotions (Rimé et al., 1998) is a substantive component of rehearsal processes (Curci et al., 2001; Finkenauer et al., 1998; Luminet et al., 2004), together with mental rumination and following the mass media coverage. According to the so-called constructivist approach (Neisser, 1982; McCloskey, Wible, & Cohen, 1988; Christianson, 1989; Wright, 1993), rehearsal processes have a constitutive role in the formation of FBMs, in that they shape their content, and make them highly modifiable and prone to decay.

Are FBMs a Special Class of Memories?

The debate about the prediction of FBMs is strictly linked with the discussion about the nature and destiny of these memory formation. Indeed, FBMs appear to have a dual nature, in that they might be considered as both collective representations shared within members of social groups and autobiographical recollections deeply anchored to the individual's life story.

According to Conway (1995), FBMs differ from ordinary autobiographical memories since they are associated with the recollection of specific sensory–perceptual details. As a consequence, they appear more vivid than any other memory. Conway maintained that FBMs arise from more densely integrated regions of the autobiographical knowledge base, thus they cannot be simply considered as ordinary memories with an unusual feature of vividness, but they appear

to be "whole" units in the space of autobiographical memory (Conway, 1995). From this approach, it follows that FBMs are a special class of memories, particularly vivid and long lasting.

On the other hand, as above outlined, the so called constructivist approach to the phenomenon stresses the role of rehearsal processes in that they might influence the subsequent evolution of these memory formations (Neisser, 1982; McCloskey et al., 1988; Christianson, 1989; Wright, 1993), or even create the general climate of expectations surrounding a public event (Bellelli, 1999). As a consequence, in spite of the sense of confidence people usually experience in association with these recollections, FBMs are not a special class of memories.

The debate on the nature of FBMs has manifest implications on the measurement of the phenomenon. If they were not more than ordinary memory formations, FBMs would easily be measured through linear models which simply sum up the number of details of the reception context remembered by individuals for a given public event (Bohannon, 1988; Pillemer, 1984; Kvavilashvili, Mirani, Schlagman, & Kornbrot, 2003). Alternatively, correlation coefficients are computed between scores corresponding to the mention of each details of the context and the theoretical construct of FBM (Finkenauer et al., 1998). On the other hand, if FBMs differed from ordinary autobiographical memories, measurement models would capture the clustered nature of the phenomenon. Thus, measurement models of FBMs clearly incorporate assumptions about both their nature and destiny. Very recently, Curci (2005) proposed a composition of this debate as regards the measurement issues. FBMs should be captured by measurement models which assume them to be very integrated memory formations, nevertheless they are not a special class of memories, as they can easily to be reconstructed or, at least, partly modified in the months and years following the relevant event. In this respect, FBMs would share a similar destiny to ordinary memories. Sophisticated data modeling is increasingly used to test specific hypotheses concerning both the nature and the formation of FBMs (Curci, 2005).

Collective Memories and Social Identities

Generational memories, reminiscence bump, and FBMs show that the memory for public events links very strictly the memories of individuals to a collective dimension. Actually, memories for public events are shared by many individuals of the same social group, and their formation and consolidation are strongly affected by sharing and social rehearsal processes. Some of them may be used as reference points (Ribot, 1882; Shum, 1998), situating in time course and giving a meaningful key to interpret personal and collective life.

How can social groups affect this selection and the accessibility of public events favoring the formation of durable "collective" memories? An important factor is the fact that the memory for public events can accomplish a function of construction and reinforcement of group identity (Rosa, Bellelli, & Bakhurst, 2000).

First, the memory for specific public events could be considered as a feature of collective identity, as well as shared heritage of the social group.

Second, shared memories can represent a strategy for the construction of collective identity. Memory for mythological events can play the same role of historical "real" events: it is not so rare that ethnical or minority groups keep imagined memories of their origins as foundations of collective identity.

Finally, the preservation of shared memories of public/collectively shared events is a process reflecting collective identification (Paez, Valencia, Besabe, Harranz, & Gonzalez, 2000).

Paez and colleagues (2000) have shown how different ethnic identities may produce different forms of collective memories, by comparing, in a trial of free rehearsal of historical events, the answers of two groups of Spanish participants with a prevalent national or ethnic identity (Basque). A high level of national identification ("I am first of all a Spanish citizen") was associated with a most frequent memory of events such as the integration of Spain within the CEE and the return to democracy. On the other hand, it was associated with a less frequent memory of other national events, such as the second republic, the bombardment of Guernica, the judgment of Burgos, ETA and political violence, the murder of Carrero Blanco, the death of Franco, the end of the dictatorship and the transition to democracy, the statute of autonomy of the Basques. To sum up, individuals with higher national identification remembered the positive events of national history more easily than the negative ones.

On the contrary, the participants with a prevalent Basque identification tended to remember better positive events such as the statute of autonomy and the transition to democracy, but remembered well also some of the negative and traumatic events such as the judgment of Burgos and Guernica.

A high level of national identification was at the origin of a better memory of the national positive events, while a high ethnic identification (Basque) produced a more accurate memory of the positive events and also in part of the negative ones. Therefore, there are memories that the group cultivates and others that the group tend to neglect.

There are circumstances for which the group tries explicitly to reinforce the memory of an event: this is the case of public ceremonies and re-evocations (Frjida, 1997). According to Frijda, commemorations origin from the desire to define the group's own collocation within a time frame of continuity, integrating the self in an experienced past and taking possession of it, and by the desire to confirm one's own identity through the group's identity.[4]

Often commemorations concern collective events that are deeply traumatic (Cole, 2004; Collins, 2004; Withehouse, 2002). Here their importance becomes even more evident. Frijda has pointed out how the rituals that accompany commemorations help people to accept their most painful emotions. Through those rites people may feel accepted in theory in the role of "moved" individuals: people who have lost dear ones or who have experienced unfairness and sufferings. But commemorations are focused on the events more than on emotions and sufferings. Commemorative rituals define the individuals' identity by assigning them their own social role as persons who have mourned or who have been offended or hurt, thus determining a greater distance with the event itself.

Not only individuals but also social groups experience difficulty in accepting their pain, which is divided between inhibition and confrontation. Durkheim (1912) has argued that rituals may reinforce emotions by strengthening cohesion and social participation of groups. From a functionalist point of view, for instance, funeral rites contribute to consolidate social order and group cohesion, by promoting collective solidarity. Studies on collective disasters confirm that funeral rites help people by strengthening relationships with the other members and to accept events giving them structure and meaning. A recent study on the March-Eleventh Madrid bombing (Paez, Rimé, & Besabe, 2005) shows that a higher level of participation in demonstrations was associated to higher national identification and collective self-esteem. The participation also predicted higher levels of subjective social support, positive affect and positive self-concept, and lower loneliness, confirming that rituals reinforce social integration and solidarity: "the process of remembering is normative in nature. It pushes people to have a social identity and to teach and learn a moral lesson" (Beristain, Paez, & Gonzalez, 2000, 5).

Oblivion and Distortions of Collective Memories

As well as memory, also the oblivion of specific events may be functional in identifying the demands of social groups. Social groups tend to recall less frequently or rather to forget negative episodes, especially the most hurtful and humiliating ones (Marques,

Paez, & Serra, 1997). For example Brossart (1992) highlights that in France the "week of blood" which occurred in 1871, the surrender to the Nazis in 1940 and Dien Bien Phu are not commemorated at all.

Sometimes to forget is the only way to avoid the powerful negative emotions awakened by an event that threatens the integrity and the dignity of the social group.[5] To forget the most negative events, those that have touched a group, gives the group itself the possibility to imagine a more favorable reelaboration of events or rather of a whole historical period (this is what often happens with dictatorships) which shifts attention from the passive acceptance of a part of the population to the heroic attitude of those people who have fought against the dictator (the resistance).

Pennebaker (1990) has clearly described the process of collective oblivion through the image of the *silent cities*. He mentions the case of Dallas and the murder of the John Fitzgerald Kennedy, on the 22nd of November 1963. Together with horror and dismay, a sense of guilt toward Dallas developed in the United States, since this city was considered responsible for what had happened.

Dallas reacted by ignoring the event as if it had never occurred. No commemoration was organized, while several other American cities organized initiatives in honour and in memory of the murdered president. Dallas became a city with no past, but at the same time it rapidly gained a new identity. Within the three years after this event Dallas experienced great economical and urban development. Between 1964 and 1968 the city changed its face. After the collective attention that was attracted by the murderers of Reverend Martin Luther King and of Robert Kennedy, suddenly and inexplicably, all the phenomena which made Dallas different from all the other American cities stopped.

To forget is essential to remember in a different way. Baumeister and Hastings (1997) have argued that oblivion is one of the ways through which a social group deceives itself. Social self-deception is performed also through other processes described by the authors. As we have seen, the first and most simple way to distort the memory of a collective negative and humiliating collective event is to selectively omit it. Dias, Marques, and Paez (2000) have carried out a study to investigate the effects of group national belonging on the memory of historical events implying shame, linked to the colonial past, by using the paradigm of serial transmission devised by Bartlett (1932).[6] They found that Portuguese participants (ingroup), made significantly more omissions than the Spanish participants (outgroup), greater assimilation and smaller accuracy.

Other devices of self-deception described by Baumeister and Hastings (1997) are the construction of false events, the exaggeration and embellishment of events, the accentuation of positive features, *linking versus detaching* in order to modify the interpretative context of events, the blaming of enemies and events, to reduce group responsibility and *contextual framing*.

Direct falsification is an extreme case, which is but frequent. The mass media plays a very important role in its construction. Knightley (1975) has shown that, starting from the American Civil War until World War II, beside battles which have never been cited there are several which have never taken place, but that despite this have received wide descriptions in the war press.

The differences between the events which refer to the ingroup and those that refer to the outgroup are great, and in general tend to maximize the successes and to minimize the losses of the ingroup. The first official communication of Pearl Harbor by the Americans was made 5 days after the event occurred and reported of few casualties while those actually suffered were far greater (Robinson, 1996).

A very common device is the embellishment and the ennobling of the event: very characteristic is the creation of mythical heroes. When real characters are involved, their most discussed features are generally omitted, while the most positive ones are highlighted in a pedagogic attempt toward younger generations. Wertsch (this volume) highlights the role of unquestionable, heroic

narratives as a distinctive feature of collective memories. The same device is produced during commemorations, especially during funeral rites, as for example happens with the funeral tombstone, where characters who were known for their violence and intolerance, are often exalted and depicted with favorable features.

Particularly interesting are those devices whose purpose is to modify the interpretative frame of the event, more than its direct distortion. Baumeister and Hastings (1997) mention what happened with the bombardment of Pearl Harbor. The Americans tend to interpret the event as a cause of the nuclear bombs dropped on Hiroshima and Nagasaki four years later. The Japanese consider these events as totally independent.

The American civil war is an example of the manipulation of the *framing*. The federal side interpreted the war by making reference to a fight against an evil institution, whose aim has been the maintenance of slavery. On the other side little importance was attributed to slavery as the rivals tended to interpret the war as a fight to defend the American right to live one's own local culture.

The role of the mass media has been already mentioned. If the role of historiography is easily recognized since it moves by definition on the ground of the past, then little attention has been dedicated yet to the role played by the mass media in influencing our knowledge of history and then our collective memory. It should not be forgotten that the mass media is the main and probably the sole source of our knowledge of public events. Paradoxically this has produced an inverse effect, since the mass media is largely considered as a neutral background, more than acknowledging its power in framing and transmitting public events (Bellelli, 1999).

Probably the role of the media has been undermined, since its activity has been considered as being anchored exclusively to the present, and it may seem queer that in some way they talk about past events. The same media (press, radio, TV, Internet) attribute a very important role to new and exclusive information (so-called scoops). Breaking news and flash news are the ordinary devices used to mark this orientation toward the present and the new. Nonetheless, journalists use history at least in three forms: *commemorations*, where past events are rehearsed, societies may mirror themselves and affirm their identity; *historical analogies*, where past events are recalled to underline, through their supposed similarity, controversial topics and attitudes of the present which engage the society's future action; and *historical contexts*, that propose to re-construct the causal context, which led to the present configuration (Edy, 1999). In this way, a "usable" (more than an "accurate") past is emerging, in order to support some identity projects in social conflict (Wertsch, this volume).

The reference to the past has important implications for collective memories. Several memorable events may be considered as such because they have produced controversies through time and thus also different interpretation and meanings associated to them. Without controversies there is no space for the negotiation of meanings. The media (first of all the press) may be an important forum for the negotiation of shared meanings, when an hegemonic point of view on the comprehension of past events has not yet emerged. We may wonder about the role of commemorations in producing a discursive space for a direct negotiation of the different meanings associated to the past.

Collectives' Memories: A Theoretical Challenge

So far we have used the term "collective" memories with a relatively restrictive meaning of "shared" memories for public/historical events. We will now try to define precisely the meaning of collective memories in a different, more qualitative, way. The focus of this last part of this chapter, in fact, is to review and discuss contributions trying to explore, starting from classic works proposed by Halbwachs (1925/1950) at the beginning of last century, this apparent paradox of attributing a memory, which does not exist independently from the individual, to an abstract entity.

Referring to the pioneering work of Maurice Halbwachs, we could find an original yet unsurpassed point of view on the complex intertwining of individual and social processes, summarized in this provocative definition. In the various works gradually shaping his interest on the field, Halbwachs (1925/1950) came to the conclusion that a memory may be defined as "collective" when it makes individuals aware of the fact that they belong to a community.

Sometimes, this awareness may arise from a deliberate effort they consciously make, as when they choose to join a commemoration. No matter what kind of ritualized activity is chosen – listening to a witness of the fact commemorated or to an old friend of the person commemorated; dedicating a monument or naming a place in honour and memory of the object of commemoration, and so on – during the time dedicated to this kind of social activity, participants are frequently reminded of the meaning that the aspect commemorated has, for their contemporary belonging to their community. Rehearsing news and info already mastered by all participants, as well as showing the emotions linked to these well-known contents (for instance, through the reactions of witnesses), commemorations accomplish, with well-scheduled timing, both a social and a personal function. On one hand, they show the importance of chosen moments to define positive characteristics of the community. On the other hand, they protect participants from the risk of missing the significance of these moments for their contemporary group belongings (Frijda, 1997).

Sometimes, on the contrary, the awareness of the relationships between one's memory and social belongings may "pop up" abruptly, without any previous choice or willingness. For instance, taking a walk with a friend, we may notice that the name of the street, commemorating an historical episode which is extremely important for our generation, sounds quite unknown to our younger friend. By experiencing this gap between our memories, we may suddenly realize that, in spite of our personal friendship, we belong to two different generational groups, sharing different historical database (Conway, 1997).

Both fictional situations considered above are similar, because both are able to make us aware of the fact that our life runs in a social context that frames our personal existence. However, they are also different, referring to the level of voluntary choice characterizing them. This difference reminds us of the classical distinction between voluntary and non-voluntary memories (Baddeley, 1990).

In one of the most famous pages of European narrative, Marcel Proust described his sudden burst of childhood memories when recognizing, in the taste of a little cake he ate, the flavor of the sweet his aunt used to give to him at teatime when he was a boy. The pleasure of these memories was doubled by the fact that the author had tried for a long time to remember this early period of his life, even beginning to think he had lost its memory for ever (Proust, 1913).

In textbooks on memory, this precious piece of narrative is often used as an example of non-voluntary memory. In fact, the failure of efforts deliberately made by Proust to remember his childhood, accessing it only by a voluntary memory quest, is an impressive demonstration of how imagination can be weak in recreating old images on command. On the other hand, the chain of involuntary memories originated by smell recognition shows how a sensory and perceptual trace may trigger an immediate access to a flourish of ancient memories. The entire episode, in short, accounts for the importance of considering mind processes as deeply rooted in body reactions.

In this sense, non-voluntary collective memories are similar to non-voluntary memories *tout court*, in showing how memory search is rooted not only in physical but also in social contexts framing mind processes. Nevertheless, this powerful analogy is also limited. In fact, in Proust's description, trigger is activated by an already experienced direct perception; collective memories, on the contrary, are rooted in the subjective capacity to recognize an abstract link between some info (as the well-known contents repeatedly offered at any commemoration time, or the name chosen for a street) and the belonging to a community.

Referring to this basic difference, we may say only in a metaphorical sense that communities "have a memory". Nevertheless, there is no doubt that any durable community "creates" a memory, by means of an *active selection of contents*, made more or less accessible in the social environment characterizing the everyday life of its members (Assmann, 1995). Therefore, contents experienced by community members as obvious or trivial, such as the name of the street in the previous example, on better consideration show themselves to be the result of a selection, meant to offer a concrete basis to convey a positive idea of the whole community. In fact, these memories are possible only because they are embodied in a preselected array of concrete intermediations: as monuments, or places, or moments dedicated to regularly commemorate events or persons meaningful for the community, or even particular body gestures, such as rising to one's feet to recognize the authority of a spiritual or political leader (Connerton, 1989).

And yet, in spite of social origins and functions, collective memories easily disclose the important role they play also on a personal level. In fact, they may be experienced as a source of insight, if people realize to what extent their meaning is at the same time societal and personal. In this sense, collective memories are an instance of how memory may act, not only as an access to past knowledge, but also as a surprising intuition about overshadowed aspects of present identity (Robinson, 1986). Therefore, a collective memory, although socially mediated, may show such a personal importance to become as a constitutive part of autobiographical memory.

Classical observations on family memories, proposed by Halbwachs, are a good example of this phenomenon. In the famous fifth chapter of *Cadres sociaux de la mémorie* (1925), describing what happens "when a family remembers". The author remarks that, when no extraneous member participates to their conversations, family members tend to frequently share memories of well-known episodes, rehearsed with an evident pleasure, as if they were admiring all together "a private treasure". These observations, that would be fully confirmed more then forty years later by sophisticated non-intrusive videotaping of spontaneous family interactions (Blum-Kulka & Snow, 1992; Miller, 1994), led Halbwachs to raise some important questions: Why people repeatedly share memory's contents already known by everyone? And why some episodes or some family members are remembered so often, while others are not? He proposes that these memories are chosen because they are able, in spite of their apparent triviality, to show to family members – and only to them. "A more or less mysterious symbol of the common ground from which they all originate their distinctive characteristics" (Halbwachs, 1925, ed. it.: 35).

By the pre-arranged selection guiding this everyday "social game", then, each family gives to its members a kind of "affective armour" that, in times of trouble or difficulty, will protect them, reminding them that they belong to a group able to cope with life and problems. In short, he proposes that these little narratives, so frequently heard, are meant to say to family members "that is the way we are".

We may therefore try to further focus more specifically our discussion on the intertwining between individual and social processes, represented in the apparently paradoxical definition of collective memory, saying that collective memories are not lived at a personal level as a recollection of already experienced moments, but as an expression of what we may literally label as re-remembering, that is, being mindful again of what we have and are as community members.

Therefore, collective memories implicitly signal a subjective adherence to a social and cultural frame of meaning. The intersection between the personal act of remembering, seen as a way to reconstruct

the meaning of past experiences (Bartlett, 1932), and the set of social and collective intermediations constituting the context in which these psychological processes are embedded, is in fact the crucible where personal and collective culture are inextricably intertwined, in a never-ending process of mutual co-construction (Barclay & Smith, 1992; Valsiner, 1987). Every voluntary act of remembering together (Middleton & Edwards, 1990) as much as every involuntary autobiographical memory helping the remembering one to seize basic features that similarly shape personal and collective identity, are therefore an indirect yet fundamental demonstration of how memory is not only a cognitive effort of the individual mind, but also the product of the access to a cultural frame, either explicitly chosen or implicitly received. Therefore, this intertwining between personal and collective culture continuously offers a set of cognitive tools, helping individual reconstruction of the meaning of the past, but also, and perhaps most importantly, an affective empowerment of individual identity (Halbwachs, 1950).

In other words, this kind of memory performs a double function. It builds up a shared reconstructive story of the community, linking today community identity to a tradition and a common ground of values. On the other hand, it offers to individuals a context of reference, which helps them to cope with stressful or difficult situations, encompassing their lives into a more comprehensive and long-term perspective. In short, collective memories may be seen as a support for both individual and community identities, intertwining inextricably them. Their same support function, however, explains their tendency towards a biased selection, saving and amplifying the aspects bound to shed a positive light on community identity. It is not by chance, for instance, that young English people may pass, absent-mindedly, through one stop of the London tube named Waterloo, and that no French passenger would find a stop in Paris underground bearing the same name.

Collective memories of wars are a good example of this kind of selective bias. By the way, among these memories, it is not defeat itself that may be a menace – here perhaps our example could be misleading. What is really dangerous, is not the defeat, but the memory of a shameful behavior, as well shown by Paez and colleagues (Paez et al., 2000). While a defeat, in fact, may be associated to an historical moment in which the community turned out to be a victim, a shameful memory is the proof that values claimed by community leaders were deceitful, and could be deliberately neglected. If it can be somehow useful, to increase the feeling of belonging to one's community, to remember that sometimes our group was badly treated by others, it can be extremely difficult to recognize that one's community has to feel shame for its past behaviors (Lewis, 1975). In this sense, as we already stressed, studying collective memory implies also understanding collective oblivion, and the reasons underlying these two processes.

A large set of empirical data, collected in very different contexts, seem to confirm the idea that collective memory is based on a selection meant to consolidate a positive community identity (Pennebaker & Banasik, 1997). The reason for this process is evident. If, as in Halbwachs' classic hypothesis described above, collective memories are meant to have a protective role, helping people to cope with challenges and problems by the feeling of being inserted in a social community sharing the same characteristics and values, a certain amount of self-serving bias is expected. Nevertheless, the same idea of selection of access for different kind of memories implies, both at a personal and a social level, a sense of *ethic commitment* to a moral responsibility (Leone, 2000). In this case, we need to understand how not only in-group but also intergroup aims may guide collective memories' selection (Mazzara & Leone, 2001).

Let us use again the example of war. Recently, we had heard frequently words we believed to be out of date: describing Christians as "Crusaders" or recording ancient fears about Muslims. There is no doubt that such a recent accessibility of these old memories is linked to the emotional climate characterizing war times, and to the growing influence of communications meant at consolidating a conflict ethos and, more generally, a threatening image of enemies (Price, 1989; Silverstein, 1992; Duck, Hogg, & Terry, 2000). However, the choice to make people feel that these old memories are contemporary is not only necessitated by the historical situation, but is also part of a conscious communicative strategy (Leone, Mazzara, Contarello, & Volpato, 2004). It is therefore subject to a moral judgment.

Many theoretical and empirical studies have been aimed at understanding how collective memories may be used to protect the identity of both groups during conflict situations, and to rationalize mutual aggression in wartime. Only recently, a small group of studies has begun to study how the selection of collective memories made salient by social activities and artefacts may help in repairing broken relationships and reconciling old enemies (Salomon & Nevo, 2002). Certainly, the study of processes of collective elaboration of Shoà, both from the point of view of victims and perpetrators, has been central in developing this new perspective. More recently, the reconciliation in South Africa, with the original experience of the Truth and Reconciliation Committees, the problem of the emergence of a super-ordinate European identity and the still unsolved situation in Middle East have been prominent cases to observe how access to collective memories may change, when intergroup relations change (Nadler, 2002). This recent field of study on collective memory may be fruitful to better understand how this issue is linked not only to the question of how the past weighs on the present, but also to the problem of how a wise selection of past memories may help us to build a peaceful future. Referring to consequences of collective memories for guiding future social activity, we need to better describe how basic processes of protecting collective identities from shameful memories may be counter-balanced by the other basic process of searching for a relational equity, recognizing past faults and atrocities (Kelman, 2001). In this new perspective, also the problem of collective oblivion may be differently discussed, being linked not only to the denial of negative experiences of collective shame and failure, but also to the positive capacity of creating relational "turning points", offering solid frames of understanding for past responsibilities, but allowing at the same time a renewal of relations between former enemies (Tavuchis, 1991).

In order to support these social efforts, a basic need to fulfill is the reconstruction of mutual trust, rooted in the will to avoid any false collective memory. Memory is scrutinized, in fact, as an expression of public responsibility. Every act of collective remembering is therefore judged, both by in group and by intergroup members, as a demonstration of ethic commitment, as a guarantee of participation to an inclusive moral standard (Nadler, 2002). It has to be accomplished, therefore, not only individually, but also in the appropriate public forums: showing how collective memory may be lived not only as a need, but also as a duty (Ricoeur, 1998).

Conclusions

To summarize what we have proposed in this chapter, we may define collective memory as the intertwining between social and individual processes. From a social point of view, a collective memory is the result of a selection of positive aspects of collective identity, made accessible and embodied in concrete mediations, as social acts or cultural artefacts. From an individual point of view, a collective memory is the expression of a personal adherence to a social and cultural frame of meaning, together with the actual importance of affective belonging to the community expressing this same frame.

Being used therefore as a support for both personal and community identity, collective

memory is implicitly based on a self-serving bias, selecting past contents functional to better advantage current social belongings. Nevertheless, this bias acts with no rigid limitations. It may be tempered with a growing psycho-social elaboration of difficult aspects of the in-group past, as in the case of shameful or traumatic memories. Moreover, it may acquire new meanings when intergroup relations change, as in the shifting from conflict to reconciliation.

Social groups, as well as individuals, feel the necessity to store the past. This means recognizing and understanding one's own identity, which sometimes is even more powerful than the same territorial borders. At the same time it is also a powerful means to justify present and future goals. The memory of the collective past is never neutral, neither is it projected simply backward, rather it moves from the present to reconstruct and interpret the past looking at the future. With some exceptions (Pennebaker, Paez, & Rimé, 1997), until now Psychology has neglected this fascinating field of research, which is intrinsically interdisciplinary (Leone, 1996; Valsiner & Rosa, this volume), since it implies different aspects and dimensions. However it is no accident that nowadays a renewed interest towards these topics is felt. This is due also to the convergent push of several circumstances. On the one hand the recent developments of the psychology of memory within the field of autobiographical memory and daily memory have led to a search for a more ecological way of doing research. On the other hand psychology and social sciences in general are experiencing a very effervescent period also within the methodological field, thus producing a significant widening of the research methods in the direction of qualitative methodology. Finally, the dramatic events which have affected the world after the Balkan war and especially after September 11th have definitely shown how illusory was the prophecy about the end of history devised some years ago by Fukuyama, thus highlighting the unstoppable ascent of ethnic identities and their rediscovery of one's own historical and sometimes mythical past.

Notes

1   Antonietta Curci wrote the paragraphs on FBMs, Giovanna Leone the last section of the chapter on collective memory, and Guglielmo Bellelli the first two and the central paragraphs on the functions and distortions of collective memories.

2   It should be considered that within the Spanish sample although there was an absence of the category "terrorism" ETA and the IRA were mentioned respectively at fourth and seventh place.

3   This is comprehensible if we consider that for a long time Italy has had the most powerful communist party in the west.

4   "Public commemorations reinforce those various aspects quite explicitly, by the joint activity and joint emotion as such, the communication of emotions both in joint listening to or looking at their public expression, and by freely manifesting one's own engagement in the issues at hand. Obviously, having and avowing a common past, and to participating in a common tradition with all the social interactions of jointly recognizing the truth of affirmations about history and the valuing of the major actors in it, form for a group the strongest glue" (Frjida, 1997, 109–110).

5   In a study carried out in Italy in 1999, none of the Italian participants, independent of age or background, mentioned among the most significant events occurring in the course of their own lives to be the episodes of violence and racism committed by the Italian soldiers during the peace campaign in Somalia, which took place a few years before and received significant (and repeated) attention in the media. (Curci, 2002).

6   Bartlett (1932) was the first to adopt a singular research paradigm, which unfortunately was neglected for a long while. He asked his participants to transmit a message to other participants. In turn these participants had to transmit the message to other participants and so on. Bartlett found a powerful effect of reconstructive transformation of memories, which were "normalized" through their adaptation to the cultural schemes of the participants.

References

Assmann, J. (1995). Collective Memory and Cultural Identity. *New German Critique*, 65, 125–33.

Baddeley, A. (1990). *Human Memory: Theory and practice*. Hove: Lawrence Erlbaum Associates.

Barclay, C. R. & Smith, T. S. 1992. Autobiographical Remembering: Creating Personal Culture. In M. A. Conway, D. C. Rubin, H. Spinnler, & W. A. Wagenaar, (Eds.), *Theoretical Perspectives on Autobiographical Memory* (pp. 75–97). Dordrecht: Kluwer Academic Press.

Bartlett, F. C. (1932). *Remembering: A Study in Experimental and Social Psychology*. Cambridge, MA: Cambridge University Press.

Baumeister, R. F. & Hastings, S. (1997). Distortions of Collective Memory: How groups flatter and deceive themselves. In J. W. Pennebaker, D. Paez, & B. Rimé, (Eds.), *Collective Memory of Political Events* (pp. 277–293). Mahwah, NJ: Lawrence Erlbaum Associates.

Bellelli, G. (1999). *Ricordo di un giudice. Uno studio sulle flashbulb memories* [Remembering a judge: A study on flashbulb memories]. Napoli: Liguori.

Bellelli, G., Curci, A. & Leone, G. (2000). Ricordi indimenticabili. Determinanti della memorabilità collettiva di eventi pubblici [Unforgettable memories. Determinants of the accessibility of public events]. *Psychofenia*, 4–5, 83–110.

Beristain, C. M., Paez, D. & Gonzalez, J. L. (2000). Rituals, social sharing, silence, emotions and collective memory claims in the case of Guatemalan genocide. *Psicothema*, 12, 117–130.

Blum-Kulka, S. & Snow, C. E. (1992). Developing Autonomy For Tellers, Tales, And Telling In Family Narrative Events. *Journal of Narrative And Life History*, 2, 187–217.

Bohannon, J. N. (1988). Flashbulb memories for the Space Shuttle disaster: A tale of two theories. *Cognition*, 29, 179–196.

Brossart, A. (1992). URSS/Polonia/RDA. El quinquagesimo aniversario del pacto germanosovietico [The 50th anniversary of the german-soviet pact]. In A. Brossart, S. Combe, J. Y. Potel, & J. C. Szurek, (Eds.), *En el Este, la memoria recuperada*. Valencia: Alfons el Magnanim.

Brown, R. & Kulik, J. (1977). Flashbulb Memories. *Cognition*, 5, 73–99.

Christianson, S. Å. 1989. Flashbulb memories: Special, but not so special. *Memory & Cognition*, 17, 435–443.

Ciompi, L. (1997). On the emotional bases of thinking. Fractal affect-logic and communication. *System families*, 10, 128–134.

Cole, J. (2004). Painful memories, ritual and the transformation of community trauma. *Culture, Medicine and Psychiatry*, 28, 87–105.

Collins, R. (2004). Rituals of solidarity in the wake of Terrorist attacks. *Sociological Theory*, 22, 53–87.

Connerton, P. (1989). *How societies remember.* Cambridge, UK: Cambridge University Press.

Conway, M. A. (1995). *Flashbulb Memories.* Hove: Erlbaum.

Conway, M. A. (1997). The inventory of experience: Memory and identity. In J. W. Pennebaker, D. Paez, & B. Rimé, (Eds.), *Collective memory of political events. Social Psychological perspectives* (pp. 21–45). Mahwah, NJ: Lawrence Erlbaum.

Conway, M. A., Anderson, S. J., Larsen, S. F., Donelly, C. M., McDaniel, M. A., McClelland, A. G. R., Rawles, R. E. & Logie, R. H. (1994). The formation of flashbulb memories. *Memory & Cognition*, 22, 326–343.

Conway, M. A. & Pleydell-Pearce, C. W. (2000). The construction of autobiographical memories in the self-memory system. *Psychological Review*, 107, 261–288.

Curci, A. (2002). *I was there. 6 studi sulle flashbulb memories* [I was there. Six studies on Flashbulb memories]. Unpublished doctoral thesis: University of Bari.

Curci, A. (2005). Latent Variable Models for the Measurement of Flashbulb Memories: A comparative approach. *Applied Cognitive Psychology*, 19, 3–22.

Curci, A., Luminet, O., Finkenauer, C. & Gisle, L. (2001). Flashbulb memories in social groups: A comparative test-retest study of the memory of French President Mitterand's death in a French and a Belgian group. *Memory*, 9, 81–101.

Dias, F. P., Marques, J. M. & Paez, D. (2000). Dealing with shame: Effects of group membership on the transmission of negative historical events, *Unpublished manuscript*, University of Porto.

Duck, J. M., Hogg, M. A. & Terry, D. J. (2000). The perceived impact of persuasive messages on "us" and "them". In D. J. Terry & M. A. Hogg, (Eds.), 2000. *Attitudes, behavior, and social context: The role of norms and group membership. Applied social research* (pp. 265–291). Mahwah, NJ: Lawrence Erlbaum Associates.

Durkheim, E. (1898). Représentations individuelles et représentations collectives. *Revue de métaphysique et de morale*, 6, 273–302.

Durkheim, É. (1912). *Les Formes élémentaires de la vie religieuse: le système totémique en Australie.* Paris: Alcan.

Edy, J. A. (1999). Journalistic uses of collective memory. *Journal of Communication*, 49, 71–85.

Er, N. (2003). A new Flashbulb memory model applied to the Marmara earthquake. *Applied Cognitive Psychology*, 17, 503–517.

Erickson, E. (1950). *Childhood and society.* New York: Norton.

Festinger, L. (1954). A theory of social comparison processes. *Human Relations*, 7, 117–140.

Finkenauer, C., Luminet, O., Gilse, L., El-Ahmadi, A., Van Der Linden, M. & Philippot, P. (1998). Flashbulb memories and the underlying mechanism of their formation: Toward an emotional-integrative model. *Memory and Cognition*, 26, 516–531.

Fitzgerald, J. M. (1988). Vivid memories and the reminiscence phenomenon: The role of self narrative. *Human Development*, 31, 261–273.

Franklin, H. C. & Holding, D. H. (1977). Personal memories at different ages. *Quarterly Journal of Experimental Psychology*, 29, 527–532.

Frijda, N. H. (1994). Universal antecedent exist, and are interesting. In P. Ekman & R. J. Davidson, (Eds.), *The nature of emotion: Fundamental questions* (pp. 155–162). New York: Oxford University Press.

Frjida, N. H. (1997). Commemorating. In J. W. Pennebaker, D. Paez & B. Rimé, (Eds.), *Collective Memory of Political Events* (pp. 103–127). Mahwah, NJ: Lawrence Erlbaum Associates.

Frijda, N. H., Kuipers, P. & ter Schure, E. (1989). Relations among emotion, appraisal, and emotional action readiness. *Journal of Personality and Social Psychology*, 57, 212–228.

Guimelli, C. (1999). *La Pensée Sociale* [The Social Thinking]. Paris: Presses Universitaires de France.

Halbwachs, M. (1925/1975). *Les cadres sociaux de la mémoire* [The social frames of memory]. Paris: Mouton.

Halbwachs, M. (1950). *La mémoire collective* [The collective memory]. Paris: Presses Universitaires de France.

Holmes, A. & Conway, M. A. (1999). Generation identity and the reminiscence bump: Memories for public and private events. *Journal of Adult Development*, 6, 21–34.

Kelman, H. C. (2001). The role of national identity in conflict resolution: experiences from Israeli-Palestinian problem-solving workshops. In R. D. Ashmore & L. Jussim, (Eds.), *Social identity, intergroup conflict, and conflict reduction. Rutgers series on self and social identity* (vol. 3, pp. 187–212). London: Oxford University Press.

Kenwyn, S. K. & Crandell, S. D. (1984). Exploring collective emotion. *American Behavioral Scientist* 27, 813–828.

Knapp, R. H. (1944). A psychology of rumour. *Public Opinion Quarterly*, 8, 22–37.

Knightley, P. (1975). *The first casualty*. New York: Harcourt Brace.

Kvavilashvili, L., Mirani, J., Schlagman, S. & Kornbrot, D. E. (2003). Comparing Flashbulb memories of September 11 and death of Princess Diana: Effects of time delays and nationality. *Applied Cognitive Psychology*, 17, 1017–1031.

Larsen, S. F. (1988). Remembering without experiencing: Memory for reported events. In U. Neisser & E. Winograd, (Eds.), *Remembering reconsidered. Ecological and traditional approaches to the study of memory* (pp. 326–355). Cambridge, UK: Cambridge University Press.

Larsen, S. F. (1992). Potential flashbulb: Memories of ordinary news as the baseline. In E. Winograd & U. Neisser, (Eds.), *Affect and accuracy in recall: Studies of "flashbulb memories"* (pp. 32–64). New York: Cambridge University Press.

Leone, G. (1996). Il futuro alle spalle. La memoria sociale e collettiva nei lavori di Bartlett, Vygotsky e Halbwachs [The Future from behind. The social and collective memory in the Bartlett, Vygotsky and Halbwachs's work]. *Rassegna di Psicologia*, XIII, 3, 91–130.

Leone G. (2000). *Cosa è sociale nella memoria?* [What is Social in memory?] In G. Bellelli, D.Bakhurst, & A. Rosa, (Eds.), *Tracce. Memoria collettiva e identità sociali* (pp. 49–69). Napoli: Liguori.

Leone, G., Mazzara, B., Contarello, A. & Volpato, C. (2004). *Monitoring the reconciliation processes: some theoretical and methodological issues.* Paper presented in the EAESP Small Group Meeting, *War and Peace Conference*, Genève, 11–13 Sept. 2004.

Lewis, B. (1975). *History: remembered, recovered, invented*. Princeton: Princeton University Press.

Livingston, R. B. (1967). Brain circuitry relating to complex behavior. In G. C. Quarton, T. Melnechuck & F. O. Schmitt, (Eds.), *The neurosciences: A study program* (pp. 499–514). New York: Rockefeller University Press.

Luminet, O., Curci, A., Marsh, E., Wessel, I., Constantin, T., Gencoz, F. & Yogo, M. (2004). The Cognitive, Emotional, and Social Impacts of the September, 11 Attacks: Group Differences in Memory for the Reception Context and the Determinants of Flashbulb Memory. *The Journal of General Psychology*, 131, 197–224.

Mannheim, K. (1928/1952). The problem of generations. In K. Mannheim, *Essays on the sociology of knowledge*. London: Routledge & Kegan.

Marques, J., Paez, D. & Serra, A. F. (1997). Social sharing, emotional climate, and the transgenerational transmission of memories: The Portuguese colonial war. In J. W. Pennebaker, D. Paez & B. Rimé, (Eds.), *Collective Memory of Political Events* (pp. 253–275). Mahwah, NJ: Lawrence Erlbaum.

Martin, L. & Tesser, A. (1989). Toward a motivational and structural theory of ruminative thought. In J. S. Ulman & J. A. Bargh, (Eds.), *Unintended thoughts* (pp. 306–326). New York: Guilford.

Mazzara B. M. & Leone G. (2001). Collective memory and intergroup relations. *Revista de Psicologia Social*, 16, 349–367.

Mc Adams, D. P. (1985). *Power, intimacy, and the life story. Personological inquiries into identity.* New York: Guilford Press.

McCloskey, M., Wible, C. G. & Cohen, N. J. (1988). Is There a Special Flashbulb-Memory Mechanism?*Journal of Experimental Psychology*, 117, 171–181.

Middleton, D. & Edwards, D., (Eds.), (1990). *Collective Remembering*. London: Sage.

Miller, P. J. (1994). Narrative Practices: Their Role In Socialization And Self-Construction, In U.Neisser & R.Fivush, (Eds.), *The Remembering Self: Construction And Accuracy In The Self-Narratives* (pp. 158–179). Cambridge, UK: Cambridge University Press.

Moscovici, S. (1976). *La psychanalyse, son image, son public*. 2nd (Ed.), Paris: Presse Universitaires de France. 1961.

Nadler, A. (2002). Post resolution processes: Instrumental and socioemotional routes to reconciliation. In G. Salomon & B. Nevo,

(Eds.), *Peace education: The concept, principles, and practices around the world* (pp. 127–141). Mahwah, NJ: Lawrence Erlbaum Associates.

Neal, A. G. (1998). *National Trauma and Collective Memory*. Armonk: M. E. Sharpe.

Neisser, U. (1982). Snapshots or benchmarks? In U.Neisser, (Ed.), *Memory observed* (pp. 43–48). San Francisco: Freeman.

Neisser, U. & Harsch, N. (1992). Phantom flashbulbs: False recollections of hearing the news about Challenger. In E. Winograd & U. Neisser, (Eds.), *Affect and accuracy in recall: Studies of "flashbulb memories"* (pp. 9–31). New York: Cambridge University Press.

Paez, D., Rimé, B. & Besabe, N. (2005). Un modelo socio-cultural de los rituals. Efectos de las traumas colectivos y procesos psico-sociales de afrontamiento con referencia a las manifestaciones del 11-M. [A socio-cultural model of rituals. Effects of collective traumas and psychosocial coping processes with reference to the March-Eleventh demonstrations]. *Revista de Psicologia Social*, 20, 369–385.

Paez, D., Valencia, J., Besabe, N., Harranz, K. & Gonzalez, J. L. (2000). Identità, comunicazione e memoria collettiva [Identity, communication and collective memory]. In G. Bellelli, D. Bakhurst & A. Rosa, (Eds.) 2000. *Tracce. Studi sulla memoria collettiva* (pp. 139–167). Napoli: Liguori.

Pennebaker, J. W. (1990). *Opening up: The healing power of confiding in others*. New York: Morrow.

Pennebaker, J. W. & Banasik, B. L (1997). On the creation and maintenance of collective memories: History as Social Psychology. In J. W. Pennebaker, D. Paez & B. Rimé, (Eds.), *Collective Memory of Political Events* (pp. 3–19). Mahwah, NJ: Lawrence Erlbaum Associates.

Pennebaker, J. W., Paez, D. & Rimé, B., (Eds.), (1997). *Collective Memory of Political Events*. Mahwah, NJ: Lawrence Erlbaum Associates.

Pennebaker, J. W., Rentfrow, J., Davis, M., Paez, D. & Bellelli, G. (2000). The Social Psychology of History: Defining the most important events of the last 10,100, and 1000 years http://homepage.psy.utexas.edu/homepage/faculty/Pennebaker/Reprints/Millennium.doc

Pillemer, D. B. (1984). Flashbulb memories of the assassination attempt on President Reagan. *Cognition*, 16, 63–80.

Price, V. (1989). Social identification and public opinion: Effects of communicating group conflict. *Public Opinion Quarterly*, 532, 197–224.

Proust, M. (1913). *Du côté de chez Swann*. Paris: Grasset.

Ribot, T. (1882). *Diseases of memory: An essay in the Positive Psychology*. New York: Appleton.

Ricoeur, P. (1998). *Dar Ratsel der Vergangenheit. – Vergessen – Verzeihen* [Remember, forget, forgive]. Gottinghen: Wallstein.

Rimé, B., Finkenauer, C., Luminet, O., Zech, E. & Philippot, P. (1998). Social sharing of emotion: New evidence and new questions. In W. Stroebe & M. Hewstone, (Eds.), *European Review of Social Psychology* (vol. 8, pp. 145–189). Chichester: Wiley & Sons Ltd.

Robinson, J. A. (1986). Autobiographical memory: An historical prologue. In D. C. Rubin, (Ed.), *Autobiographical memory* (pp. 19–24). Cambridge, UK: Cambridge University Press.

Robinson, W. P. (1996). *Deceit, delusion, and Detection*. Thousand Oaks, CA: Sage.

Rosa, A., Bellelli, G. & Bakhurst, D., (Eds.), (2000). *Memoria colectiva e identidad social* [Collective Memory and social identity]. Madrid: Biblioteca Nueva.

Rubin, D., Rahhal, T. A. & Poon, L. W. (1998). Things earned in early adulthood are remembered best. *Memory & Cognition*, 26, 3–19.

Salomon, G. & Nevo, B., (Eds.), (2002). *Peace Education: The Concept, Principles and Practices Around the World*. Mahwah, NJ: Lawrence Erlbaum Associates.

Schuman, H. & Rieger, C. (1992). Collective memory and collective memories. In M. A. Conway, D. C. Rubin, H. Spinnler & W. Wagenaar, (Eds.), *Theoretical perspectives on autobiographical memory* (pp. 323–336). Dordrecht, The Netherlands: Kluwer.

Schuman, H., & Scott, J. (1989). Generations and collective memory. *American Sociological Review*, 54, 359–381.

Scott, J. & Zac, L. (1993). Collective memories in Britain and the United States. *Public Opinion Quarterly*, 57, 315–331.

Shum, M. S. (1998). The role of temporal landmarks in autobiographical memory processes. *Psychological Bulletin*, 124, 423–442.

Silverstein, B. (1992). The psychology of enemy images. In S. Staub & P. Green, (Eds.), *Psychology and social responsibility: Facing global challenges* (pp. 145–162). New York: New York University Press.

Tait, R. & Silver, R. C. (1989). Coming to terms with major negative life events. In J. S. Uleman & J. A. Bargh, (Eds.), *Unintended thoughts* (pp. 351–382). New York: Guilford.

Tavuchis, N. (1991). *Mea culpa. A Sociology of apology and reconciliation*. Stanford, CA: Stanford University Press.

Valsiner, J. (1987). *Culture and the Development of Children's Actions. A Cultural-Historical Theory of Developmental Psychology*. Chichester: John Wiley and Sons.

Weaver, C. A., III. (1993). Do You Need a "Flash" to Form a Flashbulb Memory? *Journal of Experimental Psychology: General*, 122, 39–46.

Withehouse, H. (2002). *Arguments and Icons. Divergent modes of Religiosity*. Oxford: Oxford University Press.

Wright, D. B. (1993). Recall of the Hillsborough disaster over time: Systematic biases of 'Flashbulb' Memories. *Applied Cognitive Psychology*, 7, 129–138.

CHAPTER 32

Collective Memory

James V. Wertsch

Collective memory is an obvious and important topic for socio-cultural psychology to consider, but it has received scant attention to date, largely because it has been so little conceptualized. It is just one of several terms widely invoked in the new "memory industry" (Klein, 2000), terms such as "public memory" (Bodnar, 1991), "social memory" (Burke, 1989; Connerton, 1989), "bodily memory" (Young, 1996), and "historical consciousness" (Seixas, 2004).

Difficulties in explicating collective memory stem from the fact that it and related notions have been interpreted in a variety of ways in several disciplines, including anthropology (Cole, 2001), history (e.g., Novick, 1999), psychology (Middleton & Brown, this volume; Pennebaker, Paez, & Rimé, 1997), and sociology (e.g., Schuman, Schwartz, & D'Arcy, 2005). Further complications arise from the fact that collective memory is part of widespread, and often hotly contested debates in the public arena and the popular media. Consider, for example, disputes in Russia and the Baltics over how the Molotov-Ribbentrop Pact of 1939 should be remembered, unresolved differen-

ces in the United States over the meaning of slavery, and the conflict in Argentina over how the "disappeared" should be remembered. In all cases, these debates are intense, and they have been going on for decades, yet there is little understanding of what kind of memory is involved.

In short, collective memory is a notion that is widely invoked and discussed, but little understood. Instead of growing out of a commonly accepted definition, it is used by many different parties who often have quite different notions in mind, and these notions may overlap, conflict, or simply be unrelated. Socio-cultural psychology can play a major role in this context because it provides a kind of interdisciplinary space where various perspectives can be brought into productive contact. Instead of formulating issues in terms of whether one or another theoretical perspective is correct, thereby dismissing others in the process, the point is to identify parallels and complementarities in the insights, methods, and findings of various disciplines.

Formulating collective memory from a socio-cultural perspective requires two basic conceptual moves. First, the notion of mediation must take a central place in the formulation; this is what makes it possible to avoid some conceptual pitfalls and harness various disciplinary perspectives in an integrated fashion. Second, a few key conceptual oppositions – as opposed to a rigid definitions – are needed to guide the discussion in a productive way. These oppositions create the outlines of a conceptual field that will allow profitable engagement rather than exclusionary efforts to arrive at some sort of overriding truth.

The oppositions explored in the sections that follow are: strong vs. distributed accounts of collective memory, collective versus individual memory, history versus memory, and specific narratives versus schematic narrative templates. The notion of mediation runs throughout the discussions of these oppositions and provides a way to draw together the various threads of the discussion of collective memory.

Strong Versus Distributed Accounts of Collective Memory

When discussing collective memory, it is all too tempting to formulate issues in terms of loose analogies with memory in the individual. Many discussions of America's memory about Vietnam, for example, seem to presuppose that America is some sort of large being that has intentions, desires, memories, and beliefs just as individuals do. Such presuppositions lie behind assertions such as, "America's collective memory of Vietnam makes it very sensitive to charges that Iraq may be a quagmire."

Assumptions on this score have often been the object of legitimate critiques. Frederic Bartlett, the father of modern memory studies in psychology, was critical of the "more or less absolute likeness [that] has been drawn between social groups and the human individual" (1995, p. 293), and he warned that collectives – as collectives – do not have some sort of memory in their own right. Bartlett's critique was aimed at the French sociologist and psychologist Maurice

Halbwachs, the figure who is usually credited with founding the modern study of collective memory. As Mary Douglas (1980) has noted, Bartlett may have misinterpreted Halbwachs in this debate, but his general observation is on the mark and worth understanding.

Bartlett himself was quite concerned with the social dimension of memory. Indeed much of his argument was about how the memory of individuals is fundamentally influenced by the social context in which they function. One of his central claims in this regard was that "social organisation gives a persistent framework into which all detailed recall must fit, and it very powerfully influences both the manner and the matter of recall" (1995, p. 296). What he espoused in the end was a position that recognizes "memory *in* the group, [but] not memory *of* the group" (p. 294).

Misguided assumptions about memory "*of* the group" constitute what can be termed a "strong version" of collective memory (Wertsch, 2002). When made explicit, these claims have usually been rejected, but implicit analogies between individual and collective processes continue to slip into the discussion at many points.

An alternative that recognizes memory in the group without slipping into questionable assumptions about memory of the group is a "distributed version" of collective memory. From this perspective, memory is viewed as being distributed: (a) socially in small group interaction, as well as (b) "instrumentally" in the sense that it involves instruments of memory (Wertsch, 2002). In the case of social distribution, for example, Mary Sue Weldon (2001) has examined the "collaborative remembering" that occurs when groups of individuals work together to recall information or events from the past.

Instrumental distribution, which is the primary focus of what follows, involves active agents, on the one hand, and cultural tools such as calendars, written records, computers, and narratives, on the other. It is a notion that derives from the ideas of Lev Vygotsky about the "instrumental method" in psychology (Vygotsky, 1981) and ideas about human action such as those outlined by Aleksei N. Leont'ev (1981). Vygotsky's motivation for introducing mediation was to move beyond the "methodological individualism" (Lukes, 1977) that characterized the psychology of his day and continues to be part of the discipline now. His basic point was that human action, including mental processes, can be understood only by understanding the tools and signs incorporated into it. This attempt to avoid individualistic reductionism should not be taken to amount to a kind of "instrumental reductionism" in which active agents are left out of the picture. Instead, the point is to approach human action, including thinking, remembering, and other mental processes, from the perspective of how it involves an irreducible tension between active agent and cultural instrument (Wertsch, 1998).

What this means for the study of collective memory is that the focus must be on agents actively using cultural tools rather than on "atomistic" individuals (Taylor, 1989), on the one hand, or cognitive instruments in and of themselves, on the other. The resulting emphasis on mediated *action* means that it would be preferable to speak of collective remembering rather than collective memory, and in this connection it is noteworthy that Bartlett's classic work has "remembering" rather than "memory," in the title, and Middleton and Brown (2005) similarly insist on a focus on remembering. With this in mind, the term "remembering" will often be used in what follows, but the widespread practice of using "memory" and "collective memory" means that it is nearly impossible to avoid these terms altogether.

Given this focus on mediated action and instrumentally distributed collective memory, a crucial consideration is the type of instruments, or "cultural tools" (Wertsch, 1998) used to remember the past. Several different instruments, each suggesting a particular form of remembering, have been investigated by various scholars. While making no attempt to provide a complete inventory of these cultural tools, it is worth noting a basic divide between two forms of mediation that have emerged in this discussion.

This is the divide between explicit linguistic forms, especially narratives, that represent the past, on the one hand, and forms of mediation that rely less on explicit linguistic representation and more on embodied practices, on the other.

In many accounts of collective remembering it is automatically assumed that narrative or other linguistic forms are the basic tools involved, and indeed language will be the focus of much of what follows. However, it is worth noting the critique of this assumption that has been leveled by analysts such as Paul Connerton. In *How Societies Remember* (1989) Connerton noted the strong bias toward assuming recollection is "something that is inscribed." He viewed this as a limitation that derives from a linguistic bias in hermeneutic scholarship, arguing that "although bodily practices are in principle included as possible objects of hermeneutic inquiry, in practice hermeneutics has taken inscription as its privileged object" (p. 4).

Connerton built on this critique by outlining a notion of "habit memory," the rationale being, "If there is such a thing as social memory . . . , we are likely to find it in commemorative ceremonies; but commemorative ceremonies prove to be commemorative only in so far as they are performative; performativity cannot be thought of without a concept of habit; and habit cannot be thought without a notion of bodily automatisms" (pp. 4–5). Like Halbwachs, Connerton derives crucial aspects of his account of memory from the social theory of Emile Durkheim, something that led to a focus on ritual and ritualistic practice. This line of reasoning bears many similarities with that outlined by Middleton and Brown (this volume).

Notions of habit memory, ritual, and so forth clearly deserve a place in the study of collective remembering. Nonetheless, the bulk of the work on this topic has focused on linguistic mediation, especially in the form of narrative, and this will be the focus in what follows. Jerome Bruner (1990) has noted that narratives occupy a particularly important place in the "tool kit" of human cognition in general, and they can also be expected to be a crucial cultural tool for representing the past, both in history and in memory. From this perspective, what makes collective memory collective is the fact that members of a group share the same narrative resources. By harnessing and discussing these narrative resources, the group is transformed into what Brian Stock (1990) has called a "textual community."

The centrality of narratives and other forms of linguistic mediation in a distributed version of collective remembering has several implications. To say that narratives and other forms of linguistic mediation do some of the remembering for us would suggest the sort of instrumental reductionism rejected earlier, but this way of formulating things does provide a reminder of how central cultural tools are in the process.

The philosopher and literary analyst Mikhail Mikhailovich Bakhtin provides some insight into the nature of these claims. In his analysis of Dostoevsky's novels, Bakhtin outlined some ways that the Russian author was influenced by historically situated genres. In particular, Bakhtin argued for the influence of Menippean satire on Dostoevsky's writing. The origins of this genre are traced back to Menippius of Gadara an author from third century Greece, who developed a literary form characterized by its mockery of serious forms, unexpected digressions, and humorous exaggeration.

As is the case in virtually all instances of linguistic mediation, in order to produce utterances (in this case written ones) Dostoevsky had to employ existing forms, and this is the first point worth nothing in Bakhtin's analysis. The very act of speaking and writing involves the use of words and other linguistic forms that have been used by others, the result being that every utterance is inherently situated in socio-cultural space.

In pursuing this line of reasoning, Bakhtin went on to argue that words and other linguistic forms such as genres have a sort of memory of their own. This is a point that applies to utterances in general, but especially to the stylized writing of a novel.

"Does this mean that Dostoevsky proceeded *directly* and *consciously* from the ancient menippea? Of course not. In no sense was he a *stylizer* of ancient genres. Dostoevsky linked up with the chain of a given generic tradition at that point where it passed through his own time ... Speaking somewhat paradoxically, one could say that it was not Dostoevsky's subjective memory, but the objective memory of the very genre in which he worked, that preserved the peculiar feature of the ancient menippea" (1984, p. 121).

The implication is that just as Dostoevsky's writing was shaped by the "objective memory" of genres with their long and complex history, collective remembering is shaped by forms of linguistic mediation, especially in the form of narratives. These narratives with their long history of use are often not part of the "subjective memory" of the people who use them, but they often introduce a powerful perspective that shapes the memories we have, even though we are not consciously aware of this.

Collective Versus Individual Remembering

The study of collective and individual remembering differs greatly in terms of the disciplines involved, the methods employed, and the findings accumulated. Individual memory has been a central topic in psychology for over a century, and the result is that relatively well-established and accepted terms and methods have emerged. To be sure, there are major disagreements among psychologists on many issues, but their discussion begins with the assumption that terms like "short-term memory," "long-term memory," "semantic memory," and "episodic memory" can be used with some shared understanding.

There are two additional defining features of the psychological study of individual memory worth noting when contrasting it with the study of collective memory. The first is the assumption that memory can be studied in isolation from other aspects of mental life, and the second is that a basic metric for assessment is accuracy. Assuming that memory can be studied in isolation is consistent with views of it as a faculty or specialized skill, sometimes coupled with claims about specific regions of the brain or neural networks. But even more important than such conceptual commitments are the methods employed in psychology to study memory. As in the study of cognition, attention, and other aspects of mental functioning, the disciplinary norm for examining memory is to employ experimental settings where variables can be controlled and hypotheses tested.

As outlined below, this control of variables approach introduces some important limitations to the study of remembering. But it has yielded major conceptual and empirical breakthroughs. As an example of this consider the phenomenon of "memory distortion" outlined by Henry Roediger and Kathleen McDermott (1995). Using carefully controlled lists of words and experimental conditions, these researchers demonstrated that subjects are likely to systematically, but falsely recognize certain words in recall and recognition experiments. For instance, when presented with a list such as: *door, glass, pane, ledge, sill, house, open, curtain, frame, view, breeze, sash, screen*, and *shutter*, subjects are likely to "remember" that *window* was in the list – even when they are explicitly warned that they would be tempted to include incorrect items.

Because the experimental method employed by Roediger and McDermott is grounded in the careful control of variables, it was able to produce a reliable finding that would otherwise have been hard to substantiate. As is the case for much of the psychological research on memory, the methodological standards employed in this case are linked to the assumption that memory is a distinct phenomenon that can be studied in relative isolation from other mental functions. From this perspective it is entirely legitimate, indeed preferable to study memory in and of itself, and it is also assumed that there are settings in which individuals can engage in remembering strictly for the sake of remembering.

Such assumptions stand in clear opposition to ideas that guide most discussions of collective memory. Instead of assuming that one can find and study remembering as an isolated phenomenon that occurs strictly for the sake of remembering, the guiding assumption is that it is invariably bound up with something else. Partly for this reason, collective remembering seldom lends itself to being studied with a methodology grounded in the control of variables. Instead, it is viewed as existing in a complex setting and in the service of providing a "usable past." The usable past is almost invariably part of some identity project such as mobilizing a nation to come together in the face of a perceived threat. As such, collective remembering is taken to be part of some broader agenda, and any attempt to consider it in isolation or view it as amenable to an experimental paradigm would be viewed as destroying the very phenomenon to be studied.

These observations are related to an additional point that distinguishes the study of individual and collective memory – what will be termed here the "accuracy criterion." The very notion of memory presupposes some representation (in the broadest sense) of the past, and it is usually assumed that this representation makes some claim to being accurate. As already noted in the case of collective remembering, however, other competing functions and hence other criteria for assessing the appropriateness and power of memory may be involved. The issue, then, is the degree to which accuracy is a criterion by which to assess a memory performance.

In the psychological study of individual memory the accuracy criterion takes a front seat. This is not to claim that psychologists believe individual memory to be particularly accurate. If anything, several decades of research have shown myriad ways that memory can be *in*accurate. The power of schemas, implicit theories, encoding biases, and so forth to systematically reduce the accuracy of memory has been well documented. But the point remains that the basic metric by which memory is usually assessed in psychology is accuracy. One cannot talk about memory "distortion" (Schacter, 1995), "false" memory (Schacter, 1996, chapter 9), or many other major topics in the field without presupposing accurate representation of past events as a starting point.

Things stand somewhat differently when it comes to the study of collective remembering. As already noted, most research traditions concerned with this topic have assumed that collective remembering can only be understood as part of a larger whole. For example, in studies that focus on socially distributed (as opposed to instrumentally distributed) memory, David Middleton and his colleagues (Middleton & Edwards, 1990) have argued that remembering often occurs in the context of the discursive negotiation of social differences and identity. And in another line of research concerning "public memory," John Bodnar (1992) views remembering as part of a struggle between "official culture" and "vernacular culture" in a societal setting.

The larger picture of which collective memory is a part is usually formulated in terms of conflict and negotiation rather than approximation to accuracy. Such conflict and negotiation occur in the social and political sphere (Bodnar, 1992; Wertsch, 2002) of "memory politics" (Hacking, 1996) and are carried out in the service of providing a usable past that serves some identity project. This is not to say that accuracy is not important or is not assumed by those doing the remembering, but it does mean that accuracy is of secondary importance and may be sacrificed to the extent required to serve other functions.

A psychologist whose research of individual memory provides a sort of bridge to this discussion in collective memory studies is Martin Conway (e.g., Conway & Playdell-Pearce, 2000). In contrast to many analyses in psychology that assume memory can be studied in isolation from other aspects of mental life, Conway and Playdell-Pearce have argued for the need to examine autobiographical memory as part of a larger system of self and life goals. Another researcher who has developed a related line of research is Michael Ross (1989), who has argued that the "implicit theories" we have about ourselves shape our autobiographical memory. Like many psychologists, Ross assumes that remembering is often not particularly accurate, at least with regard to details, but he goes beyond many others in viewing the recall of personal histories as being systematically shaped by powerful biasing factors, including implicit theories.

In sum, the study of collective memory stands in contrast to research on individual memory in several ways, many of which have to do with disciplinary differences and the methods associated with them. Psychological research on individual memory has tended to rely on laboratory methods that allow for controlled experimentation, and this has encouraged it to focus on memory as an isolated mental process. Furthermore, it has encouraged the privileging of the criterion of accuracy when formulating research questions. In contrast, the study of collective remembering has tended to focus on how memory is part of social and political processes such as negotiating group identity, and this has led it to view remembering from the perspective of contestation and negotiation. This focus, in turn, has placed issues of accuracy in a secondary position.

The different methods employed in the study individual and collective remembering have given rise to different notions of what remembering is, but several scholars have provided analyses that seem to serve both orientations. Perhaps the most prescient of these was provided by Frederic Bartlett, the father of the modern memory studies in psychology. He emphasized that the active processes of remembering involves an "effort after meaning" (1995, p.20), a formulation that applies to the kind of laboratory experiments by Roediger and McDermott as well as the account of public memory outlined by Bodnar.

History Versus Memory

The nature and understanding of history and memory have themselves undergone transformation over the past several centuries. In particular, the rise of mass literacy and the mental habits associated with it have had a profound impact on human memory. Literacy makes possible what cognitive scientists call the "off-loading" of information (Bechtel & Abrahamsen, 1991) into written texts, and the history of this process has been explored by analysts such as Malcolm Donald (1991). The crucial point in what follows, however, is that the emergence of literacy – especially its widespread dissemination during the Enlightenment – has been associated with privileging new forms of critical thought and discourse. This, in turn, has been associated with a new way of representing the past.

This way of representing the past is usually termed "history" and stands in opposition to memory. In the 1920s Halbwachs (1980, 1992) formulated a version of this opposition, and in one form or another it continues to be a part of the discussion today. As Kerwin Lee Klein formulates this point, "much current historiography pits memory against history even though few authors openly claim to be engaged in building a world in which memory can serve as an alternative to history" (2000, p. 128).

As a starting point for discussing this distinction, consider the following comments by the historian Peter Novick (1999), who built on the ideas of Halbwachs to argue:

> To understand something historically is to be aware of its complexity, to have sufficient detachment to see it from multiple perspectives, to accept the ambiguities, including moral ambiguities, of protagonists' motives and behavior. Collective memory simplifies; sees events from a single, committed perspective; is impatient with ambiguities of any kind; reduces events to mythic archetypes. (pp. 3–4)

Contemporary discussions of how history differs from memory have been at the heart of recent debates carried on by Pierre Nora (1989), who has argued that "real memory" has been largely pushed aside, if not eradicated by the practices of creating critical historical accounts of the past. The result is that "we speak so much of memory because there is so little of it left" (p. 7), and we have a felt need to create *lieux de mémoire* (sites of memory) "because there are no longer *milieux de mémoire*, real environments of memory" (p. 7).

In Nora's view, memory and history are not just different; they stand in fundamental opposition. For him memory "remains in permanent evolution" and is "unconscious of its successive deformations, vulnerable to manipulation" (p. 8). In contrast, "history, because it is an intellectual and secular production, calls for analysis and criticism . . . At the heart of history is a critical discourse that is antithetical to spontaneous memory" (pp. 8–9). The nature of this opposition is such that "history is perpetually suspicious of memory, and its true mission is to suppress and destroy it" (p. 9). Nora's line of reasoning does not entail that analytic history simply supplants memory. Instead, the implicit contrast with history resulted in an ongoing differentiation and redefinition of what memory is, and the struggle over this issue continues in the renewed debates that have been carried out over the past few decades.

The upshot of this ongoing differentiation of history from memory is that it is often quite difficult to categorize an account of the past unequivocally as either one or other. For example, official histories produced by modern states include elements of collective remembering as well as history. Indeed, scholars such as Louis Mink (1978) and Hayden White (1987) have raised questions about whether *any* representation of the past – including those generated by academic historians – can be genuinely distanced and objective and hence whether this distinction can be maintained.

But even those who are most critical of the distinction between history and memory accept that it must be accepted in some form. For example, Novick (1988), a figure who has produced a major critique of the "noble dream" of objectivity in history, contrasts history's willingness to deal with complexity and multiple perspectives with the tendency of collective memory to simplify, to see events from a "single committed perspective," and to be "impatient with ambiguities of any kind" (1999, pp. 3–4).

In developing his version of the distinction between history and collective memory Novick goes so far as to assert that the latter "is in crucial senses ahistorical, even antihistorical" (p. 3). This is so because:

> *Historical consciousness, by its nature, focuses on the* historicity *of events – that they took place then and not now that they grew out of circumstances different from those that now obtain. Memory, by contrast, has no sense of the passage of time; it denies the "pastness" of its objects and insists on their continuing presence. Typically a collective memory, at least a significant collective memory, is understood to express some eternal or essential truth about the group – usually tragic. A memory, once established, comes to define that eternal truth, and, along with it, an eternal identity, for the members of the group. (p. 4)*

Recent studies of commemoration, a practice closely tied to collective memory, have made similar points about the tendency to eschew ambiguity and to present the past from a single committed perspective. In his discussion of the distinction between the commemorative voice and the historical voice in history museum exhibits, for example, Edward Linenthal (1996) touched on this point. He did so in connection with the dispute over the Enola Gay exhibit in the National Air and Space Museum in 1995, a case that escalated into a "history war" (Linenthal & Engelhardt, 1996). His analysis led Linenthal to argue that accepting a single committed perspective results in viewing the museum as a "temple" (p. 23), whereas encouraging the exploration of ambiguity presupposes that the museum is a "forum." In the museum as a forum there is a tendency to take into consideration the "complicated motives of actions and consequences often hardly considered at the moment of the event itself" (pp. 9–10). Instead of being a "reverently held story," it should involve

"later reappraisal" (p. 10) of these complicated motives, actions, and consequences.

In another analysis of the forces that gave rise to the history wars around the Enola Gay exhibit, the historian John Dower (1996) provided additional insight into how history differs from commemoration. Specifically, he discussed "two notions that most historians take for granted: that controversy is inherent in any ongoing process of historical interpretation, and that policymaking is driven by multiple considerations and imperatives" (p. 80). In formulating ways in which commemoration and collective memory stand in opposition to history Dower outlined a notion of heroic narrative as being inherently hostile to the assumptions guiding the historian.

> *Heroic narratives demand a simple, unilinear story line. In popular retellings, that simple line often takes the form of an intimate human-interest story . . . In the case of the atomic bombs, the American narrative almost invariably gravitates to Colonel Paul W. Tibbets, Jr., who piloted the famous plane, and his crew – brave and loyal men, as they surely were. And the pilot and his crew tell us, truthfully, what we know they will: that they carried out their mission without a second thought in order to save their comrades and help end the war. Such accounts . . . tell us little if anything about how top-level decisions were made – about who moved these men, who gave them their orders, and why. To seriously ask these questions is to enter the realm of multiple imperatives. (pp. 80–81)*

By way of summarizing these points, consider a set of oppositions that can be used to distinguish collective memory from history. At the risk of reinforcing the mistaken impression that the two can be easily and neatly separated, these are set out below. It is essential to keep in mind that the oppositions outlined here are *tendencies* and *aspirations* of collective memory and history rather than ironclad attributes and that the opposing tendencies often operate in tension with one another.

Collective Memory	History
"Subjective"	"Objective"
• single committed perspective	• distanced from any particular perspective
• reflects a particular group's social framework	• reflects no particular social framework
• unself-conscious	• critical, reflective stance
• impatient with ambiguity about motives and the interpretation of events	• recognizes ambiguity
Denies "pastness" of events	Focus on historicity
• links the past with the present	• differentiates the past from the present
• ahistorical, antihistorical	• views past events as "then and not now"
Commemorative voice	Historical voice
• museum as a temple	• museum as a forum
• unquestionable heroic narratives	• disagreement, change, controversy as part of historical interpretation

Specific Narratives Versus Schematic Narrative Templates

As noted earlier, narratives provide a crucial form of linguistic mediation in a distributed version of collective remembering. This is part of a larger claim about how central narrative is to human consciousness, something that has been explored by scholars such as Bruner (1990) and the moral philosopher Alisdair MacIntyre (1984). In the latter's view, "man is in his actions, and practice, as well as in his fictions, essentially a story-telling animal... Hence there is no way to give us an understanding of any society, including our own, except through the stock of stories which constitute its initial dramatic resources" (p. 216).

In order to build a general account of the role of narrative in collective remembering, it is important to differentiate between various senses of narrative, something that is extremely difficult as witnessed by writings on the topic. Rather than trying to review the various definitions that have been put forth, the focus here will be on one distinction that is particularly useful in the discussion of collective remembering. This is the distinction and between "specific narratives" and "schematic narrative templates." Under the heading of specific narratives I have in mind items in MacIntyre's stock of stories such as "stories about wicked stepmothers, lost children, good but misguided kings, wolves that suckle twin boys, youngest sons who receive no inheritance but must make their own way in the world and eldest sons who waste their inheritance on riotous living and go into exile to live with the swine" (p. 216). These are narratives in the Western tradition that have specific settings, characters, and events.

Such specific narratives contrast with more generalized, abstract versions, or what can be termed "schematic narrative templates" (Wertsch, 2002). The notion of a schematic narrative template derives from several influences, the most important of which is perhaps the Russian folklorist Vladimir Propp (1968). In developing his account of Russian folk tales, Propp argued for the need to focus on the generalized "functions" that characterize an entire set of narratives, as opposed to the particular events and actors that occur in specific ones. From this perspective, "recurrent constants," or functions "of dramatis personae are basic components of the tale" (p. 21). This focus on abstract function means that several specific events and actors may fit under the heading of a function in a narrative. In this view, *"Functions of characters serve as stable, constant elements of a tale, independent of how and by whom they are fulfilled"* (p. 21, italics in the original).

Propp identified an extensive network of generalized functions, including items such

as "THE VILLAIN RECEIVES INFORMA-
TION ABOUT HIS VICTIM" (p. 28) and
"THE VILLAIN IS DEFEATED" (p. 53).
When exploring the implications of Propp's
ideas for collective remembering, what is
crucial is his general line of reasoning rather
than his detailed claims about particular
functions – claims that were developed in
connection with Russian folk tales.

Switching from folklore to psychology, a
related line of reasoning may be found in the
writings of Bartlett (1995). Although there
is no reason to assume that he was familiar
with Propp's writings, Bartlett did develop
some strikingly similar claims. In his view
remembering is usually more of a "constructive" process (p. 312) than a product of stimuli, and this led him to examine the generalized patterns or "schemata" brought to
this process by the agent doing the constructing.

The writings of Propp and Bartlett contribute different points to an understanding of schematic narrative templates. The
common points that can be extracted from
their ideas are: (a) narrative templates are
schematic in the sense that they concern
abstract, generalized functions of the sort
that Propp discussed in his structural analysis
of folk tales or that Bartlett discussed under
the heading of schema-like knowledge structures; (b) the organizing form is narrative,
a point that is explicit in Propp's writings
and consistent with what Bartlett proposed;
and (c) the notion of template is involved
because these abstract structures can underlie an entire set of specific narratives, each of
which has a particular setting, cast of characters, dates, and so forth.

The writings of Propp and Bartlett suggest a couple of additional properties worth
keeping in mind when dealing with narrative
templates. First, they are not some sort of
universal archetypes. Instead, they are specific to particular narrative traditions that
can be expected to differ from one socio-
cultural setting to another. And second, narrative templates are not readily available to
consciousness. As Bartlett noted they are
used in an "unreflective, unanalytical and
unwitting manner" (1995, p. 45).

The writings of Vygotsky (1987), Bakhtin
(1986), and others suggest that schematic
narrative templates emerge out of the repeated use of standard narrative forms used in
the family, schools, popular media, and elsewhere. The narrative templates that emerge
from this process are effective in shaping
what we can say and think because: a) they
are largely unnoticed, or "transparent" to
those employing them, and b) they are a
fundamental part of the identity claims of
a group. The result is that these templates
act as an unnoticed, yet very powerful "co-
author" when we attempt to simply tell
what "really happened" in the past (Wertsch,
2002, chapter 1).

Schematic Narrative Templates:
An Illustration

Consider a schematic narrative template
that has been outlined by Wertsch (2002).
It is one that occupies a place of particular importance in Russians' understanding of crucial historical episodes, and as
such it imposes a basic plot structure on
a range of specific characters, events, and
circumstances. This is the "triumph-over-
alien-forces" schematic narrative template
and includes the following elements:

1. an "initial situation" (Propp, 1968, p. 26)
    in which the Russian people are living
    in a peaceful setting where they are no
    threat to others is disrupted by:
2. the initiation of trouble or aggression by
    alien forces, which leads to:
3. a time of crisis and great suffering by the
    Russian people, which is:
4. overcome by the triumph over the alien
    force by the Russian people, acting hero-
    ically and alone.

At first glance it may appear that there is
nothing peculiarly Russian about this narrative template. For example, by replacing
"Russian" with "American," it would seem
to provide a foundation for American collective memory of the Japanese attack on Pearl
Harbor in 1941. The claim is not that this

narrative template is available only to members of the Russian narrative tradition or that it is the only one available to this group. However, there are several indications that this template plays a particularly important role and takes on a particular form in the Russian narrative tradition and collective remembering.

The first of these concerns its ubiquity. Whereas the United States and many other societies have accounts of past events that are compatible with this narrative template, it seems to be employed more widely in the Russian tradition than elsewhere. In this connection consider the comments of Musatova (2002) about the cultural history of Russia. In remarking on the fate of having to learn "the lessons of conquests and enslavement by foreigners" (p. 139), she lists several groups who are viewed as having perpetrated similar events in Russia's history: "Tartars, Germans, Swedes, Poles, Turks, Germans again" (p. 139). She does this in a way that suggests that while the particular actors, dates, and setting may change, the same basic plot applies to all these episodes. They have all been stamped out of the same basic template.

Some observers would go so far as to say that the triumph-over-alien-forces narrative template is *the* underlying story of Russian collective remembering, and this provides a basic point of contrast with other groups. For example, it is strikingly different from American items such as the "mystique of Manifest Destiny" (Lowenthal, 1994, p. 53) or a "quest for freedom" narrative (Wertsch, 1994; Wertsch and O'Connor, 1994). The triumph-over-alien-forces template clearly plays a central role in Russian collective memory, even in instances where it would not seem relevant, at least to those who are not "native speakers" (Lotman & Uspenskii, 1985) of this tradition.

As Wertsch (2003) has argued, this schematic narrative template has had a powerful impact on the state-sponsored official history in Soviet and post-Soviet Russia. It has yielded a striking continuity in this history (which, like all state-sponsored official histories, functions as part of an identity project and hence incorporates ingredients

of memory as well as history). For example, it provides a foundation for interpreting and then "repairing" accounts of episodes such as the Molotov-Ribbentrop Pact that would otherwise seem to be exceptions to the basic narrative template.

The Social Organization of Collective Remembering

By definition collective remembering involves a collective of some sort, and hence social processes. But the organization of these processes is envisioned quite differently by various scholars. The distributed version of collective remembering outlined above begins with the assumption that a memory community is built around a shared set of textual means, especially narratives. This does not mean, however, that everyone in the community has equal knowledge or beliefs about these narrative texts, a point that echoes the claims of Brian Stock (1990) that "textual communities" are shaped by internal differentiation and institutionalization as by the texts around which they are formed. Instead a variety of social and political dynamics typically give rise to a complex, differentiated collective.

In some cases scholars highlight these dynamics to such a degree that collective remembering is viewed primarily as a matter of political negotiation and contestation. For example, in his account of "public memory" the historian Bodnar (1992) views remembering primarily in terms of the struggle between "official culture" and "vernacular culture," one result being that the accuracy criterion that guides such a central role in psychological studies plays a distinctly secondary role.

Considerations of social structure have long been part of the sociological study of collective remembering. For example, in his classic article "The Problem of Generations," first published in 1928, Karl Mannheim (1952) argued that each generation develops a distinctive picture of political and social reality depending on the experiences it has during the formative years of young adulthood. Included in this line of reasoning was the claim that a generation is a social rather than a biological construct, and one upshot of this is that distinctive generations may not appear in traditional societies where novel events may be rare and change slow.

Howard Schuman and Jacqueline Scott (1989) used Mannheim's notions to formulate hypotheses about different generations would recall events like World War II, the Vietnam War, and the Civil Rights Era. They found that American subjects recalled as especially important events that occurred in their teens or early twenties, hence supporting the generational hypothesis that memories of important political events and social changes are structured by age.

Complementing such studies in sociology is research in psychology on reminiscence. Studies by Joseph Fitzgerald (1988, 1995) and others have resulted in account of the "reminiscence bump" that challenges usual assumptions about how memories decay over the life span. Instead of a steady decline in memories for more distant events, this research has consistently shown that older adults' memories for events that occurred during their young adult years are more detailed than are memories for events that happened before or after this formative age. The cause of the reminiscence bump is still being debated, but analyses have focused on issues of self and identity development (Conway & Playdell-Pearce, 2000) and crucial stages in the formation of a living narrative (Fitzgerald, 1988). Regardless of the final outcome of this debate in life span psychology, this is one topic on which this discipline has the potential of coming into productive collaboration with sociological analyses of collective remembering.

More recently, Howard Schuman, Barry Schwartz, and Nancy D'Arcy (2005) have outlined other dimensions of social structure that influence collective remembering. Analyzing responses from a national sample of Americans, they identified varying ideas about Columbus and his place in American history based on race, religion, and nonnormative critical stance toward the United States. For example, they concluded that "among white respondents, the characterization of Columbus as villainous draws on a larger receptivity to non-normative beliefs generally, presumably in a liberal or radical direction" (p. 16).

What is perhaps most interesting about the study by Schuman and colleagues, however, is how little change there has been in Americans' ideas about Columbus over the past few decades, even in the face of radically new, critical portrayals of him in connection with the 500th anniversary of his arrival in the Americas. They report that "most Americans continue to admire Columbus because, as tradition puts it, "he discovered America," though only a small number of mainly older respondents speak of him in the heroic terms common in earlier years" (p. 2).

This "inertia of memory" noted by Schuman and colleagues is a more general phenomenon that has struck several investigators of collective remembering. For example, Wertsch (2003) has suggested that schematic narrative templates seem to introduce an important element of conservatism that makes collective remembering quite resistant to change. This perhaps should come as no surprise, given the extent to which memory is typically tied to identity and the threat that changes in collective accounts to the past could pose to the group. In contrast to analytic history, where enough countervailing evidence at least on occasion gives rise to a new narrative, collective memory seems to be nearly impervious to such transformation.

This appears to be the case even in the face of major revisions of official history, revisions such as those that occurred in how Columbus is presented in U.S. education (Schuman et al., 2005) and those that occurred in the radical rewriting of Russian history after the Soviet period. In the latter case Wertsch (2002) has documented a radical rewriting of specific narratives, but in the end the triumph-over-alien-forces schematic narrative template has continued to exert such a strong impact on textbook writing and other discussions among the elite that some initial rewritings have been "repaired" by moving back toward this narrative template.

For example, in the post-Soviet period newly acknowledged facts about the Molotov-Ribbentrop Pact of 1939 were clearly embarrassing to the basic premises of this narrative template, but these facts did not create the kind of fundamental and permanent transformation in it that had long been envisioned by people in the Baltic countries and elsewhere. Instead, after an initial period of confusion and prevarication, characterized by what Wertsch (2003) termed "narrative rift," this schematic narrative template re-asserted its power and gave rise to reinterpretations that once again were quite consistent with the old narrative template.

Conclusion

Collective remembering is a topic that could play a major role in socio-cultural studies, but to date it has not received the attention it deserves. Given that a major reason for this is that collective remembering has been so little conceptualized, a major goal of this chapter is to lay out a framework for pursuing theoretical and empirical studies. Rather than trying to provide a definition of collective remembering – which would inevitably be overly simple and rigid at this point – the goal has been to lay out a few basic oppositions that shape the current debate: strong versus distributed versions of collective memory, individual versus collective remembering, history versus memory, and specific narratives versus schematic narrative templates.

The strong version of collective memory is often implicitly introduced into discussions of the topic, but it has long been suspect because of its vague formulation. It was criticized by the father of modern psychological studies of memory, Frederic Bartlett, in the 1930s, and despite Bartlett's reading to the contrary, a strong version was also eschewed by the father of collective memory studies, Maurice Halbwachs. Distributed versions of collective memory are grounded in a basic notion of sociocultural psychology: semiotic mediation. From this perspective, collective remembering is viewed as involving active agents employing mediational means such as narratives, and what makes collective memory collective is the fact that a "textual community" shares the same mediational means.

Arguing that collective memory involves semiotic mediation does not in itself differentiate it from individual memory. As outlined in this chapter the study of individual memory has generated an extensive body of literature as well as rough agreement on basic terms, two accomplishments that stand in contrast to the yet underdeveloped field of collective memory studies. Collective and individual memory studies are also separated by their methodological orientations and by the accuracy criterion that underlies most psychological studies of individual memory. In contrast to using accuracy as the starting point, collective memory studies tend to focus on the role of representations of the past in creating and defending identity claims that underlie the formation and maintenance of collectives.

The opposition between history and collective memory is another issue that involves different orientations toward identity claims. In contrast to history, which aspires to provide a balanced, objective account of the past – one that is devoid of identity commitments, collective memory is subjective, grounded in a particular group's perspective, and impatient with ambiguity that might threaten its identity claims. There are those who question whether a distinction between history and collective memory can be maintained in theory, but in practice the contrasting tendencies of the two ways of relating to the past are distinct and must be maintained not only for analytic, but also for ethical reasons. If analytic history were to collapse into collective memory, there would be little other than power relationships to adjudicate disputes about the past, something that would be dangerous for all who subscribe to the Enlightenment project. One way of summarizing this distinction is to note that analytic history is willing, at least in principle, to give up a narrative in light of established evidence, whereas collective memory tends to give up evidence in light of an established narrative.

A final conceptual opposition outlined in this chapter is that between specific narratives and schematic narrative templates. Given the central role of narrative in mediating collective remembering, some differentiation among types of narratives becomes essential, and this one seems particularly useful when trying to understand other aspects of collective memory such as its conservative nature and resistance to change. Evidence suggests that even when the specific narratives shared by a collective undergo significant change, the schematic narrative template that underlies the group's interpretive framework remains largely the same, thus reining in temporary changes at the surface level.

In sum, collective memory is a natural topic for the future of sociocultural studies. This is so first of all because its study is inherently interdisciplinary in ways familiar to sociocultural analysis. Furthermore, once the power of ideas of Vygotsky, Bakhtin, Leont'ev, and others becomes apparent, the appropriateness of sociocultural analysis for the study of collective memory becomes all the more obvious. Indeed, it may only be the interdisciplinary, theoretically rich tradition of sociocultural studies that can offer the possibility of bringing rigorous critical insight into the study of collective remembering in future years.

References

Bakhtin, M. M. (1984). *Problems of Dostoevsky's poetics*. Minneapolis: University of Minnesota Press. (Edited and translated by C. Emerson)

Bakhtin, M. M. (1986). The problem of the text in linguistics, philology, and the human sciences: An experiment in philosophical analysis. In Bakhtin, M.M. (1986). *Speech genres & other late essays*. Austin: University Texas Press, (pp. 103–131). (Translated by Vern W. McGee; edited by Caryl Emerson and Michael Holquist).

Bartlett, F. C. (1995). *Remembering: A study in experimental and social psychology*. Cambridge: Cambridge University Press. (First published in 1932).

Bechtel, W. & Abrahamsen, A. (1991). *Connectionism and the mind: An introduction to parallel processing in networks*. Oxford: Blackwell.

Bodnar, J. (1992). *Remaking America: Public memory, commemoration, and patriotism in the twentieth century*. Princeton: Princeton University Press.

Burke, P. (1989). History as social memory. In T. Butler, (Ed.), *Memory: History, culture and the mind* (pp. 97–113). Oxford: Basil Blackwell.

Bruner, J. (1990). *Acts of meaning*. Cambridge, MA: Harvard University Press.

Chang, I. (1997). *The rape of Nanking: The forgotten holocaust of World War II*. Harmondsworth, England: Penguin.

Cole, J. (2001). *Forget colonialism? Sacrifice and the art of memory in Madagascar*. Berkeley: University of California Press.

Connerton, P. (1989). *How societies remember*. Cambridge: Cambridge University Press.

Conway, M. A. (1997). The inventory of experience: Memory and identity. In J. W. Pennebaker, D. Paez, & B. Rimé, (Eds.), *Collective memory of political events: Social psychological perspectives*, pp. 21–45.

Conway, M. A. & Playdell-Pearce, C. W. (2000). The construction of autobiographical memories in the self-memory system. *Psychological review*, 107(2), 261–288.

Donald, M. (1991). *Origins of the modern mind*. Cambridge, MA: Harvard University Press.

Douglas, M. (1980). Introduction: Maurice Halbwachs (1877–1945). In Halbwachs, M. (1980). *The collective memory*. New York: Harper & Row. (Translated by Francis J. Didder, Jr. and Vida Yazdi Ditter)

Dower, J. W. (1996). Three narratives of our humanity. In Linenthal, E. T. & Engelhardt, T. (Eds.), *History wars: The Enola Gay and other battles for America's past* (pp. 63–96). New York: Metropolitan Books.

Fitzgerald, J. M. (1988). Vivid memories and the reminiscence phenomenon: The role of a self narrative. *Human Development*, 31, 261–273.

Fitzgerald, J. M. (1995). Intersecting meanings of reminiscence in adult development and aging. In D. C. Rubin, (Ed.), *Remembering our past: Studies in autobiographical memory* (pp. 360–383). Cambridge: Cambridge University Press.

Hacking, I. (1996). Memory sciences, memory politics. In P. Antze & M. Lambek, (Eds.), *Tense past: Cultural essays in trauma and memory* (pp. 67–87). New York: Routledge.

Halbwachs, M. (1980). *The collective memory*. New York: Harper & Row. (Translated by Francis J. Didder, Jr. and Vida Yazdi Ditter)

Halbwachs, M. (1992). *On collective memory*. Chicago : University of Chicago Press. (Edited, translated, and with an introduction by Lewis A. Coser)

Klein, K. L. (2000). On the emergence of *memory* in historical discourse. *Representations, 69*, Winter 2000, pp. 127–150.

Leont'ev, A. N. (1981). The problem of activity in psychology. In J.V. Wertsch, (Ed.), *The concept of activity in Soviet psychology* (pp. 37–71). Armonk, NY: M.E. Sharpe.

Linenthal, E. T. (1996). Anatomy of a controversy. In Linenthal, E.T. & Engelhardt, T. (Eds.), (1996). *History wars: The Enola Gay and other battles for America's past* (pp. 9–62). New York: Metropolitan Books.

Linenthal, E.T. & Engelhardt, T. (Eds.), (1996). *History wars: The Enola Gay and other battles for America's past*. New York: Metropolitan Books.

Lotman, Yu. M. & Uspenskii, B.A. (1985). Binary models in the dynamics of Russian culture (to the end of the eighteenth century). In A.D. Nakhimovsky & A.S. Nakhimovsky, (Eds.), *The semiotics of Russian cultural history. Essays by Iurii M. Lotman, Lidiia Ia. Ginsburg, Boris A. Uspenskii* (pp. 30–66). Ithaca: Cornell University Press.

Lowenthal, D. (1994). Identity, heritage, and history. In J.R. Gillis, (Ed.), *Commemorations: The politics of national identity* (pp. 41–57). Princeton: Princeton University Press.

Lukes, S. (1977). Methodological individualism reconsidered. In S. Lukes, (Ed.), *Essays in social theory* (pp. 177–186). New York: Columbia University Press.

MacIntyre, A. (1984). *After virtue: A study in moral theory*. Notre Dame, IN: University of Notre Dame Press.

Mannheim, K. (1952). The problem of generations. Chapter VII. In: K. Mannheim. *Essays on the sociology of knowledge* (pp. 276–320). London: Routledge & Kegan Paul Ltd. (Edited by Paul Kecskemeti)

Middleton, D. & Edwards, D. (1990). Conversational remembering: A social psychological approach. In D. Middleton & D. Edwards, (1990), (Eds.), *Collective remembering* (pp. 23–45). London: Sage Publications.

Middleton, D. & Brown, S. D. (2005). *Social psychology of experience: Studies in remembering and forgetting*. New York: Sage.

Mink, L. O. (1978). Narrative form as a cognitive instrument. In R.H. Canary and H. Kozicki (Eds.), *The writing of history: Literary form and historical understanding* (pp. 129–149). Madison: University of Wisconsin Press.

Musatova, M. M. (2002). "Uzkie uchastki" ekonomicheskogo rosta Rossii v usloviyakh globalizatskii. ["Narrow sectors" of economic growth in Russia in conditions of globalization]. Sb. Nauch. Tr – Novosibirsk; NGU [Collected Scientific Works – Novosibirsk; Novosibirsk State Uiversity], pp. 108–114.

Nora, P. (1989). Between memory and history: Les lieux de mémoire. *Representations*, Spring 1989, 26, 7–25.

Novick, P. (1999). *The Holocaust in American life*. Boston: Houghton Mifflin Company.

Pennebaker, J. W., D. Paez, & B.Rimé, (Eds.), (1997). *Collective memory of political events: Social psychological perspectives*. Mahwah, NJ: Lawrence Erlbaum Associates.

Propp, V. (1968). *Morphology of the folktale*. Austin, TX: University of Texas Press. (Translated by Laurence Scott)

Roediger, H. L. & K.B. McDermott (1995). Creating false memories: Remembering words not presented in lists. *Journal of Experimental Psychology: Learning, Memory, and Cognition, 21*, 803–814.

Ross, M. (1989). Relation of implicit theories to the construction of personal histories. *Psychological Review, 96*(2), 341–357.

Schacter, D. L., (Ed.), (1995). *Memory distortion: How minds, brains, and societies reconstruct the past*. Cambridge, MA: Harvard University Press.

Schacter, D. L. (1996). *Searching for memory: The brain, the mind, and the past*. New York: Basic Books.

Schudson, M. (1992). *Watergate in American memory: How we remember, forget, and reconstruct the past*. New York: Basic Books.

Schuman, H., B. Schwartz, & H. D'Arcy. (2005). Elite revisionists and popular beliefs: Christopher Columbus, hero or villain? *Public Opinion Quarterly, 69*(1), spring 2005, 2–29.

Schuman, H. & J. Scott. (1989). Generations and collective memories. *American Sociological Review, 4*(54, June), 359–381.

Seixas, P. (Ed.), (2004). *Theorizing historical consciousness*. Toronto: University of Toronto Press.

Stock, B. (1990). *Listening for the text: On the uses of the past*.Philadelphia: University of Pennsylvania Press.

Taylor, C. (1989) *Sources of the self: The making of modern identity*. Cambridge, MA: Harvard University Press.

Vygotsky, L. S. (1981). The instrumental method in psychology. In J.V. Wertsch, (Ed.), *The concept of activity in Soviet psychology* (pp. 134–143). Armonk, NY: M.E. Sharpe.

Vygotsky, L. S. (1987). *The collected works of L.S. Vygotsky. volume 1. Problems of general psychology. Including the Volume Thinking and speech.* New York: Plenum. (Edited and translated by N. Minick)

Weldon, M. S. (2001). Remembering as a social process. In D.L. Medin, (Ed.), *The psychology of learning and motivation* (pp. 67–120). San Diego: Academic Press.

Wertsch, J. V. (1994). Struggling with the past: Some dynamics of historical representation. In M. Carretero & J.F. Voss, (Eds.), *Cognitive and instructional processes in history and the social sciences* (pp. 323–338).

Wertsch, J. V. & O'Connor, K. (1994). Multivoicedness in historical representation: American college students' accounts of the origins of the U.S. *Journal of Narrative and Life History*, 4(4), 295–310.

Wertsch, J. V. (1998). *Mind as action*. New York: Oxford University Press.

Wertsch, J. V. (2002). *Voices of collective remembering*. New York: Cambridge University Press.

Wertsch, J. V. (2003). Filling in the blank spots in history: The Molotov-Ribbentrop Pact in Russian collective memory. Paper presented at the conference "Memory and War" at the Massachusetts Institute of Technology, January, 2003.

White, H. (1987). *The content of the form: Narrative discourse and historical representation*. Baltimore: The Johns Hopkins University Press.

Young, A. (1996). Bodily memory and traumatic memory. In P. Antze & M. Lambek, (Eds.), *Tense past: Cultural essays in trauma and memory* (pp. 89–102). New York: Routledge.

CHAPTER 33

Issues in the Socio-Cultural Study of Memory

Making Memory Matter

David Middleton and Steven D. Brown

Our concern in this chapter is to examine how we can approach memory as a topic of study in socio-cultural psychology. This will involve approaching remembering and forgetting as public, social activities where individual experience is necessarily mediated by collective experience. Now we are by no means the first to have envisaged a social turn in the psychological study of memory. There have been numerous contributions by sociocultural researchers, such as Brockmeier (2002); Bruner and Feldman (1996); Cole (1996); Hirst and Manier (1996); Middleton and Edwards (1990); and Wertsch (2002), along with ecologically orientated psychology, notably Barclay (1994), Neisser (1982), Neisser and Winograd (1988); social psychology such as Bangerter (2000, 2002); Wegner (1986) and Weldon (2001); Weldon and Bellinger (1997); Middleton and Brown (2005), and discourse analysis such as Norrick (2000). In addition, within psychology there is Bartlett's (1932) classic work on remembering, in which he aimed to put the study of memory on a properly social footing. We will discuss some of this work in more detail later in this chapter, but we should also note at this point that memory has been a fertile field for debate about the social basis of psychological functioning for as long as psychology has been established as a discipline.

William James (1890/1950), for instance, devotes considerable space in his *The Principles of Psychology* to discussing the basis whereby our consciousness becomes endowed with a form of continuity. For James, the question of memory is caught up in his distinctive and well-known account of human self-awareness as a 'stream of consciousness'. Memory is, then, to be approached in terms of the ability to connect together aspects of our experience as they appear in the ongoing flow of awareness. This implies some form of selectivity, we must exercise choice in relation to the nature of the connections to be made in order that our recollections can be best fitted to our current concerns and activities. Hence, "in the practical use of our intellect, forgetting is as important a function as recollecting" (James, 1950, 679).

We can turn back yet further than this to John Locke's (1690/1975) description of a "forensic self" defined by memory, which some authors (for example, Douglas, 1992; Hacking, 1995) see as laying the foundations for the modern concept of selfhood. Locke argued – contrary to the dominant tradition of English idealism – that memory was every bit as powerful as perception, and that chains of memories and responsibilities linking the present into the depths of the past were the precondition of selfhood. Without such a "forensic" link, the idea of justice or merely holding some person accountable for their past deeds has no meaning. In this philosophical tradition inherited by psychology, there is, then, a series of deep conceptual links between persistence of the past into the present, the idea of selfhood, the possibility of judgment and social responsibility. What this all suggests is that "memory" should not be regarded as a psychological function like any other. Rather, it is a key site where questions of personal identity and social order are negotiated. Witness, for example, the often-fraught legal and scientific arguments fought around the issue of recovered memories (see Ashmore, Mac-Millan, & Brown, 2004). What is at stake in these "memory wars" ranges from particular concerns with justice for the abuse and trauma suffered by individuals to far broader concerns with the nature of the modern family, the status and standing of therapy, authentic versions of selfhood and so on (Pezdek & Banks, 1996).

In saying that we wish to approach memory as a socio-cultural phenomenon, we are essentially "knocking at an open door." Public debate about the apparently flexible and contingent manner in which governments and official bodies construct past "truths" rages in most Western nations (for instance, the debate at the time of writing about what was or was not known by the Bush and Blair administrations concerning the actual existence of weapons of mass destruction in Iraq during the preparations for war in 2003). At the same time, a routine engagement with commemorative activities, be they purely nostalgic (such as the recycling of popular culture from the 1970s and 1980s) or highly sensitive (Ronald Reagan's laying a wreath at

they Bitburg Cemetery where Nazi SS soldiers are buried during his presidential state visit to the then West Germany in 1985, for example) is part of the fabric of much daily life. They are both part of "symbolic politics" (see Hedetoft and Moghaddam this volume). In each case, the thoroughly social character of memory is a pure truism for a great many people, whether or not they are immediately touched by controversies such as the memory wars. Barbara Misztal's 2003 book *Theories of Social Remembering* argues that what is required to understand this social landscape of everyday remembering is an approach that eschews both psychological and sociological reductionism. As with other sociological arguments (such as Schudson, 1992; Zerubavel, 1996, 1997), Misztal begins by attempting to clarify who is remembering what version of the past and to which end. The importance of such sociological concerns is its emphasis on the social organization and mediation of individual memory. Although it is the individual who is seen as the agent of remembering, the nature of what is remembered is profoundly shaped by "what has been shared with others," such that what is remembered is always a "memory of an intersubjective past, of past time lived in relation to other people" (Misztal, 2003: 6). This shared intersubjective memory is forged, Misztal states, by means of social processes such as language, rituals, and other commemorative practices and in relation to common memorial sites.

The insights provided by this intersubjective turn within sociological studies of memory are clear. They allow us to see that the work of remembering – and, hence, producing ourselves as people who have a past, a personal history – necessarily intersects with, and is shaped by, the groups and cultural forms we inhabit. However, at the same time, we need to grasp why it is that, despite the obvious influence of these social dimensions, for most of us the act of remembering still feels like a highly personal act. We feel that we "own" our personal memories and speak them of our free will without undue influence from others. Ian Hacking (1995) argues that the modern experience of remembering takes this form because our self understandings have been so profoundly shaped by psychology as a "science of memory" that we find it difficult to grasp memory in any other way. This is to say that everyday practices of remembering have been recruited into psychologists' versions of what it means to remember and forget. Doubtless it is the case that psychology in its myriad forms has acquired tremendous cultural authority over matters of self-knowledge, at least in North America and Europe (for a detailed account of this rise of the "psy complex," see the work of Nikolas Rose, 1989, 1996). It is doubtless also the case that, as Danziger (2002) points out, this authority has led to a narrowing and constriction of the common stock of metaphors and cultural models by means of which memory has traditionally been understood. However, rather than simply dismiss psychology as being guilty of brute reductionism, we need instead to focus more clearly on this central paradox: why it is that an activity that is so thoroughly public and social feels so intensely private and personal. We need, in other words, to get a handle on the complex and often ambiguous forms experience that are central to how remembering and forgetting is performed.

We will look to a range of approaches to memory in psychology, social anthropology, history, and socio-cultural studies. We aim to use these approaches as diagnostic tools to help shed light on our understanding of memory as a site where both the singularity and collectivity of experience intersect.

A Conversation With Bartlett – Social Organization of Remembering in Communicative Action

A key starting point for us was the work of Frederick Bartlett. Although his work is frequently cited as a pivotal historical moment in the experimental study of memory, its influence extends well beyond the disciplinary concerns of psychology. Indeed, as Rosa (1996) argues, Bartlett's research career was forged in the use of psychological methods to pursue anthropological questions concerning the "conventionalization" of cultural materials – that is, how individuals and groups borrow, modify, and adapt materials that are foreign or new to them. These ideas still generate contemporary interest in anthropological work on remembering and forgetting (Cole, 1998, 2001). However, the significance of Bartlett's focus on culture as the ongoing and highly particular production and reconstruction of meaning has not been fully exploited in contemporary social and cognitive psychology. As Kashima (2000: 384) notes, the tendency has been to treat culture as 'a repository of meaningful symbolic structures that structure people's experience' rather than a dynamic process of transmission and transformation.

Take, for example, Bartlett's celebrated and much quoted 1932 book, *Remembering: A study in experimental and social psychology*. This reports empirical studies and develops theoretical arguments concerning the dynamics of succession and change. Bartlett opens by questioning the reductionist strategy of aiming to isolate any form of simple mental faculty or processes occurring independently of each other. He rejects the Ebbinghaus (1885/1964) tradition of memory research. That tradition sought to eliminate the personal and idiosyncratic responses people might make to material that they are requested to memorize and recall under the controlled conditions of memory experiments. This is achieved by means of short and meaningless written material. Bartlett questions this strategy of paralyzing the accompanying human responses. He doubts the general appropriateness of such a strategy that loses "the special character" of human action – namely, the ability to render situations sensible for the purposes of current and future concerns. He argues that the improvised settings of experiments moulded in the Ebbinghaus image do not, as was supposed, allow us to see psychological capacities in their pure state by removing all extraneous social variables. Rather, they simply present a different kind of social context for the complex human organism to respond to.

Bartlett's description of psychological experimentation then emphasizes that experiments are no less socially located than any other form of social setting (see Edwards & Middleton, 1986). Indeed, his celebrated use of the serial reproduction technique was more than a simple documentation of the power of conventional symbols in dictating individual perception, as many introductory textbook summaries on psychology would imply. Rather, its aim was to try and capture, on the fly, the actual cultural process of "conventionalization." The remarkable feature of this concern with the practices of conventionalization is that it allows us to see not only that remembering is a constructive activity, where what is recalled is transformed in the act of communication, but also that such recollection involves selection and exclusion. In other words, what is not remembered, not passed on to another, is just as important as what is recalled and transmitted onwards.

Most contemporary citations of Bartlett's work, while not actually denying a place for these kinds of "social" factors, tend to regard them as another set of independent variables that can be grafted on to procedures when appropriate (see, for example, Conway, 1992; Stephenson, Kniveton, & Wagner, 1991). However, to treat conventionalization in this way is to create exactly the kind of dualism between the individual and the social settings in which they act that Bartlett strove to resist. A significant issue here is the way one of the key terms in Remembering – "schema" – has come to be understood. In classic cognitive science texts (Neisser, 1967; Rumelhart, 1975; Schank, 1982), the term schema is defined as some form of knowledge structure stored in the brain or mind of the individual to assist in the interpretation of experience. Schemata allow for a quick pattern matching of perception against a summary of prior experience, such that rapid judgments can be made. This results in an overall reduction in expenditure of cognitive effort, but can increase the possibilities of error (as in the case of unwarranted stereotyping) if the schemata in use become too inclusive or rigid (see especially Neisser, 1967). Such a definition is, however, at odds with the use Bartlett makes of the word. He defines it instead as the ongoing dynamic adaptation between people and their physical and social environments. That is, as sociocultural arrangements that blur the boundaries between individuals and their social world. Bartlett's preferred definition (1932, 201) was then of schemas as "organized settings":

> "I strongly dislike the term 'schema'. It is at once too definite and too sketchy... it suggests some persistent but fragmentary, 'form of arrangement' and it does not indicate what is very essential to the whole notion, that the organised mass results of past changes of position and posture are actively doing something all the time; are so to speak carried along with us, complete, though developing, from moment to moment. It would probably be best to speak of 'active developing patterns'; but the word 'pattern'... has its own difficulties; and it like 'schema' suggests a greater articulation of detail than is normally found. I think probably the term 'organised setting' approximates most closely and clearly to the notion required."

It is striking, given the individualistic ways in which the notion of schema is typically used in cognitive and social psychology, just how highly critical Bartlett is of his own use of the term. However, if Bartlett has difficulty in arriving at the idea of an "organized setting," it is because what he is pursuing is a complex and challenging account of psychological functioning. Very roughly, Bartlett states that our conscious awareness – or "attitude" – stands in a dynamic relation, to the direction and range of concerns – or "interests" – that characterize our ongoing relations with the social worlds we inhabit. As these relations are subject to continuous transformation, at least within certain parameters, it follows that our attitudes and interests are themselves evolving. An organized setting is, then, a complex of cognition and emotion that is located within, and dependent on, the cultural and material particularities of the local environment. We cannot then separate out the mental from the social in any clear-cut manner.

What Bartlett tries to capture is the essential integration of individual mentality and culture, of the interdependency of cognition, affect, and cultural symbols. It is within this model of psychological functioning that Bartlett develops his account of remembering. For Bartlett, remembering is indicative of the kind of liberty that schemata, as organized settings, afford us. To exist within an organized setting is to have some of the burden of being forced to continuously adjust to the changing vicissitudes of the environment removed. Organized settings render the world stable, they free us from the "chronological determinism" (Bartlett, 1932: 202) of the present moment, but, at the same time, they do not rigidly determine our thinking. Bartlett (1932, 208) argues that the "special character" of human psychological functioning emerges as the human organism 'discovers how to turn round upon its own "schemata," or, in other words, it becomes conscious. To be conscious is to have a reflexive awareness of the organized setting in which one's thoughts and actions are situated. From this it follows that schema are "not merely something that works the organism, but something with which the organism can work" (Bartlett, 1932, 208). It is this ability to turn around on schema that constitutes remembering as a constructive process of living development – in other words, as a kind of ongoing dialogue between our thinking and the cultural symbols that feature in a given organized setting. By remembering, we are then able to reconstruct and transform "our daily modes of conduct." This occurs via an interesting synthesis of sensory and symbolic issues – what can be termed as "cross-modal remembering" (Edwards & Middleton, 1986). The terms "mode" and "cross-modal" do not refer to the sense organs, but the forms of symbolization or representation in which the materials that are the subject of attention are experienced and later re-presented or remem-

bered. Bartlett clearly recognized the importance of studying how we put experience into words and the significance of conventional symbols in conscious activity. He also recognized the function of conversational discourse, where, for example, remembering occurs as people talk with one another. In such contexts, the purposes of communicative action very often take precedence over notions of reproductive accuracy (Bartlett, 1932, 96):

> The actions and reproductions of everyday life come largely by the way, and are incidental to our main preoccupations. We discuss with other people what we have seen, in order that they may value or criticise our impressions with theirs. There is ordinarily no directed and laborious effort to secure accuracy. We mingle interpretation with description, interpolate things not originally present, transform without effort and without knowledge.

The prevailing consensus in studies of memory – be they ecological (such as Neisser, 1982; Neisser & Winograd, 1988) or concerned with information processing (such as Atkinson & Schiffrin, 1968; Baddeley, 1982; Neisser, 1967) – has been a concern with issues of verity in remembering as the indices of structure, content and process – how to sort "genuine" memories from "distorted" ones (for example, Loftus, 1979) and there have been heated debates about what has been termed false memory syndrome (Loftus & Ketchum, 1994). However, as we see in the previous extract, Bartlett argues strenuously that issues of accuracy are less important than addressing our "main preoccupations" – that is, settling current matters at hand as they emerge in communicative action. Indeed, he even goes so far as to argue that, 'in a world of constantly changing environment, literal recall is extraordinarily unimportant' (1932, 204).

What Bartlett then calls for is an understanding of remembering as primarily concerned with how the past is constructed in the present to serve the needs of whatever actions we are currently engaged in.

Rather than view what people remember as a window on to the content and structure of individual minds or strident attempts to retell original experience, we ought instead to be concerned with how people construct versions of the past, their position in so doing and their use of the very notion of what it is to remember. Moreover, as Bartlett makes clear in both *Remembering* and, later on, in *Thinking* (1958), this reconstruction of the past is done by means of conversation. Talk is a fundamental aspect of "everyday thinking" or, as Bartlett (1958: 164) terms it, "immediate communication thinking."

It might be argued that this is all well and good, but the real topic remains what people really do with their minds or really can remember, not just what they can report. However, as has been previously argued (Edwards & Potter, 1992), this is an empirically difficult distinction to maintain. Descriptions of experience are endlessly variable. In addition to this, one of the main functions of such talk is to establish what it is that might have actually, possibly or definitely happened. In a sense germane to the psychology of participants, the truth of original events is the outcome, not the input, to the reasoning displayed in talk. The turn to a discursive analysis of remembering – to understand the way in which remembering is organized for and accomplished within the pragmatics of communicative action – is a legacy of Bartlett's concerns. Conversational remembering is a fundamental aspect of conduct in socially ordered settings.

The Impact of Bartlett's Discursive Agenda Beyond Psychology

Bartlett's work has had a significant impact beyond the discipline of psychology. We will now discuss briefly in turn several bodies of work that may be organized according to four key themes from Bartlett: commemoration; conventionalization; objectification and mediation. Following this we will summarize how these themes converge on the key notion of *individual and collective experience situated within organized settings*.

Commemoration

The *Social Memory* monograph (1992) by anthropologist James Fentress and historian Chris Wickham gives a thorough demonstration of Bartlett's point that memory is reconstructed in the process of its articulation and transmission (or, as Bartlett succinctly put it, the "effort after meaning" that characterizes recollection).

Fentress and Wickham (1992, X) approach memory in terms of the way in which "individual consciousness" relates to "the collectivities those individuals make up." They argue that membership of a social group subtly inflects the form that memory takes for group members. In particular, it inflects the precise manner in which individuals are able to talk or write about the past. For example, in a detailed analysis of the medieval poem "Chanson de Roland," they show that the structure of the poem sets up a montage of visual images for the listener rather than a clear narrative continuity. The past recalled by the poem is, then, experienced as highly stylized and vivid visual dramatizations of past events.

There are two key points to be made here. First, that the local techniques available for retelling the past – such as poems, stories, legends, or folklore – profoundly shape the way in which individuals can gain access to their own history. "Chanson de Roland," for instance, uses a great deal of formulaic language. This, Fentress and Wickham argue, is the "mnemonic armature" (1992, 53) that makes the poem memorable and recognizable across the occasions of its telling. So long as the performer retains this armature, precise narrative details can be altered or excised. Second, that, in the process of being told, the poem transmits a set of cultural values and social meanings rather than a clear record of historical moments. Seen in this way, "Chanson" is a poor record of empirical events, but an excellent vehicle of collectively held ideas. Commemoration, then, for

Fentress and Wickham (1992: 59) is "not stable as information; it is stable, rather, at the level of shared meanings and remembered images."

This analysis of commemoration clearly follows Bartlett in exploring memory not merely as a faculty with which individuals are endowed – that is, a property or thing (a "noun") – but also as an activity – a set of social techniques or procedures (as a "verb"). Fentress and Wickham are concerned with the manner in which social groups make available for members ways of connecting their present lives and concerns with the past. What this means is that "the way we order and structure our ideas in our memories, and the way we transmit these memories, is a study of the way we are" (1992, 7).

Commemoration is as much about establishing who we are now, as social beings, as it is about settling what happened in the past. Indeed, for Fentress and Wickham, the lesson to be learnt from "Chanson" is that the power of such commemoration is "little affected by its truth." In one sense, it does not matter whether the events recalled did or did not happen in the way in which they are retold. What does matter is that the commemoration takes a form that is sufficiently consonant with the group's collectively held values that members may affirm it without finding it "strictly believable." Put slightly differently, "memory is validated in and through actual practice" (1992, 24).

This appears to suggest that groups can continuously remake the past – at least, within certain limits. Now this may be all well and good when we are considering medieval social memory, as exemplified by "Chanson," but what of modern forms of commemoration? Michael Schudson directly addresses this point in his 1992 book *Watergate in American Memory: How We Remember, Forget and Reconstruct the Past.*

Schudson begins from a pragmatic position – Watergate is not a myth or a legend, it is a definite historical event. Watergate is the name given to the political scandal resulting from the complicity of the then American President, Richard Nixon, in the cover-up of an attempted break-in during 1972 at the Democrat National Committee Headquarters in the Watergate Office Complex in Washington, DC, with apparent intention to fix a malfunctioning wire tap. Newspaper and then formal Senate investigations led to impeachment proceedings and the infamous eventual resignation of Nixon in 1974. This, Schudson (1992: 55) argues, is "something [that] happened, and on that, not on interest or values or free interpretation, hangs a tale. Tracing the consequences of "something happened" is what an interest in the past is all about." The point, for the study of social memory, is to establish not what did or did not actually occur, but to understand how Watergate lends itself to various forms of interpretation and narration over time.

There are, of course, numerous versions of and points of view about 'what happened' around Watergate. For Schudson, it is precisely these kinds of debates and disagreements that constitute what we can term "collective memory." He (1992: 50) aims to "show how different views of Watergate have warred with one another through the past decades and to analyze how different forms and forums have carried these views on in American memory." What matters is how individuals then orientate themselves to Watergate as a topic, make it salient as a "memorable" and "tellable" event and engage with others in such debate. However, one of the peculiarities of Watergate is that, at the time, there were other events – such as the energy crisis of the early 1970s – that would have appeared far more vivid and memorable.

Californians, for example, would have directly experienced the spectacle of sitting in "gasoline lines." Watergate, by contrast, would have been experienced at a distance, as events reported in a newspaper. If we add to this that there is no formal commemorative practice featuring Watergate (no annual "Nixon day," for instance) then the persistence of the event in North American social memory is all the more puzzling.

The answer, Schudson claims, is to understand Watergate as a process rather than an event. Central to this is not what Water-gate was, but, rather, what it has now become (and continues to become) as it serves as the source material for a variety of informal commemorative practices. For example, Nixon's resignation may be taken as a metaphor for the victory of the common people (in this case, the Washington Post reporters who pursued the case) over the powerful (the machinations of Nixon and his White House advisers). As such, Watergate can be used to express or support a variety of projects in the present. Schudson refers to these practices as the "cultural vehicles" or "resources" by means of which collective memory is woven. It is via such cultural vehi-cles that the past comes to us and informs our personal and collective sense of who we are – "the forms of collective memory, attached to human or humanly constructed vehicles, are an aspect of human culture through which time travels" (1992, 5).

Barry Schwartz's book, *Abraham Lincoln and the Forge of National Memory* (2000), takes a similar approach. Schwartz is also interested in the gap between matters of his-torical record – in his case, the presidency of Abraham Lincoln – and how that his-tory is reconstructed as social memory – the ups and downs of how Lincoln's "reputation" and "legacy" have been interpreted.

Once again, the point of departure is Bartlett's insight that remembering both preserves and transforms in the transmission of the past. If Schudson alerts us to the dan-ger of placing too much weight on interpre-tation (we cannot change our recollection of "what happened" on a whim), then Schwartz points out the equivalent danger of imag-ining that the past determines the present, that we are directly constituted by our his-tory. Instead, Schwartz (2000, 18) argues, we should see the past as acting as a "model" for the present in two distinct ways – as "a template that organizes and animates behav-ior and a frame within which people locate and find meaning for their present experi-ence. Collective memory affects social real-ity by reflecting, shaping, and framing it." Seen in this way, collective remembering is a continuous dialogue between present and past, where what is recalled is used as a "framework of meaning" for understanding the present without determining the direc-tion of the future.

In Schwartz's analysis, "frameworks of meaning" are subject to processes of suc-cession and change. Each generation inher-its a given framework, but, at the same time, typically recognizes potential shortcomings within it and the need for revision. What he (2000: 25) then calls the "lineaments of commemorative persistence and change" are central to how Schwartz approaches prac-tices of collective remembering. For exam-ple, a physical monument may have been erected in order to preserve some past event (such as a war), but the meaning given to that monument by successive generations will pass through a series of modifications. See for example, Scott Sandage's exemplary analysis of the ways in which the Lincoln Memorial in Washington, DC has been sub-jected to successive forms of appropriation in relation to the emergence of the Civil Rights movement between 1939 and 1963. This example also points to the significance of the tools and symbols for commemoration that are passed on in the course of history. We inherit a rich set of materials in which prior choices about which aspects of our col-lective past are worth preserving are already embedded. Our contemporary forms of col-lective remembering are then forced to con-front these tools and symbols, and are set the challenge of deciding whether or not they have any form of meaning for us, in the here and now.

Conventionalization

Schwartz's work points us towards a second theme from Bartlett – the manner in which cultural materials are modified and adapted as they are put to use in the work of remem-bering. It might be argued that this idea is strongly echoed in the approach to memory adopted in the overlapping fields of cognitive psychology and neuroscience. As Schachter (1996) describes it, the emerging view of memory here is as a subjective, multilevel process, where past memories are subtly modified in the present. Thus, in the same way that Bartlett emphasizes the contingency between what is granted to us by the cultural materials we use in remembering and what we then subsequently go on to recall, so the cognitive system itself is seen to do the work of reorganization and transformation based on the way in which the past has been recorded and stored in the neural architecture of the cortex.

Much as an awareness of the contingency of remembering on the part of cognitive neuroscience is to be welcomed, for many critics outside the discipline, the direction and force of Bartlett's argument remains generally misunderstood by psychologists. For example, Maurice Bloch (1998: 69) points out that:

> The problem with psychologists' approach to memory in the real world comes ... from their failure to grasp the full complexity of the engagement of the mind in culture and history and, in particular, their failure to understand that culture and history are not just something created by people but that they are, to a certain extent, that which creates persons.

The problem, as Bloch sees it, is that psychologists make an overly firm distinction between the "inner world" of the cognitive system and the "outside world" reached via human perception. If one begins to study memory in this way, then attention is quite naturally focused on how the external world becomes represented and encoded by the cognitive system. What we call "memories" are then subjective symbolic transformations of some external reality, rendered fit for cognitive-neural processing. From here it is only a short leap to imagine that what is called "culture" is simply a set of techniques that have evolved to assist humans in this process of the subjective symbolization of the world and the secondary coordination of such symbols in the public domain. As Bloch (1998, 69) has it, standard psychology textbooks on memory (such as Baddeley, 1976; Cohen, 1990) view "socially instituted practices of memory as merely a primitive form of artificial intelligence" that are tasked with simply

translating our private individual representations into public representations and then archiving them accordingly.

Bloch's point is that such a view arrives at the rather perverse notion that "culture" and "history" are creations of the cognitive system, designed for its own convenience, rather than the more plausible notion that these terms mark wider processes within which our self-consciousness emerges and has meaning. In fact, it is this direction of influence – from the cultural to the personal – that Bartlett was seeking to elaborate in his discussion of how cultural materials, such as myth, serve to inform and resource our acts of remembering. Although Bartlett's early research was conducted as part of anthropological studies, it is perhaps ironic, given his long career as a psychologist, that it is now anthropologists rather than psychologists who enact the intellectual project of the founder of the Cambridge Psychological Laboratory.

An informative example here is the work of Jennifer Cole (1998, 2001). Drawing on material from her ethnographic work among the Betsimisaraka people, who are located in the small town of Ambodiharina in east Madagascar, Cole (2001: 1) argues for an analysis of how "individual and social memory are woven together." For Cole, there is a complex set of interdependencies between personal consciousness and public representations. For example, within Madagascar, there are strong reminders of the legacy of colonial rule in the form of public architecture and other physical symbols. This legacy may be considered painful – Ambodiharina, for instance, witnessed outbreaks of extreme violence and brutality during the transition to the post-colonial period. One of Cole's most remarkable findings was that memories of this period appeared to be almost completely absent from the descriptions given by her informants of their lives and families. Nor were such memories present in the ritual forms of commemoration adopted by Betsimisaraka. Why should this be so? Is it possible that the individual Betsimisaraka have simply "forgotten" the past?

In fact, as Cole discovered, this was not to remain the case. She witnessed and recorded "an explosion of memories" concerning political violence and people's emotional reactions to them. These were occasioned by the developing circumstances of a presidential election in the early 1990s. Opposing parties directly invoked memories from political change of previous times when reminding the electorate of differing ethnic groups of the consequences of voting or aligning themselves in one way or another. Anxieties and past rivalries of political and economic ascendancy were used to rekindle the potential for intercommunity violence.

The lesson that Cole takes from this example is that memory is considerably more than simply the storage of past events and experiences. Indeed, the term used by the Betsimisaraka – mahatsiaro – translates as "make not set apart." This refers to neither a "thing" nor "capacity," but rather the activity of renewing some sort of ancestral connection. For example, one family reported an ancestor as having been saved from bandits by the distracting cry of a bird. That bird does not form part of that family's diet. The memory then becomes embedded in a concrete social practice enacted by family members – or, as Cole (2001: 111) puts it, "memories of those ancestors come to dwell in the very bodies of their descendants." To use Bartlett's term, we would say that the symbolic properties of dietary ingredients become conventionalized to enable the commemoration of family lineage.

Moreover, this conventionalization is an ongoing achievement. The Betsimisaraka also engage in a practice of reburial, where individual remains are broken apart and reconfigured into two male and female collected ancestors. Cole (2001, 288) argues that this process provides for a way of thinking about how memories become gathered up together and "of the transformations that occur as people work to secure their ties to the past, thereby themselves, quite literally, the many who will not be sundered." By literally rearranging the skeletons of the dead, families reconfigure their relationships to ancestors and knot the present more firmly to a clearly defined version of the past.

Cole uses the term "memoryscape" (made popular by Geertz, 1973) to denote the two directions pointed out in this work of conventionalization. On the one hand, there is the constitution of a diachronic succession between ancestors and descendants forged by the rearranging of bones. On the other hand, there is a synchronic gathering up of relationships between family members as relatives at the burial site argue the significance of which bones should be arranged and the manner and reasons for their selection. Put more simply, the work of revisiting the past is also a work of transforming the present.

A memoryscape is, then, something like a shared space where social and individual memory meet and the identity of family members in relation to a collective past is worked out. This is another way of thinking about the relationship Bartlett identifies between individual experience and organized settings. We see in Cole's work that what is key to an organized setting is how memory is collectively configured, and that this configuration involves ways of thinking and acting in concert with one another, along with formal social practices (reburial among the Betsimisaraka).

Finally, Cole also confirms Bartlett's point that participation in an organized setting involves an emotional investment (a mixing of "affect" with "attitude"). Recollection, for the Betsimisaraka, is not an abstract cognitive act, but, rather, occurs in a "fuzzy space between thinking and feeling," as a "feeling memory" (Cole, 2001: 281). To experience the past in the reburial of ancestors or the ritual sacrifice of cattle is to feel the significance of memory within the present, to sense both a connection to what has gone before and an orientation towards the present and what ought to be.

Objectification

Anthropological work, such as Cole's, captures something of what Bartlett is striving for in the various descriptions he offers of "schemas" as dynamic "developing patterns" or "orientations" between the organism and the "organized mass of past changes." What such work also underscores is the physical or embodied nature of such an orientation to the past. Now, the experimental psychological study of memory is typically concerned with remembering as a cognitive act, as a work of pure thought (even if that thought is often in "error"). If the body is invoked in such work, then it is only in terms of the physical state of the cortex, which itself is understood purely as the "hardware" on which the cognitive architecture is supported.

Consider for a moment, however, what it feels like to take part in a generic memory experiment. One is usually asked to sit in small, barren room for a prolonged period of time and concentrate on a range of meaningless digits or words flashed up on a brightly lit computer screen. This is certainly a most peculiar experience – from the potential physical discomfort of, and ongoing ambiguity about, the nature of the task to the uneasy awareness that one's performance is being monitored and recorded by the unseen experimenter – with whom contact is limited to a few words of greeting, direction, and farewell and the signing of consent forms. In short, there are a wide variety of embodied experiences involved in this activity that are simply not registered in formal psychological theories of memory.

In fact, it is rare to find any systematic accounts of these embodied dimensions of remembering. One significant exception is Edward Casey's (1987) *Remembering: A Phenomenological Study*. Casey presents detailed philosophical arguments using phenomenological data for going beyond the analysis of memory as an exclusively mental phenomenon. He argues that a disembodied account of remembering has its roots in the classical Cartesian view of space as an "empty," homogeneous medium in which our actions happen to occur. For example, the cubicle in which the experiment takes place is simply a convenient space in which

subjects can be monitored as they respond to computer-presented stimuli. For the experimenter, the space is considered to have no intrinsic meaning – it is "dead," so to speak.

However, there are other ways in which to think about the way we inhabit space. We typically find our environments to be rich in meaning, particularly those places in which we routinely work and dwell. Such places are "alive" – they provide the boundaries and significant markers within which our experiences are contained. As Casey (1987, 182) states, as our experience "takes place in place and nowhere else, so our memory of what we experience is likewise place specific: it is bound to place as its own basis." We have a living, embodied relationship to the places we inhabit – even to the supposedly "dead" spaces we have occasion to pass through – that affords and shapes our relationship to the past. If this is so, then we must think of memory as extending out into the world (Casey, 1987, 259):

> The mind of memory is already in the world: *it is in reminders and reminiscences, in acts of recognition and in the lived body, in places and in the company of others.*

Our acts of remembering are interdependent on the places and people that make up our everyday experiences. A familiar sight may serve as the basis for a recollection, just as a conversation might afford a particular reminiscence. In both instances, our memories point outside of ourselves. They are part of an ongoing relationship with place and to others. Casey captures this interdependency with his notion that "adverbs" rather than "nouns" or "substantives" best express how we remember. We recollect "with" the embodied utterances and gestures we make, "through" the commemorative practices and routines we engage in, and "around" the significant and meaningful features of the environment in which we dwell. "Withness," "throughness" and "aroundness" then denote three modes of participation that concern, respectively, bodies, practices, and places. For Casey, these modes of participation are the relational aspects of remembering that are precisely the ones missing from the disembodied, purely mentalistic study of memory.

Casey is, in effect, arguing that much of what we take to be personal and private is, in fact, embedded in our actual concrete engagement with other people and things. In so doing, the inner character of our experiences becomes necessarily extended outwards and reflected back at us – in other words, *objectified*. What is more, this objectification is part of the full richness of being – our memories become deepened and expanded as a result. However, is it not also possible that certain modes of participation may act to restrict or constrain remembering? Paul Connerton's (1989) book *How Societies Remember* explores this possibility. Connerton is primary concerned with "ritual" forms of commemoration. He (1989: 59) argues that, as rituals typically involve a highly stylized, repetitive set of movements and actions on the part of performers, this results in a restriction of meanings that arise in the performance, leaving little space for individual interpretation:

> *One kneels or one does not kneel, one executes the movement necessary to perform the Nazi salute or one does not. To kneel in subordination is not to state subordination, nor is it just to communicate a message of submission. To kneel in subordination is to display it through the visible, present substance of one's body.*

As James Wertsch (this volume) also points out such rituals are, in essence, performative. What they seek to accomplish – submission, assent to authority, religious piety – is achieved in the very doing of the act. The space for arguing otherwise or withholding consent is effaced as soon as one begins to participate. Connerton notes that this performative character means that rituals have a compelling effect on participants. To take part in a commemorative ritual is to be recruited into the significance of the event being collectively recalled (particularly when the ritual involves some form of re-enactment, such as when an annual

march traces a particular geographical route or flowers are lain at a monument). A principal difference, then, between ritual and the kinds of narrative forms of commemoration studied by Schudson and Schwartz is that, while it always possible to ironize a narrative in the act of its telling, it is extremely difficult, in the course of an organized commemorative ritual, to kneel "ironically" in submission or perform an "ironic" Hitler salute. As Connerton (1989: 59) deadpans, "the limited resources of ritual posture, gesture, and movement strip communication clean of many of hermeneutic puzzles." Moreover, there are, Connerton (1989, 54) argues, "certain things that can be expressed only in ritual." For example, the nexus of meanings contained in the transubstantiation of Christ's body within the Catholic ritual of Communion are not adequately expressed in a verbal account given outside of the activity itself.

The key to ritual commemoration is the use of a "bodily substrate" for the preservation of collective memory. By training and disciplining bodily movements by means of what Connerton calls "incorporating practices" as diverse as "good" table manners, "nice" writing, "correct" sitting positions, or "proper" marching, a moral order can be established as a matter of habit. Once acquired, such habitual activities all but demand to be performed correctly – we find it troubling to not write properly or eat with our mouths open and are disturbed to see such lapses on the part of others. This is, once again, a reiteration of Bartlett's point that organized settings/schemas create an "affective disposition" on the part of members. What Connerton adds to this is that, as the habitual activities that accompany such dispositions are freighted not only with their own moral orders but also with a burden of the past (what it means to "sit nicely," "smile politely," "stand to attention properly," and so on), we are more or less impelled to transmit a set of collective values that we might otherwise seek to question. Thus, rituals are particularly well suited to the preservation of those collective memories that are critical for securing group identities (Connerton, 1989, 102):

> *Every group, then, will entrust to bodily automatisms the values and categories which they are anxious to conserve. They will know how well the past can be kept in mind by a habitual memory sedimented in the body.*

Both Connerton and Casey, then, offer useful counterweights to the narrowly cognitive or mentalist approach to memory by demonstrating how the past becomes objectified in our habitual actions and routine embodied relationships with the world. However, this still leaves open the question of just how this objectification is achieved – that is, the nature of tools or resources that enable the modes of participation. It is to this final theme that we will now turn.

Mediation

As we described earlier, Bartlett's work on remembering is situated within a project of creating a distinctive psychological approach to anthropological issues. Bartlett's concern with the conventionalization of cultural materials aimed to show that access to the past is never direct – it always passes by way of a set of resources that are derived from the broader cultural and social landscape. These resources then inevitably shape and restructure whatever is remembered.

Although Bartlett's insight has, by and large, not been adopted within the experimental psychology of memory, socio-cultural studies are one place where there is a systematic approach to the use of cultural resources in higher psychological functions. Of particular interest here being Vygotsky's analysis of higher mental functioning as mediated forms of psychological activity (Vygotsky, 1987). In brief, Vygotsky worked within the intellectual space of Soviet communism, deployed techniques of dialectical thinking to analyze human development in terms of collective accomplishments. Such accomplishments are structured as distinct social practices that have their own histori-

cal trajectories. Individual development, as Vygotsky saw it, is then a matter of the participation of a given person with these already established sets of practices, who becomes transformed as a consequence.

One of the key terms in socio-cultural research is mediation. Human action is understood as involving the use of tools – both literal tools or artefacts and symbolic tools, such as language – in order to reach its goals. Tools then mediate between action and the objects towards which it strives and, in so doing, expand the range and complexity of what humans are able to achieve. For many socio-cultural researchers (such as Daniels, 2001; Engeström, 1987), an "activity" is then decomposable into a complex of agents, outcomes and mediational devices.

In Vygotsky's work (1987, for example), the psychological significance of this complex is that mediation not only expands the range of human actions but also has a "reverse action" on the human agent. Mediation – notably in the form of signs and symbols – becomes a way in which agents can "master" their own minds and behavior "from the outside" (see Daniels, 1996). What we call higher-order psychological functions are then, in Vygotsky's terms, actions that are first performed publicly and then secondarily acquired as private "mental operations."

James Wertsch's (2002) *Voices of Collective Remembering* is a key illustration of a systematic sociocultural approach to memory. Wertsch argues for an understanding of collective remembering where mediated action constitutes the basic unit of analysis. By this, he intends to draw attention to the range of "cultural tools" that people employ in accomplishing remembering activities. What counts as a tool, for Wertsch, is quite broad – language qualifies, as do written texts and technologies such as electronic search agents. These tools are always relative to the cultural and historical settings in which they are fashioned and produced.

To begin to use a tool is to become connected, in advance of the accomplishment of the act, with a broader socio-historical collectivity. For example, Wertsch discusses at some length how Russians have traditionally used a particular form of schematic narrative – or "narrative template" – as a cultural tool that makes it possible to represent their historical trajectory in terms of contemporary circumstances. This template consists of a rudimentary storyline where the peaceful existence of the Russian people is threatened by an aggressor leading to a dire crisis that is only overcome by the heroism of the Russian people. The functionality of this template – which Wertsch calls "triumph-over-evil-forces" – is that a range of characters and events can be slotted into the narrative without losing the basic plot line. Soviet accounts of the 1918–1920 Russian civil war, for instance, position Western imperialism, in the guise of "White Russians," as the aggressor, defeated by the valor of the Communist Party, which stands for the Russian people. Post Soviet accounts adjust the timeframe such that it was the initial rise of the communist party in the October revolution that constitutes the tragedy and the Russian people are now seen as distinct actors rather than subsumed by the Party. In this way, Wertsch shows how, despite the successive changes in historical consciousness that have occurred in the transition into and out of the Soviet period, the cultural tool provides for a kind of continuity.

In part of his discussion of history textbooks and generational differences in collective remembering, Wertsch (2002, 97) displays how the continuity in the accounts of the past produced by the generation who grew up in post Second World War Soviet Russia can be further indexed to a massive state control of history education where:

across all 11 time zones of that massive state students in the same grade were literally on the same page of the same history textbook on any given day of the school year, and the official history taught allowed little room for competing voices.

Control over mediational resources is a means of ensuring that what can be collectively remembered is shaped to fit official, state-sponsored versions of the past.

The point Wertsch underscores here is the fit between mediational tools and the contexts in which they are used, such as the history classroom or the "kitchen table" where alternative underground samizdat photo-copied texts were furtively discussed. These contexts are never neutral – they are sites where collective remembering as a practice rubs up against the state production of "official history." As Wertsch shows, in Soviet Russia this confrontation was often marked by an all-pervading sense of distrust of the narratives and resources provided by the state. In particular, the regular excision or "airbrushing" of Party members who had fallen from favor from official historical accounts and even, notoriously, photographic records, was well recognized by Soviet citizens, even if it could not be publicly discussed (Wertsch, 2002, 77):

For ordinary citizens as well as for major actors on the Soviet scene, keeping track of which truth was current was a deadly serious task, but it also gave rise to bits of Soviet humour such as the aphorism that "Nothing is so unpredictable as Russia's past."

What this cynicism with regard to official narratives reflects is what Wertsch refers to as a more general "tension" between individuals and the mediational tools that resource their activity. Tools expand the range of what we are able to achieve, but rarely express the intentions of the actors involved in their entirety. Just as the literal act of writing slows down and "disciplines" the writer, so the narrative tools available for remembering organize and frame what can be remembered. Just as the writer may experience this slowing down as a frustrating inability to get the words out quickly enough, so the individual who is forced to use the official narrative resources may equally feel a tension between what can be expressed via these resources and other "competing voices."

The tension between agent and tool can be expressed in a variety of ways, from the efforts by the agent to "master" the mediational means to attempts at "resistance" or rejection. It is within the interplay of these activities that Wertsch locates the changing dynamics of collective remembering and, ultimately, the generational discontinuities between the memories of younger post glasnost Russians and their Soviet-educated forebears.

Conclusion

Our purpose in this chapter was not to provide a detailed summary of the extensive literature on memory addressing social and cultural issues. There are excellent summaries already available in the literature (see, for example, Antze & Lambek, 1996; Irwin-Zarecka, 1993; Klein, 2000; Misztal, 2003; Olick & Robbins, 1998; Wertsch, 2002; Zelizer, 1992, 1995; Zerubavel, 1996). Rather, our aim has been to identify a range of issues that could equip us to take forward the socio-cultural study memory.

Based on our brief review of a variety of work from across the social sciences, it has become clear to us that the kind of study that needs to be pursued must be capable of addressing at least four sets of concerns. It must be able to show how issues of succession and change in the transmission of collective memory are handled in commemorative practices. In particular, we need to establish the manner in which transformation occurs – how it is that certain elements of the past become reconstructed while others are disposed of. It must also be able to display how individuals and groups engage in the conventionalization of cultural resources. That is, how they borrow, modify, reconstruct, pass on, or destroy narrative, symbols, and artefacts as part of their ongoing practices of recalling the past in the present. Moreover, it must be able to provide an account of remembering as objectification of experience. This requires the study of our living, embodied engagement with other people, with objects that hold meaning and with the particularities of the places in which we dwell. Finally, it must provide for a focus on the ambiguous nature of mediation. In other words, how the reach and depth of our remembering activities becomes expanded beyond ourselves by means of cultural tools and, at the same time, how mediation acts back on us as individuals, and the effects this "reverse action" has on what we can achieve.

Acknowledgments

This chapter is an adaptation of material previously published in Middleton and Brown (2005). We gratefully acknowledge Alberto Rosa's and Jaan Valsiner's helpful editorial comments.

References

Antze, P., & Lambek, M. (Eds.), (1996). *Tense past: Cultural essays in trauma and memory*. New York; London: Routledge.

Ashmore, M., MacMillan, K., & Brown, S. D. (2004). It's a scream: Professional hearing and tape fetishism. *Journal of Pragmatics, 36*, 349–374.

Atkinson, R. C., & Schiffrin, R. M. (1968). Human memory: A proposed system and its control processes. In K. Spence & J. Spence (Eds.), *The psychology of learning and motivation*, Vol. 2. New York: Academic Press.

Baddeley, A. D. (1976). *The psychology of memory*. London: Harper & Row.

Baddeley, A. D. (1982). Domains of recollection. *Psychological Review, 89*, 708–729.

Bangerter, A. (2000). Identifying individual and collective acts of remembering in task related communication. *Discourse Processes, 30*, 237–264.

Bangerter, A. (2002). Maintaining task continuity: The role of collective memory processes in redistributing information. *Group Processes and Intergroup Relations, 5*, 203–219.

Barclay, C. R. (1994). Collective remembering. *Semiotica, 101*(3/4), 323–330.

Bartlett, F. C. (1932). *Remembering: A study in experimental and social psychology*. Cambridge: Cambridge University Press.

Bartlett, F. C. (1958). *Thinking: An experimental and social study*. London: George Allen & Unwin.

Bloch, M. E. (1998). *How we think they think: Anthropological approaches to cognition, memory and literacy*. Boulder, Colorado: Westview Press.

Brockmeier, J. (2002). Remembering and forgetting: Narrative as cultural memory. *Culture and Psychology, 8*(1), 15–43.

Bruner, J. S., & Feldman, C. (1996). Group narrative as a cultural context of autobiography. In D. Rubin (Ed.), *Remembering our past: Studies in autobiographical memory*, Cambridge: Cambridge University Press.

Casey, E. S. (1987). *Remembering: A phenomenological study*. Bloomington & Indianapolis: Indiana University Press.

Cohen, G. (1990). *Memory and the real world*. London: Lawrence Erlbaum Associates.

Cole, M. (1996). *Cultural psychology: A once and future discipline*. Cambridge, Massachusetts: The Belknap Press of the Harvard University Press.

Cole, J. (1998). The work of memory in Madagascar. *American Ethnologist*, 25(4), 610–633.

Cole, J. (2001). *Forget colonialism? Sacrifice and the art of memory in Madagascar*. Berkeley: University of California Press.

Connerton, P. (1989). *How societies remember*. Cambridge: Cambridge University Press.

Conway, M. A. (1992). In defense of everyday memory. *American Psychologist*, 46, 19–26.

Daniels, H. (1996). *An introduction to Vygotsky*. London: Routledge.

Daniels, H. (2001). *Vygotsky and pedagogy*. London: Routledge.

Danziger, K. (2002). How old is psychology, particularly concepts of memory. *History and Philosophy of Psychology*, 4(1), 1–12.

Douglas, M. (1992). The person in an enterprise culture. In S. H. Heap & A. Ross (Eds.), *Understanding the enterprise culture: Themes in the work of Mary Douglas* (pp. 41–62). Edinburgh: Edinburgh University Press.

Ebbinghaus, H. (1885/1964). *Memory: A contribution to experimental psychology*. New York: Dover.

Edwards, D., & Middleton, D. (1986). Text for memory: Joint recall with a scribe, *Human Learning*, 5, 125–138.

Edwards, D., & Potter, J. (1992). *Discursive psychology*. London: Sage.

Engeström, Y. (1987). *Learning by expanding*. Helsinki: Orienta-Konsultit Oy.

Fentress, J., & Wickham, C. (1992). *Social memory*. Oxford: Basil Blackwell.

Geertz, C. (1973). *The interpretation of cultures*. New York: Basic Books.

Hacking, I. (1995). *Rewriting the soul: Multiple personality and the sciences of memory*. Princeton, New Jersey: Princeton University Press.

Hirst, W., & Manier, D. (1996). Opening vistas for cognitive psychology. In L. Martin, B. Rogoff, K. Nelson & E. Tolbach (Eds.), *Sociocultural Psychology* (pp. 89–124). Cambridge: Cambridge University Press.

Irwin-Zarecka, I. (1993). *Frames of remembrance: social and cultural dynamics of collective memory*. New Brunswick, New Jersey: Transaction.

James, W. (1890/1950). *The principles of psychology*. New York: Dover.

Kashima, Y. (2000). Recovering Bartlett's social psychology of cultural dynamics. *European Journal of Social Psychology*, 30, 383–403.

Klein, K. L. (2000). On the emergence of memory in historical discourse. *Representations*, 69 (Winter), 127–150.

Locke, J. (transcribed and edited by P. H. Niddtch) (1690/1975). *Essay concerning human understanding*. Oxford: Oxford University Press.

Loftus, E. F. (1979). *Eyewitness testimony*. Cambridge, MA: Harvard University Press.

Loftus, E. F., & Ketchum, K. (1994). Tricked by memory. In Jaclyn Jeffrey and Glenace Edwall (Eds.), *Memory and history: Essays on recalling and interpreting experience* (pp. 17–32). Boston: University Press of America.

Middleton, D., & Brown, S. D. (2005). *The social psychology of experience: Studies in remembering and forgetting*. London: Sage Publications

Middleton, D., & Edwards, D. (1990). *Collective remembering*. London: Sage.

Misztal, B. A. (2003). *Theories of social remembering*. Buckingham: Open University Press.

Neisser, U. (1967). *Cognitive psychology*. New York: Appleton-Century-Crofts.

Neisser, U. (1982). *Memory observed: Remembering in natural contexts*. San Francisco: W. H. Freeman and Company.

Neisser, U., & Winograd, E. (1988). *Remembering reconsidered: Ecological and traditional approaches to the study of memory*. Cambridge: Cambridge University Press.

Norrick, N. R. (2000). *Conversational Narrative: Story telling in everyday conversation*. Amsterdam: John Benjamins Publishing Company.

Olick, J. K., & Robbins, J. (1998). Social memory studies: From 'collective memory' to the historical sociology of mnemonic practices. *Annual Review of Sociology*, 24, 105–140.

Pezdek, K., & Banks, W. P. (Eds.), (1996). *The recovered memory/false memory debate*. London: Academic Press.

Rosa, A. (1996). Bartlett's psycho-anthropological project. *Culture & Psychology*, 2(2), 355–378.

Rose, N. (1989). *Governing the soul: The shaping of the private self*. London: Routledge.

Rose, N. (1996). *Inventing our selves: Psychology, power and personhood*. Cambridge: Cambridge University Press.

Rumelhart, D. E. (1975). Notes on a schema for stories. In D. G. Brobrow and A. M. Collins. (Eds.), *Representation and understanding: Studies in cognitive science*. New York: Academic Press.

Sandage, S. (1993). A Marble House Divided: The Lincoln Memorial, the Civil Rights Movement and the Politics of Memory, 1939–1963. *Journal of American History*, 80:1, 135–67.

Schacter, D. L. (1996). *Searching for memory: The brain, the mind, and the past*. New York: Basic Books.

Schank, R. C. (1982). *Dynamic memory: A theory of reminding and learning in computers and people*. Cambridge: Cambridge University Press.

Schudson, M. (1992). *Watergate in American memory: How we remember, forget and reconstruct the past*. New York: Basic Books.

Schwartz, B. (2000). *Abraham Lincoln and the forge of national memory*. Chicago: University of Chicago Press.

Stephenson, G. M., Kniveton, B. H., & Wagner, W. (1991). Social influences on remembering: Intellectual, interpersonal and intergroup components. *European Journal of Social Psychology*, 21(6), 463–475.

Vygotsky, L. S. (1987). *Thought and language*. Cambridge, MA: MIT Press.

Wegner, D. (1986). Transactive memory. In B. Mullen & G. Goethals (Eds.), *Theories of group behavior*. New York: Springer-Verlag.

Weldon, M. S. (2001). Remembering as a social process. In D. L. Medin. (Ed.), *The psychology of learning and motivation* (pp. 67–120). San Diego: Academic Press.

Weldon, M. S., & Bellinger, K. D. (1997). Collective memory: Collaborative and individual processes in remembering. *Journal of Experimental Psychology: Learning, Memory & Cognition*, 23, 1160–1175.

Wertsch, J. V. (2002). *Voices of collective remembering*. Cambridge: Cambridge University Press.

Zelizer, B. (1992). *Covering the body: The Kennedy assassination, the media, and the shaping of collective memory*. Chicago: University of Chicago Press.

Zelizer, B. (1995). Reading the past against the grain: The shape of memory studies. *Critical Studies in Mass Communication*, 12, 214–239.

Zerubavel, E. (1996). Social memories: Steps to a sociology of the past. *Qualitative Sociology*, 19(3), 283–299.

Zerubavel, E. (1997). *Social mindscapes: An invitation to cognitive sociology*. Cambridge, MA: Harvard University Press.

CHAPTER 34

The Social Basis of Self-Reflection

Alex Gillespie

Self-reflection can be defined as a temporary phenomenological experience in which
self becomes an object to oneself. According
to theorists like Mead and Vygotsky, self-
reflection is a defining feature of humans,
and fundamental to the higher mental functions. Central to a socio-cultural perspective
is the idea that this distancing, from both
self and the immediate situation, occurs
using semiotic mediators (Valsiner, 1998).
Naming (i.e., using a semiotic mediator to
pick out) an affective experience or a situation distances the individual from that
experience or situation. Furthermore, such
distance enables self to act upon self and the
situation. For example, in order to obtain
dinner one must first name either one's
hunger or the fact that it is dinner time.
This naming, which is a moment of self-
reflection, is the first step in beginning to
construct, semiotically, a path of action that
will lead to dinner.

What triggers this process of semiotic
mediation? Exactly how do semiotic mediators enable distancing in general, and self-
reflection in particular? What is it in the
structure of semiotic mediators, or signs, that
enables this "stepping out" from immediate experience? And how are these signs
combined into complex semiotic systems
(representations, discourses, cultural artifacts, or symbolic resources) that provide
even greater liberation from the immediate
situation?

In order to address these questions, the
present chapter begins with a review of
socio-cultural theories of the origins self-
reflection. Four types of theory can be distinguished: rupture theories, mirror theories,
conflict theories, and internalization theories. In order to address the limitations of
these theories, Mead's theory of the social
act is advanced. These theories are then evaluated against an empirical instance of self-
reflection and a novel conception of complex
semiotic systems is proposed.

Rupture Theories

Rupture theories of self-reflection posit that
self-reflection arises when one's path of

action becomes blocked or when one faces a decision of some sort. Peirce provides an early articulation of this idea:

> If for instance, in a horse-car, I pull out my purse and find a five-cent nickel and five coppers, I decide, while my hand is going to the purse, in which way I will pay my fare. [...] To speak of such a doubt as causing an irritation which needs to be appeased, suggests a temper which is uncomfortable to the verge of insanity. Yet looking at the matter minutely, it must be admitted that, if there is the least hesitation as to whether I shall pay the five coppers or the nickel (as there will sure to be, unless I act from some previously contracted habit in the matter), though irritation is too strong a word, yet I am excited to such small mental activities as may be necessary in deciding how I shall act. [...] Images pass rapidly through consciousness, one incessantly melting into another, until at last, when all is over – it may be in a fraction of a second, in an hour, or after long years – we find ourselves decided as to how we should act. (1878/1998, 141–2)

According to Peirce, the problematic situation stimulates reflective thought. Even a small irritation, or rupture, can stimulate a stream of thought. This is a phenomenological experience that many people would be inclined to agree with. But why should a rupture spontaneously generate the semiotic system necessary for distancing?

Dewey (1896), developing Peirce's ideas, argued that in the ruptured situation the object ceases, from the perspective of the actor, to be objective and becomes, so to speak, subjective. Specifically, the object becomes subjective because the actor has two or more responses toward the object. Dewey gives the example of a child reaching for a flame. The child is attracted to the flame because it looks like something to play with; but the child is also afraid of the flame because of a previous burn. Thus there are two contradictory responses in the child: to reach toward the flame *and* to withdraw from the flame. It is due to the disjunction

between these two responses, Dewey argues, that self-reflection arises.

Mead (1910) criticized this theory arguing that there is nothing in having two contradictory responses which necessarily leads to self-reflection. In non-human animals there are conflicting responses, yet there is no self-consciousness. Pavlov (1951), for example, conditioned dogs to salivate upon seeing a circle and not to salivate upon seeing an ellipse. In successive trials he reduced the difference between the two contradictory stimuli, until the ellipse was almost a circle. When the stimuli became difficult to differentiate, thus evoking two contradictory responses, the dogs, usually placid, became frantic and remained disturbed for weeks afterward. Pavlov called this "experimental neurosis." Assuming that these dogs did not become self-reflective (and there is no evidence to suggest they did), then these experiments show that contradictory responses can co-exist without leading to self-reflection.

Piaget (1970) offers a more contemporary variant of the rupture theory. According to Piaget the child is forced to abstract and reorganize his/her developing schemas when those schemas lead to unfulfilled expectations. For example, the child expects the consequence of action X to be Y, but instead the consequence of action X is Z. Like the other rupture theorists, Piaget points to a proximal cause of self-reflection, namely a problematic situation, but he does not give us much purchase on the semiotic processes through which self-reflection arises. Again one can ask, why should a rupture stimulate the emergence of semiotic mediators? In order to address this question we need to move beyond the subject-object relation that Peirce, Dewey and Piaget were working with, and examine the self-other social relation.

Mirror Theories

The defining feature of mirror theories of self-reflection, compared to the rupture theories, is the presence of an other. These theories assume that the other perceives more about self than self can perceive. The reflective distance from self which self-reflection entails first exists in the mind of other. This "surplus" (Bakhtin, 1923/1990; Gillespie, 2003) can be fed back to self by other, such that self can learn to see self from the perspective of other. In this sense, mirror theories assume that the other provides feedback to self in the same way that a mirror provides feedback about appearance that we cannot perceive unaided. An early variant of this theory can be found in the writings of Adam Smith:

> Were it possible that a human creature could grow up to manhood in some solitary place, without any communication with his own species, he could no more think of his own character, of the propriety or demerit of his own sentiments and conduct, of the beauty or deformity of his own mind, than the beauty or deformity of his own face. All of these are objects which he cannot easily see, which naturally he does not look at, and with regard to which he is provided with no mirror which can present them to his view. Bring him into society, and he is immediately provided with the mirror which he wanted before. It is placed in the countenance and behaviour of those he lives with. (1759/1982, 110)

For Adam Smith it is "fellow man" who teaches self the value of self's actions, who is a "mirror" redirecting self's attention to the meaning of self's own actions. Growing up alone, without such a mirror, Smith writes, there is nothing to make a person reflect upon him/herself. The "mirror" is the "countenance and behaviour" of other.

The metaphor of society as a mirror, leading to self-reflection, was elaborated in Cooley's (1902, 184) concept of the "looking-glass self." According to Cooley, the self is a social product formed out of three elements: "the imagination of our appearance to the other person; the imagination of his judgment of that appearance, and some sort of self-feeling, such as pride or mortification." Interestingly, self-reflection for Cooley is always entwined with judgments, leading

to emotions such as pride, shame, guilt, or gloating. Unfortunately, much of the literature which has taken up Cooley's ideas has become mired in examining the extent to which self is "actually" able to take the perspective of the other (Shrauger & Schoeneman, 1979; Lundgren, 2004).

Psychoanalysts, on the other hand, have bypassed this trivial question, and have developed a sophisticated theory based on the mirror metaphor. According to Lacan (1949/1977), before the mirror stage the child is fragmented: feelings, desires and actions are unconnected. Within this scheme the mirror reveals the child to him/herself as a bounded totality, a *gestalt*. The self, by perceiving itself as bounded, and thus isolated, becomes alienated through self-reflection. This idea of mirroring is still current in psychoanalytic theories of child development (e.g., Gergely & Watson, 1996).

The feedback theories, despite articulating a proximal cause of self-reflection, encounter three problems if extended into a theory of the origin and nature of self-reflection. First, many non-human animals live in complex societies, and are constantly exposed to feedback from others, yet they do not have a consciousness of self. Presumably the difference between humans and other animals is that humans take the perspective of the other in the mirroring process. However, this only raises the second problem, namely, how does self take the perspective of the other? This seems to be assumed rather than explained. The third problem is the apparently neutral nature of the other in mirror theories. The idea that the other is a passive mirror, neutrally reflecting self back to self, is problematized by the third group of theories dealing with self-reflection, namely, the conflict theories.

Conflict Theories

According to the conflict theories, self-reflection arises through a social struggle. Hegel's theory of self-consciousness as exemplified in the master-slave allegory is a paradigmatic example (Marková, 1982).

Self-consciousness, Hegel argues, arises through gaining recognition from an other who is not inferior to self. According to the master-slave allegory, initially, self and other treat each other as physical objects, and thus deny any recognition to each other. Due to this mutual denial, self and other enter into a struggle, the outcome of which is a relation of domination and subordination, that is, the master-slave relation. The master dominates the slave and in that sense is free, while the slave, having lost the struggle, is in bondage to the master and is, thus, not free. The slave is in the service of the master and sees the master as superior, while the master sees the slave as inferior. According to Hegel's logic of recognition, the paradoxical outcome of this situation is that the slave can get recognition from the master, but the master cannot get recognition from the slave. The slave struggles for recognition from the master, and thus is led to develop new skills and competencies, which when recognized by the master create new domains of self-consciousness for the slave. The master, on the other hand, cannot satisfy the need for recognition because recognition by the slave is worthless. The interesting dynamic that Hegel describes is that self-consciousness, and thus self-reflection, arise through *struggling* for recognition from the other. In socio-cultural psychology one can find variations on this basic idea at the levels of interaction, institution, and representation.

At the interactional level, for example, the tradition of research on socio-cognitive conflict has clearly established that conflict between self and other over how to proceed in a joint task can lead to cognitive development (Doise & Mugny, 1984). Moreover, recent research has shown that a key component of durable cognitive development results from social interaction that takes the form of 'explicit recognition' (Psaltis & Duveen, under review), which is defined as the interaction or conversation where new acquired knowledge for self is recognized by other and self – that is to say, the interaction produces mutual self-reflection. However, it is also clear that such self-reflection can also position self negatively, as some-

one who is unable to learn or who should not learn, and thus stifle cognitive development. Sigel's Psychological Distancing Theory expresses a similar dynamic. Sigel (2002, 197–8) asserts that discrepancies introduced by the utterances of others can put a cognitive demand on the child which can in turn lead to representational work and thus distancing. In this case the utterances of others conflict with the child's initial impulses, and draw the child out of those impulses to reflect upon them. Stimulating the child to self-reflection in this way is a form of scaffolding, in which social others are intricately involved in the child's development.

Moving to the institutional level, activity theorists posit that contradictions between different components of an activity system lead to reflection. Activity Theory has much in common with Dewey's ideas (Tolman & Piekkola, 1989), but it differs from Dewey by extending the definition of the problematic situation to include problems introduced by the perspective of others. This is quite clear in Engeström's (1987; see also Cole & Engeström, Chapter 17, this volume) concept of "expansive learning," which refers to participants within an activity system prompting each other to reflect upon the conditions and rules of their ongoing interaction. The roots of expansive learning are to be found in "disturbances, ruptures and expansions" which arise in communication within an activity system (Engeström, Brown, Christopher, & Gregory, 1977, 373).

Finally, at the level of representation, recent work in social representations theory emphasizes the contradictions between different bodies of knowledge circulating in modern societies (Moscovici, 1984; Duveen, Chapter 26, this volume). Bauer and Gaskell (1999) argue that people become aware of representations at the points at which they overlap or contradict each other. "It is through the contrast of divergent perspectives that we become aware of representations, particularly when the contrast challenges our presumed reality" (Bauer & Gaskell, 1999, 169). Divergent representations, sustained by different groups, in different domains of practice, can come together and clash in the public sphere (Jovche-lovitch, 1995). When this occurs, individuals and groups may come to participate in conflicting representations. According to Bauer and Gaskell, it is this conflict which produces awareness of representations. This co-existence of multiple forms of knowledge in society, and consequently, in the individual minds of members of society engenders a state of "cognitive polyphasia" (e.g., Wagner, Duveen, Themel, & Verma, 1999), which can, but does not necessarily, lead to self-reflection.

Examining the conflict theories critically, one could say that they have the same basic structure as the rupture theories. In the rupture theories, tension is introduced through a problematic self-object relation, while in the conflict theories tension is introduced through a problematic self-other relation. In both cases the dynamic is similar, and thus the conflict theories are vulnerable to the same critiques as are posed to the rupture theories, namely, they identify a proximal cause of self-reflection (i.e., social conflict), but do little to elucidate the actual semiotic process through which self-reflection arises. The question to ask is: what is it about the social situation (self-other relation) that is not present in the practical situation (self-object relation) and which can account for the process of self-reflection? One possible answer to this question is provided by the internalization theories.

Internalization Theories

The idea that thought is a self-reflective internal dialogue with absent others goes back, at least, to Plato (e.g., *Sophist*, 263e; *Theaetetus*, 190). Forms of internalization are evident in the theories of Freud (in the formation of the superego), Bakhtin, and Vygotsky. Today this line of theory is carried forward by Hermans (2001), and Josephs (2002). Within this line of theorizing, one can conceptualize self-reflection as arising through internalizing the perspective that the other has upon self, followed by self taking the perspective of other upon self.

Or more generally, one could think of self-reflection as arising through the internal dialogue between internalized perspectives.

There are, however, problems over how the metaphor of "internalization" should be understood (Matusov, 1998). Wertsch and Stone (1985, 163) call the idea that social relations are simply "transmitted" into psychological structure "uninteresting and trivial." While some theorists make this mistake, Vygotsky (1997, 106) himself emphasized that the process of internalization is a process of "transformation," rather than simple "transmission" (see also Lawrence and Valsiner, 1993). The process of transformation is clearly evident Vygotsky's analysis of the emergence of pointing (1997, 104–5).

According to Vygotsky, the child becomes able to point only when he/she is able to reflect upon the meaning of the pointing from the standpoint of others. How does this come about? "Initially," Vygotsky (1997, 104) writes, "the pointing gesture represents a simply unsuccessful grasping movement directed toward an object and denoting a future action." At first the child is not self-conscious of pointing, and thus is not trying to communicate anything. Rather, the child is simply reaching for something out of reach. However, from the perspective of the mother, the child's reaching is meaningful, it indicates that the child desires the reached-for object. Vygotsky (1997, 105) states: "In response to the unsuccessful grasping movement of the child, there arises a reaction not on the part of the object, but on the part of an other person." The grasping first has the meaning of pointing for the mother, and only later has meaning for the child. It is only when the grasping becomes a meaningful gesture for the child that we can say the child is pointing, for it is only then that the child knows the meaning of his/her gesture for others. The child, Vygotsky (1997, 105) writes, "becomes for himself what he is in himself through what he manifests for others." That is to say, the child becomes self-aware of his/her own being through how he/she appears to others.

Summarizing the emergence of self-reflective meaning through internalization,

Vygotsky (1997, 105) writes: "Every higher mental function was external because it was social before it became an internal, strictly mental function; it was formerly a social relation of two people." Social relations, like conversations, become internalized and constitute the higher mental functions. Self-reflection, for example, can be understood as a change of perspective within the individual (analogous to the change of perspective between people taking turns in a conversation). "I relate to myself as people related to me. Reflection is a dispute" (Vygotsky, 1989, 56–7).

The tale that turns grasping into pointing can also be used to articulate Vygotsky's concept of the sign. According to Vygotsky (1997), signs are first used to mediate the behavior of others, and are later used to talk about self, reflect upon self and mediate the behavior of self. The child learns to point, first in order to direct the attention of others, and later to direct his own attention (for example, using his/her finger to keep his/her eyes focused upon the text). Equally, the child learns to ask questions of others before he/she asks questions of him/herself. But what is it in the structure of the sign that enables humans, on the one hand to communicate, and on the other hand to self-reflect?

The difference between grasping and pointing is that grasping is a response (to the stimulus of the desired object), while pointing is a response that is also a stimulus to both self and other. While grasping may be a stimulus to other, it is not a stimulus to self. Pointing becomes a sign when it is *not just a response but also a stimulus to self in the same way that it is a stimulus to other*. Thus, signs differ from other stimuli because "they have a reverse action," that is, signs are responses which can also be stimuli (Vygotsky & Luria, 1930/1994, 143). The classic example of "reverse action" is tying a knot in a handkerchief as a mnemonic aid. Self ties a knot in a handkerchief (a response), so that later, the knot will function as a stimulus, reminding self that something must be remembered. The idea of "reverse action" is fundamental to Vygotsky's concept of

the sign, which he initially theorized as a "reversible reflex" (1925/1999).

Only human actions and their products possess the key property of "reverse action." A naturally occurring tree might be a stimulus, but it is not a response. A dog might bare its teeth in response to the stimulus of a wolf. The baring of teeth may be a stimulus to the wolf, but it will never become a stimulus to the dog itself – thus the dog cannot know the meaning of this action for the wolf. A human's angry gesture is a response which may become a stimulus to the other. But crucially, the angry gesture may also become a stimulus to self, in the same way that it is a stimulus to other. To the other person the angry gesture may be evidence of an impulsive personality, and self may also become aware of this possible meaning of his/her angry gesture. If the gesture becomes a stimulus with the same meaning for self as it has for other, then it is a sign. Thus the man may shake his fist, not meaning to hit the other person, but simply to communicate his anger.

Vygotsky's conception of the sign is astonishingly close to Mead's concept of the significant symbol. Mead (1922) defines the significant symbol as a gesture which self experiences both from the perspective of self and from the perspective of other. As Mead (1922, 161) writes: "It is through the ability to be the other at the same time that he is himself that the symbol becomes significant." The key point of similarity is that both Mead and Vygotsky conceive of the sign (or significant symbol) as comprising two perspectives. On the one hand there is the embodied actor perspective (the response) toward some object (e.g., the reaching child desires the object). On the other hand, there is the distance introduced by the observer perspective of the other on the action (e.g., the mother sees the child's grasping as indicating desire). When the child takes both his/her own grasping perspective and the mother's perspective toward that grasping, then the grasping becomes pointing. Thus there is an equivalence between Vygotsky's concept of "reverse action" and Mead's concept of taking the perspective of the other.

Vygotsky's theory of the sign, and Mead's theory of the significant symbol, are fundamentally different from the theories of Peirce, Saussure, Bühler, and Morris (Gillespie, 2005). The latter all have monological theories of the sign. Simply put, they conceive of the sign as representing something or some relation to the world. However, according to the present reading of Vygotsky and Mead, the sign (or significant symbol) is a composite of two different perspectives, namely, an actor perspective and an observer perspective. Thus the sign (or significant symbol) is fundamentally intersubjective: *it evokes both actor and observer perspectives in both self and other.*

The fruitful consequences of the present conception of the sign are immediately evident when one tries to explain the role of the sign in either empathizing or self-reflection. In empathy, the sign carries the empathizer from an observer perspective (on, for example, the suffering of the other) to an actor perspective (participating in that suffering). In self-reflection, or distanciation, the sign carries the person from an actor perspective (a fully absorbed action orientation toward something) to an observer perspective (reacting to the absorbed action orientation), which can reconstruct the course of action, leading to absorption in a new actor perspective. And thus the absorption-distanciation cycle continues. The point being made, however, is that theorizing semiotics in terms of significant symbols, begins to make this cyclical movement explicable.

In the context of the present review of theories of self-reflection, Vygotsky's theory of the sign, and Mead's concept of the significant symbol, are landmark contributions, because both theories specify precisely the semiotic structure that can account for self-reflection. However, a lacuna remains. How does the child come to react to his/her own grasping in the same way that the mother responds? If the sign is a composite of the perspectives of self and other, then how does this composite form? How are these two perspectives brought together? In order to address this question we need to turn to Mead's theory of the social act.

The Social Act

Mead's theory of the social act is a theory of institutional structures (Gillespie, 2005). The first defining feature of humans for Mead is that they move amongst positions within a relatively stable social, or institutional, structure. Of course social structure is not unique to humans. Within an ant colony one will find the queen, workers, foragers, nurses, and soldiers. But it is not simply the existence of social structure that is fundamental for Mead. Rather, it is *position exchange within the institutional structure.* In non-human societies there is a division of labor, but there is never frequent position exchange. However, humans frequently exchange position within institutional structures. For example, people sometimes host parties and at other times attend parties. The perspectives of host and guest are quite divergent. If these social positions were never exchanged, or reversed, then it is unlikely that either would be able to take the perspective of the other. However, because people are sometimes hosts and sometimes guests this means that most adults have experience of both perspectives, and thus are able to take the perspective of the other when they are in either social position.

Additional social acts in which frequent position exchange occurs include: buying/selling, giving/receiving, suffering/helping, grieving/consoling, teaching/learning, ordering/obeying, winning/losing, and stealing/punishing. Each of these social acts entails reciprocal actor and observer positions, and importantly, because most people have had enacted both social positions, they have the both the actor and observer perspectives for each social act and thus are able to take the perspective of each other within a social act. The self then, is dialogical (see Salgado & Gonçalves, Chapter 30, this volume) – it contains a multitude of different perspectives originating in the social positions of a given society. Returning to the example of pointing, the child cannot learn the meaning of his/her own pointing without first having been in the social position of responding to the pointing of others.

However, having previously been in the social position of the other, within a social act, does not mean that self will necessarily take the perspective of the other. Why should the perspective of other be evoked in self when self is not in the social position of the other? The problem is that most of the stimuli for self and other are quite divergent. The child, who desires the object and is grasping toward it, is in a completely different situation to the mother, who is attentive to the child's grasping. Even if the child had previously responded to the grasping of others, why should the child now respond to his/her own grasping? The feeling of grasping is quite different to the sight of someone else grasping. What is common in these two situations that could serve to unite these two perspectives in the mind of the child? Mead (1912; Farr, 1997) points to the peculiar significance of the vocal gesture. Stimuli in the auditory modality (like vocal gestures) sound the same for self as they do for other. Accordingly, the vocal gesture is ideally poised to integrate both actor and observer perspectives. Because self hears self speak in the same way that self hears other speak, so self can react to self's utterances in the same way that self reacts to other. This is more than a mirror theory of self-reflection, it is not that self sees self in the mirror of the other, but rather self *hears* self in the same way that self hears other.

It is often asserted that self and other co-emerge in ontogenesis. However, Mead would disagree with this, arguing that the other exists for self before self exists for self. First self reacts to other, then self changes social position with the other, and finally self is able to react to self (in the same way that self previously reacted to other). Empirical evidence for rejecting the co-emergence thesis, in favor of Mead's theory, is found in studies of children's use of words denoting self and other, which have shown that chil-

dren talk about other before talking about self (e.g., Cooley, 1908; Bain, 1936).

Mead's theory of the social act fits closely with his theory of the significant symbol. The structure of the significant symbol (or sign) is a pairing of an actor perspective engaged in some action with an observer perspective reacting to that action. The social act is the institution that first provides individuals with roughly equivalent actor and observer experiences, and second, integrates these perspectives within the minds of individuals.

When both actor and observer perspectives within the significant symbol (or sign) are evoked, then there is self-reflection, because self is both self and other simultaneously. The question then is: what can trigger this double evocation? Simply, there are two ways in which self can arrive at an observer perspective on self (i.e., self-reflection). The process can begin with either an actor perspective engaged in some action, or an observer perspective on someone else's action. Either of these perspectives can evoke, via the structure of the significant symbol (or sign), the complementary actor and observer perspectives, thus leading to self-reflection. Self-reflection triggered by an actor perspective I call self-mediation. Self-reflection triggered by an observer perspective on an actor I call short-circuiting. The next section illustrates these two forms of self-reflection.

Two Processes of Self-Reflection: An Illustration

The following analysis is taken from a study on the interactions between tourists and Ladakhis, in northern India (Gillespie, 2006). Ladakh, on the border of Tibet, is a popular backpacker destination. Tourists are led to Ladakh by representations of the Himalayan mountains, spirituality and traditional culture. Usually the tourists in Ladakh reject the idea of package tourism, and claim to be searching for something more authentic. In the following exchange, an English university student is explaining, to me and another tourist, how she wants to have an authentic experience of Ladakh

> Laura: "I wanted to come up here for longer, to do voluntary work, to be more part of it, rather than just a tourist passing through, taking photos and buying things, eh, eh, I am quite disappointed I haven't, I don't know, eh, in eight days you can't, em, [. . .] it's just, having been with a family in the first place, I now want everything to be personal, to see proper India rather than just the India that everyone – that sounds rather clichéd – but that tourists see (pause) – (sigh) so I am a tourist really."

The actor perspective that Laura is initially embedded in is that of wanting "to be more part of" Indian life, and wanting "to see proper India." This desire for an authentic experience is positioned against the other tourists who are merely "passing through" and touring "the India that everyone [. . .] sees." Before traveling to Ladakh Laura had spent two months in south India, living with an Indian family, thus having seen the "proper India." Although she had planned to stay in Ladakh for longer, and even do voluntary work, she is now planning to leave Ladakh after just eight days. Accordingly, it is difficult for her to claim the position of someone who has experienced the "proper" Ladakh. The reality is that she, like the other tourists, is merely "passing through." The contradiction becomes apparent and leads to two inter-related, but theoretically distinct, movements of self-reflection: self-mediation and short-circuiting.

Self-Mediation

The first movement of self-reflection, which culminates in the utterance "that sounds rather clichéd," is quite straightforward. Laura begins in the actor perspective of wanting an authentic experience of India and Ladakh, and then, in the self-reflective utterance ("that sounds rather clichéd") switches to an observer perspective on her previous actor perspective. She ends up reflecting upon herself, suggesting that such a

search for the "proper" Ladakh is in fact a tourist cliché. How can this self-mediation be explained?

The rupture theories are obviously inadequate, because there is no pragmatic subject-object rupture. The mirror theories have more to contribute, because this self-reflection is embedded in a social situation. Laura is speaking to me and another tourist, and her self-reflection may have been stimulated by social feedback. For example, she may have perceived skeptical looks concerning her search for authenticity, thus triggering this self-reflection. Her utterance ("that sounds rather clichéd") is pejorative. Such a cliché is an embarrassment. Thus we could describe Laura as struggling for recognition from her audience. However, such an analysis, while insightful, does not explain the semiotic process underlying Laura's self-reflection. The internalization theories, on the other hand, do provide a model. According to these theories one could argue that Laura became self-aware by taking the perspective of her audience. But how does she take the perspective of her audience? The answer, I suggest, is to be found in Mead's concept of the vocal gesture.

Laura's phrase, "that sounds rather clichéd," is particularly revealing because according to Mead (1912) it is precisely the sound of her previous utterances that trigger self-reflection. The peculiar significance of vocal gestures is that they sound the same to self as they do to other. Laura hears her own utterances (expressing a desire to see the "proper India") in the same way as her audience. Accordingly, she is able to react to her own utterance as if it were the utterance of an other. Presumably, if Laura heard another tourist talking about finding the "proper India" she would think that it sounded clichéd. Using Vygotsky's terminology, one could say that Laura's initial utterance is not only a response to my question, it is also a stimulus to herself. In short, she becomes self-aware because she reacts to herself in the same way that she reacts to others. The key process underlying this instance of self-reflection is a movement from an actor perspective to an observer perspective on self. The vocal gesture is the semiotic means that carries Laura from being embedded in an actor perspective (searching for the "proper" India), to an observer perspective upon herself (that what she says sounds clichéd).

Short-Circuiting

The second movement of self-reflection culminates in the utterance, "so I am a tourist really." This movement begins with the contradiction between Laura's criticism of tourists "passing through, taking photos and buying things" and the fact that she only spent eight days in Ladakh (and, as she mentioned elsewhere, that she took many photos and bought many souvenirs). This movement is analytically distinct from the first instance of self-reflection, because here, the movement is from an observer perspective on other tourists (criticizing them for having a shallow experience) to an observer perspective on self (recognizing that self is the same as other).

The rupture theories again are of little use in this analysis because there is no subject-object rupture. Both the mirror and conflict theories can contribute an understanding of the proximal cause of Laura's self-reflection. One could speculate that the gaze of the audience made the contradiction salient, thus leading to a collapse of the self-other distinction. But again, this does not explain the semiotic process through which this might occur. Interestingly, the internalization theories also have little to contribute. Laura is not taking the perspective of the other, *rather she is taking her own perspective upon the other tourists and turning this upon herself.*

Vygotsky's theory of the sign and Mead's theory of the significant symbol, however, can begin to unpack this movement of self-reflection. When Laura is criticizing the other tourists, she is using signs (or significant symbols) to describe the other. She says that other tourists are just "passing through, taking photos and buying things." In the moment of speaking, Laura is blind to the fact that this is exactly what she has done. However, because signs are pairings of actor and observer perspectives, describing the other always evokes an empathetic actor response in self. In Laura's case, this empathetic response "resonates" with her own experiences. She hesitates ("eh, eh") and begins to speak ("I am quite disappointed I haven't") and then hesitates again ("I don't know, eh") and finally we discover what it is that is welling up in her mind, namely, that she has only spent eight days in Ladakh (and was leaving the next day). The significance of this takes time to manifest explicitly, and when it does, Laura can only say that, despite her wishes, she is a tourist just like any other tourist in Ladakh ("so I am a tourist really"). I call this form of self-reflection 'short-circuiting,' because it begins with an emphasis on the difference between self and other, and then this difference collapses and self becomes equivalent to other.

Mead's theory of the social act takes the analysis even further. *Laura's short-circuit can only occur because of frequent exchange of social positions within the social act.* If Laura had not been in the actual social position of the other tourists, if she had not been merely "passing through," taking photos and buying souvenirs, then the self-reflection could not have occurred. Stating the case even more forcefully, position exchange is a necessary precondition for this type of self-reflection. In this type of self-reflection, one can see clearly that self and other do not co-emerge, but rather that the characteristics first associated with "they" become recognized as characteristics of "me." First there is action, second, there is observing the other doing the same action, and finally, in the combination of these two perspectives, there is self-reflection.

Complex Semiotic Systems

The analysis of Laura's self-reflection, as outlined so far, could be criticized on two fronts: first it is too individualistic (isn't Laura's self-reflection part of a larger cultural pattern?), and second, it is overly concerned with individual signs (what about more complex semiotic systems?). Both of these criticisms are well placed. Laura is not the first tourist to hypocritically criticize other tourists (Prebensen, Larsen, & Abelsen, 2003). Moreover, Laura's description of other tourists as just "passing through, taking photos and buying things" is a complex collective and historical product. Neither Vygotsky nor Mead provides an adequate theory of the more complex trans-individual semiotic systems that circulate in society. One of the significant advances of socio-cultural psychology, since the work of Mead and Vygotsky, has been the theorization of these complex semiotic systems in a variety of ways: as social representations (Moscovici, 1984), cultural artifacts (Cole, 1996), symbolic resources (Zittoun, Duveen, Gillespie, Ivinson, & Psaltis, 2003; Zittoun, Chapter 16, this volume), narratives (Bruner, 1986), interpretive repertoires (Potter & Wetherell, 1987), and discourses with subject positions (Harré & Van Langehove, 1991).

Laura participates in a collective and historical discourse that contains several subject positions. First, there is the subject position of the tourist dupe. This is the tourist who just passes through, takes photos, and buys souvenirs. Most tourists willingly ascribe this subject position to other tourists, yet few ascribe this position to themselves. Instead, tourists try to occupy one of the more favorable subject positions, like that of adventurer, spiritual searcher, or reflexive post-tourist. Laura, for example, tries to occupy the position of having authentic encounters with the local population, as evidenced by her aspirations to do voluntary work and live with a local family.

The question is: How can these complex semiotic systems be used to help explain the semiotics of self-reflection? The interesting thing about the discourse is not simply that it has several subject positions, but that Laura claims, in discourse, one position, while enacting, in action, a different position. On the one hand, Laura's actions conform to typical tourist practices. She has been led, by various representations, to a tourist destination where the only obvious paths of action are to sightsee, take photos and buy souvenirs. On the other hand, Laura participates in a discourse that conceives of these typical tourist actions as shallow, and instead aspires to less attainable subject positions (i.e., having authentic encounters). Thus Laura is caught in a contradictory stream of cultural meanings. This collectively produced, and historically sustained, fault-line makes both self-mediation and short-circuiting immanent.

Using the theory of the sign, outlined above, we can further this analysis. This fault-line in the cultural stream corresponds to the structure of the sign. The contradiction is between the semiotic guidance of tourist action (actor perspective) and the criticism of other tourists (observer perspective). There is, at the level of discourses and representations, then, a lack of integration between actor and observer perspectives. It must be emphasized that this is not simply a contradiction between two semiotic systems (i.e., a conflict theory of self-reflection), rather it concerns a very specific contradiction, namely between actor and observer perspectives. The position that self claims and the position that self enacts are disjunctive. This is what Ichheiser (1949) called a mote-beam divergence. The prevalence of this divergence reveals that the lack of integration between actor and observer perspectives is not simply something that occurs at the level of individual signs, but something that is played out in much more macro semiotic dynamics. The point, then, is that the structure of the sign (or significant symbol), is not only evident at the level of individual words or gestures, but is evident in the macro-structure of whole complex semiotic systems.

Conclusion

Returning to the questions raised at the outset of this chapter, it is now possible to offer some concise answers. The proximal reasons for self-reflection are diverse. Humans can be led to self-reflection by ruptures (problems with the subject-object relation), social feedback (where the other acts as a mirror), social conflict (in the struggle for recognition), and internal dialogues (through internalizing the perspective of the other on self). Moreover, there is a cultural level to the analysis; the complex semiotic systems in which people are embedded contain contradictions that can make self-reflection immanent. These different theoretical traditions are not in opposition. Rather they theorize different proximal paths leading toward self-reflection, and entail different dynamics of thought (e.g., distinction, similarity, contrast, and internal dialogical relations). However, beyond differentiating these proximal routes toward self-reflection, the present chapter has tried to explicate the semiotic conditions underlying any self-reflection in terms of the structure of the sign, or significant symbol.

Before the formation of the sign (or significant symbol) there is undifferentiated experience (level o experience in Valsiner's (2001) terminology). But this experience is structured by social acts: it contains experience belonging to both actor and observer perspectives. The magic of the social act is that it integrates these actor and observer experiences, or perspectives, into the formation of signs – enabling higher levels of semiotic mediation. Conceiving of the sign as this integration of perspectives elucidates the logic of self-reflection. Whenever one uses a sign to describe self's own actor experience, the sign may carry self from an actor perspective to an observer perspective on that experience (as illustrated by Laura's self-mediation). Equally, whenever one uses a sign to describe, or observe, the actions of others, the sign may carry self from this observer perspective to an empathetic actor participation in the actions of the other (which in Laura's case leads to a short-circuit).

Introducing the concept of the sign (or significant symbol) into our conception of complex semiotic systems entails abandoning the assumption that the complex semiotic systems "mirror" the world, and instead conceptualizing these semiotic systems as architectures of intersubjectivity (Rommetveit, 1974) which enable the translation between actor and observer perspectives within a social act. Such a conception gives us considerable purchase on complex semiotic systems.

Consider, for example, narratives. It has been argued by Nelson (2000) that the key to self-consciousness is awareness of self in time, and that this implies narratives. According to Nelson, the developing child is offered self-narratives, and by appropriating these, the child is able to conceptualize him/herself in time. Combining this with the present theoretical approach, we can say that before appropriating a narrative a child will have certain fields of undifferentiated (actor perspective) experience. For example, the child may have experienced the loss of a loved one, but have not reflective articulation of this experience. The narrative offered to the child provides an observer's perspective on this actor experience of loss. And it is the integration of actor and observer perspectives, that enables the child to distanciate from the experience, and thus to become self-conscious of the loss (raising the level of semiotic mediation to levels 1 and 2 in Valsiners (2001) terminology).

A similar dynamic is evident in Zittoun's (Chapter 16, this volume) analysis of Emma Bovary's use of novels as a symbolic resource. Initially, Emma is embedded in the actor perspective of being in love. She feels exalted and has no self-reflective awareness of this experience. Then she thinks of some romance novels that she read. These provide her with an observer's perspective on an other's love. Combining the actor perspective (elation) with the observer perspective (on the love of others) results in the self-reflective awareness of herself being in love. Thus the narrative is not just a narrative that is analogical to self's own experience, it is an intersubjective structure that enables translations between actor and observer perspectives.

Partially integrated actor and observer perspectives are the pre-condition for self-reflection. Rupture, feedback, and social conflict can cause self-reflection because of a pre-existing, and only partially integrated, architecture of intersubjectivity. These social dynamics can provide the impetus for self-reflection, and thus have a part to play in constructing the architecture of intersubjectivity. However, these social dynamics, in themselves, cannot explain the semiotic process underlying self-reflection. For that we need a theory of semiotics. The origin of self-reflection is not just in social interaction, but in social acts, or institutions, which provide structured actor and observer perspectives, and a mechanism for integrating these perspectives in the minds of individuals, and thus for the formation of semiotic mediators.

References

Bain, R. (1936). The self-and-other words of a child. *The American Journal of Sociology*, 41(6), 767–775.

Bakhtin, M. (1923/1990). Author and hero in aesthetic activity (Translated by V. Liapunov). In M. Holquist & V. Liapunov (Eds.), *Art and answerability: early philosophical essays by M. M. Bakhtin* (Vol. 9). Austin, Texas: University of Texas Press.

Bauer, M. W., & Gaskell, G. (1999). Towards a paradigm for research on social representations. *Journal for the Theory of Social Behaviour*, 29(2), 163–186.

Bruner, J. (1986). *Actual minds, possible worlds*. Cambridge, MA: Harvard University Press.

Cole, M. (1996). *Cultural psychology: A once and future discipline*. Cambridge, MA: Harvard University Press.

Cooley, C. H. (1902). *Human nature and the social order*. New York: Charles Scribner's Sons.

Cooley, C. H. (1908). A study of the early use of the self-words by a child. *Psychological Review*, 15, 339–357.

Dewey, J. (1896). The reflex arc concept in psychology. *Psychological Review*, 3(July), 357–370.

Doise, W., & Mugny, G. (1984). *The social development of the intellect*. Oxford: Pergammon.

Engeström, Y. (1987). *Learning by expanding: An activity-theoretical approach to developmental research*. Helsinki: Orienta Konsultit.

Engeström, Y., Brown, K., Christopher, L. C., & Gregory, J. (1997). Coordination, cooperation and communication in the courts: Expansive transitions in legal work. In M. Cole & Y. Engestrom & O. Vasquez (Eds.), *Mind, culture and activity: Seminal papers from the Laboratory of Comparative Human Cognition* (pp. 369–385). Cambridge: Cambridge University Press.

Farr, R. M. (1997). The significance of the skin as a natural boundary in the sub-division of psychology. *Journal for the Theory of Social Behaviour*, 27(2–3), 305–323.

Gergely, G., & Watson, J. S. (1996). The social biofeedback theory of parental affect-mirroring: The development of emotional self-awareness and self-control in infancy. *International Journal of Psychoanalysis*, 77(6), 1181–1212.

Gillespie, A. (2003). Surplus & supplementarity: Moving between the dimensions of otherness. *Culture & Psychology*, 9(3), 209–220.

Gillespie, A. (2005). G. H. Mead: Theorist of the social act. *Journal for the Theory of Social Behaviour*, 35(1), 19–39.

Gillespie, A. (2006). *Becoming other: From social interaction to self-reflection*. Greenwich, CT: Information Age Publishing.

Harré, R., & Van Langenhove, L. (1991). Varieties of positioning. *Journal for the Theory of Social Behaviour*, 21(4).

Hermans, H. J. M. (2001). The Dialogical Self: Toward a theory of personal and cultural positioning. *Culture & Psychology*, 7(3), 243–281.

Ichheiser, G. (1949). Misunderstandings in human relations: A study in false social perception. *American Journal of Sociology*, 55 (suppl.), 1–72.

Josephs, I. E. (2002). 'The Hopi in Me': The construction of a voice in the dialogical self from a cultural psychological perspective. *Theory & Psychology*, 12(2), 161–173.

Jovchelovitch, S. (1995). Social Representations in and of the public sphere: Towards a theoretical articulation. *Journal for the Theory of Social Behaviour*, 25, 81–102.

Lacan, J. (1949/1977). The mirror stage as formative of the function of the I as revealed in psychoanalytic theory, *Ecrits: A selection*. London: Tavistock Publications.

Lawrence, J. A., & Valsiner, J. (1993). Conceptual roots of internalization: From transmission to transformation. *Human Development*, 36, 150–167.

Lundgren, D. C. (2004). Social feedback and self-appraisals: Current status of the Mead-Cooley hypothesis. *Symbolic Interaction*, 27(2), 267–286.

Marková, I. (1982). *Paradigms, thought and language*. Chichester: Wiley.

Matusov, E. (1998). When solo activity is not privileged: Participation and internalization models of development. *Human Development, 41*, 326–354.

Mead, G. H. (1910). Social consciousness and the consciousness of meaning. *Psychological Bulletin, 6*, 401–408.

Mead, G. H. (1912). The mechanism of social consciousness. *The Journal of Philosophy, Psychology and Scientific Methods, 9*(15), 401–406.

Mead, G. H. (1922). A behavoioristic account of the significant symbol. *Journal of Philosophy, 19*(6), 157–163.

Moscovici, S. (1984). The phenomenon of social representations. In R. Farr & S. Moscovici (Eds.), *Social Representations*. Cambridge: Cambridge University Press.

Nelson, K. (2000). Narrative, time and the emergence of the encultured self. *Culture & Psychology, 6*(2), 183–196.

Pavlov, I. P. (1951). *Psychopathology and psychiatry: Selected works* (D. Myshne & S. Belsky, Trans.). Moscow: Foreign Languages Publishing House.

Peirce, C. S. (1878/1998). *Charles S. Peirce: The essential writings* (Edited by Edward C. Moore). New York: Prometheus Books.

Perret-Clermont, A. N. (1980). *Social interaction and cognitive development in children*. London: Academic Press.

Piaget, J. (1970). Piaget's theory. In P. H. Mussen (Ed.), *Carmichael's manual of child psychology* (3rd ed., pp. 703–732). New York: John Wiley and Sons.

Potter, J., & Wetherell, M. (1987). *Discourse and social psychology*. London: Sage Publications.

Prebensen, N. K., Larsen, S., & Abelsen, B. (2003). I'm not a typical tourist: German tourists' self-perception, activities, and motivations. *Journal of Travel Research, 41*(4), 416–420.

Psaltis, C., & Duveen, G. (under review). Social relations and cognitive development: The influence of conversation type and representations of gender. *European Journal of Social Psychology*.

Rommetveit, R. (1974). *On message structure: A framework for the study of language and communication*. London: John Wiley and Sons.

Shrauger, J. S., & Schoeneman, T. J. (1979). Symbolic interactionist view of self-concept. *Psychological Bulletin, 86*, 549–573.

Sigel, I. E. (2002). The psychological distancing model: A study of the socialization of cognition. *Culture & Psychology, 8*(2), 189–214.

Smith, A. (1759/1982). *The theory of moral sentiments* (Edited by D. D. Raphael & A. L. Macfie). Indianapolis, IN: Liberty Fund.

Tolman, C. W., & Piekkola, B. (1989). John Dewey and dialectical materialism: Anticipations of activity theory in the critique of the reflex arc concept. *Activity Theory, 1*(3–4), 43–46.

Valsiner, J. (1998). *The Guided Mind*. Cambridge, MA: Harvard University Press.

Valsiner, J. (2001). Process structure of semiotic mediation in human development. *Human Development, 44*, 84–97.

Vygotsky, L. S. (1925/1999). Consciousness as a problem in the psychology of behavior. In N. N. Veresov (Ed.), *Undiscovered Vygotsky: Etudes on the pre-history of cultural-historical psychology*. Bern: Peter Lang Publishing.

Vygotsky, L. S., & Luria, A. (1930/1994). Tool and symbol in child development. In R. Van de Veer & J. Valsiner (Eds.), *The Vygotsky Reader*. Oxford: Blackwell.

Vygotsky, L. S. (1989). Concrete human psychology. *Soviet Psychology, 27*(2), 53–77.

Vygotsky, L. S. (1997). *The collected works of L. S. Vygotsky (Volume 4, edited by R. W. Rieber)* (Translated by M. J. Hall). New York: Plenum Press.

Wagner, W., Duveen, G., Themel, M., & Verma, J. (1999). The modernization of tradition: thinking about madness in Patna, India. *Culture & Psychology, 5*, 413–445.

Wertsch, J. V., & Stone, C. A. (1985). The concept of internalization in Vygotsky's account of the genesis of higher mental functions. In J. V. Wertsch (Ed.), *Culture, communication and cognition*. Cambridge: Cambridge University Press.

Zittoun, T., Duveen, G., Gillespie, A., Ivinson, G., & Psaltis, C. (2003). The use of symbolic resources in developmental transitions. *Culture & Psychology, 9*(4), 415–448.

Socio-Cultural Psychology on the Move

Semiotic Methodology in the Making

Alberto Rosa and Jaan Valsiner

"I am now changing sails and seeking an untrod land. To be sure, the voyage will probably find its end before [reaching] the coast. At least, what happens to so many of my colleagues shall not happen to me: to settle down comfortably in the ship itself so that eventually they think that the ship itself is the new land."

Georg Simmel to Marianne Weber, Berlin/Westend, Dec, 9, 1912 . (Wolf, 1959)

A research field is indeed similar to a ship. It sails somewhere – sometimes only the direction may be known, but not the route, nor the harbor of arrival. At times, the goals are set in terms that look appealing – discovering a Westward route to India, or curing a dangerous disease. The reality of arrival may be much less grandiose than ever expected – instead of the golden land one may arrive at some tropical island that fits future potentials for sugar cane and slavery; or after arriving at a cure for a disease that very cure may trigger new diseases. Development of open systems – biological, psychological, social, and epistemological – is always wrought

with unexpected expansions into new areas of challenges.

Simmel's words are most appropriate for the general conclusions of this first handbook on socio-cultural psychology. Socio-cultural reality, like the sea, is always moving, encompassing storms and hiding various dangerous reefs and floating icebergs. One has to adjust the course and continuously set the sails to reach to a coast that always seems to be beyond immediate reach. The temptation for the sailors of this sea – socio-cultural researchers – are in danger for becoming involved in a discourse within their own community, and leave the complex problems of the cultural realities to face their own storms, and floating icebergs. Surely, the new discipline of socio-cultural psychology that – as the readers of this Handbook could observe – gives so much promise for new understanding of complex realities – should not become the *Titanic* of the social sciences.

To avoid the gloriously sad fate of a sinking ship, a synthesis of currently existing and historically prominent key ideas is in order. We hope that this Handbook fulfills the needs for such synthesis that for a decade has been attempted on the pages of the core journal in the field – *Culture & Psychology* (Valsiner, 1995, 2001, 2004). However, every new synthesis is a slow and inherently ambivalent achievement. The reader may observe the authors rambling around some complex idea, showing off their positioning by all too frequent use of it – and failing to link it with the phenomena that are under investigation. How, then, can we – as Editors of the Handbook – view its accomplishments and gaps in our building up of the new and promising continent of basic understanding?

This book presented an overview of the main aspects of current research within the field and offers a line of thought that runs throughout the chapters that unifies the different contributions. Collectively the contributions to this book break the tradition of separating research from theory – a phenomenon we can often observe in contemporary social sciences where different versions of blind empiricism reign. Some of these versions are pseudo-empirical:

> ... *psychological research tends to be pseudoempirical, that is, it tends to involve empirical studies of relationships which follow logically from the meanings of the concepts involved. An example would be studying whether all bachelors are really male and unmarried.* (Smedslund, 1995, p. 196)

Pseudo-empiricism can be countered by careful elucidation of theoretical assumptions and their linkages with those research questions that can provide the investigator new knowledge that cannot be derived from the meanings of the terms in use.

The alternative to the dominance of "blind" and "pseudo"- empiricism is the saturation of the social sciences by various forms of ideologies-bound perspectives. This tendency is also visible in the field. Instead of treating a theory as an epistemic tool that allows the researcher a different perspective upon the object of investigation, theories become ossified as orthodoxies – as political, rather than scientific, standpoints. Examples of such diversion can be found in the history of the parts of the socio-cultural area – excessive arguments about topics like "this is not *true* Vygotskian view" or "activity theory *is right*" are examples of superfluous side-stepping from the main issue – how to study socio-cultural phenomena?

New Discourse Topics in Socio-Cultural Psychology

Looking back at our experiences in editing this Handbook, we come to the realization that it has presented a story. It is obviously a multi-voiced story where the narration passes through a jungle of psychological, sociological, philosophical, and ethical issues.

It seems to be that when new ideas are produced some version of an evolutionary process is operating. Social transaction around such ideas produces states of equilibriae – key sub-areas of scientific discourse– which sometimes became agents, actors, and then authors of their own life and life-story. For this to happen, both the individuals – the scientists– and their environments – immediate networks and wider social contexts– have to adjust to each other, and re-construct each other. The outcome is the creation of new environmental ambience for the management of conduct, so that changes in the distribution of agency take place. Thus, statements like "theory X tells us to do Y" are examples of outward projection of the constructions of the minds of the researchers into their intellectual environments where the agency is attributed to these constructs.

A number of sub-concepts emerge in the field at our present time and are prominent in a number of chapters here – dynamic systems, conventionalization of objects and movements, uncertainty, religious experience, dialogical self, social representing, networks of actants, are some of them. A few of them come from recent contributions of neighboring disciplines. Others are recovered from the past of Psychology and examined with a new regard. A comment on some of them is at issue.

SYMBOLIC RESOURCES

Real-life psychological phenomena are culturally made through utilization of resources – material and symbolic. Symbolic resources are important parts of cultural life. They mediate what groups and individuals can do and understand when involved in social practices. Symbols are also susceptible to change their meanings as they are subjected to novel uses. When new generations are trained in cultural practices and in the use of these symbols, new groups appear and these practices and meanings are transformed. The result is a continuous commerce between social and personal cultures, in which both are transformed, producing changes in values, feelings of belonging, identity and the self. One of the consequences of these changes is an increase in uncertainty. Past experiences have to be recalled, reviewed, and updated, so memory and self-reflection become resources for resolving current problems and preparing a future.

When examining the intricacies of the working of the symbolic market, Bourdieu (1991) discusses the issue of symbolic power, and warns about the naivety of thinking of the existence of a sort of *linguistic communism*. Neither has everybody the same resources for choosing, nor all the shops offer goods at affordable prices. Distribution systems do not reach everybody either. One has to negotiate the situation with the resources s/he has at hand, and to choose between different options. Retreating into the safe heaven of traditional life, into forming groups which offer personal comfort (sects or gangs), or going into the pains of facing the inclemency of life and devise her or his own way of increasing his/her symbolic capital, are among the available options. But sometimes there is room for one to build one's own virtues, a sort of internal moral drive either to increase one's own capability for enjoying life, or to excel in the performance of his/her actuations in society. And sometimes both. There is no doubt that contingencies are at play when these options are made, as the prices to pay before and after one option is taken are also different.

THE NOTION OF ACTUATION

Culture is the means for transformation of nature by mankind. It also leads to developing new means for the direction and understanding of human behavior. Something that is done by the change of use of natural objects, or the production of new ones (tools). The notion of actuation (chapters 10 and 14) is a new addition to the theoretical repertoire. Actuations are structured sets of actions regulated by a semiotic logic. They are a result of the biological function of orientation which evolves into intentionality and purpose, and eventually in goal-oriented behavior. Actuations develop into scripts capable of changing their functionality to attain new goals, producing novel uses of actions and objects, and so make new abilities to appear. Conventional symbolic resources are a result of this process. The nature of actuations upon the world and upon the others then changes. Once this process is underway inter-actuations can be negotiated through communicative actuations mediated by conventional symbols.

Social norms develop through these interactions as well as they regulate how to perform actuations and interactuations mediated by these objects. These norms are an instantiation of how action can be adapted to the affordances (both physical and social) of these new objects. This requires the attunement of interactuations, and so new mediating symbols are developed, as well as new rules for their use, and so setting a historical process into motion which is peculiar of each particular group. The social structure of the group varies as the complexity of production processes increases, and so subgroups (social classes, gender groups, etc.) appear, each one with its peculiar tools for mediating their work and rules for using them and regulating their inter-actuating scripts, with their own systems of norms and values to make possible to have the shared representations indispensable for cooperation. Newcomers to these subgroups (children and immigrants) are directed in ways that shape their intentional schemas and scripts, and so they follow a developmental path devised to fit their psychological resources so that they can come to sharing the experiences produced in the working of the group.

The Cultural Construction of the World, Reason and the Person

Once this historical process of cultural evolution is on the move, some consequences happen which are worthy of being taken into account. The *world* at large appears as a structured whole that goes beyond actual lived experiences. Myths, Philosophy, and other epistemic devices and practices develop, producing a *Weltanschauung* typical of a particular cultural group. Scripts for actuation then not only have a sense, they have a shared meaning, which may be taken to transcend what is immediately felt. The actor becomes a character in an on-going drama, and so becomes a *persona* with a role to play, and some norms and values to be embodied in his or her actions. She or he is presented with some moral norms to follow, with some goals for excellence, with some virtues to attain.

The beliefs about the world, the artifacts and artificial symbols, the social structure and norms, the personalities of the members of the group, the performed actuations, and the meaning of experiences and of the tasks to be carried out are all tightly knitted in a network which can be expressed as a set of *rationes*, of proportions, as a set of formulae to navigate within the complexities of life. It can then be said that the transformations happened within the group along time shape a *reason* (González, 1997). A reason that no doubt develops from the rationale of the natural encounters of particular shaped organisms and their *Umwelt*, but that also takes a particular form as a result of how the social and cultural changes of the group have proceeded along the times. In sum, the human *reason* so developed is on the one hand, universal (natural), but on the other it takes some particularities that fits the needs and resources developed within the cultural group. This particularity is a specification of natural structures adapted to particular tools, to a concrete social structure and some specific cultural practices. It is a situated rea-

son that can only be explained by taking into account both, the natural encounters of organisms and their environment, and the particular ways in which contingencies have played in a particular cultural milieu so that teleonomy has been turned into teleology by a set of particular human actuations.

DEVELOPMENTAL EXPLANATION
In order to account for how this reason came into existence, one should look, first, into how evolution provided with the organic structures which shape the human body to actuate upon the environment (phylogenesis); then, on how human actuations in the past has transformed the environment, created new objects and shape a socio-cultural *Umwelt* (i.e., cultural history); and, finally how an individual born in such a group gets psychologically shaped along its physical maturation through an immersion in the practices of the socio-cultural cradle she or he grows within (ontogenesis). How a human being actually actuates before a new task to be carried out in a particular instant (microgenesis) can only be accounted for by looking into her or his life-history, and the actual demands of the task at hand, as well as to the constraints and resources available for actuation; that is, combining an ecological and socio-cultural (and historical) approach.

Culture is both natural and artificial – it results from human social action, and as such invention – acts as guidance for what being human is, what humans can do, and how to reflect upon what they are doing – in ways which are particular for each social group. A human being is enmeshed in a network of social relationships, tools, communicative signs, and discourses that regulate his/her actuations, s/he is regulated by discourses which give a sense to what is being done at that moment, since they are actuating towards a socio-culturally set goal, that the actor is making his/her own, and so incorporating into her/his personal motivational structure. In sum, an on-going dramaturgical actuation can be described using the analytical and explanatory device that Engeström (1987) calls an *activity system* (see Cole & Engeström, chapter 23, this volume).

So viewed, the historical evolution of a cultural group puts into motion a process of co-construction of social structures and institutions, tools, symbols, discourses, rituals and practices, as well as it shapes the psychological structure of its members. Thus, persons, moral codes, and the world at large get mutually constituted along this process. The culture provides cultural systems of sense (Gillespie, 2006, and chapter 34, this volume; Rosa & Monserrat, 2003; Zittoun, 2006, and Chapter 16, this volume) which provide individual performing actuations and scripts with sense and reasons, set a moral, and so makes accountability possible. Since each individual occupies a particular position within the socio-cultural structure, is expected to perform some particular tasks in concrete settings, has some particular resources and constraints for his/her actuations, and also s/he is continuously developing him/herself along this process, it can be said that his/her performing actuations are always within a co-constructed "zonified"[1] milieu (Valsiner, 1997).

REASON, SENSE, AND MORALITY

Moral norms and personal accountability result from social norms that connect together scripts for actuation and discourses describing the world as a meaningful system of meanings. Everything to be done, and everything actually done, has then a social meaning beyond personal sense, and so can be termed as morally right, wrong, or indifferent, and so to be praised or corrected. Moral accountability so appears, since everyone is urged to judge how to conciliate personal desires and sense with social norms and meanings, and face the consequence of his/her choices.

The tightly knit cultural tissue weaves together a view of what the world at large is like, of what the social group and humanity is (linked to being one of us, of our particular way of being human), and so produces resources and set constraints about what to make sense of what is felt and sensed: about how to have meaningful experiences. Feelings and emotions are so attributed meanings which fit within the cultural cradle for

providing experiences with personal sense (Choi, Han, & Kim – chapter 15, this volume). As well as sensorial experiences are taken to be signs of particular objects made to exist in each culture (mythical entities, idols, virtual objects, etc.). So, empirical experience is made to fit the constructed view of the world, and so it reinforces the meaning of everything in life. The result is that any alternative view would not only shed doubts about the received view of the world, but also threatens the social order, as well as going against the social norms: it is immoral. Trespassers of these limits are then sinners, if not blasphemous or insane, and in any case to be corrected, or even outcast. They talk and act against reason. Or should one say *beyond reason*?

SEARCHING FOR "THE TRUTH" – NEVER TO FIND IT

The creation of a view of the world at large is done via the use of artificial symbols and discourses. The world so viewed is then a *world of paper* (Latour, 1987) a world as it is represented in discourses (irrespectively of whether they are oral or written). Meaningful experience connects what is felt when performing actuations upon the milieu with that view of the world. This makes possible that mismatches occur – leading to disequilibration. The search for something called *truth* becomes then an issue – people, social groups, and sometimes whole countries become involved in "soul-searching" of some kind. Meaningfully framed experience and reason, in addition to (and sometimes in spite of) moral constructs – become criteria to sort out what is "true" (or "false").

Social dynamics provide plenty of examples of these kinds of disequilibria. These often result from the historical development of a group, and become increasingly frequent as groups turn into large societies, or even into civilizations. When a collective culture expands throughout a large territory and sets up communalities, its homogenizing function is weakened as a result of local syncretisms which introduce ever-new varieties to human social lives. When this happens disequilibria may become more frequent, producing crises that may produce revolutionary historical changes (e.g., as happened in Western modernity when science appeared, or in European religious Reformation and Counter-Reformation – Pettegree, 2005).

Contact between different societies also produces commerce of symbols and discourses (aside from goods) and so threatens the delicate equilibrium on which a society or a civilization lives, or even produce the risk of dangerous clashes (Huntington, 1996). It is therefore no surprise that political systems eagerly create boundaries – walls in the middle of a city or around a neighboring country, radio jamming practices, newspaper censorship, and public discreditation campaigns – to maintain their order. These efforts lead to counter-efforts to topple that order – a boundary created by one is a challenge for another to overcome, tear down, and – replace by some other boundary of one's own.

These three processes – historical evolution, revolutionary crises and cultural clashes – set the stage for permanent situations of uncertainty that – at the level of personal experiences – are full of ambivalence (Frenkel-Brunswik, 1949; Valsiner & Abbey, 2006a). Received views and norms do not suffice, and new forms of interpretation – new semiosis, actuations, scripts, views of the world, social norms, and personal virtues – have to be devised. Social and personal instabilities lead to efforts to overcome those – and lead to new instabilities.

Struggling With Uncertainty

One of the consequences of modernity was the breaking of cultural isolation. A historical process which has not stopped since – nor can it ever do so. Closed socio-cultural realms, with monopolistic production and distribution systems of symbolic goods and commodities, could not keep themselves closed to foreign influence. Open societies (Popper, 1945) flourished. They resulted from new forms of equilibria in which the public and the private intersected in new ways as a result of the development of symbolic markets (Bourdieu, 1991).

The tight fabric of culture above described, that made possible a stability of the world, the social structure, and the self, could not keep its splendid isolation. Traditional society from being a resource for social and personal life turned, either into a cherished imagined past which provided a nostalgic safe heaven for the uncertainties now to be faced, or into a suffocating Leviathan one wants to get rid off so that opting among newly available choices become possible. And sometimes both.

John Locke's *Letter concerning tolerance* (1689) and Immanuel Kant's critical philosophy were among the voices which called for a new way of conceiving society, knowledge, civil law, and ethics. Private life and the public realm so could be separated. Personal beliefs, what the world may be, and civil law could so to start to be liberated from each other. This new way of approaching the intersection of nature, society, culture, and the person has a revolutionary potential whose development we are still witnessing. Rather than claiming that one's own view of the world and moral positions are the only bearers of truth, and so justify the struggle for imposing them in order to illuminate and save the others (even in spite of themselves), one is urged by new norms which call to de-center oneself from one's own position, and consider oneself as another among many with whom to negotiate how to live in common.

The results of this change are far-reaching. Reason has to be negotiated, and so rationality can be made to appear (González, 1997). Rationality results from reason, but also transcends any particular cultural reason. It is a drive towards an increased understanding of experience, and for the guidance of behavior in a moving world. It is also an ethical impulse that goes beyond any particular given moral code. It is more a virtue to be cultivated than a set of rules to be applied. It is a drive to empower individuals and groups on how to manage choices for knowing and acting, at the same time as a constant effort to keep harmony between diversity and social cooperation. It is a search for concealing maximum objectivity with personal freedom. Something that at first look may seem to some to be a contradiction in terms. But that we do not believe to be so. What we take it for certain is that to reach such goal a price has to be paid.

The Central Role of Ambivalence

One has to face a world of ambivalence and ambiguities, where choices have to be continuously made. Activities make Reason to turn into itself and to be confronted with other reasons. A continuous struggle for developing new rules of reason then starts, even if it is known that any attained outcome will soon become obsolete. Reason then turns into *Rationality*, into an effort for understanding and actuating better. Rationality then gives birth to *Ethics* out of moral norms. Ethics is a form of morality that goes into the struggle to liberate itself from particular socio-cultural situated moral codes, and so urges one to act along the lines of rationality, which then becomes itself a kind of cause and result of Ethics. The World also cannot not escape from these transformations. It cannot anymore be represented through images taken from mythical constitutions, it becomes *Objectivity*. Something that transcends experience and can only be glimpsed and never reached by the interpretation of signs provided by experience and interpreted with the mediational means available at each moment.

Rationality, Ethics, and Objectivity are then impossible to be disentangled from each other. They are delicate creatures that only exist by transforming themselves. They, rather than offering a fixed network of sacred meanings one has to worship and live within, offer suggestions, but give no commands. They provide transitory guidance for understanding but offer no security, and so make one insecure, but accountable for one's own actuations. They exist and are useful for the *community of knowledge* within which they thrive. That is why *virtues of citizenship* (Cerezo, 2005; Slunecko & Hengl – chapter 2, this volume) are to be cultivated and

cherished, because it is in the effort of perfecting one's humanity within an open sociocultural environment where the seeds for reaching objectivity, freedom, and accountability lay. Teleology then is now in full motion.

Human sciences evolved from the moral sciences, and came a long way. They have proved themselves able to reasonably describe many different ways of being moral. However, they cannot avoid searching for new ethical ways of suggesting how to be, but always keeping aware of what a risky business is to offer final prescriptions. The cultural experiments of the 20th century (the bloodiest of human history) should make us wary of the dangers of worshiping the idols produced by modernity. Reverting to one's morals is a sin against the rational ethics, as also is reverting rationality into *one* situated reason. Science cannot but be an ethical endeavor.

Rationality and Society

The open society with an open symbolic market forces one to abandon the safety of the warm womb of a closed cultural group. It makes one to move from being a member of a group, a class, or a community of believers – a status that provides a clear-cut views on the world and identity, as well as with moral rules for conduct– to be an individual who has to device how to act facing inclemency. When this happens, one faces the "open market" – one's abilities needed for mastering the use of the cultural tools to join social life, the symbols and discourses which provide one with food for thought – are all needed for adaptation. These choices makes one a consumer, but also a producer of cultural products (de Certeau, 1984).

The individual has to move between the different stands in the market, and continuously change between the roles of producer, consumer, and distributor of cultural products. Suddenly one becomes aware of being playing many different social roles, sometimes even performing scripts which may be morally contradictory, and so feeling forced to wearing many different persona masks in the same day, as one moves between different sceneries for actuation. Guilt becomes then a price to pay. When this happens identity and the *self* become an issue. If one tries to conciliate these different positions, sometimes at a great personal cost, then she or he is not just simply playing received scripts, but also devising something new. This person is creating a new *activity* (González, 1997), navigating between ambivalences, making choices and solving problems and so creating new paths for personal and cultural development.

Activities are thus beyond scripts. They evolve from previous scripts as a result of circular reactions (in James Mark Baldwin's sense) – and make new scripts that are immediately overcome. Activities make it possible for new abilities to develop. Problem-solving develops into full-fledged thinking and planning, leading to new actions– and so new forms of creativity appear. The architect builds a cathedral – or an outhouse – with some initial spur of an image, followed by a plan, and finally – adjusting the plan to the conditions of the building site. Activity makes new cultural products to appear in the market of rules for actuation, providing further grounds for new activities to happen.

BECOMING THE AUTHOR OF ONE'S LIFE
Activities change the actor into an author. One is not any more a character playing a role. One has to construct an image of oneself that transcends all these different sceneries. One is forced to be the author of one's own life, as lived, as well as narrated. Constructing one's own self becomes then a necessity, and sometimes a personal moral dictum. One looks at oneself, not only as an object to be understood, but also as an object which has to widen its capabilities for carrying out activities. If this is done, freedom of choice increases, as also accountability does. Then it is no surprise that one feels under stress, that identity crisis abound, that a new notion of *saturated self* appears (Gergen, 1991) that saturates the theoretical world of the social sciences (Rosa, Castro, & Blanco, 2006), and so psychology becomes a valued socio-cultural practice since it is one of the devices for dealing with the distressed selves which populate society (Rose, 1996).

Whatever the case, the author of a life is faced with the task of constructing its own self. As Ricoeur (1991) argues, the modern self gets shaped throughout a process in which *selfness* and *selfhood* have to be negotiated. This can only be done in a dialogue not only with the voices of actually present interlocutors, but also with voices coming from the arts, the sciences, and the media (Bakhtin, 1981, Wertsch, 1991). The result is a *dialogical self* (Salgado & Gonçalves, chapter, 30, this volume): an object that gets shaped, sedimented, and transformed through ever on-going dialogues. Parts of public culture become then constituents of personal culture (Barclay & Smith, 1992; Valsiner, 1998), and one's own self is a sort of crossroads where discourses operate (Slunecko & Hengl – Chapter 2, this volume).

Agency, Rationality, Ethics, and Objectivity

With the emerging authorship, a radical redistribution of agency has then happened. The actor then gets enmeshed in a network of objects and actants (Callon, 1986, 1991), and agency is distributed between objects, organisms and networks, with a prominent role of the calculation centers, where information and power are concentrated (Latour, 1987). But one is not an inane puppet anymore. One is simultaneously placed in different knots of the network. So that one can think of oneself with the means and interlocutors one has available. A whole range of possibilities are open between conceiving of oneself as author of one's own life, or as simply an actor playing a received script. Nevertheless, there is always behind a background in which unmanageable and unknown forces play beyond the harnessing power of anyone.

Explaining and Understanding Experiences: Objectivity Through the Self

Our story constructed through this Handbook aims at explicating the consequences of the view of *Psyche* presented in Chapter 1 of this volume. We described how physical autocatalytic processes turned into life, and how life produces action with meaning-making capacities. Meaning is then a product of natural process, but can only be explained historically. In order to do so, we have gone into the pains of essaying a narrative which combined the empirical evidence conveyed by particular empirical studies reviewed within this volume, with conceptual evidence taken from different disciplines (mainly from philosophy, psychology, semiotics, and sociology). This is what a historical narrative does (Danto, 1985).

Any historical account is a cultural construction. It includes an ordered sequence of events which transit from one to the next has to be explained. Both, the happenings that make up an event and the causes that make one event to follow an other, have to be documented. The first going into the sources which provide the empirical material, the latter by borrowing explanatory devices from other disciplines which so act as auxiliary disciplines for history. The final outcome is a story in which each event has to be explained by the necessary presence of documented antecedent elements, and linked by explanatory principles which must provide sufficient causes for each event to happen. The task of the historian is that of gathering data, explaining changes, and producing a story which has as many elements as necessary as to account for the changes and as few as suffice for making the interpretation of sense possible (Danto, 1985).

Changes are happenings which break canonicity. This is what catches the attention of historians. The expected continuity of a "steady state" of a life of a social system is no news[2]. Historians – as well as journalists, evolutionary biologists, paleontologists or developmental psychologists – are interested in breaking points, in describing, explaining, and making sense of their significance for the future of each particular event. Events are selected because of their significance, because they are needed for the explanation of others events placed in a future

which now is a past for the historian. All psychology is idiographic science (Molenaar & Valsiner, 2005) – generalizations are made on the basis of single cases that are studied systemically in their time-ordered sequences of transformation.

THE MINDSET OF HISTORY

Final causes are forbidden in history – like teleology is disallowed in evolutionary theory. Both are constructed time-free explanations. In contrast – once a story in formed by linking events into a series, something new appears: events become meaningful, each gets a sense within the framework of the historical story at large. This does not mean that the happened events had a particular purpose or were following a teleology when they happened. On the contrary, human History tells us how often events have unexpected outcomes, some times contrary to the purposes of the agents who triggered them. However, historical stories produce specific meanings, and also convey a morale (White, 1973). And this is what makes history to be a valuable cultural practice offering useful products to society.

History is not a natural science. It makes use of scientific methods for gathering evidence and for providing explanations, but its purpose is interpreting what happened, so we can make sense of the present in order to act towards the future. As Collingwood said time is the substance of history (1946), since it is by traveling through time that events get provided with sense. Something that does not imply any kind of final cause, nor any immanent teleology.

History is constructed by moving from the watch towers of the present into images of reconstructed pasts. One looks into the remains the past left in our present in order to imagine a non-visitable past event. This is obviously made by using the epistemological and cognitive devices available when performing this imagined historical journey. The result is a fascinating exercise in which the play of contingencies is retraced and the vertigo of the play of randomness and necessity (Monod, 1970) is felt, as one feels that the world one can now experience, and even one self as a being, is the result of a chain of events, sometimes resulting from decisions taken by others in the past, and some others to happenings not far from a long sequence of random dice throws.

Understanding and Explaining in Socio-Cultural Psychology

Historical reconstruction (from the present to the past) goes into the task of imagining what things were at the very beginning (without resorting to their future for its explanation, but also having the advantage of knowing what happened afterwards), and so to retrace how the immediate future of a given past could happen, and proceed up to our present. This is what makes historical narratives to have abductive capacities (Danto, 1985) – the course of the story takes a turn that leads to a "jump" in the meaning for the recipient. This feature of communicative messages – be those poems, fables, short stories, or theatre performances – fascinated the young Vygotsky when he charted out the process of affective synthesis as the central object of psychological investigation (Vygotsky, 1971).

Narratives set entities into dynamic relationships. Hence entities can only be conceived by processes, and processes can only happen because of encounters between entities. The result is that the natural history of the development of the capacity of experiencing parallels that of the creation of objective entities. This is meant in a radical evolutionary way. It is not that one can only know what can currently experience and explain – something that is indisputable, and so is an evolutionary triviality when comparing different species currently leaving with us, although it is extremely important when looking into ontogenesis. What is meant, is that new entities evolved because of the competitive advantage the meaning-making capacities provided them with. This takes one to an important consequence: actuating capacities and physical structures create each other, in a sort of shuffling movement, something already suggested by Darwin

before the genetically oriented and material reductionist neo-Darwinism eloped with his heritage (Fernández, 2005; Richards, 1987, 2002; Sánchez & Loredo, 2005).

Taking the argument further it can be said that in evolution the semiotic function plays a role in transforming the materiality of the world. Or if one were into the mood of being provocative, one could say that spirit (itself a natural force) has always had some agency in the changes of the Objective and in shaping the materiality of our perceived world. The reverse is also true. Matter (structures) and Spirit (processes) are thus inextricably united. They cannot be separated from each other. This is a peculiar feature of the biological sciences – as far as psychology can be taken to belong to them. As Wundt made it clear, psychology is bi-faced. It is as much a natural science as a science of the spirit. We believe that the time is ripe for it not to be separated in two irreconcilable halves. The biological bases of the body work through the cultural experience, that further modifies the body. The "spirit" is "embodied" – while the body is "enspirited" – it is functioning under the leadership of constantly active mind that creates meaningfulness. Each step in the process of description and explanation should go into the pains of laboring in the two directions of the double spiral, without attempting to reduce one direction to the other. The idiographic nature of phenomena is constantly compared with the generalization that is inherent in the systemic model – inductive and deductive strategies should go hand in hand in a continuous shuffling movement that results in abduction.

Socio-cultural psychology leads to a new look at hypotheses generation – and testing. The propositions to be tested empirically – otherwise called hypotheses – are set up within the whole of the methodology cycle. An empirical proof of a hypothesis is productive only if it leads to a new idea – rather than confirms an existing one. Deductively generated (that is – theories'-based) hypotheses would highlight the role of empirical investigation for science. Yet the focus here is not in the proof (or disproof) of a hypothesis, but the evocation of new structures as those emerge in the research process. Social scientists are not investigating the "world out there" – but due to their own immediate participation in the "world we are all in" they study the adaptation of the social systems to various challenges.

Reality in science is not immediately perceived, but distantly interpreted – yet in ways that remain true to that reality. Hence we need to accept a semiotic interpretation of "the data." Data are constructed new signs that present selected features of the phenomena. Hence all empirical work is semiotic through its epistemological credo. The adequacy of the constructed signs as representations of the selected phenomena is the crucial feature of all data-as-signs, and needs to be under careful scrutiny (see Knorr-Cetina, 1999, for examples of how such scrutiny happens in different natural sciences). It is sufficient to undertake one unwarranted step in the transformation of phenomena into signs (data) that the value of the latter is wiped out in full.

Psychology – The Science of Human Cultural Experience

As becomes clear from this Handbook, socio-cultural psychology has been for a while changing its course. From being predominantly concerned with the study of action has been steering to take a course which combines this concern with that of studying sense and meaning. This focus situates the area of research in the realm of the study of experience. As a product of consciousness, human experience is a hard nut to crack in this research endeavor. The processes of experiencing are what allow us interpreting and understanding what is going on around us; and once one is proficient in the use of conventional symbolic languages to speak and so shape and produce communicable knowledge.

Socio-cultural psychology is concerned with the study of human actions and experiences as those are culturally organized. The development of new tools, the change in

social practices, the constant arising of new goals and senses make it to be always uncompleted, and always searching for new methods. *Methodos* is a Greek word which means *road*. But the goal the socio-cultural research strives to reach changes its place before one can finish the journey. No road, no method could ever exhaust such a subject-matter. A never ending collective endeavor will keep moving through different alleys which crisscross the complex geography of society and culture.

It is apparent that a theoretically guided reflexive perspective is the backbone that unifies the various contributions to this volume, together with the focus on the development of meanings, their transformations in activity contexts, and various forms of mediation of the human *psyche* through signs. Hence the semiotic ideas of C.S. Peirce figure prominently among various contributions to this Handbook. This is not surprising – in the work of Peirce the boundaries of the natural and social sciences vanish. What remains to be accomplished, of course, is the creation of new semiotic methodology for the field.

Methodology Cycle as the Knowledge Construction Process

The methods and the data are constructed by the researcher on the basis of the specific structure of the process cycle. Methodology here is equal to the cyclical process of general knowledge construction, where different parts of the cycle feed differentially into other parts. The axiomatic look at the phenomena is based on the experience of the phenomena together with abstracted general ideas about them. Theories gain input from the axiomatic ideas and serve as a translation point of those ideas into methods – which, as those are made to relate with the phenomena, produce data as a "side effect" of the methodology process. The data are selective, theory-and-method based representations of some selected aspects of the phenomena – that feed forward to the further construction of theoretical kind. We are on the road to this restoration of epistemic unity in the middle of diversity. The "methodology

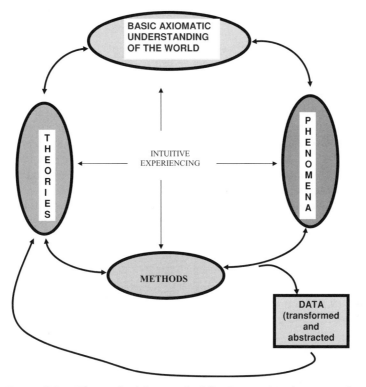

Figure GC.1. The methodology cycle (after Branco & Valsiner, 1997).

cycle" (Branco & Valsiner, 1997) becomes the basis for reflexivity about how new knowledge is being constructed (Figure GC.1).

It would be adequate to depict Figure GC.1 not merely as a cycle, but as a helix – there is never a full return to the previously generated knowledge, even if there may be outward resemblance between what is new and what is old (see also Chapter 1, Figure 1.3). Such helical development of scientific knowledge allows us to benefit from the history of ideas – detecting a need at our present time to make sense of a basic issue (such as development) leads us to look back into the history of our disciplines for times when similar needs were detected.

A Way to Look at Culturally Directed Psychological Phenomena

We set up our research efforts within the framework of wide general perspectives – frames of reference (see Chapter 1). Frames of reference are general conceptual position-

ing devices within the minds of researchers, who set up their research questions and construct methods in ways that unify different levels of the methodology cycle. The same phenomenon can be studied very differently – from the different perspectives specified by the different reference frames.

Frames of reference narrow down the focus of empirical research efforts. These frames are like the selection of magnification levels in a microscope – while some details become better observable in selecting a particular frame, others vanish from the view. The reference frames are necessary and needed "blinders" – theoretical general orientation tools that make focusing on our desired object possible, while eliminating the "noise". Out of the four frames (Valsiner, 2000, Chapter 5) the *individual-socioecological* – is fitting for socio-cultural psychology. It includes:

(a) an active person,
(b) environment,

(c) person's acting towards the environment,

(d) the guiding role of the acting by somebody else (be it a person, social institution, or a symbolic object within the environment), and

(e) the transformation of the person as a result of this socially guided action by the person oneself.

In the case of the individual-socioecological frame, the researcher needs to analyze the structure of social suggestions that exists in the particular episode of encounter between the person and the environment. Some of these suggestions are encoded into the environment itself, others are produced by the other persons who are active in the same environment, regulating the person's conduct in it. The Method of Double Stimulation that was created by Lev Vygotsky in the 1920s (van der Veer & Valsiner, 1991) is an example of the ways in which the general scheme of individual-socio-cultural reference frame can be put into practice.

EXPERIMENT IN THE REALM OF
SOCIO-CULTURAL PSYCHOLOGY

All methods in psychology are derivates from the basic human encounter with the world – in terms of perception and attention. Scientists are guided in their professional identity development to assume different positions in relation to the phenomena they study – to look at them from a distance (observe and contemplate), or study them through direct impact (experiment, interview, taking the "native's perspective" by immersion in the cultural worlds of "the others" in anthropology).

Some of the methods used in psychology are hybrids of these distant versus close positioning of the researcher – for instance, a paper-and-pencil method (test, questionnaire, rating scale) may be brought to the actors to be studied by the researcher in direct contact. For instance, the researcher administers one's questionnaires to a group of participants, yet the method entails providing distant answers the format of which is pre-set by the method constructor. The

marks the person makes on the piece of paper provided – or on a computer screen – refer to intra-psychologically complex phenomena that lose their reality after the answer is given.

The experimental method is crucial for most sciences – yet in each of them it has its own specific features. Figure GC.2 provides its generic overview. The innovative moment here is to link this mental process registration tradition with experimental manipulation of semiotic kind – it is through the insertion of some meaning change ("meaning block" in Figure GC.2) while the Subject is moving towards a previously set meaningful goal that the access to the phenomena is created. The person's action plan is expected to be interrupted, and s/he begins to use new – created or imported – meanings for dealing with the meaning disturbance. The "rupture" is created by way of counter-suggestive signs.

Concluding Words: A Caravan Moving Towards Objectivity

Objectivity in science emerges on the basis of a deeply subjective process of generalization. The basic scientific creativity takes place in the subjective world of the knowledge maker – scientist or artist. The scientist is constantly operating on the basis of one's intra-mental understanding of what it is that is being studied, how to study it, and what to expect. Here the role of a philosopher and psychologist converge – both rely upon their powers of thinking to make sense of some phenomenon.

The construction of basic knowledge in the social sciences depends not upon the sophistication of the analytic techniques in the treatment of the phenomena, but on the general strategies for *where* to look, *which comparisons to make*, and *what to assume* about the phenomena before the actual analytic techniques are put into use. It is an illusion in psychology to think that – due to researchers being similar to the persons they study – the phenomena are immediately

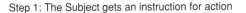

Step 1: The Subject gets an instruction for action

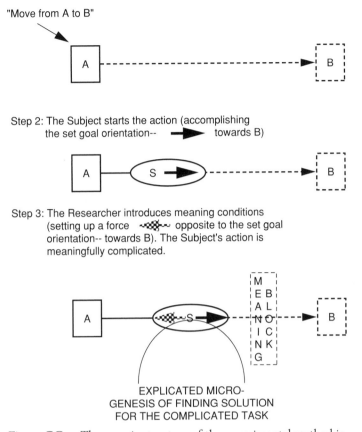

Step 2: The Subject starts the action (accomplishing the set goal orientation-- ➤ towards B)

Step 3: The Researcher introduces meaning conditions (setting up a force ⟶ opposite to the set goal orientation-- towards B). The Subject's action is meaningfully complicated.

EXPLICATED MICRO-GENESIS OF FINDING SOLUTION FOR THE COMPLICATED TASK

Figure GC.2. The generic structure of the experimental method in socio-cultural psychology.

accessible to the psychologist. In reality, the inquiry into the minds and feelings of the person next to oneself may be as inaccessible as the realities of far-away galaxies are for astrophysicists.

The socio-cultural field is in active movement. Yet its methodology requires further innovation. The centrality of the author – the scientist, the meaning maker – is being restored to its central role. Ever new computer or laboratory technology – will never solve basic scientific problems – only their constructors and users might. Constructing scientific knowledge entails creating new stories about reality – hopefully those that present that reality in general ways. Scientific knowledge is semiotic in its nature.

Where socio-cultural psychology is going can not be known before it moves. Still, as we saw in this Handbook, it is a burgeoning new interdisciplinary field that moves on as a carnevalesque caravan in the middle of the mundane funding policies of national governments. The Colombian novelist Alvaro Mutis (2002, p. 625). made one of his characters to speak about the movement of caravans:

I believe that both of us have always known that the goal we throw ourselves into searching, without measuring obstacles nor fearing dangers, is completely out of reach. It is what I once said about caravans.

A caravan symbolizes or represents nothing. A caravan exhaust its meaning in its own movement. Our mistake is in thinking that it goes somewhere or comes from somewhere else. The beasts which make it up know that, caravaneers do not.

Notes

1   "zonified" = area divided into various zones, with boundaries of different openness/closedness and plasticity/rigidity.
2   It would be somewhat comic to imagine a news broadcast where all items reported are of the kind "nothing has happened in X since Y, and here is our reporter on the site to cover *the latest news."*

References

Bakhtin, M. M. (1981). *The dialogical imagination.* Austin: The University of Texas Press.

Barclay, C. R., & Smith, T. S. (1992). Autobiographical Remembering: Creating Personal Culture. In M. A. Conway; D. C. Rubin; H. Spinnler & E. A. Wagenaar (Eds.), (1992). *Autobiographical memory* (pp. 75–97). Dordrecht: Kluwer Academic Publisher.

Bourdieu, P. (1991). *Language and symbolic power.* Cambridge, MA: Harvard University Press.

Branco, A. U., & Valsiner, J. (1997). Changing methodologies: A co-constructivist study of goal orientations in social interactions. *Psychology and Developing Societies,* 9, 1, 35–64.

Callon, M. (1986). Some Elements of a Sociology of Translation: Domestication of the Scallops and the Fishermen of St Brieuc Bay. In John Law (Ed.), *Power, Action and Belief: A New Sociology of Knowledge* (pp. 196–233). London: Routledge & Kegan Paul.

Callon, M. 1991. Techno-economic networks and irreversibility. In John Law (Ed.), *A Sociology of Monsters: Essays on Power, Technology and Domination* (pp. 132–165). London: Routledge.

Cerezo, P. (Ed.), (2005). *Democracia y virtudes civicas.* Madrid: Biblioteca Nueva.

Choi, S., Han, G., & Kim, C. (2007). Analysis of Cultural Emotion: Understanding of Indigenous Psychology for Universal Implications. In J. Valsiner & A. Rosa (Eds.), *The Cambridge Handbook of Socio-Cultural Psychology* (pp. 310–342). New York: Cambridge University Press.

Cole, M., & Engeström, Y. (2007). Cultural-Historical Approaches to Designing for Development. In J. Valsiner & A. Rosa (Eds.), *The Cambridge Handbook of Socio-Cultural Psychology* (pp. 434–507). New York: Cambridge University Press.

Collingwood, R. J. (1946/1976). *The idea of History.* New York: Oxford University Press.

Danto, A. C. (1985). *Narration and Knowledge.* New York: Columbia University Press.

de Certeau, M. (1984). *The practice of everyday life.* Berkeley: University of California Press.

Engeström, Y. (1987). *Learning by Expanding.* Helsinki: Orienta-Konsultit Oy.

Fernández, T. R. (2005). Sobre la Historia Natural del Sujeto y su lugar en una Historia de la Ciencia. A propósito de Robert J. Richards y el Romanticismo de Darwin. *Estudios de Psicología,* 26 (1), 67–104.

Frenkel-Brunswik, E. (1949). Intolerance of ambiguity as an emotional and perceptual personality variable. *Journal of Personality,* 18, 108–143.

Gergen, K. (1991). *The saturated self, Dilemmas of identity in contemporary life.* New York: Basic Books.

Gillespie, A. (2006). *Becoming other: From social interaction to self-reflection.* Greenwich, Ct.: Information Age Publishers, Inc.

González, A. (1997). *Estructuras de la praxis. Ensayo de una filosofía primera.* Madrid: Trotta.

Huntington, S. P. (1996). *The clash of civilizations and the remaking of world order.* New York: Simon & Schuster.

Knorr Cetina, K. (1999). *Epistemic Cultures: How the sciences make knowledge.* Cambridge, MA: Harvard University Press.

Latour, B. (1987). *Science in action.* Cambridge, MA: Harvard University Press.

Locke, J. (1689). *Epistola de Tolerantia.* http:// oregonstate.edu/instruct/phl302/texts/locke/ locke2-locke-t/locke`toleration.html.

Molenaar, P. C. M., & Valsiner, J. (2005). How generalization works through the single case: A simple idiographic process analysis of an individual psychotherapy case. *International Journal of Idiographic Science,* 1, 1–13. [www. valsiner.com]

Monod, J. (1970). Le hasard et la nécessité: essai sur la philosophie naturelle de la biologie moderne. Paris: Seuil.

Mutis, A. (2002). *Empresas y tribulaciones de Maqroll el gaviero.* Madrid: Alfaguara.

Pettegree, A. (2005). *Reformation and the culture of persuasion.* Cambridge: Cambridge University Press.

Popper, K. (1945). *The Open Society and Its Enemies.* (2 Vols). London: Routledge.

Richards, R. J. (1987). *Darwin and the emergence of evolutionary theories of mind and behavior.* Chicago: The University of Chicago Press.

Richards, R. J. (2002). *The Romantic conception of life. Science and Philosophy in the age of Goethe.* Chicago: The University of Chicago Press.

Ricoeur, P. (1991). Narrative identity. In D. Wood (Ed.), *On Paul Ricoeur: Narrative and Interpretation.* Londres:Routledge.

Rosa, A., Castro, J., & Blanco, F. (2006). Otherness in historic situated self-experiences. In L. Simão and J. Valsiner (Eds.), *Otherness in question: Labyrinths of the self.* Greenwich, Ct: Information Age Publishers.

Rosa, A., & Monserrat, J. (2003). Cultural symbols, social discourses and the personal sense of actions. Paper presented at the Biennial Conference of the International Society for Theoretical Psychology. Istanbul.

Rose, N. (1996). *Inventing Our Selves.* Cambridge: Cambridge University Press.

Salgado, J., & Gonçalves, M. (2007). The Dialogical Self: Social, Personal, and (Un)Conscious. In J. Valsiner & A. Rosa (Eds.), *The Cambridge Handbook of Socio-Cultural Psychology.* New York: Cambridge University Press.

Sánchez, J. C., & Loredo, J. C. (2005). Psicologías para la evolución. Catálogo y crítica de los usos actuales de la Selección Orgánica. *Estudios de Psicología* 26 (1), 105–126.

Simão, L. M., & Valsiner, J. (Eds.), (2006). *Otherness in question: Labyrinths of the self.* Greenwich, CT: Information Age Publishers.

Slunecko, T., & Heingl, S. (2007). Language, Cognition, Subjectivity – A Dynamic Constitution. In J. Valsiner & A. Rosa (Eds.), *The Cambridge Handbook of Socio-Cultural Psychology.* New York: Cambridge University Press.

Smedslund, J. (1995). Psychologic: Common sense and the pseudoempirical. In J. A. Smith, R. Harré, and L. van Langenhove (Eds.), *Rethinking psychology* (pp. 196–206). London: Sage.

Valsiner, J. (1995). Editorial: Culture and Psychology. *Culture & Psychology, 1,1,* 5–10.

Valsiner, J. (1997). *Culture and the development of children's Action.* 2nd ed. New York: Wiley.

Valsiner, J. (1998). *The Guided Mind.* Cambridge, MA: Harvard University Press.

Valsiner, J. (2000). *Culture and human development.* London: Sage

Valsiner, J. (2001). The first six years: Culture's adventures in psychology. *Culture & Psychology, 7, 1,* 5–48.

Valsiner, J. (2004). Three years later: Culture in psychology – between social positioning and producing new knowledge. *Culture & Psychology, 10, 1,* 5–27.

Valsiner, J., & Abbey, E. (2006). Ambivalence in focus: Remembering the life and work of Else Frenkel-Brunswik. *Estudios de Psicologia, 27, 1,* 9–17.

Van Der Veer, R., & Valsiner, J. (1991). *Understanding Vygotsky: A quest for synthesis.* Oxford: Basil Blackwell.

Vygotsky, L. S. (1971). *Psychology of art.* Cambridge, MA: MIT Press.

Wertsch, J. V. (1991). *Voices of the Mind.* Cambridge, MA: Harvard University Press.

White, H. (1973). *Metahistory.* Baltimore: The John Hopkins University Press.

Wolf, K. A. (Ed.), (1959). *Georg Simmel, 1858–1918.* Columbus: The Ohio State University Press.

Zittoun, T. (2006). *Transitions: Symbolic resources in development.* Greenwich, CT: Information Age Publishing, Inc.

Index